TEACHER'S EDITION

3

Auténtico

Go **Online** to practice

PEARSON realize™

PearsonSchool.com/Autentico

 AUDIO VIDEO WRITING  SPEAK/RECORD  MAPA GLOBAL AUTÉNTICO  FLASHCARDS ETEXT 2.0 GAMES

Peggy Palo Boyles
OKLAHOMA CITY, OK

Myriam Met
EDGEWATER, MD

Richard S. Sayers
LONGMONT, CO

 **Pearson**

Boston, Massachusetts   Chandler, Arizona
Glenview, Illinois   New York, New York

TEACHER'S EDITION

3

Auténtico

Go Online to practice

PEARSON realize™

PearsonSchool.com/Autentico

 AUDIO   VIDEO   WRITING  SPEAK/RECORD  MAPA GLOBAL  AUTÉNTICO  FLASHCARDS   ETEXT 2.0   GAMES

Professional Development Handbook

Table of Contents

» Go online at www.PearsonSchool.com/Autentico.
Each *capítulo* is supported wtih video, audio, activities,
games, and more.

PEARSON realize™

World-Readiness Standards

ACTFL's World-Readiness Standards (the 5 C's) encompasses five goal areas for language learning and instruction: Communication, Cultures, Connections, Comparisons, and Communities. Within Communication, ACTFL identifies three modes of communication: Interpersonal, Interpretive, and Presentational. The emphasis of these revised Standards is for learners to use the target language to explore the products, practices, and perspectives of the target culture, make connections with other disciplines, compare the language and culture of Spanish-speaking countries with their own, and explore opportunities to use their Spanish language skills in their own community. *Auténtico* provides users with culturally authentic resources for students to view, listen to, or read to better meet these standards. As students gain skills and confidence in the target language, they are encouraged to apply their learning beyond the classroom and become active participants in the global community.

GOAL AREAS	STANDARDS		
COMMUNICATION Communicate effectively in more than one language in order to function in a variety of situations and for multiple purposes	**Interpersonal Communication** Learners interact and negotiate meaning in spoken, signed, or written conversations to share information, reactions, feelings, and opinions.	**Interpretive Communication** Learners understand, interpret, and analyze what is heard, read, or viewed on a variety of topics.	**Presentational Communication:** Learners present information, concepts, and ideas to inform, explain, persuade, and narrate on a variety of topics using appropriate media and adapting to various audiences of listeners, readers, or viewers.
CULTURES Interact with cultural competence and understanding	**Relating Cultural Practices to Perspectives** Learners use the language to investigate, explain, and reflect on the relationship between the practices and perspectives of the cultures studied		**Relating Cultural Products to Perspectives** Learners use the language to investigate, explain, and reflect on the relationship between the products and perspectives of the cultures studied
CONNECTIONS Connect with other disciplines and acquire information and diverse perspectives in order to use the language to function in academic and career-related situations	**Making Connections** Learners build, reinforce, and expand their knowledge of other disciplines while using the language to develop critical thinking and to solve problems creatively		**Acquiring Information and Diverse Perspectives** Learners access and evaluate information and diverse perspectives that are available through the language and its cultures
COMPARISONS Develop insight into the nature of language and culture in order to interact with cultural competence	**Language Comparisons** Learners use the language to investigate, explain, and reflect on the nature of language through comparisons of the language studied and their own.		**Cultural Comparisons** Learners use the language to investigate, explain, and reflect on the concept of culture through comparisons of the cultures studied and their own.
COMMUNITIES Communicate and interact with cultural competence in order to participate in multilingual communities at home and around the world	**School and Global Communities** Learners use the language both within and beyond the classroom to interact and collaborate in their community and the globalized world		**Lifelong Learning** Learners set goals and reflect on their progress in using languages for enjoyment, enrichment, and advancement.

Proficiency

A ttention to communication and proficiency is consistently emphasized in guidelines and standards developed by the American Council on the Teaching of Foreign Languages (ACTFL), such as the ACTFL World-Readiness Standards, the ACTFL Proficiency Guidelines 2012, and the ACTFL Performance Descriptors for Language Learners. Expectations regarding the functional use of language and the level of proficiency students are expected to achieve are clearly stated within the NCSSFL-ACTFL Global Can-Do Benchmarks.

The Can-Do Benchmarks reflect a change in measuring proficiency, a way to guide curriculum development, and a shift in classroom emphasis onto the learner. The Can-Do Statements provide assessment guidelines for both the instructor and the learner. Written in a checklist style, these statements express what the learner "can do," and they place a shared responsibility for learning and assessment onto both instructor and student. Using these benchmarks with your students helps them to become more independent learners and gives them the skills for life-long learning.

What are the Can-Do Statements?

The Can-Do Statements incorporate a context and purpose for second language learning in a checklist format. The result of a collaboration between the NCSSFL[1], developers of LinguaFolio®, a learner-directed portfolio assessment instrument, and ACTFL, the Can-Do Statements provide specific language tasks within proficiency guidelines broken down into five levels of language ability, from the beginning of language instruction through advanced language study and use. The three base levels of Novice, Intermediate and Advanced are further broken down into Low, Mid, and High levels.

To use *Auténtico* with the Can-Do Statements, refer to the following level alignment. The level of your class or curriculum may vary from these suggestions:

Auténtico, Level 1: Novice Low/Novice Mid to Novice High

Auténtico, Level 2: Novice High/Intermediate Low to Intermediate Mid

Auténtico, Level 3: Intermediate Low/Intermediate Mid to Intermediate High

Auténtico and the Can-Do Statements

The three Modes of Communication—Interpersonal, Interpretive, and Presentational—are at the core of

the Can-Do Statements and also form the foundation of learning and practice within *Auténtico*. The Can-Do statements provide the framework and contexts for language use in a learner's everyday life. The same contexts can be found throughout the themes of *Auténtico*.

How to use *Auténtico* with the Can-Do Statements

As an instructor, you may wish to use the NCSSFL-ACTFL Can-Do Statements to set goals for your students and to guide their assessment. Ask students to be responsible for their own personal lists of Can-Do's, which they can monitor and refer to throughout the year.

Auténtico provides you and your students a series of tools and resources to help you create additional individual goals that fit into your curriculum benchmarks or students' learning plans. These tools include chapter and section objectives, end-of chapter personal self-assessments, and rubrics.

Use the Chapter Objectives to set personal goals. These objectives are highlighted on the first page of each chapter, and are easily aligned to the three Modes of Communication:

Interpretive: Listen and read ...

Presentational: Talk and write about ...

Interpersonal: Exchange information ...

Objectives also appear at the beginning of each section in the chapter. These objectives are the steps and contexts that support the overarching chapter goals.

On the first page of each chapter, the section "You will demonstrate what you know and can do" directs students to the end of the chapter, *Preparación para el examen,* where self-assessment tasks relate back to the Chapter Objectives. These tasks are written and labeled so that students can directly assess what they "can do" as they progress through the chapter, and where they need to go in the chapter if they need more practice.

The following pages show the Global Can-Do Benchmarks for each proficiency mode and the main Can-Do indicators that correspond to Auténtico, Level 3. The benchmarks are aligned with pages in *Auténtico* that support these proficiencies and indicators. This is not meant to be a complete correlation, but rather a guide for you as you plan your lessons.

[1]National Council of State Supervisors for Languages

Performance Indicators for Language Learners

AUTÉNTICO supports the Global Can-Do Benchmarks across all levels. Use this chart to track where the global benchmarks and progress indicators are addressed throughout the Student and Teacher Edition for this level of the program. This is not meant to be a complete correlation, but rather a guide for you as you plan your lessons.

Interpersonal Communication

Intermediate Low	
I can participate in conversations on a number of familiar topics using simple sentences. I can handle short social interactions in everyday situations by asking and answering simple questions.	
I can have a simple conversation on a number of everyday topics.	pp. 4, 183, 191, 209
I can ask and answer questions on factual information that is familiar to me.	pp. 16, 135, 168
I can use the language to meet my basic needs in familiar situations.	pp. 129, 177

Intermediate Mid	
I can participate in conversations on familiar topics using sentences and series of sentences. I can handle short social interactions in everyday situations by asking and answering a variety of questions. I can usually say what I want to say about myself and my everyday life.	
I can start, maintain, and end a conversation on a variety of familiar topics.	pp. 17, 44, 143, 255
I can talk about my daily activities and personal preferences.	pp. 3, 41, 67, 95
I can use my language to handle tasks related to my personal needs.	pp. 35, 120, 183
I can exchange information about subjects of special interest to me.	pp. 83, 98, 282

Intermediate High	
I can participate with ease and confidence in conversations on familiar topics. I can usually talk about events and experiences in various time frames. I can usually describe people, places, and things. I can handle social interactions in everyday situations, sometimes even when there is an unexpected complication.	
I can exchange information related to areas of mutual interest.	pp. 120, 137, 255, 352, 365
I can use my language to do a task that requires multiple steps.	pp. 14, 125
I can use my language to handle a situation that may have a complication.	pp. 35, 155, 195, 473

Presentational Speaking

Intermediate Low

I can present information on most familiar topics using a series of simple sentences.	
I can talk about people, activities, events, and experiences.	pp. 14, 29, 185
I can express my needs and wants.	pp. 195, 219
I can present information on plans, instructions, and directions.	pp. 125, 135, 147, 159
I can present songs, short skits, or dramatic readings.	pp. 46, 93, TE 104, TE 180
I can express my preferences on topics of interest.	pp. 67, 83, 89, 143

Intermediate Mid

I can make presentations on a wide variety of familiar topics using connected sentences.	
I can make a presentation about my personal and social experiences.	pp. 49, 51, 63, 399
I can make a presentation on something I have learned or researched.	pp. TE 16-b, 147, 351, 387
I can make a presentation about common interests and issues and state my viewpoint.	pp. 15, 99, 491, 495

Intermediate High

I can make presentations in a generally organized way on school, work, and community topics, and on topics I have researched. I can make presentations on some events and experiences in various time frames.	
I can present information on academic and work topics.	pp. TE 111-b, 111, 303, 447
I can make a presentation on events, activities, and topics of particular interest.	pp. 291, 347, 351, TE 489
I can present my point of view and provide reasons to support it.	pp. 195, 243, 435, 483

Presentational Writing

Intermediate Low

I can write briefly about most familiar topics and present information using a series of simple sentences.	
I can write about people, activities, events, and experiences.	pp. 9, 35, 44, 49
I can prepare materials for a presentation.	pp. 14, 15, TE 16-b
I can write about topics of interest.	pp. 67, 87, 95
I can write basic instructions on how to make or do something.	pp. 124, 129, 146
I can write questions to obtain information.	pp. 29, 129, 134

Presentational Writing, *continued*

Intermediate Mid

I can write on a wide variety of familiar topics using connected sentences.	
I can write messages and announcements.	pp. 244–245, 255, 388–389, 436–437
I can write short reports about something I have learned or researched.	pp. 251, 292–293, TE 291, TE 304-b
I can compose communications for public distribution.	pp. 52–53, 101–102, 111, 148–149, 340–341, 495

Intermediate High

I can write on topics related to school, work, and community in a generally organized way. I can write some simple paragraphs about events and experiences in various time frames.	
I can write about school and academic topics.	pp. 196–197, TE 256-b, TE 352-b, TE 400-b
I can write about work and career topics.	pp. 82, TE 101, 139, 242, 244–245
I can write about community topics and events.	pp. 16, 399, 447, 484–485
I can write about an entertainment or social event.	pp. 9, 10, 44, 95

Interpretive Listening

Intermediate Low

I can understand the main idea in short, simple messages and presentations on familiar topics. I can understand the main idea of simple conversations that I overhear.	
I can understand the basic purpose of a message.	pp. 63, 146, 231
I can understand messages related to my basic needs.	pp. 23, 159
I can understand questions and simple statements on everyday topics when I am part of the conversation.	pp. 89, 143, 183

Intermediate Mid

I can understand the main idea in messages and presentations on a variety of topics related to everyday life and personal interests and studies. I can understand the main idea in conversations that I overhear.	
I can understand basic information in ads, announcements, and other simple recordings.	pp. 31, 87, 167, 215
I can understand the main idea of what I listen to for personal enjoyment.	pp. 207, 321, 338, 347
I can understand messages related to my everyday life.	pp. 39, 266

Interpretive Listening, *continued*

Intermediate High

I can easily understand the main idea in messages and presentations on a variety of topics related to everyday life and personal interests and studies. I can usually understand a few details of what I overhear in conversations, even when something unexpected is expressed. I can sometimes follow what I hear about events and experiences in various time frames.	
I can easily understand straightforward information or interactions.	pp. 71, 81, 91, 230
I can understand a few details in ads, announcements, and other simple recordings.	pp. 41, 50, 234
I can sometimes understand situations with complicating factors.	pp. 194, 242, 303, 374

Interpretive Reading

Intermediate Low

I can understand the main idea of short and simple texts when the topic is familiar	
I can understand messages in which the writer tells or asks me about topics of personal interest.	pp. 8, 10, 131
I can identify some simple information needed on forms.	pp. 89, 99 ,176, 183
I can identify some information from news media.	pp. 38, 63, 431

Intermediate Mid

I can understand the main idea of texts related to everyday life and personal interests or studies.	
I can understand simple personal questions.	pp. 172, 176, 182
I can understand basic information in ads, announcements, and other simple texts.	pp. 35, 83, 220, 230
I can understand the main idea of what I read for personal enjoyment.	pp. 13, 94, 194, 458
I can read simple written exchanges between other people.	pp. 120, 140, 179

Intermediate High

I can easily understand the main idea of texts related to everyday life, personal interests, and studies. I can sometimes follow stories and descriptions about events and experiences in various time frames.	
I can understand accounts of personal events or experiences.	pp. 232, 310–311, 486–489
I can sometimes follow short, written instructions when supported by visuals.	pp. 150–153, 187
I can understand the main idea of and a few supporting facts about famous people and historic events.	pp. 192–193, 240–241, 480–481

Using Authentic Materials in the Spanish Classroom
Focusing on the Interpretive Mode of Communication

The ACTFL World-Readiness Standards

1.2 Interpretive **Communication**

Learners understand, interpret, and analyze what is heard, read, or viewed on a variety of topics.

When language learners first interact with native speakers they may feel intimidated by the speed of the language or the amount of unfamiliar vocabulary. Frequent and regular exposure to authentic materials in the classroom, however, can build students' skills and give them the confidence to take their language learning beyond the classroom. Each chapter of *Auténtico* features opportunities for students to view, read, and listen to authentic materials that were created by native speakers of Spanish for native speakers of Spanish. As students become accustomed to interpreting these materials, they develop the skills necessary to use their Spanish in the real world.

Choose the right material

It can be difficult to choose level-appropriate authentic content for students in the earliest stages of language learning. While students at the beginning levels will not understand everything, encountering some familiar vocabulary will help them access the content and increase their confidence in their ability to understand native speakers. Choosing video, audio, and texts that are thematically related to what students are already learning will offer a sense of familiarity and provide students with a connection to the material.

Prepare students

Preparing students before watching an authentic video, listening to audio, or reading authentic content is essential to success.

- **Activate background knowledge** Ask questions to uncover what students already know about the topic in the authentic material. This will help students connect their prior knowledge to the new content.

- **Provide context** Before watching the video, give students an overview of the type of content that they will be viewing. Talk about cultural elements that would be commonly understood by a native speaker viewing the material but that may be unfamiliar to language learners.

- **Introduce key vocabulary** Pre-teach vocabulary that is key to understanding the content.

Tailor the viewing or listening task

One of the most important aspects of using authentic material with language learners is to make sure that the task is level appropriate so students can succeed. Tasks will vary according to the type of authentic resource. Tasks that are appropriate for early learners include:

ALL GENRES

- **Write down cognates** Ask students to write down any cognates that they encounter.

- **Focus on main ideas and key details** Provide students with graphic organizers to help them identify main ideas. Do a Concept Map or Webbing activity with the class to identify the main concepts and related details. Or have students do a Scavenger Hunt, in which students watch or listen for key ideas or cultural details.

- **Predict** Ask students to predict what they might see, hear, or read based on the type of reading or the general topic.

- **Discuss cultural context** Have students focus on cultural elements or the cultural context of the resource. Discuss with them cultural details that were unexpected or impressed them in some way.

- **Create individual vocabulary lists** Ask each student to make a list of five words they heard or saw that they didn't know and want to learn, have students compare lists. Teach students how to look up words they may not know how to spell.

VIDEO

- **Assign group work** As students become more comfortable with authentic materials, let them work as a group to dissect a video, discuss with their partners, then present what they learned to the class.

- **Turn off the sound** Show the video first without audio and have students focus on the visuals, ask them to write words they think they might hear, then put a checkmark next to any they hear when you play the video with sound.

AUDIO

- **Give students control** have students listen to the audio alone on a computer where they can pause and rewind as many times as they like.

READING

- **Focus on common features of the reading genre** Ask students to guess the meaning of new vocabulary by considering what type of information is expected. When reading a web page, for example, students can reasonably guess that the *Buscar* button next to the search box means "search" because they are familiar with navigating web pages.

After viewing or listening

Take the time after working with authentic materials, either as a class or as homework, to reflect on the content.

- **Consider cultural perspectives** Ask students to consider the relationship between the products and practices in the authentic material and the perspectives of the culture of the intended audience.
- **Personalize understanding** Give students the opportunity to think critically about the content and to personalize their understanding.
- **Provide a self-assessment rubric** Create a simple rubric for students to assess their understanding of a resource.

Assign varying points for criteria such as: Can I identify the main idea? Can I understand supporting details? Can I infer meaning of new words from the context? Can I identify cultural products or practices, and the related cultural perspectives?

Revisit the content

Throughout the course of the school year, have students watch previously viewed videos or listen to an audio selection from an earlier chapter. Assign students a new task for their second encounter with the same content. Ask students to discuss or write about how their understanding of the content changed over time.

Authentic Resources in AUTÉNTICO

Auténtico **feature in the Student Edition** *Auténtico pages* in the Student Edition feature strategies that build students' language skills and increase their confidence by watching, listening to, and reading carefully-curated authentic resources. ▼

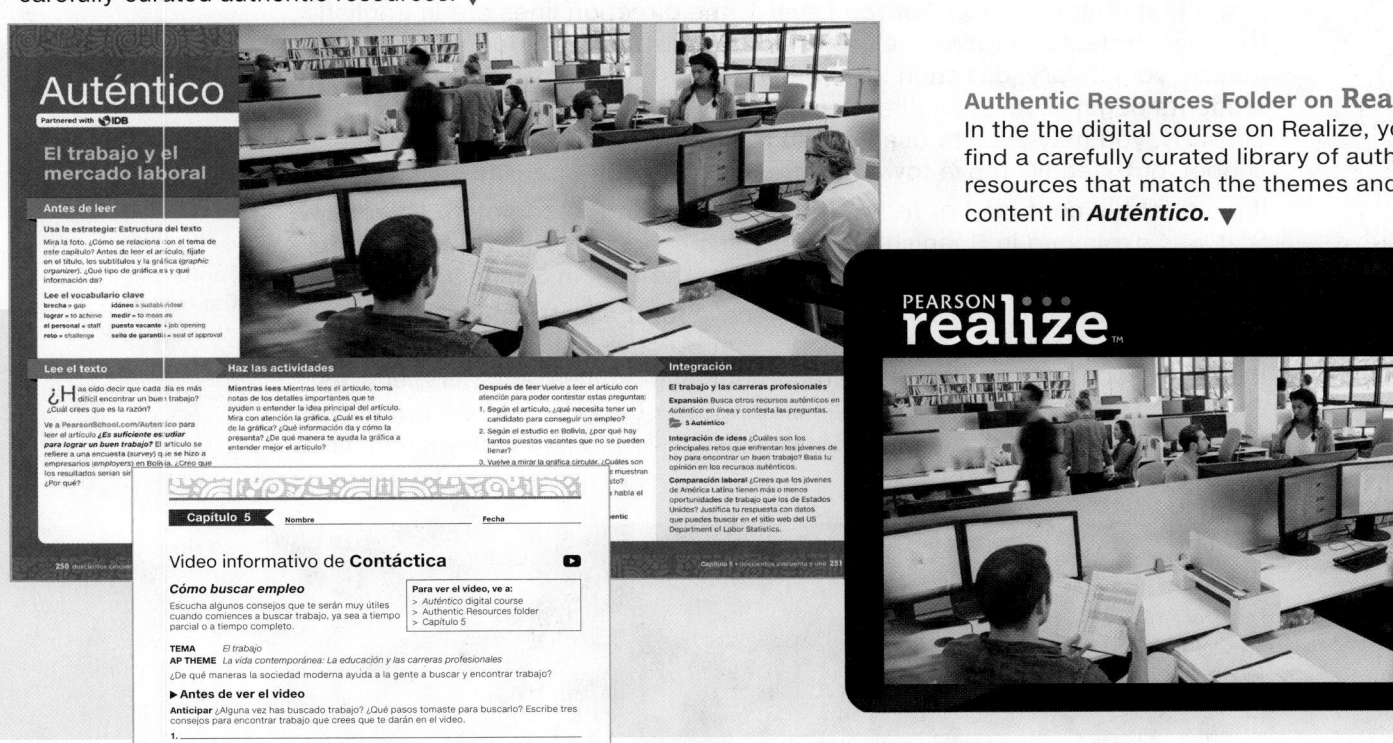

Authentic Resources Folder on Realize In the the digital course on Realize, you'll find a carefully curated library of authentic resources that match the themes and content in *Auténtico.* ▼

◄ **Authentic Resources Workbook** The ***Authentic Resources Workbook*** offers two pages of activities for every resource in the Authentic Resources Library on Realize. These activities will prepare your students to watch the authentic video, listen to the audio, or read the authentic reading selection. Activities help students focus their attention on key elements of the video, audio, or text. Post-viewing, post-listening, and post-reading activities check comprehension.

Reaching 90% Spanish in the Classroom

The goal of most Spanish teachers is to get students speaking Spanish in the classroom so that students will develop the language proficiency and cultural understanding necessary to use the language beyond the classroom. This is a challenging goal to meet, especially in the earliest stages of language learning. Here are some strategies to help you and your students spend as much of your instructional time as possible speaking Spanish.

Use English Strategically

• At the beginning of the year, set an expectation as to when English will be allowed in the classroom. As students develop their vocabulary and improve their fluency, reset expectations. Students can be expected to rely less on English in Levels 2 and 3 than they do at the beginning of Level 1.

• Present the Lesson Objectives and the standards that will be taught in the lesson in English so students have a clear idea of the expectations. Also review lesson objectives/standards at end of each class to make sure goals were met.

• In the first chapters of **Auténtico** Level 1, the direction lines are in English to allow students to focus their attention on the task. As students acquire a basic vocabulary, direction lines begin to shift to Spanish. By the time students begin Level 2, all direction lines for activities are in Spanish. Similarly, you may wish to use English to set the task in the first few weeks of school, but steadily move toward more instruction in Spanish.

• If a student is confused or frustrated and struggling to complete an activity that was explained in Spanish, using English may decrease frustration and help the student be more receptive to doing the task in Spanish.

• Consider when using English is more effective for the instructional goal, for example, when learning about concepts that go beyond the language level of the class, such as discussing cultural products, practices, and perspectives. Encourage students to use the Spanish language they know to describe a piece or art or a type of food, but allow English discussion for higher level concepts.

Use strategies that help students access the content

- Focus on the chapter communicative objectives and the key phrases in the chapter vocabulary that support those objectives. For example: A Chapter 1A objective is: Talk and write about what you and others like to do. The key phrases from Chapter 1A vocabulary to meet that goal are:

    ¿Qué te gusta hacer?

    ¿A mí (no) me gusta....?

    ¿Y a tí?

- These key phrases are used to present the vocabulary lexically in each chapter, and are repeated in the *Vocabulario en uso* activities. They help guide students in communicating in Spanish right from the start of each chapter.
- Use gestures and body language to help communication.
- Speak slowly and simplify.
- Read the models aloud with students or show the *Videomodelos.*
- Use the video and audio program for listening exercises so students become accustomed to hearing and understanding different Spanish speakers.
- Repeat key phrases.
- Restate things in different ways.
- Provide visual support for your instruction.
- Use simple familiar phrases when possible.
- Use cognates.
- Encourage personalization and student use of language.
- Check often for understanding.
- Use the *En voz alta* feature to have students explore authentic poetry and song lyrics.

Provide students with the support they need to keep classroom conversation in Spanish

- Start the year with the *Para empezar* chapter. It provides a quick review of key vocabulary and grammar.

- Write key phrases or sentence frames that link to the objectives on the board.
- Post word walls and language ladders to help students with reminders of language they can use to negotiate meaning with each other.
- Write sentence starters on the board for challenging activities.
- Use the Differentiated Instruction suggestions in the Teacher's Edition to tailor activities to students' learning needs so students can complete tasks at their proficiency level.
- Create word walls with the *Expresiones útiles para conversar* in the back of the Student Edition so that students can refer to these expressions during conversations.
- Use frequent comprehension checks.
- Teach key words for comprehension checks – *¿Comprenden? ¿Verdad? ¿Están de acuerdo?*
- Model ways students can ask for clarification or help.

Assign tasks that require English as homework

- Assign vocabulary and grammar presentations and receptive practice activities as homework so that class time is free for communicative activities.
- Have students read the *Presentación oral* assignment the night before they do the work together in class. Provide language ladders on the wall or on the whiteboard to provide students with the language they need to negotiate who is playing each role and other discussions around the task.

Use technology to provide additional support

- Assign the grammar explanations in the textbook or online course as homework. Ask students to read the explanations then watch the Grammar Tutorial Videos. When students come to class, you can briefly review the grammar in Spanish or have students work immediately on the communicative grammar activities.
- Use the Interactive Whiteboard activities to present the *Vocabulario en contexto.*
- Encourage students to use the online flashcards and games at home for vocabulary practice.

Integrating 21st Century Skills in the Spanish Classroom

Spanish teachers recognize the need for students to interact effectively with the many Spanish speakers in the United States and across the globe. Today's world languages curriculum and instruction are based upon the 5Cs (Communication, Cultures, Connections, Comparisons, and Communities) with the goal of building communicative proficiency and cultural understanding. World languages learners are 21st Century Learners. However, as today's students enter into an increasingly global economy, it is important that they have a diverse range of skills to succeed. The Partnership for 21st Century Skills, a national organization that advocates for 21st century readiness for every student, has developed a Framework for 21st Century Learning. This document fuses the traditional 3Rs with what they call the 4Cs:

• Critical thinking and problem solving

• Communication

• Collaboration

• Creativity and innovation

World Languages 21st Century Skills Map

The American Council on the Teaching of Foreign Languages (ACTFL) has worked with the Partnership for 21st Century Skills to create a 21st Century Skills Map that describes the integration of World Languages and 21st Century Skills. This map provides concrete examples of how 21st Century Skills can be integrated into all world language classrooms.

By combining the 5Cs of the ACTFL World-Readiness Standards for Learning Languages with the 4Cs from the Partnership for 21st Century Skills, world languages teachers now have a unique opportunity. As schools, districts, and states expand assessment and instruction to focus on 21st Century Skills, we can further prepare students for their future. The 4Cs can be seamlessly integrated on a daily basis within the world languages classroom.

Auténtico and the 21st Century World Languages Classroom

Teachers using *Auténtico* will easily be able to integrate 21st Century Skills into daily instruction due to the series' pedagogical framework, the alignment of assessment and instruction, and the integration of print and digital resources. In *Auténtico*:

• Each chapter is built around thematic instruction based upon real-world tasks and authentic sources.

• Instruction is learner-centered; students take responsibility for the learning and creation of new content.

• Technology is integrated with instruction and assessment to support and enhance learning.

• Instruction and assessment are differentiated to meet the needs of individual learners.

• Assessment is focused on what students can do with the language; students know what they will be asked to do and how they will be assessed.

• Instruction and assessment of culture focuses on the relationship between the products, practices, and perspectives of the target culture as well as comparisons between cultures.

• Students explore opportunities to use the language outside of the classroom.

Auténtico and the 4 Cs

Auténtico provides a wide range of resources, activities, and assessments that support the 4Cs. At the beginning of each Tema in the Teacher's Edition for Levels 1–3, the "b" page contains a chart with recommended activities and assessments in each chapter that build the skills outlined on the 21st Century Skills Map for World Languages.

For further information about the Partnership for 21st Century Skills, please visit their Web site: www.p21.org.

AUTÉNTICO prepares your students for success on the College Board's AP Spanish Language and Culture Examination.

Each chapter of the Student Edition features academically challenging Integration activities that require students to integrate ideas from multiple authentic sources. ▼

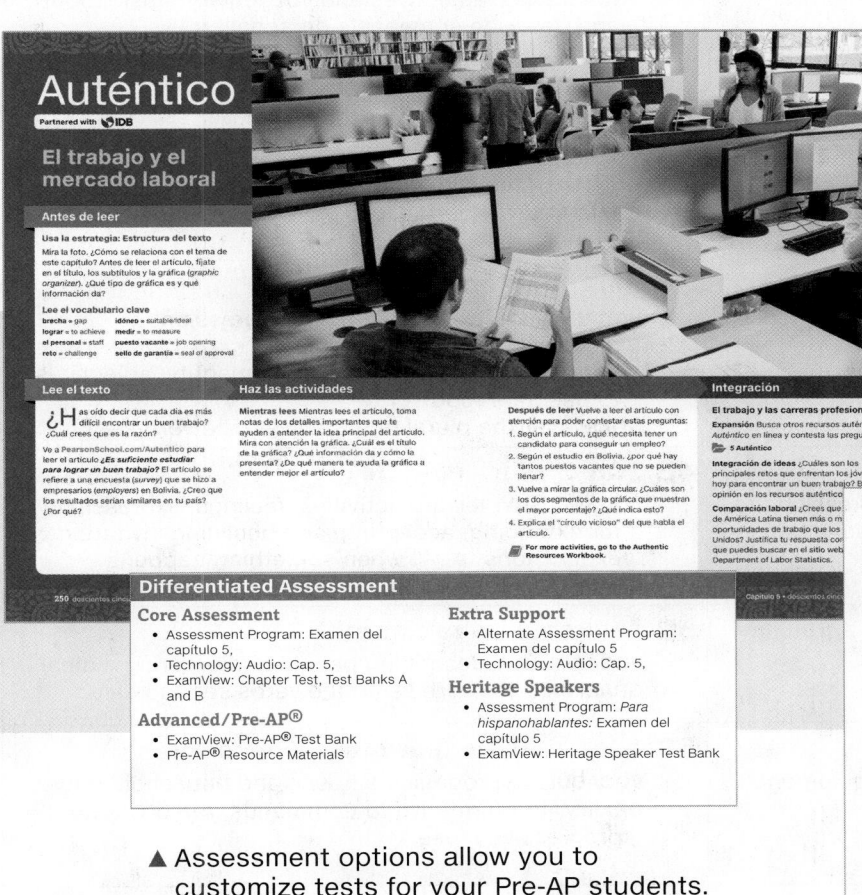

Differentiation suggestions and Pre-AP Integration ideas are included throughout the Teacher's Edition. ▼

Differentiated Instruction

Students with Learning Difficulties

Before playing the audio selection for *Actividad* 6, help students preview some of the target language for which they will be listening. Discuss the illustration with them. Point out and briefly describe the characters, and invite students to add details.

Challenge/Pre-AP®

Some students may enjoy creating informal quizzes and exercises for other students. Monitor their work carefully for spelling, grammar, and punctuation. Help them write clear and concise instructions, and teach them over time to make their activities neither too difficult nor too easy for their peers.

Pre-AP® Integration

- **Learning Objective:** Interpersonal Speaking
- **Activity:** Have pairs of students prepare and present mini-dialogues. One partner plays the role of an applicant and asks questions about the job. The other plays the prospective employer and answers the questions.
- **Pre-AP® Resource Materials:** Comprehensive guide to Pre-AP® vocabulary skill development

Differentiated Assessment

Core Assessment
- Assessment Program: Examen del capítulo 5,
- Technology: Audio: Cap. 5,
- ExamView: Chapter Test, Test Banks A and B

Advanced/Pre-AP®
- ExamView: Pre-AP® Test Bank
- Pre-AP® Resource Materials

Extra Support
- Alternate Assessment Program: Examen del capítulo 5
- Technology: Audio: Cap. 5,

Heritage Speakers
- Assessment Program: *Para hispanohablantes:* Examen del capítulo 5
- ExamView: Heritage Speaker Test Bank

▲ Assessment options allow you to customize tests for your Pre-AP students.

Interpretive: Reading

Teaching students to read in Spanish presents a unique challenge. For many students, reading is a difficult exercise in decoding and translating. It is important to teach students to read for overall meaning from the very beginning, and to avoid trying to translate every word. Do not develop or use activities that require them to extract every minute detail from the reading. Instead, point out to them that a global understanding is sufficient at first. As their reading fluency develops, they become better prepared to take on a passage for a deeper understanding. Once they are equipped with the right strategies to master texts at their reading level, they will want to read for enjoyment or information. Practice will result in fluency, which will help students advance their reading level. For success on the interpretive reading section of the AP® Exam, students must be able to know the content and vocabulary, but they must also have strong strategies to apply to material that may be above their reading level. Therefore, your two main goals as a teacher should be to instill useful strategies in students' reading practices and to promote fluency to make reading Spanish less intimidating for them.

are focusing on a developing plot and characters, while in the other they are looking to gain factual information. Students may have already been taught about various texts in their Language Arts classes, and may already be aware of how to treat each type of text. Remind them to use these practices in Spanish, too.

A third important factor in gauging how much students will comprehend from a given text is their background knowledge. When presenting students with a text (fiction or non-fiction), try to access the information that they already know. If you find that they are limited in background knowledge for a particular text, be sure to provide them with comprehensible information that they can use to better understand the text.

Finally, it is recommended that you carefully examine a reading selection prior to presenting it to the class. This way, you can choose to focus on a selected set of vocabulary and/or structures that are present in the reading. Make sure that students are familiar with the vocabulary and grammar in the reading. By using the vocabulary from the chosen text in other activities prior to doing the reading, students will feel less intimidated. The same is true for syntax. If a reading is particularly heavy with a certain type of structure, extract some samples of the structure from the reading and use them to practice the structure before doing the actual reading.

The Role of Pre-reading

Teaching Tips

Pre-reading at all levels
Regardless of the reading level of the assigned text or the students' abilities, it is always important to prepare them for what they will be reading. Use visuals around a text and the title of the passage to provide indications to students about the content of the passage.

Also, remind students to notice what type of text they are going to be working with, and encourage them to handle it appropriately. For example, students would not approach a short story with the same reading skills as they would an informational text. In one, they

Activities

Student Strategy
Encourage students to scan the last paragraph or sentence of a passage before they begin reading. By doing this, students can form expectations for the content of the text, which will help them focus more on the content when they do go back and read it.

Two possibilities
Have students read the last sentence or paragraph of any text you may assign to them. Based on what they read in that segment, have students conjecture two possible details about the body of the text. Ask them to write these

Pre-AP® Resource Book ▬ *Reading* **19**

Additional Pre-AP Resources on **Realize** ▶ feature thematic planning charts, teaching tips, a focus on pre-AP activities per chapter, and additional practice.

Scope and Sequence

TEMA	CAPÍTULO	
Para empezar	• En la escuela: greetings; introductions; leave-takings; numbers; time; body parts • En la clase: classroom, dates, asking for help • El tiempo: weather, seasons	
1 **Mis amigos y yo**	**1A ¿Qué te gusta hacer?** **VOCABULARY:** activities and expressions for saying what you like and don't like to do **GRAMMAR:** infinitives; making negative statements	**1B Y tú, ¿cómo eres?** **VOCABULARY:** adjectives and vocabulary to ask about and describe someone's personality **GRAMMAR:** adjectives; definite and indefinite articles; word order
2 **La escuela**	**2A Tu día en la escuela** **VOCABULARY:** classroom items and furniture; parts of the classroom; prepositions of location **GRAMMAR:** subject pronouns; the present tense of -ar verbs	**2B Tu sala de clases** **VOCABULARY:** classroom items and furniture; parts of the classroom; prepositions of location **GRAMMAR:** the verb estar; plurals of nouns and articles
3 **La comida**	**3A ¿Desayuno o almuerzo?** **VOCABULARY:** foods; beverages; adverbs of frequency; expressions to show surprise **GRAMMAR:** present tense of -er and -ir verbs; me gusta(n), me encanta(n)	**3B Para mantener la salud** **VOCABULARY:** food; beverages; expressions to discuss health; expressions to discuss preferences, agreement, disagreement, and quantity; adjectives to describe food **GRAMMAR:** the plural of adjectives; the verb ser
4 **Los pasatiempos**	**4A ¿Adónde vas?** **VOCABULARY:** leisure activities; places; expressions to tell where and with whom you go; expressions to talk about when things are done **GRAMMAR:** the verb ir; interrogative words	**4B ¿Quieres ir conmigo?** **VOCABULARY:** leisure activities; feelings; expressions for extending, accepting, and declining invitations; expressions to tell when something happens **GRAMMAR:** ir + a + infinitive; the verb jugar
5 **Fiesta en familia**	**5A Una fiesta de cumpleaños** **VOCABULARY:** family and parties **GRAMMAR:** the verb tener; possessive adjectives	**5B ¡Vamos a un restaurante!** **VOCABULARY:** describing people and ordering a meal **GRAMMAR:** the verb venir; the verbs ser and estar
6 **La casa**	**6A En mi dormitorio** **VOCABULARY:** bedroom items; electronic equipment; colors; adjectives to describe things **GRAMMAR:** comparisons and superlatives; stem-changing verbs: poder and dormir	**6B ¿Cómo es tu casa?** **VOCABULARY:** rooms in a house and household chores **GRAMMAR:** affirmative tú commands; the present progressive tense
7 **De compras**	**7A ¿Cuánto cuesta?** **VOCABULARY:** clothing; shopping; numbers 200–1,000 **GRAMMAR:** stem-changing verbs: pensar, querer, and preferir; demonstrative adjectives	**7B ¡Qué regalo!** **VOCABULARY:** places to shop; gifts; accessories; buying and selling **GRAMMAR:** preterite of -ar, -car, and -gar verbs; direct object pronouns lo, la, los, las
8 **Experiencias**	**8A De vacaciones** **VOCABULARY:** vacation places; activities; modes of transportation **GRAMMAR:** preterite of -er and -ir verbs; preterite of ir; the personal a	**8B Ayudando en la comunidad** **VOCABULARY:** recycling and volunteer work; places in a community **GRAMMAR:** the verb decir; indirect object pronouns; preterite of hacer and dar
9 **Medios de comunicación**	**9A El cine y la televisión** **VOCABULARY:** television shows; movie genres; giving opinions **GRAMMAR:** acabar de + infinitive; gustar and similar verbs	**9B La tecnología** **VOCABULARY:** computers; communication; computer-related activities **GRAMMAR:** the verbs pedir and servir; saber and conocer

AUTÉNTICO A covers the same content as the *Para empezar* section and *Temas* 1–4.

TEMA	CAPÍTULO	
Para empezar	• En la escuela: greetings; introductions; leave-takings; numbers; time; body parts • En la clase: classroom, dates, asking for help • El tiempo: weather, seasons	
1 **Mis amigos y yo**	**1A ¿Qué te gusta hacer?** **VOCABULARY:** activities and expressions for saying what you like and don't like to do **GRAMMAR:** infinitives; making negative statements	**1B Y tú, ¿cómo eres?** **VOCABULARY:** adjectives and vocabulary to ask about and describe someone's personality **GRAMMAR:** adjectives; definite and indefinite articles; word order
2 **La escuela**	**2A Tu día en la escuela** **VOCABULARY:** classroom items and furniture; parts of the classroom; prepositions of location **GRAMMAR:** subject pronouns; the present tense of *-ar* verbs	**2B Tu sala de clases** **VOCABULARY:** classroom items and furniture; parts of the classroom; prepositions of location **GRAMMAR:** the verb *estar*; plurals of nouns and articles
3 **La comida**	**3A ¿Desayuno o almuerzo?** **VOCABULARY:** foods; beverages; adverbs of frequency; expressions to show surprise **GRAMMAR:** present tense of *-er* and *-ir* verbs; *me gusta(n), me encanta(n)*	**3B Para mantener la salud** **VOCABULARY:** food; beverages; expressions to discuss health; expressions to discuss preferences, agreement, disagreement, and quantity; adjectives to describe food **GRAMMAR:** the plural of adjectives; the verb *ser*
4 **Los pasatiempos**	**4A ¿Adónde vas?** **VOCABULARY:** leisure activities; places; expressions to tell where and with whom you go; expressions to talk about when things are done **GRAMMAR:** the verb *ir;* interrogative words	**4B ¿Quieres ir conmigo?** **VOCABULARY:** leisure activities; feelings; expressions for extending, accepting, and declining invitations; expressions to tell when something happens **GRAMMAR:** *ir + a* + infinitive; the verb *jugar*

AUTÉNTICO B provides a review section called *Para empezar* and continues with *Temas* 5–9.

TEMA	CAPÍTULO	
5 **Fiesta en familia**	**5A Una fiesta de cumpleaños** **VOCABULARY:** family and parties **GRAMMAR:** the verb *tener;* possessive adjectives	**5B ¡Vamos a un restaurante!** **VOCABULARY:** describing people and ordering a meal **GRAMMAR:** the verb *venir;* the verbs *ser* and *estar*
6 **La casa**	**6A En mi dormitorio** **VOCABULARY:** bedroom items; electronic equipment; colors; adjectives to describe things **GRAMMAR:** comparisons and superlatives; stem-changing verbs: *poder* and *dormir*	**6B ¿Cómo es tu casa?** **VOCABULARY:** rooms in a house and household chores **GRAMMAR:** affirmative *tú* commands; the present progressive tense
7 **De compras**	**7A ¿Cuánto cuesta?** **VOCABULARY:** clothing; shopping; numbers 200–1,000 **GRAMMAR:** stem-changing verbs: *pensar, querer,* and *preferir;* demonstrative adjectives	**7B ¡Qué regalo!** **VOCABULARY:** places to shop; gifts; accessories; buying and selling **GRAMMAR:** preterite of *-ar, -car,* and *-gar* verbs; direct object pronouns *lo, la, los, las*
8 **Experiencias**	**8A De vacaciones** **VOCABULARY:** vacation places; activities; modes of transportation **GRAMMAR:** preterite of *-er* and *-ir* verbs; preterite of *ir;* the personal *a*	**8B Ayudando en la comunidad** **VOCABULARY:** recycling and volunteer work; places in a community **GRAMMAR:** the verb *decir;* indirect object pronouns; preterite of *hacer* and *dar*
9 **Medios de comunicación**	**9A El cine y la televisión** **VOCABULARY:** television shows; movie genres; giving opinions **GRAMMAR:** *acabar de* + infinitive; gustar and similar verbs	**9B La tecnología** **VOCABULARY:** computers; communication; computer-related activities **GRAMMAR:** the verbs *pedir* and *servir; saber* and *conocer*

Scope and Sequence

AUTÉNTICO 2

Auténtico 2 uses a recursive Scope and Sequence that revisits the themes from *Auténtico A, B,* or *1.* This natural recycling allows for important review and reteaching. In addition, students expand their vocabulary, grammar, and cultural understanding as they revisit each theme in greater depth.

TEMA	CAPÍTULO	
Para empezar	**A. ¿Cómo eres tú?** *Repaso:* describing people; asking for information; nationalities; adjective agreement; the verb *ser* **B. ¿Qué haces?** t*Repaso:* leisure activities; seasons of the year; regular *-ar, -er,* and *-ir* verbs	
1 **Tu día escolar**	**1A ¿Qué haces en la escuela?** **VOCABULARY:** classroom items, activities, and rules **GRAMMAR:** *(Repaso)* stem-changing verbs; affirmative and negative words	**1B ¿Qué haces después de las clases?** **VOCABULARY:** extracurricular activities **GRAMMAR:** making comparisons; *(Repaso)* the verbs *saber* and *conocer; hace* + time expressions
2 **Un evento especial**	**2A ¿Cómo te preparas?** **VOCABULARY:** daily routines, getting ready for an event **GRAMMAR:** reflexive verbs; *(Repaso)* the verbs *ser* and *estar;* possessive adjectives *mío, tuyo, suyo*	**2B ¿Qué ropa compraste?** **VOCABULARY:** shopping vocabulary, prices, money **GRAMMAR:** *(Repaso)* the preterite of regular verbs; demonstrative adjectives
3 **Tú y tu comunidad**	**3A ¿Qué hiciste ayer?** **VOCABULARY:** running errands; locations in a downtown; items purchased **GRAMMAR:** *(Repaso)* direct object pronouns; the irregular preterite of the verbs *ir, ser, hacer, tener, estar, poder*	**3B ¿Cómo se va . . . ?** **VOCABULARY:** places in a city or town; driving terms; modes of transportation **GRAMMAR:** *(Repaso)* direct object pronouns: *me, te, nos;* irregular affirmative *tú* commands; *(Repaso)* present progressive: irregular forms
4 **Recuerdos del pasado**	**4A Cuando éramos niños** **VOCABULARY:** toys; play terms; describing children **GRAMMAR:** the imperfect tense: regular verbs and irregular verbs; *(Repaso)* indirect object pronouns	**4B Celebrando los días festivos** **VOCABULARY:** expressions describing etiquette; holiday and family celebrations **GRAMMAR:** the imperfect tense: describing a situation; reciprocal actions
5 **En las noticias**	**5A Un acto heroico** **VOCABULARY:** natural disasters; emergencies; rescues; heroes **GRAMMAR:** the imperfect tense: other uses; the preterite of the verbs *oír, leer, creer,* and *destruir*	**5B Un accidente** **VOCABULARY:** parts of the body; accidents; events in the emergency room **GRAMMAR:** the irregular preterites: *venir, poner; decir, traer;* the imperfect progressive and preterite
6 **La televisión y el cine**	**6A ¿Viste el partido en la televisión?** **VOCABULARY:** watching television programs; sporting events **GRAMMAR:** the preterite of *-ir* stem-changing verbs; other reflexive verbs	**6B ¿Qué película has visto?** **VOCABULARY:** movies; making a movie **GRAMMAR:** verbs that use indirect objects; the present perfect
7 **Buen provecho**	**7A ¿Cómo se hace la paella?** **VOCABULARY:** cooking expressions; food; appliances; following a recipe; giving directions in a kitchen **GRAMMAR:** negative *tú* commands; the impersonal *se*	**7B ¿Te gusta comer al aire libre?** **VOCABULARY:** camping and cookouts; food **GRAMMAR:** *Usted* and *ustedes* commands; uses of *por*
8 **Cómo ser un buen turista**	**8A Un viaje en avión** **VOCABULARY:** visiting an airport; planning a trip; traveling safely **GRAMMAR:** the present subjunctive; irregular verbs in the subjunctive	**8B Quiero que disfrutes de tu viaje** **VOCABULARY:** staying in a hotel; appropriate tourist behaviors; traveling in a foreign city **GRAMMAR:** the present subjunctive with impersonal expressions; the present subjunctive of stem-changing verbs
9 **¿Cómo será el futuro?**	**9A ¿Qué profesión tendrás?** **VOCABULARY:** professions; making plans for the future; earning a living **GRAMMAR:** the future tense; the future tense of irregular verbs	**9B ¿Qué haremos para mejorar el mundo?** **VOCABULARY:** environment; environmental issues and solutions **GRAMMAR:** the future tense: other irregular verbs; the present subjunctive with expressions of doubt

AUTÉNTICO 3

Auténtico 3 offers ten thought-provoking thematic chapters that integrate rich vocabulary groups and a thorough presentation of grammar. Chapter activities combine communication, culture, and cross-curricular content with authentic literature and poetry.

CAPÍTULO	Each thematic chapter is divided into two sections. Each of these sections (1 and 2) present and practice vocabulary and grammar.	
Para empezar	**1. Tu vida diaria** *Repaso:* daily routines; school life; leisure activities; present tense verbs; reflective verbs **2. Días especiales** *Repaso:* weekend activities; celebrations; special events; verbs like *gustar*: possessive adjectives	
	1	**2**
1 **Días inolvidables**	**VOCABULARY:** hiking objects, activities, and perils; weather **GRAMMAR:** *(Repaso)* preterite verbs with the spelling change *i–y; (Repaso)* preterite of irregular verbs; *(Repaso)* preterite of verbs with the spelling change *e–i* and *o–u*	**VOCABULARY:** getting ready for an athletic or academic competition; emotional responses to competition; awards and ceremonies **GRAMMAR:** *(Repaso)* the imperfect; uses of the imperfect
2 **¿Cómo te expresas?**	**VOCABULARY:** describing art and sculpture; tools for painting; describing what influences art **GRAMMAR:** *(Repaso)* the preterite vs. the imperfect; *estar* + participle	**VOCABULARY:** musical instruments; describing dance; describing drama **GRAMMAR:** *(Repaso) ser* and *estar;* verbs with special meanings in the preterite vs. the imperfect
3 **¿Qué haces para estar en forma?**	**VOCABULARY:** nutrition; illnesses and pains; medicine; habits for good health **GRAMMAR:** *(Repaso)* affirmative *tú* commands; *(Repaso)* affirmative and negative commands with *Ud.* and *Uds.*	**VOCABULARY:** exercises; getting and staying in shape; health advice **GRAMMAR:** *(Repaso)* the subjunctive: regular verbs; *(Repaso)* the subjunctive: irregular verbs; *(Repaso)* the subjunctive with stem changing *-ar* and *-er* verbs
4 **¿Cómo te llevas con los demás?**	**VOCABULARY:** personality traits; interpersonal behavior; friendship **GRAMMAR:** *(Repaso)* the subjunctive with verbs of emotion; *(Repaso)* the uses of *por* and *para*	**VOCABULARY:** expressing and resolving interpersonal problems; interpersonal relationships **GRAMMAR:** commands with *nosotros;* possessive pronouns
5 **Trabajo y comunidad**	**VOCABULARY:** after-school work; describing a job **GRAMMAR:** *(Repaso)* the present perfect; *(Repaso)* the past perfect	**VOCABULARY:** volunteer activities; the benefits and importance of volunteer work **GRAMMAR:** the present perfect subjunctive; demonstrative adjectives and pronouns
6 **¿Qué nos traerá en el futuro?**	**VOCABULARY:** jobs and professions; qualities of a good employee **GRAMMAR:** *(Repaso)* the future; *(Repaso)* the future of probability	**VOCABULARY:** technology; inventions; jobs in the future **GRAMMAR:** the future perfect; *(Repaso)* the use of direct and indirect object pronouns
7 **¿Mito o realidad?**	**VOCABULARY:** archaeological terms and activities; describing archaeological sites **GRAMMAR:** the present and past subjunctive in expressions of doubt	**VOCABULARY:** myths and legends; ancient beliefs; pre-Columbian scientific discoveries **GRAMMAR:** the subjunctive in adverbial clauses
8 **Encuentro entre culturas**	**VOCABULARY:** architecture and history of Spain **GRAMMAR:** the conditional	**VOCABULARY:** Spain in the Americas; the encounter between Cortés and the Aztecs; family heritage **GRAMMAR:** the past subjunctive; the past subjunctive with *si* clauses
9 **Cuidemos nuestro planeta**	**VOCABULARY:** caring for the environment **GRAMMAR:** present subjunctive with conjunctions (*mientras, tan pronto como,* etc.); relative pronouns *que, quien, lo que*	**VOCABULARY:** environmental issues; endangered animals **GRAMMAR:** present subjunctive with other conjunctions (*a menos que, sin que, para que,* etc.)
10 **¿Cuáles son tus derechos y responsabilidades?**	**VOCABULARY:** rights and responsibilties **GRAMMAR:** the passive voice: *ser* + past participle; the present vs. the past subjunctive	**VOCABULARY:** government; the role of government; individual rights **GRAMMAR:** the past perfect subjunctive; the conditional perfect

Program Components for Students

AUTÉNTICO The digital course puts the complete student edition, workbooks, audio, video, songs, flashcards, games, and more right at your students' fingertips.

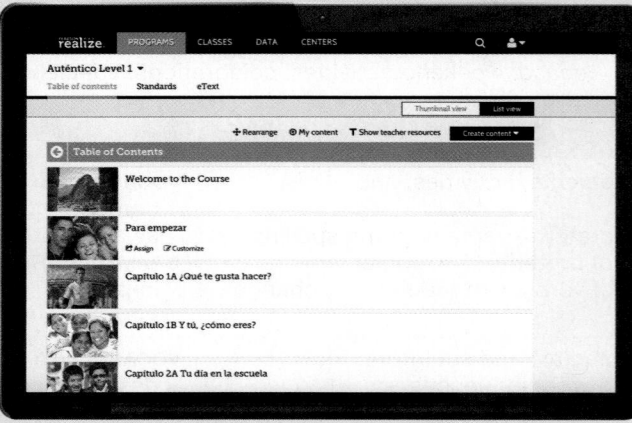

PEARSON realize™

The digital course on Realize!

The program's digital course on Realize puts engaging standards-aligned content, embedded assessments, instant data, and flexible tools at your fingertips.

📖 ETEXT 2.0
The complete interactive textbook online with audio and video files

📂 AUTÉNTICO
A folder of curated authentic resources that relate to each theme

🔊 AUDIO
Audio files for Student Edition, Communication Activities and *Canciones de hip hop*

▶ VIDEO
Videonovela *¡Pura vida!*

Videohistoria Vocabulary video to help present the new vocabulary

Grammar Tutorials Clear explanations of grammar with comparisons to English

Videodocumentario

 WORKBOOKS
Available in print and as part of the digital course on Realize

Leveled Vocabulary and Grammar Workbook
Part 1
Guided Workbook
Vocabulary clip art and study sheets
Step-by-step grammar activities
Simplified reading, speaking, and writing activities
Part 2
Core Workbook
Focused practice for vocabulary and grammar
End-of-chapter Crossword Puzzle and Organizer

Authentic Resources Workbook
Strategies to help students access the authentic materials
Key vocabulary lists for each resource
Pre- and post-viewing, reading, and listening activities

Literacy Skills Workbook
Standards-based skills practice
Two to three thematically linked readings per *Capítulo*

Also available as part of the digital course on **Realize:**
Flashcards, Communication Activities, Test Preparation, *Para hispanohablantes,* Grammar Study Guide, Games, *Mapa global interactivo*

Program Components for Teachers

A wide variety of planning, teaching, and assessment options for **AUTÉNTICO** are available in the print Teacher Edition and online at PearsonSchool.com/Autentico.

 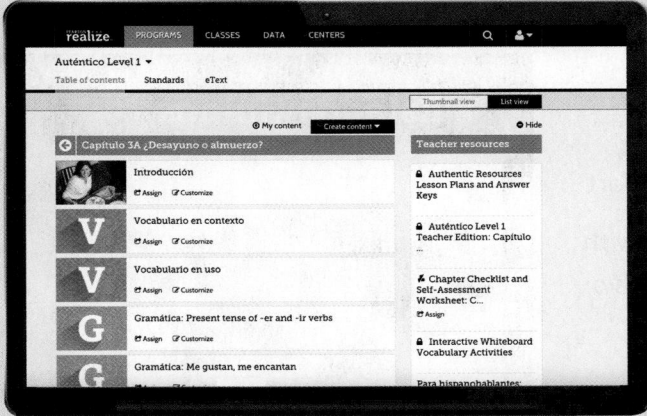

PLAN

Digital Teacher's Edition

Authentic Resources Lesson Plans

PDF Files of Student Resources

Pre-AP® Resource Materials

Para hispanohablantes Printable PDF Worksheets and Answer Key

Communicative Pair Activities

Project-based Learning for each *Tema* (Levels 1 and 2) or *Capítulo* (Level 3)

Situation Cards

School-to-Home Letters

Input Scripts

Vocabulary Clip Art

Audio and Video Scripts

Answer Keys for Workbooks and *Mapa global interactivo*

Editable Rubrics

PRESENT

Activities and Tools for Interactive Whiteboards for use with or without a SMART™ Interactive Whiteboard

Interactive practice activities for vocabulary and grammar

Teaching suggestions, extensions, and answers

Vocabulary images and clip art

Videohistoria Vocabulary presentation videos

Videomodelo Videos that model speaking tasks

¡Pura vida! Videonovela

Videodocumentario

Student Edition audio

ASSESS

Pruebas for Vocabulary Recognition (auto-graded)

Pruebas with remediation for Vocabulary Production and Grammar (auto-graded)

Examen del capítulo (auto- and teacher-graded)

Speak and Record Speaking Tasks: *Presentación oral, Examen del capítulo,* Integrated Performance Assessments

Alternate Assessment Program

Assessment Program for Heritage Speakers

Four editable test banks per chapter: two for core assessment, one for heritage speakers, one for Pre-AP® learners

Zip file of project and assessment rubrics

Assessment audio

Students get started in **AUTÉNTICO 3** with these colorful reference and introductory sections:

Mapas▶

Colorful atlas pages support geography skills. Students can explore more online with

 Mapa global interactivo

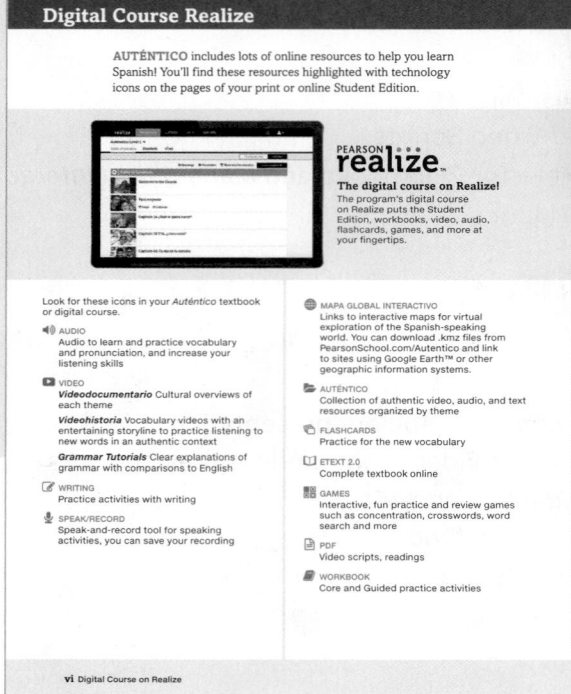

The Digital Course ▲

Students get a complete overview of the online resources available on the digital course on Realize.

◀ Using Authentic Resources

Students are introduced to the types of authentic resources that they will learn from in *Auténtico.*

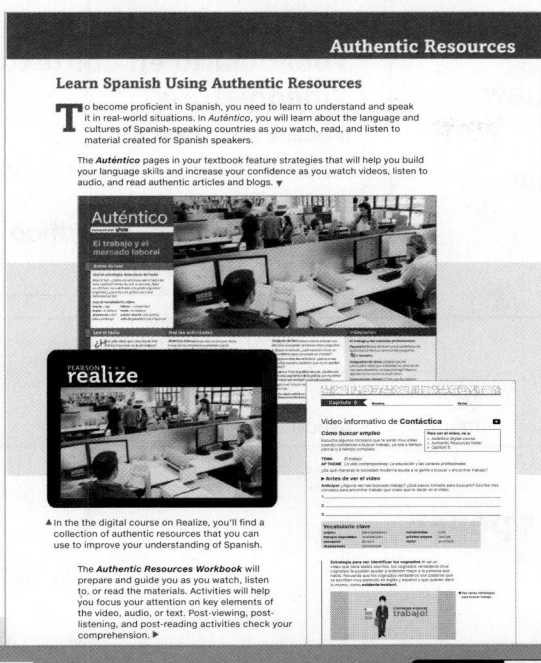

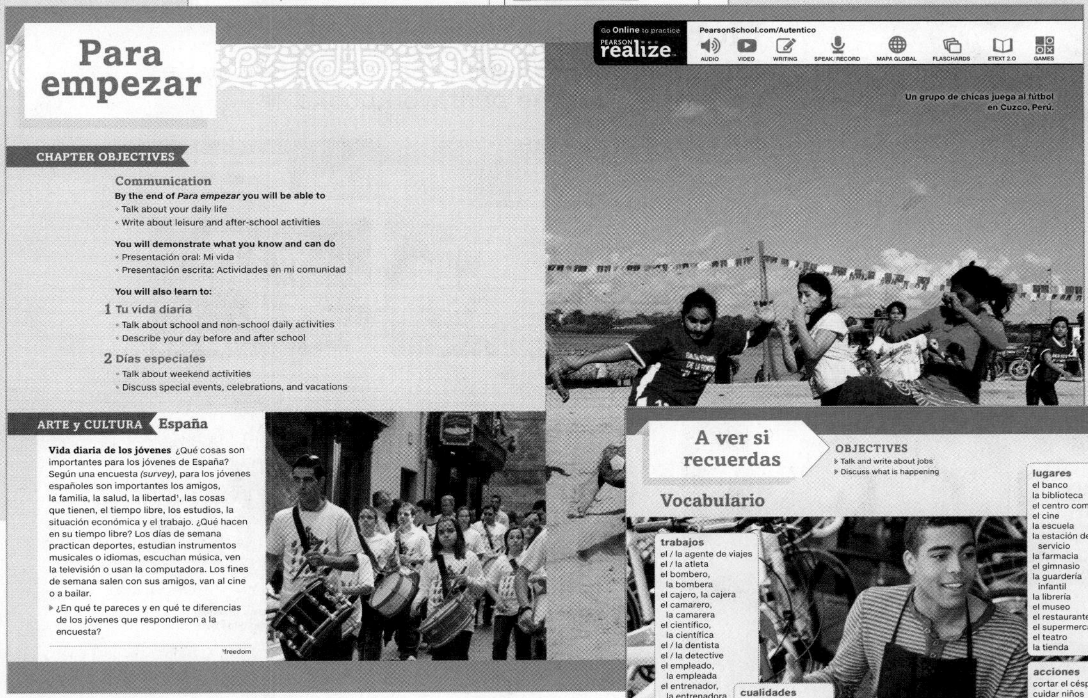

Learn Spanish Using Authentic Resources

To become proficient in Spanish, you need to learn to understand and speak it in real-world situations. In *Auténtico*, you will learn about the language and cultures of Spanish-speaking countries as you watch, read, and listen to material created for Spanish speakers.

The *Auténtico* pages in your textbook feature strategies that will help you build your language skills and increase your confidence as you watch videos, listen to audio, and read authentic articles and blogs. ▼

▲ In the the digital course on Realize, you'll find a collection of authentic resources that you can use to improve your understanding of Spanish.

The *Authentic Resources Workbook* will prepare and guide you as you watch, listen to, or read the materials. Activities will help you focus your attention on key elements of the video, audio, or text. Post-viewing, post-listening, and post-reading activities check your comprehension. ▶

Para empezar ▲

This bridge section gives students a quick review of key content from Level 2.

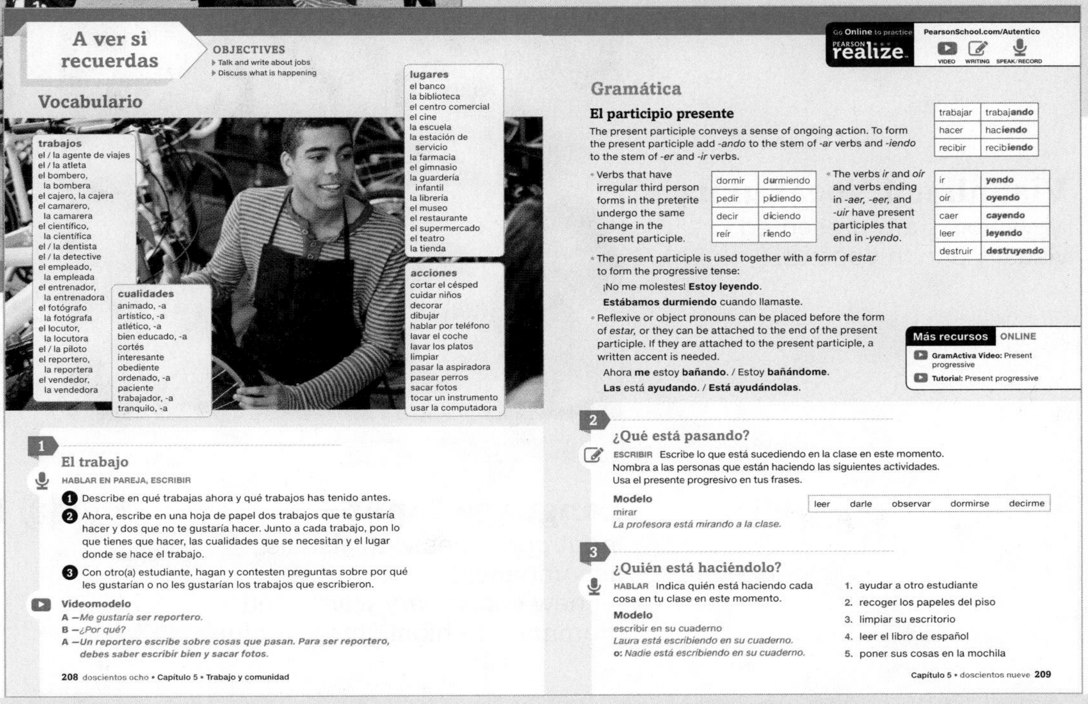

A ver si recuerdas ▶

This section helps students review the key vocabulary and grammar learned in first- and second-year Spanish as it relates to the themes for the upcoming chapter.

Para empezar

CHAPTER OBJECTIVES

Communication

By the end of *Para empezar* you will be able to
- Talk about your daily life
- Write about leisure and after-school activities

You will demonstrate what you know and can do
- Presentación oral: Mi vida
- Presentación escrita: Actividades en mi comunidad

You will also learn to:

1 Tu vida diaria
- Talk about school and non-school daily activities
- Describe your day before and after school

2 Días especiales
- Talk about weekend activities
- Discuss special events, celebrations, and vacations

ARTE y CULTURA ◀ España

Vida diaria de los jóvenes ¿Qué cosas son importantes para los jóvenes de España? Según una encuesta (*survey*), para los jóvenes españoles son importantes los amigos, la familia, la salud, la libertad¹, las cosas que tienen, el tiempo libre, los estudios, la situación económica y el trabajo. ¿Qué hacen en su tiempo libre? Los días de semana practican deportes, estudian instrumentos musicales o idiomas, escuchan música, ven la televisión o idiomas, escuchan música. Los fines de semana salen con sus amigos, van al cine o a bailar.

▶ ¿En qué te pareces y en qué te diferencias de los jóvenes que respondieron a la encuesta?

¹*freedom*

Un grupo de chicas juega al fútbol en Cuzco, Perú.

A ver si recuerdas

OBJECTIVES
- Talk and write about jobs
- Discuss what is happening

Vocabulario

trabajos
el / la agente de viajes
el / la atleta
el bombero, la bombera
el cajero, la cajera
el camarero, la camarera
el científico, la científica
el / la dentista
el / la detective
el empleado, la empleada
el entrenador, la entrenadora
el fotógrafo, la fotógrafa
el locutor, la locutora
el / la piloto
el reportero, la reportera
el vendedor, la vendedora

cualidades
animado, -a
artístico, -a
atlético, -a
bien educado, -a
cortés
interesante
obediente
ordenado, -a
paciente
trabajador, -a
tranquilo, -a

lugares
el banco
la biblioteca
el centro comercial
el cine
la escuela
la estación de servicio
la farmacia
el gimnasio
la guardería infantil
la librería
el museo
el restaurante
el supermercado
el teatro
la tienda

acciones
cortar el césped
cuidar niños
decorar
dibujar
hablar por teléfono
lavar el coche
lavar los platos
limpiar
pasar la aspiradora
pasear perros
sacar fotos
tocar un instrumento
usar la computadora

Gramática

El participio presente

The present participle conveys a sense of ongoing action. To form the present participle add *-ando* to the stem of *-ar* verbs and *-iendo* to the stem of *-er* and *-ir* verbs.

trabajar	trabaj**ando**
hacer	hac**iendo**
recibir	recib**iendo**

- Verbs that have irregular third person forms in the preterite undergo the same change in the present participle.

dormir	durmiendo
pedir	pidiendo
decir	diciendo
reír	riendo

- The verbs *ir* and *oír* and verbs ending in *-aer*, *-eer*, and *-uir* have present participles that end in *-yendo*.

ir	yendo
oír	oyendo
caer	cayendo
leer	leyendo
destruir	destruyendo

- The present participle is used together with a form of *estar* to form the progressive tense:

¡No me molestes! **Estoy leyendo.**

Estábamos durmiendo cuando llamaste.

- Reflexive or object pronouns can be placed before the form of *estar*, or they can be attached to the end of the present participle. If they are attached to the present participle, a written accent is needed.

Ahora **me estoy bañando.** / Estoy **bañándome.**

Las está ayudando. / Está **ayudándolas.**

Más recursos ONLINE
- **GramActiva Video:** Present progressive
- **Tutorial:** Present progressive

---

1 El trabajo

HABLAR EN PAREJA, ESCRIBIR

1 Describe en qué trabajas ahora y qué trabajos has tenido antes.

2 Ahora, escribe en una hoja de papel dos trabajos que te gustaría hacer y dos que no te gustaría hacer. Junto a cada trabajo, pon lo que tienes que hacer, las cualidades que se necesitan y el lugar donde se hace el trabajo.

3 Con otro(a) estudiante, hagan y contesten preguntas sobre por qué les gustarían o no les gustarían los trabajos que escribieron.

Videomodelo
A —Me gustaría ser reportero.
B —¿Por qué?
A —Un reportero escribe sobre cosas que pasan. Para ser reportero, debes saber escribir bien y sacar fotos.

2 ¿Qué está pasando?

ESCRIBIR Escribe lo que está sucediendo en la clase en este momento. Nombra a las personas que están haciendo las siguientes actividades. Usa el presente progresivo en tus frases.

Modelo
mirar
La profesora está mirando a la clase.

| leer | darle | observar | dormirse | decirme |

3 ¿Quién está haciéndolo?

HABLAR Indica quién está haciendo cada cosa en tu clase en este momento.

Modelo
escribir en su cuaderno
Laura está escribiendo en su cuaderno.
o: Nadie está escribiendo en su cuaderno.

1. ayudar a otro estudiante
2. recoger los papeles del piso
3. limpiar su escritorio
4. leer el libro de español
5. poner sus cosas en la mochila

Chapter Organization

Vocabulario en contexto and Videohistoria

This four-page section gives students a "first look" at the new vocabulary and grammar and focuses on the interpretive mode of communication through comprehensible input that integrates visuals and text with audio and video.

Chapter Sequence
- Vocabulario en contexto
- Videohistoria
- Vocabulario en uso
- Gramática y vocabulario en uso
- Cultura, Lectura, Presentaciones, Auténtico
- Repaso del capítulo

Go **Online** to practice
PEARSON realize™

PearsonSchool.com/Autentico

 AUDIO   VIDEO   WRITING  SPEAK/RECORD  MAPA GLOBAL   AUTÉNTICO   FLASHCARDS   ETEXT 2.0   GAMES

◀ **Chapter opener**
Capítulo 5

More Practice
Extra practice is available on the digital course on Realize or in the print workbooks. ▼

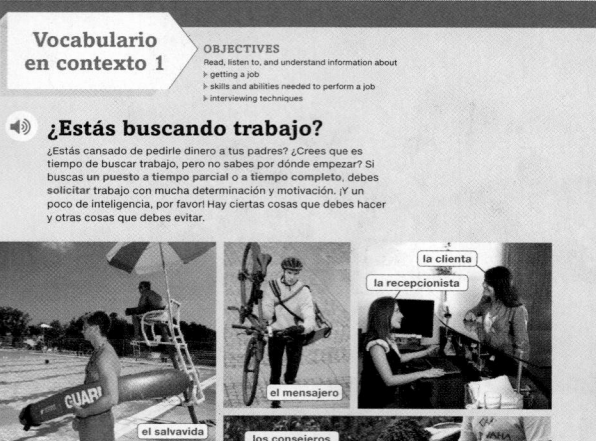

Visualized Vocabulary ▶
New words are presented visually and in context.

Language Input ▲
Input continues with visuals accompanied by narrative. All new vocabulary words and grammar are highlighted in **blue**.

◀)) **Listening Comprehension** ▲
Short interpretive listening activities check comprehension.

Reading and Language Input

The input of new vocabulary and grammar continues with an example of an interpersonal exchange in spoken or written conversation, followed by a short activity to check comprehension. ▼

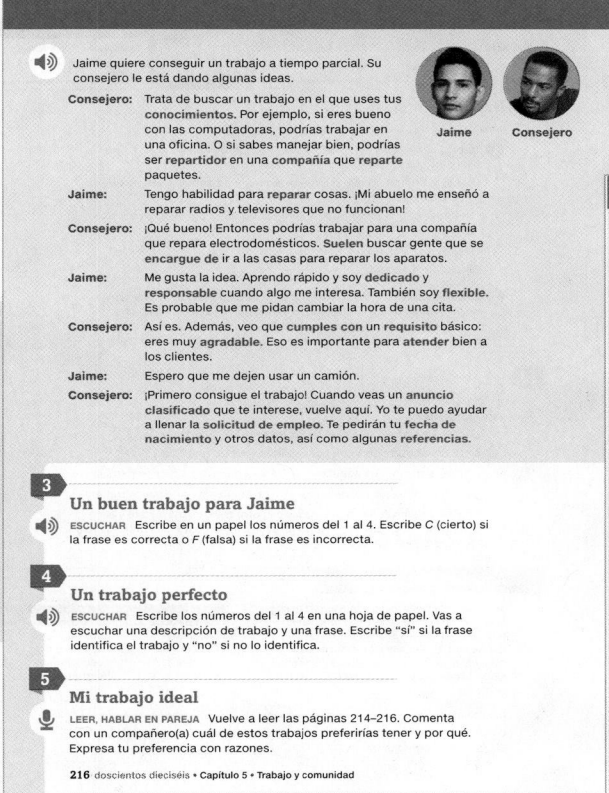

Jaime quiere conseguir un trabajo a tiempo parcial. Su consejero le está dando algunas ideas.

Consejero: Trata de buscar un trabajo en el que uses tus **conocimientos**. Por ejemplo, si eres bueno con las computadoras, podrías trabajar en una oficina. O si sabes manejar bien, podrías ser repartidor en una compañía que reparte paquetes.

Jaime: Tengo habilidad para reparar cosas. ¡Mi abuelo me enseñó a reparar radios y televisores que no funcionan!

Consejero: ¡Qué bueno! Entonces podrías trabajar para una compañía que repara electrodomésticos. Suelen buscar gente que se encargue de ir a las casas para reparar los aparatos.

Jaime: Me gusta la idea. Aprendo rápido y soy dedicado y responsable cuando algo me interesa. También soy flexible. Es probable que me pidan cambiar la hora de una cita.

Consejero: Así es. Además, veo que cumples con un requisito básico: eres muy agradable. Eso es importante para atender bien a los clientes.

Jaime: Espero que me dejen usar un camión.

Consejero: ¡Primero consigue el trabajo! Cuando veas un anuncio clasificado que te interese, vuelve aquí. Yo te puedo ayudar a llenar la solicitud de empleo. Te pedirán tu fecha de nacimiento y otros datos, así como algunas referencias.

3 Un buen trabajo para Jaime

ESCUCHAR Escribe en un papel los números del 1 al 4. Escribe C (cierto) si la frase es correcta o F (falsa) si la frase es incorrecta.

4 Un trabajo perfecto

ESCUCHAR Escribe los números del 1 al 4 en una hoja de papel. Vas a escuchar una descripción de trabajo y una frase. Escribe "sí" si la frase identifica el trabajo y "no" si no lo identifica.

5 Mi trabajo ideal

LEER, HABLAR EN PAREJA Vuelve a leer las páginas 214–216. Comenta con un compañero(a) cuál de estos trabajos preferirías tener y por qué. Expresa tu preferencia con razones.

216 doscientos dieciséis • Capítulo 5 • Trabajo y comunidad

Strategies

Pre-viewing and viewing strategies and activities help students access the content in the *Videohistoria.* Post-viewing activities check comprehension and encourage students to consider the cultural products, practices, and perspectives in the video. ▼

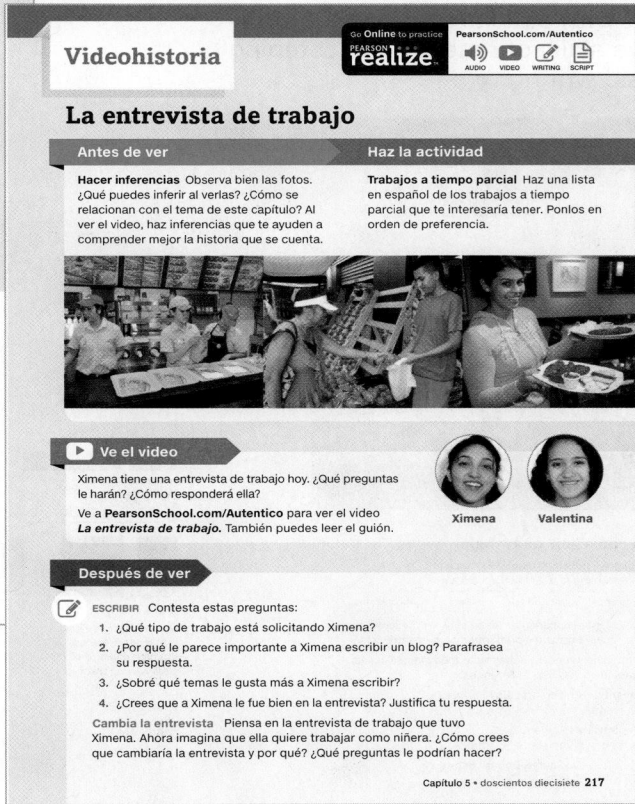

Go **Online** to practice   PearsonSchool.com/Autentico

PEARSON **realize**   AUDIO VIDEO WRITING SCRIPT

Videohistoria

La entrevista de trabajo

Antes de ver

Hacer inferencias Observa bien las fotos. ¿Qué puedes inferir al verlas? ¿Cómo se relacionan con el tema de este capítulo? Al ver el video, haz inferencias que te ayuden a comprender mejor la historia que se cuenta.

Haz la actividad

Trabajos a tiempo parcial Haz una lista en español de los trabajos a tiempo parcial que te interesaría tener. Ponlos en orden de preferencia.

Ve el video

Ximena tiene una entrevista de trabajo hoy. ¿Qué preguntas le harán? ¿Cómo responderá ella?

Ve a **PearsonSchool.com/Autentico** para ver el video *La entrevista de trabajo.* También puedes leer el guión.

Ximena   Valentina

Después de ver

ESCRIBIR Contesta estas preguntas:

1. ¿Qué tipo de trabajo está solicitando Ximena?
2. ¿Por qué le parece importante a Ximena escribir un blog? Parafrasea su respuesta.
3. ¿Sobré qué temas le gusta más a Ximena escribir?
4. ¿Crees que a Ximena le fue bien en la entrevista? Justifica tu respuesta.

Cambia la entrevista Piensa en la entrevista de trabajo que tuvo Ximena. Ahora imagina que ella quiere trabajar como niñera. ¿Cómo crees que cambiaría la entrevista y por qué? ¿Qué preguntas le podrían hacer?

Capítulo 5 • doscientos diecisiete **217**

▶ Videos and Language Input ▲

Students continue to develop their interpretive listening skills with the *Videohistoria.* Characters from Spanish-speaking families around the United States interact with each other, their local friends and family, and relatives throughout the Spanish-speaking world. The characters participate in video calls and share authentic content with each other online.

Chapter Organization

Vocabulario en uso and Gramática

Students begin to actively use the chapter's new vocabulary and grammar.

Chapter Sequence
- Vocabulario en contexto
- Videohistoria
- **Vocabulario en uso**
- **Gramática y vocabulario en uso**
- Cultura, Lectura, Presentaciones, Auténtico
- Repaso del capítulo

▶ **Videomodelo** Students can view videos that model the conversation.

🎤 **PAIRED STUDENTS** can record their conversations online!

Focused Practice
Students start with activities that focus on the interpretive skills of reading and listening and some basic writing. ▼

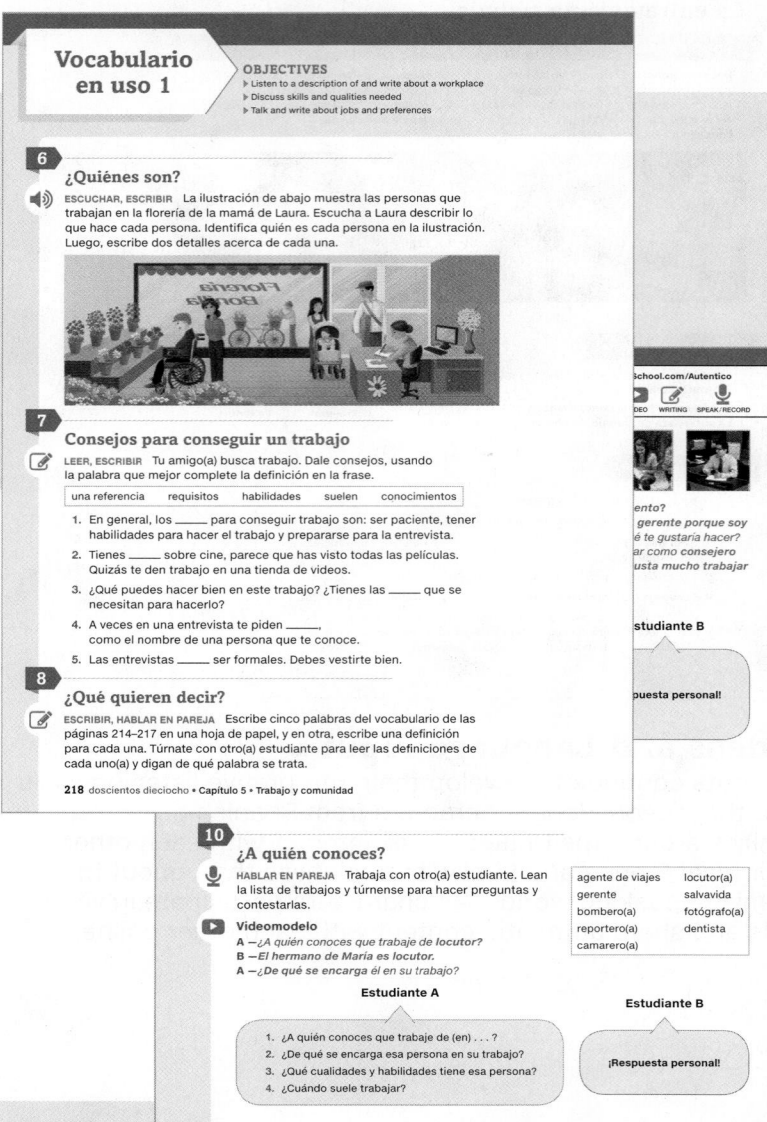

Vocabulario en uso 1

OBJECTIVES
▶ Listen to a description of and write about a workplace
▶ Discuss skills and qualities needed
▶ Talk and write about jobs and preferences

6 ¿Quiénes son?

🔊 ESCUCHAR, ESCRIBIR La ilustración de abajo muestra las personas que trabajan en la florería de la mamá de Laura. Escucha a Laura describir lo que hace cada persona. Identifica quién es cada persona en la ilustración. Luego, escribe dos detalles acerca de cada una.

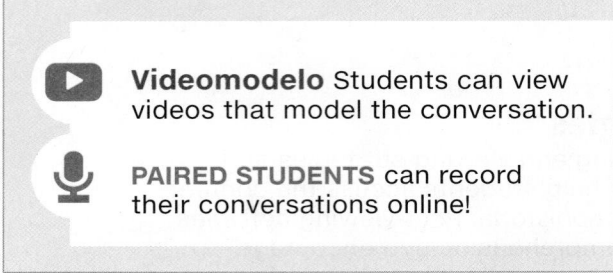

7 Consejos para conseguir un trabajo

📝 LEER, ESCRIBIR Tu amigo(a) busca trabajo. Dale consejos, usando la palabra que mejor complete la definición en la frase.

| una referencia | requisitos | habilidades | suelen | conocimientos |

1. En general, los _____ para conseguir trabajo son: ser paciente, tener habilidades para hacer el trabajo y prepararse para la entrevista.
2. Tienes _____ sobre cine, parece que has visto todas las películas. Quizás te den trabajo en una tienda de videos.
3. ¿Qué puedes hacer bien en este trabajo? ¿Tienes las _____ que se necesitan para hacerlo?
4. A veces en una entrevista te piden _____, como el nombre de una persona que te conoce.
5. Las entrevistas _____ ser formales. Debes vestirte bien.

8 ¿Qué quieren decir?

📝 ESCRIBIR, HABLAR EN PAREJA Escribe cinco palabras del vocabulario de las páginas 214–217 en una hoja de papel, y en otra, escribe una definición para cada una. Túrnate con otro(a) estudiante para leer las definiciones de cada uno(a) y digan de qué palabra se trata.

218 doscientos dieciocho • Capítulo 5 • Trabajo y comunidad

10 ¿A quién conoces?

🎤 HABLAR EN PAREJA Trabaja con otro(a) estudiante. Lean la lista de trabajos y túrnense para hacer preguntas y contestarlas.

▶ **Videomodelo**
A —¿A quién conoces que trabaje de locutor?
B —El hermano de María es locutor.
A —¿De qué se encarga él en su trabajo?

agente de viajes	locutor(a)
gerente	salvavida
bombero(a)	fotógrafo(a)
reportero(a)	dentista
camarero(a)	

Estudiante A
1. ¿A quién conoces que trabaje de (en) . . . ?
2. ¿De qué se encarga esa persona en su trabajo?
3. ¿Qué cualidades y habilidades tiene esa persona?
4. ¿Cuándo suele trabajar?

Estudiante B
¡Respuesta personal!

Capítulo 5 • doscientos diecinueve **219**

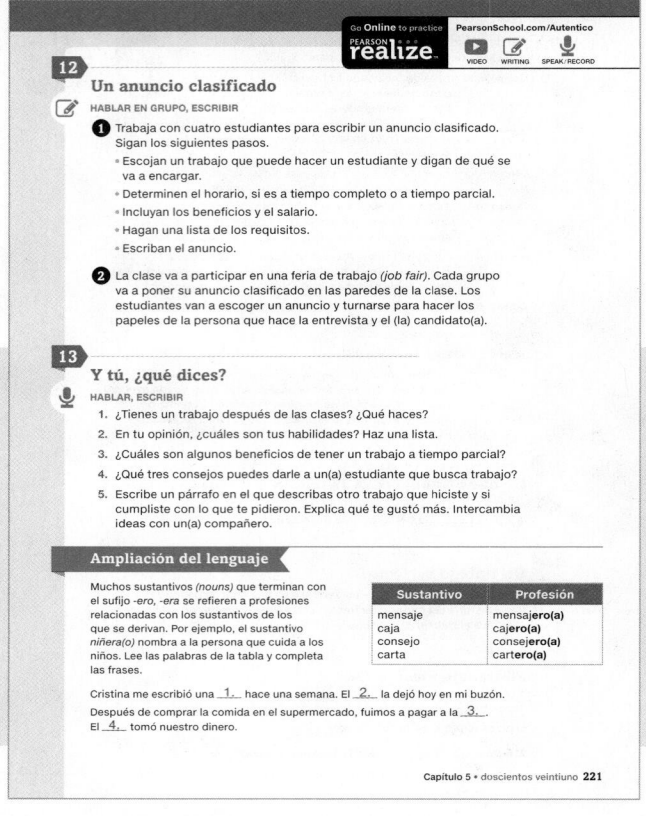

Go Online to practice PearsonSchool.com/Autentico
PEARSON **realize**
VIDEO WRITING SPEAK/RECORD

12 Un anuncio clasificado

📝 HABLAR EN GRUPO, ESCRIBIR

❶ Trabaja con cuatro estudiantes para escribir un anuncio clasificado. Sigan los siguientes pasos.
- Escojan un trabajo que puede hacer un estudiante y digan de qué se va a encargar.
- Determinen el horario, si es a tiempo completo o a tiempo parcial.
- Incluyan los beneficios y el salario.
- Hagan una lista de los requisitos.
- Escriban el anuncio.

❷ La clase va a participar en una feria de trabajo (job fair). Cada grupo va a poner su anuncio clasificado en las paredes de la clase. Los estudiantes van a escoger un anuncio y turnarse para hacer los papeles de la persona que hace la entrevista y el (la) candidato(a).

13 Y tú, ¿qué dices?

🎤 HABLAR, ESCRIBIR

1. ¿Tienes un trabajo después de las clases? ¿Qué haces?
2. En tu opinión, ¿cuáles son tus habilidades? Haz una lista.
3. ¿Cuáles son algunos beneficios de tener un trabajo a tiempo parcial?
4. ¿Qué tres consejos puedes darle a un(a) estudiante que busca trabajo?
5. Escribe un párrafo en el que describas otro trabajo que hiciste y si cumpliste con lo que te pidieron. Explica qué te gustó más. Intercambia ideas con un(a) compañero.

Ampliación del lenguaje

Muchos sustantivos (nouns) que terminan con el sufijo -ero, -era se refieren a profesiones relacionadas con los sustantivos de los que se derivan. Por ejemplo, el sustantivo niñera(o) nombra a la persona que cuida a los niños. Lee las palabras de la tabla y completa las frases.

Sustantivo	Profesión
mensaje	mensajero(a)
caja	cajero(a)
consejo	consejero(a)
carta	cartero(a)

Cristina me escribió una _1_ hace una semana. El _2_ la dejó hoy en mi buzón. Después de comprar la comida en el supermercado, fuimos a pagar a la _3_. El _4_ tomó nuestro dinero.

Capítulo 5 • doscientos veintiuno **221**

Personal Responses ▲
The sequence of exercises culminates with personalized speaking and writing activities.

◀ Interpersonal Practice
Students transition to paired practice activities that focus on the new vocabulary in the interpersonal mode of communication.

Grammar Integrated with Communication

The complete grammar presentation features clear explanations helping students to acquire accuracy of expression. ▼

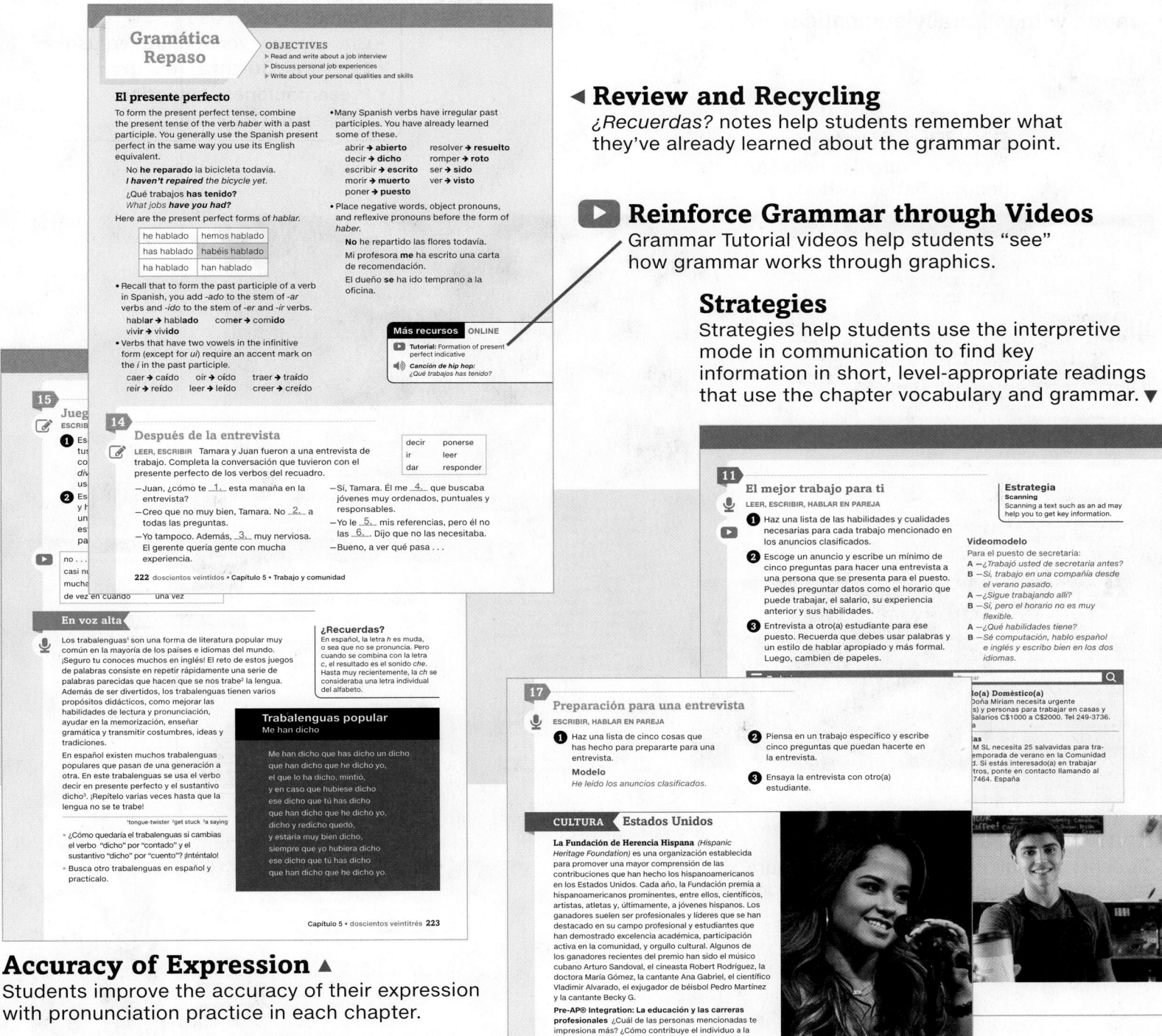

◄ Review and Recycling
¿Recuerdas? notes help students remember what they've already learned about the grammar point.

▶ Reinforce Grammar through Videos
Grammar Tutorial videos help students "see" how grammar works through graphics.

Strategies
Strategies help students use the interpretive mode in communication to find key information in short, level-appropriate readings that use the chapter vocabulary and grammar. ▼

Gramática Repaso

OBJECTIVES
▶ Read and write about a job interview
▶ Discuss personal job experiences
▶ Write about your personal qualities and skills

El presente perfecto

To form the present perfect tense, combine the present tense of the verb *haber* with a past participle. You generally use the Spanish present perfect in the same way you use its English equivalent.

No **he reparado** la bicicleta todavía.
I haven't repaired the bicycle yet.
¿Qué trabajos **has tenido?**
What jobs have you had?

Here are the present perfect forms of *hablar*.

he hablado	hemos hablado
has hablado	habéis hablado
ha hablado	han hablado

- Recall that to form the past participle of a verb in Spanish, you add *-ado* to the stem of *-ar* verbs and *-ido* to the stem of *-er* and *-ir* verbs.
  habl**ar** → habl**ado**   com**er** → com**ido**
  viv**ir** → viv**ido**
- Verbs that have two vowels in the infinitive form (except for *ui*) require an accent mark on the *i* in the past participle.
  caer → caído   oír → oído   traer → traído
  reír → reído   leer → leído   creer → creído

- Many Spanish verbs have irregular past participles. You have already learned some of these.

abrir → **abierto**	resolver → **resuelto**
decir → **dicho**	romper → **roto**
escribir → **escrito**	ser → **sido**
morir → **muerto**	ver → **visto**
poner → **puesto**	

- Place negative words, object pronouns, and reflexive pronouns before the form of *haber*.
  No he repartido las flores todavía.
  Mi profesora **me** ha escrito una carta de recomendación.
  El dueño **se** ha ido temprano a la oficina.

Más recursos ONLINE
▶ **Tutorial:** Formation of present perfect indicative
🔊 **Canción de hip hop:** *¿Qué trabajos has tenido?*

---

14 Después de la entrevista

LEER, ESCRIBIR Tamara y Juan fueron a una entrevista de trabajo. Completa la conversación que tuvieron con el presente perfecto de los verbos del recuadro.

decir	ponerse
ir	leer
dar	responder

—Juan, ¿cómo te __1__ esta mañana en la entrevista?
—Creo que no muy bien, Tamara. No __2__ a todas las preguntas.
—Yo tampoco. Además, __3__ muy nerviosa. El gerente quería gente con mucha experiencia.

—Sí, Tamara. Él me __4__ que buscaba jóvenes muy ordenados, puntuales y responsables.
—Yo le __5__ mis referencias, pero él no las __6__. Dijo que no las necesitaba.
—Bueno, a ver qué pasa . . .

222 doscientos veintidós • Capítulo 5 • Trabajo y comunidad

---

15 Jue...
ESCRIB...

① Es...
tu...
co...
div...
us...

② Es...
y h...
un...
es...
pa...

no . . .
casi n...
mucha...
de vez en cuando   una vez

En voz alta ◄

Los trabalenguas¹ son una forma de literatura popular muy común en la mayoría de los países e idiomas del mundo. ¡Seguro tú conoces muchos en inglés! El reto de estos juegos de palabras consiste en repetir rápidamente una serie de palabras parecidas que hacen que se nos trabe² la lengua. Además de ser divertidos, los trabalenguas tienen varios propósitos didácticos, como mejorar las habilidades de lectura y pronunciación, ayudar en la memorización, enseñar gramática y transmitir costumbres, ideas y tradiciones.

En español existen muchos trabalenguas populares que pasan de una generación a otra. En este trabalenguas se usa el verbo decir en presente perfecto y el sustantivo dicho³. ¡Repítelo varias veces hasta que la lengua no se te trabe!

¹tongue-twister ²get stuck ³a saying

- ¿Cómo quedaría el trabalenguas si cambias el verbo "dicho" por "contado" y el sustantivo "dicho" por "cuento"? ¡Inténtalo!
- Busca otro trabalenguas en español y practícalo.

¿Recuerdas?
En español, la letra *h* es muda, o sea que no se pronuncia. Pero cuando se combina con la letra *c*, el resultado es el sonido *che*. Hasta muy recientemente, la *ch* se consideraba una letra individual del alfabeto.

Trabalenguas popular
Me han dicho

Me han dicho que has dicho un dicho
que han dicho que he dicho yo,
el que lo ha dicho, mintió,
y en caso que hubiese dicho
ese dicho que tú has dicho
que han dicho que he dicho yo,
dicho y redicho quedó,
y estaría muy bien dicho,
siempre que yo hubiera dicho
ese dicho que tú has dicho
que han dicho que he dicho yo.

Capítulo 5 • doscientos veintitrés **223**

---

11 El mejor trabajo para ti

LEER, ESCRIBIR, HABLAR EN PAREJA

① Haz una lista de las habilidades y cualidades necesarias para cada trabajo mencionado en los anuncios clasificados.

② Escoge un anuncio y escribe un mínimo de cinco preguntas para hacer una entrevista a una persona que se presenta para el puesto. Puedes preguntar datos como el horario que puede trabajar, el salario, su experiencia anterior y sus habilidades.

③ Entrevista a otro(a) estudiante para ese puesto. Recuerda que debes usar palabras y un estilo de hablar apropiado y más formal. Luego, cambien de papeles.

Estrategia
Scanning
Scanning a text such as an ad may help you to get key information.

Videomodelo
Para el puesto de secretaria:
A —¿Trabajó usted de secretaria antes?
B —Sí, trabajo en una compañía desde el verano pasado.
A —¿Sigue trabajando allí?
B —Sí, pero el horario no es muy flexible.
A —¿Qué habilidades tiene?
B —Sé computación, hablo español e inglés y escribo bien en los dos idiomas.

---

17 Preparación para una entrevista

ESCRIBIR, HABLAR EN PAREJA

① Haz una lista de cinco cosas que has hecho para prepararte para una entrevista.

Modelo
He leído los anuncios clasificados.

② Piensa en un trabajo específico y escribe cinco preguntas que puedan hacerte en la entrevista.

③ Ensaya la entrevista con otro(a) estudiante.

o(a) Doméstico(a)
Doña Miriam necesita urgente
s) y personas para trabajar en casas y
Salarios C$1000 a C$2000. Tel 249-3736.

as
M SL necesita 25 salvavidas para tra-
emporada de verano en la Comunidad
d. Si estás interesado(a) en trabajar
tros, ponte en contacto llamando al
7464. España

CULTURA Estados Unidos

La Fundación de Herencia Hispana *(Hispanic Heritage Foundation)* es una organización establecida para promover una mayor comprensión de las contribuciones que han hecho los hispanoamericanos en los Estados Unidos. Cada año, la Fundación premia a hispanoamericanos prominentes, entre ellos, científicos, artistas, atletas y, últimamente, a jóvenes hispanos. Los ganadores suelen ser profesionales y líderes que se han destacado en su campo profesional y estudiantes que han demostrado excelencia académica, participación activa en la comunidad, y orgullo cultural. Algunos de los ganadores recientes del premio han sido el músico cubano Arturo Sandoval, el cineasta Robert Rodriguez, la doctora María Gómez, la cantante Ana Gabriel, el científico Vladimir Alvarado, el exjugador de béisbol Pedro Martínez y la cantante Becky G.

Pre-AP® Integration: La educación y las carreras profesionales ¿Cuál de las personas mencionadas te impresiona más? ¿Cómo contribuye el individuo a la sociedad hispana?

La cantante Becky G

224 doscientos veinticuatro • Capítulo 5 • Trabajo y comunidad

---

Accuracy of Expression ▲
Students improve the accuracy of their expression with pronunciation practice in each chapter.

Language and Culture ▶
Culture is woven together with language practice.

▲ Pre-AP Integration
Integration activities accompany the culture notes. These level-appropriate activities encourage students to think critically and to compare the culture being studied to their own.

Chapter Organization

Lectura

Students apply their language skills in the interpretive mode with culturally authentic readings.

Chapter Sequence
- Vocabulario en contexto
- Videohistoria
- Vocabulario en uso
- Gramática y vocabulario en uso
- **Lectura, Cultura, Integración**
- Presentaciones, Auténtico
- Repaso del capítulo

Reading Strategies

Reading strategies help students become better readers. ▼

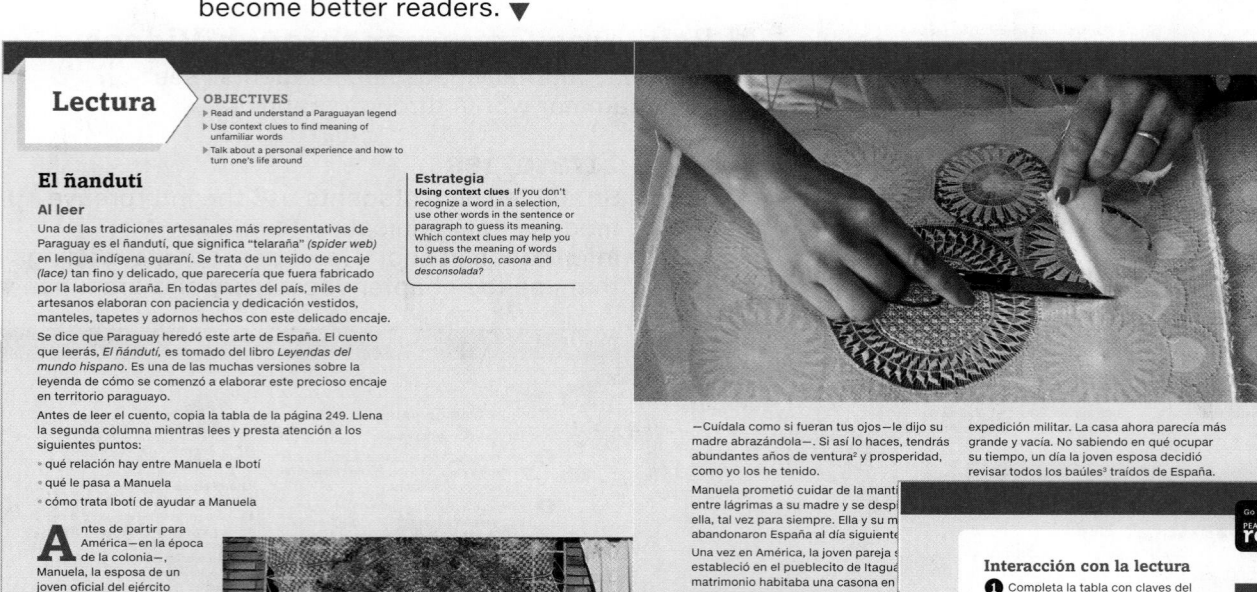

Lectura

OBJECTIVES
▸ Read and understand a Paraguayan legend
▸ Use context clues to find meaning of unfamiliar words
▸ Talk about a personal experience and how to turn one's life around

El ñandutí

Al leer

Una de las tradiciones artesanales más representativas de Paraguay es el ñandutí, que significa "telaraña" *(spider web)* en lengua indígena guaraní. Se trata de un tejido de encaje *(lace)* tan fino y delicado, que parecería que fuera fabricado por la laboriosa araña. En todas partes del país, miles de artesanos elaboran con paciencia y dedicación vestidos, manteles, tapetes y adornos hechos con este delicado encaje.

Se dice que Paraguay heredó este arte de España. El cuento que leerás, *El ñandutí*, es tomado del libro *Leyendas del mundo hispano*. Es una de las muchas versiones sobre la leyenda de cómo se comenzó a elaborar este precioso encaje en territorio paraguayo.

Antes de leer el cuento, copia la tabla de la página 249. Llena la segunda columna mientras lees y presta atención a los siguientes puntos:

- qué relación hay entre Manuela e Ibotí
- qué le pasa a Manuela
- cómo trata Ibotí de ayudar a Manuela

Estrategia

Using context clues If you don't recognize a word in a selection, use other words in the sentence or paragraph to guess its meaning. Which context clues may help you to guess the meaning of words such as *doloroso, casona* and *desconsolada?*

A ntes de partir para América—en la época de la colonia—, Manuela, la esposa de un joven oficial del ejército español destinado al Paraguay, fue a decir adiós a su madre. El encuentro fue muy doloroso, pues no sabían si volverían a verse en vida. Entre las muchas cosas que la madre le dio en aquella ocasión para su nuevo hogar, había una de especial belleza: una mantilla[1] de un encaje exquisito.

[1]lace scarf

246 doscientos cuarenta y seis • Capítulo 5 • Trabajo y comunidad

—Cuídala como si fueran tus ojos—le dijo su madre abrazándola—. Si así lo haces, tendrás abundantes años de ventura[2] y prosperidad, como yo los he tenido.

Manuela prometió cuidar de la manti[...] entre lágrimas a su madre y se despi[...] ella, tal vez para siempre. Ella y su m[...] abandonaron España al día siguiente[...]

Una vez en América, la joven pareja s[...] estableció en el pueblecito de Itagua[...] matrimonio habitaba una casona en [...] del pueblo. Al poco de su llegada, er[...] vivir con ellos una muchacha guaran[...] Ibotí ayudaría a Manuela con las tare[...] casa. Pronto nació entre ambas muje[...] amistad sincera y un cariño profundo[...] el corazón bañado de nostalgia, Mar[...] de la muchacha su confidente. Se se[...] las dos en el patio al atardecer, a la s[...] de algún árbol, y Manuela abría su al[...] recuerdos. Le hablaba a Ibotí de su p[...] de su madre. ¡Qué gran consuelo era[...] poder desahogar de esa manera el c[...]

En cierta ocasión, el marido de Man[...] que ausentarse del hogar, con motiv[...]

expedición militar. La casa ahora parecía más grande y vacía. No sabiendo en qué ocupar su tiempo, un día la joven esposa decidió revisar todos los baúles[3] traídos de España.

Interacción con la lectura

1. Completa la tabla con claves del contexto.

2. Trabaja en grupo. Completen sus tablas. Usen las palabras clave para decir cuál creen que es el significado de las palabras desconocidas. Escriban el significado de cada palabra.

3. Comenta con tu grupo lo que escribieron en sus tablas y contesta las preguntas.
   - Parafrasea la idea principal y los detalles de apoyo del cuento. ¿Cuál es el tema?
   - ¿Qué significa tenía la mantilla en la vida de Manuela?

4. ¿Conoces otras leyendas sobre el origen de una tradición, arte o costumbre? Escribe un párrafo sobre alguna leyenda que conozcas.

CLAVES DEL CONTEXTO		
palabra desconocida	palabras clave	significado
desahogar		
entrañable		
fregó		
esperanzada		
desengañaba		
palpitó		
asombrada		
cansancio		
recuperó		

Go **Online** to practice
PearsonSchool.com/Autentico
PEARSON realize
WRITING

Real-world Readings ▲

Students are able to connect to the cultural richness and diversity in the Spanish-speaking world.

CULTURA ◂ Estados Unidos

CONTEXTO

Vuelta de hoja La vida de Luis Rodríguez iba por un camino peligroso. A los 7 años, ya era un ladrón. No pasaba de los 13 años, cuando estuvo en un centro de detención juvenil[1] y a los 15, dejó la escuela. Pero a los 18 años "comencé a darle vuelta a mi vida", recuerda Rodríguez. Con ayuda, empezó a trabajar. "Pero a lo largo de todo, leí todo lo que pude. Los libros salvaron mi vida", dice Rodríguez.

En diciembre del 2001, Rodríguez abrió al noreste de Los Ángeles el Café Cultural Tía Chucha, para los jóvenes hispanohablantes y sus familias. Allí tienen charlas de historia y libros, presentaciones musicales y exhibiciones de películas. Rodríguez quiere ayudar a otros jóvenes a desarrollar sus habilidades y a curarse[2] ellos mismos, tal como él se curó. Él es un escritor y activista mexicano-americano que nació en El Paso, Texas. Su padre, Alfonso, un director de escuela en México, fue quien fomentó su amor por los libros.

- ¿Conoces algún centro de la comunidad en tu barrio que te haya ayudado a ti o a algún(a) joven que conoces? ¿Cómo los(as) ayudó?
- ¿Por qué crees que el café de Rodríguez puede gustarles a los jóvenes? ¿Qué otras cosas crees que puede añadir al café?

[1]juvenile detention center [2]to heal

▲ Luis Rodríguez en el Café Cultural Tía Chucha

Capítulo 5 • doscientos cuarenta y nueve **249**

▼ Building a Bridge to Culture

Puente a la cultura High-interest cultural readings deepen cultural perspectives.

Puente a la cultura

OBJECTIVES
▶ Read about Hispanic American contributions to U.S. society
▶ Identify key information to improve understanding

Go Online to practice
PEARSON realize.
PearsonSchool.com/Autentico
VIDEO   WRITING

Los Estados Unidos . . . en español

Desde el origen de nuestro país, los hispanohablantes han hecho importantes contribuciones. Ya en 1776, el capitán Jorge Ferragut había venido desde España para luchar por la independencia. Hoy día los hispanohablantes son una importante parte de la población[1] y sus contribuciones se pueden observar en todas las áreas de la sociedad.

La población

Según datos de la oficina del censo en el año 2010, la población hispanohablante representa el 15 por ciento del total de la población y es el grupo minoritario más grande de los Estados Unidos. Del año 2000 al año 2010 la población hispana aumentó en un 43 por ciento. Según el último censo del año 2010, el 13 por ciento de la población total (50.5 millones de personas) habla español en casa. Como el número de hispanohablantes sigue aumentando cada año, el español tiene cada vez más fuerza e influye en muchos campos del país. Por eso podemos decir que el español es ahora parte importante de la cultura de los Estados Unidos.

La política

Julián Castro es el decimosexto Secretario del Departamento de Vivienda y Desarrollo Urbano. Antes de aceptar el puesto en 2014, era alcalde de San Antonio, Texas, donde el 63% de la población es de origen mexicano. Su misión es "crear comunidades fuertes, sostenibles y de inclusión..."

Sonia Sotomayor es la primera jueza hispana de la Corte Suprema de los Estados Unidos y la tercera mujer en conseguir este puesto, en el año 2009. Sus padres se mudaron a Nueva York desde Puerto Rico. Sotomayor nació y se crió en el barrio neoyorquino del Bronx, donde hay una gran comunidad puertorriqueña. Estudió derecho en la Universidad de Yale, una de las más prestigiosas del país.

[1]population [2]grew

Estrategia

Reading for comprehension Read without stopping at unknown words. Then go back, decide if the words are important, and see if you can guess the meaning. If you do not understand the meaning, then look at the footnotes or a dictionary.

Online Cultural Reading

Go to Auténtico
ONLINE to read and understand a website about organizations in a Latin American country that help homeless children.

▲ Sonia Sotomayor

240 doscientos cuarenta • Capítulo 5 • Trabajo y comunidad

Hilda Solís, nacida en Los Ángeles de padres inmigrantes, fue la primera mujer hispana que trabajó como miembro del Senado de California y como Secretaria de Trabajo en el gobierno de Obama. La californiana de origen mexicano Rosa Gumataotao es la sexta latina en ocupar el puesto de Tesorera de los Estados Unidos, que obtuvo en el año 2009.

Los negocios[3]

De las 500 compañías que la revista *Fortune* considera las más importantes de los Estados Unidos, nueve tienen hispanohablantes como directores generales.

Linda G. Alvarado además de ser directora general de su propia compañía, Alvarado Construction, es también dueña de los Colorado Rockies. Es la primera mujer hispana que compró un equipo de béisbol de las ligas mayores.

Las ciencias

Los hispanohablantes se han destacado[4] también como científicos. Por ejemplo, el Dr. Luis W. Álvarez recibió el Premio Nobel de Física por sus estudios sobre partículas elementales[5] y el Dr. Mario J. Molina ganó el Premio Nobel de Química por sus estudios sobre la capa de ozono.

[3]business [4]have stood out [5]elementary particles

▲ Rosa Gumataotao

▲ Linda G. Alvarado

¿Comprendiste?

1. ¿Puede decirse que la población hispanohablante es una minoría importante en Estados Unidos? ¿Por qué? ¿Qué ha pasado con esta población desde los años noventa?

2. ¿En qué campos trabajan y hacen importantes contribuciones los hispanohablantes de Estados Unidos?

3. ¿Los hispanohablantes participan en la política de Estados Unidos? Da un ejemplo.

Escribe tu opinión

Después de leer el artículo, piensa có... aprender español a una persona que... un párrafo en el que expliques cómo... ayudar a esa persona a encontrar un...

Videodocumentario Un voluntario en la...

Integrated Skills Activity ▶

Students expand multiple skills as they write or speak on current topics using information from audio recordings and readings.

Pre-AP® Integración

OBJECTIVES
▶ Listen to and read about two community centers
▶ Write a cover letter to apply for a job

¿Qué me cuentas?: En busca de empleo

En tu colegio, ¿es necesario cumplir con un número de horas de servicio comunitario? Escucha una entrevista en una organización que busca voluntarios.

1 Vas a escuchar una narración en tres partes. Después de cada parte, vas a oír una o dos preguntas. Escoge la respuesta que corresponda a cada pregunta.

1. a. comedor de beneficencia	b. hogar de niños	c. centro recreativo
2. a. llevarlas a la entrevista	b. pedirlas a los ancianos	c. leerlas
3. a. si tenía responsabilidad	b. si le gustaba ser voluntario	c. si sabía cocinar
4. a. de horario flexible	b. sólo a tiempo parcial	c. fácil
5. a. si donan fondos	b. cuál es el salario	c. ¡Felicitaciones!

2 Ahora lee el folleto sobre otro lugar.

Centro Comunitario San Felipe: Ayudamos a nuestra gente

En el Centro Comunitario San Felipe, siempre necesitamos voluntarios para...

• revisar los alimentos y la ropa que se ha donado
• repartir alimentos de La Bodega
• ayudar a la gente
• ayudar a juntar fondos y donaciones de comida y ropa
• dar orientación legal y económica
• donar tiempo, comida o dinero

Buscamos a voluntarios que sean...

• amables y sinceros
• organizados y responsables
• trabajadores
• bilingües

En el Centro Comunitario San Felipe ayudamos a la gente de la comunidad con programas de salud y educación, y con orientación legal y económica. También repartimos alimentos y ropa entre la gente más necesitada y ofrecemos un lugar seguro para los jóvenes después del horario escolar. Para educar a la gente, ofrecemos clases de español e inglés. El centro está abierto los siete días de la semana y ayuda a casi 2000 familias.

Si quiere donar fondos, comida, ropa o su tiempo voluntariamente, por favor llame al 805-123-9876.

3 En una lista, compara y contrasta las dos oportunidades de trabajo voluntario. Luego, escoge un lugar y escribe una carta al director. Explica por qué te gustaría trabajar allí como voluntario y cuánto tiempo puedes dedicar. ¿Qué cualidades o habilidades puedes ofrecer? ¿Qué experiencias anteriores has tenido que te sirven como voluntario? Usa las siguientes expresiones para conectar tus ideas.

me interesaría	en cuanto (as soon as)	mientras
me encantaría	para empezar	durante

242 doscientos cuarenta y dos • Capítulo 5 • Trabajo y comunidad

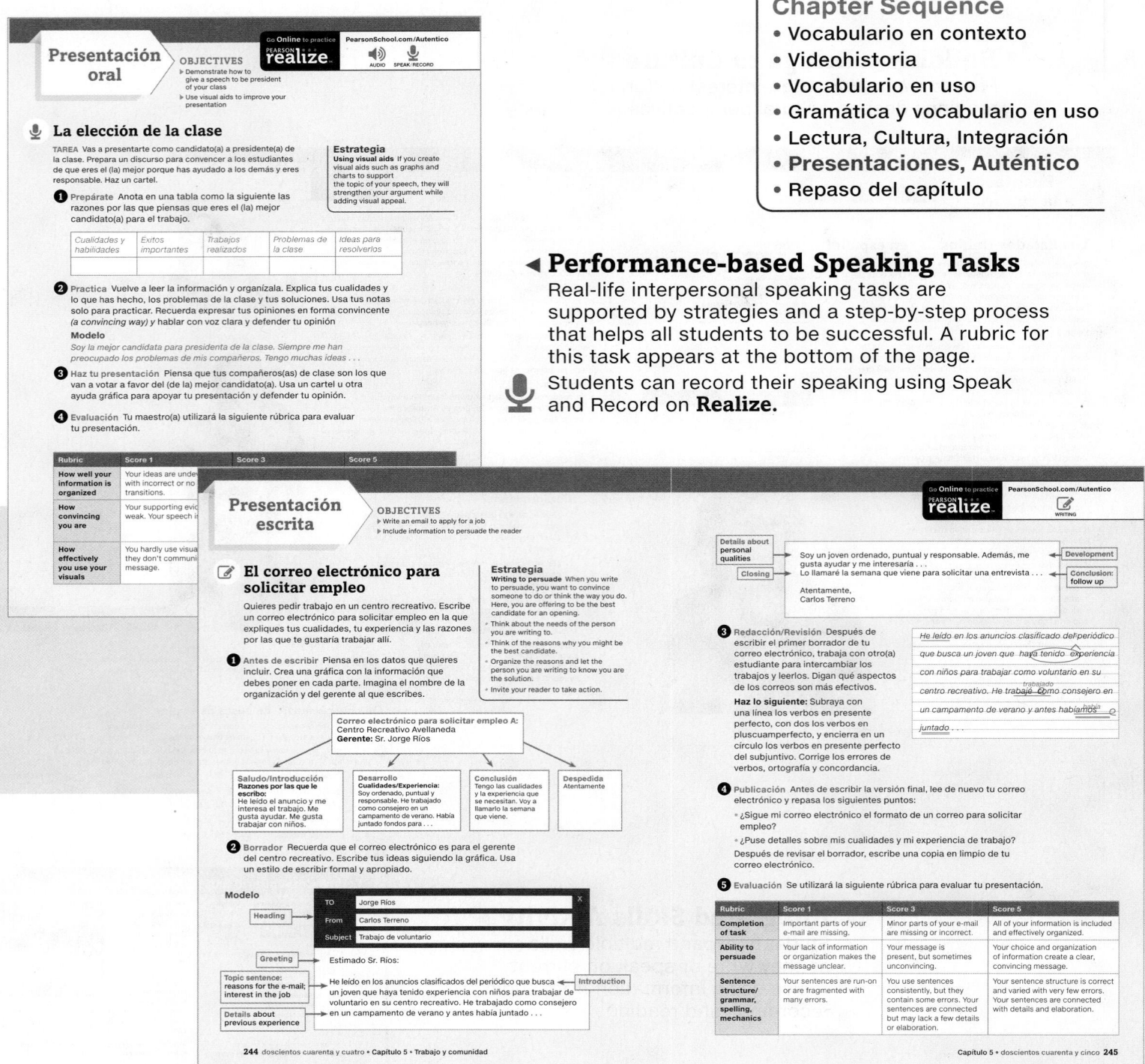

Chapter Sequence
- Vocabulario en contexto
- Videohistoria
- Vocabulario en uso
- Gramática y vocabulario en uso
- Lectura, Cultura, Integración
- **Presentaciones, Auténtico**
- Repaso del capítulo

◄ **Performance-based Speaking Tasks**
Real-life interpersonal speaking tasks are supported by strategies and a step-by-step process that helps all students to be successful. A rubric for this task appears at the bottom of the page.

Students can record their speaking using Speak and Record on **Realize.**

▲ **Performance-based Writing Tasks**
Students become better writers with real-life tasks that are supported with the writing process and focused strategies. As with the speaking tasks, a rubric has been specially written for each *Presentación escrita*.

Students can submit writing tasks on **Realize** for easy teacher grading!

Auténtico

Students use the interpretive mode of communication to comprehend culturally authentic video, audio, and readings.

Partnered with IDB

Students watch, listen to, and read content that was created by native speakers for native speakers. ▼

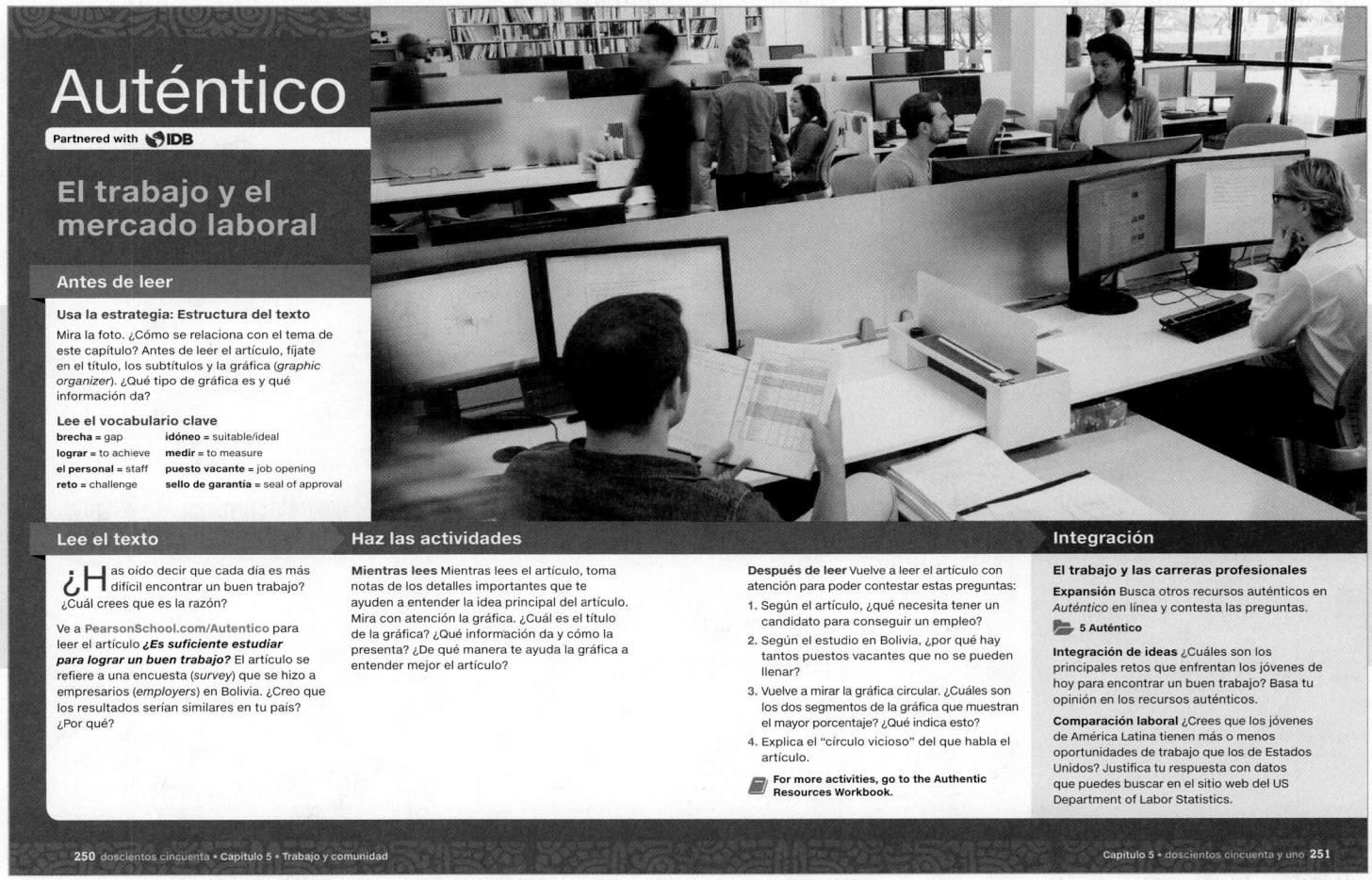

Auténtico
Partnered with ●IDB

El trabajo y el mercado laboral

Antes de leer

Usa la estrategia: Estructura del texto

Mira la foto. ¿Cómo se relaciona con el tema de este capítulo? Antes de leer el artículo, fíjate en el título, los subtítulos y la gráfica (*graphic organizer*). ¿Qué tipo de gráfica es y qué información da?

Lee el vocabulario clave

brecha = gap	**idóneo** = suitable/ideal
lograr = to achieve	**medir** = to measure
el personal = staff	**puesto vacante** = job opening
reto = challenge	**sello de garantía** = seal of approval

Lee el texto

¿**H**as oído decir que cada día es más difícil encontrar un buen trabajo? ¿Cuál crees que es la razón?

Ve a **PearsonSchool.com/Autentico** para leer el artículo *¿Es suficiente estudiar para lograr un buen trabajo?* El artículo se refiere a una encuesta (*survey*) que se hizo a empresarios (*employers*) en Bolivia. ¿Creo que los resultados serían similares en tu país? ¿Por qué?

Haz las actividades

Mientras lees Mientras lees el artículo, toma notas de los detalles importantes que te ayuden a entender la idea principal del artículo. Mira con atención la gráfica. ¿Cuál es el título de la gráfica? ¿Qué información da y cómo la presenta? ¿De qué manera te ayuda la gráfica a entender mejor el artículo?

Después de leer Vuelve a leer el artículo con atención para poder contestar estas preguntas:

1. Según el artículo, ¿qué necesita tener un candidato para conseguir un empleo?

2. Según el estudio en Bolivia, ¿por qué hay tantos puestos vacantes que no se pueden llenar?

3. Vuelve a mirar la gráfica circular. ¿Cuáles son los dos segmentos de la gráfica que muestran el mayor porcentaje? ¿Qué indica esto?

4. Explica el "círculo vicioso" del que habla el artículo.

📖 **For more activities, go to the Authentic Resources Workbook.**

Integración

El trabajo y las carreras profesionales

Expansión Busca otros recursos auténticos en *Auténtico* en línea y contesta las preguntas.

📂 **5 Auténtico**

Integración de ideas ¿Cuáles son los principales retos que enfrentan los jóvenes de hoy para encontrar un buen trabajo? Basa tu opinión en los recursos auténticos.

Comparación laboral ¿Crees que los jóvenes de América Latina tienen más o menos oportunidades de trabajo que los de Estados Unidos? Justifica tu respuesta con datos que puedes buscar en el sitio web del US Department of Labor Statistics.

250 doscientos cincuenta • Capítulo 5 • Trabajo y comunidad

Capítulo 5 • doscientos cincuenta y uno **251**

Authentic Resources Workbook ▲

The digital course on Realize features a library of authentic materials. Students use the accompanying **Authentic Resources Workbook** (in print or on Realize) to guide them through the content with tasks that are appropriate for their level of proficiency.

Integration ▲

Students respond to open-ended questions that require them to integrate their thoughts on a variety of authentic materials. Additional authentic resources for each chapter are available on Realize.

Chapter Organization

Repaso del capítulo

These two pages provide complete review and preparation for the chapter test.

Chapter Sequence
- Vocabulario en contexto
- Videohistoria
- Vocabulario en uso
- Gramática y vocabulario en uso
- Cultura, Lectura, Presentaciones, Auténtico
- **Repaso del capítulo**

Vocabulary List
Chapter vocabulary is listed as language functions and with English translations. ▼

Grammar Summary
Chapter grammar is conveniently summarized. ▼

◀ Additional Review
Flashcards, Tutorials and *Canciones de hip hop* for this chapter are available online.

Complete Test Preparation ▶
This spread prepares students for the proficiency and culture sections of the chapter test. Students are told how they will be tested, what the task might be like, and how to review.

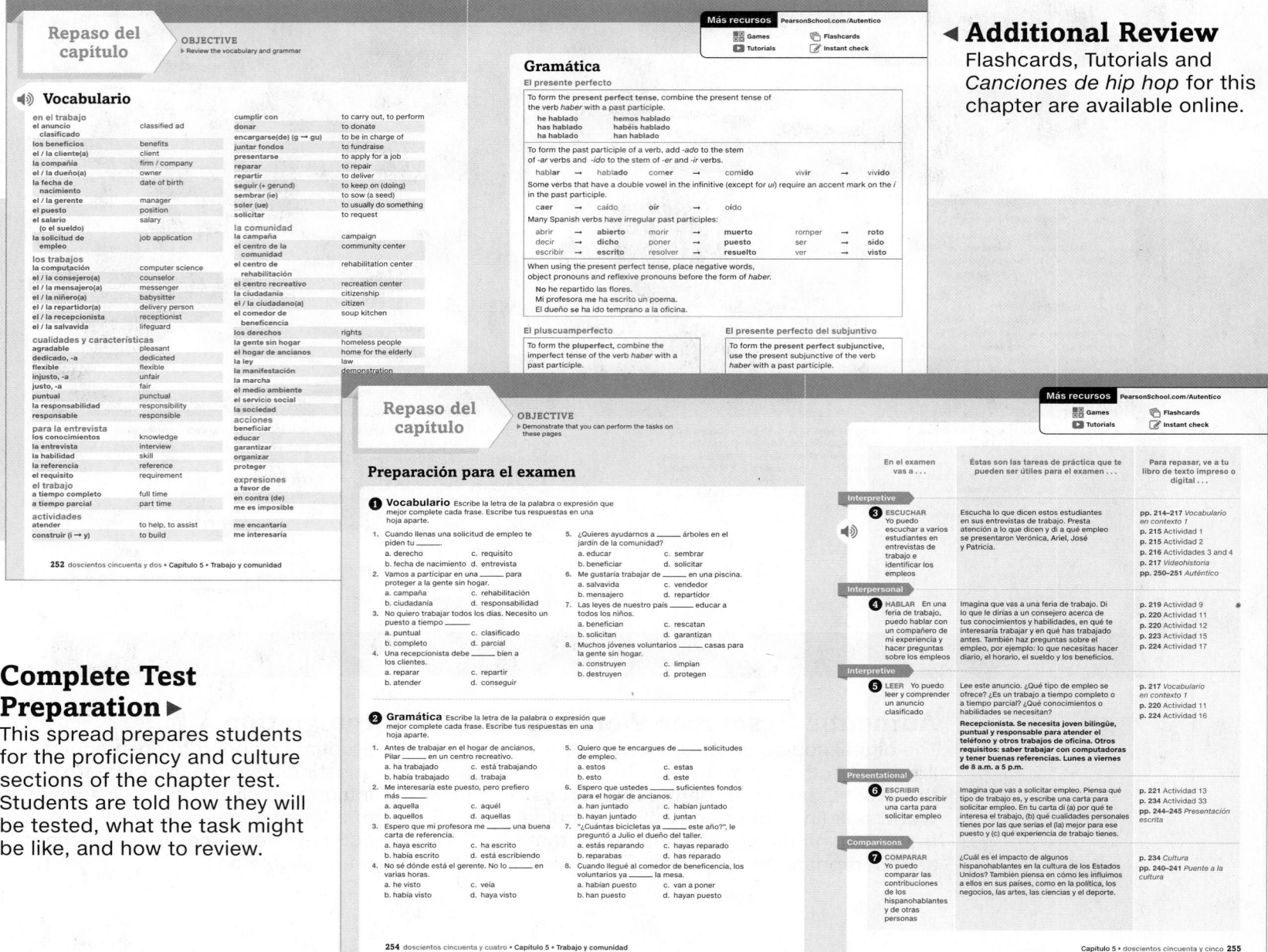

Additional Thematic Vocabulary

Useful lists provide additional thematic vocabulary. ▼

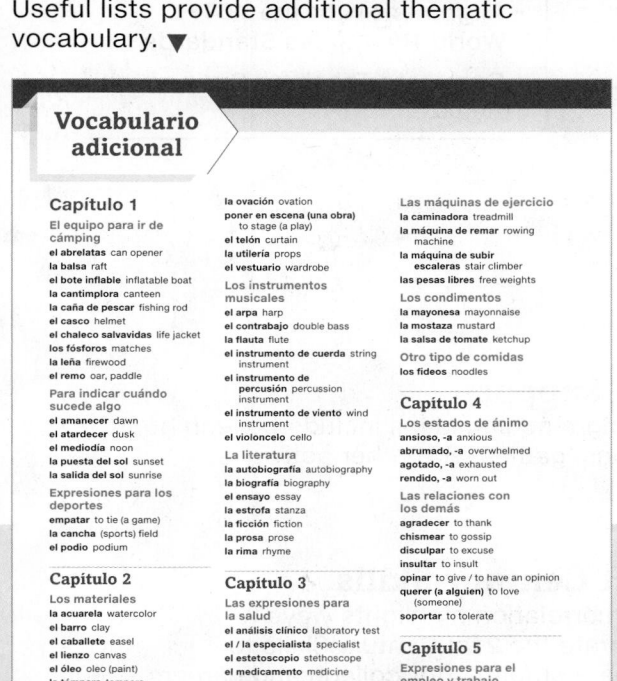

Vocabulario adicional

Capítulo 1

El equipo para ir de cámping

el abrelatas can opener
la balsa raft
el bote inflable inflatable boat
la cantimplora canteen
la caña de pescar fishing rod
el casco helmet
el chaleco salvavidas life jacket
los fósforos matches
la leña firewood
el remo oar, paddle

Para indicar cuándo sucede algo

el amanecer dawn
el atardecer dusk
el mediodía noon
la puesta del sol sunset
la salida del sol sunrise

Expresiones para los deportes

empatar to tie (a game)
la cancha (sports) field
el podio podium

Capítulo 2

Los materiales

la acuarela watercolor
el barro clay
el caballete easel
el lienzo canvas
el óleo oleo (paint)
la témpera tempera

Las expresiones de teatro

la escenografía set design
la iluminación lighting
la ovación ovation
poner en escena (una obra) to stage (a play)
el telón curtain
la utilería props
el vestuario wardrobe

Los instrumentos musicales

el arpa harp
el contrabajo double bass
la flauta flute
el instrumento de cuerda string instrument
el instrumento de percusión percussion instrument
el instrumento de viento wind instrument
el violoncelo cello

La literatura

la autobiografía autobiography
la biografía biography
el ensayo essay
la estrofa stanza
la ficción fiction
la prosa prose
la rima rhyme

Capítulo 3

Las expresiones para la salud

el análisis clínico laboratory test
el / la especialista specialist
el estetoscopio stethoscope
el medicamento medicine
los minerales minerals
la presión arterial blood pressure
los primeros auxilios first aid
la respiración breathing
el síntoma symptom
el termómetro thermometer

Las máquinas de ejercicio

la caminadora treadmill
la máquina de remar rowing machine
la máquina de subir escaleras stair climber
las pesas libres free weights

Los condimentos

la mayonesa mayonnaise
la mostaza mustard
la salsa de tomate ketchup

Otro tipo de comidas

los fideos noodles

Capítulo 4

Los estados de ánimo

ansioso, -a anxious
abrumado, -a overwhelmed
agotado, -a exhausted
rendido, -a worn out

Las relaciones con los demás

agradecer to thank
chismear to gossip
disculpar to excuse
insultar to insult
opinar to give / to have an opinion
querer (a alguien) to love (someone)
soportar to tolerate

Capítulo 5

Expresiones para el empleo y trabajo voluntario

comunitario, -a community related

Resumen de gramática

Grammar Terms

Adjectives describe nouns: *a **red** car.*

Adverbs usually describe verbs: *He read it **quickly.*** Adverbs can also describe adjectives or other adverbs: ***very** tall, **quite** well.*

Articles are words in Spanish that can tell you whether a noun is masculine, feminine, singular, or plural. In English, the articles are ***the, a,*** and ***an.***

Commands are verb forms that tell people to do something: ***Work!***

Comparatives compare people or things: *more . . . than.*

Conditional tense is used to express what a person would do or what a situation would be like: *I **would like** to write a book.*

Conjugations are verb forms that add endings to the stem in order to tell who the subject is and what tense is being used: *escrib**o**, escrib**iste.***

Conjunctions join words or groups of words. The most common ones are ***and, but,*** and ***or.***

Direct objects are nouns or pronouns that receive the action of a verb: *I read **the book.** I read **it.***

Future tense is used to talk about actions in the future: *Tomorrow we **will begin** working.*

Gender in Spanish tells you whether a noun, pronoun, or article is masculine or feminine.

Imperfect tense is used to talk about actions that happened repeatedly in the past; to describe people, places, and situations in the past; to talk about a past action or situation where no beginning or end is specified; and to describe an ongoing action in the past.

Imperfect progressive tense is used to describe something that was taking place over a period of time in the past: *He **was skiing** when he broke his leg.*

Indicative mood refers to present, past or future actions or states based on reality: *It **snowed** all night. **It's snowing** right now. **Will it snow** tomorrow?*

Indirect objects are nouns or pronouns that tell you to whom / what or for whom / what something is done: *I gave **him** the book.*

Infinitives are the basic forms of verbs. In English, infinitives have the word "to" in front of them: ***to walk.***

Interrogatives are words that ask questions: ***What** is it? **Who** is he?*

Nouns name people, places, or things: ***students, Mexico City, books.***

Number tells you if a noun, pronoun, article, or verb is singular or plural.

Past participles are verb forms that are used with forms of *haber* to form compound tenses: ***He escrito** una carta.* When a participle is used with *estar*, it functions as an adjective: *La mesa **está puesta.***

Prepositions show relationship between their objects and another word in the sentence: *He is **in** the classroom.*

Present tense is used to talk about actions that always take place, or that are currently happening: *I always **take** the bus; I **study** Spanish.*

Present perfect tense is used to say what a person *has done: We **have seen** the new movie.*

Present progressive tense is used to emphasize that an action is happening *right now: I **am doing** my homework; he **is finishing** dinner.*

Preterite tense is used to talk about actions that were completed in the past: *I **took** the train yesterday.*

Pronouns are words that take the place of nouns: ***She** is my friend.*

Reflexive verbs are used to say that people do something to or for themselves: *I **wash my** hair.* Reflexive verbs often describe a change in emotional or physical state, and express the idea that someone "gets" or "becomes": *They **became** angry.*

Subjects are the nouns or pronouns that perform the action in a sentence: ***John** sings.*

Subjunctive mood is used to say that one person influences the actions of another: ***I recommend that you study** more.* It is also used after verbs and expressions of doubt or uncertainty: ***It's possible that there's** enough food.*

Verbs show action or link the subject with a word or words in the predicate (what the subject does or is): *Ana **writes;** Ana **is** my sister.*

Nouns, Number, and Gender

Nouns refer to people, animals, places, things, and ideas. Nouns are singular or plural. In Spanish, nouns have gender, which means that they are either masculine or feminine.

Singular Nouns	
Masculine	Feminine
libro	carpeta
pupitre	casa
profesor	noche
lápiz	ciudad

Plural Nouns	
Masculine	Feminine

Grammar Summary and Charts

This quick reference guide helps students build a strong grammar foundation.

Expresiones útiles para conversar

Making an Apology

Perdóname. Forgive me.
Lo siento mucho. I'm very sorry.
Fue un malentendido. It was a misunderstanding.
Hagamos las paces. Let's make up.
Reconciliémonos. Let's reconcile.
Te pido perdón. I'm asking for your forgiveness.
Estoy equivocado, -a. I'm wrong.
Pongámonos de acuerdo. Let's come to an agreement.
Yo tengo la culpa. It's my fault.

Talking about Friendship

Tenemos mucho en común. We have a lot in common.
Te acepto tal como eres. I accept you just the way you are.
Tengo celos. I'm jealous.
No me hace caso. He / She doesn't pay any attention to me.
Sólo piensa en sí mismo, -a. He / She only thinks about himself / herself.
Confío en ti. I trust you.
Cuento contigo. I count on you.
Sé guardar un secreto. I can keep a secret.
Resolvamos este conflicto. Let's resolve this conflict.
Tenemos una diferencia de opinión. We disagree.
Me identifico contigo. I identify with you.
De hoy en adelante . . . From now on . . .
Ten en cuenta . . . Keep in mind . . .
Tengo derecho a . . . I have a right to . . .

Expressing Disagreement

Qué va. No way.
Yo no fui. I didn't do it.
No es cierto que . . . It's not true that . . .
No es verdad que . . . It's not true that . . .
No estoy de acuerdo. I disagree.
Me parece que no tienes razón. I think you're wrong.

Expressing Interest

Me es posible. I can.
Me gustaría . . . I'd like to . . .
Me encantaría . . . I'd love to . . .

Expressing Certainty or Possibility

Es cierto que . . . It's true that . . .
Estoy seguro, -a que . . . I'm sure that . . .
Es probable que . . . It's probable that . . .
Puede ser que . . . It's possible that . . .
Es posible que . . . It's possible that . . .
Es evidente que . . . It's clear that . . .
Quizás . . . Perhaps . . .

Expressing Doubt or Uncertainty

Dudo que . . . I doubt that . . .
No creo que . . . I don't think that . . .
No estoy seguro, -a que . . . I'm not sure that . . .
Es imposible que . . . It's impossible that . . .

Talking about How You Feel Physically

Me siento fatal. I feel awful.
Me caigo de sueño. I'm exhausted.
Estoy resfriado, -a. I have a cold.
Tengo tos. I have a cough.
Estornudo mucho. I'm sneezing a lot.
Tengo gripe. I have the flu.
Tengo fiebre. I have a fever.
Tengo alergia a . . . I'm allergic to . . .

Talking about How You Feel Emotionally

Estoy en la luna. I'm daydreaming.
No puedo concentrarme. I can't concentrate.
No aguanto más. I can't take it anymore.
Estoy de buen humor. I'm in a good mood.
Estoy de mal humor. I'm in a bad mood.
Estoy estresado, -a. I'm stressed out.
Me preocupo por . . . I'm worried about . . .
Me emociono mucho. I'm very emotional.
Estoy orgulloso, -a de . . . I'm proud of . . .
Estoy animado, -a. I'm excited.
Tengo confianza en mí mismo, -a. I have confidence in myself.
Me vuelvo loco, -a. I'm going crazy.
He cambiado de opinión. I've changed my mind.
Me doy cuenta de que . . . I realize that . . .
Me vuelvo . . . I'm getting / becoming . . .
Haré lo que me dé la gana. I'll do whatever I want.

Talking about Personal Goals

Alcancé mi meta. I achieved my goal.
Hice un esfuerzo. I made an effort.
Salí campeón. I won (I was the winner).
¡Felicitaciones! Congratulations!
Eres mi fuente de inspiración. You're my inspiration.

Describing Things or People

Se parece a . . . It / He / She looks like . . .
Suena a . . . It / He / She sounds like . . . .
Está basado, -a en . . . It's based on . . .
Se destaca. It / He / She stands out.
Está a cargo de . . . He / She is in charge of . . .

Expressions for Communication ▶

This handy list can help students become better communicators.

Vocabulario español-inglés

The *Vocabulario español-inglés* contains all active vocabulary from the text, including vocabulary presented in the grammar sections.

A dash (—) represents the main entry word. For example, **pasar la —** after **la aspiradora** means **pasar la aspiradora.**

The number following each entry indicates the chapter in which the word or expression is presented. A Roman numeral (I) indicates that the word was presented in AUTÉNTICO 1. A Roman numeral (II) indicates that the word was presented in AUTÉNTICO 2.

The following abbreviations are used in this list: *adj.* (adjective), *dir. obj.* (direct object), *f.* (feminine), *fam.* (familiar), *ind. obj.* (indirect object), *inf.* (infinitive), *m.* (masculine), *pl.* (plural), *prep.* (preposition), *pron.* (pronoun), *sing.* (singular).

A

a to (*prep.*) (I)
— **... le gusta(n)** he / she likes (I)
— **... le encanta(n)** he / she loves (I)
— **casa** (to) home (I)
— **causa de** because of (II)
— **favor de** in favor of (5-2)
— **la derecha (de)** to the right (of) (I)
— **la izquierda (de)** to the left (of) (I)
— **la parrilla** on the grill (II)
— **la una de la tarde** at one (o'clock) in the afternoon (I)
— **las ocho de la mañana** at eight (o'clock) in the morning (I)
— **las ocho de la noche** at eight (o'clock) in the evening, at night (I)
— **mano** by hand (II)
— **medida que** as (10-2)
— **menos que** unless (9-2)
— **menudo** often (I)
— **pesar de** despite (10-2)
— **mí también.** I do (like to) too. (I)
— **mí tampoco.** I don't (like to) either. (I)
¿— **qué hora?** (At) what time? (I)
— **tiempo** on time (II)
— **tiempo completo** full time (5-1)
— **tiempo parcial** part time (5-1)
— **través de** through (2-1)
— **veces** sometimes (I)
— **ver.** Let's see. (I)
abdominales crunches (3-2)
abierto, -a open (II)
el abogado, la abogada lawyer (II, 6-1)
abordar to board (II)
abrazar(se) to hug (II)
el abrigo coat (I)
abril April (I)
abrir to open (I)
abstracto, -a abstract (2-1)
el abuelo, la abuela grandfather, grandmother (I)
los abuelos grandparents (I)
aburrido, -a boring (I)
aburrir to bore (I)
aburrirse to get bored (II)
me aburre(n) it bores me (they bore me) (I)
el abuso abuse (10-1)
acabar de + *inf.* to have just... (I)
el accidente accident (II)
el aceite cooking oil (II)
aceptar to accept (4-1)
— **tal como (soy)** to accept (me) the way (I am) (4-1)
acercarse a to approach (1-1)
acompañar to accompany (II)
aconsejar to advise (3-2)
acostarse (o → ue) to go to bed (II)
las actividades extracurriculares extracurricular activities (II)
el actor actor (I)
la actriz, *pl.* **las actrices** actress (I)
la actuación acting (II)
actuar to perform (2-2)
el acueducto aqueduct (8-1)
acuerdo:
Estoy de —. I agree. (I)
No estoy de —. I don't agree. (I)
el acusado, la acusada accused (10-2)
acusar to accuse (4-2)
adecuado, -a adequate (10-1)
además de in addition to, besides (II, 6-1)
¡Adiós! Good-bye! (I)
la adolescencia adolescence (10-1)
el / la adolescente adolescent (10-1)
¿Adónde? (To) where? (I)
adoptar to adopt (8-2)
la aduana customs (II)
el aduanero, la aduanera customs officer (II)
el aeropuerto airport (II)
el aerosol aerosol (9-2)
afectar to affect (9-2)
afeitarse to shave (II)
el aficionado, la aficionada fan (II)
afortunadamente fortunately (II)
africano, -a African (8-2)
la agencia de viajes travel agency (II)
el / la agente de viajes travel agent (II)
agitado, -a agitated (II)

End Glossaries ▲

Helpful Spanish-English and English-Spanish glossaries are located at the end of the book

Students can listen to pronunciation on **Realize.**

Using the Teacher's Edition

Teaching the Theme

The Teacher's Edition provides complete planning support for teaching the themes.

Go Online to practice
PEARSON realize™

Use the Lesson Plans, teacher resources, and program content on Realize to plan for instruction and assign activities.

- Teaching the Theme
- Planning for Instruction
- Alignment with the ACTFL World-Readiness Standards
- Complete Teaching Support on Realize

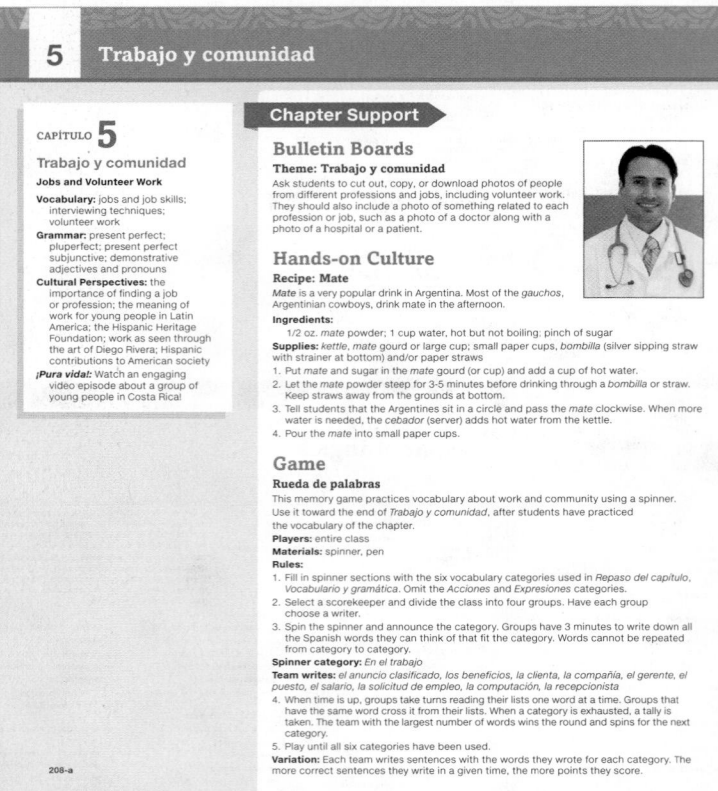

◀ Theme Support

Time-saving teaching ideas include bulletin board suggestions, games, and other activities.

▼ 21st Century Skills

This correlation highlights ways to integrate the 21st Century Skills to prepare students for college and careers.

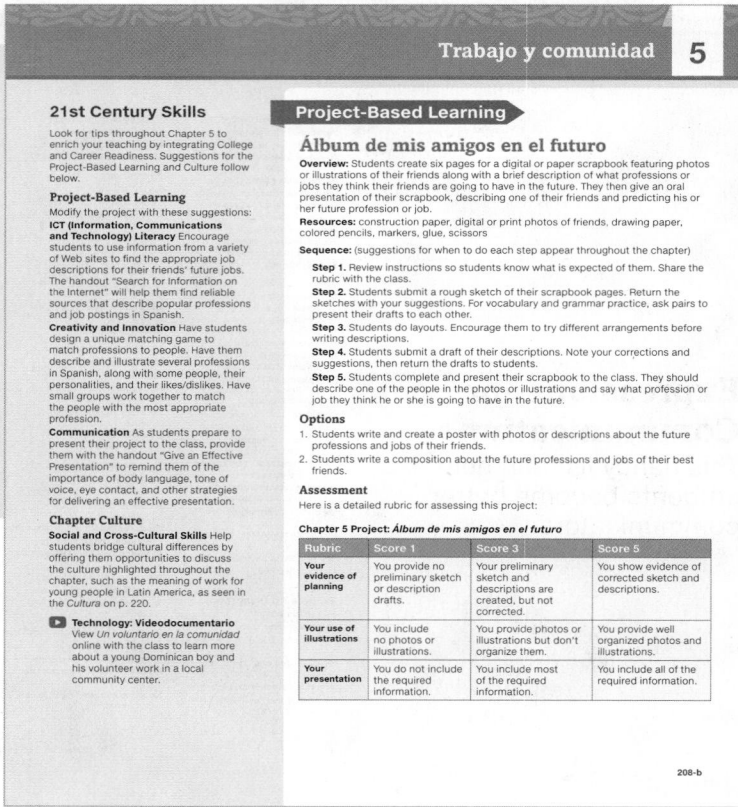

Project-Based Learning ▶

Each theme includes a learning project divided into manageable steps. The rubric is at the bottom of the page as well as on Realize.

Planning for Instruction

The Teacher's Edition provides four pages of planning support interleaved at the beginning of each chapter.

▼ Chapter Overview

This section gives a quick overview of each chapter.

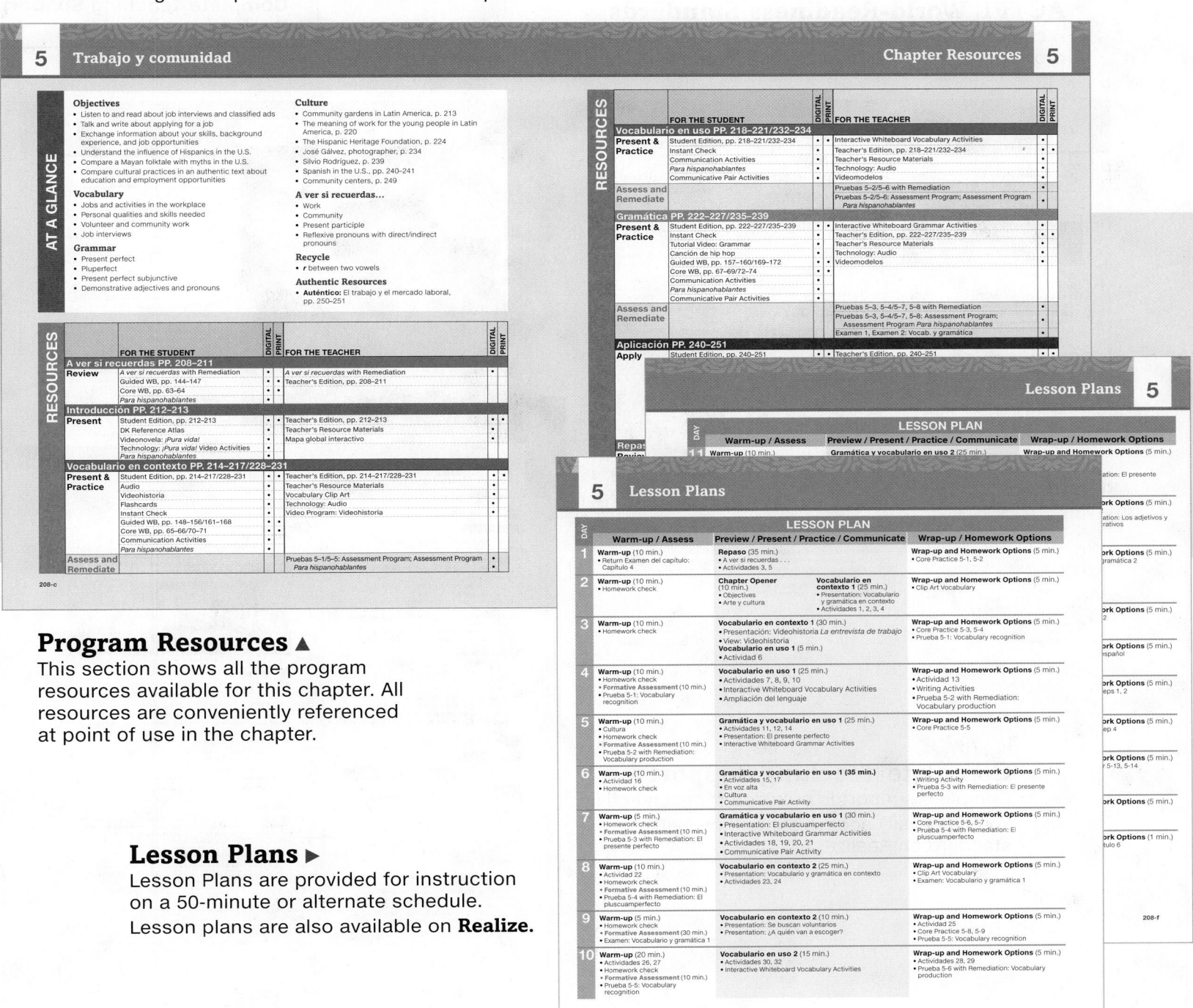

Program Resources ▲

This section shows all the program resources available for this chapter. All resources are conveniently referenced at point of use in the chapter.

Lesson Plans ▶

Lesson Plans are provided for instruction on a 50-minute or alternate schedule.
Lesson plans are also available on **Realize**.

Alignment with the ACTFL World-Readiness Standards

AUTÉNTICO provides complete coverage of the ACTFL World-Readiness Standards for Learning Languages.

- Teaching the Theme
- Planning for Instruction
- **Alignment with the ACTFL World-Readiness Standards**
- **Complete Teaching Support on Realize**

▼ ACTFL World-Readiness Standards

A complete correlation of chapter activities to the standards is provided at the beginning of each chapter.

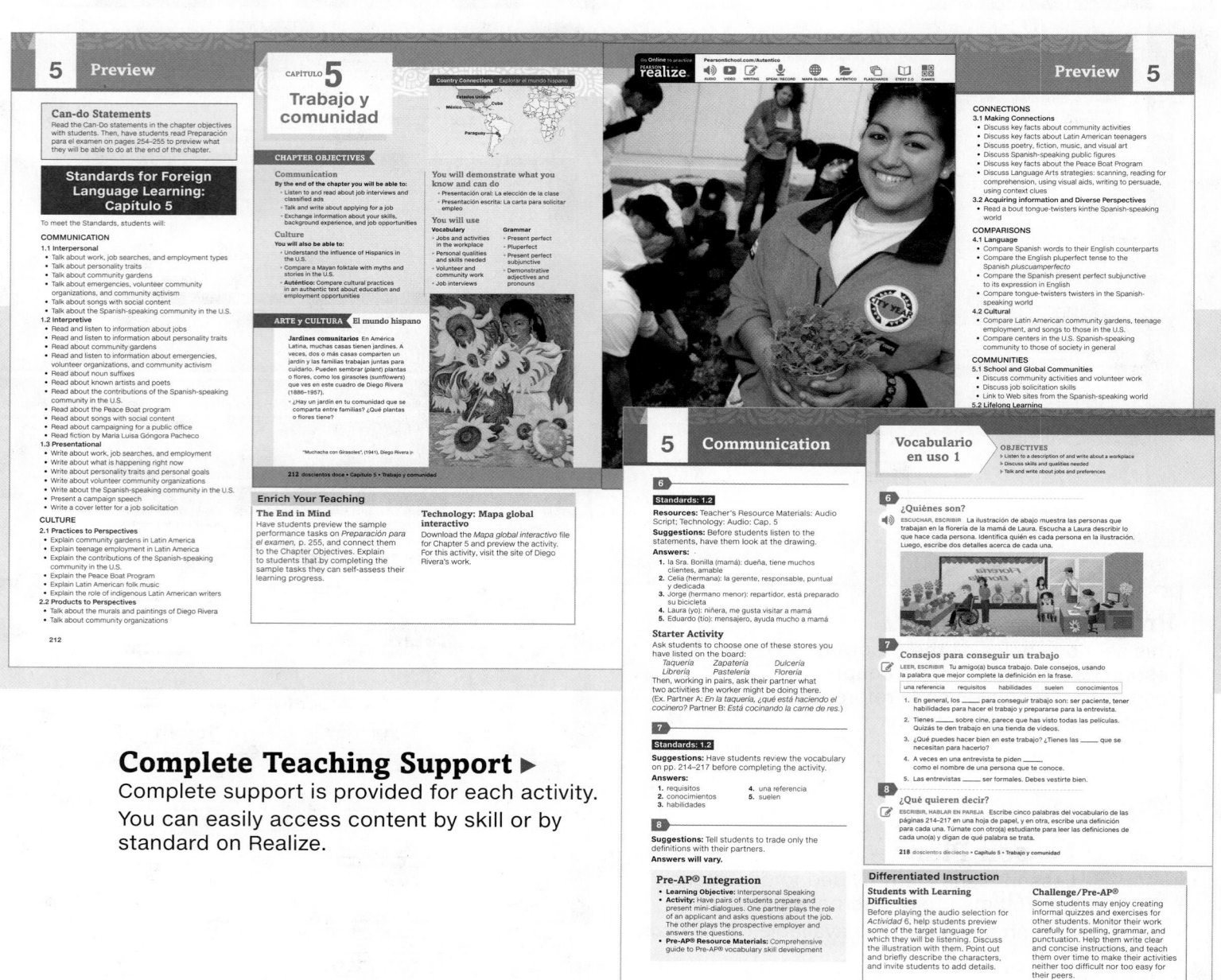

Complete Teaching Support ▶

Complete support is provided for each activity. You can easily access content by skill or by standard on Realize.

Complete Teaching Support

AUTÉNTICO provides teachers with complete instructional support in both print and technology formats.

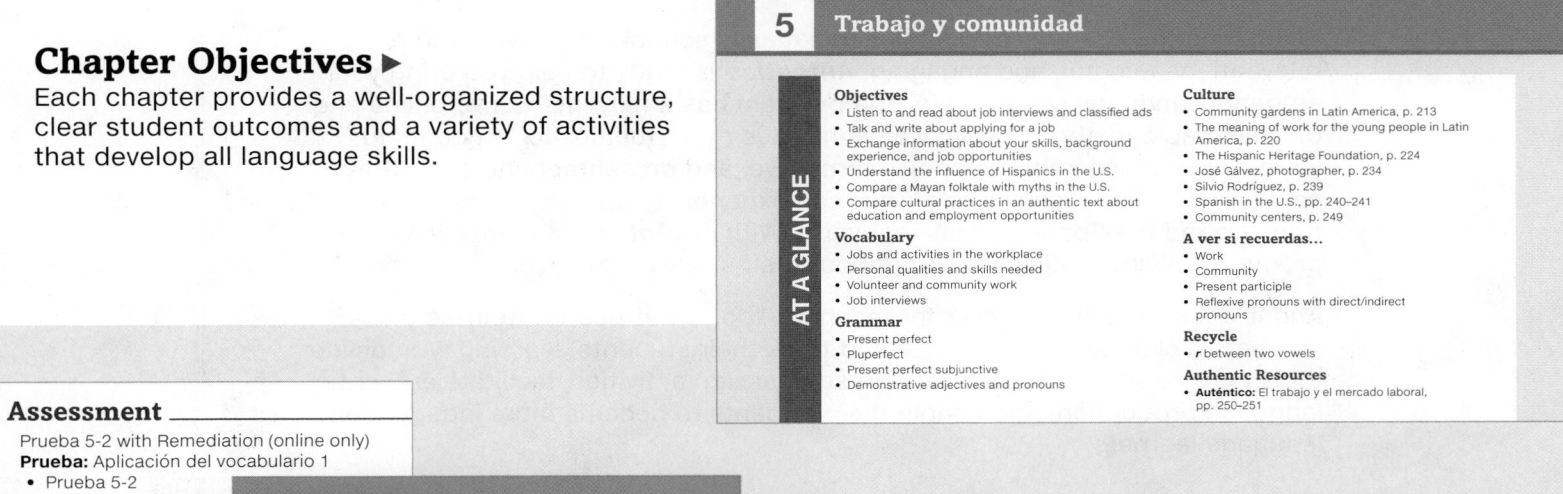

Chapter Objectives ▶
Each chapter provides a well-organized structure, clear student outcomes and a variety of activities that develop all language skills.

5 Trabajo y comunidad

AT A GLANCE

Objectives
- Listen to and read about job interviews and classified ads
- Talk and write about applying for a job
- Exchange information about your skills, background experience, and job opportunities
- Understand the influence of Hispanics in the U.S.
- Compare a Mayan folktale with myths in the U.S.
- Compare cultural practices in an authentic text about education and employment opportunities

Vocabulary
- Jobs and activities in the workplace
- Personal qualities and skills needed
- Volunteer and community work
- Job interviews

Grammar
- Present perfect
- Pluperfect
- Present perfect subjunctive
- Demonstrative adjectives and pronouns

Culture
- Community gardens in Latin America, p. 213
- The meaning of work for the young people in Latin America, p. 220
- The Hispanic Heritage Foundation, p. 224
- José Gálvez, photographer, p. 234
- Silvio Rodríguez, p. 239
- Spanish in the U.S., pp. 240–241
- Community centers, p. 249

A ver si recuerdas…
- Work
- Community
- Present participle
- Reflexive pronouns with direct/indirect pronouns

Recycle
- *r* between two vowels

Authentic Resources
- **Auténtico:** El trabajo y el mercado laboral, pp. 250–251

Assessment
Prueba 5-2 with Remediation (online only)
Prueba: Aplicación del vocabulario 1
- Prueba 5-2

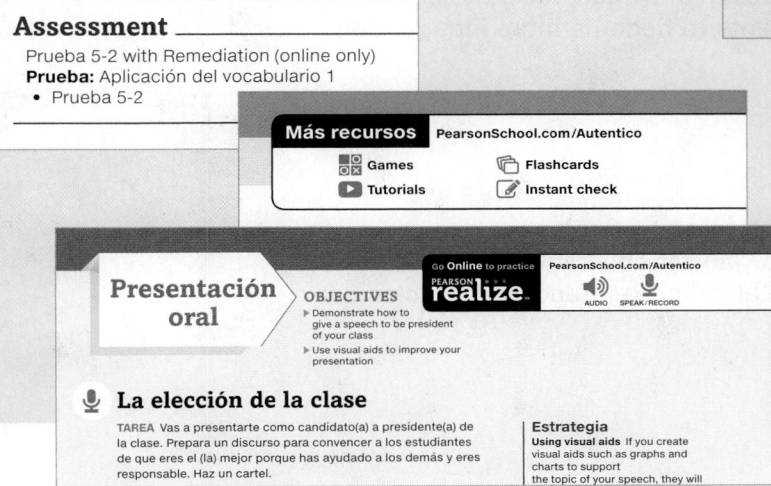

Más recursos PearsonSchool.com/Autentico
- Games
- Tutorials
- Flashcards
- Instant check

Presentación oral

OBJECTIVES
▶ Demonstrate how to give a speech to be president of your class
▶ Use visual aids to improve your presentation

Go **Online** to practice
PEARSON **realize** PearsonSchool.com/Autentico
AUDIO SPEAK/RECORD

La elección de la clase

TAREA Vas a presentarte como candidato(a) a presidente(a) de la clase. Prepara un discurso para convencer a los estudiantes de que eres el (la) mejor porque has ayudado a los demás y eres responsable. Haz un cartel.

Estrategia
Using visual aids If you create visual aids such as graphs and charts to support the topic of your speech, they will

Assessment ▲
Teachers are provided with multiple print and technology tools that measure student progress in listening, speaking, reading, and writing. The program also offers an Integrated Performance Assesssment for each chapter.

Differentiated Instruction

Students with Learning Difficulties
Allow students who have difficulty reciting in front of others to record their recitations of the Machado poem on p. 223. You may wish to have them recite only one stanza of the poem.

Advanced Learners
Have students use the present perfect tense to tell about five things they have done that qualify them either for the job they actually have or for a job they would like to have: *Quiero ser cajera. He trabajado de cajera en la tienda de mis padres. Mi papá me ha enseñado a usar la caja…*

Differentiated Assessment

Core Assessment
- Assessment Program: Examen del capítulo 5,
- Technology: Audio: Cap. 5,
- ExamView: Chapter Test, Test Banks A and B

Advanced/Pre-AP®
- ExamView: Pre-AP® Test Bank
- Pre-AP® Resource Materials

Extra Support
- Alternate Assessment Program: Examen del capítulo 5
- Technology: Audio: Cap. 5,

Heritage Speakers
- Assessment Program: *Para hispanohablantes:* Examen del capítulo 5
- ExamView: Heritage Speaker Test Bank

Differentiated Instruction ▲
Auténtico provides teaching suggestions to help all students learn Spanish. Each level also provides differentiated assessment.

Instructional Planning and Support
Auténtico provides complete planning and teaching support. The Teacher's Edition and the teacher resources on Realize provide time-saving teaching tools to help you teach all your students.

From wireless communication tools to the virtual world, technology has changed the lives of today's students. Access to technology in schools and society is integrated into their lives, and their world has expanded through laptops, handhelds, cell phones, and whiteboards. While using the electronic tools, they have the chance to learn, practice skills, and explore. They can contribute to the online community through outlets like social media, wikis, and podcasts.

Embracing the changes to digital media makes school coursework more relevant, meaningful, and engaging. *Auténtico* is ready to help you bring your students' language study to life. The program has a fully interactive online and downloadable textbook, as well as numerous opportunities for students to learn and practice interpersonal, interpretive, and presentational skills. They can learn from storyline videos. They can experience authentic resources from around the Spanish-speaking world. With *Auténtico*, students will make progress toward proficiency throughout their study of Spanish.

And it will be easier than ever for teachers, too. *Auténtico* on **Realize** gives teachers a chance to personalize and track their students' learning with online tools and reports. They can plan, present, assign activities, facilitate authentic language production, and enable their students to become more independent language learners.

PEARSON • • •
realize™

Go online for links to national professional organizations, regional conferences, Web sites of interest, and Listservs. You will also find references to articles on instruction and assessment.

Integrating Tech

AUTÉNTICO is delivered via **Realize** and is organized into a simple learning model that can be seamlessly incorporated into your classroom instruction.

Present

Everything you need to teach key concepts to your students in the classroom, or at home, including offline access to your eText.

Selected Examples

Videohistoria Brand new videos to engage your students

Interactive Whiteboard Presentations Engage students in new grammar points and vocabulary

Practice and Communicate

Let your students practice what they've learned, with activities you assign for classroom or at-home work.

eText activities, all activities in the SE can be done online
Speak-and-Record tasks
Grammar tutorials for preview, learning, or review
GramActiva activities, to reinforce instruction

More Practice

Additional practice resources are here to help reinforce the concepts of each chapter.
Vocabulary App, a fun way for students to practice chapter vocabulary
Videomodelos, for students to watch and re-watch vocabulary in context
Culture Reading Activity, support for engaging *Lectura* in the student book and etext

Assess

Test your students' knowledge as they progress through a chapter with auto-corrected quizzes and assigned remediation activities. At the end of each chapter, assess your students' ability to show what they've learned with communicative, gradable tests.

Lesson quizzes with remediation, so you and your students can check understanding
Chapter Tests and Cumulative Tests, for summative assessment
Situation Cards, for students to demonstrate authentic use of new vocabulary and grammar skills
Integrated Performance Assessment, alternative assessment in authentic contexts
ExamView® Assessment Suite, editable banks of test items

More Resources

Do your students need more help or different help? Each chapter includes a *Más Recursos* folder with many differentiated resources to help your struggling students.

Leveled Vocabulary and Grammar Workbook: Guided Practice, for more practice designed to help students at all levels of proficiency; in print and online
Para hispanohablantes, support for your heritage speakers

Looking for authentic Spanish resources?

Each chapter includes an Auténtico folder with videos, audio recordings, and articles from our partners Univision, NBC Learn, EFE News, and the Inter-American Development Bank.

UNIVISION®
COMMUNICATIONS INC

Assessment

Topics Covered

- Assessing Student Progress
- Purposes of Assessment
- Forms of Assessment
- **AUTÉNTICO** and the standards
- Integrating Technology with Assessment on **Realize**
- Assessment Resources in **AUTÉNTICO**

An assessment program in a second language classroom should be based on the premise that the main purpose of learning a language is to communicate in a meaningful and culturally appropriate way. As you begin to teach a unit of instruction, you might want to start by asking a few key questions: What do I expect my students to learn? What do I want them to be able to do? How can I assess what I am looking for in student performance?

Assessing Student Progress

The role of assessment in the world languages classroom is to provide both the teacher and students with a measure of progress toward achieving predetermined outcomes. It is an integral and ongoing part of the learning process. Here are key factors to consider as you develop curriculum that aligns assessment with instruction:

- Focus assessment on what students can do in the language (not just what they know).
- Performance tasks should be based upon real-world, authentic activities.
- Consider the principles of backward design to align assessment with instruction: determine outcomes, decide upon the evidence of transfer (performance tasks), and then create the learning activities.
- Give students multiple opportunities to show what they can do with the language that take into consideration cultures, learning styles, languages, and individual abilities.
- Use rubrics to evaluate performance tasks. This tool measures specific criteria against a defined scale. Provide the rubric to students in advance of the performance task.
- Provide students with anchors, or representative samples, of the performance task so that they can better understand the desired outcomes.
- Utilize both formative and summative assessments to provide ongoing feedback to students.
- Provide opportunities for students to self-evaluate and reflect upon their learning and progress.
- Provide an opportunity for students to create a portfolio of representative work. This could be in a physical or online location. With a portfolio, students can see progress throughout the year. If your school allows, you might save students' portfolios across the years of language study as well.

Purposes of Assessment

The following chart outlines the various purposes for assessment:

Purposes of Assessment	
Entry-level assessment	• Analyzes students' ability to communicate as a basis for placing students at an appropriate level in an established world languages program
Formative assessment	• Provides real-time feedback during the instructional process • Can take many different forms in the classroom • Helps the teacher and student determine the next steps to further learning • Takes place prior to the summative assessment
Summative assessment	• Documents and evaluates students' learning or success at a point in time such as the end of a unit, chapter, or course of study

Forms of Assessment

Achievement tests determine what students know by evaluating them on specific, previously learned material, such as the names of items of clothing or the conjugation of -*ar* verbs. Students are tested on discrete bits of information. Achievement tests are used to measure the incremental steps involved in learning a second language—for example, to cover what was taught in a specific chapter. Achievement may be quizzed or tested with some frequency as proof of regular progress for both student and teacher.

Performance-based assessment measures what students can do with this knowledge and how well they can perform in the language. These tasks do not involve testing specific items; rather they are performance-based, checking how well students integrate what they have learned. Their characteristic open-endedness permits students to use what they know to receive or communicate a message, since the emphasis is on communication needs. Performance-based assessment addresses this question: How well and at what level can the student use the language to receive and express meaningful communication?

Performance-based presentational writing task in *Auténtico 3 Capítulo 5* ▶

▼ Performance-based presentational speaking task in *Auténtico 3 Capítulo 5*

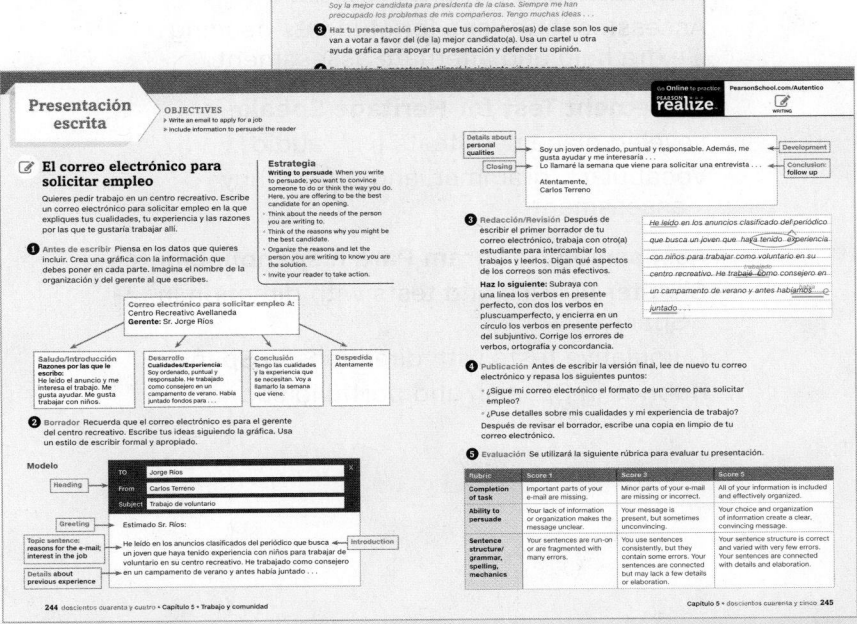

Assess Standards and Demonstrate Understanding

Auténtico is fully aligned to the ACTFL World-Readiness Standards for Learning Languages. The standards are organized around five goal areas: Communication, Culture, Connections, Comparisons, and Communities. The three modes of communication (Interpersonal, Interpretive, and Presentational) encompass a number of skills, including reading, writing, speaking, and listening. These skills are best practiced through authentic situations and through working with materials from a variety of authentic sources.

Auténtico has been carefully written to provide activities that develop and assess communication at levels appropriate to the students' proficiency. The last page in each chapter of Levels 1–3, called *Preparación para el examen,* provides an overview of the chapter outcomes and performance tasks organized around the interpretive, interpersonal, and presentational modes of communication. Numerous online activities on **Realize** provide opportunities for formative and summative assessment of all three modes of communication.

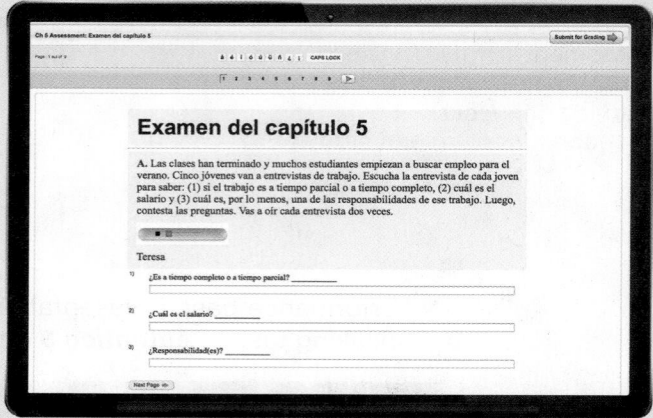

PEARSON
realize™

Assessment Resources on Realize

Auténtico offers a wide range of assessment resources for teachers and students on **Realize.** Or create your own test using the **Exam***View*® Test Bank CD-ROM.

Assessment Program
Placement test
Chapter quizzes and tests
Cumulative tests
Rubrics and portfolio support

Alternate Assessment Program
Assessment options for students needing extra help and alternate assessment

Placement Test for Heritage Speakers
Leveled placement tests with audio
Vocabulary, grammar, and proficiency assessment

Assessment Program Para hispanohablantes
Chapter quizzes and tests with direction in Spanish
Cumulative tests with directions in Spanish
Rubrics in Spanish and portfolio support

🎤 SPEAK / RECORD
Use the Speak and Record feature on Realize to evaluate your students' interpersonal and presentation skills.

 GAMES
Who says learning can't be fun? Each chapter of *Auténtico* offers a variety of games on Realize that help students monitor their learning.

 INTERACTIVE WHITEBOARD
Get your students talking using the *¡Cuéntame!* and *Encuesta* Interactive Whiteboard Activities.

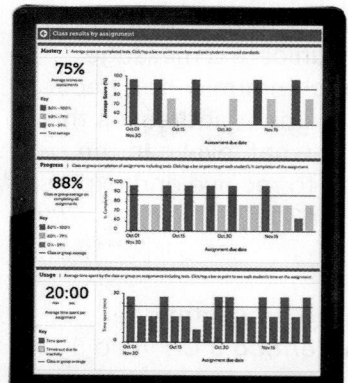

◀ **Mastery Reports**
Grading and reporting data is available for individual students and classroom instruction. Real-time data helps provide remediation and ensures student mastery and understanding of the standards.

Assessment Resources in AUTÉNTICO

Assessment Resources	Self-Evaluation	Formative	Summative: Achievement	Summative: Performance
Student Edition				
Actividades (various)		✖		✖
Presentación oral				✖
Presentación escrita				✖
Preparación para el examen				✖
Print and Digital Resources				
Literacy Skills Workbook Two to three thematically linked readings per *Tema*				✖
Examview® Computer Test Generator Test Banks			✖	
PEARSON realize™				
Placement Tests				✖
Actividades with Speak and Record	✖	✖		✖
Presentación oral				✖
Communicative Pair Activities		✖		
Instant Checks	✖	✖		
Situation Cards				✖
Interactive Whiteboard Activities		✖		✖
Chapter Quizzes	✖	✖		
Practice Tests				✖
Chapter Tests with Speak and Record			✖	✖
Integrated Performance Assessments with Speak and Record				✖
Cumulative Tests			✖	✖
Rubrics				✖
Chapter Checklist and Self-Assessment worksheet	✖			
Pre-AP® Activities				✖
Mobile Apps				
Auténtico eText		✖		✖
Vocabulary App	✖	✖		

Differentiated Instruction

Topics Covered

- Success in Teaching All Students
- Effective Instructional Strategies
- Teaching Today's Students
- Teaching Spanish to Students with Learning Disabilities
- Accommodating Instruction
- Accommodations for Students with Special Needs
- Accommodation in AUTÉNTICO
- Heritage Speakers
  - Teaching Heritage Speakers
  - Teaching Heritage Speakers with *Para hispanohablantes*
  - Teaching Heritage Speakers with AUTÉNTICO 3
- Teaching All Students: Summary

All students are capable of and can benefit from learning a second language. However, today's students bring into the classroom a wide range of needs, interests, motivations, home languages, and literacy levels. This diversity presents heightened challenges to both curriculum and instruction. It should be clearly acknowledged that individual needs of some students require additional specialized support. However, the goal of a comprehensive program remains the provision of teaching all students to develop proficiency in Spanish. All students should have access to a communicative and culturally rich program in addition to whatever specialized intervention may be required. *Auténtico* has been developed especially to meet the diverse needs of students in Spanish classrooms.

Success in Teaching All Students

All students are able to access learning when teachers provide curriculum and instruction in ways that allow all learners in the classroom to participate and achieve the instructional and behavioral goals of general education, as well as those of the core curriculum. Success is achieved in classrooms that consistently and systematically integrate instructional strategies that are responsive to the needs of all learners with a special focus on students that need extra help—students with learning difficulties, heritage speakers, and students who are eligible for and receiving special education services.

Effective Instructional Strategies

Here are general strategies that deliver effective instruction for all learners in the Spanish classroom.

- **Clarify the objectives for a chapter.** Students need to understand the outcomes for which they will be assessed.

- **Provide "thinking time" before students have to talk.** You may want to ask a question and then count to 10 before expecting a response. If a student is struggling, state that you want him/her to think about it, and indicate that you'll be back for the response in a minute. Move on to another student, and then return to the student for his/her response.

- **Write all assignments on the board.** Assignments given both verbally and visually are clearer to all students.

- **Use visuals throughout the lesson.** Present vocabulary visually. Use charts to present grammar. Use video that provides visual support (such as vocabulary words highlighted on the screen) and grammar videos that visualize grammar patterns. Use graphic organizers whenever possible. Connect communicative tasks to photos, art, and realia.

- **Assist in time management.** When requiring students to complete projects or long-term assignments, provide a calendar that breaks down requirements by due dates. Many students experience significant difficulties in self-managing the time needed to complete complex projects.

- **Build in opportunities for reteaching and practicing vocabulary words and grammar.** Students need many opportunities to learn new concepts and need to practice in a variety of formats.

- **Build vocabulary skills by teaching the patterns of language.** Teach the meaning of prefixes, suffixes, and the role of cognates. Point out connections between English, Spanish, and Latin.

- **Work with students based on their strengths rather than their weaknesses.** Allow students to experience success by using their strengths while working on areas of weakness.

- **Consider alternative means for demonstrating understanding.** Think beyond the common modes of reading and writing. Students could present information orally, create a poster or visual representation of work, record their ideas on an audio file, or act out their understanding.

- **Have students begin all work in class.** Prior to class dismissal, check to ensure that each student has a good start and understands what is expected.

- **Assign work on Realize or create a class Web page.** Homework assignments could be posted and easily accessed by parents and students outside of school hours.

Teaching Today's Students

The strategies presented on these pages provide an overview of instructional strategies that are effective with all learners. Today's students need instruction that enables them to see how learning is relevant, that helps them organize their time and learning, that provides focus on what is important (either within instructional materials or with classroom activities), that provides multiple opportunities to learn utilizing different modalities, and that assures students know what is expected of them whether in the classroom or for homework.

" All students are **capable** of and can **benefit** from learning a second language. **"**

Differentiated Instruction

Teaching Spanish to Students with Learning Disabilities

There are many reasons why students may experience difficulties in learning a second language. In general, these difficulties may be characterized by the inability to spell or read well, problems with auditory discrimination and in understanding auditory input, and difficulty with abstract thinking. Research by Ganchow and Sparks (1991) indicates that difficulties with one's first language are a major factor in foreign language learning difficulties.

It is not always evident which students will experience difficulties with learning a second language. Many times these students are bright and outgoing. They may have experienced reading or spelling problems in elementary school, but they have learned to compensate over time. Ask students what problems they may have experienced with their first language, especially in the areas of reading and dictation.

Accommodating Instruction

Students with learning disabilities can develop a level of proficiency in a second language with some modifications to instruction and testing. These learners benefit from a highly structured approach that teaches new content in context and in incremental amounts. Teach, practice, and assess using multi-sensory strategies. Many students benefit when instruction combines seeing, hearing, saying, and writing. For example, a teacher would first show a visual of a word and say it aloud. This is followed by using the new word in context. The teacher then writes the word on the board. Students would say the word aloud with the teacher. They then write it down and say it aloud again. In subsequent days, many students benefit from frequent reviews of learned auditory materials.

Accommodations for Students with Special Needs

Here are suggestions for instruction for students with special needs. For additional support, see the *Auténtico* Alternate Assessment Program.

Hearing impairments

- Help students comprehend oral information or instructions. Provide written directions/materials and/or visual cues to support what is presented orally. Face the students when speaking, repeat as needed, and speak clearly. Seat these students in the front of the classroom. Provide outlines of lectures or oral presentations. Have another student take notes and make copies of notes available to all students. Use the audio and video scripts on **Realize.** Turn the close-caption feature on.

- Allow students to refer to their textbooks or to other written materials during oral presentations.

- Limit background noises that may distract students. Avoid seating these students where they may hear extraneous noise.

- Change listening activities and assessments to reading/writing activities. In activities that require aural/oral skills, let students demonstrate skills through alternative responses such as writing.

- Provide access to the audio and video materials on **Realize.** The eText provides pronunciation support, access to all Student Edition listening activities, and access to the vocabulary and grammar videos.

Visual perception problems

- Help students access information provided visually. Allow for preferred seating in the front of the class, including providing space for a guide dog, if necessary. Avoid seating students where they will be distracted by extraneous auditory or visual stimuli. Give students additional time to review visual input prior to an oral or written task. Highlight important information by providing key words, visuals, and simple outlines.

- Provide support for accessing printed information. Make sure the print is easy to read. The readings should be designed to maximize readability: easy-to-read font, layout, and design. Teach reading strategies that highlight the visual aspects of a selection: text organization, use of visuals, titles and headers, and the use of color. Provide copies of reading selections with additional support: underline key words/sentences/concepts or magnify the text in duplication.

- Teach, practice, and assess using multi-sensory strategies.

ADHD/ADD

- Provide additional support that enables students to focus. Present information in small "chunks." This includes new content, short instructions or directions, and shorter assignments, or break assignments into steps. Limit extraneous auditory and visual stimulation. Provide visual and written support for aural instructions or input. Repeat and explain (again) as needed. Provide outlines of oral presentations. Support readings with strategies similar to those for students with visual perception problems. Use graphic organizers.

- Verify that students "got it." Check that students are looking at you (eye contact) when providing oral instructions. Ask students to repeat what you just told them. Move closer to students to increase attention. Provide preferential seating that allows you to monitor students' focus and attention. Allow extra wait time when students are responding.

- Provide a variety of different learning activities that reach different learning styles. This will also allow for frequent changes of activities within a class. Provide for hands-on activities, vocabulary clip art, and grammar manipulatives.

- Use technology to provide interactive learning. These students will benefit from using the online resources on **Realize.**

- Be predictable. Establish a daily routine for managing the classroom and be consistent. Avoid surprises with these students.

- Help students organize themselves and their learning. Ask students to maintain notebooks that are organized by dividers. Provide study guides, summary sheets, and organizers for daily or weekly assignments.

Accommodation in *Auténtico*

Auténtico 3 provides a wide range of support for accommodating instruction.

STUDENT EDITION

- Clean design and layout of pages

- Visualized presentation of vocabulary

- Step-by-step scaffolding of activities

- Online vocabulary and grammar tutorials and extra practice available on **Realize**

TEACHER'S EDITION

- Differentiated Instruction article

- Differentiated Instruction suggestions

LEVELED VOCABULARY AND GRAMMAR WORKBOOK: GUIDED PRACTICE

- Vocabulary clip art to create flashcards

- Focused vocabulary practice

- Simplified grammar instruction

- Answer Key in Teacher's Resource Materials on **Realize**

ALTERNATE ASSESSMENT PROGRAM ON **REALIZE**

- Additional suggestions for accommodating assessment for students needing extra help

Heritage Speakers

Teaching Heritage Speakers

A diverse background Those who have a home language other than English bring a wider range of language abilities to the classroom. These abilities range from minimal functioning in the language to complete fluency and literacy. It is important for teachers to assess the language skills of the different heritage speakers in the classroom. This diversity includes:

- Students who are able to understand the spoken language, but are unable to respond in the language beyond single-word answers.

- Students who are able to understand the language and communicate at a minimal level. These students may be able to read some items, but because of their limited vocabulary, they may not comprehend much information. They may write what they are able to sound out, but errors are evident.

- Students who can speak the language fluently but who have little to no experience with the language in its written form.

- Students who have come to the United States from non-English-speaking countries. They can understand and speak the language fluently; however, their reading and writing skills may be limited due to lack of a formal education in their country of origin.

- Fluent bilingual students who can understand, speak, read, and write another language very well and have possibly received formal instruction in that language in the United States or in another country.

Program goals Heritage speakers bring rich home language experiences to the classroom that can serve as a foundation for learning. Because of their language background, these students have the potential to be bilingual, biliterate, and bicultural. Heritage speakers need to be exposed to a program that can improve and maintain the home language. Students need to study the grammar and focus on vocabulary development. Emphasis should be placed on building reading and writing skills. It is important that students develop a sensitivity to when standard and non-standard language should be employed and comfortably adjust their language accordingly. In addition, students should be exposed to the diverse cultures within the Spanish-speaking community while developing a sense of pride in their own heritage. Heritage speakers need to reach a high level of proficiency and accuracy that will ensure success at the advanced level of language study and testing. These students should also be ready to transition into a focused study of Spanish in specific professional areas.

Focus on individual needs Due to their diverse backgrounds, heritage speakers differ greatly in language skills and may need individualized instruction. In many of today's classrooms, teachers encounter classes that contain a mixture of beginning-level students and heritage speakers. These groups need different materials, different instructional approaches, and different objectives. Here are several strategies that may be helpful for heritage speakers:

- Build upon their background knowledge. Develop instructional units around themes and topics that relate to their life experiences. Encourage students to use these experiences as the foundation for building language skills through vocabulary development, reading, and writing.

- Help students connect aural with written language. If students don't understand a word in a reading, have them read it aloud or ask a friend or teacher to read it aloud. Often they can recognize the word once they hear it. Allow for opportunities for students to follow along as a story is read aloud.

- Use strategies that are effective in a language arts classroom, such as building schema, teaching language-learning strategies, using graphic organizers, and incorporating pre- and post-reading tasks. Use the writing process to develop good writers.

- Encourage students to begin communicating, especially in writing. Have them write down their thoughts in the way they sound to them. Then have students work with the teacher or another student for corrections. Students can also look through textbooks and dictionaries to assist with error correction.

- Maintain high standards. Require students to focus on accuracy and proficient communication. Many heritage speakers experience frustration with reading and writing in the home language when they have good aural/oral skills. Building language skills takes time.

Teaching Heritage Speakers with *Auténtico 3*

Auténtico 3 offers the ideal solution for heritage speakers. It is recommended that teachers use **Auténtico 3,** *Para hispanohablantes,* with these students. This gives teachers three options: (1) the student textbook; (2) the companion all-Spanish worktext on Realize; or (3) a combination of both.

Teaching All Students: Summary

The diverse needs of today's Spanish students pose a challenge to teachers, curriculum developers, and school administrators as they design programs to ensure that all students develop language proficiency. With **Auténtico,** teachers have at their disposal a variety of materials and strategies to enable them to provide access to Spanish for all learners. Clearly, some students will require additional tutoring and specialized services to reach their full learning potential. However, the activities and materials that accompany **Auténtico,** coupled with instructional strategies described within this article, constitute a viable framework for reaching and teaching all learners.

Teaching Heritage Speakers with *Para hispanohablantes*

Auténtico 3 provides extensive support for teaching heritage speakers.

STUDENT EDITION

- Focused vocabulary and grammar
- Integrated language and culture
- Extensive reading and writing

PARA HISPANOHABLANTES ON **REALIZE**

- All-Spanish companion worktext available as downloadable PDFs
- All-Spanish grammar explanations
- Companion PDFs for each section of Student Edition
- Increased emphasis on reading and writing
- Accompanying Teacher's Guide on Realize

ASSESSMENT PROGRAM: *PARA HISPANOHABLANTES* ON **REALIZE**

- Direction lines in Spanish
- Complete assessment support
- Rubrics in Spanish

PLACEMENT TEST ON **REALIZE**

- Leveled Placement Test with audio
- Vocabulary, grammar, and proficiency assessment

Index of Cultural References

The numbers following each entry indicate the pages on which a reference to that topic is made; an *i* following a number indicates that the reference appears on that page in an illustration, photograph, or artwork; an *m* indicates that the reference appears in a map.

Cancha maya en Chichén Itzá

Index of Cultural References

Index of Cultural References

Index of Cultural References

La Catedral de Sevilla, España

Index of Cultural References

Una Calle de Antiqua

Auténtico

Pearson

Boston, Massachusetts   Chandler, Arizona
Glenview, Illinois   New York, New York

Auténtico

3

Go **Online** to practice

PEARSON
realize™

PearsonSchool.com/Autentico

 AUDIO VIDEO  WRITING  SPEAK/RECORD  MAPA GLOBAL  AUTÉNTICO FLASCHARDS ETEXT 2.O GAMES

Peggy Palo Boyles
OKLAHOMA CITY, OK

Myriam Met
EDGEWATER, MD

Richard S. Sayers
LONGMONT, CO

 Pearson

Auténtico Authors

Peggy Palo Boyles

During her foreign language career of over forty years, Peggy Palo Boyles has taught elementary, secondary, and university students in both private and public schools. She is currently an independent consultant who provides assistance to schools, districts, universities, state departments of education, and other organizations of foreign language education in the areas of curriculum, assessment, cultural instruction, professional development, and program evaluation. She was a member of the ACTFL Performance Guidelines for the K–12 Learners task force and served as a Senior Editor for the project. She served on the Advisory Committee for the ACTFL Assessment for Performance and Proficiency of Languages (AAPPL). Peggy is a Past-President of the National Association of District Supervisors of Foreign Language (NADSFL) and was a recipient of ACTFL's K–12 Steiner Award for Leadership in K–12 Foreign Language Education.

Myriam Met

For most of her professional life, Myriam (Mimi) Met has worked in the public schools, first as a high school teacher in New York, then as K–12 supervisor of language programs in the Cincinnati Public Schools, and finally as a Coordinator of Foreign Language in Montgomery County (MD) Public Schools. After a long career in the public schools, she joined the National Foreign Language Center, University of Maryland, where she worked on K–12 language policy and infrastructure development. She currently works with schools and school districts as an independent consultant.

Richard S. Sayers

Rich Sayers has been involved in world languages education since 1978. He taught Spanish at Niwot High School in Longmont, CO for 18 years, where he taught levels 1 through AP Spanish. While at Niwot High School, Rich served as department chair, district foreign language coordinator, and board member of the Colorado Congress of Foreign Language Teachers and the Southwest Conference on Language Teaching. In 1991, Rich was selected as one of the Disney Company's Foreign Language Teacher Honorees for the American Teacher Awards. Rich has served as a world languages consultant for Pearson since 1996. He is currently the Vice President of Humanities in Pearson's Sales division.

Contributing Writers

Eduardo Aparicio
Chicago, IL

Daniel J. Bender
New Trier High School, Winnetka, IL

Marie Deer
Bloomington, IN

Leslie M. Grahn
Howard County Public Schools, Ellicott City, MD

Thomasina Hannum
Albuquerque, NM

Nancy S. Hernández
World Languages Supervisor, Simsbury (CT) Public Schools

Patricia J. Kule
Fountain Valley School of Colorado, Colorado Springs, CO

Jacqueline Hall Minet
Upper Montclair, NJ

Alex Paredes
Simi Valley, CA

Martha Singer Semmer
Breckenridge, CO

Dee Dee Drisdale Stafford
Putnam City Schools, Oklahoma City, OK

Christine S. Wells
Cheyenne Mountain Junior High School, Colorado Springs, CO

Michael Werner
University of Chicago, Chicago, IL

Digital Course Realize

AUTÉNTICO includes lots of online resources to help you learn Spanish! You'll find these resources highlighted with technology icons on the pages of your print or online Student Edition.

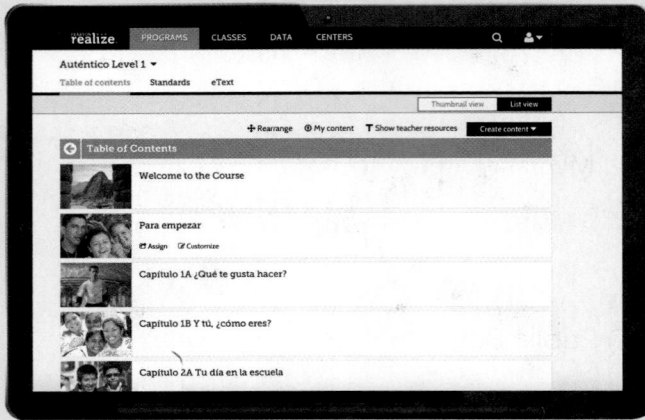

PEARSON **realize**™

The digital course on Realize!
The program's digital course on Realize puts the Student Edition, workbooks, video, audio, flashcards, games, and more at your fingertips.

Look for these icons in your *Auténtico* textbook or digital course.

🔊 **AUDIO**
Audio to learn and practice vocabulary and pronunciation, and increase your listening skills

▶ **VIDEO**
Videodocumentario Cultural overviews of each theme

Videohistoria Vocabulary videos with an entertaining storyline to practice listening to new words in an authentic context

Grammar Tutorials Clear explanations of grammar with comparisons to English

✏️ **WRITING**
Practice activities with writing

🎤 **SPEAK/RECORD**
Speak-and-record tool for speaking activities, you can save your recording

🌐 **MAPA GLOBAL INTERACTIVO**
Links to interactive maps for virtual exploration of the Spanish-speaking world. You can download .kmz files from PearsonSchool.com/Autentico and link to sites using Google Earth™ or other geographic information systems.

📁 **AUTÉNTICO**
Collection of authentic video, audio, and text resources organized by theme

🗂 **FLASHCARDS**
Practice for the new vocabulary

📖 **ETEXT 2.0**
Complete textbook online

🎮 **GAMES**
Interactive, fun practice and review games such as concentration, crosswords, word search and more

📄 **PDF**
Video scripts, readings

📓 **WORKBOOK**
Core and Guided practice activities

Learn Spanish Using Authentic Resources

To become proficient in Spanish, you need to learn to understand and speak it in real-world situations. In *Auténtico*, you will learn about the language and cultures of Spanish-speaking countries as you watch, read, and listen to material created for Spanish speakers.

The **Auténtico** pages in your textbook feature strategies that will help you build your language skills and increase your confidence as you watch videos, listen to audio, and read authentic articles and blogs. ▼

▲ In the the digital course on Realize, you'll find a collection of authentic resources that you can use to improve your understanding of Spanish.

The **Authentic Resources Workbook** will prepare and guide you as you watch, listen to, or read the materials. Activities will help you focus your attention on key elements of the video, audio, or text. Post-viewing, post-listening, and post-reading activities check your comprehension. ▶

Tabla de materias

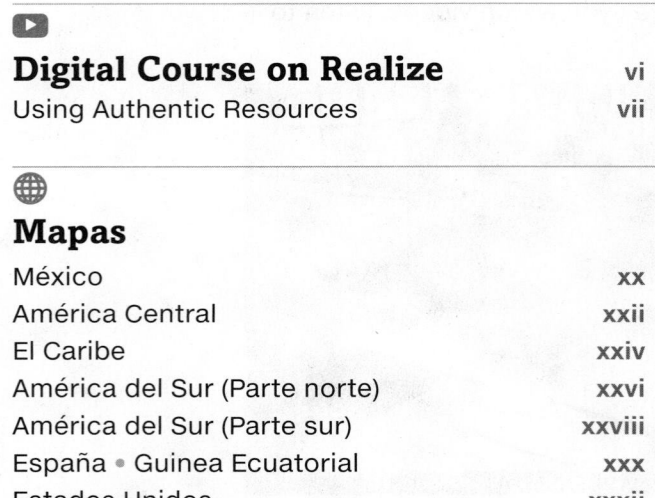

Días inolvidables

CAPÍTULO 2
¿Cómo te expresas?

¿Qué haces para estar en forma?

CAPÍTULO 4
¿Cómo te llevas con los demás?

CAPÍTULO 5

Trabajo y comunidad

¿Qué nos traerá el futuro?

¿Mito o realidad?

Encuentro entre culturas

Cuidemos nuestro planeta

CAPÍTULO 10
¿Cuáles son tus derechos y deberes?

México

ESTADOS UNIDOS

Tijuana

Ciudad
Juárez

Río Bravo
del Norte

30° N

Chihuahua

SIERRA MADRE OCCIDENTAL

Baja California

Golfo de California
(Mar de Cortés)

Nuevo
Laredo

Río Grande

Monterrey

SIERRA MADRE ORIENTAL

Golfo de México

Trópico de Cáncer

LEYENDA
Elevación

Metros Pies
3,000   9,840
2,000   6,560
1,000   3,280
500   1,640
200   656

Frontera nacional
⬨ Capital
● Ciudad
▲ Volcán o montaña

0   200 Millas
0   200 Kilómetros
Proyección cónica conforme de Lambert

20° N

N
O   E
S

Guadalajara

Querétaro

Mérida

Península de
Yucatán

Paracutín ▲

Ciudad de
México

⬨ Iztaccíhuatl
▲ ● Puebla
Popocatépetl

Veracruz

Oaxaca

ISTMO DE
TEHUANTEPEC

BELICE

Acapulco

SIERRA MADRE DEL SUR

GUATEMALA

OCÉANO PACÍFICO

EL SALVADOR

Celebración del equinoccio de primavera,
Teotihuacán, México

México

Capital México, D.F.

Población 121.7 millones

Área 758,449 mi cuadradas / 1,964,375 km cuadrados

Idiomas español (idioma oficial), náhuatl, varios idiomas mayas y de otros grupos indígenas

Gobierno república federal

Moneda peso mexicano

Exportaciones productos manufacturados, petróleo y sus derivados, plata, café, algodón, frutas, verduras

América Central

MÉXICO

Parque Nacional Tikal ▪

Lago Petén Itzá

BELICE

Golfo de Honduras

JAMAICA

Quetzaltenango •

GUATEMALA

Ciudad de Guatemala ✪

Copán ■

San Pedro Sula •

HONDURAS

Santa Rosa de Copán •

Lago de Izabal

Antigua •

Cerro El Pital ▲

Tegucigalpa ✪

Mar Caribe

Volcán de Santa Ana ▲

Santa Ana •

San Salvador ✪

La Libertad •

Santa Rosa de Lima •

CORDILLERA ISABELIA

EL SALVADOR

Golfo de Fonseca

NICARAGUA

CORDILLERA CHONTALEÑA

Lago de Managua

92° O

Managua ✪ Masaya •

Granada •

Lago de Nicaragua

Los Chiles •

COSTA RICA

Puerto Limón •

San José ✪

Golfo de Nicoya

OCÉANO PACÍFICO

Colón •

Ciudad de Panamá ✪

Canal de Panamá

PANAMÁ

Golfo de Panamá

Parque Nacional Darién ▪

Golfo Dulce

88° O

84° O

80° O

COLOMBIA

16° N

12° N

8° N

LEYENDA
Elevación

Metros	Pies
3,000	9,840
2,000	6,560
1,000	3,280
500	1,640
200	656

— Frontera nacional

✪ Capital

• Ciudad

▲ Volcán o montaña

▪ Zona arqueológica

0   100 Millas

0   100 Kilómetros

Proyección azimutal equivalente de Lambert

Guatemala

Capital Ciudad de Guatemala

Población 14.9 millones

Área 42,042 mi cuadradas / 108,889 km cuadrados

Idiomas español (idioma oficial), quiché y otros idiomas indígenas

Gobierno república democrática constitucional

Moneda quetzal, dólar

Exportaciones café, azúcar, petróleo, ropa, textiles, plátano

El Salvador

Capital San Salvador

Población 6.1 millones

Área 8,124 mi cuadradas / 21,041 km cuadrados

Idiomas español (idioma oficial), nahua

Gobierno república

Moneda dólar

Exportaciones elaboración de productos con materiales fabricados en el extranjero, café, azúcar, textiles, productos químicos

Honduras

Capital Tegucigalpa

Población 8.7 millones

Área 43,278 mi cuadradas / 112,090 km cuadrados

Idiomas español (idioma oficial), idiomas indígenas

Gobierno república democrática constitucional

Moneda lempira

Exportaciones café, plátano, camarón, langosta, ropa, oro, madera

Go **Online** to practice PEARSON realize
PearsonSchool.com/Autentico
MAPA GLOBAL

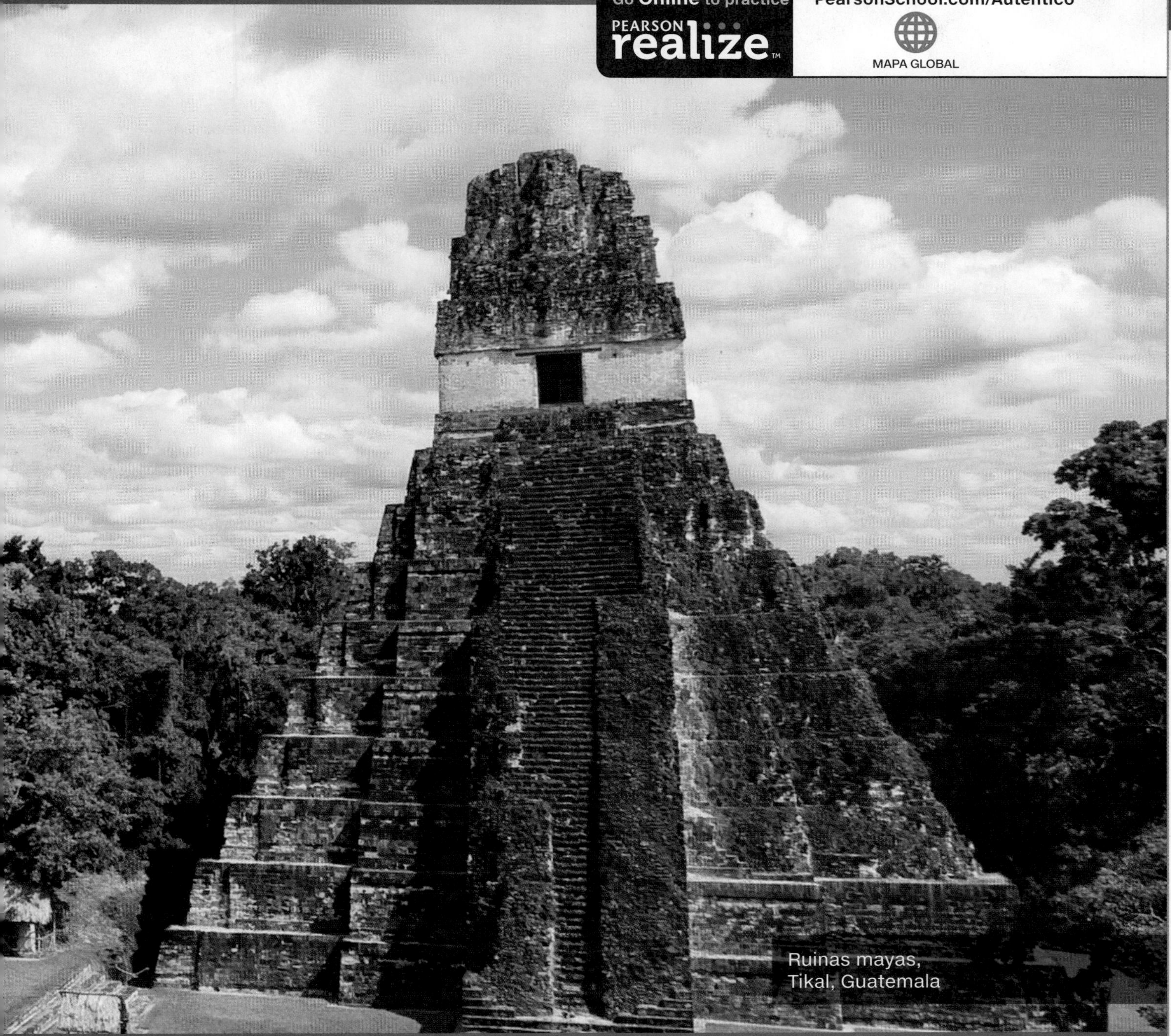

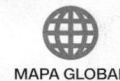

Ruinas mayas, Tikal, Guatemala

Nicaragua

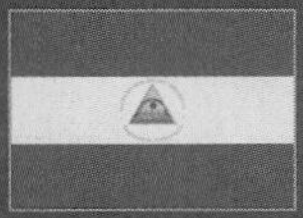

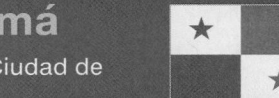

Capital Managua

Población 5.9 millones

Área 50,336 mi cuadradas / 130,370 km cuadrados

Idiomas español (idioma oficial), inglés, miskito y otros idiomas indígenas

Gobierno república

Moneda córdoba

Exportaciones café, camarón, langosta, algodón, tabaco, carne, azúcar, oro

Costa Rica

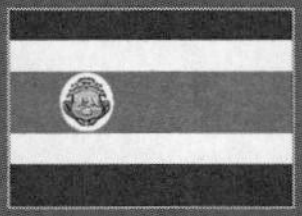

Capital San José

Población 4.8 millones

Área 19,730 mi cuadradas / 51,100 km cuadrados

Idiomas español (idioma oficial) e inglés

Gobierno república democrática

Moneda colón

Exportaciones café, plátano, azúcar, piña, componentes electrónicos

Panamá

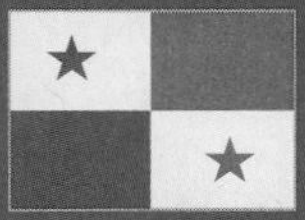

Capital Ciudad de Panamá

Población 3.7 millones

Área 29,120 mi cuadradas / 75,420 km cuadrados

Idiomas español (idioma oficial), idiomas indígenas

Gobierno democracia constitucional

Moneda balboa, dólar

Exportaciones fruta, fruto seco, pescado, sobrante de hierro y acero, madera

El Caribe

ESTADOS UNIDOS

Golfo de México

ISLAS BAHAMAS

Estrecho de la Florida

24° N
Trópico de Cáncer

La Habana

CUBA

OCÉANO ATLÁNTICO

Isla de la Juventud

Guantánamo

Santiago de Cuba

REPÚBLICA DOMINICANA

20° N

Bahía de Samaná

PUERTO RICO (E.E.U.U.)

HAITÍ

VIEQUES

San Juan

Ponce

El Yunque

JAMAICA

Santo Domingo

LEYENDA
Elevación

Metros	Pies
3,000	9,840
2,000	6,560
1,000	3,280
500	1,640
200	656

— Frontera nacional
✪ Capital
● Ciudad
▲ Volcán o montaña

0   100 Millas
0   100 Kilómetros

Proyección azimutal equivalente de Lambert

Mar Caribe

16° N

80° O   76° O   72° O   68° O

Cuba

Capital La Habana

Población 11 millones

Área 42,803 mi cuadradas / 110,860 km cuadrados

Idiomas español (idioma oficial)

Gobierno estado comunista

Moneda peso cubano

Exportaciones azúcar, níquel, tabaco, mariscos, productos médicos, cítricos, café

República Dominicana

Capital Santo Domingo

Población 10.5 millones

Área 18,792 mi cuadradas / 48,670 km cuadrados

Idiomas español (idioma oficial)

Gobierno república democrática

Moneda peso dominicano

Exportaciones azúcar, oro, plata, cacao, tabaco, carne

Puerto Rico

Capital San Juan

Población 3.6 millones

Área 5,325 mi cuadradas / 13,791 km cuadrados

Idiomas español e inglés (idiomas oficiales)

Gobierno estado libre asociado de Estados Unidos

Moneda dólar estadounidense

Exportaciones productos químicos, productos electrónicos, ropa, atún enlatado, concentrados de bebidas

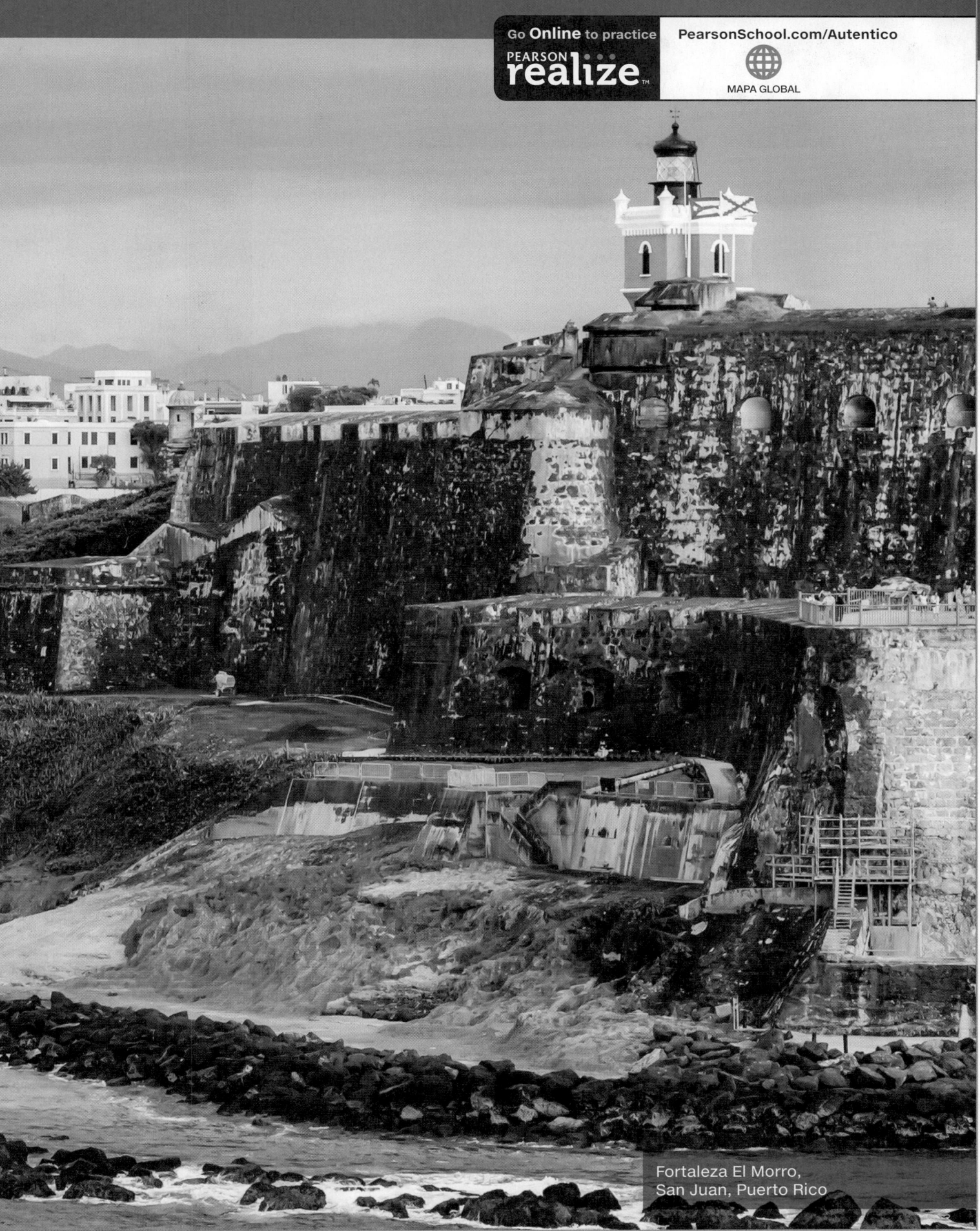

Fortaleza El Morro,
San Juan, Puerto Rico

América del Sur (PARTE NORTE)

Mar Caribe

Cartagena
Maracaibo
Caracas

Río Orinoco

VENEZUELA

Medellín
Río Magdalena

Cali
Bogotá
COLOMBIA

ECUADOR
Quito
Ecuador
0°

Chimborazo
Guayaquil

BRASIL

ISLAS
GALÁPAGOS
(Ecuador)

Golfo de
Guayaquil

PERÚ

Huascarán

Callao
Lima

Machu
Picchu
Cuzco

BOLIVIA

OCÉANO
PACÍFICO

Lago
Titicaca

La Paz
Cochabamba

Nevado
Sajama
Sucre
Potosí

PARAGUAY
20° S

LEYENDA
Elevación

Metros	Pies
3,000	9,840
2,000	6,560
1,000	3,280
500	1,640
200	656

— Frontera nacional
✪ Capital
● Ciudad
▲ Volcán o montaña
■ Zona arqueológica

0   400 Millas

0   400 Kilómetros

Proyección azimutal
equivalente de Lambert

CHILE

Trópico de Capricornio

ARGENTINA

URUGUAY

OCÉANO
ATLÁNTICO

40° S

N
O   E
S

Colombia

Capital Bogotá

Población 46.7 millones

Área 439,736 mi cuadradas /
1,138,910 km cuadrados

Idiomas español (idioma oficial)

Gobierno república

Moneda peso colombiano

Exportaciones petróleo, carbón,
café, esmeraldas, plátano, flores,
níquel

Ecuador

Capital Quito

Población 15.9 millones

Área 109,483 mi cuadradas /
283,561 km cuadrados

Idiomas español (idioma oficial),
quechua y otros idiomas indígenas

Gobierno república

Moneda dólar

Exportaciones petróleo, plátano,
flores, camarón, cacao, café, madera

Go **Online** to practice PEARSON realize

PearsonSchool.com/Autentico

MAPA GLOBAL

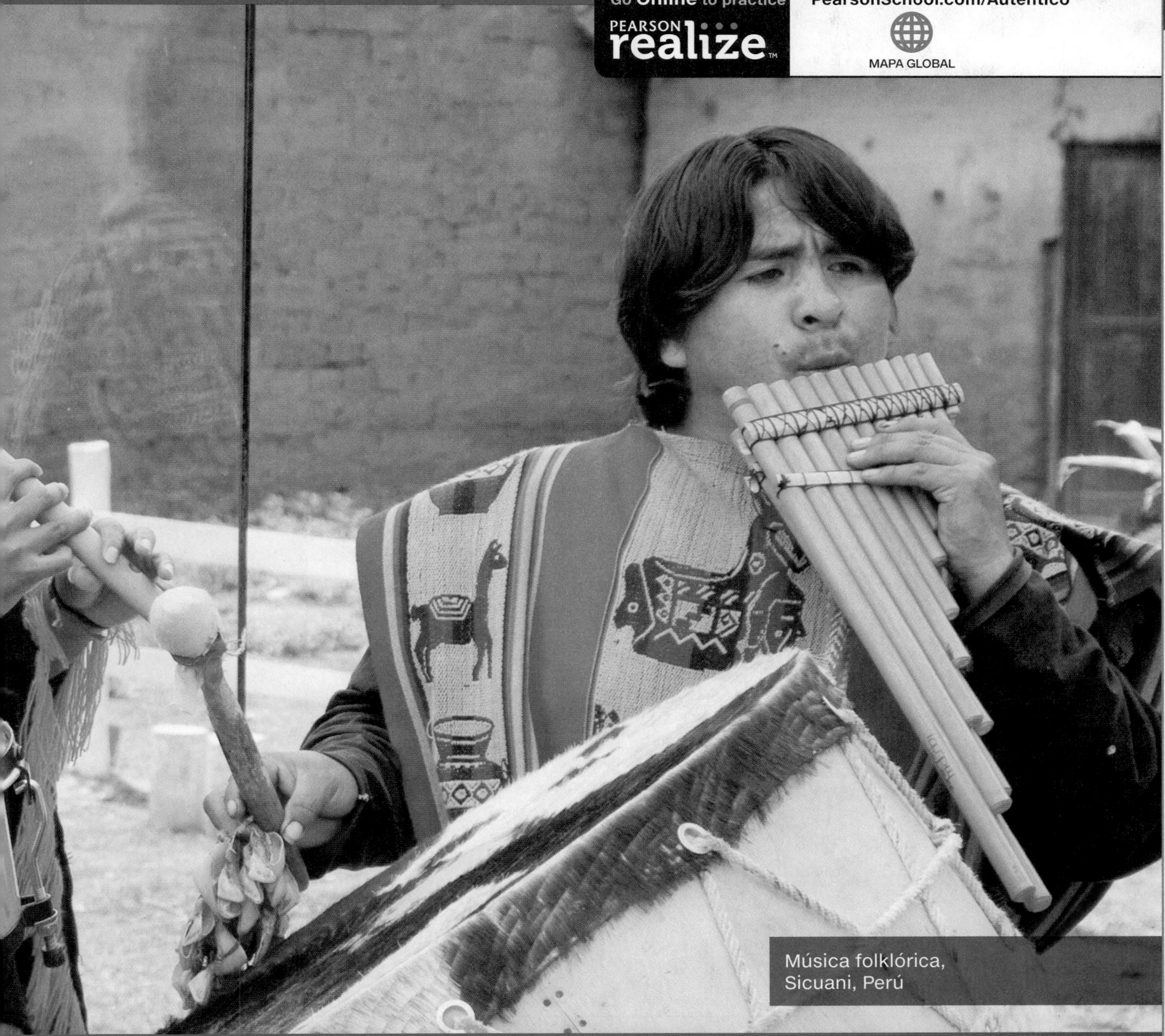

Música folklórica, Sicuani, Perú

Perú

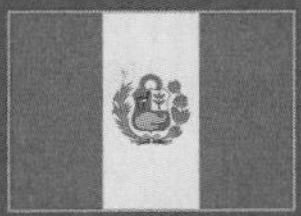

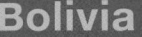

Capital Lima

Población 30.4 millones

Área 496,225 mi cuadradas / 1,285,216 km cuadrados

Idiomas español, quechua, aymara (idiomas oficiales) y otros idiomas indígenas

Gobierno república constitucional

Moneda nuevo sol

Exportaciones oro, cinc, cobre, pescado y productos de pescado

Venezuela

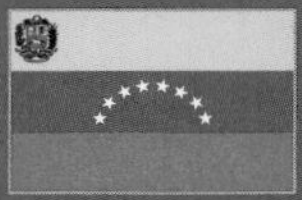

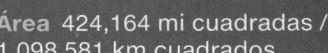

Capital Caracas

Población 29.3 millones

Área 352,144 mi cuadradas / 912,050 km cuadrados

Idiomas español (idioma oficial), idiomas indígenas

Gobierno república federal

Moneda bolívar fuerte

Exportaciones petróleo y productos de petróleo, aluminio, mineral, productos químicos

Bolivia

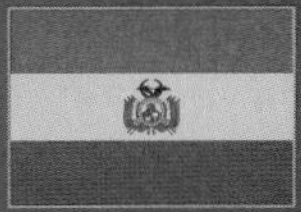

Capitales La Paz, Sucre

Población 10.8 millones

Área 424,164 mi cuadradas / 1,098,581 km cuadrados

Idiomas español, quechua, aymara, guaraní (idiomas oficiales) y otros idiomas

Gobierno república (estado unitario social)

Moneda boliviano

Exportaciones soja y productos de soja, gas natural, estaño, oro

América del Sur (PARTE SUR)

Mar Caribe

VENEZUELA

COLOMBIA

Ecuador

ECUADOR

0°

PERÚ

BRASIL

OCÉANO
PACÍFICO

BOLIVIA

ALTIPLANO

CORDILLERA DE LOS ANDES

Río Paraguay

20° S

LEYENDA
Elevación

GRAN CHACO

PARAGUAY

Asunción ✪

Cataratas
del Iguazú

Trópico de Capricornio

Metros	Pies
3,000	9,840
2,000	6,560
1,000	3,280
500	1,640
200	656

CHILE

Río Paraná

— Frontera nacional

✪ Capital

● Ciudad

▲ Volcán o montaña

ARGENTINA

Viña del Mar ●
Valparaíso ●✪
Santiago

Cerro
Aconcagua

Rosario ●

URUGUAY

Montevideo
●✪
Punta del
Este

0   400 Millas

0   400 Kilómetros

Proyección azimutal
equivalente de Lambert

Buenos Aires ●✪

PAMPAS

Río de la Plata

Mar del Plata ●

OCÉANO
ATLÁNTICO

40° S

Cerro de
San Valentín ▲

PATAGONIA

Torres del
Paine ▲

TIERRA DEL
FUEGO

Estrecho de
Magallanes

● Cabo de Hornos

Chile

Capital Santiago

Población 17.5 millones

Área 291,933 mi cuadradas /
756,102 km cuadrados

Idiomas español (idioma oficial),
inglés e idiomas indígenas

Gobierno república

Moneda peso chileno

Exportaciones cobre, pescado,
fruta, papel y pulpa, productos
químicos, vino

Go **Online** to practice

PearsonSchool.com/Autentico

PEARSON
realize™

MAPA GLOBAL

Esquiar en las montañas, Chile

Paraguay

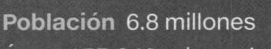

Capital Asunción

Población 6.8 millones

Área 157,048 mi cuadradas / 406,752 km cuadrados

Idiomas español y guaraní (idiomas oficiales)

Gobierno república constitucional

Moneda guaraní

Exportaciones soja, algodón, carne, aceite comestible, madera, cuero

Argentina

Capital Buenos Aires

Población 43.4 millones

Área 1,073,518 mi cuadradas / 2,780,400 km cuadrados

Idiomas español (idioma oficial), inglés, francés, italiano, alemán e idiomas indígenas

Gobierno república

Moneda peso argentino

Exportaciones soja y productos de soja, petróleo, gas, vehículos

Uruguay

Capital Montevideo

Población 3.3 millones

Área 68,037 mi cuadradas / 176,215 km cuadrados

Idiomas español (idioma oficial), portuñol/brasilero

Gobierno república constitucional

Moneda peso uruguayo

Exportaciones carne, celulosa, soja, arroz, trigo, madera, productos lácteos, lana

España
Guinea Ecuatorial

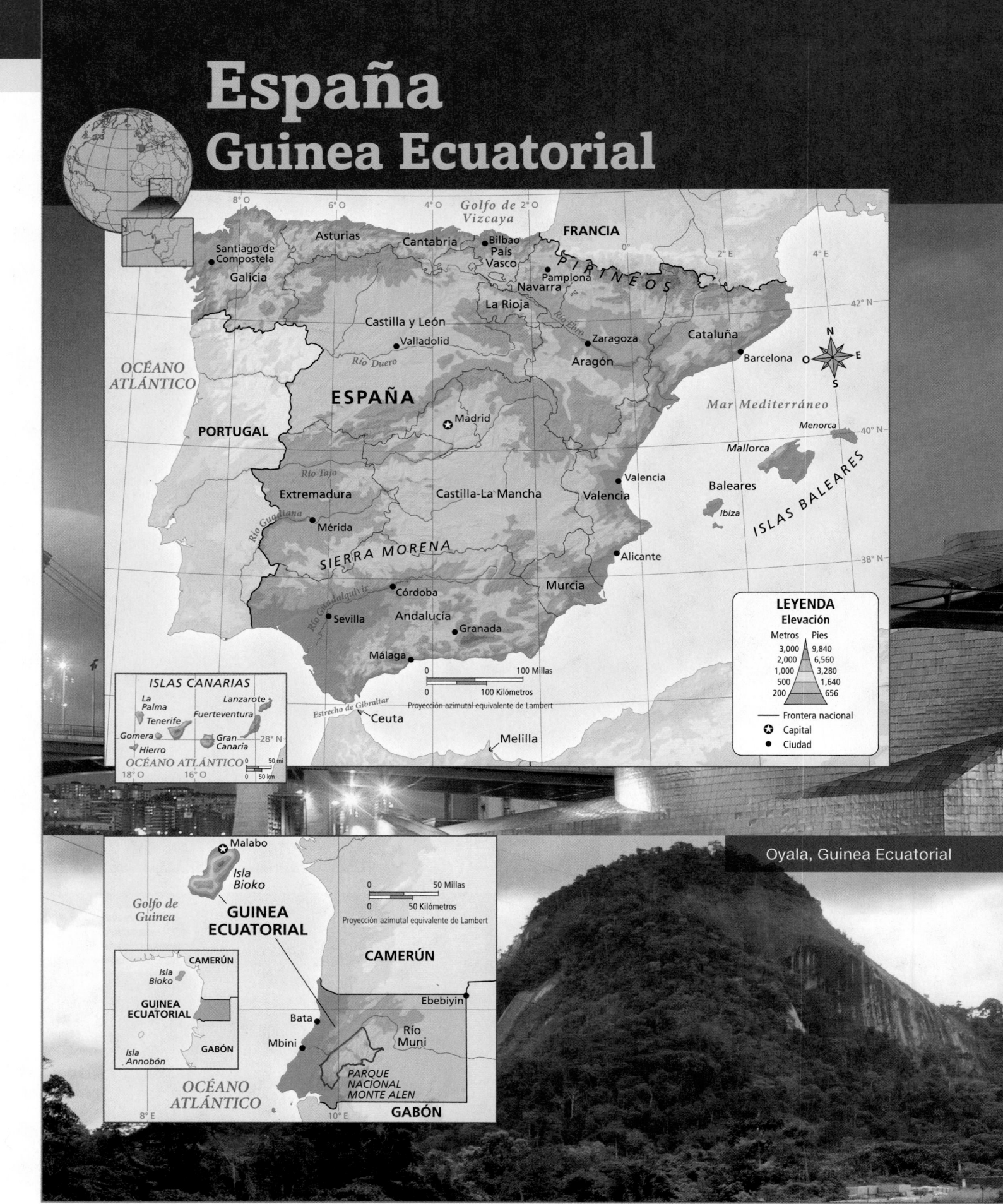

FRANCIA

Golfo de Vizcaya

Asturias
Cantabria
Santiago de Compostela
Bilbao
País Vasco
PIRINEOS
Galicia
Pamplona
Navarra
La Rioja
Río Ebro
Castilla y León
Zaragoza
Cataluña
Valladolid
Aragón
Barcelona

OCÉANO ATLÁNTICO

Río Duero

ESPAÑA

Madrid

PORTUGAL

Mar Mediterráneo

Menorca

Mallorca

Río Tajo

Extremadura
Castilla-La Mancha
Valencia
Valencia
Baleares
Ibiza
ISLAS BALEARES

Río Guadiana
Mérida

SIERRA MORENA

Alicante

Murcia

Córdoba
Río Guadalquivir
Sevilla
Andalucía
Granada

Málaga

0   100 Millas
0   100 Kilómetros
Proyección azimutal equivalente de Lambert

Estrecho de Gibraltar
Ceuta

Melilla

ISLAS CANARIAS

La Palma
Lanzarote
Tenerife
Fuerteventura
Gomera
Gran Canaria
Hierro
OCÉANO ATLÁNTICO
0   50 mi
0   50 km
18° O   16° O   28° N

LEYENDA
Elevación

Metros	Pies
3,000	9,840
2,000	6,560
1,000	3,280
500	1,640
200	656

—— Frontera nacional
⊛ Capital
● Ciudad

Malabo
Isla Bioko
Golfo de Guinea
GUINEA ECUATORIAL
CAMERÚN
Isla Bioko
GUINEA ECUATORIAL
GABÓN
Isla Annobón
CAMERÚN
Ebebiyin
Bata
Mbini
Río Muni
0   50 Millas
0   50 Kilómetros
Proyección azimutal equivalente de Lambert
PARQUE NACIONAL MONTE ALEN
OCÉANO ATLÁNTICO
8° E   10° E   GABÓN

Oyala, Guinea Ecuatorial

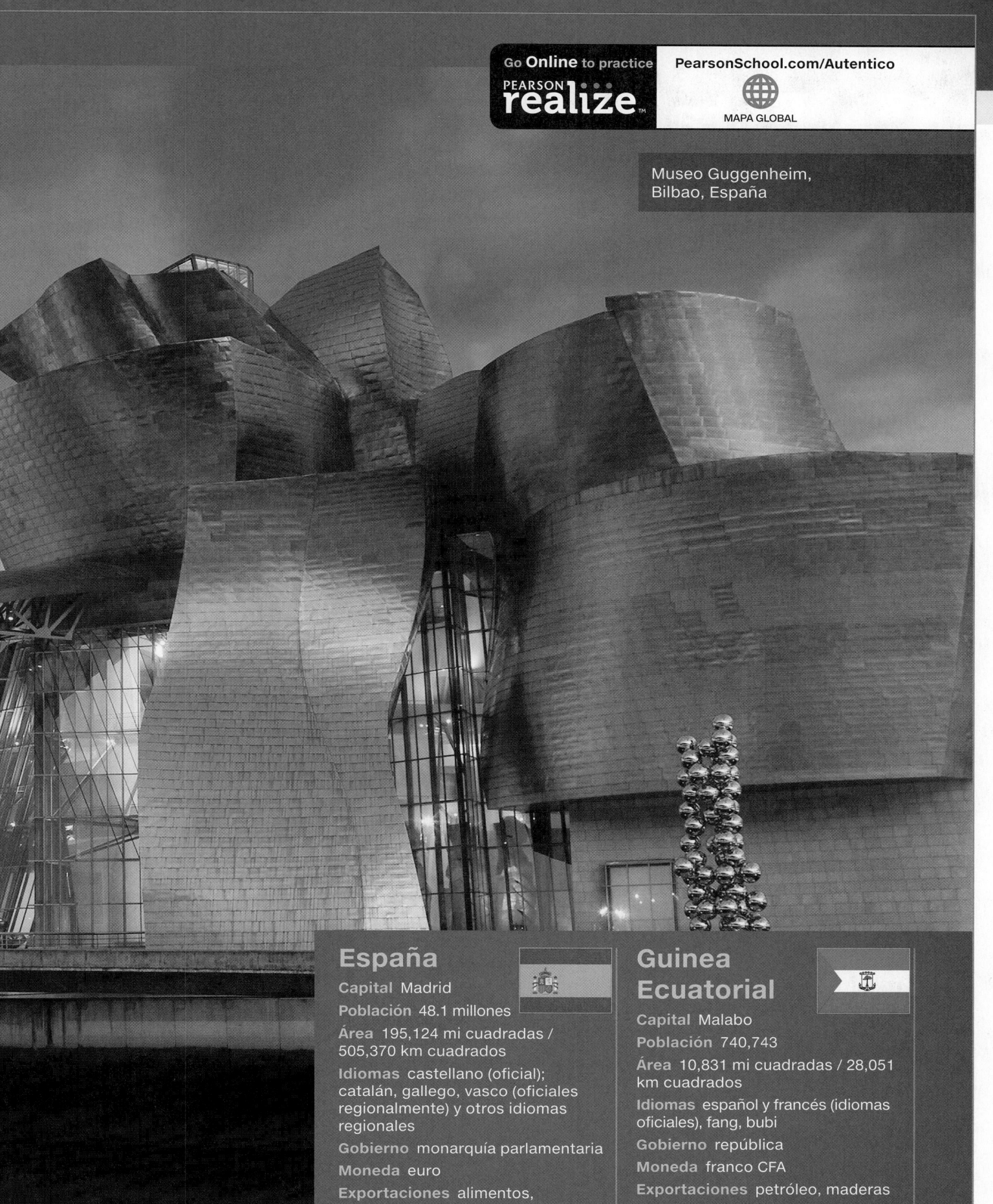

Museo Guggenheim,
Bilbao, España

España

Capital Madrid

Población 48.1 millones

Área 195,124 mi cuadradas /
505,370 km cuadrados

Idiomas castellano (oficial);
catalán, gallego, vasco (oficiales
regionalmente) y otros idiomas
regionales

Gobierno monarquía parlamentaria

Moneda euro

Exportaciones alimentos,
maquinaria, vehículos, medicina

Guinea Ecuatorial

Capital Malabo

Población 740,743

Área 10,831 mi cuadradas / 28,051
km cuadrados

Idiomas español y francés (idiomas
oficiales), fang, bubi

Gobierno república

Moneda franco CFA

Exportaciones petróleo, maderas

Estados Unidos

120° O 110° O 100° O 90° O 80° O 70° O 50° N

CANADÁ

Seattle

MONTAÑAS ROCOSAS

GRANDES LLANURAS

Grandes Lagos

40° N

Minneapolis

Boston

San Francisco

Denver
Mt. Elbert

ESTADOS UNIDOS

Chicago

Detroit

Cleveland

Nueva York

Filadelfia

Washington, D.C.

MONTES APALACHES

OCÉANO ATLÁNTICO

Los Ángeles

San Diego

Phoenix

St. Louis

OCÉANO PACÍFICO

Río Grande

Dallas

Atlanta

30° N

Houston

San Antonio

MÉXICO

Golfo de México

CUBA

Miami

Estrecho de la Florida

Trópico de Cáncer

20° N

LEYENDA
Elevación

Metros	Pies
3,000	9,840
2,000	6,560
1,000	3,280
500	1,640
200	656

—— Frontera nacional
⊛ Capital
● Ciudad
▲ Volcán o montaña

0   400 Millas
0   400 Kilómetros
Proyección cónica conforme de Lambert

ALASKA
Mt. McKinley
CANADÁ
70° O
60° N
Mar de Bering
Golfo de Alaska
0   300 Millas
0   300 Kilómetros
160° O   150° O

160° O   158° O   OCÉANO PACÍFICO
22° N
HAWÁI
20° N
0   100 Millas
0   100 Kilómetros

San Antonio Riverwalk, Texas

Estados Unidos

Capital Washington, D.C.

Población 321.4 millones

Área 3,796,742 mi cuadradas / 9,833,517 km cuadrados

Idiomas inglés, español, idiomas indígenas, idiomas asiáticas y del Pacífico Sur, otros idiomas

Gobierno república federal

Moneda dólar estadounidense

Exportaciones vehículos automotores, medicinas, equipos de telecomunicaciones, equipos electrónicos, productos químicos, soja, fruta, maíz

1 TU VIDA DIARIA

School and non-school daily activities

Vocabulary: daily activities; household chores; errands

Grammar: present tense of irregular verbs; present tense of stem-changing verbs; reflexive verbs

Cultural Perspectives: daily activities of young people in Spain

2 DÍAS ESPECIALES

Weekend activities and special events and celebrations

Vocabulary: entertainment; special events and celebrations; television and movies; travel

Grammar: verbs that conjugate like *gustar*; possessive adjectives

Cultural Perspectives: skiing in Bariloche, Argentina

Chapter Support

Bulletin Boards

Theme: Días especiales

Ask students to cut out, copy, or download photos or pictures of special celebrations and holidays in different countries. They can also include their own photos. Cluster pictures by country.

Game

Preguntas y respuestas

This game practices making questions and answers, using verbs in the present tense.

Players: the entire class

Materials: 3" x 5" index cards, cut in half, small paper bag

Steps:

1. Give students two halves of an index card and ask them to write a question in the present tense on one half and an answer on the other. Questions can be funny, silly, or serious. The answers should include as many details as possible. For example:
   Q: ¿Cómo ayudas a tu mamá cuando regresas de la escuela?
   A: Voy al supermercado con ella y la ayudo a cocinar.
2. Place answers in a bag and mix them up. Each student selects a card from the bag.
3. The first player reads his / her question aloud. A student who thinks he / she has the correct answer reads it to the class. If correct, this student reads the next question. If incorrect, another player reads an answer. If, after three tries, no one presents the correct answer, the player who wrote the original question says the answer and chooses someone to read the next question. The game is over when all questions are read.

Hands-on Culture

Craft: Piñata

A *piñata* is a decorated container filled with candy and toys that is suspended from a height. Children take turns trying to break it open with a stick while blindfolded. The *piñata* is a Mexican custom that has existed for many centuries. Original *piñatas* were made of clay, and then replaced by cardboard.

Materials:

medium-size round balloon, string and scissors, newspapers, white liquid glue and water, old tablespoon for measuring, small bowl for glue, bowl to hold the balloon, brush for glue, tissue paper in assorted colors, wrapped candy and/or small toys, masking tape (optional)

Steps:

1. Blow up the balloon and tie it with a string. Do not cut the string ends.
2. In a bowl, dilute six tablespoons of white liquid glue with three tablespoons of water.
3. Tear off small pieces of tissue paper. Brush diluted glue over the balloon, a small section at a time, and paste on the paper pieces. Overlap the pieces and brush more glue on top. Continue to cover the balloon, making large patches of different colors, overlapping them at edges. Leave a 2" patch uncovered around the knot.
4. Use the string to hang the balloon upside down. Let dry overnight.
5. Paste two more layers of paper pieces on the balloon, letting it dry overnight between each layer.
6. Cut the knotted end off, pull the balloon out and discard it.
7. Fill the piñata with wrapped candies. Paste tissue paper pieces to cover the opening.
8. When is dry, paint and decorate the *piñata*.
9. Use the string to hang up the *piñata* outside.

21st Century Skills

Look for tips throughout *Para empezar* to enrich your teaching by integrating 21st Century Skills Cross-Disciplinary Standards. Suggestion for the Project-based Learning and Chapter support follow below.

Project-Based Learning

Modify the Project-Based learning with one or more of these suggestions:

Critical Thinking and Problem Solving

As students begin preparations for the Project-Based Learning Project, have them make a list of the interrogative words and phrases they know in Spanish. Make sure they integrate their Spanish interrogative words and phrases into their script for the student interview.

Collaboration
Encourage students to work with a partner or in a small group to share the responsibility of preparing the interview questions. They should take turns playing the role of interviewer and interviewee by asking and answering the questions they created as a rehearsal for the recording of the interview.

Communication
Have students interview an older family member or a person in their community from another culture about a similar daily time schedule. They can conduct the interview in English, then report back to the class in Spanish. Have students circulate around the room to compare their schedules with the schedules they have gathered from people outside the class. What are the similarities and differences?

Chapter Culture

Social and Cross-Cultural Skills Have students compare their responses to the question in the *Cultura* note on page xxxvi with a partner. What similarities or differences are there between their responses? Ask them to consider what these similarities or differences might be attributed to: culture? economics? other influences? Ask them to identify the most important element to them from the list (friends, family, health, etc.), and to comment on their choices.

Project-Based Learning

La entrevista

Overview: Students write a television script for an interview program about all the things a student does everyday from the time he / she wakes up. They also create a time schedule showing all the things the interviewee (a student) does. They then perform the interview and record it for the class to view.

Resources: design tools for print or screen, poster board, markers, video equipment

Sequence: suggestions for when to do each step are found throughout the unit)

Step 1. Review instructions so students know what is expected of them. Share the rubric with the class.

Step 2. Students write a rough draft of their interview. They then exchange scripts with a partner for peer editing. Students make corrections based on their partner's comments.

Step 3. Students create a time schedule. The time schedule should show the different things the student says he / she does during the day. After completing the schedules, students could add illustrations to make it more interesting.

Step 4. Students rehearse their interview with a partner. Partners give students feedback about the content, accuracy, and presentation of the subject.

Step 5. Students record their interview. Show videos to the class.

Options

1. Students present their interviews to the class "live" instead of recording them.
2. Students give a presentation of the everyday activities of a student.

Assessment

Here is a detailed rubric for assessing this project:

Para empezar Project: *La entrevista*

Rubric	Score 1	Score 3	Score 5
Your evidence of planning	You do not include a written draft.	Your draft is written, but not corrected.	You provide evidence of corrected draft.
Your use of illustrations	You do not include a time schedule.	Your time schedule is difficult to read, incomplete, and / or inaccurate.	Your time schedule is easy to read, complete, and accurate.
Your interview presentation	You do not include the majority of the required elements.	You include some of the following: greeting, questions, answers, and descriptions.	You include the following: greeting, questions, answers, and descriptions.

AT A GLANCE

Objectives
- Talk about your daily life
- Write about leisure and after-school activities
- Talk about school and non-school daily activities
- Describe your day before and after school
- Talk about weekend activities
- Discuss special events, celebrations, and vacations

Vocabulary
- Daily activities (school related and non-school related)
- Help around the house and errands
- Entertainment, television, and movies
- Events and celebrations
- Traveling

Grammar
- Irregular verbs
- Stem-changing verbs in the present tense
- Reflexive verbs
- Verbs that conjugate like **gustar**
- Possessive adjectives

Culture
- Daily activities of young people, p. xxxvi
- Skiing in Bariloche, p. 12

Recycle
- Foods and beverages
- Health and exercise

RESOURCES

	FOR THE STUDENT	DIGITAL	PRINT	FOR THE TEACHER	DIGITAL	PRINT
Plan				Teacher's Edition, pp. xxxvi-a–15	•	•
				Teacher's Resource Materials, pp. 1–10	•	
				Lesson Plans	•	•
				Mapa global interactivo	•	
Introducción pp. xxxvi–1						
Present	Student Edition, pp. xxxvi–1	•	•	Teacher's Edition, pp. xxxvi–1	•	•
	DK Reference Atlas	•		Teacher's Resource Materials	•	
	Para hispanohablantes	•		Mapa global interactivo	•	
Tu vida diaria pp. 2–7						
Present & Practice	Student Edition, pp. 2–7	•	•	Interactive Whiteboard Grammar Activities	•	
	Audio	•		Teacher's Edition, pp. 2–7	•	•
	Instant Check	•		Teacher's Resource Materials	•	
	Guided WB, pp. 1–10	•	•	Communicative Pair Activities	•	
	Core WB, pp. 1–3	•	•	Technology: Audio		
	Communication Activities	•				
	Para hispanohablantes	•				
	Communicative Pair Activities	•				
Assess and Remediate				Prueba P–1 with Remediation	•	
				Prueba P–1: Assessment Program	•	
				Para hispanohablantes	•	

RESOURCES

	FOR THE STUDENT	DIGITAL	PRINT	FOR THE TEACHER	DIGITAL	PRINT
Días especiales pp. 8–13						
Present & Practice	Student Edition, pp. 8–13	•	•	Interactive Whiteboard Grammar Activities	•	
	Instant Check	•		Teacher's Edition, pp. 8–13	•	•
	Tutorial Video: Grammar	•		Teacher's Resource Materials	•	
	Guided WB, pp. 11–14	•	•	Technology: Audio	•	
	Core WB, pp. 4–6	•	•			
	Communication Activities	•				
	Para hispanohablantes, pp. 6–9	•				
Assess and Remediate				Prueba P–2 with Remediation	•	
				Prueba P–2: Assessment Program	•	
				Para hispanohablantes	•	
Presentación oral, Presentación escrita pp. 14–15						
Application	Student Edition, pp. 14–15	•	•	Teacher's Edition, pp. 14–15	•	•
	Para hispanohablantes	•				

LESSON PLAN

DAY	Warm-up / Assess	Preview / Present / Practice / Communicate	Wrap-up / Homework Options
1	**Warm-up** (10 min.) • Chapter Opener • Arte y cultura	**Tu vida diaria** (35 min.) • Presentation: Tu vida diaria • Actividad 1 • Presentation: Gramática-Repaso • Interactive Whiteboard Grammar Activities • Actividades 3, 4, 5, 6 • Audio Activity 1 • Presentation: Gramática-Repaso	**Wrap-up and Homework Options** (5 min.) • Actividades 2, 7, 8, 9 • Core Practice P-1 • Clip Art Vocabulary
2	**Warm-up** (10 min.) • Homework check	**Tu vida diaria** (35 min.) • Actividad 10 • Audio Activity 2 • Presentation: Gramática-Repaso • Actividad 11 • Audio Activity 3 • Communicative Pair Activity	**Wrap-up and Homework Options** (5 min.) • Actividad 12 • Core Practice P-2, P-3 • Prueba P-1 with Remediation
3	**Warm-up** (10 min.) • Homework check • **Formative Assessment** • Prueba P-1 with Remediation	**Días especiales** (35 min.) • Presentation: Días especiales • Actividad 13 • Actividades 15, 16 • Audio Activity 4 • Presentation: Gramática-Repaso • Interactive Whiteboard Grammar Activities • Actividades 17, 18 • Audio Activity 5	**Wrap-up and Homework Options** (5 min.) • Actividad 14 • Core Practice P-4 • Prueba P-2 with Remediation
4	**Warm-up** (10 min.) • Homework check • **Formative Assessment** • Prueba P-2 with Remediation	**Días especiales** (20 min.) • Presentation: Gramática-Repaso • Actividades 19, 20, 21 • Cultura **Assessment** (15 min.) • Presentación oral • Communicative Pair Activity	**Wrap-up and Homework Options** (5 min.) • Core Practice P-5 • Presentación oral
5	**Warm-up** (3 min.) • **Formative Assessment** (32 min.) • Presentación oral	• **Formative Assessment** (14 min.) • Presentación escrita	**Wrap-up and Homework Options** (1 min.) • Presentación escrita

ALTERNATE LESSON PLAN

DAY	Warm-up / Assess	Preview / Present / Practice / Communicate	Wrap-up / Homework Options
1	**Warm-up** (10 min.) • Chapter Opener • Arte y cultura	**Tu vida diaria** (25 min.) • Presentation: Tu vida diaria • Actividad 1 • Presentation: Gramática-Repaso • Interactive Whiteboard Grammar Activities • Actividades 3, 4, 5, 6 • Audio Activity 1 • Presentation: Gramática-Repaso • Actividades 8, 9, 10 • Audio Activity 2 • Presentation: Gramática-Repaso • Actividad 11 • Audio Activity 3 • Communicative Pair Activity	**Wrap-up and Homework Options** (5 min.) • Actividades 2, 7, 12 • Core Practice: P-1, P-2, P-3 • Clip Art Vocabulary • Prueba P-1 with Remediation
2	**Warm-up** (10 min.) • Actividad 6 • Homework check • **Formative Assessment** • Prueba P-1 with Remediation	**Días especiales** (60 min.) • Presentation: Días especiales • Actividades 13, 15, 16 • Audio Activity 4 • Presentation: Gramática-Repaso • Interactive Whiteboard Grammar Activities • Actividades 17, 18 • Audio Activity 5 • Presentation: Gramática-Repaso • Actividades 20, 21 **Assessment** (15 min.) • Presentación oral	**Wrap-up and Homework Options** (5 min.) • Actividades 14, 19 • Core Practice: P-4, P-5 • Presentación oral • Prueba P-2 with Remediation
3	**Warm-up** (10 min.) • Actividad 10 • Homework check • **Formative Assessment** • Prueba P-2 with Remediation	• **Formative Assessment** (60 min.) • Presentación oral • Presentación escrita	**Wrap-up and Homework Options** (20 min.) • Cultura • Communicative Pair Activity

Para empezar

Can-Do Statements
Read the Can-Do Statements in the chapter objectives with students.

Standards for Para empezar

To achieve the goals of the Standards, students will:

COMMUNICATION

1.1 Interpersonal
- Talk about the activities of Spanish young people
- Talk about daily routines, pastimes, and chores
- Talk about TV programs, entertainment, special days, and vacations
- Talk about Bariloche, Argentina

1.2 Interpretive
- Read about the activities of Spanish young people
- Read and listen to information about daily routines, pastimes, and household chores
- Read and listen to information about TV programs, entertainment, special days, and vacations
- Read about Bariloche, Argentina
- Read about speech and composition preparation

1.3 Presentational
- Write and present information orally about daily routines, pastimes, and household chores
- Write and present information orally about TV programs, entertainment, special days, and vacations
- Write about activities for visiting foreign students

CULTURE

2.1 Practices to Perspectives
- Understand lifestyles and values of Spanish young people
- Understand the vacation practices of Spanish-speaking peoples

2.2 Products to Perspectives
- Learn about the ski resort of Bariloche, Argentina

CONNECTIONS

3.1 Making Connections
- Learn key facts about Spanish youth
- Learn key facts about an Argentine town
- Learn Language Arts Strategies: evaluate your lead

COMPARISONS

4.1 Language
- Compare the use of *encantar, gustar, importar,* and *interesar* to that of their English counterparts
- Compare Spanish words to their English counterparts

4.2 Cultural
- Compare the activities of young people in Spain to those in the United States

COMMUNITIES

5.1 School and Global Communities
- Link to Web sites from the Spanish-speaking world

CHAPTER OBJECTIVES

Communication

By the end of *Para empezar* you will be able to
- Talk about your daily life
- Write about leisure and after-school activities

You will demonstrate what you know and can do
- Presentación oral: Mi vida
- Presentación escrita: Actividades en mi comunidad

You will also learn to:

1 Tu vida diaria
- Talk about school and non-school daily activities
- Describe your day before and after school

2 Días especiales
- Talk about weekend activities
- Discuss special events, celebrations, and vacations

ARTE y CULTURA ► España

Vida diaria de los jóvenes ¿Qué cosas son importantes para los jóvenes de España? Según una encuesta *(survey)*, para los jóvenes españoles son importantes los amigos, la familia, la salud, la libertad[1], las cosas que tienen, el tiempo libre, los estudios, la situación económica y el trabajo. ¿Qué hacen en su tiempo libre? Los días de semana practican deportes, estudian instrumentos musicales o idiomas, escuchan música, ven la televisión o usan la computadora. Los fines de semana salen con sus amigos, van al cine o a bailar.

▶ ¿En qué te pareces y en qué te diferencias de los jóvenes que respondieron a la encuesta?

[1]freedom

Enrich Your Teaching

The End in Mind
Have students preview the *Presentación oral* and *Presentación escrita* tasks on pages 14–15 and connect them to the Chapter Objectives. Explain to students that by completing these sample tasks they can self-assess their learning progress.

Technology: Mapa global interactivo
Download the *Mapa global interactivo* files for *Para empezar* and preview the activity. For this activity, travel to Bariloche, the gateway to Patagonia in Argentina.

Preview | **PE**

Un grupo de chicas juega al fútbol
en Cuzco, Perú.

Para empezar • uno **1**

Chapter Opener

Para empezar is designed to give a quick re-entry into the new school year by allowing students to talk about what they enjoy doing. It reviews fundamental structures and basic vocabulary. Additional review of vocabulary and structures will be woven throughout the book in the *A ver si recuerdas* sections as well as in the regular chapters. You may also want to incorporate any favorite activities or materials from *Auténtico* 1 and 2 that deal with the same topics or structures.

Suggestions: Introduce yourself to students who don't know you. Provide a brief description of yourself (where you are from and some activities you enjoy). Then have each student turn to a partner he or she doesn't know to find out his or her name and some favorite activities.

ARTE Y CULTURA ◀

Standards: 1.1, 1.2, 2.1, 3.1, 4.2

Suggestions: After students read the information silently, guide them to answer the question by saying: *¿Hay cosas que son importantes para los jóvenes españoles que no son importantes para ti? ¿Cuáles son?*

Answers will vary.

Culture Note

Soccer is the world's most popular sport. According to FIFA, the international governing body for the game of soccer, there are over 270 million male and female players and officials involved in the game of soccer worldwide. This represents almost four per cent of the world's population.

 Technology: Mapa global interactivo, Actividad 1 Discover Bariloche, the gateway to Patagonia in Argentina.

Project-Based Learning

Actividades que hacen los jóvenes

As students read about the different activities presented in *Para empezar,* have them take notes of those that young people in their own community might participate in, such as going to the movies, playing a sport, working out, shopping, and so on. Then tell students to use their notes to complete the writing activity in *Presentación escrita* on p.15.

PE   Interpretive

Tu vida diaria 1

Standards: 1.2

Resources: Teacher's Resource Materials: Input Script, Audio Script, Technology: Audio para empezar

Suggestions: After students have read the blogs, say the activities aloud and have volunteers pantomime the actions.

 Technology: Interactive Whiteboard

Grammar Activities, Para Empezar Use the whiteboard activities in your Teacher Resources as you progress through the grammar practice with your class.

1

Standards: 1.1, 1.2

Suggestions: Have students write down words and phrases to answer the questions. Have them use these notes as they answer orally in complete sentences.

Common Errors: Students may forget to change first-person forms to the third-person when answering. Model correct verb forms and have students repeat.

Answers:
1. Rosa trabaja 3 horas al día en el supermercado.
2. Va con su novio al parque para jugar con su perro.
3. Nacho juega al fútbol y al béisbol.
4. Por la noche Nacho hace la tarea y ayuda a su hermano con las matemáticas.
5. Answers will vary.

2

Standards: 1.3

Suggestions: Encourage students to include details, such as times and descriptive adjectives, in their answers.

Answers will vary.

---

1 Tu vida diaria

OBJECTIVES
▸ Talk and write about your daily routine
▸ Discuss school and extracurricular activities

¿Cómo pasan los días los jóvenes?

ROSA

" Durante la semana trabajo de las 3 a las 6 en el supermercado y por la noche tengo que estudiar. Me gusta poner música cuando hago la tarea para la escuela. Los fines de semana mi novio y yo vamos al parque para jugar con el perro. En el invierno nos gusta pasar tiempo en el gimnasio. Tienen una piscina excelente. "

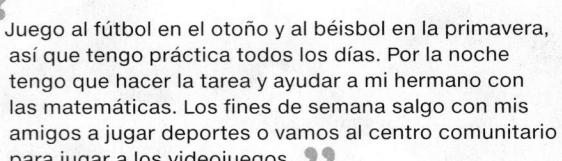

" Juego al fútbol en el otoño y al béisbol en la primavera, así que tengo práctica todos los días. Por la noche tengo que hacer la tarea y ayudar a mi hermano con las matemáticas. Los fines de semana salgo con mis amigos a jugar deportes o vamos al centro comunitario para jugar a los videojuegos. "

NACHO

1

¿Qué hacen?

 LEER, HABLAR EN PAREJA   Contesta las preguntas sobre los blogs de los jóvenes.
1. ¿Cuántas horas trabaja Rosa y dónde?
2. ¿Adónde va para jugar con el perro y con quién?
3. ¿Qué deportes juega Nacho?
4. ¿Qué hace Nacho por la noche?
5. ¿Con qué elementos de la vida de Nacho y Rosa te identificas?

2

Tu vida diaria

 ESCRIBIR   ¿Qué haces durante el día? Completa las frases con lo que haces en un día típico.

1. Voy . . .	3. Tomo . . .	5. Pongo . . .	7. Miro . . .	9. Estudio . . .
2. Hago . . .	4. Juego . . .	6. Salgo . . .	8. Ayudo . . .	10. Escucho . . .

2 dos • Para empezar • Tu vida diaria

Differentiated Instruction

Bodily/Kinesthetic Learner
Have students group themselves, pantomime an action, and conjugate one verb accordingly. For example, one student pantomimes and says: *Yo tomo el desayuno.* Another joins him or her and they say: *Nosotros tomamos el desayuno.* Another addresses them and says: *Uds. toman el desayuno,* and so on.

Advanced Learners
Have students interview a classmate on the subject of his or her daily activities on a typical day. Then ask them to convert the interviewee's answers to the third-person and present an oral report of the person's typical day.

Verbos irregulares

Remember that some verbs in Spanish are irregular in the first person singular of the present tense. Look at the following examples. Note that other verbs you know that are conjugated like *conocer* are *obedecer, ofrecer,* and *parecer*.

conocer	cono**zco**	poner	pon**go**	traer	trai**go**
dar	**doy**	saber	**sé**	ver	**veo**
hacer	ha**go**	salir	sal**go**	caer	cai**go**

Also, there are some verbs in Spanish that are irregular in all the persons of the present tense:

ser

soy	somos
eres	sois
es	son

ir

voy	vamos
vas	vais
va	van

decir

digo	decimos
dices	decís
dice	dicen

estar

estoy	estamos
estás	estáis
está	están

oír

oigo	oímos
oyes	oís
oye	oyen

tener

tengo	tenemos
tienes	tenéis
tiene	tienen

Más recursos ONLINE

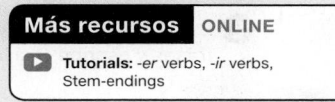 **Tutorials:** -*er* verbs, -*ir* verbs, Stem-endings

3

¿Qué haces tú?

 HABLAR EN PAREJA No todas las personas hacen las mismas actividades durante el día. Trabaja con otro(a) estudiante para hablar sobre las actividades que hacen usando los verbos del recuadro. Usen *¿qué?, ¿cómo?, ¿cuándo?, ¿dónde?, ¿para qué?, ¿a qué hora?,* y *¿por qué?* para hacer las preguntas.

 Videomodelo
A —*¿A qué hora* **desayunas**?
B —*Yo* **desayuno** *a las ocho de la mañana.*

comer	ir de compras	ir a la escuela
estudiar	hacer la tarea	llegar
ir al gimnasio	hacer/practicar un deporte	tomar (lecciones)
ver la tele	hablar por teléfono	navegar en la Red
salir de paseo	tomar el desayuno	

Enrich Your Teaching

Culture Note

In most places in Latin America, school sports are not as heavily funded and organized as they are in United States schools. However, this doesn't mean young people there don't play league sports. Rather, sports enthusiasts belong to neighborhood teams sponsored by local merchants or parents' organizations.

21st Century Skills

ICT (Information, Communications and Technology) Literacy Direct students to the online tutorials available in **Realize** for self-directed review of the grammar topics recycled in this chapter. These tools will help them monitor their own understanding and learning needs. Remind them that each tutorial is followed by a quick comprehension check.

Gramática: Repaso

Suggestions: Conduct a rapid interchange, moving through the class with questions to which students invent answers on the spot:
—*María, ¿de dónde sales por la mañana?*
—*Salgo de la casa.*
—*Pedro, ¿de dónde sale María?*
—*Sale de la casa.*
—*¿Y tú? ¿De dónde sales por la tarde?*
—*Salgo de la escuela.*
—*Y Pedro, ¿qué pones en la mochila?*
—*Pongo mis libros.*

3

Standards: 1.1

Suggestions: Have students conduct the activity twice, switching roles, so that each partner can practice the first-person forms.

Answers will vary.

Extension: Ask students questions about their partner's activities, and then about their own:
—*Belinda, ¿qué dice Tomás sobre la tarea?*
—*Tomás hace su tarea después de la cena.*
—*¿Y tú? ¿Cuándo haces tu tarea?*
—*Yo hago mi tarea antes de la cena.*

Teacher-to-Teacher

Have students socialize on the first day of class by interviewing four classmates. Ask them to find out the names, ages, favorite classes, and favorite activities of the people to whom they speak. Encourage students to take notes. Call on volunteers to report their findings to the class.

Additional Resources

 Technology: Online Resources
• Communication Activities
• Teacher's Resource Materials: Audio Script, Technology: Audio, Para empezar

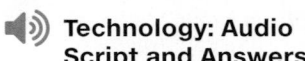

Standards: 1.2

Resources: Teacher's Resource Materials: Audio Script, Technology: Audio, Para empezar

Suggestions: Before playing the audio for Step 2, ask questions with **quién:** *¿Quién corta el césped?* Have students respond with complete sentences.

🔊 Technology: Audio Script and Answers

1. La mamá y el papá de Elena limpian el garaje juntos. (F)
2. Elena limpia la sala con su hermano mayor. (F)
3. El hermano arregla el jardín de la escuela de la comunidad. (F)
4. La mamá hace la cena y la sirve. (F)
5. El papá prepara el desayuno. (C)
6. Elena hace las compras del supermercado. (F)

5

Standards: 1.1, 1.3

Suggestions: Encourage students to use Elena's account in *Actividad 4* as a model for their own accounts of household chores.

Answers will vary.

6

Standards: 1.1, 1.3

Suggestions: Point out to students that they should concentrate on verbs involved in performing the activity, in order to adequately describe it. For *lavar el coche,* for example, suitable verbs might be *llenar* or *usar*.

Answers will vary.

Teacher-to-Teacher

Time pair work and group work activities with a kitchen timer. When the alarm sounds, stop the activity, address any questions students may have, and move on. Timed activities will help you greatly in designing and sticking to your lesson plans.

4

Elena y su familia

 LEER, ESCUCHAR

1 Lee la siguiente descripción de Elena de los quehaceres que hace cada miembro de su familia.

En mi familia todos ayudamos con los quehaceres de la casa. Cada uno de nosotros tiene una tarea específica.

Mamá:
- *preparar el almuerzo*
- *limpiar la cocina y el baño*
- *lavar la ropa*

Yo:
- *arreglar mi cuarto*
- *dar de comer al perro*
- *poner la mesa*

Papá:
- *hacer el desayuno*
- *cortar el césped*
- *lavar el coche*

Mi hermano mayor:
- *preparar la cena*
- *arreglar su cuarto y hacer la cama*
- *pasar la aspiradora*

Como todos ayudamos con los quehaceres, las tareas se hacen más rápido y tenemos más tiempo libre.

2 Escribe los números del 1 al 6 en una hoja. Escucha las frases y escribe *C* si la frase es cierta y *F* si es falsa.

5

En tu familia

 ESCRIBIR, HABLAR EN PAREJA

1 Escribe una breve descripción sobre quiénes hacen los quehaceres en tu casa y qué hace cada uno. Escribe la información en forma de frase.

2 Trabaja con un(a) compañero(a) para comparar las descripciones que escribieron. Decidan qué actividades tienen en común y por qué.

6

Tu actividad favorita

 ESCRIBIR, HABLAR EN GRUPO

1 Describe cuál es tu actividad favorita. No digas qué es. Usa oraciones conectadas con detalles y elaboradas.

Modelo
Leo mis libros. Escribo muchas cosas.

2 En grupo, cada uno(a) lee su descripción. El resto debe adivinar de qué actividad se trata.

Modelo
Tu actividad favorita es hacer la tarea.

4 cuatro • Para empezar • Tu vida diaria

Differentiated Instruction

Students with Learning Difficulties

Have students work with partners who are kinesthetic learners. The partners can pantomime doing household chores while students name the chore being pantomimed.

Advanced Learners

Have students with cameras create photo essays of people, preferably their families, doing household chores. Each picture of a chore should be accompanied by a one-sentence caption saying who is doing the chore.

Gramática Repaso

Interpersonal PE

Presente de los verbos con cambios de raíz

Remember that in Spanish there are three groups of stem-changing verbs. The stem change occurs in all forms except the *nosotros(as)* and *vosotros(as)* forms. Here are the present-tense forms of *perder (ie), poder (ue)* and *pedir (i)*.

perder (e ➜ ie)

p**ie**rdo	perdemos
p**ie**rdes	perdéis
p**ie**rde	p**ie**rden

poder (o ➜ ue)

p**ue**do	podemos
p**ue**des	podéis
p**ue**de	p**ue**den

pedir (e ➜ i)

p**i**do	pedimos
p**i**des	pedís
p**i**de	p**i**den

Other verbs like *perder* are: *empezar, querer, preferir, pensar, divertirse, despertarse, sentirse, mentir, cerrar, comenzar, entender.*

Other verbs like *poder* are: *jugar (u → ue), contar, costar, encontrar, recordar, volar, dormir, volver, devolver, acostarse, almorzar.*

Other verbs like *pedir* are *servir, repetir, reír, sonreír, seguir, vestirse.*

> **Más recursos** ONLINE
>
> ▶ **Tutorial:** Conjugation of stem-changing verbs

7

Vida deportiva

LEER , ESCRIBIR Lee lo que escribió Carmen sobre su equipo de fútbol Completa el párrafo con la forma correcta del verbo apropiado en el presente.

Después de la escuela yo __1.__ (*preferir / dormir*) ir al club para jugar al fútbol. Mis compañeras y yo __2.__ (*recordar / jugar*) bastante bien pero nuestra entrenadora __3.__ (*poder / pensar*) que el equipo rival __4.__ (*empezar / jugar*) mejor. A veces nosotras __5.__ (*perder / servir*) un partido, pero cuando nuestro equipo __6.__ (*poder / comenzar*) meter un gol es fabuloso.

8

Actividades de la semana

ESCRIBIR Haz planes con otro(a) estudiante por texto. Usa los verbos del recuadro.

Modelo

A —¿Qué quieres hacer después de la escuela? ¿Vamos al cine?

B —No puedo. Tengo que estudiar.

servir	perder
dormir	sentirse
querer	jugar
poder	preferir

Para empezar • cinco **5**

Gramática: Repaso

Un poco más de repaso

Suggestions: Ask students to write sentences that contain two verbs from each of the three lists in the *Gramática*. Tell them not to use **nosotros** or **vosotros** forms.

7

Standards: 1.2

Suggestions: Remind students to pay attention to the subject of each sentence before they write their answer.

Answers:

1. prefiero
2. jugamos
3. piensa
4. juega
5. perdemos
6. puede

8

Standards: 1.3

Suggestions: Encourage students to refer as often as necessary to the verb conjugations in the *Gramática* while they complete the activity.

Answers will vary.

Additional Resources

📶 **Technology: Online Resources**
- Guided, Core, Audio, Writing practice
- Communication Activities
- *Para hispanohablantes*
- Teacher's Resource Materials: Audio Script; Technology: Audio Para empezar

Print
- Guided WB pp. 5-6
- Core WB p. 1

Enrich Your Teaching

Teacher-to-Teacher

Have students get acquainted with the book at the outset of the school year. Make a list of features for students to find as quickly as they can. These might include: maps of the Spanish-speaking world, English-Spanish and Spanish-English vocabulary lists, a *¿Recuerdas?* box, a Go Online feature, a *Repaso* section, the first *Lectura,* and so on. Have students write down the page numbers of the various features. This could be done as a whole-class activity or as a race between groups of students.

9

Standards: 1.2, 1.3

Common Errors: Some students may forget to make the spelling changes when they use forms of verbs that have them. Point out that the spelling changes affect the pronunciation of the forms as well. Model correct pronunciation where the spelling changes occur. Have students repeat, or correct their spelling if the error was written.

Suggestions: Help students focus on the content of the reading by having them copy the chart to their own paper before they read.

Answers will vary.

Starter Activity

Write logical sentences by unscrambling these words and conjugating the verb appropriately.

1) una ensalada/preferir/mis amigos/para el almuerzo

2) ocho horas/dormir/mi hermanito/todos los días

3) a veces/arroz con pollo/servir/mi mamá

10

Standards: 1.3

Suggestions: Point out to students that they can skip around when choosing their cues. They don't have to use the cues in a straight, horizontal line.

Answers will vary.

Active Classroom

After students have written their paragraphs, put them in pairs. Have each student exchange paragraphs. The partner is to write six *Cierto/Falso* statements about the information. Each student reads the statements to the partner who will agree or correct the incorrect information.

9

Roberto y Lucas

 LEER, ESCRIBIR

1 Imagina que conoces a dos hermanos muy diferentes entre sí *(from each other)*. Observa las fotos y lee el texto.

Roberto y Lucas son hermanos. Ellos son muy diferentes entre sí. Los fines de semana, Roberto duerme hasta las siete de la mañana. A las ocho, juega al fútbol con sus amigos y a las diez vuelve a casa. Lucas prefiere levantarse tarde. No entiende cómo su hermano puede levantarse temprano. A Lucas le gusta tocar la guitarra. Sonríe mucho cuando escucha música, porque le encanta. Cuando Lucas toca la guitarra muy alto *(loudly)*, Roberto se vuelve loco. Lucas se vuelve loco cuando Roberto enciende la luz y lo despierta.

2 ¿Te pareces más a Roberto o a Lucas? Indica con una *X* quién hace cada una de estas actividades y si tú también las haces. Luego, escribe un párrafo comparándote a ti mismo con Roberto y Lucas.

Modelo
Lucas y yo preferimos escuchar música que hacer deportes.

Actividad	Roberto	Lucas	Yo
jugar al fútbol			
tocar la guitarra			
sonreír al escuchar música			
preferir levantarse tarde			
encender la luz temprano			

10

¿Y qué haces tú?

 ESCRIBIR Imagina que estás en una reunión de amigos y comienzan a hablar de lo que hacen. Escribe frases usando las palabras de las tres columnas.

Modelo
yo / cortarse / el pelo
Yo me corto el pelo todos los meses.

A	B	C
yo	ayudar	autobús
tú	correr	de paseo
Carlos	desayunar	en el parque
nosotros	hacer	quehaceres
ustedes	salir	tarea de la escuela
mis amigos	tomar	temprano / tarde

6 seis • Para empezar • Tu vida diaria

Differentiated Instruction

Students with Learning Difficulties

Help students orientate themselves when using the chart in *Actividad* 9. Slide your finger across the first row of the chart and explain that all the information in that row has to do with playing football. Repeat this procedure for each row of the chart.

Students with Special Needs

Provide hearing-impaired students with a seat near the speakers, or with headphones if possible, whenever conducting recorded listening activities.

Gramática
Repaso

 Go **Online** to practice
PEARSON **realize**™

PearsonSchool.com/Autentico

 WRITING

Interpersonal   PE

Los verbos reflexivos

To say that people do something to or for themselves, you use reflexive verbs. A reflexive verb has two parts: a reflexive pronoun (*me, te, se, nos, os*) and a verb form. Here are all the present-tense forms of *levantarse*:

me levanto	**nos** levantamos
te levantas	**os** levantáis
se levanta	**se** levantan

Many reflexive verbs in Spanish describe daily routine actions:

acostarse (ue), afeitarse, arreglarse, bañarse, cepillarse, despertarse (ie), ducharse, lavarse, pintarse, ponerse, secarse, vestirse (i).

Except for *se,* the reflexive pronouns are the same as the indirect object pronouns. They usually come before the verb, but they may also be attached to an infinitive.

> **Me lavo** la cara.
>
> Voy a **lavarme** la cara.

Remember that with reflexive verbs, you usually use the definite article with parts of the body or articles of clothing.

> Me pongo **la** chaqueta.
>
> Me cepillo **los** dientes.

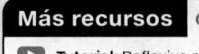

Más recursos   ONLINE

▶ **Tutorial:** Reflexive pronoun forms

11

Lo opuesto a ti

 ESCRIBIR   Imagina que tienes hermanos(as) muy diferentes a ti. Lo que a ti te gusta hacer, a ellos(as) no. Escribe frases comparándose.

Modelo
secarse el pelo
Mi hermana no se seca el pelo antes de salir de la casa pero yo sí.

1. lavarse la cara
2. cepillarse los dientes
3. vestirse con ropa moderna
4. cortarse el pelo todos los meses
5. despertarse
6. acostarse

12

A las 7:00 . . .

 ESCRIBIR   Describe lo que haces cada mañana desde que abres los ojos hasta que sales para ir a la escuela.

Modelo
7:00: Me despierto. 7:05: Me levanto de la cama.

Para empezar • siete **7**

Gramática: Repaso

Un poco más de repaso

Suggestions: Use the reflexive verbs in sentences about what you are going to do tomorrow. Have students respond by saying that they perform the action every day. —*Mañana, voy a despertarme a las seis y media.* —*Yo me despierto a las seis y media todos los días.* Pantomime the action and have students do likewise.

11

Standards: 1.3

Suggestions: Point out to students that for this activity, all reflexive pronouns should precede the verb.

Answers: Family members will vary. Students will use the following verb forms (with singular subjects).

1. se lava	3. se viste	5. se despierta
2. se cepilla	4. se corta	6. se acuesta

12

Standards: 1.1, 1.3

Suggestions: Have students list all their morning activities. Suggest that they refer to the *Gramática* for reminders. Then have them convert their list into a final draft that includes the times and complete sentences. As they make their final draft they can include other activities that were not in their lists.

Answers will vary.

Additional Resources

 Technology: Online Resources
- Instant Check
- Guided, Core, Listening, Writing, Reading
- Communication Activities
- Teacher's Resource Materials: Audio Script, Communicative Pair Activity, Technology: Audio Para empezar
- *Para hispanohablantes*

Print
- Guided WB pp. 7-10
- Core WB pp. 2-3

Assesment

Prueba P-1 with Remediation (online only)
Prueba: Tu vida diaria
- Prueba P-1

Enrich Your Teaching

Teacher-to-Teacher

Conduct an information exchange. Prepare a worksheet with students' names in the left column and in the right column a list of daily activities with their times of day, such as ***almorzar a la una.*** Give each student a slip of paper with a daily activity and time from the right column of the worksheet written on it. Have students complete the worksheet by circulating around the room and asking each other questions about the right column: *¿Tú almuerzas a la una?* The first to match all the names and daily activities on his or her worksheet wins.

Días especiales 2

Standards: 1.2

Resources: Teacher's Resource Materials: Input Script, Audio Script, Technology: Audio Para empezar

Suggestions: Draw or display a four-column graphic organizer. Enter the names *Margarita, Laura,* and Manuel at the tops of the first three columns. Leave the fourth column empty. Ask guiding questions to elicit information about each of the three people and record students' answers in the appropriate column. For example, if you ask *¿A quién le gustan las celebraciones para los acontecimientos importantes?* students should say *a Manuel.* Under **Manuel** on the chart, write *celebraciones.* Continue until all information for each person is recorded.

 Technology: Interactive Whiteboard

Grammar Activities PE Use the whiteboard activities in your Teacher Resources as you progress through the the grammar practice with your class.

13

Standards: 1.2, 1.3

Suggestions: Ask students to answer the questions in complete sentences, using their own words as much as possible.

Answers:

1. El día favorito de Margarita es el día de su cumpleaños. El de Manuel es el día que la familia entera se reúne.
2. Se reúnen para celebrar algún acontecimiento importante, como una boda o una graduación.
3. Se arregla con sus amigas en la casa de una de ellas.
4. Lo mejor para Margarita es pasar la noche bailando con sus amigos.
5. Manuel tiene que cuidar a sus hermanos y primos más pequeños.
6. En los dos días favoritos, la gente baila.

2 Días especiales

OBJECTIVES
▸ Write and talk about special events and activities
▸ Exchange information about favorite movies, TV programs, and sports
▸ Write about and discuss vacations

 Todos los años, la revista *Familia* hace una encuesta. A continuación aparecen algunas de las respuestas más interesantes a la encuesta "¿Cuál es tu día de fiesta favorito?".

MARGARITA — Mi día de fiesta favorito es el día de mi cumpleaños. Siempre hacemos una fiesta. Mis padres y yo decoramos la casa con globos y luces. Mi mamá siempre me prepara un pastel. Pero lo mejor es que todos mis amigos vienen y traen música y nos pasamos la noche bailando.

LAURA — Lo que más me gustan son las fiestas especiales, como las quinceañeras y las bodas. Me gustan porque puedo charlar con mis amigos y bailar. Además me encanta arreglarme para las fiestas. Con mis amigas siempre nos reunimos en una de las casas para prepararnos e ir juntas.

MANUEL — Mi día preferido es el día que la familia entera se reúne para celebrar algún evento importante, como una boda o una graduación. La abuela prepara una gran cena pero todos ayudamos con algo. Yo tengo la tarea de cuidar a mis primos y hermanos más pequeños.

13

Los días de fiesta

 LEER, ESCRIBIR Contesta las preguntas sobre los jóvenes de la encuesta.

1. ¿Cuál es el día favorito de Margarita? ¿Y el de Manuel?
2. ¿Por qué se reúnen Manuel y sus parientes?
3. ¿Cómo se arregla Laura para las fiestas especiales?
4. ¿Qué es lo mejor para Margarita?
5. ¿Qué tarea tiene Manuel en las fiestas?
6. ¿En qué se parecen los días favoritos de Margarita y Laura?

8 ocho • **Para empezar** • **Días especiales**

Differentiated Instruction

Heritage Speakers

Invite students to share information about special days they celebrate with their families. What is the occasion? What activities take place? Are there decorations? Are any special foods prepared?

Students with Learning Difficulties

As students read the information about each person, point to appropriate parts of the accompanying photo to help them associate words and meanings.

14

Actividades de una joven

LEER, ESCRIBIR, HABLAR EN GRUPO

1 Lucía participa en una encuesta. Lee la siguiente gráfica que indica cuántas veces Lucía realiza cada actividad.

Actividad	1 a 3 veces por semana	1 vez al mes	1 a 3 veces al año	Nunca
ir a bailar		X		
practicar deportes	X			
ir al cine		X		
ver la televisión	X			
ir a una fiesta de sorpresa			X	
tocar un instrumento musical	X			
reunirse con amigos	X			
ir de vacaciones			X	
tener una cita		X		
ir a una boda				X
hacer una audición		X		

2 Copia la gráfica y úsala para hacer la encuesta a tres estudiantes.

Videomodelo
A —¿Cuántas veces al mes o al año vas a bailar?
B —Voy a bailar una vez al mes.

3 Con los resultados que obtengas, escribe cinco frases sobre las actividades de tus compañeros.

15

Tu día favorito

LEER, ESCRIBIR

1 Por medio de textos, haz planes con un(a) amigo(a) para un día de fiesta. Incluye con quién van a celebrar, qué prepararán y qué harán.

2 Basándote en tus textos, escribe un párrafo usando oraciones conectadas con detalles y elaboración, para describir tu día favorito del año y decir cuál es. Cuenta lo que ocurre ese día.

Para empezar • nueve **9**

14

Standards: 1.1, 1.3

Suggestions: Explain that for Step 2, students should write the names of each student they interview in the appropriate space, rather than using Xs.
Answers will vary.

15

Standards: 1.3

Suggestions: Remind students before they complete Step 2, that the first sentence of their paragraph should announce which favorite day they are going to describe.
Answers will vary.

Extension: Invite volunteers to read their completed paragraphs to the class.

Culture Note

In Mexico, a girl's fifteenth birthday celebration, her *quinceañera,* is often one of the biggest of her life. (The term *quinceañera* is used to refer to the girl herself, as well as to the celebration.) It is often a huge family affair. Traditionally, this day marks the transition from girlhood to womanhood. Depending on the family, it may begin with a religious celebration, often a Catholic Mass. Urban families might lease a banquet hall and have a formal gala dinner. Rural families might have a more casual celebration, perhaps outdoors, with plenty of food, music, and relaxing fun for everyone.

Enrich Your Teaching

Teacher-to-Teacher

Have students write a note describing themselves (name, favorite classes, and activities). Then have them write four questions to ask someone in the class. Place the notes in a box and have students randomly draw a note. Have them read the information then respond in writing to the questions and return the note to the appropriate person.

21st Century Skills

Social and Cross-Cultural Skills Ask students to bring into class a picture or a drawing of a favorite holiday occasion they have celebrated with their family and friends. Working in small groups, have them name the occasion, the people in attendance, special food and preparations, and any other details they would like to share with their classmates about the celebration.

16

Standards: 1.2, 1.3

Suggestions: Review some of the adjectives suggested in Step 2 before students complete the activity. Use exaggerated gestures and pantomime to clarify the meanings of adjectives such as *horrible, violento, emocionante,* and *artístico.* Meanings of other adjectives can be taught by using them in sentences.

Answers:

Step 1
1. Possibilities include: los personajes, el argumento, la música, los efectos especiales
2. Sandra dice que la película no muestra los personajes tan bien como el libro. También dice que tiene menos detalles que el libro.
3. A Lucas le gustan los actores y le gusta la imaginación del director. No le gusta el argumento.

Step 2
Answers will vary.

16

Las películas

LEER, ESCRIBIR

1 Una actividad que le gusta hacer a casi todo el mundo es ir al cine. Lee lo que dicen estos jóvenes venezolanos de la película *El señor de los anillos* y contesta las preguntas que siguen.

1. Nombra tres cosas que le gustan a Pedro de la película.
2. ¿Qué cree Sandra sobre cómo la película se compara al libro?
3. Nombra una cosa que le gusta y una cosa que no le gusta a Lucas.

¿Recuerdas?

Para hablar de las películas:
un drama
una comedia
una película de ciencia ficción
una película policíaca
una película romántica
una película de horror

¿Qué estás pensando?

Ana Casas *El señor de los anillos* me parece fabuloso. ¿Qué opinan?

Pedro Rosas Es una película impresionante. Me encantan los personajes y el argumento. La música y los efectos especiales son fantásticos. La gente no se aburre de verla. Su director es un genio.
–A Emilia y a Fede les gusta. ☺

Sandra Gómez La película es interesante pero los actores no me gustan. No muestran (show) bien cómo son los personajes del libro. El director no cuenta la historia con detalles y es difícil de entender. La gente que no conoce el libro no puede entender de qué trata.

Lucas Pérez La película no se parece al libro, pero mantiene la misma idea. Me gusta la imaginación del director. Los actores hacen un buen trabajo, pero el argumento no me fascina. Recomiendo la película para pasar un buen momento.

---

2 Piensa en una película que te gusta mucho o que no te gusta nada. Escribe una descripción de la película. Puedes usar las palabras del recuadro.

inolvidable	artístico(a)	emocionante
típico(a)	talentoso(a)	exagerado(a)
estupendo(a)	despacio(a)	horrible
bello(a)	divertido(a)	violento(a)

10 diez • **Para empezar** • **Días especiales**

Differentiated Instruction

Students with Learning Difficulties

Make a set of index cards containing the adjectives in Step 2 of *Actividad* 16. Go through the movie section of a local newspaper. Help students match the various adjectives with appropriate movies. Then ask them to make a sentence about each movie using the adjective on the card.

Advanced Learners

Ask students to write their own opinion about a film they have recently seen. Have them use the opinions in *Actividad* 16 as models.

Go **Online** to practice   PearsonSchool.com/Autentico

VIDEO   WRITING   SPEAK/RECORD

Verbos que se conjugan como *gustar*

You already know several verbs that always use the indirect object pronouns *me, te, le, nos, os, les*:

encantar	*to love*	**importar**	*to matter*
gustar	*to like*	**interesar**	*to be interested in*

These verbs all use the same construction:
indirect object pronoun + verb + subject.

Me gusta el fútbol.   **¿Te interesan** las pinturas?

Remember, in the sentences above, the verb forms *gusta* (singular) and *interesan* (plural) agree with the subjects *fútbol* and *pinturas*. The words *me* and *te* are indirect object pronouns.

Más recursos   ONLINE

 Tutorial: *Gustar* and similar verbs

17

Los programas de televisión

 HABLAR EN PAREJA ¿Qué programas te gustan? Trabaja con un(a) compañero(a) para hablar sobre sus programas favoritos. Usa *gustar, encantar,* e *interesar*.

Videomodelo

A —¿*Te interesan los programas de noticias?*
B —*Sí, me interesan mucho. Me gusta saber lo que pasa en el mundo.*
o: —*No, no me gustan porque son aburridos.*

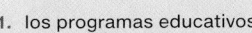

Estudiante A

1. los programas educativos
2. los programas de la vida real
3. los programas de dibujos animados
4. los programas de deportes
5. las telenovelas

Estudiante B

¡Respuesta personal!

18

Programas de deportes

 HABLAR EN PAREJA Trabaja con otro(a) estudiante para hacer y contestar preguntas sobre tus deportes favoritos y otras actividades que haces en tu vida diaria. Usa los verbos *gustar, encantar, importar* e *interesar*.

Enrich Your Teaching

Culture Note

The use of social media sites on the Internet has grown exponentially in the Spanish-speaking world. By 2011, more than 130 million accounts had been registered in Spain and Latin America in one social network alone. Besides Facebook and *Facebook en español,* other popular social media sites include Tuenti and Orkut.

21st Century Skills

Critical Thinking and Problem Solving
Discuss with students the issue of digital versus print sources of information about movies or other entertainment materials. Do they ever read reviews about movies they are interested in via websites, blogs, or Facebook pages? Do they ever read a printed review in the arts section of a newspaper? Ask them for their opinions about the advantages and disadvantages of both mediums for obtaining entertainment news, for example.

Gramática: Repaso

Suggestions: Have students practice the verbs by talking about things that please, enchant, interest, or matter to them. Remind them that in a sentence such as: *Me gusta el perro,* the subject is **perro.** The construction moves in the opposite direction from the English sentence "I like the dog."

Starter Activity

Label two columns on the board:
        Divertido/Aburrido
Brainstorm as a class to place different types of TV shows in the appropriate column to reflect the class opinion.

17

`Standards: 1.1`

Suggestions: Tell Student B to "bounce" the question back to Student A with a question such as: *¿Y a ti?* or *¿Y qué piensas tú?* This way both students can practice the verbs like **gustar** in a natural, flowing conversation.

Answers will vary.

18

`Standards: 1.1`

Suggestions: Suggest that students talk about sports they enjoy watching as well as those they enjoy playing, so they can extend the activity for further practice.

Answers will vary.

Additional Resources

 **Technology: Online Resources**
- Instant Check
- Guided, Core, Listening, Writing, Reading
- Communication Activities
- Teacher's Resource Materials: Audio Script, Technology: Audio Para empezar
- *Para hispanohablantes*

Print
- Guided WB pp. 11-12
- Core WB p. 4

Gramática: Repaso

Un poco más de repaso

Suggestions: Have students practice the possessive adjectives by describing their own home, then that of a friend or relative. Ask guiding questions to elicit the various pronouns: —*¿Y cómo es el jardín de tu abuelo?* —*Su jardín es muy hermoso*.

19

Standards: 1.2

Suggestions: Have students scan the entire blog first for meaning before they begin to write their answers.

Answers:

1. mi	6. mis
2. nuestro	7. Mis
3. nuestros	8. mi
4. Nuestro	9. su
5. nuestras	10. sus

CULTURA

Standards: 1.1, 1.2, 3.1

 Technology: Mapa global interactivo, Actividad, Visit Bariloche, the gateway to Patagonia in Argentina.

Suggestions: Before students read the information, show Bariloche, Argentina on a map. It is a bit more than halfway down the length of Argentina, in the Andes Mountains, near the Chilean border.

Answers will vary.

Gramática Repaso

Adjetivos posesivos

Remember that possessive adjectives in Spanish agree in gender and number with the nouns they describe. They are placed in front of the noun.

Singular		Plural	
mi, tu, su, nuestro, vuestro	vuelo	mis, tus, sus, nuestros, vuestros	vuelos
mi, tu, su, nuestra, vuestra	maleta	mis, tus, sus, nuestras, vuestras	maletas

Since *su* and *sus* have many meanings, use the prepositional phrase *de* + name/pronoun instead for clarity or emphasis.

Sus pantalones son elegantes.
¿Los pantalones **de ella**?
No, los **de usted**.

Más recursos ONLINE

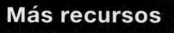 **Tutorial:** Possessive adjectives

19

¡A esquiar!

 LEER, ESCRIBIR Pablo sale mañana para esquiar con su familia en Bariloche, Argentina. Él está muy emocionado (*excited*) y escribe cómo se siente en su blog. Lee lo que escribe y llena los espacios con la forma correcta del adjetivo posesivo apropiado.

Mañana voy con __1.__ familia a esquiar en Bariloche. Estamos un poco nerviosos porque __2.__ vuelo sale muy temprano y todavía tenemos que recoger __3.__ boletos en el aeropuerto. __4.__ agente de viajes nos dice que __5.__ reservaciones están confirmadas, y yo le creo.

Estoy muy emocionado con esquiar. ¡Hace una semana que están hechas __6.__ maletas! __7.__ padres y __8.__ hermana mayor tienen maletas muy grandes a causa de __9.__ ropa. Mi hermano menor también lleva una maleta grande a causa de __10.__ juguetes... ¡tiene muchos!

CULTURA Argentina

Esquiar en Bariloche Cuando hay nieve, mucha gente aprovecha (*takes advantage*) para practicar su deporte preferido: esquiar. En Bariloche, Argentina, se encuentra uno de los centros de esquí más famosos de Latinoamérica. Esquiadores de todas partes del mundo, tanto profesionales como principiantes (*beginners*), llegan a este lugar cada año. Aquí pueden disfrutar de modernas pistas de esquí y también de los impresionantes paisajes (*scenery*) que hay a su alrededor. Bariloche es un lugar ideal para hacer deportes y conocer las bellezas naturales que nos ofrece nuestro planeta.

Pre-AP® Integration La identidad nacional: Se dice que Bariloche es la Suiza de América del Sur. ¿Qué regiones de Norteamérica se identifican con características similares?

 Mapa global interactivo Explore Bariloche e investiga su clima y su geografía.

12 doce • Para empezar • Días especiales

Differentiated Instruction

Students with Learning Difficulties

Have students work with single objects and pairs of similar objects, such as a pencil and a pair of pencils. Hand the object or objects to various individuals or pairs and ask students to say sentences such as: *Son sus lápices. Son mis lápices. Es mi lápiz. Es tu lápiz.*

Advanced Learners

Have students pretend they are on a trip to a vacation spot of their choice in Spain or Latin America. Ask them to research the place and write a postcard as if they were there, telling about some of its attractions. Tell them to use at least two possessive adjectives.

20

Días de vacaciones

LEER, ESCRIBIR

1 Lee esta tarjeta postal que Rosa le escribe a una amiga sobre sus vacaciones de verano.

2 Escribe un párrafo con oraciones conectadas con detalles y elaboración. Incluye todas las cosas que hace Rosa en sus vacaciones.

Modelo
Rosa se levanta tarde, desayuna y va a la playa. Después...

Querida Sara:

¿Cómo estás? Te escribo desde la playa, en Miami. ¡Me encanta estar de vacaciones! Todos los días me levanto tarde, desayuno y voy a la playa con mi familia. Mis hermanos y yo nos bañamos en el mar todo el día, y a veces salimos a dar vueltas por la ciudad en nuestras bicicletas. Mi hermano también se encuentra con sus amigos. Todas las noches, después de cenar, voy con mi hermano y sus amigos al cine o a comer helado. Nuestro hotel también es fantástico. Hay un vendedor que vende artesanías en la playa y me encanta mirar sus aretes de plata. ¡Qué divertido!

Saludos, Rosa

21

Unas preguntas sobre tus vacaciones

ESCRIBIR, HABLAR EN PAREJA

1 Piensa en las cosas que haces durante tus vacaciones. En una hoja de papel escribe las respuestas a estas preguntas.

1. ¿Qué haces durante tus vacaciones?
2. ¿Te quedas en la ciudad todo el tiempo?
3. ¿Viajas con tu familia o amigos a algún lugar? ¿Adónde?
4. ¿Qué haces generalmente en un día de vacaciones?
5. ¿A qué hora te levantas? ¿Y a qué hora te acuestas?
6. ¿Qué lugar te gusta más para irte de vacaciones?

2 Trabaja con otro(a) estudiante para hablar sobre las vacaciones. Usen las preguntas anteriores como modelo para su conversación. Usa oraciones conectadas con detalles y elaboración para escribir un párrafo sobre los eventos de tus vacaciones.

Para empezar · trece **13**

20

Standards: 1.2

Suggestions: Instruct students to mention with whom Rosa does the activities, so they practice using plural possessive adjectives.

Answers will vary.

21

Standards: 1.1, 1.3

Suggestions: Have students who may not go on vacations themselves write about their partner's vacation or that of someone they know.

Answers will vary.

Additional Resources

📶 **Technology: Online Resources**
• Instant Check
• Guided, Core, Listening, Writing, Reading
• Communication Activities
• *Para hispanohablantes*
Print
• Guided WB pp. 13-14
• Core WB pp. 5-6

Assessment

Prueba P-2 with Remediation (online only)
Prueba: Días especiales
• Prueba P-2

Enrich Your Teaching

Culture Note

The founding of Bariloche, Argentina is attributed to a man named Carlos Weitherholdt. He built a house and began regular trade in wool, leather, potatoes, cheese, butter, and other products. German influence can still be seen in some of the architecture in the older parts of the town.

21st Century Skills

Communication Have students write an e-mail or a postcard to a friend in which they describe their summer vacation. Direct them to use the questions in *Actividad* 21 to guide their writing. Students can use the postcard in *Actividad* 20 as a model for their correspondence.

Presentación oral

Suggestions: Help students decide on which task they will do. Review the four-step approach with them. Review the rubric with the class (see *Assessment* below) to explain how you will grade the performance task. Encourage them to use a graphic organizer, such as a column chart or a concept web in Step 1, as an aid to organizing their ideas.

Digital Portfolio

Make video or audio recordings of student presentations in class, or assign the Speak and Record activity so they can record their presentations online. Include the recording in their portfolios.

Additional Resources

 Technology: Online Resources
  • *Para hispanohablantes*

Assessment

Presentación oral

Review the rubric with students. Go over the descriptions of the different levels of performance. After assessing students, help individuals understand how their performance could be improved. (See Teacher's Resource Materials for suggestions on using rubrics in assessment.)

Presentación oral

🎤 Mi vida

TAREA Imagina que tienes que hacer una presentación oral en español. Escoge uno de estos aspectos de tu vida y expresa tus preferencias. Incluye detalles para defender y apoyar tu opinión.

• Un día en la escuela. ¿Qué haces antes de ir a la escuela? ¿Te diviertes en tu escuela? ¿Cómo son tus amigos? ¿Qué actividades haces después de la escuela?

• Tu película o programa de televisión favorito. ¿Quiénes son los personajes del programa o de la película? ¿Qué problemas tienen? ¿Qué hacen para resolverlos?

• El deporte que practicas. ¿Por qué te gusta ese deporte? ¿Con quiénes practicas ese deporte? ¿Dónde lo practicas? ¿Qué se necesita para ser un buen jugador?

▲ Estudiantes comen pizza después de la escuela en la República Dominicana.

1 **Prepárate** Contesta las preguntas o escribe frases y palabras que te van a ayudar a hacer tu presentación.

2 **Practica** Vuelve a leer la información que escribiste y piensa cómo la vas a presentar. Puedes usar tus notas para practicar, pero no al hablar ante la clase. Después, vas a ir donde están los estudiantes que hablarán del mismo tema para practicar.

3 **Haz tu presentación** Habla de tu tema con tu grupo como ayuda para pensar en más ideas. Al final, cada estudiante debe presentar el tema ante la clase.

4 **Evaluación** Tu profesor(a) utilizará la siguiente rúbrica para evaluar tu presentación.

Rubric	Score 1	Score 3	Score 5
How well you organize your ideas	You have too few ideas. Your ideas aren't organized.	Some organizational problems make your speech hard to follow.	You organize ideas well, making your speech easy to follow.
How well you use details	You include no details in your speech.	You include one or two interesting details and supporting statements, but need more.	Good use of details and supporting statements makes your speech interesting.
How effectively you deliver your speech	You read your speech and make no eye contact with your audience.	You make some eye contact, and you use some intonation.	Your eye contact is good. Your intonation helps get your message across.

14 catorce• Para empezar

Differentiated Instruction

21st Century Skills

Critical Thinking and Problem Solving Ask students to review the rubrics on pages 14 and 15. Have them discuss with a partner why their teacher gives them rubrics, and how are they supposed to be used. Students should choose one of the rubrics to start with the outcome, figure out what they might need to do to get the best grade possible, and develop a plan to achieve that goal.

Presentación escrita

OBJECTIVES
▶ Create a Web page about activities and places in your community
▶ Use your lead sentence to evaluate content and add details

Go Online to practice
PEARSON realize™
PearsonSchool.com/Autentico
WRITING

✎ Actividades en mi comunidad

TAREA Imagínate que tienes que hacer una página Web describiendo las actividades que hacen los jóvenes de tu ciudad. Imagina que la leen jóvenes de otros países que planean visitar los Estados Unidos y necesitan saber qué cosas pueden hacer en tu ciudad.

① Antes de escribir Piensa en los siguientes temas:

- gimnasios
- cines y teatros
- restaurantes
- lugares para bailar o ir de compras
- escuelas de música, idiomas, computación

② Borrador Escribe tu borrador de la página Web. Usa la información de arriba. Piensa en las ilustraciones que acompañan la página Web.

③ Redacción/Revisión Trabaja con otro(a) estudiante para intercambiar los borradores de las páginas Web y leerlos. Habla de qué se puede hacer para mejorarlos. Usa oraciones conectadas con detalles y elaboración.

- ¿Incluye la página Web información sobre los temas de la sección *Antes de escribir*?
- ¿Usaste correctamente verbos y adjetivos posesivos?

④ Publicación Revisa otra vez tu borrador y escribe el texto de la página Web en una hoja grande de papel para hacer un póster. Añade fotos o ilustraciones.

⑤ Evaluación Tu profesor(a) utilizará la siguiente rúbrica para evaluar tu presentación.

Estrategia
Evaluate your lead sentence to see whether added details might help to generate more interest in your topic. Make notes to suggest areas for further development, and jot down ideas that will make the paragraphs and the information more appealing.

10:30AM
Las actividades de los jóvenes

Rubric	Score 1	Score 3	Score 5
Completion of task	Your Web page is incomplete.	Your Web page is complete, but some parts still need work.	Your Web page is complete and carefully revised.
Effective development	Your topic is undeveloped.	You have some ideas that enhance your topic.	Your ideas are all well developed and enhance your topic.
Grammar, spelling, mechanics	You make too many grammar, spelling, and/or mechanics errors.	You make some grammar, spelling, and/or mechanics errors.	You make very few grammar, spelling, and/or mechanics errors.

Enrich Your Teaching

21st Century Skills

Information Literacy Ask students to use information from a variety of online sources to plan their *Actividades en mi comunidad* Web site. Have them find reliable sources that provide accurate information about the things to do in the local area. Encourage students to include this information in their materials for the *Presentación escrita* Web page in class.

Presentación escrita

Standards: 1.2, 1.3, 3.1

Focus: Combining review vocabulary and structures in a written presentation

Suggestions: Explain the criteria you will use to evaluate students' compositions. (See Step 5, *Evaluación,* in the Student Edition, and *Assessment* below.)

Direct students' attention to the *Estrategia.* Point out that to evaluate their lead, they can simply ask classmates and other students for their opinions on the activities that they want to include on their Web page. If the people they ask don't think an activity is interesting, they should abandon that idea and think of another activity for their Web page. Point out also that talking with other people this way often generates new and better ideas. Students should write down ideas that they like and try to include them in their Web page.

In Step 2, students should concentrate on the layout of their Web page and fitting in the information they want to include.

In Step 3, students should pay closer attention to the written portions of their Web page, in particular to their use of verbs and possessive adjectives.

Evaluation

Steps 4 and 5 overlap. Students will need evaluation by you, their peers, or self-evaluation to fine-tune their drafts.

Digital Portfolio

Keep students' final drafts in their portfolios as a writing sample.

Additional Resources

 Technology: Online Resources
- *Para hispanohablantes*

Self Assessment

Presentación escrita

Review the rubric with students. Go over the descriptions of the different levels of performance. After assessing students, help individuals understand how their performance could be improved. (See Teacher's Resource Materials for suggestions on using rubrics in assessment.)

CAPÍTULO 1

Días inolvidables

Memorable outdoor experiences and competitions

Vocabulary: camping and weather; athletic events and competitions

Grammar: preterite tense of verbs with *i → y,* e → *i,* and *o → u* spelling changes; preterite tense of irregular verbs: **tener, andar, estar, poder, poner, saber, venir, decir,** and **traer**; imperfect tense; imperfect tense of irregular verbs **ir, ser,** and **ver**

Cultural Perspectives: national parks in Chile, Argentina, and Mexico; different kinds of competitions; the annual pilgrimage to the Cathedral of Santiago de Compostela in Spain; the legend of Iztaccíhuatl and Popocatépetl, two volcanoes in Mexico

¡Pura vida!: Watch an engaging video episode about a group of young people in Costa Rica!

Auténtico: Watch a culturally authentic video about outdoor activities in Puerto Rico.

Chapter Support

Bulletin Boards

Theme: Competencias diferentes

Ask students to cut out, copy or download photos of all different types of competitions from many different cultures. Arrange the pictures into three categories: team-oriented competitions, individual competitions, and personal competition.

Game

¡Vamos de cámping en las sierras!

This memory game practices camping vocabulary. Use it after completing the first *Vocabulario en contexto* section.

Players: 6 to 8

Materials: Scarf for blindfold

Rules:

1. Players sit in a circle. Choose a player to start. This player begins by saying *Para ir de cámping en las montañas, traigo _____.* Then the player proceeds to say why that item would be useful. For example: *Para ir de cámping en las montañas, traigo una linterna porque necesito ver cuando es de noche.*

2. The next player on the right then repeats the initial sentence, repeating the first player's item and adding one of his or her own plus a reason for bringing that item. For example: *Para ir de cámping en las montañas, traigo una linterna porque necesito ver cuando es de noche. También traigo una brújula para no perderme.*

3. Play continues until everyone in the circle has a chance to add an item to the list.

Variation: Play with a larger group of students and review other vocabulary such as articles of clothing and other supplies that might be useful on a camping trip.

Hands-on Culture

Recipe: Pastel de choclo

Pastel de choclo (corn pie) is one of the most popular Chilean dishes.

Ingredients: For the meat mixture: 1 chicken breast, skinned/boned; 1/4 tsp. black pepper; 8 oz. hamburger, extra lean; 1/2 cup raisins; 1/4 tsp. salt; 2 tbsp. kalamata olives, chopped

For the corn topping: 1/2 tbsp. canola oil; 1/2 cup milk, non-fat; 1/8 tsp. paprika; 1/4 tsp. cumin, ground; 1 med. onion, finely chopped; 1/4 tsp. salt; 16 oz. corn kernels, thawed; 1/4 tsp. black pepper

1. Heat oven to 400 degrees. Spray skillet with vegetable spray; place until hot. Cook chicken breast 2 minutes on each side. Remove from skillet; set aside.

2. Put beef in same skillet; cook, stirring constantly, until no longer pink. Stir in salt, pepper, raisins, and olives. Spoon 1/4 of mixture into each of 4 small, oven-proof bowls, or baking dish. Cut cooked chicken breast into quarters; place 1 quarter in each bowl.

3. Combine oil and paprika in same skillet; place over medium heat until hot. Add onion and cook, stirring frequently, until soft and translucent, about 5 minutes. While onion is cooking, combine thawed corn, milk, cumin, salt, and pepper in food processor; puree.

4. Add puréed corn mixture to cooked onion in skillet. Cook for 5 minutes. Spoon 1/4 of corn mixture over top of each bowl. Bake for 35 to 40 minutes.

21st Century Skills

Look for tips throughout Chapter 1 to enrich your teaching by integrating 21st Century Skills. Suggestions for the Chapter Project and Culture follow below.

Project-Based Learning

Modify the Project-Based Learning with one or more of these suggestions:

ICT (Information, Communications and Technology) Literacy Encourage students to use information from a variety of Web sites to plan their trip proposal. The handout "Search for Information on the Internet" will help them find reliable sources for planning an exciting trip.

Collaboration Have students work together in small groups and assume shared responsibility for researching and writing their trip proposal. Provide them with the handout "Work in Teams" to help them divide the tasks.

Critical Thinking and Problem Solving Ask students to make a list of the problems a traveler may encounter when engaged in an adventurous outdoor activity. How would this affect the clothes, medicines or other items they pack for the trip? How would weather influence what they bring?

Chapter Culture

Social and Cross-Cultural Skills Help students bridge cultural differences by offering opportunities to discuss the culture highlighted throughout the chapter. Use the information in the *Cultura* note on page 27 to discuss the importance of national parks, ecotourism, and family outings in different cultures.

▶ **Technology: Videodocumentario** View *Los deportes en el mundo hispano* online with the class to learn about the many sports and outdoor activities practiced in the Spanish-speaking world.

Project-Based Learning

Club de exploradores

Overview: Students research and create a proposal for a trip to a national park or other outdoor tourist attraction in Spain or Latin America to present to their Explorer's Club or the class. Presentations should include images of the site, each with a descriptive caption, and can be created digitally, by hand, or using a combination of resources. Students then present their proposal explaining where the park is, how club members would get there, what they would need to bring, and what there is to see and do.

Resources: online or print photos, image editing and page layout software and/or poster board, markers, glue, scissors

Sequence: (suggestions for when to do each step are found throughout the chapter)

Step 1. Review instructions so students know what's expected of them. Share the rubric with the class.

Step 2. Students submit a draft of their proposal including the name and location of their destination, what the club would need to bring, and why they might want to go there. Return the proposal with your suggestions.

Step 3. Students do a layout leaving room for photos and captions. Encourage them to try different arrangements before placing the photos.

Step 4. Students submit a draft of their photo captions. Note your corrections and suggestions, then return drafts to students.

Step 5. Students present their proposals to the class, explaining where the park is, how the club would get there, and what they could expect to see and do.

Options

1. Students write and create an article for a travel magazine with photos and captions about a national park in Spain or Latin America.
2. Students research and create a proposal for a trip back in time to an earlier civilization in Spain or Latin America.

Assessment

Here is a detailed rubric for assessing this project:

Chapter 1 Project: *Club de exploradores*

Rubric	Score 1	Score 3	Score 5
Your evidence of planning	You provide preliminary proposal or caption drafts.	Your preliminary proposal and captions are created, but not corrected.	You show evidence of corrected proposal and captions.
Your use of illustrations	You include photos.	You include photos, but layout is disorganized.	You include photos, and your presentation is easy to read and convincing.
Your presentation	You do not include the required information.	You include most of the required information.	You include all of the required information.

AT A GLANCE

Objectives
- Listen to and read about excursions and competitions
- Talk and write about nature and sports events
- Describe a trip
- Compare a famous pilgrimage route in Spain with similar trips in your community
- Understand legends about nature
- Compare cultural practices in an authentic video about an adventure park in Puerto Rico

Vocabulary
- Outdoor activities and camping
- Natural environment and weather
- Sports and competitions
- Expressing emotions

Grammar
- Verbs with spelling and stem changes in the preterite
- Irregular verbs in the preterite
- The imperfect

Culture
- The Chilean landscape, p. 21
- National parks in South America, pp. 22, 27
- Ecocamps in Chile, p. 35
- The International Olympics of Math, p. 40
- F.C. Barcelona, p. 46
- El Camino de Santiago, pp. 48–49
- Mexican legends, p. 57

A ver si recuerdas...
- Outdoor activities
- Sports and competition
- Accidents in sports
- Verbs in the preterite

Recycle
- *obtener, competir,* and *conseguir* in the preterite
- **s** and **z** before **e** and **i**

Authentic Resources
- **Auténtico:** En las montañas de Puerto Rico, pp. 58–59

RESOURCES

	FOR THE STUDENT	DIGITAL	PRINT	FOR THE TEACHER	DIGITAL	PRINT
Plan				Teacher's Edition, pp. 16–63	•	•
				Teacher's Resource Materials	•	
				Pre-AP® Resource Materials, pp. 138–140	•	
				Lesson Plans, pp. 16e–16h	•	•
				Mapa global interactivo	•	
A ver si recuerdas pp. 16–19						
Review	*A ver si recuerdas* with Remediation	•		*A ver si recuerdas* with Remediation	•	
	Guided WB, pp. 15–18	•	•			
	Core WB, pp. 7–8	•	•			
	Para hispanohablantes	•				
Introducción pp. 20–21						
Present	Student Edition, pp. 20–21	•	•	Teacher's Edition, pp. 20–21	•	•
	Videonovela: *¡Pura vida!*	•		Teacher's Resource Materials	•	
	¡Pura vida! Video Activities	•		Mapa global interactivo	•	
	Para hispanohablantes	•				
Vocabulario en contexto pp. 22–25/36–39						
Present & Practice	Student Edition, pp. 22–25/36–39	•	•	Teacher's Edition, pp. 22–25	•	•
	Technology: Audio	•		Teacher's Resource Materials	•	
	Guided WB, pp. 19–26/33–40	•	•	Technology: Audio	•	
	Core WB, pp. 9–10/14–15	•	•	Video Program: *Videohistoria*	•	
	Communication Activities	•				
	Para hispanohablantes	•				
Assess and Remediate				Pruebas 1–1/1–6: Assessment Program, *Para hispanohablantes*	•	

RESOURCES

FOR THE STUDENT	DIGITAL	PRINT	FOR THE TEACHER	DIGITAL	PRINT
Vocabulario en uso pp. 26–29/40–41					
Present & Practice Student Edition, pp. 26–29/40–41	•	•	Interactive Whiteboard Vocabulary Activities	•	
Instant Check	•		Teacher's Edition, pp. 26–29; 40–41	•	•
Communication Activities	•		Teacher's Resource Materials	•	
Para hispanohablantes	•		Technology: Audio	•	
Communicative Pair Activities	•		Videomodelos	•	
Assess and Remediate			Pruebas 1–2/1–7 with Remediation	•	
			Pruebas 1–2/1–7: Assessment Program, *Para hispanohablantes*	•	
Gramática pp. 30–35/42–47					
Present & Practice Student Edition, pp. 30–35/42–47	•	•	Interactive Whiteboard Grammar Activities	•	
Instant Check	•		Teacher's Edition, pp. 30–35; 42–47	•	•
Tutorial Video: Grammar	•		Teacher's Resource Materials	•	
Canción de hip hop	•		Technology: Audio	•	
Guided WB, pp. 29–32/41–44	•	•	Videomodelos	•	
Core WB, pp. 12–13/16–18	•	•			
Communication Activities	•				
Para hispanohablantes	•				
Communicative Pair Activities	•				
Assess and Remediate			Pruebas 1–3, 1–4, 1–5/1–8, 1–9 with Remediation	•	
			Pruebas 1–3, 1–4, 1–5/1–8, 1–9: Assessment Program, *Para hispanohablantes*	•	
Aplicación pp. 48–59					
Apply Student Edition, pp. 48–59	•	•	Teacher's Edition, pp. 48–59	•	•
Authentic Resources Workbook	•	•	Teacher's Resource Materials	•	
Authentic Resources	•		Video Program: Videodocumentario	•	
Online Cultural Reading	•		Mapa global interactivo	•	
Guided WB, pp. 45–47	•	•			
Communication Activities	•				
Para hispanohablantes	•				
Videodocumentario	•				
Auténtico, pp. 58–59	•	•			
Repaso del capítulo pp. 60–63					
Review Student Edition, pp. 60–63	•	•	Teacher's Edition, pp. 60–63	•	•
Core WB, pp. 19–20	•	•	Teacher's Resource Materials	•	
Communication Activities	•		Technology: Audio	•	
Para hispanohablantes	•				
Instant Check	•				
Chapter Assessment					
			Examen del capítulo 1: Assessment Program	•	
			Alternate Assessment Program	•	
			Assessment Program *Para hispanohablantes*	•	
			Technology: Audio, Cap. 1, Examen	•	
			ExamView: Test Banks A and B (questions only online)	•	
			Heritage Speaker Test Bank	•	
			Pre-AP® Test Bank	•	

LESSON PLAN

DAY	Warm-up / Assess	Preview / Present / Practice / Communicate	Wrap-up / Homework Options
1	**Warm-up** (10 min.) • Return Prueba from Para empezar	**Repaso** (35 min.) • A ver si recuerdas . . . • Actividades 1, 4 , 5	**Wrap-up and Homework Options** (5 min.) • Actividades 2, 3, 6, 7 • Core Practice 1-1, 1-2
2	**Warm-up** (10 min.) • Homework check	**Chapter Opener** (5 min.) • Objectives • Arte y cultura **Vocabulario en contexto 1** (30 min.) • Presentation: Vocabulario y gramática en contexto • Actividades 1, 2	**Wrap-up and Homework Options** (5 min.) • Clip Art Vocabulary
3	**Warm-up** (10 min.) • Homework check	**Vocabulario en contexto 1** (35 min.) • Presentation: Videohistoria: *Entre el mar, el valle y la sierra* • View: Videohistoria • Actividad 3	**Wrap-up and Homework Options** (5 min.) • Core Practice 1-3, 1-4 • Actividad 4 • Prueba 1-1: Vocabulary recognition
4	**Warm-up** (10 min.) • Homework check • **Formative Assessment** (10 min.) • Prueba 1-1: Vocabulary recognition	**Vocabulario en uso 1** (25 min.) • Interactive Whiteboard Vocabulary Activities • Actividades 6, 7, 10, 11, 13 • Ampliación del lenguaje	**Wrap-up and Homework Options** (5 min.) • Actividades 8, 9 • Writing Activities • Prueba 1-2 with Remediation: Vocabulary production
5	**Warm-up** (5 min.) • Homework check • **Formative Assessment** (10 min.) • Prueba 1-2 with Remediation: Vocabulary production	**Gramática y vocabulario en uso 1** (25 min.) • Cultura • Writing Activity • Actividades 12, 13, 14, 15 • Presentation: El pretérito de verbos con el cambio ortográfico $i \rightarrow y$ • Interactive Whiteboard Grammar Activities	**Wrap-up and Homework Options** (5 min.) • Core Practice 1-5
6	**Warm-up** (10 min.) • Homework check • **Formative Assessment** (10 min.) • Prueba 1-3 with Remediation: El pretérito de verbos con el cambio ortográfico $i \rightarrow y$	**Gramática y vocabulario en uso 1** (25 min.) • Presentation: El pretérito de los verbos irregulares • Interactive Whiteboard Grammar Activities • Actividades 16, 18	**Wrap-up and Homework Options** (5 min.) • Core Practice 1-6 • Prueba 1-4 with Remediation: El pretérito de los verbos irregulares
7	**Warm-up** (10 min.) • Activity 17 • Homework check • **Formative Assessment** (10 min.) • Prueba 1-4 with Remediation: El pretérito de los verbos irregulares	**Gramática y vocabulario en uso 1** (25 min.) • Presentation: El pretérito de verbos con los cambios $e \rightarrow i$, $o \rightarrow u$ en la raíz • Interactive Whiteboard Vocabulary Activities • Actividades 19, 20, 21, 22	**Wrap-up and Homework Options** (5 min.) • Core Practice 1-7 • Writing Activity • Communicative Pair Activity
8	**Warm-up** (5 min.) • Actividad 25 • Homework check • **Formative Assessment** (10 min.) • Prueba 1-5 with Remediation: El pretérito de verbos con los cambios $e \rightarrow i$, $o \rightarrow u$	**Vocabulario en contexto 2** (25 min.) • Presentation: Vocabulario y gramática en contexto • Actividades 26, 27	**Wrap-up and Homework Options** (5 min.) • Clip Art Vocabulary • Examen: Vocabulario y gramática 1
9	**Warm-up** (25 min.) • Homework check • **Formative Assessment** (10 min.) • Examen: Vocabulario y gramática 1	**Vocabulario en contexto 2** (10 min.) • Presentation: La voz del estudiante • Actividad 29	**Wrap-up and Homework Options** (5 min.) • Actividades 28, 30 • Core Practice 1-8, 1-9 • Prueba 1-6: Vocabulary recognition
10	**Warm-up** (10 min.) • Actividad 31 • Homework check • **Formative Assessment** (40 min.) • Prueba 1-6: Vocabulary recognition	**Vocabulario en contexto 2** (25 min.) • Actividades 32, 33, 34, 35 • Cultura	**Wrap-up and Homework Options** (5 min.) • Writing Activities • Prueba 1-7 with Remediation: Vocabulary production

LESSON PLAN

DAY	Warm-up / Assess	Preview / Present / Practice / Communicate	Wrap-up / Homework Options
11	**Warm-up** (10 min.) • Writing Activity • Homework check • **Formative Assessment** (10 min.) • Prueba 1-7 with Remediation: Vocabulary production	**Gramática y vocabulario en uso 2** (25 min.) • Presentation: El imperfecto • Interactive Whiteboard Grammar Activities • Actividades 36, 37, 38 • Writing Activity	**Wrap-up and Homework Options** (5 min.) • Core Practice 1-10 • Prueba 1-8 with Remediation: El imperfecto
12	**Warm-up** (10 min.) • Writing Activity • Homework check • **Formative Assessment** (10 min.) • Prueba 1-8 with Remediation: El imperfecto	**Gramática y vocabulario en uso 2** (25 min.) • Presentation: Usos del imperfecto • Actividades 39, 40 • El español en el mundo del trabajo	**Wrap-up and Homework Options** (5 min.) • Core Practice 1-10 • Prueba 1-9 with Remediation: Usos del imperfecto • En voz alta
13	**Warm-up** (10 min.) • Actividad 43 • Homework check • **Formative Assessment** (10 min.) • Prueba 1-9 with Remediation: Usos del imperfecto	**Gramática y vocabulario en uso 2** (25 min.) • Actividad 44 • Audio and Writing Activities • Communicative Pair Activity • Actividades 39, 40	**Wrap-up and Homework Options** (5 min.) • Examen: Vocabulario y gramática 2
14	**Warm-up** (10 min.) • Homework check • **Formative Assessment** (30 min.) • Examen: Vocabulario y gramática 2	**Aplicación** (8 min.) • Presentación oral: Step 1	**Wrap-up and Homework Options** (2 min.) • Presentación oral: Step 2
15	**Warm-up** (10 min.) • Presentación oral: Step 2	**Aplicación** (35 min.) • Presentación oral: Step 3	**Wrap-up and Homework Options** (5 min.) • El Camino de Santiago • ¿Comprendiste?
16	**Warm-up** (10 min.) • El Camino de Santiago: ¿Comprendiste? • Homework check	**Aplicación** (30 min.) • Pre-AP® Integración 1, 2, 3 • View Video	**Wrap-up and Homework Options** (5 min.) • Presentación escrita: Steps 1, 2
17	**Warm-up** (10 min.) • Homework check	**Aplicación** (15 min.) • Presentación escrita: Step 3 **Repaso** (20 min.) • Preparación para el examen: Actividades 3, 6	**Wrap-up and Homework Options** (5 min.) • Presentación escrita: Step 4 • Cultura
18	**Warm-up** (10 min.) • Homework check	**Aplicación** (35 min.) • Lectura • Interacción con la lectura • Auténtico	**Wrap-up and Homework Options** (5 min.) • Core Practice: Organizer 1-13, 1-14 • Instant Check
19	**Warm-up** (20 min.) • Preparación para el examen: Actividades 1, 2 • Homework check	**Repaso** (25 min.) • Preparación para el examen: Actividades 4, 5, 7 • Other review	**Wrap-up and Homework Options** (5 min.) • Examen del capítulo
20	**Warm-up** (5 min.) • Answer questions • **Summative Assessment** (44 min.) • Examen del capítulo		**Wrap-up and Homework Options** (1 min.) • A ver si recuerdas: Capítulo 2

DAY	Warm-up / Assess	Preview / Present / Practice / Communicate		Wrap-up / Homework Options
		ALTERNATE LESSON PLAN		
1	**Warm-up** (10 min.) • Return Prueba from Para empezar	**A ver si recuerdas** (30 min.) • Presentation: Vocabulario p. 16 • Actividad 1 • Presentation: Gramática p. 17 • Actividades 2, 3 • Presentation: Vocabulario p. 18 • Actividades 4, 5 • Presentation: Gramática p. 19 • Actividades 6, 7	**Vocabulario en contexto 1** (35 min.) • Objectives • Arte y cultura • Presentation: Vocabulario y gramática en contexto • Actividades 1, 2, 3 • Presentation: Videohistoria: *Entre el mar, el valle y la sierra* **Vocabulario en uso 1** (10 min.) • Actividades 4, 5	**Wrap-up and Homework Options** (5 min.) • Core Practice 1-1 to 1-4 • Clip Art Vocabulary • Prueba 1-1: Vocabulary recognition
2	**Warm-up** (10 min.) • Vocabulario y gramática en contexto • Homework check • **Formative Assessment** (10 min.) • Prueba 1-1: Vocabulary recognition	**Vocabulario en uso 1** (65 min.) • Actividades 6, 7, 10, 11, 13 • Interactive Whiteboard Vocabulary Activities • Ampliación del lenguaje • Cultura • Communicative Pair Activity		**Wrap-up and Homework Options** (5 min.) • Writing Activities • Prueba 1-2 with Remediation: Vocabulary production
3	**Warm-up** (10 min.) • Writing Activity • Homework check **Vocabulario en uso 1** (20 min.) • Actividad 12 • **Formative Assessment** (10 min.) • Prueba 1-2 with Remediation: Vocabulary production	**Gramática y vocabulario en uso 1** (45 min.) • Presentation: El pretérito de verbos con el cambio ortográfico *i → y* • Interactive Whiteboard Grammar Activities • Actividades 14, 15 • Presentation: El pretérito de verbos irregulares • Actividades 16, 17, 18 • Actividades 24, 25		**Wrap-up and Homework Options** (5 min.) • Core Practice 1-5, 1-6 • Pruebas 1-3, 1-4 with Remediation: El pretérito de verbos con el cambio ortográfico *i → y*, El pretérito de verbos irregulares
4	**Warm-up** (10 min.) • Writing Activity • Homework check • **Formative Assessment** (20 min.) • Pruebas 1-3, 1-4 with Remediation: El pretérito de verbos con el cambio ortográfico *i → y*, El pretérito de verbos irregulares	**Gramática y vocabulario en uso 1** (40 min.) • Presentation: El pretérito de verbos con los cambios *e → i, o → u* en la raíz • Interactive Whiteboard Grammar Activities • Actividades 19, 20, 21, 22, 23 • Writing Activity • Communicative Pair Activity **Vocabulario en contexto 2** (15 min.) • Presentation: Vocabulario y gramática en contexto • Actividades 26, 27		**Wrap-up and Homework Options** (5 min.) • Core Practice 1-7 • Prueba 1-5 with Remediation: El pretérito de verbos con los cambios *e → i, o → u* en la raíz • Examen: Vocabulario y gramática 1
5	**Warm-up** (10 min.) • Homework check • **Formative Assessment Options** (40 min.) • Prueba 1-5 with Remediation: El pretérito de verbos con los cambios *e → i, o → u* en la raíz • Examen: Vocabulario y gramática 1	**Vocabulario en contexto 2** (25 min.) • Presentation: La voz del estudiante • Actividades 28, 29, 30, 31 **Vocabulario en uso 2** (10 min.) • Actividad 32 • Interactive Whiteboard Vocabulary Activities • Cultura		**Wrap-up and Homework Options** (5 min.) • Core Practice 1-8, 1-9 • Prueba 1-6: Vocabulary recognition
6	**Warm-up** (10 min.) • Homework check • **Formative Assessment** (10 min.) • Prueba 1-6: Vocabulary recognition	**Gramática y vocabulario en uso 2** (65 min.) • Actividades 33, 34, 35 • Presentation: El imperfecto • Interactive Whiteboard Grammar Activities • Actividades 36, 37, 38		**Wrap-up and Homework Options** (5 min.) • Core Practice 1-10 • Pruebas 1-7, 1-8 with Remediation: Vocabulary production, El imperfecto

ALTERNATE LESSON PLAN

DAY	Warm-up / Assess	Preview / Present / Practice / Communicate	Wrap-up / Homework Options
7	**Warm-up** (10 min.) • Writing Activity • Homework check • **Formative Assessment** (20 min.) • Pruebas 1-7, 1-8 with Remediation: Vocabulary production, El imperfecto	**Gramática y vocabulario en uso 2** (40 min.) • Presentation: Usos del imperfecto • Interactive Whiteboard Grammar Activities • Actividades 39, 40, 41 • El español en el mundo del trabajo **Aplicación** (15 min.) • Presentación oral: Steps 1, 2	**Wrap-up and Homework Options** (5 min.) • Presentación oral: Step 2
8	**Warm-up** (15 min.) • Actividad 43 • Homework check • **Formative Assessment** (40 min.) • Presentación oral: Step 3	**Gramática y vocabulario en uso 2** (30 min.) • En voz alta • Actividades 42, 43, 44 • Communicative Pair Activity	**Wrap-up and Homework Options** (5 min.) • Core Practice 1-11, 1-12 • Prueba 1-9 with Remediation: Usos del imperfecto • Examen: Vocabulario y gramática 2
9	**Warm-up** (10 min.) • Writing Activity • Homework check • **Formative Assessment Options** (30 min.) • Prueba 1-9 with Remediation: Usos del imperfecto • Examen: Vocabulario y gramática 2	**Aplicación** (45 min.) • El Camino de Santiago • ¿Comprendiste? • Pre-AP® Integración 1, 2, 3 • View Video • Video Activities • Presentación escrita: Step 1	**Wrap-up and Homework Options** (5 min.) • Presentación escrita: Step 2 • Preparación para el examen: Actividades 1, 2
10	**Warm-up** (20 min.) • Presentación escrita: Step 3 • Homework check	**Aplicación** (35 min.) • Lectura • Interacción con la lectura • Cultura • Auténtico **Repaso** (30 min.) • Preparación para el examen: Actividades 3, 6 • Preparación para el examen: Actividades 4, 5, 7	**Wrap-up and Homework Options** (5 min.) • Presentación escrita: Step 4 • Core Practice: Organizer 1-13, 1-14 • Instant Check • Preparación para el examen: Actividades 4, 5, 7 • Examen del capítulo
11	**Warm-up** (10 min.) • Homework check • **Summative Assessment** (45 min.) • Examen del capítulo	**Theme Game** (20 min.) **A ver si recuerdas – Capítulo 2** (10 min.) • Presentation: Vocabulario • Presentation: Gramática	**Wrap-up and Homework Options** (5 min.) • A ver si recuerdas – Capítulo 2 • Actividades 1–6

Vocabulario: Repaso

Standards: 1.1, 1.2

Un poco más de repaso

Suggestions: Before presenting the material in this review section, consider testing your students' command of the material by assigning the Remediation. Students will automatically be given additional practice of the material they have not yet mastered, and you can focus your review based on the class's overall performance on the post-test.

Have students copy the headings for each category on a sheet of paper. With the book closed, students work in groups of two and list as many words as they can remember in each category.

Standards: 1.1, 1.3

Suggestions: Remind students to use the word web as a source for ideas. Encourage them to use vocabulary and expressions that they might know which are not on the list.

Common Errors: Following English logic, some students may talk about weather conditions attempting to use **estar** + adjective when **hacer** + noun would more commonly be used in Spanish. Provide repeated models of the **hacer** construction.

Extension: Have students take notes on what their partner says and later use the notes to write a paragraph with complete sentences.

Answers will vary.

Active Classroom

Have students break into groups of four. Taking turns, each student has to stand up and pantomine a vocabulary word from the word web. The other students in the group have to guess the word. Alternate students acting out words until all the words have been used or you call time.

A ver si recuerdas

OBJECTIVES
▶ Write about and discuss outdoor activities
▶ Exchange information about past actions and vacations

Vocabulario

El tiempo
llueve (llover)
nieva (nevar)
hace . . .
  buen tiempo
  calor
  frío
  mal tiempo

Lugares
el campo
el lago
el mar
las montañas
el parque
la playa
el río

Otras actividades
hacer . . .
  esquí acuático
  moto acuática
  surf de vela
  una fogata
  una parrillada
  un picnic

Actividades
dar una caminata
ir de pesca
ir de vacaciones
ir de viaje
montar en bicicleta
montar a caballo
tomar el sol

Animales / Insectos
las hormigas
el mono
los mosquitos
el oso
el pájaro
los peces

 1

¿Adónde vas?

 ESCRIBIR, HABLAR EN PAREJA

1 Escoge dos lugares de la lista adonde a veces vas de vacaciones. Escribe dos actividades que haces allí, el tiempo que hace y los animales que puedes encontrar.

2 Ahora trabaja con otro(a) estudiante para hablar de sus vacaciones. Usen palabras de las listas y las preguntas modelo para elaborar frases sobre sus vidas diarias.

• Y tú, ¿adónde vas de vacaciones generalmente?
  Voy a . . .
• ¿Qué actividades te gusta hacer allí?
  Me gusta . . .
• ¿Qué tiempo hace?
  Hace . . .

16 dieciséis • Capítulo 1 • Días inolvidables

Differentiated Instruction

Heritage Speakers

Assign students one or more of the following from the *Actividades* list: **dar un(a), ir de, montar en/a,** or **tomar.** Ask them to think of as many expressions as they can that begin with their assigned word(s), such as **dar una vuelta, ir de compras, montar en bicicleta,** or **tomar precauciones.**

Advanced Learners

Have students apply the same expressions to other situations: *¿Adónde vas los fines de semana?*

Go **Online** to practice

PEARSON
realize™

PearsonSchool.com/Autentico

WRITING SPEAK/RECORD

Recycle | **1**

Gramática

El pretérito de los verbos

You use the preterite to talk about things that happened in the past.
Here are the regular preterite forms of verbs ending in -*ar*, -*er*, and -*ir*:

caminar

caminé	caminamos
caminaste	caminasteis
caminó	caminaron

comer

comí	comimos
comiste	comisteis
comió	comieron

vivir

viví	vivimos
viviste	vivisteis
vivió	vivieron

Here are the preterite forms of the irregular verbs *hacer, dar,* and *ver*:

hacer

hice	hicimos
hiciste	hicisteis
hizo	hicieron

dar

di	dimos
diste	disteis
dio	dieron

ver

vi	vimos
viste	visteis
vio	vieron

2

El fin de semana pasado

 LEER, ESCRIBIR Carmen describe lo que hizo su familia durante el fin de semana. Completa las siguientes frases con la forma correcta del pretérito de los verbos.

hacer	visitar	correr	dar
pasear	comer	aprender	ver

1. (Yo) _____ a mis abuelos.
2. Mis hermanos _____ en bote.
3. Tú _____ muchas películas.
4. Nosotros _____ a montar a caballo.
5. Mi padre _____ caminatas.
6. Mis primos _____ por la playa.
7. Tú y yo _____ helados.
8. Mi hermana _____ ejercicio.

3

Las vacaciones

 ESCRIBIR, HABLAR EN PAREJA

1 Haz una lista de ocho actividades que tú y otras personas hicieron durante las vacaciones pasadas.

Modelo
Caminé por la playa.
Mi familia y yo hicimos un picnic en el campo.

2 Con otro(a) estudiante hablen de sus vacaciones. Recuerden usar las expresiones apropiadas y un estilo menos formal cuando hablen.

Capítulo 1 • diecisiete **17**

Gramática: Repaso

Un poco más de repaso

Suggestions: Refer students who are having difficulty with the preterite of verbs to the *GramActiva* video from Level 2 Chapter 2B, and to the online tutorials. Allow students a few minutes to read through the grammar review on their own. Continue by using verbal cues to elicit preterite forms of regular verbs such as ***ayer, anoche, la semana pasada,*** or ***el año pasado.***

2

Standards: 1.2

Suggestions: After students complete the activity, have them check their answers with a partner.

Common Errors: Students commonly confuse first- and third-person preterite endings. Provide them with this mnemonic device: The first-person endings are -*e* as in the English first-person **"me"** and -*i* as in English first-person **"I."**

Answers:

1. visité
2. pasearon
3. viste
4. aprendimos
5. dio
6. corrieron
7. comimos
8. hizo

3

Standards: 1.1

Suggestions: Remind students that they can use the verbs on p. 16 to complete this activity.
Answers will vary.
Extension: Ask students to write a list of activities they did at another time in the past: ***ayer en la clase...; el fin de semana pasado....***

Enrich Your Teaching

Teacher-to-Teacher

Have students work in pairs to practice preterite verb forms. Student A cues Student B by asking if he or she is doing something in the present. Student B gives a negative response, adds that he or she did that thing yesterday, and asks Student A another question:

A —*¿Hablas con Rita hoy?*
B —*No, pero hablé con ella ayer.*
B —*¿Vemos una película en clase hoy?*
A —*No, pero vimos una película en clase ayer.*

Vocabulario: Repaso

Standards: 1.1, 1.2

Un poco más de repaso

Suggestions: Have students use the vocabulary to talk about the photo. For names of parts of the body, use a picture from a magazine or bring in a doll. Point to various parts of the body and have students name them.

 4

Standards: 1.1, 1.2

Suggestions: Model intonation as necessary and encourage students to speak with intonation that is appropriate for the sentence.

Answers will vary.

Extension: Have each student write two sentences that are similar to the exercise items: one about a positive occurrence and one about a negative one. Then have partners take turns reading and reacting to their sentences.

 5

Standards: 1.2, 1.3

Suggestions: Have students check their answers with a partner orally. Reading the items aloud will provide additional pronunciation practice.

Answers:

1. a   **2.** d   **3.** b   **4.** e   **5.** c

Extension: Invite students who wrote stories to read them aloud. Encourage those who wrote dialogues to act them out with you or a partner.

A ver si recuerdas

OBJECTIVES
▸ Talk and write about sports and competitions
▸ Write about where you and others went and what you did

Vocabulario

Deportes
correr
esquiar
jugar al fútbol
montar en monopatín
nadar
navegar
patinar

El cuerpo
el brazo
el codo
el dedo
el hueso
la mano
la muñeca
el músculo
el pie
la pierna
la rodilla
el tobillo

Acciones
ganar
jugar
participar
perder
practicar

Accidentes
caerse
cortarse
lastimarse
romperse
torcerse

Reacciones
¡Fantástico!
¡Genial!
¡Increíble!
Lo siento.
¡Qué lástima!
¡Qué pena!
¡Uy!

Competencias
el campeón, la campeona
el campeonato
la competencia
competir
el concurso
el equipo
el jugador, la jugadora
el partido
el premio
el tanteo

 4

El campeonato

LEER, HABLAR EN PAREJA Trabaja con otro(a) estudiante para leer y reaccionar a los comentarios siguientes. Usen gestos apropiados para expresar más emoción.

1. ¡Ganamos cinco a cero!
2. El jugador se cayó y se lastimó.
3. Me torcí el tobillo.
4. Nuestro equipo quedó campeón.

Videomodelo
A —Perdimos el partido.
B —¡Qué lástima!

5. Les metimos tres goles.
6. ¡Perdimos el campeonato!
7. Hoy llovió y no pudimos jugar.

 5

Definiciones

 LEER, ESCRIBIR Empareja cada definición con la palabra correspondiente. Luego, escribe un diálogo o un cuento usando cuatro de las palabras o expresiones de la segunda columna.

1. una parte del cuerpo que usas para jugar al fútbol
2. un grupo de personas que juegan un partido
3. la persona que siempre gana una competencia
4. lo que dices si te caes
5. un tipo de accidente

a. el pie
b. el campeón / la campeona
c. torcerse la muñeca
d. un equipo
e. ¡Uy!

18 dieciocho • Capítulo 1 • Días inolvidables

Differentiated Instruction

Students with Special Needs

Students with hearing disabilities may not be able to distinguish between the sounds of **-car** and **-gar**, or between **-qué** and **-gué.** Such minimal pairs may require exaggerated emphasis on the first consonant sound.

Students with Learning Difficulties

Using vocabulary clip art, have students sort vocabulary into appropriate categories: **la rodilla** goes in **partes del cuerpo** and so on.

Gramática

El pretérito de los verbos *ir* y *ser*, y de los verbos que terminan en *-car, -gar* y *-zar*

The preterite forms of *ir* and *ser* are exactly the same.

Carlos **fue** de vacaciones a las montañas. (ir)

Mi equipo **fue** campeón escolar el año pasado. (ser)

Remember that verbs ending in *-car, -gar,* or *-zar* have a spelling change in the *yo* form in the preterite. The other forms of these verbs are regular.

fui	fuimos
fuiste	fuisteis
fue	fueron

buscar	yo bus**qué**	investigar	yo investi**gué**	almorzar	yo almor**cé**
chocar	yo cho**qué**	navegar	yo nave**gué**	comenzar	yo comen**cé**
practicar	yo practi**qué**	jugar	yo ju**gué**	cruzar	yo cru**cé**
sacar	yo sa**qué**	llegar	yo lle**gué**	empezar	yo empe**cé**

6 El partido ayer

LEER, ESCRIBIR Completa las siguientes frases sobre el partido de ayer con el pretérito de *ser* o *ir*. Indica si usaste una forma del verbo *ser* o del verbo *ir*.

Modelo
Yo no *fui* al partido ayer. *(Ir)*

1. El partido de fútbol _____ ayer por la noche.
2. Todos los padres _____ al estadio.
3. Tú _____ el mejor jugador del equipo.
4. El partido _____ muy emocionante.
5. Este equipo _____ campeón hace dos años.
6. Durante el partido, nosotros _____ a comprar unas salchichas.
7. El partido duró más de tres horas. _____ muy largo.
8. Después del partido, los campeones _____ a celebrar a un restaurante.

7 La tarea

LEER, ESCRIBIR Luisa no pudo hacer la tarea. Completa este correo electrónico que le escribió a su profesora con la forma correcta del verbo apropiado.

> Estimada Srta. Herrera:
>
> Perdón, yo no pude hacer la tarea, por eso no la _1_ *(entregar / llegar)*. Ayer pensaba jugar al tenis pero no _2_ *(caminar / jugar)*. Por la mañana _3_ *(salir / llegar)* al club deportivo. Después _4_ *(buscar / pintar)* mi raqueta y la _5_ *(llevar / sacar)* del bolso. Cuando yo _6_ *(ganar / empezar)* a jugar _7_ *(comenzar / ir)* a llover. Entonces _8_ *(cantar / tropezar)* y me lastimé la mano. Esta nota la escribió mi hermano.
>
> Gracias, Luisa

Capítulo 1 • diecinueve **19**

Gramática: Repaso

Un poco más de repaso

Suggestions: Refer students who are having difficulty with the preterite of irregular verbs, and with verbs with spelling changes in the preterite, to the *GramActiva* videos from Level 1 Chapters 7A and 8A, and to the online tutorials. Assign one verb from the charts to each student and ask them to use their verb in two sentences with two different subjects. Ask students to spell the ending of each verb form.

6

Standards: 1.2

Suggestions: Have students read their completed activity items aloud.

Answers:

1. fue/ser
2. fueron/ir
3. fuiste/ser
4. fue/ser
5. fue/ser
6. fuimos/ir
7. Fue/ser
8. fueron/ir

Common errors: Students tend to misspell **fueron.** Remind them there is no **"i"** in **fue** or **fueron.**

Extension: Ask students to use **ser** and **ir** to create and share two additional sentences about yesterday's soccer match.

7

Standards: 1.2

Suggestions: Point out the reason for the spelling change in **-car** and **-gar** verbs: it allows the **c** and **g** consonants to retain their "hard" sound before the vowel **e**.

Answers:

1. entregué
2. jugué
3. salí
4. busqué
5. saqué
6. empecé
7. comenzó
8. tropecé

Additional Resources

 Technology: Online Resources
- *A ver si recuerdas* with Remediation
- Guided, Core, Audio, Writing practice
- *Para hispanohablantes*

Print
- Guided WB pp. 15–18
- Core WB pp. 7–8

Assessment

A ver si recuerdas with Remediation (online only)

After reviewing material on these pages, assign the *A ver si recuerdas* with Remediation to evaluate students' mastery of the material. Additional practice is available online.

Can-Do Statements

Read the Can-Do Statements in the chapter objectives with students. Then, have students read *Preparación para el examen* on pp. 62–63 to preview what they will be able to do at the end of the chapter.

Standards for Capítulo 1

To meet the Standards, students will:

COMMUNICATION

1.1 Interpersonal

- Talk about national parks, camping, and vacations
- Talk about competitive events
- Talk about geographic locations and weather events
- Talk about fine art
- Talk about a party and opinions
- Talk about childhood memories
- Talk about ancient pilgrimages and Aztec myths

1.2 Interpretive

- Read and listen to information about national parks, camping, and outdoor vacations
- Read and listen to information about competitive events
- Read about geographic locations and weather events
- Read about fine art
- Read about a professional translator
- Read about childhood memories
- Read about ancient pilgrimages and Aztec myths

1.3 Presentational

- Write and present information orally about national parks, camping, and outdoor vacations
- Write and present orally about competitive events
- Write about geographic locations
- Write about a party and childhood memories
- Write and present information orally about Aztec myths
- Present information orally about ancient pilgrimages

CULTURE

2.1 Practices to Perspectives

- Interpret pilgrimages in Spain
- Interpret the effects of Aztec myths in Mexico

2.2 Products to Perspectives

- Discuss Matilde Pérez and her paintings
- Discuss *El Camino de Santiago*
- Discuss *Iztaccíhuatl* and *Popocatépetl*

CONNECTIONS

3.1 Making Connections

- Talk about an artist and her work: Matilde Pérez
- Explain Language Arts strategies: cause and effect, describing events, using prior knowledge, choosing a topic, adding details, making predictions
- Use the skill of using graphic organizers
- Describe constellations in the southern hemisphere
- Discuss key facts about Mexico and Spain

CAPÍTULO **1**
Días inolvidables

España
México · Cuba
Puerto Rico
Chile · Argentina

CHAPTER OBJECTIVES

Communication

By the end of the chapter you will be able to:

- Listen and read about excursions and competitions
- Talk and write about nature and sports events
- Describe a trip

Culture

You will also be able to:

- Compare a famous pilgrimage route in Spain with similar trips in your community
- Understand the relationship between legends and nature
- Compare cultural practices in an authentic video about an adventure park in Puerto Rico

You will demonstrate what you know and can do

- Presentación oral, Una experiencia inolvidable
- Presentación escrita, Aventuras bajo el sol

You will use

Vocabulary
- Outdoor activities and camping
- Natural environment
- Sports and competitions
- Expressing emotions and impressions

Grammar
- Verbs with spelling and stem changes in the preterite
- Irregular verbs in the preterite
- The imperfect

ARTE y CULTURA ◄ Chile

Paisaje chileno Imagínate un lugar que tiene el desierto más árido del mundo, glaciares eternos, volcanes, un inmenso océano y además majestuosas montañas. Pues este lugar no está solo en tu imaginación. Se llama Chile y sus diversos paisajes han inspirado a famosos artistas. Entre ellos está la pintora Matilde Pérez (1920-2014), quien escogió el tema de la Cordillera de los Andes para crear este cuadro.

▶ ¿Qué paisaje es típico de la región donde vives? ¿Y cómo te hace sentir?

 Mapa global interactivo Explora Chile y compara el desierto de Atacama con regiones similares en los Estados Unidos.

"Paisaje chileno", Matilde Pérez

20 veinte • Capítulo 1 • Días inolvidables

Enrich Your Teaching

The End in Mind

Have students preview the sample performance tasks on *Preparación para el examen*, p. 63, and connect them to the Chapter Objectives. Explain to students that by completing the sample tasks they can self-assess their learning progress.

Technology: Mapa global interactivo

Download the *Mapa global interactivo* files for Chapter 1 and preview the activities. In Activity 1, travel to the Atacama Desert in Chile. Activity 2 takes you to national parks in Argentina. In Activity 3, locate astronomical observatories in both hemispheres. Activity 4 follows the route of pilgrims from France to northern Spain. In Activity 5, locate the two volcanoes in a Mexican legend.

El Glaciar Grey en el Parque
Nacional Torres del Paine, Chile

 Videonovela ¡Pura vida!

Capítulo 1 • veintiuno **21**

3.2 Acquiring information and Diverse Perspectives
- Read popular cheers for the Barcelona soccer team
- Discuss how indigenous peoples have affected the language of Mexico
- Discuss how ancient pilgrimages have shaped travel practices in Spain today

COMPARISONS
4.1 Language
- Compare Spanish words to their English counterparts
- Compare Spanish and English commands
4.2 Cultural
- Compare ancient ball games to modern ones
- Compare Spanish and Latin American teen magazines and their readership to those in the United States

COMMUNITIES
5.1 School and Global Communities
- Link to Web sites from the Spanish-speaking world
5.2 Lifelong Learning
- Talk about important facts about healthy lifestyles
- Talk about important facts about scientific studies
- Develop an appreciation for the art of songwriting
- Read an authentic Spanish-language text

Chapter Opener

Suggestions: Introduce the chapter theme and objectives. Use *Mapa global interactivo* to locate featured countries.

▶ **Technology: Videonovela ¡Pura vida!** View this stand-alone storyline video online about five young adults in San José, Costa Rica with your class.

ARTE Y CULTURA ◀

Standards: 1.1, 1.2, 2.2, 3.1, 4.2

Suggestions: Tell students Matilde Pérez painted realistic scenes, but became famous for her abstract art. Have them do an Internet search for **arte cinética.**

Answers will vary.

⊕ **Technology: Mapa global interactivo, Actividad 1** Travel to the Atacama Desert in Chile.

Teaching with Art
Ask students to list the landscape features they see in the photo.

Differentiated Instruction

Un momento especial
As students work through the chapter during the week, have them take notes of the activities they have participated in. Tell them to include the details and any pertinent information, such as location, special moments, and so on. Explain that they can use the notes to help them select their most unforgettable experience to complete the *Presentación oral* on p. 51.

Vocabulario en contexto 1

Standards: 1.2

Resources: Teacher's Resource Materials: Input Script, Clip Art, Audio Script, Technology: Audio Cap. 1

Suggestions: The next three pages present new vocabulary and grammar in context using visuals. Each page can be presented separately, but they complement each other. Use the audio to present new vocabulary. Have students read along as you play it. Ask what each item is used for. Check comprehension by asking questions. See the Input Script in the *Teacher's Resource Materials* for examples.

Starter Activity

Ask students to refer to pp. xxviii–xxix to locate Chile on the map and share facts about the country. (Use Map Transparency *América del Sur/parte sur.*)

 Technology: Interactive Whiteboard

> **Vocabulary Activities 1-1** Use the whiteboard activities in your Teacher Resources as you progress through the vocabulary practice with your class.

1

Standards: 1.2

Resources: Teacher's Resource Materials: Audio Script, Technology: Audio Cap. 1

Suggestions: Use the audio or read the script aloud to students.

Common Errors: Remind students not to try to understand every word they hear during listening comprehension activities. They should let the language "flow through" as a stream.

 Technology: Audio Script and Answers

1. Está muy oscuro en el bosque. Vas a tener que llevar la linterna. *(lógica)*
2. ¿Me prestas la brújula? Quiero observar esos pájaros que están en el árbol. *(ilógica)*
3. ¡Ay, cómo molestan estos mosquitos! Dame el repelente de insectos, por favor. *(lógica)*
4. Vamos a explorar el valle un poco. Llevamos la tableta con brújula para no perdernos. *(lógica)*
5. Ya es tarde y todos estamos cansados. ¿Dónde están los sacos de dormir? *(lógica)*
6. Quiero usar los nuevos binoculares para grabar lo que veo en el desierto. *(lógica)*

Vocabulario en contexto 1

OBJECTIVES
Read, listen to, and understand information about
▶ Camping activities
▶ Features of the natural environment

 ¡Cámping!

Ir de cámping es una buena manera de explorar la **naturaleza**. Sin embargo, antes de ir al **bosque**, **valle** o **desierto** es necesario tener el equipo apropiado. En la actualidad, la tecnología ofrece opciones increíbles.

el repelente de insectos

la linterna

el bosque

los binoculares

la brújula

el valle

el desierto

la tienda de acampar

el saco de dormir

> " Cuando vas de cámping, puedes llevar una **linterna** con radio y un cargador (charger) para tu teléfono, una tableta con **brújula**, termómetro y GPS o unos **binoculares** con grabadora. **Así** puedes grabar un video de todo lo que ves. "

22 veintidós • Capítulo 1 • Días inolvidables

Differentiated Instruction

Heritage Speakers

Invite students to research information they have about camping abroad. They might describe national parks or comment on differences between the camping experience in the United States and in other places.

Students with Learning Disabilities

Remind students that the new vocabulary is presented in blue. Use the visuals and context to determine meaning.

Go **Online** to practice
PEARSON
realize
PearsonSchool.com/Autentico

AUDIO

" Todos los años miles de personas van de cámping a **las sierras** chilenas y **lo pasan muy bien.** ¡Los **paisajes** son **hermosos!** Éstas son unas fotos de una familia y sus maravillosas vacaciones. "

la naturaleza

Al amanecer, mi familia y yo dimos un paseo a caballo.

Durante nuestro viaje nos gustaba escalar rocas.

Al anochecer las estrellas se veían muy claras y cercanas.

1

Equipo de cámping

ESCUCHAR En una hoja de papel escribe los números del 1 al 6. Vas a escuchar a unos jóvenes hablar sobre el equipo de cámping. Escucha cada frase y escribe si es lógica o ilógica.

2

Ir de cámping

ESCUCHAR En una hoja de papel escribe los números del 1 al 5. Escucha cada frase y escribe C (cierta) o F (falsa), según las fotos. Vas a oír cada frase dos veces.

Capítulo 1 • veintitrés **23**

Enrich Your Teaching

Culture Note

Ecotourism has become an important industry in Latin America. The beauty and variety of climate, landscape, flora, and fauna attract visitors from around the world. In recent years, countries such as Costa Rica, Venezuela, and Brazil have become internationally renowned ecotourism hotspots.

21st Century Skills

Critical Thinking and Problem Solving
Have teams of students discuss which outdoor activities are most popular in their area. What national or state parks are nearby? What problems might arise with an increase in popularity of outdoor activities in these parks? Why? How could these problems be avoided or minimized?

2

Standards: 1.2

Resources: Teacher's Resource Materials: Audio Script, Technology: Audio Cap. 1

Suggestions: Use the audio or the script. Remind students that this listening activity is based on the vocabulary on pp. 22–23.

Technology: Audio Script and Answers

1. Al amanecer, la familia dio un paseo por el bosque. (F)
2. Mucha gente va de cámping al desierto. (F)
3. Dieron un paseo a caballo por la mañana. (C)
4. Al anochecer, comieron salchichas. (F)
5. Escalaron las rocas durante sus vacaciones. (C)

Extension: On the board, copy as models two or three statements from the Audio Script. Have each student write two statements like the models, one true and one false. Ask volunteers to read aloud one of their statements. After each statement, ask another volunteer to determine whether it is *cierto* or *falso.*

Pre-AP® Integration

- **Learning Objective:** Interpersonal Speaking
- **Activity:** Ask students to make up a mini-story using one of the photos as an illustration. They should give names to the people and create sentences using the preterite to relate their story. Have students share their story with classmates.
- *Pre-AP® Resource Material:* Comprehensive guide to Pre-AP® vocabulary skill development

Teacher-to-Teacher

Have students write a note to a friend asking for advice on what they need for a camping trip, focusing on basic needs such as clothing, food, and shelter. Have them exchange notes with a classmate who will write a response. Ask students to hand in the notes if you wish to assess the activity.

Starter Activity

On the board, begin a word web with the expression ***ir de cámping*** at the center. Invite students to share what they know about camping and to tell about outdoor experiences they have had. Add camping and outdoors-related vocabulary that students use to the web.

Vocabulario en contexto 1

Standards: 1.2

Resources: Teacher's Resource Materials: Input Script, Audio Script, Technology: Audio Cap. 1

Suggestions: Pre-reading: Point out to students that identifying cause and effect relationships can help them understand what they are reading. Provide a few examples, such as the following: *Causa:* Empezó a llover. *Efecto:* Fuimos a casa. Then tell students to think about the cause and effect relationships as they read the dialogue.

Reading: Have students read along as they listen. Have them look at each of the visuals to aid comprehension. Allow them to listen more than once. Model pronunciation of the words in boldface. Check comprehension by asking questions. See the Input Scripts in the *Teacher's Resource Materials* for specific questions.

Post-reading: Complete *Actividad 3* to check comprehension.

Extension: Have students rewrite Jairo's account as a third-person narrative.

3 ▬▬▬▬▬▬▬▬▬▬▬▬

Standards: 1.1, 1.2, 1.3

Suggestions: Review the answers with the class. Then tell students to correct the false statements.

 Technology: Audio Script and Answers

1. Jairo y sus amigos fueron de paseo al mar. (F)
2. Jairo y sus amigos encontraron refugio en una caverna. (C)
3. Miguel perdió el equilibrio y se lastimó una pierna. (F)
4. Jairo y sus amigos no pudieron volver a su tienda de acampar. (F)

Project-Based Learning

Share the Chapter 1 Project-Based Learning outline and rubric from p. 16-b. Explain the task to them, and have them perform Step 1. (For more information, see p. 16-b.)

 Jairo le cuenta a su mamá cómo le fue en su paseo por la sierra.

Jairo / Mamá

Mamá:	Hola hijo, ¿qué tal te fue en tu paseo?
Jairo:	Nos divertimos mucho, mami. ¡Pero no te imaginas lo que nos pasó!
Mamá:	¿Qué **sucedió**?
Jairo:	Cuando estábamos escalando una montaña, vimos **relámpagos** y oímos un **trueno**. ¡Luego comenzó a **caer granizo**!
Mamá:	¡No me digas! ¿Y qué hicieron?
Jairo:	**Nos refugiamos** en una caverna. **Una vez allí**, nos sentamos a hablar mientras pasaba el mal tiempo. Nos **impresionó** el tamaño del granizo. ¡Parecían bolas de golf!
Mamá:	¡Qué bueno que encontraron **refugio**!
Jairo:	Sí, pero ahí no terminó todo. Cuando **dejó de** llover salimos de la caverna y comenzamos a bajar la montaña. El suelo estaba mojado y Miguel **perdió el equilibrio,** pero no se cayó.
Mamá:	¡Ay, qué bien! ¿Y entonces qué pasó?
Jairo:	Bajamos la montaña y **anduvimos** por **un rato** hasta que **nos acercamos** a un bosque grande. Habíamos olvidado la linterna y la brújula en la caverna. ¡Yo sabía que íbamos a **perdernos**!
Mamá:	¿Y cómo volvieron entonces?
Jairo:	Al rato **apareció** un guardabosques *(park ranger)* que nos mostró **hacia** dónde ir. Llegamos a la tienda al anochecer.
Mamá:	¡Ay, hijo, tus aventuras me **asustan** mucho!

3 ▬

La aventura de Jairo y sus amigos

 ESCUCHAR En una hoja de papel escribe los números del 1 al 4. Escucha cada frase y escribe *C* si es cierta o *F* si es falsa.

24 veinticuatro • Capítulo 1 • Días inolvidables

Differentiated Instruction

Culture Note

A backpacking or camping trip to the mountains in the southern part of South America would probably include sightings of the guanaco or its cousin the vicuña. These wild herd animals are related to the camel, but smaller. The llama and the alpaca, domestic animals used in the Andes, are descendants of the guanaco.

21st Century Skills

Collaboration Ask students working collaboratively in small groups to create a Spanish interview program about outdoor survival adventures called *¡Sobrevivientes!* Have one of the students interview the others in the group, who will play people who have survived an unforgettable wilderness experience, and explain how their adventure ended.

Videohistoria

Go **Online** to practice
PEARSON
realize.
AUDIO VIDEO WRITING SCRIPT

PearsonSchool.com/Autentico

Interpretive 1

Entre el mar, el valle y la sierra

Antes de ver

Usar las imágenes como contexto Piensa en qué información te dan estas fotos. ¿Qué clase de lugar muestra cada una? ¿Qué hacen las personas? Al ver el video, usa las imágenes para inferir palabras y frases desconocidas.

Haz la actividad

En medio de la naturaleza Haz una lista de distintos tipos de actividades y deportes que se pueden hacer en medio de la naturaleza. Comienza con las actividades que se muestran en las fotos.

▶ Ve el video

Teo y Camila hablan de dos divertidas actividades al aire libre: una es en el mar, la otra en el valle y la sierra. ¿Qué actividades pueden ser?

Ve a **PearsonSchool.com/Autentico** y busca el video *Entre el mar, el valle y la sierra*. También puedes leer el guión[1].

Camila **Teo**

Después de ver

 ESCRIBIR Contesta las siguientes preguntas:

1. ¿De qué actividad comienzan a hablar Teo y Camila?
2. ¿Por qué Camila le habla a Teo del paseo que hicieron a la sierra?
3. ¿Qué imágenes te ayudan a entender mejor de qué habla Camila?
4. Parafrasea lo que Daniel dice en el video.
5. ¿Por qué crees que el video se llama *Entre el mar, el valle y la sierra*?

Tu opinión ¿Qué te parece más divertido, hacer surfing o ir de camping? ¿Por qué? Da razones específicas.

[1]script

Capítulo 1 • veinticinco **25**

Enrich Your Teaching

Culture Note

Mancora, located in northwestern Peru, is considered one of the best surfing destinations in the South Pacific coast. Surfers from around the world flock to this charming beach town each year, especially between the months of December and January when the winds are optimum for powerful waves.

21st Century Skills

Creativity and Innovation Invite students to work with a partner to create a simple video script in Spanish describing an outdoor activity. Guide them through the following steps:

1. Select the outdoor activity.
2. Select the people that will appear in the video.
3. List the main idea and the important details of the story you are telling.
4. Plan the actions and the images that will be needed.
5. Write a draft of the script.

Tecnología: Video

Standards: 1.2

Resources: Teacher's Resource Materials: Video Script

Antes de ver

Review the previewing strategy and activity with the students. Invite them to observe and discuss the photos. Lead them to conclude that they illustrate outdoor activities in different natural settings. Suggest that they use the images on the video to infer the meaning of unfamiliar phrases.

Ve el video

Show the video once without pausing. Show it again, stopping to check comprehension. Guide students to notice the different segments in which this Videohistoria could be divided: 1. Camila and Teo talking about surfing. 2. Camila and Teo remembering the camping trip. 3. Video of Daniel talking about surfing in Peru. 4. Camila and Teo commenting Daniel's experiences.

Después de ver

Standards: 1.2

Suggestions: Discuss the questions with the class. Invite volunteers to paraphrase the important details in Daniel's video.

Answers

1. de surfing
2. para que recuerde a Daniel, quien fue con ellos a la sierra
3. las imágenes del camping y del surfing
4. Answers will vary but should include how popular surfing is in Peru.
5. Answers will vary.

Tu opinión: Answers will vary.

Have students go to Realize for additional video activities.

Additional Resources

📶 **Technology: Online Resources**
- Instant Check
- Guided, Core, Video, Audio
- *Para hispanohablantes*

Print
- Guided WB pp. 33–40
- Core WB pp. 14–15

Assessment _____

Quiz: Vocabulary Recognition
- Prueba 1-6

25

4

Recycle: reflexive pronouns, preterite forms
Suggestions: Refer students to pp. 22–25 for vocabulary.
Answers:

1. Al amanecer
2. dar un paseo
3. Una vez allí
4. un rato
5. relámpagos
6. truenos
7. hacia
8. nos refugiamos

5

Suggestions: Ask students to check their answers with a partner.
Answers:

1. f
2. c
3. d
4. a
5. e
6. b

6

Recycle: expressions with the infinitive
Suggestions: Point out that only seven camping items are pictured. Students must come up with their own eighth item in Step 1.
Possible Answers:

1. linterna; ver por donde caminar
2. tienda de acampar; dormir y descansar
3. binoculares; ver animales
4. agua; beber
5. brújula; no perderme
6. sartén; cocinar pescado
7. mochila; llevar cosas

Vocabulario en uso 1

4

Un paseo en bicicleta

LEER, ESCRIBIR Completa el blog con las palabras correctas.

un rato	una vez allí	relámpagos
dar un paseo	truenos	nos refugiamos
al amanecer	hacia	

El blog de Jóse

___1.___ nos levantamos y preparamos las bicicletas para ___2.___ por el campo. ___3.___ paramos para descansar y almorzar. Después de ___4.___ empezó a llover. Vimos ___5.___ y oímos unos ___6.___ que nos asustaron mucho. Corrimos ___7.___ una casa donde ___8.___. ¡Fue un día inolvidable!

5

Definiciones

ESCRIBIR Empareja cada palabra o frase con su definición. Escribe después un cuento breve usando algunas palabras de la primera columna.

1. suceder
2. perder el equilibrio
3. refugiarse
4. acercarse a
5. al anochecer
6. al amanecer

a. ir cerca de
b. cuando empieza la mañana
c. caerse
d. esconderse
e. cuando empieza la noche
f. pasar

6

¿Qué vas a llevar?

ESCRIBIR, HABLAR EN PAREJA

1 Vas de cámping este fin de semana. Haz una lista de siete cosas que necesitas llevar y explica para qué las necesitas.

2 Dejaste en casa algunas cosas que necesitas para ir de cámping. Usa la lista que escribiste para hablar con otro(a) estudiante.

lo que necesitas	para qué lo necesitas
linterna	*ver cuando está oscuro*

Videomodelo

A —¡Ay, caramba! Dejé la **linterna** en casa.
B —¡Qué pena! Ahora **no puedes caminar por el bosque por la noche.**

1  **2**  **3**

4  **5**  **6**  **7**

Differentiated Instruction

Students with Learning Difficulties

For *Actividad* 4, have students copy the word bank to their papers. As they complete each item, tell them to check off or cross out the item they used from the word bank in order to minimize their choices for the remaining items.

Advanced Learners

Have students use the preterite to write their own paragraph about a real or imagined outdoor experience. Invite them to read their paragraphs aloud in a small group and discuss similarities and differences among their outdoor experiences.

7

Al mal tiempo buena cara

HABLAR EN PAREJA Habla con otro(a) estudiante de las excursiones que hicieron a varios lugares y de lo que les sucedió.

Videomodelo

A —¿Qué hicieron en **el océano**?
B —**Navegamos todo el día**.

A —¿Y luego, qué sucedió?
B —**Oímos truenos y llovió**.

navegar / oír truenos

1. observar pájaros / ver relámpagos

2. dar un paseo / caer granizo

3. escalar rocas / perder el equilibrio y caerse

4. dar un paseo a caballo / perderse

5. nadar / empezar a llover

6. **¡Respuesta personal!**

CULTURA ◄ Chile • Argentina

Parques nacionales de América del Sur En la última década las visitas a los parques nacionales de América del Sur, especialmente de Chile y Argentina, aumentaron mucho. Esto se debe a[1] un creciente[2] interés por estar en contacto con la naturaleza y disfrutar de actividades al aire libre. ¿Quiénes son los visitantes? Familias, grupos de jóvenes recién egresados[3] de la escuela secundaria, grupos de estudiantes en excursiones de estudio y personas de todas las edades interesadas en conocer nuevas especies de animales y plantas y estar en contacto con la naturaleza. La gran variedad de parques nacionales atrae[4] a todo tipo de gente. En la Argentina hay selvas tropicales en el Parque Nacional Baritú, enormes cataratas[5] en el Parque Nacional Iguazú y hasta glaciares en el Parque Nacional Perito Moreno.

Pre-AP Integration: Los viajes y el ocio ¿Por qué crees que ha aumentado el número de personas que visita los parques nacionales de Chile y Argentina?

 Mapa global interactivo Explora la geografía del Parque Nacional Perito Moreno e investiga los procesos relacionados con sus glaciares.

[1]is due to [2]growing [3]graduated [4]attracts [5]waterfalls

Las Cataratas del Iguazú, en el Parque Nacional Iguazú, Argentina

Capítulo 1 • veintisiete **27**

7

Standards: 1.1

Suggestions: Direct students to use the pictures and clues to guide them.

Answers:
1. ¿Qué hicieron en el bosque?/Observamos los pájaros./Vimos relámpagos.
2. ¿...en el valle?/Dimos un paseo./Cayó granizo.
3. ¿...en la sierra? Escalamos rocas./Perdimos el equilibrio y nos caímos.
4. ¿...en el desierto?/Dimos un paseo a caballo./Nos perdimos.
5. ¿...en el lago?/Nadamos./Empezó a llover.
6. Answers will vary.

Starter Activity

Have students refer to the pictures in Actividad 7 and be prepared to say what the weather might be like in each location. (Ex. *En la playa, hace sol.*)

CULTURA ◄

Standards: 1.2, 3.1

Suggestions: After students read the paragraph, ask them to talk about activities in which visitors to national parks frequently engage.

Answers:

Los parques atraen a todo tipo de gente: familias, grupos de jóvenes recién egresados de la escuela secundaria, estudiantes en excursiones de estudio y personas de todas las edades.

A los visitantes les interesa conocer nuevas especies de animales y plantas y ponerse en contacto con la naturaleza. También quieren disfrutar de actividades al aire libre.

 Technology: Mapa global interactivo, Actividad 2 Explore a glacier and a tropical national park in Argentina.

Enrich Your Teaching

Culture Note

One of Venezuela's national parks, Canaima, is the home of the world's highest waterfall, **El Salto Ángel** (Angel Falls). It plunges off a **tepuy,** a flat-topped mountain, to fall for more than 2,400 feet. There are more than 100 **tepuys** in the area of **el Salto Ángel,** all with vertical sides of sandstone shaped by heavy rainfalls.

21st Century Skills

ICT Literacy Have students research the national parks of Chile and Argentina. Ask them to brainstorm the list of keywords they will use in their search. How can they decide which websites will give them reliable and accurate information?

AMPLIACIÓN DEL LENGUAJE

Standards: 1.2, 4.1

Suggestions: Ask volunteers to supply the verbs that correspond with the nouns in the second part. Ask other volunteers to use the **ir de...** expressions in complete sentences.

Answers:

comprar	visitar
cazar	viajar

8

Standards: 1.3

Suggestions: In addition to using the word or expression in parentheses in a sentence, encourage students to supply an extra detail or two, as the model does.

Answers will vary.

9

Standards: 1.2, 1.3

Suggestions: Remind students that paying attention to cause and effect will help them write their e-mail messages.

Answers will vary.

10

Standards: 1.1, 1.2

Suggestions: After students have done their role-play once through with the narration, ask them to do it again and describe what is happening.

Answers will vary.

Ampliación del lenguaje   ‹ Ir de . . .

Muchas acciones en español se pueden expresar usando *ir de* más un sustantivo *(noun)* de la misma familia que el verbo. Por ejemplo:

ir de pesca	pescar
ir de paseo	pasear

Como puedes ver, el sustantivo *pesca* y el verbo *pescar* pertenecen a la misma familia de palabras.

¿Puedes adivinar *(guess)* cuáles son los verbos que corresponden a las siguientes expresiones con *ir de . . .* ?

ir de compras
ir de caza *(hunting)*
ir de visita
ir de viaje

8

¿Qué pasó?

 LEER, ESCRIBIR Imagina lo que pasó en cada situación y escribe una frase usando los verbos entre paréntesis.

Modelo
Fuimos de pesca el sábado. *(perder)*
Perdimos el equilibrio en el bote y nos caímos al agua.

1. Mis padres fueron de paseo. *(acercarse)*
2. Mi hermana fue de compras. *(pasarlo bien)*
3. Fui de viaje con mi familia. *(impresionar)*
4. Fuimos de caza al amanecer. *(asustar)*
5. Mis abuelos fueron de visita. *(perderse)*

9

¡Fue un desastre!

 ESCRIBIR Acabas de regresar de una excursión de cámping desastrosa. Quieres escribir un mensaje electrónico a un(a) amigo(a) para decirle cómo lo pasaste. Escribe cinco frases para describir tu experiencia. Escoge entre las siguientes palabras y expresiones:

Modelo
Durante toda la noche cayó granizo sobre la tienda de acampar.

una vez allí	aparecer	dejar de
caer granizo	llover	relámpago
trueno	así	impresionar
perderse	refugiarse	

10

Juego

 HABLAR EN GRUPO Trabaja con un grupo de cuatro estudiantes y escojan uno de los mensajes electrónicos que escribieron para la Actividad 9. Actúen el mensaje mientras otro grupo cuenta lo que pasó. Usen gestos y expresiones apropiados.

Differentiated Instruction

Students with Learning Difficulties

Point out to students that **ir de** is very similar to the English expression "to be going." Like that expression, **ir de** is often used to talk about future events. Provide examples, such as: *¿Qué vas a hacer el sábado? Voy de pesca.*

Advanced Learners

Have students work in a group to develop one of the situations from *Actividad* 9 into a skit about an outdoor experience. One student can narrate in the past tense, while the others act out the scene(s) and engage in dialogue that uses preterite forms and new vocabulary.

Las estrellas del sur

11

LEER, ESCRIBIR Lee este párrafo para aprender sobre las estrellas del hemisferio sur y contesta las preguntas.

Conexiones ◄ Las ciencias

Desde América del Sur, por estar en otra latitud, el cielo se ve diferente. Solo en la línea ecuatorial[1] se ve todo el cielo durante todo el año. Esto crea un problema para los astrónomos, porque solo pueden ver una parte del cielo si no están en el ecuador. Por ejemplo, solamente en el hemisferio sur se ve la constelación de la Cruz del Sur.

• ¿Adónde puedes ir para ver las estrellas?
• ¿Qué constelaciones puedes ver donde tú vives?

 Mapa global interactivo Explora algunos observatorios en el mundo hispanohablante y averigua la importancia de su ubicación.

[1]Equator

▲ La Cruz del Sur

Lugares para explorar

ESCRIBIR, HABLAR EN GRUPO

1 Piensa en un lugar que te gustaría explorar: el desierto, el océano, el mar, el bosque, la sierra o una selva tropical. Escribe un texto a un(a) amigo(a) y pregúntale sus planes. Él o ella te contesta con su preferencia.

Modelo
A—*¿Dónde quieres explorar primero?*
B—*Quiero ir a la sierra porque me gusta el paisaje.*

2 Forma un grupo con otros estudiantes que escogieron el mismo lugar que tú. Conversen sobre sus preferencias personales.

3 Usa las ideas del grupo para escribir una breve conversación explicando tus razones para explorar ese lugar.

4 Expresa tu preferencia a la clase. Recuerda explicar por qué recomiendas ese lugar.

Y tú, ¿qué dices?

ESCRIBIR, HABLAR

1. Imagina que estás haciendo planes para ir a un parque nacional. Envía un texto a un(a) compañero(a) con preguntas. Él o ella te dirá lo que necesitas hacer y por qué.

Modelo
A—*¿Qué hago en la noche?*
B—*Necesitas ver las estrellas. Son increíbles.*

2. Los parques nacionales son refugios de muchos animales como osos, coyotes y búfalos. ¿Alguna vez se acercó a ti uno de estos animales? ¿Te asustó? ¿Qué hiciste? Relata una ocasión en que algo te asustó y describe tu reacción. Usa oraciones conectadas con detalles y elaboración.

Capítulo 1 • veintinueve **29**

Enrich Your Teaching

Culture Note

The beautiful colored lights of the aurora borealis sometimes appear in the night sky of the Northern Hemisphere. The aurora australis is found in the Southern Hemisphere. Both phenomena occur when electrons and protons from the sun are drawn toward the poles by Earth's magnetic field.

21st Century Skills

Communication Encourage students to articulate their thoughts and ideas clearly and effectively as they respond to the questions in *Actividades* 12 and 13. Ask them to pay special attention to the adjectives and descriptive phrases they could use to make their descriptions more vivid. Students will use both oral and written communication skills in these activities.

Interpersonal | 1

11

Standards: 1.1, 1.2, 3.1

Suggestions: Remind students that cognates, such as *latitud* and *ecuatorial,* are a valuable aid to understanding new material.

Answers will vary.

 Technology: Mapa global interactivo, Actividad 3 See the location of astronomical observatories in both hemispheres.

Starter Activity

Have students share what is studied in various science classes (*biología, química, ciencias naturales*). List on the board.

12

Standards: 1.1, 1.3, 3.1

Suggestions: Encourage students to use a graphic organizer such as a concept web to help them develop their presentation.

Answers will vary.

13

Standards: 1.1, 1.2, 1.3, 3.1

Suggestions: Assign or have students choose one or more of the options, depending on time and ability. Option 3 is the most challenging.

Answers will vary.

Additional Resources

 Technology: Online Resources
• Communication Activities
• Teacher's Resource Materials: Communicative Pair Activity, Audio Script, Technology: Audio Cap. 1

Assessment

Prueba 1-2 with Remediation (online only)
Prueba: Aplicación del vocabulario 1
• Prueba 1-2

Gramática: Repaso

Un poco más de repaso

Suggestions: Point out the *i* to *y* changes in the paradigm. Have students write out the verbs that follow the same pattern.

 Technology: Interactive Whiteboard

> **Grammar Activities 1-1** Use the whiteboard activities in your Teacher Resources as you progress through the grammar practice with your class.

14

Standards: 1.2

Suggestions: Ask volunteers to spell aloud the verb forms they wrote.

Answers:

Step 1

1. dimos	4. vimos	7. empezó
2. oyó	5. oímos	8. Cayó
3. creyó	6. se cayó	9. corrimos

Step 2
Answers will vary.

15

Standards: 1.2

Resources: Teacher's Resource Materials: Audio Script, Technology: Audio Cap. 1

Focus: Practicing listening comprehension and writing accuracy.

 Technology: Audio

(For the script, see Teacher's Resource Materials.)

Answers: Step 1

1. se cayeron	3. destruyó	5. creyó
2. oímos	4. leyó	

Step 2
1. Tres árboles se cayeron.
2. Uno de los árboles destruyó un puente.
3. La hermana no creyó la historia. Ella no estaba allí.

Assessment

Prueba 1-3 with Remediation (online only)
Prueba: El pretérito de verbos con el cambio *i → y*
• Prueba 1-3: p. 17

Gramática Repaso

OBJECTIVES
▸ Talk and write about outdoor adventures
▸ Listen to and write about what happened

El pretérito de los verbos con el cambio ortográfico *i → y*

Verbs ending in *-uir,* such as *destruir,* have a spelling change in the preterite. The *i* becomes *y* in the *Ud. / él / ella* and *Uds. / ellos / ellas* forms.

Other verbs, such as *leer, creer, oír,* and *caerse,* follow a similar pattern.

destruí	destruimos		leí	leímos
destruiste	destruisteis		leíste	leísteis
destruyó	destruyeron		leyó	leyeron

Note that the *i* is only accented in the *yo* form.

In these verbs, the *i* is always accented.

Más recursos ONLINE

▶ **Tutorial:** Spelling Changes in the Preterite

14

 En el bosque

LEER, ESCRIBIR

1 En una hoja de papel escribe los números del 1 al 9. Completa este cuento con el pretérito del verbo apropiado.

2 Ahora, con otro(a) estudiante, escribe un final para el cuento.

El verano pasado, Tomás y yo __1.__ *(dar / leer)* un paseo por el bosque. Nos sentamos a descansar, cuando de repente, Tomás __2.__ *(creer / oír)* un ruido arriba de un árbol. Tomás __3.__ *(creer / caerse)* que era un mono, pero cuando nos acercamos al árbol, nosotros no __4.__ *(ver / comer)* ni __5.__ *(oír / destruir)* nada. Pero entonces, Tomás perdió el equilibrio y __6.__ *(creer / caerse).* Afortunadamente, no se lastimó mucho. Un poco después __7.__ *(empezar / hacer)* a llover. __8.__ *(caer / leer)* granizo. Nosotros __9.__ *(correr / vivir)* a refugiarnos pero . . .

15

 Después de la tormenta

ESCUCHAR, LEER, ESCRIBIR

1 Escucha lo que pasó después de una tormenta y escribe los verbos.

Ayer, después de la tormenta, __1.__ tres árboles en el parque. Hicieron un ruido tremendo. Nosotros estábamos en el lago, pero lo __2.__ claramente. Uno de los árboles __3.__ un puente. Esta mañana, mi hermana __4.__ la noticia en el periódico. Ella no estaba con nosotros en el lago y no __5.__ la historia hasta que vio la noticia.

2 Ahora parafrasea la idea principal, el tema y los detalles. Usa las preguntas para ayudarte.

1. ¿Cuántos árboles se cayeron?
2. ¿Qué destruyó uno de los árboles?
3. ¿Quién no creyó esta historia? ¿Por qué?

Differentiated Instruction

Heritage Speakers

Have students review the irregular preterite forms in the *Gramática* on p. 31 in groups. Ask them to work together to think of other words that have irregular preterite forms and write the forms in tables like the one in the *Gramática.* Encourage them to check their spelling using the Student Edition or an online dictionary.

Advanced Learners

Have students write five sentences that use verbs with the *i* to *y* change in the preterite. Ask them to read their sentences aloud to a partner. The partner who listens writes down the preterite verb he or she hears in each sentence. Partners can then check their spelling of the preterite verb forms with each other.

Gramática Repaso

Go Online to practice
PearsonSchool.com/Autentico

PEARSON realize

AUDIO VIDEO WRITING

OBJECTIVES
▶ Listen to and write about a rafting adventure
▶ Talk and write about what people did
▶ Exchange information about camping activities

El pretérito de los verbos irregulares

Some verbs have irregular stems in the preterite.

tener	andar	estar	poder	poner	saber	venir
tuve	anduve	estuve	pude	puse	supe	vine
tuviste	anduviste	estuviste	pudiste	pusiste	supiste	viniste
tuvo	anduvo	estuvo	pudo	puso	supo	vino
tuvimos	anduvimos	estuvimos	pudimos	pusimos	supimos	vinimos
tuvisteis	anduvisteis	estuvisteis	pudisteis	pusisteis	supisteis	vinisteis
tuvieron	anduvieron	estuvieron	pudieron	pusieron	supieron	vinieron

The verbs *decir* and *traer* also have irregular stems in the preterite.

decir		traer	
dije	dijimos	traje	trajimos
dijiste	dijisteis	trajiste	trajisteis
dijo	dijeron*	trajo	trajeron*

*Note that the Uds./ellos/ellas endings for decir and traer are slightly different from the verbs listed above.

Más recursos ONLINE

▶ **Tutorial:** Stem Changes in the Preterite

 Canción de hip hop: *Un viaje a la sierra*

16 Un paseo en balsa

 ESCUCHAR, LEER, ESCRIBIR

1 Escucha esta descripción de un viaje en balsa *(raft)*. Lee las preguntas y levanta la mano derecha si escoges la opción **a**, y la mano izquierda si escoges la opción **b**.

1. ¿Los chicos pusieron **a. las balsas** o **b. las mochilas** encima del coche?
2. ¿El guía vino **a. unos minutos después** o **b. una hora después**?
3. ¿El guía les dijo que iban a ir **a. al centro de Santiago** o **b. al río Maipo**?
4. ¿Los chicos tuvieron que llevar las balsas **a. al río** o **b. al coche**?
5. Antes de comenzar el viaje, ¿los chicos se pusieron **a. las gorras** o **b. los trajes de baño**?
6. Después del viaje, ¿todos estuvieron de acuerdo en que **a. lo pasaron bien** o en que **b. lo pasaron mal**?

2 Ahora, parafrasea la idea principal del audio. Incluye el tema y los detalles más importantes.

Capítulo 1 • treinta y uno **31**

Enrich Your Teaching

Teacher-to-Teacher

English speakers often wonder why there are two forms of "you" in Spanish. Explain that the answer begins with Latin's second-person plural: *vos.* In the fourth century, the Romans began to use this form as a sign of respect for individuals. The custom carried over to languages that evolved from Latin. (Spanish *vosotros* is a vestige, although it is a plural form.) In the eighteenth century, Spain's upper classes refined rules of address for individuals. *Vos* (a singular form) became *vuestra merced,* which underwent such variations as *vuesarcé* and *ucé* until it became *usted.* This was later used by the nobility with the third-person singular verb forms.

Gramática: Repaso

Un poco más de repaso

Suggestions: Have students practice listening comprehension of the verb forms by providing them with models that use the forms. Then ask questions in the preterite for students to answer. Point out the irregular stems and the endings they all share.

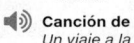 **Technology: Interactive Whiteboard**

Grammar Activities 1-1 Use the whiteboard activities in your Teacher Resources as you progress through the grammar practice with your class.

16

Standards: 1.2

Resources: Teacher's Resource Materials: Audio Script, Technology: Audio Cap. 1

Suggestions: Have students read through the questions before they hear the audio. Remind students to use verbs in the preterite.

 Technology: Audio

(For the audio script, see Teacher's Resource Materials.)

Answers:
Step 1

1. a	**3.** b	**5.** b
2. a	**4.** a	**6.** a

Step 2
1. Pusieron las balsas encima del coche.
2. Vino unos minutos después.
3. Les dijo que iban a ir al Río Maipo.
4. Tuvieron que llevar las balsas al río.
5. Se pusieron los trajes de baño.
6. Estuvieron de acuerdo en que lo pasaron bien.

Common Errors: Some students regularly forget to use reflexive pronouns. Take advantage of *Actividad* 16 to remind students of how strongly these pronouns can affect meaning. Point out the difference in meaning between *pusieron* in item 1 and *se pusieron* in item 5.

Project-Based Learning

Students can perform Step 2 at this point. Be sure they understand your corrections and suggestions. (For more information, see p. 16-b.)

Additional Resources

Technology: Online Resources
• Instant Check
• Guided, Core, Audio
• *Para hispanohablantes*
Print
• Guided WB pp. 27–28
• Core WB pp. 11

17

Standards: 1.3

Suggestions: Tell students that, besides targeting verb forms, this activity examines their comprehension of the sentence parts that they must put together.

Answers:
1. Yo no pude venir.
2. Nosotros trajimos la comida.
3. Perla se puso el traje de baño.
4. Raúl y Silvia estuvieron muy ocupados.
5. Tú viniste en bicicleta.
6. Todos dijimos "¡Claro que sí!"

Starter Activity

Form groups of six students. Taking turns around the circle, each student uses one of the forms of *decir* in the preterite to say what different people said about the past summer's activities.

18

Standards: 1.1, 1.2

Un poco más de repaso

Recycle: time expressions, daily routines

Suggestions: Tell students they should listen carefully to their partner's question, and answer using the same verb that the question contained.

Answers will vary.

Additional Resources

Technology: Online Resources
- Instant Check
- Guided, Core, Reading, Writing
- *Para hispanohablantes*

Print
- Guided WB pp. 29–30
- Core WB pp. 12

Assessment

Prueba 1-4 with Remediation (online only)
Prueba: El pretérito de los verbos irregulares
- Prueba 1-4

17

Una invitación a la playa

ESCRIBIR Carolina invitó a sus amigos a ir con ella a la playa. Describe cómo respondió cada amigo(a) usando el pretérito del verbo entre paréntesis y las palabras apropiadas del recuadro.

Modelo
José *(venir)* / después de un rato.
José **vino después de un rato.**

el traje de baño	muy ocupados(as)	venir
en bicicleta	la comida	"¡Claro que sí!"

1. Yo no *(poder)*   3. Perla *(ponerse)*   5. Tú *(venir)*
2. Nosotros *(traer)*   4. Raúl y Silvia *(estar)*   6. Todos *(decir)*

18

En el Campamento Amistad

 LEER, HABLAR EN PAREJA Los consejeros del Campamento Amistad hablan de las actividades que hicieron los niños. Trabaja con otro(a) estudiante para hablar del horario. Puedes usar los verbos *andar, estar, poder, poner, venir, tener* y *traer*.

 Videomodelo
A —*¿Dónde estuvo Daniel a las 11:00?*
B —*Estuvo en la piscina.*
A —*¿Qué tuvo que hacer Julián a la 1:00?*
B —*Tuvo que servir la comida.*

Horario del grupo "Los piratas" para el 15 de julio					
Nombre	9:00 a 10:30	11:00 a 12:30	1:00 a 1:15	3:00 a 5:00	6:00 a 7:00
Daniel	campo de deportes/jugar al fútbol	piscina/traer el traje de baño	comedor/lavar los platos	playa/bucear	sala/usar la computadora
Marta	campo de deportes/jugar al tenis	piscina/traer las toallas	comedor/traer el pan	lago/navegar	sala/poner flores
Estela	campo de deportes/jugar al tenis	bosque/andar por los senderos	comedor/poner la mesa	campo/montar a caballo	jardín/traer los binoculares
Julián	en cama/enfermo	lago/navegar	comedor/servir la comida	playa/nadar	playa/hacer una fogata

Differentiated Instruction

Heritage Speakers

Have students list in chronological order five activities that they did today before they arrived to Spanish class. Have them exchange lists with a partner and check each other's work for errors in spelling or placement of accent marks.

Students with Learning Difficulties

Help students better understand the schedule in *Actividad* 18. Reproduce the schedule on the board with clock faces at the top to show the time periods. Point out that the time gets later as students read from left to right in the schedule.

Gramática Repaso

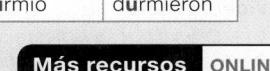

OBJECTIVES
▶ Talk and write about past family trips
▶ Exchange information about parties and excursions
▶ Write about excursions and places in Chile

Go **Online** to practice
PEARSON realize ™
PearsonSchool.com/Autentico

VIDEO   WRITING   SPEAK/RECORD

El pretérito de los verbos con los cambios e → i, o → u en la raíz

Stem changing -ir verbs in the present tense also have a stem change in the preterite tense. The changes are e → i and o → u and take place in the *Ud. / él / ella* and *Uds. / ellos / ellas* forms only.

Here are the preterite forms of *pedir, sentir,* and *dormir:*

pedí	pedimos
pediste	pedisteis
pidió	pidieron

sentí	sentimos
sentiste	sentisteis
sintió	sintieron

dormí	dormimos
dormiste	dormisteis
durmió	durmieron

Other verbs like *pedir (i)* and *sentir (i)* are: *divertirse, preferir, sugerir, vestirse.* Another verb like *dormir (u)* is: *morir.*

Más recursos   ONLINE

▶ **Tutorial:** Irregular Preterite Forms

19

¿Qué pasó en el picnic?

LEER, ESCRIBIR   La familia Suárez hizo un picnic en la playa. Completa las frases con el pretérito del verbo apropiado.

1. Yo *(preferir / dormir)* ir a la playa.
2. Mis hermanitos *(morirse / pedir)* de miedo cuando hicieron moto acuática.
3. Fuimos de pesca y *(morirse / divertirse).*
4. Mi hermanita *(pedir / dormir)* más postre.
5. Después de comer mis hermanos y yo *(dormir / servir)* una siesta.

20

¿Cómo lo pasaron?

HABLAR EN PAREJA   Una semana después, los hermanos Suárez fueron de cámping por cinco días. Habla con otro(a) estudiante de su experiencia.

 **Videomodelo**
¿A qué hora? / dormirse
A —¿A qué hora **se durmieron**?
B —**Se durmieron a las siete.**

Estudiante A

1. ¿Por dónde? / andar los hermanos
2. ¿Dónde? / dormir los hermanos
3. ¿Qué? / tener el hermano menor
4. ¿Qué? / traer los chicos para beber

Estudiante B

Capítulo 1 • treinta y tres **33**

Gramática: Repaso

Un poco más de repaso
Suggestions: Have students use the vocabulary from pp. 22–23 and write sentences with the preterite forms of three of the verbs listed.

 Technology: Interactive Whiteboard

Grammar Activities 1-1 Use the whiteboard activities in your Teacher Resources as you progress through the grammar practice with your class.

19

Standards: 1.2

Suggestions: Have students write the answers. Then call on volunteers to read the answers aloud and spell the verb forms. Write the answers on the board.

Answers:
Step 1
1. preferí
2. se murieron
3. nos divertimos
4. pidió
5. dormimos

Common errors: Students often forget the third-person stem change. Review this change using the transparency.

20

Standards: 1.1

Suggestions: Remind students to use the pictures to help them answer the questions.

Answers:
1. —¿Por dónde anduvieron los hermanos?
   —Anduvieron por el sendero.
2. —¿Dónde durmieron los hermanos?
   —Durmieron en una tienda de acampar.
3. —¿Qué tenía el hermano menor?
   — Tenía una mochila para guardar sus cosas.
4. —¿Qué trajeron los chicos para beber?
   —Trajeron agua para beber.

Enrich Your Teaching

Teacher-to-Teacher

Students can create a conversation that revolves around a bad experience with a food server. For example, Student A tells B how the server kept bringing the wrong food, how the food was overcooked, and so on. Student B can ask for more details with questions such as *¿Y después? ¿Qué pidieron Uds. de postre?*

21st Century Skills

Media Literacy Remind students of the various digital tools available in **Realize** to help them monitor their own understanding and learning needs, such as the eText with embedded audio files and online tutorials.

21

Standards: 1.1, 1.3

Suggestions: For Step 2, encourage students to use their questions as notes for a naturally flowing conversation like the one in the model.

Answers will vary, but should include correct spellings of the verb forms used.

22

Standards: 1.1, 1.3

Suggestions: In Step 3, encourage students to practice using expressions such as **Teresa me dijo que** when reporting to the class about their partner.
Answers will vary.

23

Standards: 1.1, 3.1

Suggestions: Have students read through the passage and determine how to set up and solve the equation. Then ask them for the answer and have them explain the steps they took to arrive at it.

Answers:

Cantidad mensual:
5 mm al año ÷ 12 meses = 0,42 mm al mes.
Cantidad del 12 de julio de 1997 (95 mm) ÷ cantidad mensual (0,42 mm) = 226 meses o casi 19 años.

Pre-AP® Integration

- **Learning Objective:** Presentational Writing
- **Activity:** Have students bring a picture to class (from a magazine, a personal photo) representing one of the outdoor locations presented in this chapter. Have them write a paragraph telling about five actual or fabricated activities/chores that they or others in the photo did. Encourage them to use the preterite tense and connector words.
- **Pre-AP® Resource Materials:** Comprehensive guide to Pre-AP® writing skill development

---

21

¿Cómo lo pasaron?

 ESCRIBIR, HABLAR EN PAREJA

1 Escribe cinco preguntas que puedes hacerle a otro(a) estudiante sobre cómo lo pasó en una fiesta. Usen los verbos del recuadro.

divertirse	servir	preferir	sugerir
sentirse	vestirse	estar	poder

Modelo
estar
¿Estuvo buena la fiesta de Ernesto?

2 Ahora, usando las preguntas que escribiste en el Paso 1, habla con otro(a) estudiante sobre cómo lo pasaron en la fiesta.

Videomodelo
A —*¿Estuvo buena la fiesta de Ernesto?*
B —*Sí, bailé toda la noche. Lo pasé muy bien. ¿Y tú?*

22

Una excursión al aire libre

 HABLAR EN PAREJA

1 Piensa en la última vez que hiciste una excursión y contesta las preguntas.

1. ¿Adónde fuiste?
2. ¿Quién te sugirió el lugar?
3. ¿Cómo te vestiste?
4. ¿Qué tuviste que traer?
5. ¿Qué hiciste?
6. ¿Te divertiste o no?

2 Ahora manda un texto a otro(a) estudiante con cuatro de las preguntas modelo y escribe dos nuevas preguntas. El otro estudiante te mandará sus respuestas.

3 Presenta las respuestas a la clase.

23

Lluvia en el desierto

 ESCRIBIR, HABLAR EN PAREJA ¿Sabías que a veces llueve en los desiertos? Lee la siguiente información sobre el desierto de Atacama y resuelve el problema con otro(a) estudiante.

Conexiones ‹ **Las matemáticas**

El desierto de Atacama, al norte de Chile, generalmente recibe sólo 5 mm de precipitación al año. Pero, el 12 de julio de 1997 cayeron 95 mm de agua en solo 15 horas.

Si en los próximos años recibe la precipitación habitual, ¿cuántos meses hay que esperar hasta llegar a la cantidad de precipitación del 12 de julio de 1997?

Desierto de Atacama, Chile

34 treinta y cuatro • Capítulo 1 • Días inolvidables

Differentiated Instruction

Heritage Speakers

Ask students who have lived in a heritage country to choose a place there in which it would be a good idea to have an ecocamp. Have them explain the attractions of the location. In what ways would that particular place benefit from having an ecocamp?

Students with Learning Difficulties

Help students deal with the numerical information in *Actividad* 23. Have them first establish how many numbers there are in the text. (*five*) Ask which numbers measure water. (*95 mm, 5 mm*) Remind them that they must use one more number, 12, the number of months in a year, to do the problem.

24

Una caminata por Torres del Paine

✎ **LEER, ESCRIBIR** Imagina que vas a ir a hacer una excursión como la que se describe en este anuncio turístico del Parque Nacional Torres del Paine. Escribe un correo electrónico a un(a) compañero(a) y pregúntale lo que necesitas hacer para participar en cada actividad. Él o ella te contestará con lo que necesitas o lo que tienes que hacer y por qué.

25

Los Ecocamps de Torres del Paine

✎ **LEER, ESCRIBIR** Lee el texto sobre el Parque Nacional Torres del Paine y los Ecocamps y contesta las siguientes preguntas.

El Parque Nacional Torres del Paine, situado en la zona patagónica de Chile, es uno de los lugares más hermosos de nuestro planeta. Los senderos del parque ofrecen vistas magníficas del paisaje patagónico: montañas, bosques, ríos, glaciares, lagos y abundante flora y fauna. Este parque, remoto y misterioso, atrae a miles de turistas y aventureros de todo el mundo que vienen cada año a hacer caminatas, montar a caballo o navegar. Y la gran demanda por visitar el parque ha generado problemas serios de impacto ecológico y en la calidad de los servicios turísticos en general.

Una solución a este problema ha sido cambiar los hoteles por "Ecocamps", tiendas de acampar modernas, cómodas y transportables. Los "Ecocamps" permiten a los visitantes estar más cerca de la naturaleza y producen menos basura que los hoteles.

1. ¿Qué tipos de paisajes ofrece el Parque Nacional Torres del Paine?

2. ¿Qué solución ofrecen los Ecocamps para mejorar los problemas de impacto ecológico?

3. ¿Qué crees que puedes hacer tú para ayudar a cuidar lugares como éste?

Viaje Parque Nacional

TORRES DEL PAINE

- Caminatas de entre 4 a 7 horas por día
- Navegar en el lago
- Escalar el Glaciar Grey
- Montar a caballo por el Valle del Ascencio
- Acampar en el exclusivo Ecocamp

PRECIO: USD $1,500 7 días, 6 noches

24

Standards: 1.2, 1.3

Suggestions: Have students tell about what they themselves did on the trip, what one other person did, and what the whole group did.

Answers will vary.

25

Standards: 1.1, 1.2, 3.1

Suggestions: Have students read the passage at least twice to comprehend the main idea and important details. Ask them to write their answers in one or more complete sentences.

Common Errors: Some students tend to answer every question that begins with *¿Qué crees...?* or *¿Crees que...?* with *Creo que....* Point out that, although grammatically correct, it is not necessary and can become monotonous.

Answers:

1. Ofrece montañas, bosques, ríos, glaciares y lagos.
2. Los Ecocamps producen menos basura que los hoteles.
3. Answers will vary.

Additional Resources

📶 **Technology: Online Resources**
- Instant Check
- Guided, Core, Reading, Writing
- *Para hispanohablantes*
Print
- Guided WB pp. 31–32
- Core WB p. 13

Assessment

Prueba 1-5 with Remediation (online only)
Prueba: El pretérito de verbos con los cambios e → i, o → u
- Prueba 1-5
Examen: Vocabulario y gramática 1
- Examen 1
- ExamView: Examen 1

Enrich Your Teaching

Culture Note

The Atacama desert extends from the Pacific Ocean to the Andes Mountains. It is 600 miles long and a little less than 100 miles wide in most places. It is the most arid place on Earth—so arid, in fact, that scientists believe it may have a lot in common with Mars. A robot that will be sent to Mars is being tested in the Atacama desert.

21st Century Skills

Critical Thinking and Problem Solving Encourage students to exercise sound reasoning and use their reading strategies when reading these short Spanish passages. Remind them to preview the comprehension questions first before reading *Los Ecocamps de Torres del Paine.*

Vocabulario en contexto 2

Standards: 1.2

Resources: Teacher's Resource Materials: Input Script, Clip Art, Audio Script, Technology: Audio Cap. 1

Suggestions: Have students read along as you play the audio to present the new vocabulary. Model the pronunciation of the new vocabulary words. Have students repeat in chorus. Make sure they read the information on the poster. Check for comprehension by asking questions. See the Input Scripts in the *Teacher's Resource Materials* for specific questions.

 Technology: Interactive Whiteboard

Vocabulary Activities 1-2 Use the whiteboard activities in your Teacher Resources as you progress through the vocabulary practice with your class.

Vocabulario en contexto 2

OBJECTIVES
Read, listen to, and understand information about
▶ Athletic events
▶ Other kinds of competitions
▶ Goals and prizes

🔊 **Cómo alcanzar tus metas**

El blog de María

MARIA

Mi vida cambió cuando **obtuve una medalla** después de terminar mi primera **carrera** de 5k. No quería **salir campeona**. Me conozco: nunca iba a recibir un **trofeo**. Siempre quería correr pero cada vez que **hice un esfuerzo**, terminé llorando. Fue **duro** y no pude. Así que hice un plan.

MI PLAN

1 **Inscribirme en una carrera de 5K**
Cuando completé la **inscripción** me sentí motivada para ponerme en forma. ¡Tenía una meta que **alcanzar**!

CARRERA FAMILIAR DE 5 KILÓMETROS
SÁBADO 10 DE AGOSTO

¡Todos los participantes reciben premios!

 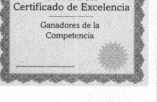 

la medalla   el certificado   el trofeo

Inscripciones: Carrera 5K.com

36 treinta y seis • Capítulo 1 • Días inolvidables

Differentiated Instruction

Culture Note

The *Desierto de los leones* was declared Mexico's first national park in 1917. Unlike its name, the park is located in the mountains outside of Mexico City and filled with pine and oak forests. It is a favorite of runners, hikers, and mountain bikers.

Challenge/Pre-AP®

Have students write an interview with María. Challenge them to use her blog as a basis for questions, such as *¿Por qué decidiste participar en una carrera de 5K? ¿Cómo te preparaste? ¿Cómo te sentiste después de la carrera?*

2 **Completar el entrenamiento** Estaba muy **animada, sin embargo** fue muy duro. **Al principio**, solo caminaba. Después empecé a correr 30 segundos y a caminar 2 o 3 minutos durante 20 minutos. Después de unas semanas, **me di cuenta** de que podía correr más y más tiempo. Corría cuatro o cinco veces por semana.

3 **Tener paciencia** Cuando no podía ni siquiera *caminar* los 5 kilómetros, me sentía muy **desanimada**. Pero sabía que con un poco de paciencia podía mejorar. La **carrera** de 5k **tuvo lugar** en agosto. Empecé a **entrenarme** en enero. Así que fueron 7 meses DUROS de levantarme temprano, comer bien y salir a correr en el frío, el calor o el mal tiempo.

4 **Aceptar las felicitaciones** No terminé en primer lugar. No me importa. **Me emocioné** mucho al final. Estoy muy **orgullosa** porque logré mi **meta**. Ahora estoy más feliz, más sana y ¡SOY CORREDORA!

26

¿Qué pasó?

 ESCRIBIR Completa cada oración con la palabra o frase correcta.

1. Su primera (carrera/medalla) era de 5k.
2. No recibió un(a) (trofeo/medalla).
3. Quería correr pero era (duro/fácil).
4. Quería alcanzar un(a) (meta/plan).
5. Su vida cambió cuando (salió campeona/obtuvo una medalla).

27

¿Cuál era el plan?

 ESCUCHAR Escribe en una hoja los números del 1 al 7. Escucha las frases. Escribe *C* (cierto) o *F* (falso) para cada frase.

Capítulo 1 • treinta y siete **37**

26

Standards: 1.2

Suggestions: Explain to students that the activity focuses on María's blog on pages 36 and 37. Remind them to read the flyer as well, which also contains important information.

Answers:
1. carrera
2. trofeo
3. duro
4. meta
5. obtuvo una medalla

27

Standards: 1.2

Teacher's Resource Materials: Audio Script, Technology: Audio Cap. 1

Suggestions: Before using the audio or the script for this activity, allow students a few minutes to reread pp. 36–37.

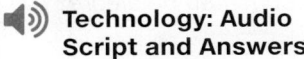 **Technology: Audio Script and Answers**

1. Gané mi primera carrera de 5 kilómetros. Soy campeona. *(F)*
2. Estuve 7 meses entrenándome. *(C)*
3. Estaba triste al final porque no terminé en primer lugar. *(F)*
4. Al principio del entrenamiento, corría mucho. *(F)*
5. Mi meta era correr 5 kilómetros. *(C)*
6. Hice un esfuerzo muy grande para alcanzar mi meta. *(C)*
7. La carrera tuvo lugar en el Club de Atletismo. *(F)*

Extension: Read the script or play the audio again. Ask students to correct the false statements.

Project-Based Learning

Students can perform Step 3 at this point. (For more information, see p. 16-b.)

Vocabulario en contexto 2

Standards: 1.2

Teacher's Resource Materials: Input Script, Clip Art, Audio Script, Technology: Audio Cap. 1

Suggestions:

Pre-reading: Have students use the titles and pictures to predict what each story is about.
Reading: Play the audio or read aloud from the script. Have students read along as they listen. Allow them to listen more than once.
Post-reading: Check comprehension by asking questions.

28

Standards: 1.3

Suggestions: Have students give the answers orally before writing them. If they have difficulty, rephrase the question, embedding the answer. For item 1, for example, ask: *¿Qué concurso no ganaron los estudiantes: el concurso de ajedrez o el partido de fútbol?*

Answers:

1. Los estudiantes de la escuela no ganaron el concurso de ajedrez.
2. Los jóvenes poetas estaban muy contentos al final de la ceremonia.
3. El año pasado el equipo de fútbol de la escuela quedó eliminado del campeonato.
4. Las chicas del equipo del Liceo San Martín perdieron el partido de fútbol.
5. Answers will vary.

Pre-AP® Integration

- **Learning Objective:** Interpretive: Print and Audio
- **Activity:** This activity helps students practice key print and audio interpretative skills. Have students follow along as you read the selection aloud or play the audio. Have students create multiple choice questions to check their comprehension. Then, have them confirm their answers by reading the text.
- **Pre-AP® Resource Materials:** Comprehensive guide to Pre-AP® vocabulary skill development

---

 **LA VOZ** del ESTUDIANTE

Santiago, 23 de septiembre

Nuestros jóvenes maestros

Diez estudiantes de nuestra escuela participaron en el concurso de ajedrez. **Desafortunadamente**, nuestra escuela no ganó el primer premio, pero **estamos orgullosos de** nuestros **representantes**.

POESÍA	DEPORTES

CERTIFICADO DE EXCELENCIA

GANADORES DE LA COMPETENCIA ESTATAL DE POESÍA

Profesora Loida Grossman

El poder de las palabras

¡Felicitaciones a nuestros poetas estudiantiles! **La ceremonia** de **entrega de premios** tuvo lugar la semana pasada en el teatro de la escuela. Al final de la ceremonia los ganadores estaban muy contentos.

¡Campeonas de fútbol!

¿Recuerdan cuando el año pasado **eliminaron** a nuestro equipo del campeonato de fútbol? Pues este año, con mucho **entrenamiento** y esfuerzo, las chicas del equipo de nuestra escuela jugaron **contra** el equipo rival del Liceo San Martín y **vencieron** 3 a 1. ¡FELICITACIONES, CAMPEONAS!

28

¿Comprendiste?

 ESCRIBIR

1. ¿Qué concurso no ganaron los estudiantes de la escuela?
2. ¿Cómo se sintieron los jóvenes poetas al final de la ceremonia?
3. ¿Qué le pasó el año pasado al equipo de fútbol de la escuela?
4. ¿Quién perdió el partido de fútbol este año?
5. ¿Por qué crees que los estudiantes están orgullosos de sus jugadores de ajedrez?

38 treinta y ocho • Capítulo 1 • Días inolvidables

Differentiated Instruction

Heritage Speakers

Ask students to think of other information that could be included in one of the articles from *La voz del estudiante.* Encourage them to invent names for teams and individual players, and include details about highlights during an event. Have them rewrite the article incorporating their new information.

Advanced Learners

Invite students to write their own brief articles for a school newspaper. They should report on an actual recent competitive event or awards ceremony at your school. Collaborative efforts can be combined into a Spanish-language school newspaper. Have students place sketches where photos would go.

29

¡Salimos campeonas!

 ESCUCHAR Escucha las siguientes frases e indica a qué dibujo se refiere cada una. Cada dibujo puede referirse a más de una frase.

Estrategia

Order of events Determining the order of events in a story will help you understand it better. When you listen to a story in Spanish, pay attention to words such as *antes, al principio, durante, después, más tarde,* and *finalmente* to determine the sequence.

Go **Online** to practice
PearsonSchool.com/Autentico
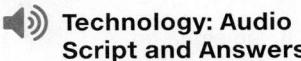
AUDIO WRITING SPEAK/RECORD

30

Ordena tus notas

 LEER, ESCRIBIR Imagina que eres reportero(a) de *La Voz del Estudiante*. Acabas de tomar unas notas sobre el partido de básquetbol, pero tus notas no están en orden. Escribe las frases en orden.

- Durante el partido tuvimos que hacer un gran esfuerzo porque el otro equipo era muy bueno.
- Más tarde, tuvimos un empate de 42 a 42.
- Cuando nos dieron el trofeo, todas nos emocionamos mucho.
- Antes del partido, nuestra entrenadora nos hizo practicar con la pelota.
- Finalmente, pudimos vencer a nuestras rivales 68 a 62.

31

Evalúa las actividades

 HABLAR EN PAREJA En el periódico se habla de tres actividades en las que participan los estudiantes. Con un(a) compañero(a), expresen sus preferencias personales sobre las actividades. Expliquen por qué piensan así. Usen:

Prefiero . . .

No disfruto mucho . . . porque. . .

No me gusta . . .

Enrich Your Teaching

Teacher-to-Teacher

After students complete and check *Actividad* 29, ask them to say which elements in each picture helped them decide on the answer.

21st Century Skills

Social and Cross-Cultural Skills Have students discuss how media messages are conveyed in a student newspaper like *La voz del estudiante* on page 38. Who is the intended audience? What is the purpose of each article? How is this newspaper similar to or different from their school newspaper?

29

Standards: 1.2, 3.1

Teacher's Resource Materials: Audio Script, Technology: Audio Cap. 1

Suggestions: Review the *Estrategia* with students.

Technology: Audio Script and Answers

1. Al principio, nos entrenábamos todos los días. Queríamos salir campeonas. *(1)* **2.** Finalmente, pudimos vencer a nuestras rivales. Recibimos un trofeo por nuestros esfuerzos. *(3)* **3.** Durante el partido, tuvimos que hacer un gran esfuerzo para vencer al otro equipo. *(2)* **4.** Más tarde, cuando nos entregaron los premios, todas nos sentimos muy emocionadas. *(3)* **5.** Antes del partido, nuestra entrenadora nos hizo practicar con la pelota. *(1)* **6.** El otro equipo jugaba muy bien. Sin embargo, nosotras no estábamos desanimadas. *(2)*

30

Standards: 1.2

Suggestions: Have students use the transitions in the *Estrategia* to sequence the events.

Answers:

Antes del partido, nuestra entrenadora nos hizo practicar con la pelota. Durante el partido tuvimos que hacer un gran esfuezo porque el otro equipo era muy bueno. Más tarde, tuvimos un empate de 42 a 42. Finalmente, pudimos vencer a nuestras rivales 68 a 62. Cuando nos dieron el trofeo, todas nos emocionamos mucho.

31

Standards: 1.1

Suggestions: Remind students that the expressions they are using to begin their sentences introduce statements of opinion.

Answers will vary.

Additional Resources

Technology: Online Resources
- Instant Check
- Guided, Core, Audio, Reading, Writing
- *Para hispanohablantes*

Print
- Guided WB pp. 33–40
- Core WB pp. 14–15

Assessment

Prueba: Aplicación del vocabulario 2
- Prueba 1-6

Vocabulario en uso 2

OBJECTIVES
▶ Talk and write about sports competitions and prizes
▶ Listen to a report about a tennis competition
▶ Write about and discuss a sports event

32

Standards: 1.2

Suggestions: Encourage students to quickly read over the entire passage first in order to have an idea of what it is about.

Answers:

1. representantes
2. meta
3. Desafortunadamente
4. eliminaron
5. desanimados
6. Sin embargo
7. se dio cuenta
8. alcanzar
9. orgulloso
10. animados

Starter Activity

Unscramble the following words for prizes:

fotroe   icerfcatido   demalal   olrfes

(Answers: *trofeo/certificado/medalla/flores*)

CULTURA

Standards: 1.2, 3.1, 4.2

Suggestions: Many high-level competitions use the word "Olympic" in their title. Ask students why they think this is so. They might say it's because the Olympic Games are the height of sports competition, because there are participants from many different places, and so on.

Answers will vary.

Note Both *Matemática* and *Matemáticas* are correct uses of this noun.

Active Classroom

Inside-Outside Circles. Have each student write two questions to ask a partner on a sheet of paper or index card that relate to an event or competition. Have students count off by twos. One partner goes to the "inside circle" and faces out. The second partner goes to the "outside circle" and faces in. The partners ask their questions and after about one minute, you call time and everyone moves two spaces. Repeat.

32

El concurso

 LEER, ESCRIBIR Completa los párrafos con las palabras de los recuadros.

desafortunadamente eliminaron desanimados meta representantes

Los __1.__ de mi escuela organizaron un concurso de música. Su __2.__ era obtener suficiente dinero para construir un nuevo teatro. Todos los padres de la escuela participaron. Vendieron refrescos y galletas. __3.__ nuestra banda no llegó a los finales y nos __4.__ de la competencia. Todos nos sentimos muy __5.__ .

animados orgulloso sin embargo se dio cuenta alcanzar

__6.__ , al día siguiente, tuvimos una gran sorpresa. El director de la escuela __7.__ de que con la venta de galletas pudimos __8.__ nuestra meta. Después, dijo que estaba muy __9.__ de los esfuerzos de nuestro equipo. Esta vez, todos nos sentimos muy __10.__ .

CULTURA El mundo hispano

La Olimpíada Iberoamericana de Matemática Cada año, chicos y chicas de América Latina y España participan en la Olimpíada Iberoamericana de Matemática. Es una competencia para jóvenes de escuela secundaria. Las olimpíadas tienen como meta estimular el estudio de las matemáticas y el desarrollo[1] de jóvenes con talento para esta ciencia, a través de[2] la resolución ingeniosa de problemas matemáticos en un tiempo limitado.

¿Dónde y cuándo? La Olimpíada Iberoamericana de Matemática tiene lugar cada año en un país diferente de América Latina o en España. Otros países del mundo también tienen olimpíadas de matemáticas.

Pre-AP Integration: La ciencia y la tecnología ¿Crees que esta competencia ha impulsado el desarrollo o la innovación en las matemáticas? ¿Cómo?

[1]development [2]through

Differentiated Instruction

Heritage Speakers

Ask students to research the ***Olimpíada Iberoamericana de Matemática*** on the Internet. Have them prepare brief reports in which they share the information they find, such as where the next event will be held and what kinds of events it will involve.

Advanced Learners

Invite students to browse through sports magazines or sports-related websites and describe situations and events they see in pictures about competitive events. Encourage them to talk about the events in the past tense.

33

La entrega de premios

🎤 **HABLAR** Di qué premios obtuvieron los atletas en la ceremonia de entrega de premios.

Modelo
el atleta que salió en tercer lugar
El atleta que salió en tercer lugar obtuvo una camiseta.

¿Recuerdas?
El verbo *obtener* tiene las mismas terminaciones en el pretérito que *tener*.

1. el equipo campeón

2. el atleta que ganó la carrera

3. el atleta que salió en segundo lugar

4. todos los participantes

5. los entrenadores

34

El campeonato de tenis

🔊 **ESCUCHAR, ESCRIBIR** Escucha el reportaje sobre el campeonato de tenis. Luego contesta las preguntas.

1. ¿Qué significa la expresión "tuvo lugar"? ¿Qué otras palabras te ayudaron con el significado?
2. ¿Cómo fue el partido?
3. ¿Cuándo hizo un gran esfuerzo María?
4. ¿Quién ganó?
5. ¿Qué recibió como premio la campeona?
6. ¿Cómo se sintieron las dos tenistas al final?

35

El festival deportivo

🎤 **ESCRIBIR, HABLAR EN PAREJA**

❶ Imagina que fuiste a un festival deportivo en el que había partidos de diferentes deportes, comida y premios. Un(a) estudiante te entrevista para aprender un poco más del festival. Contesta sus preguntas.

1. ¿Cuándo y dónde tuvo lugar el festival?
2. ¿Cuánto costó la inscripción?
3. ¿Qué eventos deportivos había?
4. ¿En cuáles participaste tú?
5. ¿Jugaste con un equipo? ¿Contra quién jugaste?
6. ¿Participaste en alguna carrera?

7. ¿Ganaste algún premio? Si es así, ¿qué ganaste?
8. ¿Cómo se sintieron los participantes después de la ceremonia de entrega de premios?
9. ¿Cómo lo pasaste?

❷ Trabaja con otro(a) estudiante para hacer y contestar preguntas sobre el festival.

Un partido de béisbol en Cuba

Capítulo 1 • cuarenta y uno **41**

Enrich Your Teaching

Culture Note
Point out that the suffix ***ibero-*** is often used in words having to do with Spain and the Spanish-speaking world. ***América Latina*** is often called ***Iberoamérica,*** and Spain itself is sometimes still referred to as ***Iberia.*** These appellations tend to be used by Spaniards rather than Latin Americans. ***Iberia*** and its variations come from the name the ancient Greeks gave to the peninsula comprising what are now Spain and Portugal ***(la Península Ibérica).*** The Greeks got the name ***Iberia*** from a river on the peninsula that they called the Iber River, which many believe to be the Ebro, one of Spain's major rivers.

33

Standards: 1.1

Recycle: irregular preterite stems, sports
Suggestions: First refer students to the *¿Recuerdas?* before doing the exercise.

Answers:

1. obtuvo un trofeo
2. obtuvo una medalla
3. obtuvo una medalla
4. obtuvieron un certificado
5. obtuvieron flores

34

Standards: 1.2, 1.3

Resources: Teacher's Resource Materials: Audio Script, Technology: Audio Cap. 1

🔊 **Technology: Audio**

Script: El campeonato de tenis tuvo lugar el 25 de agosto, en Madrid. Sandra Vásquez jugó contra María Reyes. Las dos tenistas se entrenaron por meses para participar en el campeonato. El partido fue muy largo y duro. Al principio, parecía que Sandra iba a ganar. Iba 5 a 2 en el primer set. Sin embargo, en el último set, María hizo un gran esfuerzo y logró vencer a su oponente 6 a 4. La campeona obtuvo como premio un trofeo de plata. Al final del partido, las dos tenistas se sintieron muy orgullosas de sus esfuerzos.

Answers:

1. Tuvo lugar es "ocurrió". El 25 de agosto en Madrid.
2. El partido fue muy largo y duro.
3. Hizo un gran esfuerzo en el último set.
4. María ganó el partido.
5. Recibió un trofeo de plata.
6. Se sintieron muy orgullosas.

35

Standards: 1.1, 1.2, 1.3

Suggestions: Encourage students to write their answers based on real events.

Answers will vary.

Additional Resources

📶 **Technology: Online Resources**
- Communication Activities
- Teacher's Resource Materials: Audio Script, Communicative Pair Activity, Technology: Audio Cap 1

Assessment

Prueba 1-7 with Remediation (online only)
Prueba: Aplicación del vocabulario 2
- Prueba 1-7

Gramática: Repaso

Un poco más de repaso

Suggestions: Refer students to the *¿Recuerdas?* Challenge them to create sentences in the imperfect that use the expressions listed there.

Starter Activity

Have students write the infinitive form of four verbs in Spanish to represent what they used to do in elementary school.

 Technology: Interactive Whiteboard

> **Grammar Activities 1-2** Use the whiteboard activities in your Teacher Resources as you progress through the grammar practice with your class.

36

Recycle: regular and irregular verbs, imperfect tense

Suggestions: Before students write their answers, ask them to point out expressions in the exercise that are similar to those in the *¿Recuerdas?* above.

Answers:

1.	era	**6.**	pedían
2.	tenía	**7.**	molestaba
3.	íbamos	**8.**	devolvían
4.	leía/sacaba	**9.**	enojaba
5.	leía/sacaba	**10.**	eran

Gramática Repaso

El imperfecto

Use the imperfect tense to talk about actions that happened regularly. In English you often say "used to" or "would" to express this idea.

> Todos los meses, mi escuela **organizaba** una carrera.
> Nuestro equipo nunca **perdía**.

¿Recuerdas?
Expresiones como *generalmente, a menudo, muchas veces, todos los días, siempre* y *nunca* indican el uso del imperfecto.

estar

estaba	estábamos
estabas	estabais
estaba	estaban

tener

tenía	teníamos
tenías	teníais
tenía	tenían

vivir

vivía	vivíamos
vivías	vivíais
vivía	vivían

• Stem-changing verbs do not have a stem change in the imperfect.
Quería participar en el campeonato pero no **me sentía** bien.

The verbs *ir, ser,* and *ver* are the only irregular verbs in the imperfect. Here are their forms:

ir

iba	íbamos
ibas	ibais
iba	iban

ser

era	éramos
eras	erais
era	eran

ver

veía	veíamos
veías	veíais
veía	veían

Más recursos ONLINE
▶ **Tutorial:** Uses of the Imperfec
🔊 **Canción de hip hop:** *Cuando era niño*

• The imperfect form of *hay* is *había* ("there was / were, there used to be").
Generalmente, no **había** muchos participantes en el campeonato.

36

 Recuerdos de mi niñez

✏️ **LEER, ESCRIBIR** Completa con la forma del imperfecto del verbo.

ir	tener	ser	leer	sacar

Cuando yo __1.__ niño, me gustaba mucho leer. Yo __2.__ más de cien libros. Todos los sábados, mi hermana y yo __3.__ a la biblioteca. Mi hermana __4.__ libros de historia. Yo, en cambio, __5.__ los libros de aventura.

molestar	devolver	pedir	enojar	ser

A veces, mis amigos me __6.__ prestado un libro. A mí no me __7.__ compartir los libros, pero cuando ellos no los __8.__, entonces yo me __9.__ mucho. Los libros __10.__ mis mejores amigos.

Differentiated Instruction

Students with Learning Difficulties

Some students may need extra help in order to understand verb form paradigms like those in the *Gramática* on this page. Copy some of the paradigms on the board, including the subject pronouns, so students can associate subjects with verb forms.

Challenge/Pre-AP®

Invite students to prepare and deliver a short presentation in which they practice using the imperfect. They can tell about a situation that occurred regularly in the past, such as a summer camp they attended, a vacation spot their family repeatedly visited, a pastime they engaged in, or a class they attended in grade school.

37 Campeonatos escolares

 LEER, HABLAR EN PAREJA Marilú recuerda los deportes y las actividades que hacía de niña en la escuela primaria. Depués de leer su descripción, trabaja con otro(a) estudiante para hacer y contestar preguntas sobre los recuerdos de Marilú.

"Cuando yo asistía a la escuela primaria, jugaba en un equipo de fútbol que siempre vencía a los demás. Mis compañeras y yo nos entrenábamos todos los días y nuestros entrenadores nos ayudaban mucho. Nuestros padres siempre nos animaban para alcanzar nuestra meta, que era hacer el mejor esfuerzo posible para ganar.

Un año, salimos campeonas del estado y nos dieron un trofeo.

—¡Felicitaciones campeonas! —nos decían todos durante la entrega de premios. Nos emocionamos mucho".

▶ **Videomodelo**
A —¿A qué deporte jugaba Marilú de niña?
B —Marilú jugaba al fútbol.

38 ¿Qué hacías de niño(a)?

 ESCRIBIR, HABLAR EN PAREJA

1 Escribe una descripción de tu vida cuando eras niño(a). Incluye:
- los juegos
- los deportes
- la familia
- los programas de televisión
- la comida
- los(as) amigos(as)

2 Ahora, pregúntale a otro(a) estudiante si hacía las mismas cosas que tú. Toma notas de sus respuestas.

▶ **Videomodelo**
A —*De niño(a) yo leía libros de cuentos.* ¿Tú también leías libros de cuentos?
B —Sí, a mí me gustaba leer libros de cuentos.

3 Preséntale a la clase una comparación entre tu vida de niño(a) y la de tu compañero(a).

Modelo
Los dos comíamos cosas dulces. Yo prefería chocolate y él prefería helado.

Capítulo 1 • cuarenta y tres **43**

Enrich Your Teaching

Teacher-to-Teacher
Students enjoy talking about movie or TV characters. Have them choose one such character and prepare a brief description, telling about where the character lived, what he or she was like, what activities he or she did, and what makes this character stand out.

21st Century Skills
Media Literacy Remind students of the various digital tools available in **Realize** to help them monitor their own understanding and learning needs, such as the eText with embedded audio files, audio activities, and online tutorials.

37
Standards: 1.1, 1.2

Suggestions: Before students work in pairs, ask them to look through Marilú's description for verbs that are in the preterite rather than the imperfect. Discuss the difference between actions that happened at one specific time in the past and those that happened regularly.
Answers will vary.
Extension: Ask students to write their questions about Marilú's description on slips of paper. Place the slips in a hat or other container. Have students take turns drawing one question at a time, reading it aloud, and answering it orally.

38
Standards: 1.1, 1.3

Recycle: games and pastimes, food, family members
Suggestions: In Step 1, tell students they should write at least one sentence about each of the items. Point out that, as students are interviewing each other in Step 2, they should offer suggestions to help keep the conversation flowing and take notes they can use in Step 3.
Answers will vary.

Project-Based Learning
Students can perform Step 4 at this point. Be sure they understand your corrections and suggestions. (For more information, see p. 16-b.)

Additional Resources
Technology: Online Resources
- Instant Check
- Guided, Core, Reading, Writing
- *Para hispanohablantes*
Print
- Guided WB pp. 41–42
- Core WB p. 16

Assessment
Prueba 1-8 with Remediation (online only)
Prueba: El imperfecto
- Prueba 1-8

43

Gramática: Repaso

Un poco más de repaso

Suggestions: Ask for additional examples of each use of the imperfect.

 Technology: Interactive Whiteboard

Grammar Activities 1-2 Use the whiteboard activities in your Teacher Resources as you progress through the grammar practice with your class.

39

Standards: 1.1, 1.2

Recycle: household chores, leisure activities
Suggestions: After students write their sentences, have them share their recollections with the class.
Answers will vary.

40

Standards: 1.1, 1.2, 1.3

Suggestions: Tell students that the event they choose to talk about with their partners can be real or imaginary. In Step 2, encourage students to write in complete sentences in paragraph form.
Answers: will vary.

Alternative Assessment: Use the written report from Step 2 of *Actividad* 40 to assess students' writing skills. Students' oral presentations of their reports can likewise be used to assess speaking skills.

Pre-AP® Integration

- **Learning Objective:** Interpersonal Speaking
- **Activity:** This *Entrevista* activity helps students practice key interpersonal skills. Remind students to practice strategies for effectively sustaining conversations.
- **Pre-AP® Resource Materials:** Comprehensive guide to Pre-AP® speaking skill development

---

Gramática Repaso

OBJECTIVES
▸ Write about regular past actions
▸ Talk and write about athletes and competitions

Usos del imperfecto

You have learned to use the imperfect to describe something that used to take place regularly. You also use the imperfect

Más recursos ONLINE
▶ **Tutorial:** Uses of the Imperfect

- to describe people, places, and situations in the past.

  Hacía mucho calor. El estadio **estaba** lleno. Los espectadores **gritaban.**

- to talk about a past action that was continuous or that kept happening.

  Los atletas se **entrenaban** en el gimnasio.

- to describe the date, time, age, and weather in the past.

  Era el 5 de noviembre. **Eran** las seis de la mañana pero ya **hacía** calor.

39

Los sábados del pasado

 ESCRIBIR   Hazle preguntas sobre su vida diaria a un(a) compañero(a) por correo eléctronico. Pregúntale qué hacía los sábados cuando era pequeño. Él o ella te responde con los verbos *ir, ver* o *ser*.

1. Por las mañanas, mis hermanos y yo . . .
2. Por las tardes, yo . . .
3. Muchas veces, yo . . .
4. Mis padres . . .
5. Los quehaceres . . .
6. Por la tarde, mis amigos . . .

40

Entrevista

 HABLAR EN PAREJA, ESCRIBIR

❶ Entrevista a un(a) compañero(a). Hazle preguntas sobre alguna competencia a la que asistió o en la que participó. Toma notas de sus respuestas.

1. ¿Dónde tuvo lugar la competencia de . . . ?
2. ¿A qué hora era?
3. ¿Cómo era el auditorio / estadio / salón / gimnasio?
4. ¿Quiénes eran los participantes?
5. ¿Quiénes asistieron al evento?
6. ¿Cómo se sintió el público?
7. ¿Qué premios entregaron a los ganadores?
8. ¿Cómo se sentían los ganadores después de recibir sus premios?

❷ Escribe un reportaje basado en las notas de la entrevista que hiciste. Usa oraciones conectadas con detalles y elaboración. Luego, lee tu reportaje a la clase.

44 cuarenta y cuatro • Capítulo 1 • **Días inolvidables**

Differentiated Instruction

Students with Learning Difficulties

Help students better understand the concept of completed actions vs. continuous actions in the past. Have them first focus on a completed action they did earlier in the day: "I ate breakfast." Then ask them to think of something that was happening while they performed that action: "It was raining." Translate their sentences to Spanish.

Advanced Learners

Have students prepare and present brief oral presentations about an important event they experienced in the past. Their presentations should include the imperfect and preterite tenses. They should use the imperfect to "set the scene" of the event and to describe people, places, or things, and the preterite to tell about the event itself.

Interpersonal   1

Un atleta olímpico

✎ **LEER, ESCRIBIR**

1 Completa la biografía del atleta olímpico Leonel Manzano con el pretérito o el imperfecto del verbo en paréntesis.

Leonel __1.__ (nacer) en México y __2.__ (mudarse) a Texas con su familia cuando __3.__ (tener) cuatro años. __4.__ (Comenzar) a correr a una edad temprana. __5.__ (Ganar) nueve campeonatos del estado de Texas para Marble Falls High School. Luego, __6.__ (competir) para la Universidad de Texas y __7.__ (ser) el primer estudiante en la historia de la escuela de conseguir una posición en el equipo olímpico de los Estados Unidos para la carrera de 1,500m. En 2012, __8.__ (lograr) su sueño y __9.__ (conseguir) una medalla de plata en los Juegos Olímpicos. Después, Leonel __10.__ (enviar) un tweet "¡La medalla de plata! Siento como gané representando dos países, Estados Unidos y México". En 2014, __11.__ (ser) campeón de la carrera USTAF al aire libre de 1,500m en un tiempo de 3:38.63.

2 Contesta las preguntas sobre Leonel Manzano.

1. ¿Qué características personales crees que ayudaron a Leonel a triunfar?

2. ¿Por qué crees que dijo que se sentía ganador cuando quedó en segundo lugar?

3. ¿Qué importancia tiene la medalla olímpica de Leonel para otros jóvenes hispanohablantes de los Estados Unidos?

4. ¿Conoces a otros(as) campeones(as) olímpicos(as) de habla hispana? ¿Qué hacen?

¿Recuerdas?
Los verbos *competir* y *conseguir* tienen el cambio e → i en el pretérito.

▲ Leonel Manzano

El español en el mundo del trabajo

El español y el fútbol americano

"Hoy en día, muchos latinoamericanos que viven en los Estados Unidos disfrutan del fútbol americano. Algunas cadenas[1] de televisión transmiten sus programas sobre fútbol americano también en español. Mi labor es traducir[2] lo que dicen los jugadores y locutores. Pero ese deporte no se practica mucho en América Latina ni en España, por eso a veces es difícil buscar la palabra que exprese en español la jugada, el error o la regla que no existe en nuestro idioma. Muchas veces hay que inventar la palabra o expresión que necesitamos. Traducir es hacer que dos culturas distintas puedan conversar . . . hasta de deportes".

[1]networks [2]translate

Standards: 1.2, 1.3

Focus: Practicing the preterite and imperfect tenses in a cloze exercise; writing to demonstrate comprehension of a reading passage

Recycle: sports, personality traits

Suggestions: After students complete the activity on their own, have them take turns reading through it aloud together. Have them give their reasons for choosing the preterite or imperfect. In Step 2, point out to students that not all the questions have explicit answers. They must use their critical thinking skills and background knowledge to answer the questions.

Answers:
Step 1
1. nació
2. se mudó
3. tenía
4. Comenzó
5. Ganó
6. competió
7. Fue
8. logró
9. Consiguió
10. envió
11. fue
Step 2
Answers will vary.

Starter Activity
Have students write two sentences telling what was going on in the classroom when they entered today.

El español en el mundo del trabajo

Standards: 1.2, 5.2

Suggestions: Explain that translation *(la traducción)* rests in the domains of reading and writing. Most translators *(los traductores)* read in the foreign language and write the translation in their own language. Interpretation *(la interpretación)* is a more immediate oral activity. Interpreters *(los intérpretes)* listen to the foreign language and speak the interpretation in their own language.

Enrich Your Teaching

Culture Note
Rio de Janeiro is the first South American city to host the Summer Olympics. Hosting an Olympic event is an enormous expense (an estimated $12 billion in 2016). However, these expenses include a large-scale revitalization project of the city's waterfront, a new tram from the airport and other public works renovations upgrading the water supply, sanitation, electricity, and so on.

21st Century Skills
Thinking and Problem Solving
Encourage students to watch and/or listen online to a soccer game in Spanish and try to determine the Spanish expressions used for certain sports terms, such as *goal, penalty kick, score a point,* or *goalie.* What similarities can they find between these English and Spanish terms?

42

Standards: 1.2, 1.3

Suggestions: Point out that the information in *En voz alta* continues the story of the same soccer match.

Answers:

Step 1

1. Era	**6.** eran	**11.** paró
2. Llovía	**7.** eran	**12.** dio
3. hacía	**8.** comenzó	**13.** tuvo
4. Era	**9.** iba	**14.** llegó
5. Jugaban	**10.** parecía	**15.** estaban

Step 2

Answers will vary.

En voz alta

Standards: 1.2, 3.1, 3.2, 5.2

Teacher's Resource Materials: Audio Script, Technology: Audio Cap. 1

Suggestions: Have students silently read the information. Ask comprehension questions: *¿Cuántos años tiene el equipo de Barcelona? ¿Qué dice el primer cántico acerca de la relación entre el equipo y los aficionados?*
Direct student's attention to the information in the *¿Recuerdas?* Allow them a few minutes to practice with a partner. Explain that Catalan uses the *s* sound for the letter *c* before *e* and *i*. In Catalan, the *cedilla*, *ç* is also pronounced like the *s* in English. You may want to share with the class the second cheer in Catalan and discuss the similarities between the two versions: *O le le , o la la, ser de Barça es, el millor que hi ha.*
Discuss with the class the second comprehension question. Brainstorm possible meanings for the Catalan phrase *Força Barça*, then explain that it means "force" or "strength to Barça." In English, a similar cheer would be "Go Barça!"

Project-Based Learning

Students can perform Step 5 at this point. Record their presentations for inclusion in their portfolio. (For more information, see p. 16-b.)

42

Un partido inolvidable

🖉 LEER, ESCRIBIR

1 Completa esta descripción de un famoso partido de fútbol que tuvo lugar en 1928 en España, con el pretérito o el imperfecto del verbo entre paréntesis.

____1.____ *(ser)* el 28 de mayo de 1928. __2.__ *(llover)* y __3.__ *(hacer)* viento. __4.__ *(ser)* un día muy especial para Santander. __5.__ *(jugar)* el Barcelona y La Real Sociedad. Platko y Samitier __6.__ *(ser)* las grandes estrellas del Barcelona. Las estrellas de la Real __7.__ *(ser)* Zaldúa y Cholín. Por fin __8.__ *(comenzar)* el partido. En un momento en que la Real __9.__ *(ir)* hacia el área del Barcelona,

Cholín avanzó[1] hasta el arco[2]. Cuando el gol __10.__ *(parecer)* inevitable, el guardameta[3] Platko se arrojó[4] sobre el pie de Cholín y __11.__ *(parar)* la pelota. Sin embargo, el pie de Cholín __12.__ *(dar)* contra la cabeza de Platko, quien __13.__ *(tener)* que salir del campo, con la frente[5] llena de sangre. A los pocos minutos se __14.__ *(llegar)* al descanso, con un empate de cero a cero. Los aficionados del Barcelona __15.__ *(estar)* desanimados. ¿Cómo podían ganar el campeonato sin Platko, su gran guardameta?

---
[1]moved forward [2]goal [3]goalkeeper [4]leaped [5]forehead

2 Ahora, contesta las preguntas.

1. ¿Crees que Platko era valiente? ¿Por qué?

2. ¿Qué pensaban los aficionados del Barcelona sobre Platko? ¿Cómo lo sabes?

3. ¿Alguna vez te sentiste como los aficionados del Barcelona? ¿Por qué?

En voz alta

🔊 ¿Sabes cómo terminó el partido? Platko volvió al juego. Su equipo ganó uno de los encuentros más emocionantes de la historia del fútbol.

El equipo de Barcelona tiene unos cánticos[1] que son conocidos en todo el mundo. Se cantan en catalán, el idioma de la región de Cataluña. La mayoría de los cánticos utilizan melodías de música conocidas. Uno se puede imaginar que los aficionados de Barcelona cantaron estos cánticos muchas veces durante este partido inolvidable.

Escucha los cánticos, unos traducidos al español, y trata de repetirlos. Luego, contesta las preguntas.

• ¿Qué palabras o frases se repiten? ¿Cuál es el efecto de esta repetición?

• ¿Cuál de los tres cánticos está en catalán? En tu opinión, ¿qué significa?

¿Recuerdas?

En América Latina y en partes de España, la c antes de las vocales e e i, y la z antes de una vocal se pronuncian como la s en inglés de la palabra *sink*. En otras regiones de España esas letras se parecen al sonido de th en la palabra *think*.
Pronuncia estas palabras usando los dos sonidos de la letra c y escucha la diferencia: *nació, Barcelona*.

Cánticos del Fútbol Club Barcelona

Cántico 1
1899, nació el club que llevo en el corazón,
azulgrana[2] son los colores,
¡Fútbol Cluuub Barceloona!
Le le le le le leeee,
le le le le le leeeee,
¡Fútbol Cluuub Barcelooona!

Cántico 2
O le le le, o la la la
Ser del Barça es, el mejor que hay.

Cántico 3
Força Barça!

---
[1]cheers [2]blue and scarlet

Differentiated Instruction

Heritage Speakers

Have students pick a sport and recall the most thrilling game they ever saw, either live or on TV. Ask them to write about the game's most exciting moment or moments and to describe in detail one or two events that made the game so thrilling.

Students with Learning Difficulties

On the board, create a T-chart. Label the left side **pretérito** and the right side **imperfecto.** Write a few examples of one-time, completed actions on the left and longer, "background" actions on the right. Allow students to use the chart as a reference as they complete *Actividad* 42.

43

Una competencia artística

ESCRIBIR Fuiste a una competencia artística y tuviste que escribir un informe para presentar en tu clase. Usa los dibujos para escribir lo que sucedió. Usa las formas correctas del pretérito y del imperfecto.

Estrategia

Describing events When you describe a sequence of events, it is useful to write words such as *primero* (first), *luego* (next), *después* (then), *al final* (finally) to describe the order in which these events have occurred.

El Palacio de las Artes

44

Un cuento en grupo

ESCRIBIR, HABLAR EN GRUPO

1 Usa tu imaginación para completar este cuento con cuatro de tus compañeros(as). Traten de incorporar en su cuento el vocabulario y la gramática que aprendieron en este capítulo.

1. Había una vez un(a) . . .
2. Era una persona muy . . . y . . .
3. Vivía en . . . con su(s) . . . y su(s) . . .
4. Siempre le gustaba . . . y . . .
5. Un día, al amanecer, (nombre) fue . . .
6. Era un lugar . . . y . . .
7. De repente, oyó / vio . . .
8. ¡Era un(a) . . . !
9. Cuando el / la . . . se acercó, (nombre) empezó a . . .
10. Pero entonces, se dio cuenta de . . . y . . . a pasear por . . .
11. Al final, (nombre) . . .
12. Fue una aventura muy . . .

2 Trabajen en grupo para leer, comentar y corregir el cuento que escribieron. ¿Usaron el pretérito y el imperfecto correctamente? ¿Las oraciones están conectadas? ¿Hay suficiente elaboración? Añadan más detalles si es necesario.

3 Presenten su cuento a la clase. La clase va a votar por el cuento más imaginativo, el más divertido y el mejor cuento de horror.

Capítulo 1 • cuarenta y siete **47**

43

44

Starter Activity

On the board, draw a simple compass rose and use it to review direction words, such as **norte, sur, este, oeste,** and the intermediate points. Point to a place on the compass rose and ask students to say which direction it is.

Puente a la cultura

Standards: 3.1

Suggestions

Pre-reading: Ask a volunteer to read the title of the passage aloud. Read the *Estrategia* aloud together and have students answer the questions. Have students read the captions and describe what they see in the pictures.

Reading: Encourage students to read once through the entire passage silently, without stopping at problem words or to ask questions. Then have them read it again, stopping after each paragraph to address comprehension issues.

Post-reading: Ask the *¿Comprendiste?* questions to check comprehension.

COUNTRY CONNECTION

Standards: 1.1, 1.2, 1.3, 2.1, 2.2, 3.1

 Technology: Mapa global interactivo, Actividad 4 Follow the route of pilgrims from France to northern Spain.

Suggestions

Display a map of Spain and point out that it is comprised of 17 **regiones autónomas,** including **las Islas Canarias** and **las Islas Baleares.** Remind students that, besides the **castellano** they are learning, four other languages are spoken in Spain: **vascuence** in **el País Vasco, catalán** in **Cataluña, valenciano** in **la Comunidad Valenciana**, and **gallego** in **Galicia**, the region in which Santiago de Compostela is located.

Online Cultural Reading

Standards: 2.1

Suggestion: After doing the online activity, ask students to identify and list three activities popular in Chile that differ from those that they might do in their own communities. Suggest that they compare and contrast the cultural practices.

Puente a la cultura

OBJECTIVES
▶ Read about a famous pilgrimage route in Spain
▶ Apply your prior knowledge of pilgrims to understand the reading
▶ Compare a pilgrimage to your own travel experiences

El Camino de Santiago

Los peregrinos de Plymouth, Massachusetts, buscaban la libertad religiosa. Otros peregrinos viajan en busca de algo sagrado o religioso, como los peregrinos musulmanes que viajan a La Meca y los peregrinos judíos y cristianos que viajan a Jerusalén.

Hace más de mil años, en el extremo noroeste de España se descubrió la tumba del apóstol Santiago[1], una figura fundamental de la religión católica. Empezaron a viajar peregrinos de toda Europa al lugar del descubrimiento en donde se fundó la ciudad de Santiago de Compostela. La ruta sagrada que seguían los peregrinos se dio a conocer[2] como El Camino de Santiago y terminaba en el portal de la Catedral de Santiago de Compostela.

A lo largo de[3] la ruta construyeron iglesias y albergues[4] para recibir a los peregrinos. Algunos peregrinos venían de lugares tan lejanos como Rusia y tardaban años para completar su viaje a pie.

Hoy en día muchas personas viajan a Santiago por la misma razón que los peregrinos de hace mil años: por motivos[5] religiosos. Otros lo recorren[6] como turistas o por motivos culturales debido a su importancia histórica.

[1]the apostle Saint James [2]became known as [3]All along
[4]hostels [5]reasons [6]travel along

Estrategia

Activating prior knowledge
A *peregrino* (pilgrim) is a person who makes a trip for spiritual reasons. To better understand the selection, think of other pilgrims you might know of. Why did the Pilgrims come from England to Plymouth, Massachusetts in the 17th century? Why did they found a colony? Look at the maps on these pages to see the route of another group of pilgrims.

Online Cultural Reading

Go to **Auténtico ONLINE** to read and understand a website for tourists.

Estrategia Use visuals: Use images to figure out what unfamiliar language means.

¡Inténtalo! Look at the website. Can you figure out words that you don't understand by looking at the pictures? List the words or phrases that you just learned.

Jóvenes en camino hacia Santiago de Compostela

48 cuarenta y ocho • Capítulo 1 • Días inolvidables

En la Catedral de Santiago de Compostela está la tumba del apóstol Santiago.

Differentiated Instruction

Heritage Speakers

Ask students to research and report on a pilgrimage that takes place in Latin America or the southwestern United States. They might also report on a major shrine, such as the **Basílica de la Virgen de Guadalupe** in Mexico City.

Advanced Learners

Invite students to research **el Camino de Santiago** and report back to the class. They can look for information such as the names and locations of **albergues juveniles,** the costs and procedures involved when staying there, tour groups, and distances between towns along the pilgrimage.

Muchos de los que hacen este viaje son jóvenes. Algunos lo hacen a pie, otros en bicicleta y otros ¡hasta a caballo! Por eso mismo, hay muchos albergues juveniles que ofrecen servicios muy baratos. Para quedarte en ellos, debes llevar tu propia comida. Los albergues son lugares excelentes para conocer a chicos y chicas de todo el mundo.

◄ Un peregrino de la antigüedad

▲ Uno de los albergues del Camino de Santiago

¿Comprendiste?

1. Nombra los cuatro grupos de peregrinos que se mencionan en la lectura. En general, ¿qué buscan los peregrinos?

2. ¿De dónde eran los peregrinos que iban a Santiago?

3. ¿Cuáles son tres motivos para seguir el Camino de Santiago hoy en día?

4. ¿Qué atractivos tiene el Camino para una persona joven?

Mi propio camino

1 Piensa en un viaje o una excursión que hiciste el año pasado. ¿Adónde fuiste? ¿Por qué fuiste allí? ¿Cómo fuiste? ¿Qué tuviste que llevar? ¿Dónde te quedaste? ¿Cómo era el lugar? ¿Qué había allí? ¿A quién(es) conociste?

2 Ahora compara tu experiencia con el recorrido que hacen muchos jóvenes a Santiago de Compostela. ¿En qué se parecen? ¿En qué se diferencian?

 Videodocumentario Los deportes en el mundo hispano

 Mapa global interactivo Explora el camino que tomaron los peregrinos y haz conexiones con su historia y tradiciones.

Capítulo 1 • cuarenta y nueve **49**

¿Qué me cuentas?

Standards: 1.1, 1.2, 1.3

Resources: Teacher's Resource Materials: Audio Script, Technology: Audio Cap. 1

AP® Skills: Integration of listening, reading, and writing to comprehend and synthesize information from spoken and written sources.

Suggestions: For Step 1, use the audio or read the descriptions aloud. Allow students to hear both descriptions twice through: the first time to write their answers, the second time to check them. For Step 2, have students identify significant details as they read and then summarize the main points of the article.

Encourage students to use each of the suggested expressions in their written responses for Step 3.

 Technology: Audio Script and Answers

Step 1

No era un día muy bueno para ir de cámping. Había algunas nubes y hacía frío. Pero decidimos dar un paseo por el valle. Anduvimos por los senderos hasta llegar al pie de una montaña.

1. ¿Qué tiempo hacía? (a)
2. ¿Por dónde dieron un paseo? (b)
3. ¿Hasta dónde llegaron? (c)

De repente, aparecieron muchísimos mosquitos. Desafortunadamente, ninguno de nosotros tenía el repelente de insectos, así que empezamos a correr para buscar refugio. Por suerte no nos perdimos y pudimos encontrar nuestra tienda de acampar. Unos minutos después de entrar en la tienda, empezó a llover y caer granizo. Fue una gran aventura.

4. ¿Qué aparecieron de repente? (a)
5. ¿Qué es lo que no tenían los chicos? (b)
6. ¿Qué sucedió después de regresar a la tienda? (a)

Steps 2–3
Answers will vary.

Extension: As students do Step 2, have them also write three multiple-choice questions about the article, like the ones they answered in Step 1. Remind them to make their distractors (the incorrect answers) different from the correct answers. Have them ask their questions orally before they begin Step 3.

Additional Resources

 Technology: Online Resources
• *Para hispanohablantes*

**Pre-AP®
Integración**

OBJECTIVES
▸ Listen to and read about an excursion and a sports competition
▸ Write a comparison of two past events

¿Qué me cuentas?: Dos aventuras

El fin de semana pasado hubo dos eventos en el Parque Nacional Tierra del Fuego. Compara lo que sucedió en cada uno. Primero escucha una descripción del paseo. Anota las respuestas a las preguntas y guárdalas para usarlas en el paso 3.

 1 Escucha las siguientes descripciones. Después de cada descripción vas a oír tres preguntas. Escoge la mejor respuesta para cada pregunta.

1. a. no hacía buen tiempo	**b.** hacía calor	**c.** llovía
2. a. por el bosque	**b.** por el valle	**c.** por la playa
3. a. hasta una roca	**b.** hasta un árbol	**c.** hasta el pie de una montaña
4. a. mosquitos	**b.** pájaros	**c.** peces
5. a. binoculares	**b.** repelente de insectos	**c.** brújula
6. a. empezó a llover	**b.** empezó a nevar	**c.** cayeron relámpagos

2 Ahora lee un artículo sobre la competencia que ocurrió el mismo día.

El maratón vuelve a Ushuaia

Domingo, 30 de marzo   ★ ★ ★ ★ ★ commentarios (569)

Ushuaia, Arg. — Hacía frío cuando los atletas empezaron a correr en el maratón que tuvo lugar ayer en el Parque Nacional Tierra del Fuego. Más de 250 atletas, representantes de unos veinte países, se inscribieron en la carrera. La carrera fue dura, no solo por las temperaturas bajas, sino también por el viento fuerte. Los competidores corrieron por un camino de roca que cruzaba el bosque y contra un viento que a veces superaba los 65 kilómetros por hora. Mientras los atletas corrían los últimos veinte kilómetros, empezó a llover y a caer granizo. Sin embargo, el público estaba animado y se emocionó cuando los primeros atletas alcanzaron la meta.

Los vientos de Ushuaia deforman los árboles

 3 Escribe dos párrafos y compara los dos eventos del fin de semana pasado. Piensa en el tiempo que hacía en el parque y en lo que sucedió en cada aventura. ¿Qué esfuerzo hicieron los participantes en cada aventura? ¿Cómo crees que se sentían y por qué? Mientras escribes, usa estas expresiones para conectar tus ideas.

al principio	una vez allí
entonces	más tarde
al final	de repente
sin embargo	durante

50 cincuenta • Capítulo 1 • Días inolvidables

Differentiated Instruction

Heritage Speakers
After students complete Step 2 on p. 50, ask them to think of a sporting or other event they have witnessed that was affected by unexpected weather. Have them tell what happened. Encourage them to use both the preterite and imperfect tenses.

Bodily-Kinesthetic Learner
For Step 3, help students think about how the people in Steps 1 and 2 felt. Ask them to recall a similar experience of their own. Encourage them to imagine the sensory details, including sights, sounds, and smells that will help them remember how they felt under similar circumstances.

Presentación oral

OBJECTIVES
- Demonstrate how to tell a story about a personal experience
- Use the information you know about your audience to choose a topic

Go **Online** to practice
PearsonSchool.com/Autentico

 PEARSON **realize**™

 AUDIO   WRITING   SPEAK/RECORD

Una experiencia inolvidable

TAREA Trabajas en un campamento para niños. Cuéntales a los niños de una experiencia inolvidable que tuviste.

❶ **Prepárate** Responde a las preguntas de la tabla.

¿Adónde fuiste?	
¿Cómo era el lugar?	
¿Qué había allí?	
¿Qué sucedió?	
¿Cómo te sentiste?	
¿Cómo terminó?	

❷ **Practica** Vuelve a leer la información que anotaste en la tabla. Practica varias veces tu presentación. Puedes usar tus notas para practicar, pero no al hablar ante la clase. Recuerda:

- describir claramente todo lo que sucedió
- mirar directamente al público
- usar el vocabulario que aprendiste en esta lección
- usar oraciones conectadas con detalles y elaboración

❸ **Haz tu presentación** Imagina que tus compañeros son los niños del campamento. Cuéntales tu experiencia inolvidable usando oraciones conectadas con detalles y elaboración.

❹ **Evaluación** Tu profesor(a) utilizará la siguiente rúbrica para evaluar tu presentación.

Estrategia

Choosing a topic When giving an oral presentation, think about your audience as you choose a topic. Make a list of details that support your main idea and make sure you have enough interesting information.

Modelo

Hace un tiempo, fui a acampar al valle. El paisaje era impresionante. Había flores de todos los colores. Después de caminar un rato, me perdí. Entonces me di cuenta de que no tenía mi brújula. Sentí miedo. Después de un rato oí unas voces. ¡Eran mis amigos!

Rubric	Score 1	Score 3	Score 5
How well you narrate the event	You don't include narration or have incomplete narration.	You present an idea for narration, but it needs more elaboration.	Your narration uses connected sentences with details and elaboration.
How well you use chapter vocabulary	Your chapter vocabulary is absent.	You used one or two chapter vocabulary items.	You used several chapter vocabulary items appropriately.
How effectively you deliver your speech	You have no eye contact with the audience. There is little or no intonation.	You made some eye contact. You used intonation, but not convincingly.	You have good eye contact with the audience. Intonation and gestures made the narration interesting.

Capítulo 1 • cincuenta y uno **51**

Presentational 1

Presentación oral

Standards: 1.1, 1.2, 1.3, 3.1

Suggestions: Review the task and the rubric with students. Before they write their questions, direct students' attention to the *Estrategia*. Do a presentation of your own (called an anchor) to model a top-scoring presentation.

Pre-AP® Integration

- **Learning Objective:** Presentational Speaking
- **Activity:** Remind students to focus on the presentational speaking skills used in this task such as fluency, pronunciation, and comprehensibility.
- **Pre-AP® Resource Materials:** Comprehensive guide to Pre-AP® speaking skill development

Digital Portfolio

Make audio or video recordings of student oral presentations in class, or assign the Speak and Record activity so they can record their presentations online. Include the recording in their portfolios.

Additional Resources

 Technology: Online Resources
- *Para hispanohablantes*

Self Assessment

Presentación oral
- **Assessment Program: Rubrics**

Review the rubric with students. Go over the descriptions of the different levels of performance. After assessing students, help individuals understand how their performance could be improved. (See Teacher's Resource Materials for suggestions on using rubrics in assessment.)

Enrich Your Teaching

Teacher-to-Teacher

Record your own model presentation online. This way, students can view the model as often as they wish while they prepare and practice their presentations. Some students show a marked improvement when they have a readily accessible model to study. Remind them that it is only a model and that their presentations should not include any content taken directly from it.

21st Century Skills

Communication As they do this *Presentación oral* task, students should try to use sensory information (sights, sounds, and smells, etc.) to provide additional detail and interest as they describe their unforgettable summer camp experience.

Language Arts Connection
Creative Writing

Standards: 3.1

Explain to students that the five-step writing process presented on these two pages will be used consistently throughout *Auténtico*. Point out that this is the same process they most likely use for writing assignments in their Language Arts classes. They can apply the skills and strategies they learn there to their writing in Spanish and vice versa.

Presentación escrita

Standards: 1.3, 3.1

Suggestions: Explain at the start the criteria you will use to evaluate students' compositions. (See Step 5, *Evaluación* and *Assessment* on the next page.) During Step 1, circulate and consult with students. Use questions and suggestions to help them limit their topic. For example, a student will have trouble bringing life to a composition on a topic as broad as **un verano en Chiapas.** Help him or her narrow the topic to one important or interesting incident that happened that summer.

During Step 2, direct students' attention to the *Estrategia.* Point out that focusing on details requires them to stretch their vocabulary and grammar skills because they will include more ideas and images in their sentences.

Pre-AP® Integration

- **Learning Objective:** Presentational Writing
- **Pre-AP® Resource Materials:** Comprehensive guide to Pre-AP® writing skill development

---

Presentación escrita

OBJECTIVES
▸ Narrate a special experience in the past tense
▸ Add details in order to improve the story

Aventuras bajo el sol

Imagínate que acabas de participar en una de las actividades que muestran las fotos de este capítulo. Escribe un cuento sobre esa aventura. ¿Quiénes participaron? ¿Cómo era el lugar? ¿Qué querían ver? ¿Cómo lo pasaron? ¿Fue emocionante? ¿Qué opinas de la actividad? ¿La recomiendas a otras personas?

Estrategia
Adding details Adding details to our writing makes it more interesting. If you say *"oí un ruido y me asusté,"* the reader cannot imagine the setting very well. But if you write: *"En la oscuridad de la noche, sentí un ruido como de un trueno . . . comencé a gritar,"* your reader will have a better picture of what happened.

1 **Antes de escribir** Usa una red de palabras para organizar tus ideas.

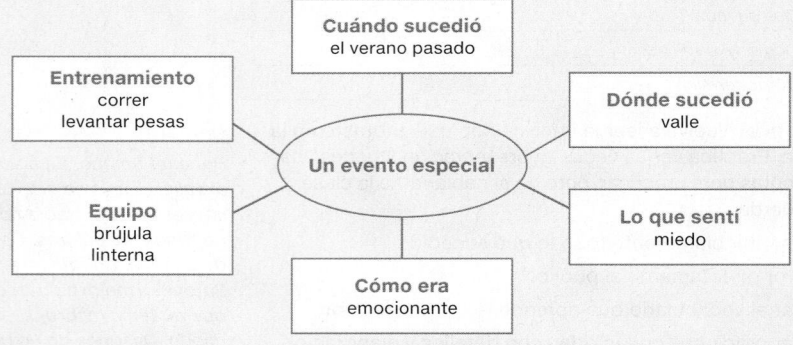

2 **Borrador** Escribe tu borrador. Usa el pretérito y el imperfecto y el vocabulario de esta lección en oraciones conectadas con detalles y elaboración. Escribe tus ideas en orden lógico, así tu cuento va a ser más interesante y más fácil de entender.

Modelo

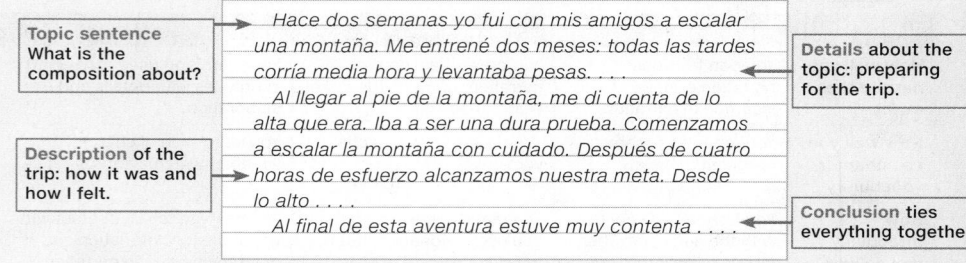

Differentiated Instruction

Heritage Speakers

These students are sometimes used as reference sources by those who are not heritage speakers. This arrangement can be beneficial to both parties, and many heritage language learners are happy to provide help. Set limits, however, to make sure their own work is not unduly interrupted.

Students with Learning Difficulties

To stress the importance of details in a narrative, ask students to "freeze" the action of the characters in their minds, as if they had pressed the "pause" button on a video or DVD. While the characters are frozen tell them to concentrate on the details in the scene, such as clothing and background objects.

Go **Online** to practice
PearsonSchool.com/Autentico
PEARSON
realize™
WRITING

Presentational 1

3 Redacción/Revisión Después de escribir el primer borrador de la composición, trabaja con otro(a) estudiante para intercambiar los trabajos y leerlos. Decidan qué aspectos son más efectivos. Fíjense en cómo el escritor del modelo incluyó detalles en su composición. Cada persona puede decir qué se puede hacer para mejorar la composición que leyó.

Haz lo siguiente: Subraya con una línea los verbos en pretérito y con dos líneas los verbos en imperfecto.

• ¿Hay concordancia *(agreement)* entre cada sujeto y verbo?

• ¿El pretérito y el imperfecto están empleados correctamente?

• ¿Están las oraciones conectadas con detalles y elaboración?

> *fui*
> Hace dos semanas ~~yo fueron~~ con mis
>
> amigos a escalar una montaña. Me entrené dos
> *corría*
> meses: todas las tardes ~~corrían~~ media hora y
>
> levantaba pesas.

4 Publicación Antes de crear la versión final, lee de nuevo tu borrador y repasa los siguientes puntos:

• ¿Sigue mi cuento un orden lógico?

• ¿Tiene un argumento, con un principio, un cuerpo y un final?

• ¿Incluí recomendaciones y detalles que defienden mi opinión?

• ¿Hay otros detalles que debo poner en mi composición? ¿Hay algo que debo quitar?

Después de revisar el borrador, escribe tu composición en limpio.

5 Evaluación Se utilizará la siguiente rúbrica para evaluar tu presentación.

Rubric	Score 1	Score 3	Score 5
Completion of task	You don't highlight any special event.	Your idea for narration is present but needs development.	Your special event is clearly narrated and made prominent.
Organization and level of detail	Your ideas aren't presented in logical order nor with detail.	You have some organizational problems. One or two details are provided.	Your organization is easy to follow. You use good details.
Sentence structure	Your sentences are run-on or are fragmented with many errors.	You use sentences consistently, but with some errors.	Your sentence structure is correct with few errors.

Suggestions (Cont'd):
During Step 3, encourage students to add details to their writing, focusing on sentence structure and transitions as they work in added details. During their peer consultations, remind them to follow the suggestions shown. Remind them that now is the time to think about a title to give their finished work.
Evaluation: Steps 4 and 5 overlap. Students will need evaluation by you, their peers, or self-evaluation to fine-tune and polish their drafts.

Digital Portfolio
Keep students' final drafts in their portfolios as a writing sample.

Teacher-to-Teacher
e-amigos: Pair students to be *e-amigos.* Have them use e-mail to send each other the compositions they wrote for the *Presentación escrita.* Ask students to include an introduction to the composition and ask their partner's opinion of the story. Have students print out their e-mails or send them to you for review.

Additional Resources
 Technology: Online Resources
• *Para hispanohablantes*

Self Assessment _____
Presentación escrita
• **Assessment Program:** Rubrics
Review the rubric with students. Go over the descriptions of the different levels of performance. After assessing students, help individuals understand how their performance could be improved. (See Teacher's Resource Materials for suggestions on using rubrics in assessment.)

Enrich Your Teaching

21st Century Skills
Productivity and Accountability
Students will have to use their written language for the purpose of narrating a special experience in the past. Have students create a list of words and expressions that signal sequence of events, such as *primero, después, luego,* and *finalmente.* These can serve as good transitions between the events in their story.

Lectura

Standards: 1.2, 1.3, 2.2, 3.1, 3.2, 5.2

 Technology: Mapa global interactivo, Actividad 5 Locate two Mexican volcanoes, which are the source of a popular legend.

Suggestions

Pre-reading: Read aloud the title of the passage. Model the pronunciation of the names **Iztaccíhuatl** and **Popocatépetl** and have students repeat. Ask if anyone knows from what Native American culture these unusual names come. If necessary, explain that they are **náhuatl** names. **Náhuatl** is the language of the Aztecs. Before the arrival of the conquistadors, the Aztecs had a great civilization that included the area around what is today Mexico City. Tell students they will come across other **náhuatl** words as they read the selection. Ask students to share what they know about the two volcanoes near Mexico city named **Iztaccíhuatl** and **Popocatépetl.** Tell them they are going to read an Aztec legend that explains how these two mountains were created and got their names. Before reading, direct students' attention to the *Estrategia* and to the *Al leer* section. Have them answer the questions there and copy the graphic organizer from p. 57.

Starter Activity

Have students share the name of a legend that they remember from childhood and a one-sentence description of what happened in it.

Active Classroom

After reading the *Lectura,* assign each student a paragraph for which he or she must write four questions. Have students circulate around the class asking and answering the questions related to each of their paragraphs. This should help students comprehend the story in more detail.

Lectura

OBJECTIVES
- Read and understand a Mexican legend
- Make predictions to increase interest
- Discuss legends that explain natural phenomena

El Iztaccíhuatl y el Popocatépetl

Al leer

El cuento que vas a leer es una leyenda mexicana que relaciona una historia de amor con dos volcanes en México. Copia la gráfica organizadora de la página 57. Mientras lees la selección, llena todos los espacios de la gráfica con la información del cuento.

Mientras lees, presta atención a los siguientes puntos:

- el conflicto entre las dos familias
- la relación entre los personajes principales y la naturaleza

   Hace mucho tiempo, en la gran ciudad de Teotihuacán, había un rey tolteca que tenía una hija muy hermosa. El pelo de la princesa era tan negro y suave como una noche de verano, sus ojos eran tan grandes y oscuros como las aguas de un lago secreto y su sonrisa era tan bonita que decían que el sol miraba por las montañas todas las mañanas para ser el primero en verla.

Muchos príncipes ricos y famosos venían de todas partes de la región tolteca para ganar el amor de la princesa, pero ella no se enamoraba de ninguno. El rey, que quería para su hija un esposo rico de buena posición en la sociedad tolteca, ya estaba impaciente. A veces le preguntaba a la princesa qué esperaba.

—No sé —contestaba la muchacha—. Sólo sé que mi esposo va a ser alguien que voy a amar desde el principio y para siempre.

Un día llegó a la ciudad un príncipe chichimeca. Los chichimecas no tenían una civilización tan espléndida como la de los toltecas. Vivían de la caza[1] y la pesca en las montañas. Los toltecas pensaban que los chichimecas vivían como perros, y se reían de ellos.

[1] hunting

Estrategia

Making predictions Making predictions about what will happen in a story allows us to focus on what we read and increases our interest in the story.
- Do you know any stories that explain a natural phenomenon?
- Look at the picture of the volcanoes. What do you think this story will explain?

Differentiated Instruction

Students with Special Needs

To help the hearing-impaired understand these names, say them aloud slowly several times (note that final **-l** is hardly pronounced): Popocatépetl (poh-poh-ca-TEH-pehtl), Iztaccíhuatl (is-tahs-IH-wahtl), Teotihuacán (tah-oh-tee-hwah-KAHN), chichimeca (chee-chee-MEH-kuh), náhuatl (NAH-wahtl).

Advanced Learners

Invite students to write a narrative about a volcanic eruption from the point of view of a Toltec or Chichimec person. Encourage them to try to portray the emotions such a person might feel at such a moment.

Reading: Allow students time to read silently through the entire selection on their own. You might assign this task for homework. Then go back and read the selection again together, either aloud or silently, depending on time.

During the second reading, pause at regular intervals, such as after each paragraph, in order to address any comprehension issues students may bring up. Ask your own comprehension questions to help students focus on the main idea and important details of each section.

Here are some possible questions you might ask about the second paragraph of the passage. Note that some of them are accompanied by a partner question with a lower level of difficulty:

¿Quiénes venían de todas partes de la región tolteca?

¿Por qué venían los príncipes? ¿Venían para ver los volcanes o para ganar el amor de la princesa?

¿La princesa se enamoraba de algún príncipe?

¿Qué quería el rey para su hija? ¿Qué tipo de esposo quería para ella?

Cierto o falso: El rey estaba impaciente porque su hija se enamoró de dos príncipes.

Remind students to fill out their charts as they read the passage.

Teacher-to-Teacher

Try timing students for their initial silent reading of a longer passage. Give them three to four minutes per page, and call out these increments as they read. This forces them to keep moving and to get an overview of the entire passage, including spots that might be problematic, without getting bogged down on any one word or sentence.

El príncipe chichimeca venía para visitar el gran mercado de Teotihuacán, donde vendían hermosísimos objetos de oro, ropa de brillantes colores, animales exóticos y muchas otras cosas.

Ese mismo día, la princesa tolteca estaba en el mercado comprando canastas[2], telas y alfombras para su palacio. Pasó que, de repente, entre toda la gente y el ruido del mercado, el príncipe y la princesa se fijaron[3] uno en el otro. Sin una palabra, desde el principio y para siempre, el príncipe y la princesa se enamoraron.

Los dos sabían muy bien que su amor era prohibido. Cada uno debía casarse con alguien de su pueblo y su clase: la princesa tolteca con un príncipe tolteca y el príncipe chichimeca con una princesa chichimeca.

Las señoras que acompañaban[4] a la princesa se dieron cuenta de lo que pasaba, y rápidamente llevaron a la princesa a su palacio. El príncipe también regresó al suyo en las montañas. Trató de olvidar a la bella princesa, pero no pudo.

Después de un tiempo, el príncipe decidió volver a Teotihuacán, a pedir la mano de la princesa. Un día se vistió de su ropa más fina y fue al palacio del rey tolteca. Allí mandó[5] a sus mensajeros a hablar con el rey para pedirle a su hija como esposa.

Cuando oyó las palabras de los mensajeros del príncipe, el rey tembló[6] de furia y gritó: —¡Mi hija sólo se va a casar con un príncipe tolteca, nunca con un chichimeca que vive en las montañas como un animal!

---

[2]large round basket [3]they noticed [4]escorted [5]sent [6]shook

Capítulo 1 • cincuenta y cinco 55

Enrich Your Teaching

Culture Note

Teotihuacán was home to a culture that flourished from the first century A.D. until the middle of the sixth—before the Toltecs arrived. With 200,000 people, it was one of the largest cities in the entire world. Nevertheless, very little is known about the people who lived there, not even what language they spoke.

21st Century Skills

ICT (Information, Communications and Technology) Literacy Have students use the digital technology within **Realize** to access extra reading support. Computer corrected activities employ different strategies to help students build their vocabulary and progress at their own pace through the reading.

Interpretive Reading

Suggestions (Cont'd):

Post-reading: Once students have read and discussed the passage section by section, allow them time for another silent reading. This allows them to apply their prior knowledge about the topic, as well as the information they have learned from class discussion. During a final silent reading, students can approach the passage with more confidence and iron out any final comprehension problems they may have.

Pre-AP® Integration

- **Learning Objective:** Presentational Speaking (Cultural Comparison)
- **Background:** This task prepares students for the Spoken Presentational Communication tasks that focus on cultural comparisons.
- **Activity:** Have students prepare a two-minute (maximum) presentation on the following topic: Different views about the natural world are reflected in the legends of different cultures. Students may use the Mexican legend in this reading as a basis for the comparison. They should then comment on a legend they know from another culture, explaining the similarities and differences between the two.
- **Pre-AP® Resource Materials:** Comprehensive guide to Pre-AP® writing skill development

---

Cuando la princesa oyó todo esto, se sintió muy triste. Le tenía mucho respeto a su papá, pero sabía que no podía vivir sin el amor del príncipe chichimeca. Salió de su palacio y se reunió con el príncipe para decirle que sí quería casarse con él. Se fueron a las montañas, y esa noche se casaron.

Al día siguiente, la princesa regresó a Teotihuacán y le dijo a su padre que ya era la esposa del príncipe chichimeca. Le pidió perdón y esperó la comprensión de su padre. Pero el rey estaba furioso: —¿Cómo pudiste hacerme eso? —le preguntó a su hija—. ¡Vete de aquí y no vuelvas nunca! ¡Y no le pidas ni comida ni casa a ningún tolteca, que no te va a dar nada! ¡Lo prohíbo!

Lo mismo le pasó al príncipe cuando volvió a su palacio. Su padre le gritó: —¿Te casaste con una tolteca? ¡Ya no eres mi hijo, ni eres chichimeca! ¡No esperes nunca la ayuda de ningún chichimeca!

Con el corazón muy triste, el príncipe y la princesa se reunieron y empezaron a buscar dónde vivir en las montañas. Nadie los quería ayudar o darles un lugar para descansar y refugiarse de los vientos fríos. Comían sólo hierbas[7] y frutas, porque el príncipe no tenía nada con qué cazar o pescar. Poco a poco, los esposos se estaban muriendo.

Una noche muy fría y larga, el príncipe se dio cuenta de que pronto se iban a morir los dos. Estaban en un valle pequeño desde donde podían ver la ciudad de Teotihuacán. La princesa pensaba en su casa, y el príncipe la miraba con tristeza y amor, sabiendo lo que pensaba.

—Mi bella princesa —le dijo—, ya nos vamos a morir. Nos vamos a separar ahora en este mundo para estar siempre juntos en el otro. Duerme por última vez en mis brazos esta noche. En la mañana, tú te vas a ir a la montaña más baja que mira sobre tu ciudad, y yo me voy a ir a la montaña más alta que también mira sobre tu ciudad. Allí vamos a

descansar, allí te voy a cuidar para siempre y nuestros espíritus[8] van a ser un solo espíritu. Al día siguiente los dos se separaron, y cada uno empezó a subir su montaña. La princesa subió la montaña Iztaccíhuatl y el príncipe subió la montaña Popocatépetl.

Cuando la princesa llegó a la cumbre[9] de su montaña, se durmió y la nieve la cubrió[10]. El príncipe se puso de rodillas, mirando hacia la princesa y la nieve también lo cubrió.

De esta manera podemos ver hoy al príncipe y a la princesa, en la cumbre del Iztaccíhuatl y el Popocatépetl. A veces hay grandes ruidos desde muy dentro del Popocatépetl. Es el príncipe llorando por su princesa.

---

[7]grass [8]spirits, souls [9]summit [10]covered

Differentiated Instruction

Students with Learning Difficulties

Help students deal with long reading passages by "jigsawing" the reading process. Divide the passage into sections and have individuals or pairs work on reading comprehension for their assigned section only. Then have students meet and share what they have learned about their section.

Advanced Learners

Mt. Popocatéptl is an active volcano which has recently seen an increase in activity. Encourage students to research and report on these eruptions and on the status of the volcano today.

Interpretive Reading

1

Interacción con la lectura

1 Llena el organizador gráfico con detalles del argumento.

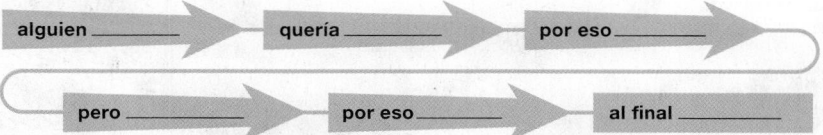

alguien _____ ➝ quería _____ ➝ por eso _____

pero _____ ➝ por eso _____ ➝ al final _____

2 Trabaja con otro(a) estudiante para comparar la información de sus organizadores. Contesten las preguntas y añadan a sus organizadores cualquier otro detalle interesante que recuerden.

- ¿Cómo conoció el príncipe a la princesa? ¿Por qué no podían casarse?
- ¿Qué hicieron los jóvenes? ¿Crees que hicieron bien?
- ¿Qué emociones expresan los personajes al comienzo, después y al final del cuento?
- ¿Cómo terminó la historia? ¿Pudo tener otro final?

3 Ahora parafrasea la idea principal, el tema y los detalles del cuento basándote en el organizador gráfico.

4 Trabaja con un grupo para contestar estas preguntas.

- ¿Qué cuentos, obras de teatro o películas conocen que cuentan una historia similar?
- ¿Por qué en casi todas las culturas hay historias de jóvenes enamorados a quienes sus padres no comprenden?

CULTURA ‹ **México**

Los indígenas americanos vivían en íntimo contacto con la naturaleza. Algunos de sus mitos y leyendas explicaban fenómenos naturales como los eclipses, las tormentas y las erupciones volcánicas. La leyenda de Iztaccíhuatl y Popocatépetl explica la formación de dos volcanes cerca de la Ciudad de México. Iztaccíhuatl, el volcán más antiguo, tiene la forma de una mujer reclinada. En efecto, su nombre en la lengua náhuatl quiere decir "mujer dormida". Popocatépetl, el volcán más joven, es todavía activo. Su nombre náhuatl significa "montaña que humea" (*smoking mountain*).

- ¿Qué otra leyenda conoces que explique un fenómeno natural? Compara la leyenda con la de los dos volcanes.

El volcán Popocatépetl

 Mapa global interactivo Examina el área de México donde vivía la civilización chichimeca y haz conexiones entre los volcanes y las leyendas mexicanas.

Capítulo 1 • cincuenta y siete **57**

Interacción con la lectura

Standards: 1.2

Suggestions: This four-step process helps guide students toward better comprehension of the reading passage. It also develops their speaking, listening, and writing skills by using the passage as a vehicle for pair and group discussions and a writing assignment.

Answers:

Step 1

Answers will vary, but should follow a story line somewhat like the following:

La princesa tolteca y el príncipe chichimeca se enamoraron. Por eso querían casarse.

Pero sus padres prohibieron el matrimonio. Por eso los enamorados tuvieron que buscar dónde vivir.

Al final, subieron a dos montañas para estar cerca el uno del otro, y dormir para siempre juntos.

Steps 2–4

Answers will vary.

CULTURA ‹

Standards: 1.1, 1.2, 2.1, 3.1, 4.1

Suggestions: If students have difficulty coming up with legends concerning natural phenomena, ask them if they have ever heard of the following legends: In Greek myth, the Cyclopes—giant, one-eyed monsters—were responsible for giving thunder and lightning to Zeus, the ruler of all the gods. In Navajo lore, Changing Woman is responsible for the creation of light.

Ask these questions about the photo:

¿Por qué tienen los volcanes estos nombres?

¿Qué pueblo les puso los nombres a los volcanes?

¿Desde qué ciudad se pueden ver? ¿Son volcanes activos?

Answers will vary.

Additional Resources

Technology: Online Resources
- Guided, Writing, Reading
- *Para hispanohablantes*
- Cultural Reading Activity

Print
- Guided WB pp. 46–47
- Literacy Skills WB

Enrich Your Teaching

Culture Note

Perhaps the most famous volcano in Mexico is Parícutin. It was born in 1943, when a farmer discovered a crack in his cornfield. Soon ashes covered the area. A year later, the village of San Salvador Parícutin had been overrun by lava. The last eruption was in 1952. By then the volcano had grown to an altitude of 424 meters, or about 1,300 feet.

21st Century Skills

Media Literacy Have students do online research about other legends that try to explain a natural phenomenon. They can research legends from any ancient civilizations they have previously studied, or legends from indigenous groups in the world today.

Auténtico

Standards: 1.2

Resources: Authentic Resources Wkbk, Cap. 1

Authentic Resources: Cap 1: Videoscript

AP®Theme: *La vida contemporánea: Los viajes y el ocio*

Antes de ver

Invite students to look at the image of the woman zip-lining and ask them to express in Spanish what she is doing and in what type of place she might be. Then refer students to the *Estrategia*. Tell them to pay close attention to the places and activities shown in the video, which will provide key details to help them grasp the main idea. Then review the key vocabulary with the class.

Technology: Ve el video

Before starting the video, direct students' attention to the *Mientras ves* activity. Have them complete the activity page from the Authentic Resources Workbook.

Play the video completely through once, without pausing. Tell students that the main objective with this first viewing is to use the images to get a general idea of the video's topic and theme. Since this video contains images of several locations in Puerto Rico, you can gauge the students' overall comprehension right after the initial viewing. Replay the video, stopping as necessary for students to complete the listening activity. Show the video a final time without pausing.

Haz las actividades

Mientras ves

Standards: 1.2

Suggestions: Have students work with a partner to talk about the video. Then, discuss the questions with the whole class. To start, divide the video into segments and list them on the board:

1. Presentación del video: presentador y presentadora
2. Introducción: reportera
3. Descripción de los atractivos de Puerto Rico: Jorge
4. Aventuras en la montaña y el río: Jorge, reportera y turistas

---

Auténtico

Partnered with UNIVISION COMMUNICATIONS INC

En las montañas de Puerto Rico

Antes de ver

Usa la estrategia: Identificar la idea principal y los detalles

Mira la foto del video. ¿En qué lugar crees que fue tomada? Al ver el video, trata de identificar la idea principal, el tema y los detalles importantes. Usa las imágenes para entender mejor lo que oyes.

Lee el vocabulario clave

lugar idóneo = ideal place
adentrarse = to go deeper
charla de seguridad = safety talk
cueva = cave
cuerpo de agua = body of water
corriente = current

▶ Ve el video

Cuando piensas en una isla del Caribe seguro imaginas playa, mar y palmas, ¿verdad? Pero, ¿sabías que también puede haber montañas, selvas y ríos?

Ve a **PearsonSchool.com/Autentico** para ver el video *Parques de aventura en las montañas de Puerto Rico.* Descubre qué opciones de ecoturismo se ofrecen en esta isla del Caribe, también conocida como Borinquen y la Isla del Encanto.

Haz las actividades

Mientras ves Fíjate muy bien en las distintas secciones del video y en qué dice cada persona en cada sección. ¿Cómo empieza el video? ¿Qué sigue después? ¿Y más adelante? Identifica quién habla en cada sección. Cada sección te da detalles que te ayudan a entender la idea principal del video.

Differentiated Instruction

Heritage Speakers

Invite students to research an island from their heritage country or a neighboring country. Ask them to focus on the natural features that attract tourists to islands, such as beaches, mountains, rivers, etc. Invite students to share their findings with the class using illustrations or video clips, if possible. Encourage them to select a nickname for their island, such as *La isla del sol, La isla de las palmas, La isla misteriosa,* or whatever name seems appropriate for their chosen island.

Advanced Learners

Ask students to create a brochure in Spanish advertising the natural beauties and formations of Puerto Rico's central mountains. To perform this task, ask them to watch the video carefully one more time, focusing on the comments about the mountain, the jungle, and the river. If necessary, suggest that students obtain additional information online. Encourage them to use plenty of adjectives in their descriptions and to illustrate their brochures with photos from the Internet or magazine clippings.

41
6:23p   61°

UNIVISION®
COMMUNICATIONS INC

Integración

Después de ver Vuelve a ver el video una o dos veces más para poder contestar estas preguntas:

1. Parafrasea la idea principal, el tema y los detalles importantes del video.

2. Según lo que dice el video, ¿qué oportunidades turísticas ofrece Puerto Rico?

3. Compara las actividades turísticas de Puerto Rico con las que tú conoces.

4. Parafrasea lo que dice la reportera sobre las piedras que hay en el río.

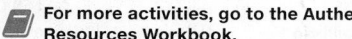 **For more activities, go to the Authentic Resources Workbook.**

El ocio y la naturaleza

Expansión Busca estos recursos en *Auténtico* en línea y contesta las preguntas.

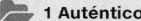 **1 Auténtico**

Integración de ideas ¿Qué relación hay entre las formaciones y bellezas de la naturaleza con nuestras actividades de ocio *(leisure activities)*? Respalda tu respuesta con detalles.

Comparación cultural: Investiga sobre un parque nacional de Estados Unidos, como el Gran Cañón o Yellowstone. Compara las actividades turísticas que se ofrecen allí con las que se ofrecen en las montañas de Puerto Rico.

Después de ver

Standards: 1.2, 1.3, 4.2

Suggestions: Guide students to infer the main idea of the video with questions such as *¿Cuál es el título del video? ¿Cuál es la información más importante que da?* Then invite volunteers to paraphrase the main idea, the key details and the theme off the video. For the third question, guide discussion to the fact that Spanish speakers sometimes borrow terms from English that might not have a defined equivalent in Spanish, such as *zip-lining* and *rappelling*.

Answers:

1. Idea principal: En las montañas de Puerto Rico hay parques de diversiones. Detalles: Hay actividades en la selva y el río. Tema: Ecoturismo.
2. Puerto Rico tiene todo: sol, playa, monte y río.
3. Answers will vary.
4. tienen líneas que han sido formadas por la corriente

For more Authentic Resources: Assign the Authentic Resources Workbook activities for homework, so that students can play the video on their own and complete the workbook activities at their own pace.

Pre-AP® Integration

Resources: Authentic Resources Wkbk, Cap. 1
Authentic Resources: Cap 1 Videoscript

Suggestions: Before completing the Pre-AP® activity, have students go to the workbook and complete the worksheets for the additional resources.

Integración de ideas
Demonstrate understanding of culturally authentic audiovisual materials in a variety of contexts.

Comparación cultural
Suggestions: Call on volunteers to share the activities they would like to do in both locations.

Enrich Your Teaching

Teacher to Teacher
You might want to teach additional vocabulary in Spanish related to "zip-lining" and "rappelling." Make a list on the board of words related to these two activities, such as *cable, tensión, deslizarse, cruzar, bosque, montaña, bajar,* and their equivalent in English. Then have students categorize them as words that go with zip-lining or rappelling. Finally, have students use the words to describe each activity in Spanish.

Using Authentic Resources
Have students create a personal vocabulary list with terms from the authentic resources that are related to ecotourism.

Review Activities

Para hablar de actividades al aire libre, cámping y el tiempo/Para describir la naturaleza/Para indicar que sucede algo y cuándo sucede algo:
Show a five-minute segment of an adventure film or recorded TV show set in the outdoors. Tell students to open their books to this page. Ask them to think of ways to use as many vocabulary items as they can to talk about what they saw. Play the segment again, pausing frequently to allow students to make their comments. Ask questions to elicit words and expressions they have not yet included in their comments.

Make It a Game: The above review strategy can also be set up as a game. Divide the class into two teams. Choose two students as neutral "readers." After showing the recorded segment, give teams ten minutes to use as many vocabulary items as they can in comments about the segment. Have them write their comments as a single list of sentences. Only accurate and sensible comments count. Collect the two lists, and have the readers take turns reading one comment at a time. Keep a tally. The team that uses the most vocabulary items wins.

Para prepararse para un evento deportivo/ Para hablar de competencias deportivas/Para expresar emociones e impresiones
Have pairs of students create comic strips about a character or characters involved in a sporting event. Their strips should include at least one scene each involving training, the event itself, and a victory or awards ceremony. The strips should include narrative lines and speech and/or thought balloons for the characters. Display completed comic strips in the classroom.

Otras palabras y expresiones: Students can use these words and expressions as they do the review activities for the other categories.

Repaso del capítulo

🔊 Vocabulario

para hablar de actividades

acercarse a	to approach
andar	to walk, to move
dar un paseo	to take a walk, stroll
dejar de	to stop (doing something)
escalar	to climb (a rock or mountain)
perderse	to get lost
refugiarse	to take shelter

para describir la naturaleza

el bosque	wood, forest
el desierto	desert
hermoso, -a	beautiful
la naturaleza	nature
el paisaje	landscape
el refugio	refuge, shelter
la roca	rock
la sierra	sierra, mountain range
el valle	valley

para hablar de cámping

los binoculares	binoculars
la brújula	compass
la linterna	flashlight
el repelente de insectos	insect repellent
el saco de dormir	sleeping bag
la tienda de acampar	tent

para hablar del tiempo

caer granizo	to hail
el granizo	hail
el relámpago	lightning
el trueno	thunder

para indicar que sucede algo

suceder	to occur
tener lugar	to take place

para indicar cuándo sucede algo

al amanecer	at dawn
al anochecer	at dusk
al principio	at the beginning
un rato	a while
una vez allí	once there

para prepararse para un evento deportivo

el entrenamiento	training
entrenarse	to train
hacer un esfuerzo	to make an effort
inscribirse	to register
la inscripción	registration

para hablar de competencias deportivas

alcanzar	to reach
la carrera	race
la ceremonia	ceremony
el certificado	certificate, diploma
contra	against
eliminar	to eliminate
la entrega de premios	awards ceremony
¡Felicitaciones!	Congratulations!
la medalla	medal
la meta	goal
obtener	to obtain, get
el / la participante	participant
el / la representante	representative
salir campeón, campeona	to become the champion
el trofeo	trophy
vencer	to beat

para expresar emociones e impresiones

animado, -a	excited
asustar	to scare
darse cuenta de	to realize
desafortunadamente	unfortunately
desanimado, -a	discouraged
duro, -a	hard
emocionarse	to be moved
estar orgulloso / orgullosa de	to be proud of
impresionar	to impress
pasarlo bien / mal	to have a good / bad time

otras palabras y expresiones

aparecer	to appear
así	this way
hacia	toward
perder el equilibrio	to lose one's balance
sin embargo	however

Differentiated Instruction

Linguistic Learner

Ask a volunteer with good acting skills to say the items in the ***emociones e impresiones*** list and exaggerate the corresponding intonation. Have the other students repeat chorally, imitating the intonation.

Students with Learning Difficulties

Given the importance of the element of time when dealing with the past tenses, students may find it easier to retain vocabulary—and use the proper tense—if they add a few words when reviewing the lists of preterite and imperfect verbs. For example: *Yo leí un libro ayer. ¿Qué tiempo hacía ayer?*

Gramática

Más recursos PearsonSchool.com/Autentico

- Games
- Flashcards
- Instant check
- Tutorials

el pretérito

destruir *to destroy*

destruí	destruimos
destruiste	destruisteis
destruyó	destruyeron

leer *to read*

leí	leímos
leíste	leísteis
leyó	leyeron

The verbs *creer, oír,* and *caerse* follow the same pattern as *leer.*

tener *to have*

tuve	**tuv**imos
tuviste	**tuv**isteis
tuvo	**tuv**ieron

Other verbs that have an irregular stem in the preterite and share the same endings as *tener* are: *andar, estar, poder, poner, venir.*

decir *to tell*

dije	**dij**imos
dijiste	**dij**isteis
dijo	**dij**eron

The verb *traer* follows the same pattern as *decir.*

pedir (i) *to ask for*

pedí	pedimos
pediste	pedisteis
pidió	pidieron

The verbs *sentir, divertirse, preferir, sugerir,* and *vestirse* follow the same pattern as *pedir.*

dormir (u) *to sleep*

dormí	dormimos
dormiste	dormisteis
durmió	durmieron

The verb *morir* follows the same pattern as *dormir.*

el imperfecto

estar (-ar) *to be*

est**aba**	est**ábamos**
est**abas**	est**abais**
est**aba**	est**aban**

tener (-er) *to have*

ten**ía**	ten**íamos**
ten**ías**	ten**íais**
ten**ía**	ten**ían**

vivir (-ir) *to live*

viv**ía**	viv**íamos**
viv**ías**	viv**íais**
viv**ía**	viv**ían**

ir *to go*

iba	íbamos
ibas	ibais
iba	iban

ser *to be*

era	éramos
eras	erais
era	eran

ver *to see*

veía	veíamos
veías	veíais
veía	veían

The imperfect of *hay* is *había.*

Enrich Your Teaching

Teacher-to-Teacher

Try "jigsawing" the verb form review from the column on this page. Give one different verb form to each student and allow them five minutes to work. Each student comes up with as much information as he or she can about the assigned verb form and the verb to which it belongs. Then students come together to share their information. Listeners can fill in information they think is missing.

Pretérito e imperfecto

At random, say one preterite or imperfect form of any verb. Ask students to say as much as they can about that verb form and the verb to which it belongs. For example:

Teacher: **pedí**
Student A: *Es el pretérito de pedir.*
Student B: *Es la primera persona: Yo pedí.*
Student C: *Las formas de la tercera persona son irregulares: pidió, pidieron.*
Student D: *Las demás formas en el pretérito son pediste, pedimos y pedisteis.*
Student E: *Las formas del imperfecto son pedía, pedías, pedía...*

This "working backward" approach to reviewing verb forms challenges students and encourages them to look back through the chapter for answers.

Alternative Assessment Options

The above activity can be used as a way to assess students' assimilation of the chapter grammar points.

Digital Portfolio

Invite students to review the activities they completed in this chapter, including written reports, posters or other visuals, tapes of oral presentations, and other projects. Have them select one or two items that they feel best demonstrate their achievements in Spanish. Include these products in students' portfolios. Have them include this with the Chapter Checklist and Self-Assessment Worksheet.

Additional Resources

 Technology: Online Resources
- Instant Check
- *Para hispanohablantes*
- Teacher's Resource Materials: Situation Cards, Clip Art

Assessment

Prueba 6-2 with Remediation (online only)
Prueba: Chapter Checklist and Self-Assessment Worksheet

 Technology: *¡Pura vida!* is a storyline video that is independent of chapter content and an ideal support for expanding listening skills. The 14 episodes are available within **Realize.** Student activities and Teacher support are also assignable within **Realize.**

Performance Tasks

Standards: 1.1, 1.2, 1.3, 2.1

Teacher's Resource Materials: Audio Script, Technology: Audio Cap. 1

1. Vocabulario

Suggestions: Encourage students to review the vocabulary from the *Vocabulario en contexto* sections on pp. 22–25 and 36–38 before they complete the activity.

Answers:

1. d	**5.** c
2. b	**6.** b
3. c	**7.** a
4. a	**8.** d

2. Gramática

Suggestions: Remind students that the main ideas of the grammar presentations in *Capítulo* 1 were the forms and uses of the preterite and the imperfect.

Answers:

1. d	**5.** b
2. a	**6.** c
3. b	**7.** a
4. a	**8.** d

Repaso del capítulo

OBJECTIVE
▶ Demonstrate that you can perform the tasks on these pages

Preparación para el examen

❶ Vocabulario Escribe la letra de la palabra o expresión que mejor complete cada frase. Escribe tus respuestas en una hoja aparte.

1. Me levanté muy temprano, _____, para ir de cámping.
   a. por la tarde
   b. al anochecer
   c. por la noche
   d. al amanecer

2. Cuando fuimos al bosque, Luis trajo _____ porque no había mucha luz.
   a. unos binoculares
   b. una linterna
   c. un repelente de insectos
   d. un saco de dormir

3. El paisaje era impresionante. _____ mucho cuando vi las montañas.
   a. Me cansé
   b. Me asusté
   c. Me emocioné
   d. Me aburrí

4. Cuando gané el campeonato mis padres me dijeron que estaban muy _____ de mis esfuerzos.
   a. orgullosos
   b. desanimados
   c. asustados
   d. tristes

5. Buscamos un refugio porque _____.
   a. perdí el equilibrio
   b. nos eliminaron
   c. comenzó a caer granizo
   d. no dormimos bien

6. Cuando llegué tarde a casa mis padres me preguntaron: "¿Qué te _____?"
   a. dieron
   b. sucedió
   c. rompiste
   d. pusiste

7. Antes de participar en el campeonato, la chica _____ por tres meses.
   a. se entrenó
   b. se perdió
   c. se divirtió
   d. se durmió

8. Fue un partido muy _____. Todos tuvimos que hacer un gran esfuerzo para ganar.
   a. agitado
   b. fácil
   c. aburrido
   d. duro

---

❷ Gramática Escribe la letra de la palabra o expresión que mejor complete cada frase. Escribe tus respuestas en una hoja aparte.

1. Leí en el diario que la tormenta _____ muchos árboles.
   a. destruye
   b. destruía
   c. destruyendo
   d. destruyó

2. No puedo creer que te olvidaste la mochila. ¿Por qué no la _____?
   a. trajiste
   b. traen
   c. trajeron
   d. traían

3. _____ la una de la tarde cuando llegamos al campamento.
   a. Fue
   b. Era
   c. Eran
   d. Estaban

4. El sábado pasado, los chicos _____ dos horas por los senderos.
   a. anduvieron
   b. andaban
   c. andan
   d. anduviste

5. Anoche, después del partido, el campeón _____ diez horas porque estaba cansado.
   a. dormía
   b. durmió
   c. está durmiendo
   d. duerme

6. De niña, a menudo yo _____ a los partidos de tenis con mis tíos.
   a. voy
   b. fui
   c. iba
   d. iban

7. El atleta que salió en primer lugar _____ un trofeo.
   a. obtuvo
   b. obtiene
   c. obtenía
   d. obtuviste

8. Generalmente, ¿cómo _____ cuando tu equipo perdía un partido?
   a. te sientes
   b. te sentiste
   c. se sentían
   d. te sentías

Differentiated Instruction

Students with Learning Difficulties

Before students complete the tasks, have them review the Vocabulario on p. 60 and make flash cards for any words that they do not know. Have them use the cards for practice in pairs with partners who are more confident.

Advanced Learners

Ask students to serve as tutors for classmates who are struggling. Give tutors specific targets to work on. Some students may consider these requests an unfair imposition and extra work. Consider these feelings, while at the same time working towards maintaining an atmosphere of cooperation.

En el examen vas a . . .	Éstas son las tareas de práctica que te pueden ser útiles para el examen . . .	Para repasar, ve a tu libro de texto impreso o digital . . .
Interpretive		
3 ESCUCHAR Yo puedo escuchar y comprender la descripción de una excursión a un parque nacional.	Un amigo(a) te deja un mensaje por teléfono sobre una excursión que hizo a un parque nacional. (a) ¿Adónde fue? (b) ¿Qué vio? (c) ¿Qué hizo allí? (d) ¿Qué le sucedió? (e) ¿Cómo lo pasó?	**pp. 22–25** *Vocabulario en contexto 1* **p. 23** *Actividades 1–2* **p. 24** *Actividad 3* **p. 30** *Actividad 15*
Interpersonal		
4 HABLAR Yo puedo hablar con un compañero sobre una excursión que hizo mi clase.	Tu clase fue de excursión a un lugar especial. Cuéntale lo que pasó a un(a) compañero(a) que no pudo ir. Él o ella te hará preguntas que incluyen: quiénes fueron, adónde fueron, qué había allí, qué tiempo hacía, qué hicieron y cómo lo pasaron. Usa una forma de hablar amistosa y menos formal.	**p. 50** *¿Qué me cuentas?* **p. 51** *Presentación oral*
Interpretive		
5 LEER Yo puedo leer y comprender un anuncio sobre un concurso.	Lee el anuncio que apareció en el periódico de la escuela y decide: (a) qué tipo de concurso es; (b) cuándo es la inscripción; (c) quiénes pueden participar; (d) cuándo es la audición; (e) qué premio va a obtener el / la ganador(a). ***Concurso de Música*** *Invitamos a todos los estudiantes de tercer y cuarto año a participar en nuestro concurso.* **Fecha de inscripción:** *6 de octubre* **Audición:** *9 de octubre* **Primer premio:** *dos entradas* (tickets) *para un concierto en el teatro San Martín*	**pp. 36–39** *Vocabulario en contexto 2* **p. 40** *Cultura* **p. 41** *Actividades 33, 35*
Presentational		
6 ESCRIBIR Yo puedo escribir un artículo sobre un evento deportivo importante para el periódico de la escuela.	Imagina que eres reportero del periódico de la escuela. Tienes que escribir un artículo sobre el último partido del año de un equipo de tu escuela. Luego, usa oraciones conectadas y elaboradas con detalles que incluyen: (a) quiénes jugaron, (b) dónde y cuándo fue, (c) si hacía buen tiempo, (d) cómo se sentían los jugadores, (e) qué sucedió, (f) cómo se sentían al final, (g) si fue un partido aburrido o emocionante y por qué.	**p. 43** *Actividad 38* **p. 44** *Actividad 40* **p. 45** *Actividad 41*
Comparisons		
7 COMPARAR Yo puedo comparar los peregrinos de hoy y de ayer.	Piensa en el viaje de los peregrinos de Santiago de Compostela hace mil años. ¿Por qué quieren seguir la misma ruta muchos jóvenes hoy en día? ¿Hay lugares aquí en los Estados Unidos como Santiago de Compostela? ¿Cuáles son los motivos para viajar a estos lugares? ¿En qué se parecen? ¿En qué se diferencian?	**pp. 48–49** *Puente a la cultura*

Capítulo 1 • sesenta y tres **63**

Differentiated Assessment

Core Assessment
- Technology: Audio: Cap. 1
- ExamView: Chapter Test, Test Banks A and B

Advanced/Pre-AP®
- ExamView: Pre-AP® Test Bank
- Pre-AP® Resource Materials

Students Needing Extra Help
- Alternate Assessment Program: Examen del capítulo 1
- Technology: Audio: Cap. 1

Heritage Speakers
- Assessment Program: *Para hispanohablantes:* Examen del capítulo 1
- ExamView: Heritage Speaker Test Bank

3. Escuchar

Suggestions: Use the audio or read from the script.

Script: Hola, te habla Julián. Este fin de semana estuve en Torres del Paine. Es un parque nacional fantástico. El paisaje es impresionante. Vimos valles y montañas altísimas.
Hicimos caminatas y montamos a caballo. Me asusté un poco cuando perdí el equilibrio y me caí del caballo. Pero, por suerte, no me lastimé. En general lo pasé muy bien. Te voy a mandar una tarjeta postal. Adiós a todos.

Answers:
a. Fue al Parque Nacional Torres del Paine.
b. Vio valles y montañas altísimas.
c. Hizo caminatas y montó a caballo.
d. Perdió el equilibrio y se cayó del caballo.
e. Lo pasó muy bien.

4. Hablar

Standards: 1.1, 1.2, 1.3

Suggestions: As students take turns telling about their excursions, encourage the listeners to help the speakers by asking questions.

Answers will vary.

5. Leer

Suggestions: Tell students to refer to pp. 22–25 and 36–38 if they have questions about vocabulary in the announcement.

Answers:
a. Es un concurso de música.
b. La inscripción es el 6 de octubre.
c. Todos los estudiantes de tercer y cuarto año pueden participar.
d. La audición es el 9 de octubre.
e. El (la) ganador(a) va a obtener dos entradas para un concierto en el teatro San Martín.

6. Escribir

Standards: 1.3

Suggestions: Encourage students to put their thoughts in a graphic organizer before writing.

Answers will vary.

7. Comparar

Suggestions: Ask students to write down the answers and be ready to share them with the class.

Answers will vary.

Additional Resources

 Technology: Online Resources
- Instant Check
- *Para hispanohablantes*

Print
- Core WB pp. 19–20

CAPÍTULO 2

¿Cómo te expresas?

Different artistic expressions and how to appreciate them

Vocabulary: types of art and how to describe them; music, drama and dance performances

Grammar: preterite vs. imperfect; *estar* + past participle; *ser* and *estar;* verbs with different meanings in the imperfect and the preterite

Cultural Perspectives: artistic expressions and artists in the Spanish-speaking world; the art of Mexican artists Diego Rivera and David Alfaro Siqueiros; the origins of *salsa;* the Spanish *zarzuela;* the world of Francisco de Goya

¡Pura vida!: Watch an engaging video episode about a group of young people in Costa Rica!

Chapter Support

Bulletin Boards

Theme: Las artes

Ask students to cut out, draw, or download pictures of artists from different Spanish-speaking countries and of their work. Cluster photos into categories: painting, sculpture, dance, music, and literature.

Hands-on Culture

Craft: Una máscara de tigre

In Mexico, the art of making tiger or jaguar masks has its roots in pre-Hispanic theatrical performances. The character of the tiger or jaguar is extremely popular and important in many Mexican festivals and pageants. Tiger masks are typically painted yellow with black spots in keeping with the coloring of the real animal.

Materials: water, white flour (one part flour to one part water), newspaper (uncut), aluminum foil, masking tape, strips of newspaper, poster paint, brushes

Directions:

1. Prepare paste by mixing flour and water in a large bowl until it makes a smooth paste.
2. Make a mold by forming a large round or oval shape out of balled-up sheets of dry newspaper. Next, cover the front of this shape with aluminum foil, smoothing it down so it forms to your shape. Use more balled-up newspaper to form facial features on your mold. Attach them to the aluminum foil with masking tape.
3. Dip the newspaper strips, one at a time, into the paste. Lay the coated newspaper on the mold. Smooth out the wrinkles and continue to place coated newspaper strips over the surface until it is completely covered. Continue until you have put 3 to 4 layers of newspaper strips on your mold. Allow the mask to dry for about 24 hours.
4. When the mask is dry, pull the balled-up newspaper out of it. The aluminum foil will remain attached to your mask as a lining. Paint the mask yellow and add black spots. Cut holes for the eyes and mouth.

Game

Veo, veo. ¿Qué ves?

Use this traditional children's game to practice art-related vocabulary in the *Vocabulario en uso* 1 section.

Players: entire class

Materials: Poster of a painting from a Spanish or Latin American artist.

Rules: 1. Students write their names on scraps of paper and place them in a paper bag.

2. Shake the paper bag to mix up the names. Then call on a volunteer to come to the front of the class and draw a name from the paper bag.
3. Students take turns asking the volunteer questions in order to guess an object from the painting that the volunteer has chosen.

Student 1: Veo, veo.

Student 2: ¿Qué ves?

Student 1: Una cosa.

Student 2: ¿De qué color?

Student 1: Verde.

4. When a student correctly guesses the object in the painting, he or she becomes the new volunteer. Play continues until every student asks one or two questions.

21st Century Skills

Look for tips throughout Chapter 2 to enrich your teaching by integrating 21st Century Skills. Suggestions for the Project-Based Learning and Culture follow below.

Project-Based Learning

Modify the project with these suggestions:

Information Literacy Encourage students to go online and research artists who have created self portraits or autobiographical sculptures to see how they define themselves through a variety of media. The handout "Search for Information on the Internet" will help them find reliable sources and museum Web sites to view a variety of artwork.

Creativity and Innovation Encourage students to be creative with the materials they choose to make their sculptures. Remind them of the possibilities of *collage,* such as embedding beads, small stones, or pieces of wood into their sculptures, or of using a combination of media in the same sculpture.

Communication As students prepare to present their projects, provide them with the handout "Give an Effective Presentation" to remind them of the importance of body language, tone of voice, eye contact, and other strategies for delivering an effective presentation.

Chapter Culture

Social and Cross-Cultural Skills Help students bridge cultural differences by offering opportunities to discuss the culture highlighted throughout the chapter. Use the teaching suggestions in the *Cultura* features to discuss cultural perspectives in the artistic expression of different artists and performers of the Spanish-speaking world.

▶ Technology: Videodocumentario
View *El arte en el mundo hispano* online with the class to hear different Spanish-speaking artists share their inspirations for their own work.

Project-Based Learning

Escultura personal

Overview: Students create a sculpture that will represent their personality. First they draw a draft and write how the design relates to them. Then they create the sculpture. It might be done with clay, papier-mâché, carved soap, cardboard, or other scrap materials found at home. Have them paint it or decorate it according to their taste. Finally, they give an oral presentation of the piece, explaining how it relates to them or represents them.

Resources: paper, clay, cardboard, soap, paint, markers, scrap materials found at home. Remind students that there are no restrictions on materials, as long as they are safe.

Sequence: (suggestions for when to do each step are found throughout the chapter)

Step 1. Review instructions so students know what is expected of them. Share the rubric with students.

Step 2. On a sheet of paper students draw a rough draft of their sculpture and write a few paragraphs explaining how it relates to their personality. Return their draft and text with suggestions. For vocabulary and grammar practice, ask partners to present their sketches and text to each other.

Step 3. Students create their sculpture, based on their previous drafts. Encourage them to try different materials for their work and to use as much vocabulary as possible from *Capítulo* 2 in their written text.

Step 4. Students submit a draft of their text, explaining how the sculpture relates to their personality. Write your corrections and suggestions, then return drafts to students.

Step 5. Students present their sculpture to the class, using their notes to explain how it relates to them.

Options

1. Students create a collage to represent aspects of their personality.
2. Students create a brochure about an artist of their choice.

Assessment

Here is a detailed rubric for assessing this project:

Chapter 2 Project: *Escultura personal*

Rubric	Score 1	Score 3	Score 5
Your evidence of planning	You present no draft or written text.	Your draft or text is missing.	You show evidence of a corrected draft.
Your use of materials	You provide little or no decoration.	Your structure or decoration is missing.	Your piece is well done.
Your presentation	Your presentation is short and does not relate to the sculpture.	You describe part of the sculpture.	You describe in detail your relationship with the sculpture.

AT A GLANCE

Objectives

- Listen to and read about art and music
- Talk and write about music and theater
- Discuss and explain art school activities
- Compare how artists express their ideas
- Understand the context of an artist
- Understand cross-cultural perspectives
- Compare cultural practices in an authentic video

Vocabulary

- Art forms, genres, materials and professions
- Works of art and artists
- Performing arts: music, dance, stage

Grammar

- Preterite vs. imperfect
- Verb *estar* + participle
- *Ser* and *estar*
- Verbs with different meanings in the imperfect and preterite

Culture

- Picasso and cubism, p. 68
- Miró and Dalí, p. 76
- Diego Rivera, p. 77
- David Alfaro Siqueiros, p. 80
- Lila Downs, p. 86
- El tango argentino, p. 86
- Dancing *salsa,* p. 93
- Juan Diego Flórez, p. 95
- The *zarzuela,* p. 95
- Francisco de Goya, pp. 96–97
- Esmeralda Santiago, p. 105

A ver si recuerdas...

- Arts and artists
- Colors and materials
- In the theater
- Adjectives
- Nouns and superlatives

Recycle

- Preterite and imperfect
- The letters *b* and *v*

Authentic Resources

- Auténtico: Authentic video, pp. 106–107

RESOURCES

	FOR THE STUDENT	DIGITAL	PRINT	FOR THE TEACHER	DIGITAL	PRINT
A ver si recuerdas pp. 64–67						
Review	A *ver si recuerdas* with Remediation	•		Teacher's Edition, pp. 64–67	•	
	Guided WB, pp. 48–51	•	•	A *ver si recuerdas* with Remediation	•	
	Core WB, pp. 21–22	•	•			
	Para hispanohablantes	•				
Introducción pp. 68–69						
Present	Student Edition, pp. 68–69	•	•	Teacher's Edition, pp. 68–69	•	•
	DK Reference Atlas	•		Teacher's Resource Materials	•	
	Videonovela: *¡Pura vida!*	•		Mapa global interactivo	•	
	¡Pura vida! Video Activities	•				
	Para hispanohablantes	•				
Vocabulario en contexto pp. 70–73/84–87						
Present & Practice	Student Edition, pp. 70–73/84–87	•	•	Teacher's Edition, pp. 70–73/84–87	•	•
	Audio	•		Teacher's Resource Materials	•	
	Guided WB, pp. 52–58/63–70	•	•	Vocabulary Clip Art	•	
	Core WB, pp. 23–24/28–29	•	•	Technology: Audio	•	
	Communication Activities	•		Video Program: *Videohistoria*	•	
	Para hispanohablantes	•				
Assess and Remediate				Pruebas 2–1/2–5: Assessment Program, Assessment Program *Para hispanohablantes*	•	

RESOURCES

FOR THE STUDENT	DIGITAL	PRINT	FOR THE TEACHER	DIGITAL	PRINT
Vocabulario en uso pp. 74–77/88–89					
Present & Practice — Student Edition, pp. 74–77/88–89	•	•	Interactive Whiteboard Vocabulary Activities	•	
Instant Check	•		Teacher's Edition, pp. 74–77/88–89	•	•
Communication Activities	•		Teacher's Resource Materials	•	
Para hispanohablantes	•		Technology: Audio	•	
Communicative Pair Activities	•		Videomodelos	•	
			Mapa global interactivo	•	
Assess and Remediate			Pruebas 2–2/2–6 with Remediation	•	
			Pruebas 2–2/2–6: Assessment Program, Assessment Program *Para hispanohablantes*	•	
Gramática pp. 78–83/90–95					
Present & Practice — Student Edition, pp. 78–83/90–95	•	•	Interactive Whiteboard Grammar Activities	•	
Instant Check	•		Teacher's Edition, pp. 78–83/90–95	•	•
Tutorial Video: Grammar	•		Teacher's Resource Materials	•	
Canción de hip hop	•		Technology: Audio	•	
Guided WB, pp. 59–62/71–74	•	•	Videomodelos	•	
Core WB, pp. 25–27/30–32	•	•			
Communication Activities	•				
Para hispanohablantes	•				
Communicative Pair Activities	•				
Assess and Remediate			Pruebas 2–3, 2–4/2–7, 2–8 with Remediation	•	
			Pruebas 2–3, 2–4/2–7, 2–8: Assessment Program, Assessment Program *Para hispanohablantes*	•	
			Examen 1, Examen 2: Vocab. y gramática	•	
Aplicación pp. 96–107					
Apply — Student Edition, pp. 96–107	•	•	Teacher's Edition, pp. 96–107	•	•
Authentic Resources Workbook	•	•	Teacher's Resource Materials	•	
Authentic Resources	•		Video Program: Videodocumentario	•	
Online Cultural Reading	•		Mapa global interactivo	•	
Guided WB, pp. 75–77	•		Authentic Resources Lesson Plans with scripts, answer keys	•	
Communication Activities	•				
Para hispanohablantes	•				
Videodocumentario	•				
Auténtico	•				
Repaso del capítulo pp. 108–111					
Review — Student Edition, pp. 108–111	•	•	Teacher's Edition, pp. 108–111	•	•
Core WB, pp. 33–34	•	•	Teacher's Resource Materials	•	
Communication Activities	•		Technology: Audio	•	
Para hispanohablantes	•				
Instant Check	•				
Chapter Assessment					
Assess			Examen del capítulo 2: Assessment Program, Alternate Assessment Program, Assessment Program *Para hispanohablantes*	•	
			Technology: Audio, Cap. 2, Examen	•	
			ExamView: Test Banks A and B (questions only online) Heritage Speaker Test Bank, Pre-AP® Test Bank	•	

LESSON PLAN

DAY	Warm-up / Assess	Preview / Present / Practice / Communicate	Wrap-up / Homework Options
1	**Warm-up** (10 min.) • Return Examen del capítulo: Capítulo 1	**Repaso** (35 min.) • A ver si recuerdas . . . • Actividades 5	**Wrap-up and Homework Options** (5 min.) • Core Practice 2-1, 2-2
2	**Warm-up** (10 min.) • Homework check	**Chapter Opener** (10 min.) • Objectives • Arte y cultura **Vocabulario en contexto 1** (25 min.) • Presentation: Vocabulario y gramática en contexto • Actividades 1, 2	**Wrap-up and Homework Options** (5 min.) • Clip Art Vocabulary
3	**Warm-up** (10 min.) • Homework check	**Vocabulario en contexto 1** (35 min.) • Actividades 3, 4, 5 • Presentation: Videohistoria: *Una mirada al arte de los mayas* • View: Videohistoria	**Wrap-up and Homework Options** (5 min.) • Core Practice 2-3, 2-4 • Actividad 6 • Prueba 2-1: Vocabulary recognition
4	**Warm-up** (10 min.) • Homework check • **Formative Assessment** (10 min.) • Prueba 2-1: Vocabulary recognition	**Vocabulario en uso 1** (25 min.) • Interactive Whiteboard Vocabulary Activities • Actividades 7, 8, 9, 10 • Ampliación del lenguaje	**Wrap-up and Homework Options** (5 min.) • Actividades 11, 12 • Writing Activities • Prueba 2-2 with Remediation: Vocabulary production
5	**Warm-up** (10 min.) • Homework check • **Formative Assessment** (10 min.) • Prueba 2-2 with Remediation: Vocabulary production	**Gramática y vocabulario en uso 1** (25 min.) • Actividad 13 • Presentation: Pretérito vs. imperfecto • Interactive Whiteboard Grammar Activities • Actividades 15, 16 • Writing Activity	**Wrap-up and Homework Options** (5 min.) • Core Practice 2-5
6	**Warm-up** (10 min.) • Actividad 14 • Homework check	**Gramática y vocabulario en uso 1** (35 min.) • Actividades 17, 18 • Communicative Pair Activity • Presentation: *Estar* + participio • Interactive Whiteboard Grammar Activities • Actividad 19	**Wrap-up and Homework Options** (5 min.) • Writing Activity • Prueba 2-3 with Remediation: Pretérito vs. imperfecto
7	**Warm-up** (10 min.) • Fondo cultural • Homework check • **Formative Assessment** (10 min.) • Prueba 2-3 with Remediation: Pretérito vs. imperfecto	**Gramática y vocabulario en uso 1** (25 min.) • Actividades 20, 21, 22 • El español en la comunidad • Communicative Pair Activity	**Wrap-up and Homework Options** (5 min.) • Core Practice 2-6, 2-7 • Prueba 2-4 with Remediation: *Estar* + participio
8	**Warm-up** (15 min.) • Writing Activity • Homework check • **Formative Assessment** (10 min.) • Prueba 2-4 with Remediation: *Estar* + participio	**Vocabulario en contexto 2** (20 min.) • Presentation: Vocabulario y gramática en contexto • Actividades 23, 24	**Wrap-up and Homework Options** (5 min.) • Clip Art Vocabulary • Examen: Vocabulario y gramática 1
9	**Warm-up** (15 min.) • Homework check • **Formative Assessment** (30 min.) • Examen: Vocabulario y gramática	**Vocabulario en contexto 2** (10 min.) • Presentation: Espectáculos del mundo latino • Actividad 25	**Wrap-up and Homework Options** (5 min.) • Actividad 26 • Core Practice 2-8, 2-9 • Prueba 2-5: Vocabulary recognition
10	**Warm-up** (20 min.) • Actividad 25 • Homework check • **Formative Assessment** (10 min.) • Prueba 2-5: Vocabulary recognition	**Vocabulario en uso 2** (15 min.) • Actividades 30, 31 • Interactive Whiteboard Vocabulary Activities	**Wrap-up and Homework Options** (5 min.) • Actividades 28, 29 • Prueba 2-6 with Remediation: Vocabulary production

DAY	Warm-up / Assess	Preview / Present / Practice / Communicate	Wrap-up / Homework Options
	LESSON PLAN		
11	**Warm-up** (10 min.) • Writing Activity • Homework check • **Formative Assessment** (10 min.) • Prueba 2-6 with Remediation: Vocabulary production	**Gramática y vocabulario en uso 2** (25 min.) • Presentation: *Ser y estar* • Interactive Whiteboard Grammar Activities • Actividades 32, 33, 34 • Communicative Pair Activity	**Wrap-up and Homework Options** (5 min.) • Actividad 35 • Core Practice 2-10 • Prueba 2-7 with Remediation: *Ser y estar*
12	**Warm-up** (10 min.) • Writing Activity • Homework check • **Formative Assessment** (10 min.) • Prueba 2-7 with Remediation: *Ser y estar*	**Gramática y vocabulario en uso 2** (25 min.) • Presentation: Verbos con distinto sentido en el pretérito y en el imperfecto • Interactive Whiteboard Grammar Activities • Actividades 36, 37	**Wrap-up and Homework Options** (5 min.) • Core Practice 2-11, 2-12 • Prueba 2-8 with Remediation: Verbos con distinto sentido en el pretérito y en el imperfecto
13	**Warm-up** (10 min.) • Homework check • **Formative Assessment** (10 min.) • Prueba 2-8 with Remediation: Verbos con distinto sentido en el pretérito y en el imperfecto	**Gramática y vocabulario en uso 2** (25 min.) • Actividades 38, 39 • Cultura • Communicative Pair Activity	**Wrap-up and Homework Options** (5 min.) • Examen: Vocabulario y gramática 2
14	**Warm-up** (8 min.) • Homework check • **Formative Assessment** (10 min.) • Examen: Vocabulario y gramática 2	**Aplicación** (10 min.) • Presentación oral: Steps 1, 2	**Wrap-up and Homework Options** (2 min.) • Presentación oral: Step 2
15	**Warm-up** (10 min.) • Presentación oral: Step 2	**Aplicación** (35 min.) • Presentación oral: Step 3	**Wrap-up and Homework Options** (5 min.) • El mundo de Francisco de Goya • ¿Comprendiste?
16	**Warm-up** (15 min.) • El mundo de Francisco de Goya: ¿Comprendiste? • Homework check	**Aplicación** (30 min.) • Escribe tu opinión • Pre-AP® Integración 1, 2, 3 • View Video	**Wrap-up and Homework Options** (5 min.) • Presentación escrita: Steps 1, 2
17	**Warm-up** (10 min.) • Homework check	**Aplicación** (15 min.) • Presentación escrita: Step 3 **Repaso** (20 min.) • Preparación para el examen: Actividades 3, 4	**Wrap-up and Homework Options** (5 min.) • Presentación escrita: Step 4
18	**Warm-up** (10 min.) • Homework check	**Aplicación** (35 min.) • Lectura • ¿Comprendiste? • Cultura • Auténtico	**Wrap-up and Homework Options** (5 min.) • Core Practice: Organizer 2-13, 2-14 • Instant Check
19	**Warm-up** (20 min.) • Preparación para el examen: Actividades 1, 2 • Homework check	**Repaso** (25 min.) • Preparación para el examen: Actividades 5, 6, 7 • Other review	**Wrap-up and Homework Options** (5 min.) • Examen del capítulo
20	**Warm-up** (5 min.) • Answer questions • **Summative Assessment** (44 min.) • Examen del capítulo		**Wrap-up and Homework Options** (1 min.) • A ver si recuerdas: Capítulo 3

ALTERNATE LESSON PLAN

DAY	Warm-up / Assess	Preview / Present / Practice / Communicate	Wrap-up / Homework Options
1	**Warm-up** (35 min.) • Return Examen del capítulo: Capítulo 1 • A ver si recuerdas . . . • Actividad 5 • Homework check	**Chapter Opener** (10 min.) • Objectives • Arte y cultura **Vocabulario en contexto 1** (30 min.) • Presentation: Vocabulario y gramática en contexto • Actividades 1, 2 • Actividades 3, 4, 5 • Presentation: Videohistoria: *Una mirada al arte de los mayas* • View: Videohistoria **Vocabulario en uso 1** (10 min.) • Actividades 6, 7	**Wrap-up and Homework Options** (5 min.) • Core Practice 2-3, 2-4 • Clip Art Vocabulary • Prueba 2-1: Vocabulary recognition
2	**Warm-up** (10 min.) • Actividad 8 • Homework check • **Formative Assessment** (10 min.) • Prueba 2-1: Vocabulary recognition	**Vocabulario en uso 1** (60 min.) • Actividades 9, 10, 11, 12, 13 • Interactive Whiteboard Vocabulary Activities • Ampliación del lenguaje • Communicative Pair Activity	**Wrap-up and Homework Options** (5 min.) • Writing Activities • Prueba 2-2 with Remediation: Vocabulary production
3	**Warm-up** (15 min.) • Writing Activity • Homework check • **Formative Assessment** (10 min.) • Prueba 2-2 with Remediation: Vocabulary production	**Gramática y vocabulario en uso 1** (60 min.) • Presentation: Pretérito vs. imperfecto • Interactive Whiteboard Grammar Activities • Actividades 14, 15, 16, 18 • Cultura • Audio and Writing Activities	**Wrap-up and Homework Options** (5 min.) • Core Practice 2-5 • Prueba 2-3 with Remediation: Pretérito vs. imperfecto
4	**Warm-up** (10 min.) • Actividad 17 • Homework check • **Formative Assessment** (10 min.) • Prueba 2-3 with Remediation: Pretérito vs. imperfecto	**Gramática y vocabulario en uso 1** (50 min.) • Presentation: *Estar* + participio • Interactive Whiteboard Grammar Activities • Actividades 19, 20, 21, 22 • El español en la comunidad • Communicative Pair Activity **Vocabulario en contexto 2** (15 min.) • Presentation: Vocabulario y gramática en contexto • Actividades 23, 24	**Wrap-up and Homework Options** (5 min.) • Core Practice 2-6, 2-7 • Prueba 2-4 with Remediation: *Estar* + participio • Examen: Vocabulario y gramática 1
5	**Warm-up** (10 min.) • Writing Activity • Homework check • **Formative Assessment** (40 min.) • Prueba 2-4 with Remediation: *Estar* + participio • Examen: Vocabulario y gramática 1	**Vocabulario en contexto 2** (20 min.) • Presentation: Espectáculos del mundo latino • Actividades 25, 26, 27 **Vocabulario en uso 2** (15 min.) • Actividades 30, 31 • Interactive Whiteboard Vocabulary Activities	**Wrap-up and Homework Options** (5 min.) • Core Practice 2-8, 2-9 • Prueba 2-5: Vocabulary recognition
6	**Warm-up** (20 min.) • Actividades 28, 29 • Homework check • **Formative Assessment** (10 min.) • Prueba 2-5: Vocabulary recognition	**Gramática y vocabulario en uso 2** (55 min.) • Presentation: Ser y estar • Actividades 32, 33, 34, 35 • Interactive Whiteboard Grammar Activities • Cultura • En voz alta • Writing Activities	**Wrap-up and Homework Options** (5 min.) • Core Practice 2-10 • Pruebas 2-6, 2-7 with Remediation: Vocabulary production, ser y estar

ALTERNATE LESSON PLAN

DAY	Warm-up / Assess	Preview / Present / Practice / Communicate	Wrap-up / Homework Options
7	**Warm-up** (10 min.) • Homework check • **Formative Assessment** (20 min.) • Pruebas 2-6, 2-7 with Remediation: Vocabulary production, *ser y estar*	**Gramática y vocabulario en uso 2** (40 min.) • Presentation: Verbos con distinto sentido en el pretérito y en el imperfecto • Interactive Whiteboard Grammar Activities • Actividades 36, 37, 38, 39 • Cultura **Aplicación** (15 min.) • Presentación oral: Steps 1, 2	**Wrap-up and Homework Options** (5 min.) • Presentación oral: Step 2
8	**Warm-up** (10 min.) • Writing Activity • Homework check • **Formative Assessment** (40 min.) • Presentación oral: Step 3	**Gramática y vocabulario en uso 2** (20 min.) • Communicative Pair Activity **Aplicación** (15 min.) • Presentation: El mundo de Francisco de Goya	**Wrap-up and Homework Options** (5 min.) • Core Practice 2-11, 2-12 • Prueba 2-8 with Remediation: Verbos con distinto sentido en el pretérito y en el imperfecto • Examen: Vocabulario y gramática 2
9	**Warm-up** (10 min.) • Homework check • **Formative Assessment Options** (30 min.) • Prueba 2-8 with Remediation: Verbos con distinto sentido en el pretérito y en el imperfecto • Examen: Vocabulario y gramática 2	**Aplicación** (45 min.) • El mundo de Francisco de Goya • ¿Comprendiste? • Escribe tu opinión • Pre-AP® Integración 1, 2, 3 • Presentación escrita: Step 1 • Video • Video Activities	**Wrap-up and Homework Options** (5 min.) • Presentación escrita: Step 2 • Preparación para el examen: Actividades 1, 2
10	**Warm-up** (20 min.) • Presentación escrita: Step 3 • Homework check	**Aplicación** (35 min.) • Lectura • ¿Comprendiste? • Cultura • Auténtico **Repaso** (30 min.) • Preparación para el examen: Actividades 3, 4, 6	**Wrap-up and Homework Options** (5 min.) • Presentación escrita: Step 4 • Core Practice: Organizer 2-13, 2-14 • Instant Check • Preparación para el examen: Actividades 5, 7 • Examen del capítulo
11	**Warm-up** (10 min.) • Homework check • **Summative Assessment** (30 min.) • Examen del capítulo	**Theme Game** (15 min.) **A ver si recuerdas – Capítulo 3** (10 min.) • Presentation: Vocabulario • Presentation: Gramática	**Wrap-up and Homework Options** (5 min.) • A ver si recuerdas – Capítulo 3 • Actividades 1–6 • Core Practice 3-1, 3-2

Vocabulario: Repaso

Standards: 1.1, 2.2

Suggestions: Before presenting the material in this review section, consider testing your students' command of the material by assigning the Prueba with Remediation. Students will automatically be given additional practice of the material they have not yet mastered, and you can focus your review based on the class's overall performance on the post-test.

Call out vocabulary items from the six categories in random order. Have a volunteer use the item you call out to make a statement about one or both of the paintings.

1

Standards: 1.1

Suggestions: For Step 1, make sure students choose vocabulary from various categories, rather than just one or two. Point out that the sentence starters in Steps 2 and 3 are suggestions. Encourage students to experiment with other ways to incorporate the vocabulary in their paired discussion about the paintings.

Answers will vary.

Extension: During their discussion in pairs, ask students to write down their partner's comments about the paintings. Then have students take turns reporting their partners' comments to the class: *Victoria cree que el cuadro de Velásquez es....*

Teaching with Art

To guide the discussion of the painting ask: *¿Tiene el cuadro un estilo realista? ¿Puedes explicar tu respuesta? ¿Qué elementos encuentras interesantes? ¿Te gusta el cuadro? ¿Por qué?*

Active Classroom

Have a pair of students pantomime two people with contrasting characteristics. The class should guess what is being portrayed using comparatives, superlatives, and adjective agreement.

A ver si recuerdas

OBJECTIVES
▶ Discuss and express opinions about paintings
▶ Read and write about art and artists

Vocabulario

color y luz
amarillo, -a
anaranjado, -a
azul
blanco, -a
claro, -a
gris
marrón
morado, -a
negro, -a
oscuro, -a
pastel
rojo, -a
rosado, -a
verde
vivo, -a

opiniones
a mí también /
tampoco
creo que . . .
estoy / no estoy de
acuerdo
me parece que . . .
me gusta / no me
gusta
no estoy seguro, -a
para mí, ti . . .
¿qué te parece?

el arte y los artistas
el / la artista
el cuadro
dibujar
el estilo
la estatua
el museo
pintar
el pintor,
la pintora

descripciones
aburrido, -a
bonito, -a
complicado, -a
divertido, -a
exagerado, -a
fascinante
feo, -a
horrible
interesante
mejor
moderno, -a
peor
realista
sencillo, -a
serio, -a
triste

materiales
el oro
el papel
la piedra
el plástico
la plata

comparaciones
más / menos . . . que
mejor / peor . . . que
tan . . . como

1

El arte

 ESCRIBIR, HABLAR EN PAREJA

1 Haz una lista de diez palabras que describan la obra de arte.

2 Usa la información que escribiste para describir la pintura a tu compañero(a). Usa como guía las siguientes preguntas: ¿Cómo es? ¿Qué representa?

> El cuadro de . . . es . . .
>
> El cuadro de . . . representa . . .

3 Manda un mensaje de texto para intercambiar opiniones con tu compañero(a).

• Pregúntale su opinión.
¿Qué te parece . . . ?

• Expresa tu opinión.
Yo creo que el cuadro de . . .
No estoy de acuerdo . . . porque . . .

"Paisaje hondureño de San Antonio de Oriente", (1957),
José Antonio Velásquez
Oil on canvas. 26" x 37". Collection of the Art Museum of the Americas. Organization of American States.

64 sesenta y cuatro • Capítulo 2 • ¿Cómo te expresas?

Differentiated Instruction

Students with Learning Difficulties

Have students create their own visual clues to reinforce new vocabulary. As they choose and list adjectives in *Actividad* 1, encourage them to utilize simple drawings, colored pencils, or colored chalk to help reinforce the meanings of the descriptive words they have chosen.

Advanced Learners

Have students write a paragraph describing the scene in the Velásquez painting. Encourage them to study the painting closely in order to find real-world elements that Velásquez chose to portray. Have them list the elements they recognize.

Go Online to practice
PEARSON
realize™
WRITING SPEAK/RECORD

PearsonSchool.com/Autentico

Recycle 2

Gramática

Concordancia y comparación de adjetivos

Adjectives agree in gender and number with the persons or things they describe. Masculine adjectives usually end in -o and feminine adjectives usually end in -a.

   una estatua **moderna**   un cuadro **moderno**

• Adjectives that end in -e or in a consonant may be either feminine or masculine.

   un cuadro **interesante**   una estatua **gris**

• Adjectives that end in -ista may be either masculine or feminine.

   un dibujo **realista**   una pintora **surrealista**

• To form the feminine form of adjectives that end in -or, add -a at the end.

   un niño **trabajador**   una niña **trabajadora**

• If an adjective describes a combination of masculine and feminine nouns, the masculine plural ending is used.

   Ese cuadro y esa estatua no son **feos.**

To express a comparison of similarity, use *tan* + adjective + *como.*

   El cuadro de Picasso es **tan bonito como** el cuadro de Velásquez.

To express a comparison of difference, use *más / menos* + adjective + *que.*

   El cuadro de Dalí me parece **más / menos abstracto que** el de Miró.

• These adjectives have irregular comparative forms. The words *más / menos* are not used.

| bueno(a) | **mejor (que)** | viejo(a) | **mayor (que)** |
| malo(a) | **peor (que)** | joven | **menor (que)** |

El museo de arte

LEER, ESCRIBIR Completa el diálogo con la forma correcta de los adjetivos del recuadro.

complicado	exagerado
moderno	fascinante
plástico	

A —Ayer fui a un museo de arte __1.__ y vi unos cuadros __2.__. Me gustaron mucho. Sin embargo, las estatuas de __3.__ son __4.__.

B —¿Sí? Pues yo no entiendo el arte moderno. Es muy __5.__.

En mi opinión

ESCRIBIR Usa los adjetivos para escribir un texto de cinco frases que comparen dos obras de arte. Usa *más / menos . . . que* o *tan . . . como.*

serio	moderno
realista	sencillo
bonito	

Modelo
*El cuadro de Velásquez me parece **tan interesante como** el cuadro de Picasso.*

Gramática: Repaso

Suggestions: Refer students who are having difficulty with comparisons to the *GramActiva* video from Level 2 Chapter 1B, and to the online tutorial. After students review the Gramática, write several different adjectives on the board, one at a time. Point to one adjective and say different nouns. Have students use the adjective to modify each noun, making sure it agrees in gender and number each time.

2

Standards: 1.2

Suggestions: Remind students that in noun phrases such as ***museo de arte,*** they must consider which noun is being modified in order to know which adjective form to use. In this case, since both nouns are masculine, the same adjective form can be used for either noun. But in a noun phrase such as ***sala de cuadros,*** they must decide whether they are modifying ***sala*** or ***cuadros.***

Answers:
1. moderno
2. fascinantes
3. plástico
4. exageradas
5. complicado

3

Standards: 1.1

Suggestions: Since students are comparing one ***cuadro*** with another each time, the adjective forms for the activity will all be masculine singular. This allows students to focus on the constructions ***más/menos...que*** and ***tan...como.***
Answers will vary.

Enrich Your Teaching

Teacher-to-Teacher

Display several works of art of varying styles and periods. These might be reproductions of paintings or photographs of sculptures, ceramics, or other kinds of art. Ask students to select two works of art to compare and not to reveal their choices to anyone.

Have them write sentences describing and comparing the two works of art, but not to mention either of them by name. Invite students to take turns sharing their sentences. Ask the rest of the class to decide which two works of art are being described and compared.

Starter Activity

Use the verbs in the *reacciones* section of the vocabulary to help students review the preterite. Assign each student a subject pronoun to work with, such as *nosotros* or *tu amigo y tú.* Have students use their subject and one or more of the verbs to create and share sentences about an entertainment event: *¿Tu amigo y tú se aburrieron en el concierto?*

Vocabulario: Repaso

Standards: 1.1

Suggestions: Begin by having students use the vocabulary to talk about the photos. Then play *5 preguntas*—a shortened version of 20 Questions. Each student chooses a word or expression and takes a turn at being "it." Other students ask up to five *Sí/No* questions to try to determine what the word is: *¿Es una persona? ¿Esta persona canta?*

 4

Standards: 1.2, 1.3

Suggestions: Tell students to look over the complete *mensaje* in Step 1 before writing their answers.

Answers:

Step 1

1. argumento   4. actor
2. comedia   5. galán
3. drama   6. aplaudió

Step 2

Answers will vary.

Extension: Help students practice the vocabulary under the *reacciones* and *comentarios* categories. Have them write and read aloud dialogues of two to three lines in which two people talk about an entertainment event. Provide a model like the following:

— *Anoche vi una obra de teatro inolvidable.*

—*¿Sí? ¿Te divertiste?*

— *¡Muchísimo! Después, aplaudí durante cinco minutos con todo el público.*

A ver si recuerdas

OBJECTIVES
▶ Read and write about a theater performance
▶ Discuss performing arts and compare artists

Vocabulario

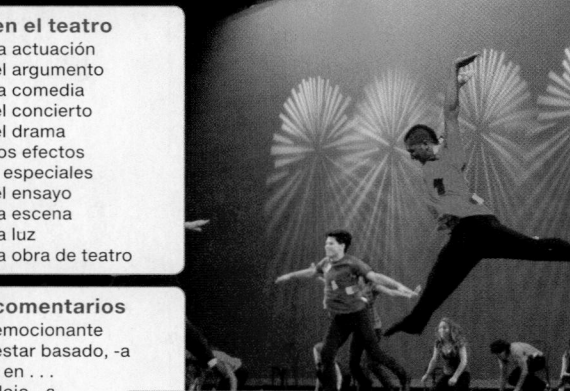

en el teatro
la actuación
el argumento
la comedia
el concierto
el drama
los efectos
  especiales
el ensayo
la escena
la luz
la obra de teatro

comentarios
emocionante
estar basado, -a
  en . . .
flojo, -a
increíble
inolvidable
largo, -a
más o menos
talentoso, -a

en el concierto
el auditorio
la banda
la canción
el coro
la música
la orquesta
la voz

participantes
el actor, la actriz
el bailarín,
  la bailarina
el / la cantante
el crítico, la crítica
el director,
  la directora
el galán
el músico, la música
el personaje

actividades
bailar
cantar
ensayar
hacer el papel de . . .
hacer el papel
  principal
tener éxito
tocar . . .
  la guitarra
  el piano

reacciones
aburrirse
aplaudir
divertirse
dormirse
gritar

4

En el teatro

LEER, ESCRIBIR

1 Completa el siguiente mensaje usando las palabras del recuadro.

| galán | drama | aplaudió | argumento | comedia | actor |

Anoche fui al teatro. Desde el principio, el de la obra me pareció muy divertido. Prefiero ir al teatro a reír con una 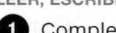 que llorar con un __3.__. El  que hacía el papel del __5.__ tuvo una actuación extraordinaria. Al final, el público __6.__ por más de cinco minutos.

2 Usa las palabras del vocabulario para escribir una descripción de estas personas. Incluye lo que hace la persona y dónde lo hace.

Modelo
un actor
Un actor hace el papel de un personaje en una película o una obra de teatro.

1. un(a) músico(a)   3. un(a) cantante
2. un(a) crítico(a)   4. un bailarín, una bailarina

Differentiated Instruction

Heritage Speakers

Have students write a description of a performing arts event that they have seen either in the United States or in their heritage country. Encourage them to use specific descriptive language in order to elaborate on each detail presented. Those who have not recently seen a performing arts event can describe one they would most like to see.

Musical Learner

Encourage students to prepare a short selection of music to share with the class. They might play an instrument, sing a song, or bring in a favorite recording. Use these as the basis for the descriptions and comparisons in *Actividad* 6 on p. 67.

Gramática

Comparación de sustantivos y el superlativo

To make a comparison or differentiation between two nouns, use *más / menos* + noun + *que.*

> Hoy hay **menos gente que** ayer en el teatro.

To make a comparison between two similar nouns, use: *tanto(a)* + noun + *como.* Since *tanto* is an adjective, it should agree with the noun in both gender (masculine or feminine) and number (singular or plural).

> Hoy hay **tanto público como** ayer en el teatro.

> Hoy hay **tantas personas como** ayer en el teatro.

The superlative is used to say something is the "most" or the "least." To express a superlative comparison use: *el / la / los / las* + noun + *más / menos* + adjective.

> **El concierto más emocionante** fue el de ayer.

> Para mí, **la obra menos divertida** es "Algún día".

- When *mejor* and *peor* are used as superlatives, the following construction is used: *el / la / los / las* + *mejor(es) / peor(es)* + noun.

> Pienso que Alejandra Ruiz es **la mejor bailarina.**

> ¡Ustedes son **los peores cantantes**!

- The preposition *de* is used after the adjective when the superlative comparison occurs within a group or category.

> El concierto de ayer fue **el más emocionante de** todos.

5

¿Qué opinas?

HABLAR EN PAREJA Un(a) compañero(a) y tú van a expresar su opinión sobre los siguientes temas.

Modelo
la mejor película del año
A —*Para ti, ¿cuál fue la mejor película del año?*
B —*Para mí, la mejor película fue "Relatos salvajes". El director es fantástico.*

a. el mejor actor de teatro
b. la peor actriz de Hollywood
c. la canción más romántica de este año
d. el baile que les gusta más a los jóvenes
e. el programa de tele más aburrido de la semana

6

La fiesta

ESCRIBIR Escribe comparaciones entre dos artistas o grupos de música. Usa los siguientes temas.

- número de canciones que grabaron
- talento que tienen
- instrumentos que tocan

Modelo
Shakira tiene más canciones en español que Jennifer López.

Enrich Your Teaching

Teacher-to-Teacher

Ask students to form small groups based on topics of shared interest. Have them talk about their common interest and create a few comparative and superlative statements about it to share with the class.

21st Century Skills

ICT (Information, Communications and Technology) Literacy Direct students to the online tutorials available in **Realize** for self-directed review of the grammar topics recycled in this chapter. Students can expand their own learning by reviewing the related English grammar first, then proceed to the new Spanish grammar point.

Gramática: Repaso

Suggestions: Refer students who are having difficulty with superlatives to the *GramActiva* video from Level 1 Chapter 6A, and to the online tutorial. On the board, write the frames for the two constructions:

más/menos + noun + *que*
el/la/los/las + noun + *más/menos* + adj.

Fill the frames with different nouns and adjectives from p. 50 that make sense and have students create sentences using the results: *Hay más público que actores en el teatro. Los bailarines son los más talentosos de todos.*

5

Standards: 1.3

Suggestions: For further practice, have students think of additional categories for their comparisons.

Answers will vary.

6

Standards: 1.1

Suggestions: Partners might share opinions or discuss their differing opinions. After they have gone through the list together, invite them to share their opinions with the rest of the class.

Answers will vary.

Extension: Ask students to collect the opinions of the class and compile the information in a chart. Consider keeping this chart and bringing it out again a few months from now to see how students' opinions have changed.

Additional Resources

 Technology: Online Resources
- *A ver si recuerdas* with Remediation
- Guided, Core
- *Para hispanohablantes*

Print
- Guided WB pp. 48–51
- Core WB pp. 21–22

Assessment

***A ver si recuerdas* with Remediation (online only)**
After presenting the review material on these pages, assign the *A ver si recuerdas* with Remediation to evaluate students' mastery of the material. Additional practice for students who need it is available online.

Can-do Statements

Read the Can-Do statements in the chapter objectives with students. Then, have students read Preparación para el examen on page 111 to preview what they will be able to do at the end of the chapter.

Standards for Capítulo 2

To meet the Standards, students will:

COMMUNICATION

1.1 Interpersonal
- Talk about the style, features, tools, and media used in the creation of works of visual, literary, and performing art
- Talk about important artists and art museums
- Talk about events in the past

1.2 Interpretive
- Read and listen to information about the style, features, tools, and media used in the creation of works of visual, literary, and performing art
- Read and listen to information about important artists
- Read about the suffix -ismo
- Read about a family party
- Read about art museums
- Read arts and entertainment reviews
- Read about events in the past
- Read song lyrics by Juan Luis Guerra

1.3 Presentational
- Write about the style, tools, and media used in the creation of visual, literary, and performing art
- Write and present information orally about artists
- Write arts and entertainment reviews
- Present orally about "the artist of the year"
- Write a review of a student audition

CULTURE

2.1 Practices to Perspectives
- Explain the practices and perspectives of important Latin American and Spanish figures in the arts

2.2 Products to Perspectives
- Discuss the work of important Latin American and Spanish figures in the visual, literary, and performing arts
- Talk about Museo del Barrio and its cultural roots
- Talk about the popular TV show *Sábado Gigante*
- Describe *salsa* music
- Discuss the song lyrics of Juan Luis Guerra

CONNECTIONS

3.1 Making Connections
- Talk about key facts about the fine arts
- Talk about key facts about the Mexican Revolution
- Talk about key facts about the history of Spain
- Discuss Language Arts strategies: using illustrations, using context clues, using visuals, organizing information, categorizing, monitoring your reading

---

CAPÍTULO 2

¿Cómo te expresas?

Country Connection Explorar del mundo hispano

España
Nueva York
Cuba
México
Puerto Rico
El Salvador
Chile
Argentina

CHAPTER OBJECTIVES

Communication

By the end of the chapter you will be able to:
- Listen and read about art and music
- Talk and write about music and theater performances
- Discuss and explain art school activities

Culture

You will also be able to:
- Compare how artists express their ideas
- Understand the historical context of a famous artist
- Understand the perspective of a person living between cultures
- Compare cultural practices in an authentic video about Mexican Talavera pottery.

You will demonstrate what you know and can do
- Presentación oral, "Artista del Año"
- Presentación escrita, El mejor candidato
- Preparación para el examen

You will use

Vocabulary
- Art forms, genres, materials and professions
- Works of art and artists
- Performing arts: Music, dance, stage

Grammar
- Preterite vs. imperfect
- Verb *estar* + participle
- *Ser* and *estar*
- Verbs with different meanings in the imperfect and preterite

ARTE y CULTURA ◄ España

Picasso y el cubismo Observa esta pintura del artista español Pablo Picasso (1881–1973). Vas a notar que el artista representa a la modelo, a la izquierda, y al pintor, a la derecha, con formas geométricas. Esta forma de expresión se conoce como cubismo, un movimiento artístico que comenzó en Francia y tuvo gran importancia en Europa y los Estados Unidos.

Pre-AP® Integration: Las artes visuales y escénicas ¿Cómo refleja el cubismo la perspectiva cultural de Europa o los Estados Unidos?

🌐 **Mapa global interactivo** Explora Málaga, España, e investiga la relación de Pablo Picasso con su ambiente.

"El pintor y su modelo", (1928), Pablo Picasso
Oil on canvas, 51 1/8 x 64 1/4 inches. The Sidney and Harriet Janis Collection, #644.19. © 2016 Estate of Pablo Picasso/Artists Rights Society (ARS), New York. Photo: © The Museum of Modern Art/Scala/Art Resource, NY.

68 sesenta y ocho • Capítulo 2 • ¿Cómo te expresas?

Enrich Your Teaching

The End in Mind

Have students preview the sample performance tasks on *Preparación para el examen,* p. 111, and connect them to the Chapter Objectives. Explain to students that by completing the sample tasks, they can self-assess their learning progress.

Technology: Mapa global interactivo

Download the *Mapa global interactivo* files for Chapter 2 and preview the activities. Activity 1 takes you to the Picasso Museum in Málaga, Spain. In Activity 2, you explore the world of Salvador Dalí in Spain. In Activity 3, discover the theaters of Madrid, Spain. In Activity 4, look at migration patterns from Puerto Rico to the United States.

Clase de música del proyecto juvenil *Por mi Barrio* en San Salvador, El Salvador

 Videonovela **¡Pura vida!**

Capítulo 2 • sesenta y nueve **69**

Project-Based Learning

Un nuevo ídolo

As students work through the chapter during the week, ask them to imagine that they will take part in a local dance contest. Have them make a list of things that they would need in order to win the contest, such as picking a song, coming up with an interesting choreography, choosing the right outfit, etc., and share it with a classmate. Encourage them to be very creative. Have them use this activity to complete the *Presentación oral* on page 99.

3.2 Acquiring information and Diverse Perspectives
• Read a famous slogan from the Mexican Revolution
• Read an advertisement for El Museo del Barrio
• Read about the cultural significance of the term *salsa*
• Read song lyrics by Juan Luis Guerra
• Read an excerpt from a work by Esmeralda Santiago

COMPARISONS

4.1 Language
• Compare Spanish words to their English counterparts
• Compare Spanish comparatives, superlatives to English
• Compare the uses of English and Spanish past tenses

4.2 Cultural
• Compare growing up in one culture to growing up in more than one culture
• Compare Goya's paintings to those of student's own world

COMMUNITIES

5.1. School and Global Communities
• Link to Web sites from the Spanish-speaking world

5.2 Lifelong Learning
• Develop an appreciation for artistic role models
• Develop an appreciation for the fine arts
• Recognize sources of artistic inspiration
• Discuss how culture impacts personality
• Read an authentic Spanish-language text

Chapter Opener

Resources: Mapa global interactivo: Regional maps

Suggestions: Introduce students to the theme and objectives of the chapter.

 Technology: Videocultura *¡Pura vida!* View this stand-alone storyline video about five young adults i San José, Costa Rica.

ARTE Y CULTURA

Standards: 1.1, 1.2, 2.2, 3.1

Resources: Map of Spain.

Technology: Mapa global interactivo, Actividad 1 Locate the Picasso Museum in Málaga,Spain.

Suggestions: Have volunteers point to various parts of the painting and say what they think they portray. Review the vocabulary of colors, shapes, and physical location so students are better able to describe the artwork.

Answers will vary, but may include American cubists such as Stuart Davis, Alfred Maurer, or Max Weber.

Teaching with Art

To guide the discussion of the painting, ask: *¿Qué puedes ver en el cuadro? ¿Qué estilo de arte es? ¿Qué elementos te interesan? ¿Te gusta el cuadro? ¿Por qué?*

Vocabulario en contexto 1

Standards: 1.2

Resources: Teacher's Resource Materials: Input Script, Clip Art, Audio Script, Technology: Audio, Cap. 2

Suggestions: Use the Input Script from the *Teacher's Resource Materials* as a source of ideas for presentation of new vocabulary and comprehensible input. Use pantomime to clarify the meaning of the adjectives **sentado(a)** and **parado(a).** For objects, use TPR. Name an object on the transparency and ask a volunteer to come and point to it. Point out that **mural, famoso(a), abstracto(a), expresar,** and **representar** are cognates.

Starter Activity

Show the painting *"El pintor y su modelo"* by Picasso, on page 68, and lead a class discussion about how many people they believe they are seeing in the painting. Mention/Point out body parts to confirm.

Technology: Interactive Whiteboard

Vocabulary Activites 2-1 Use the whiteboard activities in your Teacher Resources as you progress through the vocabulary practice with your class.

Vocabulario en contexto 1

Vocabulario en contexto 1

OBJECTIVES
Read, listen to, and understand information about
▶ Different types of art
▶ Art materials
▶ Works of art

Estrategia
Context clues When you read, try to determine the meaning of unknown words by looking at other words in the same sentence or surrounding sentences. For example, the words "él lo pintó" may help you understand that **autorretrato** is a self portrait.

 ### Arte para todos

Este fin de semana mis amigos y yo fuimos al centro para ver **obras de arte** hispanas en el museo. Había **pinturas** y **esculturas** de varios artistas **famosos** del **siglo** XX y algunas fotos de los artistas, también.

escultura abstracta

la naturaleza muerta

pincel

paleta

autorretrato

sentada

Vimos una escultura **abstracta** de Joana Vasconcelos que me fascinó y un **retrato** de Salvador Dalí, más bien un **autorretrato**, pues él lo pintó. Había una foto de la escultora argentina Dina Bursztyn **sentada** en su **taller** y otro de Fernando Botero **parado** delante de una obra suya, con **paleta** y **pincel**. También tenían una **naturaleza muerta** de Joan Miró.

70 setenta • Capítulo 2 • ¿Cómo te expresas?

Differentiated Instruction

Advanced Learners

Ask students to work together to draw and label the floor plan of the art room in your school. Encourage them to include details such as furniture, art supplies, and the various types of art that are currently on display or projects that are in progress. Then have them share the floor plan with the rest of the class. They can point out the various features of the room, tell where each of them works when they are in art class, and talk about art projects they may be currently involved in. Listeners can join in and talk about their own experiences in the art room.

El día **se volvió** aun más interesante cuando fuimos al festival de arte cerca del museo. Había muchas obras interesantes. Varias personas participaban en un proyecto muy especial: pintar un gran **mural** en el parque. Los artistas no son profesionales, pero su arte **representa** muchos estilos diferentes y **expresa** sus **sentimientos** personales. Compré una pintura hermosa con un árbol en **primer plano** y el mar en **el fondo**.

retrato
pintura

mural

fondo

primer plano

1

El festival de arte

 ESCUCHAR Escribe los números del 1 al 6 en una hoja de papel. Escucha cada frase y escribe *C* (cierto) o *F* (falso) según las fotos y la información de la lectura. Vas a oír cada frase dos veces.

2

En el museo de arte

ESCUCHAR Escucha la descripción de las obras de arte. Señala cada obra que se describe.

Capítulo 2 • setenta y uno **71**

1

Standards: 1.2

Resources: Teacher's Resource Materials: Audio Script, Technology: Audio, Cap. 2

Suggestions: Allow students a few minutes to reread pp. 70–71. Then play the audio or read the script aloud.

 Technology: Audio Script and Answers

1. Cuando vas a un festival de arte tienes la oportunidad de comprar las obras. *(C)*
2. Algunas personas pintaron un autorretrato. *(F)*
3. Varias personas pintaban un mural. *(C)*
4. Muchos pintores usan una paleta y un pincel. *(C)*
5. Había fotos de unos artistas en su taller. *(C)*
6. Solo los pintores y escultores famosos pueden participar en un festival de arte. *(F)*

2

Standards: 1.2

Resources: Teacher's Resource Materials: Audio Script, Technology: Audio, Cap. 2

Suggestions: Use the audio or read the script. Allow students to listen more than once.

Technology: Audio Script and Answers

1. Es la cara de un famoso artista pintada por él. (autorretrato)
2. Es una obra abstracta que la escultora está haciendo. (escultura abstracta)
3. Es la foto de un pintor en su taller. (pintor con pincel y paleta)
4. Es una obra de arte que varias personas están pintando. (mural)
5. Es una pintura con un árbol en primer plano. (la niña con una pintura)

Active Classroom

Have students draw a self-portrait. Then form small groups and have students ask questions about their art.

Pre-AP® Integration

- **Learning Objective:** Interpersonal Speaking
- **Activity:** Have students work in pairs to recreate the dialogue on page 72. Then record the dialogues and use them for dictation later.
- **Pre-AP® Resource Materials:** Comprehensive guide to Pre-AP® vocabulary skill development

---

Enrich Your Teaching

Culture Note

In addition to being a painter and sculptor, Joan Miró was also a printmaker. In 1938, he completed *The Black and Red Series,* a series of eight etchings. Now at the Museum of Modern Art in New York, the series shows the unique characteristics of this printing process.

21st Century Skills

Media Literacy Have students research other works by Joan Miró on the Internet. What keywords will they use in their search? Ask them to investigate different styles and mediums employed by the artist, as well as any works by Miró in museums in their area.

Vocabulario en contexto 1

Standards: 1.2

Resources: Teacher's Resource Materials: Input Script, Clip Art Audio Script, Technology: Audio, Cap. 2

Suggestions

Pre-reading: Remind students that, with the amount of Spanish they now know, they can use context clues as they read, in much the same way as they do in English.

Reading: Allow students time to read the dialogue silently first. Then play the audio or read the dialogue aloud, with students reading along as they listen. Allow them to listen more than once.

Post-reading: Complete *Actividad* 3 to check comprehension.

3

Standards: 1.2

Suggestions: Allow the students to listen to the audio once through first. Then, play it again. Pause after each phrase so they can write their answers.

 **Technology: Audio**

(See Teacher's Resource Materials for the complete script.)
Answers: 1. F   **2.** C   **3.** C   **4.** C

4

Standards: 1.1

Resources: Teacher's Resource Materials:
Suggestions: Have students to share the descriptions of their plates.
Answers will vary.

5

Standards: 1.1

Suggestions: Tell students to discuss color and light as well as the subject matter of the paintings.
Answers will vary.

Project-Based Learning

Give students copies of the project outline and rubric from the *Teacher's Resource Materials.* Explain the task to them, and have them perform Step 1. (For more information, see p. 64-b.)

 Clara toma clases de **cerámica** en el taller del profesor Torres. Hoy están hablando sobre las cerámicas que se hacen en Puebla, una ciudad de México.

Clara / Professor Torres

Profesor Torres:	**A través** de la cerámica, los artistas mexicanos **muestran** muchos aspectos de la cultura de su país. La cerámica de Puebla es parte de un **movimiento** artístico muy interesante.
Clara:	¡A mí me encanta este tipo de cerámica! Sus colores y **figuras** son increíbles.
Profesor Torres:	Así es. Mira estos platos. ¿Cuál crees que fue la **fuente de inspiración** para el artista?
Clara:	¡Las flores de México! Este país tiene flores muy lindas.
Profesor Torres:	De acuerdo. Fíjate en el plato de arriba. ¿Cómo se representan las flores aquí?
Clara:	De manera simétrica. Y por los colores azul y blanco, el artista se debió **inspirar** en las cerámicas de Talavera, que se hacen en España.
Profesor Torres:	Así es. España **influyó** mucho en este tipo de cerámica. ¿Y qué me dices de los otros dos platos?
Clara:	Las **imágenes** del plato de la mitad son realistas. Se ven claramente las flores. Las del plato de abajo son más abstractas.
Profesor Torres:	Exacto. Los tres platos tienen el **tema** de las flores pero con un estilo diferente.

3

Las cerámicas de México

 ESCUCHAR Escribe los números del 1 al 4 en una hoja. Escucha cada frase y escribe *C* (cierto) si la frase es correcta o *F* (falso) si la frase es falsa.

4

Los platos de Puebla

 HABLAR EN PAREJA Habla con un compañero(a). Elige el plato que más te guste y descríbelo. Explica por qué lo elegiste.

5

Festival de arte

 ESCRIBIR Vas a participar en un festival de arte. Escoge 5 obras que vas a incluir. Descríbelas en detalle.

72 setenta y dos • Capítulo 2 • ¿Cómo te expresas?

Differentiated Instruction

Heritage Speakers

Have students conduct an interview with a Spanish-speaking professional whose work they respect. Encourage them to prepare questions and to record the interview. Invite them to share the interview with the class.

Students with Learning Difficulties

Direct students to read for specific information about each of the artists presented. Have them create a simple chart with the following headings: ***nombre del artista, país, material, tema.*** Then have students fill in the chart with key points found in the reading.

Una mirada al arte de los mayas

Antes de ver

Usar experiencias previas Piensa en las obras de arte que ves en un museo. Piensa también en los libros, fotos y otros materiales que te ayudan a aprender de los grandes pintores y escultores del pasado. Tus experiencias previas te ayudarán a inferir palabras o frases desconocidas que encontrarás en este video.

Haz la actividad

El arte de los mayas Estas fotos muestran obras de arte hechas por la cultura maya, de México. Haz una lista de palabras en español que ya sabes para describir cada obra.

▶ Ve el video

Ximena y Seba comparten un gran interés hacia el arte. ¿De qué estarán hablando hoy? ¿Qué le mostrará Ximena a Seba?

Ve a **PearsonSchool.com/Autentico** para ver el video *Una mirada al arte de los mayas.* También puedes leer el guión.

Ximena   **Seba**

Después de ver

 ESCRIBIR Contesta las siguientes preguntas:

1. ¿Qué le muestra Ximena a Seba y porqué?
2. Identifica tres detalles claves *(key details)* sobre el arte de los mayas.
3. Usa las imágenes para inferir el significado del término "serpiente emplumada". Explica qué es en tus propias palabras.
4. ¿Qué opinión tiene Ximena sobre los dibujos que hace Seba? ¿Y a ti cómo te parecen?

Comparación cultural Compara el arte de los mayas con el de otra cultura indígena.

Capítulo 2 • setenta y tres **73**

Enrich Your Teaching

Culture Note

La serpiente emplumada, or feathered serpent, is one of the most prominent deities of the ancient cultures of Mesoamerica. Known as Kukulcán by the Mayas, Quetzalcóatl by the Aztecs, and Viracocha by the Incas, the feathered serpent is an iconoclastic symbol that is depicted in thousands of sculptures, buildings, paintings, and ceramics throughout the Americas.

21st Century Skills

Communication Ask students to discuss their favorite work of art. Encourage them to articulate their thoughts and ideas clearly and effectively. They should note the style, colors, or medium used by the artist, or the message expressed in their favorite work.

Tecnología: Video

Standards: 1.2

Resources: Teacher's Resource Materials: Video Script

Antes de ver

Review the previewing strategy and activity with the students. Activate their previous knowledge and experiences with fine art. Then ask students to describe each of the photos of Mayan art.

Ve el video

Show the video once without pausing. Ask volunteers to summarize the general idea of the video. For the second viewing, ask students to use the images to help them infer the meaning of unfamiliar words. Show the video again, stopping to check comprehension.

Después de ver

Standards: 1.2, 4.2

Suggestions: Invite students to paraphrase the theme and main idea of the video before answering the questions.

Answers

1. un video del arte de los mayas; piensa que a él le puede interesar
2. Answers will vary but may include: el estilo de los mayas se aprecia en sus murales y cerámicas; se inspira en la naturaleza; representa a sus dioses.
3. es como una serpiente con plumas
4. que los dibujos de Seba son muy lindos y únicos

Comparación cultural

Answers will vary.

Have students go to **Realize** for additional video activities.

Additional Resources

 Technology: Online Resources
- Instant Check
- Guided, Core, Video, Audio
- *Para hispanohablantes*

Print
- Guided WB pp. 52–58 • Core WB pp. 23–24

Assessment

Quiz: Vocabulary Recognition
- Prueba 2-1

6

Standards: 1.2, 1.3

Suggestions: Ask students to use the photos on pages 70–71 as a visual reference while they work on the activity.

Answers:

1. un taller
2. una naturaleza muerta
3. Un siglo
4. inspiración
5. mural

Starter Activity

Write these words on the board and have the class brainstorm items made from these materials: *el oro, la piedra, el plástico, la plata.*

7

Standards: 1.1

Suggestions: Make sure partners switch roles, so both can practice explaining the uses of the various items.

Answers:

1. **A** —El pintor usa una paleta y un pincel, ¿no?
   B —Sí, los usa para mezclar los colores.
2. **A** —Una escultora usa piedra, ¿no?
   B —Sí, la usa para crear una escultura.
3. **A** —Un(a) poeta usa papel y lápiz, ¿no?
   B —Sí, los usa para escribir sus poesías.
4. **A** —Un escritor usa una computadora, ¿no?
   B —Sí, la usa para escribir cuentos.

AMPLIACIÓN DEL LENGUAJE

Standards: 1.2, 4.1

Suggestions: Ask students to brainstorm other words they have heard that contain the *-ismo* suffix, such as *idealismo* or *modernismo.*

Answers:

impresionismo, realismo

Vocabulario en uso 1

OBJECTIVES
▶ Discuss art materials and details in paintings
▶ Talk about famous painters
▶ Write about artists and what influences them

6

Definiciones

LEER, ESCRIBIR Completa cada frase con una palabra o expresión apropiada del recuadro. Luego, escribe frases usando las palabras del recuadro.

una naturaleza muerta   inspiración   un taller   mural   un siglo

1. Los artistas generalmente trabajan en _____ .
2. Un cuadro que representa objetos, frutas o comida es _____ .
3. _____ son cien años.
4. Un artista necesita _____ para crear su obra.
5. Cuando la pintura se hace en una pared, se llama _____.

7

¿La paleta o el pincel?

HABLAR EN PAREJA En el taller de arte, los estudiantes usan diferentes materiales para crear sus obras. Lea la pregunta modelo, entonces pregunta a un(a) compañero(a) sobre lo que usa los artistas. Él o ella responde con lo que usa cada artista y para qué lo usa.

Videomodelo
los niños
A —*Los niños usan **tijeras**, ¿no?*
B —*Sí, las usan para **cortar papel**.*

Estudiante A

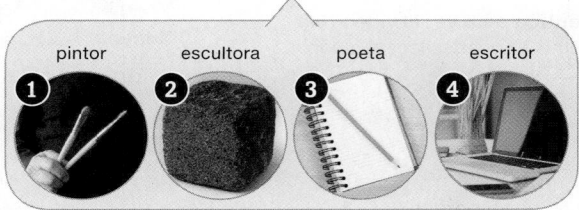

pintor   escultora   poeta   escritor
1   2   3   4

Estudiante B

¡Respuesta personal!

Ampliación del lenguaje

El sufijo *-ismo* se usa para nombrar una doctrina o un movimiento artístico. Para hablar de los pintores que hacen pinturas *románticas,* usamos la palabra *romanticismo.* Otros ejemplos son:

cubo → **cubismo**   futuro → **futurismo**   surreal → **surrealismo**

Completa cada frase.

Un pintor dijo que quería pintar la *impresión* que tenía del paisaje, por eso llamaron al movimiento __1.__ . Otros querían pintar la vida *real*, y llamaron a su movimiento __2.__ .

74 setenta y cuatro • Capítulo 2 • ¿Cómo te expresas?

Differentiated Instruction

Spatial Learner

Have students create a painting or drawing in the style of Miró, Picasso, Velázquez, or one of the other artists discussed in the chapter. Use these "original" works of art to supplement partner discussions in *Actividad* 9 on p. 75.

Advanced Learners

Have students prepare and present detailed descriptions of artistic processes such as writing a story, making a ceramic sculpture, painting a mural, or writing a song. Ask them to describe the process step by step. Remind them to use sequencing words such as **primero, segundo, después,** and **finalmente** to help listeners understand their presentations.

8

La inspiración de un joven artista

LEER, ESCRIBIR Lee la siguiente entrevista con el pintor chileno Alfonso Fernández. Después, observa el cuadro de este artista y contesta las preguntas.

Pintor chileno ⟩ Alfonso Fernández

¿Qué te gustaba hacer cuando eras joven?
"Desde joven me gustaba dibujar más que salir a bailar. Hasta los 15 años, los temas históricos fueron mi fuente de inspiración".

¿Qué artista influyó en tu obra y por qué?
"Cuando empecé a estudiar arte me inspiré en la obra del famoso pintor español Goya, porque a través de su

obra criticó el momento político y cultural en que vivió".

¿De qué época era Goya?
"Goya era del siglo XIX".

¿En qué se parece tu obra a la de Goya?
"Goya, como yo, representó al pueblo *(common people)* en su obra".

¿Qué consejo le puedes dar a un joven artista? "Es importante expresar tus sentimientos en tu obra".

"Naturaleza muerta", (1999), Alfonso Fernández

1. ¿Qué temas inspiraban a Fernández cuando era joven?

2. Más tarde, ¿qué artista influyó en su arte? ¿Cuándo vivió ese artista? ¿En qué se parecen el arte de ese artista y el de Fernández?

3. ¿Qué cree Fernández que debe hacer un joven artista?

4. ¿Tú te expresas a través del arte? ¿Cómo? ¿A través del dibujo, de la pintura o de la escultura? ¿Cuáles son tus fuentes de inspiración?

9

Describe el cuadro

HABLAR EN PAREJA Diego Rodríguez de Silva y Velázquez (1599–1660) fue el pintor de la corte del rey Felipe IV de España. "Las Meninas", un retrato de la familia real, es su obra maestra. Trabaja con otro(a) estudiante para hablar de los detalles de este cuadro. Usen las siguientes expresiones con gestos apropiados. También hablan en una manera casual, pero no muy informal.

Videomodelo
A —*¿Qué se ve a la derecha de la niña rubia?*
B —*Se ve la figura de un perro sentado.*

▲ "Las Meninas", (1656), Diego Velázquez

Estudiante A
1. en el centro, a la izquierda
2. al fondo, en la puerta
3. en primer plano
4. a la izquierda de la niña rubia
5. en la pared del fondo

Estudiante B
el pintor, parado con los pinceles y la paleta
una niña rubia de pelo largo
un hombre
un cuadro
una joven que le ofrece algo

8

Standards: 1.2, 1.3, 2.2, 3.1, 5.2

Suggestions: Remind students to pay attention to Fernández's use of the preterite and imperfect tenses.

Answers:
1. Los temas históricos lo inspiraban.
2. Goya lo influyó más tarde. Goya era del siglo XIX. Los dos artistas representan al pueblo.
3. Debe expresar sus sentimientos en su obra.
4. Answers will vary.

9

Standards: 1.1, 2.2, 3.1

Suggestions: Have students switch roles in order to practice both questioning and answering. Encourage them to elaborate on the speaking cues they are given.

Answers:
1. A —¿Qué se ve en el centro, a la izquierda?
   B —Se ve al pintor, parado con los pinceles y la paleta.
2. A —...al fondo, en la puerta?
   B —...a un hombre.
3. A —...en primer plano?
   B —...a una niña rubia de pelo largo.
4. A —...a la izquierda de la niña rubia?
   B —...a una joven que le ofrece algo.
5. A —...en la pared del fondo?
   B —Se ve un cuadro (espejo).

Enrich Your Teaching

Culture Note

Even master painters are influenced and inspired by others. Pablo Picasso, for example, was clearly influenced by the work of other Spanish masters. The connection between Picasso's portraits, such as "Lady in Blue," and the work of Diego de Silva y Velázquez is evident.

Similarly, much of the work during Picasso's Blue Period is reminiscent of the paintings of El Greco in terms of composition and style. The link between Picasso's *"Guernica"* and Goya's theme of the horror of war is also clear.

10

Suggestions: Have students refer to the photos in the student book. Have them look over the questions in *Actividad* 11 before they begin the game.

Answers will vary.

11

Suggestions: Have students answer the questions in Step 2 as a list first, before attempting to organize this information into a written comparison.

Answers:
1. Los dos artistas son de España.
2. Pintaron en el siglo XX.
3–6. Answers will vary.
7. Es arte surrealista (abstracto).
8–9. Answers will vary.

COUNTRY CONNECTION

Ask students to research on the Internet the hometowns of Joan Miró (*Barcelona, Cataluña*) and Salvador Dalí (*Figueras, Cataluña*). Have them locate these places on a map.

 Technology: Mapa global interactivo, Actividad 2 Discover Sevilla, Spain and the Explore the world of Salvador Dalí in Spain.

Teacher-to-Teacher

Have students write a note in which they express their preference for one of the two paintings in *Actividad* 11. They will then exchange notes with a partner who will respond in writing to the preference that was stated.

10

Juego

🎤 **HABLAR EN PAREJA** Escoge una de las obras de arte que se encuentran en las páginas 70 a 72. No se la muestres a tu compañero(a). Tu compañero(a) te va a hacer preguntas como las que están al final de la Actividad 11 y va a intentar adivinar la obra. ¡Después, cambien los papeles!

11

Los mundos de Miró y de Dalí

 LEER, ESCRIBIR

1 Lee este artículo sobre los artistas surrealistas Joan Miró y Salvador Dalí.

2 Ahora contesta las siguientes preguntas y usa las respuestas para escribir una comparación de los dos cuadros.

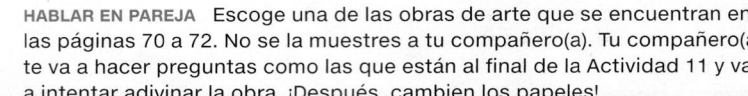

Los artistas > Surrealistas Salvador Dalí y Joan Miró

El movimiento surrealista empezó poco después de la Primera Guerra Mundial. Los pintores del surrealismo se inspiraban en temas de su propia imaginación. Querían capturar en sus cuadros ideas e imágenes del subconsciente (*subconscious*), como las que vemos en los sueños. El español Salvador Dalí (1904–1989) fue uno de los pintores más famosos de este grupo.

"Escaleras cruzan ▶ el cielo azul en una rueda de fuego", (1953), Joan Miró

Como muchos otros artistas, el español Joan Miró (1893–1983) se fue a París a principios de los años veinte. Allí lo influyeron los surrealistas, aunque su estilo es más abstracto que el de Salvador Dalí. Además, Miró usa colores vivos y figuras que recuerdan a los dibujos de un niño. Su obra es una fiesta de imaginación y colores.

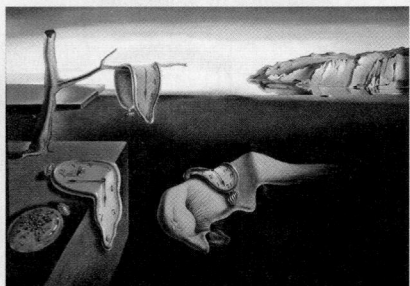

"La persistencia de la memoria", (1931), Salvador Dalí ▲

1. ¿De qué país son estos artistas?
2. ¿En qué siglo pintaron?
3. En cada cuadro, ¿qué se ve en primer plano? ¿Qué se ve al fondo?
4. ¿Qué se ve a la izquierda?
5. ¿Qué colores usa más cada artista?

6. ¿Cómo son las figuras, realistas o más abstractas?
7. ¿Qué tipo de arte es?
8. ¿Cómo te hace sentir este arte?
9. ¿Te gusta alguno de los cuadros?

 Mapa global interactivo Explora los museos en Cataluña, España e investiga la relación de Salvador Dalí con su ambiente.

Differentiated Instruction

Heritage Speakers

Students may have spelling difficulty with words involving the letters **b** and **v.** Have them identify words containing these letters. Some examples might include **obra, dibujo, abstracto(a), cubismo,** and **movimiento.** Have students separate the words into two columns and quiz each other on proper spelling.

Students with Learning Difficulties

Before they answer the questions in *Actividad* 11, have students brainstorm a bank of applicable nouns and adjectives to describe each of the paintings presented. Review the meanings of these descriptive words and have students use their word banks when answering the questions.

12

Diego Rivera: Arte y revolución

 LEER, ESCRIBIR La obra del pintor mexicano Diego Rivera (1886–1957) muestra una preocupación por los ideales de la Revolución Mexicana. Lee el siguiente artículo sobre una de las figuras principales de la obra de Rivera y contesta las preguntas.

Estrategia

Using illustrations The details in a painting or illustration can give you clues about the main theme of a text. Observe the painting on the right. What does it tell you about the main theme of this article?

Conexiones ◄ El arte y la historia

Diego Rivera creía que el arte debe ayudar a los campesinos[1] a entender su propia historia. Este panel titulado "Emiliano Zapata" representa a Zapata, el líder de los campesinos durante la Revolución Mexicana. Con el famoso lema[2] "tierra y libertad", Zapata luchó[3] por una reforma agraria a principios del siglo XX.

Diego Rivera pensaba que Zapata era un verdadero héroe de la Revolución. En este panel, que es parte de un mural del Palacio Nacional de la Ciudad de México, vemos a Zapata en primer plano y a sus revolucionarios campesinos detrás de él. En la mano derecha lleva una hoz[4] y con la mano izquierda sujeta[5] un caballo. A sus pies hay un hombre muerto.

[1]peasants [2]motto [3]fought [4]sickle [5]restrains

▲ "Emiliano Zapata" (panel de un mural), (1931), Diego Rivera

Observa los detalles del panel.

1. ¿Quién es la figura central en esta composición? ¿Cómo está vestido?
2. ¿Qué representa el caballo blanco?
3. ¿Qué representa la hoz?
4. ¿Qué comunica Rivera con los hombres que están al fondo?
5. ¿Qué representa el hombre muerto a los pies de Zapata?
6. ¿Qué crees que sucedió en esta escena?

13

Nuestra obra de arte

 ESCRIBIR, DIBUJAR, HABLAR EN PAREJA Trabaja con un(a) compañero(a) para escoger un tema histórico que les gustaría pintar. Escriban una descripción de su pintura. Si es posible, hagan un dibujo de lo que van a pintar. Usen por lo menos tres símbolos (symbols) para representar el tema que escogieron. Luego, presenten la descripción a la clase. Usen oraciones conectadas con detalles y elaboración. Incluyan la siguiente información:

• el título
• el tema y por qué lo escogieron
• qué o a quién van a mostrar en primer plano
• qué o a quién van a mostrar al fondo
• qué representan los símbolos que incluyeron

Capítulo 2 • setenta y siete **77**

12

Standards: 1.2, 1.3, 2.2, 3.1, 3.2

Suggestions: Point out to students that carefully studying the panel will help them understand the second paragraph.

Answers

1. Es Emiliano Zapata. Está vestido de blanco.
2–6. Answers will vary.

13

Standards: 1.1, 1.3

Suggestions: Ask students to make their drawings large enough for everyone to see. Point out that they will be using the future tense. Ask: *¿Qué pondrás en primer plano? ¿Y en el fondo? ¿Qué tendrá tu pintura?*

Answers will vary.

Pre-AP® Integration

• **Learning Objective:** Interpretative: Print and Audio
• **Activity:** As a pre-reading activity, distribute the questions accompanying *Actividad* 11. With books opened point to the painting from Dalí as you read aloud the first paragraph. Point to the painting from Miró as you read the second paragraph. Then, ask them to answer the questions. Finally, have students follow along in their texts as you read the selection again to confirm their answers.
• *Pre-AP® Resource Materials:* Comprehensive guide to Pre-AP® communication skill development

Additional Resources

 Technology: Online Resources
• Guided, Core, Audio
• Communication Activities
Teacher Resources
• Teacher's Resource Materials: Audio Script, Technology: Audio Cap. 2, Communicative Pair Activity

Assessment

Prueba 2-2 with Remediation (online only)
Prueba: Aplicación del vocabulario 1
• Prueba 2-2

Enrich Your Teaching

Culture Note

In 1920, Diego Rivera traveled to Italy to study the frescoes of the Renaissance. The fresco technique involves painting directly onto plaster that has been freshly applied to a wall. As the plaster dries into a hard surface, the color of the paint becomes fixed. Rivera was especially influenced by the Italian Renaissance painter Giotto.

21st Century Skills

Collaboration Have students evenly divide up the tasks of writing, drawing, and presenting in *Actividad* 13 so they can better accomplish the work. Partners work well together if they know what they want to accomplish and when each person has an equal role.

Gramática: Repaso

Suggestions: After presenting the Gramática information to students, direct their attention to the *¿Recuerdas?* Ask students to explain why each expression takes the tense that it does. For example, ***generalmente*** takes the imperfect tense because it introduces either a habitual action in the past or background details in the past. Have them give examples.

 Technology: Interactive Whiteboard

Grammar Activities 2-1 Use the whiteboard activities in your Teacher Resources as you progress through the grammar practice with your class.

14

Standards: 1.2

Suggestions: Remind students that sometimes expressions like those in the *¿Recuerdas?* will help them determine which tense to use.

Answers:
1. tomaba
2. me inscribí
3. fue
4. trabajó
5. Eran / llegamos
6. llevaba
7. visitaban

Extension: After students have completed the activity, have them compare answers and discuss the reasons for their choices.

15

Standards: 1.1

Recycle: Time expressions, things to do on a trip

Suggestions: Before doing the activity, ask: *Las actividades ocurrieron a una hora específica en el pasado. Por eso, ¿qué tiempo verbal tenemos que usar? (el pretérito)*

Answers:
1. **A** —¿Cuándo fue la maestra a comprar los boletos?
   B —Eran las 11:20 cuando fue.
2. **A** —¿Cuándo comenzaron ustedes la visita?
   B —Eran las 11:30 cuando comenzamos.
3. **A** —¿Cuándo se perdieron Juan y Lucía en el museo?
   B —Eran las 12:00 cuando se perdieron.
4. **A** —¿Cuándo se dio cuenta la maestra?
   B —Eran las 12:20 cuando se dio cuenta.
5. **A** —¿Cuándo encontraste a Juan y a Lucía?
   B —Era la 1:00 cuando los encontré.
6. **A** —¿Cuándo salieron ustedes del museo?
   B —Eran las 2:30 cuando salimos.

Gramática Repaso

OBJECTIVES
▶ Talk about activities in the past
▶ Listen to art-related activities in the past

¿Recuerdas?
Expresiones como *generalmente, a menudo* y *muchas veces* se usan frecuentemente en frases que tienen verbos en imperfecto.
Las expresiones como *ayer, la semana pasada* y *una vez* se usan en frases que llevan verbos en pretérito.

Pretérito vs. *imperfecto*

When speaking about the past, you can use either the preterite or the imperfect, depending on the sentence and the meaning you wish to convey. Compare:

> Este fin de semana **tomé** una clase de cerámica. Cuando **era** niño, **tomaba** clases de escultura.

- Use the preterite to tell about past actions that happened and are complete.

> El sábado, la clase **empezó** a las 10 de la mañana.

- Use the imperfect to tell about habitual actions in the past.

> Cuando **era** niño, las clases **empezaban** a las 5 de la tarde.

- Use the preterite to give a sequence of actions in the past.

> Cuando **llegamos,** la profesora **sacó** su pintura y sus pinceles y **empezó** a pintar.

- Use the imperfect to give background details such as time, location, weather, mood, age, and physical and mental descriptions.

> **Eran** las dos de la tarde. **Estábamos** en el parque. **Era** un día de otoño. Todos **estábamos** muy contentos.

- Use the preterite and the imperfect together when an action (preterite) interrupts another that is taking place in the past (imperfect).

> **Estábamos** en el taller cuando **entró** el profesor.

- Use the imperfect when two or more actions are taking place simultaneouly in the past.

> Mientras los niños **pintaban**, el profesor **observaba** las pinturas.

14

Una familia de artistas

 LEER, ESCRIBIR Desde niños, todos los miembros de la familia Gutiérrez participan en muchos proyectos de arte. Completa estas frases con el tiempo verbal correcto.

1. Cuando era niño *(tomé / tomaba)* clases de pintura todas las tardes.
2. Este fin de semana, *(me inscribí / me inscribía)* en un concurso de cerámica.
3. La semana pasada, mi hermano Juan *(fue / iba)* a pintar en la playa.
4. Ayer, mi mamá *(trabajó / trabajaba)* varias horas en un retrato.
5. *(Eran / Fueron)* las dos de la tarde cuando nosotros *(llegué / llegamos)* a la clase de escultura.
6. Todos los años, nuestra tía nos *(llevó / llevaba)* a ver su taller.
7. Generalmente, mis padres *(visitaron / visitaban)* el museo todos los fines de semana.

Differentiated Instruction

Students with Learning Difficulties

Students may have difficulty making the distinction between past actions that have been completed and past actions that are habitual or ongoing. Have students attempt to dramatize the examples in *Actividad 14*. Explain that the examples that are "easier" to act out (because the action is completed) require ***el pretérito.***

Challenge/Pre-AP®

Ask students to prepare a narration about a situation, real or imagined, in the past. It should include a mixture of the preterite and imperfect tenses. Allow them to prepare their narrative either as notes or as a paragraph to be read aloud. Remind them to improve their narrative by using expressions like those in the *¿Recuerdas?*

Go **Online** to practice
PEARSON
realize™
PearsonSchool.com/Autentico

AUDIO   VIDEO   WRITING   SPEAK/RECORD

Interpersonal 2

15

¿Qué pasó en el museo?

HABLAR EN PAREJA Con otro(a) estudiante, hablen de la visita de la clase al museo, la semana pasada.

Videomodelo
ustedes / llegar al museo / 11:15
A —¿Cuándo llegaron al museo?
B —Eran las 11:15 cuando llegamos.

1. la maestra / ir a comprar los boletos / 11:20
2. ustedes / comenzar la visita / 11:30
3. Juan y Lucía / perderse en el museo / 12:00
4. la maestra / darse cuenta / 12:20
5. tú / encontrar a Juan y a Lucía / 1:00
6. ustedes / salir del museo / 2:30

16

¿Imperfecto o pretérito?

ESCUCHAR, ESCRIBIR, HABLAR EN PAREJA En una hoja de papel, haz una tabla de dos columnas. Escribe *Pretérito* en la columna de la izquierda e *Imperfecto* en la columna de la derecha. Vas a escuchar una historia con los verbos en infinitivo. Cada vez que escuches un verbo, decide si debe ir en pretérito o imperfecto y escríbelo en la columna correcta. Luego, habla con otro(a) estudiante sobre las formas que escogieron.

17

Vida de artista: Remedios Varo

ESCRIBIR Completa esta corta biografía de la artista surrealista Remedios Varo con los verbos entre paréntesis. Usa la forma apropiada del pretérito o del imperfecto.

María de los Remedios Varo y Uranga __1.__ (nacer) el 16 de diciembre de 1908, en Anglés, un pequeño pueblo al norte de Barcelona, España. __2.__ (ser) hija de Rodrigo Varo y de Ignacia Uranga. Su padre __3.__ (ser) ingeniero. __4.__ (construir) canales. A causa de su trabajo, Rodrigo Varo __5.__ (llevar) a su familia por muchas partes de España y del Norte de África. Desde joven, a Remedios le __6.__ (gustar) pintar. Como otros artistas y escritores españoles de su generación, ella __7.__ (viajar) a París en 1930 en búsqueda de nuevas ideas. Allí __8.__ (encontrar) una fuente de inspiración en el movimiento surrealista. Los surrealistas __9.__ (tratar) de expresar imágenes del subconsciente. En 1936, a causa de la Guerra Civil española, Remedios __10.__ (tener) que buscar refugio en México. Allí, Remedios __11.__ (crear) algunas de las obras más originales de la pintura moderna.

"Still Life Reviving", (1963), Remedios Varo
© 2009 Artists Rights Society (ARS), New York/VEGAP, Madrid.

Capítulo 2 • setenta y nueve **79**

16

Resources: Teacher's Resource Materials: Audio Script, Technology: Cap. 2

Suggestions: Use the audio or read the script. Allow students to listen more than once.

 Technology: Audio Script and Answers

En una hoja de papel, haz un tabla de dos columnas. Escribe "Pretérito" en la columna de la izquierda e "Imperfecto" en la columna de la derecha. Vas a escuchar una historia con los verbos en infinitivo. Cada vez que escuches un verbo, decide si debe ir en pretérito o imperfecto y escríbelo en la columna correcta. Luego, habla con otro estudiante sobre las formas que escogieron. Vas a oír cada frase dos veces.

1. Todos los días, la pintora (ir) a su taller.
2. Su taller (estar) en el centro de la ciudad.
3. Un día, ella (llegar) a su taller muy tarde.
4. (Ser) las dos de la tarde cuando ella (llegar) al taller y (encontrar) cerca de su paleta y sus pinceles una caja.
5. Ella (oír) unos ruidos adentro de la caja. Al abrirla, (ver) unos gatitos que (dormir) uno junto al otro.

Pretérito	Imperfecto
llegó	iba
llegó	estaba
encontró	Eran
oyó	dormían
vio	

17

Suggestions: Have students read through the entire biography once before writing their answers.

Answers:

1. nació	5. llevó	9. trataban
2. Era	6. gustaba	10. tuvo
3. era	7. viajó	11. creó
4. Construía	8. encontró	

Enrich Your Teaching

Culture Note

In Spain and some countries in Latin America, people traditionally use two family names or surnames. The first *apellido* is the father's family name, and the second is the mother's. The two *apellidos* may be separated by *y,* as is the case for Remedios Varo y Uranga, hyphenated, or just used together.

21st Century Skills

ICT (Information, Communications and Technology) Literacy Remind students of the various digital tools available in **Realize** to help them monitor their own understanding and learning needs, such as the eText with embedded audio files and online tutorials.

18

Standards: 1.2

Suggestions: After students answer the questions, encourage them to talk about the picture further by describing the people's clothes.

Answers will vary, but should contain the following tense usage and information.

1. Eran las dos de la tarde.
2. Era probablemente el verano. Hacía buen tiempo y la gente estaba vestida de ropa de verano.
3. Las niñas saltaban a la cuerda cuando llegó la mamá.
4. El perro robó las salchichas porque tenía hambre.
5. Carlos se enojó. Él también tenía hambre.
6. Eva se reía.
7. Luis le sacaba una foto.
8. El policía se acostó debajo de un árbol para tomar una siesta.

CULTURA

Standards: 1.1, 1.2, 2.2, 3.1, 5.2

Suggestions: Remind students that all details in a mural like this one by Siqueiros are present for a reason. As they answer the questions, ask them to elaborate on details with questions such as the following: *¿Por qué muestra el artista a tantas personas en el mural? ¿Qué cosa llevan los hombres en la mano? ¿Piensas que la presencia de las mujeres es importante? ¿Por qué?*

Answers will vary.

Additional Resources

 Technology: Online Resources
• Instant Check
• Guided, Core, Audio, Writing, Reading
• *Para hispanohablantes*
Print
• Guided WB pp. 59–60
• Core WB p. 25

Assessment

Prueba 2-3 with Remediation (online only)
Prueba: Pretérito vs. imperfecto
• Prueba 2-3

Project-Based Learning

Students can perform Step 2 at this point. Be sure they understand your corrections and suggestions. (For more information, see p. 64-b.)

18

Escena en el parque

 HABLAR Contesta las preguntas. Usa las respuestas para describir lo que pasó en el parque. Incluye oraciones conectadas con detalles y elaboración.

1. ¿Qué hora era?
2. ¿Qué estación del año crees que era, probablemente? ¿Cómo lo sabes?
3. ¿Qué hacían las niñas cuando llegó la mamá?
4. ¿Quién robó las salchichas? ¿Por qué?
5. ¿Cómo se sentía Carlos? ¿Por qué?
6. ¿Qué hacía Eva?
7. ¿Qué hacía Luis mientras su papá leía?
8. ¿Quién se acostó debajo de un árbol? ¿Por qué?

CULTURA ‹ México

David Alfaro Siqueiros A principios del siglo XX, ocurrían muchos cambios sociales en México. En 1910, terminó el régimen de Porfirio Díaz, quien fue Presidente de México durante 30 años, y comenzó la Revolución Mexicana.

Junto a Rivera y Orozco, David Alfaro Siqueiros (1898–1974) fue uno de los grandes artistas del muralismo mexicano, el movimiento artístico que se inspiró en los ideales de la Revolución.

A través de su obra, Siqueiros nos habla de los tiempos y cambios que vive su país. Sus murales nos muestran una nueva realidad en la que los pobres son las figuras centrales de la historia de México.

Pre-AP® Integration: Las artes visuales y escénicas ¿Cómo crees que este mural refleja la vida y cultura de los mexicanos durante esta época?

"Del Porfirismo a la Revolución", (1906–1913),
David Alfaro Siqueiros

Museo Nacional de Historia, Castillo de Chapultepec, Mexico City, D.F., Mexico.
© 2009 Artists Rights Society (ARS), New York/ SOMAAP, Mexico City.
Photo: Schalkwijk/Art Resource, NY.

Differentiated Instruction

Heritage Speakers

Have students tell about family gatherings in their heritage country. For what types of events do families typically get together? What foods, decorations, and activities are usually involved?

Students with Learning Difficulties

Before completing the chart in *Actividad* 19 on p. 81, have students brainstorm and list the infinitive forms of verbs that would be applicable to the picture. Then lead them through the process outlined in the *Gramática*. Model, step-by-step, the conversion of each verb into the appropriate past participle form.

Gramática

OBJECTIVES
▶ Listen to the description of a family portrait
▶ Write about a description of a scene
▶ Talk about art museums and artists

Estar + participio

Many adjectives in Spanish are actually past participles of verbs. Recall that to form a past participle you add *-ado* to the root of *-ar* verbs and *-ido* to the root of *-er* and *-ir* verbs.

decor**ar**	decor**ado**	cono**cer**	cono**cido**	prefer**ir**	prefer**ido**

- The past participle is frequently used with *estar* to describe conditions that are the result of a previous action. In those cases, the past participle agrees with the subject in gender and number.

  El pintor **está sentado.**   Las paredes **estaban pintadas.**

- Recall that there are a number of cases in which the past participle is irregular.

abrir: **abierto**	escribir: **escrito**	ver: **visto**
poner: **puesto**	romper: **roto**	morir: **muerto**
decir: **dicho**	hacer: **hecho**	volver: **vuelto**
resolver: **resuelto**		

Más recursos ONLINE

▶ **Tutorial:** Past Participle Used as Adjective

🔊 *Canción de hip hop:* *Obra de arte*

19

Retrato de familia

ESCUCHAR, ESCRIBIR Rosario describe un retrato de una fiesta familiar. ¿Quiénes estaban allí? ¿Cómo estaban? En una hoja de papel, copia la siguiente tabla. Escucha la descripción del retrato y escribe cómo estaban las siguientes personas y cosas.

¿Quién? o ¿Qué?	¿Cómo estaban?
Yo	
Mi padrino	
Mi papá	
Mi tía Luisa	
Mi primo Jorge	
La mesa	
Los refrescos	
Los niños	
Mis primos más pequeños	

Capítulo 2 • ochenta y uno **81**

Enrich Your Teaching

Culture Note

Like Diego Rivera, David Alfaro Siqueiros was trained in the classic technique of fresco painting. However, Siqueiros was also known for his innovations to the technique. In addition to painting on non-conventional surfaces such as concrete and cement, Siqueiros used non-traditional oil-based paints or airbrushing to cover large areas quickly. In addition to his own painting, Siqueiros taught many other artists. One of his most famous pupils was Jackson Pollock, a painter who went on to develop his own, original technique.

Gramática

Suggestions: Point out that, just as Spanish uses past participles ending in *-ado* or *-ido* as adjectives, English also uses past participles ending in *-ed* and *-en* as adjectives: *a heated room, a typed memo, a driven student, a given answer.*

🖥 Technology: Interactive Whiteboard

Grammar Activites 2-1 Use the whiteboard activities in your Teacher Resources as you progress through the grammar practice with your class.

19

Standards: 1.2

Resources: Teacher's Resource Materials: Audio Script, Technology: Audio, Cap.2

Suggestions: Use the audio or the script. Allow students to listen more than once. Remind them to use the picture to help them.

Common Errors: In the *estar* + **participle** construction, students often forget to make the participle agree in number and gender with the subject. Correct this error with visual cues. Hold up two fingers to cue plural. Prepare a pair of flashcards with masculine and feminine symbols to cue gender.

🔊 Technology: Audio Script and Answers

Rosario: En este retrato, yo estaba sentada entre mi mamá y mi papá. El hombre que estaba parado detrás de nosotros es mi padrino. Mi papá estaba sentado a mi derecha. Mi tía Luisa estaba parada en una silla jugando con la piñata. Mi primo Jorge estaba vestido de Superman. La mesa ya estaba puesta y los refrescos estaban servidos. Pero ya eran las siete de la tarde y la fiesta no empezaba. Creo que cuando finalmente comenzó, los niños estábamos muy cansados y mis primos más pequeños ya estaban dormidos.

1. estaba sentada
2. estaba parado
3. estaba sentado
4. estaba parada
5. estaba vestido de Superman
6. estaba puesta
7. estaban servidos
8. estábamos muy cansados
9. estaban dormidos

Additional Resources

📶 **Technology: Online Resources**
- Audio, Writing, Reading
- Communication Activities

Print
- Teacher's Resource Materials: Audio Script, Communicative Pair Activities, Technology: Audio Cap. 2

Starter Activity

Before students do *Actividad* 20, help them practice using the **estar + past participle** construction. Have them perform actions and tell what they are doing. Then have them state the result of the action:

Rompo la tiza. Ahora la tiza está rota.
Abro la ventana. Ahora la ventana está abierta.
Cierro la puerta. Ahora la puerta está cerrada.
Escribo mi nombre. Mi nombre está escrito.

 20

Standards: 1.1

Suggestions: Point out to students that all of their sentences should begin with **Cuando llegué a su taller....** Therefore, they should use **estar + past participle** for all the verbs in the second part of the sentence.

Answers will vary. Endings for past participles will vary with number and gender: **abierto, dormido, hecho, roto, escondido, encendido, parado.**

 21

Standards: 1.2, 1.3, 2.2, 3.1, 5.2

Suggestions: Show students other examples of installations (collections of objects brought together by an artist) to help guide them in their discussion of the medium. Many photos of these, by Pepón Osorio and other artists, are available online and in art books and magazines.

Answers will vary.

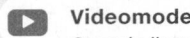 **20**

En el cuarto de la pintora

✎ **HABLAR, ESCRIBIR** Una artista te invitó a visitar su taller. Describe la escena que viste cuando llegaste. Usa el participio pasado de los siguientes verbos: *abrir, dormir, hacer, romper, esconder, encender, parar.*

▶ **Videomodelo**
*Cuando llegué a su taller, **el niño estaba sentado.***

21

Pepón Osorio, artista entre dos culturas

✎ **LEER, ESCRIBIR** ¿Cómo refleja un artista una vida entre dos culturas? Lee este artículo y contesta las preguntas.

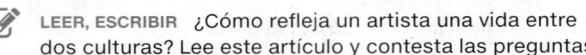 **Conexiones** ◀ **El arte**

Pepón Osorio nació en 1955, en Santurce, Puerto Rico. A los 20 años se fue a vivir a Nueva York para empezar su carrera de artista. Osorio cree que los artistas deben hacer trabajos que muestren su época y su país de origen. Gran parte de su obra representa su niñez y adolescencia en Puerto Rico, así como su experiencia multicultural como artista puertorriqueño en Nueva York. Dice que los puertorriqueños son multiculturales porque viven entre dos culturas, la puertorriqueña y la neoyorquina.

Osorio hace montajes[1] de cosas que encuentra. En "100% Boricua"[2], Osorio mezcla recuerdos turísticos de Nueva York con banderas puertorriqueñas y otros objetos típicos del Caribe.

Su objetivo es reunir los elementos de toda una comunidad en un solo lugar.

[1]assemblages [2]*Boricua* is a term Puerto Ricans use to describe themselves as natives to the island.

▲ "100% Boricua", (1991), Pepón Osorio

❶ Observa el montaje de Osorio. ¿En qué se parece un montaje a otras obras de arte? ¿En qué se diferencia?

❷ Ahora vas a planear tu propio montaje. Piensa en varios objetos que representan parte de tu historia. Escribe un corto párrafo describiendo cada objeto con detalles y elaboración. Explica por qué es importante para ti. Ponle un título y preséntalo a la clase.

82 ochenta y dos • Capítulo 2 • ¿Cómo te expresas?

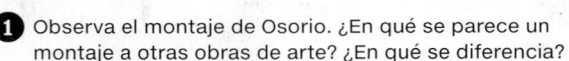 **Differentiated Instruction**

Spatial Learner

Have students select and collect objects to create their own **montajes.** Then have them explain the meaning and rationale behind the objects they have selected.

Advanced Learners

Have students create a report that compares two different kinds of visual art. They may compare two different media, such as sculpture and paintings, or two different schools, such as surrealist and kinesthetic. Ask them to research and organize their report of one of the media or styles for a class presentation.

Una visita a El Museo del Arte

🎤 LEER, HABLAR EN PAREJA

Go **Online** to practice
PEARSON
realize™
PearsonSchool.com/Autentico
▶ VIDEO ✎ WRITING 🎤 SPEAK/RECORD

1 Lee el siguiente anuncio de El Museo del Palacio de Bellas Artes y contesta las preguntas:

- ¿Dónde está el museo del Palacio de Bellas Artes?
- ¿Qué artistas presenta?
- ¿Qué puedes aprender si visitas el museo?

2 Trabaja con otro(a) estudiante para representar una visita a un museo. Hablen del museo y de las obras que tiene (autorretratos, esculturas, cerámica). Describan qué es lo que les gusta o no les gusta (tema, forma, colores). Digan cuál prefieren. Expliquen por qué, usando expresiones y una forma de hablar apropiadas.

EL MUSEO DEL PALACIO DE BELLAS ARTES

Murales
- Conoce las obras de los principales muralistas de México como Diego Rivera, José Clemente Orozco, David Alfaro Siqueiros y otros.
- Aprende más sobre los murales, los muralistas y el proyecto de conservación.

Contacto
Museo del Palacio de Bellas Artes, Eje Central Lázaro Cárdenas, Esquina con Avenida Juárez

martes a domingo
12:30 a 16:30

El español en la comunidad

El Museo del Barrio En 1969, un grupo de educadores, artistas y representantes puertorriqueños fundaron El Museo del Barrio en Harlem del Este. Su objetivo era ayudar a mantener la cultura, las tradiciones y el idioma de los puertorriqueños, y en general, de todos los latinoamericanos de Nueva York.

El Museo ha influido en la población hispanohablante de Nueva York gracias a sus programas educativos para la comunidad. Los estudiantes universitarios pueden hacer prácticas (internships) en El Museo y ser guías de visitas, ayudar a realizar talleres de orientación sobre arte y ayudar a los maestros de arte a preparar sus clases.

El Museo del Barrio es una de las instituciones culturales de la población hispanohablante más importantes de los Estados Unidos. Sirve de puente de comunicación entre los diferentes grupos latinoamericanos de Nueva York y también entre la cultura hispanohablante y la anglosajona. Ese fue el sueño de sus fundadores.

- Imagina que vas a trabajar durante el verano en El Museo del Barrio como voluntario(a). ¿Qué trabajo quieres hacer? ¿En qué crees que puedes ayudar?
- Identifica otros ejemplos de instituciones culturales que representen a las comunidades hispanohablantes en los Estados Unidos.

Capítulo 2 • ochenta y tres **83**

Standards: 1.1, 1.2, 1.3, 3.2

Suggestions: Ask partners to present to the class the conversation they come up with for Step 2.

Answers:

Eje Central Lázaro Cárdenas, Esquina con Avenida Juárez.
Presenta a Diego Rivera, José Clemente Orozco, David Alfaro Siqueiros y otros
Se puede aprender sobre los murales, los muralistas y el proyecto de conservación

El español en la comunidad

Standards: 1.1, 1.2, 5.1, 5.2

Suggestions: Have students imagine that they are starting up a museum from scratch. Ask them to think about and discuss questions such as: *¿Dónde va a estar nuestro museo? ¿Cuáles son los gastos (expenses) necesarios para empezar y mantener un museo? ¿De dónde van a venir los fondos necesarios? ¿Qué servicios va a ofrecer el museo? ¿Cómo vamos a atraer (attract) al público?*

Additional Resources

📶 **Technology: Online Resources**
- Instant Check
- Guided, Core, Audio, Writing practice
- *Para hispanohablantes*

Print
- Guided WB pp. 61–62
- Core WB pp. 26–27

Assessment

Prueba 2-4 with Remediation (online only)
Prueba: *Estar* + participio
- Prueba 2-4
Examen: Vocabulario y gramática 1
- Examen 1
- ExamView: Examen 1

Enrich Your Teaching

Culture Note

Across the United States, there are many museums and resources for Spanish and Latin American art. Some examples include the San José Center for Latino Arts, The Florida Museum of Hispanic and Latin American Art in Miami, and the Latino Museum of History, Art and Culture in Los Angeles.

21st Century Skills

Social and Cross-Cultural Skills
Encourage students to investigate another museum or cultural institution that represents the Spanish-speaking communities in the United States. Have them gather information about current exhibits, any outreach programs they have, and the Spanish-speaking communities they serve. How does it compare to the *Museo del Barrio* in New York City?

Vocabulario en contexto 2

Standards: 1.2

Resources: Teacher's Resource Materials: Input Script, Clip Art, Technology: Audio, Cap. 2

Suggestions: Use the Input Script from the Teacher's Resource Materials as a source of ideas for presentation of new vocabulary as comprehensible input. Pantomime to clarify the meaning of words and expressions such as *pararse, exagerar, el aplauso,* and l*os pasos de una danza.* Ask volunteers to point to *el tambor* and *el micrófono.*

Active Classroom

Have students work in pairs to write a short review for a cultural event similar to the models shown. Ask students to read them to the class, imitating a critic.

 Technology: Interactive Whiteboard

Vocabulary Activities 2-2 Use the whiteboard activities in your Teacher Resources as you progress through the vocabulary practice with your class.

Vocabulario en contexto 2

OBJECTIVES
Read, listen to, and understand information about
▶ Places to go when you're not in school
▶ Plans for leisure time

🔊 Los talleres de artes

El verano pasado hubo talleres de artes en la universidad. Ofrecieron clases de **danza clásica** y moderna, drama, música y literatura. Al final se organizaron unos **espectáculos**. **Las entradas** fueron gratis y asistieron muchas personas. **Las reseñas** de los participantes fueron positivas.

Carlos / Juana

el micrófono

Juana: Participé en el taller de literatura con mi hermana. Ella y yo no **actuamos**, pero leímos unos **poemas** de la famosa **poeta** y **escritora** Sandra Cisneros. Todos aplaudieron con mucho **entusiasmo**. **Me identifico** mucho con sus poemas.

el tambor

aplausos

Carlos: Mi **conjunto** tocó varias canciones. Muchas parejas empezaron a bailar al **ritmo** de la música. **Se destacó** el solo de **trompeta**. Al final el público **se paró** para darnos unos fuertes **aplausos**.

84 ochenta y cuatro • Capítulo 2 • ¿Cómo te expresas?

Differentiated Instruction

Students with Learning Difficulties

Use concrete objects and listening samples to reinforce the meaning of new vocabulary. For example, play a song from a *conjunto de salsa* so that students can hear the *ritmo.* Read aloud a poem written by *un(a) poeta.* Encourage students to bring in programs from cultural events that they have attended.

Advanced Learners

Have students work in groups to create a series of narrated pantomimes that use the vocabulary presented on pp. 84–85. Ask them to choose one student in each group as the narrator. The other members act out the actions or scenes that the narrator describes. Have them present their narrated pantomimes to the class.

Go **Online** to practice
PEARSON
realize™
PearsonSchool.com/Autentico
AUDIO   SPEAK/RECORD

Interpretive   **2**

Juana: El taller de danza fue increíble. Mi grupo de ballet **realizó una interpretación** de "Cenicienta" y otro grupo presentó una danza de hip hop. Me encantaron los **movimientos** y **los pasos** de los bailarines de hip hop.

Carlos: "¡Qué divertida fue la obra de "Don Quijote!" Cuando **interpreté** el papel de Sancho Panza, tuve que practicar mucho. Era necesario **parecerme** a un señor cómico, pero no quería **exagerar** los **gestos** y quería que la risa **sonara** real.

la danza clásica

el escenario

23

¿Estás de acuerdo?

 ESCUCHAR Escucha cada frase sobre el programa y levanta una mano si es cierta y dos manos si es falsa.

24

¡Muchas actividades!

 ESCRIBIR, HABLAR EN PAREJA Trabaja con un(a) estudiante. Si pudieras participar en tres de estos talleres, ¿cuál sería tu primera selección? ¿Y la segunda y tercera? Explica tus selecciones.

Capítulo 2 • ochenta y cinco **85**

23

Standards: 1.2

Resources: Teacher's Resource Materials: Audio Script, Technology: Audio, Cap. 2

Suggestions: Before engaging students in the listening activity, give them a few minutes to silently read about the *talleres de artes*. Then play the audio or use the script to read the activity aloud.

 Technology: Audio Script and Answers

1. Los talleres se ofrecieron en el otoño. (dos manos)
2. Juana y su hermana tocaron la trompeta. (dos manos)
3. Carlos tocó con un conjunto musical. (una mano)
4. Hubo dos presentaciones de danza, hip-hop y ballet clásico. (una mano)
5. Carlos hizo el papel de Sancho Panza. (una mano)
6. Juana leyó unos poemas de Sandra Cisneros. (una mano)

24

Standards: 1.1

Resources: Teacher's Resource Materials: Audio Script, Technology: Audio, Cap. 2

Suggestions: Ask students to share with others the three workshops they would like to participate in.
Answers will vary

Starter Activity

Write these words above columns on the board: *la danza, la música instrumental, cantante, pintor, director, escultor.* As a class brainstorm, write the names of famous people under the appropriate category.

Teacher-to-Teacher

Encourage students to bring in CD covers, posters, magazines, and ads that demonstrate their own artistic preferences. These can be used as props throughout this chapter to aid in question-and-answer sessions and discussions about the varying types of art and students' responses to them.

Project-Based Learning

Students can perform Step 3 at this point. (For more information, see p. 64-b.)

Enrich Your Teaching

Culture Note

There are many different styles of the dance we call **salsa.** The Puerto Rican Style is known for its footwork; the New York Style shows the influence of disco; the Los Angeles Style is influenced by West Coast Swing. The Cuban Style stresses the "one" and "three" beats of the music, and the rhythms are faster.

21st Century Skills

Critical Thinking and Problem Solving Encourage students to listen to salsa music online. Have them try to identify the instruments they hear in the music. Are there similarities between salsa music and other dance music they know? What are the similarities and differences?

Vocabulario en contexto 2

Standards: 1.2

Resources: Teacher's Resource Materials: Input Script, Clip Art, Audio Script, Technology: Audio, Cap. 2

Suggestions

Pre-reading: Have students read just the titles of the four descriptions. Ask them to name the kinds of art that they expect to read about.

Reading: Allow students time to read the reviews silently. Then play the audio and have students read along as they listen. Allow them to listen more than once.

Post-reading: Ask students to write down two statements about two different cultural events on pp. 86–87. Each statement should tell something that happened at the chosen event or describe how it happened. Have students take turns reading one statement at a time. Listeners identify which event is being talked about:

A. *Esta cantante cantó en Nueva York.*
B. *Es el concierto de Marc Anthony.*

Then check comprehension by having students complete *Actividades* 26 and 27.

Pre-AP® Integration

- **Learning Objective:** Interpersonal Writing
- **Activity:** Have students imagine they attended one of the three events described in *Espectáculos del mundo latino.* Based on the review, have them write an email to their parents or to a friend describing the event: where and when it occurred, who or what they saw, who did they go with, and their general impressions about the artist and the occasion.
- ***Pre-AP® Resource Material:*** Comprehensive guide to Pre-AP® writing development

Teacher-to-Teacher

To focus on the role of the *tango* and *flamenco* in the Hispanic culture, show the *Videodocumentario* video for this chapter. Play the video with and without sound to allow students to focus on the verbal and nonverbal signals in communication.

Espectáculos del mundo latino

¿Alguna vez buscaste información sobre un espectáculo en una revista, en un periódico o en la Red? Las reseñas te pueden ayudar a encontrar las películas, las obras de teatro y las exposiciones que más te interesan. ¿Qué dicen estas reseñas?

LILA DOWNS EN CONCIERTO

El 25 de octubre, la cantante mexicana Lila Downs dio un concierto en Costa Mesa, California. Nacida en Oaxaca y criada entre los EE. UU. y México, Downs es la autora de la letra y la melodía de sus canciones que combinan la música popular mexicana con poemas indígenas y el Jazz. En esta ocasión cantó las canciones de su nuevo álbum "Balas y chocolate".

MÚSICA ARGENTINA: ¡EL TANGO!

El tango en Buenos Aires ofrece muchos espectáculos de gran esplendor. En ellos se destacan los cantantes y bailarines que acompañan a la pareja central del espectáculo. Ellos, luego de actuar, enseñan a los visitantes los pasos básicos del tango.

86 ochenta y seis • Capítulo 2 • ¿Cómo te expresas?

Differentiated Instruction

Heritage Speakers

Have students compose two newspaper clips reporting on a favorite artist's exhibition or performance. Explain that one clip would appear in the newspaper before the event, and the other clip would appear after the event. Remind students to keep the time frame consistent whether they are reporting on a future or past event.

Students with Learning Difficulties

Have students preview the sentences in *Actividad* 26 on p. 87 prior to reading *Espectáculos del mundo latino.* After they have read the selection and answered true or false, have them locate and point to the sentence in the reading that proves their answer is correct.

Go **Online** to practice
PEARSON
realize™
PearsonSchool.com/Autentico
AUDIO WRITING

Interpretive 2

MARC ANTHONY

Una vez más, se vendieron todas las entradas para el concierto de Marc Anthony en el Madison Square Garden. Después de interpretar sus éxitos "Vivir mi vida" y "Te conozco bien", el público se unió a Anthony para cantar otros éxitos y bailar al compás de su música.

25

El mundo del espectáculo

 ESCUCHAR, ESCRIBIR Escribe los números del 1 al 5 en una hoja de papel. Escucha las siguientes preguntas y escribe la respuesta correcta.

26

¿Es cierto?

 LEER, ESCRIBIR Lee las frases y escribe *C* (cierto) o *F* (falso) según lo que leíste en "Espectáculos del mundo latino".

1. En los espectáculos de tango, los visitantes aprenden a bailar salsa.
2. Marc Anthony solo canta canciones en inglés.
3. Lila Downs escribe la letra y la melodía de sus canciones.
4. El tango es una música típica de Oaxaca.

27

Quisiera ir

 ESCRIBIR Después de leer estos artículos escribe una frase para cada una, diciendo por qué sí o por qué no te gustaría ir a ese espectáculo.

Capítulo 2 • ochenta y siete **87**

Enrich Your Teaching

Culture Note

Born in France, Carlos Gardel (the "Father of Tango") moved to Argentina as a young child. He went on to become one of the foremost interpreters of the Argentine tango ballad, as well as a motion picture actor. Gardel appeared in many feature films produced for Spanishspeaking audiences, such as the 1934 film *El Tango en Broadway.*

21st Century Skills

Social and Cross-Cultural Skills
Have students discuss how media messages are conveyed in announcements for cultural events, such as those on pages 86–87. What is the purpose of each announcement? Who is the intended audience? How are these articles similar to or different from the announcements they see in their own local newspapers?

25

Resources: Teacher's Resource Materials: Audio Script, Technology: Audio, Cap. 2

Suggestions: Remind students that answers to the questions they hear are found in the articles on pp. 86–87.

 Technology: Audio Script and Answers

Script:
1. Lila Downs, ¿es cantante o poeta?
2. ¿Nació en México o en los Estados Unidos?
3. El tango, ¿es más popular en Buenos Aires o en Nueva York?
4. ¿Marc Anthony se presentó en el Metropólitan o en el Madison Square Garden?
5. ¿Quién bailó al compás de la música de Marc Anthony, los bailarines de tango o el público?

Answers:
1. Es cantante.
2. Nació en México
3. Es más popular en Buenos Aires.
4. Se presentó en el Madison Square Garden.
5. El público bailó.

26

Suggestions: Have students check their answers with a partner and correct the false statements.

Answers:

1. F	3. C
2. F	4. F

27

Suggestions: Invite students to share and support their opinion with a partner.

Answers will vary.

Additional Resources

 Technology: Online Resources
• Instant Check
• Guided, Core, Audio, Writing practice
• *Para hispanohablantes*
Print
• Guided WB pp. 63–70
• Core WB pp. 28–29

Assessment

Prueba: Comprensión del vocabulario 2
• Prueba 2-5

28

Standards: 1.2, 3.1

Suggestions: When checking answers with students, ask them to say why the word they chose does not belong with the others.

Answers:

1. d	**4.** c
2. a	**5.** d
3. d	**6.** c

Starter Activity

Have students unscramble these words to make a logical sentence.

los / rió / exageró / la / se / mucho / el / gestos / político / gente / y

(**Answer:** *El político exageró los gestos y la gente se rió mucho.*)

29

Standards: 1.2, 2.2

Suggestions: Remind students that looking over the entire review first will give them an idea of what it is about and help them select the correct answers.

Answers:

1. se identifica	**5.** gestos
2. las actuaciones	**6.** entusiasmo
3. se destacan	**7.** interpretan
4. cómico	**8.** actuar

Extension: Invite students to work in groups. Have them choose a popular TV show they all know and make critical comments about it.

Vocabulario en uso 2

OBJECTIVES
▶ Read and write about different forms of entertainment
▶ Discuss a performance
▶ Talk about your favorite music

28

¡Quita la palabra!

 LEER, ESCRIBIR Escribe en una hoja de papel los números del 1 al 6. Para cada grupo de palabras, escribe en la hoja la letra de la palabra que no está relacionada con las otras. Después, haz una lista de las palabras que no están relacionadas con las demás y escribe una frase con cada una.

1. **a.** la melodía **b.** el ritmo **c.** el compás **d.** el gesto
2. **a.** el poema **b.** la danza **c.** el paso **d.** bailar
3. **a.** la actuación **b.** el gesto **c.** interpretar **d.** el conjunto
4. **a.** el escenario **b.** realizar **c.** la entrada **d.** la interpretación
5. **a.** el escritor **b.** el poeta **c.** el poema **d.** el micrófono
6. **a.** el tambor **b.** la trompeta **c.** el actor **d.** el piano

29

Una reseña

 LEER, ESCRIBIR Loreto Michea, un crítico, escribe sobre un popular programa de tele, *Sábado Gigante*. Completa la reseña con la palabra correcta.

"Sábado Gigante no era solo un programa familiar. Era un lugar donde la audiencia __1.__ *(actuaba / se identificaba)* con otros hispanohablantes, sin importar en qué lugar de América vivían. Pero los concursos, la música, el humor, __2.__ *(los pasos / las actuaciones)* y las entrevistas, no eran los elementos del programa que más __3.__ *(se destacaban / se exageraban)*. Don Francisco, su único presentador durante 53 años, era la clave *(key)* del éxito del programa. Era un animador __4.__ *(aburrido / cómico)* y con mucha energía que utilizaba sus __5.__ *(libros / gestos)*, su voz y su picardía *(wit)* para divertir al público. Su __6.__ *(entusiasmo / paso)* era impresionante, y cuando los cantantes __7.__ *(interpretaban / actuaban)* las canciones populares o los artistas aparecían en el escenario para __8.__ *(exagerar / actuar)*, la energía de Don Francisco inspiraba al público."

Differentiated Instruction

Students with Learning Difficulties

Encourage students to bring in examples of their own favorite music. After copying the chart in *Actividad* 31 on p. 89, guide students to take appropriate notes for each of the songs they hear. Have them use these to conduct the partner conversations.

Challenge/Pre-AP®

Challenge students to write six sentences, one for each item in *Actividad* 28. Each sentence should use all of the words in the row—including the word that does not belong—in a way that makes sense.

30

Un espectáculo de flamenco

ESCRIBIR, HABLAR EN PAREJA   Imagina que estuviste en el espectáculo de flamenco de la ilustración y describe la escena. Escribe frases en pretérito o imperfecto. Puedes usar las palabras y frases del recuadro. Luego, otro(a) estudiante te va a hacer preguntas sobre lo que escribiste.

Videomodelo
A —*Vi un espectáculo en el escenario.*
B —*¿Qué clase de espectáculo fue?*
A —*Fue un espectáculo de flamenco.*

el fondo	parado
al lado	el escenario
el micrófono	al frente
tocar la guitarra	a la izquierda
el cantante	los bailarines
cantar	el paso
sentado	

31

¡Viva la música!

HABLAR EN PAREJA, ESCRIBIR

1 ¿Cuál es tu álbum de música favorito? ¿Por qué? Piensa en algunas palabras que describan los diferentes elementos de tu canción o álbum de música favorito. En una hoja de papel, dibuja y completa una tabla como la siguiente.

Elemento	Álbum de música/Canción
el compás/ el ritmo	
la melodía	
la voz	
los instrumentos	
la letra	
el tema	

2 Habla con otro(a) estudiante e intercambia opiniones sobre tu canción o álbum de música favorito. Usa las palabras que escribiste en la tabla y apoya tus opiniones.

Videomodelo
A —*¿Qué te parece la melodía de la primera canción del álbum de música de Shakira?*
B —*La melodía es muy original, me gusta mucho.*
A —*¿Cómo suenan las guitarras en esta canción?*
B —*Suenan demasiado alto, no se oye la voz.*

Estudiante B

interesante	largo(a)
original	corto(a)
alegre	alto(a)
aburrido(a)	bajo(a)
tradicional	rápido(a)
	lento(a)

Estudiante A

¿Qué te parece . . . ?
¿Cómo suena . . . ?
¿Cómo es . . . ?
¿Qué canción tiene mejor . . . ?

Capítulo 2 • ochenta y nueve **89**

30

Standards: 1.1

Suggestions: Encourage students to build more than one question-and-answer exchange around each word or expression. Make sure they switch roles, so that all students have a chance to practice both asking and answering.

Answers will vary.

31

Standards: 1.1, 3.1

Suggestions: Explain to students that they should choose just one favorite album or song.

Common Errors: Some students make the assumption that all Spanish nouns ending in -a are feminine. Remind them that many nouns ending in **-a,** such as **el tema, el programa,** and **el problema,** are masculine.

Answers will vary.

Teacher-to-Teacher

Invite students to share with the class a favorite art work (part of a song, a poem or a rap, or a scene from a film) and then tell about what it means to them. Aside from any English involved, their presentations should be in Spanish. Then take the assignment one step further: request that they spend equal time showing and telling about an art form or artist from the Spanish-speaking world.

Additional Resources

Technology: Online Resources
• Audio, Writing, Reading
• Communication Activities
Print
• Teacher's Resource Materials: Audio Script, Communicative Pair Activities, Technology: Audio Cap. 2

Assessment

Prueba 2-6 with Remediation (online only)
Prueba: Aplicación del vocabulario 2
• Prueba 2-6

Enrich Your Teaching

Culture Note

Flamenco is an art form comprised of three parts: the dance, the song, and the music of the guitar. Flamenco enjoyed its "Golden Age" in the late nineteenth and early twentieth century. During this era, the art was developed in Spain's many **cafés cantantes** or musical cafés.

21st Century Skills

Social and Cross-Cultural Skills Have students investigate online music-sharing sites and find the most popular songs of the Latin genre. Have them choose a song and describe its elements, as they did in *Actividad* 31. How does this song compare to their favorite songs?

Gramática: Repaso

Standards: 4.1

Suggestions: Give other examples where the adjective has different meanings when used with **ser** or **estar**:

El niño es (está) malo. The boy is bad (sick).
Las manzanas son (están) verdes. The apples are green (unripe).

 Technology: Interactive Whiteboard

Grammar Activities 2-2 Use the whiteboard activities in your Teacher Resources as you progress through the grammar practice with your class.

32

Standards: 1.2

Suggestions: Once they are finished, encourage students to check their answers against the rules in the *Gramática* and make any necessary changes.

Common Errors: Correct usage of **ser** and **estar** is difficult for any English speaker learning Spanish. Tell students that correct usage will come with patience and practice.

Answers:

1. es	**4.** son	**7.** están
2. está	**5.** están	**8.** estamos
3. es	**6.** son	**9.** están

33

Standards: 1.2

Resources: Teacher's Resource Materials: Audio Script, Technology: Audio, Cap. 2

Suggestions: Make sure students answer in complete sentences.

Common Errors: Correct usage of **ser** and **estar** is difficult for any English speaker learning Spanish. Tell students that correct usage will come with patience and practice.

 Technology: Audio Script

(For the script, see Teacher's Resource Materials.)

Answers:

1. Es argentino.
2. Es músico.
3. Está en Chicago para dar un concierto.
4. Los otros miembros del conjunto están con él.
5. El cantante es colombiano.
6. El concierto es mañana por la noche.
7. Está un poco nervioso.

Gramática Repaso

OBJECTIVES
▶ Listen to an interview with an artist
▶ Describe a performance
▶ Write and illustrate a haiku

Ser y *estar*

Remember that *ser* and *estar* both mean "to be." They are used in different situations and have different meanings.

Use *ser*:

- to describe permanent characteristics of objects and people

  Esa canción **es** muy original.

- to indicate origin, nationality, or profession

  Mi tía **es** escritora. **Es** de Madrid.

- to indicate when and where something takes place

  El concierto **es** el viernes. **Es** en el teatro.

- to indicate possession

  La guitarra **es** de Elisa.

Use *estar*:

- to describe temporary characteristics, emotional states, or conditions

  El teatro **está** cerrado a esta hora.
  Los actores **están** muy nerviosos.

- to indicate location

  El conjunto **está** en el escenario.

- to form the progressive tense

  El bailarín **está** interpretando a Cabral.

Some adjectives have different meanings depending on whether they are used with *ser* or with *estar*.

La bailarina **es bonita.** *The dancer is pretty. (She's a pretty person.)*
La bailarina **está** muy **bonita** hoy. *The dancer looks pretty today. (She doesn't always look this pretty.)*
El cómico **es aburrido.** *(He is boring.)* El cómico **está aburrido.** *(He is bored.)*
El cantante **es rico.** *(He is wealthy.)* El postre **está rico.** *(It tastes very good.)*

Más recursos ONLINE

▶ **Tutorial:** Ser and Estar

32

Invitación a Caras y Caretas

LEER, ESCRIBIR El secretario del club de teatro mandó esta invitación por correo electrónico. Completa la invitación con la forma correcta de *ser* o *estar*.

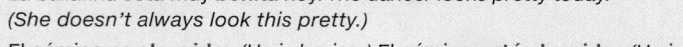

¡Atención compañeros y compañeras!

El jueves a las 3:30 __1.__ la reunión de Caras y Caretas. Nuestro club __2.__ en la sala 28, en el segundo piso. Caras y Caretas __3.__ un club que trabaja para realizar comedias y tragedias de España y América Latina. Los miembros __4.__ estudiantes, profesores y otros que __5.__ interesados en hacer teatro. Los invitados de honor __6.__ Raúl Moreno y Eva Díaz, dos jóvenes poetas mexicanos que ahora __7.__ estudiando en Nueva York. Nosotros __8.__ muy orgullosos de la obra de estos jóvenes. Todos ustedes __9.__ invitados a conocerlos. ¡Los esperamos!

90 noventa • Capítulo 2 • ¿Cómo te expresas?

Differentiated Instruction

Heritage Speakers

Have students draft an e-mail message extending an invitation to a performing arts event in their heritage country. Instruct students to identify their audience. They might be writing to a close friend or to the entire mailing list of the performing arts institution. Remind them to tailor their language accordingly.

Students with Learning Difficulties

Have students write the verb forms **es** and **está** on two separate index cards. Help them reinforce the distinction between the forms of these two verbs that both mean "to be." Provide sentences in which students must fill in the blank by holding up the appropriate card. Ask them to explain each choice.

Go Online to practice
PearsonSchool.com/Autentico
PEARSON
realize™
AUDIO VIDEO WRITING SPEAK/RECORD

Interpersonal   2

33

Entrevista en la radio

ESCUCHAR Escucha la entrevista en la radio con Carlos Galán y luego contesta las preguntas.

1. ¿De dónde es Carlos?
2. ¿Cuál es su profesión?
3. ¿Por qué está en Chicago?
4. ¿Quiénes están con Carlos?
5. ¿Quién es colombiano?
6. ¿Cuándo es el concierto?
7. ¿Cómo se siente Carlos?

34

Escena de teatro

LEER, ESCRIBIR, HABLAR EN PAREJA Tú y otro(a) estudiante están hablando de una visita que hicieron al teatro. Túrnense para combinar palabras o expresiones de las dos listas y escriban preguntas y frases completas con el imperfecto de *ser* o *estar*. Usen las formas correctas de los adjetivos para elaborar.

Videomodelo
el cantante / alto y guapo
A —¿Cómo era el cantante?
B —El cantante era alto y guapo.

1. las bailarinas
2. el micrófono
3. el teatro
4. los pasos del tango
5. la melodía
6. el concierto
7. los actores
8. nosotros

a. muy difícil
b. nervioso
c. en la calle Bolívar
d. muy bonito
e. el viernes a las ocho
f. entusiasmado con el espectáculo
g. alto
h. fondo del escenario
i. argentino

35

Poeta por un día

ESCRIBIR, DIBUJAR, HABLAR EN GRUPO Los poemas haiku tienen tres líneas. La primera tiene 5 sílabas, la segunda 7 y la tercera 5. Por lo general, hablan de la naturaleza, escenas de la vida, las artes y los sentimientos que inspiran.

1 Piensa en un lugar, cosa o situación que te gusta o no te gusta. Por ejemplo, un baile, una fiesta o un museo. ¿Qué sientes cuando estás allí? Mira el ejemplo e inspírate para escribir tu propio haiku. Usa el presente de *ser* o *estar* para escribir tus frases, y no olvides que necesitas 5, 7 y 5 sílabas.

2 Después de escribir tu haiku, haz un dibujo para ilustrarlo.

3 Ahora estás listo(a) para presentar tu haiku a la clase. Explica en qué te inspiraste para escribirlo y muestra la ilustración.

En el museo
las estatuas me miran.
Estoy perdido.

Capítulo 2 • noventa y uno **91**

34

Standards: 1.1

Suggestions: Have partners share their exchanges with the class. Ask which rule determined their use of *ser* or *estar*.

Answers will vary. The following are sensible uses of the cues given:

Answers:

1. A —¿De qué nacionalidad eran las bailarinas?
   B —Eran argentinas.
2. A —¿Dónde estaba el micrófono?
   B —Estaba al fondo del escenario.
3. A —¿Dónde estaba el teatro?
   B —Estaba en la calle Bolívar.
4. A —¿Cómo eran los pasos del tango?
   B —Eran muy difíciles.
5. A —¿Cómo era la melodía?
   B —Era muy bonita.
6. A —¿De qué era el concierto?
   B —Era de música argentina.
7. A —¿Cómo eran los actores?
   B —Eran muy altos.
8. A —¿Cómo nos sentíamos?
   B —Estábamos entusiasmados con el espectáculo.

35

Standards: 1.2, 1.3, 3.1

Suggestions: Display students' finished haikus in the classroom.

Answers will vary.

Project-Based Learning

Students can perform Step 4 at this point. Be sure they understand your corrections and suggestions. (For more information, see p. 64-b.)

Additional Resources

Technology: Online Resources
• Instant Check
• Guided, Core, Audio
• *Para hispanohablantes*
Print
• Guided WB pp. 71–72
• Core WB p. 30

Assessment

Prueba 2-7 with Remediation (online only)
Prueba: *Ser y estar*
• Prueba 2-7

Enrich Your Teaching

Culture Note

Haiku grew out of a Japanese style of poetry in which people would play a kind of word game. Today the formalized style of haiku has spread and gained popularity around the world, and haiku can be found written in a multitude of languages, including Spanish.

21st Century Skills

Creativity and Innovation As students create their haiku poems, they should try to incorporate simple yet vivid images in their descriptions. Each line can have a separate purpose: first they could state their location, then make an observation, then finish with a personal comment.

Gramática

Suggestions: Ask students to write other sentences that use the five verbs in the two tenses. Since meaning is the key here, allow them to think of an idea in English first if necessary, and then convert the idea to a Spanish sentence.

 Technology: Interactive Whiteboard

> **Grammar Activities 2-2** Use the whiteboard activities in your Teacher Resources as you progress through the grammar practice with your class.

36

Suggestions: Have students do the activity on their own. Then have volunteers take turns reading it aloud. Ask each volunteer to say in English what the sentence means, based on the Spanish verb form he or she chose.

Answers:

Step 1

1. conocía	**5.** sabía
2. conocí	**6.** pudo
3. quería	**7.** quería
4. podía	**8.** quise

Step 2

1. La conoció el verano pasado.
2. Rita dijo que quería comer algo.
3. Ricardo estaba enojado porque Rita tenía una cita con otro muchacho.

Teacher-to-Teacher

Have students work in pairs to select a song in Spanish and create a list of similarities and differences to a similar song in English. Have them play both songs for the class, present their findings, and encourage the class to add to the list.

Gramática

Verbos con distinto sentido en el pretérito y en el imperfecto

A few Spanish verbs have different meanings in the imperfect and the preterite tenses.

	IMPERFECT	PRETERITE
saber	*knew*	*found out, learned*
	¿**Sabías** que el concierto empezaba tarde?	Sí, **supe** ayer que empezaba tarde.
conocer	*knew (somebody)*	*met (somebody) for the first time*
	Pedro **conocía** muy bien a esa actriz.	Luis la **conoció** el año pasado.
querer	*wanted to*	*tried to*
	Luis **quería** comprar las entradas hoy.	Yo **quise** comprarlas, pero me enfermé.
no querer	*didn't want to*	*refused to*
	No **querían** ver esa obra de teatro.	**No quisieron** ver esa obra de teatro.
poder	*was able to, could*	*managed to, succeeded in*
	Ella **podía** aprender la letra de la canción.	Ella **pudo** aprender la letra de esa canción.

Más recursos ONLINE

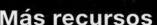 **Tutorial:** Summary of Uses of Preterite and Imperfect

 Canción de hip hop: El concierto

36

Una cita con Rita

LEER, ESCRIBIR

1 A veces las citas no resultan como queremos. Lee el blog sobre la cita que Ricardo tuvo con Rita y complétalo con el pretérito o el imperfecto de los verbos entre paréntesis.

2 Ahora, contesta las siguientes preguntas.
   1. ¿Cuándo conoció Ricardo a Rita?
   2. ¿Qué pasó cuando salieron de la escuela de danza?
   3. ¿Por qué estaba enojado Ricardo?

El blog de Ricardo

Yo no __1.__ *(conocer)* bien a Rita. Era solo nuestra segunda cita. Recuerdo que la __2.__ *(conocer)* el verano pasado en una clase de danza. Ella __3.__ *(querer)* aprender salsa, pero no __4.__ *(poder)* seguir bien los pasos. Yo le pregunté si __5.__ *(saber)* los movimientos de baile. Ella me dijo que no. Entonces, yo la ayudé y al final ella __6.__ *(poder)* aprenderlos.

Cuando salimos de la escuela de danza, Rita me dijo que __7.__ *(querer)* comer algo. Después, me dijo que ya era tarde y que tenía una cita con otro muchacho. Me invitó a ir con ellos, pero yo no __8.__ *(querer)* ir. Ya estaba bastante enojado. ¡No volví a salir con ella!

Differentiated Instruction

Heritage Speakers

Have students write out the lyrics to a favorite Spanish-language song on poster board or chart paper. Invite them to read the lyrics aloud for the class and explain unfamiliar vocabulary, then play the song so their classmates can listen and read along.

Students with Special Needs

Help students with hearing impairments experience the rhythms of salsa, merengue, and tango by exhibiting video or live examples of the dances associated with these musical genres. Encourage students to move, clap, or drum to the beat of the movements they are seeing.

CULTURA Cuba • Estados Unidos

La salsa tiene origen en el *son,* una mezcla de ritmos africanos y europeos que nació en Cuba. Al principio, el *son* se interpretaba con tambores y maracas. Luego se añadieron otros instrumentos como el bajo *(bass)* y la guitarra. El término *salsa* empezó a usarse en los años sesenta en Nueva York y sirve para definir una música que es mezcla del *son* cubano y otros ritmos del Caribe. La salsa es uno de los bailes más populares en los Estados Unidos.

• ¿Qué nombres de cantantes o grupos de salsa conoces?
• ¿Por qué crees que la salsa tiene tanto éxito en los Estados Unidos?

37

Y tú, ¿qué dices?

🎤 ESCRIBIR, HABLAR Haz y contesta preguntas con un(a) compañero(a).

1. Piensa en un momento en que quisiste hacer algo pero no pudiste. ¿Qué fue?
2. ¿Hay algo que nunca pudiste hacer bien? ¿Por qué no podías hacerlo?
3. ¿Qué poemas o canciones sabías de niño(a)? ¿Los sabías de memoria?
4. Piensa en una ocasión en que no quisiste hacer algo. ¿Qué fue?

5. ¿Conocías ya a muchos(as) de tus compañeros(as) cuando empezaste esta clase?
6. ¿Conociste a alguien famoso(a) alguna vez? ¿A quién? ¿Cómo sabías que era famoso(a)?

¿Recuerdas?
En español, las letras *b* y *v* se pronuncian igual. Al principio de una palabra, el sonido es similar a la *b* en *boy.* En otras posiciones, el sonido es más suave.

En voz alta

Juan Luis Guerra creció escuchando la música popular de la República Dominicana y a los Beatles en la radio. Más tarde, asistió al Conservatorio Nacional y al Berklee College of Music de Massachusetts, donde recibió la influencia del jazz. Con todas esas experiencias, Guerra comenzó a componer[1] canciones de merengue, el popular ritmo dominicano. Las canciones de Juan Luis Guerra son perfectas para bailar, pero su letra es mucho más rica y compleja[2] que la de los merengues tradicionales.

Escucha este fragmento de la letra de una canción de Juan Luis Guerra y luego trata de repetirla en voz alta.

¿Qué quiere decir Guerra cuando canta "haz el camino y seguiré tus huellas"?

[1]compose [2]complex

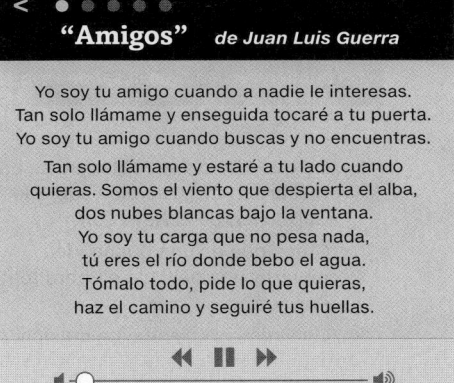

"Amigos" *de Juan Luis Guerra*

Yo soy tu amigo cuando a nadie le interesas.
Tan solo llámame y enseguida tocaré a tu puerta.
Yo soy tu amigo cuando buscas y no encuentras.

Tan solo llámame y estaré a tu lado cuando quieras. Somos el viento que despierta el alba,
dos nubes blancas bajo la ventana.
Yo soy tu carga que no pesa nada,
tú eres el río donde bebo el agua.
Tómalo todo, pide lo que quieras,
haz el camino y seguiré tus huellas.

⏪ ⏸ ⏩

🔉 ─○──────── 🔊

Capítulo 2 • noventa y tres **93**

Standards: 1.1, 1.2, 1.3, 2.2, 3.1

Suggestions: Before students read the review, direct their attention to the *Estrategia*. Remind them that using context clues will keep them reading and prevent them from getting stuck on unfamiliar words. Using context clues develops their skills in reading Spanish faster than consulting a dictionary because they are using what they already know and making associations between words and ideas.

Have students read the review silently and answer the questions on their own. Encourage them to paraphrase information drawn directly from the review, rather than stating it verbatim. Then go through the questions with the whole class. Ask students to read their answers aloud.

Answers:

1. Se habla de una obra teatral musical. Es una buena adaptación.
2. Answers will vary.
3. Se agregaron más canciones y algunas escenas dramáticas.
4. Menciona los 53 actores, el colorido vestuario y los efectos especiales.
5–6. Answers will vary.

Extension: When discussing students' answers for the questions, ask if anyone knows the original storyline of *El Rey León.* Ask any students who do to retell the story in the past tense.

Pre-AP® Integration

- **Learning Objective:** Interpretative Print
- **Activity:** As a pre-reading activity, have students prepare the following T-chart on a blank piece of paper. Have the class decide on several questions that they believe will be answered in the movie review. Then, read aloud to the class the review presented in *Actividad* 38 and ask students to take notes in column 2 as they hear their questions answered. Discuss with the class.

Preguntas sobre la reseña de El Rey León	Respuestas

- **Pre-AP® Resource Materials:** Comprehensive guide to Pre-AP® skill development

---

Una reseña de teatro

 LEER, ESCRIBIR, HABLAR Lee esta reseña de una obra musical presentada en la Ciudad de México, que fue adaptada de una película estadounidense, y luego intercambia opiniones con un(a) compañero(a) y contesten las preguntas.

Estrategia

Context clues When you read, look for cognates (words similar to English), which will make reading easier. Then, if you do not recognize a word, look at the words around it to try and guess what it means.

Reseña de un musical

El Rey León Siempre asusta el hecho de ver convertida una buena película en un musical. Sin embargo, en este caso se trata de una buena adaptación. A pesar de que se hicieron varios cambios con respecto a la película, son cambios que mejoran la adaptación musical. Por ejemplo, se agregaron más canciones y algunas escenas dramáticas. Sin dudas, el musical El Rey León es un gran éxito en la Ciudad de México.

La primera presentación del musical, traído de Broadway, es el 7 de mayo en el Teatro Telcel. Los 53 actores que trabajan en El Rey León bailan, cantan y entretienen al público con esta obra que parece hecha a medida[1] para convertirse en musical. El espectáculo lo completa el colorido vestuario[2] y los efectos especiales, que hacen que el público se sienta en la sabana[3] de África. ¡Hakuna Matata!

[1]made to measure [2]colorful wardrobe [3]savannah

1. ¿De qué tipo de espectáculo se habla en el artículo? ¿Qué dice sobre la adaptación de *El Rey León?*

2. ¿Crees que es una buena idea convertir una película en obra teatral? ¿Por qué?

3. ¿Qué cambios tiene este musical con respecto a la película?

4. ¿Qué elementos positivos del musical menciona el artículo?

5. ¿Sabes cuál es el argumento de la obra? ¿Por qué crees que el escritor de la reseña no dice cuál es el argumento o dónde ocurre la acción?

6. ¿Crees que la persona que escribió la reseña está a favor o en contra de esta comedia musical? ¿Por qué?

94 noventa y cuatro • Capítulo 2 • ¿Cómo te expresas?

Differentiated Instruction

Heritage Speakers

Have students give a brief commentary on an adaptation or translation that they have seen or read. They might choose a book that has been made into a movie, or the Spanish-language version of an English-language film, for example. Ask them to include a brief synopsis and tell which version they enjoyed more.

Students with Learning Difficulties

Have students identify and copy key words in each of the questions following *El Rey León.* Then have them locate these key words in the reading passage. Encourage them to use this connection to help find the answers to each question.

Los críticos

ESCRIBIR, HABLAR EN PAREJA

1 Trabaja con otro(a) estudiante. Escojan un espectáculo que vieron, que les gustó o que no les gustó. Escriban una lista de datos del espectáculo como los siguientes:

- tipo de espectáculo (película o musical, etc.)
- el autor o la autora
- los personajes
- el argumento
- dónde ocurría la acción
- la interpretación de los actores principales (cómica, aburrida)
- el orden de los sucesos
- con qué personajes se identificaron
- cómo reaccionó el público cuando terminó (lloró, se rió, aplaudió)

▲ Concierto de Juan Diego Flórez en el Teatro Real de Madrid

2 Escriban una reseña con los datos que juntaron. Si es posible, acompañen la reseña con fotos o anuncios del espectáculo.

Modelo

La obra de teatro "Romeo y Julieta" es un drama de William Shakespeare. Los personajes principales son . . . El problema es que . . . La acción tiene lugar en . . . En general, nos gustó . . . Los actores . . .

3 Hablen con otra pareja y expresen sus opiniones sobre las reseñas. Luego, reaccionen a las opiniones. ¿Están de acuerdo?

CULTURA España

La zarzuela ¿Ópera . . . opereta . . . obra musical de Broadway? Se parece un poco a cada una de estas formas musicales, pero es una expresión de la cultura, la historia y las costumbres de España. La zarzuela nació en el siglo XVII. En el siglo XIX se construyeron los dos teatros más famosos de la zarzuela en Madrid, el Teatro de La Zarzuela (1856) y el Teatro Apolo (1873–1929), y las compañías comenzaron a visitar América Latina. Su popularidad aumentó *(increased)* en el siglo XX, cuando varias zarzuelas se llevaron al cine.

Generalmente, la zarzuela tiene diálogos, canciones y bailes. Puede ser cómica, trágica y a veces el argumento es romántico.

- ¿Qué películas u obras de teatro similares a la zarzuela conoces? ¿Por qué crees se hizo tan popular? Sugiere dos ideas.

Mapa global interactivo Explora varios teatros en Madrid y haz comparaciones de los teatros españoles y los de tu pueblo.

Capítulo 2 • noventa y cinco **95**

39

Standards: 1.1, 1.2, 1.3, 3.1

Suggestions: Point out to students that the model review contains transitions that are an important part of clear writing. Encourage them to use similar transitions when putting together the ideas they listed in Step 1. Ask them to write a second draft of their review, paying attention to organization of ideas and sentence structure.

Answers will vary.

CULTURA

Standards: 1.1, 1.2, 2.2, 3.1

Suggestions: After students have read the information, ask comprehension questions. For example: *¿Cuáles son tres cosas que expresa la zarzuela? (Expresa la cultura, la historia y las costumbres de España.) ¿En qué siglo nació la zarzuela? (Nació en el siglo XVII.)*

Answers will vary.

Technology: Mapa global interactivo, Actividad 3 Discover the theaters of Madrid, Spain.

Additional Resources

Technology: Online Resources
- Instant Check
- Guided, Core, Audio
- *Para hispanohablantes*
- Communication Activities

Print
- Guided WB pp. 73–74
- Core WB pp. 31–32

Teacher's Resources
- Teacher's Resource Materials: Audio Script, Communicative Pair Activities, Technology: Audio Cap. 2

Project-Based Learning

Students can perform Step 5 at this point. Record their presentations for inclusion in their portfolio. (For more information, see p. 62-b.)

Assessment

Prueba 2-8 with Remediation (online only)
Prueba: Verbos con distintos sentidos en el pretérito
Examen: Vocabulario y gramática 2
- Examen 2
- ExamView: Examen 2

Enrich Your Teaching

Teacher-to-Teacher

Encourage students to keep an eye out for real-life connections to the arts. Your school might be planning an art exhibition, or the drama club rehearsing for a new production. Tap into students' interests and areas of expertise by inviting them to talk about their interests.

21st Century Skills

Communication Direct students to study other examples of movie or theater reviews in this chapter or in their local or school newspapers. Have them use them as models for their own review in *Actividad* 39.

Puente a la cultura

Standards: 1.2, 1.3, 2.1, 2.2, 3.1, 5.2

Suggestions

Pre-reading: Direct students' attention to the *Estrategia.* Use the questions there and the title of the selection to help students predict what the reading is about. Ask them to write down their predictions and to return to them as they read in order to verify whether or not they were correct. As you discuss the photos, have volunteers read the captions aloud.

Reading: Encourage students to read through the entire passage once silently, without stopping at problem words or to ask questions. Then ask volunteers to read sections aloud. Remind students to use background knowledge, cognates, and context clues to help them understand unfamiliar words and expressions as they read.

Post-reading: Ask students to comment on the predictions they wrote down in the Pre-reading. Ask questions such as: *¿Tus predicciones eran correctas? ¿Tuviste que cambiar alguna predicción? ¿Cómo? ¿Leíste algo en este artículo que no esperabas? ¿Qué fue? ¿Qué más te gustaría saber sobre Francisco de Goya?*

Common Errors: Point out to students the word ***obra*** in the first paragraph. Ask a volunteer to read aloud the sentence in which it is used. Explain that ***obra*** can refer to one single work, such as a painting, or to the work of an artist's entire life, as it does here.

Starter Activity

Show the painting *"Duquesa de Alba"* by Goya. Have students write a short paragraph telling what the woman might be doing and why.

Teacher-to-Teacher

Have students visit the official Museo del Prado Web site to find more information about Goya and his paintings.

Online Cultural Reading

Standards: 2.2, 4.2

After doing the online activity, ask students to compare the Goya paintings they see in this spread with any other paintings that they might have seen in a museum or in an art book.

Puente a la cultura

El mundo de Francisco de Goya

Francisco de Goya nació en 1746 en España. Murió en Francia en 1828, a los 82 años de edad y sordo[1], a causa de una misteriosa enfermedad. Goya es uno de los artistas más conocidos de todos los tiempos. Su obra es extensa y muy variada. Realizó murales religiosos, retratos de la corte española, dibujos de toros, cuadros sobre la guerra, y hasta sus propias pesadillas[2] que pintó en las paredes de su casa.

Uno de sus grandes triunfos artísticos fue llegar a ser Pintor de Cámara[3], o sea el pintor oficial de los reyes. Goya pintó retratos de la familia real y de otros personajes de la corte madrileña[4]. De esta época[5] son muy conocidos los retratos que hizo de la Duquesa de Alba, según algunos, una de las mujeres más hermosas de su época. Durante 18 años, Goya trabajó para la Real Fábrica de Tapices[6] de Santa Bárbara. Allí se dedicó a dibujar bocetos[7] de escenas alegres y pintorescas, que representaban la vida cotidiana[8] en Madrid. Estos bocetos luego aparecían en tapices que adornaban las paredes de los palacios reales.

[1]deaf [2]nightmares [3]Chamber Painter [4]Court of Madrid [5]period
[6]Royal Tapestry Factory [7]sketches [8]everyday

Estrategia

Using visuals Looking at the visuals before reading a selection allows us to better understand it. What do you notice about the paintings on this page and the next one? What might your observations tell you about what you will read about the painter?

Online Cultural Reading

Go to Auténtico ONLINE to read and understand a website about Goya's paintings.

"El quitasol", (1777), Francisco de Goya
Oil on canvas, 104 x 152 cm. Museo Nacional del Prado, Madrid, Spain. ▼

"Duquesa de Alba", (1795), Francisco de Goya
194 x 130 cm. Madrid, the Dukes of Alba's collection. ▼

Differentiated Instruction

Students with Learning Difficulties

Students may be overwhelmed by the amount of information contained in the biography of Francisco de Goya. To help organize this information, have them isolate the dates included in this passage. Then have them organize the dates into a timeline, adding a short caption to each significant date.

Advanced Learners

Ask students to summarize the selection by paraphrasing each paragraph in Spanish. Suggest that they begin each paraphrase with phrases such as ***El primer párrafo dice que... o Esta parte se trata de....***

Go **Online** to practice

PEARSON realize™

PearsonSchool.com/Autentico

VIDEO   WRITING

"El 3 de mayo de 1808", (1814), Francisco de Goya
Oil on canvas, 8 ft. 9 in. x 13 ft. 4 in. Museo Nacional del Prado, Madrid.
Copyright Lessing/Art Resource, NY.

La pintura de Goya cambió con el tiempo para mostrar los sucesos que ocurrían en su país. Los españoles lucharon[9] durante siete años contra las tropas francesas que Napoleón envió para invadir España. La obra más famosa de Goya sobre el tema de la guerra[10] contra Francia es el cuadro "El 3 de mayo de 1808".

Al final de su vida, Goya estuvo muy enfermo. Sus obras de esta época se llaman Pinturas Negras, ya que Goya representaba imágenes de pesadillas, como monstruos, con fondos oscuros.

Los cuadros de Goya están en los museos más importantes del mundo. Para celebrar los 250 años del nacimiento del pintor, el Museo del Prado de Madrid organizó una gran exposición en 1996. La obra de Goya sigue siendo muy popular hoy en día. ¿Por qué crees que es así?

[9]fought [10]war

 ¿Comprendiste?

1. ¿Cuándo, en qué lugar y cómo se celebraron los 250 años del nacimiento de Goya?

2. ¿Por qué podemos decir que las pinturas de la página 96 son representativas de las obras de Goya cuando era Pintor de Cámara? ¿Qué puedes inferir del significado de "Pintor de Cámara"?

3. La pintura de Goya cambió según las diferentes épocas de su vida. Da dos ejemplos y explica cómo se relacionan esas pinturas con los cambios en su vida.

4. ¿Cuáles son las razones del éxito de Goya como pintor? Explica las razones y el por qué. Presenta y defiende tu opinión frente a la clase.

 Escribe tu opinión

Acabas de leer sobre los diferentes períodos de la pintura de Goya. Basándote en la información que leíste y las obras que ves aquí, escribe si te gustaría ver más obras de Goya y explica por qué. Presenta y defiende tu opinión a la clase.

▶ **Videodocumentario** El arte en el mundo hispano.

"El sueño de la razón produce monstruos", (1799), Francisco de Goya
Plate 43 of 'Los Caprichos', published c. 1810 (color engraving). Bibliothèque Nationale, Paris, France. Archives Charmet. Bridgeman Art Library, London.

Capítulo 2 • noventa y siete **97**

¿Qué me cuentas?

Standards: 1.1, 1.2, 2.2, 3.1, 5.2

Resources: Teacher's Resource Materials: Audio Script, Technology: Audio, Cap. 3

AP® Skills: Integration of listening, reading, and writing to comprehend and synthesize information from spoken and written sources.

Suggestions: For Step 1, use the audio or read the descriptions aloud. Allow students to hear both descriptions twice through: the first time to write their answers, the second time to check them.

For Step 2, have students identify significant details as they read and then summarize the main points of the article.

In Step 3, students may need some guidance in order to discuss what they think the artists wanted to express. Circulate and listen to their discussions. If necessary, help them with questions containing embedded answers: *¿Piensas que la pintura de Irigoyen expresa la confusión o la alegría de estar en casa? ¿Y la de Picasso?*

 **Technology: Audio
Script and Answers**

1. Al fondo de este cuadro hay una alfombra con flores o estrellas.
2. Las imágenes de esta pintura representan un estilo abstracto.
3. El estilo de esta pintura es bastante realista.
4. Al primer plano de esta naturaleza muerta hay una guitarra.
5. En primer plano se ve una taza de té con una cuchara.
6. A la izquierda hay un pájaro.
7. Este cuadro muestra varios colores vivos.
8. A la derecha hay unos postres

Step 1

1. Picasso	5. Irigoyen
2. Picasso	6. Irigoyen
3. Irigoyen	7. Picasso
4. Picasso	8. Irigoyen

Step 2–3

Answers will vary.

Active Classroom

Ask each student to create a *naturaleza muerta* using colors, shapes, and images that reflect his or her personal style. Encourage creativity. Upon completion, give the painting to another student who will describe it.

Additional Resources

📶 **Technology: Online Resources**
• *Para hispanohablantes*

**Pre-AP®
Integración**

OBJECTIVES
▸ Listen to and read descriptions of paintings and the art genre of still life
▸ Discuss two paintings

🔊 ### ¿Qué me cuentas?: Naturaleza muerta

Compara el cuadro de naturaleza muerta de Irigoyen con el de Picasso. Primero escucha unas descripciones de los cuadros. Guarda lo que escribes para usarlo en el paso 3.

1 Vas a escuchar unas descripciones sobre los dos cuadros de esta página. Escribe cada descripción e indica si pertenece al cuadro de Irigoyen o de Picasso.

▲ "Naturaleza muerta/Still Life", (1910), José María de la Luz Irigoyen

▲ "Naturaleza muerta con guitarra", (1924), Pablo Picasso

2 Ahora lee la información sobre el género de naturaleza muerta.

La pintura de naturaleza muerta tiene como fuente de inspiración los objetos inanimados de la vida diaria. El pintor puede tener diferentes metas. Algunos artistas quieren hacer una representación detallada de la realidad y se concentran en la técnica de la pintura. Cuando pintan, destacan detalles en la imagen, como la textura de los objetos o los efectos de la luz. A veces los artistas quieren comunicar un mensaje e incluyen objetos simbólicos. Por ejemplo, los libros o mapas simbolizan la educación. Las frutas cortadas o flores marchitas[1] pueden simbolizar la muerte. A través de los siglos, los artistas han interpretado este género según las ideas de los movimientos artísticos de su época[2].

[1]withered [2]era

 3 Habla con otro estudiante y comparen el cuadro de Irigoyen y el de Picasso. Piensen en los títulos. ¿Por qué se llaman así? Observen las pinturas y compárenlas según el tema, los colores, las imágenes y lo que quiere expresar el artista. Expliquen cómo el artista adapta su estilo, realista o surrealista, al género de la naturaleza muerta. Usen las siguientes expresiones y hagan gestos apropiados en la interacción.

Por un lado . . . *(on the one hand)*	Esto me parece más . . .	Sin embargo . . .
Por otra parte . . . *(on the other hand)*	En primer lugar . . .	En contraste . . .

Differentiated Instruction

Heritage Speakers

Have students add a second layer to their oral presentations. In addition to explaining why a particular heritage country artist should be voted **Artista del Año.** Have them explain why a major competitor to this artist is not as qualified to receive the distinction.

Students with Learning Difficulties

Students may have difficulty organizing and recalling information for their oral presentations. To support them, have students provide you with a written copy of their presentation materials prior to the actual oral presentation. Use this information to provide guiding questions or cues if necessary.

OBJECTIVES
▶ Demonstrate how to give a presentation about your favorite artist
▶ Use key points to organize information

Go Online to practice
PEARSON realize™
PearsonSchool.com/Autentico
AUDIO SPEAK/RECORD

"Artista del Año"

TAREA Imagina que en tu clase van a seleccionar a un(a) artista como candidato(a) al premio "Artista del Año". Puede ser un(a) pintor(a), un actor, una actriz, o un(a) cantante que te guste. Explica quién debe ser el / la candidato(a) y por qué.

1 Prepárate Escoge tu artista preferido(a). Completa una tabla como ésta sobre tu candidato(a). Recuerda que puedes usar tus notas para prepararte, pero no al hacer la presentación oral.

Nombre	
Tipo de artista	
Puntos positivos	
Experiencia	
Originalidad, personalidad	

2 Practica Haz tu presentación ante el grupo. Al final, se va a hacer una votación para escoger un(a) ganador(a). Recuerda que debes:

- incluir el nombre del / de la artista, su especialidad y lo que hizo
- describir los puntos positivos del / de la candidato(a)
- decir claramente por qué debe ganar el premio
- usar el vocabulario de este capítulo

3 Haz tu presentación Haz tu presentación ante la clase. Al final, todos los estudiantes votan para elegir al / a la "Artista del Milenio".

4 Evaluación Tu profesor(a) utilizará la siguiente rúbrica para evaluar tu presentación.

Estrategia

Organize information Organize the key points you may want to talk about by listing them in a chart. This will help you give a more effective presentation.

▼ Pitbull y Enrique Iglesias

Rubric	Score 1	Score 3	Score 5
How well you provide information	You lack vital information, such as the artist's identity.	Your vital information about the artist is present.	Your information about the artist is clearly presented.
How well you support your opinion	You have little or no convincing evidence.	Your supporting evidence is present, but not developed.	Your supporting evidence is clear and convincing.
How effectively you deliver your speech	You have no eye contact with the audience.	You make some eye contact. You use intonation, but not convincingly.	You make good eye contact with the audience. You have good intonation and gestures.

Presentational | 2

Presentación oral

Standards: 1.1, 1.2, 1.3, 3.1

Suggestions: Review the task and the rubric with students. Help students decide what type of information to put in the various categories of the chart. In **Puntos positivos,** they can focus on the artist's artistic qualities. For **Experiencia,** they might list the work they know of from that artist. For **Originalidad, personalidad,** they can tell what they know about the artist's personal life.

Pre-AP® Integration

- **Learning Objective:** Presentational Speaking
- **Activity:** Remind students to focus on the presentational speaking skills used in this task such as fluency, pronunciation, and comprehensibility.
- **Pre-AP® Resource Materials:** Comprehensive guide to Pre-AP® speaking skill development

Digital Portfolio

Make audio or video recordings of student presentations in class, or assign the Speak and Record activity so they can record their presentations online. Include the recording in their portfolios.

Additional Resources

 Technology: Online Resources
- *Para hispanohablantes*

Self Assessment _____

Presentación oral
- **Assessment Program:** Rubrics

Review the rubric with students. Go over the descriptions of the different levels of performance. After assessing students, help individuals understand how their performance could be improved. (See Teacher's Resource Materials for suggestions on using rubrics in assessment.)

Enrich Your Teaching

Teacher-to-Teacher

Some students experience stress when asked to make oral presentations to the class. Allow them, at least occasionally, to record their presentations. This reduces stress for them and provides you with a handy tool for assessment.

21st Century Skills

ICT (Information, Communications and Technology) Literacy As they do this *Presentación oral* task, student should try to incorporate different types of media into their presentation, including visuals, audio, or video representations of their artist candidate. Have students determine the best media to represent their artist.

Language Arts Connection: Persuasive Writing

Remind students that in their Language Arts classes they were taught effective use of transitions in writing. As they revise their drafts in Step 3, tell them to include transitions that will warn the reader that they are changing from one main idea to another. As part of the revision process, have partners comment on one another's use of transitions.

Presentación escrita

Standards: 1.3, 3.1

Suggestions: Explain at the start the criteria you will use to evaluate students' compositions. (See Step 5, *Evaluación,* in the Student Edition.)

First, direct students' attention to the *Estrategia.* Remind them that using a graphic organizer will help them prepare their evaluations. Draw a flowchart on the board. Model filling in the information about an imaginary candidate. Make statements about the candidate's capabilities and ask students where the information should go in the web: *Sol Herrera es una buena escritora. Escribió dos cuentos cortos. Estos cuentos están publicados en revistas.* Once students determine that this information goes in the **Nombre, arte** and **Experiencia** sections of the web, fill it in on the graphic organizer. Together with students, read through the information about the imaginary candidate Vicky Lagardera in the web shown on this page. Answer any questions they may have about the graphic organizer.

Active Classroom

Encourage students to use the graphic organizer. You might have students work in small groups and share their notes.

You might ask a few students to present their notes using an overhead transparency.

Presentación escrita

OBJECTIVES
▶ Write an evaluation about a student's audition
▶ Categorize information for clarity

El mejor candidato

Imagina que te piden que des tu opinión sobre la audición de un(a) artista y por qué deben aceptarlo(a) en una escuela famosa. Escribe un informe para explicar por qué crees que será un(a) buen(a) estudiante. Recuerda defender tu opinión con declaraciones que apoyan tu manera de pensar.

Estrategia

Categorizing When writing a report you must include the greatest amount of information in the clearest way possible. If you organize the information into categories and write everything about one topic before going to the next one, the reader will have no trouble understanding your report.

1 **Antes de escribir** Contesta estas preguntas:

• ¿Qué tipo de artista es y qué experiencia tuvo? ¿Tuvo actuaciones en público? ¿Cuándo?

• Si canta, ¿sabe la letra?, ¿sigue la música? Si baila, ¿sabe los pasos?, ¿sigue el ritmo? Si hace teatro, ¿representa bien al personaje?, ¿sabe los diálogos?

• ¿Qué aptitudes naturales tiene el(la) estudiante?

Antes de escribir tu composición, usa un organizador gráfico como este para ordenar tus ideas.

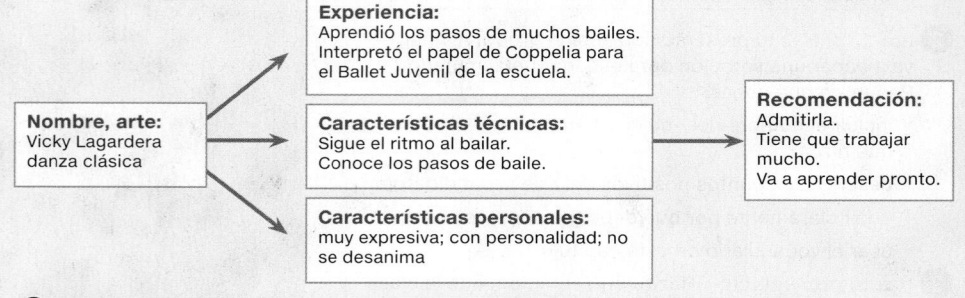

2 **Borrador** Escribe tu borrador. Escribe un informe con toda la información del organizador gráfico. Más tarde lo podrás revisar.

Modelo

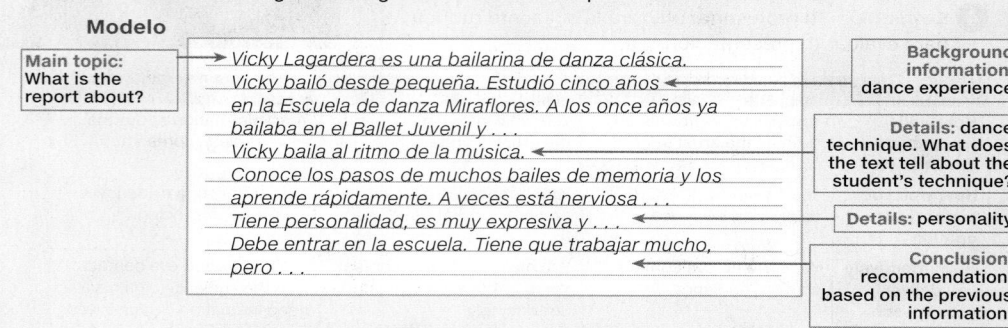

Differentiated Instruction

Heritage Speakers

Have students identify one or two specific elements of Spanish grammar that they find challenging in their writing. Direct them to focus on these specific points while revising their written presentations.

Advanced Learners

Encourage students to interview the person they are evaluating. They can ask the person for hard facts about his or her artistic experience, such as publications or exhibits. They can also ask the artist to assess his or her own strong points. They can then translate at least some of this information to Spanish and use it in their evaluations.

Go **Online** to practice
PEARSON realize.™

PearsonSchool.com/Autentico
WRITING

Presentational 2

3 **Redacción/Revisión** Después de escribir el primer borrador, trabaja con otro(a) estudiante para intercambiar los trabajos y leerlos. Luego, hagan sugerencias para mejorar sus informes.

- ¿Seguiste el plan que hiciste en tu organizador gráfico? ¿Escribiste todas las ideas que querías expresar?
- ¿Están bien organizados los párrafos? ¿Comunicaste claramente la información?
- ¿Defendiste tu opinión con oraciones que la apoyan?
- ¿Usaste los verbos y los tiempos verbales correctos?

Haz lo siguiente: Verifica si usaste correctamente los verbos en pretérito o imperfecto.

> *bailó*
> Vicky ~~bailé~~ desde pequeña. ~~Estudiaba~~ cinco
> *Estudió*
>
> años en la Escuela de danza Miraflores. A los
>
> *bailaba*
> once años ya ~~bailó~~ en el Ballet Juvenil y . . .

4 **Publicación** Antes de crear la versión final, lee de nuevo el informe y repasa los siguientes puntos:

- ¿Explica mi informe claramente lo que pienso del / de la estudiante que quiere entrar en la escuela?
- ¿Usé el vocabulario apropiado para este tema?
- ¿Debo añadir detalles importantes?

5 **Evaluación** Se utilizará la siguiente rúbrica para evaluar tu presentación.

Rubric	Score 1	Score 3	Score 5
How well you organize information	Your vital information about the candidate is missing.	You present vital information but it's unorganized.	Your information is clearly presented and organized.
How well you support your choice	You have few or no convincing details about the candidate.	Your details convince us to vote for the candidate.	Your details about the candidate are organized and convincing.
Sentence structure/ grammar, spelling, mechanics	Your sentences are run-on or are fragmented with many errors.	You use sentences effectively, but with a few errors.	Your sentence structure is varied with very few errors.

Suggestions (Cont'd)

Then, have them create on their own paper a similar, empty web and use it to prepare their evaluations of their own candidates. Once students have a rough draft ready, read through the model on this page together. Help them see how information from the web on p. 98 was incorporated into this draft and to note the additional information that was added. Point out the use of past tenses and complete sentences. Encourage them to work toward similar organization, level of detail, and language use as they revise their own drafts.

Evaluation

Steps 4 and 5 overlap. Students will need evaluation by you, their peers, or self-evaluation to fine-tune and polish their drafts.

Pre-AP® Integration

- **Learning Objective:** Presentational Writing
- **Pre-AP® Resource Materials:** Comprehensive guide to Pre-AP® writing skills development

Digital Portfolio

Keep students' final drafts in their portfolios as a writing sample.

Additional Resources

 Technology: Online Resources
- *Para hispanohablantes*

Self Assessment _____

Presentación escrita
- **Assessment Program:** Rubrics

Review the rubric with students. Go over the descriptions of the different levels of performance. After assessing students, help individuals understand how their performance could be improved. (See Teacher's Resource Materials for suggestions on using rubrics in assessment.)

Enrich Your Teaching

Teacher-to-Teacher

As students review each other's work, encourage them to begin their critiques with a positive comment or two. Remind them of how much more readily they themselves respond to positive criticism than to negative comments. Ask them to provide suggestions and additions in a constructive way.

21st Century Skills

Collaboration Have students review the rubrics they have been given (pp. 99, 101). Ask them to discuss with a partner why their teacher gives them rubrics; how are they supposed to be used? Have them work with the rubric on this page to start with the outcome, figure out what they might need to do to get the best grade possible, and develop a plan to achieve that goal.

Lectura

Standards: 1.1, 1.2, 1.3, 2.1, 2.2, 3.1, 3.2, 4.1, 4.2, 5.2

Suggestions

Pre-reading: Ask a volunteer to read the title of the passage aloud. Ask students what they think is meant by the expression *Fragmento de.* If they don't know, explain that the selection is a fragment or excerpt from a longer work.

Before reading, direct students' attention to the *Estrategia* and to the *Al leer* sections. Have them answer the questions and copy the graphic organizer from this page.

Consider having students read the information about the author of the autobiography in the *Cultura* on p. 105 before they read the selection itself. Ask them to use what they learn from that, as well as the title of the selection and the photos, to answer the question *¿De qué tratará esta lectura?*

Active Classroom

After reading the *Lectura,* ask each student to play the role of Esmeralda and do a short reading from this autobiography, perhaps one paragraph in length. Explain how it is common for authors to do "readings" of their work. Have students focus on pronunciation and personal expression, imagining how the author herself might read the selected excerpt.

Lectura

OBJECTIVES
▶ Read an excerpt of an autobiography
▶ Monitor reading to increase understanding
▶ Give your opinion about the advantages of living between two cultures

Estrategia
Monitoring your reading When you are reading a long selection, stop to ask yourself questions such as: What is the main idea? How does this idea relate to the theme of the reading? Which details are important? This strategy will help you understand better what you are reading.

Al leer

Vas a leer un fragmento de una autobiografía. Se trata de Esmeralda Santiago, una joven puertorriqueña que emigró con su familia a Nueva York. Esmeralda da una audición en la famosa escuela secundaria Performing Arts. Mientras lees, anota en la tabla de la derecha los puntos indicados.

Qué hace y cómo se siente Esmeralda	
antes de la audición	
durante la audición	
después de la audición	

Fragmento de *Cuando era puertorriqueña*

—¡Las pruebas son en menos de un mes! Tienes que aprender una escena dramática, y la vas a realizar enfrente de un jurado[1]. Si lo haces bien, y tus notas aquí son altas, puede ser que te admitan a la escuela.

El Mister Barone se encargó de prepararme para la prueba. Seleccionó un soliloquio de una obra de Sidney Howard titulada *The Silver Cord,* montada[2] por primera vez en 1926, pero la acción de la cual acontecía en una sala de estrado en Nueva York, alrededor del año 1905.

—Mister Gatti, el maestro de gramática, te dirigirá . . . Y Missis Johnson te hablará acerca de lo que te debes de poner y esas cosas.

Mi parte era la de Cristina, una joven casada confrontando a su suegra[3]. Aprendí el soliloquio fonéticamente, bajo la dirección de Mister Gatti. Mis primeras palabras eran: "You belong to a type that's very common in this country, Mrs. Phelps, a type of self-centered, self-pitying, son-devouring tigress, with unmentionable proclivities suppressed on the side".

—No tenemos tiempo de aprender lo que quiere decir cada palabra —dijo Mister Gatti—. Solo asegúrate de que las pronuncies todas.

Yo había soñado[4] con este momento durante varias semanas. Más que nada, quería impresionar al jurado con mi talento para que me aceptaran a Performing Arts High School y para poder salir de Brooklyn todos los días, y un día nunca volver.

Pero en cuanto me enfrenté con las tres mujeres bien cuidadas que formaban el jurado de la audición, se me olvidó el inglés que había aprendido y las lecciones que Missis Johnson me había inculcado sobre cómo portarme como una dama. En la agonía de contestar sus preguntas incomprensibles, puyaba[5] mis manos hacia aquí y hacia allá, formando palabras con mis dedos porque no me salían por la boca.

—¿Por qué no nos dejas oír tu soliloquio ahora? —preguntó la señora de los lentes colgantes.

Me paré como asustada, y mi silla cayó patas arriba como a tres pies de donde yo estaba

---

[1]jury panel [2]put on stage [3]mother-in-law [4]The usage of *había* with the past participle expresses what a person *had* done. *Había soñado* = I had dreamed [5]moved, pushed

Differentiated Instruction

Heritage Speakers

After previewing the selection, have students practice and present a "dramatic reading" of this literature excerpt. Tell them to imagine that their version will be broadcast on the radio. Encourage students to assume different roles, characterizations, voices, and intonations.

Students with Learning Difficulties

As students read the excerpt aloud, model for them the appropriate intonation or expression. Have students repeat and imitate your exaggerated intonation to help support the meaning of the narrative.

parada. La fui a buscar, deseando con toda mi alma que un relámpago entrara por la ventana y me hiciera cenizas allí mismo.

—No te aflijas —dijo la señora—. Sabemos que estás nerviosa.

Cerré los ojos y respiré profundamente, caminé al centro del salón y empecé mi soliloquio.

—Llu bilón tú é tayp dats beri cómo in dis contri Missis Felps. É tayp of selfcente red self pí tí in són de baurin taygrés huid on menshonabol proclibétis on de sayd.

A pesar de las instrucciones de Mister Gatti de hablar lentamente y pronunciar bien las palabras aunque no las entendiera, recité mi monólogo de tres minutos en un minuto sin respirar ni una vez.

Las pestañas[6] falsas de la señora bajita parecían haber crecido de sorpresa. La cara serena de la señora elegante temblaba con risa controlada.

La señora alta vestida de pardo me dio una sonrisa dulce.

—Gracias, querida. ¿Puedes esperar afuera un ratito?

Resistí el deseo de hacerle reverencia. El pasillo era largo, con paneles de madera angostos pegados verticalmente entre el piso y el cielo raso.

Lámparas con bombillas grandes y redondas colgaban de cordones largos, creando charcos amarillos en el piso pulido. Unas muchachas como de mi edad estaban sentadas en sillas a la orilla del corredor, esperando su turno. Me miraron de arriba a abajo cuando salí, cerrando la puerta tras de mí. Mami se paró de su silla al fondo del corredor. Se veía tan asustada como me sentía yo.

—¿Qué te pasó?

—Na'[7]—no me atrevía a hablar, porque si empezaba a contarle lo que había sucedido, empezaría a llorar enfrente de las otras personas, cuyos ojos me seguían como si

---
[6]eyelashes [7]nothing

Capítulo 2 • ciento tres **103**

Suggestions (Cont'd)

Reading: While reading the selection together with students, pause frequently to address comprehension issues that students may bring up. Ask your own comprehension questions to help them focus on the main idea and important details of each section. Here are some possible comprehension issues on pp. 102–103 for which you can provide some guidance:

- p. 102: Ask a volunteer to read aloud the excerpt that the author had to recite for her audition. Ask: *¿Este ejemplo de inglés es fácil o difícil?* Ask them to consider how much more difficult it would be for a person like the author, whose first language isn't English.
- p. 103, column 1: Tell students that the expression *No te aflijas* means the same as *No te preocupes.*
- p. 103, column 1: Explain that the paragraph beginning with *—Llu bilón...* is the phonetic rendition of English that the author refers to on the previous page. Read this aloud for students.
- p. 103, columns 1-2: Help students understand by pantomiming the actions in passages such as *La cara serena de la señora elegante temblaba...* and *...hacerle reverencia.*

Teacher-to-Teacher

Students may need some guidance in order to appreciate the humor in this selection. Point out humorous parts by asking questions such as *¿Piensan que el fragmento de una obra de teatro que eligieron los maestros de Esmeralda era adecuado* (adequate) *para su audición? ¿Por qué?/¿Por qué no? ¿Qué pasó cuando Esmeralda se levantó para decir su soliloquio? ¿Cómo se sintió ella? ¿Esmeralda dijo su soliloquio rápida o lentamente? ¿Cómo lo sabes?*

Enrich Your Teaching

Culture Note

The theme of remaining and retaining one's self in the context of a new country and culture is a popular one in contemporary U.S. literature. Some notable examples include Nicholasa Mohr's *El Bronx Remembered,* and Julia Álvarez's *How the García Girls Lost Their Accents.*

21st Century Skills

Critical Thinking and Problem Solving Encourage students to use their reading strategies when reading *Cuando era puertorriqueña.* Remind them to preview the comprehension questions first, then have them focus their attention on the use of dialogue and first person narrative as they read the story.

Suggestions (Cont'd)

Reading: Additional comprehension issues are as follows:

- p. 103, column 2: Help students through the passage about light by telling them that the key word in the passage, **charco,** means "puddle" or "pool."

- p. 103, column 2: Point out that **na** is Esmeralda's shortened, slang form of **nada.**

- p. 104, column 1: Guide students to see the humor in Esmeralda's saying **¡Presente! quiero decir, aquí...** Say: *Primero, Esmeralda habla en español, pero quiere hablar en inglés. Entonces trata de corregirse* (correct herself). *¿Qué piensan que quería decir la segunda vez?* ("Here")

- p. 105: Point out the use of the participles **jugando** and **chapurreando** in participial phrases. Remind students that they reviewed this type of usage before the reading.

Pre-AP® Integration

- **Learning Objective:** Presentational Speaking (Cultural Comparison)
- **Background:** This task prepares students for the Spoken Presentational Communication tasks that focus on cultural comparisons.
- **Activity:** Have students prepare a two-minute (maximum) presentation on the following topic: Strategies for adapting to a new culture can be varied and unexpected. Students may use Esmeralda Santiago's experiences as described in the reading as a basis for the comparison. They should comment on a cross-cultural or adaptation experience they have had or may have read about, explaining the similarities and differences between the two.
- **Pre-AP® Resource Materials:** Comprehensive guide to Pre-AP® speaking skill development

Teacher-to-Teacher

e-amigos: Have students send their e-amigos a paragraph summarizing their responses to the question in item 4 of *¿Comprendiste?* Encourage students to express their feelings in an honest and sincere way. Have students print out their e-mails or send them to you for review.

buscando señas de lo que les esperaba. Caminamos hasta la puerta de salida—. Tengo que esperar aquí un momentito.

—¿No te dijeron nada?

—No. Solo que espere aquí.

Nos recostamos contra la pared. Enfrente de nosotras había una pizarra de corcho con recortes de periódico acerca de graduados de la escuela. En las orillas, alguien había escrito en letras de bloque, "P.A." y el año cuando el actor, bailarín o músico se había graduado. Cerré mis ojos y traté de imaginar un retrato de mí contra el corcho y la leyenda "P.A. '66" en la orilla.

La puerta al otro lado del pasillo se abrió, y la señora vestida de pardo sacó la cabeza.

—¿Esmeralda?

—¡Presente! quiero decir, aquí —alcé la mano.

Me esperó hasta que entré al salón. Había otra muchacha adentro, a quien me presentó como Bonnie, una estudiante en la escuela.

—¿Sabes lo que es una pantomima? —preguntó la señora. Señalé con la cabeza que sí—. Bonnie y tú son hermanas decorando el árbol de Navidad.

Bonnie se parecía mucho a Juanita Marín, a quien yo había visto por última vez cuatro años antes. Decidimos dónde poner el árbol invisible, y nos sentamos en el piso y actuamos como que estábamos sacando las decoraciones de una caja y colgándolas en las ramas.

Mi familia nunca había puesto un árbol de Navidad, pero yo me acordaba de cómo una vez yo ayudé a Papi a ponerle luces de colores alrededor de una mata de berenjenas[8] que dividía nuestra parcela de la de Doña Ana.

Empezamos por abajo, y le envolvimos el cordón eléctrico con las lucecitas rojas alrededor de la mata hasta que no nos quedaba más. Entonces Papi enchufó otro cordón eléctrico con más luces, y seguimos envolviéndolo hasta que las ramas se doblaban con el peso y la mata parecía estar prendida en llamas.

En un ratito se me olvidó dónde estaba, y que el árbol no existía, y que Bonnie no era mi hermana. Hizo como que me pasaba una decoración bien delicada y, al yo extender la mano para cogerla, hizo como que se me cayó y se rompió. Me asusté de que Mami entraría gritándonos que le habíamos roto una de sus figuras favoritas. Cuando empecé a recoger los fragmentos delicados de cristal invisible, una voz nos interrumpió y dijo:

—Gracias.

Bonnie se paró, sonrió y se fue.

La señora elegante estiró su mano para que se la estrechara.

—Notificaremos a tu escuela en unos días. Mucho gusto en conocerte.

Le estreché la mano a las tres señoras, y salí sin darles la espalda, en una neblina silenciosa, como si la pantomima me hubiera quitado la voz y el deseo de hablar.

De vuelta a casa, Mami me preguntaba qué había pasado, y yo le contestaba, "Na'. No pasó na'," avergonzada de que, después de tantas horas de práctica con Missis Johnson, Mister Barone y Mister Gatti, después del gasto de ropa y zapatos nuevos, después de que Mami tuvo que coger el día libre sin paga para llevarme hasta Manhattan, después de todo eso, no había pasado la prueba y nunca jamás saldría de Brooklyn.

[8]eggplant bush

104 ciento cuatro • Capítulo 2 • ¿Cómo te expresas?

Differentiated Instruction

Heritage Speakers

Have students research and locate a Spanish-language play whose theme they find interesting. Have them design and rehearse a scene from this play. Remind them to consider characterization, costume, and movement. Encourage students to perform the scene for the class.

Advanced Learners

Invite students who enjoyed this selection to read the rest of Santiago's *Cuando era puertorriqueña.* If more than one student is interested, encourage them to form their own book club to discuss the book.

Epílogo: Un día de éstos

Diez años después de mi graduación de Performing Arts High School, volví a visitar la escuela. Estaba viviendo en Boston, una estudiante becada en la universidad Harvard. La señora alta y elegante de mi prueba se había convertido en mi mentora durante mis tres años en la escuela. Después de mi graduación, se había casado con el principal de la escuela.

—Me acuerdo del día de tu prueba —me dijo, su cara angular soñadora, sus labios jugando con una sonrisa que todavía parecía tener que controlar. Me había olvidado de la niña flaca y trigueña[9] con el pelo enrizado, el vestido de lana y las manos inquietas. Pero ella no. Me dijo que el jurado tuvo que pedirme que esperara afuera para poderse reír, ya que les parecía tan cómico ver a aquella chica puertorriqueña de catorce años chapurreando[10] un soliloquio acerca de una suegra posesiva durante el cambio de siglo, las palabras incomprensibles porque pasaban tan rápido.

—Admiramos el valor necesario para pararte al frente de nosotras y hacer lo que hiciste.

—¿Quiere decir que me aceptaron en la escuela no porque tenía talento, sino porque era atrevida?

Nos reímos juntas.

[9]dark haired [10]babbling

Go **Online** to practice
PEARSON realize.

PearsonSchool.com/Autentico

WRITING   MAPA GLOBAL

 ¿Comprendiste?

En parejas, revisen la tabla que completaron y luego contesten estas preguntas:

1. ¿Crees que Esmeralda se preparó bien para su audición? ¿Por qué sí o por qué no?

2. ¿Cuál fue la verdadera razón por la que la aceptaron?

3. Muchos jóvenes inmigrantes se sienten atrapados *(trapped)* entre dos culturas.

¿Cómo creía Esmeralda que podía salir de esa situación?

4. Y tú, ¿tuviste alguna vez una experiencia similar a la de Esmeralda? ¿Sentiste alguna vez que no te identificabas con un grupo? Si es así, ¿cómo resolviste el problema?

5. Parafrasea el tema, la idea principal y los detalles de la lectura. En tu opinión, ¿crees que el título del libro refleja la idea principal? ¿Cómo?

CULTURA   Puerto Rico • Estados Unidos

Esmeralda Santiago (1948-) nació en Puerto Rico y emigró con su familia a Nueva York. Fue a la escuela The High School for Performing Arts, de la cual salió con una beca *(scholarship)* para estudiar en Harvard. Dos de sus libros, *Cuando era puertorriqueña* y *Casi una mujer* son autobiográficos. Describen el proceso de adaptación a otra cultura de una joven inmigrante. Aunque escribe desde el punto de vista de otra cultura, muchos de sus lectores se identifican con sus experiencias y sentimientos.

• ¿Cuál es una ventaja *(advantage)* de vivir entre dos culturas?

 Mapa global interactivo Explora Puerto Rico e investiga los motivos de la migración de los puertorriqueños a los Estados Unidos.

Esmeralda Santiago ▶

Capítulo 2 • ciento cinco **105**

Interpretive Reading

2

¿Comprendiste?

Standards: 1.1, 1.2, 1.3

Suggestions:

Post-reading: After students revisit their chart and make changes or additions, have them share the information they included. Ask volunteers which parts of the selection help them answer the *¿Comprendiste?* questions.

Answers will vary. For question 2, guide students to see the importance of the part of the selection in which Esmeralda loses herself in her memories during the pantomime. Ask a volunteer to read that part aloud. Say: *Estos dos recuerdos (memories) deben ser importantes porque interrumpen la acción del cuento. ¿Piensas que estos recuerdos tuvieron un efecto sobre su actuación en la pantomima? ¿Qué efecto?*

CULTURA ◀

Standards: 1.2, 3.1, 4.2

Suggestions: Point out to students that this information sheds light on Santiago's purpose for writing the selection. Remind them that considering the author's purpose is a key factor in understanding what they read. Ask: *¿Cómo te puede ayudar esta información para responder a la pregunta número 5 de ¿Comprendiste?*

Answers will vary.

 Technology: Mapa global interactivo, Actividad 4 Look at migration patterns from Puerto Rico to the United States.

Teacher-to-Teacher

The excerpt by Santiago might serve as a starting point for healthy discussions between students of varying cultural backgrounds. Encourage, but never force, students to talk with each other about their cultural similarities and differences.

Additional Resources

 Technology: Online Resources
• Guided, Writing, Reading
• Cultural Reading Activity
• Communication Activities
• *Para hispanohablantes*
Print
• Guided WB pp. 76–77

Enrich Your Teaching

Culture Note

In 1936, the High School for Music and Art was founded by New York City mayor Fiorello H. LaGuardia. Its mission was to provide talented students with access to artistic training. Today's facility, The LaGuardia High School for Music and Art and Performing Arts, opened its doors in 1984, just steps away from Lincoln Center.

21st Century Skills

Social and Cross-Cultural Skills

Have students interview people from their community who may have the experience of living between two cultures. What cultures are represented? How do their experiences compare to those of Esmeralda Santiago in *Cuando era puertorriqueña?*

Auténtico

Standards: 1.2

Resources: Auténtico Resources Wkbk, Cap 2
Authentic Resources: Cap. 2; Videoscript
AP®Theme: *La belleza y la estética: Las artes visuales y escénicas*

Antes de ver

Direct students' attention to the image. Encourage them to express in Spanish what type of art this is. Then, discuss the *Estrategia* with students. Point out that in this video the images give excellent support to understand the main idea and the details.

Technology: Ve el video

Before starting the video, direct student's attention to the *Mientras ves* activity. Play the video once completely through, without pausing. Guide students to identify the main personalities: *Presentador a* (the woman who presents the video), *Experta en Talavera* (the woman who explains the origin of the Talavera pottery); *Artesanos* (the artisans/potters). As students watch the video, remind them that they will not understand every word, but that they should listen and watch for overall understanding. Replay the video, stopping as necessary to check comprehension. Show the video a final time without pausing.

Haz las actividades

Mientras ves

Standards: 1.2

Suggestions: Invite students to share their notes. It is likely that the majority of the students won't fully understand the speakers' comments, since they refer to ideas specific to their craft.

Auténtico

Partnered with UNIVISION COMMUNICATIONS INC

Puebla y su famosa Talavera

Antes de ver

Usa la estrategia: Usar las imágenes
Cuando veas el video, usa las imágenes como ayuda para entender el proceso que se explica. Esto también te ayudará a inferir el significado de palabras desconocidas.

Lee el vocabulario clave
fábrica = factory
mezcla de dos barros = clay mixture
azucarera = sugar bowl
esmalte = glaze
recipientes = containers
carbon molido = coal dust
cocer = to fire (cook) pottery
torno = pottery wheel

▶ Ve el video

¿**C**ómo debe ser una cerámica para que se convierta en una obra de arte? ¿Qué características debe tener y cómo debe ser hecha?

Ve a **PearsonSchool.com/Autentico** para ver el video *Puebla y su famosa Talavera.* Conocerás una fábrica de México en la que se crean cerámicas que son apreciadas en todo el mundo.

Haz las actividades

Mientras ves Durante el video, se explica cómo se hacen las cerámicas de Talavera. Usa las imágenes como ayuda para entender los pasos y las materiales que se usan. Presta mucha atención a cada paso del proceso y anota palabras claves *(key words)* de cada paso.

Differentiated Instruction

Heritage Speakers
Invite students to research arts and crafts from their heritage culture. Invite them to share their findings with the class.

Advanced Learners
Ask students to research the various types of designs used in the Puebla pottery. Invite them to use the information to write a paragraph in Spanish on this subject.

Después de ver

Standards: 1.2, 4.2

Suggestions: Discuss the questions with students. Evaluate their overall understanding by asking several volunteers to respond to each question.

Answers:

1. mostrar cómo se hace la cerámica de Talavera
2. de la Reina de Talavera, un sitio cerca de Toledo, España.
3. mezclar los barros blanco y negro, usar los manos para formar la cerámica en el torno, dejar secar el objeto por quince días, hornearlo, poner esmalte, cocerlo, hacer el diseño
4. Answers may vary, but can include the following: se inspiran en las cerámicas de Talavera pero al estilo mexicano; solo usan barros de Puebla

Pre-AP® Integration

Resources: Authentic Resources, Wkbk, Cap. 2
Authentic Resources: Cap. 2: Videoscript

Suggestions: Before completing the Pre-AP® activity, have students go to the workbook and complete the worksheets for the additional resources.

Comparación cultural

Suggestions: Ask students to focus on the following categories while comparing the two styles of arts or crafts: style, genre, materials used

Integración

Después de ver Vuelve a ver el video una o dos veces más para poder contestar estas preguntas:

1. ¿Cuál es el propósito principal de este video? Parafrasea la idea principal.
2. ¿De dónde viene la palabra "Talavera"?
3. Parafrasea el proceso de elaboración de las cerámicas.
4. Menciona dos características distintivas de las cerámicas de Puebla.

 **For more activities, go to the Authentic Resources Workbook.**

El arte y la cultura

Expansión Busca otros recursos auténticos en *Auténtico* en línea y contesta las preguntas.

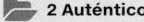 **2 Auténtico**

Integración de ideas ¿Cómo crees que el arte en sus distintas formas refleja la cultura de un país?

Comparación cultural Compara la cerámica de Puebla con algún tipo de artesanía que conozcas de Estados Unidos. ¿En qué se parecen y en qué se diferencian? ¿Qué estilo te gusta más y por qué? Da detalles que apoyen tu respuesta.

Enrich Your Teaching

Culture Note

Puebla is one of the most charming cities in Mexico. Many of its rich traditions involve food and crafts. Besides its beautiful Talavera pottery, this city is also famous for its "mole poblano," a very rich, thick sauce made with peppers and chocolate, among other ingredients. This dish is very significant to Mexico as it symbolizes the fusion of Indigenous and European cultures.

Using Authentic Resources

Have students create a personal vocabulary list with terms from the authentic resources that are related to arts and crafts.

Review Activities

Formas, géneros y materiales de arte/ Profesiones artísticas: Have partners play *Diez preguntas.* One partner chooses a word or expression from these vocabulary categories. The other partner asks up to ten *sí/no* questions to try to determine what the word or expression is. Once the vocabulary item is determined or the asker is stumped, partners switch roles.

Para describir una obra de arte: Ask students to go back through the works of art shown in this chapter of the Student Edition. Have them take turns asking and answering questions about the works of art:

A: *¿Qué fue la fuente de inspiración para esta pintura?*

B: *Pienso que fue la alegría de estar en casa.*

En el escenario/Sobre la actuación: Ask pairs of students to make a labeled sketch or computer-generated representation of a theater with actors on stage and an audience. Have them present these to other pairs, pointing out the various parts and people of the theater. For the **Sobre la actuación** category, they can make comments about the actors and the audience: *Este señor se identifica con el galán.*

Otras palabras y expresiones: Students can use these words and expressions as they do the review activities for the other categories.

Sobre la música y la danza: Have pairs of students take turns giving each other TPR commands: *Toca la trompeta. Muéstrame unos pasos de tango. Canta … .*

Pretérito e imperfecto: You will need a small foam or paper cube. Write the numbers 1–4 on four of the sides. Sides 5–6 will not count. Sides 1–4 refer to the rules in the **Pretérito e imperfecto** chart.

Divide the class into two teams. Rotate through each team so that only one student speaks for the team at a time. However, the team "speaker" can consult with teammates for up to thirty seconds before responding.

🔊 Vocabulario

formas de arte

la cerámica	pottery
la escultura	sculpture
el mural	mural
la pintura	painting

géneros de arte

el autorretrato	self-portrait
la naturaleza muerta	still life
el retrato	portrait

materiales de arte

la paleta	palette
el pincel	brush

profesiones artísticas

el / la escritor(a)	writer
el / la escultor(a)	sculptor
el / la poeta	poet

para describir una obra de arte

abstracto, -a	abstract
expresar(se)	to express (oneself)
famoso, -a	famous
la figura	figure
el fondo	background
la fuente de inspiración	source of inspiration
la imagen	image
influir (i→y)	to influence
inspirar	to inspire
la obra de arte	work of art
el primer plano	foreground
representar	to represent
el sentimiento	feeling
el siglo	century
el tema	subject

en el escenario

el aplauso	applause
la entrada	ticket
el escenario	stage
el espectáculo	show
el micrófono	microphone

otras palabras y expresiones

a través de	through
mostrar (ue)	to show
parado, -a	to be standing
pararse	to stand up
parecerse (a)	to look, seem (like)
el poema	poem
realizar	to perform, to accomplish
la reseña	review
sentado, -a	to be seated
sonar (ue) (a)	to sound like
el taller	workshop
volverse (ue)	to become

sobre la música y la danza

clásico, -a	classical
el compás	rhythm
el conjunto	band
la danza	dance
la letra	lyrics
la melodía	melody
el movimiento	movement
el paso	step
el ritmo	rhythm
el tambor	drum
la trompeta	trumpet

sobre la actuación

actuar	to perform
destacar(se)	to stand out
el entusiasmo	enthusiasm
exagerar	to exaggerate
el gesto	gesture
identificarse con	to identify oneself with
la interpretación	interpretation
interpretar	to interpret

Differentiated Instruction

Students with Special Needs

Provide concrete objects or listening examples to assist visually impaired students in their review of vocabulary from the chapter. Examples might include actual art pieces, art materials, as well as audio recordings of musical or dramatic performances.

Advanced Students

Have students use their creativity to make a video about a group of artists. Challenge them to incorporate all of the vocabulary on this page in their script. Remind them that there are many ways to do this. Some words might be seen on a sign in the background, others might occur in a letter someone reads, still others in a narration.

Gramática

pretérito e imperfecto

Use the **preterite** to tell about an action that happened once and was completed. Ayer **escribí** un poema.	Use the **imperfect** to tell about habitual actions in the past. A menudo **cantábamos** juntos.	Use the **imperfect** to give background details, like time, date and weather. **Eran** las ocho y **hacía** mucho frío.	Use the **preterite** and the **imperfect** together when an action interrupts another that is taking place in the past. **Caminábamos** por el parque cuando **empezó** a llover.

estar + participio

The **past participle** is frequently used with the verb *estar*.

El teatro **está cerrado**.	El tren **está parado**.

In the following cases, the **past participle** is irregular.

hacer: **hecho**	cubrir: **cubierto**	morir: **muerto**	escribir: **escrito**
abrir: **abierto**	decir: **dicho**	poner: **puesto**	volver: **vuelto**
descubrir: **descubierto**	romper: **roto**	ver: **visto**	resolver: **resuelto**

ser y estar

Remember that *ser* and *estar* both mean **to be** in English, but have different meanings in Spanish.	Use *ser*: to describe permanent characteristics La actriz **es** bonita. to tell the date Mañana **es** miércoles. to indicate possession Los pinceles **son** de Luis.	Use *estar*: to describe temporary characteristics El escenario **está** oscuro. to indicate location **Están** sobre la mesa. to form the progressive tenses **Estoy** dibujando un retrato.	Some adjectives have different meanings depending on whether they are used with *ser* or *estar*. Los niños **están** aburridos. (The children are bored.) Los niños **son** aburridos. (Children are boring.)

verbos con significados diferentes en el pretérito y en el imperfecto

The following Spanish verbs have different meanings in the imperfect and the preterite tenses.

Yo **conocía** ese cuadro. (I knew about that painting.)	Él **conoció** a su maestro en Perú. (He met his teacher in Perú.)
No **sabíamos** que era tan tarde. (We didn't know it was so late.)	Nunca **supe** dónde estaba. (I never found out where he/she was.)
Ellos **querían** viajar hoy. (They wanted to travel today.)	Sofía **quiso ir**, pero perdió el avión. (Sofía tried to go, but she missed the plane.)
Antes **no podía** dibujar. (Before, I couldn't draw.)	Nunca **pude** dibujar. (I was never able to draw.)

Capítulo 2 • ciento nueve **109**

Enrich Your Teaching

Teacher-to-Teacher

After students review the vocabulary on the previous page, organize a "vocabulary bee." Have all students stand in a circle around the room. Give a student one item from the list. He or she has ten seconds to come up with a Spanish definition or explanation of the vocabulary or use it correctly in a sentence that clearly shows an understanding of its meaning. Students who make a mistake or run out of time sit down. The last student standing is the winner of the bee.

(Cont'd):

Team A rolls the cube and has thirty seconds to come up with a sentence that follows the rule that was rolled. If they do, they earn a point. If their sentence is incorrect or time runs out, play passes to Team B. The team with the best score out of 21 wins.

Estar + participio: Have students work in pairs. Each partner writes down five sentences about actions completed in the past tense: *Carla abrió la ventana.* They then take turns reading one sentence at a time to each other. The listener comes up with a sentence based on the one he or she hears, that uses **estar + participio**: *La ventana está abierta.*

Ser y estar: Play a game that is set up the same way as the one for **Pretérito e imperfecto.** For rule number 4 in the chart, allow teams double the time (one minute) to come up with two sentences that contrast two different meanings of an adjective based on its use with **ser** and **estar.**

Verbos con significados diferentes en el pretérito y en el imperfecto: Have students write their own exercises modeled after *Actividad* 36 on p. 92. Their exercises need not be in story form; a numbered list is fine. Have them take each other's quizzes, and check and discuss answers.

Digital Portfolio

Invite students to review the activities they completed in this chapter, including written reports, presentations, or other projects. Have them select one or two items to include in their portfolios with the Chapter Checklist and Self-Assessment Worksheet.

Additional Resources

 Technology: Online Resources
- Instant Check
- Integrated Performance Assessment
- *Para hispanohablantes*

Teacher Resources
- Teacher's Resource Materials: Situation Cards, Clip Art

 Technology: ¡Pura vida! is a storyline video that expands listening skills and is available within **Realize.** Student activities and Teacher support are also assignable within **Realize.**

Performance Tasks

Standards: 1.1, 1.2, 1.3, 3.1

Student Resource: *Para hispanohablantes*

Teacher Resources: Teacher's Resource Materials: Audio Script, Technology: Audio, Cap. 2

1. Vocabulario

Suggestions: Encourage students to review the vocabulary from the Vocabulario en contexto sections on pp. 70–72 and 84–87 before they complete the activity.

Answers:

1. b	**5.** b
2. c	**6.** c
3. c	**7.** c
4. d	**8.** a

2. Gramática

Suggestions: Remind students of the main points of the grammar presentations in *Capítulo* 2:

- uses of the preterite and the imperfect tenses
- constructions with **estar** + past participle
- uses of **ser** vs. **estar**
- adjectives that have different meanings when used in conjunction with the imperfect or the preterite tense

Answers:

1. d	**5.** a
2. a	**6.** a
3. d	**7.** d
4. a	**8.** c

Repaso del capítulo

OBJECTIVE
▶ Demonstrate that you can perform the tasks on these pages

Preparación para el examen

❶ Vocabulario Escribe la letra de la palabra o expresión que mejor complete cada frase. Escribe tus respuestas en una hoja aparte.

1. El surrealismo fue _____ de inspiración de los pintores Miró y Dalí.
   - a. el espectáculo
   - b. la fuente
   - c. la melodía
   - d. la reseña
2. El actor principal _____ por su actuación y entusiasmo.
   - a. se interpretó
   - b. se volvió
   - c. se destacó
   - d. se inspiró
3. Si quieres bailar salsa, necesitas aprender _____ .
   - a. la letra
   - b. los gestos
   - c. los pasos
   - d. la actuación
4. La familia es _____ principal de muchos cuadros de Botero.
   - a. el estilo
   - b. el fondo
   - c. la forma
   - d. el tema
5. Picasso fue un pintor del _____ XX.
   - a. estilo
   - b. siglo
   - c. año
   - d. ritmo
6. Cuando termina una obra se oye _____ .
   - a. un paso
   - b. el micrófono
   - c. un aplauso
   - d. la paleta
7. La paleta de ese pintor _____ colores vivos como el rojo y el anaranjado.
   - a. actúa
   - b. interpreta
   - c. muestra
   - d. realiza
8. Los actores no dijeron nada pero se expresaron muy bien con _____ exagerados.
   - a. gestos
   - b. poemas
   - c. escenarios
   - d. compases

❷ Gramática Escribe la letra de la palabra o expresión que mejor complete cada frase. Escribe tus respuestas en una hoja aparte.

1. La semana pasada _____ en una clase de cerámica.
   - a. me inscribo
   - b. me inscribía
   - c. me inscribe
   - d. me inscribí
2. No te van a oír bien porque el micrófono está _____ .
   - a. roto
   - b. rotas
   - c. rompiendo
   - d. romper
3. El museo estaba _____ todos los sábados.
   - a. abrí
   - b. abriendo
   - c. abiertos
   - d. abierto
4. Marta siempre _____ nerviosa antes de un ensayo.
   - a. está
   - b. están
   - c. es
   - d. era
5. Ayer, a causa de los truenos, yo no _____ dormir en toda la noche.
   - a. pude
   - b. podía
   - c. puedo
   - d. pudo
6. ¿Dónde _____ a tu mejor amigo?
   - a. conociste
   - b. conoces
   - c. conocías
   - d. conocieron
7. Nos perdimos porque no _____ bien la ciudad.
   - a. conocemos
   - b. conocimos
   - c. conocías
   - d. conocíamos
8. Yo _____ esta mañana que la función tuvo mucho éxito.
   - a. sabía
   - b. sabe
   - c. supe
   - d. saben

Differentiated Instruction

Heritage Speakers

Have students create a brochure for their own "virtual museum." Encourage them to select artists and works from the chapter, from their own areas of interest, or from their heritage country. Remind students to tailor the language of their descriptions to the appropriate audience.

Students with Learning Difficulties

In reviewing the vocabulary and grammar of the chapter, use gestures and facial expressions to support students in their choice of the correct answer. Use TPR to support meaning of the vocabulary choices.

Más recursos — PearsonSchool.com/Autentico

Games   Flashcards   Instant check

Tutorials

En el examen vas a . . .	Éstas son las tareas de práctica que te pueden ser útiles para el examen . . .	Para repasar, ve a tu libro de texto impreso o digital . . .
Interpretive		
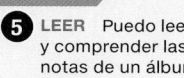 **3 ESCUCHAR** Puedo escuchar y comprender la descripción de un cuadro.	El guía de un museo está describiendo uno de los cuadros de la galería de arte moderno. (a) ¿Qué tipo de pintura describe? (b) ¿Quién es el pintor? (c) ¿Qué se ve en primer plano? (d) ¿Qué se ve al fondo? (e) ¿Cómo son los colores?	**pp. 70–71** *Vocabulario en contexto 1* **p. 75** Actividades 8–9 **p. 76** Actividad 11 **p. 77** Actividades 12, 13
Interpersonal		
4 HABLAR Puedo hablar de las actividades que tienen lugar en una escuela de arte.	Un nuevo estudiante visita por primera vez tu escuela de arte. Tu tarea es mostrarle los talleres de la escuela y explicarle lo que pasa en cada clase. Incluye en tu descripción (a) las clases que ofrecen, (b) los materiales que necesitan para cada clase, (c) las actividades que hacen en cada clase, (d) las obras que los estudiantes realizan en cada clase.	**p. 72** *Vocabulario en contexto 1* **p. 74** Actividad 7
Interpretive		
5 LEER Puedo leer y comprender las notas de un álbum musical.	Lee la reseña sobre un álbum musical y di (a) ¿cuál es el tipo de música?, (b) ¿qué cosas le gustaron al crítico?, (c) ¿qué no le gustó?, (d) ¿qué cree que puede ser mejor? La letra de las canciones del conjunto *Sol y salsa* suena a poesía. Pero creo que la interpretación puede ser mejor. El ritmo que da el tambor se destaca del de la trompeta y va bien con todo el conjunto. Me gustó mucho la melodía de la primera canción. Cuando tocan la trompeta en algunas canciones, creo que exageran. Se ve que el conjunto se inspiró mucho al tocar la música.	**pp. 84–87** *Vocabulario en contexto 2* **p. 88** Actividad 29 **p. 89** Actividad 31 **pp. 94–95** Actividades 38–39
Presentational		
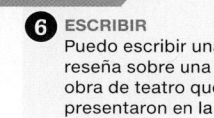 **6 ESCRIBIR** Puedo escribir una reseña sobre una obra de teatro que presentaron en la escuela.	Trabajas como reportero(a) para el periódico de la escuela y tienes que escribir una reseña sobre una obra de teatro. Incluye (a) el nombre de la obra, (b) los actores principales, (c) una breve descripción del argumento, (d) la actuación de los protagonistas.	**pp. 86–87** *Vocabulario en contexto 2* **p. 91** Actividad 34 **pp. 94–95** Actividades 38–39
Comparisons		
 **7 COMPARAR** Puedo comparar las obras de tres artistas famosos.	Piensa en las obras de Goya, Dalí o Botero. ¿Como usaron su arte para expresar sus actitudes y sus perspectivas sobre lo que pasaba en sus vidas? ¿De qué manera expresan los jóvenes de hoy sus actitudes por el arte?	**pp. 88–89** Actividades 29–31 **p. 91** Actividad 35 **pp. 96–97** *Puente a la cultura*

Differentiated Assessment

Core Assessment
- Technology: Audio: Cap. 2
- ExamView: Chapter Test, Test Banks A and B

Challenge/Pre-AP®
- ExamView: Pre-AP® Test Bank
- Pre-AP® Resource Materials

Extra Support
- Alternate Assessment Program: Examen del capítulo 2
- Technology: Audio: Cap. 2

Heritage Speakers
- Assessment Program: Para hispanohablantes: Examen del capítulo 2
- ExamView Heritage Learner Test Bank

---

3. Escuchar

Suggestions: Use the audio or read from the script.

Technology: Audio Script and Answers

El guía de un museo está describiendo uno de los cuadros de la galería de arte moderno.

(a) ¿Qué tipo de pintura describe? (b) ¿Quién es el pintor? (c) ¿Qué se ve en primer plano? (d) Qué se ve al fondo? (e) ¿Cómo son los colores?

FEMALE ADULT: El cuadro a la derecha se llama Juan Le Pins y es un paisaje de Pablo Picasso. Lo pintó en 1920, cuando tenía 41 años. Observen que la casa y los árboles que están en primer plano tienen formas casi abstractas. Al fondo podemos ver el mar Mediterráneo. Como ven, la paleta que Picasso utilizó para esta obra no incluyó colores vivos.

  a. un paisaje
  b. Pablo Picasso
  c. una casa y árboles
  d. el mar Mediterráneo
  e. los colores no son vivos

4. Hablar

Suggestions: Point out that this activity involves pair work. One partner should act as the new student, asking questions and making comments. The other should act as the student showing him or her around. The result is a dialogue.

Answers will vary.

5. Leer

Suggestions: Tell students to refer to pp. 70–72 and 84–87 if they have questions about vocabulary in the music review.

Answers:
  (a) salsa
  (b) el ritmo del tambor y la melodía de la primera canción
  (c) la trompeta en algunas canciones
  (d) la interpretación

6. Escribir

Suggestions: Encourage students to organize their thoughts in a list like the one on p. 95 before writing their reviews.

Answers will vary.

7. Comparar

Suggestions: Encourage students to put their thoughts down using a T-chart. They can label the columns *Goya, Dalí, Botero* and *artistas jóvenes.*

Answers will vary.

Additional Resources

 **Technology: Online Resources**
- Instant Check
- *Para hispanohablantes*

Print
- Guided WB pp. 33–34

CAPÍTULO **3**

¿Qué haces para estar en forma?

Health and nutrition

Vocabulary: symptoms and remedies; health food, nutrition, and fitness

Grammar: affirmative and negative *tú* commands; commands with *Ud.* and *Uds.*; subjunctive of regular, irregular, and stem-changing verbs

Cultural Perspectives: art of Rufino Tamayo; medicinal plants in Latin America; eating habits of young Spaniards; physical education in Spain; ancient sports in Mexico and Central America; Spanish and Latin American teen magazines; habits related to food and fitness; sports in ancient American civilizations

¡Pura vida!: Watch an engaging video episode about a group of young people in Costa Rica!

Chapter Support

Bulletin Boards

Theme: Pirámide de alimentos

Ask students to cut out or draw the appropriate food groups to include in the new food pyramid that they will create on the bulletin board. The left column of the pyramid should have: *pan, cereales, arroz, pasta*. Under the next two categories, they will place *vegetales* on the left side and *frutas* on the right. They will place *grasas, aceites* under the thinnest column. Products such as *leche, yogur, quesos* will be placed in the blue column, and *carne, pollo, pescado, huevos, guisantes* will be on the last column. This will be a visual guide of a healthy and complete diet.

Hands-on Culture

Recipe: Yogur de frutas helado

This Mexican recipe provides a simple and healthy way to enjoy a nutritious dessert.

Ingredients: 2 cups of lowfat yogurt (vanilla or other flavors), 2 pears or apples, 4 tablespoons of honey, 4 small serving bowls

Peel and cut the fruit into small cubes. Discard the seeds.

Fill each container halfway with yogurt.

Add the fruit to each container.

Add a tablespoon of honey.

Mix the contents in each container.

Place the bowls in the refrigerator.

Game

Síntomas y remedios

Play this game in Capítulo 3, after students have learned vocabulary related to symptoms and remedies.

Players: entire class

Materials: index cards, pen, a show box

Rules:

1. Students write names of symptoms on index cards and place them in a shoe box.
2. Shake the box to mix up the index cards. Then call on a volunteer to come to the front of the class. The volunteer draws an index card from the box and acts out the symptom.
3. Students take turns guessing the correct symptom. Once they guess the symptom they must provide a remedy or solution to alleviate it.

    Student 1: ¿Tienes gripe?

    Student 2: Sí.

    Student 1: Entonces debes tomar antibióticos.
4. The student that guesses the symptom and provides the correct remedy becomes the new volunteer. Play continues until every student has had a chance to ask one or two questions.

Variation: Instead of physical ailments, students will act out emotional states such as *"estoy en la luna," "me caigo de sueño,"* and so on.

21st Century Skills

Look for tips throughout Chapter 3 to enrich your teaching by integrating 21st Century Skills. Suggestions for the Project-Based Learning and Culture follow below.

Project-Based Learning

Modify the project with these suggestions:

ICT (Information, Communications and Technology) Literacy Ask students to go online to their favorite video-sharing site and view models of exercise programs. The handout "Analyze Media Content" will help them determine the best way to present their proposed diet and exercise plan.

Creativity and Innovation Encourage students to be creative in selecting the Spanish song to accompany their presentation. What is the role of music and exercise? What songs are used during professional sports games in this country? If they cannot find a Spanish song, encourage them to write their own song or rap.

Communication Provide students with the handout "Give an Effective Presentation" to remind them of the importance of body language, tone of voice, eye contact in a presentation.

Chapter Culture

Social and Cross-Cultural Skills Help students bridge cultural differences by offering opportunities to discuss alternative vs. traditional medicine, as presented in the *Cultura* on p. 124.

▶ **Technology: Videodocumentario** View *¿Qué haces para estar saludable?* online with the class to learn more about eating and exercise habits and medical care in the Spanish-speaking world.

Project-Based Learning

Buenos hábitos

Overview: Students create a proposal for a complete health program that consists of three parts: 1. a healthy diet, 2. a physical exercise routine, and 3. the selection of a song in Spanish to accompany their routine. They should include in their proposals the name of the artist and the country of origin. Students can create their health program digitally or by hand, or by using a combination of resources. Students then give an oral presentation of their complete program to the class.

Resources: online or print photos, image editing and page layout software and/or poster board, markers, glue, and an audio device.

Sequence: (suggestions for when to do each step are found throughout the chapter)

Step 1. Review sections of the chapter and instructions, so students know what is expected of them. Share the rubric with the class.

Step 2. Students submit a draft of the appropriate diet and matching exercises. Return the drafts with your suggestions. For vocabulary and grammar practice, ask partners to present their drafts to each other.

Step 3. Students do a layout leaving room for photos or drawings and descriptions.

Step 4. Students submit completed health programs.

Step 5. Students present their health programs to the class, play the accompanying song and explain why their program promotes health.

Options

1. Students can modify and adapt their exercise programs for body building (after appropriate research).
2. Students feature only one aspect of the health program.

Assessment

Here is a detailed rubric for assessing this project.

Chapter 3 Project: Buenos hábitos

Rubric	Score 1	Score 3	Score 5
Your evidence of planning	You have no written draft or poster layout.	Either your draft or your layout is missing.	You show evidence of corrected draft and layout.
Your use of illustrations	You have no music or song.	You are missing data about the artist.	You include music and artist's data.
Your presentation	Your presentation is weak.	Your diet and exercise program don't complement each other.	You present a coordinated program.

AT A GLANCE

Objectives
- Listen to and read about health advice and nutrition
- Talk and write about healthy eating habits and exercise
- Give advice to others about healthy lifestyles
- Compare an ancient game with a modern game
- Understand the connection between healthy habits and lifestyle in Spanish-speaking countries
- Demonstrate understanding of an authentic video about the nutritional benefits of fruits and vegetables

Vocabulary
- Symptoms and remedies
- Parts of the body
- Health, food, and nutrition
- Physical fitness and exercise
- Moods

Grammar
- Affirmative and negative *tú* commands
- Affirmative and negative *Ud.* and *Uds.* commands
- Subjunctive verbs

Culture
- Rufino Tamayo, p. 117
- Healing plants in Latin America, p. 124
- Eating habits of Spanish teenagers, p. 128
- World Health Day, p. 133
- Physical education in Spain, p. 135
- Mayan ball game, pp. 144–145
- Teen magazines, p. 153

A ver si recuerdas...
- Fruits and vegetables
- Descriptions
- Breakfast, lunch, dinner
- Direct object pronouns
- Indirect object pronouns

Recycle
- Pronunciation of the letter *d* between vowels

Authentic Resources
- Auténtico: *Un arcoiris por día*, pp. 154–155

RESOURCES

	FOR THE STUDENT	DIGITAL	PRINT	FOR THE TEACHER	DIGITAL	PRINT
A ver si recuerdas PP. 112–115						
Review	*A ver si recuerdas* with Remediation	•		Teacher's Edition, pp. 112–115	•	•
	Guided WB, pp. 78–81	•	•	*A ver si recuerdas* with Remediation	•	
	Core WB, pp. 35–36	•	•			
	Para hispanohablantes	•				
Introducción PP. 116–117						
Present	Student Edition, pp. 116–117	•	•	Teacher's Edition, pp. 116–117	•	•
	DK Reference Atlas	•		Teacher's Resource Materials	•	
	Videonovela: *¡Pura vida!*	•				
	¡Pura vida! Video Activities	•				
	Para hispanohablantes	•				
Vocabulario en contexto PP. 118–121/130–133						
Present & Practice	Student Edition, pp. 118–121/130–133	•	•	Teacher's Edition, pp. 118–121/130–133	•	•
	Audio	•		Teacher's Resource Materials	•	
	Videohistoria	•		Vocabulary Clip Art	•	
	Flashcards	•		Technology: Audio	•	
	Instant Check	•		Video Program: Videohistoria	•	
	Guided WB, pp. 82–90/97–104	•	•			
	Core WB, pp. 37–38/42–43	•	•			
	Communication Activities	•				
	Para hispanohablantes	•				
Assess and Remediate				Pruebas 3–1/3–6: Assessment Program, Assessment Program *Para hispanohablantes*	•	

RESOURCES

FOR THE STUDENT	DIGITAL	PRINT	FOR THE TEACHER	DIGITAL	PRINT
Vocabulario en uso PP. 122–124/134–135					
Present & Practice Student Edition, pp. 122–124/134–135	•	•	Interactive Whiteboard Vocabulary Activities	•	
Instant Check	•		Teacher's Edition, pp. 122–124/134–135	•	•
Communication Activities	•		Teacher's Resource Materials	•	
Para hispanohablantes	•		Technology: Audio	•	
Communicative Pair Activities	•		Videomodelos	•	
			Mapa global interactivo	•	
Assess and Remediate			Pruebas 3–2/3–7 with Remediation	•	
			Pruebas 3–2/3–7: Assessment Program, Assessment Program *Para hispanohablantes*	•	
Gramática PP. 125–129/136–143					
Present & Practice Student Edition, pp. 125–129/136–143	•	•	Interactive Whiteboard Grammar Activities	•	
Instant Check	•		Teacher's Edition, pp. 125–129/136–143	•	•
Tutorial Video: Grammar	•		Teacher's Resource Materials	•	
Canción de hip hop	•		Technology: Audio	•	
Guided WB, pp. 91–96/105–110	•	•	Videomodelos	•	
Core WB, pp. 39–41/44–46	•	•			
Communication Activities	•				
Para hispanohablantes	•				
Communicative Pair Activities	•				
Assess and Remediate			Pruebas 3–3, 3–4, 3–5/3–8, 3–9, 3–10 with Remediation	•	
			Pruebas 3–3, 3–4, 3–5/3–8, 3–9, 3–10: Assessment Program, Assessment Program *Para hispanohablantes*	•	
			Examen 1, Examen 2: Vocab. y gramática	•	
Aplicación pp. 144–155					
Apply Student Edition, pp. 144–155	•	•	Teacher's Edition, pp. 144–155	•	•
Authentic Resources Workbook	•	•	Teacher's Resource Materials	•	
Authentic Resources	•		Video Program: *Videodocumentario*	•	
Online Cultural Reading	•		Mapa global interactivo	•	
Guided WB, pp. 111–113	•	•	Authentic Resources Lesson Plans with scripts, answer keys	•	
Communication Activities	•				
Para hispanohablantes	•				
Videodocumentario	•				
Auténtico	•				
Repaso del capítulo pp. 156–159					
Review Student Edition, pp. 156–159	•	•	Teacher's Edition, pp. 156–159	•	•
Core WB, pp. 47–48	•	•	Teacher's Resource Materials	•	
Communication Activities	•		Technology: Audio	•	
Para hispanohablantes	•				
Instant Check	•				
Chapter Assessment					
Assess			Examen del capítulo 8: Assessment Program, Alternate Assessment Program, Assessment Program *Para hispanohablantes*	•	•
			Technology: Audio Cap. 8, Examen	•	
			ExamView: Test Banks A and B (questions only online) Heritage Speaker Test Bank, Pre-AP® Test Bank	• •	

LESSON PLAN

DAY	Warm-up / Assess	Preview / Present / Practice / Communicate		Wrap-up / Homework Options
1	**Warm-up** (10 min.) • Return Examen del capítulo: Capítulo 2	**Repaso** (35 min.) • A ver si recuerdas…		**Wrap-up and Homework Options** (5 min.) • Core Practice 3-1, 3-2
2	**Warm-up** (10 min.) • Homework check	**Chapter Opener** (10 min.) • Objectives • Arte y cultura	**Vocabulario en contexto 1** (25 min.) • Presentation: Vocabulario y gramática en contexto • Actividades 1, 2	**Wrap-up and Homework Options** (5 min.) • Clip Art Vocabulary
3	**Warm-up** (10 min.) • Homework check	**Vocabulario en contexto 1** (35 min.) • Presentation: Vocabulario en contexto 1 (cont.) • Actividades 3, 5 • Videohistoria		**Wrap-up and Homework Options** (5 min.) • Core Practice 3-3, 3-4 • Actividad 6 • Prueba 3-1: Vocabulary recognition
4	**Warm-up** (10 min.) • Actividad 4 • Homework check • **Formative Assessment** (10 min.) • Prueba 3-1: Vocabulary recognition	**Vocabulario en uso 1** (25 min.) • Interactive Whiteboard Vocabulary Activities • Actividades 7, 8, 9, 10 • Ampliación del lenguaje		**Wrap-up and Homework Options** (5 min.) • Writing Activities • Prueba 3-2 with Remediation: Vocabulary production
5	**Warm-up** (10 min.) • Homework check • **Formative Assessment** (10 min.) • Prueba 3-2 with Remediation: Vocabulary production	**Gramática y vocabulario en uso 1** (25 min.) • Cultura • Presentation: Mandatos afirmativos con *tú* • Interactive Whiteboard Grammar Activities • Actividades 11, 12 • Writing Activity		**Wrap-up and Homework Options** (5 min.) • Core Practice 3-5 • Prueba 3-3 with Remediation: Presentation: Mandatos afirmativos con *tú*
6	**Warm-up** (10 min.) • Actividad 11 • Homework check • **Formative Assessment** (10 min.) • Prueba 3-3 with Remediation: Mandatos afirmativos con *tú*	**Gramática y vocabulario en uso 1** (25 min.) • Presentation: Mandatos negativos con *tú* • Interactive Whiteboard Grammar Activities • Actividades 13, 14 • Communicative Pair Activity		**Wrap-up and Homework Options** (5 min.) • Core Practice 3-6 • Prueba 3-4 with Remediation: Mandatos negativos con *tú*
7	**Warm-up** (10 min.) • Writing Activity • Homework check • **Formative Assessment** (10 min.) • Prueba 3-4 with Remediation: Mandatos negativos con *tú*	**Gramática y vocabulario en uso 1** (25 min.) • Presentación: Mandatos afirmativos y negativos con *Ud.* y *Uds.* • Interactive Whiteboard Grammar Activities • Actividades 15, 16, 17, 20 • Writing Activity		**Wrap-up and Homework Options** (5 min.) • Core Practice 3-7 • Actividad 18 • Prueba 3-5 with Remediation: Mandatos afirmativos y negativos con *Ud.* y *Uds.*
8	**Warm-up** (10 min.) • Actividad 19 • Homework check • **Formative Assessment** (10 min.) • Prueba 3-5 with Remediation: Mandatos afirmativos y negativos con *Ud.* y *Uds.*	**Vocabulario en contexto 2** (25 min.) • Presentation: Vocabulario y gramática en contexto • Actividades 21, 22, 23		**Wrap-up and Homework Options** (5 min.) • Clip Art Vocabulary • Examen: Vocabulario y gramática 1
9	**Warm-up** (10 min.) • Clip Art Vocabulary • **Formative Assessment** (25 min.) • Examen: Vocabulario y gramática 1	**Vocabulario en contexto 2** (10 min.) • Presentation: ¿Qué me aconsejas? • Actividad 24 • Presentation: Día Mundial de la Salud		**Wrap-up and Homework Options** (5 min.) • Core Practice 3-8, 3-9 • Prueba 3-6: Vocabulary recognition
10	**Warm-up** (10 min.) • Homework check • Actividades 25, 26 • **Formative Assessment** (10 min.) • Prueba 3-6: Vocabulary recognition	**Vocabulario en uso 2** (25 min.) • Actividades 27, 28, 29 • Interactive Whiteboard Vocabulary Activities • Cultura • Audio and Video Activities		**Wrap-up and Homework Options** (5 min.) • Writing Activities • Prueba 3-7 with Remediation: Vocabulary production

LESSON PLAN

DAY	Warm-up / Assess	Preview / Present / Practice / Communicate	Wrap-up / Homework Options
11	**Warm-up** (10 min.) • Writing Activity • Homework check • **Formative Assessment** (10 min.) • Prueba 3-7 with Remediation: Vocabulary production	**Gramática y vocabulario en uso 2** (25 min.) • Presentation: El subjuntivo: Verbos regulares • Interactive Whiteboard Grammar Activities • Actividades 30, 31, 32 • El español en el mundo del trabajo	**Wrap-up and Homework Options** (5 min.) • Core Practice 3-10 • Prueba 3-8 with Remediation: El subjuntivo: Verbos regulares
12	**Warm-up** (10 min.) • Actividad 33 • Homework check • **Formative Assessment** (10 min.) • Prueba 3-8 with Remediation: El subjuntivo: Verbos regulares	**Gramática y vocabulario en uso 2** (25 min.) • Presentation: El subjuntivo: Verbos irregulares • Actividades 34, 35, 37 • Presentation: El subjuntivo: Verbos con cambio de raíz • Interactive Whiteboard Grammar Activities • Actividad 39	**Wrap-up and Homework Options** (5 min.) • Actividad 36 • Core Practice 3-11, 3-12 • Prueba 3-9, 3-10 with Remediation
13	**Warm-up** (10 min.) • Actividad 38 • Homework check • **Formative Assessment** (15 min.) • Pruebas 3-9, 3-10 with Remediation	**Gramática y vocabulario en uso 2** (20 min.) • Actividad 40 • En voz alta • Communicative Pair Activity	**Wrap-up and Homework Options** (5 min.) • Examen: Vocabulario y gramática 2
14	**Warm-up** (5 min.) • Writing Activity • **Formative Assessment** (30 min.) • Examen: Vocabulario y gramática 2	**Aplicación** (10 min.) • Presentación oral: Step 1	**Wrap-up and Homework Options** (5 min.) • Presentación oral: Step 2
15	**Warm-up** (10 min.) • Presentación oral: Step 2	**Aplicación** (35 min.) • Presentación oral: Step 3	**Wrap-up and Homework Options** (5 min.) • Un juego muy antiguo • ¿Comprendiste? • Usa tus conocimientos
16	**Warm-up** (15 min.) • Un juego muy antiguo: ¿Comprendiste? • Homework check	**Aplicación** (30 min.) • Pre-AP® Integración 1, 2, 3 • View Video • Video Activities 1, 2, 3	**Wrap-up and Homework Options** (5 min.) • Presentación escrita: Steps 1, 2
17	**Warm-up** (10 min.) • Video Activity 4	**Aplicación** (15 min.) • Presentación escrita: Step 3 **Repaso** (20 min.) • Preparación para el examen: Actividades 3, 4	**Wrap-up and Homework Options** (5 min.) • Presentación escrita: Step 4 • Cultura
18	**Warm-up** (10 min.) • Homework check	**Aplicación** (35 min.) • Lectura • Interacción con la lectura • Cultura • Auténtico	**Wrap-up and Homework Options** (5 min.) • Core Practice: Organizer 3-13, 3-14 • Instant Check
19	**Warm-up** (20 min.) • Preparación para el examen: Actividades 1, 2 • Homework check	**Repaso** (25 min.) • Preparación para el examen: Actividades 5, 6, 7 • Other review	**Wrap-up and Homework Options** (5 min.) • Examen del capítulo
20	**Warm-up** (5 min.) • Answer questions • **Summative Assessment** (44 min.) • Examen del capítulo		**Wrap-up and Homework Options** (1 min.) • A ver si recuerdas: Capítulo 4 • Actividades 1-4, 6

ALTERNATE LESSON PLAN

DAY	Warm-up / Assess	Preview / Present / Practice / Communicate		Wrap-up / Homework Options
1	**Warm-up** (35 min.) • Return Examen del capítulo: Capítulo 2 • A ver si recuerdas . . . • Actividad 7 • Homework check	**Chapter Opener** (10 min.) • Objectives • Arte y cultura **Vocabulario en contexto 1** (30 min.) • Presentation: Vocabulario y gramática en contexto • Actividades 1, 2 • Presentation: Vocabulario en contexto (cont.) • Actividades 3, 4, 5 • Videohistoria	**Vocabulario en uso 1** (10 min.) • Actividades 7, 8	**Wrap-up and Homework Options** (5 min.) • Core Practice 3-3, 3-4 • Clip Art Vocabulary • Prueba 3-1: Vocabulary recognition
2	**Warm-up** (15 min.) • Actividad 6 • Homework check • **Formative Assessment** (10 min.) • Prueba 3-1: Vocabulary recognition	**Vocabulario en uso 1** (60 min.) • Actividades 9, 10 • Interactive Whiteboard Vocabulary Activities • Ampliación del lenguaje • Cultura • Writing or Audio Activities • Communicative Pair Activity		**Wrap-up and Homework Options** (5 min.) • Writing Activities • Prueba 3-2 with Remediation: Vocabulary production
3	**Warm-up** (10 min.) • Writing Activity • Homework check • **Formative Assessment** (10 min.) • Prueba 3-2 with Remediation: Vocabulary production	**Gramática y vocabulario en uso 1** (65 min.) • Presentation: Mandatos afirmativos con *tú* • Interactive Whiteboard Grammar Activities • Actividades 11, 12 • Presentation: Mandatos negativos con *tú* • Actividades 13, 14 • Writing Activities		**Wrap-up and Homework Options** (5 min.) • Core Practice 3-5, 3-6 • Pruebas 3-3, 3-4 with Remediation: Mandatos afirmativos con *tú*, Mandatos negativos con *tú*
4	**Warm-up** (10 min.) • Homework check • **Formative Assessment** (20 min.) • Pruebas 3-3, 3-4 with Remediation: Mandatos afirmativos con *tú*, Mandatos negativos con *tú*	**Gramática y vocabulario en uso 1** (35 min.) • Presentation: Mandatos afirmativos y negativos con *Ud*. y *Uds*. • Interactive Whiteboard Grammar Activities • Actividades 15, 16, 17, 20 • Communicative Pair Activity **Vocabulario en contexto 2** (20 min.) • Presentation: Vocabulario y gramática en contexto • Actividades 21, 22, 23		**Wrap-up and Homework Options** (5 min.) • Actividades 18, 19 • Core Practice 3-7 • Prueba 3-5 with Remediation: Mandatos afirmativos y negativos con *Ud*. y *Uds*. • Examen: Vocabulario y gramática 1
5	**Warm-up** (10 min.) • Homework check • **Formative Options** (40 min.) • Prueba 3-5 with Remediation: Mandatos afirmativos y negativos con *Ud*. y *Uds*. • Examen: Vocabulario y gramática 1	**Vocabulario en contexto 2** (25 min.) • Presentation: ¿Qué me aconsejas? • Actividades 24, 25, 26 **Vocabulario en uso 2** (10 min.) • Actividad 29 • Interactive Whiteboard Vocabulary Activities • Cultura		**Wrap-up and Homework Options** (5 min.) • Core Practice 3-8, 3-9 • Prueba 3-6: Vocabulary recognition

ALTERNATE LESSON PLAN

DAY	Warm-up / Assess	Preview / Present / Practice / Communicate	Wrap-up / Homework Options
6	**Warm-up** (15 min.) • Actividad 28 • Homework check • **Formative Assessment** (10 min.) • Prueba 3-6: Vocabulary recognition	**Gramática y vocabulario en uso 2** (60 min.) • Actividad 27 • Presentation: El subjuntivo: Verbos regulares • Interactive Whiteboard Grammar Activities • Actividades 30, 31, 32 • Cultura • El español en el mundo del trabajo	**Wrap-up and Homework Options** (5 min.) • Core Practice 3-10 • Pruebas 3-7, 3-8 with Remediation: Vocabulary production, El subjuntivo: Verbos regulares
7	**Warm-up** (15 min.) • Actividad 33 • Homework check • **Formative Assessment** (20 min.) • Pruebas 3-7, 3-8 with Remediation: Vocabulary production, El subjuntivo: Verbos regulares	**Gramática y vocabulario en uso 2** (40 min.) • Presentation: Subjuntivo: Verbos irregulares • Presentation: Subjuntivo: Verbos con cambio de raíz • Interactive Whiteboard Grammar Activities • Actividades 34, 35, 37 • Actividad 38 **Aplicación** (15 min.) • Presentación oral: Steps 1, 2	**Wrap-up and Homework Options** (5 min.) • Presentación oral: Step 2
8	**Warm-up** (15 min.) • Actividad 36 • Homework check • **Formative Assessment** (40 min.) • Presentación oral: Step 3	**Gramática y vocabulario en uso 2** (30 min.) • En voz alta • Actividades 39, 40 • Communicative Pair Activity	**Wrap-up and Homework Options** (5 min.) • Core Practice 3-11, 3-12 • Prueba 3-9 with Remediation: El subjuntivo: Verbos irregulares • Prueba 3-10 with Remediation: El subjuntivo: Verbos con cambio de raíz • Examen: Vocabulario y gramática 2
9	**Warm-up** (10 min.) • Homework check • **Formative Assessment Options** (30 min.) • Prueba 3-9 with Remediation: El Subjuntivo: Verbos irregulares • Prueba 3-10 with Remediation: El Subjuntivo: Verbos con cambio de raíz • Examen: Vocabulario y gramática 2	**Aplicación** (45 min.) • Presentation: Un juego muy antiguo • ¿Comprendiste? • Usa tus conocimientos • Pre-AP® Integración 1, 2, 3 • View Video • Video Activities • Presentación escrita: Step 1	**Wrap-up and Homework Options** (5 min.) • Presentación escrita: Step 2 • Preparación para el examen: Actividades 1, 2
10	**Warm-up** (20 min.) • Presentación escrita: Step 3 • Homework check	**Aplicación** (35 min.) • Lectura • Interacción con la lectura • Cultura • Auténtico **Repaso** (30 min.) • Preparación para el examen: Actividades 3, 4, 6	**Wrap-up and Homework Options** (5 min.) • Presentación escrita: Step 4 • Core Practice: Organizer 3-13, 3-14 • Instant Check • Preparación para el examen: Actividades 5, 7 • Examen del capítulo
11	**Warm-up** (15 min.) • Homework check • **Summative Assessment** (45 min.) • Examen del capítulo	**Theme Game** (15 min.) **A ver si recuerdas – Capítulo 4** (10 min.) • Presentation: Vocabulario • Presentation: Gramática	**Wrap-up and Homework Options** (5 min.) • A ver si recuerdas – Capítulo 4 • Actividades 1–6 • Core Practice 4–1, 4–2

Vocabulario: Repaso

Standards: 1.1, 1.2

Suggestions: Before presenting the material in this review section, consider testing your students' command of the material by assigning the Prueba with Remediation. Students will automatically be given additional practice of the material they have not yet mastered, and you can focus your review based on the class's overall performance on the post-test.

Give students a few minutes to "create" a meal comprised of at least five of the foods from the lists. Then have them take turns describing and commenting on their "creations": *Es mi desayuno de sábado. Es muy sabroso. Tiene dos salchichas de cerdo, dos huevos fritos y pan tostado sin mantequilla. A veces como unas papas fritas. Para beber, hay café con leche y jugo de naranja.*

1

Standards: 1.1, 1.3

Suggestions: Some students may ask for suggestions on recipes they can use for Step 1. Suggest Mexican recipes with which many students will be familiar, such as **huevos rancheros, guacamole,** and **tacos**.
Answers will vary.

2

Standards: 1.1

Suggestions: Encourage students to use words from the **descripciones** category when talking about foods they like and dislike.
Answers will vary.

Active Classroom

Write each vocabulary word per category on individual slips of paper and place in a bag. Per category, ask a student to draw a word and act it out. Have the class guess the word being acted out.

A ver si recuerdas

OBJECTIVES
▶ Talk and write about food and eating habits
▶ Read and write about meals

Vocabulario

las frutas y las verduras
el aguacate
el ajo
la cebolla
las cerezas
el durazno
la ensalada
las fresas
los frijoles
los guisantes
las judías verdes
la lechuga
el maíz
el melón
la papa
la piña
la sandía
la sopa de verduras
el tomate
las uvas
la zanahoria

descripciones
bueno, -a / malo, -a
  para la salud
caliente
congelado, -a
delicioso, -a
dulce
enlatado, -a
fresco, -a
frito, -a
grasoso, -a
horrible
picante
¡Qué asco!
rico, -a
sabroso, -a

para el almuerzo o la cena
almorzar (ue)
el arroz
el bistec
el camarón
la carne de res
cenar
la chuleta de cerdo
los dulces
los espaguetis
la galleta
el helado
los mariscos
la paella
el pastel
el pavo
el pescado
el pollo
el postre

actividades
añadir
comer
cortar
probar (ue)
servir (i)

para el desayuno
el azúcar
el cereal
desayunar
el huevo
el pan con
  mantequilla
el pan tostado
las salchichas
el tocino
el yogur

1

Lista de ingredientes

ESCRIBIR, HABLAR EN PAREJA

1 Haz una lista de los ingredientes que se necesitan para preparar una comida mexicana y otra lista de los ingredientes para una comida estadounidense.

2 Con otro(a) estudiante, comparen sus listas. Trabajen juntos para preparar un menú para una comida completa.

2

Las comidas

ESCRIBIR, HABLAR EN PAREJA Escribe una lista de tus comidas favoritas y otra de las comidas que no te gustan. Usa la lista para hablar con tu compañero(a) de las comidas que les gustan y que no les gustan y de sus hábitos alimenticios *(eating habits)*. Hablen de lo que comen y por qué, cuándo y cómo lo comen.

Modelo
A—*Me gusta el yogur. Lo como con cereal todos los días en el desayuno porque es bueno para la salud.*
B—*A mí me gusta la fruta. La como en el desayuno porque tiene fibras y me hace bien.*

112 ciento doce • Capítulo 3 • ¿Qué haces para estar en forma?

Differentiated Instruction

Students with Learning Difficulties

Point to objects in the classroom and ask questions with embedded direct object pronouns. Students will restate the pronouns in their responses:
Teacher: **El libro, ¿lo ves?** Student: **Sí, lo veo**. Teacher: **El reloj, ¿lo oyes?** Student: **Sí, lo oigo**.

Advanced Learners

Have students work together to create a menu for the restaurant of their dreams. Menus should include at least three different main entrées, as well as beverages and side dishes. Ask them to be creative and dream up a restaurant that they would regularly go to. They can also describe the décor.

Gramática

Pronombres de complemento directo

Direct object pronouns tell who or what receives the action of the verb. They are used to replace a noun, in order not to repeat it. Remember that when the direct object is a person or group of people, you use the personal *a* before it.

—¿Probaste el pescado?

—Sí, **lo** probé.

—¿Ves mucho a tus amigas?

—Sí, **las** veo todos los días.

Here are all the direct object pronouns:

me	nos
te	os
lo / la	los / las

• Direct object pronouns generally go before the main verb. If there is a *no* before the verb, the pronoun goes between *no* and the verb.

—Antonio comió las uvas. **Las** comió en el desayuno. Yo no **las** comí.

• If the verb is followed by an infinitive or a present participle (present progressive), the direct object pronoun may go before the main verb or be attached to the infinitive or participle.

—¿Vas a comer el helado?

—**Lo** estoy comiendo ahora.

—Estoy comiéndo**lo** ahora.

—No, no **lo** quiero comer. / —No, no quiero comer**lo**.

3

Al restaurante

LEER, HABLAR EN PAREJA Trabaja con otro(a) estudiante. Imaginen que él (ella) fue a un restaurante con su familia. Hablen del menú y de la comida que probaron.

Videomodelo

las salchichas / mi hermano

A —¿*Alguien probó **las salchichas**?*

B —*Sí, mi hermano **las** probó.*

1. los espaguetis / mi papá
2. el helado de chocolate / mi hermanita
3. la sopa de pollo / todos
4. los pasteles / nadie
5. la chuleta de cerdo / yo
6. los huevos con tocino / mi hermanita y yo
7. el yogur de durazno / mi mamá y mi papá

4

La cena

HABLAR EN PAREJA, ESCRIBIR Planea una cena con un compañero(a). Hazle una de las siguientes preguntas y escribe su respuesta usando el pronombre de complemento correcto del recuadro.

me	nos	la	las
te	lo	los	

Modelo

A —¿Quién va a preparar **arroz**?

B —**Lo** va a preparar Luisa.

o: —*Luisa va a prepararlo.*

1. ¿Cómo vas a preparar las verduras?
2. ¿Quién va a comprar el pescado?
3. ¿Cuándo vamos a preparar la ensalada?
4. ¿Quién está cortando la fruta?
5. ¿Quieres preparar el postre?
6. ¿Quién está cortando las zanahorias?

Capítulo 3 • ciento trece **113**

Gramática: Repaso

Suggestions: Refer students who are having difficulty with direct object pronouns to the *GramActiva* videos from L2 Chapters 3A and 3B, and to the online tutorials. Cue students with sentences containing direct objects that are nouns. Have them restate each sentence, changing the direct object to a pronoun.

3

Suggestions: Have students switch roles, so both partners can practice asking and answering the questions.

Answers:

Student A's questions follow the pattern in the model. Student B's answers are as follows:

1. Sí, mi papá los probó.
2. Sí, mi hermanita lo probó.
3. Sí, todos la probamos (probaron).
4. No, nadie los probó.
5. Sí, yo la probé.
6. Sí, mi hermanita y yo los probamos.
7. Sí, mi mamá y mi papá lo probaron.

4

Suggestions: After students complete the activity, have them take turns reading the questions and their answers aloud.

Answers will vary will vary but should contain the following information:

1. las voy a preparar/voy a prepararlas
2. lo va a comprar/va a comprarlo
3. la vamos a preparar/vamos a prepararla
4. la está cortando/está cortándola
5. lo quiero preparar/quiero prepararlo
6. las está cortando/está cortándolas

Enrich Your Teaching

Teacher-to-Teacher

Students tend to confuse direct and indirect object pronouns, especially when the objects are people. This *Gramática* review focuses mainly on things as direct objects. For further review of direct objects as people, ask questions such as the following and have students respond using a direct object pronoun:

¿*Viste a* [name of student(s)] *ayer?*

¿*Conocen ustedes al (a la) señor(a)* [name of teacher]?

¿*Conoces a los (las) señores(as)* [names of teachers]?

Starter Activity

Play a game of "*Simón dice*" to review parts of the body. All students stand and listen to your (or a student leader's) commands to identify a body part: *Simón dice, "Levanta la pierna derecha."* Simón dice, *"Mueve el pie izquierdo."* Any students who fail to obey a command, or who obey a command that does not begin with the words "*Simón dice*", must sit down. The last student standing wins.

Vocabulario: Repaso

Standards: 1.1

Suggestions: Have students choose one word or expression to pantomime from the *Vocabulario*. Have them take turns presenting their pantomimes, while others say what they are doing: *A Norberto le duele el brazo. Julia tiene frío. Miguel está tomando una pastilla*. Do your own pantomimes of words and expressions that students do not elicit.

5

Standards: 1.3

Suggestions: Allow students to talk about real or imaginary illnesses they have had. Have them use the past tenses. They can also talk about an illness of another person, such as a family member, friend, or pet, in order to practice third-person forms.

Answers will vary.

Common Errors: Some students will consistently use possessive pronouns to identify parts of the body: *mi mano; mi estómago*. Remind them that, unlike English, Spanish usually uses the definite article with parts of the body. Model as necessary: *la mano; el estómago*.

A ver si recuerdas

OBJECTIVES
▸ Discuss and illustrate how you feel when you are ill
▸ Read and write about illnesses and accidents

Vocabulario

partes del cuerpo
el brazo
la cabeza
el codo
el cuello
el dedo (del pie)
la espalda
el estómago
la garganta
el hueso
la muñeca
el pie
la pierna
la rodilla
el tobillo

problemas
¡Ay!
doler (ue)
sentirse mal
tener . . .
   calor
   dolor (de)
   frío
   hambre
   sed

soluciones y medicinas
el enfermero, la enfermera
examinar
el médico, la médica
poner . . .
   la inyección
la radiografía
la receta
recetar . . .
   la medicina
   la pastilla
recomendar (ie)

para mantenerse sano
caminar
correr
descansar
dormir
hacer ejercicio
levantar pesas
mover(se)
quedarse en cama

5

Enfermo de nuevo

 DIBUJAR, ESCRIBIR, HABLAR

❶ Haz un dibujo sobre la última vez que estuviste enfermo(a). Luego, escribe:

- qué te pasaba
  Me sentía . . .
  Me dolía(n) (mucho / un poco) . . .

- qué te recomendó o recetó el médico
  Me recetó . . .
  Me recomendó . . .

- qué hiciste tú
  Tuve que . . .
  Debí . . .

❷ Muestra tu dibujo a dos estudiantes. Describe cómo te sentiste. Los(as) otros(as) estudiantes pueden hacerte preguntas.

¿Por cuánto tiempo . . . ?

¿También tuviste que . . . ?

114 ciento catorce • Capítulo 3 • ¿Qué haces para estar en forma?

Differentiated Instruction

Heritage Speakers

Students may use English or other alternative terms they have learned in place of some of the Spanish vocabulary: "prescription" instead of **receta**; "X-ray" (or **rayo equis**) instead of **radiografía**. Model the appropriate terms as necessary and have students repeat.

Musical Learner

Select a musically gifted volunteer and have him or her lead the class in a simple rap using the vocabulary for parts of the body. For example: **El brazo, el codo y la mu-ñe-ca. La cabeza, el cuello y la es-pal-da.** The rapper and the class should point to the parts of their bodies as they hear the words.

Gramática

Go **Online** to practice
PEARSON
realize™
PearsonSchool.com/Autentico
WRITING

Recycle **3**

Gramática

Pronombres de complemento indirecto

Indirect object pronouns indicate to whom or for whom an action is performed.

El médico **le** recetó unas pastillas a Eva.

Here are the indirect object pronouns:

* Sometimes you can use *a + Ud. / él / ella* or a noun to clarify to whom the indirect pronouns *le* and *les* refer.

El médico **le** dio una inyección **a ella**.
¿Quién **les** trajo las medicinas **a ustedes**?
La enfermera **le** trajo la radiografía **al doctor**.

me	nos
te	os
le	les

* If a verb is followed by an infinitive or a present participle (present progressive), the indirect object pronoun may go before the main verb or be attached to the infinitive or participle.

Le tienen que hacer una radiografía a mi perro.
Tienen que hacer**le** una radiografía a mi perro.

Les estoy dando las medicinas.
Estoy dándo**les** las medicinas.

* Remember that indirect object pronouns are used with verbs like *gustar, encantar,* and *doler.*

Me duele el brazo.   A los niños no **les** gustan las inyecciones.

6

Un accidente

 LEER, ESCRIBIR Unos(as) amigos(as) hablan de un accidente y de lo que les recetó el médico. Completa las oraciones con el pronombre de complemento indirecto *(me, te, le, nos, os, les)* que corresponda.

1. Yo no me puedo mover. _____ duele todo.
2. El médico va a poner _____ una inyección a José y a mí.
3. Y a Clara, ¿qué _____ recetó el doctor?
4. Ella se siente bien, a ella no _____ recetó nada.
5. Mi hermana está en cama. Yo _____ estoy dando las medicinas.
6. ¿Y a ti _____ duele el brazo?
7. No, a mí ahora empezaron a doler _____ las piernas.

7

Una nota

 LEER, ESCRIBIR Completa este mensaje de texto con los pronombres correctos. Luego, continúa el texto con sugerencias.

¿Cómo estás? Hace una semana que a mi hermana Teresa y a mí _1._ duele la cabeza. A mí el médico _2._ recomendó usar anteojos. _3._ pregunté si tenía que llevarlos todo el tiempo y _4._ dijo que sí. A Teresa no _5._ dio nada. ¿Qué hiciste cuando _6._ dijeron a tí?

Capítulo 3 • ciento quince **115**

Gramática: Repaso

Suggestions: Refer students who are having difficulty with indirect object pronouns to the *GramActiva* video from L2 Chapter 4A, and to the online tutorials. Have students pass around an object, such as a book. Have them use **dar** to tell about what they did, are doing, or will do: *Carlos me dio el libro. Le voy a dar el libro a María.* Change the number of recipients and guide students with questions as necessary:

¿Qué está haciendo Guillermo?
Está dándoles el libro a Gloria y a Ana.

6

Standards: 1.2

Suggestions: Remind students first to identify the indirect object in each item. This will help them determine which pronoun to use.

Answers:

1. Me	5. le
2. nos	6. te
3. le	7. me
4. le	

7

Standards: 1.2

Suggestions: Ask a volunteer to read the completed message aloud, so students can check their answers.

Answers:

1. nos
2. me
3. Le
4. me
5. le

Additional Resources

 Technology: Online Resources
* *A ver si recuerdas* with Remediation
* Guided, Core
* *Para hispanohablantes*
Print
* Guided WB pp. 78–81
* Core WB pp. 35–36

Assessment

***A ver si recuerdas* with Remediation (online only)**
After presenting the review material on these pages, assign the *A ver si recuerdas* with Remediation to evaluate students' mastery of the material. Additional practice for students who need it is available online.

Enrich Your Teaching

Teacher-to-Teacher

Give students sentences containing nouns and ask them to change all the nouns to pronouns. Remind them that subject pronouns are often eliminated completely in Spanish:
La profesora hablaba a los estudiantes./Les hablaba.

21st Century Skills

ICT (Information, Communications and Technology) Literacy Direct students to the online tutorials available in **Realize** for self-directed review of the grammar topics recycled in this chapter. Students can expand their own learning by reviewing the related English grammar first, then proceed to the new Spanish grammar point.

Can-Do Statements

Read the Can-Do Statements in the chapter objectives with students. Then, have students read Preparación para el examen on page 158 to preview what they will be able to do at the end of the chapter.

Standards for Capítulo 3

To meet the Standards, students will:

COMMUNICATION

1.1 Interpersonal

• Talk about menus, nutrition, and the preparation and quality of foods
• Talk about physical and mental health, exercise, illnesses, and remedies
• Talk about ancient Central American ball games
• Talk about Spanish and Latin American teen magazines

1.2 Interpretive

• Read and listen to information about menus, nutrition, and the preparation and quality of foods
• Read and listen to information about physical and mental health, exercise, illnesses, and remedies
• Read about word families
• Read about the career of a bilingual student advisor
• Read about ancient Central American ball games
• Read about Spanish and Latin American teen magazines
• Read lyrics from a Mexican *corrido*

1.3 Presentational

• Write about menus, nutrition, and the preparation and quality of foods
• Write about physical and mental health, exercise, illnesses, and remedies
• Write about planning a party
• Write about ancient Central American ball games

CULTURE

2.1 Practices to Perspectives

• Explain the use of natural remedies in Latin America
• Explain the physical education system in Spanish schools
• Explain the practice of ball games in ancient Central America
• Explain teen reading habits in Spain and Latin America

2.2 Products to Perspectives

• Describe a Spanish nutrition study
• Discuss *corridos* and the Mexican Revolution
• Talk about Spanish and Latin American teen magazines

CONNECTIONS

3.1 Making Connections

• Talk about key facts about health, nutrition, remedies, and physical education
• Talk about key facts about the career of a bilingual student advisor
• Talk about key facts about ancient Mexico and modern Spain

CAPÍTULO **3**

¿Qué haces para estar en forma?

Country Connection Explorar el mundo hispano

España
México

CHAPTER OBJECTIVES

Communication

By the end of the chapter you will be able to:

• Listen and read about health advice and nutrition
• Talk and write about healthy eating habits and exercise
• Give advice to others about healthy lifestyles

Culture

You will also be able to:

• Compare an ancient game with a modern game
• Understand the connection between healthy habits and lifestyle in Spanish-speaking countries
• Demonstrate understanding of an authentic video about the nutritional benefits of fruits and vegetables

You will demonstrate what you know and can do

• Presentación oral: Una vida más sana
• Presentación escrita: Por una vida más saludable

You will use

Vocabulary

• Symptoms and remedies
• Parts of the body
• Health, food, and nutrition
• Physical fitness and exercise
• Moods

Grammar

• Affirmative and negative commands with *tú*
• Affirmative and negative commands with *Ud.* and *Uds.*
• Subjunctive: Regular, stem-changing verbs, irregular verbs

ARTE y CULTURA México

Las frutas de Tamayo Rufino Tamayo (1899–1991) fue un gran pintor y muralista mexicano que nació en Oaxaca, un estado conocido por sus deliciosas frutas. Cuando Tamayo era niño, su familia vendía frutas en un mercado y él aprendió mucho de ellas. Su forma, variedad y color lo fascinaban. Sabía cuándo tenían calidad y cuándo estaban listas para comer. Él pintó muchas frutas. Decía que su único lenguaje era la pintura porque estaba hecha de formas, como las frutas.

▶ ¿Qué frutas conoces que no se producen aquí y las traen de otros países? ¿Sabes de dónde las traen?

"Sandías", Rufino Tamayo
© D.R. Rufino Tamayo/Herederos/México/2010/Fundación Olga y Rufino Tamayo, A.C./Christie's Images/Corbis.

Enrich Your Teaching

The End in Mind

Have students preview the sample performance tasks on *Preparación para el examen*, p. 158, and connect them to the Chapter Objectives. Explain to students that by completing the sample tasks, they can self-assess their learning progress.

Technology: Mapa global interactivo

Download the *Mapa global interactivo* files for Chapter 3 and preview the activities. Use Activity 1 to explore the Amazon Rain Forest. In Activity 2, discover the ruins of Chichén Itzá, where Mayans played ball games.

Go **Online** to practice
PearsonSchool.com/Autentico

PEARSON
realize™

AUDIO · VIDEO · WRITING · SPEAK/RECORD · MAPA GLOBAL · AUTÉNTICO · FLASCHARDS · ETEXT 2.0 · GAMES

Preview 3

Puesto de frutas y verduras en un mercado de Barcelona, España

Videonovela ¡Pura vida!

Capítulo 3 • ciento diecisiete **117**

- Discuss Language Arts Strategies: using prior knowledge, speech projection, persuasive writing, cause and effect

3.2 Acquiring information and Diverse Perspectives
- Read a Spanish nutrition study report
- Read an article excerpt from a Spanish magazine
- Read song lyrics from a Mexican *corrido*

COMPARISONS

4.1 Language
- Compare Spanish words to their English counterparts
- Compare Spanish and English commands

4.2 Cultural
- Compare ancient Central American ball games to modern ones
- Compare Spanish and Latin American teen magazines and their readership to those in the United States
- Compare home made remedies n the Spanish culture to those in the student's own world

COMMUNITIES

5.1 School and Global Communities
- Link to Web sites from the Spanish-speaking world
- Read about Spanish magazines for the youth

5.2 Lifelong Learning
- Discuss important facts about healthy lifestyles
- Discuss important facts about scientific studies
- Develop an appreciation for the art of songwriting
- Read an authentic Spanish-language text

Chapter Opener

Resources: Mapa global interactivo: Regional maps

Suggestions: Introduce students to the chapter theme and objectives.

▶ **Technology: Videonovela ¡*Pura vida*!** View this stand-alone storyline video about five young adults in San José, Costa Rica with your class.

ARTE Y CULTURA

Standards: 1.2, 3.1

Suggestions: Ask: *¿Qué frutas se ven en la pintura? ¿Las comes tú?*

Answers will vary, but may include mango, guava, papaya, and kiwi.

Teaching with Art

Ask students: ¿Cuál es la fruta principal que ves en la pintura? ¿Cuáles de esas frutas puedes encontrar en el área donde vives? ¿Te gustan las frutas que crecen en el área donde vives?

Project-Based Learning

Una vida saludable

As students work through the chapter during the week, ask them to create a list of healthy habits that they can share with their families and friends. Have them prepare a speech explaining why it is important to eat well and exercise often. Have them use this activity to complete the *Presentación oral* on page 147.

Vocabulario en contexto 1

Standards: 1.2

Resources: Teacher's Resource Materials: Input Script, Clip Art, Audio Script, Technology: Audio Cap. 3

Suggestions: You may want to use the Input Script from the *Teacher's Resource Materials* as a source of ideas for presentation of new vocabulary and comprehensible input. Meaning for most of the vocabulary in this lesson can be clarified either by pantomime or by TPR commands, and having students point to the objects named on pp. 118–119.

Active Classroom

Have the class stand up. Call out different vocabulary words from these two pages and have students act them out. Call them out quickly and repeat words twice or three times for reinforcement. A quick pace will make the activity fun.

Technology: Interactive Whiteboard

Vocabulary Activities 3-1 Use the whiteboard activities in your Teacher Resources as you progress through the vocabulary practice with your class.

Pre-AP® Integration

- **Learning Objective:** Interpretive: Audio
- **Activity:** Have pairs of students write a dialog between a doctor and a patient highlighting vocabulary from this chapter. In addition, have each pair write three multiple-choice questions to accompany their dialog. Have them record their dialog as well as their questions. Redistribute the recordings to other pairs. Ask each pair of other students to listen to the dialog and answer the questions.
- **Pre-AP® Resource Materials:** Comprehensive guide to Pre-AP® vocabulary skill development

---

Vocabulario en contexto 1

OBJECTIVES
Read, listen to, and understand information about
▶ Symptoms and remedies
▶ Health, food, and nutrition

La clínica comunitaria

BIENVENIDOS A LA CLÍNICA PEDROSA
Esta es la clínica de la comunidad. Aquí la gente viene a ver al médico cuando no se siente bien.

¡Algunas veces, puede tener un fuerte dolor de **oído**!

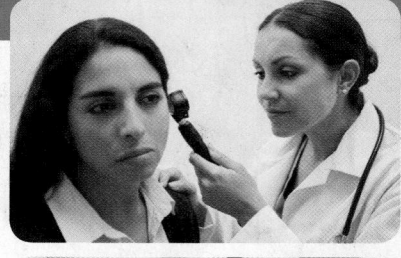

39 grados centígrados

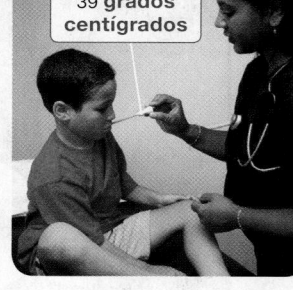

Si tiene **tos fuerte** y **estornuda**, es probable que tenga una **alergia** o un **resfriado**.

Tiene **fiebre**. Descanse y tome **aspirina**. Si tiene **gripe** y le duele **el pecho** necesitará tomar **jarabe** y **antibióticos**. Nunca **tome** remedios con el **estómago vacío**.

Nuestra clínica se especializa en nutrición

Consejo del día
Recuerde que para mantenerse sano debe evitar la **comida basura**. Coma **alimentos nutritivos**. Siempre cuide su **alimentación**.

comida basura

alimentos nutritivos

118 ciento dieciocho • Capítulo 3 • ¿Qué haces para estar en forma?

Differentiated Instruction

Heritage Speakers

Invite a student with outstanding pronunciation skills to take turns with you, randomly naming the vocabulary items during the presentation. This way, students will be exposed to variations in the pronunciation of the words and expressions.

Advanced Learners

Have students prepare and perform a skit set in a doctor's waiting room. Characters should include a doctor, a nurse, and at least two patients with different illnesses.

P: Soy un atleta profesional. ¿Qué me recomienda comer para tener una dieta rica en **calcio** y **proteínas**?

R: Los lácteos **contienen** calcio y ayudan a tener los huesos **fuertes**. Las carnes y los huevos son alimentos que contienen proteínas **aunque** no le recomiendo comerlos en grandes cantidades.

P: ¿Qué alimentos debo consumir para mejorar la cantidad de **hierro** en la sangre y tener más **energía**?

R: Las espinacas contienen un alto **nivel** de hierro. El cereal y el pan tienen **fibras** y **carbohidratos**. Ellos proveen energía.

P: Necesito darle vitaminas a mi cuerpo. ¿Qué alimentos me recomienda?

R: Coma fruta todos los días. Todas las frutas son buenas. Las naranjas tienen mucha **vitamina** C.

1

Si estás enfermo...

 ESCUCHAR Escribe los números del 1 al 6 en una hoja. Escucha las siguientes frases y escribe *C* (cierto) o *F* (falso) para cada una de ellas.

2

¿Quién es quién?

ESCUCHAR Recorta tres trozos de papel. Escribe "doctor" en uno, "paciente" en otro y "nutricionista" en el último. Escucha con atención las distintas frases y levanta el papel que corresponde a la persona que está hablando.

Capítulo 3 • ciento diecinueve **119**

Enrich Your Teaching

Culture Note

Two grains have been Latin American staples for centuries. Quinoa (KEEN-wah) was grown by the Incas; amaranth (AH-mah-rahnth) by the Aztecs. Both are highly nutritious. Moreover, they can be grown in poor soil and arid climates. Both can now be found in many United States supermarkets.

21st Century Skills

Information Literacy Have students research and come up with a list of two or three useful Internet resources for supporting sound nutritional practices, such as sites providing calorie counts for items in fast food restaurants, and the like.

1

Standards: 1.2

Resources: Teacher's Resource Materials: Audio Script, Technology: Audio Cap. 3

Suggestions: Point out to students that *Actividad* 1 focuses on the information on p. 118. Before they listen, allow students a few minutes to read over and study this page. Then play the audio or use the script to read the activity aloud.

 Technology: Audio Script and Answers

1. En la clínica de la comunidad la gente va a ver al médico cuando se siente bien.
2. Hay que tomar aspirina y descansar cuando tienes fiebre.
3. Cuando tienes alergia, tienes un resfriado.
4. Si tienes el estómago vacío no puedes tomar el jarabe.
5. Debes tomar antibióticos si estornudas.
6. Debes ir al doctor si tienes dolor de oído.

1. F	3. F	5. F
2. C	4. C	6. C

2

Standards: 1.2

Resources: Teacher's Resource Materials: Audio Script, Technology: Audio Cap. 3

Suggestions: Use the audio or the script. Allow students to listen more than once. Pause frequently to allow them to write the information. Then have students work in pairs to check their answers and each other's comprehension.

Technology: Audio Script and Answers

1. Me gustaría bajar de peso. (*paciente*)
2. Debes descansar si tienes fiebre. (*doctor*)
3. Para tener los huesos fuertes toma leche en las comidas. (*nutricionista*)
4. Debes evitar la comida basura y comer alimentos nutritivos. (*nutricionista*)
5. Me duele mucho el oído y tengo tos. ¿Qué puedo hacer? (*paciente*)
6. Nunca tomes remedios con el estómago vacío. (*doctor*)

Note: The term "comida basura" is not used in all Spanish-speaking countries. Tell your students they may also say "comida rápida" to refer to junk food.

Vocabulario en contexto 1

Standards: 1.2

Resources: Technology: Audio Cap. 3

Suggestions:

Pre-reading: Call on a volunteer to read aloud the first line. Then ask students to predict what they think Vero might say to Lucho in the text message.

Reading: Allow students time to read the information silently first. Then play the audio or read the information aloud. Allow them to listen more than once.

Post-reading: Use gestures and demonstrations to clarify the meaning of new vocabulary.

3

Standards: 1.2, 1.3

Suggestions: Have students work in pairs, so they can share strategies for learning new words and structures as well as practice writing skills.

Answers:

1. Necesita tener más energía para el deporte.
2. Es comer alimentos de todos los grupos.
3. A Lucho le gustan las papitas fritas y galletas.
4. Tiene que ir al médico para que le diga cuál es la dieta más apropiada para su edad, peso y estatura.

4

Standards: 1.1

Suggestions: Ask students to develop a plan with their partner that outlines the types of food that are part of a healthy diet.

Answers will vary.

5

Standards: 1.2

Resources: Teacher's Resource Materials: Audio Script, Technology: Audio Cap. 3

Suggestions: Allow students to listen to the audio more than once.

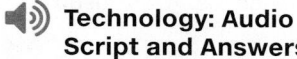 **Technology: Audio Script and Answers**

1. Comer alimentos que tengan fibra y vitaminas todos los días. *(saludable)*
2. Saltarse comidas. *(no saludable)*
3. Comer comida basura. *(saludable)*
4. Parar de comer cuando te sientas lleno. *(saludable)*

 Lucho quiere cambiar su **dieta**. Le manda un mensaje a Vero pidiéndole consejo[1].

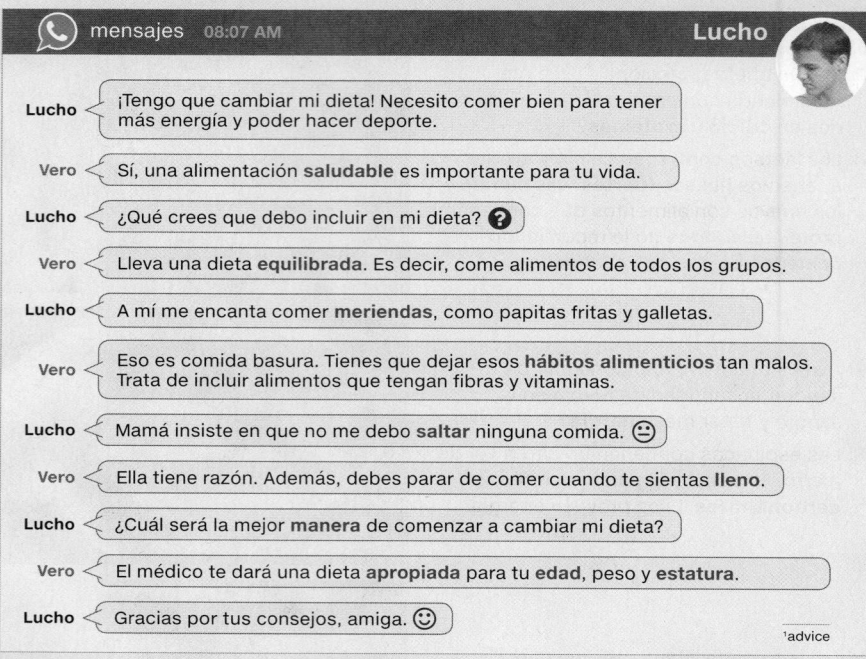

mensajes   08:07 AM   Lucho

Lucho ¡Tengo que cambiar mi dieta! Necesito comer bien para tener más energía y poder hacer deporte.

Vero Sí, una alimentación **saludable** es importante para tu vida.

Lucho ¿Qué crees que debo incluir en mi dieta?

Vero Lleva una dieta **equilibrada**. Es decir, come alimentos de todos los grupos.

Lucho A mí me encanta comer **meriendas**, como papitas fritas y galletas.

Vero Eso es comida basura. Tienes que dejar esos **hábitos alimenticios** tan malos. Trata de incluir alimentos que tengan fibras y vitaminas.

Lucho Mamá insiste en que no me debo **saltar** ninguna comida. ☺

Vero Ella tiene razón. Además, debes parar de comer cuando te sientas **lleno**.

Lucho ¿Cuál será la mejor **manera** de comenzar a cambiar mi dieta?

Vero El médico te dará una dieta **apropiada** para tu **edad**, peso y **estatura**.

Lucho Gracias por tus consejos, amiga. ☺

[1]advice

3

 Vero le da consejos a Lucho

ESCRIBIR Parafrasea el diálogo en un párrafo. Usa oraciones conectadas con detalles y elaboración.

4

 ¿Cómo es tu dieta?

HABLAR EN PAREJA Haz planes con un(a) amigo(a) para seguir una dieta más saludable.

Modelo

A —Primero, debemos comprar alimentos nutritivos.
B —Y no compraremos comida basura.

5

 ¿Es un hábito saludable?

ESCUCHAR Escucha las frases y escribe si cada hábito alimenticio que se describe es saludable o no es saludable.

Differentiated Instruction

Heritage Speakers

Ask students to tell about foods that they eat at home that are not usually part of the local United States diet. Or, in the case of foods that have become fast food, such as the *taco*, ask them to talk about how the fast-food version differs from the version they may eat at home.

Multiple Intelligences

Naturalist: Ask students to describe fruits and vegetables only in terms of touch, smell, and taste. Ask them to imagine the taste, smell, or texture and weight of each as they describe it or hear it described. Encourage them to use the Spanish they know: *El limón no es dulce.* Provide adjectives such as *ácido* if requested.

Videohistoria

Go **Online** to practice
PEARSON
realize™
AUDIO VIDEO WRITING SCRIPT

PearsonSchool.com/Autentico

Interpretive 3

La receta del abuelo

Antes de ver

Hacer predicciones Piensa en qué te hace sentir mejor cuando tienes gripe. Ahora mira las fotos. ¿Qué relación tienen con la gripe? Basándote en estas fotos, ¿de qué crees que se trata la Videohistoria que verás?

Haz la actividad

Síntomas de la gripe Trabaja con un compañero. Comenten qué sienten cuando tienen gripe. Hagan una lista de los síntomas en español.

▶ Ve el video

¿Qué pasa cuando Valentina se despierta y no se siente bien? ¿Qué hace la mamá de Valentina para tratar de que se sienta mejor?

Ve a **PearsonSchool.com/Autentico** para ver el video *La receta del abuelo.* También puedes leer el guión.

Valentina

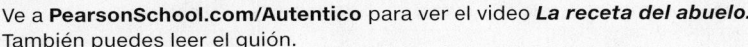

Después de ver

 ESCRIBIR Contesta las siguientes preguntas:

1. ¿Qué le duele a Valentina cuando se levanta?
2. ¿Qué cree la mamá que le pasa a Valentina?
3. ¿Qué hace la mamá para saber si Valentina tiene fiebre?
4. ¿Cuál es la receta del abuelo para aliviar la gripe? Parafrasea la receta, o explícala en tus propias palabras.

Comparación cultural Compara la receta del abuelo de Valentina con los remedios caseros *(home remedies)* y las medicinas que tus padres o abuelos usan para aliviar la gripe. Explica qué métodos crees que son más efectivos y por qué.

Capítulo 3 • ciento veintiuno **121**

Enrich Your Teaching

Culture Note

Many Latino grandmothers have an arsenal of home remedies for the flu and the common cold that might sound a little crazy in other cultures. Cutting an onion in half and leaving it by your night stand to alleviate flu symptoms, keeping a clove of garlic inside your cheek to battle congestion, and rubbing the soles of your feet with menthol paste to stop a nocturnal cough are some of the recommendations suggested by Latina grandmothers for generations.

21st Century Skills

Critical Thinking and Problem Solving Ask students to think about the rationale behind home remedies for common maladies such as cold and indigestion. For example, do they think that there is any scientifically sound reasoning behind the use of oranges, lemons, and honey to alleviate cold symptoms? How about the use of chamomile or peppermint to alleviate an upset stomach? Invite students to express their opinions in writing, using supporting statements.

Tecnología: Video

Standards: 1.2

Resources: Teacher's Resource Materials: Video Script

Antes de ver

Review the previewing strategy and activity with students. Invite them to make predictions based on the photos and the title of the video. Discuss how the photos and title of the video give clues to the content.

Ve el video

Show the video once without pausing. Ask volunteers to paraphrase the theme and main idea. Show the video again, stopping to ask volunteers to paraphrase the important details. Then show the video a final time without pausing.

Después de ver

Standards: 1.2, 1.3, 4.2

Suggestions: For question 4, guide students to understand and paraphrase the preparation of the warm orange as a home remedy for the flu. Ask them to use the images of the grandfather's hands making the concoction to infer the meaning of unfamiliar words such as *compresa, tibia, frente* and *pulpa*.

Answers

1. todo el cuerpo, pero en especial la garganta y la cabeza
2. La qmama piensa que Valentina tiene un resfriado.
3. Le pone el termómetro.
4. La naranja se calienta en el horno, se saca la pulpa y se pone en una compresa sobre la frente o el pecho.

Comparación cultural: Answers will vary.

Have students go to Realize for additional video activities.

Additional Resources

 Technology: Online Resources
- Instant Check
- Guided, Core, Video, Audio
- *Para hispanohablantes*

Print
- Guided WB pp. 82–90
- Core WB pp. 37–38
- Authentic Resources Worbook

Assessment

Quiz: Vocabulary Recognition
- Prueba 3-1

Starter Activity

Have students list three reasons they might go to the doctor.

6

Standards: 1.2

Suggestions: Have students briefly read the entire paragraph once for meaning before they write their answers.

Answers:

1. Tenía tos
2. Aunque
3. tenía fiebre
4. grados centígrados
5. tengo gripe
6. antibióticos

7

Standards: 1.1, 3.1

Suggestions: Encourage partners to ask questions and explain their answers. Remind students that everything is relative: an occasional serving of cookies and milk might be considered healthy or at least not unhealthy, but eating such foods every day is not a healthy dietary habit. Ask students to include comments about quantity and frequency as they talk about the pictures.

Answers will vary but should contain the following information:

1. Pescado frito y papas fritas; contienen proteína y carbohidratos. No son saludables.
2. Ensalada de espinacas: contiene fibra y hierro. Es saludable.
3. Cereal con leche: contiene proteína, carbohidratos, calcio y fibra. Es nutritivo y saludable.
4. Hamburguesa con papas fritas y refresco: contienen proteína y carbohidratos. No son saludables.

Project-Based Learning

Share the rubric with students. Explain the task to them and have them perform Step 1. (For more information, see p. 112-b.)

Vocabulario en uso 1

OBJECTIVES
▶ Talk about symptoms and remedies
▶ Discuss healthy eating choices
▶ Write about food and recipes

6

Llegó el otoño

LEER, ESCRIBIR En el otoño los estudiantes comienzan sus clases y todo el mundo estornuda. Completa este correo electrónico que le escribió un estudiante a su profesor con las palabras o frases del recuadro.

grados centígrados	tengo gripe
antibióticos	aunque
tenía fiebre	tenía tos

> Maestro:
>
> No puedo ir a la escuela hoy. anoche. **2.** tomé un jarabe que me recetó el doctor, no pude dormir. Hoy por la mañana tenía mucho frío, mi mamá me puso el termómetro debajo del brazo y me dijo que porque tenía 39 **4.** Ella cree que yo **5.** . En vez de recetarme **6.** , la doctora recomienda que yo descanse mucho y que beba mucha agua. ¡Siempre me pasa lo mismo en otoño! Espero regresar a clase pronto.
>
> Tomás

7

Contiene un alto nivel de . . .

HABLAR EN PAREJA Mira las fotos y explica a otro(a) estudiante lo que come cada uno de estos jóvenes y por qué es saludable o no es saludable. Usa las palabras del recuadro.

proteína	fibra	nutritivo	calcio	hierro	carbohidratos	contener

Differentiated Instruction

Logical/Mathematical Learner

Bring in empty food cans and boxes. Have students review the nutrition facts information on the labels and note the amounts of **proteína, calcio, fibra, carbohidratos,** and **hierro** in each food. Ask them to make statements comparing the nutritional contents of different foods.

Students with Learning Difficulties

Review the concept of cognates and point out examples such as **alimentación** or **nutrición** on these two pages. Ask students to name other words they see that look like English words. Help students recognize a cognate like **proteína** by writing it on the board and covering the **a.**

Ampliación del lenguaje   Familias de palabras

Las familias de palabras son grupos de palabras que tienen la misma raíz *(root)*. Muchas veces podemos saber el significado *(meaning)* de una palabra si conocemos otras palabras de la misma familia. Observa la relación entre las siguientes palabras y completa las frases.

Verbos	Sustantivos	Adjetivos
alimentar	alimentación	alimenticio
equilibrar	equilibrio	equilibrada
nutrir	nutrición	nutritivo
pesar	peso	pesado

1. Para obtener una buena _____, debemos comer alimentos nutritivos.
2. Tenemos un buen hábito _____ cuando no nos alimentamos con comida basura.

8

Preparándose para la carrera

LEER, HABLAR EN PAREJA, ESCRIBIR Trabaja con otro(a) estudiante para terminar el cuento sobre este atleta. Usa por lo menos cinco palabras del recuadro.

estar resfriado	nivel	hierro	energía
carbohidratos	hábitos	aunque	evitar

Rafa era un atleta fuerte, de peso apropiado para su edad. Iba a participar en una carrera. Tenía el estómago vacío y quería comer . . .

9

¿Qué recomienda?

HABLAR EN PAREJA Túrnate con otro(a) compañero(a) para representar la conversación entre un(a) estudiante y su maestro(a). El/La maestro(a) te expresará recomendaciones con detalles.

Videomodelo
Estudiante —*Me duele la cabeza.*
Maestro(a) —*Necesitas tomar una aspirina para reducir el dolor.*

Estudiante

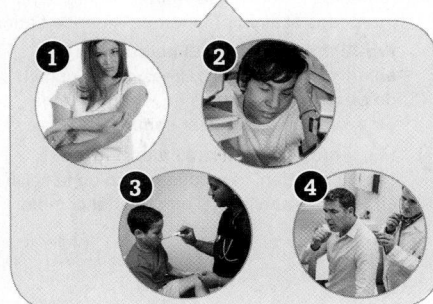

Maestro(a)

Debes . . .
Tienes que . . .
Puedes tomar . . .
El médico te puede recetar . . .

Ampliación del lenguaje

Standards: 1.2, 3.1, 4.1

Suggestions: Have groups of students use background knowledge and reference sources, such as thesauri and dictionaries, to build word families around other words: ***enfermo: enferma, enfermero(a), enfermedad, enfermería, enfermizo(a).***

Answers:
alimentación
nutritivo

8

Standards: 1.1, 1.2, 1.3

Suggestions: As an alternative to pair work, do this activity as a round-robin. The story goes around a circle, each student adding one line that makes sense after the line before it. Have a student secretary write the story on the board as it builds.

Answers will vary.

9

Standards: 1.1

Suggestions: Ask partners to present one or more of their exchanges to the class.

Answers:

Student B's answers will vary. Student A's statements should include the following vocabulary:

1. Me duele el codo.
2. Estornudo.
3. Tengo tos. Me duele el pecho.
4. Tengo fiebre.
5. Estoy cansado. (Estoy resfriado./Tengo gripe.)

Enrich Your Teaching

Teacher-to-Teacher

Invite students to view one or more segments of popular TV shows with a medical theme. Play the segments without sound. Pause frequently and ask students to comment on the action, describe some of the ailments of the patients, and discuss the actions of doctors and nurses. Another alternative is to play Spanish-language versions of these shows, available on cable channels or online, and show students all or part of an episode with sound.

3 Communication

Starter Activity

Have students refer to a metric-standard U.S. English conversion table and ask questions that help them understand the physical size and nature of measurements: *¿Cuántas libras hay en un kilo? ¿Cuántos gramos hay en una onza?*

 10

Standards: 1.1, 1.2, 1.3, 3.1

Suggestions: First, have partners work together to clear up any comprehension problems with the recipe. Remind students that for Step 2, they should discuss a recipe that involves several ingredients.

Answers will vary.

CULTURA

Standards: 1.1, 1.2, 2.1, 3.1

 Technology: Mapa global interactivo, Actividad 1 Look at the extent and importance of the Amazon Rain Forest.

Suggestions: Use the *Cultura* information to launch a discussion about the growing popularity of natural remedies. Have students consult a bilingual dictionary for names of natural remedies with which they are familiar. Possibilities include *la equinácea* (echinacea), *el ajo* (garlic), and *el hipericón (todabuena)* (St. John's wort). Ask questions such as: *¿Para qué se usa ese remedio? ¿Cómo se toma? ¿En qué forma? ¿Cuándo se toma?*

Answers will vary.

Additional Resources

 Technology: Online Resources
- Guided, Core, Audio
- Communication Activities

Teacher Resources
- Teacher's Resource Materials: Audio Script, Technology: Audio Cap. 3, Communicative Pair Activity

Assessment

Prueba 3-2 with Remediation (online only)
Prueba: Aplicación del vocabulario 1
- Prueba 3-2

10

Una receta saludable

 LEER, HABLAR EN PAREJA, ESCRIBIR

1 Ésta es una receta para preparar un postre nutritivo. Léela y explica a otro(a) estudiante por qué la receta es saludable. Habla de los ingredientes que tiene y de los que no tiene.

Modelo
El postre tiene avena. La avena es un cereal y tiene fibra, que es saludable.

2 Ahora, piensen en una comida que les gusta y escriban cinco ingredientes que contiene. Luego escriban tres frases que describen el valor *(value)* nutritivo de la comida.

Avena[1] con fresas

Ingredientes	
4 tazas de leche sabor a fresa	1 taza llena de avena
azúcar al gusto	1 cucharada de vainilla
1 raja de canela[2]	10 fresas en pedazos

Preparación:
Calentar la leche a fuego bajo, junto con el azúcar y la canela, hasta que hierva. Añadir la avena y mover la mezcla hasta que se cocine. Quitarla del fuego, añadir la vainilla, y dejarla en la olla unos diez minutos. Servirla con fresas.

[1] oatmeal [2] stick of cinnamon

CULTURA El mundo hispano

Las plantas medicinales En América Latina, es muy común tomar remedios naturales para resolver problemas menores de salud, como la tos, la fiebre y los dolores de estómago o de cabeza. Estos remedios, hechos de plantas, los comenzaron a usar los indígenas de la región por sus efectos saludables y curativos[1]. Muchas de estas plantas medicinales se preparan como una infusión o té para beber. Algunos ejemplos de plantas medicinales son la manzanilla[2], que se usa para los dolores de estómago, el girasol[3], para la tos y los resfriados, y la menta[4], para los dolores de cabeza y de estómago. Estos remedios naturales se venden en ferias y mercados al aire libre en toda América Latina.

Pre-AP® Integration: El cuidado de la salud y la medicina: ¿Crees que el cultivo de plantas medicinales en la región de la Amazonia puede causar cambios? ¿Cuáles?

Mapa global interactivo Observa los cambios recientes en una región de la selva en Bolivia y analiza los efectos del cambio.

[1]curative [2]chamomile [3]sunflower [4]mint

Unas plantas medicinales ▶

Differentiated Instruction

Heritage Speakers

Invite students to share their knowledge about folk remedies. Ask guiding questions, such as: *¿Cómo se llama el remedio? ¿Para qué se usa? Si es una planta, ¿dónde se encuentra? ¿Cómo se administra el remedio?*

Students with Learning Difficulties

Learners who have difficulty remembering the irregular *tú* commands may be helped by memorizing classic *refranes*, such as: *Dime con quien andas, y te diré quien eres. Haz bien y no mires a quien. Pon el burro delante, para que no se espante.*

Gramática Repaso

> OBJECTIVES
> ▶ Give informal advice about symptoms and remedies
> ▶ Give instructions to follow a recipe

Go **Online** to practice
PEARSON
realize.™

PearsonSchool.com/Autentico

AUDIO   VIDEO   WRITING   SPEAK/RECORD   MAPA GLOBAL

Interpersonal   3

Mandatos afirmativos con *tú*

To tell a friend or close family member to do something, use the *tú* command form. To give an affirmative command in the *tú* form, use the present indicative *Ud. / él / ella* form. This rule also applies to stem-changing verbs.

caminar → camina	comer → come	abrir → abre
jugar → juega	volver → vuelve	pedir → pide

- Some verbs have irregular tú commands.

decir → **di**	hacer → **haz**	ir → **ve**	mantener → **mantén**	poner → **pon**
salir → **sal**	ser → **sé**	tener → **ten**	venir → **ven**	

- Attach reflexive, direct, and indirect object pronouns to the end of affirmative commands. Add an accent mark to show that the stress remains in the same place.

¡**Toma** esas vitaminas! ¡**Tómalas** ahora mismo!
Siéntate aquí.

Más recursos   ONLINE

▶ **Tutorial:** Formation of regular tú commands

🔊 *Canción de hip hop:* Mamá

11

Respuestas para todo

LEER, ESCRIBIR   Verónica siempre tiene recomendaciones para todos los problemas. Completa la conversación con el mandato del verbo apropiado.

1. ¿Te duelen las piernas? _____ ejercicio. (*hacer / correr*)

2. ¿Estás muy cansada? _____ un rato. (*descansar / jugar*)

3. ¿Quieres mantener tu peso? _____ la comida basura. (*comprar / evitar*)

4. ¿Tienes malos hábitos alimenticios? _____ una dieta equilibrada. (*mantener / recetar*)

5. ¿Te sientes mal? _____ al médico. (*ayudar / ir*)

6. ¿Quieres sentirte mejor? _____ bien todos los días. (*comer / pedir*)

7. ¿No tienes energía? _____ unas vitaminas en la farmacia. (*comprar / ver*)

8. ¿Estás triste? _____ con tus amigos para divertirte. (*salir / buscar*)

12

¿Cómo se prepara?

LEER, HABLAR EN PAREJA

1 Lee la receta de la Actividad 10 y después explica a otro(a) estudiante cómo se prepara.

2 Ahora, conversa con otro(a) estudiante. Hagan planes para preparar otra receta. Usen mandatos con *tú* como el modelo.

Modelo
A —*¿Qué necesito hacer para hacer avena con fresas?*
B —*Primero, compra los ingredientes.*

Capítulo 3 • ciento veinticinco **125**

Enrich Your Teaching

Teacher-to-Teacher

Have students invent and deliver "command circuits." These are a series of commands given to a partner, beginning and ending at one point. A typical command circuit might read as follows:
Levántate. / Camina a la ventana. / Ábrela. / Ahora ciérrala. / Vuelve a tu pupitre. / Siéntate.

21st Century Skills

ICT (Information, Communications and Technology) Literacy Remind students of the various digital tools available in **Realize** to help them monitor their own understanding and learning needs, such as the online tutorials with comprehension check exercises.

Gramática: Repaso

Suggestions: Remind students that, for negative commands, regular *-ar* verb endings are used with *-er* and *-ir* verbs, and regular *-er/-ir* endings are used with *-ar* verbs.

 Technology: Interactive Whiteboard

Grammar Activities 3-1 Use the whiteboard activities in your Teacher Resources as you progress through the grammar practice with your class.

13

Standards: 1.2

Suggestions: Have students check their answers by reading each completed item aloud.

Answers:

1. hables	**3.** llegues	**5.** entregues
2. juegues	**4.** vayas	**6.** seas

14

Standards: 3.1

Suggestions: After pairs have taken turns giving commands, have students switch partners, so that they may hear a larger variety of commands.

Answers will vary. The affirmative and negative command forms are:

come, no comas; haz, no hagas; ve, no vayas; pon(te), no (te) pongas; evita, no evites; mantén, no mantengas; sal, no salgas.

Additional Resources

 Technology: Online Resources
- Instant Check
- Guided, Core, Audio, Writing, Reading
- *Para hispanohablantes*

Print
- Guided WB pp. 93–94
- Core WB p. 40

Assessment

Prueba 3-4 with Remediation (online only)
Prueba: Mandatos afirmativos con *tú*
- Prueba 3-4

Gramática Repaso

OBJECTIVES
▸ Read and write about what you shouldn't do
▸ Give informal advice about health

Mandatos negativos con *tú*

To form negative *tú* commands with regular verbs, drop the *-o* of the present tense *yo* form and add the following endings:

hablar	hablo → habl + **es**	**No hables** ahora.
comer	como → com + **as**	**No comas** tanto.
abrir	abro → abr + **as**	**No abras** la boca.

- The same rule applies to verbs whose present tense *yo* form ends in *-go, -zco, -yo,* and *-jo.*

No **salgas** si estás enferma.
No les **ofrezcas** comida basura a tus amigos.
No **escojas** comida con mucha grasa.

- The following verbs have irregular negative *tú* command forms.

dar → **no des**	ir → **no vayas**
estar → **no estés**	ser → **no seas**

- Verbs ending in *-car, -gar,* and *-zar* have the following spelling changes in the negative *tú* commands in order to keep the original sound.

sacar *(c → qu)*	saqu + es	**No saques** la basura.
llegar *(g → gu)*	llegu + es	**No llegues** tarde.
cruzar *(z → c)*	cruc + es	**No cruces** aquí.

- If you are using reflexive or object pronouns with negative commands, place them after *no.*

Estás enfermo. No **te** levantes de la cama.
No comas el pastel. No **lo** comas.

Más recursos ONLINE

▶ **Tutorial:** Formation of irregular *tú* commands

13

Lo que no debes hacer

 LEER, ESCRIBIR Luis sacó malas notas. Ayúdale a sacar mejores notas. Completa las frases con el mandato del verbo apropiado.

1. No _____ cuando la maestra está explicando algo. *(hablar / comer)*
2. No _____ con otro estudiante en clase. *(jugar / escribir)*
3. No _____ tarde a la clase. *(hacer / llegar)*
4. No _____ a la escuela sin hacer la tarea. *(ir / lavar)*
5. No _____ tu tarea sin leerla antes. *(entregar / comprar)*
6. No _____ tan impaciente. *(ser / tomar)*

14

Cuida tu salud

 HABLAR EN PAREJA Tu amiga siempre está enferma. Dale siete consejos usando los verbos del recuadro. Usa mandatos afirmativos y negativos.

Modelo
tomar
¡Toma tu medicina!

comer	hacer	ir	poner(se)
evitar	mantener	salir	

Differentiated Instruction

Heritage Speakers

Ask students to work in pairs to write sentences that demonstrate double negatives, such as No ***digas nada***. Encourage them to see how many negatives they can work into a coherent sentence: No ***digas nada de nada a nadie nunca***. Invite them to share their sentences with the class.

Challenge/Pre-AP®

Have students choose a goal that they would like to achieve, such as keeping fit or driving safely. Ask them to create advice sheets consisting of affirmative and negative commands with ***tú*** that they would give to someone in order to help them achieve this goal.

Gramática Repaso

OBJECTIVES
▸ Discuss good eating habits
▸ Read and write about a doctor's advice
▸ Write and talk about healthy living

Go **Online** to practice
PEARSON **realize**™

PearsonSchool.com/Autentico

AUDIO VIDEO WRITING SPEAK/RECORD

Mandatos afirmativos y negativos con *Ud.* y *Uds.*

To give commands to people other than *tú* and to more than one person, use the *Ud.* and *Uds* commands. To form a command with *Ud.*, remove the -*s* from a negative *tú* command form. To form a command with *Uds.*, replace the -*s* of a negative *tú* command with an -*n*.

No hables.	Hable (Ud.).	Hablen (Uds.).
No traigas la receta.	Traiga (Ud.) la receta.	Traigan (Uds.) la receta.
No vayas al consultorio.	Vaya (Ud.) al consultorio.	Vayan (Uds.) al consultorio.

• To form negative *Ud.* and *Uds.* commands just add *no* before the command.

Coma frutas, pero **no coma** muchos dulces.　　**No salten** comidas.

• Attach reflexive, direct, and indirect object pronouns to the end of affirmative *Ud.* and *Uds.* commands. Add an accent mark to show that the stress remains in the same place. In negative commands, add the pronoun between *no* and the verb.

¡**Tomen** esas pastillas! ¡**Tómenlas** ahora mismo!　　**Lleve** la receta. Por favor, **llévela.**

¡**Cepíllese** los dientes después de comer!　　**No le pidan** dulces. **Pídanle** fruta.

15

Qué dicen todos?

ESCRIBIR, HABLAR EN GRUPO

1 Intercambia mensajes de texto con dos estudiantes. Escribe un mandato afirmativo y otro negativo con Ud. y Uds. Explica por qué respondes de esa manera al mandato. Usa las expresiones, el tono y el estilo apropiados para cada lugar.

Modelo
en el consultorio
*Apaguen **el televisor**. Hay mucha gente y no se escucha nada.*
*No apaguen **el televisor**. Podemos ver la tele mientras esperamos al doctor.*

1. en la biblioteca
2. en el gimnasio
3. en una fiesta
4. en la cocina
5. en una tienda de ropa
6. en la clase de español

2 Ahora, cada pareja debe leer sus mandatos a la clase, y los demás deben decir si la frase es correcta. Si es correcta y no la tiene escrita otra pareja, gana un punto la pareja que la escribió. Gana la pareja que reúne más puntos.

Más recursos ONLINE

 Tutorials: Formation of Formal Commands
Negative Formal Commands

 Canción de hip hop: *Ejercicio*

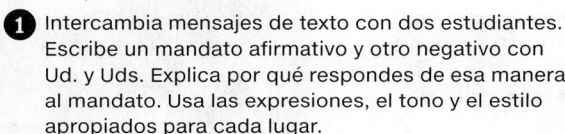

Capítulo 3 • ciento veintisiete **127**

Enrich Your Teaching

Teacher-to-Teacher

If you had students create command circuits as suggested on p. 125, have them go through them again now with a partner. Then ask them to create new command circuits that include negative commands.

21st Century Skills

Critical Thinking and Problem Solving Have students find examples of command forms used in Spanish language advertisements. Discuss why media messages use the command forms to express their intentions. What is the purpose of an advertisement? Who is the intended audience? When might they use the *tú* or *Ud./Uds.* forms?

Starter Activity

Have students create and share sentences with *tú* to help them contrast indicative and imperative forms. The first sentence is in the indicative, and the second is a *tú* command, either affirmative or negative. On the board, supply the following models:

1. *Tú tomas aspirina*. **2.** *No tomes demasiada aspirina.* OR *Toma aspirina para el dolor de cabeza.*
1. *Tú comes mucha sal.* **2.** *Come menos sal.* OR *No comas tanta sal.*

Gramática: Repaso

Standards: 4.1

Suggestions: Remind students that, just as negative *tú* commands, endings for negative *Ud.* and *Uds.* commands are also "switched." Regular -*ar* verb endings are used with -*er* and -*ir* verbs, and regular -*er*/-*ir* endings are used with -*ar* verbs.

Technology: Interactive Whiteboard
Grammar Activities 3-1 Use the whiteboard activities in your Teacher Resources as you progress through the grammar practice with your class.

15

Standards: 1.1, 1.2, 1.3

Suggestions: Students sometimes become frustrated trying to remember the command forms. Encourage them by telling them that they will learn to use the correct forms through patience and practice until the correct form "sounds right." This activity provides excellent practice, since it forces students to focus on the "switched" endings.
Answers will vary.

Project-Based Learning

Students can perform Step 2 at this point. Be sure they understand your corrections and suggestions. (see p. 112-b.)

16

Suggestions: Remind students that their commands can be negative or affirmative.

Answers will vary.

Extension: After some practice, add an element of spontaneity. After each student responds, have him or her toss a foam ball or a wadded-up sheet of paper to any other student in the group, who must say the next command.

17

Suggestions: Have students phrase their recommendations as if they were directly addressing students in Ávila, a town in the community of Castilla and León, Spain. For Advanced Learners, have students research the use and formation of ***vosotros*** commands to address the class accordingly, as though they were making suggestions directly to young people in Spain.

Answers will vary.

16

Juego

ESCRIBIR, HABLAR EN PAREJA Formen grupos de cuatro estudiantes. Cada estudiante escribe un mandato en infinitivo en un pedazo de papel y lo mete en una caja. Los estudiantes se turnan para sacar un papel de la caja. El(La) que saca el papel, lee el mandato. El(La) segundo(a) estudiante forma un mandato con *tú*. El(La) siguiente forma el mandato con *Uds.* y el(la) último(a) añade un pronombre de complemento directo o indirecto a uno de los dos mandatos. Los mandatos pueden ser negativos o afirmativos.

Modelo
Comer manzanas verdes
No comas las manzanas verdes.
No coman las manzanas verdes.
No las comas.

17

Hábitos alimenticios de los jóvenes

LEER, HABLAR Lee este artículo sobre los hábitos alimenticios de los estudiantes españoles.

Conexiones ◀ **Las ciencias**

La OMS (Organización Mundial de la Salud) recomienda a los países a reducir el consumo de azúcares libres (glucosa o azúcar de mesa) en los adultos y niños a menos de 10%.

Esto se debe al alto contenido de azúcares en la alimentación de los jóvenes.

La OMS no se refiere a los azúcares de las frutas, verduras frescas o la leche (azúcar natural), sino a los que se encuentran "ocultos" (*hidden*) en los alimentos que generalmente no se ven como "dulces", como por ejemplo la salsa de tomate.

Las recomendaciones se hacen en base a datos científicos que muestran que la gente que consume un bajo porcentaje de azúcares, reduce la obesidad y los problemas dentales.

El azúcar es importante ya que es una fuente de energía, pero es importante el control de ella en tu dieta diaria.

• Crea una lista de alimentos que comes que contienen azúcares libres. Al lado de ellos, escribe con qué alimento de azúcar natural puedes reemplazarlo (*replace*) para evitar el consumo excesivo de azúcar. Explica a la clase qué alimentos tienen que comer para tener más energía.

Differentiated Instruction

Heritage Speakers

Have students write short descriptions of their favorite breakfast food(s) and breakfast habits. Do they eat different foods on school days and on weekends? If students have lived in a heritage country, ask them to compare and contrast the foods they ate there with those they eat now.

Logical-Mathematical Learner

Have volunteers poll small groups in the class to find out what they eat for breakfast. Have them conduct their interviews in Spanish. Then have them compare their results and present their findings in a graphic organizer.

Go **Online** to practice
**PEARSON
realize** TM

PearsonSchool.com/Autentico

WRITING   SPEAK/RECORD

Interpersonal   **3**

18

Un consejo del doctor

ESCRIBIR, HABLAR EN PAREJA

1 Con un(a) compañero(a), hagan de estudiante y doctor(a). Un estudiante le pregunta al doctor acerca de tres síntomas que tiene. El doctor le responderá con mandatos. Usen las expresiones y gestos apropiados con un lenguaje más formal.

Modelo
Estudiante: Doctor, tengo mucha tos. Usted, ¿qué recomienda?
Doctor(a): Tome un jarabe.

2 Ahora tienes otros tres síntomas. Envía un correo electrónico al doctor preguntando lo que debes hacer ahora. El doctor responderá con otro mandato.

Estudiante: Ahora tengo fiebre y dolor de cabeza.
Doctor(a): Tome una aspirina. La aspirina es buena para bajar la fiebre.

19

Una gran fiesta

ESCRIBIR EN GRUPO   Imagina que tú y seis de tus amigos(as) están planeando una fiesta en tu casa. Intercambia con ellos mensajes de texto sobre qué deben hacer y para qué. Usa los verbos del recuadro con expresiones apropiadas en un tono y forma formales.

| llegar | traer | comprar | invitar | decorar | hacer |

20

Guía para una vida sana

HABLAR EN GRUPO, ESCRIBIR

1 Vas a escribir una guía para una vida sana. Trabaja con un grupo de estudiantes. Hagan una lista de ideas sobre lo que es importante hacer y evitar para mantener la salud.

Modelo
No ponga mucha sal en la comida.

2 Escriban cinco frases para la guía usando la lista de ideas. Usen expresiones apropiadas en un tono y forma formales. Incluyan mandatos con *Ud*.

3 Lean a la clase la guía que escribieron. Intercambien ideas sobre lo que recomendaron. Digan qué ideas son buenas para todas las personas, cuáles solo sirven para los jóvenes y cuáles solo para las personas mayores, y expliquen por qué.

Capítulo 3 • ciento veintinueve **129**

18

Standards: 1.1, 3.1

Suggestions: Ask students to switch roles, so that they can practice a larger variety of commands.
Answers will vary.

19

Standards: 1.3

Suggestions: Encourage students to include some commands.
Answers will vary.

20

Standards: 1.1, 1.3, 3.1

Suggestions: Have students work on their own to write sentences in Step 2.
Answers will vary.

Additional Resources

 Technology: Online Resources
- Instant Check
- Guided, Core, Audio, Writing, Reading
- *Para hispanohablantes*
- Communication Activities
- Teacher's Resource Materials: Audio Script, Communicative Pair Activities, Technology: Audio Cap. 3

Print
- Guided WB pp. 95–96
- Core WB p. 41

Assessment

Prueba 3-5 with Remediation (online only)
Prueba: Mandatos con *Ud*. y *Uds*.
- Prueba 3-5

Examen: Vocabulario y gramática 1
- Examen 1
- ExamView: Examen 1

Enrich Your Teaching

Culture Note

Although dietary habits in Spain have changed recently, much as they have in the United States, many people still enjoy a sweet breakfast of **churros y chocolate**. This is a cup of very thick hot chocolate and a small bundle of deep-fried dough sticks, whose texture resembles that of doughnuts.

21st Century Skills

Collaboration Have students browse online recipes in Spanish and work in pairs to change the ingredients to create a healthier version of the dish.

Vocabulario en contexto 2

Standards: 1.2

Resources: Teacher's Resource Materials: Input Script, Clip Art, Audio Script, Technology: Audio Cap. 3

Suggestions: Have students read along as you present the new vocabulary by playing the audio or reading aloud. Use the photos on pages 130 and 131 and clarify the meaning of new vocabulary via pantomime. Check comprehension by asking questions. See the Input Scripts in the *Teacher's Resource Materials* for specific questions.

21

Standards: 1.2

Resources: Teacher's Resource Materials: Audio Script, Technology: Audio Cap.3

Suggestions: Before engaging students in the listening activity, give them a few minutes to read over and study the advertisement for *Club Deportivo Las Fuentes.* Tell them to compare the information they hear to what they see in this announcement.

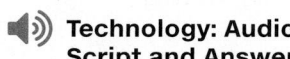 **Technology: Audio Script and Answers:**

Es bueno que te inscribas en el club deportivo Las Fuentes. Te recomiendo que vayas allí porque tienen muchos servicios, por ejemplo:

1. equipo para hacer bicicleta y cinta *(C)*
2. entrenadores profesionales *(C)*
3. clases de baile y natación *(F)*
4. está abierto 12 horas al día, 365 días al año *(F)*
5. clases de ejercicios aeróbicos y yoga *(C)*

Extension: After completing the activity, ask students to correct the false answers.

Active Classroom

Have students work in groups of 4 to 5 and create a brief speech by a fitness trainer giving tips for maintaining a healthy body. Use five expressions from this page and have the group act them out in front of the class.

 Technology: Interactive Whiteboard

Vocabulary Activities 3-2 Use the whiteboard activities in your Teacher Resources as you progress through the vocabulary practice with your class.

Vocabulario en contexto 2

OBJECTIVES
Read, listen to, and understand information about
▶ Places to go when you're not in school
▶ Plans for leisure time

¿Quieres estar en forma?

Las Fuentes te ofrece **hacer bicicleta, ejercicios aeróbicos, cinta, flexiones** y **abdominales.**

Club Deportivo Las Fuentes
¡Te ofrecemos clases personales!

¡Ven y dale a tu cuerpo **fuerza** y energía!

Abierto las 24 horas, 365 días al año.

cinta

flexiones

abdominales

ejercicios aeróbicos

hacer bicicleta

21

¡Ponte en forma!

 LEER, ESCUCHAR, ESCRIBIR Escribe en una hoja los números del 1 al 5. Escucha lo que le explica este chico a su amigo sobre el club deportivo Las Fuentes y escribe *C* (cierto) o *F* (falso) para cada frase.

Differentiated Instruction

Heritage Speakers

Have students list four favorite sports from their heritage country and then compare notes to see which two are the most popular. Encourage them to revise their lists during the discussion. Have them write a few lines explaining why they like or dislike one of those sports.

Advanced Learners

Ask students to work in a small group to prepare and present a TV commercial for a health club. Individuals can act as trainers or clients and do "sound bites" about the club's features and equipment and about correct and incorrect ways to do various exercises. Invite the group to record their commercial on video.

Go **Online** to practice
PEARSON
realize™
PearsonSchool.com/Autentico
AUDIO   WRITING

Interpretive **3**

Luciana y Sebastián **son dos de nuestros profesionales.**

Me llamo Luci. Enseño **yoga** y meditación. Con mis ejercicios la gente aprende a **relajarse, respirar** y eliminar **el estrés** que les da el colegio o el trabajo.

Me llamo Seba y entreno fútbol. El fútbol es un deporte que fortalece los **músculos** y no permite que te sientas **débil**. En mis clases enseño qué hacer para evitar **calambres** y fortalecer el **corazón**.

calambres

yoga

22

El anuncio

ESCUCHAR, HABLAR Escucha el anuncio por radio de un club deportivo. Si la foto del servicio que ofrece el club aparece en el libro, señálala. Si no está, pon la mano sobre el libro.

23

Mis favoritos

ESCRIBIR En una hoja, haz una lista de tres ejercicios que te gusta hacer que se mencionan en estas páginas y dos de los servicios del gimnasio que más te gustaría usar. Escribe un correo electrónico a un amigo(a) contándole tus elecciones. Tu amigo(a) te contesta con sus preferencias.

Modelo
A —Me gusta hacer bicicleta, flexiones y abdominales. Voy a ir a entrenar fútbol con Seba.
B —A mi me gusta hacer cinta. Voy a ir a la clase de yoga.

Capítulo 3 • ciento treinta y uno **131**

Vocabulario en contexto 2

Standards: 1.2

Resources: Teacher's Resource Materials: Input Script, Clip Art, Audio Script, Technology: Audio Cap. 3

Focus: Extending presentation of vocabulary and grammar in context

Suggestions

Pre-reading: Have students look at the photos on page 132. Tell students that one person in each of the pictures has a problem and ask if they can identify it.

Reading: Allow students time to read the presentation silently first. Then play the audio and have students read along as they listen. Allow them to listen more than once.

Post-reading: Check comprehension by asking questions. See the Input Script in the *Teacher's Resource Materials* for specific questions.

24

Standards: 1.2

Resources: Teacher's Resource Materials: Audio Script, Technology: Audio Cap. 3

Suggestions: Allow students to listen to the activity once through first. Then play the audio again, pausing after each item so students can write their answers.

 **Technology: Audio Script and Answers:**

1. ¿Te caes de sueño? Entonces debes irte a la cama. *(B)*
2. Si quieres concentrarte, tienes que estar muy preocupado. *(M)*
3. Antes de hacer ejercicio, es importante entrar en calor para evitar los calambres. *(B)*
4. Ríe cada mañana y vas a estar de mal humor todos los días. *(M)*
5. No te quejes si pierdes un partido, haz un esfuerzo para ganar. *(B)*
6. No debes relajarte ni respirar normalmente después de hacer ejercicio. *(M)*

Extension: After completing the activity, ask students to replace any bad advice they heard with helpful advice.

Escoge un buen consejo

ESCUCHAR Escribe los números del 1 al 6 en una hoja. Escucha lo que aconsejan estas personas y escribe si es un buen consejo *(B)* o un mal consejo *(M)*.

132 ciento treinta y dos • Capítulo 3 • ¿Qué haces para estar en forma?

Differentiated Instruction

Heritage Speakers

Invite students who have lived in a heritage country to tell about comic strips that are popular there. Ask questions to guide them: *¿Cómo se llaman los personajes importantes? ¿Cómo son? ¿Quién lee la tira cómica típicamente? ¿Se publica en un diario o en una revista?*

Students with Learning Difficulties

Make photocopies of page 132. Have students use these to cut out the dialogue balloons. Make other copies in which the dialogue balloons have been blanked out by covering them with a piece of paper. Give students sets of dialogue balloons and dialogue-less comic strips. Have them match the dialogues to the pictures.

Go **Online** to practice
PEARSON realize™

PearsonSchool.com/Autentico

🔊 AUDIO ✏️ WRITING 🎤 SPEAK/RECORD

🏠 🖨 ✉ 📶

Día mundial de la salud
"Por tu salud, muévete" 7 de abril

LA ACTIVIDAD FÍSICA Y LOS JÓVENES

Según la OMS (Organización Mundial de la Salud), el ejercicio es muy importante para la salud de los jóvenes. La práctica regular del ejercicio o del deporte ayuda a los niños y a los jóvenes a **desarrollar** y mantener saludables los huesos y los músculos. También ayuda a cuidar el peso, a reducir las grasas y al buen funcionamiento del corazón.

Los juegos, los deportes y otras actividades físicas permiten a los jóvenes expresarse, tener **confianza en sí mismos** y desarrollar sentimientos de éxito. Estos efectos positivos reducen el estrés de la vida de los jóvenes de hoy.

25

¿Comprendiste?

ESCRIBIR, HABLAR

1. ¿Por qué es buena la práctica regular de ejercicios?
2. ¿Cuáles son cuatro beneficios de hacer ejercicio?
3. ¿Cuáles son algunos efectos positivos de reducir el estrés con el ejercicio?
4. ¿Estás de acuerdo con que los juegos y deportes permiten a los jóvenes expresarse? Explica tu respuesta.

26

Tu propia experiencia

LEER, HABLAR EN PAREJA

Lee las frases y dile a otro(a) estudiante cuándo tienes los problemas de los que se habla aquí.

Me caigo de sueño . . .
Estoy de mal humor . . .
Me preocupo . . .
No tengo energía . . .
Estoy estresado(a) . . .
No puedo concentrarme . . .
Me quejo . . .

Modelo
Me siento fatal si no duermo bien.

Capítulo 3 • ciento treinta y tres **133**

Enrich Your Teaching

Culture Note

In a Spanish custom of long ago, girls played a game called **echar los estrechos** (pick your dear one) on the last day of each year. They wrote their names on pieces of paper and put them in a bag. Then they wrote the names of boys they knew or wished they knew and put them in another bag.

The girls drew pairs of papers and read aloud the names of each couple. If a pair of people named were already in a relationship, it was thought good luck. If they weren't, it was thought (or hoped!) that they would be before long.

25

Standards: 1.1, 1.2, 3.1

Suggestions: Have students discuss answers with a partner first.

Answers:
1. Es muy importante para la salud.
2. Ayuda a los niños y a los jóvenes a desarrollar y mantener saludables los huesos y los músculos. También ayuda a cuidar el peso, a reducir las grasas y al buen funcionamiento del corazón.
3. Permite a una persona expresarse, tener confianza en sí mismo y desarrollar sentimientos de éxito.
4. Answers will vary.

26

Standards: 1.1

Suggestions: If students don't have the problem specified, ask them to make a negative statement followed by an additional comment: *Nunca me preocupo mucho. Preocuparse mucho no resuelve ningún problema.*

Answers will vary.

Pre-AP® Integration

- **Learning Objective:** Interpersonal Writing
- **Activity:** Use the phrases in Activity 26, *Tu propia experiencia*, to write an e-mail to a friend about the things that are causing stress in your life. Be sure to ask your friend at least one question about his or her stressful problems so they can respond.
- **Pre-AP® Resource Materials:** Comprehensive guide to Pre-AP® writing skill development

Project-Based Learning

Students can perform Step 3 at this point. (For more information, see p. 112-b.)

Additional Resources

 Technology: Online Resources
- Instant Check
- Guided, Core, Audio, Writing practice
- *Para hispanohablantes*

Print
- Guided WB pp. 97–104
- Core WB pp. 42–43

Assessment

Prueba: Comprensión del vocabulario 2
- Prueba 3-6

Starter Activity

Review the vocabulary from pp. 118–120. Ask: *¿Cuáles son algunos malos hábitos alimenticios? ¿Y algunos buenos?* Reviewing this information will help students with Step 2 of *Actividad* 27.

27

Standards: 1.2

Answers:

Step 1

Some expressions are similar, and their use may vary. The following are suggestions.

1. No tengo energía.
2. Estoy en la luna.
3. No aguanto más.
4. No me puedo concentrar.
5. Me caigo de sueño.
6. Me siento fatal.

Step 2

Answers will vary.

Extension: After completing the activity, invite pairs of students to role-play one or more of the exchanges from Step 1 for the class. Encourage them to use appropriate intonation for the various expressions.

Teacher-to-Teacher

Ask students to write a note in which they complain about being out of shape. In the note, have them describe how they feel, tell why they are in such bad shape, and ask for advice about how to return to a healthier lifestyle. Have them exchange notes with a classmate who will respond with suggestions for meeting the need.

Vocabulario en uso 2

OBJECTIVES
▶ Read and write about doing exercise
▶ Discuss and give advice about health and fitness

27

En la clase de ejercicios aeróbicos

 LEER, ESCRIBIR

1 Imagina que te inscribes en una clase de ejercicios aeróbicos. Describe cómo se siente cada estudiante usando las expresiones del recuadro.

No aguanto más	No tengo energía	No me puedo concentrar
o	o	o
Me siento fatal	Me caigo de sueño	Estoy en la luna

2 Pregunta a un(a) compañero(a) por mensaje de texto lo que cree que las personas de la clase necesitan hacer en cada situación. Él o ella te responderá con sus consejos.

Differentiated Instruction

Students with Learning Difficulties

Before students complete *Actividad* 27, remind them that the third suggested sentence, ***No me puedo concentrar*** can also be stated ***No puedo concentrarme.*** They may have less difficulty understanding the alternative construction.

Advanced Learners

Ask students to work in a small group to prepare a brief skit set in a physical education class. One student can be the instructor leading an exercise session. The others can be students in the class, some having success and others having problems. Invite the group to present the skit to the class.

Go **Online** to practice
PEARSON
realize™
VIDEO   WRITING   SPEAK/RECORD

PearsonSchool.com/Autentico

Interpersonal 3

28

Nuestra entrenadora

LEER, ESCRIBIR Completa en una hoja aparte este blog de una estudiante con las palabras apropiadas del recuadro. Usa la forma apropiada de los verbos.

consejos	exigir	confianza en sí misma
débiles	corazón	estirar y flexionar
desar	rollar	

El blog de Lupe

Nuestra entrenadora es una atleta que sabe mantenerse en forma y tiene mucha __1.__. Durante las prácticas, ella nos __2.__ mucho. Primero tenemos que __3.__ los músculos. Luego levantamos pesas para __4.__ más músculos en los brazos. Nuestra entrenadora siempre nos da __5.__, como "Hagan ejercicio todos los días para cuidar su __6.__". Ella no quiere que seamos __7.__.

29

El deportista

HABLAR EN PAREJA El estudiante A hace preguntas a un(a) compañero(a). El estudiante B dice lo que debes hacer y explica por qué.

▶ **Videomodelo**
estar en forma
A —¿Cómo se puede estar en forma?
B —Se debe **hacer ejercicio.**

Estudiante A

¿Cómo se puede . . .?
1. evitar los calambres
2. quitar el mal humor
3. cuidar el corazón
4. hacer más fuertes los músculos del estómago
5. tener brazos menos débiles

Estudiante B

Se debe . . .
Se recomienda . . .

CULTURA España

¡A moverse en la calle! En abril de 2012 se celebró por primera vez en España el **Día de la Educación Física en la Calle**, una idea de los profesores que enseñan esta clase. Todo comenzó en Asturias, pero en los años siguientes se extendió por toda España. El objetivo inicial fue mostrar la importancia de la actividad física para niños y jóvenes, pero también pedir que se dedicaran más de dos horas a la educación física en las escuelas españolas. Sin embargo, hasta el año 2016, los estudiantes españoles seguían con dos horas a la semana.

Pre-AP® Integration: El cuidado de la salud y la medicina Pregunta a otros lo que se necesita hacer en las escuelas de España para mejorar esa situación. Ellos dirán lo que se tiene que hacer y sus razones.

Capítulo 3 • ciento treinta y cinco 135

28

Standards: 1.2

Suggestions: Encourage students to begin by scanning the complete paragraph.

Answers:
1. confianza en sí misma
2. exige
3. estirar y flexionar
4. desarrollar
5. consejos
6. corazón
7. débiles

29

Standards: 1.1

Suggestions: Have students switch roles to practice both parts of the dialogue.

Answers will vary.
Probable answers:
1. Se debe/Se recomienda estirar (flexionar).
2. … hacer yoga.
3. … hacer bicicleta.
4. … hacer abdominales.
5. … levantar pesas.

CULTURA

Standards: 1.1, 1.2, 3.1

Suggestions: Ask: *¿Qué problema tienen muchas escuelas españolas? ¿Qué pueden hacer los estudiantes para resolverlo?*

Answers will vary.

Additional Resources

📶 **Technology: Online Resources**
• Audio, Writing, Reading
• Communication Activities
• Teacher's Resource Materials: Audio Script, Communicative Pair Activities, Technology: Audio Cap. 3

Assessment

Prueba 3-7 with Remediation (online only)
Prueba: Aplicación del vocabulario 2
• Prueba 3-7

Enrich Your Teaching

Culture Note

About 80 percent of the people in the world rely on plants to treat illnesses. Even the other 20 percent use many prescription drugs that are plant-based. Aspirin, for example, is based on a substance found in willow bark. Plants in the rain forests of the Americas play an important part in the discovery and development of new drugs.

21st Century Skills

ICT (Information, Communications and Technology) Literacy Have students prepare a multimedia presentation in which they show how physical education class in their school is similar to and different from physical education in a school in Spain. Students can use the information in *Cultura* as a basis for their comparison.

Gramática: Repaso

Suggestions: Point out that the endings used for regular verbs in the subjunctive are the same as those used for negative command forms. Refer students to pp. 126–127 for these endings.

 Technology: Interactive Whiteboard

Grammar Activities 3-2 Use the whiteboard activities in your Teacher Resources as you progress through the grammar practice with your class.

30

Standards: 1.2

Suggestions: Ask students to pay attention to the reason for using the subjunctive in each case as they work. Then have volunteers read each sentence of the completed activity aloud, including the correct verb form.

Common Errors: Since English contains only a few vestiges of the subjunctive (such as "If I were you..."), some students have difficulty remembering to use it in Spanish. Help them by providing more examples in Spanish that require the subjunctive.

Answers:

1. comience	**4.** hagan
2. corran	**5.** estiremos
3. hablen	**6.** subamos

Extension: As students read through the completed activity aloud, ask them to state the reason why the subjunctive is required in each case.

Gramática Repaso

OBJECTIVES
▶ Read and write about a fitness class
▶ Give advice about exercise and health

El subjuntivo: Verbos regulares

To say that one person wants, suggests, or demands that someone else do something, use the *subjunctive mood*. A sentence that includes the subjunctive form has two parts, the main clause and the subordinate clause, connected by the word *que*.

Quiero que respires lentamente.   **Sugiero que bebas** agua antes de correr.
El entrenador **exige que** los atletas **estiren** los músculos.

You can also suggest more general or impersonal ideas using expressions such as *es necesario . . . , es bueno . . . ,* and *es importante . . . , followed by *que* and a form of the present subjunctive.

Es necesario que hagas ejercicio.   **Es importante que** los jóvenes **coman** bien.

To form the subjunctive, drop the *-o* ending to the *yo* form of the present tense, and add the present subjunctive endings to the stem of the verb.

saltar		**conocer**		**decir**	
salt**e**	salt**emos**	conozc**a**	conozc**amos**	dig**a**	dig**amos**
salt**es**	salt**éis**	conozc**as**	conozc**áis**	dig**as**	dig**áis**
salt**e**	salt**en**	conozc**a**	conozc**an**	dig**a**	dig**an**

Verbs ending in *-car, -gar,* and *-zar* have a spelling change in order to keep the pronunciation consistent.

buscar (c → qu)		**pagar (g → gu)**		**cruzar (z → c)**	
bus**que**	bus**quemos**	pa**gue**	pa**guemos**	cru**ce**	cru**cemos**
bus**ques**	bus**quéis**	pa**gues**	pa**guéis**	cru**ces**	cru**céis**
bus**que**	bus**quen**	pa**gue**	pa**guen**	cru**ce**	cru**cen**

Más recursos ONLINE

▶ **Tutorial:** Regular Forms of the Present Subjunctive

30

Una clase inolvidable

 LEER, ESCRIBIR ¿Tuviste alguna vez una instructora que te exigía mucho? Completa la descripción con el verbo en subjuntivo.

La instructora exige que la clase __1.__ *(comenzar / cruzar)* a tiempo y que los estudiantes __2.__ *(correr / comer)* durante diez minutos antes de comenzar la sesión. Ella no permite que ellos __3.__ *(tocar / hablar)* durante la clase. A ella tampoco le gusta que __4.__ *(hacer / tener)* ruido cuando da la clase. Prefiere que nos __5.__ *(estirar / cruzar)* y que __6.__ *(apagar / subir)* escaleras para tener más energía antes de la clase.

136 ciento treinta y seis • Capítulo 3 • ¿Qué haces para estar en forma?

Differentiated Instruction

Heritage Speakers

Have students listen to conversations between family members and focus on words or phrases in the subjunctive mood. Ask them to estimate how frequently the subjunctive is used in a brief conversation. Have them write down as many of the words as they can remember. Check for spelling and structure.

Students with Learning Difficulties

Before beginning the grammar presentation on this page, remind students that they have already seen these spelling changes in other grammatical forms. On the board, write the preterite forms of **sacar, llegar,** and **empezar**. Highlight the spelling changes in the **yo** form and remind students of the spelling change rules.

¿Qué ejercicios hago?

HABLAR EN PAREJA Imagina que eres el(la) entrenador(a) de la escuela. Habla con otro(a) estudiante para aconsejarle algo. Usen las siguientes expresiones.

Videomodelo

Me duele(n) . . . / Es necesario que . . . .

A —*Me duelen las piernas cuando corro.*

B —*Es necesario que estires los músculos antes de correr.*

Estudiante A

1. ¿Qué hago para . . . ?
2. No puedo . . .
3. Estoy muy . . .
4. Quiero desarrollar . . .
5. Necesito . . .
6. Tengo . . .

Estudiante B

Te sugiero que . . .

Es importante que . . .

Para que estés más tranquilo(a), te aconsejo que . . .

Lo mejor es que practiques . . .

Es muy bueno que vayas a . . .

Para evitar los calambres quiero que . . .

El español en el mundo del trabajo
La consejera bilingüe

De niña, María Romero Thomas solo hablaba español en su casa e inglés en la escuela. Sus padres le decían que ella no podía olvidar la cultura de sus abuelos mexicanos, pero que debía integrarse *(to integrate)* y tener éxito en la cultura estadounidense. María quiso ayudar a otros a alcanzar también esa meta y decidió estudiar para ser consejera escolar.

La función de un(a) consejero(a) escolar es muy importante para los estudiantes y para la comunidad. Estos(as) profesionales se dedican a dar apoyo a los chicos y a guiarlos al elegir la carrera que van a seguir. También aconsejan sobre temas de salud, cómo coordinar el estudio con otras actividades como recreación, trabajo y ejercicios, en las relaciones con su familia y amigos, cómo mantener un buen estado de ánimo y cómo desarrollar sus aptitudes en la escuela. Si ven que los chicos se sienten mal, no se pueden concentrar o están muy estresados, les recomiendan ir al médico, tener una alimentación saludable y cosas que pueden hacer para relajarse.

Al comienzo de los años ochenta, María Romero Thomas se convirtió en *(became)* la primera consejera bilingüe del Sequoia Union High School District, en California. En esos años, viajaba de una escuela a otra para implementar el primer programa bilingüe del distrito. También hablaba con los padres sobre la importancia que tenía para sus hijos recibir una buena educación.

Hoy en día, hay cientos de consejeros bilingües en los distritos escolares de los Estados Unidos que ayudan a los niños hispanohablantes a vivir entre dos culturas.

Go **Online** to practice
PEARSON
realize™
PearsonSchool.com/Autentico

VIDEO WRITING SPEAK/RECORD

31

Standards: 1.1

Recycle: parts of the body; *poder* + infinitive

Suggestions: Allow students a few minutes on their own to prepare the problems they are going to talk about when they play the role of Student A. As they practice the dialogue together, encourage those playing the role of Student B to respond as quickly and naturally as possible with a suggestion that makes sense.

Answers will vary.

El español en el mundo del trabajo

Standards: 1.2, 3.1, 5.1

Suggestions: Ask students, including Heritage Speakers who may have known a bilingual advisor, to talk about their experiences with him or her. Ask: *¿Cómo ayudaba el (la) consejero(a) a los estudiantes? ¿Tenía interacción con los profesores también? ¿Y con los padres? ¿Cuáles eran algunas de sus tareas?* Then ask students: *¿Les interesa tener una carrera como consejero(a) bilingüe? ¿Por qué? ¿Por qué no?*

Teacher-to-Teacher

Prepare (or ask Advanced Learners to prepare) two sets of notecards. One set contains subordinate clauses in which the verb is in the infinitive in parentheses *...que (estudiar) mucho*. The other set is a mixture of main clauses, some that require the subjunctive in the subordinate clause and some that do not, such as *Es evidente que...* or *Veo que....* Students can take turns drawing one card from each pile, determining whether or not the subjunctive is needed in the subordinate clause, and if so, what its form is. Then have them read the complete complex sentence aloud: *Veo que estudias mucho.*

Enrich Your Teaching

Culture Note

For a great many Spanish-speaking people the notion of "bilingualism" has nothing to do with English. In Mexico alone, more than a hundred languages are spoken, from the *nahuatl* of the Aztecs to *amuzgo* to *zoque*. About eight percent of those who speak an indigenous language are bilingual in Spanish. Consider all of Central and South America and the Caribbean, and the number of known languages rises to almost a thousand. Indigenous languages are so important in some countries that they have been given official standing equal to Spanish. Examples include *guaraní* in Paraguay and *quechua* in Peru.

32

Standards: 1.1

Suggestions: Remind students that the words and expressions in the word bank are to be used to begin the main clause in Student B's sentences.

Answers: Student B's sentences will vary, but should make use of the following subjunctive forms:

saques	añadas	conozcas
pongas	tomes	hagas
respires	hagas	

33

Standards: 1.1

Suggestions: Challenge students to be creative with their mixing and matching from the three columns, in order to make as many sentences as they can.

Answers will vary.

Assessment

Prueba 3-8 with Remediation (online only)
Prueba: El subjuntivo: Verbos regulares
- Prueba 3-8

32

¿Qué le aconsejas?

HABLAR EN PAREJA Trabaja con otro(a) estudiante para hablar acerca de la salud. Uno se queja de algún problema. El otro le aconseja. Usa la forma correcta del subjuntivo y las expresiones del recuadro.

sugiero	recomiendo	quiero	es importante	es necesario

Videomodelo
Me caigo de sueño. / descansar un poco
A —*Me caigo de sueño.*
B —*Sugiero que* ***descanses un poco.***

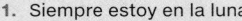

Estudiante A

1. Siempre estoy en la luna.
2. Quiero hacer más fuertes mi corazón y los músculos de mis piernas.
3. No tengo energía.
4. Estoy aburrido(a).
5. No aguanto más los juegos de mis amigos.
6. Siempre tengo sed.
7. Como demasiada comida basura.
8. Necesito hacer más ejercicio.

Estudiante B

sacar . . . de la biblioteca
poner . . .
respirar lentamente . . .
añadir más . . .
tomar . . .
hacer . . .
conocer . . .
hacer . . . y ejercicios . . .
¡Respuesta personal!

33

En el club atlético Sol y Salud

ESCRIBIR EN GRUPO Tres estudiantes son miembros de un club atlético y le envían un correo electrónico al presidente del club preguntándole qué pueden hacer para mejorar el servicio del club. El presidente y su equipo les contesta con una sugerencia. Combina palabras de las tres columnas para hacer frases con el subjuntivo.

Modelo
Queremos / Roberto / enseñar
A —*Queremos que Roberto enseñe más clases.*
B —*No hay problema. Es importante que los clientes estén contentos.*

Es importante que . . .	los entrenadores	limpiar
Sugerimos que . . .	tú	llegar a tiempo
Es mejor que . . .	David y Rita	lavar
(No) Queremos que . . .	nadie	explicar
Es necesario que . . .	ustedes	mostrar cómo
Exigimos que . . .	Julieta	no preocuparse por
	los profesores	(no) tener
	todos	aprender

Differentiated Instruction

Students with Learning Difficulties

Ask students to search for a picture in which two or more people are interacting socially. Have them write sentences using the subjunctive that the people in the picture might be saying to one another. Ask students to cut their sentences out in the shape of dialogue balloons and paste them to the picture.

Challenge/Pre-AP®

Ask students to write ten affirmative commands about eating well and keeping fit. Have them exchange sentences with a partner. Partners take turns changing the commands into suggestions, demands, or requirements that take the subjunctive: *Deja de comer comida basura./Es mejor que dejes de comer comida basura.*

OBJECTIVES
▸ Read and write about giving advice
▸ Discuss ways to solve problems

Go **Online** to practice
PearsonSchool.com/Autentico
PEARSON
realize™
VIDEO   WRITING   SPEAK/RECORD

El subjuntivo: Verbos irregulares

The following verbs are irregular in the present subjunctive:

dar	estar	haber	ir	saber	ser
dé	esté	haya	vaya	sepa	sea
des	estés	hayas	vayas	sepas	seas
dé	esté	haya	vaya	sepa	sea
demos	estemos	hayamos	vayamos	sepamos	seamos
deis	estéis	hayáis	vayáis	sepáis	seáis
den	estén	hayan	vayan	sepan	sean

34

Cambiar los hábitos

LEER, ESCRIBIR Rocío y Manuel están estresados. Escoge el verbo y completa las recomendaciones del consejero.

1. Es importante que Manuel _____ yoga dos veces por semana. *(cambiar / hacer)*

2. Les aconsejo que _____ más confianza en sí mismos. *(ser / tener)*

3. Recomiendo que los dos _____ caminatas por el campo. *(eliminar / dar)*

4. Rocío, te recomiendo que _____ más paciente con Manuel. *(estar / ser)*

35

Mensaje a la consejera sentimental

LEER, ESCRIBIR EN PAREJA

❶ Completa esta correspondencia entre una joven y una consejera con las palabras apropiadas del recuadro.

❷ Escribe un mensaje a tu compañero(a) contándole un problema similar. Él (Ella) te escribirá su sugerencia.

decir	legar	relajarse
hacer	estar	ser

Querida Ana:

Mis padres siempre me exigen demasiado. Quieren que yo siempre les __1.__ adónde voy y me exigen que __2.__ a casa antes de las 9 de la noche. Casi todos los días tenemos algún problema.

¡No aguanto más!
Frustrada en Quito

Querida Frustrada:

Primero, te aconsejo que __3.__. Es importante que __4.__ un esfuerzo para comprender lo que quieren tus padres. Ellos quieren que __5.__ segura (safe). Aunque tú quieres salir con tus amigos, es necesario que __6.__ responsable. Sé paciente y trata de hablar con tus padres y las cosas van a mejorar.
— Ana

Gramática: Repaso

Suggestions: Challenge students to create sentences using subjunctive verb forms that you call out.

 Technology: Interactive Whiteboard

Grammar Activities 3-2 Use the whiteboard activities in your Teacher Resources as you progress through the grammar practice with your class.

34

Standards: 1.2

Suggestions: Review with students the verbs in the main clause that require the subjunctive in the subordinate clause.

Answers:

1. haga
2. tengan
3. den
4. seas

35

Standards: 1.1, 1.2

Suggestions: Encourage students to look for expressions such as *querer que* and *es necesario que.* Remind them that these expressions are markers for the subjunctive.

Answers:

1. diga
2. llegue
3. te relajes
4. hagas
5. estés
6. seas

Project-Based Learning

Students can perform Step 4 at this point. Be sure they understand your corrections and suggestions. (For more information, see p. 112-b.)

Enrich Your Teaching

Teacher-to-Teacher

Invent a few scenarios in which you briefly describe an imaginary problem and ask for advice. Problem scenarios might include being tired all the time, or questions about how to create a healthy meal for guests.

21st Century Skills

Productivity and Accountability Have students create a class checklist of Spanish learning goals for the year using the subjunctive after expressions such as, *es importante que, es bueno que,* etc. Students should revisit the goals regularly through the term to track their progress.

Querida Laura . . .

 LEER, ESCRIBIR

1 Muchos jóvenes le escriben a Laura, la escritora de la columna de consejos de una revista de Madrid. Lee el texto que una joven le escribió a Laura y luego escribe la respuesta de Laura. Usa expresiones como: *te recomiendo, te sugiero, es necesario, es bueno, es importante* y la lista de sugerencias. Pon los verbos en el subjuntivo.

2 Escribe un texto a un compañero (consejero) contándole algo que prefieres hacer pero no puedes debido a algún conflicto. El consejero te contestará con una solución y sus preferencias.

4:19 PM

Ocupada hace siete minutos ✉ ☎ ★

Querida Laura:
Me encanta la clase de yoga. Siempre me siento mejor y me relajo después de ir. Pero el problema es que no tengo tiempo. Tengo mucha tarea y también estudio piano. ¿Cómo me puedo relajar y estar tranquila si no puedo ir a yoga?—*Ocupada de Burgos*

Laura hace cinco minutos ✉ ☎ ★

Querida Ocupada de Burgos:
Si tienes tanto trabajo y no puedes ir a tu clase de yoga, te recomiendo que . . .

Sugerencias
• cambiar el horario
• estar ocupada
• salir con los(as) amigos(as)
• tener tiempo para relajarse
• caminar todos los días

Intercambio de ideas

🎤 **HABLAR EN GRUPO** Imagina que tú eres la persona de las fotos. Tus compañeros(as) te van a dar sugerencias o consejos para ayudarte a resolver tus problemas. Usen los verbos del recuadro.

▶ **Videomodelo**
A —*Estoy muy aburrido, nunca hago nada interesante.*
B —*Es importante que salgas más.*
C —*Es bueno que conozcas más gente.*

ir	conocer	estar	tener	ser	saber

 **1**    **2**    **3**   **4**

140 ciento cuarenta • Capítulo 3 • ¿Qué haces para estar en forma?

Standards: 1.2, 1.3

Suggestions: Encourage students to build sentences around the *sugerencias* before they organize them into a response.

Answers will vary.

Verb forms for the *sugerencias* are as follows:
cambies
estés
salgas
tengas
camines

Standards: 1.1, 1.2

Suggestions: Have groups conduct the activity in round-robin fashion. Rotate around the circle with a different student presenting the problem each time, with others eliciting possible solutions.

Answers will vary.
Students may use the following vocabulary and subjunctive forms:

1. Me duele el codo.   **3.** Estoy de mal humor.
2. Me caigo de sueño.   **4.** Estoy estresado(a).
vayas, conozcas, estés, tengas, seas, sepa

Additional Resources

📶 **Technology: Online Resources**
• nstant Check
• Guided, Core, Audio
• *Para hispanohablantes*
Print
• Guided WB pp. 107–108
• Core WB p. 45

Assessment

Prueba 3-9 with Remediation (online only)
Prueba: El subjuntivo: Verbos irregulares
• Prueba 3-9

Differentiated Instruction

Heritage Speakers
Advice is often given in the form of popular sayings. Cite a few examples, such as **barriga llena, corazón contento** or **no todo lo que brilla es oro**. Have students ask family members what their favorite saying is and write them down. Encourage them to find out if there are similar sayings in English.

Students with Special Needs
Have visually impaired students sit with a partner who can help them complete *Actividad* 37 by explaining the scene in each of the pictures.

Gramática Repaso

OBJECTIVES
▶ Read and write about leading a healthy lifestyle
▶ Discuss suggestions for staying healthy and exercising

Go **Online** to practice

PearsonSchool.com/Autentico

VIDEO   WRITING   SPEAK/RECORD

Interpersonal   3

El subjuntivo: Verbos con cambio de raíz

In the present subjunctive, stem-changing -ar and -er verbs have the stem change in all forms except *nosotros* and *vosotros*.

jugar (u → ue)	
ju**e**gue	juguemos
ju**e**gues	juguéis
ju**e**gue	ju**e**guen

pensar (e → ie)	
pi**e**nse	pensemos
pi**e**nses	penséis
pi**e**nse	pi**e**nsen

entender (e → ie)	
enti**e**nda	entendamos
enti**e**ndas	entendáis
enti**e**nda	enti**e**ndan

• Other verbs you know that follow these patterns are:

    o → ue: contar, poder, volver, costar, probar(se), llover, doler
    e → ie: querer, sentarse, calentar, despertar(se), empezar, entender

Stem-changing *e → ie, e → i,* and *o → ue* verbs that end in *-ir* have a stem change in all forms of the subjunctive.

sentirse (e → ie)	
me s**i**enta	nos s**i**ntamos
te s**i**entas	os s**i**ntáis
se s**i**enta	se s**i**entan

pedir (e → i)	
p**i**da	p**i**damos
p**i**das	p**i**dáis
p**i**da	p**i**dan

dormir (o → ue)	
d**u**erma	d**u**rmamos
d**u**ermas	d**u**rmáis
d**u**erma	d**u**erman

• Other verbs you know that follow these patterns are:

    e → ie: divertirse, preferir
    e → i: reír, repetir, servir, vestir(se), seguir, conseguir
    o → ue: morir

38

¿Qué recomienda la entrenadora?

LEER, ESCRIBIR La entrenadora te recomienda varias cosas. Lee lo que dice y escoge el verbo para completar las frases en subjuntivo.

1. Es importante que _____ mis consejos. *(sentir / seguir)*
2. Sugiero que _____ ocho horas cada noche. *(pedir / dormir)*
3. Es importante que no _____ durante las clases de ejercicio. *(sentarse / practicar)*
4. Quiero que _____ bicicleta tres veces por semana. *(repetir / hacer)*
5. También es bueno que _____ al tenis una o dos veces por semana. *(pensar / jugar)*
6. Te aconsejo que _____ con ropa cómoda. *(seguir / vestirse)*

Capítulo 3 • ciento cuarenta y uno **141**

Enrich Your Teaching

Teacher-to-Teacher

Supply blank index cards and have pairs of students make flashcards for stem-changing verbs. They should write one verb form on each card. On the back of each card they can write the infinitive, tense, and mood. For example, "**jugar**—present subjunctive." This will help users reorganize the cards into sets.

21st Century Skills

Information Literacy The verb charts available to students in **Realize** will help students monitor their own understanding as they review the stem-changing verbs in the subjunctive. They can also find additional verb conjugation practice online.

Starter Activity

Briefly review the indicative forms of stem-changing verbs. On the board write paradigms for some of the verbs in the Gramática on this page. Leave some forms out of each paradigm and ask students to supply them, either by spelling them aloud or filling in the paradigm.

Gramática: Repaso

Suggestions: On the board, list ***...que yo ___, ...que tú ___, ...que Ud./él/ella ___, ...que nosotros(as) ___,*** and ***...que Uds./ellos/ellas ___.*** Point to these phrases at random and call out an infinitive from the *Gramática*. Ask students to supply and spell aloud the correct subjunctive form.

🔲 Technology: Interactive Whiteboard

Grammar Activities 3-2 Use the whiteboard activities in your Teacher Resources as you progress through the grammar practice with your class.

38

Standards: 1.2

Suggestions: Remind students to be extra careful with spelling, since that is the focus of the activity.

Answers:
1. sigas
2. duermas
3. te sientes
4. hagas
5. juegues
6. te vistas

Pre-AP® Integration

• **Learning Objective:** Interpersonal Speaking
• **Activity:** Working with a partner, have students use the information from Activity 36 as a model to role-play a conversation between a stressed client and a life-coach. One student will request advice for his or her stress-related problem, while the other will offer suggestions using expressions like: *te recomiendo, es necesario, es bueno,* and verbs in the subjunctive. Students may prepare a brief outline of their conversation before their role-play.
• **Pre-AP® Resource Materials:** Comprehensive guide to Pre-AP® communication skill development

39

Standards: 1.1, 1.3, 3.1

Suggestions: In Step 1, make sure students understand from the model that the two cues should be combined to make one sentence. Remind them that the subordinate *(que)* clause of each sentence should contain a subject of their choice and a subjunctive verb form. In Step 2, encourage Student B to explain in one or more sentences why he or she agrees or disagrees with the original comment.

Answers will vary.

Students should use the following expressions and subjunctive verbs:

1. Es bueno que durmamos…
2. Es mejor que perdamos…
3. Es bueno que pidamos…
4. Es bueno que volvamos…
5. Es importante que nos acostemos…
6. Es necesario que juguemos…
7. Es necesario que entendamos…
8. Es importante que sigamos…

Extension: Ask partners to report to the class on their opinions regarding a healthy lifestyle. Create a class profile by recording the information on the board.

EN VOZ ALTA

Standards: 1.2, 2.2, 3.2, 5.2

Resources: Teacher's Resource Materials: Audio Script, Technology: Audio Cap. 3

Suggestions: Have students read the information and the song silently. Have them find the rhyming words and note the pattern. Explain to students that the fighting during the Mexican Revolution started in 1910 and ended about 1920. Discuss with the class what they imagine life would have been like during that time. Ask comprehension questions: *¿Cómo son los corridos? ¿Cuáles son los temas principales? ¿Por qué cantaron corridos durante la Revolución?*

Before having students read the song aloud, direct their attention to the information in the *¿Recuerdas?* Allow them a few minutes to practice with a partner.

Answers: valiente, popular, bonita

Decisiones

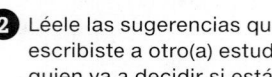

ESCRIBIR, HABLAR EN PAREJA

1 Con otro(a) estudiante, expresen sus recomendaciones por texto.

Modelo
importante / comer
Es importante que comamos verduras todos los días.

1. bueno / dormir
2. mejor / perder
3. bueno / pedir
4. bueno / volver
5. importante / acostarse
6. necesario / jugar
7. necesario / entender
8. importante / seguir

2 Léele las sugerencias que escribiste a otro(a) estudiante, quien va a decidir si está de acuerdo o no y por qué.

 Videomodelo
A —*Es importante que comamos verduras todos los días.*
B —*Estoy de acuerdo.*
o:—*No estoy de acuerdo. Es más importante que comamos comida con menos grasa.*

 En voz alta

Lee un fragmento de un corrido mexicano, un tipo de canción poética popular de México. Las letras y melodías de estas canciones son sencillas. Obtuvieron popularidad durante la Revolución Mexicana ya que servían para contar noticias, hechos importantes e historias de amor y pena. "La Adelita", uno de los más populares, cuenta de una mujer que se enamoró de un sargento y lo siguió a la guerra. La canción también representa a muchas mujeres que seguían a las tropas, les preparaban comida y cuidaban a heridos y enfermos.

Ahora, escucha la canción y trata de repetirla en voz alta.

• ¿Qué palabras que describen a Adelita pueden describir a las mujeres de la Revolución Mexicana?

¿Recuerdas?
Cuando la consonante *d* va entre vocales, su sonido es similar a la *th* en inglés de la palabra *the*.
Pronuncia estas palabras: *Adelita, acampado, además, quedar.*

"La Adelita"

En lo alto de la abrupta serranía[1]
acampado se encontraba un regimiento
y una joven que valiente lo seguía
locamente enamorada del sargento.

Popular entre la tropa era Adelita
la mujer que el sargento idolatraba
que además de ser valiente era bonita
que hasta el mismo coronel la respetaba.

Y se oía...
que decía...
aquel que tanto la quería...

Y si acaso yo muero en la guerra
y mi cuerpo en la tierra va a quedar,
Adelita por Dios te lo ruego
que por mi amor no vayas a llorar.

[1] mountainous country

Differentiated Instruction

Heritage Speakers

Have small groups review the words in *Actividad* 39 and brainstorm other words and phrases that they know are often or always used with the subjunctive. Have the groups compare lists. Then have each group write a sentence for each of the words.

Students with Learning Difficulties

Unfamiliar phrasing can make "*La Adelita*" difficult to understand. To help students follow the story told in the lyrics, have small groups rephrase each verse to retell the story in their own words.

Cómo te beneficia el ejercicio

LEER, HABLAR EN GRUPO, ESCRIBIR

1 Lee este artículo que explica diferentes clases de ejercicio aeróbico y los beneficios que tienen.

☰ **Ejercicios > Los beneficios que tienen** 🔍

Correr Un ejercicio al alcance de todos

Existen distintas formas y técnicas de correr adecuadamente, desde trotar *(jog)* suavemente, hasta dar largas zancadas *(strides)*.

Beneficios: Ayuda a adquirir resistencia, agilidad y flexibilidad.

Spinning Ejercita tu corazón y todo tu cuerpo

Esta es una clase en grupo en la que se usan bicicletas estáticas. El instructor va dando distintas indicaciones para aumentar o disminuir el nivel de resistencia y dificultad.

Beneficios: Ayuda a la capacidad cardiovascular y a tonificar todo el cuerpo, especialmente glúteos y piernas.

Zumba Ejercicio aeróbico, pero con pasos de baile

La zumba mezcla pasos de bailes como la samba, el hip-hop, la salsa y el merengue. Para hacer zumba, hay que seguir el ritmo de la música con movimientos repetitivos. Es como bailar y hacer ejercicio aeróbico a la vez.

Beneficios: Hace más fuertes los músculos, mejora la coordinación.

Zumba

2 Con otros estudiantes, hablen de cada uno de los tipos de ejercicio. ¿Están de acuerdo con lo que dice el artículo? ¿Qué otros beneficios les gustaría añadir?

3 Y a ti, ¿cuál de las clases de ejercicio prefieren tomar? Explica tu respuesta a tu grupo.

4 Conversa con otro(a) estudiante por texto. Hagan recomendaciones. Usen formas del subjuntivo y oraciones que apoyan lo que recomiendan.

Capítulo 3 • ciento cuarenta y tres **143**

Standards: 1.1, 1.2, 3.1

Suggestions: Have students read the article silently twice before opening the discussion. As they discuss the article, encourage them to paraphrase parts that support the comments they make. As students complete Step 4, ask: *¿Han cambiado sus opiniones o recomendaciones desde que empezamos este capítulo? ¿De qué manera?*

Answers will vary.

Project-Based Learning

Students can perform Step 5 at this point. Make audio or video recordings of their presentations for inclusion in their portfolio. (For more information, see p. 112-b.)

Additional Resources

📶 **Technology: Online Resources**
- Instant Check
- Guided, Core, Audio
- *Para hispanohablantes*

Print
- Guided WB pp. 109–110
- Core WB p. 46

Assessment

Prueba 3-10 with Remediation (online only)
Prueba: El subjuntivo: Verbos con cambio de raíz
- Prueba 3-10

Examen: Vocabulario y gramática 2
- Examen 2
- ExamView: Examen 2

Enrich Your Teaching

Culture Note

The **corrido** is a type of ballad that often tells the stories of heroes, natural disasters, and events. The genre originated in Mexico in the early 1800s, and was especially popular during the Mexican Revolution when it was used to spread news. The **corridos** carried on the oral tradition, and thus preserved stories.

21st Century Skills

Social and Cross-Cultural Skills

Encourage students to find online Web sites that play Mexican *corridos* and find a musical rendition of "*Adelita*" if possible. You may also ask them to listen to the lyrics of another traditional *corrido* and list any words and expressions they recognize. Are there similarities between the music of *corridos* and other folk music they know? What are the differences?

Puente a la cultura

Standards: 1.1, 1.2, 2.1, 2.2, 3.1, 5.2

Suggestions

Pre-reading: On the board, set up an **SQA** chart. This is a three-column chart with the columns labeled **Sé, Quiero saber,** and **Aprendí**. Have students duplicate the chart on their own paper. Direct their attention to the *Estrategia*. Help them access their prior knowledge on the topic by discussing the questions there. They can fill in the **Sé** column of their charts with this information. In the **Quiero saber** column, have them write at least three questions—things they would like to learn from reading **Un juego muy antiguo**.

Reading: As students read, remind them to use background knowledge, cognates, and context clues to understand unfamiliar words and expressions. Help them resolve comprehension problems by asking **sí/no** or embedded-answer questions.

Post-reading: Ask: *¿Encontraste las respuestas a todas tus preguntas en la lectura?* Have students fill in the **Aprendí** column of their **SQA** charts with any answers to the questions they wrote in the **Quiero saber** column, as well as other interesting facts they have learned.

COUNTRY CONNECTION

 Technology: Mapa global interactivo, Actividad 2 Discover the ruins of Chichén Itzá, where Mayans played ball games.

Standards: 3.1

Suggestions: Remind students that the ancient ruins found at these places are some of Mexico's major historical and tourist attractions. Assign, or ask students to choose, one of the ancient sites and research it in an encyclopedia or on the Internet. Have them report back at least three interesting facts.

Online Cultural Reading

Standards: 2.1, 3.1, 4.2

After doing the online activity, ask students to compare the ball games of our ancestors with the sports they play today.

OBJECTIVES
▸ Read about an ancient team sport played by the Native Americans in Mexico and Central America
▸ Use prior knowledge to increase comprehension

Un juego muy antiguo

La historia del juego de pelota comenzó hace unos 3,000 años alrededor del golfo de México. Los olmecas inventaron este deporte pero otros pueblos conocidos de Mesoamérica, como los mayas y los aztecas, también lo jugaban. El juego de pelota era uno de los eventos más importantes en el Nuevo Mundo.

Llamado *ullamalitzi* por los aztecas, el juego de pelota fue el primer deporte que se jugó en grupo. En la sociedad indígena, estos eventos sociales eran tanto actos religiosos como espectáculos para el público. Los pueblos indígenas creían que los dioses, la naturaleza y el ser humano no podían separarse. La vida, la astronomía y las matemáticas, la organización política y social, el arte, las guerras y hasta los deportes se relacionaban con la religión. Se cree que, para los pueblos indígenas, la competencia entre dos equipos en el juego de pelota representaba la lucha entre el Sol y otros astros[1]. Según los mayas, los dioses miraban el juego desde arriba[2]. Por eso, aunque todos podían ver el juego, solamente jugaban los nobles y los atletas entrenados por los sacerdotes[3].

Hasta hoy se han descubierto más de 600 canchas[4] de pelota en México. Todas tenían dos paredes, una en cada lado, con un anillo de piedra en el centro de cada una. Algunas eran tan grandes como una cancha de fútbol moderna. Las paredes estaban decoradas con escenas del juego.

[1]heavenly bodies [2]above [3]priests [4]courts

Estrategia

Using your prior knowledge
What do you know about competitive games in Roman and Greek times? Have you heard of the origin of games like baseball or basketball?

Remember that retrieving information you already know about the topic of your reading is always useful to help you better understand it.

Online Cultural Reading

Go to Auténtico ONLINE to read and understand a website about the types of ball games that people used to play in the past.

La cancha más grande se encuentra en Chichén Itzá, México

Differentiated Instruction

Bodily-Kinesthetic Learner

Reinforce the link between the reading and the sports context. Assign sports words by handing out papers with the words. Ask students to act out the word they received. The rest of the class calls out the appropriate sports word each time.

Advanced Learners

Encourage students to prepare more elaborate reports about the ancient site they chose in the *Country Connection*. Invite them to work together to create a bulletin board display or a graphic presentation using computer software.

Para jugar se necesitaba una pelota de caucho[5] que pesaba unas 8 libras[6] y era tan grande como una pelota de básquetbol.

La pelota no podía tocar el suelo[7] y los jugadores no podían tocarla con las manos. Usaban la cabeza, los codos, las caderas[8] y las rodillas para pasar la pelota a través de uno de los anillos.

Los atletas llevaban cascos[9] y ropa de cuero para protegerse. También llevaban uniformes especiales que se cree que formaban parte de las ceremonias religiosas anteriores al juego.

[5]rubber [6]pounds [7]ground [8]hips [9]helmets

▲ Anillo para el juego

▲ Ilustración del antiguo juego olmeca de pelota

▼ Olmec *hacha*

¿Comprendiste?

1. ¿Por qué crees que los sacerdotes eran los que entrenaban a los jugadores indígenas?
2. ¿Por qué el juego de pelota tiene un significado especial? Da una explicación de origen histórico y otra de origen religioso.
3. Di dos razones por las que crees que el juego de pelota se jugaba en la sociedad indígena, y compáralas con las que la gente tiene ahora para jugar deportes.
4. ¿A qué deportes actuales se parece más el juego de pelota? ¿En qué se parecen?

Usa tus conocimientos

Imagina que eres uno de los sacerdotes que van a entrenar a los nobles y los atletas. Piensa en una vez que te entrenaste para algo y escribe cinco ideas para explicarles cómo entrenarse, lo que es importante que hagan, cómo son las competiciones y qué deben evitar hacer.

▶ **Videodocumentario** *¿Qué haces para estar saludable?*

🌐 **Mapa global interactivo** Explora la región de Mesoamérica y observa las ruinas del campo de pelota en Chichén Itzá. Investiga la importancia de este ritual en la antigua cultura maya.

Capítulo 3 • ciento cuarenta y cinco 145

Go Online to practice
PEARSON realize.
PearsonSchool.com/Autentico
VIDEO   WRITING   MAPA GLOBAL

Culture 3

¿Comprendiste?

Standards: 1.1, 1.2, 3.1, 4.2

Suggestions: Encourage students to support their opinions with information from the reading and their own background knowledge.

Answers:

1. Los sacerdotes eran los que entrenaban a los jugadores porque los eventos sociales eran como actos religiosos para el público.
2. El juego de pelota fue el primer deporte que se jugó en grupo. Según los mayas, los dioses miraban el juego.

3-4. Answers will vary.

Usa tus conocimientos

Standards: 1.3, 3.1

Suggestions: Have students use evidence from the reading and from the pictures on these pages to help them formulate their advice. Encourage them to use the chapter vocabulary to advise the players to train for strength and endurance and to avoid injury.

Answers will vary.

Digital Portfolio

Invite students to organize their responses to *Usa tus conocimientos* and write them down in paragraph form. Keep the paragraphs in students' portfolios as a writing sample.

▶ **Technology: Videodocumentario**

Standards: 1.2

Resources: Teacher's Resource Materials: Video Script, Video Program, Cap. 3

View *¿Qué haces para estar saludable?* with the class, online in **Realize.** See the *Video Teacher's Guide* for additional suggestions.

Additional Resources

🌐 **Technology: Online Resources**
- *Videodocumentario*
- Guided, Writing, Reading
- *Para hispanohablantes*
- Cultural Reading Activity
- Communication Activities

Print
- Guided WB p. 111

Enrich Your Teaching

Culture Note

The ancient Mexicans discovered a way to process rubber around 1600 B.C. by harvesting latex from the rubber tree **(castilla elástica)**. They used it to make sandals and for waterproofing, among other things, but they generally considered rubber a ritual material.

21st Century Skills

Critical Thinking and Problem Solving Have students research the Aztec game of *ullamalitzi* and other sports of the ancient civilizations of Mexico and Central America. What was the relationship between religion and sports in the ancient civilizations? How has this relationship between religion and sports evolved in today's civilization?

¿Qué me cuentas?

Standards: 1.1, 1.2, 1.3

Resources: Teacher's Resource Materials: Audio Script, Technology: Audio Cap. 3

AP® Skills: Integration of listening, reading, and writing to comprehend and synthesize information from spoken and written sources.

Suggestions: For Step 1, use the audio or read the descriptions aloud. Allow students to hear both descriptions twice through: the first time to write their answers, the second time to check them.

For Step 2, have students summarize the main points and make inferences to show that they understand what they have read.

Encourage students to express their own opinions in addition to using information from the reading in their written responses for Step 3.

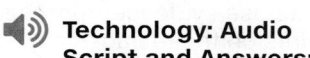 **Technology: Audio Script and Answers:**

Manuel y Vicky iban a ir al club deportivo a hacer ejercicio. Manuel siempre hace flexiones y abdominales para tener músculos más fuertes. A Vicky le gustan las clases de ejercicios aeróbicos porque son divertidos y buenos para el corazón.

1. ¿Adónde iban Manuel y Vicky? *(a)*
2. ¿Para qué hace ejercicios Manuel? *(c)*
3. ¿Qué ejercicios le gustan a Vicky? *(c)*

Justo antes de salir, Paula los llamó para ver si querían encontrarse con ella. Dijo que se sentía fatal y aburrida, porque le exigían mucho en la escuela y estaba estresada.

—¡Bueno! —dijo Vicky—, sugiero que vayamos todos al club.

—¡Sí! Tú y yo debemos hacer yoga para relajarnos y ejercicios aeróbicos para divertirnos y ponernos de buen humor —le constestó Paula.

4. ¿Qué le pasaba a Paula? *(a)*
5. ¿Qué van a hacer todos? *(c)*
6. ¿Para qué van a hacer yoga Vicky y Paula? *(c)*

Steps 2–3
Answers will vary.

Additional Resources

 Technology: Online Resources
• *Para hispanohablantes*

Pre-AP® Integración

OBJECTIVES
▸ Listen to and read about exercise routines and nutrition choices
▸ Write about nutrition advice

¿Qué me cuentas?: ¿Al club o a comer?

Tres amigos quieren hacer ejercicio y mejorar su estado físico. Escucha la conversación y luego lee unas recomendaciones. Guarda las respuestas para usar en el paso 3.

1 Vas a escuchar un cuento acerca de tres amigos que se reúnen para hacer ejercicio. Después de cada parte vas a oír tres preguntas. Escoge la respuesta correcta.

1. a. al club deportivo	b. a un restaurante	c. al doctor
2. a. para respirar	b. para dormir bien	c. para tener músculos fuertes
3. a. las flexiones	b. los abdominales	c. los ejercicios aeróbicos
4. a. se sentía fatal	b. se caía de sueño	c. tenía hambre
5. a. flexiones	b. yoga	c. ir juntos al club
6. a. para hacer lo mismo que Manu	b. para estar en la luna	c. para relajarse, divertirse y estar de buen humor

2 Ahora lee las recomendaciones para seguir una dieta sana.

Aliméntate bien y entrénate mejor }

¿Cuáles son tus razones para entrenar?
¿Sabías que una dieta apropiada mejora tu entrenamiento?

• Me entreno para estar más fuerte.
Levantar pesas quema muchas calorías y los músculos usan aún más calorías para recuperarse. Por eso, es importante que consumas más calorías de las que usas. Tu dieta debe tener alimentos ricos en proteínas, como la carne, los huevos y los lácteos[1]. Un plan de comidas ideal tiene 55% de proteínas, 25% de carbohidratos y 20% de grasas.
• Me entreno para aliviar el estrés.
Para reducir los efectos del estrés, es recomendado que incluyas entre 60% y 75% de alimentos crudos[2]. Escoge frutas y verduras frescas que tengan vitaminas B y C. También es necesario que

comas carbohidratos ricos en fibra. Toma agua y evita el café, el té, las gaseosas y los alimentos procesados.
• Me entreno para proteger el corazón.
Es importante que mantengas una dieta equilibrada. No consumas más calorías de las que quemas. Evita las grasas saturadas, pero sí incluye las grasas saludables como el aceite de oliva. No pongas demasiada sal a las comidas y evita las gaseosas porque tienen mucho sodio[3]. Consume alimentos ricos en fibra: frutas, verduras, granos[4]. Si te gustan los lácteos, escoge los que son bajos en grasa.

[1]dairy [2]raw [3]sodium [4]grains

3 Escribe unos consejos para Manuel, Vicky y Paula. Haz planes para una dieta que corresponda a sus metas de entrenamiento. Incluye los alimentos que deben comer. Usa estas expresiones para conectar tus ideas: *así, aunque, para, por eso, es importante que, es mejor que.*

146 ciento cuarenta y seis • Capítulo 3 • ¿Qué haces para estar en forma?

Differentiated Instruction

Heritage Speakers

Ask students to write a short description of a very special lunch (such as a picnic or a barbecue) that they have had with their families or friends. Have them describe the food, the setting, and anything else that made the occasion special.

Students with Learning Difficulties

Public speaking, such as the *Presentación oral* on p. 147, can be stressful for some students. Suggest that speakers pause at the end of each sentence and take a deep breath and that they use gestures to emphasize parts of what they say. Humor, and an informal approach to the subject matter are other means of reducing stress.

OBJECTIVES
▶ Demonstrate how to give advice about leading a healthy lifestyle
▶ Pay attention to your posture to give an effective presentation

Go **Online** to practice
PearsonSchool.com/Autentico
PEARSON
realize™

AUDIO   WRITING   SPEAK/RECORD

Una vida más sana

TAREA Tu escuela va a organizar un evento para que los estudiantes aprendan a tener una vida más sana. A ti te toca hacer una presentación. Busca materiales y haz un cartel.

> ### Estrategia
> **Making an oral presentation**
> When making an oral presentation make sure you face your audience at all times. You may look at the front, middle, and back rows. Remember to speak loudly enough for all to hear, and speak clearly.

1 **Prepárate** Escoge un tema y prepara un cartel.

temas	cartel
el ejercicio	deportes y tipos de ejercicio
los alimentos	alimentos nutritivos
las recetas, cómo preparar la comida	recetas saludables

2 **Practica** Vuelve a leer la información de tu cartel. Practica varias veces tu presentación para recordar los detalles. Usa mandatos con *Uds.* o recomendaciones con el subjuntivo para explicar a tus compañeros qué deben hacer. Recuerda:

• hablar con voz clara y mirar al público directamente
• hablar de cada uno de los temas en orden y explicar por qué es importante para la salud
• dar alguna recomendación

Modelo
Mi presentación es acerca de cómo tener una vida más sana. Voy a hablarles de qué ejercicios hacer para estar saludables. El ejercicio sirve para estar en forma. Hagan ejercicio por lo menos tres veces por semana.

3 **Haz tu presentación** Imagina que estás en un auditorio. Habla claro y en voz alta. Explica el tema y muestra el cartel. Al final, pregunta a los estudiantes si tienen un comentario que hacer.

4 **Evaluación** Tu profesor(a) utilizará la siguiente rúbrica para evaluar tu presentación.

Rubric	Score 1	Score 3	Score 5
How well your information is organized	Your ideas are undeveloped with incorrect or no transitions.	Some of your ideas are undeveloped. Your transitions are confusing.	Your ideas are well developed with clear transitions.
How effectively you deliver your speech	You make no eye contact with the audience. You have little intonation.	You make some eye contact and use intonation.	You make good eye contact and use intonation.
How effectively you use your visuals	Your visuals don't communicate the message.	You use visuals, but not effectively.	Your visuals are very helpful and are used effectively.

Presentación oral

Standards: 1.2, 1.3, 3.1

Suggestions: Review the task and the rubric with students. Before students begin practicing in Step 2, direct their attention to the *Estrategia*. Encourage them to practice at home before a mirror or with a partner in class to develop their public speaking skills.

Digital Portfolio

Make video or audio recordings of student presentations in class, or assign the Speak and Record activity so they can record their presentations online. Include the recording in their portfolios.

Pre-AP® Integration

• **Learning Objective:** Presentational Speaking
• **Activity:** Remind students to focus on the presentational speaking skills used in this task such as fluency, pronunciation, and comprehensibility.
• **Pre-AP® Resource Materials:** Comprehensive guide to Pre-AP® speaking skill development

Teacher-to-Teacher

Some students may prefer to use a computer and project their poster. Remind students that skillful use of visuals during a presentation is a valuable asset in many professions.

Additional Resources

 Technology: Online Resources
• *Para hispanohablantes*

Self Assessment

Presentación oral
• **Assessment Program:** Rubrics
Review the rubric with students. Go over the descriptions of the different levels of performance. After assessing students, help individuals understand how their performance could be improved. (See Teacher's Resource Materials for suggestions on using rubrics in assessment.)

Enrich Your Teaching

Teacher-to-Teacher

E-amigos: Have students send their *e-amigos* a message expressing their preferences and choices for a healthy lifestyle. Ask them to include questions about what their *e-amigos* do to satisfy the basic needs of health.

21st Century Skills

Creativity and Innovation Students will have to adapt to a variety of roles in this *Presentación oral* project. As writers, they will develop a series of persuasive suggestions for leading a healthier lifestyle. As artists, they will search for images to illustrate a poster they will design. And finally, as presenters, they will present their project effectively to the class.

Language Arts Connection:
Persuasive Writing

Standards: 3.1

Help students apply the knowledge they have about writing a persuasive essay to Spanish. Have them do their planning in Step 1 in small groups. Guide them with comments and questions such as the following:

1. *¿Quién es tu público? Es preferible elegir a un grupo específico, como los jóvenes de esta escuela, los atletas o los jóvenes que comen mucha comida basura. Si conoces bien a tu público, vas a saber mejor lo que tienes que decirle.*

2. *Hay que prestar atención a las palabras que usas. La condición física, por ejemplo, puede ser un tema delicado para mucha gente. Para persuadir a la gente, es muy importante que no la ofendas.*

Presentación escrita

Standards: 1.3, 3.1

Suggestions: Explain at the start the criteria you will use to evaluate students' compositions. (See Step 5, *Evaluación*, in the Student Edition, and *Assessment* on p. 149.)

Direct students' attention to the *Estrategia*. Ask them to share additional background information they have learned in Language Arts courses about persuasive writing. Then draw a T-chart on the board. Have students begin a similar chart on their own paper. Guide them to add other points and to develop each point with specific details. For Step 2, remind students that their persuasive essay should build through at least three arguments. They should save their strongest argument for last, rather than "bringing out the big guns" at the beginning of the article.

Presentación escrita

OBJECTIVES
▸ Write an article providing health tips
▸ Use persuasive writing to convince the audience

✎ Por una vida más saludable

Imagina que trabajas para una revista y te piden que escribas un artículo sobre cómo las personas pueden llevar una vida más saludable. Presenta y defiende tu opinión con razones para persuadir a las personas de que cambien sus hábitos para estar más saludables.

Estrategia

Persuasive writing Use persuasive writing to convince an audience about something. Use words that clearly express your opinion about an issue. Always include facts and examples to support your opinions. A persuasive composition is always addressed to a specific audience. Therefore, it is important to choose words, tone and style that are directed to your audience.

1 Antes de escribir Piensa en los elementos que ayudan a llevar una vida saludable. Describe por qué son importantes y qué ocurre si no se ponen en práctica. Crea una tabla como la de abajo.

Para llevar una vida saludable	Ventajas y problemas que se evitan
• mantener una dieta equilibrada	• se evitan las enfermedades • el cuerpo se mantiene sano
• mantenerse en forma	

2 Borrador Escribe un blog dirigido a un público específico. Usa la escritura persuasiva. Pon las ideas de tu tabla en una composición, usando el vocabulario de este capítulo, el subjuntivo con expresiones impersonales y los mandatos.

Modelo

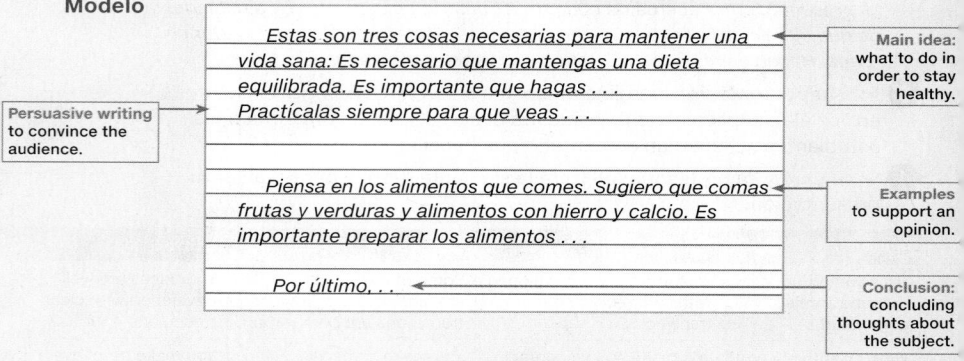

Persuasive writing to convince the audience.

Estas son tres cosas necesarias para mantener una vida sana: Es necesario que mantengas una dieta equilibrada. Es importante que hagas . . . Practícalas siempre para que veas . . .

Main idea: what to do in order to stay healthy.

Piensa en los alimentos que comes. Sugiero que comas frutas y verduras y alimentos con hierro y calcio. Es importante preparar los alimentos . . .

Examples to support an opinion.

Por último, . .

Conclusion: concluding thoughts about the subject.

Differentiated Instruction

Students with Learning Difficulties

Some students may need help understanding how to use various types of graphic organizers. Show them how the table on this page works by pointing out the titles at the top and explaining the cause-and-effect relationship between the information on the left and that on the right.

Advanced Learners

Encourage students to use their skills in Spanish to incorporate into their articles even more strategies for effective persuasive writing. Have them study persuasive articles in both English and Spanish as models.

Go **Online** to practice
PEARSON· o o
realize™
WRITING

PearsonSchool.com/Autentico

Presentational 3

3 **Redacción/Revisión** Después de escribir el primer borrador, trabaja con otro(a) estudiante para intercambiar los trabajos y leerlos. Después de leer el trabajo de tu compañero(a), sugiere cómo puede mejorarlo y dile que haga lo mismo con el tuyo. Revisen si:

• la composición se enfoca en consejos para la salud

• para persuadir al público se usan mandatos y se dan razones

• se usan expresiones impersonales para enfatizar los consejos

Haz lo siguiente: Subraya con una línea los verbos en subjuntivo, con dos líneas los mandatos, y encierra en un círculo las expresiones impersonales.

4 **Publicación** Antes de hacer la versión final, lee de nuevo tu borrador y repasa los siguientes puntos:

• ¿Di suficientes razones para apoyar mis ideas?

• ¿Usé el vocabulario apropiado para convencer al público de que lea la revista donde van a publicar el artículo?

• ¿Están conectadas las oraciones?

Presenta y defiende tu opinión con razones para persuadir al público. Los estudiantes escribirán sus reacciones a tu blog.

5 **Evaluación** Se utilizará la siguiente rúbrica para evaluar tu presentación.

Éstas son tres cosas necesarias para

mantener una vida sana: (Es necesario) que

~~mantengas~~
~~mantienes~~ una dieta equilibrada. (Es importante)

que hagas . . .

Practícalas
~~Practícala~~ siempre para . . .

Rubric	Score 1	Score 3	Score 5
Completion of task	You are missing important parts of the article.	Parts of your article are missing or incorrect.	You include all parts and it is effectively organized.
Ability to persuade	Your lack of information organization makes message unclear.	Your message is present, but sometimes unconvincing.	Your information creates a clear message.
Sentence structure/ grammar, spelling, mechanics	Your sentences are run-on or are fragmented with many grammar, spelling, and mechanics errors.	You use sentences convincingly, but with some grammar, spelling, and/or mechanics errors.	Your sentence structure is correct and varied with very few grammar, spelling, and mechanics errors.

Capítulo 3 • ciento cuarenta y nueve **149**

Suggestions (Cont'd): Once students have a rough draft ready, read through the model on this page together. Help them see how information from the chart on p. 148 was incorporated into this draft and to note the additional information that was added. Point out the use of imperative and subjunctive verb forms. Encourage them to work toward similar organization, level of detail, and language use as they revise their own drafts.

For Step 3, encourage students to focus on sentence structure, transitions, and correct use of commands and the subjunctive. Have them follow the suggestions shown.

Evaluation
Steps 4 and 5 overlap. Students will need some evaluation by you or peers or some self-evaluation to fine-tune and polish their drafts.

Pre-AP® Integration

• **Learning Objective:** Presentational Writing
• **Activity:** As a warm-up to the *Presentación escrita*, have students write a short blog about the things that cause stress in their lives. Have them describe what they do to prevent stress from taking over their lives.
• **Pre-AP® Resource Materials:** Comprehensive guide to Pre-AP® writing skill development

Digital Portfolio

Keep students' final drafts in their portfolios as a writing sample.

Additional Resources

📶 **Technology: Online Resources**
• *Para hispanohablantes*

Self Assessment ───────

Presentación escrita
• **Assessment Program:** Rubrics
Review the rubric with students. Go over the descriptions of the different levels of performance. After assessing students, help individuals understand how their performance could be improved. (See Teacher's Resource Materials for suggestions on using rubrics in assessment.)

Enrich Your Teaching

Teacher-to-Teacher

As students develop their persuasive articles, remind them that they use elements of persuasion every day. Ask them to talk about times they themselves have persuaded someone to act or think a certain way and to analyze the techniques they used.

21st Century Skills

Creativity and Innovation Students will have to use their written language for the purpose of persuading magazine readers to lead a healthier lifestyle. Have students create a list of persuasive phrases and expressions to use in their article to make their arguments more forceful and convincing.

Lectura

Standards: 1.2, 3.1

Suggestions

Pre-reading: Before reading, direct students' attention to the *Al leer* section and to the *Estrategia*. Have them answer the questions from there and copy the graphic organizer from p. 153.

Point out that each section is organized the same way, with the titles **Meta, ¡Lógralo!,** and **Nuestros consejos**. Explain that in this case *meta* means "goal" or "objective."

Ask volunteers to read the title and subtitles aloud. Based on these and the photos throughout the article, have them predict to which bulleted item on p. 150 each section of the article refers. For example: *La sección* Muy limpios *debe tratarse de la higiene personal y la salud.*

Ask students to name the items in the photos throughout the article. If they can't name an item, ask them to scan that section of the article to see if they can find it.

Active Classroom

Working in pairs, have students create a short article about a health tip following the models in the *Lectura*. Be sure they include an illustration and post it on the bulletin board.

Lectura

¡Cambia tus hábitos!

Al leer

Nuestra vida está llena de actos que repetimos todos los días, por ejemplo, comer, dormir o estudiar. Vas a leer un artículo con recomendaciones sobre cómo cambiar tus malos hábitos para llevar una vida más saludable. Copia la tabla de la página 153. Mientras lees los artículos, llena los espacios de la gráfica con causas y efectos que encuentres en el texto.

Presta atención a los siguientes puntos:

• la importancia de tener buenos hábitos alimenticios

• la higiene personal y la salud

• cómo cuidar tu espalda aprendiendo a sentarte bien

Estrategia

Cause and effect Our personality and the way we eat, sleep, or react to fear can affect our health. If we change our bad habits, we will be healthier and more productive persons. While you read this magazine article, look for other examples of cause and effect. For example, what happens if you do not eat well, you do not drink enough water, or if you do not sit correctly and comfortably?

Aliméntate bien

Meta: "Voy a desayunar todos los días".

Saltarte el desayuno no te sirve para nada. Empieza tu día con algo ligero[1], para poner a funcionar tu metabolismo. No solo da energía sino que despierta al organismo y acelera la quema de calorías durante todo el día.

¡Lógralo!

Desayuna algo aunque sea ligero, como un licuado de frutas y verduras o una fruta, pan tostado con mermelada, cereal con leche o yogur, té o un buen vaso de leche.

Nuestros consejos:

Si tienes prisa: bebe el jugo mientras caminas a la escuela. También puedes llevar un yogur que trae una porción de cereal.

[1]light

Differentiated Instruction

Heritage Speakers

Ask students to interview family members about their breakfast habits and those of other relatives or friends. How many eat a nutritious breakfast? How many have changed their eating habits over the years? Do they now eat a better breakfast than they used to, or one that is worse? Why?

Students with Learning Difficulties

If students have difficulty with the cause and effect concept in the *Estrategia*, you may wish to help them by asking guiding questions that will help them focus on the concept in English. For example: What happens if you don't allow enough time to complete a school project?

No comas comida basura

Meta: "No voy a comer tantos dulces en la escuela".

Seguro que a la hora del recreo quieres comer chocolate o una bolsa de papas fritas. Mejor escoge alimentos que echen a andar tu motor. Si comes un almuerzo nutritivo, tu rendimiento físico y mental va a ser mucho mejor y no te vas a dormir en las últimas clases.

¡Lógralo!

Lleva de tu casa zanahorias o pepinos². Las palomitas de maíz³ y las frutas deshidratadas son una buena opción en lugar de comidas fritas.

Nuestros consejos:

¡No lleves dinero! Así evitas la tentación de comprar comida basura.

²cucumbers ³popcorn

Muy limpios

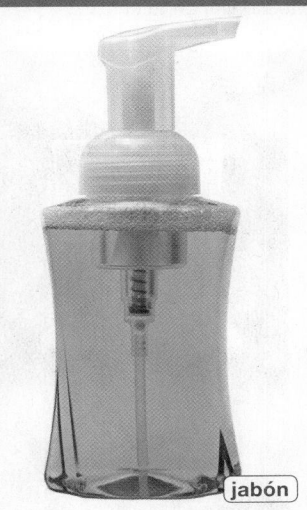

jabón

Meta: "Siempre me voy a lavar las manos y los dientes".

Muchas enfermedades del estómago se deben a las bacterias que recogemos durante el día en nuestras actividades diarias. El simple hecho de abrir la puerta para salir del baño después de lavarte las manos, ya implica una contaminación de bacterias.

¡Lógralo!

La manera más efectiva de eliminar las bacterias de las manos es lavándoselas con agua y jabón. Lleva siempre jabón en tu mochila y úsalo cada vez que vayas al baño. En cuanto a los dientes, lávalos después de cada comida.

Nuestros consejos:

Compra un cepillo de dientes de viaje (algunos incluyen una crema de dientes pequeña) y llévalo en tu mochila junto con un hilo dental. ¿Se te olvidó lavarte los dientes o no tuviste tiempo? Usa una pastilla de menta o un chicle con clorofila para evitar el mal aliento.

Capítulo 3 • ciento cincuenta y uno **151**

Suggestions (Cont'd):

Remind students that cognates and context clues can help them understand difficult passages as they read. Help them focus on cognates by saying words in English and asking them to scan a given section for the Spanish cognate. For example: *¿Cómo se dice* "dehydrated" *en español? Busquen en la sección* No comas comida basura. *(deshidratadas)*

Reading: Allow students time to read the entire selection on their own silently. You might assign this task for homework. This will allow you to capitalize on class time to read it again together with students. When reading together, pause frequently to address comprehension issues that students may bring up and to allow them to fill in their ***Causa/Efecto*** charts from p. 153. Ask your own comprehension questions to help them focus on the main idea and important details of each section. Here are some possible comprehension issues on pp. 150–151 on which you can provide some guidance:

- p. 150: *Lee la parte* Meta. *¿A qué se refiere* (refer) *la expresión* "algo ligero," *a la comida o al sueño? (a la comida)*

  ¿A qué se refiere la palabra "organismo," *a un hábito alimenticio o al cuerpo? (al cuerpo)*

- p. 151: *Lee la parte* No comas comida basura. *¿A qué se refiere la expresión* "rendimiento físico," *a tu nivel de energía o los ingredientes de una comida? (a tu nivel de energía)*

- p. 151: *Lee la parte* Muy limpios. *¿A qué se refiere la expresión* "ya implica"? *(a que eso pasa)*

Enrich Your Teaching

Teacher-to-Teacher

While reading and working through comprehension problems with students, don't forget to also focus on the content of a passage. Ask students to comment on what they are reading. For example, in the ***Muy limpios*** section, ask: *¿Quiénes deben llevar siempre jabón en la mochila?*

21st Century Skills

ICT (Information, Communications and Technology) Literacy Have students use the digital technology within **Realize** to access extra reading support. Computer corrected activities use different reading strategies to help students build their vocabulary and progress at their own pace through the reading.

3 Interpretive Reading

Suggestions (Cont'd):

Reading:

- p. 152: *Lee la parte* Más H₂O. *En la primera frase, la que empieza con "No beber …," ¿cuál es el sujeto?* (No beber suficientes líquidos durante el día) *¿Qué quiere decir esta frase en inglés?* (usando un participio presente: Not drinking enough water during the day)

  ¿Cuál es la palabra opuesta de "hidratado"? Adivina. Busca una pista en la sección No comas comida basura en la página 151. (deshidratado)

- p. 152: *Lee la parte* ¿Una siesta? *El artículo da tres categorías de causas posibles para la falta de energía después de las clases. ¿Cuáles son?* (causas fisiológicas, emocionales o relacionadas con el estilo de vida)

- p. 152: *Lee la parte* Siéntate bien. *¿Qué parte del cuerpo tienes que pegar al asiento para sentarte bien?* (toda la espalda)

Pre-AP® Integration

- **Learning Objective:** Interpretive: Print and Audio
- **Activity:** Divide the class into groups of five and assign one of the sub-titled sections to each in the group. Have each student write three true/false statements about his or her section and make four copies. Each student distributes his or her questions to other group members. Then each student will read aloud his or her section to his or her group (with textbooks closed) and allow them time to respond to the true/false statements about that section. Confirm answers.
- **Pre-AP® Resource Materials:** Comprehensive guide to Pre-AP® reading skill development

Additional Resources

 Technology: Online Resources
- *Para hispanohablantes*

Active Classroom

Bring in magazines from different Spanish-speaking countries. Have students work with a partner and find an ad related to health. Have them explain the ad to another group. Is it an effective ad?

Más H₂0

Meta: "Ahora sí voy a tomar agua".

No beber suficientes líquidos durante el día puede hacer que te sientas cansado. Los refrescos te dan energía pero solo por un momento, luego te sientes igual de cansado. Los refrescos *light* tampoco ayudan, por el contrario, te quitan energía.

¡Lógralo!

Ya te lo hemos dicho mil veces: debes tomar por lo menos 8 vasos de agua al día. No solo te mantienen hidratado, sino que ayudan al buen funcionamiento de los riñones[1].

Nuestros consejos:

¿No te gusta el agua sola? Toma jugos de fruta fresca o leche descremada durante el día.

[1]kidneys

¿Una siesta?

Meta: "Ya no voy a dormir cuando llegue de la escuela".

Nadie en tu casa entiende por qué cuando regresas de la escuela lo primero que haces es dormirte. Las causas pueden ser fisiológicas (como los niveles hormonales de la tiroides), emocionales (demasiado estrés), o estar relacionadas con tu estilo de vida (no dormir bien en las noches). Lo que debes hacer son unos cuantos ajustes en tu dieta diaria para combatir el cansancio.

¡Lógralo!

Si te sientes cansado, evita completamente las galletas, el pan dulce, los dulces, los refrescos y los jugos de fruta envasados, ya que contienen azúcares simples que te quitan energía; también evita la cafeína. Lo ideal es que comas proteínas con vegetales (como un pescado hervido con verduras).

Nuestros consejos:

Trata de hacer un poco de ejercicio para subir tus niveles de energía. O pon un disco compacto y ponte a bailar en tu cuarto.

Siéntate bien

Meta: "Me voy a sentar derecho en la silla".

No es nada fácil sentarte derecho por más de diez minutos, pero si sigues sentándote así, hundiéndote en[2] tu asiento de clases, tu cuerpo y sobre todo tu espalda se acostumbrarán y es probable que no se corrijan.

¡Lógralo!

Pega bien toda la espalda —baja, alta y lumbar— al asiento. Asegúrate de que tus pies estén bien apoyados en el piso y mantén las piernas juntas.

Nuestros consejos:

¿Se te hace muy difícil? Imagina que tienes un hilo que jala tu columna[3] hacia arriba para mantenerla derecha.

[2]sinking yourself into [3]a string that pulls your spine

Differentiated Instruction

Heritage Speakers

Have students discuss commands that their parents frequently give them at home. Ask volunteers to make signs of the four or five most common ones. Post these around the room in appropriate places. For example, *Siéntate bien* might be posted on the front wall.

Advanced Learners

Have students create a glossary of unfamiliar vocabulary for the article that lists items of students' choosing, along with a definition in Spanish. They can arrive at their definitions via discussion or by using a Spanish dictionary. Encourage them to paraphrase dictionary definitions and write them in their own words.

Go **Online** to practice
PEARSON
realize™
PearsonSchool.com/Autentico
WRITING

Interpretive Reading

3

Interacción con la lectura

1 Trabaja con un grupo de estudiantes para hacer una tabla de *causa y efecto*. Cada estudiante va a añadir las relaciones de causa y efecto que escribió mientras leía el artículo.

Causa	Efecto

2 Contesten las siguientes preguntas sobre el artículo y, si notan relaciones de causa y efecto que aún no incluyeron en la tabla, añádanlas.

- Parafrasea la idea principal, el tema y los detalles de apoyo del artículo. ¿Crees que los jóvenes en general tienen hábitos saludables? Explica tu respuesta.

- ¿Qué recomendaciones del artículo te parecen mejores o más prácticas?

- ¿Cuáles son tus recomendaciones? ¿Son similares o diferentes de las del artículo? Explica.

- Según este artículo, ¿qué tipo de comidas y bebidas debes evitar para tener más energía? ¿Cuáles debes comer o beber?

3 Trabaja con un grupo para hablar sobre estos temas. Hablen con la clase de lo que piensan sobre las causas y los efectos. En parejas, hagan los papeles de doctor y paciente. El/la paciente solicita *(requests)* recomendaciones sobre los temas del artículo y el/la doctora da consejos.

CULTURA ◀ El mundo hispano

Revistas para jóvenes Al igual que en los Estados Unidos, en España y América Latina hay muchas revistas para jóvenes. En ellas puedes encontrar los temas que les interesan a los chicos y a las chicas de esos países, cómo se visten, qué música prefieren, y cuáles son sus sueños.

Si quieres leer más artículos relacionados con la salud, si te gustan los temas culturales y científicos o quieres mantenerte al día en deportes, música, libros o cine, existe un gran número de esas revistas que te pueden interesar. Estas son algunas de ellas: *Generación 21* de Ecuador, *Revista 15 a 20* de México, y *Okapi y Muy Junior* de España.

- ¿Qué crees que significa la expresión "mantenerte al día"?

- ¿Crees que los jóvenes de otros países tienen gustos *(taste)* similares con respecto a la moda o la música? ¿Por qué?

Capítulo 3 • ciento cincuenta y tres **153**

Interacción con la lectura

Standards: 1.1, 1.2, 1.3, 3.1

Suggestions

Post-reading: After students revisit their ***Causa/Efecto*** charts and make changes or additions, have them share the information they included. Ask volunteers to read aloud or paraphrase the parts of the article that support their choices for the chart and that help them answer the *Interacción con la lectura questions*.

Answers will vary.

CULTURA ◀

Standards: 1.1, 1.2, 2.2, 4.2, 5.1

Suggestions: Ask: *¿Qué revistas estadounidenses para jóvenes puedes nombrar? ¿Cuáles de estas revistas se parecen a las que ves en Cultura? ¿Qué revistas para jóvenes lees? ¿Qué secciones de estas revistas te gustan más?* If possible, obtain some copies of the Spanish-language magazines shown and mentioned to put on display for students to peruse. Heritage Speakers may have copies of Spanish-language magazines that they are willing to lend or contribute to the class.

Answers will vary.

Teacher-to-Teacher

A comparison of Spanish-language teen magazines to ones in English from the United States will provide students with valuable cultural insight. Ask students to analyze which topics are the same in the two groups of magazines. Which are noticeably different? How are the advertisements similar or different?

Additional Resources

 Technology: Online Resources
- Guided, Writing, Reading
- Cultural Reading Activity
- Communication Activities
- *Para hispanohablantes*

Print
- Guided WB pp. 112–113
- Literacy Skills WB

Enrich Your Teaching

Culture Note

The first printing press in the Americas was established in Mexico City. At the request of Juan de Zumárraga, first Bishop of Mexico, a publishing house in Sevilla set up a branch in Mexico City. The first book printed there, in 1539, was an edition of the *Breve y más compendiosa doctrina cristiana en lengua mexicana y castellana.*

21st Century Skills

Collaboration To expand on the suggestions for the *Cultura,* have students work in small groups to review copies of the Spanish language teen magazines. Have them compare their impressions about commonalities and differences between teenagers in different countries, as illustrated by these magazines.

Auténtico

Standards: 1.2

Resources: Authentic Resources Wkbk, Cap. 3
Authentic Resources: Cap. 3: Videoscript
AP®Theme: *La ciencia y la tecnología: El cuidado de la salud y la medicina*

Antes de ver

Discuss the *Estrategia* with students. Then, point to the still image from the video and guide students to conclude that the fruits and vegetables were arranged to form a rainbow. Invite volunteers to provide the names in Spanish of the fruits and vegetables that they know, and start a bilingual list on the board. Then, review the key vocabulary with the class. Direct students to make the connection between the word *arco iris* and the title of the video, *Un arco iris por día.* Based on this connection, ask them to predict what the video will be about.

Technology: Ve el video

Before starting the video, direct student's attention to the *Mientras ves* activity. Have them use the activity page from the Authentic Resources Workbook. Explain that this video contains many true cognates, and challenge students to identify them while viewing the video.

Play the video once completely through, without pausing and evaluate student's understanding. Before replaying the video, recommend that students pay attention to the illustrations and words that appear on the screen, since these will give them clues for further comprehension.

Haz las actividades

Mientras ves

Standards: 1.2

Suggestions: Ask students how the illustrations and the text help them understand the video. Do they remember any illustrations that were especially useful? Guide them to conclude that the illustrations showing each color linked to a part of the body help viewers better grasp the concept of phytonutrients (i.e. rojo = corazón; green = células).

Lista de algunos cognados verdaderos:
color, beneficios, células, inmunidad, común

Auténtico

Partnered with 🦚 **NBC LEARN**

Un arco iris por día

Antes de ver

Usa la estrategia: Hacer predicciones

Mira la imagen del video. ¿De qué colores son las frutas y verduras que ves? ¿A qué te recuerda la forma en que están colocadas? Predice cómo se relaciona este video con tu salud.

Lee el vocabulario clave

arco iris = rainbow
estimulante cerebral = brain booster
fitonutriente = phytonutrient*
hechas al horno = baked
patatas dulces = sweet potatoes
remolachas = beets
resfriado = cold

*¿Sabías que la palabra *phyton* en griego significa "planta"?

▶ Ve el video

Con seguridad has oído decir que es importante comer frutas y verduras de distintos colores. ¿Pero sabes por qué es bueno seguir este consejo?

Ve a **PearsonSchool.com/Autentico** para ver el video *Un arco iris por día* y saber qué tiene que ver el color de las frutas y verduras con una buena salud.

Haz las actividades

Mientras ves Fíjate en las fotos e ilustraciones que aparecen a lo largo del video. Estas te ayudarán a entender el vocabulario que no conoces. Además, las palabras que van saliendo en la pantalla te darán información clave sobre el tema general del video. Anota cualquier cognado verdadero que veas. Los cognados verdaderos son palabras que se escriben muy parecido en inglés y español y que significan lo mismo, como *estimulante/stimulant*.

Differentiated Instruction

Heritage Speakers

Encourage a discussion on how the typical Hispanic diet might be different from the typical American diet. Is there a difference in the way meals are prepared? How about in the kinds of fat, vegetables, meats and spices used? Encourage students to give specific examples.

Advanced Learners

Have students create a Spanish brochure based on the nutritional information provided in the video. Suggest they use their own drawings or magazine clips to illustrate their brochures.

La nutrición
ITONUTRIENTES

Integración

Después de ver Vuelve a ver el video para poder contestar estas preguntas:

1. ¿Por qué el video se titula *Un arco iris por día*?

2. ¿Qué son los fitonutrientes y para qué sirven?

3. ¿En qué nos pueden ayudar las frutas o verduras de color rojo? ¿Y las verdes? ¿Y las de color naranja? ¿Y las moradas?

4. ¿Cuál de estos términos define mejor el tipo de video que acabas de ver?
   a. Información médica
   b. Recomendaciones de nutrición
   c. Opiniones de salud

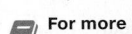 **For more activities, go to the Authentic Resources Workbook.**

La nutrición y la salud

Expansión Busca otros recursos auténticos en *Auténtico* en línea y contesta las preguntas.

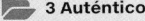 **3 Auténtico**

Integración de ideas Escribe un informe sobre la importancia de la nutrición en la salud. Incluye datos de los recursos auténticos.

Comparación Las recomendaciones de nutrición que dan los expertos cambian con el tiempo. Pregúntale a uno de tus abuelos o padres qué se consideraba "una buena alimentación" cuando ellos tenían tu edad. Escribe una comparación corta en español usando los términos "Antes" y "Ahora".

Interpret Authentic Resources 3

Después de ver

> Standards: 1.2, 1.3, 4.2

Suggestions: Discuss each question with the class and ask multiple volunteers to respond to the questions. While discussing the second question, ask students if they had heard the English term *phytonutrients,* and if that previous knowledge helped them better understand the video. Student's answers may vary based on their comprehension.

Answers:

1. Es bueno comer frutas y verduras de distintos colores, como los del arco iris.
2. sustancias químicas en las plantas que les dan color a las frutas y verduras
3. rojas: corazón; verdes: células; naranja: inmunidad; morado: cerebro
4. b: recomendaciones de nutrición

For more Authentic Resources: Assign the Authentic Resources Workbook activities for homework, so that students can watch the video on their own and complete the workbook activities at their own pace.

Pre-AP® Integration

Resources: Authentic Resources, Wkbk, Cap. 3
Authentic Resources: Cap. 3: Videoscript

Suggestions: Before completing the Pre-AP® activity, have students go to the Authentic Resources Workbook and complete the worksheets for the additional resources.

Integración de ideas
Demonstrate understanding of culturally authentic audiovisual materials in a variety of contexts.

Comparación
Suggestions: Encourage students to share their findings with the class.

Enrich Your Teaching

Culture Note
Tropical fruits loaded with vitamins and health benefits abound in Mexico, the Caribbean, and northern South America. Some of these fruits are well known in the United States, including **el coco, el mango, la papaya,** and **la piña.** Others, like **el mangostino, la pitaya,** and **el zapote** are much more exotic and are not usually imported to this country. **La guanábana,** a fruit with large seeds and pockets of soft and sweet flesh, has lately captured the worldwide attention because of its alleged anti-cancer properties.

Using Authentic Resources
Have students create a personal vocabulary list with terms from the authentic resources that are related to the link between nutrition and good health.

Review Activities

Los síntomas y las medicinas: Ask students to sort the vocabulary in this section into smaller categories of their choice. Have them use a graphic organizer, such as a columnar chart or a word web. Ask them to share their work and discuss their reasons for assigning a particular item to a category.

Partes del cuerpo: Have students sketch a basic human figure and label the parts of the body. Encourage them to include labels for other parts of the body that they previously learned, or terms such as ***columna (vertebral)*** that they learned about in the chapter.

Actividades relacionadas con la salud/La nutrición: Have students sit in a circle. Give a foam ball to a student and say one of the words from the ***actividades*** or ***nutrición*** categories. The student has ten seconds to use the word in a sentence, then tosses the ball randomly to another student in the circle and says another word from the lists. The student catching the ball uses that word in a sentence, announces the next word, and tosses the ball again. Continue until all the words in the list have been covered at least once.

Para estar en forma/Estados de ánimo: Ask pairs of students to work together using TPR commands to demonstrate comprehension of these sections of the vocabulary: *Flexiona la rodilla derecha. Ahora estírala.*

Expresiones útiles: Students can use these words and expressions as they go over the review activities for the other categories.

Teacher-to-Teacher

e-amigos: Have *e-amigos* play the role of a patient and receptionist at a doctor's office. Ask them to write an e-mail describing their symptoms and asking for an appointment. They should respond by asking appropriate questions and proposing a date and time for the appointment. Encourage students to continue the exchange until they have answered all questions and made the appointment. Have students print out their e-mails or send them to you for review.

Repaso del capítulo

🔊 Vocabulario

los síntomas y las medicinas

la alergia	allergy
el antibiótico	antibiotic
la aspirina	aspirin
estar resfriado, -a	to have a cold
estornudar	to sneeze
la fiebre	fever
el grado centígrado	centigrade degree
la gripe	flu
el jarabe	syrup
la tos	cough

partes del cuerpo

el corazón	heart
el músculo	muscle
el oído	ear
el pecho	chest

actividades relacionadas con la salud

aconsejar	to advise
contener	to contain
desarrollar	to develop
evitar	to avoid
exigir	to demand
incluir	to include
quejarse	to complain
saltar (una comida)	to skip (a meal)
tomar	to take, to drink

para estar en forma

abdominales	crunches
el calambre	cramp
débil	weak
ejercicios aeróbicos	aerobics
estar en forma	to be fit
estirar	to stretch
flexionar	to flex, to stretch
fuerte	strong
la fuerza	strength
hacer bicicleta	to use a stationary bike
hacer cinta	to use a treadmill
hacer flexiones	to do push-ups
relajar(se)	to relax
respirar	to breathe
yoga	yoga

la nutrición

la alimentación	nutrition, feeding
los alimentos	food
apropiado, -a	appropriate
el calcio	calcium
el carbohidrato	carbohydrate
la comida basura	junk food
la dieta	diet
la edad	age
la energía	energy
equilibrado, -a	balanced
la estatura	height
la fibra	fiber
el hábito alimenticio	eating habit
el hierro	iron
lleno, -a	full
la merienda	snack
nutritivo, -a	nutritious
el peso	weight
la proteína	protein
saludable	healthy
vacío, -a	empty
la vitamina	vitamin

expresiones útiles

aguantar	to endure, to tolerate
aunque	despite, even when
el consejo	advice
la manera	way
el nivel	level

estados de ánimo

caerse de sueño	to be exhausted, sleepy
concentrarse	to concentrate
confianza en sí mismo, -a	self-confidence
estar de buen / mal humor	to be in a good / bad mood
estar en la luna	to be daydreaming
el estrés	stress
estresado, -a	stressed out
preocuparse	to worry
sentirse fatal	to feel awful

156 ciento cincuenta y seis • Capítulo 3 • ¿Qué haces para estar en forma?

Differentiated Instruction

Students with Learning Difficulties

Suggest that students review the vocabulary lists in sets of three words or phrases, saying them out loud while cycling through them several times. This will also help them remember the gender of each word.

Advanced Students

Tell students to bring in a magazine photo of a scene in a hospital or doctor's waiting room, or in a gym. Have them describe the people in the scene. Then have them write a short conversation between two or more of the people.

Gramática

Mandatos afirmativos y negativos

Más recursos PearsonSchool.com/Autentico

 Games    Flashcards   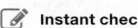 Instant check

Tutorials

Regular and stem-changing verbs, and verbs ending in -car, -gar, and -zar

	tú	Ud.	Uds.
evitar	evit**a**, no evit**es**	(no) evit**e**	(no) evit**en**
volver	vuelv**e**, no vuelv**as**	(no) vuelv**a**	(no) vuelv**an**
abrir	abr**e**, no abr**as**	(no) abr**a**	(no) abr**an**
sacar	sac**a**, no sa**ques**	(no) sa**que**	(no) sa**quen**
llegar	lleg**a**, no lle**gues**	(no) lle**gue**	(no) lle**guen**
cruzar	cruz**a**, no cru**ces**	(no) cru**ce**	(no) cru**cen**

Irregular verbs

	tú	Ud.	Uds.
decir	**di, no digas**	(no) diga	(no) digan
poner	**pon, no pongas**	(no) ponga	(no) pongan
ir	**ve, no vayas**	(no) vaya	(no) vayan
hacer	**haz, no hagas**	(no) haga	(no) hagan
tener	**ten, no tengas**	(no) tenga	(no) tengan
mantener	**mantén, no mantengas**	(no) mantenga	(no) mantengan
ser	**sé, no seas**	(no) sea	(no) sean
salir	**sal, no salgas**	(no) salga	(no) salgan

Placement of pronouns

Attach reflexive or object pronouns at the end of affirmative commands.
With negative commands, place them after the word *no*.

Toma esas vitaminas.   ¡**Tómalas** ahora mismo!   No las tomes.

El subjuntivo: Verbos regulares y verbos con cambios de raíz

saltar

salt**e**	salt**emos**
salt**es**	salt**éis**
salt**e**	salt**en**

poder (o → ue)

p**ue**da	p**o**damos
p**ue**das	p**o**dáis
p**ue**da	p**ue**dan

pedir (e → i)

p**i**da	p**i**damos
p**i**das	p**i**dáis
p**i**da	p**i**dan

El subjuntivo: Verbos irregulares

dar

dé	demos
des	déis
dé	den

haber

haya	hayamos
hayas	hayáis
haya	hayan

ir

vaya	vayamos
vayas	vayáis
vaya	vayan

estar

esté	estemos
estés	estéis
esté	estén

ser

sea	seamos
seas	seáis
sea	sean

saber

sepa	sepamos
sepas	sepáis
sepa	sepan

Capítulo 3 • ciento cincuenta y siete **157**

Mandatos afirmativos y negativos: Have individual students write a series of commands that a partner will carry out. The commands will tell the partner how to draw something. The drawing might consist of geometric shapes or of something realistic, such as a landscape or floor plan.
Then have students follow their own commands carefully, in order to create the drawing. Ask them to keep this drawing out of sight. Finally, have pairs sit back-to-back, each with pencil and paper. Students take turns reading their complete list of commands, while the partner attempts to draw based on what he or she hears. Students compare their drawings to the originals to see how well they created and followed the commands.

El subjuntivo: Have students list at least five typical health or lifestyle complaints. Have them exchange lists with a partner and write solutions to the problems with complete sentences containing the subjunctive. As a guide, write the following information on the board: Main Clause (indicative) + que + Subordinate Clause (subjunctive). This activity can be used to assess students' assimilation of rules for basic formation and use of the subjunctive.

Digital Portfolio

Invite students to review the activities and projects they completed in this chapter. Have them select one or two items that they feel best demonstrate their achievements in Spanish. Include these products in students' portfolios.

Additional Resources

 Technology: Online Resources
- Instant Check
- Integrated Performance Assessment
- *Para hispanohablantes*

Teacher Resources
- Teacher's Resource Materials: Situation Cards, Clip Art

Technology: ¡Pura vida! is a storyline video that is independent of chapter content and an ideal support for expanding listening skills. The 14 episodes are available within **Realize**. Student activities and Teacher support are also assignable within **Realize**.

Enrich Your Teaching

Teacher-to-Teacher

Have students write the infinitives of the verbs with irregular imperative forms on slips of paper and place them in a hat or other container. Have a playing cube ready. Explain that rolling an even number means ***afirmativo*** and rolling an odd number means ***negativo***. Students take turns rolling the cube, drawing a verb, and using it in either an affirmative or negative command.

Performance Tasks

Standards: 1.1, 1.2, 1.3, 2.2

Student Resource: *Para hispanohablantes*
Teacher Resources: Teacher's Resource Materials: Audio Script, Technology: Audio Cap. 3

1. Vocabulario

Suggestions: Encourage students to review the vocabulary from the *Vocabulario en contexto* sections on pp. 118–120 and 130–133 before they complete the activity.

Answers:

1. b	**5.** b
2. b	**6.** b
3. c	**7.** a
4. a	**8.** d

2. Gramática

Suggestions: Remind students of the main points of the grammar presentations in *Capítulo* 3:

- affirmative commands with **tú**
- negative commands with tú
- affirmative and negative commands with **Ud**. and **Uds**.
- the subjunctive: regular verbs
- the subjunctive: irregular verbs
- the subjunctive: stem-changing verbs

Answers:

1. b	**5.** d
2. a	**6.** a
3. a	**7.** c
4. c	**8.** d

Repaso del capítulo

OBJECTIVE
▶ Demonstrate that you can perform the tasks on these pages

Preparación para el examen

❶ Vocabulario Escribe la letra de la palabra o expresión que mejor complete cada frase. Escribe tus respuestas en una hoja aparte.

1. El médico le aconseja a Lucía que coma queso y tome leche todos los días porque contienen _____.
a. comida basura
b. calcio
c. dulces
d. fibra

2. Estoy enfermo(a) cuando _____.
a. hago yoga
b. tengo fiebre
c. hago ejercicio
d. tengo sueño

3. Te voy a recetar _____ para la tos.
a. una gripe
b. carbohidratos
c. un jarabe
d. una aspirina

4. Para evitar los calambres les recomiendo que _____.
a. estiren los músculos
b. hagan abdominales
c. hagan flexiones
d. corran rápido

5. Si _____, te aconsejo que hagas yoga.
a. estás en la luna
b. estás estresado
c. haces cinta
d. te caes de sueño

6. Doctor, _____ y tengo dolor de cabeza.
a. tengo el oído
b. me duele el pecho
c. me duele la gripe
d. estoy en forma

7. Tengo fiebre, cuando _____.
a. tengo 39° centígrados
b. evito los antibióticos
c. tengo calambres
d. mantengo mi dieta

8. ¡No aguanto más! significa que _____.
a. estás muy contento(a)
b. te gusta hacer ejercicio
c. tienes energía
d. estás muy estresado(a)

❷ Gramática Escribe la letra de la palabra o expresión que mejor complete cada frase. Escribe tus respuestas en una hoja aparte.

1. Jorge, no _____ al gimnasio hoy. Está cerrado.
a. vas
b. vayas
c. ve
d. vayan

2. Sra. Díaz, por favor _____ las vitaminas allí.
a. ponga
b. pon
c. pongan
d. pones

3. El doctor me aconseja que _____ una dieta equilibrada.
a. mantenga
b. mantén
c. mantengo
d. mantener

4. ¿Estás estresado? _____ con tus amigos para divertirte.
a. Salgas
b. Sales
c. Sal
d. Salgan

5. Es importante que ustedes _____ de buen humor durante las clases de yoga.
a. estemos
b. están
c. estamos
d. estén

6. ¡Tomen las vitaminas! ¡_____ por la mañana!
a. Tómenlas
b. Tómenlo
c. Tómalas
d. Tómenlos

7. Niños, ¡_____ comida basura a la escuela!
a. no traen
b. no traiga
c. no traigan
d. no traes

8. Quiero que tú me _____ las reglas del club.
a. explicas
b. expliquen
c. explique
d. expliques

Differentiated Instruction

Heritage Speakers

Have students create a brochure for their own "virtual museum." Encourage them to select artists and works from the chapter, from their own areas of interest, or from their heritage country. Remind students to tailor the language of their descriptions to the appropriate audience.

Students with Learning Difficulties

In reviewing the vocabulary and grammar of the chapter, use gestures and facial expressions to support students in their choice of the correct answer. Use TPR to support meaning of the vocabulary choices.

En el examen vas a . . .	Éstas son las tareas de práctica que te pueden ser útiles para el examen . . .	Para repasar, ve a tu libro de texto impreso o digital . . .
Interpretive		
3 ESCUCHAR Yo puedo escuchar y comprender un programa de radio sobre consejos para la salud.	En este programa de radio, varias personas llaman al Dr. Salvavidas para pedirle consejos. (a) ¿Qué síntomas tiene cada uno?, (b) ¿Qué tienen que tomar?, (c) ¿Qué más les aconseja el doctor?	**pp. 118–121** *Vocabulario en contexto 1* **p. 119 Actividad 2** **p. 123 Actividad 9**
Presentational		
4 HABLAR Yo puedo aconsejar a otros sobre los hábitos alimenticios.	La directora de la guardería infantil de tu barrio te pide que vengas a hablarles a los niños sobre lo importante que es tener buenos hábitos alimenticios. Haz cinco recomendaciones.	**p. 118–121** *Vocabulario en contexto 1* **p. 120 Actividad 3** **p. 122 Actividad 7** **p. 128 Actividad 17** **p. 129 Actividades 18 y 20**
Interpretive		
5 LEER Yo puedo leer y entender un anuncio.	Lucía quiere aprender a preparar alimentos nutritivos y tomar clases para tener músculos fuertes. Lee el anuncio que ella vio y dile: (a) por qué le recomiendas las clases de ejercicio y (b) por qué debe tomar las clases para preparar alimentos. **Centro Fuente de la Salud** Si estás estresado(a) y no puedes concentrarte, tenemos clases de ejercicios para ayudar a relajarte. Aprende a tener una alimentación equilibrada. Prepara galletas nutritivas y bebidas que dan energía.	**pp. 130–133** *Vocabulario en contexto 2* **p. 140 Actividad 36** **p. 140 Actividad 40**
Presentational		
6 ESCRIBIR Yo puedo escribir una carta para dar consejos.	Tu trabajo en una revista es contestar las cartas que mandan los jóvenes. En una carta, un chico te dice que siempre se siente cansado y de mal humor. Escríbele una respuesta con por lo menos cuatro consejos.	**p. 125 Actividad 11** **p. 129 Actividad 18** **p. 133 Actividad 25** **p. 139 Actividad 35** **p. 140 Actividad 36**
Comparisons		
7 COMPARAR Yo puedo comparar los antiguos juegos de los olmecas de Mesoamérica con los de la actualidad.	En tu clase puedes ganar "puntos extra" si compartes algo que aprendiste en otra clase. ¿Cómo puedes explicar el juego de pelota de los olmecas de hace 3,000 años? ¿Hoy en día hay algún juego similar? Descríbelo.	**pp. 144–145** *Puente a la cultura*

Capítulo 3 • ciento cincuenta y nueve **159**

Differentiated Assessment

Core Assessment
• Technology: Audio Cap. 3

Challenge/Pre-AP®
• ExamView: Pre-AP® Test Bank
• Pre-AP® Resource Materials

Extra Support
• Alternate Assessment Program: Examen del capítulo 3
• Technology: Audio Cap. 3

Heritage Speakers
• Assessment Program: Para hispanohablantes: Examen del capítulo 3
• ExamView Heritage Speaker Test Bank

3. Escuchar
Suggestions: Play the audio or read from the script.
Script
(For the complete script, see Teacher's Resource Materials.)
Answers:
(a) A la señorita Juana Durante le duele el estómago después del almuerzo. El señor David Ríos tiene fiebre y tos, le duelen la garganta y el pecho.
(b) La señorita Juana Durante debe cambiar sus hábitos alimenticios. El señor David Ríos debe ir al médico inmediatamente.
(c) La señorita Juana Durante debe comer más frutas y verduras y menos comida basura. El señor David Ríos debe ir al médico porque necesita antibióticos.

4. Hablar
Suggestions: Remind students that they should tailor their verb forms to the situation. Have Advanced Learners use the *vosotros* forms.

5. Leer
Suggestions: Tell students to refer to pp. 118–120 and 130–133 if they have questions about vocabulary in the review.

6. Escribir
Suggestions: Remind students that they can use either commands or sentences with the subjunctive for their advice.

7. Pensar
Suggestions: Suggest that students begin with a description of the ball game. They can then refer to this in order to compare the ancient game to modern ones.

Additional Resources

🖥 **Technology: Online Resources**
• Instant Check
• *Para hispanohablantes*
Print
• Core WB pp. 47–48

CAPÍTULO **4**

¿Cómo te llevas con los demás?

Relationships with friends and family

Vocabulary: personality traits and conflicts; friends and family relationships

Grammar: subjunctive mode with verbs of emotion; uses of *por* and *para*; commands with *nosotros*; use of possesive pronouns

Cultural Perspectives: gathering of friends and family for a "quinceañera"; love and friendship celebrations in the Spanish-speaking world; depictions of family life in the art of Carmen Lomas Garza and Pablo Picasso; love expressed through the arts in the Spanish-speaking world

¡Pura vida!: Watch an engaging video episode about a group of young people in Costa Rica!

Chapter Support

Bulletin Boards

Theme: La amistad a través del mundo

Ask students to cut out, copy, or download photos from around the world showing manifestations of friendship among teenagers in different Spanish-speaking countries and cultures. Cluster photos into categories of countries and/or cultures so that similarities and differences are evident.

Hands-on Culture

Art: Mural de la amistad

In many Latin American countries, murals are used to decorate the walls of public buildings. In schools, murals are used by students to express themselves and their feelings about events such as *el Día de la amistad*.

Materials: butcher paper, pencils, paint brushes, paint of different colors, tape

Directions:

1. Divide students into four groups. Ask each group to brainstorm a list of ideas about the meaning of friendship and choose an idea to depict in a mural.
2. Have students first draw their ideas onto two large pieces of butcher block paper that have been taped together. Then have them paint the mural.
3. Display the murals and have students explain them to the class.

Game

Busquemos el lado positivo

This game practices using positive and negative words to describe friendships and family relationships. Play it to review the vocabulary from *Capítulo* 4.

Players: the entire class, playing in pairs

Materials: index cards and colored pencils or markers

Rules:

1. On the board write positive and negative words and expressions from *Capítulo* 4. Write positive words such as *sincero(a), comprensivo(a), pedir perdón, perdonar, reaccionar, alegrarse* on the right column. On the left column, write negative words, such as *vanidoso(a), conflicto, estar equivocado(a), criticar*.
2. Ask students to write the words on their index cards, one on each card. Words from the left column should be written in blue and those from the right column should be in red.
3. Select a scorekeeper and divide the class into teams A and B. Each team A player chooses a card and thinks of a sentence that uses the negative or positive word and that can be converted to a positive or negative sentence.
4. Students go in row order, team A players alternating with players from team B. Team A player: *Una amiga que es **vanidosa** piensa sólo en ella misma.* Then, he or she says the opposite word: ***considerada.*** Team B player: *Es mejor ser amiga de alguien que es considerada y piensa en los demás.* This correct answer gives team B a turn.
5. Teams receive 1 point for each vocabulary word they use, as well as 1 point for each correct sentence. Each time they use a new word, the corresponding card is set aside.
6. If a team cannot make a sentence, it loses its turn. No word or sentence can be repeated. The team with the most points wins.

21st Century Skills

Look for tips throughout Chapter 4 to enrich your teaching by integrating 21st Century Skills. Suggestions for the Project-Based Learning and Culture follow below.

Project-Based Learning

Modify the project with these suggestions:

Critical Thinking and Problem Solving Discuss with students the purpose of their advertisement. What words, expressions, or visuals might best support this purpose for the target audience? What are the best media to use to convey their message?

Collaboration After students complete their projects, have them work together to group the students portrayed in the ads as possible roommates. Which groups of students have similar interests, likes and dislikes, eating/sleeping habits, etc.? Which pairs of students would or would not make compatible roommates?

Communication As students prepare to present their project to the class, provide them with the handout "Give an Effective Presentation" to remind them of the importance of body language, tone of voice, eye contact, and other strategies for delivering an effective presentation.

Chapter Culture

Social and Cross-Cultural Skills Help students bridge cultural differences by offering them opportunities to discuss the different cultural perspectives about the relationships between friends and family. After reading the *Cultura* on page 184, discuss the contrasts between the image of society and family life presented in soap operas and *telenovelas*.

▶ **Technology: Videodocumentario**
View *Una amistad entre hermanos* online with the class to learn more about family relationships in the Spanish-speaking world.

Project-Based Learning

Anuncio ilustrado "Busco nuevos(as) amigos(as)"

Overview: Students create an illustrated ad to look for new school friends in Latin America or Spain. The ad is for a web page of the school where they will be studying in summer. It should include the name of the student, his/her age, grade, phone number or email address, and photo.

Students include photos with captions of two of their hobbies and two of their favorite class subjects. In a paragraph, they write why they want a new friend, two personality traits they like from a new friend, and two activities they would like to do with their new friend. Students then present their ad to the class and describe the information.

Resources: online photos, image layout and page layout software

Sequence: (suggestions for when to do each step are found throughout the chapter)

Step 1. Review instructions so students know what is expected of them. Share the rubric with the class.

Step 2. Students submit a draft of their ad. Return the drafts with your suggestions. For vocabulary and grammar practice, ask partners to present their drafts to each other.

Step 3. Students do layouts, setting space for paragraphs, photos, and captions. Encourage them to try different arrangements before writing the paragraphs.

Step 4. Students submit a draft of the personal descriptions. Note your corrections and suggestions, then return drafts to students.

Step 5. Students present their ads to the class, explaining what kind of person is going to respond.

Options

1. Students create an ad for an online newspaper.
2. Students create an ad to look for a pen pal through a Web site.

Assessment

Here is a detailed rubric for assessing this project:

Chapter 4 Project: Anuncio ilustrado "Busco nuevos(as) amigos(as)"

Rubric	Score 1	Score 3	Score 5
Your evidence of planning	You provide no ad layout or written draft.	You provide layout and written draft, but it is not corrected.	You show evidence of corrected draft and layout.
Your use of illustrations	You do not include images.	You include images but layout is unorganized.	Your ad is easy to read and images are consistent with text.
Your presentation	You include little of the required information.	You include most of the required information.	You include all the required information.

AT A GLANCE

Objectives
- Listen and read about relationships
- Talk and write about conflicts
- Express opinions and emotions while discussing problems
- Emotions and art in the Hispanic world
- Compare the relationships between teens and their parents in Mexico with your own experience
- Compare cultural practices and perspectives in an authentic video about parent-child relationships

Vocabulary
- Personality traits
- Relationships
- Emotions and conflicts

Grammar
- Subjunctive with verbs of emotion
- Uses of *por* and *para*
- *Nosotros* commands
- Possessive pronouns

Culture
- Pablo Picasso, p. 164
- Spanish youth, p. 172
- *Día de la Rosa y del Libro* in Barcelona, p. 173
- Mexican teens and family relationships, pp. 182–183
- Soap operas in Latin America, p. 184
- Carmen Lomas Garza, p. 185
- A traditional Spanish children's rhyme, p. 189
- Love in the arts, pp. 192–193
- Poetry readings, p. 200

A ver si recuerdas...
- Activities
- Time
- Quantities
- Use of reflexive verbs
- Reciprocal pronouns

Recycle
- Possessive adjectives
- The letter *j*

Authentic Resources
- **Auténtico:** La amagura es contagiosa, pp. 202–203

RESOURCES

FOR THE STUDENT	DIGITAL	PRINT	FOR THE TEACHER	DIGITAL	PRINT
A ver si recuerdas pp. 160–163					
Review A ver si recuerdas with Remediation	•		A ver si recuerdas with Remediation	•	
Guided WB, pp. 114–117	•	•	Teacher's Edition, pp. 160–163		
Core WB, pp. 49–50	•	•			
Para hispanohablantes	•				
Introducción pp. 164–165					
Present Student Edition, pp. 164–165	•	•	Teacher's Edition, pp. 164–165	•	•
DK Reference Atlas	•		Teacher's Resource Materials	•	
Videonovela: ¡Pura vida!	•		Mapa global interactivo	•	
¡Pura vida! Video Activities	•				
Para hispanohablantes	•				
Vocabulario en contexto pp. 166–169/180–183					
Present & Practice Student Edition, pp. 166–169/180–183	•	•	Teacher's Edition, pp. 166–169/180–183	•	•
Audio	•		Teacher's Resource Materials	•	
Videohistoria	•		Vocabulary Clip Art	•	
Flashcards	•		Technology: Audio	•	
Instant Check	•		Video Program: Videohistoria	•	
Guided WB, pp. 118–124/129–136	•	•			
Core WB, pp. 51–52/56–57	•	•			
Communication Activities	•				
Para hispanohablantes	•				
Assess and Remediate			Pruebas 4–1/4–5: Assessment Program, Assessment Program Para hispanohablantes	•	

	FOR THE STUDENT	DIGITAL	PRINT	FOR THE TEACHER	DIGITAL	PRINT
Vocabulario en uso pp. 170–173/184–187						
Present & Practice	Student Edition, pp. 170–173/184–187	•	•	Interactive Whiteboard Vocabulary Activities	•	
	Instant Check	•		Teacher's Edition, pp. 170–173/184–187	•	•
	Communication Activities	•		Teacher's Resource Materials	•	
	Para hispanohablantes	•		Technology: Audio	•	
	Communicative Pair Activities	•		Videomodelos	•	
				Mapa global interactivo	•	
Assess and Remediate				Pruebas 4–2/4–6 with Remediation	•	
				Pruebas 4–2/4–6: Assessment Program, Assessment Program *Para hispanohablantes*	•	
Gramática pp. 174–179/188–191						
Present & Practice	Student Edition, pp. 174–179/188–191	•	•	Interactive Whiteboard Grammar Activities	•	
	Instant Check	•		Teacher's Edition, pp. 174–179/188–191	•	•
	Tutorial Video: Grammar	•		Teacher's Resource Materials	•	
	Canción de hip hop	•		Technology: Audio	•	
	Guided WB, pp. 125–128/137–140	•	•	Videomodelos	•	
	Core WB, pp. 53–55/58–60	•	•			
	Communication Activities	•				
	Para hispanohablantes	•				
	Communicative Pair Activities	•				
Assess and Remediate				Pruebas 4–3, 4–4/4–7, 4–8 with Remediation	•	
				Pruebas 4–3, 4–4/4–7, 4–8: Assessment Program, Assessment Program *Para hispanohablantes*	•	
				Examen 1, Examen 2: Vocab. y gramática	•	
Aplicación pp. 192–203						
Apply	Student Edition, pp. 192–203	•	•	Teacher's Edition, pp. 192–203	•	•
	Authentic Resources Workbook	•	•	Teacher's Resource Materials	•	
	Authentic Resources	•		Video Program: Videodocumentario	•	
	Online Cultural Reading	•		Mapa global interactivo	•	
	Guided WB, pp. 141–143	•	•	Authentic Resources Lesson Plans with scripts, answer keys	•	
	Communication Activities	•				
	Para hispanohablantes	•				
	Videodocumentario	•				
Repaso del capítulo pp. 204–207						
Review	Student Edition, pp. 204–207	•	•	Teacher's Edition, pp. 204–207	•	•
	Core WB, pp. 61–62	•	•	Teacher's Resource Materials	•	
	Communication Activities	•		Technology: Audio	•	
	Para hispanohablantes	•				
	Instant Check	•				
Chapter Assessment						
Assess				Examen del capítulo 4: Assessment Program, Alternate Assessment Program, Assessment Program *Para hispanohablantes*	•	
				Technology: Audio, Cap. 4, Examen	•	
				ExamView: Test Banks A and B (questions only online) Heritage Speaker Test Bank, Pre-AP® Test Bank	•	

DAY	LESSON PLAN		
	Warm-up / Assess	**Preview / Present / Practice / Communicate**	**Wrap-up / Homework Options**
1	**Warm-up** (10 min.) • Return Examen del capítulo: Capítulo 3	**Repaso** (35 min.) • A ver si recuerdas . . . • Actividad 5	**Wrap-up and Homework Options** (5 min.) • Core Practice 4-1, 4-2
2	**Warm-up** (10 min.) • Homework check	**Chapter Opener** (10 min.) • Objectives • Arte y cultura **Vocabulario en contexto 1** (25 min.) • Presentation: Vocabulario y gramática en contexto • Actividades 1, 2, 3, 4	**Wrap-up and Homework Options** (5 min.) • Clip Art Vocabulary
3	**Warm-up** (10 min.) • Homework check	**Vocabulario en contexto 1** (30 min.) • Presentation: Videohistoria *Unidos por una causa* • View: Videohistoria **Vocabulario en uso 1** (5 min.) • Actividad 6	**Wrap-up and Homework Options** (5 min.) • Core Practice 4-3, 4-4 • Prueba 4-1: Vocabulary recognition
4	**Warm-up** (10 min.) • Homework check • **Formative Assessment** (10 min.) • Prueba 4-1: Vocabulary recognition	**Vocabulario en uso 1** (25 min.) • Actividades 5, 7, 8 • Interactive Whiteboard Vocabulary Activities • Ampliación del lenguaje	**Wrap-up and Homework Options** (5 min.) • Actividades 9, 10 • Writing Activities • Prueba 4-2 with Remediation: Vocabulary production
5	**Warm-up** (10 min.) • Cultura • Homework check • **Formative Assessment** (10 min.) • Prueba 4-2 with Remediation: Vocabulary production	**Gramática y vocabulario en uso 1** (25 min.) • Presentation: El subjuntivo con verbos de emoción • Interactive Whiteboard Grammar Activities • Actividades 11, 13, 14, 15 • Writing Activity	**Wrap-up and Homework Options** (5 min.) • Core Practice 4-5
6	**Warm-up** (10 min.) • Actividad 12 • Homework check	**Gramática y vocabulario en uso 1** (35 min.) • Actividad 16 • Communicative Pair Activity • Presentation: Los usos de *por y para* • Interactive Whiteboard Grammar Activities • Actividad 18	**Wrap-up and Homework Options** (5 min.) • Writing Activity • Prueba 4-3 with Remediation: El subjuntivo con verbos de emoción
7	**Warm-up** (10 min.) • Homework check • **Formative Assessment** (10 min.) • Prueba 4-3 with Remediation: El subjuntivo con verbos de emoción	**Gramática y vocabulario en uso 1** (25 min.) • Actividades 17, 19, 20, 21 • Communicative Pair Activity	**Wrap-up and Homework Options** (5 min.) • Core Practice 4-6, 4-7 • Prueba 4-4: Los usos de *por y para*
8	**Warm-up** (15 min.) • Writing Activity • Homework check • **Formative Assessment** (10 min.) • Prueba 4-4 with Remediation: Los usos de *por y para*	**Vocabulario en contexto 2** (20 min.) • Presentation: Vocabulario y gramática en contexto • Actividad 22	**Wrap-up and Homework Options** (5 min.) • Clip Art Vocabulary • Examen: Vocabulario y gramática 1
9	**Warm-up** (5 min.) • Homework check • **Formative Assessment** (30 min.) • Examen: Vocabulario y gramática 1	**Vocabulario en contexto 2** (10 min.) • Presentation: Hagamos las paces • Actividad 23	**Wrap-up and Homework Options** (5 min.) • Conflictos: causas y soluciones • Core Practice 4-8, 4-9
10	**Warm-up** (20 min.) • Conflictos: causas y soluciones • Actividad 24 • Homework check • **Formative Assessment** (10 min.) • Prueba 4-5: Vocabulary recognition	**Vocabulario en uso 2** (15 min.) • Cultura • Actividades 28, 29 • Interactive Whiteboard Vocabulary Activities	**Wrap-up and Homework Options** (5 min.) • Actividades 26, 27 • Prueba 4-6 with Remediation: Vocabulary production

LESSON PLAN

DAY	Warm-up / Assess	Preview / Present / Practice / Communicate	Wrap-up / Homework Options
11	**Warm-up** (10 min.) • Actividad 25 • Homework check **• Formative Assessment** (10 min.) • Prueba 4-6 with Remediation: Vocabulary production	**Gramática y vocabulario en uso 2** (25 min.) • Actividades 30, 32 • Presentation: Mandatos con *nosotros* • Interactive Whiteboard Grammar Activities • Actividades 33, 35 • Communicative Pair Activity	**Wrap-up and Homework Options** (5 min.) • Actividad 34 • Core Practice 4-10 • Prueba 4-7 with Remediation: Mandatos con *nosotros*
12	**Warm-up** (10 min.) • Writing Activity • Homework check **• Formative Assessment** (10 min.) • Prueba 4-7 with Remediation: Mandatos con nosotros	**Gramática y vocabulario en uso 2** (25 min.) • Presentation: Pronombres posesivos • Interactive Whiteboard Grammar Activities • Actividades 36, 37, 38 • El español en el mundo del trabajo	**Wrap-up and Homework Options** (5 min.) • Core Practice 4-11, 4-12 • Prueba 4-8 with Remediation: Pronombres posesivos
13	**Warm-up** (10 min.) • Homework check **• Formative Assessment** (10 min.) • Prueba 4-8 with Remediation: Pronombres posesivos	**Gramática y vocabulario en uso 2** (25 min.) • En voz alta • Communicative Pair Activity	**Wrap-up and Homework Options** (5 min.) • Examen: Vocabulario y gramática 2
14	**Warm-up** (8 min.) • Writing Activity **• Formative Assessment** (30 min.) • Examen: Vocabulario y gramática 2	**Aplicación** (10 min.) • Presentación oral: Steps 1, 2	**Wrap-up and Homework Options** (5 min.) • Presentación oral: Step 2
15	**Warm-up** (10 min.) • Presentación oral: Step 2	**Aplicación** (35 min.) • Presentación oral: Step 3	**Wrap-up and Homework Options** (5 min.) • El amor en las artes • ¿Comprendiste?
16	**Warm-up** (15 min.) • El amor en las artes: ¿Comprendiste? • Homework check	**Aplicación** (30 min.) • Pre-AP(R) Integración 1, 2, 3 • View Video • Video Activities 1, 2, 3	**Wrap-up and Homework Options** (5 min.) • Presentación escrita: Steps 1, 2
17	**Warm-up** (10 min.) • Video Activity 4	**Aplicación** (15 min.) • Presentación escrita: Step 3 **Repaso** (20 min.) • Preparación para el examen: Actividades 3, 4	**Wrap-up and Homework Options** (5 min.) • Presentación escrita: Step 4
18	**Warm-up** (10 min.) • Homework check	**Aplicación** (35 min.) • Lectura • ¿Comprendiste? • Cultura • Auténtico	**Wrap-up and Homework Options** (5 min.) • Core Practice: Organizer 4-13, 4-14 • Instant Check
19	**Warm-up** (20 min.) • Preparación para el examen: Actividades 1, 2 • Homework check	**Repaso** (25 min.) • Preparación para el examen: Actividades 5, 6, 7 • Other review	**Wrap-up and Homework Options** (5 min.) • Examen del capítulo
20	**Warm-up** (5 min.) • Answer questions **• Summative Assessment** (44 min.) • Examen del capítulo		**Wrap-up and Homework Options** (1 min.) • A ver si recuerdas: Capítulo 5 • Actividades 1, 2, 4, 6, 7

ALTERNATE LESSON PLAN

DAY	Warm-up / Assess	Preview / Present / Practice / Communicate	Wrap-up / Homework Options
1	**Warm-up** (35 min.) • Return Examen del capítulo: Capítulo 3 • A ver si recuerdas . . . • Actividad 5 • Homework check	**Chapter Opener** (10 min.) • Objectives • Arte y cultura **Vocabulario en contexto 1** (30 min.) • Presentation: Vocabulario y gramática en contexto • Actividades 1, 2, 3, 4 • Presentation: Videohistoria *Unidos por una causa* • View: Videohistoria **Vocabulario en uso 1** (10 min.) • Actividades 6, 7 • Interactive Whiteboard Vocabulary Activities	**Wrap-up and Homework Options** (5 min.) • Core Practice 4-3, 4-4 • Clip Art Vocabulary • Prueba 4-1: Vocabulary recognition
2	**Warm-up** (15 min.) • Actividad 5 • Homework check • **Formative Assessment** (10 min.) • Prueba 4-1: Vocabulary recognition	**Vocabulario en uso 1** (60 min.) • Actividades 8, 9, 10 • Ampliación del lenguaje • Cultura • Communicative Pair Activity • Audio Activity	**Wrap-up and Homework Options** (5 min.) • Writing Activities • Prueba 4-2 with Remediation: Vocabulary production
3	**Warm-up** (15 min.) • Writing Activity • Homework check • **Formative Assessment** (10 min.) • Prueba 4-2 with Remediation: Vocabulary production	**Gramática y vocabulario en uso 1** (60 min.) • Presentation: El subjuntivo con verbos de emoción • Interactive Whiteboard Grammar Activities • Actividades 11, 12, 13, 14, 15 • Audio and Writing Activities	**Wrap-up and Homework Options** (5 min.) • Core Practice 4-5 • Prueba 4-3 with Remediation: El subjuntivo con verbos de emoción
4	**Warm-up** (10 min.) • Actividad 16 • Homework check • **Formative Assessment** (10 min.) • Prueba 4-3 with Remediation: El subjuntivo con verbos de emoción	**Gramática y vocabulario en uso 1** (50 min.) • Presentation: Los usos de *por y para* • Interactive Whiteboard Grammar Activities • Actividades 18, 19, 20, 21 • Communicative Pair Activity **Vocabulario en contexto 2** (15 min.) • Presentation: Vocabulario y gramática en contexto • Actividad 22	**Wrap-up and Homework Options** (5 min.) • Core Practice 4-6, 4-7 • Prueba 4-4: Los usos de *por y para* • Examen: Vocabulario y gramática 1
5	**Warm-up** (15 min.) • Actividad 16 • Homework check • **Formative Assessment** (40 min.) • Prueba 4-4 with Remediation: Los usos de *por y para* • Examen: Vocabulario y gramática 1	**Vocabulario en contexto 2** (20 min.) • Presentation: Vocabulario y gramática en contexto • Actividad 23 • Presentation: Conflictos: causas y soluciones • Actividad 24 **Vocabulario en uso 2** (10 min.) • Actividad 25 • Cultura • Interactive Whiteboard Vocabulary Activities	**Wrap-up and Homework Options** (5 min.) • Core Practice 4-8, 4-9 • Prueba 4-5: Vocabulary recognition
6	**Warm-up** (20 min.) • Actividades 26, 27 • Homework check • **Formative Assessment** (10 min.) • Prueba 4-5: Vocabulary recognition	**Gramática y vocabulario en uso 2** (55 min.) • Actividades 28, 29, 30, 32 • Presentation: Mandatos con *nosotros* • Interactive Whiteboard Grammar Activities • Actividades 33, 34, 35	**Wrap-up and Homework Options** (5 min.) • Core Practice 4-10 • Pruebas 4-6, 4-7 with Remediation: Vocabulary production, Mandatos con *nosotros*

ALTERNATE LESSON PLAN

DAY	Warm-up / Assess	Preview / Present / Practice / Communicate	Wrap-up / Homework Options
7	**Warm-up** (15 min.) • Actividad 31 • Homework check • **Formative Assessment** (20 min.) • Pruebas 4-6, 4-7 with Remediation: Vocabulary production, Mandatos con *nosotros*	**Gramática y vocabulario en uso 2** (35 min.) • En voz alta • Presentation: Pronombres posesivos • Interactive Whiteboard Grammar Activities • Actividades 36, 37, 38 • El español en la comunidad **Aplicación** (15 min.) • Presentación oral: Steps 1, 2	**Wrap-up and Homework Options** (5 min.) • Presentación oral: Step 2
8	**Warm-up** (15 min.) • Writing Activity • Homework check • **Formative Assessment** (40 min.) • Presentación oral: Step 3	**Gramática y vocabulario en uso 2** (15 min.) • Communicative Pair Activity **Aplicación** (15 min.) • Presentation: El amor en las artes	**Wrap-up and Homework Options** (5 min.) • Core Practice 4-11, 4-12 • Prueba 4-8: Pronombres posesivos • Examen: Vocabulario y gramática 2
9	**Warm-up** (10 min.) • Homework check • **Formative Assessment** (30 min.) • Prueba 4-8: Pronombres posesivos • Examen: Vocabulario y gramática 2	**Aplicación** (45 min.) • El amor en las artes • ¿Comprendiste? • Pre-AP® Integración 1, 2, 3 • Presentación escrita: Step 1 • View Video • Video Activities	**Wrap-up and Homework Options** (5 min.) • Presentación escrita: Step 2 • Preparación para el examen: Actividades 1, 2
10	**Warm-up** (20 min.) • Presentación escrita: Step 3 • Homework check	**Aplicación** (40 min.) • Lectura • ¿Comprendiste? • Cultura • Auténtico **Repaso** (25 min.) • Preparación para el examen: Actividades 3, 4, 6	**Wrap-up and Homework Options** (5 min.) • Presentación escrita: Step 4 • Core Practice: Organizer 4-13, 4-14 • Instant Check • Preparación para el examen: Actividades 5, 7 • Examen del capítulo
11	**Warm-up** (15 min.) • Homework check • **Summative Assessment** (45 min.) • Examen del capítulo	**Theme Game** (15 min.) **A ver si recuerdas – Capítulo 5** (10 min.) • Presentation: El amor en las artes • Presentation: Vocabulario • Presentation: Gramática	**Wrap-up and Homework Options** (5 min.) • A ver si recuerdas – Capítulo 5 • Actividades 1, 2, 4, 6, 7 • Core Practice 5-1, 5-2

Vocabulario: Repaso

Standards: 1.1, 1.2

Suggestions: Before presenting the material in this review section, consider testing your students' command of the material by assigning the Prueba with Remediation. Students will automatically be given additional practice of the material they have not yet mastered, and you can focus your review based on the class's overall performance on the post-test.

Ask students to think of one person they know well. Have them tell at least two facts about the person, using vocabulary from the three categories. Tell students that vocabulary from the *actividades* and *tiempo* categories might be used in the same sentence: *Mi hermana Jane es una persona sociable. Le gusta escribir cartas a sus amigas durante sus viajes.*

 1

Standards: 1.1, 1.3, 3.1

Suggestions: Remind students that when making their Venn diagrams in Step 1, they should fill in the overlapping parts of the diagram with qualities their friends have in common.

Common Errors: Students may forget to make an adjective agree in number and gender with the noun it modifies. Correct the error by modeling the correct form of the noun phrase and having students repeat. You can also use visual cues: hold up two fingers to elicit plural; have a flash card ready with the masculine symbol on one side and the feminine symbol on the other, and hold this up to elicit the appropriate gender.

Answers will vary.

Active Classroom

Ask each student to write a sentence of up to eight words that uses a reflexive verb in the present, past, or future tense with student(s) in the class as the subject. Put the papers in a bag. Create two teams. Alternate with individual students acting out the sentences. Allow a team up to 30 seconds to guess the sentence. Keep track of the time per sentence. The team with the lowest time wins.

A ver si recuerdas

OBJECTIVES
▶ Talk and write about personal qualities
▶ Write about daily activities and routines

Vocabulario

cualidades
artístico, -a
atlético, -a
bien educado, -a
cortés
divertido, -a
elegante
estudioso, -a
gracioso, -a
inteligente
nervioso, -a
reservado, -a
serio, -a
simpático, -a
sociable
talentoso, -a
tranquilo, -a

actividades
charlar
divertirse
encontrarse
enviar correo
 electrónico
escribir cartas
jugar juegos
llevarse bien / mal
navegar en la Red
participar
pasarlo bien
pasear
quedarse encasa
reunirse
reírse
salir

tiempo
antes (de)
después (de)
hasta
los días de semana
los fines de semana
los días festivos
durante
por la mañana
por la tarde
por la noche

 1

Cualidades que admiras

 ESCRIBIR

1 Escoge cinco cualidades que describan a tus amigos(as). Haz una lista. Compara tu lista con la de un(a) compañero(a). Luego, hagan juntos un diagrama de Venn para ver qué cualidades en común tienen sus amigos.

2 Con tu compañero(a) hablen por texto de las cualidades que sus amigos tienen en común y digan por qué las prefieren.

Modelo
Nos gustan las personas divertidas porque siempre lo pasamos bien con ellas.

160 ciento sesenta • Capítulo 4 • ¿Cómo te llevas con los demás?

Differentiated Instruction

Heritage Speakers

Invite students with exemplary pronunciation to read the vocabulary aloud as a pronunciation model. Point out any regional differences between certain pronunciations, such as /y/ or /zh/ for **ll** in the phrase **llevarse bien**.

Advanced Learners

Much of the review vocabulary can be applied to an animal, such as a pet, as well as a person. Ask students to use the vocabulary to write a brief paragraph about a pet or other animal they know: *Mi perro Jake es muy gracioso. Los fines de semana, vamos al parque y nos divertimos mucho jugando con su pelota.*

Go **Online** to practice
PEARSON
realize™
PearsonSchool.com/Autentico
▶ VIDEO ✎ WRITING

Recycle | **4**

Gramática

Otros usos de los verbos reflexivos

A verb is reflexive in Spanish when the subject receives the action of the verb. In English this is implied by the endings *-self* and *-selves.* In Spanish the reflexive pronouns are *me, te, se, nos, os, se.*

Ella **se** levanta.   *She gets **(herself)** up.*

- Many reflexive verbs in Spanish describe daily routine actions, such as *despertarse* (to wake up), *ducharse* (to take a shower), *peinarse* (to comb oneself), *vestirse* (to get dressed), and *acostarse* (to go to bed).
- Other reflexive verbs describe a physical or emotional state. Verbs of this type include *divertirse* (to enjoy oneself) and *sentirse* (to feel an emotion).
- Some reflexive verbs describe a change of state and they carry the added meaning of "to get" or "to become."

Me enojé.   *I became angry (got mad)*   **Se puso** muy nervioso.   *He became very nervous.*

- Some verbs have a different meaning when used reflexively.

ir	to go	irse	to leave	dormir	to sleep	dormirse	to fall asleep
parecer	to seem	parecerse a	to look like	quedar	to be located	quedarse	to stay
quitar	to take away	quitarse	to take off	volver	to return	volverse	to become
perder	to lose	perderse	to get lost				

- Other verbs such as *darse cuenta de* (to realize), *quejarse* (to complain), and *portarse bien* (to behave) are always reflexive.
- Placement of reflexive pronouns with commands and the present participle follow the same rules that apply to placement of direct and indirect object pronouns.

Más recursos ONLINE
▶ **Tutorial:** Reflexive pronouns

2

En familia

 ESCRIBIR Completa este párrafo con los verbos para describir lo que hace una familia los sábados.

Los sábados todos _1._ temprano. Mi hermano y mi papá _2._ con sus amigos a jugar al fútbol. Por la tarde, si hace buen tiempo, nadie quiere _3._ en casa. Todos vamos al parque a correr. A veces, después de correr, yo _4._ un poco pero nunca _5._. Lo pasamos muy bien.

quedarse
quejarse
levantarse
cansarse
irse

3

Los sábados

 ESCRIBIR Combina palabras de las dos listas para escribir lo que tú y tus amigos hacen los sábados.

Modelo
los chicos / reunirse
*Los chicos se reúnen **en la plaza.***

1.	mi amigo y yo	acostarse
2.	tú	divertirse
3.	los chicos	aburrirse
4.	yo	quedarse
5.	mi amiga	irse

Capítulo 4 • ciento sesenta y uno 161

Gramática: Repaso

Standards: 4.1

Suggestions: Refer students who are having difficulty with reflexive verbs to the online tutorial.

2

Standards: 1.2

Suggestions: Remind students that the verbs in the word bank are in the infinitive form, and therefore the reflexive pronoun **se** is attached to the end. They must detach the pronoun and adapt it and the verb form to suit the subject of the sentence, if necessary (see item 3).

Answers:
1. se levantan (nos levantamos)
2. se van
3. quedarse
4. me canso
5. me quejo

3

Standards: 1.3

Suggestions: Challenge students to compete with a partner and see who can come up with the most sentences in five minutes.

Answers will vary. Students may use the following verb forms:
1. nos acostamos/nos divertimos/nos aburrimos/nos quedamos/nos vamos
2. te acuestas/te diviertes/te aburres/te quedas/te vas
3. se acuestan/se divierten/se aburren/se quedan/se van
4. me acuesto/me divierto/me aburro/me quedo/me voy
5. se acuesta/se divierte/se aburre/se queda/se va

Vocabulario: Repaso

Standards: 1.1, 1.2

Suggestions: Hold a "gripe session" in which students think about a minor annoyance at school, work, or home. Ask them to prepare a few sentences about the annoyance, using vocabulary from as many of the categories as possible, and then share their gripe with the class.

 4

Standards: 1.3

Suggestions: Ask students to share what they have written. Encourage those listening to respond with an additional comment that makes sense, such as: *¡Uf! A mí también me molesta.*

Answers will vary.

 5

Standards: 1.1

Suggestions: Encourage students to speak with the intonation appropriate to the expression they are using.

Answers will vary. The following are suggestions:
1. ¡Déjame en paz!
2. A mí no me gusta lavar la ropa.
3. A mí tampoco.
4. Quédate tranquilo.
5. ¡Yo también!
6. Me estás volviendo loco(a).
7. Me estás poniendo nervioso(a).

A ver si recuerdas

OBJECTIVES
▶ Discuss emotions and reactions
▶ Write about personal relationships

Vocabulario

defectos
aburrido, -a
desordenado, -a
impaciente
infantil
mal educado, -a
perezoso, -a
tonto, -a

acciones
discutir
emocionarse
enojarse
gritar
importar
llorar
mentir
molestar
pelearse

reacciones
¡ay!
¡basta!
¡déjame en paz!
¡tú tampoco!
¡uf!
¡yo también!
a mí no...
a mí sí...
a mí también...
a mí tampoco...

expresiones
hablar mal (de)
llegar tarde
no pensar (en)
ponerse...
furioso, -a
nervioso, -a
quedarse
  tranquilo, -a
tener paciencia
volverse loco, -a

 4

Lo que no me gusta

ESCRIBIR Completa las frases siguientes para describir qué cosas te molestan de tus amigos.

Modelo
Me pongo nervioso(a) cuando...
*Me pongo nervioso(a) cuando **mi amiga no me llama**.*

1. Me molesta cuando...
2. No me gusta nada cuando...
3. Me enojo cuando...
4. Me pongo furioso(a) cuando...
5. Me vuelvo loco(a) cuando...

 5

Reacciona

 HABLAR EN PAREJA Trabaja con otro(a) estudiante para leer y reaccionar a los siguientes comentarios. Usa la lista de reacciones de arriba.

Videomodelo
A —Me gusta cuando la profesora está contenta con mi trabajo.
B —*A mí también.*

1. ¡Vamos! ¡Levántate, perezoso!
2. ¿Me ayudas a lavar la ropa?
3. No me gustan las fresas.
4. ¡Ten cuidado! ¡Ve más despacio!
5. ¿Al cine? ¡Sí, yo quiero ir!
6. Tengo prisa. Tenemos que llegar a las tres.
7. ¿Ya estudiaste para el examen? Dicen que va a ser difícil.

Differentiated Instruction

Bodily-Kinesthetic Learner

As you discuss conflicts and emotions, ask students to try to see situations from other people's points of view and to attempt to understand how they think and feel. Point out that paying attention to a person's body language will help them better identify that person's emotions. Invite them to share their ideas with the class.

Students with Learning Difficulties

Help students understand the concept of reciprocal actions. Invite pairs to briefly act out situations greeting someone or having a disagreement. Explain that the situations are reciprocal because both people participate. Explain that the English words "each other" signal reciprocal actions.

Gramática

Pronombres reflexivos en acciones recíprocas

To tell what people do to or for one another use the reciprocal pronouns *nos* and *se* before the first and third person plural of certain verbs.

Mis hermanos y yo no **nos** peleamos nunca.

Alonso y Fernanda **se** llaman todos los días, pero **se** ven muy poco.

In the case of a verbal phrase with an infinitive or a present participle, you may place the reciprocal pronoun either before the conjugated verb or attached to the infinitive or participle. Remember to place an accent in the third to last syllable when you add the reciprocal pronoun to a present participle.

Vamos a ver**nos** mañana.	Rodrigo y Luisa estaban abrazándo**se** en el jardín.
Nos vamos a ver mañana.	Rodrigo y Luisa **se** estaban abrazando en el jardín.

Here are some examples of reflexive verbs that are used reciprocally:

abrazarse	contarse	llamarse
ayudarse	entenderse	llevarse bien / mal
besarse	escribirse	pelearse
comprenderse	hablarse	saludarse
conocerse	leerse	verse

6

¿La pareja ideal?

 LEER, ESCRIBIR Romina siempre está hablando de la relación de su hermana Analía con su novio Nicolás. Completa las siguientes frases con el verbo que corresponda, en la forma correcta. Luego, resume en una frase qué opinas tú de la relación de esta pareja.

Analía y Nicolás...

1. _____ *(escribirse/ayudarse)* mensajes todas las mañanas.

2. _____ *(entenderse/hablarse)* muy bien y son muy felices.

3. Nunca _____ *(besarse/pelearse)* ni tienen opiniones diferentes.

4. Siempre _____ *(comprenderse/enojarse)* y _____ *(ayudarse/conocerse)*.

5. _____ *(llamarse/leerse)* todas las noches y hablan horas por teléfono.

6. _____ *(entenderse/verse)* todos los viernes y los sábados.

7. _____ *(conocerse/contarse)* desde hace muchos años.

8. _____ *(llevarse/saludarse)* muy bien.

Capítulo 4 • ciento sesenta y tres **163**

Gramática: Repaso

Suggestions: Refer students who are having difficulty with the concept of reciprocal actions to the online tutorials. Ask students to create sentences using verbs from the list at the end of the *Gramática*. If a sentence contains a verb phrase, have students practice using it both ways: with the reciprocal pronoun before the conjugated verb and with the pronoun attached to the end of the infinitive or present participle.

6

Standards: 1.3

Suggestions: Once students have written their answers, encourage them to read all the items through like a story, in order to be better able to comment on the relationship between Analía and Nicolás.

Answers:

1. Se escriben	5. Se llaman
2. Se entienden	6. Se ven
3. se pelean	7. Se conocen
4. se comprenden/se ayudan	8. Se llevan

Extension: Have students share the comments they wrote about the relationship between Analía and Nicolás. Encourage them to support their opinion with an additional comment.

Additional Resources

 Technology: Online Resources
- *A ver si recuerdas* with Remediation
- Guided, Core
- *Para hispanohablantes*
Print
- Guided WB pp. 114–117
- Core WB pp. 49–50

Assessment

***A ver si recuerdas* with Remediation (online only)**
After presenting the review material on these pages, assign the *A ver si recuerdas* with Remediation to evaluate students' mastery of the material. Additional practice for students who need it is available online.

Enrich Your Teaching

Teacher-to-Teacher

The vocabulary on these two pages is suitable to the complaints, discomforts, and frustrations that many of your students go through daily. Encourage them to think of expressions such as *¡Uf!, ¡Basta!,* and *¡Déjame en paz!* at trying times to promote connections between genuine emotion and language.

21st Century Skills

ICT (Information, Communications and Technology) Literacy Direct students to the various digital tools available in **Realize** to help them monitor their own understanding and learning needs, such as the online tutorials with comprehension check exercises. Students can review the related English grammar first, and then proceed to the new Spanish grammar point.

Can-Do Statements

Read the Can-Do Statements in the chapter objectives with students. Then, have students read *Preparación para el examen* on page 207 to preview what they will be able to do at the end of the chapter.

Standards for Capítulo 4

To meet the Standards, students will:

COMMUNICATION

1.1 Interpersonal
- Talk about friendship, interpersonal relationships, personality traits, emotions, customary behavior, conflict resolution
- Talk about known artists, musicians, and poets
- Talk about soap operas and poetry readings

1.2 Interpretive
- Read and listen to information about friendship, interpersonal relationships, personality traits, emotions, customary behavior, conflict resolution, family routines
- Read about known artists, musicians, and poets
- Read about word families
- Read about soap operas and poetry readings
- Read about bilingual children

1.3 Presentational
- Write about friendship, interpersonal relationships, personality traits, emotions, conflict resolution
- Write about a trip and a day out
- Recite song lyrics by Paulina Rubio
- Write about the theme of love in art
- Present information orally about student council
- Write about known poets and their work

CULTURE

2.1 Practices to Perspectives
- Explain artistic life in Puerto Rico
- Interpret Spanish personality demographics and Mexican family dynamics
- Explain the impact of love in Spanish-speaking cultures and their art
- Explain the practice of poetry readings in Spanish

2.2 Products to Perspectives
- Talk about known artists, musicians, and poets
- Talk about *telenovelas*

CONNECTIONS

3.1 Making Connections
- Talk about psychology, conflict resolution, and interpersonal dynamics
- Talk about known artists, musicians, and poets
- Work with percentages in surveys
- Describe holidays in Spain and Latin America
- Describe the history of the handshake
- Describe Spanish cities

CAPÍTULO 4

¿Cómo te llevas con los demás?

Country Connections Explorar el mundo hispano

España
México
El Salvador
Colombia
Chile
Argentina

CHAPTER OBJECTIVES

Communication

By the end of the chapter you will be able to:
- Listen and read about friendship and family relationships
- Talk and write about conflicts and solutions
- Express opinions and emotions while discussing problems

Culture

You will also be able to:
- Compare cultural practices in an authentic video about an adventure park in Puerto Rico
- Understand the relationship between emotions and art in the Hispanic world
- Compare how people express and react to others' emotions

You will demonstrate what you know and can do
- Presentación oral: Una sesión del consejo estudiantil
- Presentación escrita: Una relación

You will use

Vocabulary
- Personality traits
- Relationships
- Emotions and conflicts

Grammar
- Subjunctive with verbs of emotion
- Uses of *por* and *para*
- *Nosotros* commands
- Possessive pronouns

ARTE y CULTURA ▸ España

Madre e hijo La relación entre madre e hijo puede ser una relación muy íntima y especial. El artista español Pablo Picasso tiene una serie de cuadros de varios períodos y estilos que muestran las figuras de una madre y un hijo. En este cuadro se ve la influencia del arte africano. Las caras de las figuras se parecen a máscaras *(masks)* africanas. ¿Qué elementos usa Picasso para comunicar la relación entre estas dos personas?

▸ ¿Conoces a otro(a) artista que muestre relaciones entre familias? Descríbelo(a).

"Madre e hijo", (1907), Pablo Picasso ▸
© 2009 Estate of Pablo Picasso/Artists Rights Society (ARS), New York. Photo: © Réunion des Musées Nationaux/Art Resource, NY.

164 ciento sesenta y cuatro • Capítulo 4 • ¿Cómo te llevas con los demás?

Enrich Your Teaching

The End in Mind

Have students preview the sample performance tasks on *Preparación para el examen*, p. 207, and connect them to the Chapter Objectives. Explain to students that by completing the sample tasks, they can self-assess their learning progress.

Technology: Mapa global interactivo

Download the *Mapa global interactivo* files for Chapter 4 and preview the activities. In Activity 1, you travel the length of Judith Baca's mural wall in Los Angeles, CA. In Activity 2, you visit places where poet Pablo Neruda lived in Chile.

Una familia en Buenos Aires, Argentina

Videonovela ¡Pura vida!

Capítulo 4 • ciento sesenta y cinco **165**

- Discuss Language Arts strategies: compare and contrast, getting into your character, describing relationships, identifying and understanding figurative language
- Discuss conflict in fiction and drama

3.2 Acquiring information and Diverse Perspectives
- Read a Spanish youth survey
- Read poetry by known poets

COMPARISONS

4.1 Language
- Compare Spanish words to their English counterparts
- Compare English and Spanish reflexive verbs
- Compare *por* and *para* with English
- Compare *nosotros* commands with English

4.2 Cultural
- Compare Spanish and U.S. teen profiles
- Compare U.S. holidays and TV shows with those in Spanish-speaking countries
- Compare works of art

COMMUNITIES

5.1 School and Global Communities
- Link to Web sites from the Spanish-speaking world

5.2 Lifelong Learning
- Describe their own personalities
- Discuss techniques for conflict resolution
- Develop an appreciation for poetry
- Read an authentic Spanish-language text
- Listen to an authentic Spanish-language audio recording

Chapter Opener

Resources: Mapa global interactivo: Regional maps

Suggestions: Introduce students to the theme of the chapter and go over the objectives. Point out that they will learn language to help them deal with their own feelings and those of others. They will also learn about how people in other cultures deal with friends and family.

Technology: Videonovela ¡Pura vida! View this stand-alone storyline video about five young adults in San José, Costa Rica with your class.

ARTE Y CULTURA

Standards: 1.1, 1.2, 2.1, 2.2, 3.1

Suggestions: After students have read the information, ask: *¿Qué detalles nos muestran quién es la madre y quién es el hijo en la pintura?*

Project-Based Learning

Conflict Resolution
Have students take note of any conflicts or problems they encounter during the week and, if resolved, how a satisfactory outcome was reached. If the conflict is ongoing, direct students to write down possible solutions they might suggest. Have them use these notes to complete the role-play activity in *Presentación oral* on p.197.

Vocabulario en contexto 1

Standards: 1.2

Resources: Teacher's Resource Materials: Input Script, Clip Art, Audio Script, Technology: Audio Cap. 4

Suggestions: You may want to use the Input Script from the *Teacher's Resource Materials* as a source of ideas for presentation of new vocabulary and comprehensible input. Many meanings for the vocabulary in this lesson must be taught either via situations or by explanation. When explaining, use Spanish that students will readily understand:

Una persona egoísta sólo piensa en sí misma.

El joven de la foto es vanidoso, ¿verdad? Le gusta tomar fotos de si mismo todo el tiempo.

Starter Activity

Review the present subjunctive. On the board write the expressions **Es importante que…, Es bueno que…,** and **Quiero que….** Have students use these expressions in sentences about what a friend should and should not be or do. They can combine the expressions with vocabulary from pp. 160–162 and 166.

Active Classroom

In pairs, have students write a sentence describing each of the personality traits on pp. 166 and 167. Have them work with another pair, reading the descriptions to the other students who must guess the new vocabulary word.

Technology: Interactive Whiteboard

Vocabulary Activities 4-1 Use the whiteboard activities in your Teacher Resources as you progress through the vocabulary practice with your class.

Vocabulario en contexto 1

OBJECTIVES
Read, listen to, and understand information about
▶ Friendship
▶ Personality traits

🔊 La quinceañera

Una fiesta de quinceañera es la presentación formal de una niña que pasa a la edad adulta. Emilia tiene su quinceañera en unos días. Su amiga Victoria no vino para la prueba de su vestido. Emilia está triste y llama a su hermana mayor, Lola.

Emilia llamada 20 de febrero 08:00 AM

Emilia
Lola, ESTA FIESTA es el día MÁS IMPORTANTE de mi vida. ¡Es MI QUINCEAÑERA y creo que todos mis amigos **desconfían** de mí! **Temo** que no me **acepten tal como soy.**

Lola
NO ES ASÍ. Todos te quieren, Emilia.

Emilia
Victoria es mi **íntima** amiga. Hacemos muchas cosas **juntas** y **tenemos mucho en común,** pero ahora está **egoísta** y **celosa.** NO HA VENIDO HOY A AYUDARME.

Lola
Me sorprende. Victoria es muy **considerada** y **te apoya** en todo. Debes **confiar** en ella.

Emilia
Yo creía que mi amiga Mimí sabía **guardar un secreto.** Sin embargo, Victoria me dijo que es **entrometida** y **chismosa.**

Lola
Yo le tengo **confianza.** Mimí es **honesta** y **comprensiva.**

Emilia
Y mi amigo Joaquín siempre fue **cariñoso** conmigo. Desde que está con Cristina es **vanidoso** Y EGOÍSTA.

Lola
Pero es muy joven. Ojalá que cambie cuando sea un poco mayor.

166 ciento sesenta y seis • Capítulo 4 • ¿Cómo te llevas con los demás?

Differentiated Instruction

Students with Learning Difficulties

Invite students to identify the personality trait represented in each photograph on p. 166 and to use this information to figure out the meaning of some of the vocabulary words. For example: *Veo la foto del muchacho que está tomando su propia foto. Creo que "vanidoso" quiere decir* vain o stuck up.

Advanced Learners

Ask pairs of students to stretch their creativity by preparing two different pantomimes that show the meaning of each vocabulary item on this page. Have pairs present their pantomimes in random order. Those watching must guess which characteristic the partners are trying to portray.

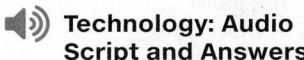
22 de febrero @ 05:00 PM

 ♡ 30

Para mi familia y mis amigos:

Quiero que todos sepan que tuve una fiesta maravillosa. Me gusta saber que mis amigos **se alegran** con las cosas buenas que me pasan. **La amistad** es muy importante en mi vida.

¡GRACIAS a todos los que compartieron este día inolvidable conmigo! ☺

—Emilia

1

¿Qué dicen Emilia y Lola?

 ESCUCHAR Escucha lo que opinian Emilia y Lola sobre estas personas. Escoge la respuesta apropiada.

1. Emilia quiere que sus amigos...
   a. desconfíen de ella
   b. la acepten como es

2. Lola piensa que Victoria es
   a. celosa
   b. considerada

3. Lola piensa que Mimí es
   a. entrometida
   b. honesta

4. Emilia dice que cuando Joaquín está con Cristina, es
   a. cariñoso
   b. vanidoso

2

Un(a) amigo(a) perfecto(a)

 ESCRIBIR, HABLAR EN PAREJA ¿Cuáles son para ti las cinco cualidades *(qualities)* más importantes que debe tener un(a) buen(a) amigo(a)? Haz una lista e intercámbiala con tu compañero(a).

Capítulo 4 • ciento sesenta y siete **167**

1

Standards: 1.2

Resources: Teacher's Resource Materials: Audio Script, Audio Program: Cap. 4

Suggestions: Before playing the audio or reading the script aloud, allow students to read over the dialogue.

 Technology: Audio Script and Answers

1. ¡Ay Lola! Estoy tan preocupada. Creo que mis amigos desconfían de mí. *(F)*
2. Victoria es tu buena amiga. Es una persona considerada. *(C)*
3. Creo que Mimí es honesta y comprensiva. *(F)*
4. Joaquín es egoísta y vanidoso cuando está con Cristina. *(C)*

2

Standards: 1.1, 1.3

Suggestions: Ask students to use vocabulary from both this and the previous page in their lists. Point out that they will have to vary the types of sentences they use. Not all sentences can have the "subject + verb + complement" structure.

Answers will vary.

Extension: Have students use the lists as a vehicle for discussion. Then they can compile the qualities into a whole-class list and report on their ideal friend.

Enrich Your Teaching

Culture Note

Explain that, as in the United States, Spanish-speaking people have varying attitudes toward punctuality. Some are sticklers and may label the person as being inconsiderate, but others have a more relaxed attitude. Arriving "fashionably late" to social occasions is usually considered acceptable behavior and rarely causes annoyance.

21st Century Skills

Media Literacy Have students research social networks that use Spanish as the target language. What keywords will they use in their search? Which social networks are most popular in different parts of the Spanish-speaking world? How do they compare to the social networks they use?

Vocabulario en contexto 1

Standards: 1.2

Resources: Teacher's Resource Materials: Input Script, Clip Art, Audio Script, Technology: Audio Cap. 4

Suggestions: Model the dialogue with a volunteer. Begin the reading again with volunteers playing the roles of Emilia and Victoria. Help students understand the new words in blue type.

Post-reading: Complete Actividad 3 to check comprehension.

3

Standards: 1.2

Suggestions: You may wish to do this as a listening activity, reading the sentences to the students.

Extension: Have students correct the false statements.

Answers: 1. C; 2. F; 3. C; 4. F

4

Standards: 1.1, 1.2, 1.3

Suggestions: If students have difficulty naming celebrations similar to the *Quinceañera,* you may wish to write the following suggestions on the board: a sweet sixteen party, a Bar Mitzvah, or a wedding. Then have students discuss the similarities and differences.

Pre-AP® Integration

- **Learning Objective:** Interpersonal Writing
- **Activity:** Have students write an e-mail to a good friend in which they express how much they value his or her friendship. Use the card in Activity 3 as a model.
- **Pre-AP® Resource Materials:** Comprehensive guide to Pre-AP® writing skill development

Performanced-Based Learning Project

Give students copies of the project outline and rubric from the *Teacher's Resource Materials.* Explain the task to them, and have them perform Step 1. (For more information, see p. 160-b.)

 ¡Emilia y Victoria tienen mucho qué comentar sobre la fiesta del día anterior! Apenas se despierta, Victoria le manda un mensaje a Emilia.

Emilia

Victoria: ¡Qué fiesta la de anoche! ☺

Emilia: Sí. Después de tanto preocuparme, salió perfecta. ¡Todo el mundo fue tan **amable** conmigo!

Victoria: ¡Tu vestido me encantó! Te veías muy linda.

Emilia: ¡Gracias! Una de las **cualidades** que más me gustan de ti es que te alegras de todo lo bueno que les pasa a tus amigos.

Victoria: No creas, a veces puedo **tener celos**. Sobre todo, si un chico que me gusta baila con mi mejor amiga.

Emilia: Ja, ja. ¿Lo dices por Mario? ¡Si solo bailé una vez con él!

Victoria: Sí, no te preocupes, no hablaba en serio. ☺

Emilia: ¿Quieres venir a mi casa en un rato? Así te puedo mostrar las fotos que tomó mi papá. ¡Están buenísimas!

Victoria: Gracias, pero estoy cansada. ¡Me duelen los pies de tanto bailar!

Emilia: Me imagino, porque no te quedaste quieta ni un minuto. Pero si **cambias de opinión**, me avisas. Voy a estar en casa todo el día.

3

 Comentarios sobre la fiesta

ESCRIBIR Lee las frases. Escribe *C* (cierto) si la frase es correcta o *F* (falso) si la frase es incorrecta.

1. Emilia quedó muy contenta con su fiesta de quinceañera.
2. Los invitados a la fiesta no fueron amables con Emilia.
3. A Victoria le gustó el vestido de Emilia.
4. Victoria aceptó ir a la casa de Emilia a ver las fotos.

4

 HABLAR La fiesta de quinceañera en muchos países latinos marca la transición de niña a mujer. Comenta con un compañero qué ritos, fiestas o celebraciones conocen que marquen la transición de niño a hombre o de niña a mujer en distintas culturas.

Differentiated Instruction

Students with Learning Difficulties

Use the chat between Victoria and Lola to review the subjunctive in context. Ask students to identify where the subjunctive is used. Challenge them to explain why the subjunctive is used in these cases and assist as needed.

Advanced Learners

Invite students to evaluate whether or not they think Emilia is a good friend to Victoria. Ask them to identify Victoria's traits and point out examples from the chat and the Vocabulario en contexto that support their opinions.

Go **Online** to practice
PEARSON
realize™
PearsonSchool.com/Autentico
AUDIO VIDEO WRITING SCRIPT

Unidos por una causa

Tecnología: Video

Standards: 1.2

Resources: Teacher's Resource Materials: Video Script

Antes de ver

Identificar a los personajes Al ver el video, concéntrate en identificar a los personajes *(characters)* y definir qué relación hay entre ellos. Esto te ayudará a entender mejor los sucesos *(events)* que se narran.

Haz la actividad

¿Qué relación tienen? Observa las fotos. ¿Qué crees que están haciendo estos chicos? ¿Qué actividad en común los une? Escribe un párrafo corto en español en el que digas qué tipo de relación podrían tener.

Antes de ver

Review the previewing strategy and activity with the students. Discuss the importance of identifying the characters, their personalities, and the connection they have. While viewing the video, ask students to pay special attention to the common interest, event, or activity the characters share.

Ve el video

▶ **Ve el video**

Valentina, Camila, Seba, Teo y Ximena participaron en un programa de voluntarios en Costa Rica. Hoy dan su testimonio de la experiencia que vivieron.

Ve a **PearsonSchool.com/Autentico** para ver el video *Unidos por una causa.* También puedes leer el guión.

Teo
Camila
Seba
Valentina
Ximena

Show the video once without pausing. Ask volunteers to identify the characters and their relationship. Show the video again, asking students to pay attention to the characters' body language, the video images, and the context of the conversation to infer the meaning of unfamiliar words and phrases. Pause the video from time to time to ask specific details about each character.

Después de ver

Standards: 1.2

Suggestions: Since the first question consists of paraphrasing important details, the answers will vary depending on comprehension and personal point of view.

Answers

1. Valentina: hizo buenos amigos; Camila: aprendió a ver otra perspectiva; Seba: perdió el miedo a las aventuras; Teo: conoció otras culturas; Ximena: ayudó a crear un mundo mejor
2. Answers will vary.
3. Answers will vary.
4. animar a otros jóvenes a que se unan al programa

Nuevas amistades: Answers will vary.

Have students go to **Realize** for additional video activities.

Después de ver

 ESCRIBIR Contesta las siguientes preguntas:

1. Parafrasea un detalle importante sobre la experiencia de cada chico(a).
2. Escribe un adjetivo que describa la personalidad de cada chico(a).
3. Seba dijo que este programa lo ayudó a ser menos egoísta. ¿Por qué crees que le pasó esto?
4. ¿Cuál fue el objetivo de los chicos al hacer el video sobre el programa?

Nuevas amistades Los chicos del video se hicieron amigos al trabajar como voluntarios. ¿Qué otros tipos de experiencias pueden ayudar a un(a) chico(a) a hacer nuevas amistades?

Capítulo 4 • ciento sesenta y nueve **169**

Additional Resources

 Technology: Online Resources
• Instant Check
• Guided, Core, Video, Audio
• *Para hispanohablantes*
Print
• Guided WB pp. 118–124
• Core WB pp. 51–52
• Authentic Resources Workbook

Assessment

Quiz: Vocabulary Recognition
• Prueba 4-1

Enrich Your Teaching

Teacher to Teacher

Guide students to analyze the meaning of *codo a codo*, the name of the organization mentioned in the video. First, call on volunteers to identify the meaning of *codo* (elbow). Then lead students to infer that *codo a codo* would be similar to *shoulder-to-shoulder*, or *side-by-side*.

Culture Note

There are several non-profit organizations that encourage young people to volunteer in international programs while making friends from around the world. Habitat for Humanity, the organization that builds homes for people in need, has programs in Costa Rica and many other countries in Central and South America.

5

Standards: 1.2

Recycle: Subjunctive forms

Suggestions: Remind students that the items, when put together, form a letter. Tell them to scan all the items first, so that they understand the situation before attempting to complete the activity.

Answers:

1. Me preocupa
2. Es una lástima
3. Es una lástima
4. Me enoja
5. Espero
6. Es triste
7. Ojalá
8. Espero

6

Standards: 1.1

Suggestions: Point out to students that the picture clues are only to elicit the various personality traits. Student B's response can be affirmative or negative. Encourage Student B to respond honestly. Make sure students switch roles, so everyone has a chance to practice both parts of the dialogue.

Answers: Student B's responses will vary. The following are possibilities for Student A's questions:

1. —Eres generoso(a), ¿verdad?
2. —... comprensivo(a), ...
3. —... honesto(a), ...
4. —... egoísta/vanidoso(a), ...
5. —... chismoso(a), ...

Teacher-to-Teacher

Tell students they are moving to a new community and have been given the name of a teen who lives there. Have them write an e-mail to socialize with this person and to seek information about the community. They should give basic information about themselves. Have them exchange e-mails and write responses. Collect the e-mails for assessment.

Vocabulario en uso 1

OBJECTIVES
▶ Read and write about relationships and personality traits
▶ Discuss friendships and family relationships
▶ Talk about your views of friendship and those of young people in Spain

5

Una carta para alguien que fue mi amigo

LEER, ESCRIBIR Federico y Roberto eran amigos íntimos hasta que se pelearon. Roberto no confía en los consejos de Federico. Cree que está celoso por su relación con Teresa, que es amiga de los dos. Lee estas frases de una carta que le escribió Federico a Roberto. Escoge las palabras que completan mejor cada frase.

1. *(Me preocupa / Me alegro de)* que no me aceptes tal como soy.
2. *(Es una lástima / Me alegro de)* que desconfíes de mí.
3. *(Es una lástima / Es bueno)* que no me comprendas.
4. *(Me alegro de / Me enoja)* que siempre cambies de opinión.
5. *(Me sorprende / Espero)* que sepas que no tengo celos.
6. *(Es triste / Es bueno)* que no nos llevemos bien.
7. *(Me alegro de / Ojalá)* que no rompamos nuestra amistad.
8. *(Espero / Temo)* que todos salgamos juntos otra vez.

6

¿Cómo te relacionas con los demás?

HABLAR EN PAREJA Trabaja con otro(a) estudiante para hablar de su relación con los amigos. Usen las fotos.

 Videomodelo
A —*Eres cariñoso(a), ¿verdad?*
B —*¡Claro que sí!, soy muy cariñoso(a).*
o:—*No, no lo soy.*
o:—*Pues, sí, a veces.*

Estudiante A

Estudiante B

¡Respuesta personal!

Differentiated Instruction

Bodily/Kinesthetic Learner

Invite students to incorporate actions or gestures into their descriptions in *Actividad* 6.

Challenge/Pre-AP®

Have students write a brief sketch of a character from a popular film or TV show. Ask them not to give away the title of the film or show or name the character, but to describe only his or her personality. Have students share their character sketches. Those listening can try to guess who the character is.

7

Amistad y cualidades

ESCRIBIR, HABLAR EN PAREJA

1 Escribe un verbo o una expresión que relacionas con cada una de estas cualidades.

Modelo
amable
ayudar a los demás

1. vanidoso(a)
2. perezoso(a)
3. entrometido(a)
4. celoso(a)
5. sincero(a)
6. considerado(a)

2 Trabaja con otro(a) estudiante para hablar de las cualidades y los verbos o las expresiones que relacionas con la amistad.

Videomodelo
A —*¿Te gusta estar con personas amables?*
B —*Sí, porque siempre se preocupan por los demás.*

3 Ahora tú y tu compañero(a) deben escoger una cualidad y escribir un párrafo sobre una persona que tenga esa cualidad.

Modelo
Luisa es muy amable porque ...

Ampliación del lenguaje Familias de palabras

Las familias de palabras son grupos de palabras relacionadas *(related)* por tener una misma raíz. Conocer familias de palabras nos ayuda a comprender mejor el significado individual de cada palabra. Para ampliar tu vocabulario debes aprender a reconocer *(recognize)* palabras que tienen la misma raíz, por ejemplo, *celos y celoso.*

Lee las familias de palabras de la tabla. Piensa en palabras que conoces, que pertenecen a esas familias. Escribe en una hoja de papel las palabras que faltan para llenar los recuadros.

Sustantivos	Adjetivos	Verbos
1. comprensión		comprender
2. alegría	alegre	
3. chisme	chismoso(a)	chismosear
4. consideración		considerar
5. sorpresa	sorprendido(a)	sorprenderse
6. reconciliación	reconciliado(a)	reconciliarse

Luego, completa las frases utilizando la palabra correcta:

1. Carlos cuenta muchos _____, por eso todos dicen que es un _____.
2. Me encanta ir a las fiestas con María, pues es muy _____. Siempre me da _____ estar con ella.
3. Mi amigo se _____ mucho cuando le hicimos una fiesta _____.

Capítulo 4 • ciento setenta y uno **171**

7

Suggestions: As students share their work in Step 2, encourage them to use additional verbs and expressions that pertain to each character trait. Point out that the more verbs and expressions they can think of, the more they will have to say about the person they write about in Step 3.
Answers will vary.

AMPLIACIÓN DEL LENGUAJE

Suggestions: Encourage students to copy the chart into their notebooks and make their additions there. Have them leave room, both horizontally and vertically, so they can add more word families and parts of speech at a later date.

Answers:
Chart
1. comprensivo (a)
2. alegrar
4. considerado (a)
Sentences
1. chismes/chismoso
2. alegre/alegría
3. sorprendió/sorpresa

Extension: Ask students to add a fourth column to their charts and title it **Adverbios.** Using background knowledge and dictionaries, have them work together to add adverbs to the word families on the chart. Model adding one adverb, such as **sorprendentemente.** Remind students that almost all Spanish adverbs end with the suffix **-mente.** Point out that not all word families in the chart will have an accompanying adverb.

Enrich Your Teaching

Teacher-to-Teacher

Consistent work with word families is an excellent way for students to increase their vocabularies on their own. Suggest that they devote an entire section of their notebooks to a word family chart like the one they began in the **Ampliación del lenguaje.**

Each week, encourage them to spend a few minutes adding words they have learned to families that already exist on their chart or sitting with a dictionary and building new word families around words of their choice.

Starter Activity

On the board, write numerical sentences and have students read them aloud. For example, "26 ÷ 100 = 0.26 (26%)" reads: *Veintiséis dividido por cien son cero punto veintiséis (o veintiséis por ciento).*

8

Standards: 1.1, 1.2, 3.1, 3.2

Suggestions: For Step 1, have students form questions to ask the class, such as (for the first survey): *¿Te consideras una persona sincera?* Have students answer each question clearly, restating the character trait to avoid confusion: *Sí, soy sincero(a).* Have them write their answers on blind ballots—folded slips of paper collected in a hat or other container. Ask volunteers to count the ballots for each question and tally the results on the board.

Common Errors: Without guidance, students would use the standard definite articles **el** and **la** instead of the neutral form **lo** in expressions like **ni lo uno ni lo otro.** Use this opportunity to habituate them to the sound and practice of using the neutral **lo.**

Answers will vary.

8

Los jóvenes viéndose a sí mismos

 LEER, HABLAR EN GRUPO, ESCRIBIR Se hizo la siguiente encuesta a jóvenes de España, para saber qué piensan sobre las cualidades de sinceridad, solidaridad y generosidad. Lee los resultados.

Encuesta sobre las cualidades de los jóvenes
¿Cuál de las siguientes cualidades define mejor a los jóvenes de hoy?

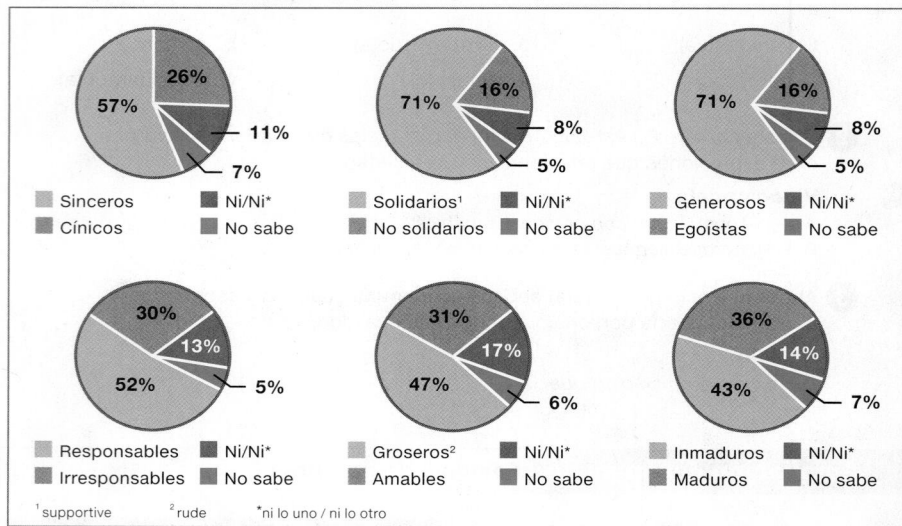

¹ supportive ² rude *ni lo uno / ni lo otro

Conexiones ◀ **Las matemáticas**

Trabaja en grupo. Hagan una encuesta a sus compañeros y comparen las respuestas de los jóvenes españoles con las de su clase.

1 Escojan un grupo de cualidades y pregúntenles a sus compañeros(as) si piensan que describen a los jóvenes de hoy.

2 Pasen los resultados a porcentajes para poder compararlos con la encuesta española. Recuerden que, para pasar los resultados de una encuesta a porcentajes, deben seguir los siguientes pasos:
Tomar el número de respuestas que quieren convertir y dividirlo por el número total de entrevistados. Luego, multiplicar el resultado por 100.

3 Comenten los resultados de las encuestas. ¿Los jóvenes de España son más o menos sinceros / solidarios / generosos que los de su clase?

Differentiated Instruction

Students with Learning Difficulties

Prepare students to understand and manipulate the information in the pie charts in *Actividad* 8. Explain that each piece of a pie chart represents a percentage or part of the total number of responses. The total of all the pieces adds up to 100 percent, which is represented by the complete circle.

Advanced Learners

Once groups complete their surveys, invite students to present visually the information that they have collected. They might show comparisons of percentages from each study through bar graphs or other graphic organizers.

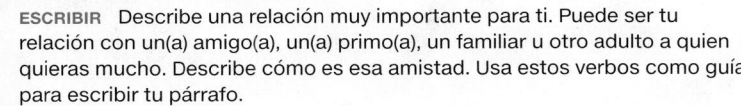
CULTURA ‹ El mundo hispano

El Día de la Rosa y del Libro Muchas tradiciones de los países hispanohablantes celebran el amor y la amistad. Por ejemplo, en Cataluña, España, se celebra el Día de la Rosa y del Libro el 23 de abril. Ese día los chicos le regalan a su novia una rosa roja, y las chicas le regalan a su novio un libro.

En algunos países latinoamericanos el Día de San Valentín, en lugar de ser el "Día de los Enamorados", es el "Día de la Amistad", y los amigos y familiares se hacen regalos y se escriben postales.

Pre-AP® Integration: Las tradiciones y los valores sociales ¿Crees que celebrar el día de la amistad o el amor tiene un impacto socio-económico en Estados Unidos? Da un ejemplo.

9
Retrato de una amistad

 ESCRIBIR Describe una relación muy importante para ti. Puede ser tu relación con un(a) amigo(a), un(a) primo(a), un familiar u otro adulto a quien quieras mucho. Describe cómo es esa amistad. Usa estos verbos como guía para escribir tu párrafo.

- conocerse
- escribirse
- contar con
- llamarse por teléfono
- enviarse mensajes electrónicos
- confiar
- apoyarse
- ayudarse
- llevarse bien
- tener en común

Modelo
Carlos y yo nos conocimos en . . . Vivíamos en el mismo barrio, pero cuando yo tenía 11 años, mi familia y yo tuvimos que irnos a . . . Ahora . . .

10
Un personaje

 ESCRIBIR Cuenta un hecho o describe a un personaje de un libro o de una película que sea un buen ejemplo de alguna de estas cualidades.

  a. cariñoso(a)   **b.** chismoso(a)   **c.** comprensivo(a)   **d.** honesto(a)

Incluye:
- sus cualidades
- cómo trata a las otras personas
- ejemplos de sus acciones

Modelo
Uno de los personajes se llama Luis. Es muy amable, generoso y divertido. Sus amigos tienen mucha confianza en él.

Capítulo 4 • ciento setenta y tres **173**

CULTURA ‹

Standards: 1.1, 1.2, 4.2

Resources: Mapa global interactivo
Suggestions: Have students locate **Cataluña** on a map of Spain. Ask: *¿Qué piensas de la costumbre del Día de la Rosa y del Libro? Imagínate que vives en Barcelona, España. ¿Te gustaría recibir un libro o una rosa en este día? ¿Cómo te sentirías?* Ask students what they think are the differences between Valentine's Day in the United States and in Latin America.

Answers will vary but should include an example that supports students' opinion.

9

Standards: 1.3

Suggestions: Remind students to use the present tense to describe the relationship and past tenses to tell about its history and how it developed.

10

Standards: 1.3

Suggestions: Ask students to share their descriptions.

Additional Resources

 Technology: Online Resources
- Guided, Core, Audio
- Communication Activities

Teacher Resources
- Teacher's Resource Materials: Audio Script, Technology: Audio Cap. 4, Communicative Pair Activity

Assessment

Prueba 4-2 with Remediation (online only)
Prueba: Aplicación del vocabulario 1
- Prueba 4-2

Enrich Your Teaching

Teacher-to-Teacher

In some subtle ways, functioning in a foreign language is like becoming a slightly different person. By Spanish 3, some students are becoming aware of how careful attention to the demands of Spanish causes them to think in different ways. You may find students in your class who are capable of talking in Spanish about topics they would not normally broach in English. This can be one of the greatest rewards a student earns after several years of language study. Praise and encourage students who demonstrate this.

Gramática: Repaso

Suggestions: Have students use the phrases in sentences with the subjunctive. Reinforce the idea of using the subjunctive with verbs of emotion by having students "act out" the expressions.

 Technology: Interactive Whiteboard

Grammar Activities 4-1 Use the whiteboard activities in your Teacher Resources as you progress through the grammar practice with your class.

11

Standards: 1.1, 1.2, 1.3

Resources: Teacher's Resource Materials: Audio Script, Technology: audio Cap. 4

Suggestions: Have volunteers write their sentences on the board with all the markings.

Answers:

Step 1
1. <u>Temo</u> que Luis (vaya) solo a la fiesta.
2. Me <u>preocupa</u> que Carmen todavía no (esté) en su casa.
3. <u>Espero</u> <u>alegrar</u> a Renata con el regalo.
4. <u>Siento</u> no <u>poder</u> ir al cine con tus amigos.
5. Ojalá que me (acepten) tal como <u>soy</u>.

Step 2
1. subjuntivo después de un verbo de emoción con cambio de sujeto
2. subjuntivo después de un verbo de emoción con cambio de sujeto
3. infinitivo con un solo sujeto
4. infinitivo con un solo sujeto
5. subjuntivo después de la expresión de emoción *ojalá*

12

Standards: 1.2

Suggestions: Have students scan the email before writing their answers.

Answers:
1. sea
2. se cuenten
3. desconfíe
4. tenga
5. lleve
6. se sienta

Gramática

OBJECTIVES
▶ Listen to a description of friendship
▶ Discuss emotions and problems in relationships
▶ Talk about the practice of shaking hands

El subjuntivo con verbos de emoción

As you already know, we use the subjunctive after verbs indicating suggestions, desire, or demands. The subjunctive is also used after verbs and impersonal phrases indicating emotion, such as *ojalá que, temo que, tengo miedo de que, me alegro de que, me molesta que, me sorprende que, siento que, es triste que,* and *es bueno que,* among others. A sentence in the subjunctive mode has two parts, the main clause and the subordinate clause. Both clauses are connected by the word *que.*

> **Tememos que** nuestros amigos **desconfíen** de nuestras palabras.

When the sentence has only one subject, we usually use the infinitive instead of the subjunctive.

> Siento no **pasar** (yo) más tiempo con mis amigas. Siento que ellas no **pasen** más tiempo conmigo.

Más recursos ONLINE

 Tutorial: Subjunctive in Noun Clauses with Verbs of Feeling and Emotions

🔊 **Canción de hip hop:** *¿Cómo te llevas?*

11

Una amiga muy cariñosa

🔊 ESCUCHAR, ESCRIBIR   Alina es una amiga muy cariñosa, aunque a veces se preocupa demasiado por todos. Escribe los números del 1 al 5 en una hoja de papel. Presta atención a lo que dice Alina y escribe las frases que escuchas.

1 Subraya con una línea los verbos en indicativo en cada frase. Subraya con dos líneas los verbos en infinitivo y encierra en un círculo los verbos en subjuntivo.

2 Explica por qué se usó el infinitivo, el indicativo o el subjuntivo.

12

Una relación complicada

✏️ LEER, ESCRIBIR   Soledad, una joven chilena, le escribió una carta a la consejera sentimental de una revista para jóvenes. Soledad se está llevando muy mal con su hermana y no sabe qué hacer. Completa la carta con el subjuntivo de los verbos del recuadro.

ser	tener
contarse	sentirse
desconfiar	llevar

> Querida Consejera:
>
> Te escribo porque mi hermana Tatiana y yo nos estamos llevando muy mal. Me preocupa que nuestra relación ya no __1.__ como antes. Creo que es importante que dos hermanas __2.__ sus problemas y sus secretos. Pero ahora temo que ella __3.__ de mí. Tatiana tiene doce años. Yo tengo quince años. A ella le molesta que yo __4.__ otros amigos de mi edad y no le gusta que yo no la __5.__ con nosotros cada vez que salimos. Es una lástima que ella __6.__ celosa de mis amigos. ¿Qué me aconsejas?

Differentiated Instruction

Students with Learning Difficulties

Prepare students for the discussion of main and subordinate clauses with the subjunctive. On the board, write English sentences, such as *She's angry that you're late. I'm afraid that we have bad news.* Explain the concepts of subject and verb and point them out in each clause.

Advanced Learners

Ask students to write the impersonal phrases that indicate emotion (see *Actividad* 13) on slips of paper and place them in a hat or other container. They can make several duplicate slips for each phrase. Have students sit in a circle and take turns drawing a phrase and using it in a sentence with the subjunctive.

13

Díganlo de dos maneras

HABLAR EN PAREJA Trabaja con un(a) compañero(a) para hablar de las relaciones con sus amigos. Tú dices frases generales usando el infinitivo y tu compañero(a) te contesta usando el subjuntivo.

Videomodelo

importante / guardar secretos
me molesta / mi amigo(a) no . . .

A —*Es importante guardar secretos.*
B —*Sí, y me molesta que mi amigo(a) no guarde mis secretos.*

Estudiante A

1. bueno / tener mucho en común con los amigos
2. malo / tener celos de los amigos
3. importante / aceptar a los demás tal como son
4. triste / desconfiar de los amigos íntimos
5. difícil / tener buenas relaciones con los amigos

Estudiante B

a. siento / mi amigo(a) y yo no . . .
b. me sorprende / mi amigo(a) . . .
c. me preocupa / tú no me . . .
d. siento / mi amigo(a) . . .
e. ojalá / todos nosotros . . .

14

Apoya a tus amigos

ESCRIBIR, HABLAR EN PAREJA

1 Con un(a) compañero(a), hagan una lista de ocho problemas que generalmente ocurren entre amigos o familiares.

Modelo
se pelean

2 Habla con tu compañero(a) de los problemas que incluyeron en la lista. Tu compañero(a) va a responder usando expresiones de emoción, gestos y en un tono apropiado.

Videomodelo

A —*Siempre me peleo con [nombre], él (ella) no me entiende.*
B —*Siento mucho que él (ella) no te entienda.*

Capítulo 4 • ciento setenta y cinco **175**

13

Standards: 1.1

Suggestions: Remind students that the determining factor for whether they use the subjunctive or an infinitive is the number of subjects in the sentence.

Answers:

1. A — Es bueno tener mucho en común con los amigos.
   B — Sí, y siento que mi amigo(a) (nombre) y yo no tengamos mucho en común.
2. A — Es malo tener ...
   B — Sí, y me sorprende que mi amigo (a) (nombre) tenga ...
3. A — Es importante aceptar ...
   B — Sí, y me preocupa que tú no me aceptes...
4. A — Es triste desconfiar ...
   B — Sí, y siento que mi amigo (a) (nombre) desconfíe ...
5. A — Es difícil tener ...
   B — Ojalá que todos nosotros tengamos...

14

Standards: 1.1

Suggestions: Ask students to "ham it up" and present one of their exchanges to the class in the form of a vignette. Encourage them to exaggerate the emotions they are portraying.

Answers will vary.

Project-Based Learning

Students can perform Step 2 at this point. Be sure they understand your corrections and suggestions. (For more information, see p. 160-b.)

Enrich Your Teaching

Teacher-to-Teacher

Have students fill out two strips of paper: one with a sentence like Student A used in *Actividad 13,* and the other with a sentence along the lines of Student B's responses. Mix them up and have each student draw one. Have students circulate and say their sentences until they find who has their corresponding sentence.

21st Century Skills

ICT (Information, Communications and Technology) Literacy Direct students to the online tutorials available in **Realize** for self-directed review of the subjunctive, its formation and uses. Students can expand their own learning by reviewing the uses of the subjunctive and doing extra verb conjugation practice on their own.

Starter Activity

Help students review negative personality traits that they will be able to use in *Actividad* 15. Have them complete the following two phrases: ***No me gusta cuando un(a) amigo(a) es... Me gusta cuando un(a) amigo(a) es....*** For the first sentence, pantomime and use gestures to elicit answers such as ***impaciente, infantil,*** or ***mal educado(a).*** Then have students complete the second sentence with the antonym of the word used in the first.

15

Standards: 1.1, 1.3

Suggestions: Ask the student pairs to prepare the chart on their own paper and to work out any comprehension problems they have with the questions in Step 1, before they interview classmates.

Answers will vary.

16

Standards: 1.1, 1.2, 3.1

Suggestions: After students have read the information once, ask them to list the cognates that helped them understand the reading. They should mention words such as ***personas, historiadores, estatua,*** and ***costumbre.***
Answers will vary.

Assessment

Prueba 4-3 with Remediation (online only)
Prueba: El subjuntivo con verbos de emoción
• Prueba 4-3

15

¿Qué te parece?

ESCRIBIR, HABLAR EN GRUPO

1 Trabaja con un(a) compañero(a) para entrevistar a cuatro estudiantes con las siguientes preguntas. Copien la tabla y complétenla con las respuestas de sus compañeros(as).

• ¿Cómo te gusta que sea tu mejor amigo(a)?
• ¿Qué no te gusta que haga tu mejor amigo(a)?
• ¿Qué te preocupa que opinen tus amigos(as) de ti?
• ¿Qué puede destruir una amistad?
• ¿Cuál es tu mejor cualidad como amigo(a)?

2 Luego, preparen una presentación para hacer ante la clase. Usen los resultados de la encuesta para apoyar sus opiniones y expliquen qué cualidades y acciones pueden fomentar *(foster)* o destruir una amistad.

	Marisa	Rafa	Luis	Ana
¿Cómo te gusta que sea . . . ?	generoso(a), comprensivo(a)			
¿Qué no te gusta . . . ?	que no me tenga confianza			
¿Qué te preocupa . . . ?				
¿Qué puede destruir . . . ?				
¿Cuál es tu mejor . . . ?				

16

Dar la mano

LEER, HABLAR ¿Sabes de dónde sale la costumbre de dar la mano para saludarse? Lee este artículo para enterarte.

> **Conexiones** ◂ **Las ciencias sociales**
>
> Nadie sabe realmente cuándo o por qué las personas comenzaron a darse la mano para saludarse. Algunos historiadores creen que todo comenzó hace 3800 años, en Babilonia. El primer día de cada año, el rey tenía que "darle la mano" a la estatua de un dios para recibir el poder *(power)*.
>
> Otros piensan que la costumbre comenzó por otra razón. Dicen que cuando dos desconocidos se encontraban en un camino o en un lugar fuera de la ciudad, se daban la mano derecha para mostrar que no tenían armas. En esos tiempos, como las mujeres no usaban armas, solo los hombres se daban la mano.

• ¿Cómo saludas a tus amigos? ¿Y a tus familiares? ¿Les das la mano? ¿Cuándo le das la mano a alguien y cuándo lo (la) abrazas?
• ¿Conoces otros gestos o palabras de saludo? ¿Sabes cuál es su origen? Explícalo a la clase.
• Conversa con tu pareja y usen los gestos apropiados. Empiecen con un saludo.

176 ciento setenta y seis • Capítulo 4 • ¿Cómo te llevas con los demás?

Differentiated Instruction

Heritage Speakers

Ask students to talk about how their family members use handshakes, kisses, or hugs to greet each other and friends, or to say good-bye. Encourage them to compare these practices with greeting and leave-taking customs in the United States.

Students with Learning Difficulties

Refer students to the list of uses for ***por*** and ***para*** as they complete *Actividad* 17. Encourage them to identify the point that explains each use of ***por*** and ***para.***

Gramática Repaso

OBJECTIVES
▶ Write and talk about friendship
▶ Discuss a conflict from different points of view

Go **Online** to practice
PEARSON
realize™
PearsonSchool.com/Autentico
VIDEO   WRITING   SPEAK/RECORD

Los usos de *por* y *para*

Both *por* and *para* are prepositions. Their usages are quite different.

Use *por* to indicate:

• length of time or distance
  Estuvieron discutiendo **por** una hora.

• place where an action takes place
  Ayer caminamos **por** el parque.

• an exchange
  Cambiamos la silla vieja **por** una nueva.

• reason or motive
  Se pelearon **por** un programa de televisión.

• substitution or action on someone's behalf
  Los padres hacen mucho **por** sus hijos.

• means of communication / transportation
  Ayer hablé con Analía **por** teléfono.

Also use *por* in certain expressions:

por ejemplo	por lo general
por la mañana (tarde, noche)	por primera (segunda) vez
por favor	por supuesto
por eso	

Use *para* to indicate:

• purpose (in order to)
  Salí temprano **para** ver a mis amigos.

• destination
  En unos minutos nos vamos **para** la playa.

• a point in time, deadline
  Debemos terminar el trabajo **para** el lunes.

• use, purpose
  Las tijeras sirven **para** cortar.

• opinion
  Para mí, no hay nada mejor que viajar.

Más recursos ONLINE

▶ Tutorial: *Por* and *para*

17

Cosas de amigas

HABLAR EN PAREJA, ESCRIBIR Hablas con un amigo(a). Completa las frases con *por* o *para*, según el contexto.

A — ¡Claro que sí! _1._ supuesto que quiero ir a la fiesta. Mañana _2._ la tarde vamos a llamar a los chicos _3._ ver si quieren ir con nosotras.

B — ¿Qué te parece si hacemos la tarea de español antes? No quiero perderme la fiesta _4._ tener que estudiar.

A — Sí, podemos pasar _5._ la casa de Anita _6._ preparar la tarea todas juntas.

18

Por dónde y para qué

ESCRIBIR, HABLAR EN PAREJA Escribe una descripción de un viaje que hiciste y léela a un(a) compañero(a). Usa *por* y *para*.

Modelo
Viajamos a Canadá por tren. Fuimos para ...

Capítulo 4 • ciento setenta y siete **177**

Enrich Your Teaching

Culture Note

For most Spanish speakers, a greeting includes saying hello as well as some physical gesture. Shaking hands is common. Women often kiss each other on the cheek. Men and women who are close friends or family also often hug and give a light kiss on the cheek.

21st Century Skills

Social and Cross-Cultural Skills Have students research how people of different cultures use different gestures or oral expressions to greet each other or say good-bye. Do they use handshakes, hugs, or kisses? What are common expressions between friends, family members, or work associates? Have students incorporate the new gestures or Spanish expressions they learn into their interactions with their classmates.

Gramática: Repaso

Suggestions: Encourage students to think of other ways to help remember some of the uses of *por* and *para*. As an example, point out that in general, when they want to say "in order to," the Spanish word they use is *para;* when they want to say "by," the word is *por.*

Technology: Interactive Whiteboard

Grammar Activities 4-1 Use the whiteboard activities in your Teacher Resources as you progress through the grammar practice with your class.

17

Standards: 1.2

Suggestions: Ask volunteers to supply other sample sentences for each of the usage rules for *por* and *para.*

Answers:

1. Por
2. por
3. para
4. por
5. por
6. para

18

Standards: 1.3

Suggestions: Ask students to read their completed sentences aloud in random order. Listeners can say the rule behind each use of *por* and *para.*

Pre-AP® Integration

• **Learning Objective:** Presentational Writing
• **Activity:** Have students write an imaginative (perhaps nonsensical) story about an incident that occurs between two friends. The story should highlight vocabulary learned in this chapter and—as a primary requirement—use *por* and/or *para* a minimum of five times. Have students share their stories.
• **Pre-AP® Resource Materials:** Comprehensive guide to Pre-AP® writing skill development

Additional Resources

Technology: Online Resources
• Instant Check
• Guided, Core, Audio, Writing, Reading
• *Para hispanohablantes*
Print
• Guided WB pp. 125–126
• Core WB pp. 53, 55

Starter Activity

Review **gustar** with various combinations of subjects and indirect object pronouns. On the board, write a model such as *A mí me gustan las galletitas.* Ask students to point out the subject *(las galletitas)* and the indirect object pronoun *(me).* Tell students you will use pictures to cue these two parts of the sentence. Use pictures from books or magazines as visual cues. Display different combinations of pictures to elicit sentences such as *A ellas les gusta la película; A nosotros nos gustan los coches,* and so on.

19

Standards: 1.1, 1.3

Suggestions: Remind students to write all their sentences about the same two real or imaginary people, so that the completed activity creates a story. If they opt to write about real people they know, ask them to be considerate and sensitive to the feelings of others.

Answers will vary.

Extension: Ask students to develop their completed sentences into a comic strip about the two friends.

20

Standards: 1.1, 1.3, 3.1

Suggestions: Allow students time to figure out individually what they plan to say for Step 1. This will ensure that they use varied and original ideas. As they fill out the Venn diagram in Step 2, have them check to see how well their partner took down the dictation and make any necessary corrections.

Answers will vary.

19

Por eso, para ellos . . .

HABLAR EN PAREJA, ESCRIBIR   Trabaja con un(a) compañero(a). Inventen una historia entre dos amigos(as) imaginarios(as) completando estas frases.

- Por lo general, ellos se divierten . . .
- La semana pasada se pelearon por . . .
- Estuvieron discutiendo por . . .
- Para [nombre] es importante . . .
- Por eso, (no) les gusta . . .
- Para llevarse bien necesitan . . .
- Por supuesto, no siempre . . .

20

¿Tienes buenos amigos?

HABLAR EN PAREJA, ESCRIBIR

1 Trabaja con un(a) compañero(a). Completa las frases para decir lo que piensas de tus amigos, mientras tu compañero(a) las escribe. Luego, tu compañero(a) completa las frases y tú las escribes.

1. Me alegro de que . . .
2. Es una lástima que . . .
3. Me preocupa que . . .
4. Me parece importante que . . .
5. Me gusta que . . .
6. Es bueno que . . .
7. Quiero que . . .
8. Temo que . . .
9. ¡Ojalá que mis amigos(as) siempre . . . !
10. Es verdad que . . .

2 Completen el diagrama de Venn con lo que piensan.

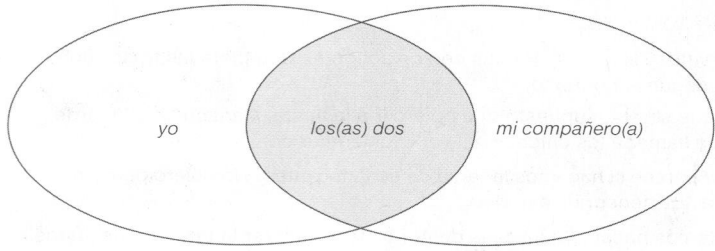

3 Escriban un breve *(short)* informe con la información de su diagrama de Venn. Presenta la información con oraciones conectadas que incluyen detalles y elaboración.

Modelo

Mi compañera Marisa y yo hablamos sobre la amistad. Las dos nos alegramos de tener muchos amigos.

178 ciento setenta y ocho • Capítulo 4 • ¿Cómo te llevas con los demás?

Differentiated Instruction

Students with Learning Difficulties

As students complete *Actividad* 19, model correct forms for completing the sentences. For example: *Por lo general, ellos se divierten jugando con su gato/nadando en el lago/jugando cartas.* Ask students to follow your model but change the content of the message.

Advanced Learners

Ask students to invent personal bios for a dating service. Their bios should use the new vocabulary and the subjunctive to provide a character sketch of an imaginary person and to explain what he or she wants and expects out of a relationship.

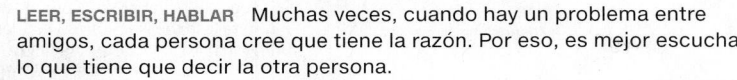

¡No me vas a creer . . . !

 LEER, ESCRIBIR, HABLAR Muchas veces, cuando hay un problema entre amigos, cada persona cree que tiene la razón. Por eso, es mejor escuchar lo que tiene que decir la otra persona.

1 Lee los relatos que hacen Luis y Manuel del mismo problema y contesta las preguntas.

1. ¿Por qué crees que Luis está tan enojado?
2. ¿Te parece sincero el relato que hace Manuel?
3. ¿Qué crees que debió hacer cada uno de los cuatro personajes para evitar este problema?
4. ¿Qué deben hacer ahora para resolver el problema que tienen?

Según Luis...

 Luis

Manuel era mi amigo más íntimo hasta ayer, pero me di cuenta de que es un entrometido. Ya no puedo confiar en él. Mi prima Laura me dijo que Manuel fue a pasear ayer con Clara, mi novia, y que los vio abrazándose. Lo llamé y le dije que estaba sorprendido de saber que salió con mi novia y que temo que nuestra amistad se rompa.

☺   💬   ➡

Según Manuel...

💬 **Manuel**

Me sorprende que Luis esté celoso de mí. Él sabe que somos amigos desde primer grado, que nos contamos nuestros secretos y nos apoyamos en todo. ¿Cómo puede sentir celos de mí? Clara me llamó porque quería pedirme un consejo sobre un problema que tenía. Ella es muy cariñosa y al saludarnos nos abrazamos, como siempre lo hacemos. Me preocupa que este problema pueda terminar con nuestra amistad.

☺   💬   ➡

2 Escribe una frase sobre cada uno de los cuatro personajes que participan en la historia, usando las palabras del recuadro.

cariñoso(a)	celoso(a)	entrometido(a)
comprensivo(a)	honesto(a)	sincero(a)

3 Imagina que eres Clara. Relata lo que sucedió desde su punto de vista.

Modelo
No me gusta que Luis esté enojado. Yo llamé a Manuel para hablar sobre un problema que tuve . . .

Capítulo 4 • ciento setenta y nueve **179**

Standards: 1.2, 1.3

Suggestions: After students have read the two accounts silently in Step 1, ask volunteers to read each one aloud. For Step 2, point out that some of the words might be used in sentences in the indicative mood describing the people; others might be used in sentences with the subjunctive, suggesting how the people should act. Have students read their completed sentences aloud and elaborate on them orally. For Step 3, have students read aloud their completed accounts by Clara.

Project-Based Learning
Students can perform Step 3 at this point. (For more information, see p. 160-b.)

Active Classroom
Have students write a short note to a personal advice columnist describing a "personal problem." Have them sign using a fake name. Collect the questions and distribute them to different students. Each student is to write a response and then read the question and response aloud.

Additional Resources

 Technology: Online Resources
- Instant Check
- Guided, Core, Audio, Writing, Reading
- *Para hispanohablantes*

Print
- Guided WB pp. 127–128
- Core WB pp. 54–55

Assessment
Prueba 4-4 with Remediation (online only)
Prueba: Los usos de *por* y *para*
- Prueba 4-4

Examen: Vocabulario y gramática 1
- Examen 1
- ExamView: Examen 1

Enrich Your Teaching

Teacher-to-Teacher
Students will learn to use prepositions more quickly if you embed the practice in a humorous context. For ***por*** and ***para,*** suggest that pairs of students prepare and present humorous dialogues in which they use the two words as often and as creatively as possible.

21st Century Skills
Critical Thinking and Problem Solving Have students analyze the problem between Luis and Manuel in *Actividad* 21. Imagine they are playing the role of a judge in a dispute between the two friends. Have them ask a question to Luis and to Manuel to better clarify each friend's point of view, then propose a solution.

Vocabulario en contexto 2

Resources: Teacher's Resource Materials: Input Script, Clip Art, Audio Script, Technology: Audio Cap. 4

Suggestions: Refer students to the *Estrategia*. Have them respond to the questions there by talking about the pictures and writing down their predictions about what happened. Then allow students time to read the presentation silently. Have students revisit the predictions. Ask questions such as the following: *¿Todas tus predicciones resultaron correctas? ¿Qué partes son distintas de tus predicciones?*

Starter Activity
Have students look at the photo on page 175 and write a short dialogue.

Active Classroom
Divide students into pairs. Assign each group section of dialogue from pages 180–181. Have students practice and then reenact the dialogues in front of the class. Remind them to focus on intonation, expression, and correct pronunciation.

 Technology: Interactive Whiteboard

> **Vocabulary Activities 4-2** Use the whiteboard activities in your Teacher Resources as you progress through the vocabulary practice with your class.

Vocabulario en contexto 2

OBJECTIVES
Read, listen to, and understand information about
▶ Conflicts and how to resolve them
▶ Friends and family relationships

Estrategia
Using illustrations to predict the outcome Before reading a text, look at the illustrations. What do you think is going to happen? What details in the illustrations support your prediction? After reading, compare your prediction with what happened at the end of the story.

🔊 La familia en vivo

La familia Aguilar se presenta en un programa de televisión para tratar de solucionar un problema familiar.

Presentador: Hoy tenemos a la familia Aguilar en nuestro programa. Lucas sacó el auto de su padre sin su permiso y lo chocó contra la puerta del garaje.

Vamos a visitar a los señores Aguilar y a sus hijos Lucas y Nacho.

¿Qué quiere decirle a su hijo, señor Aguilar?

Papá: Lucas, debes darme **una explicación.** No me gusta que **acuses** a tu hermano de algo que tú has hecho.

Presentador: Cuéntanos qué pasó, Lucas.

Lucas: Esto es un **malentendido** y mi padre **está equivocado.** Mi hermano no le hizo caso y ahora yo **tengo la culpa.**

Presentador: ¿Nacho?

Nacho: ¡Qué va! ¡Él se atrevió a sacar el auto sin permiso y lo chocó!

Nacho

Differentiated Instruction

Heritage Speakers
Remind students of strategies they can use to monitor and improve their reading comprehension. Have them pause after each section of the reading and answer *¿Qué pasó?* If they can't answer, ask them to reread the section.

Students with Learning Difficulties
Remind students that new vocabulary in the reading is identified in bold. Review the meaning of new words and phrases with them before they begin to read.

Mamá

Presentador: Señora Aguilar, ¿tiene algo que decir?

Mamá: ¡Claro! **¡Pónganse de acuerdo!** Fue solo un accidente y nadie salió lastimado. En nuestra familia siempre ha habido **armonía**. Por favor, **hagan las paces**.

Presentador: ¿Señor Aguilar?

Papá: Lucas, el auto y la puerta del garaje están rotos. Solo **piensas en ti mismo** y eso no está bien. Pero te **perdono** porque eres mi hijo y te quiero.

Presentador: Lucas, ¿qué le contestas a tu padre?

Lucas: **Reconozco** que hice mal. Yo fui el que sacó el auto del garaje sin permiso. Te **pido perdón**, papá. Voy a hacer un plan para pagar los arreglos.

Lucas y su papá

Presentador: Me gusta ver que Lucas y sus padres **resolvieron** el problema.

Esto demuestra que hablando la gente se entiende.

22

Familia en conflicto

 ESCUCHAR Escribe los números del 1 al 6 en una hoja. Vas a escuchar frases sobre el problema entre Lucas y sus padres. Escribe *C* (cierto) o *F* (falso) para cada frase.

Capítulo 4 • ciento ochenta y uno **181**

22

Standards: 1.2

Resources: Teacher's Resource Materials: Audio Script, Technology Audio Cap. 4

Suggestions: Allow students to listen to the audio once through first. Then play it again, pausing after each item, so they can write their answers.

🔊 **Technology: Audio Script and Answers**

1. La familia Aguilar consultó un psicólogo para resolver su problema. *(F)*
2. Lucas tuvo un pequeño accidente con el coche. *(C)*
3. Lucas acusa a su hermano. *(C)*
4. La mamá quiere que se pongan de acuerdo. *(C)*
5. El padre de Lucas no lo quiere. *(F)*
6. Lucas acepta responsabilidad por su error. *(C)*

Enrich Your Teaching

21st Century Skills

Critical Thinking and Problem Solving Encourage students to discuss the conflict between Nacho and Lucas. What do you think about Lucas's decision to blame his younger brother, Nacho? How do you think that made Nacho feel? Ask students if they ever blamed a sibling or another person for something that they did? What was the outcome?

Vocabulario en contexto 2

Standards: 1.2

Resources: Teacher's Resource Materials: Input Script, Clip Art, Audio Script, Technology: Audio Cap. 4

Suggestions

Pre-reading: Point out that *conflictos, criticar, ignorar, reaccionar, reconciliar,* and *colaborar* are cognates. Explain that the verb *mejorar* comes from the adjective and adverb *mejor,* which students have already learned. Write on the board *mejorar = hacer mejor* and use *mejorar* in a model sentence such as *La situación se mejoró cuando hablamos del problema.*

Reading: Have students read along as you play the audio or as you read aloud. Make sure students read the *Nota* on the next page. Use *ignorar* in model sentences like the following to demonstrate the two meanings: *Mi madre me ignora cuando grito. Mi padre no puede resolver el conflicto porque ignora los detalles.*

Post-reading: Discuss the charts and questionnaires with students and ask questions to check comprehension.

23

Standards: 1.3

Suggestions: Encourage students to cite facts from the surveys that support their answers to the questions.

Answers:

1. Muchos conflictos ocurren cuando hay diferencias de opinión entre miembros de una familia. Answers will vary.
2. Los miembros de una familia deben pensar en los demás y colaborar para tener una buena relación.

3–5. Answers will vary.

Hagamos las paces

> ¡Yo no fui!

Muchos **conflictos** ocurren cuando hay **diferencias de opinión** entre miembros de una familia.

Todas las familias tienen problemas. Pero es importante reconocer que nuestro **comportamiento** puede ayudar a mantener la armonía en la familia. Todos los miembros deben pensar en los demás y **colaborar** para tener una buena relación.

Se hizo una encuesta entre jóvenes mexicanos sobre sus relaciones con sus padres. Estas tablas muestran la información recogida en la encuesta.

Cuando hago algo que no les gusta a mis padres . . .	
Mis padres	Porcentaje
no dicen ni hacen nada	9.8 %
hablan conmigo	67.7 %
no me dejan salir	4.6 %
me **critican**	9.3 %
otra	8.6 %
Total	100.0 %

Cuando tengo algún problema con mis padres . . .			
frecuencia	lo hablo con papá	lo hablo con mamá	lo hablo con los dos
siempre	20.0 %	45.9 %	16.1 %
a veces	45.3 %	40.0 %	39.7 %
nunca	32.5 %	12.7 %	36.0 %
no quiero contestar	2.2 %	1.4 %	8.2 %

23

La armonía en la familia

ESCRIBIR, HABLAR

1. Según el artículo, ¿por qué a veces hay problemas en una familia? ¿Estás de acuerdo con esta opinión?
2. ¿Cuáles son algunas de las cosas que el artículo recomienda hacer para tener más armonía en una familia?
3. ¿Crees que por lo general las familias de esta encuesta se comunican bien o mal? ¿Por qué?
4. ¿Cómo podemos evitar conflictos?
5. Si tenemos diferencias de opinión o peleas con nuestra familia, ¿qué debemos hacer?

Differentiated Instruction

Heritage Speakers

Draw students' attention to the title *Hagamos las paces.* Invite them to share with the class other expressions that they might use to encourage harmony within their family, such as **Ya dejemos de pelear, reconciliémonos, perdón**, or **discúlpame.**

Advanced Learners

Invite students to conduct a survey similar to the one shown on p. 183. Ask them to tally the results of their surveys and to translate these into percentages, as they did on p. 172. Have them compare the results of their class with those of the students surveyed in Spain.

CONFLICTOS: Causas y soluciones

Las preguntas de estas tablas nos pueden ayudar a saber qué hacer para **mejorar** nuestra relación con las personas que más nos quieren[1].

[1] The verb *querer* in this context means "to love" or "to like."

Nota
La palabra *ignorar* tiene más de un significado. Quiere decir "no prestar atención" o "no hacer caso" y, en un contexto diferente, puede significar "no saber algo".

¿Te molesta cuando tus amigos . . .

	nunca	a veces	siempre
te **ignoran**?	○	○	○
cuentan tus secretos a otros?	○	○	○
no te **hacen caso**?	○	○	○
tienen celos?	○	○	○
no **se alegran** de tus éxitos?	○	○	○
sólo piensan en sí mismos?	○	○	○

¿Cómo reaccionas cuando tienes una pelea con un(a) amigo(a)?

	Sí	No
Gritas.	○	○
Dejas de hablarle.	○	○
Tratas de reconciliarte.	○	○
Lo(la) criticas.	○	○
Ignoras el problema.	○	○
Le **pides perdón**.	○	○

¿Cómo te reconcilias con tus padres?

	Sí	No
Hablamos del problema para resolverlo juntos.	○	○
Nos ponemos de acuerdo.	○	○
Hacemos las paces.	○	○
Reconocemos que estábamos equivocados.	○	○
Guardamos silencio hasta que pase el momento.	○	○

24

Amistad y conflicto

HABLAR EN GRUPO Trabaja con un grupo para comparar sus respuestas a las preguntas siguientes.

1. ¿Qué nos molesta?
2. ¿Por qué nos enojamos con nuestros padres?
3. ¿Qué no nos gusta que hagan nuestros amigos?
4. ¿Qué hacemos para resolver conflictos?

Capítulo 4 • ciento ochenta y tres **183**

Enrich Your Teaching

Culture Note
As in most cultures, the family forms the most important social unit for Latin Americans. The concept of family might be considered a bit different from that in the United States. In Spain and Latin America, **familia** almost always includes not only the immediate family, but grandparents, aunts, uncles, and cousins as well. In Spanish-speaking countries, it is more common for members of three generations to live together in the same house than it is in the United States.

24

Standards: 1.1, 1.2

Suggestions: Have students answer the questions individually first. Then have them meet and take turns sharing their answers. Encourage them to listen carefully to each other and to ask each other additional questions for clarification.
Answers will vary.

Pre-AP® Integration
- **Learning Objective:** Interpretive: Print and Audio
- **Activity:** Have students work in groups of three to use the photo on page 183 to create a dialogue that could be taking place between the parents and their son. Then call on groups to present their dialogues to the class.
- **Pre-AP® Resource Materials:** Comprehensive guide to Pre-AP® vocabulary skill development

Project-Based Learning
Students can perform Step 4 at this point. Be sure they understand your corrections and suggestions. (For more information, see p. 160-b.)

Teacher-to-Teacher
Have students respond to the survey on p. 183. Then have students engage in a blog to express the feelings they have in the various situations described in the survey.

Additional Resources
 Technology: Online Resources
- Instant Check
- Guided, Core, Audio, Writing practice
- *Para hispanohablantes*

Print
- Guided WB pp. 129–136
- Core WB pp. 56–57

Assessment
Prueba 4-5
Prueba: Comprensión del vocabulario 2
- Prueba 4-5

25

Standards: 1.2, 3.1

Suggestions: Point out that each possible answer has two phrases that best complete the sentence.

Answers:
1. b
2. c
3. b
4. a
5. c

Extension: Have students create their own sentences in which key vocabulary words are omitted, as in *Actividad* 25. They can exchange their sentences and have classmates complete them.

CULTURA

Standards: 1.2, 1.3, 2.1, 2.2, 4.2

Suggestions: After students read the information, ask them to compare and contrast the concept of Latin American *telenovelas* with that of U.S. soap operas. Ask: *¿En qué se parecen una telenovela y una* soap opera*? ¿En qué se diferencian? ¿Una* soap opera *dura un año o más de un año? ¿Se parecen los personajes y los argumentos? ¿En qué son diferentes?*

Answers will vary.

Vocabulario en uso 2

OBJECTIVES
▶ Read and write about conflicts and solutions
▶ Discuss relationships, problems, and reactions
▶ Describe the family relationships portrayed in a painting

25

Los opuestos

LEER, ESCRIBIR

Completa las frases con la mejor selección de palabras opuestas (*opposite*).

1. Es mejor vivir en _____ con nuestra familia y evitar los _____ .
   - a. *pelea / comportamiento*
   - b. *armonía / conflictos*
   - c. *diferencia de opinión / paces*

2. El día que _____ estaban muy enojados, pero después _____ .
   - a. *hicieron caso / ignoraron*
   - b. *perdonaron / acusaron*
   - c. *se pelearon / se reconciliaron*

3. Tú _____ , no sabes lo que dices. Alicia no quería _____ , solo ayudarte.
   - a. *haces las paces / se pelea*
   - b. *estás equivocado / criticarte*
   - c. *prestas atención / ignorarte*

4. Yo siempre _____ a lo que dice mi hermano y hago lo que nos pide, pero Pedro muchas veces lo _____.
   - a. *hago caso / ignora*
   - b. *me reconcilio / se pelea*
   - c. *pido perdón / acusa*

5. Amalia siempre _____ y ayuda a todo el mundo, pero su hermano es un egoísta que solo _____.
   - a. *acusa / se reconcilia*
   - b. *critica / colabora*
   - c. *piensa en los demás / piensa en sí mismo*

CULTURA **El mundo hispano**

Las telenovelas son la versión latinoamericana de las *soap operas* y generalmente se transmiten entre las 6 y las 10 de la noche. El argumento es siempre una historia de amor, con personajes muy buenos o muy malos que se pelean en cada programa sin resolver sus problemas. La telenovela dura menos de un año y tiene un final emocionante, donde se resuelven los conflictos, los buenos triunfan y la muchacha y el muchacho se casan.

Pre-AP® Integration: El entretenimiento y la diversión ¿Cómo influyen los productos culturales, como las telenovelas, en la vida de la gente en los países latinoamericanos y los Estados Unidos?

Jauma Mateu y Michelle Renaud, ▶
Pasión y poder

Differentiated Instruction

Heritage Speakers

Have students write a brief scene from a **telenovela** they know or one of their invention. The script should include one of the features mentioned in the *Cultura*. Encourage them to perform their scenes for the class. Remind them that **telenovelas** are usually quite dramatic. Encourage them to "ham it up!"

Challenge/Pre-AP®

Ask students to prepare a general overview of a soap opera they know. Have them describe the setting, the main characters, and some long- and short-term conflicts. If students are also familiar with any **telenovelas,** have them include an overview for these programs too.

Go **Online** to practice
PEARSON
realize™
PearsonSchool.com/Autentico

WRITING

Interpersonal 4

26

Más consejos, ¡por favor!

 LEER, ESCRIBIR

1 Un chico que participó en un salón de chat escribió este mensaje. Completa el mensaje con las palabras del recuadro.

Estoy colaborando con un grupo de estudiantes para hacer un informe, pero uno de mis compañeros es muy egoísta. Cuando nos debemos reunir, dice que no puede porque tiene un partido de fútbol o clases de tenis. ¡No _1._ en nada! ¡Este chico solo _2._ ! Ya tuvimos varias _3._ porque temo que recibamos una mala nota, pero no _4._ y siempre que le pedimos algo él responde: " _5._ ".

hace caso
piensa en sí mismo
¡Qué va!
colabora
peleas

2 Con otro(a) estudiante, da un buen consejo a la persona que escribió el mensaje. Incluyan las razones en su mensaje.

27

Lomas Garza: La gran familia chicana

 LEER, ESCRIBIR   La obra de Carmen Lomas Garza es como un retrato de familia de la comunidad chicana, es decir, mexicano-americana, de los Estados Unidos.

Conexiones ▸ El arte

Carmen Lomas Garza (1948 –) es una artista chicana de Texas. Lomas Garza se inspiró en el Movimiento Chicano de los años sesenta, y desde entonces trata de representar en su obra la cultura de los chicanos. En sus cuadros, Lomas Garza ilustra las costumbres, las fiestas y la vida interesante y complicada de las personas que viven entre dos culturas, la mexicana y la estadounidense. Observa su cuadro "Cascarones" (*Eggshells*), de 1989, y contesta las preguntas.

- ¿Te parece que hay armonía o conflicto en esta familia?

- ¿Por qué crees que hay una figura más grande que las otras en el cuadro? ¿Qué quiso expresar la pintora con ese detalle?

- Imagínate algo que pasa entre los miembros de esta familia. Usa las palabras del recuadro para contar lo que sucede.

colaborar   hacer caso   malentendido   explicación   comportamiento

"Cascarones", (1989), Carmen Lomas Garza
Gouache painting. 15 x 20 inches. © 1989 Carmen Lomas Garza.
Photo by: Wolfgang Dietze. Collection of Gilbert Cardenas, Notra Dame, IN.

Capítulo 4 • ciento ochenta y cinco **185**

26

Standards: 1.1, 1.2

Recycle: Past tenses, subjunctive

Suggestions: Explain to students that a clear understanding of the character description in the first part of the message will help them fill in the blanks in the second part. For Step 2, encourage students to use expressions that take the subjunctive.

Answers:
1. colabora
2. piensa en sí mismo
3. peleas
4. hace caso
5. ¡Qué va!

Starter Activity

Have students unscramble these letters to form words for family members:

aleuba   ineto   damarsart   hormone

(**Answers:** *abuela, nieto, madrastra, hermano*)

27

Standards: 1.1, 1.2, 2.1, 2.2, 3.1

Suggestions: Remind students that they can refer to *Capítulo* 2 if they need to review the fine art vocabulary used in the reading passage.

Answers will vary.

Enrich Your Teaching

Culture Note

Besides her paintings, Carmen Lomas Garza also makes prints, installations (mixed-media artworks in three dimensions, often incorporating movement), and paper and metal cutouts. Her installations tend to focus on the Day of the Dead **(el Día de los Muertos),** a Mexican feast day celebrated on November 1. Behind all of Garza's artwork lies pride in her Chicana heritage.

28

Standards: 1.1

Suggestions: Remind students that the *¡Respuesta personal!* at the end of Student B's cues is an invitation for them to invent their own reactions as well as to practice those cues.

Answers will vary. Student B can use the following verb forms:

me alegro
me enojo
doy/pido una explicación
lloro
me pongo (feliz, furioso(a), contento(a))
reconozco el error/pido perdón
digo "¡Qué va!"/ "Yo no fui"

29

Standards: 1.1, 1.2

Suggestions: As students are preparing the paper slips for the drawing, ask them to read all of the items and think about the dramatization they will do if they select it.

Answers will vary.

30

Standards: 1.1

Suggestions: Encourage students to supply their own personal reasons for disagreements with people they know.

Answers will vary.

28

¿Cómo reaccionas cuando . . . ?

 **HABLAR EN PAREJA** Con un(a) compañero(a), habla sobre tu comportamiento en las situaciones siguientes.

▶ **Videomodelo**
tu amigo te ignora
A —*¿Cómo reaccionas cuando tu amigo te ignora?*
B —*Generalmente le pido una explicación.*

Estudiante A

1. tu amigo dice que estás equivocado(a)
2. tu hermano(a) te acusa de algo
3. tus padres te critican
4. tus padres te preguntan "¿por qué?"
5. alguien no te hace caso
6. alguien no quiere hacer las paces

Estudiante B

alegrarse
enojarse
dar / pedir una explicación
llorar
ponerse (feliz, furioso, contento)
reconocer el error / pedir perdón
decir "¡Qué va!" / "Yo no fui"
¡Respuesta personal!

29

Juego

✏ **ESCRIBIR, HABLAR EN GRUPO** Trabaja con un grupo y pide a cada persona que escriba una de las siguientes frases en una tira de papel. Luego, pónganlos todos en una caja o bolsa y tomen turnos para sacarlos. Dos personas del grupo actúen en una conversación la frase que sacaron. Usen gestos y expresiones apropiados. ¡Sé dramático(a)!

1. Explícale a tu padre por qué llegaste tarde anoche.

2. Tuviste una pelea y te das cuenta de que estabas equivocado(a).

3. Crees que tu maestro(a) está equivocado(a). ¿Qué dices / haces? Sé muy cortés.

4. Tú y tu amigo(a) se pelearon. Hay que reconciliarse. ¿Qué dices para reconciliarte?

5. Tu hermano(a) te acusa de algo que tú no hiciste. ¿Cómo reaccionas?

6. Tu hermano(a) menor se portó mal en la tienda. ¿Qué le dices?

30

Diferencias de opinión

HABLAR EN PAREJA Trabaja con otro(a) estudiante y explícale por qué a veces peleas con estas personas. Usa las palabras del recuadro. Después, intercambien papeles.

criticar	ignorar
reconocer	hacer
acusar de	atreverse
tener la culpa	

Modelo
hermano mayor
*Peleo con mi hermano mayor cuando **no me deja escuchar MP3**.*

1. papá 3. hermano(a) 5. mejor amigo(a) 7. compañero(a) de clase

2. mamá 4. hermano(a) menor 6. primo(a)

Differentiated Instruction

Heritage Speakers

Have students write a paragraph about one aspect of their family that they really enjoy. They might write about a relationship with a certain family member, a special family tradition, a celebration, or a memory that is important to them. Allow students to write about a close, personal friend as an option.

Advanced Learners

Ask students to interview students and teachers from other classes about their conflicts with others and how they resolve them. Have them prepare their interviews in advance by writing four or five questions they will ask. They can conduct their interviews in English and report back to the class in Spanish.

Go **Online** to practice
PearsonSchool.com/Autentico

PEARSON
realize™

VIDEO   WRITING   SPEAK/RECORD

Interpersonal   4

31

Encuesta: ¿Para qué necesitas permiso?

 LEER, ESCRIBIR   Lee en la tabla la información recogida en una encuesta que se hizo entre jóvenes mexicanos con respecto a sus padres. Después, contesta las preguntas.

Actividades	Prohibido	Necesito permiso	Yo decido Chicos	Yo decido Chicas	No aplica	No contestó	Total
Tener novio(a)	9.3%	33.0%	35.2%	16.5%	5.2%	0.8%	**100%**
Salir con amigos	5.5%	65.1%	19.9%	7.4%	1.8%	0.3%	**100%**
Vestirte como quieres	2.9%	10.5%	43.3%	42.0%	0.9%	0.4%	**100%**
Llegar tarde a casa	15.2%	60.1%	16.7%	5.0%	2.6%	0.4%	**100%**
Ponerte aretes	45.5%	8.0%	9.7%	6.1%	30.2%	0.5%	**100%**

1. ¿Qué actividad se prohíbe más? ¿Cuál se prohíbe menos?

2. ¿Qué información de la tabla te sorprende? ¿Por qué?

3. Mira la columna con el título "Yo decido". ¿Qué te dice esa información?

4. Un(a) chico(a) tiene prohibido llegar tarde a casa pero nunca hace caso. ¿Cómo crees que van a reaccionar los padres?

5. ¿Qué puede hacer después ese(a) chico(a) para resolver el conflicto con sus padres?

6. Si ese(a) mismo(a) chico(a) llegó tarde a casa porque no pasó el autobús, ¿crees que los padres deben enojarse? ¿Por qué?

32

Los conflictos

 ESCRIBIR, HABLAR EN GRUPO

1. Escribe una lista de, por lo menos, tres conflictos o malentendidos que suceden a veces en una familia. Por ejemplo: alguien no arregló su cuarto o alguien llegó muy tarde a casa.

2. ¿Quiénes son las personas que participan en cada conflicto?

3. ¿Qué pueden hacer para mejorar la situación?

4. Con otro(a) estudiante, representen el conflicto ante la clase.

5. Basándote en los consejos del cartel, sugiere una solución para uno de los conflictos.

 PARA RESOLVER UN CONFLICTO

 1. hablen para resolver el problema

 2. sugieran soluciones posibles

 3. sean sinceros

 4. expliquen lo que pasó

Capítulo 4 • ciento ochenta y siete **187**

 31

Suggestions: When students have had some time to study the chart, ask additional questions: *¿Qué porcentaje de los jóvenes necesita permiso para salir con amigos?* (65.1)

Answers:

1. Más: Ponerte aretes. Menos: vestir como tú quieres.
2–6. Answers will vary.

32

Suggestions: For item 3, ask students to think of their own ways to resolve the problems. Remind them that they do not need to have personal experience with some of the ways they mention.

Answers will vary.

Additional Resources

 Technology: Online Resources
• Audio, Writing, Reading
• Communication Activities
• Teacher's Resource Materials: Audio Script, Communicative Pair Activities, Technology: Audio Cap. 4

Assessment

Prueba 4-6 with Remediation (online only)
Prueba: Aplicación del vocabulario 2
• Prueba 4-6

Enrich Your Teaching

Culture Note

Young single adults in much of Latin America tend to live with their parents longer than their counterparts in the United States. Reasons for this vary. Sometimes they are economical; sometimes they have to do with employment; but in many cases they spring from cultural traditions that place a high value on a strong bond between the generations within a family. As in all cultures, such traditions and values are changing.

Gramática

Standards: 4.1

Suggestions: Have students write more examples using the **vamos a + infinitive** construction. Ask them to include some suggestions that use stem-changing verbs and one or more of the pronouns referred to in the *Gramática*. Have them take turns reading their suggestions aloud. Ask volunteers to convert each one to the **nosotros** command form with correct spelling and pronoun placement.

 Technology: Interactive Whiteboard

Grammar Activities 4-2 Use the whiteboard activities in your Teacher Resources as you progress through the grammar practice with your class.

33

Standards: 1.2

Suggestions: Ask students to practice the **nosotros** commands, but remind them that the **vamos a + infinitive** construction is also an option for the items.

Answers will vary.

1. Hablemos, veamos
2. Pidámosle, prometamos
3. Ignoremos, perdonémosla
4. Démosle, terminemos

34

Standards: 1.1, 1.2

Suggestions: Call on volunteers to read aloud their exchanges.

Answers will vary.

Gramática

OBJECTIVES
▶ Read and write about conflict resolution
▶ Discuss suggestions for doing activities with other people

Mandatos con *nosotros*

There are two ways to suggest that others do some activity with you *(Let's . . .)*.

You can use the construction *Vamos a +* infinitive.

> **Vamos a hacer** las paces. ***Let's*** *make up.*

You can also use a command with a *nosotros* form. The *nosotros* command form is the same as the *nosotros* form of the present subjunctive.

> **Resolvamos** el conflicto.
> No **reaccionemos** tan rápido.

Remember that stem-changing verbs whose infinitive ends in *-ir* have a stem change of e → *i*, or o → *u* in the *nosotros* form.

> **Pidamos** perdón por el malentendido.
> No **durmamos** al aire libre.

Verbs whose infinitive ends in *-car, -gar,* or *-zar* have a spelling change in the *nosotros* form of the present subjunctive, and consequently of the *nosotros* command.

> No **critiquemos** a nuestros padres.
> **Empecemos** a pensar un poco en ellos.

Direct and indirect object pronouns are attached at the end of affirmative *nosotros* commands, but precede the negative *nosotros* command form.

> **Celebremos** la amistad. **Celebrémosla**.
> **Digámosle** todo. **No le mintamos**.

When attaching reflexive or reciprocal pronouns at the end of a *nosotros* command, drop the final *-s* of the command before the pronoun.

> ¡**Alegrémonos** con sus éxitos!
> **Atrevámonos** a darles nuestras opiniones.

Más recursos ONLINE

▶ **Tutorial:** *Nosotros* Commands (Subjunctive)

🔊 **Canción de hip-hop:** *Conflictos*

33

Encontremos la solución

✏️ **LEER, ESCRIBIR** Miriam y Leonor se pelearon con Tamara, su hermana mayor. Completa las frases con el mandato con *nosotros* del verbo apropiado para saber qué sugieren para reconciliarse con Tamara.

1. _____ (*acusar / hablar*) con papá y _____ (*ver / ignorar*) cómo reacciona.

2. _____ (*pedirle / criticar*) perdón y _____ (*perder / prometer*) no mentir nunca más.

3. _____ (*mejorar / ignorar*) todo y _____ (*decirle / perdonarla*).

4. _____ (*darle / reaccionar*) una explicación y _____ (*terminar / reaccionar*) la pelea.

34

Un plan para el sábado

✏️ **ESCRIBIR** Imagina que el sábado quieres ir al cine con un(a) amigo(a). Escribe tres preguntas por texto para sugerir lo que pueden hacer. Ahora, tu amigo(a) escribe las respuestas a tus preguntas. Pueden usar las palabras del recuadro.

> comer antes
> cenar después
> invitar a Juana
> ver la primera o la segunda película
> ir en autobús

Modelo

A —¿Adónde quieres ir el sábado?
B —Escojamos una película para ver.

A —¿Cuándo compramos las entradas?
B —Lleguemos al cine temprano.

188 ciento ochenta y ocho • Capítulo 4 • ¿Cómo te llevas con los demás?

Differentiated Instruction

Heritage Speakers

Provide extra support to students as you discuss the letters *j* and *h* in *¿Recuerdas?* Although they rarely mispronounce Spanish words with *h,* students often make errors in spelling these words. Briefly review common errors that you see, such as misspelling **a ver** and **haber.**

Students with Special Needs

Pair advanced learners with visually impaired students in order to complete *Actividad* 35. The former can describe the actions shown in each scene. Their partners can then suggest other activities to do.

35

¿Y ahora qué hacemos?

HABLAR EN PAREJA Raúl y Rosalía nunca se ponen de acuerdo. Con otro(a) estudiante, hagan los papeles de Raúl y Rosalía. Uno(a) sugiere lo que aparece en el dibujo y el (la) otro(a) sugiere hacer otra cosa.

Videomodelo
A —*Caminemos por el parque.*
B —*Dijeron que va a llover.*
   Volvamos a casa.

En voz alta

Hay una rima tradicional que los niños en Colombia y otros países de América Latina usan para jugar. Se llama *Juguemos en el bosque.* Un niño del grupo es el "lobo", mientras que los demás niños se toman de las manos y dan vueltas cantando la rima. Cuando el lobo se termina de vestir, les anuncia a los niños que ya va a salir. Entonces los demás niños salen corriendo para que el lobo no los pueda alcanzar. Escucha la rima, luego trata de repetirla en voz alta. ¿Conoces rimas, canciones o juegos similares de tu cultura?

¿Recuerdas?
En español la letra *j* se pronuncia como la letra *h* en la palabra *hat* pero con un sonido más fuerte. Escucha y repite esta palabra: *juguemos.*
En español la letra *h* casi nunca suena: *hablemos.*

< • • • • •

Juguemos en el bosque

Juguemos en el bosque, mientras el lobo no está.
—¿Lobo estás?
—Me estoy poniendo los pantalones.
Bailemos en el bosque, mientras el lobo no está.
—¿Lobo estás?
—Me estoy poniendo el chaleco.
Caminemos en el bosque, mientras el lobo no está.
—¿Lobo estás?
—Me estoy poniendo el sombrerito.
Corramos en el bosque, mientras el lobo no está.
—¿Lobo estás?
—¡Sí y salgo a perseguirlos[1]!

◀◀ ❚❚ ▶▶
◀—◯———

[1] chase

Capítulo 4 • ciento ochenta y nueve **189**

Gramática

Suggestions: On the board, write this model: *Aquellas llaves son tuyas. Aquí tengo las mías.* Ask students to refer to other individual objects or groups of objects around the classroom and make similar pairs of sentences using possessive adjectives and pronouns.

 Technology: Interactive Whiteboard

Grammar Activities 4-2 Use the whiteboard activities in your Teacher Resources as you progress through the grammar practice with your class.

36

Standards: 1.1, 1.2

Suggestions: Have students first read through the entire email for meaning. Ask them to identify the noun that is replaced by each possessive pronoun.

Answers:

1. mías
2. míos
3. mía
4. suyo
5. tuyos

37

Standards: 1.1

Suggestions: Have students practice third-person forms by reporting to the class on their partner's statements.

Answers will vary, but students will use the following possessive forms:

mi ropa: la tuya, la mía
mi perro: el tuyo, el mío
mi computadora: la tuya, la mía
nuestro coche: el tuyo, el nuestro
mis comidas favoritas: las tuyas, las mías
mis abuelos: los tuyos, los míos
mi hermano(a): el (la) tuyo(a), el (la) mío(a)
mi familia: la tuya, la mía
nuestros(as) amigos(as): los (las) tuyos(as), los (las) míos(as)

Gramática

Pronombres posesivos

To form the possessive pronouns, use the long form of possessive adjectives preceded by the definite article. Both the article and the possessive must agree in number and gender with the noun they replace.

Mis padres son muy serios. ¿Y **los tuyos**? **Los míos** son bastante divertidos.

Tu familia es muy pequeña. **La mía** es bastante grande.

We often omit the article between the verb *ser* and the possessive pronoun.

Esas maletas **son nuestras**.
Mi hermano siempre dice que toda la culpa **es mía**.

¿Recuerdas?
The long form possessive adjectives are used for clarity or emphasis.

1st, 2nd, and 3rd Person Sing.
mío(s)	mía(s)	*my, mine*
tuyo(s)	tuya(s)	*your, yours*
suyo(s)	suya(s)	*your, yours his, her, hers*

1st, 2nd, and 3rd Person Plural
nuestro(s)	nuestra(s)	*our, ours*
vuestro(s)	vuestra(s)	*your, yours*
suyo(s)	suya(s)	*your, yours their, theirs*

36

¿Cuándo vamos al cine?

 LEER, ESCRIBIR

1 Débora se enojó con Pablo porque él no pudo ir al cine con ella y le escribió un mensaje de texto diciéndoselo. Entonces, Pablo le escribió un correo electrónico para reconciliarse. Completa el correo electrónico de Pablo con las formas correctas de los pronombres posesivos del recuadro. Algunas se pueden usar más de una vez.

tuyo
mío
suyo

Hola Débora,

Leí tu mensaje de texto. Entiendo tus razones pero yo tengo las __1.__ para no ir al cine. Tus padres te dejan ir al cine siempre, pero los __2.__ nunca me dejan. Ayer tu mamá llamó a la __3.__ para pedirle que me dejara ir a tu casa, pero mi mamá dijo que su coche no funciona. Tu mamá dijo que podía llevarme en el __4.__, pero mi mamá no quiso. Yo quiero mucho a mis padres, pero me gustaría que fueran como los __5.__. Espero que me perdones. Creo que el sábado que viene sí me van a dejar ir contigo. ¡Nos vamos a divertir!

Pablo

2 Ahora escríbele un correo electrónico a un compañero(a) diciéndole adónde prefieres ir tú el sábado. El compañero te responde con sus preferencias para salir juntos.

190 ciento noventa • Capítulo 4 • ¿Cómo te llevas con los demás?

Differentiated Instruction

Students with Learning Difficulties

Write on the board the following sentences: *These are my books. These are mine.* Guide students to understand that *mine* is a pronoun that takes the place of *my books.* Point out that English, like Spanish, uses different words for possessive adjectives and pronouns. (my/mine, your/yours, and so on.)

Advanced Learners

As students complete *Actividad* 36, ask them to tell why each form is correct. Have them say to which noun each possessive pronoun refers, identifying its number and gender. Then ask students to add two more sentences containing possessive pronouns from Pablo's letter.

37

Los míos, los tuyos, los nuestros

HABLAR EN PAREJA Con otro(a) estudiante, hablen sobre los siguientes aspectos de su vida.

- mi computadora
- nuestro coche
- mis comidas favoritas

- mis abuelos
- mi familia
- nuestros(as) amigos(as)

- mi ropa
- mi perro

▶ **Videomodelo**

mis padres

A —*Mis padres son serios, pero comprensivos. ¿Cómo son los tuyos?*

B —*Los míos son muy generosos, y siempre piensan en los demás.*

38

Retrato de familia

ESCRIBIR, HABLAR EN PAREJA

1 Piensa en una familia de una película, un libro o un programa de televisión que conoces. Imagina que eres un miembro de esa familia. Con un compañero(a), hagan y contesten preguntas por texto acerca de la familia.

    1. ¿Cómo es tu familia? (cuántos son, quiénes son, cómo es cada uno)

    2. ¿Quién piensa siempre en los demás y quién piensa más en sí mismo?

    3. ¿Quién se pelea con los demás? ¿Quién trata de mantener la armonía?

    4. ¿Cómo resuelven los conflictos?

2 Basándote en las respuestas a las preguntas anteriores, escribe una descripción de tu familia imaginaria.

3 Con otro(a) estudiante, hablen de las descripciones que escribieron y comparen sus familias imaginarias.

El español en la comunidad

Niños bilingües En muchas familias latinas de los Estados Unidos los niños aprenden el nuevo idioma más rápido que los adultos, y son los intérpretes, o traductores, de la familia.

A veces, esto ayuda a la armonía de la familia, pues todos colaboran para adaptarse a la nueva cultura. Pero otras veces hay conflictos, porque los padres sienten que pierden control sobre los hijos y los hijos piensan que sus padres no los entienden.

Ahora que tú sabes hablar español, puedes servir de intérprete de los nuevos estudiantes hispanohablantes y así ser útil a tu comunidad.

Enrich Your Teaching

Culture Note

Spanish is quickly becoming an important part of many communities in the United States. According to one study, the Hispanic population has grown faster over the past two decades than that of any immigrant group in the history of the United States. Experts predict that this rapid growth will probably continue for several decades.

21st Century Skills

ICT (Information, Communications and Technology) Literacy Remind students of the various digital tools available in **Realize** to help them monitor their own understanding and learning needs, such as the online tutorials with comprehension check exercises.

38

Suggestions: Have students begin their family descriptions by identifying themselves: *Me llamo Joselito. Soy el hijo menor de la familia Cartwright....*
Answers will vary.

El español en la comunidad

Suggestions: Ask students to consider what it would be like to be a parent or child in a bilingual family. If your class includes heritage speakers, they may have a lot to offer to this discussion.

Project-Based Learning

Students can perform Step 5 at this point. Make audio or video recordings of their presentations for inclusion in their portfolio. (For more information, see p. 160-b.)

Additional Resources

🖥 **Technology: Online Resources**
- Instant Check
- Guided, Core, Audio
- *Para hispanohablantes*
- Communication Activities

Print
- Guided WB pp. 139–140
- Core WB pp. 59–60

Teacher's Resources
- Teacher's Resource Materials: Audio Script, Communicative Pair Activities, Technology: Audio Cap. 4

Assessment

Prueba 4-8 with Remediation (online only)
Prueba: Pronombres posesivos
- Prueba 4-8

Examen: Vocabulario y gramática 2
- Examen 2
- ExamView: Examen 2

Puente a la cultura

Standards: 1.1, 1.2, 1.3, 2.1, 2.2, 3.1, 3.2

Suggestions

Pre-reading: Refer students to the *Estrategia*. Ask them to apply their background knowledge about poetry, music, and visual arts. Talk about what different kinds of love are expressed in the art they know and how it is expressed.

Reading: Encourage students to read through the entire passage once silently, without stopping at problem words or to ask questions. Remind them to use background knowledge, cognates, and context clues to help them understand unfamiliar words and expressions.

Post-reading: Ask volunteers to paraphrase the main idea and important details from the three main sections of the reading, including the introduction.

COUNTRY CONNECTION

Standards: 3.1

Suggestions: Display a map of Spain. Point out the Spanish cities mentioned in the reading. Assign a different city to small groups. Ask them to research their city and report back to the class with three facts about its history, important industries, and famous sites.

 Technology: Mapa global interactivo, Actividad 1 Travel the length of Judith Baca's mural wall in Los Angeles, CA.

Teacher-to-Teacher

e-amigos: Have students choose an expression of love or friendship from a Spanish-language song. Ask them to send their *e-amigos* the quote and comment on the feelings expressed.

Online Cultural Reading

Standards: 2.2

Suggestion: After doing the online activity, ask students to describe two traits that represent their personalities.

Puente a la cultura

OBJECTIVES
▶ Read about expressions of love in Latin American and Spanish arts
▶ Compare and contrast different historical and cultural expressions of love

El amor en las artes

A través de su arte y literatura, los países de América Latina y España han expresado siempre la importancia que tiene el amor. Esta característica de la cultura del mundo hispanohablante se mantuvo a través de los siglos y sigue viva hoy.

El amor en la pintura

Quizá el sentimiento de amor más importante en la cultura latinoamericana y española es el amor a la madre. Además de poemas y estatuas, el amor a la madre ha inspirado a muchos pintores. Uno de ellos es Diego Rivera (1886–1957). Este famoso pintor y muralista disfrutaba pintando mujeres con niños, especialmente mujeres indígenas a quienes presentaba con hermosos niños, y vestidas de brillantes colores.

La pintura en murales ha sido otra forma de expresión artística del amor, el amor a la comunidad. Judith Francisca Baca es una artista de California que ha fundado programas de creación de murales. Con su arte ha ayudado a embellecer la comunidad, a hacer conocer otras culturas y a alentar[1] a miles de jóvenes a interesarse en las artes. En la creación de uno de sus murales, *"The Great Wall"*, participaron más de 400 jóvenes de 14 a 21 años de edad.

[1] to encourage

Estrategia

Compare and contrast To compare, look for ways that people, events, things, or ideas are the same. To contrast, think about ways they are different. Think about their use, color, size, and shape, or other characteristics.

Online Cultural Reading

Go to Auténtico
ONLINE to read and understand a website with a personality quiz from the Spanish-speaking world.

Estrategia: Use the structure: When you are familiar with the genre of a website, you can predict what kind of information it will provide.

¡Inténtalo! Scan the website. Have you encountered sites with a similar format? What do you think the purpose of this site is?

"The Great Wall of Los Angeles", (1976–1984), Judith Baca

Differentiated Instruction

Students with Special Needs

Pair advanced learners with visually impaired students. Advanced learners can describe the Diego Rivera painting, focusing on how the painter demonstrates the love between mother and child. Advanced learners will also benefit from this analysis of the artwork.

Advanced Learners

Ask students to prepare an oral report about an important poem, song, or painting from the Spanish-speaking world that has love as a theme. This might be a work of art they have studied in earlier chapters of *Auténtico*. Have them tell about the kind of love expressed and how it is expressed.

Go **Online** to practice
PEARSON
realize
VIDEO   WRITING   MAPA GLOBAL

PearsonSchool.com/Autentico

Culture **4**

El amor en la música

La música es otra de las artes que se han usado para expresar el amor. Se escucha siempre en los grandes festivales y eventos patrióticos, en las elegantes bodas, en paseos y en funerales.

Agustín Lara (1897–1970), uno de los grandes compositores mexicanos, compuso la letra y la melodía de más de 600 canciones y sus éxitos suman cientos. La fuente de inspiración de la mayoría de sus canciones fue el amor a la mujer, ya que su vida estuvo llena de romances. Pero Agustín también fue un enamorado de España y dedicó canciones a las ciudades de Sevilla, Toledo, Navarra, Murcia, Valencia y Madrid. Su canción "Granada" ha dado la vuelta al mundo en las voces de los más famosos artistas.

El amor en la poesía

De todas las formas de expresar el amor en la literatura, quizás la más apropiada es la poesía. Un ejemplo es la obra del gran poeta español Gustavo Adolfo Bécquer (1836–1870). Cuando la escuela en donde estudiaba náutica cerró, Gustavo Adolfo se mudó a Madrid donde fundó la revista "España Artística" con algunos amigos. Allí empezó a tener problemas económicos y de salud, lo que lo llevó a instalarse en el Monasterio de Veruela en donde escribió, entre otras obras, las famosas "Cartas desde mi celda". Su escritura era simple y sentimental. Una de sus obras más reconocidas es "Rimas", un conjunto de poemas breves. Gustavo Adolfo Bécquer fue sin duda un escritor romántico.

Amor eterno

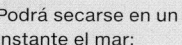

Podrá nublarse el sol
eternamente;
Podrá secarse en un
instante el mar;
Podrá romperse el eje[1] de la tierra
Como un débil cristal.
¡Todo sucederá! Podrá la muerte
Cubrirme con su fúnebre crespón[2];
Pero jamás en mí podrá apagarse
La llama[3] de tu amor.

[1]axis   [2]black cloak   [3]flame

¿Comprendiste?

1. Según el artículo, ¿en qué manifestaciones del arte de los países hispanohablantes se nota la importancia del amor? Da algunos ejemplos.

2. En el artículo se dice que el amor a la madre es el sentimiento más importante en la cultura hispanohablante. ¿Qué lugar crees que tiene en tu cultura? ¿Por qué?

3. Da ejemplos de otros sentimientos de amor que pueden expresarse en las artes.

4. Piensa en una expresión de amor de una canción, un poema o una pintura que conozcas. Escribe una composición para comparar tu ejemplo con el del artículo y di en qué se parecen y en qué se diferencian.

 Videodocumentario Una amistad entre hermanos

 Mapa global interactivo Explora el mural "La gran muralla de Los Ángeles", de Judith Baca, en Los Ángeles, California. Investiga las conexiones entre el arte público y la vida de las comunidades.

Capítulo 4 • ciento noventa y tres **193**

Enrich Your Teaching

Culture Note

Although Mother's Day **(el Día de la Madre)** is celebrated in much of Latin America as it is in the United States, it is especially important in Mexico. There, it is celebrated on May 10, and schools are closed. During the weeks before the holiday, Mexican students spend time rehearsing elaborate performances they will put on.

21st Century Skills

Media Literacy Encourage students to do online research on the artists, poets, and musicians featured in this cultural reading. They can search the keywords: *Agustín Lara, Diego Rivera, Judith Francisca Baca,* or *Juana de Ibarbourou.* Have students identify another work from one of these artists that represents another interpretation of love.

¿Comprendiste?

Standards: 1.2, 1.3, 2.1, 2.2, 3.1, 5.2

Suggestions: Have students read aloud or paraphrase the sections of the reading that support their answers to the first question. Use the other questions for discussion with the class.

Answers:

1. Se nota en la pintura, en la música y en la poesía. Unos ejemplos son las pinturas y los murales de Diego Rivera, las canciones de Agustín Lara y la poesía de Juana de Ibarbouru.

2–4. Answers will vary.

Teaching with Art

Suggestions: Help students talk about the Baca mural by asking: *¿Te gusta esta pintura? ¿Por qué? ¿Por qué no?*

 Technology: Videodocumentario

Standards: 1.2

View *Una amistad entre hermanos* with the class to learn more about family relationships. Access the video online in **Realize.** See the *Video Teacher's Guide* for additional suggestions.

Active Classroom

After the class has completed the reading, assign each student the number 1, 2, or 3. Each number represents a topic in the reading (1–***pintura;*** 2–***música;*** 3–***poesía***). Students are to write four questions about their section. Randomly create groups of 1s, 2s, and 3s. In these groups, have them ask each other their questions.

Additional Resources

 Technology: Online Resources
• Technology: *Videodocumentario*
• Guided, Writing, Reading
• *Para hispanohablantes*
• Cultural Reading Activity
• Communication Activities
Print
• Guided WB p. 141

¿Qué me cuentas?

Standards: 1.1, 1.2, 1.3

AP® Skills: Integration of listening, reading, and writing to comprehend and synthesize information from spoken and written sources.

Suggestions:

For Step 1, use the audio or read the descriptions aloud. Allow students to hear both descriptions twice through: the first time to write their answers, the second time to check them.

For Step 2, have students summarize the main points and make inferences to show that they understand what they have read.

Encourage students to express their own opinions in addition to using information from the reading in their written responses for Step 3.

 Technology: Audio Script and Answers

(For the complete script, see Teacher's Resource Materials.)

Step 1

1. b	**3.** b	**5.** a
2. a	**4.** a	**6.** b

Steps 2–3

Answers will vary.

Teacher-to-Teacher

Have students imagine they had an argument with their best friend. Have them write a note to the friend to explain how upset they are, to tell how important their friendship is, and to apologize for the dispute. Have students exchange the notes with another student who will respond in the role of the best friend. Ask students to focus on how a friendship satisfies their basic needs.

Additional Resources

 Technology: Online Resources
  • *Para hispanohablantes*

Pre-AP® Integración

OBJECTIVES
▶ Listen to and read about a description of a relationship
▶ Talk about the conflict and its solutions

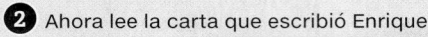 **¿Qué me cuentas?: Conflictos con y sin solución**

¿Qué consejos das a los demás? Primero escucha una versión de un conflicto que pasó entre dos jóvenes. Anota las respuestas a las preguntas y guárdalas para usarlas en el paso 3.

1 Vas a escuchar lo que ocurrió entre Laura y Enrique. Después de cada descripción, vas a oír dos preguntas. Escoge la respuesta correcta para cada pregunta.

1. a. Fueron a ver una película en el cine.
   b. Fueron a dar un paseo por el barrio.
2. a. tres meses
   b. nueve meses
3. a. de que la cena no estaba hecha
   b. de que no tenía su bolsa
4. a. Regresó al parque para ver si encontraba la bolsa.
   b. Fue a la casa de Enrique para ver si él tenía la bolsa.
5. a. a Enrique con otra chica
   b. a una chica con su bolsa
6. a. que lo perdonaba
   b. "¡Adiós!"

2 Ahora lee la carta que escribió Enrique.

❧ *Diana Dice* ❧

DIFERENCIA DE OPINIÓN

Estimada Diana: Necesito que me ayude con un problema. Laura y yo llevamos tres meses de novios. Es una chica fantástica y me encanta pasar tiempo con ella. Pero la verdad es que soy joven (tengo solo 16 años), y quiero conocer más chicas. Hace poco, pasé un día entero con Laura y nos divertimos mucho, pero por la noche tenía una cita con una amiga nueva. Fui con ellla al parque para conversar cuando de repente pasó Laura y nos vio. Se enojó y salió corriendo. Laura ya no contesta mis llamadas ni me habla en el colegio. Normalmente es una chica muy comprensiva. Quiero reconciliarme con ella, pero temo que ella ya no confíe en mí. No creo que la culpa sea mía, y quiero que hagamos las paces. ¿Qué hago?

—*Malentendido en Santiago*

3 Habla con un(a) compañero(a) sobre el conflicto entre Laura y Enrique. ¿Qué opinan de cada joven? ¿Qué aconsejan a Enrique? ¿Está equivocado? ¿Debe pedirle perdón a Laura? ¿Y qué aconsejan a Laura? ¿Debe confiar en Enrique? ¿Deben seguir de novios? Presenten sus recomendaciones a la clase. Si no están de acuerdo, expliquen sus diferencias de opinión. Usen las expresiones para conectar sus ideas.

cuando
entonces
porque
importante que
es una lástima que

194 ciento noventa y cuatro • Capítulo 4 • ¿Cómo te llevas con los demás?

Differentiated Instruction

Heritage Speakers

Some students with a particularly strong command of spoken Spanish may be able to skip Step 1 of the *Presentación oral* on the next page and offer problems and solutions orally without writing them down.

Students with Learning Difficulties

Before students begin the first part of *¿Qué me cuentas?*, review the directions, emphasizing that they will hear three descriptions and two questions after each description. Suggest that after answering questions 1 and 2, they put down their pencils and listen to the next description. The same applies after questions 3 and 4, and 5 and 6.

Presentación oral

OBJECTIVES
▸ Demonstrate how to discuss and solve problems
▸ Get into the character you are representing to improve your performance

Go **Online** to practice
PEARSON
realize™
PearsonSchool.com/Autentico
 AUDIO    SPEAK/RECORD

Una sesión del consejo estudiantil

TAREA Un consejo estudiantil *(student council)* es un grupo de estudiantes que ayuda a resolver problemas en la escuela. Trabaja con un grupo para representar ante la clase una sesión del consejo estudiantil.

1 **Prepárate** Al reunirse el consejo, algunos miembros deben presentar un problema y otros deben expresar sus recomendaciones para resolver el problema y justificar su opinión. Anoten sus ideas en una tabla como ésta.

Problemas	Soluciones posibles
•	•

> **Estrategia**
>
> **Getting into your character** In some cases, your oral presentation will require you to act something out. Keep in mind the character you are representing and try to act, look, and speak in the same way your character would using culturally appropriate expressions, gestures, and register.

2 **Practica** Uno(a) de ustedes explica un problema y otro(a) sugiere soluciones. Lean lo que escribieron en la tabla y asignen turnos para que todos presenten por lo menos un problema o una solución.

Modelo

Miembro del consejo 1: *El problema que quiero presentar es el siguiente: Los estudiantes de los grados 10 y 11 siempre discuten en el gimnasio. Todos quieren jugar al básquetbol a la vez.*

Miembro del consejo 2: *Hablemos con el director para que tengamos recreos más largos y a horas diferentes.*

Miembro del consejo 3: *Pongámonos de acuerdo con ellos y tomemos turnos para usar el gimnasio.*

3 **Haz tu presentación** Hagan la representación ante la clase. Usen oraciones conectadas con detalles y elaboración. El estudiante cuenta en detalle el problema. Si lo desea, puede ponerse de pie.

4 **Evaluación** Tu profesor(a) utilizará la siguiente rúbrica para evaluar tu presentación.

Rubric	Score 1	Score 3	Score 5
How well you presented a problem	You presented no problem, or your problem could not be understood.	You mentioned a problem but it wasn't clearly presented.	Your problem was clearly and completely presented.
How well you presented solutions	You offered no solutions.	You offered some recommendations, but they need more supporting statements.	Your solutions were clearly and completely presented.
How well you portrayed your characters	Your speakers said very little. You offered no character portrayal.	Your speakers read their lines.	Your speakers clearly portrayed realistic characters.

Presentación oral

Standards: 1.1, 1.3, 3.1

Suggestions: Review the task and the four-step approach with students. Review the rubric with the class (see *Assessment* below). Before students begin practicing in Step 2, direct their attention to the *Estrategia*. Encourage them to practice at home before a mirror or with a partner in class to develop their drama skills.

Digital Portfolio

Make video or audio recordings of student presentations in class, or assign the Speak and Record activity so they can record their presentations online. Include the recording in their portfolios.

Pre-AP® Integration

- **Learning Objective:** Presentational Speaking
- **Activity:** Remind students to focus on the presentational speaking skills used in this task such as fluency, pronunciation, and comprehensibility.
- **Pre-AP® Resource Materials:** Comprehensive guide to Pre-AP® speaking skill development

Active Classroom

You might want to set up the presentation in a way similar to a trial as seen on Court TV. Record each scene and encourage one of the students to "introduce" each episode.

Additional Resources

 Technology: Online Resources
- *Para hispanohablantes*

Self Assessment

Presentación oral
- **Assessment Program:** Rubrics

Review the different levels of performance. After assessing students, help individuals understand how their performance could be improved. (See Teacher's Resource Materials for suggestions on using rubrics in assessment.)

Enrich Your Teaching

21st Century Skills

Productivity and Accountability Have students clearly define the tasks they need to accomplish for this "mock" student council presentation. Have them evenly divide up the tasks so each person has an equal role in defining the problem, determining the solution, and presenting to the class.

Language Arts Connection: Expository Writing

Standards: 3.1

Ask students to revisit stories they have read in their Language Arts classes. Have them study scenes in which two characters interact and ask: *¿Cómo se portan los dos personajes cuando hay un conflicto? ¿Cómo nos demuestran sus cualidades? ¿Cómo influyeron las cualidades de los personajes en la resolución del conflicto?*

Presentación escrita

Standards: 1.2, 1.3, 3.1

Suggestions: Begin by explaining the criteria you will use to evaluate students' compositions. (See Step 5, *Evaluación*, in the Student Edition, and *Assessment* on the following page.)

Direct students' attention to the *Estrategia*. Ask them to consider how a character's actions, words, and thoughts are closely linked to what he or she is like. Ask: *Si un personaje es entrometido, ¿qué va a hacer si ve a dos personas que hablan? Si un personaje es comprensivo, ¿qué va a hacer si un amigo le pide perdón?* On their own paper, have students begin a chart like the one shown on this page. Point out that for this assignment, students need to tell about an event that happened between the two characters that helps readers better see what they are like.

Active Classroom

Collect the first drafts and write sentences that show examples of errors. Distribute these to pairs of students to find and fix the errors. Do not identify which papers the errors came from. This will help them become more aware of common errors and assist them with self-editing.

Presentación escrita

OBJECTIVES
▸ Write a description of a relationship
▸ Use the characters' actions to describe them

Estrategia
Describing relationships
Good writers help readers deduce the relationships between characters from their actions, words, and thoughts.

✎ Una relación

Piensa en algún cuento sobre la amistad entre dos personas. Escribe una composición sobre los personajes. Describe cómo son, qué cosas tienen en común, en qué son diferentes y cómo es su relación.

1 **Antes de escribir** Para ayudarte a recordar a los personajes de tu composición, puedes hacerte las siguientes preguntas.

• ¿Quiénes eran los personajes? ¿Qué cualidades tenían?
• ¿Qué cosas tenían en común? ¿En qué se diferenciaban?
• ¿Tuvieron algún problema? ¿Cómo lo resolvieron?

Completa la tabla para preparar tu composición. En la primera columna, apunta los nombres de los personajes. En la segunda, haz una lista de sus cualidades. En la tercera, apunta las acciones de los personajes que contribuyen *(contribute)* a la armonía o al conflicto. En la cuarta, describe por qué los personajes hacen lo que hacen y, finalmente, en la quinta, saca conclusiones sobre cómo sus acciones y cualidades influyen en la relación que tienen.

Personajes	Cualidades	Acciones	¿Por qué?	¿Cómo influyen en la relación?
Sandra	generosa, alegre, habla mucho, hace bromas	alguien dijo que ella se había copiado en un examen	hacía muchas bromas	
Paola	callada, honesta	le dijo a Sandra que hablara con la profesora	sabía que era un malentendido	

2 **Borrador** Escribe tu borrador. Para empezar, describe a los personajes. Luego cuenta qué problema tuvieron y cómo lo resolvieron. Por último, saca conclusiones sobre la relación.

Modelo

Presenting the main characters: Describe the characters using specific words.

Conflict resolution: Explain the consequences of the characters' actions.

Sandra y Paola son amigas. Sandra es generosa y alegre. Paola es callada y honesta. Le preocupa que Sandra tenga problemas por hacer tantas bromas. Alguien le contó a la profesora que Sandra se había copiado en la prueba. Paola estaba segura de que era una broma. Luego . . .
Sandra fue a hablar con la profesora para resolver el malentendido.
Creo que estas chicas tienen una buena amistad. Lo que hizo Paola muestra que piensa en los demás, y que Sandra le hizo caso muestra que tiene confianza en su amiga.

Main conflict: Describe the characters' actions.

Conclusion: Draw conclusions about the relationship.

Differentiated Instruction

Heritage Speakers

Students may sometimes confuse the letters **b** and **v** in their writing since these letters are often pronounced the same way in Spanish. As part of the revision process, have students use a dictionary to be sure that they have spelled all words with **b** and **v** correctly.

Advanced Learners

Ask students to write a short scene or part of a scene from a play in which two characters are in conflict. Students do not have to resolve the conflict in this scene. Have them share their scenes with other students, who tell what the characters are like, based on what they do, say, or think in the scene.

3 **Redacción/Revisión** Después de escribir el borrador, intercambia tu trabajo con el de un(a) compañero(a) y hagan sugerencias para mejorarlo. Revisen si:

• usaron palabras específicas para describir a los personajes

• hay concordancia *(agreement)* entre sustantivos, adjetivos, verbos y pronombres

Haz lo siguiente: Subraya con una línea los sustantivos, con dos líneas los adjetivos y encierra en un círculo los verbos. Asegúrate de que en cada oración haya concordancia.

Sandra es generosa y alegre. Paola es callado y
_____ callada

honesta. Le preocupan que Sandra tenga
_____ preocupa

problemas por hacer muchas bromas. Alguien

le contó a la profesora que Sandra copió en la

prueba.

---

4 **Publicación** Antes de hacer la versión final, lee tu borrador y repasa los siguientes puntos:

• ¿Describí claramente a los personajes?

• ¿Expliqué el conflicto y las acciones de los personajes?

• ¿Corresponde la conclusión a la descripción de los personajes?

Después de revisar el borrador, escribe una copia en limpio y ponle un título.

5 **Evaluación** Se utilizará la siguiente rúbrica para evaluar tu presentación.

Rubric	Score 1	Score 3	Score 5
Your completion of task	Your lack of information or organization makes the writing unclear.	You offer descriptions, but important information is missing.	Choice and organization of information creates a convincing message.
Your description of characters	Your characters are not identified or described.	Your character descriptions need more development.	Your characters are clearly portrayed.
Sentence structure/ grammar, spelling, mechanics	Your sentences are run-on or are fragmented. There are many grammar, spelling, and mechanics errors.	You use sentences consistently, but some grammar, spelling, and/or mechanics errors are present.	You use correct structure. There are few grammar, spelling, and mechanics errors. Your sentences are connected and contain details and elaboration.

Capítulo 4 • ciento noventa y siete **197**

Enrich Your Teaching

21st Century Skills

Social and Cross-Cultural Skills
Have the students brainstorm a list of famous relationships as seen in modern day television shows, movies, or books they all know. Discuss how each relationship is portrayed in the media (in the spoken language, gestures or body language, conflicts, music, etc.) and how the media may influence how we perceive each relationship.

Suggestions (Cont'd): Once students have a rough draft ready, read through the model on this page together. Help them see how information from the chart on the previous page was incorporated into this draft and note the additional information that was added. Point out uses of the subjunctive and of ***por*** and ***para.*** Encourage them to work toward similar organization, level of detail, and language use as they revise their own drafts.

Common Errors: Students often have difficulty effectively organizing their writing. Guide them to follow these steps in their composition:

A. Give a general description of the characters.
B. Introduce a conflict.
C. Show how the characters acted in the conflict.
D. Show how the conflict was resolved.

Evaluation
Steps 4 and 5 overlap. Students will need some evaluation by you, their peers, or some self-evaluation to polish their drafts.

Digital Portfolio
Keep students' final drafts in their portfolios as a writing sample.

Pre-AP® Integration

• **Learning Objective:** Presentational Writing
• **Activity:** As a warm-up to the *Presentación escrita,* ask students to brainstorm a list of five or more qualities of a healthy friendship and five or more qualities of an unhealthy relationship.
• **Pre-AP® Resource Materials:** Comprehensive guide to Pre-AP® writing skill development

Additional Resources

 Technology: Online Resources
• *Para hispanohablantes*

Self Assessment

Presentación escrita
• **Assessment Program:** Rubrics
Review the different levels of performance. After assessing students, help individuals understand how their performance could be improved. (See Teacher's Resource Materials for suggestions on using rubrics in assessment.)

Lectura

 Technology: Mapa global interactivo, Actividad 2 Visit places where poet Pablo Neruda lived in Chile.

Suggestions

Pre-reading: Before reading, direct students' attention to the *Al leer* section and to the *Estrategia*. Address any difficulties they may have understanding the concepts of ***la metáfora*** and ***el símil,*** and provide additional examples as necessary. Copy the graphic organizer from p. 203 and read the instructions that accompany it. Tell students that they will first work with a partner to record the examples of figurative language they find. Later, the class will compile their findings.

Reading: Have students work in pairs to read each poem using this procedure:

- Read the poem silently.
- Discuss comprehension problems, find examples of figurative language, and record these on the chart.
- Read the poem again silently.

Besides the instances of figurative language mentioned in the *¿Comprendiste?* on the next page, the following are other instances found in *Poema No. 15* that students should notice:

Metáfora

mariposa en arrullo (line 10)

Símil

Eres como la noche (line 15)

Starter Activity

As a class, brainstorm a list of words to describe personality traits of good friends. (*honesto, cariñoso, etc.*)

Lectura

OBJECTIVES
- Read about poems of love and friendship
- Identify figurative language to understand a poem
- Express your opinion about rap and rap poetry readings

La poesía, expresión de amor y amistad

Al leer

En la cultura del mundo hispanohablante la poesía es una de las formas preferidas para expresar lo que sentimos. Para crear sus poemas, los poetas usan figuras retóricas *(figures of speech)* como la metáfora y el símil.

El símil es una comparación que se hace entre dos cosas usando la palabra *como.* Por ejemplo, el poeta Pablo Neruda habla de un "silencio claro como una lámpara". Con las metáforas también se hacen comparaciones entre dos cosas, pero sin usar la palabra *como.* Por ejemplo, cuando el poeta llama a la mujer que ama "mariposa de sueño", la está comparando con una mariposa. Copia la tabla de la página 195. Mientras lees los poemas, completa los espacios en blanco de la tabla.

Presta atención a los siguientes puntos:

- cómo los poemas expresan amor o amistad
- el uso de las metáforas y los símiles
- las imágenes que usa el o la poeta

Estrategia

Identifying and understanding figurative language When somebody says *He ruffled his friend's feathers,* do you think that the friend is a bird? Of course not. This is a figurative language expression that means "to bother" or "to annoy". To identify figurative language, pay attention to phrases that connect two different kinds of things, for example *cheeks like roses,* or *life is a river.* Then, to figure out what the poet is trying to communicate, think what characteristics of one of those things can be used to describe the other.

Poema No.15

Pablo Neruda

Me gustas cuando callas[1] porque estás como ausente[2],
y me oyes desde lejos, y mi voz no te toca.
Parece que los ojos se te hubieran volado[3] y
parece que un beso te cerrara la boca.

Como todas las cosas están llenas de mi alma[4]
emerges de las cosas, llena del alma mía.
Mariposa de sueño[5], te pareces a mi alma,
y te pareces a la palabra melancolía.

Me gustas cuando callas y estás como distante.
Y estás como quejándote, mariposa en arrullo[6].
Y me oyes desde lejos, y mi voz no te alcanza:
déjame que me calle con el silencio tuyo.

Déjame que te hable también con tu silencio
claro como una lámpara, simple como un anillo.
Eres como la noche, callada y constelada.
Tu silencio es de estrella, tan lejano y sencillo.

Me gustas cuando callas porque estás como ausente.
Distante y dolorosa como si hubieras muerto.
Una palabra entonces, una sonrisa bastan[7]. Y
estoy alegre, alegre de que no sea cierto.

[1]you are quiet [2]absent [3]had flown [4]soul [5]dream butterfly [6]cooing [7]suffice

---

Differentiated Instruction

Heritage Speakers

Have students select a Latin American artist whose works express love or friendship. They may choose a poem, a song, or a piece of visual art. Ask them to write a paragraph about how the artist expresses his or her love or friendship. Have them also mention what they like and don't like about the work.

Visual/Spatial Learner

Invite students to close their eyes as you read the poems out loud. Then invite them to share the mental images that the poets' words evoked.

Go **Online** to practice
PEARSON
realize™
PearsonSchool.com/Autentico
✍ WRITING 🌐 MAPA GLOBAL

Homenaje a los padres chicanos

Abelardo Delgado

Con el semblante[1] callado,
con el consejo bien templado[2],
demandando siempre respeto,
con la mano ampollada[3] y el orgullo repleto,
así eres tú y nosotros te hablamos este día,
padre, papá, apá, jefito, dad, daddy . . . father,
como acostumbremos llamarte, eres el mismo.
La cultura nuestra dicta[4]
        que el cariño que te tenemos
lo demostremos poco
        y unos hasta creemos
que father's day
        es cosa de los gringos
                pero no . . .
tu sacrificio es muy sagrado
para dejarlo pasar hoy en callado.
Tu sudor[5] es agua bendita[6]
y tu palabra sabia[7],
derecha como esos surcos[8]
que con fe unos labran[9] día tras día,
nos sirve de alimento espiritual
y tu sufrir por tierras

y costumbres extrañas,
tu aguante[10], tu amparo[11], tu apoyo,
todo eso lo reconocemos y lo agradecemos
y te llamamos hoy con fuerza
        para que oigas
aun si[12] ya estás muerto,
        aun si la carga fue mucha
o la tentación bastante y
        nos abandonaste
aun si estás en la cárcel[13]
o en un hospital . . .
óyeme, padre chicano, oye también a mis
hermanos, hoy y siempre, papá, te veneramos.

---

[1]face [2]tempered [3]blistered [4]dictates [5]sweat [6]holy water [7]wise [8]grooves [9]plow [10]endurance [11]protection [12]even if [13]jail

¿Comprendiste?

Trabaja con un grupo para hablar de las poesías y contestar estas preguntas:

1. ¿Qué quiere decir el poeta con "Me gusta cuando callas porque estás como ausente"?

2. ¿Qué te parece que quiere decir Neruda con "tu silencio claro como una lámpara, simple como un anillo"?

3. ¿Por qué se alegra el poeta en la última estrofa del "Poema No. 15"?

4. ¿Qué crees que quiere decir Delgado con "con la mano ampollada y el orgullo repleto"?

5. Describe las características de los padres que admira Delgado.

Mapa global interactivo Explora la ubicación de las tres casas de Pablo Neruda en Chile.

Capítulo 4 • ciento noventa y nueve **199**

Enrich Your Teaching

Culture Note

Pablo Neruda (1904–1973), a Chilean poet and diplomat, won the Nobel Prize for Literature in 1971. He was politically active, holding various positions as Chilean consul to Burma, Argentina, and Mexico. In 1943, he was elected to the Chilean Senate. Much of Neruda's writing reflects political struggles, and he became known as the people's poet. Neruda is also greatly admired for his love poems. His poetry is more widely read than that of any other Latin American poet.

Suggestions (Cont'd):
Reading: Besides the instances of figurative language mentioned in the *¿Comprendiste?*, the following are other instances found in *Homenaje a los padres chicanos* that students should notice:

Metáfora
Tu sudor es agua bendita (line 13)

Símil
tu palabra sabia, / derecha como esos surcos / que con fe unos labran día tras día (lines 14–16)

AP® Literature: Pablo Neruda is an AP® Literature author. You may want to suggest that students read additional works by this author.

¿Comprendiste?

Standards: 1.1, 1.2

Suggestions: Remind students that understanding every word in the poems is less important than understanding the main ideas and the imagery the poets use to create impressions and to stir our emotions.

Answers will vary.

Pre-AP® Integration

- **Learning Objective:** Presentational Speaking (Cultural Comparison)
- **Background:** This task prepares students for the Spoken Presentational Communication tasks that focus on cultural comparisons.
- **Activity:** Have students prepare a two-minute (maximum) presentation on the following topic: Different views about fathers vary between cultures. Students may use Abelardo Delgado's view of the Chicano father as presented in his poem, *"Homenaje a los padres chicanos"* as a basis for the comparison. They should then comment on another poem or song from their own culture, explaining the similarities and differences between the two.
- **Pre-AP® Resource Materials:** Comprehensive guide to Pre-AP® speaking skill development

Suggestions (Cont'd):

Interpretive: Besides the instances of figurative language mentioned in the *¿Comprendiste?* on the next page, the following are other instances that students should notice:

El amor en preguntas:

Metáfora

volver a nacer (line 5)
inventar la gente (line 6)
crecer otra vez (line 9)

Point out that these are all metaphors the poet uses to describe what one must do to love and be loved. None of them are meant to be taken literally; instead they refer metaphorically to actions of the spirit.

Como tú:

Metáfora

el paisaje celeste de los días de enero (lines 3–4)
Mi sangre bulle (line 5)

Símil

la poesía es como el pan (line 9)

Pre-AP® Literature: Gustavo Adolfo Bécquer is an Pre-AP® Literature author. You may want to suggest that students read additional works by this author.

Teaching with Art

Suggestions: To guide discussion of the painting, ask: Who is present in the painting? What are the decorations like? What story does the picture tell? What feelings does the artist convey, and how?

El amor en preguntas

Elizabeth Torres (15 años)

¿Qué me hace falta para amar?
¿Qué es necesario para ser amado,
para entender la vida y saber soñar?
Tengo acaso que obtener permisos,
girar el mundo,
volver a nacer,
inventar la gente,
dar para merecer[1],
responder preguntas,
crecer[2] otra vez?

¿O se necesita estar inspirado,
abarcar[3] el mundo,
ser iluminado?

Estallar[4] el alma . . .
¡sólo para amar!

[1]to deserve [2]to grow [3]to cover [4]to burst

"La salchichona", (1917), Pablo Picasso
Oil on canvas, 116 x 89 cm. Musée Picasso, Barcelona, Spain.
© 2009 Estate of Pablo Picasso/Artists Rights Society (ARS), New York.
Photo: Giraudon/Art Resource, NY.

Rimas

Gustavo Adolfo Bécquer

XXI

¿Qué es poesía? —dices mientras clavas[1]
 en mi pupila tu pupila azul—.
¿Qué es poesía? ¿Y tú me lo preguntas?
 Poesía . . . eres tú.

XXIII

Por[2] una mirada, un mundo;
por una sonrisa, un cielo,
por un beso . . . , ¡yo no sé
qué te diera[3] por un beso!

XXVIII

Los suspiros[4] son aire y van al aire.
Las lágrimas[5] son agua y van al mar.
Dime, mujer: cuando el amor se
olvida, ¿sabes tú a dónde va?

[1]fix [2]in exchange for [3]I would give [4]sighs [5]tears

Como tú

Roque Dalton

Yo, como tú,
amo el amor, la vida, el dulce encanto
de las cosas, el paisaje
celeste de los días de enero.

También mi sangre bulle[1]
y río por los ojos que
han conocido el brote[2] de las lágrimas.

Creo que el mundo es bello,
que la poesía es como el pan, de todos.

Y que mis venas[3] no terminan en mí
sino en la sangre unánime
de los que luchan por la vida,
el amor,
las cosas,
el paisaje y el pan,
la poesía de todos.

[1]boils [2]outpouring [3]veins

Differentiated Instruction

Heritage Speakers

Invite students with exemplary pronunciation to read aloud one stanza of each poem. After each reading, point out words that are linked together in spoken language. For example, in the first line of **Rimas,** the **e** sound in **qué** is elided with the first sound of the next word, **es.**

Advanced Learners

Ask students to read another poem by one of the poets studied and give a brief interpretation of its meaning and its use of figurative language.

Go **Online** to practice

PearsonSchool.com/Autentico

PEARSON
realize

WRITING

Interpretive Reading

4

Interacción con la lectura

Trabaja con la clase para completar una tabla como la de al lado y comentar lo que cada poeta quiere decir.

• Identifiquen y apunten todas las metáforas y símiles que encuentren en los poemas.

• Hablen acerca de lo que quiere trasmitir el poeta con cada uno(a).

Metáfora	Símil

¿Comprendiste?

1. Parafrasea la idea principal de cada poema. Incluye el tema y los detalles más importantes.

2. Según Bécquer, ¿la poesía está en las palabras de un poema? ¿Estás de acuerdo con el poeta? ¿Por qué?

3. En la "Rima XXVIII", ¿qué comparación hace el autor entre los suspiros, las lágrimas y el amor?

4. Después de leer el poema de Elizabeth Torres, ¿crees que es necesario hacer cosas extraordinarias para ser amado por las otras personas? ¿Por qué?

5. ¿Qué quiere decir Roque Dalton cuando escribe "mis venas no terminan en mí"?

6. ¿Cuál de los poemas te gustó más? ¿Por qué?

7. Forma un grupo con tres compañeros(as) para dar su opinión sobre estos temas:

   • ¿Qué medios usan los jóvenes para expresar sus sentimientos? Hagan una lista.

   • ¿De qué manera esas expresiones de sentimientos benefician a la comunidad?

CULTURA ◀ **El mundo hispano**

La lectura de poemas por sus propios autores es una costumbre muy popular en bibliotecas y librerías de toda España y América Latina. De igual manera, en los Estados Unidos se realiza una actividad cultural similar; en muchos centros comunitarios[1] se hacen concursos de poesía y rap, en los cuales los poetas leen sus obras ante el público. Por ejemplo, en la Ciudad de Nueva York, el *Nuyorican Poet's Cafe,* organiza concursos literarios y lecturas en español y en inglés.

• Muchas personas creen que el rap es una forma de poesía. ¿Estás de acuerdo? ¿Por qué?

• ¿Te interesa asistir a un concurso en el que los poetas de rap recitan sus poemas? ¿Por qué?

• ¿Te interesa asistir a un concurso de poesía que no sea rap? ¿Por qué?

[1]community centers

Capítulo 4 • doscientos uno **201**

Interacción con la lectura

Standards: 1.1, 1.2, 3.1

Suggestions

Pre-reading: Have students compile the examples of figurative language they and their partners have found into a class chart. Use this activity as a basis for further discussion of the poems.

¿Comprendiste?

Standards: 1.1, 1.2, 1.3, 3.2

Suggestions: For item 7, ask the small groups to divide the task in such a way that everyone participates in reporting orally.

Answers will vary.

CULTURA ◀

Standards: 1.1, 1.2, 2.1

Suggestions: After reading and discussing the information, ask interested students to work together to prepare and present a poetry reading. Students can research Spanish-language poetry at libraries and on the Internet, then present readings of the poems. Encourage them to accompany each reading with a brief interpretation of the poem's meaning.

Answers will vary.

Additional Resources

Technology: Online Resources
• Guided, Writing, Reading
• Cultural Reading Activity
• Communication Activities
• *Para hispanohablantes*
Print
• Guided WB pp. 142–143
• Literacy Skills WB pp. 34–44

Enrich Your Teaching

Culture Note

As students read about love in Spanish literature, explain the origins of the appellation "Don Juan." Never an actual person, Don Juan is a legendary character of Spanish folklore. The earliest-known dramatization of a Don Juan story, **El burlador de Sevilla,** was written by Tirso de Molina in 1630.

21st Century Skills

ICT (Information, Communications and Technology) Literacy Have students use the digital technology within **Realize** to access extra reading support. Computer corrected activities use reading strategies to help students build their vocabulary and progress at their own pace through the reading.

Auténtico

Standards: 1.2

Resources: Authentic Resources Wkbk, Cap. 4
Authentic Resources: Cap. 4: Videoscript
AP®Theme: *La vida contemporánea: Las relaciones personales*

Antes de ver

Discuss the *Estrategia* with students. Invite them to look at the image from the video and ask them to express in Spanish what emotions the man reveals in his face. Then review the key vocabulary with the class. Tell students that *taconazos* comes from the word *tacón*, which means *high heel*.

Technology: Ve el video

Before starting the video, direct students' attention to the *Mientras ves* activity. Have students use the activity page from the Authentic Resources Workbook.

Play the video through, without pausing. Ask students to pay special attention to the role of each person in the video. Guide them to identify the format of the piece: one person presents the main information about emotions, and the other four people on the panel express their opinions on that same subject. Replay the video, pausing as necessary.

Haz las actividades

Mientras ves

Standards: 1.2

Suggestions: Discuss the questions with the class. Ask volunteers to respond to each question to determine overall understanding.

Answers:

- La presentadora que habla al comienzo.
- El hombre llamado Ismael.
- Complementar la información que da Ismael.

Auténtico

Partnered with UNIVISION COMMUNICATIONS INC

La amargura es contagiosa

Antes de ver

Usa la estrategia: Lenguaje corporal

Mira la imagen del video. ¿Qué emoción expresa esta persona? Al ver el video, pon atención a los gestos de las personas que hablan. Esto te ayudará a inferir el significado de palabras o términos que no conoces.

Lee el vocabulario clave

amargura = bitterness
inconsciente = unconscious [could also be "unaware"]
entorno = surroundings
dar taconazos = stomp one's feet
apacible = peaceful
carcajada = fit of laughter

▶ Ve el video

¿Crees que las emociones son contagiosas? Por ejemplo, ¿crees que si una persona que está junto a ti se enoja, tú también puedes llegar a sentirte enojado(a)?

Ve a **PearsonSchool.com/Autentico** para ver el video *¡Toma nota!: la amargura de los demás sí se contagia.* Conocerás los resultados de una interesante investigación sobre este tema.

Haz las actividades

Mientras ves Mientras ves el video, identifica a las personas que hablan. Hazte estas preguntas:

- ¿Quién hace las preguntas?
- ¿Quién da la información más importante?
- ¿Qué papel tienen las demás personas del panel?

Differentiated Instruction

Heritage Speakers

Invite students to discuss in Spanish situations where their emotions spread to others or when someone else's emotions affected their own. They should describe the emotions and the situation.

Challenge

For a more challenging activity, invite volunteers to role-play the panelists that appear on the video. Ask them to paraphrase in Spanish the opinions given in the video.

¿TE ESTÁS CONTAGIANDO DE LA AMARGURA
DE LAS PERSONAS QUE TE RODEAN?

UNIVISION®
COMMUNICATIONS INC

Después de ver

Standards: 1.2, 4.2

Suggestions: Discuss the questions with the class and enlist several volunteers to respond to each question to gauge overall understanding. Students may need some guidance with the first question. Tell them to think about how both the flu and one's emotions can spread from one person to another.

Answers:

1. se transmite igual de rápido
2. Las neuronas espejo replican las emociones de los demás.
3. alguien da taconazos y otros se ponen ansiosos; alguien se ríe y otros se ríen
4. tratar de imitar a las personas con buena actitud

Pre-AP® Integration

Resources: Authentic Resources Wkbk, Cap. 4
Authentic Resources: Cap. 4: Videoscript

Suggestions: Before completing the Pre-AP® activity, have students go to the workbook and complete the worksheets for the additional resources.

Comparación cultural

Interpretive: Compare and contrast cultural practices from authentic audiovisual materials.

Suggestions: Have students provide specific examples of how they express their emotions in particular situations and how people they know from other backgrounds express theirs.

Integración

Después de ver Vuelve a ver el video para poder contestar estas preguntas:

1. Según la presentadora del video, ¿qué tiene que ver la gripe con las emociones?
2. ¿Qué explicación científica da Ismael sobre cómo se contagian las emociones?
3. Parafrasea los dos ejemplos que da Ismael sobre cómo se contagian las emociones.
4. ¿Cómo podemos aprovechar el contagio de las emociones de manera positiva?

For more activities, go to the Authentic Resources Workbook.

Las emociones humanas

Expansión Busca otros recursos auténticos en *Auténtico* en línea y contesta las preguntas.

 4 Auténtico

Integración de ideas ¿Qué circunstancias internas y externas pueden afectar las emociones que siente una persona? Respalda tu respuesta con detalles.

Comparación cultural ¿Qué diferencias puede haber entre el modo en que tú expresas tus emociones y el modo en que las expresa alguien de otro país o cultura?

Enrich Your Teaching

Culture Note

Introduce students to the following or similar expressions in Spanish related to human emotions:

- **¡Trágame tierra!** = I wish I could disappear!
- **¡Me saca de mis casillas!** = It gets on my nerves
- **¡Estoy en las nubes!** = I have my head in the clouds.

Encourage students to start a personal dictionary of Spanish idioms.

Using Authentic Resources

Have students create a personal vocabulary list with terms from the authentic resources that are related to human emotions.

Review Activities

Cualidades: Have students create a T-chart with the left column titled **Cualidades positivas** and the right titled **Cualidades negativas.** Ask them to sort the vocabulary from the **cualidades** list into these two categories and to write a brief Spanish definition for each word.

Sustantivos: Build a story using the nouns in this section of the *Vocabulario.* Have students sit in a circle. One student begins the story with a sentence that includes the word **amistad.** The student to his or her left continues by repeating that sentence and adding another that uses the word **armonía,** and so on. A variation on this is to write the words on slips of paper and place them in a hat or other container. This is passed around the circle. Students must build the story by adding a sentence that includes the word they draw from the hat.

Verbos: Have students work in pairs to invent mini-dialogues that use the verbs in the list. Each dialogue should use at least one of the verbs. Encourage them to use the verbs in different tenses, in the subjunctive, and with different subjects, in order to practice with different forms.

Expresiones: Play charades using the expressions from this list. Write the expressions on slips of paper and place them in a hat or other container. Students take turns drawing an expression and getting its meaning across to the others any way they can without speaking or writing. Use body language and strategies of traditional charades such as tugging at the ear to mean **suena como** or holding up two fingers to mean **dos palabras,** or invent your own rules.

El subjuntivo con verbos de emoción: On the board, write several subordinate **(que)** clauses, using a variety of verbs in the subjunctive. Vary the subjects of your clauses in order to use different verb forms. Precede each subordinate clause with a blank: ___ **que vayas.** ___ **que Uds. vayan a llegar tarde.** Have students supply verbs or expressions of emotion that make sense: *Te sugiero que vayas. Temo que Uds. vayan a llegar tarde.*

Repaso del capítulo

OBJECTIVE
▶ Review the vocabulary and grammar

🔊 Vocabulario

cualidades

amable	kind
cariñoso, -a	loving, affectionate
celoso, -a	jealous
chismoso, -a	gossipy
comprensivo, -a	understanding
considerado, -a	considerate
egoísta	selfish
entrometido, -a	meddlesome, interfering
honesto, -a	honest
íntimo, -a	intimate
sincero, -a	sincere
vanidoso, -a	vain, conceited

sustantivos

la amistad	friendship
la armonía	harmony
el comportamiento	behavior
la confianza	trust
el conflicto	conflict
la cualidad	quality
la explicación	explanation
el malentendido	misunderstanding
la pelea	fight
el secreto	secret

verbos

acusar	to accuse
alegrarse	to be delighted
apoyar(se)	to support, to back (each other)
atreverse	to dare
colaborar	to collaborate
confiar (i → í)	to trust
contar con	to count on
criticar	to criticize
desconfiar (i → í)	to mistrust
esperar	to hope (for)
estar equivocado, -a	to be mistaken
guardar (un secreto)	to keep (a secret)

ignorar	to ignore
mejorar	to improve
pedir perdón	to ask for forgiveness
perdonar	to forgive
ponerse de acuerdo	to reach an agreement
reaccionar	to react
reconciliarse	to become friends again
reconocer (c → zc)	to admit, recognize
resolver (o → ue)	to resolve
sorprender(se)	to (be) surprised
temer	to fear

expresiones

aceptar tal como (soy)	to accept (me) the way (I am)
cambiar de opinión	to change one's mind
la diferencia de opinión	difference of opinion
hacer caso	to pay attention / to obey
hacer las paces	to make peace (with)
juntos, -as	together
ojalá	I wish, I hope
pensar en sí mismo(a)	to think of oneself
¡Qué va!	No way!
tener en común	to have in common
tener celos	to be jealous
tener la culpa	to be guilty
¡Yo no fui!	It wasn't me!

Differentiated Instruction

Students with Learning Difficulties

Whenever possible, provide students with memory clues for retaining vocabulary. For example, say: **"Egoísta** looks like the English word 'egotistic.' Someone who is egotistic thinks a lot of him or herself and is probably selfish." Invite students to share their own memory devices.

Advanced Learners

Have students write a short e-mail to a friend that uses vocabulary and structures from the chapter. E-mails can be one of two types: either thanking the friend for his or her positive role in resolving a problem, or reproaching the friend for an undesirable action. Have students look back through the chapter for models of similar letters, such as the ones on pp. 169 and 179.

Gramática

Más recursos PearsonSchool.com/Autentico

- Games
- Tutorials
- Flashcards
- Instant check

El subjuntivo con verbos de emoción

Use the *subjunctive* following verbs indicating suggestions, desire or demands.	Use the *subjunctive* after verbs and impersonal phrases indicating emotion.	When the sentence has only one subject, we usually use the *infinitive* instead of the subjunctive.
Te sugiero que **vengas.** **Esperamos** que **llueva.** **Nos exigió** que **estudiemos.** **¡Ojalá** que **se diviertan!**	**Tememos** que nuestros amigos **desconfíen** de nosotros. **Es una lástima** que no **hagan** las paces.	**Espero ir** mañana al cine. **Espero ver** esa película.

Los usos de *por* y *para*

Use *por* to indicate: length of time or distance, where an action takes place, an exchange, a reason or motive, an action on behalf of someone, a means of communication or transportation.	Use *por* in certain expressions:	Use *para* to indicate: purpose, destination, a point in time, use, opinion.
Bailamos **por** varias horas. Busqué **por** todos los pasillos. Te cambio el café **por** un dulce. Me puse muy feliz **por** tu llegada. Fue a una marcha **por** la paz. Mandó la carta **por** avión.	**por** ejemplo **por** eso (tanto) **por** la (mañana, tarde, noche) **por** favor **por** lo general **por** primera (segunda, tercera, última) vez **por** supuesto	Estudio **para** tener un buen futuro. Salimos **para** la ciudad dentro de una hora. **Para** las ocho ya estaban allí. Ponte la chaqueta **para** no tener frío. **Para** ustedes todo es divertido.

Mandatos con *nosotros*

Regular verbs		Stem-changing verbs whose infinitive ends in *–ir*		Verbs ending in *–car, –gar,* and *–zar*	
olvidar	**olvidemos**	ped**ir**	**pidamos**	criti**car**	**critiquemos**
pensar	**pensemos**	dorm**ir**	**durmamos**	pa**gar**	**paguemos**
reconocer	**reconozcamos**			empe**zar**	**empecemos**

Direct and indirect pronouns are attached at the end of affirmative *nosotros* commands but precede the negative *nosotros* command form.	To attach reflexive or reciprocal pronouns at the end of a *nosotros* command, drop the final *–s* of the command before the pronoun.
Digámosle toda la verdad. No **les mintamos.**	**Alegrémonos** con nuestro éxito. **Abracémonos** uno al otro.

Pronombres posesivos

To form the **possesive pronouns,** use the long form possessive adjectives preceded by the definite article.

Mis padres son muy serios. ¿Y **los suyos**?
Su vestido es grande. **El nuestro** es pequeño.

We often omit the article between the verb *ser* and the possessive pronoun.

Esas maletas **son nuestras**, pero la mochila **es suya.**

Los usos de *por* y *para*: Have pairs write their own fill-in-the-blank quiz on the uses of **por** and **para.** Their quizzes should contain ten sentences in which one of the words is required. Tell students to include a variety of items in order to target the various rules of usage. They should make two copies, and they should also create an answer key. Then have pairs exchange their quizzes with another pair, take each other's quizzes, and check their work.

Mandatos con *nosotros*: Have students write three problems that need solving, such as *Mi computadora no funciona bien.* Have partners take turns reading these to each other and replying with a **nosotros** command that makes sense: *Llamemos a un técnico de computadoras.*

Pronombres posesivos: Have students create two sets of note cards. One set names individuals or groups of people, such as **María** or **los abuelos.** The other set names single or multiple nouns, such as **los problemas** or **el secreto.** Collect the cards and shuffle each set. Have students take turns drawing one card from each pile and making a sentence with a possessive pronoun: *María/los problemas: Los problemas son suyos.*

Digital Portfolio

Invite students to review the activities and projects they completed in this chapter. Have them select one or two items that they feel best demonstrate their achievements in Spanish. Include these products in students' portfolios with the Chapter Checklist and Self-Assessment Worksheet.

Additional Resources

 Technology: Online Resources
- Instant Check
- Integrated Performance Assessment
- *Para hispanohablantes*

Teacher Resources
- Teacher's Resource Materials: Situation Cards, Clip Art

 Technology: ¡Pura vida! is a storyline video that is independent of chapter content and an ideal support for expanding listening skills. The 14 episodes are available within **Realize.** Student activities and Teacher support are also assignable within **Realize.**

Enrich Your Teaching

Teacher-to-Teacher

By creating their own tools for learning, students can benefit twice: once as they are creating the tool and again as they are using it. When asking students to make tools such as flashcards, for example, make sure that your instructions are clear and give several examples so students understand exactly what is needed.

21st Century Skills

ICT (Information, Communications and Technology) Literacy Remind students of the various digital tools available in **Realize** to help them monitor their own understanding and learning needs, such as the online tutorials with comprehension check exercises, games, flashcards, and practice tests.

Performance Tasks

`Standards: 1.1, 1.2, 1.3, 2.1`

Student Resource: *Para hispanohablantes*
Teacher Resources: Teacher's Resource Materials: Audio Script, Technology: Audio Cap. 4

1. Vocabulario

Suggestions: Encourage students to review the vocabulary from the *Vocabulario en contexto* sections on pp. 166–168 and 180–183 before they complete the activity.

Answers:

1. a	**5.** c
2. b	**6.** b
3. d	**7.** d
4. b	**8.** a

2. Gramática

Suggestions: Remind students of the main points of the grammar presentations in *Capítulo* 4:

- the subjunctive with verbs of emotion
- uses of **por** and **para**
- **nosotros** commands
- possessive pronouns

Answers:

1. c	**5.** a
2. a	**6.** d
3. b	**7.** b
4. b	**8.** a

3. Escuchar

Suggestions: Use the audio or read from the script.

Script

El locutor de un canal de televisión entrevistó a varios jóvenes sobre lo que piensan de sus amigos. Escucha lo que dijo cada joven y, según lo que dijo, decide: (a) qué cualidades tiene su mejor amigo o amiga; (b) qué le molesta de su amigo o amiga; (c) qué tienen en común. Vas a oír cada conversación dos veces.
(For the complete script, see Teacher's Resource Materials.)

Answers:
Jorge:
- **a.** Su mejor amigo es muy comprensivo. Lo acepta tal como es y siempre puede contar con él.
- **b.** A veces es un poco entrometido y quiere saber todo lo que hace.
- **c.** A los dos les gusta jugar al béisbol.

Cristina:
- **a.** Su mejor amiga es muy sincera y considerada. Siempre le da consejos y nunca la critica.
- **b.** A veces es un poco vanidosa.
- **c.** Las dos toman clases de danza clásica y también les gusta mucho hacer yoga.

Repaso del capítulo

OBJECTIVE
▶ Demonstrate that you can perform the tasks on these pages

Preparación para el examen

1 Vocabulario Escribe la letra de la palabra o expresión que mejor complete cada frase. Escribe tus respuestas en una hoja aparte.

1. Mis sobrinos siempre me besan y me abrazan. Son muy _____.
   a. cariñosos c. entrometidos
   b. sinceros d. honestos

2. Cuando dos amigos se reconcilian, _____.
   a. piensan en sí mismos c. piensan en los demás
   b. hacen las paces d. tienen la culpa

3. Una persona _____ no sabe guardar secretos.
   a. vanidosa c. celosa
   b. egoísta d. chismosa

4. Beto y Graciela son _____. Nunca mienten.
   a. armonía c. amables
   b. sinceros d. comprensivos

5. Cuando acusé a mi amigo de romper mi cámara, él me contestó, "_____. ¡Yo no fui!"
   a. ¡Qué lástima! c. ¡Qué va!
   b. ¡Ojalá! d. ¡Tienes razón!

6. Mis padres nunca me _____. Me aceptan tal como soy.
   a. hacen caso c. temen
   b. critican d. piden perdón

7. Mis amigos y yo tenemos _____. Nos gusta montar en monopatín y jugar videojuegos.
   a. celos c. muchas peleas
   b. mucha confianza d. mucho en común

8. El cariño y la confianza son dos _____ importantes en una amistad.
   a. cualidades c. consejos
   b. conflictos d. explicaciones

2 Gramática Escribe la letra de la palabra o expresión que complete mejor cada frase. Escribe tus respuestas en una hoja aparte.

1. Me molesta que ustedes _____ tan chismosos.
   a. son c. sean
   b. seas d. es

2. Ojalá que ella me _____.
   a. perdone c. perdona
   b. perdonado d. perdonando

3. Es triste _____ nuestra amistad.
   a. rompa c. roto
   b. romper d. rompo

4. Fernando y Pedro _____ todos los días.
   a. nos escribíamos c. les escribí
   b. se escribían d. se escribió

5. Mis hermanas y yo _____ contábamos todos los secretos.
   a. nos c. se
   b. me d. lo

6. Después de pelearse con su mejor amigo, Jorge le dijo: "_____ las paces".
   a. hacíamos c. hicimos
   b. hacemos d. hagamos

7. "¿Nos reconciliamos?", preguntó Ana. "Sí, _____," contestó Gaby.
   a. reconciliarme c. reconciliémosnos
   b. reconciliémonos d. reconciliamos

8. Mis padres son muy comprensivos. ¿Cómo son _____?
   a. los tuyos c. las tuyas
   b. tuyos d. tuyas

Differentiated Instruction

Heritage Speakers

Remind students to take their time during both the chapter review and the actual exam. Point out that, even though they may have the necessary language skills to do well, they will have a higher chance of success if they read carefully and follow all directions.

Students with Learning Difficulties

Review test-taking strategies to prepare students for the exam. Remind them to read the directions before they begin each section. Practice using the process of elimination in items that resemble multiple-choice items on a test. Remind students that when deciding between two possible answers, first instincts are often correct.

Más recursos PearsonSchool.com/Autentico

 Games   Flashcards
Tutorials   Instant check

En el examen vas a . . .	Éstas son las tareas de práctica que te pueden ser útiles para el examen . . .	Para repasar, ve a tu libro de texto impreso o digital . . .
Interpretive 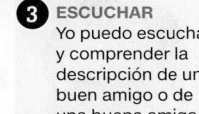 **3 ESCUCHAR** Yo puedo escuchar y comprender la descripción de un buen amigo o de una buena amiga.	El locutor de un canal de televisión entrevistó a varios jóvenes sobre lo que piensan de sus amigos. Escucha lo que dijo cada joven y, según lo que dijo, decide: (a) qué cualidades tiene su mejor amigo(a); (b) qué le molesta de su amigo(a); (c) qué tienen en común.	pp. 160–163 *Vocabulario en contexto 1* pp. 164–165 **Actividades 6–7** p. 166 **Actividad 8**
Interpersonal 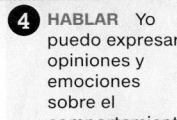 **4 HABLAR** Yo puedo expresar opiniones y emociones sobre el comportamiento de otra persona.	Estás cuidando a tu hermano menor que a veces se porta bien y a veces bastante mal. Dile a tu hermano lo que piensas y sientes acerca de su comportamiento. Usa por lo menos cinco frases. Por ejemplo, puedes decir: *Me alegro de que no tengas celos de nuestra hermanita. Es triste que no le hagas caso a mamá.*	p. 168 *El subjuntivo con verbos de emoción* p. 169 **Actividades 13–14** p. 181 **Actividad 32**
Interpretive 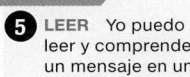 **5 LEER** Yo puedo leer y comprender un mensaje en un salón de chat.	Lee este mensaje que una joven puso en un salón de chat. Decide por qué tiene tantos conflictos con sus amigos y qué debe hacer para mejorar su relación con ellos. **No entiendo por qué mis amigos están enojados conmigo. Ana dice que nunca le presto mis revistas. Lucía está enojada porque le conté a su mamá que sacó una mala nota. Luis está furioso porque llegué dos horas tarde al cine y no pudimos ver la película. En fin, ¡mi vida es un desastre! ¿Qué puedo hacer?**	p. 160–163 *Vocabulario en contexto 1* p. 168 **Actividad 12** p. 173 **Actividad 21** pp. 174–177 *Vocabulario en contexto 2*
Presentational 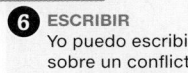 **6 ESCRIBIR** Yo puedo escribir sobre un conflicto entre amigos(as).	Escribe sobre un conflicto que ocurre entre dos amigos(as) en una película que viste o entre amigos(as) de la vida real. Explica por qué se rompe la armonía y cómo se reconcilian esas personas. Incluye oraciones conectadas con detalles y elaboración.	p. 170 **Actividad 15** p. 172 **Actividad 20** p. 173 **Actividad 21** p. 179 **Actividad 26** p. 181 **Actividad 32**
Comparisons 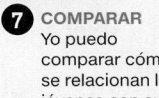 **7 COMPARAR** Yo puedo comparar cómo se relacionan los jóvenes con sus familias.	En México se hizo una serie de encuestas sobre la vida de los jóvenes y sus familias. Piensa en la información que leíste sobre este tema en el capítulo y compara las respuestas de los jóvenes mexicanos con tu propia experiencia.	pp. 176–177 **Actividades 23–24** p. 181 **Actividad 31**

Capítulo 4 • doscientos siete **207**

4. Hablar

Standards: 1.1

Suggestions: Tell students to first write down five good and bad ways in which the little brother behaves. Then they can more easily come up with their comments about his behavior.

Answers will vary.

5. Leer

Suggestions: Tell students to refer to pp. 166–168 and 180–183 if they have questions about vocabulary in the review.

Answers will vary, but should make use of these subjunctive forms:

prestes/no cuentes/llegues/puedas

6. Escribir

Standards: 1.3

Suggestions: Remind students to be sensitive to the privacy of others if they choose to write about real-life events.

Answers will vary.

7. Comparar

Suggestions: Have students share their thoughts with each other and compare their perceptions about young people and family life in the United States.

Answers will vary.

Additional Resources

Technology: Online Resources
• Instant Check
• *Para hispanohablantes*
Print
• Core WB pp. 61–62

Differentiated Assessment

Core Assessment
• Technology: Audio Cap. 4
• ExamView: Chapter Test, Test Banks A and B

Advanced/Pre-AP®
• ExamView: Pre-AP® Test Bank
• Pre-AP® Resource Materials, pp. 147–149

Extra Support
• Alternate Assessment Program: Examen del capítulo 4
• Technology: Audio Cap. 4

Heritage Speakers
• Assessment Program: Para hispanohablantes: Examen del capítulo 4
• ExamView: Heritage Speaker Test Bank

CAPÍTULO 5

Trabajo y comunidad

Jobs and Volunteer Work

Vocabulary: jobs and job skills; interviewing techniques; volunteer work

Grammar: present perfect; pluperfect; present perfect subjunctive; demonstrative adjectives and pronouns

Cultural Perspectives: the importance of finding a job or profession; the meaning of work for young people in Latin America; the Hispanic Heritage Foundation; work as seen through the art of Diego Rivera; Hispanic contributions to American society

¡Pura vida!: Watch an engaging video episode about a group of young people in Costa Rica!

Bulletin Boards

Theme: Trabajo y comunidad

Ask students to cut out, copy, or download photos of people from different professions and jobs, including volunteer work. They should also include a photo of something related to each profession or job, such as a photo of a doctor along with a photo of a hospital or a patient.

Hands-on Culture

Recipe: Mate

Mate is a very popular drink in Argentina. Most of the *gauchos*, Argentinian cowboys, drink mate in the afternoon.

Ingredients:

1/2 oz. *mate* powder; 1 cup water, hot but not boiling; pinch of sugar

Supplies: *kettle*, *mate* gourd or large cup; small paper cups, *bombilla* (silver sipping straw with strainer at bottom) and/or paper straws

1. Put *mate* and sugar in the *mate* gourd (or cup) and add a cup of hot water.
2. Let the *mate* powder steep for 3-5 minutes before drinking through a *bombilla* or straw. Keep straws away from the grounds at bottom.
3. Tell students that the Argentines sit in a circle and pass the *mate* clockwise. When more water is needed, the *cebador* (server) adds hot water from the kettle.
4. Pour the *mate* into small paper cups.

Game

Rueda de palabras

This memory game practices vocabulary about work and community using a spinner. Use it toward the end of *Trabajo y comunidad*, after students have practiced the vocabulary of the chapter.

Players: entire class

Materials: spinner, pen

Rules:

1. Fill in spinner sections with the six vocabulary categories used in *Repaso del capítulo*, *Vocabulario y gramática*. Omit the *Acciones* and *Expresiones* categories.
2. Select a scorekeeper and divide the class into four groups. Have each group choose a writer.
3. Spin the spinner and announce the category. Groups have 3 minutes to write down all the Spanish words they can think of that fit the category. Words cannot be repeated from category to category.

Spinner category: *En el trabajo*

Team writes: *el anuncio clasificado, los beneficios, la clienta, la compañía, el gerente, el puesto, el salario, la solicitud de empleo, la computación, la recepcionista*

4. When time is up, groups take turns reading their lists one word at a time. Groups that have the same word cross it from their lists. When a category is exhausted, a tally is taken. The team with the largest number of words wins the round and spins for the next category.
5. Play until all six categories have been used.

Variation: Each team writes sentences with the words they wrote for each category. The more correct sentences they write in a given time, the more points they score.

21st Century Skills

Look for tips throughout Chapter 5 to enrich your teaching by integrating 21st Century Skills. Suggestions for the Project-Based Learning and Culture follow below.

Project-Based Learning

Modify the project with these suggestions:

ICT (Information, Communications and Technology) Literacy Encourage students to use information from a variety of Web sites to find the appropriate job descriptions for their friends' future jobs. The handout "Search for Information on the Internet" will help them find reliable sources that describe popular professions and job postings in Spanish.

Creativity and Innovation Have students design a unique matching game to match professions to people. Have them describe and illustrate several professions in Spanish, along with some people, their personalities, and their likes/dislikes. Have small groups work together to match the people with the most appropriate profession.

Communication As students prepare to present their project to the class, provide them with the handout "Give an Effective Presentation" to remind them of the importance of body language, tone of voice, eye contact, and other strategies for delivering an effective presentation.

Chapter Culture

Social and Cross-Cultural Skills Help students bridge cultural differences by offering them opportunities to discuss the culture highlighted throughout the chapter, such as the meaning of work for young people in Latin America, as seen in the *Cultura* on p. 220.

▶ **Technology: Videodocumentario**
View *Un voluntario en la comunidad* online with the class to learn more about a young Dominican boy and his volunteer work in a local community center.

Project-Based Learning

Álbum de mis amigos en el futuro

Overview: Students create six pages for a digital or paper scrapbook featuring photos or illustrations of their friends along with a brief description of what professions or jobs they think their friends are going to have in the future. They then give an oral presentation of their scrapbook, describing one of their friends and predicting his or her future profession or job.

Resources: construction paper, digital or print photos of friends, drawing paper, colored pencils, markers, glue, scissors

Sequence: (suggestions for when to do each step appear throughout the chapter)

Step 1. Review instructions so students know what is expected of them. Share the rubric with the class.

Step 2. Students submit a rough sketch of their scrapbook pages. Return the sketches with your suggestions. For vocabulary and grammar practice, ask pairs to present their drafts to each other.

Step 3. Students do layouts. Encourage them to try different arrangements before writing descriptions.

Step 4. Students submit a draft of their descriptions. Note your corrections and suggestions, then return the drafts to students.

Step 5. Students complete and present their scrapbook to the class. They should describe one of the people in the photos or illustrations and say what profession or job they think he or she is going to have in the future.

Options

1. Students write and create a poster with photos or descriptions about the future professions and jobs of their friends.
2. Students write a composition about the future professions and jobs of their best friends.

Assessment

Here is a detailed rubric for assessing this project:

Chapter 5 Project: *Álbum de mis amigos en el futuro*

Rubric	Score 1	Score 3	Score 5
Your evidence of planning	You provide no preliminary sketch or description drafts.	Your preliminary sketch and descriptions are created, but not corrected.	You show evidence of corrected sketch and descriptions.
Your use of illustrations	You include no photos or illustrations.	You provide photos or illustrations but don't organize them.	You provide well organized photos and illustrations.
Your presentation	You do not include the required information.	You include most of the required information.	You include all of the required information.

AT A GLANCE

Objectives
- Listen to and read about job interviews and classified ads
- Talk and write about applying for a job
- Exchange information about your skills, background experience, and job opportunities
- Understand the influence of Hispanics in the U.S.
- Compare a Mayan folktale with myths in the U.S.
- Compare cultural practices in an authentic text about education and employment opportunities

Vocabulary
- Jobs and activities in the workplace
- Personal qualities and skills needed
- Volunteer and community work
- Job interviews

Grammar
- Present perfect
- Pluperfect
- Present perfect subjunctive
- Demonstrative adjectives and pronouns

Culture
- Community gardens in Latin America, p. 213
- The meaning of work for the young people in Latin America, p. 220
- The Hispanic Heritage Foundation, p. 224
- José Gálvez, photographer, p. 234
- Silvio Rodríguez, p. 239
- Spanish in the U.S., pp. 240–241
- Community centers, p. 249

A ver si recuerdas...
- Work
- Community
- Present participle
- Reflexive pronouns with direct/indirect pronouns

Recycle
- *r* between two vowels

Authentic Resources
- **Auténtico:** El trabajo y el mercado laboral, pp. 250–251

RESOURCES

	FOR THE STUDENT	DIGITAL	PRINT	FOR THE TEACHER	DIGITAL	PRINT
A ver si recuerdas PP. 208–211						
Review	*A ver si recuerdas* with Remediation	•		*A ver si recuerdas* with Remediation	•	
	Guided WB, pp. 144–147	•	•	Teacher's Edition, pp. 208–211		
	Core WB, pp. 63–64	•	•			
	Para hispanohablantes	•				
Introducción PP. 212–213						
Present	Student Edition, pp. 212–213	•	•	Teacher's Edition, pp. 212–213	•	•
	DK Reference Atlas	•		Teacher's Resource Materials	•	
	Videonovela: *¡Pura vida!*	•		Mapa global interactivo	•	
	Technology: *¡Pura vida!* Video Activities	•				
	Para hispanohablantes	•				
Vocabulario en contexto PP. 214–217/228–231						
Present & Practice	Student Edition, pp. 214–217/228–231	•	•	Teacher's Edition, pp. 214–217/228–231	•	•
	Audio	•		Teacher's Resource Materials	•	
	Videohistoria	•		Vocabulary Clip Art	•	
	Flashcards	•		Technology: Audio	•	
	Instant Check	•		Video Program: Videohistoria	•	
	Guided WB, pp. 148–156/161–168	•	•			
	Core WB, pp. 65–66/70–71	•	•			
	Communication Activities	•				
	Para hispanohablantes	•				
Assess and Remediate				Pruebas 5–1/5–5: Assessment Program; Assessment Program *Para hispanohablantes*	• •	

	FOR THE STUDENT	DIGITAL	PRINT	FOR THE TEACHER	DIGITAL	PRINT
Vocabulario en uso PP. 218–221/232–234						
Present & Practice	Student Edition, pp. 218–221/232–234	•	•	Interactive Whiteboard Vocabulary Activities	•	
	Instant Check	•		Teacher's Edition, pp. 218–221/232–234	•	•
	Communication Activities	•		Teacher's Resource Materials	•	
	Para hispanohablantes	•		Technology: Audio	•	
	Communicative Pair Activities	•		Videomodelos	•	
Assess and Remediate				Pruebas 5–2/5–6 with Remediation	•	
				Pruebas 5–2/5–6: Assessment Program; Assessment Program *Para hispanohablantes*	•	
Gramática PP. 222–227/235–239						
Present & Practice	Student Edition, pp. 222–227/235–239	•	•	Interactive Whiteboard Grammar Activities	•	
	Instant Check	•		Teacher's Edition, pp. 222–227/235–239	•	•
	Tutorial Video: Grammar	•		Teacher's Resource Materials	•	
	Canción de hip hop	•		Technology: Audio	•	
	Guided WB, pp. 157–160/169–172	•	•	Videomodelos	•	
	Core WB, pp. 67–69/72–74	•	•			
	Communication Activities	•				
	Para hispanohablantes	•				
	Communicative Pair Activities	•				
Assess and Remediate				Pruebas 5–3, 5–4/5–7, 5–8 with Remediation	•	
				Pruebas 5–3, 5–4/5–7, 5–8: Assessment Program; Assessment Program *Para hispanohablantes*	•	
				Examen 1, Examen 2: Vocab. y gramática	•	
Aplicación PP. 240–251						
Apply	Student Edition, pp. 240–251	•	•	Teacher's Edition, pp. 240–251	•	•
	Online Cultural Reading	•		Teacher's Resource Materials	•	
	Guided WB, pp. 173–175	•	•	Video Program: Videodocumentario	•	
	Communication Activities	•		Mapa global interactivo	•	
	Para hispanohablantes	•		Authentic Resources Lesson Plans with scripts, answer keys	•	
	Videodocumentario	•				
	Auténtico	•				
	Authentic Resources Workbook	•	•			
	Authentic Resources	•				
Repaso del capítulo pp. 252–255						
Review	Student Edition, pp. 252–255	•	•	Teacher's Edition, pp. 252–255	•	•
	Online Games	•		Teacher's Resource Materials	•	
	Core WB, pp. 75–76	•	•	Technology: Audio	•	
	Communication Activities	•				
	Para hispanohablantes	•				
	Instant Check	•				
Chapter Assessment						
Assess				Examen del capítulo 5: Assessment Program; Alternate Assessment Program; Assessment Program *Para hispanohablantes*	• • •	
				Technology: Audio Cap. 5, Examen	•	
				ExamView: Test Banks A and B (questions only online) Heritage Speaker Test Bank Pre-AP® Test Bank	• • •	

RESOURCES

LESSON PLAN

DAY	Warm-up / Assess	Preview / Present / Practice / Communicate	Wrap-up / Homework Options
1	**Warm-up** (10 min.) • Return Examen del capítulo: Capítulo 4	**Repaso** (35 min.) • A ver si recuerdas . . . • Actividades 3, 5	**Wrap-up and Homework Options** (5 min.) • Core Practice 5-1, 5-2
2	**Warm-up** (10 min.) • Homework check	**Chapter Opener** (10 min.) • Objectives • Arte y cultura **Vocabulario en contexto 1** (25 min.) • Presentation: Vocabulario y gramática en contexto • Actividades 1, 2, 3, 4	**Wrap-up and Homework Options** (5 min.) • Clip Art Vocabulary
3	**Warm-up** (10 min.) • Homework check	**Vocabulario en contexto 1** (30 min.) • Presentación: Videohistoria *La entrevista de trabajo* • View: Videohistoria **Vocabulario en uso 1** (5 min.) • Actividad 6	**Wrap-up and Homework Options** (5 min.) • Core Practice 5-3, 5-4 • Prueba 5-1: Vocabulary recognition
4	**Warm-up** (10 min.) • Homework check • **Formative Assessment** (10 min.) • Prueba 5-1: Vocabulary recognition	**Vocabulario en uso 1** (25 min.) • Actividades 7, 8, 9, 10 • Interactive Whiteboard Vocabulary Activities • Ampliación del lenguaje	**Wrap-up and Homework Options** (5 min.) • Actividad 13 • Writing Activities • Prueba 5-2 with Remediation: Vocabulary production
5	**Warm-up** (10 min.) • Cultura • Homework check • **Formative Assessment** (10 min.) • Prueba 5-2 with Remediation: Vocabulary production	**Gramática y vocabulario en uso 1** (25 min.) • Actividades 11, 12, 14 • Presentation: El presente perfecto • Interactive Whiteboard Grammar Activities	**Wrap-up and Homework Options** (5 min.) • Core Practice 5-5
6	**Warm-up** (10 min.) • Actividad 16 • Homework check	**Gramática y vocabulario en uso 1** (35 min.) • Actividades 15, 17 • En voz alta • Cultura • Communicative Pair Activity	**Wrap-up and Homework Options** (5 min.) • Writing Activity • Prueba 5-3 with Remediation: El presente perfecto
7	**Warm-up** (5 min.) • Homework check • **Formative Assessment** (10 min.) • Prueba 5-3 with Remediation: El presente perfecto	**Gramática y vocabulario en uso 1** (30 min.) • Presentation: El pluscuamperfecto • Interactive Whiteboard Grammar Activities • Actividades 18, 19, 20, 21 • Communicative Pair Activity	**Wrap-up and Homework Options** (5 min.) • Core Practice 5-6, 5-7 • Prueba 5-4 with Remediation: El pluscuamperfecto
8	**Warm-up** (10 min.) • Actividad 22 • Homework check • **Formative Assessment** (10 min.) • Prueba 5-4 with Remediation: El pluscuamperfecto	**Vocabulario en contexto 2** (25 min.) • Presentation: Vocabulario y gramática en contexto • Actividades 23, 24	**Wrap-up and Homework Options** (5 min.) • Clip Art Vocabulary • Examen: Vocabulario y gramática 1
9	**Warm-up** (5 min.) • Homework check • **Formative Assessment** (30 min.) • Examen: Vocabulario y gramática 1	**Vocabulario en contexto 2** (10 min.) • Presentation: Se buscan voluntarios • Presentation: ¿A quién van a escoger?	**Wrap-up and Homework Options** (5 min.) • Actividad 25 • Core Practice 5-8, 5-9 • Prueba 5-5: Vocabulary recognition
10	**Warm-up** (20 min.) • Actividades 26, 27 • Homework check • **Formative Assessment** (10 min.) • Prueba 5-5: Vocabulary recognition	**Vocabulario en uso 2** (15 min.) • Actividades 30, 32 • Interactive Whiteboard Vocabulary Activities	**Wrap-up and Homework Options** (5 min.) • Actividades 28, 29 • Prueba 5-6 with Remediation: Vocabulary production

LESSON PLAN

DAY	Warm-up / Assess	Preview / Present / Practice / Communicate	Wrap-up / Homework Options
11	**Warm-up** (10 min.) • Cultura • Homework check • **Formative Assessment** (10 min.) • Prueba 5-6 with Remediation: Vocabulary production	**Gramática y vocabulario en uso 2** (25 min.) • Actividades 31, 33 • Presentation: El presente perfecto del subjuntivo • Interactive Whiteboard Grammar Activities • Cultura • Actividad 35	**Wrap-up and Homework Options** (5 min.) • Actividad 34 • Core Practice 5-10 • Prueba 5-7 with Remediation: El presente perfecto del subjuntivo
12	**Warm-up** (15 min.) • Actividad 36 • Homework check • **Formative Assessment** (10 min.) • Prueba 5-7 with Remediation: El presente perfecto del subjuntivo	**Gramática y vocabulario en uso 2 (20 min.)** • Presentation: Los adjetivos y los pronombres demostrativos • Interactive Whiteboard Grammar Activities • Actividades 37, 39	**Wrap-up and Homework Options** (5 min.) • Core Practice 5-11, 5-12 • Prueba 5-8 with Remediation: Los adjetivos y los pronombres demostrativos
13	**Warm-up** (10 min.) • Cultura • Homework check • **Formative Assessment** (10 min.) • Prueba 5-8 with Remediation: Los adjetivos y los pronombres demostrativos	**Gramática y vocabulario en uso 2** (25 min.) • Actividad 38 • Communicative Pair Activity • El español en la comunidad	**Wrap-up and Homework Options** (5 min.) • Examen: Vocabulario y gramática 2
14	**Warm-up** (5 min.) • Writing Activity • **Formative Assessment** (30 min.) • Examen: Vocabulario y gramática 2	**Aplicación** (10 min.) • Presentación oral: Step 1, 2	**Wrap-up and Homework Options** (5 min.) • Presentación oral: Step 2
15	**Warm-up** (10 min.) • Presentación oral: Step 2	**Aplicación** (35 min.) • Presentación oral: Step 3	**Wrap-up and Homework Options** (5 min.) • Estados Unidos . . . en español • Escribe tu opinión • ¿Comprendiste?
16	**Warm-up** (15 min.) • Estados Unidos . . . en español: ¿Comprendiste? • Homework check	**Aplicación** (30 min.) • Pre-AP® Integración 1, 2, 3 • View Video • Video Activities 1, 2, 3	**Wrap-up and Homework Options** (5 min.) • Presentación escrita: Steps 1, 2
17	**Warm-up** (10 min.) • Video Activity 4	**Aplicación** (15 min.) • Presentación escrita: Step 3 **Repaso** (20 min.) • Preparación para el examen: Actividades 3, 4	**Wrap-up and Homework Options** (5 min.) • Presentación escrita: Step 4
18	**Warm-up** (10 min.) • Homework check	**Aplicación** (35 min.) • Lectura • Interacción con la lectura • Cultura • Auténtico	**Wrap-up and Homework Options** (5 min.) • Core Practice: Organizer 5-13, 5-14 • Instant Check
19	**Warm-up** (20 min.) • Preparación para el examen: Actividades 1, 2 • Homework check	**Repaso** (25 min.) • Preparación para el examen: Actividades 5, 6, 7 • Other review	**Wrap-up and Homework Options** (5 min.) • Examen del capítulo
20	**Warm-up** (5 min.) • Answer questions • **Summative Assessment** (44 min.) • Examen del capítulo		**Wrap-up and Homework Options** (1 min.) • A ver si recuerdas: Capítulo 6 • Actividades 4, 5, 8

ALTERNATE LESSON PLAN

DAY	Warm-up / Assess	Preview / Present / Practice / Communicate	Wrap-up / Homework Options
1	**Warm-up** (35 min.) • Return Examen del capítulo: Capítulo 4 • A ver si recuerdas . . . • Actividad 3, 5 • Homework check	**Chapter Opener** (10 min.) • Objectives • Arte y cultura **Vocabulario en contexto 1** (30 min.) • Presentation: Vocabulario y gramática en contexto • Actividades 1, 2, 3, 4, 5 • Presentación: Videohistoria *La entrevista de trabajo* • View: Videohistoria	**Wrap-up and Homework Options** (5 min.) • Core Practice 5-3, 5-4 • Clip Art Vocabulary • Prueba 5-1: Vocabulary recognition
2	**Warm-up** (15 min.) • Actividad 8 • Homework check • **Formative Assessment** (10 min.) • Prueba 5-1: Vocabulary recognition	**Vocabulario en uso 1** (60 min.) • Actividades 6, 7, 9, 10, 11, 12, 13 • Interactive Whiteboard Vocabulary Activities • Cultura • Ampliación del lenguaje	**Wrap-up and Homework Options** (5 min.) • Writing Activities • Prueba 5-2 with Remediation: Vocabulary production
3	**Warm-up** (15 min.) • Writing Activity • Homework check • **Formative Assessment** (10 min.) • Prueba 5-2 with Remediation: Vocabulary production	**Gramática y vocabulario en uso 1** (60 min.) • Presentation: El presente perfecto • Actividades 14, 15, 17 • Interactive Whiteboard Grammar Activities • En voz alta • Cultura • Audio or Writing Activities	**Wrap-up and Homework Options** (5 min.) • Core Practice 5-5 • Prueba 5-3 with Remediation: El presente perfecto
4	**Warm-up** (10 min.) • Actividad 16 • Homework check • **Formative Assessment** (10 min.) • Prueba 5-3 with Remediation: El presente perfecto	**Gramática y vocabulario en uso 1** (45 min.) • Presentation: El pluscuamperfecto • Interactive Whiteboard Grammar Activities • Actividades 18, 20, 21, 22 • Communicative Pair Activity **Vocabulario en contexto 2** (15 min.) • Presentation: Vocabulario y gramática en contexto • Actividades 23, 24	**Wrap-up and Homework Options** (5 min.) • Core Practice 5-6, 5-7 • Prueba 5-4 with Remediation: El pluscuamperfecto • Examen: Vocabulario y gramática 1
5	**Warm-up** (10 min.) • Actividad 19 • Homework check • **Formative Assessment** (40 min.) • Prueba 5-4 with Remediation: El pluscuamperfecto • Examen: Vocabulario y gramática 1	**Vocabulario en contexto 2** (20 min.) • Presentation: Vocabulario y gramática en contexto • Actividades 25, 26 • Presentation: ¿A quién van a escoger? • Actividad 27 **Vocabulario en uso 2** (10 min.) • Actividad 30 • Interactive Whiteboard Vocabulary Activities	**Wrap-up and Homework Options** (5 min.) • Core Practice 5-8, 5-9 • Prueba 5-5: Vocabulary recognition

ALTERNATE LESSON PLAN

DAY	Warm-up / Assess	Preview / Present / Practice / Communicate	Wrap-up / Homework Options
6	**Warm-up** (20 min.) • Actividad 28, 29 • Homework check • **Formative Assessment** (10 min.) • Prueba 5-5: Vocabulary recognition	**Gramática y vocabulario en uso 2** (55 min.) • Actividades 31, 32, 33 • Cultura • Presentation: El presente perfecto del subjuntivo • Interactive Whiteboard Grammar Activities • Actividades 34, 35, 36	**Wrap-up and Homework Options** (5 min.) • Core Practice 5-10 • Pruebas 5-6, 5-7 with Remediation: Vocabulary production, El presente perfecto del subjuntivo
7	**Warm-up** (15 min.) • Writing Activity • Homework check • **Formative Assessment** (20 min.) • Pruebas 5-6, 5-7 with Remediation: Vocabulary production, El presente perfecto del subjuntivo	**Gramática y vocabulario en uso 2** (35 min.) • Presentation: Los adjetivos y los pronombres demostrativos • Interactive Whiteboard Grammar Activities • Actividades 37, 38, 39 • El español en la comunidad • Cultura **Aplicación** (15 min.) • Presentación oral: Steps 1, 2	**Wrap-up and Homework Options** (5 min.) • Presentación oral: Step 2
8	**Warm-up** (15 min.) • Writing Activity • Homework check	**Aplicación** (40 min.) • Presentación oral: Step 3 **Gramática y vocabulario en uso 2** (15 min.) • Communicative Pair Activity **Aplicación** (15 min.) • Presentation: Estados Unidos . . . en español	**Wrap-up and Homework Options** (5 min.) • Core Practice 5-11, 5-12 • Prueba 5-8: Los adjetivos y los pronombres demostrativos • Examen: Vocabulario y gramática 2
9	**Warm-up** (10 min.) • Homework check • **Formative Assessment** (30 min.) • Prueba 5-8 with Remediation: Los adjetivos y los pronombres demostrativos • Examen: Vocabulario y gramática 2	**Aplicación** (45 min.) • Estados Unidos . . . en español • ¿Comprendiste? • Escribe tu opinión • View Video • Video Activities • Pre-AP® Integración 1, 2, 3 • Presentación escrita: Step 1	**Wrap-up and Homework Options** (5 min.) • Presentación escrita: Step 2 • Preparación para el examen: Actividades 1, 2
10	**Warm-up** (20 min.) • Presentación escrita: Step 3 • Homework check	**Aplicación** (40 min.) • Lectura • Interacción con la lectura • Cultura • Auténtico **Repaso** (25 min.) • Preparación para el examen: Actividades 3, 4, 6	**Wrap-up and Homework Options** (5 min.) • Presentación escrita: Step 4 • Core Practice: Organizer 5-13, 5-14 • Instant Check • Preparación para el examen: Actividades 5, 7 • Examen del capítulo
11	**Warm-up** (15 min.) • Homework check • **Summative Assessment** (45 min.) • Examen del capítulo	**Theme Game** (15 min.) **A ver si recuerdas – Capítulo 6** (10 min.) • Presentation: Vocabulario • Presentation: Gramática	**Wrap-up and Homework Options** (5 min.) • A ver si recuerdas – Capítulo 6 • Actividades 4, 5, 8 • Core Practice 6-1, 6-2

Vocabulario: Repaso

Standards: 1.1, 1.2

Suggestions: Before presenting the material in this review section, consider testing your students' command of the material by assigning the Prueba with Remediation. Students will automatically be given additional practice of the material they have not yet mastered, and you can focus your review based on the class's overall performance on the post-test.

On the board, write the following sentence: *En el (la)* lugar, *conozco a un(a)* trabajo *muy* cualidad *que* acción. Have students fill in the blanks with items from the four categories of the *Vocabulario* to create sentences that make sense: *En la* biblioteca, *conozco a una* empleada *muy* ordenada *que* usa la computadora.

Standards: 1.1, 1.3

Suggestions: Help students create a T-chart. Encourage students to base their discussion on real-life situations as much as possible. If a job they actually have is not included in the *Vocabulario*, have them find out the Spanish term for it either in a bilingual dictionary or by asking heritage speakers. For Step 3, point out that students should be commenting on the jobs their partners wrote about.

Answers will vary.

A ver si recuerdas

OBJECTIVES
▶ Talk and write about jobs
▶ Discuss what is happening

Vocabulario

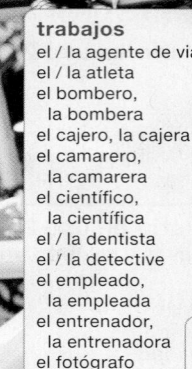

trabajos
el / la agente de viajes
el / la atleta
el bombero,
  la bombera
el cajero, la cajera
el camarero,
  la camarera
el científico,
  la científica
el / la dentista
el / la detective
el empleado,
  la empleada
el entrenador,
  la entrenadora
el fotógrafo
  la fotógrafa
el locutor,
  la locutora
el / la piloto
el reportero,
  la reportera
el vendedor,
  la vendedora

cualidades
animado, -a
artístico, -a
atlético, -a
bien educado, -a
cortés
interesante
obediente
ordenado, -a
paciente
trabajador, -a
tranquilo, -a

lugares
el banco
la biblioteca
el centro comercial
el cine
la escuela
la estación de
  servicio
la farmacia
el gimnasio
la guardería
  infantil
la librería
el museo
el restaurante
el supermercado
el teatro
la tienda

acciones
cortar el césped
cuidar niños
decorar
dibujar
hablar por teléfono
lavar el coche
lavar los platos
limpiar
pasar la aspiradora
pasear perros
sacar fotos
tocar un instrumento
usar la computadora

El trabajo

 HABLAR EN PAREJA, ESCRIBIR

❶ Describe en qué trabajas ahora y qué trabajos has tenido antes.

❷ Ahora, escribe en una hoja de papel dos trabajos que te gustaría hacer y dos que no te gustaría hacer. Junto a cada trabajo, pon lo que tienes que hacer, las cualidades que se necesitan y el lugar donde se hace el trabajo.

❸ Con otro(a) estudiante, hagan y contesten preguntas sobre por qué les gustarían o no les gustarían los trabajos que escribieron.

 Videomodelo
A —*Me gustaría **ser reportero**.*
B —*¿Por qué?*
A —*Un reportero escribe sobre cosas que pasan. Para ser reportero, debes saber escribir bien y sacar fotos.*

208 doscientos ocho • Capítulo 5 • Trabajo y comunidad

Differentiated Instruction

Students with Special Needs
Help hearing impaired students complete Step 3 of *Actividad* 1, by having them work with a partner and write out the dialogue instead of speaking it.

Advanced Learners
Have students choose one ***lugar*** from the *Vocabulario* and prepare a brief oral presentation telling about the different kinds of jobs encountered there, actions typically done, and one desirable quality for people to have who work there.

Go **Online** to practice

PearsonSchool.com/Autentico

PEARSON
realize™

▶ VIDEO ✎ WRITING 🎤 SPEAK/RECORD

Gramática

El participio presente

The present participle conveys a sense of ongoing action. To form the present participle add *-ando* to the stem of *-ar* verbs and *-iendo* to the stem of *-er* and *-ir* verbs.

trabajar	trabaj**ando**
hacer	hac**iendo**
recibir	recib**iendo**

- Verbs that have irregular third person forms in the preterite undergo the same change in the present participle.

dormir	d**u**rmiendo
pedir	p**i**diendo
decir	d**i**ciendo
reír	r**i**endo

- The verbs *ir* and *oír* and verbs ending in *-aer, -eer,* and *-uir* have present participles that end in *-yendo.*

ir	**yendo**
oír	**oyendo**
caer	**cayendo**
leer	**leyendo**
destruir	**destruyendo**

- The present participle is used together with a form of *estar* to form the progressive tense:

  ¡No me molestes! **Estoy leyendo**.

  Estábamos durmiendo cuando llamaste.

- Reflexive or object pronouns can be placed before the form of *estar*, or they can be attached to the end of the present participle. If they are attached to the present participle, a written accent is needed.

  Ahora **me** estoy **bañando**. / Estoy **bañándome**.

  Las está **ayudando**. / Está **ayudándolas**.

Más recursos ONLINE

▶ **GramActiva Video:** Present progressive

▶ **Tutorial:** Present progressive

2

¿Qué está pasando?

ESCRIBIR Escribe lo que está sucediendo en la clase en este momento. Nombra a las personas que están haciendo las siguientes actividades. Usa el presente progresivo en tus frases.

Modelo
mirar
La profesora está mirando a la clase.

| leer | darle | observar | dormirse | decirme |

3

¿Quién está haciéndolo?

HABLAR Indica quién está haciendo cada cosa en tu clase en este momento.

Modelo
escribir en su cuaderno
Laura está escribiendo en su cuaderno.
o: *Nadie está escribiendo en su cuaderno.*

1. ayudar a otro estudiante
2. recoger los papeles del piso
3. limpiar su escritorio
4. leer el libro de español
5. poner sus cosas en la mochila

Gramática: Repaso

Suggestions: Refer students who are having difficulty with the present progressive and the present participle to the online tutorial. Have students practice with present participles by contrasting the simple present with the present progressive tense. Ask them to tell about actions they do regularly and then say whether or not they are doing them at this moment: *Escucho música a menudo, pero no estoy escuchando música en este momento.*

2

Standards: 1.3

Suggestions: Have students switch roles, so both partners can practice asking and answering the questions.

Answers will vary, but students will use the following present participles:

leyendo	mirando
dándole	durmiéndose
observando	diciéndome

3

Standards: 1.1

Suggestions: Ask students to use compound subjects in some of their answers, so that they can practice with plural forms of the present progressive tense.

Answers will vary, but students will use the following present participles:

1. ayudando
2. recogiendo
3. limpiando
4. leyendo
5. poniendo

Enrich Your Teaching

Teacher-to-Teacher

Remind students that Spanish speakers use the present progressive in slightly different situations than do English speakers. Unless the action is happening right at the moment, Spanish speakers generally use the simple present tense. However, to emphasize that an action is taking place now, the present progressive can be used. Many English speakers tend to overuse the present progressive when speaking Spanish. Encourage students to avoid this habit and use the simple present.

Vocabulario: Repaso

Standards: 1.1, 1.2

Suggestions: Have students sit in a circle. Give one student a foam ball and have him or her give a definition of a vocabulary item that you choose from one of the lists. That student tosses the ball to another and names an item from a different *Vocabulario* category. The student who catches the ball gives a brief definition of that item and tosses the ball to another student, and so on.

Standards: 1.3

Suggestions: If students finish the task early, encourage them to add an extra ***trabajo*** done at a given location.

Answers will vary.

Extension: Have students trade their chart with a partner. The partner reports orally on the information he or she sees there: *Marina dice que en el hospital uno juega con los niños enfermos.*

Standards: 1.1

Suggestions: Make sure students switch roles in order to practice both parts of the dialogue. Remind them to include the personal *a* when referring to the people they are helping.

Answers will vary.

A ver si recuerdas

OBJECTIVES
▶ Talk and write about community work
▶ Discuss volunteer jobs

Vocabulario

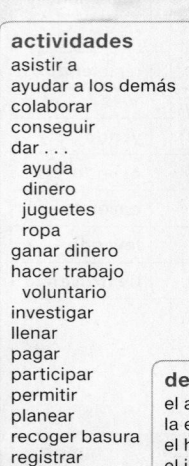

actividades
asistir a
ayudar a los demás
colaborar
conseguir
dar . . .
  ayuda
  dinero
  juguetes
  ropa
ganar dinero
hacer trabajo
  voluntario
investigar
llenar
pagar
participar
permitir
planear
recoger basura
registrar

desastres
el accidente
la explosión
el huracán
el incendio
la inundación
el terremoto
la tormenta

personas
los ancianos
la gente pobre
el niño, la niña
el paramédico,
  la paramédica
la víctima
el voluntario,
  la voluntaria

lugares
el aeropuerto
la agencia de viajes
el club atlético
el consultorio
el laboratorio
el mercado
el quiosco
el salón de belleza

expresiones
¿cómo se hace . . .?
ganarse la vida
no te olvides de . . .
seguir una carrera

Para la comunidad

 ESCRIBIR Haz una tabla como la siguiente. Escribe tres lugares de tu comunidad donde se pueda hacer trabajo voluntario. Al lado de cada lugar escribe qué trabajo se puede hacer y para qué o quién.

Lugar	Para quién / qué	Trabajo
el hospital	jugar	los niños enfermos

Trabajo voluntario

 HABLAR EN PAREJA Tu compañero(a) trabaja como voluntario(a).

1 Pregúntale:
- dónde trabaja
- qué hace allí
- a quién ayuda

2 Tu compañero(a) te invita a trabajar con él (ella). Acepta la invitación o da una excusa.

Differentiated Instruction

Heritage Speakers

Invite students who have lived in a heritage country to tell about volunteer work there. Encourage them to tell about the qualities needed in a person who does that kind of work.

Students with Learning Difficulties

If students have difficulty completing the chart independently, provide them with a partially completed chart and give some clues to help them finish it. For example, complete the ***Lugar*** column and then ask: *¿Qué trabajo se puede hacer allí?*

Go **Online** to practice
PEARSON
realize™
VIDEO | WRITING
PearsonSchool.com/Autentico

Gramática

Dónde van los pronombres reflexivos y de complemento

Reflexive pronouns, as well as direct and indirect object pronouns, may be placed either before a verb or after it.

- When there are two verbs, as with a participle or an infinitive, the pronoun may come either before the first verb or after the second verb.

- If the sentence is negative, place the pronoun between *no* and the verb.

- In affirmative commands, pronouns are attached to the end of the verb

- In negative commands, place the pronoun between *no* and the verb.

- Notice that written accent marks must often be added when a pronoun is attached to a verb.

Estamos divirtiéndo**nos** mucho.
Nos estamos divirtiendo mucho.
Voy a acostar**me** temprano.
Me voy a acostar temprano.

No **me** estoy aburriendo.
No **las** voy a comprar.

Carlos, despiérta**te**.   Chicos, láven**se** las manos.
¿Los niños? Cuída**los**.   ¿El parque? Límpie**lo**.

Esa película es mala. No **la** veas.

Recoge la basura.   **Recógela**.
Estoy lavando los platos.   Estoy **lavándolos**.

Más recursos ONLINE

▶ **Tutorials:** Indirect object pronouns, Placement of indirect object pronouns, Placement of reflexive pronouns

---

6

Según el director

LEER, ESCRIBIR El señor Díaz es el director de un centro de ayuda y da muchos mandatos. Usa los verbos y el pronombre apropiado para completar los mandatos que les dio a sus voluntarios.

| recoger | limpiar | servir | abrir | ayudar | lavarse |

Modelo
¿Los libros? _____ en la biblioteca.
¿Los libros? ***Pónganlos*** *en la biblioteca.*

1. ¿La comida? _____ al mediodía y _____ las manos antes de servirla.

2. ¿Las ventanas? No _____ ahora.

3. ¿La basura? No _____ ahora.

4. ¿Los niños? _____ con la tarea.

5. ¿El comedor? _____ después del almuerzo.

7

Metas personales

ESCRIBIR Escribe cinco metas *(goals)* que quieres alcanzar *(reach)* este año. Usa los pronombres apropiados.

Modelo
No voy a quejarme. / No me voy a quejar.
Quiero ayudar a los niños. / Quiero ayudarlos.

Enrich Your Teaching

Teacher-to-Teacher

Assign a different everyday object to each student. Have them write as many commands as they can telling one person typical things to do and not do with the object, using a direct object pronoun each time: ***la botella***—*Ábrela. Ciérrala. Llénala. Vacíala. Lávala. Recíclala. No la tires a la basura.*

21st Century Skills

ICT (Information, Communications and Technology) Literacy Direct students to the online tutorials available in **Realize** for self-directed review of the grammar topics recycled in this chapter. Students can expand their own learning by reviewing the related English grammar first, and then proceeding to the new Spanish grammar point.

Gramática: Repaso

Suggestions: Refer students who are having difficulty with the placement of pronouns to the online tutorials. Say sentences that contain direct or indirect objects as nouns. Ask students to say each sentence again, changing the direct and/or indirect object to a pronoun. Include affirmative and negative commands in your sentences:
Teacher: *Lee el libro* or *No leas el libro.*
Student: *(No) Lo estoy leyendo/Estoy leyéndolo.*

6

Standards: 1.2

Suggestions: Remind students to include an accent mark in the appropriate syllable whenever necessary.

Answers:
1. Sírvanla, lávense
2. las abran
3. la recojan
4. Ayúdenlos
5. Límpienlo

7

Standards: 1.3

Common Errors: Since students are concentrating on positioning the pronouns, they may forget to make them agree in number and gender. When checking answers aloud, provide a correct model as necessary and have students repeat.

Suggestions: Have students write the sentences twice, with the pronouns in the alternative positions, whenever possible.

Answers will vary.

Additional Resources

 Technology: Online Resources
- *A ver si recuerdas* with Remediation
- Guided, Core, Audio, Writing practice
- *Para Hispanohablantes*
Print
- Guided WB pp. 144–147
- Core WB pp. 63–64

Assessment

A *ver si recuerdas* with Remediation (online only)
After reviewing the material on these pages, assign the *A ver si recuerdas* with Remediation to evaluate students' mastery of the material. Additional practice is available online.

Can-do Statements

Read the Can-Do statements in the chapter objectives with students. Then, have students read Preparación para el examen on pages 254–255 to preview what they will be able to do at the end of the chapter.

Standards for Capítulo 5

To meet the Standards, students will:

COMMUNICATION

1.1 Interpersonal
- Talk about work, job searches, and employment types
- Talk about personality traits
- Talk about community gardens
- Talk about emergencies, volunteer community organizations, and community activism
- Talk about songs with social content
- Talk about the Spanish-speaking community in the U.S.

1.2 Interpretive
- Read and listen to information about jobs
- Read and listen to information about personality traits
- Read about community gardens
- Read and listen to information about emergencies, volunteer organizations, and community activism
- Read about noun suffixes
- Read about known artists and poets
- Read about the contributions of the Spanish-speaking community in the U.S.
- Read about the Peace Boat program
- Read about songs with social content
- Read about campaigning for a public office
- Read fiction by María Luisa Góngora Pacheco

1.3 Presentational
- Write about work, job searches, and employment
- Write about what is happening right now
- Write about personality traits and personal goals
- Write about volunteer community organizations
- Write about the Spanish-speaking community in the U.S.
- Present a campaign speech
- Write a cover letter for a job solicitation

CULTURE

2.1 Practices to Perspectives
- Explain community gardens in Latin America
- Explain teenage employment in Latin America
- Explain the contributions of the Spanish-speaking community in the U.S.
- Explain the Peace Boat Program
- Explain Latin American folk music
- Explain the role of indigenous Latin American writers

2.2 Products to Perspectives
- Talk about the murals and paintings of Diego Rivera
- Talk about community organizations

CAPÍTULO 5

Trabajo y comunidad

Country Connections Explorar el mundo hispano

Estados Unidos
México
Cuba
Paraguay

CHAPTER OBJECTIVES

Communication

By the end of the chapter you will be able to:
- Listen to and read about job interviews and classified ads
- Talk and write about applying for a job
- Exchange information about your skills, background experience, and job opportunities

Culture

You will also be able to:
- Understand the influence of Hispanics in the U.S.
- Compare a Mayan folktale with myths and stories in the U.S.
- **Auténtico:** Compare cultural practices in an authentic text about education and employment opportunities

You will demonstrate what you know and can do
- Presentación oral: La elección de la clase
- Presentación escrita: La carta para solicitar empleo

You will use

Vocabulary
- Jobs and activities in the workplace
- Personal qualities and skills needed
- Volunteer and community work
- Job interviews

Grammar
- Present perfect
- Pluperfect
- Present perfect subjunctive
- Demonstrative adjectives and pronouns

ARTE y CULTURA   El mundo hispano

Jardines comunitarios En América Latina, muchas casas tienen jardines. A veces, dos o más casas comparten un jardín y las familias trabajan juntas para cuidarlo. Pueden sembrar (*plant*) plantas o flores, como los girasoles (*sunflowers*) que ves en este cuadro de Diego Rivera (1886–1957).

- ¿Hay un jardín en tu comunidad que se comparta entre familias? ¿Qué plantas o flores tiene?

"Muchacha con Girasoles", (1941), Diego Rivera ▶

Enrich Your Teaching

The End in Mind

Have students preview the sample performance tasks on *Preparación para el examen,* p. 255, and connect them to the Chapter Objectives. Explain to students that by completing the sample tasks they can self-assess their learning progress.

Technology: Mapa global interactivo

Download the *Mapa global interactivo* file for Chapter 5 and preview the activity. For this activity, visit the site of Diego Rivera's work.

Go **Online** to practice
PEARSON
realize™

PearsonSchool.com/Autentico

🔊 AUDIO ▶ VIDEO ✏ WRITING 🎤 SPEAK/RECORD 🌐 MAPA GLOBAL 📁 AUTÉNTICO 🗂 FLASCHARDS 📖 ETEXT 2.0 🎮 GAMES

Preview 5

▶ Videonovela ¡Pura vida!

Proyecto de ayuda a la comunidad en Miami, Florida

Capítulo 5 • doscientos trece **213**

CONNECTIONS

3.1 Making Connections
- Discuss key facts about community activities
- Discuss key facts about Latin American teenagers
- Discuss poetry, fiction, music, and visual art
- Discuss Spanish-speaking public figures
- Discuss key facts about the Peace Boat Program
- Discuss Language Arts strategies: scanning, reading for comprehension, using visual aids, writing to persuade, using context clues

3.2 Acquiring information and Diverse Perspectives
- Read a bout tongue-twisters kinthe Spanish-speaking world

COMPARISONS

4.1 Language
- Compare Spanish words to their English counterparts
- Compare the English pluperfect tense to the Spanish *pluscuamperfecto*
- Compare the Spanish present perfect subjunctive to its expression in English
- Compare tongue-twisters twisters in the Spanish-speaking world

4.2 Cultural
- Compare Latin American community gardens, teenage employment, and songs to those in the U.S.
- Compare centers in the U.S. Spanish-speaking community to those of society in general

COMMUNITIES

5.1 School and Global Communities
- Discuss community activities and volunteer work
- Discuss job solicitation skills
- Link to Web sites from the Spanish-speaking world

5.2 Lifelong Learning
- Develop an appreciation for poetry and fiction
- Discuss the value of community activity
- Discuss campaigning for a public office
- Read an authentic Spanish-language text

Chapter Opener

Suggestions: Discuss the chapter theme and objectives with students.

▶ **Technology: Videonovela ¡Pura vida!** View this stand-alone storyline video about five young adults in San José, Costa Rica with your class.

ARTE Y CULTURA ◀

Standards: 1.1, 1.2, 2.1, 3.1, 4.2

Suggestions: Ask students if they are familiar with a community garden.

Teaching with Art

Suggestions: After students have read the information, ask: ¿Cuántos años crees que tiene la mujer de la pintura? ¿Cómo crees que se siente? ¿De qué manera ese sentimiento se refleja en la pintura?

Project-Based Learning

Un trabajo para un bilingüe

As students work through the chapter during the week, ask them to create a list of jobs that interest them. Encourage students to think about how they can use their Spanish-language skills in any of these jobs and determine which jobs are the best fit based on their qualities and experience. Have them use the information to complete the *Presentación escrita* on pages 244–245.

213

Vocabulario en contexto 1

Resources: Teacher's Resource Materials: Input Script, Clip Art, Audio Script, Technology: Audio, Cap. 5

Suggestions: *El/la salvavidas* is another common form of *el/la salvavida.* Some heritage speakers may be more familiar with the former version. For visualized vocabulary such as *la salvavida, la recepcionista, la clienta,* and *el mensajero,* point to the picture in the book, say the word, and have students repeat. Meaning of other vocabulary can be clarified through demonstration or explanations in Spanish. For example: *El salario es el dinero que gana una persona cuando trabaja.*

Starter Activity

Write these places on the board:

un hospital	*una escuela primaria*
una biblioteca	*un parque*

Working in pairs, have students brainstorm types of voluntary activities that one can do at any two of the places listed and share with the class.

Teacher-to-Teacher

Have students brainstorm a list of businesses where speaking Spanish would be a valuable asset. Lists may include airline companies, travel agencies, FBI, CIA, radio and television, etc. Divide the class into groups and have them research how they could request information about possible employment opportunities. You might ask students to follow through and inquire about specific information and share their results with the class. You might create a bulletin board based on their research.

 Technology: Interactive Whiteboard

> **Vocabulary Activities 5-1** Use the whiteboard activities in your Teacher Resources as you progress through the vocabulary practice with your class.

Project-Based Learning

Share the rubric and instructions with the class. Explain the task and have them perform Step 1. (For more information, see p. 208-b.)

Vocabulario en contexto 1

OBJECTIVES

Read, listen to, and understand information about
▶ getting a job
▶ skills and abilities needed to perform a job
▶ interviewing techniques

¿Estás buscando trabajo?

¿Estás cansado de pedirle dinero a tus padres? ¿Crees que es tiempo de buscar trabajo, pero no sabes por dónde empezar? Si buscas **un puesto a tiempo parcial** o **a tiempo completo**, debes **solicitar** trabajo con mucha determinación y motivación. ¡Y un poco de inteligencia, por favor! Hay ciertas cosas que debes hacer y otras cosas que debes evitar.

el salvavida

el mensajero

la clienta
la recepcionista

la niñera

los consejeros

Differentiated Instruction

Students with Learning Difficulties

Help students improve their reading comprehension by discussing the boldfaced vocabulary items prior to reading each paragraph. After previewing the vocabulary, have them predict what information will be discussed in the paragraph. After reading, help them confirm and correct their predictions.

Lo que debes hacer

el gerente

Es mejor conocer tus **habilidades** y buscar trabajos que te interesen. A este joven le gusta **la computación**, así que **solicitó** trabajo en tiendas donde venden computadoras.

Debes ir bien vestido a **la entrevista**. Ella consiguió el trabajo porque **se presentó** bien vestida ante **el gerente** y dejó una buena impresión.

Lo que no debes hacer

la dueña

Debes ser **puntual**. Nunca debes llegar tarde a las entrevistas o **seguirás buscando** trabajo por mucho tiempo.

En tu entrevista, no le preguntes a **la dueña** inmediatamente sobre **el salario** o **los beneficios**.

1

¿En qué trabaja?

 ESCUCHAR   Escucha las frases e indica sobre qué trabajo habla cada una de las personas. Usa las ilustraciones.

2

¿Qué debes hacer?

 ESCUCHAR   En una hoja de papel, escribe los números del 1 al 5. Escucha lo que dice cada persona. Escribe *C* si la información es cierta o *F* si es falsa.

Capítulo 5 • doscientos quince **215**

Enrich Your Teaching

Culture Note

Point out that many Latin American and Spanish work schedules differ from those in the United States. The workday starts later, the lunch break is longer, and the day ends later. Although the total hours worked are about the same, they are more spread out. Many workers still go home to have lunch together with their families. A work day that ends later coincides with the custom in many countries of eating dinner at a later hour than in the United States, often as late as ten o'clock.

Interpretive 5

1

Standards: 1.2

Resources: Teacher's Resource Materials: Audio Script, Technology: Audio, Cap. 5

Suggestions: Allow students to listen more than once. Remind them not to try to listen to every word, but rather for key words that will help them determine the main idea. Pause frequently to allow them to write the information.

Technology: Audio Script and Answers:

1. Se solicitan personas que quieren trabajar en un campamento. Si te gusta estar activo y trabajar con niños, este trabajo es para ti. El trabajo es solo para el verano. *(consejero)* **2.** ¿Te gustan los bebés y niños pequeños? ¿Puedes trabajar después de la escuela, los fines de semana o en la noche? El trabajo es de tiempo parcial. *(niñero/a)* **3.** Para este puesto se necesita una persona de tiempo completo para entregar paquetes y cartas. Puede usar bicicleta o coche. *(mensajero)* **4.** Este es un trabajo de tiempo completo en la playa. Se requieren las habilidades de nadar y rescatar personas en el mar. *(salvavidas)*

2

Standards: 1.2

Resources: Teacher's Resource Materials; Audio Script, Technology: Audio, Cap. 5

Suggestions: Use the audio or read the script aloud. Pause to check students' progress after each item.

Technology: Audio Script and Answers:

1. Siempre consigues el trabajo si le preguntas al dueño sobre tu salario inmediatamente. *(F)* **2.** Es necesario ser puntual y estar bien vestido. *(C)* **3.** La muchacha dejó una buena impresión ante el gerente y consiguió el trabajo. *(C)* **4.** Al joven le gustan los videojuegos y buscaba trabajos de consejero. *(F)* **5.** Si llegas tarde a las entrevistas, seguirás buscando trabajo por mucho tiempo. *(C)*

Teacher-to-Teacher

Have students do a search under categories like bilingual employment possibilities to find professional organizations to request information about possible employment opportunities. Web sites that may be helpful include: HispanicJobs. com, LatPro.com, and Bilingual.Jobs.com. In addition, the federal government posts many bilingual jobs at FederalJobSearch.com.

215

Vocabulario en contexto 1

Standards: 1.2

Resources: Teacher's Resource Materials: Audio Script, Technology: Audio, Cap. 5

Suggestions

Pre-reading: Have students listen to the audio two times. Ask students to identify the theme of the conversation.

Reading: Allow students time to read the dialogue silently. Play the audio one more time and have students read along as they listen.

Post-reading: Use gestures and explanations to clarify the meaning of the new vocabulary.

3

Standards: 1.1, 1.2

Suggestions: Make sure students understand that the statements pertain to the dialogue on p. 216.

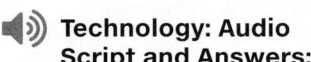 **Technology: Audio Script and Answers:**

1. Jaime es muy bueno para reparar cosas. *(C)* **2.** El consejero le dice a Jaime que él podría ser bueno para cuidar niños. *(F)* **3.** Jaime no cree que pueda cumplir con los requisitos del trabajo. *(F)* **4.** En la solicitud de empleo Jaime tendrá que dar su fecha de nacimiento. *(C)*

4

Standards: 1.2

Suggestions: Use the audio or the script. Allow students to listen more than once. Remind them not to try to listen to every word, but rather for key words that will help them determine the main idea.

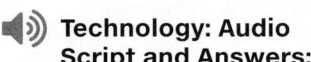 **Technology: Audio Script and Answers:**

1. Paso el día cuidando niños. Soy niño. *(no)* **2.** Tengo un negocio de equipo deportivo. Soy dueña. *(sí)* **3.** Uso un camión para repartir cartas. Soy escritora. *(no)* **4.** Voy a una tienda para comprar algo. Soy cliente. *(sí)*

5

Standards: 1.1

Suggestions: Encourage students to answer honestly. Tell them to express their personal preferences using supporting statements.

 Jaime quiere conseguir un trabajo a tiempo parcial. Su consejero le está dando algunas ideas.

Jaime   Consejero

Consejero: Trata de buscar un trabajo en el que uses tus **conocimientos**. Por ejemplo, si eres bueno con las computadoras, podrías trabajar en una oficina. O si sabes manejar bien, podrías ser **repartidor** en una **compañía** que **reparte** paquetes.

Jaime: Tengo habilidad para **reparar** cosas. ¡Mi abuelo me enseñó a reparar radios y televisores que no funcionan!

Consejero: ¡Qué bueno! Entonces podrías trabajar para una compañía que repara electrodomésticos. **Suelen** buscar gente que se **encargue de** ir a las casas para reparar los aparatos.

Jaime: Me gusta la idea. Aprendo rápido y soy **dedicado** y **responsable** cuando algo me interesa. También soy **flexible**. Es probable que me pidan cambiar la hora de una cita.

Consejero: Así es. Además, veo que **cumples con** un **requisito** básico: eres muy **agradable**. Eso es importante para **atender** bien a los clientes.

Jaime: Espero que me dejen usar un camión.

Consejero: ¡Primero consigue el trabajo! Cuando veas un **anuncio clasificado** que te interese, vuelve aquí. Yo te puedo ayudar a llenar la **solicitud de empleo**. Te pedirán tu **fecha de nacimiento** y otros datos, así como algunas **referencias**.

3

Un buen trabajo para Jaime

 ESCUCHAR   Escribe en un papel los números del 1 al 4. Escribe *C* (cierto) si la frase es correcta o *F* (falsa) si la frase es incorrecta.

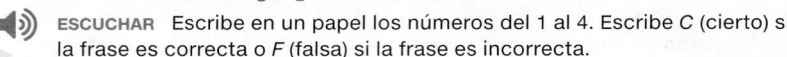

4

Un trabajo perfecto

 ESCUCHAR   Escribe los números del 1 al 4 en una hoja de papel. Vas a escuchar una descripción de trabajo y una frase. Escribe "sí" si la frase identifica el trabajo y "no" si no lo identifica.

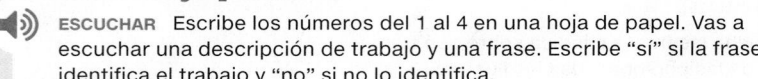

5

Mi trabajo ideal

 LEER, HABLAR EN PAREJA   Vuelve a leer las páginas 214–216. Comenta con un compañero(a) cuál de estos trabajos preferirías tener y por qué. Expresa tu preferencia con razones.

Differentiated Instruction

Students with Learning Difficulties

For *Actividad* 4, help students with listening comprehension by playing each speaker's statement once, then pointing out key vocabulary that students should listen for before playing it a second time.

Advanced Learners

Invite students to evaluate whether or not the *Consejero* gives Jaime good advice about his job searching. Ask them to identify Jaime's skills and point out examples from the chat that support their opinions.

Videohistoria

Go **Online** to practice
PEARSON
realize™
AUDIO VIDEO WRITING SCRIPT

PearsonSchool.com/Autentico

Interpretive 5

La entrevista de trabajo

Antes de ver

Hacer inferencias Observa bien las fotos. ¿Qué puedes inferir al verlas? ¿Cómo se relacionan con el tema de este capítulo? Al ver el video, haz inferencias que te ayuden a comprender mejor la historia que se cuenta.

Haz la actividad

Trabajos a tiempo parcial Haz una lista en español de los trabajos a tiempo parcial que te interesaría tener. Ponlos en orden de preferencia.

▶ Ve el video

Ximena tiene una entrevista de trabajo hoy. ¿Qué preguntas le harán? ¿Cómo responderá ella?

Ve a **PearsonSchool.com/Autentico** para ver el video *La entrevista de trabajo.* También puedes leer el guión.

Ximena   **Valentina**

Después de ver

 ESCRIBIR Contesta estas preguntas:

1. ¿Qué tipo de trabajo está solicitando Ximena?
2. ¿Por qué le parece importante a Ximena escribir un blog? Parafrasea su respuesta.
3. ¿Sobré qué temas le gusta más a Ximena escribir?
4. ¿Crees que a Ximena le fue bien en la entrevista? Justifica tu respuesta.

Cambia la entrevista Piensa en la entrevista de trabajo que tuvo Ximena. Ahora imagina que ella quiere trabajar como niñera. ¿Cómo crees que cambiaría la entrevista y por qué? ¿Qué preguntas le podrían hacer?

Capítulo 5 • doscientos diecisiete **217**

Enrich Your Teaching

Culture Note

Spanish speakers, specially young people, are borrowing more and more English terms related to technology and social media. That is the case for *blog*, for which there is no specific equivalent in Spanish. Other digital jargon commonly used by Spanish speakers is *hashtag, selfie, webinar, e-mail,* and *smartphone.*

21st Century Skills

Communication Invite students to write a blog entry in Spanish on interviewing techniques and send it to a classmate, who will write a short comment in response to the blog.

Tecnología: Video

Standards: 1.2

Resources: Teacher's Resource Materials: Video Script

Antes de ver

Review the previewing strategy and activity with the class. Guide students to infer that the photos on this page are related to part-time jobs. Encourage them to continue making inferences while viewing the video. Explain that taking clues from the video and adding what they already know from their own experiences will help them with comprehension.

Ve el video

Play the video once without pausing and ask volunteers to summarize the main idea. Replay it with pauses to check comprehension. Suggest students use the visual clues and the context to infer the meaning of unfamiliar words. Then show the video a final time without pausing.

Después de ver

Standards: 1.2, 1.3

Suggestions: To guide students with the second question, read from the script where Ximena expresses her opinion about the importance of a blog. Then, ask volunteers to paraphrase what she says and say if they agree with her.

Answers

1. un trabajo para escribir un blog
2. Ximena dice que un blog puede servir de inspiración a chicos de todo el mundo.
3. sobre historia y ciencia
4. Answers will vary.

Cambia la entrevista: Answers will vary.

Have students go to Realize for additional video activities.

Additional Resources

🖥 **Technology: Online Resources**
- Instant Check
- Guided, Core, Video, Audio
- *Para hispanohablantes*

Print
- Guided WB pp. 148–156
- Core WB pp. 65–66
- Authentic Resources Workbook

Assessment _____

Quiz: Vocabulary Recognition
- Prueba 5-1

Vocabulario en uso 1

OBJECTIVES
▶ Listen to a description of and write about a workplace
▶ Discuss skills and qualities needed
▶ Talk and write about jobs and preferences

6

Standards: 1.2

Resources: Teacher's Resource Materials: Audio Script; Technology: Audio: Cap. 5

Suggestions: Before students listen to the statements, have them look at the drawing.

Answers:

1. la Sra. Bonilla (mamá): dueña, tiene muchos clientes, amable
2. Celia (hermana): la gerente, responsable, puntual y dedicada
3. Jorge (hermano menor): repartidor, está preparado su bicicleta
4. Laura (yo): niñera, me gusta visitar a mamá
5. Eduardo (tío): mensajero, ayuda mucho a mamá

Starter Activity

Ask students to choose one of these stores you have listed on the board:

Taquería	*Zapatería*	*Dulcería*
Librería	*Pastelería*	*Florería*

Then, working in pairs, ask their partner what two activities the worker might be doing there. (Ex. Partner A: *En la taquería, ¿qué está haciendo el cocinero?* Partner B: *Está cocinando la carne de res.*)

7

Standards: 1.2

Suggestions: Have students review the vocabulary on pp. 214–217 before completing the activity.

Answers:

1. requisitos	4. una referencia
2. conocimientos	5. suelen
3. habilidades	

8

Standards: 1.1, 1.3

Suggestions: Tell students to trade only the definitions with their partners.

Answers will vary.

Pre-AP® Integration

- **Learning Objective:** Interpersonal Speaking
- **Activity:** Have pairs of students prepare and present mini-dialogues. One partner plays the role of an applicant and asks questions about the job. The other plays the prospective employer and answers the questions.
- **Pre-AP® Resource Materials:** Comprehensive guide to Pre-AP® vocabulary skill development

---

6

¿Quiénes son?

 ESCUCHAR, ESCRIBIR La ilustración de abajo muestra las personas que trabajan en la florería de la mamá de Laura. Escucha a Laura describir lo que hace cada persona. Identifica quién es cada persona en la ilustración. Luego, escribe dos detalles acerca de cada una.

7

Consejos para conseguir un trabajo

 LEER, ESCRIBIR Tu amigo(a) busca trabajo. Dale consejos, usando la palabra que mejor complete la definición en la frase.

una referencia	requisitos	habilidades	suelen	conocimientos

1. En general, los _____ para conseguir trabajo son: ser paciente, tener habilidades para hacer el trabajo y prepararse para la entrevista.

2. Tienes _____ sobre cine, parece que has visto todas las películas. Quizás te den trabajo en una tienda de videos.

3. ¿Qué puedes hacer bien en este trabajo? ¿Tienes las _____ que se necesitan para hacerlo?

4. A veces en una entrevista te piden _____, como el nombre de una persona que te conoce.

5. Las entrevistas _____ ser formales. Debes vestirte bien.

8

¿Qué quieren decir?

 ESCRIBIR, HABLAR EN PAREJA Escribe cinco palabras del vocabulario de las páginas 214–217 en una hoja de papel, y en otra, escribe una definición para cada una. Túrnate con otro(a) estudiante para leer las definiciones de cada uno(a) y digan de qué palabra se trata.

Differentiated Instruction

Students with Learning Difficulties

Before playing the audio selection for *Actividad* 6, help students preview some of the target language for which they will be listening. Discuss the illustration with them. Point out and briefly describe the characters, and invite students to add details.

Challenge/Pre-AP®

Some students may enjoy creating informal quizzes and exercises for other students. Monitor their work carefully for spelling, grammar, and punctuation. Help them write clear and concise instructions, and teach them over time to make their activities neither too difficult nor too easy for their peers.

Go **Online** to practice

PearsonSchool.com/Autentico

PEARSON
realize™

AUDIO VIDEO WRITING SPEAK/RECORD

Interpersonal 5

9

¿En qué te gustaría trabajar?

HABLAR EN PAREJA Imagina que estás haciendo planes para conseguir un trabajo. Con otro(a) estudiante, piensen en varios trabajos a tiempo parcial, digan cuáles les gustaría hacer y por qué. Decidan qué tipo de trabajo les gustaría más conseguir.

Estudiante A

1
2
3
4

Videomodelo

A —*Dime, ¿qué te gustaría más, trabajar de **gerente** o de **consejero de campamento**?*

B —*Me gustaría trabajar de **gerente** porque soy **responsable**. Y a ti, ¿qué te gustaría hacer?*

A —*A mí me gustaría trabajar como **consejero de campamento**. Me gusta mucho trabajar con niños.*

Estudiante B

¡Respuesta personal!

10

¿A quién conoces?

HABLAR EN PAREJA Trabaja con otro(a) estudiante. Lean la lista de trabajos y túrnense para hacer preguntas y contestarlas.

Videomodelo

A —*¿A quién conoces que trabaje de **locutor**?*
B —*El hermano de María es **locutor**.*
A —*¿De qué se encarga él en su trabajo?*

agente de viajes	locutor(a)
gerente	salvavida
bombero(a)	fotógrafo(a)
reportero(a)	dentista
camarero(a)	

Estudiante A

1. ¿A quién conoces que trabaje de (en) . . . ?
2. ¿De qué se encarga esa persona en su trabajo?
3. ¿Qué cualidades y habilidades tiene esa persona?
4. ¿Cuándo suele trabajar?

Estudiante B

¡Respuesta personal!

Capítulo 5 • doscientos diecinueve **219**

9

Recycle: constructions with *gustar*

Suggestions: As you go over the model with students, point out the way in which Student B politely bounces Student A's question back after answering it. Remind students that there are many ways to sustain a conversation. Encourage them to be creative and try different ways whenever they practice dialogues in which the roles are switched.

Common Errors: Some students will try to change *salvavida* to *"salvavido"* in an attempt to give it a masculine gender form. Tell them that, just as with the word *artista,* the word ends in *-a* when applied to either gender. Point out that it is a compound word made from a form of *salvar* plus *vida.*

Answers will vary.

Student A might inquire about the following jobs based on the picture clues:

1. ...de niñero(a) o de mensajero(a)?
2. ...de salvavida o de reportero(a)?
3. ...de repartidor(a) o de camarero(a)?
4. ...de vendedor(a) o de cajero(a)?

10

Suggestions: Have students take turns reading the questions aloud and answering them. Encourage them to help each other when they have difficulty answering.

Answers will vary.

Enrich Your Teaching

Teacher-to-Teacher

When students work with partners to practice dialogues and target language, end the activity by inviting pairs to present their dialogues if time allows. When practicing with the understanding that they will make a presentation, many students are inclined to extend their conversations and stretch their abilities.

21st Century Skills

Communication Have pairs of students discuss which part-time jobs are most popular for young people in their community. Where do young people work in the summer or after school? Which jobs are popular with girls or with boys? What job do they currently have or would like to have?

Starter Activity

Review **seguir** + present participle by asking questions about their activities: *Edward, ¿sigues tocando el piano?* Have them reply in a complete sentence: *Sí, sigo tocando el piano.* Students may use the **seguir** + present participle construction in *Actividad* 11.

11

Standards: 1.1, 1.2, 1.3

Suggestions: Refer students to the *Estrategia*. Remind them that classified ads are written for the convenience of the reader: they are categorized, and the information is presented in a similar order each time. Have them scan the ads with these things in mind.

Answers will vary.

CULTURA

Standards: 1.1, 1.2, 2.1, 4.2

Suggestions: After students have read the information, ask: *¿Cuál es la edad oficial para poder empezar a trabajar en los Estados Unidos? En general, ¿qué creen los padres latinoamericanos que es más importante para los jóvenes: que estudien o que ganen dinero? ¿Cómo gastan los jóvenes latinoamericanos el dinero que ganan? ¿Piensan que lo gastan de la misma manera que los jóvenes de los Estados Unidos?*

Answers will vary.

11

El mejor trabajo para ti

LEER, ESCRIBIR, HABLAR EN PAREJA

1 Haz una lista de las habilidades y cualidades necesarias para cada trabajo mencionado en los anuncios clasificados.

2 Escoge un anuncio y escribe un mínimo de cinco preguntas para hacer una entrevista a una persona que se presenta para el puesto. Puedes preguntar datos como el horario que puede trabajar, el salario, su experiencia anterior y sus habilidades.

3 Entrevista a otro(a) estudiante para ese puesto. Recuerda que debes usar palabras y un estilo de hablar apropiado y más formal. Luego, cambien de papeles.

Estrategia
Scanning
Scanning a text such as an ad may help you to get key information.

Videomodelo
Para el puesto de secretaria:
A —¿Trabajó usted de secretaria antes?
B —Sí, trabajo en una compañía desde el verano pasado.
A —¿Sigue trabajando allí?
B —Sí, pero el horario no es muy flexible.
A —¿Qué habilidades tiene?
B —Sé computación, hablo español e inglés y escribo bien en los dos idiomas.

☰ **Trabajos** ⌕ [Buscar] 🔍

Secretario(a) Recepcionista
Requisitos indispensables: Experiencia mínima de 2 años, extremadamente responsable y puntual, 2 cartas de recomendación con número telefónico, nivel intermedio de inglés y de preferencia domicilio particular cercano a nuestra zona en Distrito Federal, México.

Mensajero(a) / Repartidor(a)
Se necesitan personas activas, excelente orientación de servicio, con iniciativa y muy responsables, para cumplir funciones de mensajero(a) y repartidor(a) motorizado(a). Se requiere la licencia de manejar correspondiente. Enviar currículum. Santiago, Chile

Empleado(a) Doméstico(a)
Agencia Doña Miriam necesita urgente niñeros(as) y personas para trabajar en casas y cocinar. Salarios C$1000 a C$2000. Tel 249-3736. Nicaragua

Salvavidas
AQUASWIM SL necesita 25 salvavidas para trabajar la temporada de verano en la Comunidad de Madrid. Si estás interesado(a) en trabajar con nosotros, ponte en contacto llamando al tlf. 605587464. España

---

CULTURA ◀ **El mundo hispano**

El trabajo y la juventud En América Latina, la edad oficial para poder empezar a trabajar suele ser 15 años. Pero socialmente no se ve bien que un joven trabaje porque los padres piensan que interfiere con la vida escolar. En todo caso, se ven jóvenes haciendo trabajos a tiempo parcial, tales como llenar bolsas para los clientes en el supermercado o servir en los restaurantes de comida rápida. Los jóvenes usan el dinero de sus salarios para salir a divertirse o comprarse cosas.

• ¿Qué piensa la gente en los Estados Unidos de los jóvenes que tienen un trabajo a tiempo parcial?

Differentiated Instruction

Heritage Speakers

Invite students who have lived in heritage countries to share their background knowledge about typical employment for young people there. Encourage them to tell about the duties, schedules, and pay rates of the various kinds of jobs.

Students with Learning Difficulties

Give each student a photocopy of one of the classified ads. Have them use a colored highlighter to shade the key words and phrases in their ad. Then have them exchange ads with a partner and analyze the partner's markings. Finally, have them scan an unmarked ad and orally share the key information.

Go **Online** to practice   PearsonSchool.com/Autentico

PEARSON
realize

VIDEO

WRITING

SPEAK/RECORD

Interpersonal 5

12

Un anuncio clasificado

HABLAR EN GRUPO, ESCRIBIR

1 Trabaja con cuatro estudiantes para escribir un anuncio clasificado. Sigan los siguientes pasos.

• Escojan un trabajo que puede hacer un estudiante y digan de qué se va a encargar.

• Determinen el horario, si es a tiempo completo o a tiempo parcial.

• Incluyan los beneficios y el salario.

• Hagan una lista de los requisitos.

• Escriban el anuncio.

2 La clase va a participar en una feria de trabajo *(job fair)*. Cada grupo va a poner su anuncio clasificado en las paredes de la clase. Los estudiantes van a escoger un anuncio y turnarse para hacer los papeles de la persona que hace la entrevista y el (la) candidato(a).

13

Y tú, ¿qué dices?

HABLAR, ESCRIBIR

1. ¿Tienes un trabajo después de las clases? ¿Qué haces?

2. En tu opinión, ¿cuáles son tus habilidades? Haz una lista.

3. ¿Cuáles son algunos beneficios de tener un trabajo a tiempo parcial?

4. ¿Qué tres consejos puedes darle a un(a) estudiante que busca trabajo?

5. Escribe un párrafo en el que describas otro trabajo que hiciste y si cumpliste con lo que te pidieron. Explica qué te gustó más. Intercambia ideas con un(a) compañero.

Ampliación del lenguaje

Muchos sustantivos *(nouns)* que terminan con el sufijo *-ero, -era* se refieren a profesiones relacionadas con los sustantivos de los que se derivan. Por ejemplo, el sustantivo *niñera(o)* nombra a la persona que cuida a los niños. Lee las palabras de la tabla y completa las frases.

Sustantivo	Profesión
mensaje	mensaj**ero(a)**
caja	caj**ero(a)**
consejo	consej**ero(a)**
carta	cart**ero(a)**

Cristina me escribió una __1.__ hace una semana. El __2.__ la dejó hoy en mi buzón.

Después de comprar la comida en el supermercado, fuimos a pagar a la __3.__. El __4.__ tomó nuestro dinero.

Capítulo 5 • doscientos veintiuno **221**

12

Standards: 1.1, 1.3

Suggestions: For Step 2, have students build their interviews around an ad that another group wrote.

Answers will vary.

13

Standards: 1.1, 1.3

Suggestions: Have students discuss the questions orally first. This will prepare them for writing their answers. For item 1, be prepared to help students name their job in Spanish. You might have to consult a dictionary, a colleague, or another source.

Answers will vary.

Extension: Assign two or more students to be reporters of the **feria de trabajo** in *Actividad* 12. The group can videotape the various interviews and present them in the format of a news feature about the **feria.** Ask them to provide a brief introduction and a conclusion.

AMPLIACIÓN DEL LENGUAJE

Standards: 1.2, 4.1

Focus: Understanding the noun suffixes *-ero* and *-era*

Suggestions: For each example, ask students to use both the noun and the noun + *-ero(a)* suffix in a sentence: *Un cartero reparte cartas.*

Answers:

1. carta
2. cartero
3. caja
4. cajero

Additional Resources

Technology: Online Resources
• Audio, Writing practice
• Teacher's Resource Materials: Audio Script, Communicative Pair Activity, Technology: Audio Cap. 5

Assessment

Prueba 5-2 with Remediation (online only)
Prueba: Aplicación del vocabulario 1
• Prueba 5-2

Enrich Your Teaching

Teacher-to-Teacher

Group projects like the feria de trabajo in Actividad 12 elicit language that goes far beyond the task at hand. In order to work together, students will need to make affirmative and negative commands and to use the subjunctive in order to express necessities and preferences. Monitor them as they work and provide models of language that will help them in task-oriented communication.

Gramática: Repaso

Standards: 4.1

Suggestions: Ask students to write complete, original sentences in the present perfect tense using the irregular past participles shown in the *Gramática*.

 Technology: Interactive Whiteboard

Grammar Activities 5-1 Use the whiteboard activities in your Teacher Resources as you progress through the grammar practice with your class.

14

Standards: 1.2

Suggestions: Have students check their answers by reading each completed item aloud. Remind them that the initial *h-* in the forms of *haber* is always silent.

Answers:
1. ha ido
2. he respondido
3. me he puesto
4. ha dicho
5. he dado
6. ha leído

Project-Based Learning

Students can perform Step 2 at this point. Be sure they understand your corrections and suggestions. (For more information, see p. 208-b.)

Gramática Repaso

OBJECTIVES
▶ Read and write about a job interview
▶ Discuss personal job experiences
▶ Write about your personal qualities and skills

El presente perfecto

To form the present perfect tense, combine the present tense of the verb *haber* with a past participle. You generally use the Spanish present perfect in the same way you use its English equivalent.

No **he reparado** la bicicleta todavía.
I haven't repaired the bicycle yet.

¿Qué trabajos **has tenido?**
*What jobs **have you had?***

Here are the present perfect forms of *hablar*.

he hablado	hemos hablado
has hablado	habéis hablado
ha hablado	han hablado

• Recall that to form the past participle of a verb in Spanish, you add *-ado* to the stem of *-ar* verbs and *-ido* to the stem of *-er* and *-ir* verbs.

habl**ar** → habl**ado**   com**er** → com**ido**
viv**ir** → viv**ido**

• Verbs that have two vowels in the infinitive form (except for *ui*) require an accent mark on the *í* in the past participle.

caer → caído   oír → oído   traer → traído
reír → reído   leer → leído   creer → creído

• Many Spanish verbs have irregular past participles. You have already learned some of these.

abrir → **abierto**   resolver → **resuelto**
decir → **dicho**   romper → **roto**
escribir → **escrito** ser → **sido**
morir → **muerto**   ver → **visto**
poner → **puesto**

• Place negative words, object pronouns, and reflexive pronouns before the form of *haber*.

No he repartido las flores todavía.

Mi profesora **me** ha escrito una carta de recomendación.

El dueño **se** ha ido temprano a la oficina.

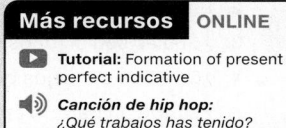

Más recursos ONLINE

▶ **Tutorial:** Formation of present perfect indicative

🔊 *Canción de hip hop:* ¿Qué trabajos has tenido?

14

Después de la entrevista

 LEER, ESCRIBIR Tamara y Juan fueron a una entrevista de trabajo. Completa la conversación que tuvieron con el presente perfecto de los verbos del recuadro.

decir	ponerse
ir	leer
dar	responder

—Juan, ¿cómo te __1.__ esta mañana en la entrevista?

—Creo que no muy bien, Tamara. No __2.__ a todas las preguntas.

—Yo tampoco. Además, __3.__ muy nerviosa. El gerente quería gente con mucha experiencia.

—Sí, Tamara. Él me __4.__ que buscaba jóvenes muy ordenados, puntuales y responsables.

—Yo le __5.__ mis referencias, pero él no las __6.__. Dijo que no las necesitaba.

—Bueno, a ver qué pasa . . .

Differentiated Instruction

Students with Learning Difficulties

Allow students who have difficulty reciting in front of others to record their recitations of the Machado poem on p. 223. You may wish to have them recite only one stanza of the poem.

Advanced Learners

Have students use the present perfect tense to tell about five things they have done that qualify them either for the job they actually have or for a job they would like to have: *Quiero ser cajera. He trabajado de cajera en la tienda de mis padres. Mi papá me ha enseñado a usar la caja....*

Go **Online** to practice
PearsonSchool.com/Autentico

PEARSON
realize.™

VIDEO

WRITING

SPEAK/RECORD

Interpersonal 5

Juego

 ESCRIBIR, HABLAR EN GRUPO Vas a jugar con los(as) compañeros(as) de tu clase.

1 Escribe siete preguntas para saber si tus compañeros(as) han hecho o no cosas como *trabajar en un parque de diversiones.* Para hacer tus preguntas, usa el presente perfecto de los verbos.

2 Escribe un texto a otro(a) estudiante y haz y contesta las preguntas. Usa una forma de hablar informal con un estilo apropiado. Incluye las siguientes palabras o expresiones.

no . . . todavía	varias veces
casi nunca	algunas veces
muchas veces	casi siempre
de vez en cuando	una vez

3 La clase forma dos círculos concéntricos con los estudiantes cara a cara. Al oír música, los estudiantes se mueven a la derecha. Al parar la música, deben parar y hacerle una pregunta al (a la) estudiante que tienen enfrente usando el presente perfecto. Al terminar el juego, el profesor te va a hacer preguntas sobre las respuestas de tus compañeros(as).

Videomodelo
A —*¿Has trabajado en un parque de diversiones alguna vez?*
B —*Sí, trabajé una vez en el verano.*

En voz alta

Los trabalenguas[1] son una forma de literatura popular muy común en la mayoría de los países e idiomas del mundo. ¡Seguro tú conoces muchos en inglés! El reto de estos juegos de palabras consiste en repetir rápidamente una serie de palabras parecidas que hacen que se nos trabe[2] la lengua. Además de ser divertidos, los trabalenguas tienen varios propósitos didácticos, como mejorar las habilidades de lectura y pronunciación, ayudar en la memorización, enseñar gramática y transmitir costumbres, ideas y tradiciones.

En español existen muchos trabalenguas populares que pasan de una generación a otra. En este trabalenguas se usa el verbo decir en presente perfecto y el sustantivo dicho[3]. ¡Repítelo varias veces hasta que la lengua no se te trabe!

[1]tongue-twister [2]get stuck [3]a saying

* ¿Cómo quedaría el trabalenguas si cambias el verbo "dicho" por "contado" y el sustantivo "dicho" por "cuento"? ¡Inténtalo!
* Busca otro trabalenguas en español y practícalo.

¿Recuerdas?
En español, la letra *h* es muda, o sea que no se pronuncia. Pero cuando se combina con la letra *c*, el resultado es el sonido *che*. Hasta muy recientemente, la *ch* se consideraba una letra individual del alfabeto.

Trabalenguas popular
Me han dicho

Me han dicho que has dicho un dicho
que han dicho que he dicho yo,
el que lo ha dicho, mintió,
y en caso que hubiese dicho
ese dicho que tú has dicho
que han dicho que he dicho yo,
dicho y redicho quedó,
y estaría muy bien dicho,
siempre que yo hubiera dicho
ese dicho que tú has dicho
que han dicho que he dicho yo.

Standards: 1.1, 1.3

Suggestions: By Step 3, students should be ready to ask one of the questions they wrote or responded to in the earlier steps. Since they have had some practice, encourage them to invent new, spontaneous questions when they are in the double-circle formation.

Answers will vary.

EN VOZ ALTA

Standards: 1.2, 1.3, 2.1, 3.1, 3.2, 4.1, 5.2

Resources: Teacher's Resource Materials: Audio Script, Technology: Audio Cap. 5

Suggestions: Have students read the information and the tongue-twister silently. Ask comprehension questions: *¿Qué es un trabalenguas? ¿Qué propósitos didácticos puede tener un trabalenguas?*

Before having students say the tongue-twister, direct their attention to the information in the *¿Recuerdas?* Have students repeat some Spanish words that begin with *h* such as *hermano,* and *hola.* Then invite them to practice the *ch* sound with words such as *chico* and *chocolate.* Finally, allow students a few minutes to practice saying the tongue-twister with a partner.

Answers will vary.

Active Classroom

After completing *En voz alta,* have students work in groups to write their own one-line tongue-twisters. Call on each group to present their tongue-twisters to the class.

Enrich Your Teaching

Culture Note
The Carnaval de Cadiz, one of the most important carnivals in Spain, features humorous groups that perform satirical pieces in which tongue-twisters are very common.

Teacher-to-Teacher
Many students take pleasure in the practice and perfection of the sounds of a new language. Encourage them by setting up a regularly scheduled recital period. Aside from pronunciation practice, regular recitals or readings of poetry, song lyrics, or fiction excerpts strengthen students' reading skills.

16

Standards: 1.2, 1.3

Suggestions: Remind students that in real life a paragraph like the one they are writing has the value of creating a favorable first impression.

Answers will vary.

17

Standards: 1.1, 1.2, 1.3

Suggestions: For Step 3, remind students that most Spanish speakers would address each other with *Ud.* rather than *tú* during an interview.

Answers will vary.

CULTURA

Standards: 1.1, 1.2

Suggestions: After students have read the information, ask them to name other prominent people of Spanish or Latin American heritage in the United States. Have them tell what each person does or has done.

Answers will vary.

Additional Resources

 Technology: Online Resources
- Instant Check
- Guided, Core, Audio, Writing, Reading
- *Para hispanohablantes*

Print
- Guided WB pp. 157–158
- Core WB p. 67

Assessment

Prueba 5-3 with Remediation (online only)
Prueba: El presente perfecto
- Prueba 5-3

¿Cómo te describes a ti mismo?

LEER, ESCRIBIR Imagina que estás buscando trabajo y lees en línea este anuncio clasificado. Para contestar al anuncio, escribe un breve párrafo sobre tus cualidades y las cosas que has hecho hasta ahora. Si no te interesa este trabajo, escoge uno de los trabajos que se anuncian en la página 220. Usa oraciones conectadas con detalles y elaboración.

Modelo
Mi nombre es Enrique y he trabajado con niños desde los 12 años. Siempre he sido responsable, puntual y he cumplido con mi trabajo.

> ☰ **Anuncios** 🔍
>
> Se busca joven responsable y cortés para trabajar en un campamento de verano. Debe gustarle la naturaleza y los niños. Enviar un párrafo breve describiendo sus cualidades y lo que ha hecho en materia de trabajo y estudio.

Preparación para una entrevista

🎤 **ESCRIBIR, HABLAR EN PAREJA**

1 Haz una lista de cinco cosas que has hecho para prepararte para una entrevista.

Modelo
He leído los anuncios clasificados.

2 Piensa en un trabajo específico y escribe cinco preguntas que puedan hacerte en la entrevista.

3 Ensaya la entrevista con otro(a) estudiante.

CULTURA ‹ Estados Unidos

La Fundación de Herencia Hispana *(Hispanic Heritage Foundation)* es una organización establecida para promover una mayor comprensión de las contribuciones que han hecho los hispanoamericanos en los Estados Unidos. Cada año, la Fundación premia a hispanoamericanos prominentes, entre ellos, científicos, artistas, atletas y, últimamente, a jóvenes hispanos. Los ganadores suelen ser profesionales y líderes que se han destacado en su campo profesional y estudiantes que han demostrado excelencia académica, participación activa en la comunidad, y orgullo cultural. Algunos de los ganadores recientes del premio han sido el músico cubano Arturo Sandoval, el cineasta Robert Rodríguez, la doctora María Gómez, la cantante Ana Gabriel, el científico Vladimir Alvarado, el exjugador de béisbol Pedro Martínez y la cantante Becky G.

Pre-AP® Integration: La educación y las carreras profesionales ¿Cuál de las personas mencionadas te impresiona más? ¿Cómo contribuye el individuo a la sociedad hispana?

La cantante Becky G

Differentiated Instruction

Heritage Speakers

Have students pretend they are announcers presenting a Hispanic Heritage Award to an accomplished member of the Hispanic American community in the United States. Encourage them to use target language from the chapter. Provide feedback on errors they may make.

Students with Learning Difficulties

Have students work with a partner to complete Steps 1 and 2 of *Actividad* 17. Allow partners to prepare one set of questions that can be used twice.

OBJECTIVES
▸ Read and write about looking for a job
▸ Exchange information about past work experiences

Go **Online** to practice
PEARSON
realize™
PearsonSchool.com/Autentico
WRITING   SPEAK/RECORD

El pluscuamperfecto

You use the pluperfect tense to describe an action in the past that occurred *before* another action in the past. To form the pluperfect tense, combine the imperfect tense of the verb *haber* with a past participle. You generally use the Spanish pluperfect in the same way you use its English equivalent.

Cuando llegué a la oficina, el gerente ya **había leído** mis cartas de recomendación

*When I arrived in the office, the manager **had** already **read** my letters of recommendation.*

Después de la entrevista, yo estaba muy nerviosa porque la dueña de la compañía me **había pedido** referencias.

*After the interview, I was feeling nervous because the owner of the company **had asked** me for references.*

Here are the pluperfect forms of *hablar*:

había hablado	habíamos hablado
habías hablado	habíais hablado
había hablado	habían hablado

Más recursos ONLINE

▶ **Tutorial:** Use of Pluperfect Indicative

18

En la agencia de empleos

 LEER, ESCRIBIR Jorge y Agustín fueron a una agencia de empleos a pedir trabajo. Completa las siguientes frases con los verbos del recuadro en la forma correcta del pluscuamperfecto.

encargarse	tener	escribir	llenar
pedir	atender	cumplir	solicitar

1. Antes de ir a la agencia, Jorge y Agustín _____ varias solicitudes de empleo.

2. Antes de llenar las solicitudes, Agustín ya _____ una lista de sus habilidades.

3. El año pasado, durante varios meses, Jorge _____ de cuidar niños.

4. Estaban sorprendidos porque la recepcionista los _____ muy rápido.

5. Poco después de entrar a la oficina, el gerente les _____ cartas de recomendación y les _____ referencias.

6. En un momento durante la entrevista, les preguntó qué salario ellos _____ en sus otros trabajos.

7. Cuando terminó la entrevista, la recepcionista ya _____ con su trabajo.

Capítulo 5 • doscientos veinticinco **225**

Gramática: Repaso

Standards: 4.1

Suggestions: Tell students you will say two events that happened in the past. Ask them to combine your two sentences into one using the pluperfect tense.

Teacher: *Primero, entré en la cocina. Después, sonó el teléfono.*

Student: *Había entrado en la cocina cuando sonó el teléfono.*

 Technology: Interactive Whiteboard

Grammar Activities 5-1 Use the whiteboard activities in your Teacher Resources as you progress through the grammar practice with your class.

18

Standards: 1.2

Suggestions: Remind students to look over the exercise carefully first in order to decide how best to use the answers in the word bank.

Common Errors: Some students will try to make the past participle agree in number with the subject: ***habían idos.*** Remind them that the verb ***haber*** is the only part of the verb phrase that must agree in number with the subject: ***habían ido.***

Answers:
1. habían llenado
2. había escrito
3. se había encargado
4. había atendido
5. había solicitado/había pedido
6. habían tenido
7. había cumplido

Extension: For extra practice, have students rewrite the subordinate clauses of the sentences using the preterite tense. For example: *Jorge y Agustín llenaron varias solicitudes de empleo.*

Enrich Your Teaching

Teacher-to-Teacher

Set up a situation, such as a family going to bed at night. Use an adverbial clause such as ***antes de acostarse....*** Ask students to tell one thing that each member of the family had done before retiring. Then have them write sentences using the pluperfect: *Antes de acostarse, papá había apagado las luces.*

21st Century Skills

ICT (Information, Communications and Technology) Literacy Remind students of the various digital tools available in **Realize** to help them monitor their own understanding and learning needs, such as the online tutorials with comprehension check exercises, the flashcards, and the audio files.

19

Standards: 1.2

Suggestions: Point out that for this activity, students already know the tense they need to use each time. All they need to focus on is choosing the correct verb and forming the pluperfect tense correctly. Ask volunteers to take turns reading the completed story aloud, so students have a chance to concentrate on meaning.

Answers:

1. había buscado
2. había conseguido
3. había preparado
4. había estado
5. se había presentado
6. se había levantado
7. había andado
8. había querido

20

Standards: 1.1, 1.3

Suggestions: Invite students to use this activity as an opportunity to get to know someone better. Suggest that they learn something about a parent or other family member by using him or her as the subject of their paragraph in Step 2.

Answers will vary.

19

Trabajos en bicicleta

 LEER, ESCRIBIR

Ayer Andrés empezó a trabajar. Lee lo que le sucedió y completa el relato con el pluscuamperfecto del verbo apropiado.

Andrés __1.__ *(buscar / creer)* trabajo por mucho tiempo. Finalmente __2.__ *(destruir / conseguir)* un trabajo como mensajero en bicicleta, en la compañía donde trabajaba su amigo Luis. Ayer era su primer día. Él __3.__ *(preparar / comer)* sus cosas desde el día anterior para no llegar tarde. Esa mañana, Luis lo __4.__ *(oír / estar)* esperando en la parada del autobús para irse juntos a trabajar. Como Andrés no llegaba, Luis lo llamó a la casa. Andrés nunca antes __5.__ *(presentarse / entrar)* tarde a una cita. La mamá le dijo que Andrés __6.__ *(levantarse / acostarse)* hacía diez minutos y se estaba duchando. Luis se fue entonces solo en autobús. Cuando llegó a la compañía, Andrés ya estaba allí. Él __7.__ *(correr / andar)* en bicicleta hasta allí. Más tarde, Andrés le explicó que __8.__ *(caer / querer)* dar una buena impresión el primer día.

20

Una persona que trabaja

 ESCRIBIR, HABLAR EN PAREJA

1 Piensa en una persona que conozcas bien y que tenga un trabajo. Haz una línea de tiempo como la de abajo para indicar qué había hecho esa persona antes de conseguir este trabajo. Responde a las siguientes preguntas como ayuda.

- ¿De qué trabaja esa persona ahora?
- ¿Qué trabajo o responsabilidades tenía el año pasado?
- ¿De qué otras responsabilidades se había encargado antes?

Había trabajado de empleado.	Era gerente de otra tienda	Es gerente en una tienda de zapatos
Antes	**El año pasado**	**Hoy**

2 Escribe un párrafo describiendo a esta persona y sus experiencias en el mundo del trabajo. Usa oraciones conectadas con detalles y elaboración.

3 Intercambia papeles con otro(a) estudiante. Háganse preguntas sobre las experiencias de la persona que han descrito.

Differentiated Instruction

Students with Special Needs

Ask an advanced learner to describe the Rivera painting on p. 227 in detailed language for visually impaired students.

Advanced Learners

Ask students to interview their parents or other adults about things they had already done by the time they were the student's age. Then have students report back to the class in Spanish. For example: *Antes de tener dieciséis años, mi mamá había viajado en avión.*

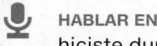

Mi trabajo el año pasado

 HABLAR EN PAREJA Habla con otro(a) estudiante y dile tres cosas que hiciste durante el año pasado. Luego, dile si habías hecho lo mismo años anteriores.

▶ **Videomodelo**

A —*El año pasado ganamos el campeonato de fútbol.*
B —*¿Habían ganado el campeonato antes?*

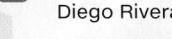

El trabajo en el arte

 LEER, ESCRIBIR El tema del trabajo siempre estuvo presente en la obra de Diego Rivera, el gran pintor de México.

Conexiones ⟩ El arte

En los años 1920, el tema principal de la pintura de Diego Rivera fue los campesinos mexicanos. Sin embargo, en los Estados Unidos Rivera pintó obras en las que el trabajador estadounidense era el tema central. Ya en 1930, Rivera había pintado obras importantes en San Francisco y era un artista conocido en los Estados Unidos.

Henry Ford, el dueño de la compañía Ford, y su hijo Edsel, pidieron a Rivera que pintara un mural en el Detroit Institute of Arts. Rivera comenzó a pintarlo en 1932. Había escogido a los trabajadores de Ford como tema de su obra.

Desde 1930, las ideas políticas que Rivera expresaba en sus obras habían causado muchas críticas. Cuando terminó su obra del Detroit Institute en 1933, muchos la criticaron por esa razón. Pero gracias al apoyo de Edsel Ford, el mural sigue hoy en su lugar.

• Mira el detalle *(detail)* del mural que aparece en esta página. ¿Qué crees que nos quiere decir el artista?

• ¿Conoces otro artista al que han criticado por las ideas políticas que expresa en sus obras? ¿Qué piensas tú sobre su obra?

 Mapa global interactivo Explora la ubicación de tres ciudades en los Estados Unidos asociadas con la obra de Diego Rivera. Investiga la relación del artista con el ambiente de una de ellas.

▲ Detalle del mural del Detroit Institute of Arts

Detroit Industry, (1933), Diego Rivera. © 2010 Banco de México Diego Rivera & Frida Kahlo Museums Trust, México, D.F./Artists Rights Society (ARS)/ Detroit Institute of the Arts/Bridgeman Art Library.

Capítulo 5 • doscientos veintisiete **227**

21

Standards: 1.1

Suggestions: Encourage students to talk naturally.
Answers will vary.

22

Standards: 1.1, 1.2, 2.2, 3.1

Suggestions: Ask comprehension questions. For example: *¿Qué había pintado Diego Rivera antes de 1930? El mural del Detroit Institute of Arts sigue hoy en su lugar. ¿Gracias a quién?*
Answers will vary.

🌐 **Technology: Mapa global interactivo,**
Actividad Visit the site of artist Diego Rivera's work.

Pre-AP® Integration

• **Learning Objective:** Interpretive: Print and Audio
• **Activity:** If available, show the entire Diego Rivera painting, *Detroit Industry.* Have students write brief descriptions of small sections of the scene.
• **Pre-AP® Resource Materials:** Comprehensive guide to Pre-AP® communication skill development

Additional Resources

🔲 **Technology: Online Resources**
• Instant Check
• Guided, Core, Audio, Reading
• *Para hispanohablantes*
• Teacher's Resource Materials: Audio Script, Communicative Pair Activity, Technology: Audio Cap. 5
Print
• Guided WB pp. 159–160
• Core WB pp. 68–69

Project-Based Learning

Students can perform Step 3 at this point. (For more information, see p. 208-b.)

Assessment

Prueba 5-4 with Remediation (online only)
Prueba: El pluscuamperfecto
• Prueba 5-4: p. 110

Examen: Vocabulario y gramática 1
• Examen 1
• ExamView: Examen 1

Enrich Your Teaching

Culture Note

Diego Rivera believed art should not be hidden in museums, but displayed openly for the public to appreciate and enjoy. Rivera was commissioned to create a large fresco mural for the 1940 Golden Gate International Exposition in San Francisco. After the fair closed, the mural was supposed to be installed in a new library at what is now the City College of San Francisco. The library was never built, so the mural was boxed and stored. 20 years later, it was finally installed in the lobby of the campus theater where it can be enjoyed and appreciated as the artist had intended.

Vocabulario en contexto 2

Standards: 1.2

Resources: Teacher's Resource Materials: Input Script, Clip Art, Audio Script, Technology: Audio, Cap. 5

Suggestions: Have students read along as you present the new vocabulary by playing the audio or reading the text aloud. As you read about each situation shown in the book, ask students to point at it in their books.

Starter Activity

Have the class brainstorm a list of "needs" that a community might have following a natural disaster.

 Technology: Interactive Whiteboard

Vocabulary Activities 5-2 Use the whiteboard activities in your Teacher Resources as you progress through the vocabulary practice with your class.

Vocabulario en contexto 2

OBJECTIVES
Read, listen to, and understand information about
▶ Volunteer work opportunities in your community
▶ How you can help your community

🔊 30 obras buenas en 30 días

¡Hacer algo para **beneficiar** a las personas de tu comunidad es una experiencia inolvidable! Necesitamos tu ayuda durante los próximos 30 días.

FUNDACIÓN DE VOLUNTARIOS

¿Quieres **proteger el medio ambiente**? Entonces tal vez **te encantaría** participar en **una manifestación** en contra de la contaminación e ir a **la marcha** a la capital. ¿**Te es imposible** ir a la capital? Entonces, este fin de semana puedes reunirte con otros voluntarios a plantar árboles y **sembrar** verduras en el jardín público. Hay cientos de posibilidades de colaborar como voluntario.

Escoge una de estas oportunidades que te interesaría y que va con tus habilidades:

Servir comida en **el comedor de beneficencia**

Compartir tu talento en **el hogar de ancianos**

Differentiated Instruction

Heritage Speakers

Have students create original announcements to post on the *Fundación de voluntarios* website. Encourage them to consider volunteer opportunities in their community and in places they have visited. Provide feedback on errors in Spanish and then invite them to share their work with the class.

Advanced Learners

Ask small groups of students to obtain leaflets or flyers from community organizations, preferably in Spanish. Have students scan the papers for words and pictures that relate to the new vocabulary, cut them out, and create a collage.

Go **Online** to practice
PearsonSchool.com/Autentico
PEARSON realize™
AUDIO WRITING

Donar objetos para el **centro de la comunidad**

Organizar actividades para el **centro recreativo**

Ayudar a los veteranos del **centro de rehabilitación**

Esperamos que esta página haya sido una inspiración para ayudar a tu comunidad. Para más oportunidades e información, haz clic en estos enlaces:

 Organizar eventos

 Juntar fondos

 Ayudar a la gente sin hogar

 Más ideas

23

 ### Dónde puedes ayudar

ESCUCHAR, ESCRIBIR Escribe los números del 1 al 5 en una hoja. Escucha la descripción de estos lugares y escribe el nombre del lugar.

24

 ### ¿Quieres ser voluntario?

ESCRIBIR Escribe un texto a un amigo(a) sobre cómo quieren ayudar a su comunidad. Intercambien sus ideas usando expresiones apropiadas como *me encantaría* o *me es imposible*.

Capítulo 5 • doscientos veintinueve **229**

23

Standards: 1.2

Resources: Teacher's Resource Materials: Audio Script, p. 13; Technology: Audio, Cap. 5

Suggestions: Use the audio or read the script aloud. Pause to check students' progress after each item. Remind students that they should focus on the vocabulary for volunteer work opportunities, and that they should not worry about understanding every word.

🔊 **Technology: Audio Script and Answers:**

Escribe los números del 1 al 5 en una hoja. Escucha la descripción de estos lugares y escribe el nombre del lugar. Vas a oír cada frase dos veces.

1. En este lugar les dan de comer a personas pobres. *(comedor de beneficiencia)*
2. Aquí vienen niños y adultos a hacer ejercicio y a divertirse. *(centro recreativo)*
3. En este lugar hay salones para eventos de la comunidad. *(centro de la comunidad)*
4. Éste es un lugar donde atienden a los ancianos. *(hogar de ancianos)*
5. Los pacientes asisten a este lugar para sentirse mejor y hacer ejercicio. *(centro de rehabilitación)*

24

Standards: 1.1, 1.3

Suggestions: Explain to students that there are different ways to help in their community. They should come up with ideas and exchange them using expressions such as: *me encantaría* or *me es imposible*.

Answers will vary.

Vocabulario en contexto 2

Standards: 1.2

Resources: Teacher's Resource Materials: Input Script, Clip Art, Audio Script, Technology: Audio, Cap. 5

Suggestions

Pre-reading: Present the readings on this and the next page one at a time, along with their respective activities.

Reading: Allow students time to read each presentation silently first before they listen to the audio.

Post-reading: Check comprehension by asking questions.

25

Standards: 1.2

Suggestions: Have students share and discuss their answers.

Answers:
1. Pueden ayudarlos a llenar los formularios y a estudiar para el examen de ciudadanía.
2–3. Answers will vary.

26

Standards: 1.2

Resources: Teacher's Resource Materials: Audio Script, Technology: Audio, Cap. 5, Track 14

Suggestions: Before students hear the conversation, have them read items 1–4 and the choices offered in parentheses. In this way they will be better prepared for the task and know what to listen for.

 Technology: Audio Script:

(For the complete script, see Teacher's Resource Materials.)

Answers:
1. solicitar la ciudadanía
2. llenar los formularios
3. la historia del país
4. es imposible

Se buscan voluntarios hispanohablantes para ayudar a inmigrantes

¿No sabes qué hacer con tu tiempo libre? Ayuda a un inmigrante a hacerse **ciudadano**.

Buscamos voluntarios para dar clases a inmigrantes. El objetivo de las clases es **educar** a los inmigrantes para conseguir **la ciudadanía**.

¿Qué hacen los voluntarios en las clases?

Un abogado explica **las leyes** de inmigración y luego, los voluntarios ayudan a las personas a llenar los formularios y a estudiar para el examen de ciudadanía.

★ ★ ★ ★ ★   **Para más información, visítanos en Roosevelt Ave. y 84th St., Queens, NY**

25

¿Comprendiste?

 ESCRIBIR

1. ¿Qué pueden hacer los voluntarios para beneficiar a los inmigrantes?
2. ¿Por qué es importante que los inmigrantes comprendan las leyes antes de obtener la ciudadanía?
3. ¿Crees que todos debemos ayudar y educar a las personas que lo necesitan? ¿Por qué?

26

Ayuda a inmigrantes

 ESCUCHAR   Escucha la conversación de unos jóvenes voluntarios. Luego, completa cada frase según lo que dijeron los jóvenes.

1. Un abogado explicó cómo (*llenar los formularios / solicitar la ciudadanía*).
2. Los voluntarios ayudaron a (*hacer el examen / llenar los formularios*).
3. Paola tuvo que estudiar (*las leyes de inmigración / la historia del país*).
4. A Luis le (*es imposible / encantaría*) ayudar en las clases para inmigrantes.

Differentiated Instruction

Heritage Speakers

Ask students to research the United States citizenship test on the Internet. Then have them prepare a mini-lesson in which they act as volunteer teachers for Spanish-speaking immigrants and the rest of the class acts as the immigrants.

Students with Learning Difficulties

Have students list the main ideas from the paragraphs about the candidates on this page. This will help them focus on key language for *Actividad* 27. Allow them to refer to their lists as they complete the activity.

Go **Online** to practice

PEARSON
realize

PearsonSchool.com/Autentico

AUDIO   WRITING

Interpretive   **5**

¿A quién van a escoger?

La Sociedad de Beneficencia Manuel García

La Sociedad es una organización que tiene un hogar de ancianos y un hospital para niños. Cada cuatro años se hace una **campaña** para elegir *(elect)* un presidente. Lee sobre los candidatos de este año y sus causas, es decir, lo que piensan que es más importante.

Soy María Luna de Soto. Estoy **a favor de** proteger **los derechos** de todos los niños, por eso quiero que haya más programas de **servicio social**. Debemos **garantizar** los fondos para comprar medicinas para nuestros ciudadanos más jóvenes, los niños, y buscar voluntarios que ayuden a las personas que lo necesitan. Es **injusto** que sólo algunas personas reciban cuidado y ayuda.

Soy Mauricio Gutiérrez. Pienso que ser presidente de la Sociedad de Beneficencia es una gran **responsabilidad.** Estoy a favor de comprar equipo médico y garantizar así una mejor atención a la salud de nuestros pacientes. También quiero **construir** un centro recreativo junto al hogar de ancianos. Me parece **justo** que los ancianos tengan un lugar donde descansar y recibir todo el cuidado que ellos necesitan.

27

¿Quién está a favor de esto?

ESCUCHAR   En una hoja, escribe los números del 1 al 6. Después de leer sobre los dos candidatos, escucha estas frases y escribe *Mauricio* o *María* según quién haya expresado esa idea.

Capítulo 5 • doscientos treinta y uno **231**

Enrich Your Teaching

Culture Note

Many volunteer organizations protect the rights and aid in the welfare of children throughout Latin America and Spain. Some of them are worldwide organizations, while others are based in individual countries. Some examples are the Homeless Children's Network, Amnesty International, and Doctors Without Borders.

Teacher-to-Teacher

Invite volunteers to perform dramatic readings of the paragraphs about María Luna de Soto and Mauricio Gutiérrez. After they read their speeches, invite the class to ask questions about their positions on issues mentioned in the paragraph. Readers can improvise their answers.

27

Standards: 1.2

Resources: Teacher's Resource Materials: Audio Script, Technology: Audio, Cap. 5

Suggestions: Prepare students for the listening activity by asking comprehension questions about the main points of each candidate's statements.

Technology: Audio Script:

1. Está a favor de proteger los derechos de los niños. **2.** Está a favor de comprar más equipo médico. **3.** Le importan mucho los ciudadanos más jóvenes: los niños. **4.** Piensa construir un nuevo centro recreativo junto al hogar de ancianos. **5.** Le parece injusto que solo algunas personas reciban cuidado y ayuda. **6.** Quiere que haya más programas de servicio social.

Answers:

1. María   4. Mauricio
2. Mauricio   5. María
3. María   6. María

Pre-AP® Integration

• **Learning Objective:** Interpretive: Print and Audio
• **Activity:** *Actividad* 27 helps students practice key audio and print interpretive skills. Ask students to follow along as you read the selection aloud or play the audio. Have students create three multiple-choice questions to check their comprehension. Then, have them confirm their answers by reading the text.
• **Pre-AP® Resource Materials:** Comprehensive guide to Pre-AP® communication skill development

Project-Based Learning

Students can perform Step 4 at this point. Be sure they understand your corrections and suggestions. (For more information, see p. 208-b.)

Additional Resources

Technology: Online Resources
  • Instant Check
  • Guided, Core, Audio, Reading, Writing practice
  • *Para hispanohablantes*
  Print
  • Guided WB pp. 161–168
  • Core WB pp. 70–71

Assessment

Prueba: Comprensión del vocabulario 2
  • Prueba 5–5

28

Recycle: preterite tense, imperfect tense

Suggestions: Encourage students to read the entire paragraph before filling in the blanks. When they have finished, have students read the paragraph again and make sure they understand Rocío's description of her efforts.

Answers:

1. responsabilidad
2. ciudadana
3. campaña
4. servicio social
5. dona
6. juntar fondos
7. sociedad
8. comedores de beneficencia
9. donen
10. construir
11. gente sin hogar

Starter Activity

Have students write the appropriate preterite form for the following verbs:

saber (yo)	buscar (Uds.)
pensar (él)	pedir (nosotros)
decidir (tú)	

29

Recycle: *nosotros* forms of *-ar* verbs

Suggestions: After students have read the announcement, ask them to discuss whether they think the ad is successful in its objective.

Answers:

1. La responsibilidad de los ciudadanos es la de votar.
2. El objetivo principal es juntar fondos para la campaña para votar.
3. Beneficia a los ancianos para que entiendan sus derechos y ayuda a los inmigrantes a solicitar la ciudadanía.
4. Answers will vary.

Vocabulario en uso 2

28

Ayudar es fácil

 LEER, ESCRIBIR

Completa la entrevista sobre la campaña de Rocío Hernández.

servicio social	campaña
dona	responsabilidad
ciudadana	juntar fondos

Cuando supe que 24,000 personas en el mundo mueren de hambre cada día y que el 75% son niños, pensé que era mi _1._, como _2._ del mundo, ayudar a eliminar el hambre. Decidí crear una _3._ de _4._ con el nombre de "Ayudachicos". Allí buscamos diferentes maneras de ayudar. Por ejemplo, encontramos un sitio en la Red que se llama "Hunger Site". Cada vez que haces un clic, se _5._ comida a los ciudadanos de un país pobre. También hicimos una marcha para _6._ que luego enviamos a UNICEF.

comedores de beneficencia	gente sin hogar
donen	sociedad
construir	

Además, escribimos a varias compañías de comida enlatada[1] para que donen parte de sus productos a la _7._ de Aldeas Infantiles SOS. En nuestro pueblo, pedimos donaciones de comida y las llevamos a los _8._. Ahora, vamos a solicitar a arquitectos y a compañías de construcción que _9._ materiales y proyectos de construcción a "Hábitat para la humanidad", que se encarga de _10._ casas para la _11._.

[1]canned food

29

Jóvenes ciudadanos

 LEER, ESCRIBIR Lee este anuncio de una organización que beneficia a la comunidad y contesta las preguntas.

1. ¿Cuál es la responsabilidad de los ciudadanos?
2. ¿Cuál es el objetivo principal de esta organización?
3. ¿A qué dos grupos beneficia esta organización? ¿Cómo los ayuda?
4. ¿Te interesaría participar en este proyecto? ¿Estás a favor o en contra de su causa? Intercambia tu opinión con un/a compañero/a y explica por qué.

¡CAMPAÑA PARA VOTAR!

¿Quiere cumplir con su responsabilidad como ciudadano?

- Educamos a los ancianos a entender sus derechos.
- Ayudamos a los inmigrantes a solicitar la ciudadanía.
- Juntamos fondos para la campaña.

Reuniones cada jueves a las 5:00 PM
931 E. Market St. Salinas, CA 93905

 **Proyecto ¡Vote!**
Beneficiamos a la sociedad.

Differentiated Instruction

Students with Learning Difficulties

To help students complete *Actividad* 28, encourage them to read each sentence and fill in the blank with a word or phrase that they think would make sense. Then have them search the choices for a word or phrase that is similar to their own idea.

Advanced Learners

Have students contact a community organization that employs Spanish speakers as staff or volunteers. Ask students to arrange for someone from the organization to speak to the class about volunteer work and areas in which Spanish-speaking volunteers are needed.

Go **Online** to practice

PearsonSchool.com/Autentico

PEARSON
realize™

 VIDEO   WRITING  SPEAK/RECORD

Interpersonal 5

30

El servicio social

HABLAR EN PAREJA Habla con un(a) compañero(a) sobre el servicio social. Expresa tus preferencias y explica por qué piensas así.

▶ **Videomodelo**

A —¿*Te interesaría hacer servicio social en* **una escuela primaria**?

B —*Sí, me encantaría porque* **me gusta** **encargarme de los niños**.

o: *No, me es imposible porque* **tengo miedo de** **hablar frente a un grupo**.

Estudiante A

Estudiante B

Me encantaría
Me interesaría
No me gustaría
Me es imposible
¡Respuesta personal!

31

Compañeros voluntarios . . .

ESCRIBIR, HABLAR EN PAREJA, DIBUJAR

1 Haz una lista de cinco acciones que recomiendas y que benefician a la sociedad, tales como *donar ropa a la gente sin hogar*.

2 En grupos de cuatro, hablen de las acciones que todos escribieron. ¿Cuáles creen que son las cinco recomendaciones más importantes? ¿Por qué?

▶ **Videomodelo**

A —*Es importante donar ropa a la gente sin hogar.*

B —*Estoy de acuerdo, pero para mí es más importante* *que los niños tengan comida.*

3 En grupo, escriban las acciones en orden de importancia (1 = lo más importante; 5 = lo menos importante). Escojan las tres acciones que a ustedes les parecen más importantes y hagan un cartel para animar a otros(as) jóvenes a hacer trabajo voluntario.

Capítulo 5 • doscientos treinta y tres **233**

30

Standards: 1.1

Suggestions: Have partners practice all the dialogues, switching roles. Then ask them to choose one dialogue to present to the class.

Answers will vary. Student A will use the following vocabulary:

1. un hogar de ancianos
2. un centro de rehabilitación
3. un centro de la comunidad
4. un centro recreativo
5. un comedor de beneficencia
6. un jardín comunitario

31

Standards: 1.1, 1.3

Suggestions: Remind students that expressions such as *es importante que* take the subjunctive. Point out that their announcement in Step 3 should include either subjunctive expressions, infinitive expressions, or imperatives.

Answers will vary.

Enrich Your Teaching

Teacher-to-Teacher

If your school has a charitable organization or a club that contributes to such efforts, ask your students to create a Spanish-language poster for it. Obtain permission to place several of these on the school grounds. The posters will help the organization, and your students will benefit from the experience.

21st Century Skills

Collaboration Have students work together to identify different volunteer opportunities in their own community, or in different parts of the world. They can connect via technology to learn more about projects that interest them in their own communities, or in a Spanish-speaking country.

32

Standards: 1.2

Resources: Teacher's Resource Materials: Audio Script, Technology: Audio, Cap. 5

Suggestions: Have students listen to the report and read the sentences. Then play it again, pausing after each item, so they can write their answers.

 **Technology: Audio Script:**

Radio News Report: Caracas, Venezuela. El señor Nicolás Sepúlveda, dueño de la compañía "El Salvador," donó un millón de bolívares a la Campaña "Educar es nuestra responsabilidad." Gracias a la generosa donación va a ser posible construir una escuela para adultos, que va a beneficiar a los ancianos de esta ciudad. Al hablar de las razones para hacer esta donación, Sepúlveda dijo "siento la responsabilidad de ayudar a todos los ciudadanos."

Answers:
1. la compañía "El Salvador"
2. un millón de bolívares
3. es nuestra responsabilidad
4. los ancianos de esta ciudad
5. siente la responsabilidad de ayudar a todos los ciudadanos

33

Standards: 1.1, 1.2

Suggestions: Remind students that when talking about opinions and values, the subjunctive is often required.

Answers will vary.

CULTURA

Standards: 1.1, 1.2, 2.1, 3.1, 5.1

Suggestions: Ask students to research José Gálvez and his work on the Internet and hold a follow-up discussion in which they tell about their findings.

Answers will vary.

Additional Resources

 Technology: Online Resources
• Teacher's Resource Materials: Audio Script, Communicative Pair Activity, Technology: Audio Cap. 5

Assessment

Prueba 5–6 with Remediation (online only)
Prueba: Aplicación del vocabulario 2
• Prueba 5–6

 32

Un reportaje especial

ESCUCHAR, ESCRIBIR Imagina que estás en Caracas, Venezuela y que escuchas este reportaje en la radio. Completa las frases siguientes con la información del reportaje. Luego, usa esta información para hacer un resumen.

1. Sepúlveda es dueño de _____.
2. Donó _____.
3. La campaña se llama "Educar _____".
4. La escuela va a beneficiar a _____.
5. Sepúlveda decide ayudar porque _____.

 33

Y tú, ¿qué dices?

ESCRIBIR, HABLAR

1. ¿Qué servicios sociales hay en la comunidad donde vives? ¿A quién(es) beneficia(n)? En tu opinión, ¿cuál es el más importante? ¿Por qué?
2. ¿En cuál de estos servicios sociales participas o has participado? Si no has participado en ninguno, ¿en cuál te gustaría participar?
3. Imagina que vas a crear una organización de servicio social. ¿Qué organización recomiendas para tu comunidad? ¿Por qué? Intercambia ideas con un(a) compañero(a).

CULTURA ◂ Estados Unidos

José Gálvez, fotógrafo En todos los tiempos, los artistas han utilizado el arte como una forma de protesta social. Hoy en día puedes ver arte de artistas chicanos que expresan posiciones a favor de algo o en su contra.

José Gálvez creció en Tucson, Arizona. Era fotógrafo para los periódicos *The Arizona Daily Star* y *The Los Angeles Times*. Su cámara siempre ha estado preparada para capturar la experiencia de la comunidad hispanohablante. En 1984 ganó el Premio Pulitzer por una serie de fotos sobre la experiencia mexicano-americana en Los Ángeles. En 2015 Gálvez presentó su exhibición de fotografías "Nosotros estamos aquí", que retrata la vida de los latinos en Estados Unidos. Gálvez dice que el verdadero concepto de la fotografía se ha perdido con los avances tecnológicos y las llamadas "selfies".

• Compara la protesta social de los artistas con la de las personas que participan en una marcha o una manifestación. ¿En qué se parecen y en qué se diferencian?

• Habla con otros(as) estudiantes sobre personas que han logrado cambios con protestas sociales.

José Gálvez

Differentiated Instruction

Heritage Speakers

Students may be familiar with additional expressions of emotion that require the present perfect subjunctive. Invite them to share other expressions that are not listed in *Capítulo* 4 by using them in sentences.

Musical Learner

Help students obtain first-hand knowledge about Latin American musicians whose work has a social message. Have them listen to a song of your choice by the contemporary Mexican band Los Tigres del Norte and discuss the message of the song.

Gramática

OBJECTIVES
▶ Read and write about voluntary work
▶ Discuss volunteer opportunities

Go **Online** to practice
PEARSON realize TM
PearsonSchool.com/Autentico
AUDIO WRITING

El presente perfecto del subjuntivo

The present perfect subjunctive refers to actions or situations that may have occurred before the action in the main verb.

Me alegro de que **hayas trabajado** de voluntario.
*I'm glad that you **have worked** as a volunteer.*

Ojalá que ellos **hayan juntado** mucho dinero.
*I hope that they **have collected** a lot of money.*

Siento que no **hayan participado** en la campaña.
*I'm sorry that you **haven't participated** in the campaign.*

To form the present perfect subjunctive, we use the present subjunctive of the verb *haber* with a past participle. Here are the present perfect subjunctive forms of *trabajar.*

haya trabajado	hayamos trabajado
hayas trabajado	hayáis trabajado
haya trabajado	hayan trabajado

The present perfect subjunctive uses the same regular and irregular past participles as the other perfect tenses you have learned. To review irregular past participles see pages 222–225.

Más recursos ONLINE

▶ **Tutorial:** Formation of the Present Perfect Subjunctive

🔊 *Canción de hip hop: Voluntario*

34

 La bienvenida al comedor

ESCRIBIR, LEER

1 Santiago es el presidente de un comedor de beneficencia. Completa lo que dice a los voluntarios con el presente perfecto del subjuntivo del verbo apropiado.

juntar	escribir	decidir	tener
colaborar	organizar	enviar	

2 Imagina que eres Santiago y escribe dos frases más en un texto a los voluntarios. Usa el presente perfecto del subjuntivo y las expresiones con un estilo y una forma de escribir apropiados. Otro(a) estudiante hace el papel de un voluntario y reponda a tu texto.

Para	Todos los voluntarios	X
Sujeto	La labor del comedor	

Queridos voluntarios,

Me alegro de que ustedes __1.__ trabajar como voluntarios en el comedor. Creo que es justo que los ancianos y la gente sin hogar __2.__ esta oportunidad de recibir alimentos todos los días. Es muy bueno que un voluntario __3.__ fondos para comprar alimentos y espero que nosotros __4.__ para hacer más fácil su trabajo. Ojalá que cuando termine este año, nosotros __5.__ mejor la forma de servir la comida. Estoy contento de que ustedes __6.__ sus comentarios y los __7.__ a la dirección electrónica que les di.

Santiago

 ✎ ▾ B I TI ≛ ☰ ☰ ☰ ↱ ↰ ☺

Capítulo 5 • doscientos treinta y cinco **235**

Starter Activity

Before presenting the present perfect subjunctive, have students create sentences using expressions of emotion and the present subjunctive. Examples can be found in *Capítulo 4* on p. 174.

Gramática

Standards: 4.1

Suggestions: Have students use vocabulary from pp. 228–229 in sentences with ***Ojalá*** and the present perfect subjunctive: *Ojalá que muchos hayan participado en la manifestación.*

🔲 **Technology: Interactive Whiteboard**

Grammar Activities 5-2 Use the whiteboard activities in your Teacher Resources as you progress through the grammar practice with your class.

34

Standards: 1.1, 1.2, 1.3

Suggestions: Have students read the entire message before completing the activity. Ask them to point out verbs of emotion that require the subjunctive.

Answers:

Step 1

1. hayan decidido
2. hayan tenido
3. haya juntado
4. hayamos colaborado
5. hayamos organizado
6. hayan escrito
7. hayan enviado

Step 2

Answers will vary.

Pre-AP® Integration

- **Learning Objective:** Interpersonal Writing
- **Activity:** Using Actividad 34 as a model, ask students to write an e-mail to thank students at their own school who have a local community organization. Expand the task by asking students to include at least one question for the volunteer/recipient to answer with the communication.
- **Pre-AP® Resource Materials:** Comprehensive guide to Pre-AP® writing skill development

35

Standards: 1.1

Suggestions: In Step 1, remind students that in most Spanish-speaking countries, people in this situation would address each other using **Ud.** Have them use the **Ud.** forms for their conversations.
Answers will vary.

36

Standards: 1.1, 1.3

Suggestions: Encourage students to be honest when creating their lists in Step 1. This will contribute to a realistic assessment of the group during the discussion in Step 2.
Answers will vary.

Active Classroom
Actividad 36: Have students work in groups of 4 or 5. On strips of paper, have one student write out the four expressions in *Actividad 36.* Place them face down in one pile. Then have each student write out on three separate strips of paper any subject and any infinitive: *David/trabajar.* Place in a second pile, face down. One student is to select a strip from each pile and create a sentence, receiving a point if the sentence is correct and makes sense. Place strips at the bottom of each pile and continue to play. The winner is the student with the most points.

Additional Resources
 Technology: Online Resources
- Instant Check
- Guided, Core, Audio
- *Para hispanohablantes*

Print
- Guided WB pp. 169–170
- Core WB p. 72

Assessment
Prueba 5-7 with Remediation (online only)
Prueba: Presente perfecto del subjuntivo
- Prueba 5-7

 35

¿Qué hacen cada día?

ESCRIBIR, HABLAR EN PAREJA

1 Imagina que eres voluntario(a) de un centro de rehabilitación. Escribe cinco preguntas que puedes hacerle al (a la) director(a) del centro para saber lo que ha pasado y lo que necesitas hacer.

2 Trabaja con otro(a) estudiante. Hagan los papeles del (de la) director(a) y el (la) voluntario(a). El (la) director(a) explica lo que no se ha hecho todavía y por qué es importante que se haga. Recuerda que debes usar un estilo culturalmente apropiado en tu diálogo. La conversación debe ser más formal entre un(a) director(a) y un estudiante.

Modelo
A —¿Los pacientes han hecho sus ejercicios de rehabilitación? ¿Deben hacer sus ejercicios?
B —No sé. Espero que ya los hayan hecho. Es importante que hagan sus ejercicios todos los días. Deben hacer sus ejercicios.

 36

Ayudando a otros

ESCRIBIR, HABLAR EN GRUPO

1 Haz una lista de trabajos que hayas hecho para ayudar a otros.
   Modelo
   He atendido a ancianos.
   He cocinado para mis catorce primos.

2 Trabaja con un grupo de estudiantes. Comenten lo que han hecho y escriban una lista de todos los trabajos. Observen la lista y piensen en algunos trabajos que no hayan hecho y que pueden ayudar a la comunidad. Usen las expresiones siguientes para comentar sobre lo que han hecho y lo que no han hecho.

estoy orgulloso(a) de . . .	me alegro de . . .
es una lástima que . . .	me sorprende que . . .

   Modelo
   Me alegro de que varios estudiantes hayan donado ropa a la gente sin hogar. Me sorprende que nadie haya trabajado como voluntario en un hogar de ancianos.

Differentiated Instruction

Challenge/Pre-AP®
Ask students to think of a scene in which something has gone wrong. For example: *Un coche está parado en la calle y le está saliendo humo del motor.* Other students tell what has happened using verbs of emotion and the present perfect subjunctive: *Es una lástima que se haya descompuesto el coche.*

Visual/Spatial Learner
Ask students to create visuals to help them remember demonstrative pronouns and adjectives. Tell them to include either a caption or speech bubble that shows which word they are illustrating.

Gramática Repaso

OBJECTIVES
▶ Read and write about volunteer jobs
▶ Discuss preparations for a demonstration
▶ Point out objects

Los adjetivos y los pronombres demostrativos

Remember that you use demonstrative adjectives to point out people or things that are nearby and farther away. A demonstrative adjective always comes before the noun and agrees with it in gender and number.

Me gusta **este** centro recreativo.
*I like **this** recreation center.*

¿Quién donó **esa** comida?
*Who donated **that** food?*

Voy a ayudar a **aquellos** pacientes.
*I'm going to help **those** patients.*

▲ Éste es un perro marrón.

Demonstrative adjectives can also be used as pronouns to replace nouns. To distinguish them from demonstrative adjectives, they have a written accent*.

No puedo trabajar para **este** candidato, pero me gustaría trabajar para **ése**.
*I can't work for **this** candidate, but I would like to work for **that one**.*

¿Ves **esas** bolsas? Por favor, recoge **ésa**, pero no recojas **aquélla**.
*Do you see those bags? Please pick up **that one**, but don't pick up **that one over there**.*

▲ Ése es un perro blanco.

To refer to an idea, or something that has not been identified, use the demonstrative pronouns *esto, eso,* or *aquello.* None of them has an accent mark.

Esto es injusto.
This is unfair.

Me encantaría **eso**.
I would love that.

¿Qué es **aquello**?
What is that (over there)?

Here are all the demonstrative adjectives and pronouns.

▲ Aquél es un perro negro.

	Close to you		Closer to the person you are talking to		Far from both of you	
Adjectives	este	estos	ese	esos	aquel	aquellos
	esta	estas	esa	esas	aquella	aquellas
Pronouns	éste	éstos	ése	ésos	aquél	aquéllos
	ésta	éstas	ésa	ésas	aquélla	aquéllas

*Note that accents on demonstrative pronouns are no longer required by Spain's Royal Academy. However, many people continue to use them for purposes of clarity. Anything written before 2009 will include accents on demonstrative pronouns.

Gramática

Standards: 4.1

Suggestions: Have students talk in pairs about classroom objects using demonstrative adjectives and pronouns. Then ask students to make cards for the chapter vocabulary. Two or three cards are needed for each vocabulary item. Place the cards around the room. Students can stand in one position and create a series of sentences that use the vocabulary along with demonstrative adjectives and pronouns: *Trabajo en este centro recreativo. Ese centro recreativo es donde trabaja mi hermano. Me gustaría saber quién trabaja en aquel centro recreativo.*

Note: *According to the Real Academia Española, the use of accent marks is no longer necessary for demonstrative pronouns. The Real Academia suggests that accent marks only be used on demonstrative pronouns as needed to distinguish them from demonstrative adjectives. In this section, we teach students to use a written accent mark on demonstrative pronouns so they learn to recognize and use the two different types of words.*

Technology: Interactive Whiteboard

Grammar Activities 5-2 Use the whiteboard activities in your Teacher Resources as you progress through the grammar practice with your class.

Enrich Your Teaching

Teacher-to-Teacher

Write the demonstrative adjectives on note cards. Have students take turns drawing a card and using the demonstrative adjective in a sentence. Sentences should refer to an object whose relative distance makes it clear that the student understands the adjective. Students can also use the demonstrative adjective in a comparison in order to make the meaning clear: *Me gusta más esta obra de arte que aquélla al lado de la puerta.*

Standards: 1.2

Suggestions: Tell students that they must carefully consider accent marks and gender and number agreement as they complete this activity.

Answers:
1. Esta/Aquélla
2. Éstos/este
3. aquello
4. Aquel/ése
5. Aquéllas
6. este
7. Éstas
8. esto
9. esas/Ésta
10. Éste

El español en la comunidad

Standards: 1.2, 3.1

Suggestions: Once students have read the information, ask comprehension questions. For example: *¿Por qué se ofrecen clases de español a bordo del Peace Boat? (Se ofrecen clases de español porque muchos de los participantes no hablan español, pero el barco visita muchos países hispanohablantes.) ¿Cuál es el objetivo principal del Peace Boat? (El objetivo es ayudar a grupos que promueven los derechos humanos, la paz y la protección del medio ambiente.)*

Project-Based Learning

Students can perform Step 5 at this point. Make audio or video recordings of their presentations for inclusion in their digital portfolio. (For more information, see p. 208-b.)

 37

¿Éste o aquél?

LEER, ESCRIBIR Margarita es voluntaria en el centro de la comunidad. El supervisor del centro le dice lo que tiene que hacer. Completa las siguientes frases con el adjetivo demostrativo o el pronombre demostrativo correcto.

1. *(Esta / Ésta)* lista no es la de los nuevos ciudadanos. *(Aquella / Aquélla)* es la lista.
2. *(Estos / Éstos)* son los fondos que juntó el centro *(este / estos)* mes.
3. Todo *(aquel / aquello)* beneficia al centro que organiza la marcha.
4. *(Aquel / Aquél)* escritorio no es el tuyo, *(esa / ése)* es el tuyo.
5. *(Aquéllas / Esas)* son las donaciones de alimentos que trajo la gente.
6. Debes leer *(esto / este)* artículo sobre el medio ambiente.
7. *(Esas / Éstas)* son las plantas que deben sembrarse en el parque.
8. Tenemos que publicar en nuestro informe *(esto / esos)* que dice el artículo sobre los servicios sociales.
9. No tienes que leer todas *(ésas / esas)* páginas. *(Esta / Ésta)* es la más importante.
10. *(Éste / Este)* es el informe que tienes que leer.

El español en la comunidad

Profesores voluntarios por la paz, los derechos humanos y el medio ambiente

Peace Boat es una organización no gubernamental (ONG) que tiene como objetivo ayudar a grupos que promueven *(promote)* los derechos humanos, la paz y la protección del medio ambiente en distintos países. Para alcanzar su objetivo, *Peace Boat* organiza viajes en un barco alrededor del mundo para visitar países donde se pueda dar ayuda.

Como muchos de los países que el barco visita son hispanohablantes, y muchos de los participantes no hablan español, en el barco se ofrecen clases de español todos los días durante el viaje. Todos los profesores de español de *Peace Boat* son voluntarios. La organización paga solamente el boleto, la comida y las medicinas para los profesores. Todos los pasajeros pueden asistir a las clases, que se ofrecen en un "curso intensivo" para las personas que tienen bastante tiempo para estudiar. Y pueden participar en "clases libres" los pasajeros que no tienen tiempo para estudiar todos los días pero quieren disfrutar y aprender un poquito de español. Es una hermosa manera *(way)* de enseñar español, promover la paz y los derechos humanos y ayudar a proteger el medio ambiente, todo a la misma vez.

Differentiated Instruction

Students with Learning Difficulties

Help students understand demonstrative adjectives and pronouns by making spatial relationships clear. On three cards, write, for example, **esta, esa,** and **aquella.** Place each card beside three similar objects, such as chairs, that are arranged at three different distances from the student. Ask the student to remain in place, point, and say or repeat sentences such as *Esta es una silla. Esa también es una silla. Aquella silla está lejos.*

38

Ésta, ésa, aquélla

🎤 **HABLAR** Imagina que te estás preparando para participar en una manifestación. Habla con un(a) compañero(a) sobre los preparativos *(preparations)*. Usa los pronombres demostrativos apropiados.

Estudiante A

1. carteles
2. banderas
3. anuncios
4. tambores
5. libros
6. camisetas de la manifestación

Videomodelo

artículo / en la página 2 del periódico

A —¿Cuál es el artículo **que habla sobre la manifestación?**

B —**Éste, el que está** en la página 2 del periódico.

Estudiante B

en el piso   sobre la mesa
en el armario   allí
de color azul   al lado de la puerta

39

A sugerir soluciones

🎤 **ESCRIBIR, HABLAR EN GRUPO**

1 La clase va a dividirse en dos grupos. Un grupo cree que el trabajo voluntario debe ser obligatorio para la graduación; el otro piensa que no. Cada grupo trata de convencer al otro. Hablen sobre:
- tipos de trabajo
- cuándo deben hacer el trabajo (después de clases, fines de semana)
- si debe ser parte del currículum o no
- los beneficios futuros que puede tener

2 Formen grupos y preparen la representación de una marcha o una manifestación. Decidan
- a favor o en contra de qué o de quiénes protestan
- qué exigen o qué resultados esperan
- qué pasará si no consiguen lo que quieren

3 Uno o dos estudiantes pueden representar a reporteros de televisión y entrevistar a los que protestan.

CULTURA Cuba

Silvio Rodríguez es el cantante más importante del "Movimiento de la Nueva Trova", un movimiento musical que apareció en Cuba en los años 60 y tuvo gran influencia en América Latina. Aunque ha escrito canciones de amor, frecuentemente en sus letras habla de los problemas de la sociedad, de lo que cree que es justo o injusto, de las causas que apoya.

Pre-AP® Integration: La conciencia social ¿Qué cantante o grupo musical conoces que hable en sus canciones de la sociedad? ¿Cuáles son los problemas sociales de que canta?
- Pregunta a un(a) compañero(a) lo que se debería hacer para resolver algunos de estos problemas. Él o ella te dirá sus ideas, incluyendo información que apoye sus razones.

Silvio Rodríguez

38

Standards: 1.1

Suggestions: Encourage students to point to the objects mentioned, thus indicating the distance that corresponds to the demonstrative pronoun they have chosen.

Answers will vary. Student B will choose from among the following:

1. Éstos/Ésos/Aquéllos
2. Éstas/Ésas/Aquéllas
3. Éstos/Ésos/Aquéllos
4. Éstos/Ésos/Aquéllos
5. Éstos/Ésos/Aquéllos
6. Éstas/Ésas/Aquéllas

39

Standards: 1.1

Suggestions: As students do their planning, circulate and help them come up with meaningful ways to use the present perfect subjunctive.

Answers will vary.

CULTURA

Standards: 1.1, 1.2, 2.1, 4.2, 5.2

Suggestions: Explain that *trova* means "ballad." A person who sings *trovas* is a *trovador(a)*. This comes from the same Latin root as the English "troubadour."

Answers will vary.

Additional Resources

📶 **Technology: Online Resources**
- Instant Check
- Guided, Core, Audio
- *Para hispanohablantes*
- Teacher's Resource Materials: Audio Script, Communicative Pair Activities, Technology: Audio Cap. 5

Print
- Guided WB pp. 171–172
- Core WB pp. 73–74

Assessment

Prueba 5-8 with Remediation (online only)
Prueba: Los demostrativos
- Prueba 5–8

Examen: Vocabulario y gramática 2
- Examen 2
- ExamView: Examen 2

Enrich Your Teaching

Culture Note
Cuban music has seen a resurgence in popularity in recent years in the United States and Europe. Many different kinds of Cuban music, including **Nueva Trova, son, mambo, rumba, danzón,** and **cha cha chá,** have been a vital cultural force in popular music worldwide for the better part of a century.

21st Century Skills
Social and Cross-Cultural Skills
Encourage students to go online to learn more about the **Nueva Trova** and **Nueva Canción** movements, and to hear music by artists such as Silvio Rodríguez, Joan Manuel Serrat, or Mercedes Sosa. Have them find lyrics to one song that may deal with a commentary on a social problem. Does the music remind them of other singers they know? What are the similarities or differences?

Puente a la cultura

Suggestions

Pre-reading: Refer students to the *Estrategia*. Remind them to use their knowledge of cognates, word families, and context clues to keep reading through difficult parts of passages.

Reading: Help students resolve comprehension problems by asking **sí/no** or embedded-answer questions: *¿Julián Castro es el Secretario del Departamento de Vivienda y Desarrollo Urbano o alcalde de San Antonio, Texas? (Es el Secretario del Departamento de Vivienda y Desarrollo Urbano; antes fue alcalde de San Antonio, Texas.) ¿Linda G. Alvarado es la primera jueza hispana de la Corte Suprema? (No. La primera jueza hispana es Sonia Sotomayor.)*

Post-reading: On the board, begin a concept web with the words **contribuciones de los hispanohablantes** in the center. Use the web as a vehicle to discuss the article. Record in it students' responses about the people mentioned in the article, as well as other information they may supply from their background knowledge.

COUNTRY CONNECTION

Resources: Mapa global interactivo

Suggestions: Remind students that Sonia Sotomayor is Puerto Rican. Ask a volunteer to locate Puerto Rico on Mapa global interactivo. Remind students that the island is the only United States territory where **Cristóbal Colón** actually set foot. He landed there on his second voyage to the Americas in 1493. Puerto Rico is a commonwealth associated with the United States. Large numbers of Puerto Ricans have made permanent homes in Florida, New York City, and elsewhere on the mainland.

Online Cultural Reading

Suggestions: After doing the online activity, ask students to take a look at some of the organizations in their community that offer help to families and children in need. Are there volunteer opportunities for them?

Puente a la cultura

Los Estados Unidos . . . en español

Desde el origen de nuestro país, los hispanohablantes han hecho importantes contribuciones. Ya en 1776, el capitán Jorge Ferragut había venido desde España para luchar por la independencia. Hoy día los hispanohablantes son una importante parte de la población[1] y sus contribuciones se pueden observar en todas las áreas de la sociedad.

La población

Según datos de la oficina del censo en el año 2010, la población hispanohablante representa el 15 por ciento del total de la población y es el grupo minoritario más grande de los Estados Unidos. Del año 2000 al año 2010 la población hispana aumentó en un 43 por ciento. Según el último censo del año 2010, el 13 por ciento de la población total (50.5 millones de personas) habla español en casa. Como el número de hispanohablantes sigue aumentando cada año, el español tiene cada vez más fuerza e influye en muchos campos del país. Por eso podemos decir que el español es ahora parte importante de la cultura de los Estados Unidos.

La política

Julián Castro es el decimosexto Secretario del Departamento de Vivienda y Desarrollo Urbano. Antes de aceptar el puesto en 2014, era alcalde de San Antonio, Texas, donde el 63% de la población es de origen mexicano. Su misión es "crear comunidades fuertes, sostenibles y de inclusión..."

Sonia Sotomayor es la primera jueza hispana de la Corte Suprema de los Estados Unidos y la tercera mujer en conseguir este puesto, en el año 2009. Sus padres se mudaron a Nueva York desde Puerto Rico. Sotomayor nació y se crió en el barrio neoyorquino del Bronx, donde hay una gran comunidad puertorriqueña. Estudió derecho en la Universidad de Yale, una de las más prestigiosas del país.

[1]population [2]grew

Sonia Sotomayor ▶

Differentiated Instruction

Students with Learning Difficulties

Some students may be intimidated by long reading passages. Provide a jigsawing option for small groups in which each student reads one section of the passage and reports key information to the rest of the group.

Advanced Learners

Ask students to choose one of the people mentioned in the article or another Spanish speaker for further research. Have them present brief oral reports about their choice. Students can also make posters with photos that can be placed in the classroom or around the school.

Go **Online** to practice PearsonSchool.com/Autentico

PEARSON
realize.

VIDEO   WRITING

Hilda Solís, nacida en Los Ángeles de padres inmigrantes, fue la primera mujer hispana que trabajó como miembro del Senado de California y como Secretaria de Trabajo en el gobierno de Obama. La californiana de origen mexicano Rosa Gumataotao es la sexta latina en ocupar el puesto de Tesorera de los Estados Unidos, que obtuvo en el año 2009.

Los negocios[3]

De las 500 compañías que la revista *Fortune* considera las más importantes de los Estados Unidos, nueve tienen hispanohablantes como directores generales.

Linda G. Alvarado además de ser directora general de su propia compañía, Alvarado Construction, es también dueña de los Colorado Rockies. Es la primera mujer hispana que compró un equipo de béisbol de las ligas mayores.

Las ciencias

Los hispanohablantes se han destacado[4] también como científicos. Por ejemplo, el Dr. Luis W. Álvarez recibió el Premio Nobel de Física por sus estudios sobre partículas elementales[5] y el Dr. Mario J. Molina ganó el Premio Nobel de Química por sus estudios sobre la capa de ozono.

▲ Rosa Gumataotao

---

[3]business [4]have stood out [5]elementary particles

▲ Linda G. Alvarado

 ¿Comprendiste?

1. ¿Puede decirse que la población hispanohablante es una minoría importante en Estados Unidos? ¿Por qué? ¿Qué ha pasado con esta población desde los años noventa?

2. ¿En qué campos trabajan y hacen importantes contribuciones los hispanohablantes de Estados Unidos?

3. ¿Los hispanohablantes participan en la política de Estados Unidos? Da un ejemplo.

Escribe tu opinión

Después de leer el artículo, piensa cómo puede servirle aprender español a una persona que no lo habla. Escribe un párrafo en el que expliques cómo el español puede ayudar a esa persona a encontrar un trabajo.

Dr. Mario Molina

▶ **Videodocumentario** Un voluntario en la comunidad

Capítulo 5 • doscientos cuarenta y uno **241**

¿Comprendiste?

Standards: 1.2

Suggestions: Have students paraphrase the parts of the article they use to support their answers. Point out that for item 3 they must use their critical thinking skills.

Answers:

1. Sí, la población hispanohablante es una minoría importante en los Estados Unidos. Representa el 14 por ciento de la población. Durante los años noventa, esta población aumentó más del 60 por ciento. **2.** Además de la cultura y los deportes, los hispanohablantes trabajan y hacen importantes contribuciones en el campo de la política, los negocios y las ciencias. **3.** Sí, los hispanohablantes participan en la política de los Estados Unidos. **Answers will vary.**

Escribe tu opinión

Standards: 1.3, 5.2

Suggestions: Encourage students to use chapter vocabulary and structures, such as the pluperfect tense and present perfect subjunctive in their paragraphs.

Answers will vary.

Digital Portfolio

Keep students' paragraphs from *Escribe tu opinión* in their digital portfolios as a writing sample.

▶ **Technology: Videodocumentario**

Standards: 1.2

Resources: Teacher's Resource Materials: Video Script, Technology: Video Program: Cap. 5

View *Un voluntario en la comunidad* with the class online in **Realize**. See the *Video Teacher's Guide* for additional suggestions.

Additional Resources

 Technology: Online Resources
• Technology: *Videodocumentario*
• Guided, Writing, Reading
• *Para hispanohablantes*
• Cultural Reading Activity
Print
• Guided WB p. 173

Enrich Your Teaching

Culture Note

Linda G. Alvarado is a role model in the Hispanic American community and for women in general. Her field of construction is traditionally male, and she has overcome many obstacles in her career. Alvarado began her construction company in 1976 with a loan of $2,500 from her parents. Today it is one of the fastest growing general contracting firms in the country.

21st Century Skills

ICT (Information, Communications and Technology) Literacy Have student search the Internet for more information on the individuals featured in this reading. Ask students to identify other Hispanic Americans who have made important contributions to the United States in the areas of politics, business, or the sciences.

¿Qué me cuentas?

Standards: 1.1, 1.2, 1.3

Resources: Teacher's Resource Materials: Audio Script, Technology: Audio, Cap. 5

AP® Skills: Integration of listening, reading, and writing to comprehend and synthesize information from spoken and written sources.

Suggestions:

For Step 1, use the audio or read the dialogue aloud. Allow students to hear it twice through: the first time to write their answers, the second time to check them.

For Step 2, have students identify points that will allow them to compare the volunteer opportunity presented in the reading to the one they heard about in Step 1.

Encourage students to express their own opinions and to cite specific information from Steps 1 and 2 in their written responses for Step 3.

Answers:

Step 1

1. a	**3.** b	**5.** b
2. a	**4.** a	

Steps 2–3

Answers will vary.

Active Classroom

Have student work in pairs to write ten statements that are **cierto** or **falso** about the brochure in Step 2. Have them partner with another pair and take turns reading their statements. Each pair has to determine whether the other pair's statements are **cierto** or **falso.**

Additional Resources

 Technology: Online Resources
  • *Para hispanohablantes*

Pre-AP® Integración

OBJECTIVES
▸ Listen to and read about two community centers
▸ Write a cover letter to apply for a job

◀») ¿Qué me cuentas?: En busca de empleo

En tu colegio, ¿es necesario cumplir con un número de horas de servicio comunitario? Escucha una entrevista en una organización que busca voluntarios.

1 Vas a escuchar una narración en tres partes. Después de cada parte, vas a oír una o dos preguntas. Escoge la respuesta que corresponda a cada pregunta.

1. **a.** comedor de beneficencia **b.** hogar de niños **c.** centro recreativo
2. **a.** llevarlas a la entrevista **b.** pedirlas a los ancianos **c.** leerlas
3. **a.** si tenía responsabilidad **b.** si le gustaba ser voluntario **c.** si sabía cocinar
4. **a.** de horario flexible **b.** sólo a tiempo parcial **c.** fácil
5. **a.** si donan fondos **b.** cuál es el salario **c.** ¡Felicitaciones!

2 Ahora lee el folleto sobre otro lugar.

Centro Comunitario San Felipe: Ayudamos a nuestra gente

En el Centro Comunitario San Felipe, siempre necesitamos voluntarios para...

• revisar los alimentos y la ropa que se ha donado
• repartir alimentos de La Bodega
• ayudar a la gente
• ayudar a juntar fondos y donaciones de comida y ropa
• dar orientación legal y económica
• donar tiempo, comida o dinero

Buscamos a voluntarios que sean...

• amables y sinceros
• organizados y responsables
• trabajadores
• bilingües

En el Centro Comunitario San Felipe ayudamos a la gente de la comunidad con programas de salud

y educación, y con orientación legal y económica. También repartimos alimentos y ropa entre la gente más necesitada y ofrecemos un lugar seguro para los jóvenes después del horario escolar. Para educar a la gente,

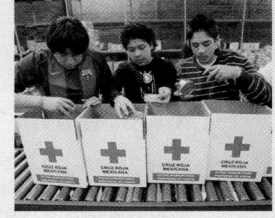

ofrecemos clases de español e inglés. El centro está abierto los siete días de la semana y ayuda a casi 2000 familias.

Si quiere donar fondos, comida, ropa o su tiempo voluntariamente, por favor llame al 805–123–9876.

 3 En una lista, compara y contrasta las dos oportunidades de trabajo voluntario. Luego, escoge un lugar y escribe una carta al director. Explica por qué te gustaría trabajar allí como voluntario y cuánto tiempo puedes dedicar. ¿Qué cualidades o habilidades puedes ofrecer? ¿Qué experiencias anteriores has tenido que te sirven como voluntario? Usa las siguientes expresiones para conectar tus ideas.

me interesaría	en cuanto *(as soon as)*	mientras
me encantaría	para empezar	durante

Differentiated Instruction

Heritage Speakers

Invite students to create a brochure or Web site in Spanish for a volunteer organization in the community, using the brochure in Step 2 as a guide. You may want to present the finished product to the organization for their use.

Students with Learning Difficulties

Students who find it difficult to create their own letter will benefit from working with an advanced learner first. Together they can complete the list in Step 3 before splitting off to write their letters individually.

Presentación oral

OBJECTIVES
▸ Demonstrate how to give a speech to be president of your class
▸ Use visual aids to improve your presentation

Go **Online** to practice
PEARSON
realize™
PearsonSchool.com/Autentico
🔊 AUDIO   🎤 SPEAK/RECORD

La elección de la clase

TAREA Vas a presentarte como candidato(a) a presidente(a) de la clase. Prepara un discurso para convencer a los estudiantes de que eres el (la) mejor porque has ayudado a los demás y eres responsable. Haz un cartel.

Estrategia
Using visual aids If you create visual aids such as graphs and charts to support the topic of your speech, they will strengthen your argument while adding visual appeal.

1 Prepárate Anota en una tabla como la siguiente las razones por las que piensas que eres el (la) mejor candidato(a) para el trabajo.

Cualidades y habilidades	Éxitos importantes	Trabajos realizados	Problemas de la clase	Ideas para resolverlos

2 Practica Vuelve a leer la información y organízala. Explica tus cualidades y lo que has hecho, los problemas de la clase y tus soluciones. Usa tus notas solo para practicar. Recuerda expresar tus opiniones en forma convincente *(a convincing way)* y hablar con voz clara y defender tu opinión

Modelo
Soy la mejor candidata para presidenta de la clase. Siempre me han preocupado los problemas de mis compañeros. Tengo muchas ideas . . .

3 Haz tu presentación Piensa que tus compañeros(as) de clase son los que van a votar a favor del (de la) mejor candidato(a). Usa un cartel u otra ayuda gráfica para apoyar tu presentación y defender tu opinión.

4 Evaluación Tu maestro(a) utilizará la siguiente rúbrica para evaluar tu presentación.

Rubric	Score 1	Score 3	Score 5
How well your information is organized	Your ideas are undeveloped with incorrect or no transitions.	You leave some ideas undeveloped, with some confusing details.	Your ideas are well developed with clear, consistent transitions.
How convincing you are	Your supporting evidence is weak. Your speech is read.	Some of your evidence is convincing. You make some eye contact with audience.	All your evidence is convincing. You have good eye contact and use of gestures.
How effectively you use your visuals	You hardly use visuals, or they don't communicate the message.	You use visuals sometimes, but they're not always effective.	Your visuals are very helpful and are used effectively.

Capítulo 5 • doscientos cuarenta y tres **243**

Enrich Your Teaching

Teacher-to-Teacher
After students listen to the presentations, have them write a note to name their preferences for the top two candidates and give reasons for their choice. Have them exchange notes with another student. They should respond in writing, telling why they agree or disagree with the writer's preferences.

21st Century Skills
Communication Have students browse video-sharing sites to view nomination speeches for class president by students in Spanish. Remind them that they are "selling" themselves as candidates in this oral presentation. Encourage them to be creative in finding the best way to appeal to the target audience—their classmates.

Presentación oral

Standards: 1.2, 1.3, 3.1

Suggestions: Review the task and the four-step approach with students. Before students begin, direct their attention to the *Estrategia.* Encourage them to design their visual aid to be simple, clear, and large enough to be seen by everyone in their audience. Help them organize their information by using a chart, such as the one shown in the activity, with five columns.

Digital Portfolio
Make video or audio recordings of student presentations in class, or assign the Speak and Record activity so they can record their presentations online. Include the recording in their digital portfolios.

Pre-AP® Integration
• **Learning Objective:** Presentational Speaking
• **Activity:** Remind students to focus on the presentational speaking skills used in this task such as fluency, pronunciation, and comprehensibility.
• **Pre-AP® Resource Materials:** Comprehensive guide to Pre-AP® speaking skill development

Additional Resources
 Technology: Online Resources
• *Para hispanohablantes*

Self Assessment _____
Presentación oral
• **Assessment Program:** Rubrics
Review the rubric with students. Go over the descriptions of the different levels of performance. After assessing students, help individuals understand how their performance could be improved. (See Teacher's Resource Materials for suggestions on using rubrics in assessment.)

Language Arts Connection: Informational Writing

Remind students that in today's busy world, the most important qualities for messages such as the letter they are writing are clarity and brevity. Have them consult reference sources from their Language Arts classes for models of a persuasive cover letter. They can use and adapt information from those models for this assignment.

Presentación escrita

Standards: 1.2, 1.3, 3.1, 5.1

Suggestions: Begin by explaining the criteria you will use to evaluate students' compositions. (See Step 5, *Evaluación,* in the Student Edition, and *Assessment* on the following page.)

Direct students' attention to the *Estrategia*. Ask them to share additional background information they have learned in Language Arts courses about persuasive writing. Remind them that they also developed some effective persuasion strategies in the *Presentación oral* on the previous page. Draw on the board a web graphic organizer and write the main idea in the center. Use the outer boxes for each part of the letter.

Presentación escrita

OBJECTIVES
▶ Write an email to apply for a job
▶ Include information to persuade the reader

✎ El correo electrónico para solicitar empleo

Quieres pedir trabajo en un centro recreativo. Escribe un correo electrónico para solicitar empleo en la que expliques tus cualidades, tu experiencia y las razones por las que te gustaría trabajar allí.

1 **Antes de escribir** Piensa en los datos que quieres incluir. Crea una gráfica con la información que debes poner en cada parte. Imagina el nombre de la organización y del gerente al que escribes.

Estrategia

Writing to persuade When you write to persuade, you want to convince someone to do or think the way you do. Here, you are offering to be the best candidate for an opening.

• Think about the needs of the person you are writing to.

• Think of the reasons why you might be the best candidate.

• Organize the reasons and let the person you are writing to know you are the solution.

• Invite your reader to take action.

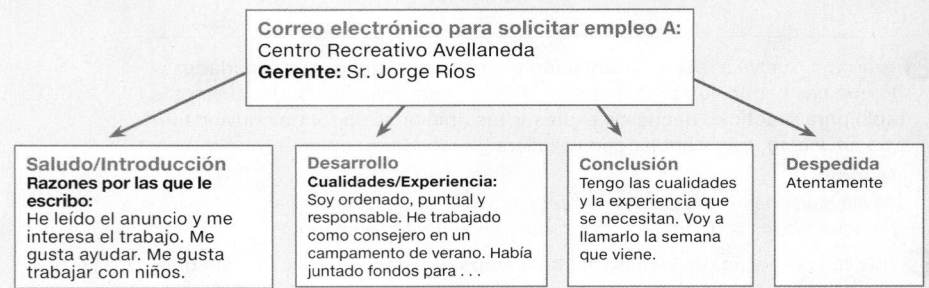

Correo electrónico para solicitar empleo A:
Centro Recreativo Avellaneda
Gerente: Sr. Jorge Ríos

Saludo/Introducción	**Desarrollo**	**Conclusión**	**Despedida**
Razones por las que le escribo: He leído el anuncio y me interesa el trabajo. Me gusta ayudar. Me gusta trabajar con niños.	**Cualidades/Experiencia:** Soy ordenado, puntual y responsable. He trabajado como consejero en un campamento de verano. Había juntado fondos para . . .	Tengo las cualidades y la experiencia que se necesitan. Voy a llamarlo la semana que viene.	Atentamente

2 **Borrador** Recuerda que el correo electrónico es para el gerente del centro recreativo. Escribe tus ideas siguiendo la gráfica. Usa un estilo de escribir formal y apropiado.

Modelo

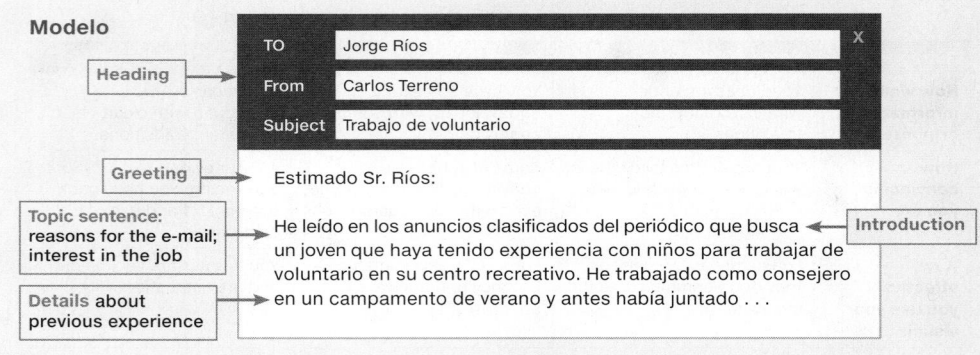

Heading →	TO	Jorge Ríos	X
	From	Carlos Terreno	
	Subject	Trabajo de voluntario	

Greeting → Estimado Sr. Ríos:

Topic sentence: reasons for the e-mail; interest in the job → He leído en los anuncios clasificados del periódico que busca ← Introduction
un joven que haya tenido experiencia con niños para trabajar de voluntario en su centro recreativo. He trabajado como consejero
Details about previous experience → en un campamento de verano y antes había juntado . . .

Differentiated Instruction

Students with Special Needs

Allow students with fine motor skill difficulties to dictate their ideas to another student. The second student also benefits from this arrangement, since he or she is exposed to new ideas.

Advanced Learners

Have pairs of students create a humorous skit about a person who lacks the qualities they described in their letters interviewing for a job. Ask them to act out their "How Not to Get a Job" skits for the class.

Go **Online** to practice

PEARSON
realize

PearsonSchool.com/Autentico

WRITING

Presentational 5

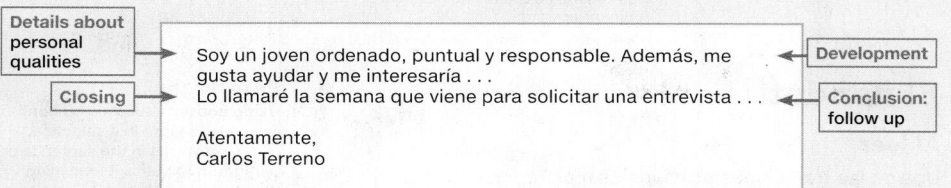

Details about personal qualities

Closing

Soy un joven ordenado, puntual y responsable. Además, me gusta ayudar y me interesaría . . .
Lo llamaré la semana que viene para solicitar una entrevista . . .

Atentamente,
Carlos Terreno

Development

Conclusion: follow up

3 **Redacción/Revisión** Después de escribir el primer borrador de tu correo electrónico, trabaja con otro(a) estudiante para intercambiar los trabajos y leerlos. Digan qué aspectos de los correos son más efectivos.

Haz lo siguiente: Subraya con una línea los verbos en presente perfecto, con dos los verbos en pluscuamperfecto, y encierra en un círculo los verbos en presente perfecto del subjuntivo. Corrige los errores de verbos, ortografía y concordancia.

He leído en los anuncios clasificados del periódico que busca un joven que haya tenido experiencia con niños para trabajar como voluntario en su centro recreativo. He trabajé Como consejero en un campamento de verano y antes habíamos juntado . . .

trabajado

había

4 **Publicación** Antes de escribir la versión final, lee de nuevo tu correo electrónico y repasa los siguientes puntos:

• ¿Sigue mi correo electrónico el formato de un correo para solicitar empleo?

• ¿Puse detalles sobre mis cualidades y mi experiencia de trabajo?

Después de revisar el borrador, escribe una copia en limpio de tu correo electrónico.

5 **Evaluación** Se utilizará la siguiente rúbrica para evaluar tu presentación.

Rubric	Score 1	Score 3	Score 5
Completion of task	Important parts of your e-mail are missing.	Minor parts of your e-mail are missing or incorrect.	All of your information is included and effectively organized.
Ability to persuade	Your lack of information or organization makes the message unclear.	Your message is present, but sometimes unconvincing.	Your choice and organization of information create a clear, convincing message.
Sentence structure/ grammar, spelling, mechanics	Your sentences are run-on or are fragmented with many errors.	You use sentences consistently, but they contain some errors. Your sentences are connected but may lack a few details or elaboration.	Your sentence structure is correct and varied with very few errors. Your sentences are connected with details and elaboration.

Capítulo 5 • doscientos cuarenta y cinco 245

Enrich Your Teaching

21st Century Skills

Communication Students will use their writing skills for the purpose of convincing a prospective employer that they are the best candidate for a particular job. Have students create a list of persuasive words and expressions to use in a cover letter. Ask them to write a list of reasons why they are the perfect candidate for this particular job. Make sure they invite the employer to take action on the job position.

Suggestions (Cont'd): In Step 2, students should concentrate on how to develop the ideas in the chart from Step 1 and include them in the appropriate sequence in a letter. Explain that the three parts of their chart called ***Introducción, Desarrollo,*** and ***Conclusión*** should each become a paragraph in their letter.

For Step 3, encourage students to focus on sentence structure, transitions, use of the pluperfect tense and the present perfect subjunctive, and use of demonstrative adjectives and pronouns. In this step, they should also include and arrange the ***Saludo, Despedida,*** date, and necessary addresses in their letter. Have them follow the suggestions shown.

Evaluation
Steps 4 and 5 overlap. Students will need evaluation by you, their peers, or self-evaluation to fine-tune and polish their drafts.

Digital Portfolio

Keep students' final drafts in their digital portfolios as a writing sample.

Pre-AP® Integration

• **Learning Objective:** Presentational Writing
• **Activity:** Have students write an e-mail to a prospective employer in which they express their interest in a job posting. Be sure students ask the prospective employer at least one question about the job, and summarize their own qualifications for the job.
• **Pre-AP® Resource Materials:** Comprehensive guide to Pre-AP® writing skill development

Additional Resources

Technology: Online Resources
  • *Para hispanohablantes*

Self Assessment

Presentación escrita
• **Assessment Program:** Rubrics
Review the rubric with students. Go over the descriptions of the different levels of performance. After assessing students, help individuals understand how their performance could be improved. (See Teacher's Resource Materials for suggestions on using rubrics in assessment.)

Lectura

Standards: 1.2, 2.2, 3.1, 3.2

Suggestions:

Pre-reading: Before reading, direct students' attention to the *Al leer* section. Have them copy the graphic organizer from p. 249 and make sure they understand how they will use it. Address any comprehension problems they may have with the three points at the end of *Al leer*, and remind them to focus on these points as they read. Also refer them to the *Estrategia*. In order to answer the question there, ask them to watch for the words **doloroso, casona** and **desconsolada** as they read.

Starter Activity

Have students write a sentence about the illustration on page 247. Ask them to describe what they see and what they think the picture shows.

COUNTRY CONNECTION

Standards: 3.1

Resources: Mapa global interactivo

Suggestions: After reading the *Al leer* section, refer students to a map of Paraguay. Point out the capital city of Asunción and explain that Itaguá is located about 30 kilometers away. Explain that this city is also called "Ciudad del Ñanduti" because of its art of "ñanduti", a special type of lace resembling a spider web. Its current population is only about 90,000.

Lectura

OBJECTIVES
▶ Read and understand a Paraguayan legend
▶ Use context clues to find meaning of unfamiliar words
▶ Talk about a personal experience and how to turn one's life around

El ñandutí

Al leer

Una de las tradiciones artesanales más representativas de Paraguay es el ñandutí, que significa "telaraña" *(spider web)* en lengua indígena guaraní. Se trata de un tejido de encaje *(lace)* tan fino y delicado, que parecería que fuera fabricado por la laboriosa araña. En todas partes del país, miles de artesanos elaboran con paciencia y dedicación vestidos, manteles, tapetes y adornos hechos con este delicado encaje.

Se dice que Paraguay heredó este arte de España. El cuento que leerás, *El ñándutí,* es tomado del libro *Leyendas del mundo hispano.* Es una de las muchas versiones sobre la leyenda de cómo se comenzó a elaborar este precioso encaje en territorio paraguayo.

Antes de leer el cuento, copia la tabla de la página 249. Llena la segunda columna mientras lees y presta atención a los siguientes puntos:

• qué relación hay entre Manuela e Ibotí
• qué le pasa a Manuela
• cómo trata Ibotí de ayudar a Manuela

Estrategia

Using context clues If you don't recognize a word in a selection, use other words in the sentence or paragraph to guess its meaning. Which context clues may help you to guess the meaning of words such as *doloroso, casona* and *desconsolada?*

Antes de partir para América—en la época de la colonia—, Manuela, la esposa de un joven oficial del ejército español destinado al Paraguay, fue a decir adiós a su madre. El encuentro fue muy doloroso, pues no sabían si volverían a verse en vida. Entre las muchas cosas que la madre le dio en aquella ocasión para su nuevo hogar, había una de especial belleza: una mantilla[1] de un encaje exquisito.

---
[1] lace scarf

Differentiated Instruction

Heritage Speakers

Have students ask family members about legends from their heritage country, and invite them to share these tales with the class. Some family members might even enjoy visiting the class and sharing these legends themselves.

Students with Learning Difficulties

Stop periodically and help students summarize what they have read so far. By breaking up the selection into smaller chunks, you provide students with a better chance for successful reading comprehension.

—Cuídala como si fueran tus ojos—le dijo su madre abrazándola—. Si así lo haces, tendrás abundantes años de ventura[2] y prosperidad, como yo los he tenido.

Manuela prometió cuidar de la mantilla, besó entre lágrimas a su madre y se despidió de ella, tal vez para siempre. Ella y su marido abandonaron España al día siguiente.

Una vez en América, la joven pareja se estableció en el pueblecito de Itaguá. El matrimonio habitaba una casona en el centro del pueblo. Al poco de su llegada, empezó a vivir con ellos una muchacha guaraní, Ibotí. Ibotí ayudaría a Manuela con las tareas de la casa. Pronto nació entre ambas mujeres una amistad sincera y un cariño profundo. Todavía el corazón bañado de nostalgia, Manuela hizo de la muchacha su confidente. Se sentaban las dos en el patio al atardecer, a la sombra de algún árbol, y Manuela abría su alma a los recuerdos. Le hablaba a Ibotí de su patria y de su madre. ¡Qué gran consuelo era para ella poder desahogar de esa manera el corazón!

En cierta ocasión, el marido de Manuela tuvo que ausentarse del hogar, con motivo de una expedición militar. La casa ahora parecía más grande y vacía. No sabiendo en qué ocupar su tiempo, un día la joven esposa decidió revisar todos los baúles[3] traídos de España. Ibotí participaba en esta labor. Muchas cosas hermosas salieron a la luz: tejidos, vestidos, manteles, cubiertos, candelabros, joyas. Entre tanto objeto bello, el recuerdo más entrañable seguía siendo la mantilla. Manuela no pudo evitar lágrimas al verla, acordándose de su madre.

Sin embargo, el tiempo no había pasado en balde[3] desde su salida de España: la mantilla estaba amarilla y un poco gastada. Manuela pensó en devolverle su blancura y antiguo esplendor. Pidió a Ibotí que la lavara con agua y jabón, recomendándole que fuera muy cuidadosa. La muchacha la fregó con toda delicadeza y cariño; no obstante, al sacarla del agua, vio desconsolada que la mantilla estaba completamente deshilachada[4]. Cuando Manuela supo lo ocurrido, sintió que una parte de su memoria se había perdido, y lloró con angustia.

[2]fortune [3]trunks [4]unravelling

Suggestions (Cont'd):

Reading: Allow students time to read the entire selection on their own silently. You might assign this task for homework. This will allow you to capitalize on class time to read it again together with students. When reading together, pause frequently to address comprehension issues that students may bring up and to allow them to fill in their **Claves del contexto** charts from p. 249. The following questions and possible thought processes refer to the three words mentioned in the *Estrategia*. Encourage students to use similar reasoning as they complete the rest of the chart.

• p. 246: *¿Qué claves del contexto usaste para comprender la palabra* **doloroso?** *(Manuela tiene que decir adiós a su madre y dice que no sabía si volverían a verse. Es una situación triste. La palabra* **doloroso** *viene de la palabra* **dolor** *que significa "pain" y "-oso" es un sufijo que quiere decir "full of." Así que creo que* **doloroso** *debe significar "painful.")*

• p. 247: *¿Qué claves del contexto usaste para comprender la palabra* **casona?** *(Es un lugar donde vive el matrimonio.* **Casona** *viene de la palabra "casa" y tiene la terminación "-ona" que significa "grande". Así que una* **casona** *debe ser una casa grande.)*

• p. 247: *¿Qué claves del contexto usaste para comprender la palabra* **desconsolada?** *(Cuando Manuela vio que la mantilla estaba deshilachada, creo que se sintió triste. La palabra* **desconsolada** *tiene el prefijo* **des-** *que quiere decir algo negativo. La palabra* **consolada** *significa "comforted" así que* **desconsolada** *debe significar "to feel dispair" o "heartbroken".)*

Teacher-to-Teacher

A successful strategy for teaching reading skills is articulating your thoughts in words, as if you were thinking aloud in order to answer a question. In Spanish, this process not only guides students in how to implement a reading strategy; it provides excellent listening practice.

Enrich Your Teaching

Culture Note

The Spaniards introduced the art of making embroidery lace to Paraguay during the colonial period. Ñanduti means "spider web" in Guarani, an indigenous language of Paraguay. The structure of the lace resembles a spider web or the rays of the sun. An annual "Ñanduti Festival" is held in the city during the summer and showcases the region's art, crafts, food, and music.

21st Century Skills

ICT (Information, Communications and Technology) Literacy Have students use the digital technology within **Realize** to access extra reading support. Computer corrected activities use different reading strategies to help students build their vocabulary and progress at their own pace through the reading.

Suggestions (Cont'd):

Reading: The following questions can be used to help students comprehend the reading:

¿Por qué crees que la madre de Manuela le dio una mantilla? (Se la dio como un recuerdo de ella.)

¿Qué le pasó a la mantilla? ¿Por qué? ¿Fue culpa de Ibotí? (La mantilla se deshizo cuando Ibotí la lavó. Ibotí la fregó con cuidado pero la mantilla era vieja y muy delicada.)

¿Qué significa la expresión "Empezaba su trabajo cada anochecer con ilusión; pero cada amanecer la desengañaba"? (Ibotí empezaba el tejido con mucho entusiasmo cada noche, pero no lograba tejer la mantilla.)

Post-reading: As students discuss the story and complete the activities in *Interacción con la lectura* on the next page, ask them to think about the ways that Iboti's gift helped Manuela. You might wish to begin a discussion about how the mantilla not only helped her reconnect with her mother and her past, but also how the mantilla represents the web of connections we all weave in our lives.

Pre-AP® Integration

- **Learning Objective:** Presentational Speaking (Cultural Comparison)
- **Background:** This task prepares students for the Spoken Presentational Communication tasks that focus on cultural comparisons.
- **Activity:** Have students prepare a two-minute (maximum) presentation on the following topic: Different views about the value and importance of family heirlooms or other things our parents give us. Students may use the mantilla as a basis for comparison. They should then comment on the importance of items passed down from generation to generation from their own culture, explaining the similarities and differences between the two.
- **Pre-AP® Resource Materials:** Comprehensive guide to Pre-AP® speaking skill development

Active Classroom

After the class has read the story, create "story experts." Divide the story in four sections and give students numbers 1, 2, 3, or 4. This "expert" is to create five questions about his or her section of the story. Create groups of four students, each with a different "expert." Have them direct their questions to other members of the group.

Un extraño presentimiento anidó[5] entonces en el pecho de la mujer. Además, los días pasaban y no se tenían noticias del esposo. Una mañana, Manuela despertó con los ojos aterrados. En sueños, había revivido las palabras de despedida de su madre. Ahora estaba convencida de que su marido corría peligro. La tristeza más absoluta empezó a residir en la casona. El silencio se alojaba[6] en cada habitación. Y seguía sin tener noticias del oficial español. Ibotí trataba de animar a su señora. Era imposible.

Una noche, Ibotí soñó con el encaje de la mantilla. ¡Lo veía clarísimamente! Los dibujos se arremolinaban[7] en el agua. Después, los remolinos se tranquilizaron y grabaron en las ondas de un riachuelo[8] los trazos exactos del encaje. La joven despertó agitada. "¡Tejeré una mantilla igual que la de la señora!", se dijo esperanzada.

A partir de aquel momento, no hubo noche en que Ibotí no trabajara tejiendo una mantilla. Empezaba su trabajo cada anochecer con ilusión; pero cada amanecer la desengañaba. Nada de lo que hacía era como lo que había soñado. Nada de lo que hacía era como la mantilla deshecha de su señora. Y Manuela estaba más y más triste, más y más enferma.

Una noche de hermosa luna y cálido aire, Ibotí salió al patio a calmar su pena. Ya no sabía qué hacer. De pronto, un rayo de luna doró la tela que una arañita tejía. El corazón de la buena Ibotí palpitó violentamente. ¡Las líneas que aquella araña dibujaba eran como las de la mantilla de Manuela! Durante las siguientes semanas, todas las tardes Ibotí salía al patio y observaba la tela de la araña. Tan pronto como oscurecía, corría a su habitación y se ponía a tejer la mantilla. Tejía y tejía, y no conocía el cansancio. Por fin, una madrugada, poco antes del alba[9], el trabajo estuvo acabado.

Aquella mañana, cuando despertó Manuela, vio ante sus ojos una mantilla prácticamente idéntica a la que se había perdido. Creía estar soñando.

—¡Ibotí!, ¿qué es esto?—preguntó asombrada—. ¿De dónde ha salido esta mantilla?

—Es "ñandutí", tela de araña. La he tejido yo misma—contestó Ibotí modesta y risueña[10].

Manuela recuperó gran parte de su alegría. Se sentía casi feliz. Y aquella misma tarde su dicha fue completa, pues tuvo noticias de su querido esposo: estaba bien y pronto vendría a casa.

Ibotí, por su parte, encontró su camino. Siguió tejiendo y fabricó otras muchas mantillas maravillosas. También enseñó a hacerlas a las jóvenes guaraníes del lugar. Desde entonces, el pueblo de Itaguá es conocido por sus bellos tejidos de ñandutí, o "tela de araña".

[5]nestled [6]to harbor (a feeling or sensation) [7]to wrap around [8]stream [9]dawn [10]cheerful

Differentiated Instruction

Interpersonal/Social Learner

Invite students to discuss ways they can use their interpersonal skills to better the community by working with people of their own age. In small groups, they can brainstorm community needs and possible solutions that they and groups from other schools can help bring about.

Advanced Learners

Students who enjoyed reading this legend might wish to use the Internet to find out more the art and history of Ñanduti lace in Paraguay. Students may also be interested in reading other legends that surround Ñanduti lace.

Interacción con la lectura

Go **Online** to practice

PEARSON
realize™

PearsonSchool.com/Autentico

WRITING

1 Completa la tabla con claves del contexto.

2 Trabaja en grupo. Completen sus tablas. Usen las palabras clave para decir cuál creen que es el significado de las palabras desconocidas. Escriban el significado de cada palabra.

3 Comenta con tu grupo lo que escribieron en sus tablas y contesta las preguntas.

• Parafrasea la idea principal y los detalles de apoyo del cuento. ¿Cuál es el tema?

• ¿Qué significa tenía la mantilla en la vida de Manuela?

4 ¿Conoces otras leyendas sobre el origen de una tradición, arte o costumbre? Escribe un párrafo sobre alguna leyenda que conozcas.

CLAVES DEL CONTEXTO		
palabra desconocida	palabras clave	significado
desahogar		
entrañable		
fregó		
esperanzada		
desengañaba		
palpitó		
asombrada		
cansancio		
recuperó		

CULTURA ▸ Estados Unidos

Vuelta de hoja La vida de Luis Rodríguez iba por un camino peligroso. A los 7 años, ya era un ladrón. No pasaba de los 13 años, cuando estuvo en un centro de detención juvenil[1] y a los 15, dejó la escuela. Pero a los 18 años "comencé a darle vuelta a mi vida", recuerda Rodríguez. Con ayuda, empezó a trabajar. "Pero a lo largo de todo, leí todo lo que pude. Los libros salvaron mi vida", dice Rodríguez.

En diciembre del 2001, Rodríguez abrió al noreste de Los Ángeles el Café Cultural Tía Chucha, para los jóvenes hispanohablantes y sus familias. Allí tienen charlas de historia y libros, presentaciones musicales y exhibiciones de películas. Rodríguez quiere ayudar a otros jóvenes a desarrollar sus habilidades y a curarse[2] ellos mismos, tal como él se curó. Él es un escritor y activista mexicano-americano que nació en El Paso, Texas. Su padre, Alfonso, un director de escuela en México, fue quien fomentó su amor por los libros.

• ¿Conoces algún centro de la comunidad en tu barrio que te haya ayudado a ti o a algún(a) joven que conoces? ¿Cómo los(as) ayudó?

• ¿Por qué crees que el café de Rodríguez puede gustarles a los jóvenes? ¿Qué otras cosas crees que puede añadir al café?

[1]juvenile detention center [2]to heal

CONTRIBUT

▲ Luis Rodríguez en el Café Cultural Tía Chucha

Enrich Your Teaching

Culture Note

In addition to being a successful and important community leader, Luis Rodríguez is a renowned writer. He has published memoirs, fiction, nonfiction, children's literature, and poetry. Rodríguez named his café after his aunt, who was an inspiration to him.

21st Century Skills

ICT (Information, Communications and Technology) Literacy Remind students of the various digital tools available in **Realize** to help them monitor their own understanding and learning needs, such as the online tutorials with comprehension check exercises, interactive puzzles, flashcards, and practice tests.

Interacción con la lectura

Standards: 1.1, 1.2, 4.2

Suggestions: After students share the thought processes they followed to complete the **Claves del contexto** chart, encourage them to go back and read over sections of the story, now that they have a better understanding of the vocabulary.

Answers:

Steps 1, 2, 4
Answers will vary.

Step 3
Una leyenda que describe cómo un nido de araña (ñanduti) inspiró a una muchacha de Itaguá, Paraguay, para tejer una mantilla.

Answers will vary for the remaining bulleted questions.

CULTURA ▸

Standards: 1.1, 1.2, 5.1, 5.2

Suggestions: After students have read the information silently, ask comprehension questions. For example: *Da unos ejemplos del "camino peligroso" por donde iba Luis Rodríguez durante la primera parte de su vida. (Era ladrón y miembro de una pandilla. Estuvo en un centro de detención juvenil. Se dedicó a la violencia y a las drogas.) ¿Qué ocurre típicamente en el Café Cultural Tía Chucha? (charlas, presentaciones musicales y exhibiciones de películas)*

Answers will vary.

Teacher-to-Teacher

Help students personalize the information about Luis Rodríguez. Use it as a vehicle for discussion about social issues that affect them and your community.

Additional Resources

Technology: Online Resources
• Guided, Writing, Reading
• *Para hispanohablantes*
• Cultural Reading Activity
Print
• Guided WB p. Lectura, pp. 174–175
• Literacy Skills WB

Auténtico

Standards: 1.2

Resources: Authentic Resources Wkbk, Cap. 5
Authentic Resources: Cap 5; Audioscript
AP® Theme: *La vida contemporánea: La educación y las carreras profesionales*

Antes de leer

Discuss the *Estrategia* with students. Ask them what elements help a reader to better understand the main idea and the important details in a nonfiction text. Guide them to name in Spanish those elements, including *títulos, subtítulos, ilustraciones* and *gráficas*. Point to the circular graphic in the Authentic article, and ask students what kind of graphic it is and how does it present the data. Then review the key vocabulary with the class. Check comprehension by asking questions.

Lee el texto

Before asking students to read the article, direct their attention to the *Mientras lees* activity. Have them use the activity page from the Authentic Resources Workbook. Point out that the lead of an article—the first sentence or paragraph—usually gives key information to the reader.

Have students silently read the entire article. Ask them to share with a partner the general idea of the article. Then invite students to reread the article, this time paying more attention to the details and the information provided by the graphic.

Complete the Activities

Mientras lees

Standards: 1.2

Suggestions: Invite students to share and discuss their notes. Ask volunteers to paraphrase the important details in the article that support the main idea. Then, direct attention to the graph. Point out that it illustrates the perspective of the employer. If needed, help them understand the meaning of each segment of the graph.

Answers:
1. Dificultades para encontrar personal
2. La gráfica explica las causas por las que los empleadores no encuentran personal; cada segmento, o causa, tiene un color distinto.

Auténtico

Partnered with **IDB**

El trabajo y el mercado laboral

Antes de leer

Usa la estrategia: Estructura del texto

Mira la foto. ¿Cómo se relaciona con el tema de este capítulo? Antes de leer el artículo, fíjate en el título, los subtítulos y la gráfica (*graphic organizer*). ¿Qué tipo de gráfica es y qué información da?

Lee el vocabulario clave

brecha = gap	**idóneo** = suitable/ideal
lograr = to achieve	**medir** = to measure
el personal = staff	**puesto vacante** = job opening
reto = challenge	**sello de garantía** = seal of approval

Lee el texto

¿**H**as oído decir que cada día es más difícil encontrar un buen trabajo? ¿Cuál crees que es la razón?

Ve a **PearsonSchool.com/Autentico** para leer el artículo ***¿Es suficiente estudiar para lograr un buen trabajo?*** El artículo se refiere a una encuesta (*survey*) que se hizo a empresarios (*employers*) en Bolivia. ¿Creo que los resultados serían similares en tu país? ¿Por qué?

Haz las actividades

Mientras lees Mientras lees el artículo, toma notas de los detalles importantes que te ayuden a entender la idea principal del artículo. Mira con atención la gráfica. ¿Cuál es el título de la gráfica? ¿Qué información da y cómo la presenta? ¿De qué manera te ayuda la gráfica a entender mejor el artículo?

Differentiated Instruction

Heritage Speaker

Encourage students to imagine that they are recruiting employees for a company located in their heritage country. Invite them to imagine the type of company. Then, ask them to write a paragraph in Spanish describing the kind of workers needed for such a company. What abilities, studies, and experience are they looking for? Do the prospects need to be fluent in more than one language?

Logical-Mathematical Learner

Invite students to go on line and research the unemployment rates in Spain or one of the Latin American countries. Ask them to gather figures by age, gender and socioeconomic background, if available. Then invite students to present the information in the form of a graphic and share their findings with the class.

Después de leer

Standards: 1.2, 4.2

Suggestions: Discuss questions with the class. For the third one, guide students to analyze the information provided by the graphic. Read the label for each colored segment and help them interpret its meaning using the context. Answers may vary based on comprehension.

Answers:

1. una educación de calidad y experiencia laboral
2. Los empleadores no encuentran el tipo de personal que necesitan.
3. El segmento rosado muestra el mayor porcentaje, con un 31%. El segundo más grande es el azul claro, con un 25%. Esto indica que la falta de habilidades y de experiencia son las principales causas de que los empleadores no encuentren el personal que necesitan.
4. Sin experiencia, no se consigue trabajo. Si no se consigue trabajo, no se puede tener experiencia.

For more Auténtico Resources: Assign the Authentic Resources Workbook activities for homework, so that students can read the article one more time and complete the workbook activities at their own pace.

Pre-AP® Integration

Resources: Authentic Resources Wkbk, Cap. 43; Authentic Resources: Cap 3; Text transcript

Suggestions: Before completing the Pre-AP® activity, have students go to the workbook and complete the worksheets for the additional resources.

Comparación laboral

Suggestions: Have students work in pairs to research the information on the web site. Then call on volunteers to present their comparisons to the class.

Integración

Después de leer Vuelve a leer el artículo con atención para poder contestar estas preguntas:

1. Según el artículo, ¿qué necesita tener un candidato para conseguir un empleo?
2. Según el estudio en Bolivia, ¿por qué hay tantos puestos vacantes que no se pueden llenar?
3. Vuelve a mirar la gráfica circular. ¿Cuáles son los dos segmentos de la gráfica que muestran el mayor porcentaje? ¿Qué indica esto?
4. Explica el "círculo vicioso" del que habla el artículo.

 For more activities, go to the Authentic Resources Workbook.

El trabajo y las carreras profesionales

Expansión Busca otros recursos auténticos en *Auténtico* en línea y contesta las preguntas.

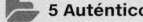 **5 Auténtico**

Integración de ideas ¿Cuáles son los principales retos que enfrentan los jóvenes de hoy para encontrar un buen trabajo? Basa tu opinión en los recursos auténticos.

Comparación laboral ¿Crees que los jóvenes de América Latina tienen más o menos oportunidades de trabajo que los de Estados Unidos? Justifica tu respuesta con datos que puedes buscar en el sitio web del US Department of Labor Statistics.

Enrich Your Teaching

Teacher to Teacher

You might want to simplify the information presented in the article's graph to make it more clear for students. Copy the graph on the board, replacing the labels for each category with a simpler version. For example: "Falta de habilidades, 31%;" "Falta de experiencia, 25%;" "Salario insuficiente, 15%;" and so on.

Using Authentic Resources

Have students write a personal vocabulary list of Spanish terms related to jobs and careers from the authentic resources.

Review Activities

En el trabajo/Los trabajos/Para la entrevista:
Have students prepare their own Spanish definition for each vocabulary item in these categories. Then have teams of two students play against each other in a game of "Password." One student on a team gives his or her partner a definition. The partner must name the vocabulary item defined to earn a point. If he or she cannot, the other team gets a chance at the same definition. The team that correctly matches the greatest number of definitions and vocabulary items wins.

Cualidades y características: Have students work in pairs. One student describes a personality trait of someone he or she knows: *Tengo una hermana que nunca llega tarde.* The partner responds by restating the information using an appropriate adjective: *Así es, tienes una hermana muy puntual.*

Actividades/Acciones: Have students write their own cloze exercises for the items in this category. Explain that, to make a cloze exercise, they use the word or expression correctly in a sentence, then delete the word or expression and replace it with a blank. Ask them to make an answer key to accompany their exercise. Students might enjoy creating their exercises using computer word-processing software. Have partners trade exercises, complete them, and check their work together.

La comunidad: Have students work in pairs and play "Hangman" using the words and expressions in this category.

Expresiones: Students can use these words and expressions as they do the review activities for the other categories.

El presente perfecto: Have students write five sentences in the present perfect tense about the actions of five different people they know or people in the news during the past week. Tell students not to name the people in their sentences, and encourage them to vary the subject each time. Have them share their sentences with other students, who must identify who the subject is: *Hemos ganado el partido de básquetbol contra Wilford Heights. (los miembros del equipo de básquetbol de nuestra escuela)*

Repaso del capítulo

🔊 Vocabulario

en el trabajo

el anuncio clasificado	classified ad
los beneficios	benefits
el / la cliente(a)	client
la compañía	firm / company
el / la dueño(a)	owner
la fecha de nacimiento	date of birth
el / la gerente	manager
el puesto	position
el salario (o el sueldo)	salary
la solicitud de empleo	job application

los trabajos

la computación	computer science
el / la consejero(a)	counselor
el / la mensajero(a)	messenger
el / la niñero(a)	babysitter
el / la repartidor(a)	delivery person
el / la recepcionista	receptionist
el / la salvavida	lifeguard

cualidades y características

agradable	pleasant
dedicado, -a	dedicated
flexible	flexible
injusto, -a	unfair
justo, -a	fair
puntual	punctual
la responsabilidad	responsibility
responsable	responsible

para la entrevista

los conocimientos	knowledge
la entrevista	interview
la habilidad	skill
la referencia	reference
el requisito	requirement
el trabajo	
a tiempo completo	full time
a tiempo parcial	part time

actividades

atender	to help, to assist
construir (i → y)	to build

cumplir con	to carry out, to perform
donar	to donate
encargarse(de) (g → gu)	to be in charge of
juntar fondos	to fundraise
presentarse	to apply for a job
reparar	to repair
repartir	to deliver
seguir (+ gerund)	to keep on (doing)
sembrar (ie)	to sow (a seed)
soler (ue)	to usually do something
solicitar	to request

la comunidad

la campaña	campaign
el centro de la comunidad	community center
el centro de rehabilitación	rehabilitation center
el centro recreativo	recreation center
la ciudadanía	citizenship
el / la ciudadano(a)	citizen
el comedor de beneficencia	soup kitchen
los derechos	rights
la gente sin hogar	homeless people
el hogar de ancianos	home for the elderly
la ley	law
la manifestación	demonstration
la marcha	march
el medio ambiente	environment
el servicio social	social service
la sociedad	society

acciones

beneficiar	to benefit
educar	to educate
garantizar	to guarantee
organizar	to organize
proteger	to protect

expresiones

a favor de	in favor of
en contra (de)	against
me es imposible	It is impossible for me. . .
me encantaría	I would love to. . .
me interesaría	I would be interested . . .

Differentiated Instruction

Students with Learning Difficulties

Have students write down words or phrases they are having difficulty remembering. Place these in a hat. Then invite a volunteer to choose two words from the hat and work with a more advanced learner to come up with a sentence using the two words. Students can share their sentences with the class.

Advanced Learners

Invite students to create and trade crossword puzzles using the chapter vocabulary. Tell them they can be creative with their clues, but they must be accurate. You may wish to provide or have students use computer software to make the crossword puzzles.

Más recursos PearsonSchool.com/Autentico

- Games
- Tutorials
- Flashcards
- Instant check

Gramática

El presente perfecto

To form the **present perfect tense**, combine the present tense of the verb *haber* with a past participle.

he hablado	hemos hablado
has hablado	habéis hablado
ha hablado	han hablado

To form the past participle of a verb, add *-ado* to the stem of *-ar* verbs and *-ido* to the stem of *-er* and *-ir* verbs.

hablar	→	hablado	comer	→	comido	vivir	→	vivido

Some verbs that have a double vowel in the infinitive (except for *ui*) require an accent mark on the *í* in the past participle.

caer	→	caído	oír	→	oído

Many Spanish verbs have irregular past participles:

abrir	→	**abierto**	morir	→	**muerto**	romper	→	**roto**
decir	→	**dicho**	poner	→	**puesto**	ser	→	**sido**
escribir	→	**escrito**	resolver	→	**resuelto**	ver	→	**visto**

When using the present perfect tense, place negative words, object pronouns and reflexive pronouns before the form of *haber*.

No he repartido las flores.
Mi profesora **me** ha escrito un poema.
El dueño **se** ha ido temprano a la oficina.

El pluscuamperfecto

To form the **pluperfect**, combine the imperfect tense of the verb *haber* with a past participle.

había hablado	habíamos hablado
habías hablado	habíais hablado
había hablado	habían hablado

El presente perfecto del subjuntivo

To form the **present perfect subjunctive**, use the present subjunctive of the verb *haber* with a past participle.

haya trabajado	hayamos trabajado
hayas trabajado	hayáis trabajado
haya trabajado	hayan trabajado

Los adjetivos y los pronombres demostrativos

	Close to you		Closer to the person you are talking to		Far from both of you	
Adjectives	este	estos	ese	esos	aquel	aquellos
	esta	estas	esa	esas	aquella	aquellas
Pronouns	éste	éstos	ése	ésos	aquél	aquéllos
	ésta	éstas	ésa	ésas	aquélla	aquéllas

To refer to an idea, or something that has not been identified, we use the demonstrative pronouns *esto, eso,* or *aquello.*

Enrich Your Teaching

Teacher-to-Teacher

Building on activities within the same context, as in the first three activity suggestions on this Teacher's Edition page, is an excellent way to clarify the meaning of verb tenses and moods and show how they interrelate.

El pluscuamperfecto: Students can use the sentences they wrote in the previous activity. This time, listeners add a fact about what had happened previously: *Hemos ganado el partido de básquetbol contra Wilford Heights. Antes no habíamos ganado ni un solo partido.*

El presente perfecto del subjuntivo: Have students continue using the same contexts from the previous two activities. This time, they use **Ojalá que** and the present perfect subjunctive to make an additional statement: *Hemos ganado el partido de básquetbol contra Wilford Heights. Antes no habíamos ganado ni un solo partido. Ojalá que nuestro equipo se haya entrenado mejor y no haya sido solo suerte.*

Los adjetivos y los pronombres demostrativos: Have partners choose three objects to refer to. Pairs take turns giving demonstrations using the demonstrative adjectives and pronouns. They place the objects around the room, stand at opposite ends, and make sentences: *Estas llaves (las que están aquí cerca de mí) son mías. Ésas (las que están cerca de ti)…*

Technology: Digital Portfolio

Invite students to review the activities and projects they completed in this chapter. Have them select one or two items that they feel best demonstrate their achievements in Spanish. Include these products in students' digital portfolios with the Chapter Checklist and Self-Assessment Worksheet.

Additional Resources

Technology: Online Resources
- Instant Check
- Integrated Performance Assessment
- *Para hispanohablantes*

Teacher Resources
- Teacher's Resource Materials: Situation Cards, Clip Art
- **Assessment Program:** Chapter Checklist and Self-Assessment Worksheet

Technology: ¡Pura vida! is a storyline video that is independent of chapter content and an ideal support for expanding listening skills. The 14 episodes are available within **Realize**. Student activities and Teacher support are also assignable within **Realize**.

Performance Tasks

Standards: 1.1, 1.2, 1.3

Teacher Resources: Teacher's Resource Materials: Audio Script, Technology: Audio, Cap. 5

1. Vocabulario

Suggestions: Encourage students to review the vocabulary on pp. 214–217 and 228–231 before they complete the activity.

Answers:

1. b	**5.** c
2. a	**6.** a
3. d	**7.** d
4. b	**8.** a

2. Gramática

Suggestions: Remind students of the main points of the grammar presentations in *Capítulo* 5:

- the present perfect tense
- the pluperfect tense
- the present perfect subjunctive
- demonstrative adjectives and pronouns

Answers:

1. b	**5.** c
2. c	**6.** b
3. a	**7.** d
4. a	**8.** a

Repaso del capítulo

OBJECTIVE
▸ Demonstrate that you can perform the tasks on these pages

Preparación para el examen

❶ Vocabulario Escribe la letra de la palabra o expresión que mejor complete cada frase. Escribe tus respuestas en una hoja aparte.

1. Cuando llenas una solicitud de empleo te piden tu _____.
   a. derecho   c. requisito
   b. fecha de nacimiento   d. entrevista

2. Vamos a participar en una _____ para proteger a la gente sin hogar.
   a. campaña   c. rehabilitación
   b. ciudadanía   d. responsabilidad

3. No quiero trabajar todos los días. Necesito un puesto a tiempo _____.
   a. puntual   c. clasificado
   b. completo   d. parcial

4. Una recepcionista debe _____ bien a los clientes.
   a. reparar   c. repartir
   b. atender   d. conseguir

5. ¿Quieres ayudarnos a _____ árboles en el jardín de la comunidad?
   a. educar   c. sembrar
   b. beneficiar   d. solicitar

6. Me gustaría trabajar de _____ en una piscina.
   a. salvavida   c. vendedor
   b. mensajero   d. repartidor

7. Las leyes de nuestro país _____ educar a todos los niños.
   a. benefician   c. rescatan
   b. solicitan   d. garantizan

8. Muchos jóvenes voluntarios _____ casas para la gente sin hogar.
   a. construyen   c. limpian
   b. destruyen   d. protegen

❷ Gramática Escribe la letra de la palabra o expresión que mejor complete cada frase. Escribe tus respuestas en una hoja aparte.

1. Antes de trabajar en el hogar de ancianos, Pilar _____ en un centro recreativo.
   a. ha trabajado   c. está trabajando
   b. había trabajado d. trabaja

2. Me interesaría este puesto, pero prefiero más _____.
   a. aquella   c. aquél
   b. aquellos   d. aquellas

3. Espero que mi profesora me _____ una buena carta de referencia.
   a. haya escrito   c. ha escrito
   b. había escrito   d. está escribiendo

4. No sé dónde está el gerente. No lo _____ en varias horas.
   a. he visto   c. veía
   b. había visto   d. haya visto

5. Quiero que te encargues de _____ solicitudes de empleo.
   a. estos   c. estas
   b. esto   d. este

6. Espero que ustedes _____ suficientes fondos para el hogar de ancianos.
   a. han juntado   c. habían juntado
   b. hayan juntado   d. juntan

7. "¿Cuántas bicicletas ya _____ este año?", le preguntó a Julio el dueño del taller.
   a. estás reparando c. hayas reparado
   b. reparabas   d. has reparado

8. Cuando llegué al comedor de beneficencia, los voluntarios ya _____ la mesa.
   a. habían puesto   c. van a poner
   b. han puesto   d. hayan puesto

254 doscientos cincuenta y cuatro • Capítulo 5 • Trabajo y comunidad

---

Differentiated Instruction

Heritage Speakers

Ask students to write down changes that have occurred in their Spanish due to what they have learned in *Capítulo* 5. These might include corrections of grammar or spelling errors, improvements in vocabulary or pronunciation, or elimination of Anglicisms. Have them keep a running list of such changes in their digital portfolios.

Students with Learning Difficulties

Before asking students to complete each activity on p. 255, review with them the chapter material that pertains to the activity. If students still have difficulty, encourage them to review together in study groups.

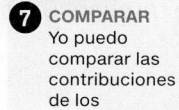

En el examen vas a . . .	Éstas son las tareas de práctica que te pueden ser útiles para el examen . . .	Para repasar, ve a tu libro de texto impreso o digital . . .
Interpretive		
3 ESCUCHAR Yo puedo escuchar a varios estudiantes en entrevistas de trabajo e identificar los empleos	Escucha lo que dicen estos estudiantes en sus entrevistas de trabajo. Presta atención a lo que dicen y di a qué empleo se presentaron Verónica, Ariel, José y Patricia.	**pp. 214–217** *Vocabulario en contexto 1* **p. 215** Actividad 1 **p. 215** Actividad 2 **p. 216** Actividades 3 and 4 **p. 217** *Videohistoria* **pp. 250–251** *Auténtico*
Interpersonal		
4 HABLAR En una feria de trabajo, puedo hablar con un compañero de mi experiencia y hacer preguntas sobre los empleos	Imagina que vas a una feria de trabajo. Di lo que le dirías a un consejero acerca de tus conocimientos y habilidades, en qué te interesaría trabajar y en qué has trabajado antes. También haz preguntas sobre el empleo, por ejemplo: lo que necesitas hacer diario, el horario, el sueldo y los beneficios.	**p. 219** Actividad 9 **p. 220** Actividad 11 **p. 220** Actividad 12 **p. 223** Actividad 15 **p. 224** Actividad 17
Interpretive		
5 LEER Yo puedo leer y comprender un anuncio clasificado	Lee este anuncio. ¿Qué tipo de empleo se ofrece? ¿Es un trabajo a tiempo completo o a tiempo parcial? ¿Qué conocimientos o habilidades se necesitan? **Recepcionista. Se necesita joven bilingüe, puntual y responsable para atender el teléfono y otros trabajos de oficina. Otros requisitos: saber trabajar con computadoras y tener buenas referencias. Lunes a viernes de 8 a.m. a 5 p.m.**	**p. 217** *Vocabulario en contexto 1* **p. 220** Actividad 11 **p. 224** Actividad 16
Presentational		
6 ESCRIBIR Yo puedo escribir una carta para solicitar empleo	Imagina que vas a solicitar empleo. Piensa qué tipo de trabajo es, y escribe una carta para solicitar empleo. En tu carta di (a) por qué te interesa el trabajo, (b) qué cualidades personales tienes por las que serías el (la) mejor para ese puesto y (c) qué experiencia de trabajo tienes.	**p. 221** Actividad 13 **p. 234** Actividad 33 **pp. 244–245** *Presentación escrita*
Comparisons		
7 COMPARAR Yo puedo comparar las contribuciones de los hispanohablantes y de otras personas	¿Cuál es el impacto de algunos hispanohablantes en la cultura de los Estados Unidos? También piensa en cómo les influimos a ellos en sus países, como en la política, los negocios, las artes, las ciencias y el deporte.	**p. 234** *Cultura* **pp. 240–241** *Puente a la cultura*

Differentiated Assessment

Core Assessment
- Assessment Program: Examen del capítulo 5,
- Technology: Audio: Cap. 5,
- ExamView: Chapter Test, Test Banks A and B

Advanced/Pre-AP®
- ExamView: Pre-AP® Test Bank
- Pre-AP® Resource Materials

Extra Support
- Alternate Assessment Program: Examen del capítulo 5
- Technology: Audio: Cap. 5,

Heritage Speakers
- Assessment Program: *Para hispanohablantes:* Examen del capítulo 5
- ExamView: Heritage Speaker Test Bank

3. Escuchar

Suggestions: Use the audio or read from the script.

Technology: Audio

Script:

Male Adult: ¿Y puedes bañar a los perritos, si es necesario?

Verónica: ¡Sí! Y me gustaría trabajar aquí porque me encantan los perros y los gatos y tengo experiencia con animales. He trabajado con un veterinario y antes había atendido al gatito de mi vecina.

Ariel: Me gusta mucho ayudar, señora López. Puedo leerles el periódico a los ancianos y ayudar a servir la comida. Puedo trabajar de voluntario a tiempo parcial, desde las cinco hasta las ocho.

José: He trabajado de salvavida el verano pasado en otro club deportivo, y antes había hecho varios cursos de natación. Me interesaría el trabajo porque el club está cerca de mi casa.

Patricia: He trabajado atendiendo el teléfono. También sé usar computadoras y hacer todas las tareas de oficina.

Answers:

Verónica: empleada en una tienda de animales **Ariel:** voluntario en un hogar de ancianos **José:** salvavida **Patricia:** recepcionista

4. Hablar

Suggestions: Remind students that in this situation they would most likely address the people to whom they are speaking with *Ud.*

Answers will vary.

5. Leer

Suggestions: Tell students to refer to pp. 214–217 and 228–231 if they have questions about vocabulary in the review.

Answers:

Recepcionista. Es un trabajo a tiempo completo. Se necesita ser bilingüe, puntual y responsable. Hay que saber trabajar con computadoras y tener buenas referencias.

6. Escribir

Suggestions: Tell students to use their own cover letters in their digital portfolios as a model.

Answers will vary.

6. Comparar

Suggestions: Ask students if their perceptions of the Spanish-speaking population have changed in any way because of what they have learned.

Answers will vary.

Additional Resources

 Technology: Online Resources
- Instant Check
- *Para hispanohablantes*

Print
- Core WB pp. 75–76

CAPÍTULO **6**

Chapter Overview

Careers, professions, and technology

Vocabulary: careers and professions; plans for the future; impact of science and technology

Grammar: future; future of probability; future perfect; uses of direct and indirect object pronouns

Cultural Perspectives: Chilean surrealist painter Roberto Matta; living arrangements of young people in Spain; internships in Washington, D.C., for young Spanish speakers; the international baccalaureate program; Spanish and Latin American architects

¡Pura vida!: Watch an engaging video episode about a group of young people in Costa Rica!

Chapter Support

Bulletin Boards

Theme: ¿Qué nos traerá el futuro?

Ask students to cut out, copy, or download photos or pictures of projects or things for the future, and people whose careers are related to the future. Cluster photos or pictures according to these themes. Add brief captions to the photos or pictures explaining the project or item for the future.

Hands-on Culture

Recipe: Gallo pinto

The national dish of Costa Rica is *gallo pinto*, which is refried rice and beans and is served at breakfast, lunch, or dinner, with fried eggs, sour cream, and hot *tortillas.*

Ingredients:

1 cup white rice	1-3⁄4 cups water
1 tablespoon olive oil	1 medium onion, diced
1/2 red bell pepper, seeded and diced	1 jalapeño pepper, seeded and minced
2 cloves garlic, minced	1 handful chopped cilantro leaves
16 ounces canned black beans, drained	Salt to taste
1 teaspoon Tabasco sauce	2 tablespoons Worcestershire sauce

Supplies: frying pan, 2 qt. saucepan, serving dish

1. Wash the rice in cold water, drain, and put it in a pot with the water and a pinch of salt. Bring the rice to a boil, stir, cover, and lower the heat to a simmer. Cook until the water is absorbed, about 20 minutes. Let stand for 10 minutes, then fluff it with a fork.
2. Heat the olive oil in a skillet over medium-high heat. Add the onions and peppers and sauté, stirring for 5 minutes. Stir in the garlic and sauté for 2 minutes. Add the cilantro and sauté for 1 minute more.
3. Spoon the rice and beans into the skillet, mix well, and heat everything through. Season with salt and a combination of Worcestershire sauce and Tabasco sauce.

Game

Cosas del futuro

This game practices grammar and vocabulary about the future. Use it toward the end of the chapter, after students have practiced the chapter vocabulary.

Players: entire class

Materials: paper, pencils, markers, pen

Rules:

1. Divide the class into small groups. Have each group think of an invention for the future, such as a special machine that does homework for students.
2. Ask students draw a picture of the invention and to write a clue about its function.
3. Call on a group to show its drawing and read aloud the clue.
4. The rest of the students take turns asking the members of the group *sí/no* questions in an attempt to determine what the object is used for.
5. When a student correctly guesses what the object is, his or her group gets one point and is the next one to come to the front of the class and show their drawing. Play continues in this manner until every group has had the chance of showing their drawings and answering questions. The group with more points wins the game.

Variation: Instead of drawing the objects, students can write clues in the form of sentences so students guess what the object is.

21st Century Skills

Look for tips throughout Chapter 6 to enrich your teaching by integrating 21st Century Skills. Suggestions for the Project-Based Learning and Culture follow below.

Project-Based Learning

Modify the project with these suggestions:

ICT (Information, Communications and Technology) Literacy Encourage students to access a variety of Web sites to use as a model for designing their own Web page. Have them evaluate the layout of various sites to gather ideas for creating their own.

Communication As students prepare to start the project, provide them with the handout "Compare and Contrast" to help them organize their ideas about how to describe the evolution of their product from the moment of invention to the present, and projecting to the future.

Creativity and Innovation Have students be as creative as possible when describing the stages of development of their featured products. How many ways could they present and organize this information using visuals, descriptive text, audio or video footage? How do the products affect the lives of people who use them? How will this change in the future?

Chapter Culture

Social and Cross-Cultural Skills Direct students to review the information and their answers to the questions in the *Cultura* notes on pages 272, 281, and 297. Promote a discussion about the different cultural perspectives that young people would learn if they participated in these programs. In what ways would they need to adapt to the opportunities provided by them?

 Technology: Videodocumentario
View *La tecnología en la carrera de un profesional* online with the class to learn more about a photography professor and his class at the New England School of Photography.

Project-Based Learning

La evolución de los inventos

Overview: Students create a Web page featuring items that have evolved throughout time and will continue to change in the future. Students should show when each item was invented, what it looked like then, what it looks like now, and what it is going to look like in the future. They should insert a brief description of the changes in the history of each product. Students then present their Web page to the class, describing all the information featured on the page.

Resources: digital or print photos, image editing and page layout software, bilingual dictionary

Sequence: (suggestions for when to do each step appear throughout the chapter)

Step 1. Review instructions so students know what is expected of them. Share the rubric with the class.

Step 2. Students submit a rough draft of their Web page. Return the drafts with your suggestions. For vocabulary and grammar practice, ask students to work in pairs and present their drafts to each other.

Step 3. Students create layouts. Encourage students to try different arrangements before writing descriptions. Ask them to use as much of the vocabulary from *Capítulo* 6 as possible in the descriptions. Also, have them use a bilingual dictionary for any words they would like to use but do not yet know.

Step 4. Students submit a draft of their descriptions. Note your corrections and suggestions, then return the drafts to students.

Step 5. Students complete and present their Web page to the class. They describe all the information featured on the page.

Options

1. Students create a poster for their school instead of a Web page.
2. Students write an article for the school newspaper about the inventions.

Assessment

Here is a detailed rubric for assessing this project:

Chapter 6 Project: *La evolución de los inventos*

Rubric	Score 1	Score 3	Score 5
Your evidence of planning	You provide no written draft or page layout.	Your draft was written and layout created, but not corrected.	You show evidence of corrected draft and layout.
Your use of illustrations	You include photos or visuals.	Your photos or visuals were included, but the layout was unorganized.	Your Web page was easy to read, complete, and accurate.
Your presentation	You include little of the required information.	You include most of the required information.	You include all of the required information.

AT A GLANCE

Objectives
- Listen and read about future plans and predictions
- Talk and write about future problems and advances
- Explain your career goals for the future
- Understand how Hispanic architects are shaping the future
- Compare living situations of college graduates from Spain and U.S.
- Compare cultural practices and perspectives in an authentic video about the banker of the future

Vocabulary
- Professions and careers
- Personal qualities
- Future ideas and actions
- Careers of the future

Grammar
- Future
- Future of probability
- Future perfect tense
- Uses of the direct and indirect pronouns

Culture
- Surrealism in art, p. 261
- Living situations of Spanish young people, p. 267
- Hispanic youth working in Washington, D.C., p. 272
- Technology of the future, pp. 276–277
- International baccalaureate, p. 281
- Life in the future, p. 282
- Architecture in the future, pp. 288–289
- Virtual school in Mexico, p. 297

A ver si recuerdas...
- Career and jobs
- Technology and environment
- *Saber* and *conocer*
- Impersonal *se*

Recycle
- Combining letters when speaking
- Verbs with irregular participles

Authentic Resources
- **Auténtico:** *La banca del futuro,* pp. 298–299

RESOURCES

	FOR THE STUDENT	DIGITAL	PRINT	FOR THE TEACHER	DIGITAL	PRINT
A ver si recuerdas pp. 256–259						
Review	*A ver si recuerdas* with Remediation	•		*A ver si recuerdas* with Remediation	•	
	Guided WB, pp. 176–179	•	•	Teacher's Edition, pp. 256–259	•	•
	Core WB, pp. 77–78	•	•			
	Para hispanohablantes	•				
Introducción pp. 260–261						
Present	Student Edition, pp. 260–261	•	•	Teacher's Edition, pp. 260–261	•	•
	DK Reference Atlas	•		Teacher's Resource Materials	•	
	Videonovela: *¡Pura vida!*	•		Mapa global interactivo	•	
	¡Pura vida! Video Activities	•				
	Para hispanohablantes	•				
Vocabulario en contexto pp. 262–265/276–279						
Present & Practice	Student Edition, pp. 262–265/276–279	•	•	Teacher's Edition, pp. 262–265/276–279	•	•
	Audio	•		Teacher's Resources Materials	•	
	Videohistoria	•		Vocabulary Clip Art	•	
	Flashcards	•		Technology: Audio	•	
	Instant Check	•		Video Program: Videohistoria	•	
	Guided WB, pp. 180–188/193–200	•	•			
	Core WB, pp. 79–80/84–85	•	•			
	Communication Activities	•				
	Para hispanohablantes	•				
Assess and Remediate				Pruebas 6–1/6–5: Assessment Program, Assessment Program *Para hispanohablantes*	•	

RESOURCES

	FOR THE STUDENT	DIGITAL	PRINT	FOR THE TEACHER	DIGITAL	PRINT
Vocabulario en uso pp. 266–269/280–282						
Present & Practice	Student Edition, pp. 266–269/280–282	•	•	Interactive Whiteboard Vocabulary Activities	•	
	Instant Check	•		Teacher's Edition, pp. 266–269/280–282	•	•
	Communication Activities	•		Teacher's Resource Materials	•	
	Para hispanohablantes	•		Technology: Audio	•	
	Communicative Pair Activities	•		Videomodelos	•	
Assess and Remediate				Pruebas 6–2, 6–6 with Remediation	•	
				Pruebas 6–2, 6–6: Assessment Program, Assessment Program *Para hispanohablantes*	•	
Gramática pp. 270–275/283–287						
Present & Practice	Student Edition, pp. 270–275/283–287	•	•	Interactive Whiteboard Grammar Activities	•	
	Instant Check	•		Teacher's Edition, pp. 270–275/283–287	•	•
	Tutorial Video: Grammar	•		Teacher's Resource Materials	•	
	Canción de hip hop	•		Technology: Audio	•	
	Guided WB, pp. 189–192/201–204	•	•	Videomodelos	•	
	Core WB, pp. 81–83/86–88	•	•			
	Communication Activities	•				
	Para hispanohablantes	•				
	Communicative Pair Activities	•				
Assess and Remediate				Pruebas 6–3, 6–4, 6–7, 6–8 with Remediation	•	
				Pruebas 6–3, 6–4, 6–7, 6–8: Assessment Program, Assessment Program *Para hispanohablantes*	•	
				Examen 1, Examen 2: Vocab. y gramática, pp. 133–135/142–144	•	
Aplicación pp. 288–299						
Apply	Student Edition, pp. 288–299	•	•	Teacher's Edition, pp. 288–299	•	•
	Authentic Resources Workbook	•	•	Teacher's Resource Materials	•	
	Authentic Resources	•		Video Program: Videodocumentario	•	
	Online Cultural Reading	•		Mapa global interactivo	•	
	Guided WB, pp. 205–207	•	•	Authentic Resources Lesson Plans with scripts, answer keys	•	
	Communication Activities	•				
	Para hispanohablantes	•				
	Videodocumentario	•				
Repaso del capítulo pp. 300–303						
Review	Student Edition, pp. 300–303	•	•	Teacher's Edition, pp. 300–303	•	•
	Core WB, pp. 89–90	•	•	Teacher's Resource Materials	•	
	Communication Activities	•		Technology: Audio	•	
	Para hispanohablantes	•				
	Instant Check	•				
Chapter Assessment						
Assess				Examen del capítulo 6: Assessment Program, Alternate Assessment Program, Assessment Program *Para hispanohablantes*	•	
				Technology: Audio, Cap. 6, Examen	•	
				ExamView: Test Banks A and B (questions only online) Heritage Speaker Test Bank, Pre-AP® Test Bank	•	

	LESSON PLAN		
DAY	**Warm-up / Assess**	**Preview / Present / Practice / Communicate**	**Wrap-up / Homework Options**
1	**Warm-up** (10 min.) • Return Examen del capítulo: Capítulo 5	**Repaso** (35 min.) • A ver si recuerdas . . . • Actividades 1, 2, 3, 6, 7	**Wrap-up and Homework Options** (5 min.) • Core Practice 6-1, 6-2
2	**Warm-up** (10 min.) • Homework check	**Chapter Opener** (10 min.) • Objectives • Arte y cultura **Vocabulario en contexto 1** (25 min.) • Presentation: Vocabulario y gramática en contexto • Actividades 1, 2, 3	**Wrap-up and Homework Options** (5 min.) • Clip Art Vocabulary
3	**Warm-up** (10 min.) • Homework check	**Vocabulario en contexto 1** (30 min.) • Presentation: Videohistoria ¿Cuáles son mis aptitudes? • View: Videohistoria **Vocabulario en uso 1** (5 min.) • Interactive Whiteboard Vocabulary Activities • Actividades 4, 5	**Wrap-up and Homework Options** (5 min.) • Core Practice 6-3, 6-4 • Actividad 6 • Prueba 6-1: Vocabulary recognition
4	**Warm-up** (10 min.) • Homework check • **Formative Assessment** (10 min.) • Prueba 6-1: Vocabulary recognition	**Vocabulario en uso 1** (25 min.) • Actividades 7, 8, 9 • Cultura • Ampliación del lenguaje	**Wrap-up and Homework Options** (5 min.) • Actividad 10 • Writing Activities • Prueba 6-2 with Remediation: Vocabulary production
5	**Warm-up** (15 min.) • Homework check • Communicative Pair Activity • Audio Activity • **Formative Assessment** (10 min.) • Prueba 6-2 with Remediation: Vocabulary production	**Gramática y vocabulario en uso 1** (20 min.) • Presentation: El futuro • Interactive Whiteboard Grammar Activities • Actividades 11, 12, 13 • Writing Activity	**Wrap-up and Homework Options** (5 min.) • Core Practice 6-5
6	**Warm-up** (10 min.) • Homework check	**Gramática y vocabulario en uso 1** (35 min.) • Actividades 14, 15 • Cultura • Presentation: El futuro de probabilidad • Interactive Whiteboard Grammar Activities • Actividades 16, 17	**Wrap-up and Homework Options** (5 min.) • Core Practice 6-6, 6-7 • Prueba 6-3 with Remediation: El futuro
7	**Warm-up** (10 min.) • Homework check • **Formative Assessment** (10 min.) • Prueba 6-3 with Remediation: El futuro	**Gramática y vocabulario en uso 1** (25 min.) • Actividades 18, 19 • Communicative Pair Activity • En voz alta	**Wrap-up and Homework Options** (5 min.) • Writing Activity • Prueba 6-4 with Remediation: El futuro de probabilidad
8	**Warm-up** (10 min.) • Homework check • **Formative Assessment** (10 min.) • Prueba 6-4 with Remediation: El futuro de probabilidad	**Vocabulario en contexto 2** (25 min.) • Presentation: Vocabulario y gramática en contexto • Actividades 20, 21	**Wrap-up and Homework Options** (5 min.) • Clip Art Vocabulary • Examen: Vocabulario y gramática 1
9	**Warm-up** (5 min.) • Homework check • **Formative Assessment** (30 min.) • Examen: Vocabulario y gramática 1	**Vocabulario en contexto 2** (10 min.) • Presentation: Tres campos que tienen futuro • Actividad 22	**Wrap-up and Homework Options** (5 min.) • Actividad 23 • Core Practice 6-8, 6-9 • Prueba 6-5: Vocabulary recognition
10	**Warm-up** (20 min.) • Homework check • **Formative Assessment** (10 min.) • Prueba 6-5: Vocabulary recognition	**Vocabulario en uso 2** (15 min.) • Actividades 24, 25, 26 • Cultura	**Wrap-up and Homework Options** (5 min.) • Actividades 27, 28

LESSON PLAN

DAY	Warm-up / Assess	Preview / Present / Practice / Communicate		Wrap-up / Homework Options
11	**Warm-up** (15 min.) • Homework check	**Vocabulario en uso 2** (15 min.) • Interactive Whiteboard Vocabulary Activities • Actividad 29 • Writing Activity	**Gramática y vocabulario en uso 2** (15 min.) • Presentation: El futuro perfecto • Interactive Whiteboard Grammar Activities • Actividades 30, 32	**Wrap-up and Homework Options** (5 min.) • Core Practice 6-10 • Prueba 6-6 with Remediation: Vocabulary production
12	**Warm-up** (10 min.) • Homework check • **Formative Assessment** (10 min.) • Prueba 6-6 with Remediation: Vocabulary production	**Gramática y vocabulario en uso 2 (25 min.)** • Actividad 32 • Presentation: Uso de los complementos directos e indirectos • Interactive Whiteboard Grammar Activities • Writing Activity • Actividades 33, 34 • El español en la comunidad		**Wrap-up and Homework Options** (5 min.) • Core Practice 6-11, 6-12 • Prueba 6-7 with Remediation: El futuro de probabilidad
13	**Warm-up** (10 min.) • Homework check • **Formative Assessment** (10 min.) • Prueba 6-7 with Remediation: El futuro de probabilidad	**Gramática y vocabulario en uso 2** (25 min.) • Actividades 35, 36, 37 • Audio Activity • Writing Activity		**Wrap-up and Homework Options** (5 min.) • Writing Activity • Prueba 6-8 with Remediation: Uso de los complementos directos e indirectos
14	**Warm-up** (10 min.) • Communicative Pair Activity • **Formative Assessment** (10 min.) • Prueba 6-8 with Remediation: Uso de los complementos directos e indirectos	**Aplicación** (25 min.) • La arquitectura del futuro • ¿Comprendiste? • El futuro de la comunidad • Presentación oral: Step 1		**Wrap-up and Homework Options** (5 min.) • Examen: Vocabulario y gramática 2
15	**Warm-up** (5 min.) • Answer questions • **Formative Assessment** (25 min.) • Examen: Vocabulario y gramática 2	**Aplicación** (15 min.) • Presentación oral: Step 2		**Wrap-up and Homework Options** (5 min.) • Presentación oral: Step 3
16	**Warm-up** (5 min.) • Homework check	**Aplicación** (40 min.) • Presentación oral: Step 3 (half class) • Pre-AP® Integración 1, 2, 3		**Wrap-up and Homework Options** (5 min.) • Presentación escrita: Steps 1, 2
17	**Warm-up** (10 min.) • Homework check	**Aplicación** (35 min.) • Presentación oral: Step 3 (half class) • View Video • Video Activities 1, 2, 3 • Presentación escrita: Step 3		**Wrap-up and Homework Options** (5 min.) • Presentación escrita: Step 4 • Preparación para el examen: 1, 2
18	**Warm-up** (10 min.) • Homework check	**Repaso** (10 min.) • Preparación para el examen: Actividades 3, 4 **Aplicación** (25 min.) • Lectura • Cultura • ¿Comprendiste? • Auténtico		**Wrap-up and Homework Options** (5 min.) • ¿Comprendiste? • Core Practice: Organizer 6-13, 6-14 • Instant Check
19	**Warm-up** (15 min.) • Homework check	**Repaso** (30 min.) • Preparación para el examen: Actividades 5, 6, 7 • Other review		**Wrap-up and Homework Options** (5 min.) • Examen del capítulo
20	**Warm-up** (5 min.) • Answer questions • **Summative Assessment** (44 min.) • Examen del capítulo			**Wrap-up and Homework Options** (1 min.) • A ver si recuerdas: Capítulo 7

ALTERNATE LESSON PLAN

DAY	Warm-up / Assess	Preview / Present / Practice / Communicate	Wrap-up / Homework Options
1	**Warm-up** (35 min.) • Return Examen del capítulo: Capítulo 6 • A ver si recuerdas . . . • Homework check	**Chapter Opener** (10 min.) • Objectives • Arte y cultura **Vocabulario en contexto 1** (30 min.) • Presentation: Vocabulario y gramática en contexto • Actividades 1, 2, 3 • Presentation: Videohistoria: ¿Cuáles son mis aptitudes? • View: Videohistoria **Vocabulario en uso 1** (10 min.) • Interactive Whiteboard Vocabulary Activities • Actividades 4, 5, 6	**Wrap-up and Homework Options** (5 min.) • Core Practice 6-3, 6-4 • Clip Art Vocabulary • Prueba 6-1: Vocabulary recognition
2	**Warm-up** (20 min.) • Homework check • Actividades 7, 8, 9 • **Formative Assessment** (10 min.) • Prueba 6-1: Vocabulary recognition	**Vocabulario en uso 1** (55 min.) • Actividad 10 • Ampliación del lenguaje • Audio Activity • Writing Activity • Communicative Pair Activity	**Wrap-up and Homework Options** (5 min.) • Prueba 6-2 with Remediation: Vocabulary production
3	**Warm-up** (5 min.) • Homework check • **Formative Assessment** (10 min.) • Prueba 6-2 with Remediation: Vocabulary production	**Gramática y vocabulario en uso 1** (70 min.) • Presentation: El futuro • Interactive Whiteboard Grammar Activities • Actividades 11, 12, 13, 14, 15 • Cultura • Writing Activity	**Wrap-up and Homework Options** (5 min.) • Actividad 15: Step 3 • Core Practice 6-5 • Prueba 6-3 with Remediation: El futuro
4	**Warm-up** (10 min.) • Homework check • **Formative Assessment** (10 min.) • Prueba 6-3 with Remediation: El futuro	**Gramática y vocabulario en uso 1** (50 min.) • Presentation: El futuro de probabilidad • Interactive Whiteboard Grammar Activities • Actividades 16, 17, 18, 19 • En voz alta • Writing Activity • Communicative Pair Activity **Vocabulario en contexto 2** (15 min.) • Presentation: Vocabulario y gramática en contexto • Actividades 20, 21	**Wrap-up and Homework Options** (5 min.) • Core Practice 6-6, 6-7 • Prueba 6-4 with Remediation: El futuro de probabilidad • Examen: Vocabulario y gramática 1
5	**Warm-up** (10 min.) • Homework check • **Formative Assessment Options** (40 min.) • Prueba 6-4 with Remediation: El futuro de probabilidad • Examen: Vocabulario y gramática 1	**Vocabulario en contexto 2** (20 min.) • Presentation: Tres campos que tienen futuro • Actividades 22, 26 **Vocabulario en uso 2** (15 min.) • Interactive Whiteboard Vocabulary Activities • Actividades 25, 26	**Wrap-up and Homework Options** (5 min.) • Core Practice 6-8, 6-9 • Actividades 27, 28 • Clip Art • Prueba 6-5: Vocabulary recognition
6	**Warm-up** (35 min.) • Homework check • Actividades 26, 29 • Audio Activity • Writing Activity • Communicative Pair Activity • **Formative Assessment** (10 min.) • Prueba 6-5: Vocabulary recognition	**Gramática y vocabulario en uso 2** (40 min.) • Presentation: El futuro perfecto • Interactive Whiteboard Grammar Activities • Actividades 30, 31, 32 • Writing Activities	**Wrap-up and Homework Options** (5 min.) • Core Practice 6-10 • Pruebas 6-6, 6-7 with Remediations: Vocabulary production, El futuro perfecto

DAY	ALTERNATE LESSON PLAN		
	Warm-up / Assess	**Preview / Present / Practice / Communicate**	**Wrap-up / Homework Options**
7	**Warm-up** (10 min.) • Homework check • **Formative Assessment** (20 min.) • Pruebas 6-6, 6-7 with Remediations: Vocabulary production, El futuro perfecto	**Gramática y vocabulario en uso 2** (40 min.) • Presentation: El uso de los complementos directos e indirectos • Interactive Whiteboard Grammar Activities • Actividades 33, 34, 35, 36, 37 • Audio Activity • Writing Activity • El español en la comunidad **Aplicación** (15 min.) • Presentación oral: Steps 1, 2	**Wrap-up and Homework Options** (5 min.) • Core Practice 6-11, 6-12 • Prueba 6-8 with Remediation: El uso de los complementos directos e indirectos • Presentación oral: Step 2
8	**Warm-up** (15 min.) • Communicative Pair Activity • Homework check • **Formative Assessment** (10 min.) • Prueba 6-8 with Remediation: El uso de los complementos directos e indirectos	**Gramática y vocabulario en uso 2** (35 min.) • Presentación oral: Step 3 **Aplicación** (25 min.) • Presentation: La arquitectura del futuro • ¿Comprendiste? • El futuro de tu comunidad	**Wrap-up and Homework Options** (5 min.) • ¿Comprendiste? • El futuro de tu comunidad • Examen: Vocabulario y gramática 2
9	**Warm-up** (5 min.) • Homework check • **Formative Assessment Options** (30 min.) • Examen: Vocabulario y gramática 2	**Aplicación** (50 min.) • Pre-AP® Integración 1, 2, 3 • View Video • Video Activities • Presentación escrita: Step 1	**Wrap-up and Homework Options** (5 min.) • Presentación escrita: Step 2 • Preparación para el examen: Actividades 1, 2
10	**Warm-up** (20 min.) • Homework check • Presentación escrita: Step 3	**Aplicación** (35 min.) • Lectura • ¿Comprendiste? • Cultura • Auténtico **Repaso** (30 min.) • Preparación para el examen: Actividades 3, 4, 6	**Wrap-up and Homework Options** (5 min.) • Presentación escrita: Step 4 • Core Practice: Organizer 6-13, 6-14 • Instant Check • Preparación para el examen: Actividades 5, 7 • Examen del capítulo
11	**Warm-up** (15 min.) • Homework check • **Summative Assessment** (45 min.) • Examen del capítulo	**Theme Game (15 min.)** **A ver si recuerdas – Capítulo 7** (10 min.) • Presentation: Vocabulario • Presentation: Gramática	**Wrap-up and Homework Options** (5 min.) • A ver si recuerdas – Capítulo 7 • Actividades 1–6 • Core Practice 7-1, 7-2

Vocabulario: Repaso

Standards: 1.1, 1.2

Suggestions: Before presenting the material in this review section, consider testing your students' command of the material by assigning the Prueba with Remediation. Students will automatically be given additional practice of the material they have not yet mastered, and you can focus your review based on the class's overall performance on the post-test.

Have students copy the names of the five categories onto their own paper. With books closed, have students work in pairs and list as many words as they can for each category.

1

Standards: 1.1

Suggestions: Encourage students to use vocabulary and structures from previous chapters in Step 2. For example, they might use the present perfect tense when referring to the experiences needed for a particular profession: *Si alguien ha trabajado mucho con los animales, puede estudiar para ser veterinario(a).*

Common Errors: Some students may use a feminine article when they refer to a male ***artista, policía,*** or ***dentista.*** Remind them that although these nouns end in ***-a,*** they apply to either gender. Students should use them with masculine articles when talking about males: *Conozco a un artista que se llama Guillermo.*

Answers:
Step 1

1. e	**3.** a	**5.** c
2. d	**4.** b	

Step 2
Answers will vary.

Active Classroom

Extend *Actividad* 1 by asking students to write clues or associations for ten additional jobs. Have them read the list to a partner who will try to guess the job being described.

A ver si recuerdas

OBJECTIVES
▶ Discuss professions and needed qualifications
▶ Talk and write about things and people we know

Vocabulario

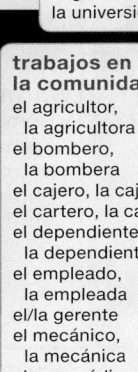
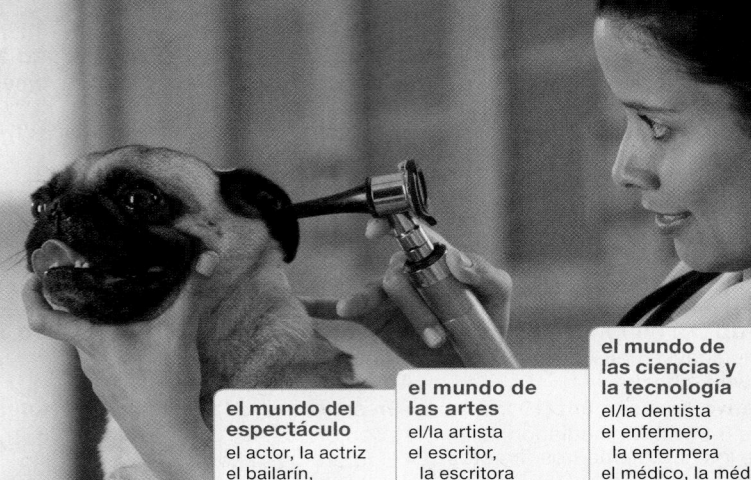

los estudios
la graduación
la universidad

trabajos en la comunidad
el agricultor, la agricultora
el bombero, la bombera
el cajero, la cajera
el cartero, la cartera
el dependiente, la dependienta
el empleado, la empleada
el/la gerente
el mecánico, la mecánica
el paramédico, la paramédica
el/la policía
el político, la política
el secretario, la secretaria

el mundo de las ciencias y la tecnología
el/la dentista
el enfermero, la enfermera
el médico, la médica
el técnico, la técnica
el veterinario, la veterinaria

el mundo del espectáculo
el actor, la actriz
el bailarín, la bailarina
el/la cantante
el crítico, la crítica

el mundo de las artes
el/la artista
el escritor, la escritora
el escultor, la escultora
el pintor, la pintora

1

Las profesiones

 HABLAR EN PAREJA

1 Empareja cada actividad o área de trabajo con una profesión.

1. actuar, el teatro	a. policía
2. los animales, las ciencias naturales	b. escritor(a)
3. cuidar y proteger a la gente	c. abogado(a)
4. los libros, escribir	d. veterinario(a)
5. las leyes, las ciencias sociales	e. actor, actriz

2 Con un(a) compañero(a), habla de las profesiones de las listas de Vocabulario y da recomendaciones.

Modelo
A —*A mí me gusta investigar.*
B —*Entonces, creo que debes ser científico.*

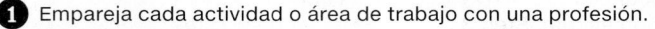

Differentiated Instruction

Bodily-Kinesthetic Learner

Have students play a game of charades in which they physically act out the movements associated with different professions. After the professions have been identified, have all students review by performing the actions while repeating the vocabulary.

Advanced Learners

Have students choose one profession from the *Vocabulario* and prepare a brief oral presentation telling what a person in that profession does, where he or she works, and what skills and studies he or she needs.

Gramática

Saber vs. conocer

Go **Online** to practice
PEARSON
realize™
PearsonSchool.com/Autentico

VIDEO   WRITING   SPEAK/RECORD

Both *saber* and *conocer* mean "to know."

You use *saber* to talk about knowing facts or information.

> Nadie **sabe** la fecha del examen.
> ¿**Saben** Uds. quién es ese actor?

Saber followed by an infinitive means "to know how to do something."

> Por supuesto, yo **sé usar** la computadora.
> No, mi hermanito no **sabe manejar**.

Conocer means "to know" in the sense of being familiar with a person, place, or thing.

> **Conocemos** al Dr. Fernández y a toda su familia.
> ¿**Conocen** Uds. el jardín zoológico?

In the preterite, *conocer* means "to meet someone for the first time."

> **Conocí** a dos críticos que trabajan para el periódico.
> ¿Los **conociste** en la conferencia?

> **Más recursos** ONLINE
>
> ▶ **GramActiva:** *Saber* and *conocer*
> ▶ **Tutorial:** *Saber* and *conocer*

2

¿Qué debe saber?

🎤 **HABLAR EN PAREJA** Túrnate con un(a) compañero(a) para preguntar y contestar lo que se debe saber hacer en cuatro profesiones.

Modelo
A —¿Qué debe hacer un periodista?
B —Un periodista **debe saber escribir** bien. Debes seguir cursos de escritura.

3

¿Saber o conocer?

🎤 **HABLAR EN PAREJA** Túrnate con tu compañero(a) para hacer y contestar preguntas usando *saber* y *conocer*.

▶ **Videomodelo**
el número de teléfono de (nombre) . . .
A —¿Sabes el número de teléfono de Alex?
B —Sí, lo sé, es 555-1719. / No, no lo sé.

- la fecha de hoy
- la respuesta
- al profesor (nombre)
- la Ciudad de México
- alguna canción en español
- montar en bicicleta
- alguna mujer de negocios
- a qué hora abre el museo

4

La fiesta

✏️ **LEER, ESCRIBIR** Dos amigos hablan en una fiesta. Completa la conversación con el verbo *saber* o *conocer* según corresponda.

A —¿ __1.__ quién es esa señora?
B —Es la doctora Rubio. Yo __2.__ a sus hijos.
A —¿De veras? ¿Dónde los __3.__ ?
B —En la universidad. Ellos __4.__ a mi amiga.

Gramática: Repaso

Standards: 1.4

Suggestions: Refer students who are having difficulty with *saber* and *conocer* to the online tutorial. Call out words or phrases and have students associate them with the correct verb.
Teacher: *la dirección*
Student: *saber*

2

Standards: 1.1

Suggestions: Encourage students to say more than one thing a person should know how to do for each profession.
Answers will vary.

3

Standards: 1.1

Suggestions: Remind students that Student A's question tells Student B which verb to use.
Answers:

saber	saber
saber	saber
conocer	conocer
conocer	saber

4

Standards: 1.3

Suggestions: Remind students to make each verb agree in person and number with the subject, and to watch for correct use of tense.
Answers:

1. Sabes   3. conociste
2. conozco   4. conocen

Enrich Your Teaching

Teacher-to-Teacher

Always have a few review targets ready, and use creative ways—informal questions or comments—to elicit them from students as they walk in the door each day. You don't need to do this with all students. One or two comments or questions a day, to different students each time, will have them thinking in Spanish as they come into your classroom.

6 Recycle

Vocabulario: Repaso

Standards: 1.1, 1.2

Suggestions: Ask students to create sentences that use items from at least two of the categories in the *Vocabulario*. For example: *Me gusta mi computadora portátil porque la puedo llevar conmigo y trabajar en casa o en la escuela.*

5

Standards: 1.1, 1.3

Suggestions: As students share their sentences, encourage them to elaborate on each other's comments.

Answers will vary.

Extension: Ask students to say what changes they have made in their personal lives due to the changes in their community: *He tenido que cambiar mi rutina de la mañana. Hoy día es necesario que salga más temprano.*

6

Standards: 1.1

Suggestions: Point out to students that **había** remains singular, even if they are referring to plural objects: *... no había videos.*

Answers will vary.

A ver si recuerdas

OBJECTIVES
▸ Discuss and write about how things have changed
▸ Express ideas about people and things in general

Vocabulario

la tecnología
la computadora
la computadora
  portátil
el correo electrónico
el disco compacto
la página Web
la Red
el salón de chat
el televisor
el video

la ciudad
el apartamento
el barrio
la calle
la casa
la comunidad
el edificio de
  apartamentos
la gente
el tráfico

**el medio
ambiente**
el agua
el aire
los animales
limpio, -a
la naturaleza
puro, -a
sucio, -a

acciones
beneficiar
cambiar
construir
crear
darse cuenta de
eliminar
mejorar
obtener
preocuparse
proteger
realizar
tener lugar

para comparar
ahora
antes
desafortunadamente
hace . . . que
hasta
más . . . (que)
mejor
menos . . . (que)
peor
pero

5

Cambios en mi barrio

 ESCRIBIR, HABLAR   Haz una lista de cuatro cosas que hayan cambiado en tu barrio o comunidad en los últimos años. Luego escribe frases comparando cómo son las cosas ahora y cómo eran antes. Usa las palabras de la lista. Comparte tus frases con un(a) compañero(a).

Modelo
tráfico
El tráfico en mi comunidad es ahora peor que antes porque hay más gente que vive en el barrio.

6

En el pasado

 HABLAR EN PAREJA   Túrnate con un(a) compañero(a) para decir qué había o no había en los períodos de tiempo indicados. Usen las palabras o expresiones de las listas.

Modelo
Hace 50 años . . .
Hace 50 años había televisión pero no había discos compactos.

1. Hace 40 años . . .
2. En 1975 . . .
3. El año pasado . . .
4. Hace 10 años . . .
5. En 1930 . . .
6. Hace 20 años . . .

258 doscientos cincuenta y ocho • Capítulo 6 • ¿Qué nos traerá el futuro?

Differentiated Instruction

Heritage Speakers

Ask students who have lived in a heritage country to discuss changes that have taken place there as well as in their current community. Have them predict future changes.

Students with Learning Difficulties

Help students organize their sentence ideas for *Actividad* 5. On a piece of paper, have them label two columns **antes** and **ahora.** Ask them to write a simple sentence in each column. Then guide them to connect the two ideas into a complex sentence.

258

Go **Online** to practice

PearsonSchool.com/Autentico

PEARSON
realize

VIDEO WRITING SPEAK/RECORD

Recycle | **6**

Gramática

El *se* impersonal

In English you often use *they, you, one,* or *people* in an impersonal or an indefinite sense meaning "people in general." In Spanish you use *se* + the *Ud. / él / ella* or the *Uds. / ellos / ellas* form of the verb.

Se habla español.   **Se** venden computadoras baratas.

• Note that you don't know who performs the action. The word that follows the verb determines whether the verb is singular or plural.

Se creó una página web.   **Se crearon** páginas web.

• When the word following the conjugated verb is an infinitive, the verb form is singular.

Se necesita construir un nuevo edificio.

Más recursos ONLINE

 Tutorial: Impersonal *se*

7

Lugares y actividades

 HABLAR EN PAREJA Trabaja con otro(a) estudiante para hacer la pregunta *¿Dónde . . . ?* y contestarla. Luego inventen y contesten tres preguntas más con *¿Dónde?*

 Videomodelo
escribir reseñas
A —*¿Dónde se escriben reseñas?*
B —*En el periódico se escriben reseñas.*

1. ver mucha gente tomando el sol
2. no permitir sacar fotos
3. vender ropa barata
4. poder esquiar
5. comer muy bien
6. **¡Respuesta personal!**

8

En el periódico

 ESCRIBIR Trabajas en la sección de anuncios clasificados de un periódico. En una hoja aparte escribe títulos para anuncios usando los siguientes verbos y las palabras de abajo. Recuerda que si la palabra que va después del verbo es plural el verbo debe ir en plural.

vender	reparar	alquilar
necesitar	buscar	comprar

1. un coche
2. computadoras
3. apartamento nuevo
4. personas con experiencia

5. bicicletas usadas
6. joven cortés
7. casas viejas
8. videos y discos compactos

Capítulo 6 • doscientos cincuenta y nueve **259**

Enrich Your Teaching

Teacher-to-Teacher

As an extension of *Actividad* 8, bring in and photocopy a page from the classified section of a Spanish-language newspaper. Before making copies, scan the ads to make sure no unwanted topics or language are present. Ask students to find examples of the use of the impersonal *se.*

21st Century Skills

ICT (Information, Communications and Technology) Literacy Direct students to the online tutorials for self-directed review of the grammar topics recycled in this chapter. Students can expand their own learning by reviewing the related English grammar first then proceed to the new Spanish grammar point. Each tutorial is followed by a quick comprehension check.

Gramática

Standards: 4.1

Suggestions: Refer students who are having difficulty with the impersonal *se* to the *GramActiva* video from Level 2 Chapter 7A and the online tutorial. Explain that in most cases the **se** construction can also be compared to the English passive voice. Provide examples, such as "Spanish is spoken here." *(Aquí se habla español.)*

7

Standards: 1.1

Common Errors: Students may treat the word **gente** as plural. Remind them that **gente** is always singular and takes singular forms of verbs, adjectives, and articles: *La gente está tomando el sol.*

Answers:

Student B's answers will vary. Student A's questions will use the following verb forms:

1. se ve
2. no se permite
3. se vende

4. se puede
5. se come
6. Answers will vary.

8

Standards: 1.3

Suggestions: Remind students that, as in English, Spanish ad titles often omit smaller function words, such as articles.

Answers will vary, but may include:

1. Se vende coche.
2. Se reparan computadoras.
3. Se alquila apartamento nuevo.
4. Se buscan personas con experiencia.
5. Se compran bicicletas usadas.
6. Se necesita joven cortés.
7. Se reparan casas viejas.
8. Se venden videos y discos compactos.

Additional Resources

 Technology: Online Resources
• *A ver si recuerdas* with Remediation
• Guided, Core, Audio, Writing practice
• *Para hispanohablantes*
Print
• Guided WB pp. 176–179
• Core WB pp. 77–78

Assessment

A ver si recuerdas with Remediation (online only)
After reviewing the material on these pages, assign the *A ver si recuerdas* with Remediation to evaluate students' mastery of the material. Additional practice is available online.

Can-Do Statements

Read the Can-Do Statements in the chapter objectives with students. Then, have students read Preparación para el examen on page 302 to preview what they will be able to do at the end of the chapter.

Standards for Capítulo 6

To meet the Standards, students will:

COMMUNICATION

1.1 Interpersonal
• Talk about careers and professions
• Talk about virtual and physical communities
• Talk about past, present, and future changes
• Talk about lifestyles of Spanish youth
• Talk about educational organizations

1.2 Interpretive
• Read and listen to information about careers and professions and necessary qualities for them
• Read about virtual and physical communities
• Read and listen about past, present, future changes
• Read about lifestyles of Spanish youth
• Read about educational organizations
• Read about word families in the world of professions
• Read poetry by Bécquer and fiction by Balzarino
• Read about online Spanish-language newspapers
• Read about speech preparation and compare and contrast essays

1.3 Presentational
• Write and present information orally about careers and professions and necessary qualities for them
• Write and present information orally about past, present, and future changes
• Recite poetry by Gustavo Adolfo Bécquer

CULTURE

2.1 Practices to Perspectives
• Explain the lifestyles of Spanish youth
• Explain the work of educational organizations
• Explain the readership of online newspapers
• Explain the changing roles of Mexican television
• Explain the perspectives of Spanish-speaking architects

2.2 Products to Perspectives
• Discuss the poetry of Bécquer and fiction of Balzarino
• Discuss the products of Spanish-speaking architects

CONNECTIONS

3.1 Making Connections
• Discuss key facts about Spanish youth
• Discuss key facts about educational organizations
• Discuss key facts about the poetry of Gustavo Adolfo Bécquer and the fiction of Ángel Balzarino
• Discuss employment demographics and futurology
• Discuss Spanish speakers' use of the Internet and T.V.
• Discuss key facts about architecture

CAPÍTULO **6**

¿Qué nos traerá el futuro?

Country Connections Explorar el mundo hispano

CHAPTER OBJECTIVES

Communication

By the end of the chapter you will be able to:
• Listen and read about future plans and predictions
• Talk and write about future problems and advances
• Explain your career goals for the future

Culture

You will also be able to:
• Compare cultural practices and perspectives in an authentic video about the banker of the future
• Understand how architects from the Hispanic world are shaping the architecture of the future

• Compare the living situations of many Spanish college graduates with those of graduates in the U.S.

You will demonstrate what you know and can do
• Presentación oral: Mi escuela del futuro
• Presentación escrita: El futuro según el presente

You will use

Vocabulary
• Professions and careers
• Personal qualities
• Future ideas and actions
• Careers of the future

Grammar
• Future
• Future of probability
• Future perfect tense
• Uses of the direct and indirect pronouns

ARTE y CULTURA · Chile

Matta y el surrealismo El surrealismo fue un movimiento literario y artístico muy importante de la primera mitad *(half)* del siglo XX. Entre sus artistas principales se destaca el pintor chileno Roberto Matta (1911–2002). Matta vivió la mayor parte de su vida en Europa y los Estados Unidos, y sus influencias más importantes fueron Dalí y Picasso. Sus obras se caracterizan por el uso de figuras abstractas, el espacio, la transparencia, el movimiento, la energía y los colores brillantes *(bright)*. Este cuadro es un ejemplo de la pintura surrealista.

▶ ¿Cómo crees que se diferencia el realismo del surrealismo en la pintura?

"L'Étang de No", (1958), Roberto Matta ▲

L'Étang de No (1958) by Roberto Matta-Echaurren/© Artists Rights Society (ARS), New York/ADAGP, Paris/Musée national d'art moderne, Centre Georges Pompidou/Photo Credit: CNAC/MNAM/Dist. Réunion des Musées Nationaux/Art Resource, NY.

260 doscientos sesenta • Capítulo 6 • ¿Qué nos traerá el futuro?

Enrich Your Teaching

The End in Mind

Have students preview the sample performance tasks on *Preparación para el examen,* p. 303, and connect them to the Chapter Objectives. Explain to students that by completing the sample tasks they can self-assess their learning progress.

Technology: Mapa global interactivo

Download the *Mapa global interactivo* files for Chapter 6 and preview the activity. In this activity, you will look at some of the tallest buildings in Mexico City.

Go **Online** to practice
PEARSON
realize.

PearsonSchool.com/Autentico

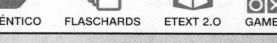

AUDIO   VIDEO   WRITING   SPEAK/RECORD   MAPA GLOBAL   AUTÉNTICO   FLASCHARDS   ETEXT 2.O   GAMES

Preview 6

El Metropol Parasol en Sevilla, España

▶ Videonovela **¡Pura vida!**

Capítulo 6 • doscientos sesenta y uno **261**

- Use Language Arts Strategies: circumlocution, compare and contrast, mapping your speech using main idea and details, coping with unknown words

3.2 Acquiring information and Diverse Perspectives
- Read a university workshop announcement
- Read poetry by Bécquer and fiction by Balzarino

COMPARISONS

4.1 Language
- Compare impersonal se to the passive in English
- Compare Spanish and English future tenses
- Compare Spanish words to their English counterparts

4.2 Cultural
- Compare lifestyles of young people in Spain and U. S.
- Compare the roles of T. V. in Mexico and the U. S.
- Compare distance education in Puerto Rico and U. S.

COMMUNITIES

5.1 School and Global Communities
- Link to Web sites from the Spanish-speaking world
- Describe strategies for obtaining employment and keeping up with employment trends
- Discuss distance education and study abroad

5.2 Lifelong Learning
- Discuss important facts about going to college
- Prepare for the future
- Develop an appreciation for poetry and fiction
- Read an authentic Spanish-language text

Chapter Opener

Resources: Mapa global interactivo: Regional maps

Suggestions: Introduce students to the chapter theme and objectives.

▶ **Technology: Videonovela ¡Pura vida!** View this stand-alone storyline video about five young adults in San José, Costa Rica with your class.

ARTE Y CULTURA ◄

Standards: 1.1, 1.2, 2.2, 3.1

Suggestions: Ask comprehension questions. For example: *¿Qué artistas tuvieron una gran influencia en la obra de Matta?*

Answers will vary but may include Dalí and Picasso.

Project-Based Learning

La biblioteca del futuro

As students go through the chapter during the week, ask them to make a list of all the things that they might see if they walked into a library of the future. Encourage them to think about the ways in which technological inventions will change the way we read and use books. Have them use this information to complete the *Presentación oral* on page 291.

261

Vocabulario en contexto 1

Standards: 1.2

Resources: Teacher's Resource Materials: Input Script, Clip Art, Audio Script, Technology: Audio Cap. 6

Suggestions: Before students read pages 262–263, say the names of visualized vocabulary items, have students repeat, and ask students to point to the appropriate image in their book. For non-visualized vocabulary such as *diseñar, cuidadoso(a),* and *eficiente,* give an explanation and ask students to identify the vocabulary item explained: *Una persona que hace su trabajo con mucho cuidado es una persona ... (cuidadosa).*

Starter Activity

Have students choose a word to complete these sentences from the board:

1) *El _____ (dependiente/bombero) ayudó a las víctimas de un incendio.*
2) *Mi padre era _____ (mecánico/gerente) en el almacén El Corte Inglés.*
3) *El _____ (paramédico/agricultor) investigó nuevos métodos de cultivar el maíz.*
4) *La _____ (política/cajera) anunció su plan para reducir el uso de gasolina en la ciudad.*
5) *Espero al _____ (cartero/crítico) que me va a traer el paquete de mis abuelos.*

Active Classroom

Have students work in pairs to draw two illustrations similar to the photos on these pages to represent two additional jobs. Have one pair of students exchange drawings with another group. Each group will write a description for the illustrations using the descriptions on these two pages as models. Have the pairs then read their descriptions to each other.

📱 Technology: Interactive Whiteboard

Vocabulary Activities 6-1 Use the whiteboard activities in your Teacher Resources as you progress through the vocabulary practice with your class.

Vocabulario en contexto 1

OBJECTIVES

Read, listen to, and understand information about professions and future plans.

🔊 Haz lo que amas…Ama lo que haces

Una investigación hecha por **científicos** descubrió que las personas que son felices, son mejores trabajadores. Con esa idea, un grupo de estudiantes **emprendedores** de la clase de sociología buscaron las personas más felices en su trabajo.

los cocineros

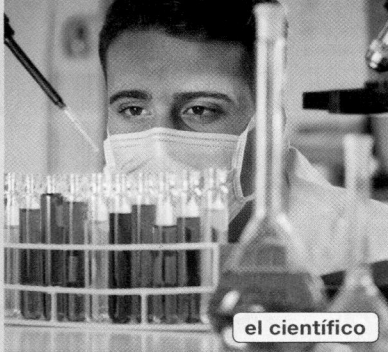
el científico

la arquitecta

la jueza

el abogado

el peluquero

el redactor

la mujer de negocios

Differentiated Instruction

Students with Learning Difficulties

Using note cards, have students write words associated with each profession. Tell them not to write the names of the professions. Shuffle the cards and read them aloud. Have students identify the profession associated with each word they hear. Remind them that some words might pertain to more than one profession.

Advanced Learners

Ask students to talk about a person they know whose profession is one of those in the *Vocabulario.* Have them tell the person's profession, some of the activities he or she does, and at least one quality necessary for that type of work.

🏠 🖨 ✉   www...   ↺   🔊 📶

Lo que dijeron

la programadora

Edmundo

❝Soy un profesional **capaz de** manejar el dinero de compañías importantes. Siempre me han fascinado las **finanzas**.❞

la diseñadora

Claudia

❝¡Tengo el mejor trabajo del mundo! Hay que ser **eficiente** y **cuidadoso** con los detalles, pero puedo jugar en mi computadora todo el día.❞

el banquero

Sara

❝Soy una persona artística y me encanta **diseñar** mi propia ropa. ¡Los colores brillantes me hacen feliz!❞

 Es la hora de **tomar decisiones** acerca de tu futuro. ¿Qué tipo de trabajo buscarás después de **graduarte**? **Además de** buscar una carrera interesante, recuerda elegir lo que te hace feliz.

1

¿Qué trabajo?

 ESCUCHAR Escucha lo que dicen las personas de sus trabajos y lo que les hace felices. Señala la foto para indicar sobre qué profesión habla cada una.

Capítulo 6 • doscientos sesenta y tres **263**

1

Standards: 1.2

Resources: Teacher's Resource Materials: Audio Script, Technology: Audio Cap. 6

Suggestions: Remind students to listen for key words that will help them determine the answers. Use the audio or read the script. Allow students to listen more than once.

 Technology: Audio Script and Answers:

1. Puedo pasar horas y horas en el laboratorio. Me fascina la investigación. *(científica)*
2. Lo que más me gusta de mi trabajo es ver lo que he escrito en una revista o en línea. *(redactor)*
3. Las horas de mi trabajo son largas pero no me importa. Estoy feliz cuando veo que a las personas les gusta mi comida. *(cocinero)*
4. Esta casa la diseñé yo. Estoy muy orgulloso de mi trabajo. *(arquitecto)*

Teacher-to-Teacher

Have pairs of students engage in a written exchange in which they describe their preferred professions and the reasons for their preference.

Enrich Your Teaching

Culture Note

One of the world's most renowned fashion designers, Oscar de la Renta, is a Spanish speaker. He was born in Santo Domingo, Dominican Republic. As a young man, he left home to study painting in Madrid. There, he started his career in design by drawing for fashion houses. De la Renta worked with accomplished designers in Paris before establishing himself at Elizabeth Arden in New York City. In 1965, de la Renta started his own company, known for fashions, accessories, and fragrances.

Vocabulario en contexto 1

Standards: 1.2

Resources: Technology: Audio Cap. 6

Suggestions: Model the dialogue with a volunteer. Begin the reading again with volunteers playing the roles of Manuela and Alejandra.

Post-reading: Complete Actividad 2 to check comprehension.

2

Standards: 1.2

Suggestions: Have students read aloud or paraphrase the sections of the reading that support their answers.

Answers:
1. en una empresa que construya edificios
2. quiere ser traductora
3. para pagar sus estudios
4. con sus abuelitos

3

Standards: 1.2

Resources: Teacher's Resource Materials: Audio Script, Technology: Audio Cap. 6

Suggestions: Point out that there may be more than one way to correct the illogical sentences.

 **Technology: Audio Script and answers:**

1. Me gustan mucho los autos, creo que voy a ser peluquero. (ilógico)
2. No quiero estar soltera. Por eso, nunca me casaré. (ilógico)
3. Me interesan las finanzas y el dinero. Pienso ser contador. (lógico)
4. Después de terminar la escuela, iré a Madrid a estudiar más español. Seré traductora y redactora. (lógico)
5. Siempre me ha interesado la salud, así que me dedicaré a la mecánica. (ilógico)

Pre-AP® Integration

- **Learning Objective:** Interpretive: Print and Audio
- **Activity:** Have students read the quotes on p. 263 the night before. In class the next day, read only a portion of each quote as a dictation. After the students finish writing, point out the selections that you read in the book and have students correct their answers.
- **Pre-AP® Resource Materials:** Comprehensive guide to Pre-AP® vocabulary skill development

---

 Manuela y Alejandra hablan sobre sus planes para cuando terminen la escuela secundaria.

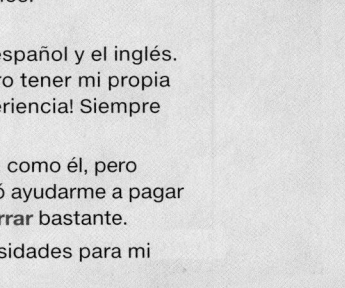 **Manuela**

 **Alejandra**

Manuela: ¿Qué planes tienes para los **próximos** años?

Alejandra: Tú sabes que soy muy **ambiciosa** y quiero llegar muy alto. Quiero ser **ingeniera** y **desempeñar un cargo** en una **empresa** que construya edificios. ¿Y qué planes tienes tú?

Manuela: Quiero **seguir una carrera** en la que use el español y el inglés. **Así que** creo que **me haré traductora**. Quiero tener mi propia empresa y ser mi propia **jefa**. ¡Ya tengo experiencia! Siempre les **traduzco** todo a mis abuelitos.

Alejandra: A mi papá le gustaría que yo fuera **contadora**, como él, pero sabe que yo quiero ser ingeniera. Me prometió ayudarme a pagar mis estudios, pero yo también tengo que **ahorrar** bastante.

Manuela: Yo tengo que **averiguar** si hay buenas universidades para mi carrera por aquí. Mamá no quiere que me **mude** lejos de ella.

Alejandra: ¡Pero si tú siempre **hacías lo que se te daba la gana**!

Manuela: Sí, pero ya soy mayor y más **madura**. **Por lo tanto**, escucho lo que me dice mamá.

Alejandra: ¡Ojalá las dos podamos **lograr** nuestras metas mientras somos **solteras** y **nos dedicamos** solo a la carrera! Una vez **casadas** será más difícil.

Manuela: ¡Para eso falta mucho!

2

 Los planes de Alejandra y Manuela

ESCRIBIR Contesta las siguientes preguntas:

1. ¿En qué tipo de empresa le gustaría trabajar a Alejandra?
2. ¿A qué se quiere dedicar Manuela?
3. ¿Por qué Alejandra tiene que ahorrar dinero?
4. ¿Con quiénes practica Manuela para la carrera que quiere seguir?

3

 Planes para el futuro

 ESCUCHAR En una hoja escribe los números del 1 al 5. Después, escucha lo que dicen las personas y escribe si es lógico o ilógico. Corrige las oraciones ilógicas.

Differentiated Instruction

Heritage Speakers

Ask students if any of them have considered a career that would utilize their language skills. Some examples might include translator, court interpreter, teacher, international business person, or diplomat. Ask them to share the stories of people they know who utilize two or more languages on the job.

Students with Learning Difficulties

After students have read the dialogue, ask them to identify just the questions by pointing to them in the text. Then ask students to provide personal responses to the questions.

Videohistoria

Go **Online** to practice

PEARSON **realize**™

🔊 AUDIO ▶ VIDEO ✎ WRITING 📄 SCRIPT

PearsonSchool.com/Autentico

¿Cuáles son mis aptitudes?

Antes de ver

Personalizar Piensa en qué te gustaría hacer en el futuro. Ahora mira las fotos. ¿Te interesa alguna de estas profesiones? Al ver la Videohistoria, establece conexiones entre tus experiencias y lo que dicen los chicos.

Haz la actividad

Tu futura carrera Piensa en qué carrera te gustaría seguir. Haz una lista en español de las aptitudes que crees que se requieren para esa carrera.

▶ Ve el video

Valentina, Camila y Teo hicieron pruebas de aptitudes que les indicarán qué tipo de carreras deben seguir. ¿Cuáles serán los resultados?

Ve a **PearsonSchool.com/Autentico** para ver el video *¿Cuáles son mis aptitudes?* También puedes leer el guión.

Valentina

Camila

Teo

Seba

Después de ver

 ESCRIBIR Contesta las siguientes preguntas:

1. ¿Qué aptitudes tiene Teo? Parafrasea los detalles de su prueba.

2. Según la prueba, Camila tiene aptitudes para ser ingeniera, científica o programadora. ¿Qué pueden tener en común estas tres carreras?

3. ¿Por qué a Teo no le recomiendan ser científico, redactor ni traductor?

4. ¿Qué carrera quiere seguir Valentina y por qué?

Expresa tu opinión ¿Crees que las pruebas de aptitudes son o no son un buen indicador de las carreras que debe seguir una persona? ¿Por qué? Justifica tu opinión.

Capítulo 6 • doscientos sesenta y cinco **265**

Enrich Your Teaching

Teacher to Teacher

If additional support is needed for comprehension, have students form three groups. Assign each group one of the Videohistoria characters: Teo, Valentina, or Camila. Ask students in each group to take notes only on their character's comments. Then, invite each group to discuss their notes and come up with a summary of what was said by their character. Finally invite a student from each group to share the summary with the rest of the class.

21st Century Skills

Social and Cross-Cultural Skills Have students research on the Internet one of the careers mentioned on pp. 262–264. What courses and certifications would be needed to become a professional in those fields? What institutions in their area would provide the necessary training? Have students report their findings to the class.

Tecnología: Video

Standards: 1.2

Resources: Teacher's Resource Materials: Video Script

Antes de ver

Review the previewing strategy and activity with students and point out that personalizing the content may help them with comprehension. Generate a brief discussion of the students' plans after graduating from high school.

Ve el video

Show the video once without pausing. Show it again, pausing after each of the characters finishes talking. Then show it a final time without pausing. Ask volunteers to paraphrase the main idea and the key details.

Después de ver

Standards: 1.2

Suggestions: Invite volunteers to discuss and paraphrase the supporting details from the video. You may want to create a three column chart on the board with the names Teo, Valentina, and Camila, and call on volunteers to complete it with information collected as students watch.

Answers

1. Es emprendedor y puede ser bueno como banquero, hombre de negocios o peluquero.
2. Answers will vary, but may include that the three careers require attention to detail and math skills.
3. En esas carreras tendría poco contacto con la gente.
4. Quiere ser chef porque es buena cocinera.

Expresa tu opinión: Answers will vary.

Have students go to **Realize** for additional video activities.

Additional Resources

 Technology: Online Resources
• Instant Check
• Guided, Core, Video, Audio
• *Para hispanohablantes*
Print
• Guided WB pp. 180–188
• Core WB pp. 79–80
• Authentic Resources Workbook

Assessment

Quiz: Vocabulary Recognition
• Prueba 6-1

OBJECTIVES
▶ Listen to classified ads
▶ Discuss professions, qualifications, and plans for the future
▶ Read about summer workshops and job hunting

4

Standards: 1.1, 1.2

Resources: Teacher's Resource Materials: Audio Script, Technology: Audio Cap. 6

Suggestions: Remind students that some of the ads they will hear are missing definite and indefinite articles. Have them listen to the audio more than once.

 Technology: Audio Script:

1. Se busca una persona madura y con experiencia para desempeñar el cargo de jefe del departamento de finanzas. Llamar al cinco, cinco, cinco, siete, dos, ocho, cuatro.
2. Salón de belleza necesita un peluquero con las siguientes cualidades: capaz de trabajar rápido; amable y sociable. Si tienes estas cualidades, visítanos en la calle Independencia, número cincuenta.
3. Importante periódico necesita un redactor con experiencia. Se busca una persona emprendedora y responsable, capaz de trabajar en equipo. Favor de enviar solicitud de empleo por correo electrónico diarioelsol, arroba punto com.
4. El restaurante Cuatro Caminos necesita cocinero eficiente y creativo para trabajar por las noches. Los interesados deberán presentarse con una carta de recomendación y solicitud de empleo entre las diez y once de la mañana. Llamar al cinco, cinco, cinco, cinco, tres, tres, dos.

Answers:
1. jefe; persona madura, con experiencia
2. peluquero; capaz de trabajar rápido, amable y sociable
3. redactor; con experiencia, emprendedor y responsable, capaz de trabajar en equipo
4. cocinero; eficiente y creativo

5

Standards: 1.2

Suggestions: Have students review the vocabulary on pp. 262–264 before completing the activity.

Answers:
1. próximo
2. Además de
3. por lo tanto
4. casado
5. soltero

6

Standards: 1.1, 1.3, 3.1

Recycle: adjectives describing personality

Suggestions: Refer students to the *Estrategia.* Remind them that you often use circumlocution when introducing new vocabulary to the class.

Answers will vary.

266

4

Las cualidades necesarias

 ESCUCHAR, ESCRIBIR, HABLAR EN PAREJA   En una hoja, escribe los números del 1 al 4. Escucha los anuncios clasificados y escribe la profesión y la cualidad o las cualidades que se necesitan para cada trabajo. Compara tu lista con la de otro(a) estudiante.

5

Los 17 años

 ESCRIBIR, LEER   A los 17 años, los jóvenes también tienen nuevas responsabilidades y problemas. Completa lo que dicen estos dos amigos sobre esta edad.

| por lo tanto | casado(a) | soltero(a) | además de | próximo |

—¿Sabes a qué universidad vas a asistir el año __1.__, Roberto?

—No lo sé todavía, Luisa. __2.__ la Universidad San Ignacio, he escrito a cuatro universidades. Todas están lejos de aquí, __3.__ sé que voy a tener que mudarme.

—Me dicen que en San Ignacio te ayudan a alquilar apartamento si estás __4.__ porque reconocen que es más difícil para dos personas.

—Pues a mí no me importa eso. Voy a estar __5.__ hasta cumplir los 30 años.

—¡Yo también!

6

¿Cómo se dice?

 ESCRIBIR, HABLAR EN PAREJA

1 Imagina que te olvidaste de estas palabras. Escribe frases que quieran decir lo mismo.

Modelo
responsable
persona que es capaz de tomar decisiones y desempeñar un cargo

1. amable
2. emprendedor
3. ambicioso
4. honesto
5. capaz
6. maduro
7. cuidadoso
8. puntual

Estrategia
Circumlocution
When you can't remember or don't know a word, you can use circumlocution to describe or exemplify it without naming it (e.g., *the thing you open a door with for doorknob*).

2 Con otro(a) estudiante, decidan qué características deben tener los siguientes profesionales: ingeniero(a), contador(a), hombre / mujer de negocios, mecánico(a), peluquero(a).

266 doscientos sesenta y seis • Capítulo 6 • ¿Qué nos traerá el futuro?

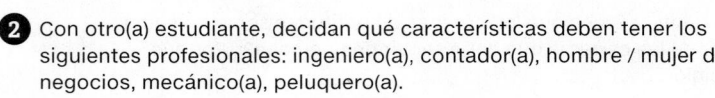

Differentiated Instruction

Heritage Speakers
In addition to definitions, have students brainstorm synonyms for the adjectives in *Actividad* 6. For example: ***amable/simpático(a); capaz/talentoso(a).*** Invite students to share their synonyms with the class.

Advanced Learners
Ask students to write their own classified ad. In it, they should name the position they are trying to fill and briefly describe the qualities of an ideal candidate.

Go **Online** to practice

PearsonSchool.com/Autentico

PEARSON
realize™

AUDIO VIDEO WRITING SPEAK/RECORD

¿Qué quieres ser?

HABLAR EN PAREJA

1 ¿Qué trabajo prefieres? Con un(a) compañero(a) hablen sobre los trabajos.

Videomodelo

A —*¿Te gustaría ser banquero?*
B —*Sí, porque me fascinan los números.*
o: *¿Yo? ¡Qué va! No me interesan nada los números.*

Estudiante A

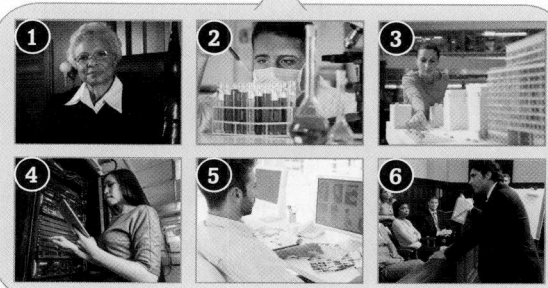

Estudiante B

organizado(a)
eficiente
responsable
creativo(a)
capaz
amable
ambicioso(a)
emprendedor(a)

¡Respuesta personal!

2 Con otro(a) compañero(a), hagan los papeles de estudiante y consejero. El estudiante le envía un e-mail al consejero preguntándole lo que necesita hacer para seguir dos carreras que le gustan. El consejero le responde. Apoya tus ideas.

Modelo:

A —*Me gustaría estudiar computación y diseño gráfico. ¿Qué hago?*
B —*Necesitas tomar cursos en los dos. Así podrás combinar las dos carreras.*

CULTURA España

En casa de mamá Según un estudio, casi el 80% de los jóvenes españoles menores de 30 años vive con sus padres. Hay varias razones importantes. En España es bastante difícil conseguir un empleo que les permita vivir solos. Además, no es fácil conseguir una casa o un apartamento barato para mudarse. Otros dicen que el problema es que los jóvenes no quieren tener responsabilidades y por eso viven con sus padres. También hay quienes piensan que en la cultura española la familia y padres son muy importantes para los jóvenes.

Pre-AP® Integration: Los estilos de vida

• ¿Por qué viven muchos jóvenes españoles con sus padres? ¿Cómo influye esta práctica en la vida contemporánea?
• Compara la situación de los jóvenes españoles y los estadounidenses. ¿Qué tienen en común? ¿Cuál es la diferencia?

Capítulo 6 • doscientos sesenta y siete **267**

Standards: 1.1

Suggestions: For Step 1, encourage students to switch roles and to read each dialogue more than once. Student B's response should be different each time.

Answers will vary. Students will use the following vocabulary:

1. juez
2. científico(a)
3. diseñador(a)
4. programador(a)
5. redactor(a)
6. contador(a)

CULTURA

Standards: 1.1, 1.2, 2.1, 3.1, 4.2

Suggestions: After students have read the information, ask: *¿Qué piensas de esta información? ¿A ti te gustaría vivir con tus padres tanto tiempo? ¿Cuáles son los beneficios posibles de este estilo de vida? ¿Cuáles son los puntos negativos?*

Answers:

Una razón es porque es difícil encontrar un empleo que les permita ganar el dinero necesario para vivir solos. Otra es que no es fácil conseguir una casa o un apartamento barato.

Other answers will vary.

Starter Activity

Have students unscramble these words for professions:

> tarodnoc
> equlupero
> zujea
> corenico
> tordacre

(**Answers:** *contador, peluquero, jueza cocinero, redactor*)

Enrich Your Teaching

Culture Note

Children in Spain attend elementary school from ages 6 to 12 and secondary school from ages 12 to 16. After secondary school, students may either go on to one to two years of vocational study or complete the *bachillerato,* a two-year course that prepares them for university study.

Teacher-to-Teacher

When students do pair work, such as in *Actividad 7,* encourage them to work with a different partner each time, and avoid the habit of the same partners working together day after day. Working with new partners is a good strategy for keeping students on task.

8

Standards: 1.1, 1.2, 3.2

Suggestions: Assist students as needed with the meaning of any unknown vocabulary.

Answers:

1. Negociación y debate
2. Danza contemporánea
3. Negociación y debate
4. Negociación y debate
5. Danza contemporánea
6. Danza contemporánea

Starter Activity

Step 3 of *Actividad* 9 asks students to make recommendations for which they will need to use the subjunctive. Prepare them for this by asking them to make up sentences with **Es necesario que...** and the subjunctive.

9

Standards: 1.1, 1.2

Suggestions: Ask groups to appoint a spokesperson to report the results of their discussion to the class.

Answers will vary.

8

Talleres de verano

 LEER, HABLAR EN GRUPO Trabaja con un grupo de tres estudiantes para decidir a que taller(es) quisieras asistir si quieres ser:

1. escritor(a)
2. actor / actriz en obras musicales
3. hombre / mujer de negocios
4. político(a)
5. bailarín / bailarina
6. coreógrafo(a)

UNIVERSIDAD RODRIGO CABEZAS

Departamento de actividades culturales
Facultad de humanidades

Talleres de verano
6 de diciembre al 12 de febrero

DANZA CONTEMPORÁNEA
Profesor: Lucía Suárez,
bailarina y coreógrafa

NEGOCIACIÓN Y DEBATE
Profesor: Olivero Rojas,
periodista, licenciado en
Comunicación Social

Inscripciones e informaciones
hasta el 2 de diciembre en San
Martín 301

9

Hablar sobre el trabajo

 LEER, HABLAR EN GRUPO

1 La búsqueda de trabajo es un tema sobre el que todo el mundo tiene diferentes opiniones. Lee la siguiente encuesta *(survey)* que se hizo a un grupo de jóvenes sobre de qué depende encontrar un trabajo.

¿De qué depende encontrar un buen trabajo? ¿Y en segundo lugar?		
	Primer lugar (%)	Segundo lugar (%)
De estar bien preparado.	50	27
De tener buenas recomendaciones.	28	30
De la buena suerte.	16	23
De saber hablar bien.	3	11
De ser guapo(a).	2	7
No sé.	1	2

2 Trabaja con un grupo de estudiantes para hablar de la encuesta y responder a las siguientes preguntas.

1. ¿Están de acuerdo con los resultados de la encuesta? ¿Por qué? Den ejemplos de algunas personas que conocen.

2. ¿Pueden añadir alguna otra razón a la lista?

3 Habla con un(a) compañero(a) y pregúntale lo que debe hacer una persona que quiere seguir una carrera o comenzar una nueva profesión. Él/ella debe incluir sus razones en su respuesta.

Differentiated Instruction

Logical-Mathematical Learner

Have groups of students conduct their own polls on the topic of what it takes to find a good job. Have them record their data and present it in the form of a chart. Invite different groups to compare their results.

Students with Learning Difficulties

Distribute props or pictures associated with the professions listed in *Ampliación del lenguaje.* Ask students to say three simple sentences to accompany their props: *Yo soy cocinero(a). Yo cocino. Aquí está la cocina.* Redistribute props among male and female students, so they can practice both masculine and feminine endings.

Y tú, ¿qué dices?

ESCRIBIR, HABLAR

1. ¿A qué se dedican tus padres? ¿Vas a seguir la misma carrera? ¿Por qué?

2. ¿Cuál es el sueño que quieres alcanzar? ¿Qué quieres lograr en el futuro?

3. ¿Te gustaría mudarte a otra ciudad, otro estado u otro país? ¿Por qué?

4. Imagina que no necesitas ahorrar dinero. ¿A qué te gustaría dedicarte después de graduarte de la universidad?

5. ¿Qué carreras no te gustaría seguir? ¿Por qué?

6. ¿Qué te gustaría hacer con tu tiempo libre?

7. ¿Cuáles son las mayores responsabilidades que tienes a tu edad? ¿Y los problemas? ¿Qué quieres cambiar o lograr en el futuro?

Ampliación del lenguaje

Profesiones En español hay varios sufijos que indican profesión. Muchas palabras que terminan con los sufijos *-or/-ora, -ero/-era, -ario/-aria* nombran profesiones que tienen relación con los verbos o sustantivos de los que derivan.

Verbo	Sustantivo	Profesión
vender	venta	vendedor(a)
traducir	traducción	traductor(a)
escribir	escrito	escritor(a)
programar	programa	programador(a)
redactar	redacción	redactor(a)
dirigir	dirección	director(a)
diseñar	diseño	diseñador(a)
	biblioteca	bibliotecario(a)
	carta	cartero(a)
cocinar	cocina	cocinero(a)
	banco	banquero(a)

Lee las palabras de la tabla y escribe ocho frases en las que uses las profesiones y los verbos o sustantivos relacionados.

Modelo
vender / vendedor(a)
*Un **vendedor** trabaja tratando de **vender** cosas a otras personas.*

carta / cartero(a)
*Mi tío es **cartero**. Entrega **cartas** en las casas y apartamentos de nuestra ciudad.*

Capítulo 6 • doscientos sesenta y nueve **269**

10

Standards: 1.1, 1.3

Suggestions: This activity is ideal as a homework assignment. Encourage students to take the questions seriously and sit in a quiet place to answer them, giving them careful thought. Then invite them to share their answers with the class during a subsequent session.

Answers will vary.

AMPLIACIÓN DEL LENGUAJE

Standards: 1.2, 1.3, 3.1, 4.1

Suggestions: Ask students to use more than one variation of the word in the same sentence. Encourage them to make it clear from their sentences that they understand the meaning of each word.

Answers will vary.

Additional Resources

Technology: Online Resources
• Guided, Core, Audio
• Communicative Pair Activity
Teacher Resources
• Teacher's Resource Materials: Audio Script, Technology: Audio Cap. 6

Assessment

Prueba 6-2 with Remediation (online only)
Prueba: Aplicación del vocabulario 1
• Prueba 6-2

Enrich Your Teaching

Teacher-to-Teacher

Regularly refer to and isolate word parts such as prefixes and suffixes, and ask students to do the same. Such attention to meaningful chunks of words is an excellent way for language learners to expand their vocabularies. Once students know that suffixes like those shown in the *Ampliación del lenguaje* indicate professions, they can experiment with them on their own to build new words. Parallels can often be drawn between Spanish and English word parts. For example, the suffixes shown in the *Ampliación del lenguaje* can be compared to English *-er,* as in "teacher" or "baker."

Gramática: Repaso

Suggestions: Ask students to take turns telling about their plans for next summer, using the future tense. If necessary, cue them with questions that elicit verbs of various kinds, including those with the irregular stems shown in the *Gramática*.

 Technology: Interactive Whiteboard

Grammar Activities 6-1 Use the whiteboard activities in your Teacher Resources as you progress through the grammar practice with your class.

11

Standards: 1.2

Suggestions: Remind students to first look over the entire paragraph about Lorena in order to get an idea of its meaning.

Answers:

1. haré	**7.** podré
2. iré	**8.** regresaré
3. realizaré	**9.** llamará
4. Estudiaré	**10.** diseñaré
5. pasaré	**11.** tendré
6. visitaré	**12.** disfrutarán

Extension: Conduct a question-and-answer session with students, using the completed activity as a base. Teacher: *¿Qué decidió Lorena hoy? Student: Decidió lo que hará el año próximo.*

Active Classroom

Have students work in pairs to practice the different irregular forms of the future. Have one student select an infinitive and then provide different subject pronouns. The partner has to quickly provide the correct verb conjugation. Switch roles with each verb.

Gramática Repaso

OBJECTIVES
▶ Discuss and write about plans for the future
▶ Discuss relationships with family and friends in the future

El futuro

You can express the future in Spanish in three ways: by using *ir + a +* infinitive, the present tense, or the future tense. In the future tense, all verbs have the same endings. For most verbs, attach the endings to the infinitive.

Here are the future tense forms of the regular verbs *pasar, comer,* and *pedir:*

pasar**é**	comer**é**	pedir**é**
pasar**ás**	comer**ás**	pedir**ás**
pasar**á**	comer**á**	pedir**á**
pasar**emos**	comer**emos**	pedir**emos**
pasar**éis**	comer**éis**	pedir**éis**
pasar**án**	comer**án**	pedir**án**

Some verbs have irregular stems in the future tense. Note that their future endings (*-é, -ás, -á, -emos, -éis, -án*) are the same as those of regular verbs.

haber	→	habr-	
poder	→	podr-	
querer	→	querr-	-é
saber	→	sabr-	-ás
poner	→	pondr-	-á
salir	→	saldr-	-emos
tener	→	tendr-	-éis
venir	→	vendr-	-án
decir	→	dir-	
hacer	→	har-	

Más recursos ONLINE

▶ **Tutorials:** Formation of Regular Future Tense
Use of Future Tense
Verbs with Irregular Stems in Future Tense

◀)) *Canción de hip hop: El futuro*

11

Los sueños

 ESCRIBIR, LEER Lorena escribe en su diario sobre sus experiencias y sueños para el futuro. Completa este fragmento de su diario con el futuro de los verbos del recuadro.

poder	estudiar	hacer	visitar
pasar	alcanzar	ir	

Hoy, después de regresar del parque, decidí lo que __1.__ el año próximo. Yo __2.__ a una universidad famosa y allí __3.__ mi sueño. __4.__ arquitectura. Después de estudiar, __5.__ unos años en Japón y __6.__ los parques más famosos. Así __7.__ aprender mucho.

disfrutar	regresar	llamar
diseñar	tener	

Finalmente, __8.__ a este país para crear mi propia empresa. Se __9.__ "Parques y jardines de oriente" y yo __10.__ los jardines. Estoy segura de que __11.__ mucho éxito y muchas personas __12.__ de mis jardines y parques.

270 doscientos setenta • Capítulo 6 • ¿Qué nos traerá el futuro?

Differentiated Instruction

Heritage Speakers

Have students with exemplary pronunciation model the pronunciation of future verb forms. Ask them to be especially aware of the written accent on the last syllable on all but the **nosotros** forms, and have all students repeat.

Challenge/Pre-AP®

Ask students to talk about habits they or someone they know used to have but now no longer engage in. For the old habit they use the imperfect tense, and for the change they use the future tense: *Antes solía charlar mucho en la cafetería. No charlaré más allí porque no tengo tiempo.*

Go **Online** to practice

PearsonSchool.com/Autentico

PEARSON
realize™

AUDIO   VIDEO   WRITING   SPEAK/RECORD

Interpersonal **6**

12

En el futuro

🎤 **HABLAR EN PAREJA** ¿Sabes lo que quieres hacer en el futuro? Pregúntale a otro(a) estudiante sobre sus planes. Después, intercambien papeles.

▶ **Videomodelo**

mudarse a otra ciudad para estudiar

A —¿*Te mudarás* a otra ciudad para estudiar en la universidad?

B —*No, iré a la universidad de mi ciudad.*

Estudiante A

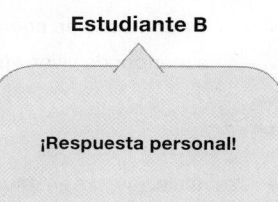

1. seguir una carrera después de graduarse
2. dedicarse a hacer trabajo de voluntario
3. averiguar información sobre la carrera de ingeniería
4. ir a ver a un consejero
5. hacer lo que le dé la gana
6. tener un trabajo y ahorrar mucho dinero
7. estudiar finanzas en unos años
8. tomar decisiones importantes para una empresa

Estudiante B

¡Respuesta personal!

13

¿Qué hará . . . ?

 LEER, ESCRIBIR Piensa en personas de tu escuela, familia, comunidad o programa de televisión favorito que correspondan a estas descripciones. ¿Qué harán en el futuro? Usa el futuro de los verbos del recuadro para escribir frases sobre lo que hará cada persona.

hacerse . . .	dedicarse a . . .	lograr ser . . .	trabajar como / en . . .
tener . . .	estudiar para ser . . .	ser . . .	mudarse a . . .

Modelo

Pinta cuadros muy bonitos.
Santiago será un pintor famoso.

1. Le encanta arreglarles el pelo a sus amigas.
2. Le gusta planear y construir caminos y puentes.
3. Le gustan los animales.
4. Es cuidadoso(a) y escribe muy bien.
5. Le gustan las matemáticas.
6. Me fascina traducir textos.
7. Tiene mucho talento artístico.
8. Le interesan los negocios y las finanzas.

12

Standards: 1.1

Suggestions: Point out to students that in the future tense, reflexive and object pronouns are placed in the same position in relation to the verb as they are in other tenses of conjugated verb forms.

Answers: Student B's responses will vary. Student A's questions will use the following verb forms:

1. Seguirás
2. Te dedicarás
3. Averiguarás
4. Irás
5. Harás
6. Tendrás
7. Estudiarás
8. Tomarás

13

Standards: 1.2, 1.3

Suggestions: Tell students to demonstrate their comprehension of new vocabulary by making a logical connection between each cue and the future plans of their chosen person. Remind them that some of their sentences can be negative.

Answers will vary. Third-person, singular future forms of the verbs in the word bank are as follows:

se hará	logrará
tendrá	será
se dedicará	trabajará
estudiará	se mudará

Project-Based Learning

Students can perform Step 2 at this point. Be sure they understand your corrections and suggestions. (For more information, see p. 256-b.)

Enrich Your Teaching

Teacher-to-Teacher

Young people are as interested in making New Year's resolutions as many adults. You can take advantage of this custom at any time of the year. An enjoyable way to help them practice using the future tense is to ask them to make a short list of resolutions for the coming week or month. At the end of the time period, check back with students to see whether they kept their resolutions, giving them an opportunity to review the past tenses.

6 Communication

14

Standards: 1.1

Suggestions: Ask Student B to think of real people and to provide an additional detail or two, as the model does.

Answers: Students A and B will use the following verb forms respectively:

1. se escribirán/nos escribiremos
2. asistirán/asistiremos
3. tendrán/tendremos
4. sabrán/sabremos
5. saldrán/saldremos
6. recordarán/recordaremos

15

Standards: 1.1, 1.3

Suggestions: Tell students to use **nosotros** forms in the left column of the chart in Step 2. The right column will most likely contain a negative statement about one partner and an affirmative one about the other.

Answers: Students will use the following verb forms for Step 1:

me quedaré/me mudaré	viajaré
asistiré/encontraré	me casaré/seguiré
seguiré	tendré

Steps 2–3

Answers will vary.

CULTURA

Standards: 1.1, 1.2, 3.1

Suggestions: After students have read the information, ask: *¿Te gustaría trabajar en un programa como éste? ¿Trabajarás para el gobierno en el futuro?*

Answers will vary.

Additional Resources

 Technology: Online Resources
- Instant Check
- Guided, Core, Audio, Writing, Reading
- *Para hispanohablantes*

Print
- Guided WB pp. 189–191
- Core WB p. 83

Assessment

Prueba 6-3 with Remediation (online only)
Prueba: El futuro
- Prueba 6-3

14

Después de . . .

 HABLAR EN PAREJA Con un(a) compañero(a), hablen de cómo serán sus relaciones en el futuro usando las frases de abajo. Hablen de sus relaciones con los amigos, la familia o las personas de la escuela o de la comunidad.

Videomodelo

verse cada semana
A —*En diez años, ¿tus amigos y tú **se verán** cada semana?*
B —*No, no nos veremos cada semana pero quizás cada mes.*

1. escribirse por correo electrónico
2. asistir a la misma universidad
3. tener mucho en común
4. saber dónde viven sus amigos de la escuela
5. salir juntos los fines de semana
6. recordar todo lo que pasó en la escuela secundaria

15

¿Cómo será tu vida en el futuro?

 ESCRIBIR, HABLAR EN GRUPO

1 Escribe sobre tu futuro. Incluye la siguiente información:
- quedarse en la misma ciudad o mudarse
- asistir a la universidad o encontrar trabajo
- seguir una carrera
- viajar y adónde
- casarse o seguir soltero(a)
- tener hijos y cuántos

2 Ahora, compara tus respuestas con las de un(a) compañero(a). Completen una tabla como la siguiente con las semejanzas y las diferencias.

SEMEJANZAS	DIFERENCIAS

3 Usa la tabla para escribir un párrafo acerca de tu futuro y el futuro de tu compañero(a).

CULTURA Estados Unidos

Jóvenes hispanohablantes en Washington El *Congressional Hispanic Caucus Institute,* CHCI, selecciona todos los años a unos 50 jóvenes para participar en su programa de pasantías[1]. Los seleccionados trabajan en Washington, D.C., disfrutando de las ventajas de poder observar al gobierno en acción. "CHCI me ha enseñado que tengo el poder de ser un agente de cambio y me ha dado las técnicas para ser un líder en mi comunidad", dijo Pablo Galindo-Payan, un participante del programa.
- ¿Por qué es importante para los estudiantes participar en un programa de pasantías?

[1]internships

Differentiated Instruction

Heritage Speakers

In preparation for the *Gramática* on p. 273, ask students to prepare a short skit portraying a situation in which there is some element of doubt. Instruct them to use the future tense to express this uncertainty at least once in the dialogue. A possible theme might be *¿Dónde estará mi tarea para mañana?*

Students with Learning Difficulties

Before students begin *Actividad* 14, allow them time to make notes on the future forms of the verbs presented. Point out that they will be using the **Uds.** and **nosotros** forms. Give students similar time and guidance for *Actividad* 15.

OBJECTIVES
▶ Express the probability of something occurring
▶ Make predictions about careers and accomplishments

El futuro de probabilidad

In Spanish, you use the future tense to express uncertainty or probability in the present.

¿Qué hora será?
I wonder what time it is.

Serán las seis.
It's probably six o'clock.

Estarán debajo de tu cama.
They must be under your bed.

The English equivalents in these cases are *I wonder, it's probably, it must be,* and so on.

¿Dónde estarán mis calcetines?
Where can my socks *be?*

Más recursos ONLINE

▶ **Tutorial:** Use of Future Tense

16

 Probablemente . . .

LEER, ESCRIBIR En una fiesta, conoces a las siguientes personas y comienzas a imaginarte qué cosas tendrán o qué harán en sus trabajos. Lee las siguientes frases. Escribe una segunda frase relacionada con la primera. Usa la forma correcta de los verbos del recuadro en el futuro para indicar probabilidad.

Modelo
Marcela es escritora.
Tendrá muchos libros.

tener	saber	vender	comprar	trabajar
estudiar	dedicarse	ser	aprender	seguir

1. El Sr. Paz es abogado.
2. Carmen es una mujer de negocios.
3. Andrés quiere ser traductor.
4. La Sra. Dávila es peluquera.
5. Héctor espera ser ingeniero.

6. Los hermanos González son agricultores.
7. Roberto quiere ser diseñador.
8. Margarita quiere ser científica.
9. El Sr. Pérez es juez.
10. Jaime y Elena quieren ser cocineros.

Enrich Your Teaching

Teacher-to-Teacher

Making a connection between a grammar point and something in students' everyday lives leads to meaningful language practice and helps students solidify their understanding of the grammar point. Remind students that we frequently make predictions as we look forward to elections, sports events, or award ceremonies.

Choose an upcoming school event, such as a sports match, and ask students to write their predictions about it. Take a survey to see how many of them predict each possible outcome. After the event, ask students to state whether their predictions were correct.

Gramática: Repaso

Standards: 4.1

Suggestions: Have students talk about the picture using the future tense to express uncertainty: *¿Qué estará buscando el chico de la foto? Estará buscando...*

Technology: Interactive Whiteboard

Grammar Activities 6-1 Use the whiteboard activities in your Teacher Resources as you progress through the grammar practice with your class.

16

Standards: 1.3

Suggestions: To avoid confusion, remind students that the meaning of the word **conoces** in the first line of the instructions is "to meet someone" rather than "to know someone."

Answers will vary. Students will choose from the following verb forms, depending on the subject of their sentence:

tendrá/tendrán
estudiará/estudiarán
sabrá/sabrán
se dedicará/se dedicarán
venderá/venderán
será/serán
comprará/comprarán
aprenderá/aprenderán
trabajará/trabajarán
seguirá/seguirán

Extension: Once students have completed the activity, challenge them to add another logical sentence about each person. They can use a verb from the word bank or another verb of their choice in the future tense.

Pre-AP® Integration

- **Learning Objective:** Interpersonal Speaking
- **Activity:** Have students bring in magazine pictures that show one or more people. Ask them to share with a partner a mini-story using the future of probability to indicate what they believe might be or is probably happening.
- **Pre-AP® Resource Materials:** Comprehensive guide to Pre-AP® communication skill development

EN VOZ ALTA

Standards: 1.2, 1.3, 2.2, 3.1, 3.2, 5.2

Resources: Teacher's Resource Materials: Audio Script, Technology: Audio Cap 6

Suggestions: Have students read the information and the poem silently. Help them understand the complicated syntax. For example, point out that **volverán** in the first line is only part of a verb phrase. Ask: *¿Cuáles son las demás palabras que completan esta frase? (a colgar)* Remind them that for effect, poets like Bécquer often invert the positions of subjects and verbs.

Before having students recite the poem, direct their attention to the information in *¿Recuerdas?* Then allow them a few minutes to practice reciting the poem excerpt with a partner.

Common Errors: When working with pronunciation in *¿Recuerdas?*, students may interrupt the elision of the vowel sounds with a glottal stop (a stoppage of air at the back of the throat). Model pronouncing the word groups without interruption and have students repeat.

Extension: Gustavo Adolfo Bécquer is an AP® Literature author. You may want to suggest that students read additional works by this poet.

17

Standards: 1.1, 1.3

Suggestions: Tell students that their predictions must be at least one complete sentence in length. They need not make all their predictions about the same person or persons.

Answers will vary. The following are third-person singular and plural forms of the verbs in the word bank:

será/serán	realizará/realizarán
logrará/lograrán	hará/harán
trabajará/trabajarán	se mudará/se mudarán
estará/estarán	ahorrará/ahorrarán
se dedicará/se dedicarán	desempeñará/desempeñarán
tendrá/tendrán	podrá/podrán

En voz alta

El poeta español Gustavo Adolfo Bécquer nació en Sevilla en 1836. Era hijo de un pintor famoso que murió cuando Bécquer tenía sólo 5 años. Desde joven, Bécquer comenzó a escribir poesía. A los 22 años conoció a Julia Espín, la mujer que inspiró la mayoría de sus famosas *Rimas*. El poeta murió en 1870, a los 34 años de edad.

Bécquer fue quizás el último de los poetas románticos. Sus *Rimas* fueron durante mucho tiempo los poemas de amor más famosos en el mundo hispanohablante.

Lee este fragmento de la "Rima LIII" y luego trata de repetirlo en voz alta.

"Rima LIII"
de Gustavo Adolfo Bécquer

Volverán las oscuras golondrinas[1]
en tu balcón sus nidos[2] a colgar[3],
y otra vez con el ala[4] a sus cristales
  jugando llamarán.

Pero aquellas que el vuelo refrenaban[5] tu
hermosura y mi dicha[6] a contemplar, aquellas
que aprendieron nuestros nombres . . .
  Ésas . . . ¡no volverán!

[1]swallows [2]nests [3]hang [4]wing [5]slowed down [6]happiness

¿Recuerdas?
Al hablar en voz alta muchas veces se combinan la última vocal de una palabra con la primera vocal de la siguiente en una sola sílaba. Por ejemplo: *que aprendieron; que el.*

17

¿Dónde estarán en diez años?

ESCRIBIR, HABLAR EN PAREJA

1 Haz predicciones sobre tus amigos, profesores, artistas o políticos famosos. Completa la tabla usando por lo menos seis verbos de la lista en futuro.

ser	trabajar	dedicarse	realizar	mudarse	desempeñar
lograr	estar	tener	hacer	ahorrar	poder

¿Cuándo?	Predicción
El próximo año	(Nombre) tendrá. . .
En cinco años	
En diez años	
En veinte años	

2 Ahora, habla con un(a) compañero(a) sobre las predicciones que hizo cada uno. Escojan una de ellas, digan si están de acuerdo o no, y vuelvan a contarla añadiendo más detalles. Usen su imaginación y añadan todos los detalles que puedan.

Modelo
en diez años / mi amiga Ana
A —*En diez años, mi amiga Ana será una actriz famosa.*
B —*Sí, primero se mudará a Hollywood y logrará un papel importante. Será muy popular.*

274 doscientos setenta y cuatro • Capítulo 6 • ¿Qué nos traerá el futuro?

Differentiated Instruction

Students with Special Needs

Help hearing impaired students appreciate the rhythm and style of *"Rima LIII"* by Gustavo Adolfo Bécquer. After the class has read the poem aloud, ask students to compose a series of rhythmic gestures to accompany the text. Invite everyone to participate in the movements.

Advanced Learners

Ask students to imagine that they will be attending their ten-year high school reunion. Have them use the future tense in as many sentences as they can to describe their classmates as they might appear ten years from now. Monitor for appropriate language usage.

18

Go **Online** to practice

PearsonSchool.com/Autentico

PEARSON
realize

WRITING

SPEAK/RECORD

¿Qué lograrás?

ESCRIBIR ¿Qué harás en las siguientes situaciones? Completa las frases de una manera original usando el futuro.

Modelo

Si ahorro mucho dinero, . . .
Si ahorro mucho dinero, podré viajar a Guinea Ecuatorial.

1. Si consigo el empleo de mis sueños, . . .
2. Si conozco a un(a) chico(a) que me gusta mucho, . . .
3. Si encuentro un millón de dólares en la calle, . . .
4. Si logro entrar en la universidad, . . .
5. Si me ofrecen estudiar en el extranjero, . . .
6. Si mis padres se mudan a otro estado, . . .
7. Si logro tener mi propia empresa, . . .
8. Si me piden trabajar como voluntario(a), . . .

> **Nota**
> Cuando una frase comienza con *si* + presente indicativo, generalmente es seguida de una frase que usa el futuro.

19

Los trabajos del futuro

LEER, HABLAR EN PAREJA

1 ¿Qué profesiones serán importantes para el año 2036? Lee el artículo y haz una lista con un(a) compañero(a).

2 Expliquen de qué hablan las predicciones del artículo. Busquen ejemplos que apoyen estas opiniones.

3 Escojan dos profesiones y pregunta a tu compañero(a) por texto lo que él o ella piensa que se necesita para obtener estas carreras. Él o ella te responderá con su opinión y sus razones.

PROFESIONES DEL FUTURO

Según un artículo de la revista Forbes, entre las diez profesiones del futuro está el granjero eólico *(wind farmer)*, diseñador de vehículos alternativos y el nanomédico. Dicen también que los médicos, paramédicos, enfermeros, cocineros y maestros no perderán su importancia. Esto se debe a que las personas no dejarán de enfermarse y siempre necesitarán comer y estudiar. Incluso con el avance del tiempo estas profesiones tendrán más importancia que ahora.

Capítulo 6 • doscientos setenta y cinco **275**

Enrich Your Teaching

Culture Note

In addition to writing poetry, Gustavo Adolfo Bécquer composed music, wrote **zarzuelas,** and painted. He was influenced by **coplas,** two-to-three-line poems, usually sung, that were a popular poetic style of the time. Bécquer composed 76 **rimas** in all.

21st Century Skills

Social and Cross-Cultural Skills Have students search the Internet for more information on Gustavo Adolfo Bécquer and his poetry. Have them find sites where they can listen to the poems from the *Rimas* collection being recited by native speakers.

18

Standards: 1.3

Suggestions: Once students have prepared their answers, encourage them to share them. They can invite others' responses with questions such as **Y tú, ¿qué harás si...?**

Answers will vary.

19

Standards: 1.1, 1.2

Suggestions: Before students read the information, have them predict what they think will be important jobs or professions in the future.

Answers:

Step 1
granjero eólico (wind farmer), diseñador de vehículos alternativos y el nanomédico

Steps 2–3

Answers will vary.

Project-Based Learning

Students can perform Step 3 at this point. (For more information, see p. 256-b.)

Additional Resources

Technology: Online Resources
- Instant Check
- Guided, Core, Audio
- *Para hispanohablantes*
- Teacher's Resource Materials: Audio Script, Communicative Pair Activity, Technology: Audio Cap. 6

Print
- Guided WB pp. 192
- Core WB pp. 82–83

Assessment

Prueba 6-4 with Remediation (online only)
Prueba: El futuro de probabilidad
- Prueba 6-4

Examen: Vocabulario y gramática 1
- Examen 1
- ExamView: Examen 1

Vocabulario en contexto 2

Standards: 1.2

Resources: Teacher's Resource Materials: Input Script, Clip Art, Audio Script, Technology: Audio Cap. 6

Suggestions: Ask students to look at the photos on these pages. Ask: *¿Estas fotos tratan sobre avances tecnológicos o avances artísticos? (tecnológicos)* Play the audio or read the text and have students follow along. Point out cognates that will aid in comprehension, such as *inventos, máquinas, satélite, reducir,* and *energía,* among others. Use circumlocution to explain the meaning of other vocabulary: *¿Qué palabra significa el lugar donde se producen cosas como coches? (fábrica)*

Starter Activity

Have students complete this sentence on a sheet of paper and be prepared to defend their ideas with the class.

Yo creo que el problema más grande para el futuro es _____.

Active Classroom

Have students work in pairs to write out definitions of five of the words on these two pages. This will practice the skill of circumlocution. Have them work with another pair of students. Each pair will read aloud the definitions. The other pair has to guess the word being described.

 Technology: Interactive Whiteboard

Vocabulary Activities 6-2 Use the whiteboard activities in your Teacher Resources as you progress through the vocabulary practice with your class.

Vocabulario en contexto 2

OBJECTIVES
Read, listen to, and understand information about
▸ Changes in technology
▸ The impact of technology on our lives

🔊 Ya vivimos en el futuro

La tecnología tiene un papel importante en el trabajo y el tiempo de **ocio**. Hoy podemos **curar** enfermedades y **prolongar** la vida de las personas. Además, con el uso de nueva tecnología, los científicos **han descubierto** nuevas **fuentes de energía** y mejores maneras de **comunicarse**, por ejemplo **vía satélite**.

Eduardo   **Ana**

la realidad virtual

Eduardo: ¡Qué fabuloso! La tecnología de **realidad virtual** es algo increíble.

Ana: Estoy de acuerdo. Es una experiencia **como si fuera** real. Pero hay muchos más inventos interesantes en el siglo 21.

Ana: Eduardo, ¿sabías que en 2010, Bernhardt Smilde **inventó** nubes que pueden formarse adentro de las **viviendas** u otros lugares? Sé que **desaparecen** rápido, pero, qué interesante, ¿no?

Eduardo: Pues, no tanto. ¿Por qué necesito nubes en mi casa? Para mí **el invento** más espectacular es el coche híbrido porque no **contamina** y **reduce** nuestro impacto al medio ambiente. **Predigo** que pronto **reemplazará** a los coches con **motores** que usan gasolina.

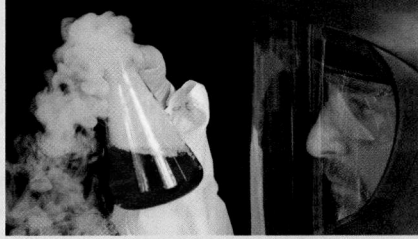

Differentiated Instruction

Students with Learning Difficulties

Encourage students to use the photographs on these two pages to help predict the main idea of each paragraph. Ask embedded-answer questions to help them understand the passages: *¿Quién hará muchos trabajos peligrosos en el futuro, la gente o las máquinas?*

Advanced Learners

Have students brainstorm and "invent" a technological advancement that might be possible 100 years from now. Individuals or small groups should describe in detail their prediction and include a drawing that can be shown to the class.

Ana: En medicina también hubo nuevos e interesantes **avances tecnológicos.**

Eduardo: Bueno, sé que ha habido avances con el estudio de **los genes** y **la genética** en general.

Ana: Me enteré que de **hoy en adelante** las personas sin uso de las piernas pueden usar un aparato robótico que les permita caminar.

Eduardo: ¡Fenomenal! Primero empezaron los robots en **las fábricas** y ahora los hay por todas partes. Ya estamos viviendo en el futuro.

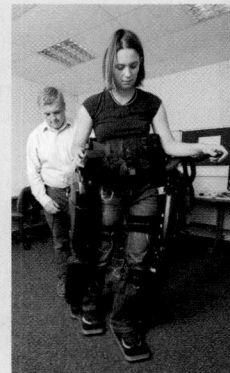

máquinas robóticas

20

Avances científicos

 ESCUCHAR   Escribe los números del 1 al 6. Vas a escuchar lo que se dice sobre unos avances científicos. Escucha cada frase y escribe si es lógica o ilógica.

21

¿Qué invento te gusta?

 ESCRIBIR   Escribe un texto a un(a) compañero(a) y pregúntale sobre qué invento cree que es más útil y cuál le gustaría usar. Tu compañero(a) responde con su opinión.

Capítulo 6 • doscientos setenta y siete **277**

20

Standards: 1.2

Resources: Teacher's Resource Materials: Audio Script, Technology: Audio Cap. 6

Suggestions: Remind students that they are only commenting on whether or not each statement is logical. Then play the audio or use the script to read the activity aloud.

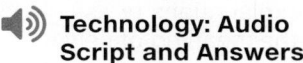 **Technology: Audio Script and Answers:**

1. Se puede usar el invento de Bernard Schmidt para entrenar pilotos. *(ilógica)*
2. La nueva tecnología robótica puede ayudar a las personas. *(lógica)*
3. Ana cree que los coches híbridos van a reemplazar a los coches con motores. *(lógica)*
4. Desafortunadamente no habrá más avances en el área de la genética. *(ilógica)*
5. A Eduardo le encanta la realidad virtual. *(lógica)*
6. Ahora hay nuevas fuentes de energía y mejores maneras de comunicarse debido a la nueva tecnología. *(lógica)*

21

Standards: 1.3

Suggestions: Ask students to use complete sentences to describe their favorite invention, rather than copying it verbatim from the *Vocabulario* presentation.

Answers will vary.

Enrich Your Teaching

Culture Note

In 1950, with its population growing rapidly, Mexico City began work on a modern transportation system. The first line of the Mexico City Metro was opened in 1969. Today the system is still expanding and modernizing to meet the needs of the future. Plans are currently in place to introduce light rail lines into the suburbs.

21st Century Skills

Collaboration Have students work in pairs or small groups to discuss the inventions that they selected in *Actividad* 21. Then, ask them to compare them and select the most important one for improving their environment over the next few years.

Vocabulario en contexto 2

Standards: 1.2

Resources: Teacher's Resource Materials: Input Script, Clip Art, Audio Script, Technology: Audio Cap. 6

Suggestions

Pre-reading: Have students look at the photos and talk about what they see. Ask a volunteer to describe the photos. Give explanations or ask questions that help clarify the meaning of new vocabulary.

Reading: Allow students time to read the information on this and the next page silently first. Then play the audio and have students read along as they listen. Allow them to listen more than once.

Post-reading: Check comprehension by asking questions, including those found in *Actividad* 23.

Pre-AP® Integration

- **Learning Objective:** Interpersonal Writing
- **Activity:** Have students write an e-mail to a friend in which they predict what will be the most popular profession of the future. Have students explain whether they would be interested in following this particular career path, and their reasons for it. Be sure students ask their friend their opinion about the profession of the future.
- **Pre-AP® Resource Materials:** Comprehensive guide to Pre-AP® writing skill development

Tres campos que tienen futuro

Según estudios de los últimos años, para el año 2050 habrá desaparecido la mayoría de los trabajos que ahora existen. Aunque habrá demanda de médicos, abogados y economistas, estos son los campos con más futuro:

1 Informática Con el uso de las computadoras y de la Red, la informática es la profesión del futuro. Por todo el mundo, los ingenieros de sistemas y programadores se dedican al **desarrollo** de nuevos y mejores programas de computación.

2 Hospitalidad La hospitalidad se ha vuelto una **industria**. Habrá mucho trabajo en hoteles y empresas turísticas. Se necesitarán cocineros, agentes de viaje, camareros y administradores.

3 Servicios Las **empresas** en general tendrán menos empleados, pero necesitarán de los servicios de profesionales como vendedores, secretarios y diseñadores gráficos.

Differentiated Instruction

Heritage Speakers

Ask students if they have ever had the opportunity to help a physically challenged person. Have them discuss the circumstances in which that happened, and share what they learned from that experience. What was the main challenge? How will technology improve the lives of physically challenged people in the future?

Students with Special Needs

Provide visually impaired students with a partner who can verbally describe the photographs under *Tres campos que tienen futuro.* Instruct the partners to focus on details associated with the profession being discussed.

Go **Online** to practice

PEARSON
realize.

PearsonSchool.com/Autentico

AUDIO   WRITING

Interpretive   6

Las personas que trabajan en el campo de **mercadeo** desarrollan **estrategias** para vender **productos**.

La demanda de traductores **aumentará** porque habrá más comercio entre los diferentes países.

Agencia Traduce

TRADUCCIONES

- Traducciones bilingües: inglés-español y español-inglés
- Especializados en documentos legales, informes de mercadeo, libros científicos
- Servicio rápido y eficiente
- Traductores certificados

Tel: 111-555-5555
www.agenciatraduce.cr

22

Campos de trabajo

 ESCUCHAR Escribe los números del 1 al 5 en una hoja de papel. Escucha la descripción de cada trabajo y escribe a qué campo se refiere.

23

¿Comprendiste?

 ESCRIBIR, HABLAR

1. ¿Qué empleados(as) se necesitarán para ofrecer servicios a empresas?
2. Según lo que leíste, ¿cuál es la profesión del futuro? Parafrasea las detalles que te ayudan a explicar por qué crees eso.
3. ¿Por qué se necesitarán más traductores en el futuro?
4. ¿Por qué crees que habrá más demanda de empleados en la industria de la hospitalidad?
5. ¿Puedes describir una estrategia de mercadeo que se usa para vender un producto que conoces?

Capítulo 6 • doscientos setenta y nueve **279**

Enrich Your Teaching

Culture Note

Some students involved in the **Bachillerato Internacional** go on to special programs of study for careers in interpretation and translation. Students involved in these programs study the difference between *simultaneous* interpretation, listening and speaking at the same time, and *consecutive* interpretation, waiting for

pauses every two to three sentences. They also master *phrase* interpretation, which is word-for-word translation, and *summary* interpretation, providing the main idea of what a speaker has said. Students often develop an expertise in a particular field, such as court interpretation or medical translation.

22

Standards: 1.2

Resources: Teacher's Resource Materials: Audio Script, Technology: Audio Cap. 6

Suggestions: Before students listen, make sure they understand the meaning of the word **campo,** since it is a key word in the activity. Give examples of its two most common meanings: *El campo sembrado de maíz es muy bonito. En el campo de la hospitalidad, la gente trabaja en hoteles y restaurantes.*

 Technology: Audio Script:

1. Los y las profesionales de este campo planean estrategias para vender los productos.
2. Es la profesión del futuro gracias al uso de las computadoras y la Red.
3. Los cocineros y cocineras, los camareros y camareras, y los agentes de viajes trabajan en esta industria.
4. Los profesionales de este campo se dedican a traducir de un idioma a otro.
5. Muchos secretarios y secretarias, diseñadores gráficos y diseñadoras gráficas, y vendedores y vendedoras se dedican a ayudar a las empresas.

Answers:

1. el mercadeo
2. la informática
3. la industria de la hospitalidad
4. la traducción
5. los servicios a empresas

23

Standards: 1.3

Suggestions: Have students answer the questions on their own. Then invite them to share their responses.

Answers:

1. Se necesitarán vendedores(as), secretarios(as) y diseñadores(as) gráficos(as).
2. La informática es la profesión del futuro. Los (Las) ingenieros(as) de sistemas y programadores(as) desarrollarán nuevos y mejores programas de computadora.
3. Se necesitarán más traductores porque habrá más comercio entre los diferentes países.

4–5. Answers will vary.

Additional Resources

Technology: Online Resources
- Instant Check
- Guided, Core, Audio, Writing practice
- *Para hispanohablantes*

Print
- Guided WB pp. 193–200
- Core WB pp. 84–85

24

Standards: 1.2

Suggestions: Remind students to refer back to pp. 276–279 to review the vocabulary, if necessary.

Answers:
1. b
2. c
3. a
4. b
5. a

25

Standards: 1.2

Suggestions: Have students read the entire paragraph before completing it.

Answers:

1. predecir
2. el uso
3. reemplazar
4. los inventos
5. la realidad virtual
6. como si fuera
7. los avances
8. el campo
9. tener en cuenta

Starter Activity

As you call out these actions, have students respond aloud with the *nosotros* form of the verb in the future:

dar	ver
tener	hacer
ser	mudar
trabajar	

Active Classroom

After completing *Actividad* 27, have students share and summarize the most popular responses to the different questions. Then have students write a short "news report" about the results of this class survey.

Vocabulario en uso 2

24

¿Nos ayudarán los robots?

 ESCRIBIR Muchas personas creen que el uso del robot cambiará mucho nuestra vida en el futuro. Completa cada frase con la palabra correcta.

1. En el futuro, ¿nos darán los robots más tiempo para dedicarlo al _____ y al descanso?

   a. uso **b.** ocio **c.** avance

2. La _____ de las fábricas ya tienen o pronto tendrán robots para hacer gran parte del trabajo allí.

   a. máquina **b.** tecnología **c.** mayoría

3. La _____ para vender los robots al público será a través de la Red.

   a. estrategia **b.** informática **c.** vía satélite

4. Veremos robots en muchas _____ también. Los usarán en casas y apartamentos para los trabajos diarios.

   a. demandas **b.** viviendas **c.** enfermedades

5. Muchas personas que predicen el futuro creen que el robot será uno de los _____ tecnológicos más importantes del siglo.

   a. avances **b.** genes **c.** campos

25

Una vida diferente

 ESCRIBIR ¿Qué piensas acerca de las computadoras? Completa el párrafo con las palabras o expresiones del recuadro.

el uso	reemplazar	predecir	la realidad virtual	los inventos
como si fuera	los avances	el campo	tener en cuenta	

Es imposible __1.__ el futuro, pero no hay duda de que __2.__ de la tecnología va a aumentar. Cada día, los ingenieros de sistemas escriben programas que cambian nuestra vida. Claro, las computadoras nunca van a __3.__ a las personas, pero __4.__ como __5.__, muestran cómo una computadora puede funcionar __6.__ una persona. Pero con todos __7.__ en __8.__ de la informática, es importante __9.__ que las computadoras nunca serán personas.

Differentiated Instruction

Students with Learning Difficulties

Model for students the process of elimination by guiding them to try out each multiple-choice answer in *Actividad* 24. If they are having difficulty with new vocabulary, have them review the *Vocabulario en contexto* sections to find and reread the words in other contexts.

Challenge/Pre-AP®

Have students tell about the future of their own current field of employment or that of someone they know. They should mention whether or not they think the type of employment will be more or less common in years to come and give reasons for their opinion.

Las profesiones del mañana

LEER, ESCRIBIR, HABLAR EN PAREJA

1 En otro papel, escribe los números del 1 al 8. Escribe la información apropiada para cada espacio en blanco de la tabla.

2 Con otro(a) estudiante hablen de cuál o cuáles de esos trabajos recomiendan y por qué.

3 Habla con tu compañero(a) sobre la importancia de estas profesiones ahora y en el futuro.

Industria	Profesión	Servicio / Producto
transporte	ingeniero	1
medios de comunicación	2.	teléfono celular
finanzas	3.	cajero automático
4.	5.	programa de computación
medicina	6.	7.
8.	mujer de negocios	estrategias para vender productos

27

Y tú, ¿qué dices?

ESCRIBIR, HABLAR Imagina que vas a vivir solo(a) durante ocho semanas en un observatorio, en medio del desierto. Haz una lista de los aparatos, la tecnología o los inventos que te gustaría tener allí.

1. ¿Cuáles te parecen más importantes? ¿Cuáles crees que usarás más frecuentemente?

2. ¿Cuáles de esos aparatos o inventos crees que desaparecerán en el futuro? ¿Por qué?

3. ¿Cuáles crees que serán los mejores avances que verás en el futuro?

4. ¿Qué cosas piensas que habrá en el futuro que no te gustarán? ¿Qué crees que se puede hacer para evitarlas?

CULTURA ◀ **El mundo hispano**

Bachillerato Internacional El Bachillerato Internacional es un programa de estudios común para las escuelas preparatorias de América Latina y otros países. Actualmente[1], más de 4,276 colegios[2] de todo el mundo forman parte del programa. Tiene una gran ventaja[3] para los estudiantes que cambian de país con frecuencia ya que pueden ir, sin problemas, de un colegio que ofrece Bachillerato Internacional a otro.

Los programas se enseñan en el idioma del país. Por ejemplo, un estudiante de Francia que estudia en España tiene el mismo currículum que el de su país, pero lo aprende en español. El programa empezó en 1968 y es reconocido por universidades de todo el mundo. Busca la excelencia académica, desarrolla el pensamiento crítico y ayuda a la comprensión intercultural entre los jóvenes de todos los países.

- ¿Has oído hablar del Bachillerato Internacional? ¿Conoces alguna escuela que ofrece este programa?

- ¿Qué opinas de un programa de estudios que es igual en todo el mundo? ¿Es buena idea? ¿Por qué? ¿Por qué no?

[1]Currently [2]high schools [3]advantage

Capítulo 6 • doscientos ochenta y uno **281**

Go **Online** to practice

PEARSON
realize™

PearsonSchool.com/Autentico

WRITING SPEAK/RECORD

26

Standards: 1.1

Suggestions: Draw a T-chart on the board as a reference while students fill in the chart for Step 1.

Answers will vary.

27

Standards: 1.3

Suggestions: Point out that questions 1 and 2 deal with the desert observatory situation. Questions 3 and 4 require more open-ended, personal responses.

Answers will vary.

CULTURA ◀

Standards: 1.1, 1.2, 3.1, 5.1, 5.2

Suggestions: After students read the information, ask comprehension questions such as the following: *¿Qué tipo de escuela forma parte del Bachillerato Internacional? ¿Cómo beneficia el programa a los jóvenes?*

Common Errors: Some students will assume that ***actualmente*** means the same as the English "actually." Remind them that this is a false cognate and means "currently."

Answers will vary.

Project-Based Learning

Students can perform Step 4 at this point. Be sure they understand your corrections and suggestions. (For more information, see p. 256-b.)

Enrich Your Teaching

Teacher-to-Teacher

Play "Concentration." Prepare twenty notecards. On ten of them, write the name of an area of employment or a profession. On the other ten, write a word or expression that is clearly associated with each area. Example: ***el (la) abogado(a)/la ley.*** Write the numbers 1–20 in random order on the back of the cards. Tape them to the board in numerical order in a grid. Divide students into two teams. A player from Team A chooses two cards, which are turned over and read aloud. If they match, they are removed from the grid. Team A scores a point and goes again. If the cards don't match, they are returned to their positions and it is Team B's turn.

Standards: 1.1, 1.2

Suggestions: Refer students to p. 260 for forms of the future tense.

Answers:

Step 1

1. reemplazarán	**6.** Nos enteraremos
2. curarán	**7.** Desaparecerán
3. Nos comunicaremos	**8.** Inventarán
4. prolongarán	**9.** aumentarán
5. reducirán	**10.** descubrirán

Step 2

Answers will vary.

Standards: 1.1, 1.2, 3.1

Suggestions: For Step 1, students can read the article in pairs. Ask them to help each other with any comprehension problems they may have.

Answers will vary.

Additional Resources

 Technology: Online Resources
  • Teacher's Resource Materials: Audio Script, Communicative Pair Activity, Technology: Audio Cap. 6

Assessment

Prueba 6-6 with Remediation (online only)
Prueba: Aplicación del vocabulario 2
  • Prueba 6-6

282

Predicciones

 ESCRIBIR, HABLAR EN PAREJA

1 Averigua qué piensan tus compañeros(as) sobre cómo será la vida en 50 años. Completa las siguientes preguntas con el futuro del verbo correcto.

aumentar	comunicarse	curar	desaparecer	descubrir
enterarse	inventar	prolongar	reducir	reemplazar

1. ¿Los robots _____ a los empleados de las fábricas?

2. En el campo de la medicina, ¿_____ a las personas que sufren de cáncer?

3. ¿_____ nosotros con extraterrestres?

4. ¿Nuevas medicinas _____ la vida hasta los cien años?

5. ¿Nuevos métodos tecnológicos _____ la contaminación del aire?

6. ¿_____ nosotros de las causas del cáncer?

7. ¿_____ las enfermedades, como el resfriado común?

8. ¿_____ los ingenieros nuevos aparatos que harán más fáciles los quehaceres diarios?

9. ¿Los autobuses eléctricos _____ el ahorro de gasolina?

10. ¿Los científicos _____ nuevas fuentes de energía en el medio ambiente?

2 Con otro(a) estudiante preparen respuestas para tres de las preguntas y expliquen por qué dieron esas respuestas.

Los futurólogos predicen . . .

LEER, HABLAR EN PAREJA

1 Lee estos fragmentos de un artículo sobre la vida en el año 2050.

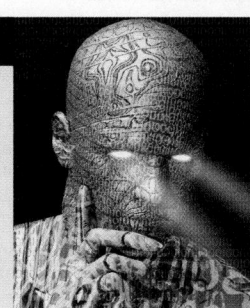

LA VIDA EN EL 2050

Los futurólogos no son adivinos, son científicos que basan sus predicciones en el estado de la ciencia y la sociedad del presente. Predicen que en el 2050 los robots realizarán las tareas de la casa y toda clase de operaciones médicas. La realidad virtual nos permitirá visitar lugares o amigos en el otro lado del mundo, en segundos. La prensa escrita desaparecerá por completo y tambien los libros y revistas. Las energías limpias pasarán a ser comunes en nuestras vidas. Los carros y el transporte público serán eléctricos además de automáticos. También la realidad virtual tendrá muchas utilidades: por ejemplo, como una herramienta para aprender en las escuelas.

2 Habla con otro(a) estudiante sobre cómo será más fácil la vida y cómo podremos hacer más rápidamente las cosas, según el artículo.

3 Expliquen por qué son positivos o negativos los cambios que se mencionan en el artículo.

Differentiated Instruction

Heritage Speakers

Have students exchange papers and edit each other's work for *Actividad* 30. Direct them to focus on the correct placement of accent marks, as well as the correct spelling of past participles. Allow students to discuss their editorial changes with their partners.

Students with Learning Difficulties

Help students divide *Actividad* 28 into several steps. First, have them read over each sentence for meaning. Second, have them identify the subject of the sentence. Third, have them choose the appropriate verb from the word bank. Finally, have them write the correct future verb form in the blank.

Gramática

> OBJECTIVES
> ▶ Read about future accomplishments
> ▶ Discuss inventions and predictions

Go **Online** to practice
PEARSON realize.™   PearsonSchool.com/Autentico

AUDIO   VIDEO   WRITING

El futuro perfecto

Use the future perfect tense to express what will have happened by a certain time. To form the future perfect, use the future of the verb *haber* with the past participle of the verb.

Here are all the future perfect tense forms of *inventar*:

habré inventado	habremos inventado
habrás inventado	habréis inventado
habrá inventado	habrán inventado

Para el año 2050 los científicos **habrán descubierto** otras fuentes de energía.
*By 2050, scientists **will have discovered** other energy sources.*

• The future perfect tense is often used with *dentro de* + time.

Dentro de cinco años, **habremos aprendido** mucho sobre la genética.
*In five years, we **will have learned** a lot about genetics.*

• You also use the future perfect tense to speculate about something that may have happened in the past.

—Laura no me llamó. ¿Qué le **habrá pasado**?
—**Se habrá enterado** de que no ibas.

—*Laura didn't call me. What **could have happened** to her?*
—***Perhaps she found out** you were not coming.*

¿Recuerdas?

Varios verbos tienen participios irregulares, como *escribir, escrito* y *volver, vuelto.* Los participios pasados de los verbos *descubrir* y *resolver* también son irregulares: *descubierto, resuelto.*

Más recursos   ONLINE

▶ **Tutorials:** Formation of Future Perfect
Use of Future Perfect

🔊 *Canción de hip hop:*
Los misterios del mundo

 30

¿Qué habremos logrado para el año . . .?

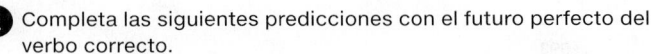
ESCRIBIR

1 Completa las siguientes predicciones con el futuro perfecto del verbo correcto.

1. En unos diez años, la mejor estudiante de geología de mi clase _____ (descubrir / desaparecer) nuevos materiales de la Luna.

2. Dentro de veinte años, nuestra amiga escritora _____ (conseguir / permitir) el Premio Nobel de Literatura.

3. Para las próximas Olimpiadas, mi patinadora favorita _____ (inventar / reemplazar) a la campeona mundial.

4. Si sigo estudiando, dentro de dos años _____ (aumentar / eliminar) mi vocabulario de español.

2 Envía un texto a un estudiante de tu clase y hazle 4 preguntas con algunos de los verbos de la Parte 1. El otro estudiante debe contestar tu texto expresando su opinión más allá de la vida diaria.

Capítulo 6 • doscientos ochenta y tres **283**

Interpersonal   6

Starter Activity

Before presenting the future perfect forms of *haber* in the *Gramática* on this page, review with students the present tense and imperfect forms. Have students use these forms in sentences in the present perfect and past perfect tenses.

Gramática

Standards: 4.1

Suggestions: Refer students to the *¿Recuerdas?* Have them list other irregular past participles that they can remember. Point out that all the perfect tenses they have learned so far use the auxiliary verb *haber.* Explain that this verb's conjugated forms are most often used in perfect tenses.

 Technology: Interactive Whiteboard

Grammar Activities 6-2 Use the whiteboard activities in your Teacher Resources as you progress through the grammar practice with your class.

 30

Standards: 1.1, 1.2

Suggestions: Tell students to complete Step 1 in steps. First, choose the verb that makes sense. Second, convert the verb to its past participle form. Third, add the appropriate future tense form of *haber* before the participle.

Answers:

Step 1
1. habrá descubierto
2. habrá conseguido
3. habrá reemplazado
4. habré aumentado

Enrich Your Teaching

Culture Note

According to The Second World Assembly on Aging, which met in Madrid in 2002, there will be two billion people over the age of 60 in the world in the year 2050, and for the first time, the number of people over 60 will outnumber those under 14. Ask students to discuss the implications of this trend.

Teacher-to-Teacher

Ask students to write three sentences using the future perfect tense to tell what they will have done one week from now, one month from now, and one year from now.

31

Standards: 1.1, 1.3

Suggestions: As part of their discussion, ask students to compute the year in which the use of each invention became widespread.

Answers will vary.

32

Standards: 1.1

Suggestions: As students discuss their predictions, encourage them to choose a secretary for the group who notes down students' comments by category.

Answers will vary.

Extension: After students' discussions, have them report to the class on what other members of their group said. This will elicit third-person forms of the future perfect tense.

Additional Resources

 Technology: Online Resources
- Instant Check
- Guided, Core, Audio
- *Para hispanohablantes*

Print
- Guided WB pp. 201–202
- Core WB p. 86

Assessment

Prueba 6-7 with Remediation (online only)
Prueba: El futuro perfecto
- Prueba 6-7

31

Más y más rápido

 LEER, HABLAR EN PAREJA Muchas veces, pasan años antes de que la gente empiece a usar los inventos. Lee la tabla siguiente. Con otro(a) estudiante, piensa por qué unos inventos habrán tardado mucho *(taken a long time)* en usarse mientras que otros inventos habrán tardado poco. Escojan cuatro inventos y preparen explicaciones.

▶ **Videomodelo**
electricidad / 46 años
A —¿Por qué habrán pasado 46 años entre el invento de la electricidad y su uso masivo?
B —Habrá pasado mucho tiempo porque . . .

▲ Coche antiguo

Más y más rapido		
Invento	**Fecha**	**Años para su uso masivo (widespread)**
Electricidad	1873	46
Teléfono	1876	35
Coche	1886	55
Radio	1906	22
Televisión	1927	26
La Red	1991	7
Teléfono inteligente	1992	5
Tableta electrónica	1993	17

32

Predicciones para el año 2030

 HABLAR EN PAREJA En grupos de cuatro, hagan predicciones para el año 2030. ¿Qué habrá pasado en el mundo? ¿Qué pasará? Piensen en sus metas, su escuela, su comunidad, sus viajes de vacaciones, los deportes, la moda y los alimentos.

Modelo
Para el año 2030, habré terminado una carrera y estaré trabajando como abogada.

284 doscientos ochenta y cuatro • Capítulo 6 • ¿Qué nos traerá el futuro?

Differentiated Instruction

Students with Learning Difficulties

Guide students to focus on the first sentence or clause of each item in *Actividad* 33. Instruct them to copy the noun that will become an object pronoun in the second part of the item. Then have them convert each noun to the appropriate object pronoun, insert it in the second part of the sentence, and read the entire item aloud.

Advanced Learners

Ask students to use the Internet to investigate other technological advances like those in *Actividad* 31. They might research the creation and widespread use of smartphones, DVDs, e-readers, or tablets. Have them prepare brief reports telling when the device was invented and about what year its use became widespread.

OBJECTIVES
▶ Read about plans for the future and advances in technology
▶ Talk about people and about giving things to other people

Uso de los complementos directos e indirectos

You already know the direct object pronouns *(me, te, lo, la, nos, os, los, las)* and the indirect object pronouns *(me, te, le, nos, os, les)* in Spanish.

When you use a direct and an indirect object pronoun together, place the indirect object pronoun before the direct object pronoun.

—Si necesitas un teléfono celular, yo **te lo** doy. ¿Quién **te** prestará la computadora?

—Octavio **me la** prestará.

When the indirect object pronoun *le* or *les* comes before the direct object pronoun *lo, la, los,* or *las,* change *le* or *les* to *se.* In these cases, you often add the prepositional phrase *a Ud., a él, a ella,* etc. or *a* + a noun or a person's name for clarification.

—¿A quién **le** comunicarán la noticia del descubrimiento?

—**Se la** comunicaremos **a Carlos**.

—José y Adela quieren leer los libros sobre el nuevo invento. ¿Puedes **prestárselos**?

When you attach two object pronouns to an infinitive, a command, or a present participle, you must add an accent mark to preserve the original stress.

—Quiero ver las fotos que van a usar para el mercadeo. **Dámelas**, por favor.

—No puedo **dártelas** hoy, espera hasta mañana.

33

Sobre el futuro

 LEER, ESCRIBIR Completa las oraciones con los complementos apropiados.

1. Laura quiere que le preste mi libro sobre genética pero no *(se lo / me lo)* _____ voy a prestar.

2. ¿Viste el programa vía satélite sobre la importancia del español en el mundo? *(Se lo / Te lo)* _____ recomiendo.

3. No recibimos la información sobre los nuevos aparatos eléctricos. El gerente de la empresa dice que *(nos la / se la)* _____ enviará la próxima semana.

4. Sé que ustedes comprarán una televisión digital. *(Me la / Se la)* _____ pediré prestada.

5. Quiero leer el artículo sobre informática. ¿*(Me lo / Te lo)* _____ das?

6. Nos explicaron la tarea sobre las nuevas fuentes de energía que habrá en el 2040, pero no *(te la / nos la)* _____ explicaron muy bien.

7. Me compré un programa de realidad virtual. *(Se lo / Te lo)* _____ mostraré cuando vengas a casa.

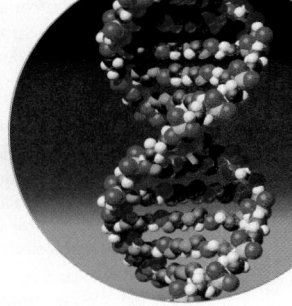
Una cadena de ADN

Gramática: Repaso

Suggestions: On the board or a transparency, cue students with sentences of various types that contain both a direct and an indirect object as nouns. Ask students to restate the sentences, changing the objects to pronouns.

 Technology: Interactive Whiteboard

Grammar Activities 6-2 Use the whiteboard activities in your Teacher Resources as you progress through the grammar practice with your class.

33

Standards: 1.2

Suggestions: Remind students to use the *se* form of the third-person indirect object pronoun. Point out that Spanish never has the pronoun combinations *le lo, le la, le los,* or *le las.*

Answers:

1. se lo
2. Te lo
3. nos la
4. Se la
5. Me lo
6. nos la
7. Te lo

Enrich Your Teaching

Teacher-to-Teacher

Using one word per sheet of paper, write the sentence *Juan da el libro a María* and the direct and indirect object pronouns, including **se.** Distribute to students. Say the sentence in English. Students who have the words stand in the correct order. Then say, "Juan gives it to María." The student with **lo** comes up, the one with **el libro** sits down.

21st Century Skills

Initiative and Self-Direction Have students working in small groups come up with a proposal for a new invention. Their invention can be serious or fanciful, but must be geared towards improving possible future living conditions. Have students share their ideas with the class.

Standards: 1.1

Suggestions: Encourage students to practice alternative placements of object pronouns: *Voy a dársela a Marta./Se la voy a dar a Marta.*

Answers will vary.

Standards: 1.1

Suggestions: As students have their group discussions, ask them to be ready to report to the rest of the class on their donation strategy.

Answers will vary.

El español en la comunidad

Standards: 1.2, 5.1

Suggestions: Once students have read the information, ask comprehension questions. For example: *¿Cuál es la idea principal de esta lectura? ¿Cómo ayudan los diarios digitales a los hispanohablantes en los Estados Unidos?*

Pre-AP® Integration

- **Learning Objective:** Interpersonal Speaking
- **Activity:** Have students bring to class a donation item such as a CD, a book, etc. Moving around the classroom, have them interact with other students asking if they would like to exchange "gifts" with them. Use this model:
  A. *¿Quieres mi disco compacto de Shakira?*
  B. *No, gracias. Dáselo a Marcos, o Sí, dámelo.*
  Following the activity, students can keep the "gift" or, as a class, donate all of the items to a local charity.
- **Pre-AP® Resource Materials:** Comprehensive guide to Pre-AP® communication skill development

---

34

¿Qué les darás?

🎤 **HABLAR EN PAREJA**

▶️

1 Imagina que vas a mudarte a un apartamento muy pequeño. Haz una lista de las cosas que no vas a necesitar y que les puedes regalar a tus amigos.

2 Intercambia tu lista con la de un(a) compañero(a). Tu compañero(a) te va a preguntar a quién le darás cada una de tus cosas.

Videomodelo
la televisión
A —*¿A quién le vas a dar la televisión?*
B —*Voy a dársela a Marta.*

35

¿Qué les podemos ofrecer?

🎤 **HABLAR EN GRUPO**

1 Tú y tus amigos van a donar cosas a las siguientes personas que las necesitan. Para cada persona, escribe una cosa que le puedes ofrecer.

Modelo
un paciente de un centro de rehabilitación
unas revistas o una novela

2 Trabaja con otro(a) estudiante. Hablen de las cosas que pueden ofrecer, cuándo las donarán y cómo las entregarán.

- un inmigrante que acaba de llegar
- una mujer sin hogar
- una persona de un hogar de ancianos
- un niño de un centro de rehabilitación

▶️ **Videomodelo**

A —*¿Qué le podemos ofrecer a un paciente de un centro de rehabilitación?*
B —*Le podemos ofrecer unos refrescos.*
A —*¡Buena idea! ¿Cuándo podemos llevárselos?*
B —*Se los podemos llevar este fin de semana.*

El español en la comunidad

Diarios digitales Las personas hispanohablantes en los Estados Unidos siempre han querido enterarse de las noticias de sus países de origen. Es lógico, allí tienen sus raíces y parte de sus familias. Algunas de las fuentes de información en español más usadas son los periódicos y canales de televisión en español de los Estados Unidos.

Además, gracias a los diarios digitales que hay en la Red, los hispanohablantes pueden leer periódicos de sus países todos los días.

La Red también les ofrece a los estudiantes de español la oportunidad de practicar el idioma y aprender sobre los países hispanohablantes. Pueden saber, por ejemplo, no sólo las noticias importantes de Quito, sino también qué restaurante está de moda, qué película es más popular o qué obra de teatro están poniendo. La Red hace del mundo un lugar verdaderamente pequeño.

Differentiated Instruction

Heritage Speakers

Ask students who have lived in a heritage country to discuss the role of television there. What are some of the most popular programs? Who are some of the most popular actors or personalities? Ask them to express their opinion on the influence of television. Do they find it positive or negative?

Students with Learning Difficulties

After students have chosen their topics for *Actividad* 36, instruct them to reread sections of the chapter pertaining to that topic. Help them find these sections and suggest that they write down vocabulary and phrases that might be useful to their presentations.

Las cosas que traerá el futuro

✎ HABLAR EN GRUPO, ESCRIBIR, ESCUCHAR

1 Trabaja con un grupo de tres o cuatro estudiantes. Escojan uno de los temas de la lista y hagan predicciones sobre ese tema. Luego, preparen una pequeña presentación para la clase. Mientras escuchan las presentaciones de los demás grupos, tomen notas.

- la vivienda
- los medios de comunicación
- la tecnología
- el ocio
- las carreras
- los alimentos

2 Con tu compañero(a), usen sus notas para intercambiar sus opiniones personales sobre lo que dijeron los demás grupos. Escriban algunas frases que digan si las predicciones de los(as) demás estudiantes son lógicas o ilógicas y por qué.

37

Cómo la televisión hizo historia

✎ LEER, ESCRIBIR Pocos avances tecnológicos han tenido una influencia tan grande como la televisión. En México, la televisión ha sido un agente de cambio que ha jugado papeles muy diferentes en distintos momentos históricos.

Conexiones ‹ Las ciencias sociales

La primera transmisión de televisión en México para el público fue el 16 de mayo de 1935, y tuvo lugar en la sede[1] del partido político que gobernó[2] ese país por más de 70 años. Los líderes del partido pensaban que con la televisión en sus manos podían decidir qué ideas, noticias y opiniones iba a recibir el pueblo. Por mucho tiempo, la televisión fue un instrumento de los líderes del país.

- Envíale un mensaje de texto—más allá de la vida diaria—a un compañero(a) para preguntarle sobre su opinión del papel que juega la televisión en la política de los Estados Unidos. Tu compañero(a) te responderá con otro mensaje de texto.

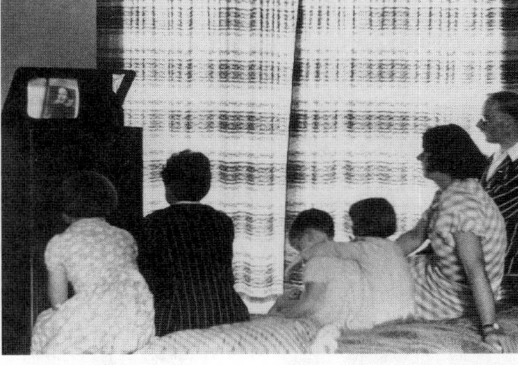

[1]headquarters [2]ruled

Standards: 1.1, 1.3

Suggestions: As students plan in Step 1, have them brainstorm a list of details associated with their topic that they can use to develop their presentation.

Answers will vary.

Standards: 1.2, 3.1, 4.2

Suggestions: Have students read the information silently once. Then ask volunteers to read it aloud in sections. Before students begin their texts to each other, address any reading comprehension issues.

Answers will vary.

Project-Based Learning

Students can perform Step 5 at this point. (For more information, see p. 256-b.)

Additional Resources

 Technology: Online Resources
- Instant Check
- Guided, Core, Audio
- *Para hispanohablantes*
- Teacher's Resource Materials: Audio Script, Communicative Pair Activity, Technology: Audio Cap. 6
Print
- Guided WB pp. 203–204
- Core WB p. 87–88

Assessment

Prueba 6-8 with Remediation (online only)
Prueba: Uso de los complementos
- Prueba 6-8

Examen: Vocabulario y gramática 2
- Examen 2
- ExamView: Examen 2

Enrich Your Teaching

Teacher-to-Teacher

Prepare students for *Actividad* 35 by briefly reviewing vocabulary associated with volunteer work and community centers. This can be found in the *Vocabulario en contexto* 2 section of *Capítulo* 5.

21st Century Skills

ICT (Information, Communications and Technology) Literacy Remind students that whenever they do a speaking activity, as in *Actividades* 34 and 35, they will have the opportunity to first watch and listen to native speakers in the *Videomodelos*. This way, they can use a native-speaker model to monitor their own progress.

Puente a la cultura

Standards: 1.1, 1.2, 2.2, 3.1

Suggestions

Pre-reading: Refer students to the *Estrategia* and have them answer the questions there. Then, based on the title of the selection, pictures, and captions, ask: *Después de leer este artículo, ¿qué tipo de comparación piensas que podremos hacer? (Podremos comparar ejemplos de la arquitectura del futuro; Podremos comparar la arquitectura del futuro con la de hoy día.)*

Reading: Encourage students to read through the entire passage once silently, without stopping at problem words or to ask questions. Then, for the second time through, ask volunteers to read sections aloud. Remind students to use background knowledge, cognates, and context clues to help them understand unfamiliar words and expressions as they read.

Post-reading: Ask students to work in small groups to complete a graphic organizer, such as a chart or a concept web, that shows the reading's main ideas and important supporting details.

Online Cultural Reading

Standards: 2.1

Suggestion: After completing the online activity, ask students to describe what kind of careers they think they will have 10 years from now.

COUNTRY CONNECTION

Standards: 3.1

 Technology: Mapa global interactivo Look at some of the tallest buildings in Mexico City.

Suggestions: Remind students that Luis Barragán is from Mexico. Tell them that Monterrey, Mexico's third-largest city, is not only the country's leading industrial center, but also home to seven universities.

Puente a la cultura

OBJECTIVES
▸ Read about the architecture of the future and the architects from the Hispanic world who are shaping it
▸ Compare and contrast different modern buildings
▸ Make predictions about the architecture of the future

La arquitectura del futuro

¿Te has preguntado alguna vez cómo serán los edificios del futuro? La mayoría de los arquitectos están de acuerdo en que serán más eficientes, mejores y más inteligentes pero, ¿qué quiere decir eso?

Seguramente, los edificios del futuro usarán menos ladrillo[1] y piedra, pues tendrán materiales como el titanio y las fibras de carbón y grafito[2], siguiendo el ejemplo de los aviones y coches. Cada vez habrá más edificios "inteligentes", en otras palabras, edificios en los que una computadora central controla todos los aparatos y servicios para aprovechar[3] mejor la energía eléctrica, la calefacción y el aire acondicionado en el interior.

El argentino César Pelli es uno de los arquitectos que diseñan edificios futuristas. Una de sus obras más importantes son las Torres Petronas, en Kuala Lumpur, Malasia, consideradas entre los edificios más altos del mundo. Estas torres, con su planta en forma de estrella y construídas de cristal, acero[4] y concreto, tienen un diseño que es a la vez futurista e influenciado por la arquitectura islámica.

Otro edificio futurista es el Faro del Comercio, en Monterrey, México, diseñado por el arquitecto mexicano Luis Barragán. La arquitectura de Barragán reúne en un mismo diseño líneas simples y modernas con el uso de colores, texturas y materiales que recuerdan la cultura popular mexicana y los colores de la naturaleza.

[1]brick [2]titanium, and carbon and graphite fibers [3]to utilize [4]steel

Estrategia

Look at Illustrations Pictures, photographs, and other graphics are often used to emphasize a written message.

You can anticipate what the content of a text will be by examining the illustrations.

The article on this page is about architecture. Look at the photos on these pages and think about the style of the buildings. What might the article be about?

Online Cultural Reading

Go to Auténtico
ONLINE to read and understand a website with online classified advertising for employment opportunities.

Hotel Camino Real, México

Faro del Comercio, México

Torres Petronas, Malasia

Differentiated Instruction

Students with Learning Difficulties

Before they read **La arquitectura del futuro,** have students create a chart with the following headings: **nombre del arquitecto, edificio, ciudad, diseño.** After an initial read, have them re-read to find the information necessary to complete the chart.

Advanced Learners

As a group project, have students design and then talk about a futuristic building of their own creation. They should illustrate or discuss how the building will be used, what its appearance will be, and so on.

La Ciudad de Nueva York

Go **Online** to practice

PEARSON
realize™

WRITING   MAPA GLOBAL   AUDIO

PearsonSchool.com/Autentico

Ricardo Legorreta, otro reconocido arquitecto mexicano, ha diseñado el Hotel Camino Real en Polanco, México. La arquitectura de Legorreta se caracteriza por ambientes con diseños geométricos, una armoniosa combinación de espacio y color y un uso funcional y decorativo de la luz.

Un edificio que impresiona por su estilo futurístico es el intercambiador de transportes *(transit hub)* del World Trade Center en la Ciudad de Nueva York, diseñado por el arquitecto español Santiago Calatrava. Este edificio se destaca por su forma única que combina elementos de arte y arquitectura.

 ## ¿Comprendiste?

1. ¿Qué materiales se usarán para construir los edificios del futuro? ¿Por qué crees que se usarán esos materiales?

2. ¿Qué influencias se pueden ver en las Torres Petronas y en el Faro del Comercio? ¿Conoces algún edificio similar? Explica las razones para diseñarlo así.

3. Compara un edificio de estas páginas con algún edificio moderno que te guste. ¿En qué se parecen? ¿En qué se diferencian?

El futuro de tu comunidad

Usa la información del texto y las fotos para hacer predicciones sobre los edificios del futuro de tu comunidad. ¿Cómo será la escuela?, ¿la biblioteca?, ¿el hospital? Escribe un párrafo sobre alguno de esos edificios.

 Videodocumentario La tecnología en la carrera de un profesional

 Mapa global interactivo Explora dos ejemplos de arquitectura moderna en Monterrey y la Ciudad de México. Compáralos con edificios similares en tu ciudad o área.

Capítulo 6 • doscientos ochenta y nueve **289**

¿Comprendiste?

Standards: 1.2, 1.3

Suggestions: Tell students that questions 1 and 2 are fact-based, and the answers to them can be found in the reading. Question 3 is more open-ended. Encourage them to talk about their personal tastes and values while answering question 3.

Answers:

1. Se usarán titanio y fibras de carbón y grafito. Seguirán el ejemplo de los aviones y coches.
2. Se pueden ver las influencias futuristas. Answers will vary.
3. Answers will vary.

El futuro de tu comunidad

Standards: 1.3

Suggestions: Encourage students to use chapter vocabulary and structures, such as the future perfect tense, in their paragraphs. Remind them of other technological advances, such as those in electronics.

Answers will vary.

Digital Portfolio

Keep students' paragraphs from *El futuro de tu comunidad* in their portfolios as a writing sample.

 Technology: Videodocumentario

Standards: 1.2

Resources: Teacher's Resource Materials: Video Script

View *La tecnología en la carrera de un profesional* with the class online in **Realize.** See the *Video Teacher's Guide* for additional suggestions.

Additional Resources

Technology: Online Resources
- *Videodocumentario*
- Guided, Writing, Reading
- *Para hispanohablantes*
- Cultural Reading Activity

Print
- Guided WB p. 205

Enrich Your Teaching

Culture Note

César Pelli has also designed many performing arts centers in the United States. The Aronoff Center in Cincinnati features the use of brick and stone, traditional building materials for the area. Pelli's design for the Performing Arts Center of Greater Miami reflects the city's tropical climate and multicultural ambience.

21st Century Skills

Media Literacy Have students search the Internet for more information on the individuals featured in this reading. They can search the keywords: *Santiago Calatrava, César Pelli, Luis Barragán,* and *Ricardo Legorreta.* Ask students to identify other Spanish-speaking architects who have made important contributions in today's world.

¿Qué me cuentas?

Standards: 1.1, 1.2, 1.3

Resources: Teacher's Resource Materials: Audio Script, Technology: Audio Cap. 6

AP® Skills: Integration of listening, reading, and writing to comprehend and synthesize information from spoken and written sources.

Suggestions:

For Step 1, use the audio or read the descriptions aloud. Allow students to hear the descriptions twice through: the first time to write their answers, the second time to check them.

For Step 2, have students identify significant details as they read and make appropriate inferences about the type of person that would be best suited for each of the jobs.

For Step 3, encourage students to use each of the suggested expressions, and to support their arguments with specific information from both the listening in Step 1 and the reading in Step 2.

Answers:

Step 1

1. b	**3.** a	**5.** b
2. c	**4.** c	**6.** b

Steps 2–3
Answers will vary.

Active Classroom

Ask each student to write five false statements about the article. Place the students in pairs. Have them read the sentences to each other with the other student correcting each of the false statements.

Additional Resources

 Technology: Online Resources
  • *Para hispanohablantes*

Pre-AP® Integración

OBJECTIVES
▶ Listen to and read about professional careers
▶ Discuss professions and the necessary qualifications

¿Qué me cuentas?: Cuando sea mayor

Escucha cómo un profesor describe a sus estudiantes. Anota el nombre de cada estudiante mientras contestas las preguntas. Luego, lee las descripciones de carreras profesionales y decide qué carrera será apropiada para cada estudiante.

1 Vas a escuchar una serie de descripciones. Después de cada descripción, vas a oír dos preguntas. Escoge la respuesta correcta para cada pregunta.

1. **a.** avances tecnológicos   **b.** programas de dibujos animados   **c.** productos de mercadeo
2. **a.** insectos   **b.** medios de comunicación   **c.** cómo curar enfermedades
3. **a.** el mercadeo   **b.** las comunicaciones   **c.** la medicina
4. **a.** una gerente   **b.** una cocinera   **c.** una arquitecta
5. **a.** un disco digital   **b.** una calculadora   **c.** un teléfono celular
6. **a.** una contadora   **b.** una actriz cómica   **c.** una abogada

2 Ahora lee este artículo sobre carreras profesionales.

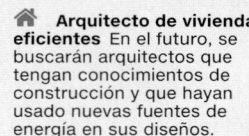

> ☰   Considera ❯ **Carreras del futuro**
>
> 🏠 **Arquitecto de viviendas eficientes** En el futuro, se buscarán arquitectos que tengan conocimientos de construcción y que hayan usado nuevas fuentes de energía en sus diseños.
>
> 🖥 **Diseñador de juegos virtuales educativos** En el futuro, los diseñadores tendrán que tener experiencia como programadores. Los candidatos ideales serán artísticos pero lógicos y cuidadosos en su trabajo.
>
> ⚙ **Vendedores de productos tecnológicos** Se necesitarán representantes amables y emprendedores. Estos vendedores tendrán que buscar nuevos clientes y ofrecerles nuevos productos. Será necesario que sean bilingües o hasta trilingües.
>
> 🚢 **Gerentes de turismo y hotelería** Se buscarán personas maduras que puedan tomar decisiones. Es importante que se lleven bien con todo tipo de clientes y que tengan un buen sentido de humor.
>
> 🧪 **Científico** Las empresas farmacéuticas necesitarán personas que estén informadas sobre los últimos avances tecnológicos de genética y que tengan experiencia en el campo de la medicina.
>
> 📖 **Contador** Las compañías internacionales necesitarán contadores con conocimientos de finanzas y de leyes internacionales. Se buscarán personas capaces de trabajar en forma independiente. Será necesario que tengan experiencia en el extranjero.

 3 Trabaja con un(a) compañero(a) y empareja cada estudiante del paso 1 con una carrera del paso 2. Considera estas preguntas: ¿Qué tendrá que estudiar cada estudiante para seguir esa carrera? ¿Qué cualidades y habilidades serán necesarias para esa carrera? Presenten su análisis a la clase. Usen las siguientes expresiones para conectar sus ideas. Recuerden de incluir detalles que apoyan su análisis.

así que	por lo tanto	mientras
además que	por eso	aunque

Differentiated Instruction

21st Century Skills

Critical Thinking and Problem Solving Have students categorize the six highlighted careers based on the Multiple Intelligences. You may need to explain the categories: linguistic, logical/mathematical, musical/rhythmic, visual/spatial, bodily/kinesthetic, and naturalist. Then, have them write about which career might suit them best and why.

Students with Learning Difficulties

Help students organize information for their oral presentations. Model how to turn each question in the chart into an informative sentence. *¿Quiénes darán las clases? Los estudiantes darán las clases.*

OBJECTIVES
▸ Demonstrate how to give a speech about adapting a school's technology
▸ Map your speech using a main idea and supporting details

Go Online to practice
PearsonSchool.com/Autentico
PEARSON
realize.
AUDIO SPEAK/RECORD

Mi escuela del futuro

TAREA Imagina que dentro de 10 años regresas a tu escuela y que serás el(la) nuevo(a) director(a). ¿Qué cambios harás para adaptar la escuela a los nuevos avances tecnológicos? Tienes que preparar un discurso para decir lo que harás.

1 Prepárate Responde a las preguntas sobre los cambios que harás en tu escuela. Usa una tabla como ésta.

¿Quiénes darán las clases y cómo las darán?	
¿Qué materias enseñarán?	
¿Qué cambios harás en el edificio?	
¿Cómo harán sus tareas los estudiantes?	
¿Cómo se comunicarán los estudiantes?	

2 Practica Vuelve a leer la información de la tabla. Recuerda:
• usar oraciones conectadas con detalles y elaboración
• mirar directamente al público al hablar
• usar los tiempos futuros y el vocabulario del capítulo

Modelo

Los estudiantes podrán estudiar desde sus casas. Por las tardes, un robot ayudará a todos los estudiantes con sus tareas. Cada estudiante tendrá una computadora muy avanzada, casi humana . . .

3 Haz tu presentación Imagina que las personas que escuchan no saben cómo será tu escuela en el futuro. Descríbeles la situación y narra con detalles y elaboración las cosas que harás para adaptar tu escuela a los avances del futuro. Usa oraciones conectadas.

4 Evaluación Se utilizará la siguiente rúbrica para evaluar tu presentación.

Rubric	Score 1	Score 3	Score 5
How well your information is organized	Your ideas are undeveloped or not addressed at all.	You tend to skip around from idea to idea.	Your ideas are presented in a logical, planned order.
How well you support your main ideas	Your supporting evidence is absent.	Some of your supporting evidence is weak.	All your main ideas are supported with interesting details.
How effectively you deliver your speech	You read your speech. You have no eye contact with the audience and little or no intonation.	You make some eye contact. You use intonation, but not convincingly.	You have good eye contact with the audience. Your intonation helps get the message across.

Capítulo 6 • doscientos noventa y uno **291**

Estrategia

Mapping your speech using main idea and details To organize a speech you can *map* it in advance. Think of your presentation as an organized way to communicate your ideas. You should start with an opening statement of the main idea. Then, use the items in the chart you wrote as subtopics. As you speak, introduce each subtopic one at a time, and elaborate on it by adding details. End your presentation with a closing statement that reinforces the main idea or your opinion about it.

Presentación oral

Standards: 1.2, 1.3, 3.1

Suggestions: Review the task and the four-step approach with students. Review the rubric (see *Assessment* below) to explain how you will grade the performance task. Before students begin, direct their attention to *Estrategia.* Point out that the chart in Step 1 is one way of mapping a speech. Use a T-chart as a model. Show students how to set up their own charts by copying the questions into the left column. Leave plenty of space between questions and tell students to use that space to write their answers in the right column of their own charts. The answers they write will be the details they use to support each main idea in their speech.

Pre-AP® Integration

• **Learning Objective:** Presentational Speaking
• **Activity:** Remind students to focus on the presentational speaking skills used in this task such as fluency, pronunciation, and comprehensibility.
• **Pre-AP® Resource Materials:** Comprehensive guide to Pre-AP® speaking skill development

Digital Portfolio

Make video or audio recordings of student presentations in class, or assign the Speak and Record activity so they can record their presentations online. Include the recording in their portfolios.

Additional Resources

 Technology: Online Resources
• *Para hispanohablantes*

Self Assessment

Presentación oral
• **Assessment Program: Rubrics**
Review the rubric with students. Go over the descriptions of the different levels of performance. After assessing students, help individuals understand how their performance could be improved. (See Teacher's Resource Materials for suggestions on using rubrics in assessment.)

Enrich Your Teaching

Teacher-to-Teacher

e-amigos: Have students send their *e-amigos* a written summary of their *Presentación oral.* Encourage students to defend their suggestions and to respond to those of their *e-amigos.*

21st Century Skills

Media Literacy In preparation for their presentations, have students browse the Internet using keywords such as *futuristic schools* and *future learning.* Encourage students to integrate available images of futuristic school buildings, classrooms, and learning technologies into their presentations to illustrate their visionary plans for their schools.

Language Arts Connection: Expository Writing

Standards: 3.1

Point out to students that there are two ways they can organize their compare and contrast essay. They can tell all about one period of time first, then compare it to the other in another paragraph. Or they can go back and forth between one period of time and the other, showing how they are alike or different in various ways. Remind them that this latter alternative will require them to use more transitions in their writing.

Presentación escrita

Standards: 1.2, 1.3, 3.1

Suggestions: Begin by explaining the criteria you will use to evaluate students' compositions. (See Step 5, *Evaluación,* in the Student Edition, and *Assessment* on the following page.)

Direct students' attention to the *Estrategia.* Ask them to share additional background information they have learned in Language Arts courses about comparing and contrasting. Use a Venn diagram to model brainstorming and recording ideas for a comparison and contrast essay.

Pre-AP® Integration

- **Learning Objective:** Presentational Writing
- **Pre-AP® Resource Materials:** Comprehensive guide to Pre-AP® writing skill development

---

Presentación escrita

OBJECTIVES
▸ Write a comparison of the past and the present
▸ Use a Venn diagram to organize similarities and differences

El futuro según el presente

 El futuro es siempre incierto *(uncertain)*. Tenemos una idea de lo que sucederá pero no podemos estar completamente seguros de ello. Podemos hacer predicciones. Para la gente que vivió en tiempos pasados el futuro también fue incierto. Escoge un período del pasado y compáralo con el presente. Escribe un ensayo *(essay)* con tus comparaciones, teniendo en cuenta la pregunta: "¿El futuro será siempre mejor que el presente?"

1 Antes de escribir Usa un diagrama como éste para anotar las semejanzas y las diferencias *(similarities and differences)* entre el período del pasado que escogiste y el presente.

Siglo XIX
- mucha gente no iba a la escuela
- había muchas enfermedades
- no había medios de comunicación muy avanzados

(intersección)
- curiosidad por el futuro
- importancia de la familia

Presente
- importancia de la educación
- avances en los descubrimientos para curar enfermedades
- comunicaciones muy avanzadas

Estrategia

Compare and contrast If you want to compare issues, use signal words to mark their similarities and their differences.
You can say, for instance, *"En el pasado había muchas enfermedades, pero hoy, con los avances en la medicina, podemos curarlas"* or *"Antes, los viajes tardaban mucho tiempo, pero ahora tardan sólo unas horas."* Other expressions are: *"Antes . . . pero ahora . . .", "en el pasado, ambos . . . y hoy . . .", "ni entonces ni ahora . . . ."*
Signal words give you clues about the structure of the passage.

2 Borrador Escribe tu borrador en forma de ensayo. Comienza con la pregunta de la introducción y presenta las épocas *(time periods)* que vas a describir. Explica las diferencias y semejanzas entre los dos períodos, según lo que escribiste en el diagrama de Venn. Usa expresiones como *pero* y *sin embargo* para comparar y contrastar.

Modelo

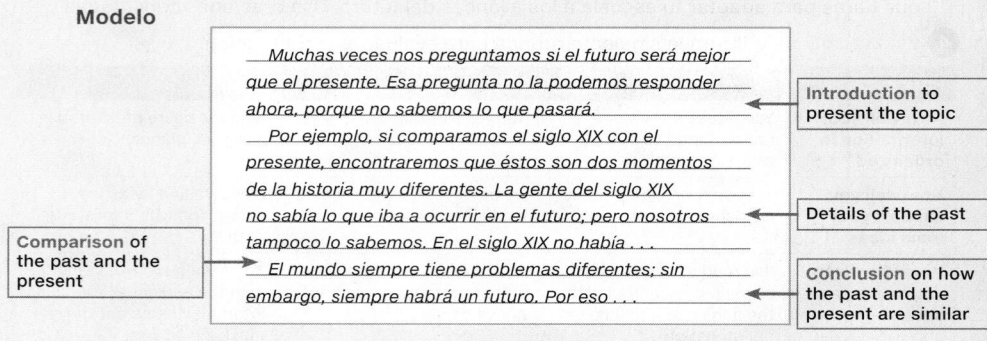

Muchas veces nos preguntamos si el futuro será mejor que el presente. Esa pregunta no la podemos responder ahora, porque no sabemos lo que pasará.

Por ejemplo, si comparamos el siglo XIX con el presente, encontraremos que éstos son dos momentos de la historia muy diferentes. La gente del siglo XIX no sabía lo que iba a ocurrir en el futuro; pero nosotros tampoco lo sabemos. En el siglo XIX no había . . .

El mundo siempre tiene problemas diferentes; sin embargo, siempre habrá un futuro. Por eso . . .

Introduction to present the topic

Details of the past

Conclusion on how the past and the present are similar

Comparison of the past and the present

Differentiated Instruction

Heritage Speakers

Students may have difficulty correctly placing commas in complex sentences. Have students trade drafts of their essay with a partner and read the drafts aloud. Remind students that in many cases, when they sense a pause in the text, a comma should be inserted.

Advanced Learners

Ask students to imagine they have taken a trip back in time to a point of their choice. Have them explain to a person of that period how one or more aspects of everyday life will have changed. Challenge them to focus on something they take for granted that didn't exist during their chosen period of the past.

❸ Redacción/Revisión Después de escribir el primer borrador de tu ensayo, intercambia tu trabajo con el de otro(a) estudiante. Léanlos y hagan sugerencias sobre cómo mejorarlos. Decidan qué aspectos de los ensayos son más o menos efectivos. Fíjense en cómo el escritor del modelo conectó las oraciones e incluyó detalles en su ensayo. Hagan sugerencias sobre cómo mejorar los ensayos.

Haz lo siguiente: Subraya con una línea los verbos en presente y con dos los verbos en futuro.

- ¿Hay concordancia entre los verbos y el sujeto?

- ¿El presente y el futuro están empleados correctamente?

> nos preguntamos ~~será~~
> Muchas veces ~~preguntamos~~ si el futuro ~~es~~
> el presente
> mejor que ~~presente~~ No sabemos lo que
> pasarán en 50 años. Ignoramos lo que se habrá
> descubierto entonces. Esa pregunta no la
> podemos
> ~~podremos~~ responder ahora, ya que . . .

❹ Publicación Antes de escribir la versión final, lee de nuevo tu borrador y repasa los siguientes puntos:

- ¿Sigue mi ensayo un orden lógico?

- ¿Comparé claramente los dos períodos?

- ¿Añadí detalles a mis descripciones?

- ¿Usé oraciones conectadas con detalles y elaboración?

- ¿La conclusión es resultado de lo que dice el ensayo?

Después de revisar el borrador, escribe una copia en limpio de tu ensayo.

❺ Evaluación Se utilizará la siguiente rúbrica para evaluar tu presentación.

Rubric	Score 1	Score 3	Score 5
Completion of task	Your main idea is unclear, not stated, or not developed.	Your main idea is stated, but development is weak.	Your main idea is clearly stated and developed.
Development of comparison and contrast	Your essay does not present two time periods for comparison and contrast.	You presented two time periods, but few details are compared or contrasted.	You compared and contrasted time periods clearly with good use of supporting detail.
Sentence structure/ grammar, spelling, mechanics	Your sentences run on or are fragmented with many grammar, spelling, mechanics errors.	You used sentences consistently. You have some grammar, spelling, and/or mechanics errors.	Your sentence structure is correct and varied with few grammar, spelling, mechanics errors.

Capítulo 6 • doscientos noventa y tres **293**

Suggestions (Cont'd):

In Step 2, students should decide on the organization of their essays. Will they make a side-by-side comparison, or will they describe one time period all at once and then compare and contrast the other in a separate paragraph? Explain that the organization strategy they choose depends on how much they have to say about each time period. If they are comparing several details, suggest that they use the latter strategy, focusing on one period at a time, in separate paragraphs.

For Step 3, encourage students to focus on sentence structure, transitions, and use of past, present, and future tenses. Have them follow the suggestions shown.

Evaluation

Steps 4 and 5 overlap. Students will need evaluation by you, their peers, or self-evaluation to fine-tune and polish their drafts.

Digital Portfolio

Keep students' final drafts in their portfolios as a writing sample.

Additional Resources

Technology: Online Resources
- *Para hispanohablantes*

Self Assessment

Presentación escrita
- **Assessment Program:** Rubrics

Review the rubric with students. Go over the descriptions of the different levels of performance. After assessing students, help individuals understand how their performance could be improved. (See Teacher's Resource Materials for suggestions on using rubrics in assessment.)

Enrich Your Teaching

21st Century Skills

Communication Students will have to use their written language for the purpose of comparing and contrasting a time period in the past with the present. As a warm-up to this task, have students make a list of the Spanish words and expressions they use to discuss similarities and differences between two topics, as well as common transition words and phrases.

Lectura

Standards: 1.2, 1.3, 2.2, 3.1, 3.2, 5.2

Suggestions:

Pre-reading: Before reading, direct students' attention to the *Al leer* section. Have them copy the graphic organizer from p. 297 and make sure they understand how they will use it. Also refer students to the *Estrategia*. Remind them that, besides using context clues as suggested, they know other strategies to help them understand difficult words and passages: they can use their knowledge of cognates and word families.

Reading: When reading together with students, pause frequently to address comprehension issues they may have and to allow them to fill in their *Elementos del cuento* charts from p. 297. Here are some possible comprehension issues on this page for which you can provide some guidance:

- After students have read the first part of the story, ask: *¿Cuántos personajes están presentes al principio del cuento? ¿Cómo se llaman? ¿Qué relación existe entre ellos? ¿Son miembros de la misma familia? ¿Son amigas? ¿Trabajan juntas? ¿De qué gran cambio están hablando? (Son tres: Rosa, Betty y Carmen; trabajan juntas; hablan del cambio de puesto de Rosa.)*
- *En esta escena, ¿cómo tratan de ayudar Betty y Carmen a Rosa? (Tratan de animarla, de hacerla sentirse mejor.)*
- *Mira las dos primeras preguntas en la sección Al leer. ¿Cómo las puedes contestar ahora?*

Starter Activity

Write these words for parts of a computer on the board:

> teclado   pantalla   ratón

Have students write one sentence for each using the following format:

El/La _____ sirve para_____.

Lectura

OBJECTIVES
- Read and understand a short story about today's world
- Use context to infer the meaning of unknown words
- Express your opinion about virtual education

Estrategia
Coping with unknown words When you encounter a word you don't know, try to infer its meaning from the context of the sentence. If you can't guess the meaning, skip the word and continue reading. If the word is essential and the reading doesn't help you understand it, look it up in the dictionary.

Al leer

Vas a leer un cuento de Ángel Balzarino, escritor argentino nacido en 1943. Al leer el cuento verás que el autor no nos explica dónde ocurre la acción, ni nos dice claramente quiénes son o qué hacen los personajes. De esta manera, el autor añade un elemento de suspenso. Lee el cuento una primera vez para tener una idea general de lo que pasa. Luego, copia la tabla que aparece al final de la lectura. Mientras lees por segunda vez, completa la tabla. Presta atención a los siguientes puntos:

- quiénes son los personajes
- las emociones de los personajes al principio del cuento
- la importancia de trabajar y la satisfacción de un trabajo bien realizado
- el final sorprendente (*surprising*)

Control de Datos Generales

Rosa

—¡Hoy es el día! —el tono de Rosa expresó cierta zozobra[1], la sensación de una derrota[2] ineludible—. ¿Por qué habrán decidido eso?

—Nadie lo sabe, querida —respondió Betty.

—Así es. Son órdenes[3] superiores —Carmen pareció resignada[4] ante esa realidad—. Simplemente debemos obedecer.

Aunque la explicación resultaba clara y sencilla, no logró convencer a Rosa. Ya nada la consolaría[5]. Ahora solo deseaba sublevarse[6], expresar abiertamente la indignación que sentía desde hacía una semana, cuando le comunicaron la orden increíble de sacarla de allí.

---

[1]uneasiness, anxiety [2]defeat [3]orders [4]resigned
[5]would comfort [6]to revolt

294 doscientos noventa y cuatro • Capítulo 6 • ¿Qué nos traerá el futuro?

Differentiated Instruction

Heritage Speakers

After students have read the selection for comprehension, assign them the roles of the different characters in the story and have them prepare a dramatic reading. Encourage them to focus on pronunciation and expression.

Students with Learning Difficulties

Some students may have difficulty keeping track of the characters in the story. On a piece of paper, have them copy the names **Rosa, Betty,** and **Carmen.** After reading each paragraph, have them stop and record a key phrase related to the character who has just spoken or been described.

—¡No quiero separarme de ustedes! —ahora su voz tuvo el carácter de un ruego angustioso[7]—. ¡No puedo aceptarlo!

—Nosotras tampoco lo deseamos, Rosa.

—Posiblemente te lleven a un sitio más importante —dijo Carmen dulcemente, tratando de animarla—. Tus antecedentes son extraordinarios. Sin duda los han tenido en cuenta para esa resolución.

—Por supuesto —confirmó Betty—. ¿Adónde te gustaría trabajar ahora?

Se produjo un largo silencio; embargada[8] por la duda, Rosa demoró[9] una respuesta concreta, como si aún no hubiera contemplado esa posibilidad.

—No lo sé. No tengo ambiciones. Me gusta estar aquí.

—Pero ya estuviste mucho tiempo, ¿no te parece?

—Tal vez sí. ¡Cuarenta y tres años! —la pesadumbre[10] de Rosa se transformó de pronto en una ráfaga de orgullo[11]—. Fui la primera que empezó a trabajar en el Control de Datos Generales. Siempre me encargaron las tareas más complicadas. Nunca tuve un problema, nadie me ha hecho una corrección.

—Lo sabemos, Rosa.

—¡Una trayectoria realmente admirable!

—Por eso querrán trasladarte. Necesitarán tus servicios en otra parte. Quizá te lleven al Centro Nacional de Comunicaciones.

Las palabras de Betty reflejaron un vibrante entusiasmo, casi tuvieron una mágica sonoridad[12]. Trabajar en ese lugar constituía un hermoso privilegio. A pesar de ser un anhelo[13] común, todas comprendían que eran remotas las posibilidades de realizarlo, como si debieran recorrer un camino lleno de escollos[14]. Preferían, tal vez para evitar una desilusión, descartar la esperanza[15] de ser escogidas.

—A cualquiera le gustaría estar allí —dijo Rosa sin énfasis—. Pero creo que ya soy demasiado vieja.

—Precisamente por eso te habrán escogido —dijo Betty con fervor—. Para trabajar allí se necesita tener mucha experiencia.

—Las cosas están cambiando, Rosa —confirmó Carmen—. Todo se presenta bajo un aspecto nuevo, casi sorprendente. Es un proceso de reestructuración. Ellos parecen decididos a dar a cada cosa el lugar que le corresponde. Sin duda comprendieron que era hora de darte una merecida recompensa[16].

—Quizá tengan razón —dijo Rosa modestamente—. Cuarenta y tres años de eficiente labor tienen un gran significado. Aunque nunca me interesó recibir un premio. Simplemente me dediqué a trabajar de la mejor manera.

—Siempre serás un ejemplo para nosotras, Rosa.

—Nadie será capaz de reemplazarte. Estamos seguras.

—Sin embargo, desearía saber a quién pondrán en mi lugar.

---

[7]anguished plea [8]overwhelmed [9]delayed
[10]sorrow [11]burst of pride

[12]harmony [13]yearning [14]stumbling blocks
[15]to leave aside any hope [16]deserved reward

Capítulo 6 • doscientos noventa y cinco **295**

Suggestions (Cont'd):

Reading: Here are some possible comprehension issues on this page for which you can provide some guidance:

- *En tus propias palabras, ¿qué pasa en el cuento al principio de esta página? (Alguien se acerca.)*
- *En la seguna columna, ¿qué palabra se parece a la palabra* annihilation *en inglés y tiene el mismo significado? (aniquilación)*
- *¿Con qué van a reemplazar a Rosa, con otra máquina o con un ser humano? (un ser humano)*

Post-reading: Have students discuss the ending of the story and share their thoughts. Did they expect the ending to turn out as it did?

Pre-AP® Integration

- **Learning Objective:** Presentational Writing
- **Activity:** Have students focus on the various services that Rosa mentions she has efficiently performed for the company. Then ask each student to imagine that they are a current-day "machine" that will some day be useless. Have each write a brief paragraph arguing several reasons why they should be retained. (Coche: *Siempre lo llevé a su trabajo por la lluvia y la nieve. No gasté mucha gasolina.*) Share with the class.
- **Pre-AP® Resource Materials:** Comprehensive guide to Pre-AP® writing skill development

Active Classroom

Have students work in groups of three and present this story to the class as a play. Without a narrator (a voice to describe the action), they are to present the dialogue between Rosa, Betty, and Carmen. Ask them to focus on portraying the emotions between the three characters. Have the play end at the line *"¡Mucha suerte en tu nuevo trabajo, Rosa!"*

Las palabras de Rosa quedaron de repente superadas[17] por el ruido de unos pasos cada vez más cercanos; entonces, algo sobresaltadas[18] por esa señal que parecía anunciar una grave amenaza[19], las tres se quedaron a la expectativa.

—¡Allí vienen!

—Sí —Rosa no se preocupó en disimular su consternación—. ¡Ha llegado el momento!

Carmen y Betty se vieron contagiadas[20] por ese estado de ánimo; después, con forzada exaltación, sólo pudieron decir a modo de despedida:

—¡Mucha suerte en tu nuevo trabajo, Rosa!

La puerta se abrió de repente y cuatro hombres jóvenes, de cuerpos esbeltos y vigorosos, entraron en el lugar donde se amontonaban[21] diversas máquinas y pantallas a las que las luces incandescentes les daban un aspecto limpio, reluciente, casi de implacable frialdad[22].

—¿Cuál es? —preguntó uno de ellos.

El Suplente pasó lentamente la vista a su alrededor, en una especie de reconocimiento, hasta que extendió una mano.

—Aquélla. Se la conoce con el nombre de Rosa.

Los tres hombres se acercaron con pasos firmes y decididos hacia la computadora más grande, cuyo material parecía algo deteriorado por el uso y los años.

—¿La llevamos al lugar de costumbre?

—Sí, a la Cámara[23] de Aniquilación.

—Está bien.

Mientras los hombres llevaban la vieja y pesada computadora, el Suplente fue a ocupar su puesto. Entonces no pudo evitar una franca sonrisa de seguridad, de absoluto triunfo al comprender que ya estaba a punto de finalizar la Era de las Máquinas.

[23]Chamber

[17]overcome [18]alarmed [19]serious threat [20]infected [21]piled up [22]coldness

Differentiated Instruction

Heritage Speakers

Have students debate the following topic with a partner: *La computadora es el avance tecnológico más importante del siglo XX.* Instruct one student to agree with the statement, and the other to disagree. Encourage those who have lived in heritage countries to consider the role of computers there.

Advanced Learners

Ask students to pretend they are writing a longer story about the future. Invite them to write one scene from the story. This could be a dialogue between two or more characters or a description of a futuristic setting.

Interacción con la lectura

1 Llena la tabla con información del cuento.

ELEMENTOS DEL CUENTO	
nombre del personaje principal	
dos palabras que describen al personaje	
una frase que dice cuál es el problema	
una frase que dice cuál es el final	

2 Trabaja con un grupo de estudiantes para comentar lo que escribieron en sus tablas.

- Parafrasea la idea principal del cuento. Incluye el tema y los detalles que la apoyan.
- Carmen dice que quizás lleven a Rosa a un lugar más importante. ¿Lo habrá hecho porque lo cree o para animar a Rosa?
- ¿Cómo apoyan a Rosa sus compañeras? ¿Te parece que así debe ser?
- ¿Cuál será el futuro de Rosa? ¿Por qué habrá dicho que no tiene ambiciones?
- ¿Qué te parece el final del cuento? ¿Te parece optimista o pesimista? Explica por qué.

3 Trabaja con tu grupo para buscar palabras de la lectura que no conocían o no recordaban. Hablen sobre cómo lograron determinar o recordar el significado de esas palabras para entender mejor la lectura.

4 Y tú, ¿qué piensas? ¿Somos en realidad "arquitectos de nuestro propio futuro"? ¿O crees que otras personas deciden todo por nosotros?

CULTURA ◄ México

La Nueva Escuela Virtual del Departamento de Educación de México sigue buscando maestros. En su Salón Virtual el maestro creará sus grupos de estudiantes y dará sus clases totalmente en línea.

Los interesados deben tener habilidades para el trabajo con computadoras, y tener cuentas (*accounts*) privadas de acceso a la Red.

- ¿Crees que en el futuro toda la educación será a distancia?
- ¿Cuáles serán las ventajas (*advantages*) de estos cursos? ¿Cuáles serán las desventajas?
- ¿Has pensado alguna vez en tomar clases a distancia? ¿Conoces alguna universidad o escuela que las ofrezca?

Capítulo 6 • doscientos noventa y siete **297**

Interacción con la lectura
Standards: 1.1, 1.2, 1.3, 3.1

Suggestions: Point out to students that what they are doing in Step 3 is sharing learning strategies. Provide help as necessary by reminding students of names for the strategies they use, such as *usar claves de contexto, considerar familias de palabras,* or *reconocer cognados.*

Answers:

Step 1

Rosa

vieja, trabajadora

Le comunicaron la orden increíble de sacarla de allí.

Los hombres llevaban la vieja y pesada computadora.

Steps 2–4

Answers will vary.

CULTURA ◄
Standards: 1.1, 1.2, 3.1, 5.1

Suggestions: After students have read the information silently, ask comprehension questions. For example: *¿Está buscando el Departamento de Educación de México maestros o estudiantes?* (maestros) *¿Será un buen candidato una persona que no tiene computadora? Explica tu respuesta.* (*No. Un buen candidato tiene que tener habilidades para el trabajo con computadora y acceso a la Red.*)
Answers will vary.

Teacher-to-Teacher

Invite students to tell what they know about existing distance education programs. Encourage them to explain how the programs work and what their advantages and disadvantages are.

Additional Resources

Technology: Online Resources
- Guided, Writing, Reading
- Cultural Reading Activity

Print
- Guided WB pp. 206–207

Enrich Your Teaching

Culture Note

Today it is possible to study and travel "virtually." Distance-learning programs allow students to take courses throughout the world. International chat rooms create a place to meet and practice language skills. Many cultural and tourist destinations have their own Web sites.

21st Century Skills

Critical Thinking and Problem Solving Have students discuss the challenges that a foreign language student might face when enrolling in a distance learning program. What are the advantages and disadvantages of learning Spanish in a virtual classroom? How might a distance learning program help them learn Spanish? Are there some skills that they could practice more than others?

Auténtico

Standards: 1.2

Resources: Authentic Resources Wkbk, Cap. 6
Authentic Resources: Cap. 6: Videoscript
AP®Theme: *Los desafíos mundiales: Los temas económicos*

Antes de ver

Direct student's attention to the video image and ask them what they see and how they interpret it. What idea has the illustrator tried to convey about banking with this illustration? Then refer students to the *Estrategia*. Explain that by paraphrasing small parts of the video as they watch it, they will have a better understanding of the video as a whole. Then review the key vocabulary with the class. Ask students to identify the financial terms.

Technology: Ve el video

Before starting the video, direct students' attention to the *Mientras ves* activity. Have them complete the activity page from the Authentic Resources Workbook. Ask them to be ready to take notes while they watch the video.

Play the video once without pausing. Ask students to pay attention to the animation as a way to grasp the concepts of the video. Replay the video, this time stopping at key points to allow students to paraphrase that part. For example, pause after the conventional banker has been introduced, pause after the banker of the future has been introduced, pause after the connection with the past has been made, and so on. Then show the video a final time without pausing.

Haz las actividades

Mientras ves

Standards: 1.2

Suggestions: Invite students to share what they paraphrased with a partner. Then discuss the questions posed in the *Mientras ves* activity and guide students to infer the answers.

Answers:
- banquero convencional y banquero del futuro
- mostrar cómo será el banquero del futuro
- en blanco y negro para mostrar que la banca convencional es un trabajo mecánico; a color y como mujer para mostrar que la banca del futuro será más activa y abrirá más puertas a la mujer

---

Auténtico

Partnered with 🌐IDB

La banca del futuro

Antes de ver

Usa la estrategia: Resumir *(summarize)*

Mira la imagen. ¿Qué relación puede tener con la banca del futuro? Al ver el video, haz pausas para resumir lo que has entendido. Al final, parafrasea el tema, las ideas principales y los detalles.

Lee el vocabulario clave

banca = banking
ahorros = savings
préstamos = loans
canalizar = to channel
a corto plazo = short-term
accionistas = shareholders
ganancias = profit
vocación de servicio = spirit of service
inversión = investment

▶ Ve el video

¿Cómo crees que serán los banqueros del futuro? ¿Qué habilidades y talentos especiales deberán tener? ¿Qué servicios ofrecerán?

Ve a **PearsonSchool.com/Autentico** para ver el video **La banca del futuro** y conocer una interesante perspectiva sobre cómo serán los banqueros del mañana.

Haz las actividades

Mientras ves Mientras ves el video, pon mucha atención a los dibujos animados y al texto que ves en la pantalla porque te servirán de guía para inferir el significado de las palabras que no conoces. Toma notas de las ideas y los detalles que te ayuden a parafrasear cada parte. Guíate por estas preguntas:
- ¿Qué se compara en el video?
- ¿Cuál es el propósito del video?
- ¿Por qué se representa a la banca convencional en blanco y negro y a la banca del futuro como mujer y a color?

Differentiated Instruction

Heritage Speakers

Invite students to write a paragraph expressing their insights for the future of their heritage country. Guide them with questions such as: *¿De qué modo los trabajadores del mañana podrán ayudar a que el país tenga un mejor futuro?*

Advanced Learners

Invite students to work with a partner. One will be the conventional banker and the other will be the banker of the future. Ask them to watch the video one more time paying special attention to the way in which each type of banker is represented. Then encourage partners to have a debate in Spanish on who is doing a better job and why. Each student will support his or her position with ideas from the video.

Suggestions: Discuss each question with the students. For the first question, make a two-column chart on the board with the headings *Banquero convencional* and *Banquero del futuro*. Ask students to copy and complete the chart with information from the video.

Answers may vary:

1. Banquero convencional: Sus clientes son como números; trabaja de forma mecánica; su meta es obtener máximas ganancias. Banquero del futuro: Le preocupa la comunidad y el medio ambiente; quiere que sus clientes tomen buenas decisiones; es un agente de cambio social y económico.
2. El banquero del futuro ayudará más al cliente. Se preocupará por el impacto de sus decisiones en el medio ambiente. Será agente de cambio social y económico.
3. En el video hay dibujos animados que muestran pilas de dinero que van subiendo. Esto simboliza más dinero o máximas ganancias.

For more Authentic Resources: Assign the Authentic Resources Workbook activities for homework so that students can play the video on their own and complete the workbook activities at their own pace.

Pre-AP® Integration

Resources: Authentic Resources Wkbk, Cap. 6
Authentic Resources: Cap. 6: Videoscript

Suggestions: Before completing the Pre-AP® activity, have students go to the workbook and complete the worksheets for the additional resources.

Comparación cultural
Suggestions: Call on students to provide specific examples of the similarities and differences between banks in the United States and those in Latin America.

Integración

Después de ver Vuelve a ver el video y contesta estas preguntas.

1. Haz una tabla de dos columnas. En la primera, anota tres características del banquero convencional y en la segunda tres características del banquero del futuro.
2. Usa la información de la tabla para parafrasear el video. Incluye el tema, los detalles y las ideas principales.
3. Explica cómo los dibujos animados del video te ayudaron a inferir el significado de la frase "obtener las máximas ganancias".

For more activities, go to the Authentic Resources Workbook.

Desafíos mundiales y trabajos del futuro

Expansión Busca estos recursos en *Auténtico* en línea y contesta las preguntas.

 **6 Auténtico**

Integración de ideas ¿De qué manera los trabajos del futuro podrán contribuir a solucionar algunos de los desafíos *(challenges)* mundiales que enfrentamos hoy?

Comparación cultural ¿Crees que el trabajo de los banqueros es similar en América Latina y Estados Unidos? Justifica tu respuesta con datos del video y tus concimientos previos.

Enrich Your Teaching

21st Century Skills

Leadership and Responsibility Invite students to write a couple of paragraphs in Spanish describing how a concept from the past could be rediscovered or reinvented in favor of a better future. As an example, remind them of how the video refers to the *vocación de servicio* as a concept from the past that can be reclaimed by the banking of the future. What other concept, custom, or way of doing something in the past would be valuable for a better society in the future?

Using Authentic Resources

Have students create a personal vocabulary list with terms from the authentic resources that are related to job prospects for the future.

Review Activities

Profesiones y oficios/Sustantivos asociados con el futuro: Have students prepare cards or slips of paper for each vocabulary item in these categories. Divide students into groups and assign each group a section of the vocabulary items. Place the cards or slips from each category into two separate containers. Have students take turns drawing an item from each pile. If there is an obvious connection between the two items drawn, the student makes that connection in a sentence that uses both items. If there is not, the student tells about a connection that might exist in the future. For example: ***el (la) peluquero(a)/el aparato*** – *Una peluquera usa varios aparatos eléctricos en su trabajo.* ***el (la) peluquero(a)/el gen*** – *El peluquero del futuro cambiará los genes de sus clientes para que tengan el pelo perfecto.*

Cualidades/Campos y carreras del futuro: Have students use these items in sentences that make it clear they understand their meanings.

Verbos: Have students work in pairs. Partners take turns using a verb in a sentence that either makes sense or doesn't. If the sentence makes sense, the other partner says so and goes to the next verb. If the sentence does not make sense, the partner must explain why it doesn't or correct it so that it does.

Otras palabras y expresiones: Students can use these words and expressions as they go over the review activities for the other categories.

El futuro: Have students pretend they are a wizard from 300 years ago who is very good at making accurate predictions about what life will be like in the twenty-first century. Have them tell about life today: *Cada casa tendrá una caja mágica que da visiones de las cosas que pasan en otras partes del mundo. En vez de leer libros, la gente mirará las imágenes en la caja mágica.*

Repaso del capítulo

🔊 Vocabulario

profesiones y oficios

el / la abogado(a)	lawyer
el / la arquitecto(a)	architect
el / la banquero(a)	banker
el / la científico(a)	scientist
el / la cocinero(a)	cook
el / la contador(a)	accountant
el / la diseñador(a)	designer
la empresa	business
las finanzas	finance
el hombre de negocios, la mujer de negocios	businessman, businesswoman
el / la ingeniero(a)	engineer
el / la jefe(a)	boss
el / la juez(a)	judge
el / la peluquero(a)	hairstylist
el / la programador(a)	programmer
el / la redactor(a)	editor
el / la traductor(a)	translator

cualidades

ambicioso, -a	ambitious
capaz	able
cuidadoso, -a	careful
eficiente	efficient
emprendedor, -a	enterprising
maduro, -a	mature

verbos

ahorrar	to save
aumentar	to increase
averiguar	to find out
comunicarse	to communicate
contaminar	to pollute
curar	to cure
dedicarse a	to dedicate oneself to
desaparecer	to disappear
descubrir	to discover
desempeñar un cargo	to hold a position
diseñar	to design
enterarse	to find out
graduarse (u → ú)	to graduate
hacerse	to become
inventar	to invent

lograr	to achieve, to manage (to)
mudarse	to move to
predecir	to predict
prolongar	to prolong, to extend
reducir (zc)	to reduce
reemplazar	to replace
seguir una carrera	to pursue a career
tomar decisiones	to make decisions
traducir	to translate

sustantivos asociados con el futuro

el aparato	gadget
el avance	advance
el desarrollo	development
la enfermedad	illness
la fábrica	factory
la fuente de energía	energy source
el gen, *pl.* los genes	gene
la genética	genetics
el invento	invention
la máquina	machine
la mayoría	the majority
los medios de comunicación	media
el ocio	free time
la realidad virtual	virtual reality
tecnológico, -a	technological
el uso	use
vía satélite	via satellite
la vivienda	housing

otras palabras y expresiones

así que	therefore
además de	in addition to
casado, -a	married
como si fuera	as though it were
de hoy en adelante	from now on
haré lo que me dé la gana	I'll do as I please
por lo tanto	therefore
próximo, -a	next
soltero, -a	single
tener en cuenta	to take into account

Differentiated Instruction

Students with Learning Difficulties

To help students reinforce vocabulary comprehension, have them create their own flashcards. On one side of the card, have them write a vocabulary word. On the other side, they can draw a picture or write a Spanish synonym or other clue.

Advanced Learners

Invite students to create a video about a profession of the future. This could be a future version of a profession that exists today or one that is yet unheard of. Have one or more students dramatize the profession while a narrator explains it.

Más recursos | PearsonSchool.com/Autentico

⊞ **Games**   ▤ **Flashcards**   ✏ **Instant check**   ▶ **Tutorials**

campos y carreras del futuro

el campo	field	la informática	information technology
la demanda	demand	el mercadeo	marketing
la estrategia	strategy	el producto	product
la hospitalidad	hospitality	el servicio	service
la industria	industry		

Gramática

el futuro

To express the future in Spanish, you can use *ir + a* + infinitive, the present tense, or the future. For most verbs, attach the endings (*-é, -ás, -á, -emos, -éis, -án*) to the infinitive.

pasar *to pass*

pasar**é**	pasar**emos**
pasar**ás**	pasar**éis**
pasar**á**	pasar**án**

comer *to eat*

comer**é**	comer**emos**
comer**ás**	comer**éis**
comer**á**	comer**án**

pedir *to ask*

pedir**é**	pedir**emos**
pedir**ás**	pedir**éis**
pedir**á**	pedir**án**

Other verbs have irregular stems in the future but have the same endings as the regular verbs.

haber	**habr-**
hacer	**har-**
saber	**sabr-**
tener	**tendr-**
poder	**podr-**
decir	**dir-**
salir	**saldr-**
querer	**querr-**
poner	**pondr-**
venir	**vendr-**

el futuro de probabilidad

In Spanish the future tense can express uncertainty or probability in the present.

¿Qué hora **será**? *(I wonder what time it is.)*

el futuro perfecto

Use the future perfect tense to express what will have happened by a certain time. To form the future perfect, use the future of the verb *haber* with the past participle of the verb.

pasar *to pass*

ha**bré** pasado	ha**bremos** pasado
ha**brás** pasado	ha**bréis** pasado
ha**brá** pasado	ha**brán** pasado

el uso de los complementos directos e indirectos

The indirect object pronoun goes before the direct object pronoun.

Te los traduciré. (los libros)

In the third person, the indirect objects *le / les* become **se** before the indirect objects *lo / la, los / las.* You can add the prepositional phrase *a Ud., a él, a ella,* etc., or *a* + a noun / name for clarification.

Se los traduciré a ella.

When the object pronouns are attached to an infinitive, a command, or a present participle, you must add an accent mark to keep the stress: *traducírmelos, tradúcemelos, traduciéndomelos.*

El futuro de probabilidad: Have students work in pairs, sitting back to back. One partner performs a simple action that the other can't see. Actions might include writing, holding up a number of fingers, or putting on a hat. The other partner tries to guess the action using the future tense: *¿Escribirás algo? ¿No tendrás unos dedos en el aire? ¿Llevarás puesto tu sombrero?*

El futuro perfecto: Have students make predictions about things that will have happened by the year 2110: *Habremos colonizado otros planetas. Gracias a la genética, todas las enfermedades habrán desaparecido.*

El uso de los complementos directos e indirectos: Have students work in groups of three. Individually, they think of two sentences describing actions that they can perform in the group. Each action should involve a direct object and refer to one or both of the other students as the indirect object. For example: *Les digo un secreto a Uds. dos* or *Le doy mi cuaderno a Mark.* Have them take turns saying their sentences. The other two protest and turn the sentence into a negative command using pronouns: *¡No, no nos lo digas! ¡No, no se lo des!*

Digital Portfolio

Invite students to review the activities, reports and projects they completed in this chapter, including written reports, posters or other visuals, recordings of oral presentations, and other projects. Have them select one or two items that they feel best demonstrate their achievements in Spanish. Include these products in students' portfolios with the Chapter Checklist and Self-Assessment Worksheet.

Pre-AP® Integration

- **Learning Objective:** Interpersonal Speaking
- **Activity:** Remind students to focus on the speaking skills used in this task such as fluency, pronunciation, and comprehensibility.
- **Pre-AP® Resource Materials:** Comprehensive guide to Pre-AP® speaking skill development

Additional Resources

 Technology: Online Resources
- *Para hispanohablantes*

Teacher Resources
- Teacher's Resource Materials: Situation Cards, Clip Art

 Technology: ¡Pura vida! is a storyline video that is independent of chapter content and an ideal support for expanding listening skills. The 14 episodes are available within **Realize.** Student activities and Teacher support are also assignable within **Realize.**

Enrich Your Teaching

Teacher-to-Teacher

Using imperative forms and pronouns are some of the most difficult skills your students have to learn, and yet they are a common part of everyday speech. Provide students with plenty of accurate models and give them every opportunity possible to practice using these structures.

21st Century Skills

ICT (Information, Communications and Technology) Literacy Remind students of the various digital tools available in **Realize** to help them monitor their own understanding and learning needs, especially as a review of the chapter. There are online tutorials with comprehension check exercises, interactive puzzles, flashcards, and self-tests.

Performance Tasks

Standards: 1.1, 1.2, 1.3, 4.2

Student Resource: *Para hispanohablantes*

Teacher Resources: Teacher's Resource Materials: Audio Script, Technology: Audio Cap. 6

1. Vocabulario

Suggestions: Encourage students to review the vocabulary from the *Vocabulario en contexto* sections on pp. 262–264 and 276–279 before they complete the activity.

Answers:

1. b	**5.** c
2. b	**6.** c
3. a	**7.** a
4. a	**8.** b

2. Gramática

Suggestions: Remind students of the main points of the grammar presentations in *Capítulo* 6:

- the future tense
- the future tense used for probability
- the future perfect tense
- use of direct and indirect object pronouns together

Answers:

1. b	**5.** a
2. b	**6.** a
3. c	**7.** a
4. d	**8.** d

Repaso del capítulo

OBJECTIVE
▶ Demonstrate that you can perform the tasks on these pages

Preparación para el examen

❶ Vocabulario Escribe la letra de la palabra o expresión que mejor complete cada frase. Escribe tus respuestas en una hoja aparte.

1. Tengo que _____ qué cursos ofrecen en la universidad.
   a. desarrollar   c. inventar
   b. averiguar   d. prolongar

2. Después de terminar sus estudios, mi hermano piensa _____ a otro estado.
   a. dedicarse   c. enterarse
   b. mudarse   d. comunicarse

3. Cuando una persona sabe hacer algo bien, se dice que es _____.
   a. capaz   c. madura
   b. entrometida   d. sincera

4. Gracias a _____ como el teléfono celular podemos comunicarnos desde muchos lugares.
   a. aparatos   c. campos
   b. transportes   d. servicios

5. Los avances en la genética harán posible curar _____.
   a. la contaminación   c. las enfermedades
   b. las viviendas   d. el ocio

6. La _____ te permite vivir una experiencia como si fuera real.
   a. vivienda   c. realidad virtual
   b. genética   d. informática

7. A Jorge le gusta resolver problemas y tomar decisiones sin ayuda. Es muy _____.
   a. emprendedor   c. honesto
   b. cuidadoso   d. puntual

8. Creo que _____ me voy a dedicar a la medicina.
   a. así que   c. tener en cuenta
   b. de hoy en adelante   d. como si fuera

❷ Gramática Escribe la letra de la palabra o expresión que mejor complete cada frase. Escribe tus respuestas en una hoja aparte.

1. El año próximo _____ mi sueño de viajar por todo el mundo.
   a. realicé   c. realizo
   b. realizaré   d. estoy realizando

2. Andrés quiere ser traductor. El año que viene _____ en las Naciones Unidas.
   a. trabaja   c. está trabajando
   b. trabajará   d. trabajaba

3. No tengo reloj. ¿Qué hora _____?
   a. estará   c. será
   b. saldrá   d. era

4. Si necesitas un texto de genética, yo _____ prestaré.
   a. te la   c. se lo
   b. te los   d. te lo

5. ¿Vio usted el programa sobre los inventos del siglo XX? _____ prestaré.
   a. Se lo   c. Me lo
   b. Se la   d. Te la

6. Quiero ver las fotos que sacaste ayer. _____ por favor.
   a. Dámelas   c. Déle
   b. Dáselas   d. Déselas

7. Dentro de 20 años, ya _____ otras fuentes de energía.
   a. habrán descubierto   c. descubrieron
   b. han descubierto   d. están descubriendo

8. Para el año 2020, muchos aparatos que ahora se usan ya _____.
   a. han desaparecido   c. están desapareciendo
   b. desaparecen   d. habrán desaparecido

Differentiated Instruction

Heritage Speakers

Ask students to draft their own set of multiple-choice review questions based on the vocabulary and grammar points of the chapter. Have them trade questions with a partner. Students should not only choose the correct answer, but also proofread their partner's questions for errors.

Students with Special Needs

Give hearing impaired students a transcribed or illustrated version of the conversation in the listening section of the exam. Have students work in pairs and track the appropriate text as the dialogue is played.

Más recursos PearsonSchool.com/Autentico

⊞ Games ▱ Flashcards ☑ Instant check

▶ Tutorials

En el examen vas a . . .	Éstas son las tareas de práctica que te pueden ser útiles para el examen . . .	Para repasar, ve a tu libro de texto impreso o digital . . .
Interpretive		
3 ESCUCHAR Yo puedo escuchar y comprender una conversación entre dos jóvenes.	Félix y Carmen hablan sobre sus planes para el futuro. Escucha su conversación y di (a) qué intereses y habilidades tiene cada uno; (b) cuáles son sus planes para después de graduarse de la escuela secundaria; (c) cuáles son sus sueños para su carrera.	**pp. 262–264** *Vocabulario en contexto* 1 **p. 263** Actividad 1 **p. 264** Actividad 3 **p. 265** *Videohistoria* **p. 279** Actividad 22 **pp. 298–299** *Auténtico*
Interpersonal		
4 HABLAR Yo puedo hablar de mis preferencias y de lo que quiero hacer en el futuro.	Imagina que te entrevistas con una consejera que te ayudará a decidir qué carrera debes estudiar y a qué universidad debes ir. Explícale cuáles son tus intereses y cualidades, qué trabajo te gustaría tener, qué sueños quieres realizar, qué quieres lograr, en fin, explícale qué quieres hacer con tu vida.	**p. 268** Actividad 9 **p. 269** Actividad 10 **p. 271** Actividad 12
Interpretive		
5 LEER Yo puedo leer y comprender las predicciones de un futurólogo.	Lee este fragmento del artículo de un futurólogo. ¿Esta persona cree que el futuro será mejor o peor que el presente? ¿Por qué? *En el futuro viviremos en paz, pues en unos años habrá nuevos inventos y aparatos que permitirán una mejor comunicación entre las personas. Además, gracias a ciencias nuevas como la informática y la genética, en 50 ó 60 años no habrá hambre ni enfermedades. Todos vivirán 100 años y trabajarán mucho menos que nosotros.*	**pp. 276–279** *Vocabulario en contexto* 2 **p. 280** Actividad 25 **p. 282** Actividades 28, 29 **p. 287** Actividad 36
Presentational		
6 ESCRIBIR Yo puedo escribir sobre los avances que habrá en el futuro.	Escribe sobre los principales avances y problemas que crees que habrá en los 50 años que vienen. Di dos cosas que crees que habrán ocurrido. ¿Cómo cambiará la vida de la gente? ¿Cuáles serán los problemas más difíciles que tendrán que resolver?	**p. 277** Actividad 21 **p. 279** Actividad 23 **p. 281** Actividad 27 **p. 283** Actividad 30
Comparisons		
7 COMPARAR Yo puedo comparar la actitud de los jóvenes norteamericanos con la de algunos jóvenes españoles que prefieren vivir con sus padres al terminar de estudiar.	Piensa por qué te gustará o no te gustará vivir con tus padres cuando termines tus estudios. Compara tus razones con las de algunos jóvenes españoles.	**p. 267** *Cultura* **p. 272** Actividad 15 **p. 292** *Presentación escrita*

Differentiated Assessment

Core Assessment
- Technology: Audio Cap. 6
- ExamView: Chapter Test, Test Banks A and B

Challenge/Pre-AP®
- ExamView: Pre-AP® Test Bank
- Pre-AP® Resource Materials

Extra Support
- Alternate Assessment Program: Examen del capítulo 6
- Technology: Audio Cap. 6

Heritage Speakers
- Assessment Program: Para hispanohablantes: Examen del Capítulo 6
- ExamView: Speaker Learner Test Bank

3. Escuchar

Suggestions: Use the audio or read from the script.

(See Teacher's Resource Materials for script.)

Answers:

a. Intereses y habilidades: Félix: finanzas, banca; eficiente, emprendedor Carmen: le gustan los libros, es bilingüe

b. Carmen y Félix piensan seguir estudiando para ser traductora y banquero.

c. Sus sueños:
Félix: ganar mucho dinero y hacer lo que le dé la gana. Quiere ser banquero. Carmen: Quiere ser traductora. Quiere viajar al extranjero y aprender más sobre los países del mundo.

4. Hablar

Suggestions: Point out that this activity requires students to use a variety of tenses. They might use the present tense to talk about their personal qualities and the future tenses and subjunctive mood to tell about their plans for the future.

Answers will vary.

5. Leer

Suggestions: Tell students to refer to pp. 262–265 and 276–279 if they have questions about vocabulary in the review.

Answers:

Esta persona cree que el futuro será mejor que el presente.

Answers will vary.

6. Escribir

Suggestions: After students have completed their writing, ask them how their perceptions of the future have changed since they began *Capítulo* 6.

Answers will vary.

7. Comparar

Suggestions: Encourage students to write down their thoughts in a T-chart with the two columns entitled **A favor de** and **En contra de.**

Answers will vary.

Additional Resources

📶 **Technology: Online Resources**
- Instant Check
- *Para hispanohablantes*

Print
- Core WB pp. 89–90

CAPÍTULO 7

¿Mito o realidad?

Myths, legends, and mysterious events

Vocabulary: archeaological discoveries and mysteries; description of objects; myths and legends;

Grammar: present and present perfect subjunctive after expressions of doubt, uncertainty, or disbelief; uses of *pero* and *sino*; subjunctive in adjective clauses

Cultural Perspectives: prehispanic civilizations as viewed in the art of Diego Rivera; two wonders of Peru: the Inca Trail and Machu Picchu; Aztec myths and legends; contributions of the Mayan and Aztec civilizations; mysteries of pre-Columbian civilizations

¡Pura vida!: Watch an engaging video episode about a group of young people in Costa Rica!

Chapter Support

Bulletin Boards

Theme: Las culturas indígenas latinoamericanas

Ask students to cut out, copy, or download images of the Aztecs, Mayas, or other indigenous groups in Latin America. Images can include examples of clothing, folk art, crafts, and food. Cluster photos around the name of each group that is chosen.

Hands-on Culture

Music: Songs from Spain and Latin America

The fusion of old and new music styles has revived many traditional beats and sounds, such as flamenco, salsa, and cumbia.

Directions:

1. Type out names of Hispanic musical artists and distribute copies to students. Some artists to look for are: Gypsy Kings and Carlos Villalobos (flamenco), Gloria Estefan (salsa), Tito Puente (salsa, boleros, cumbia), and Inti Illimani (Andean).
2. Divide students into four groups. Assign two students with artistic skills to each group.
3. Ask students to do research about their artist on the Internet and record music clips.
4. Each group types out a fact sheet about their artist with information from the research and makes copies for the class. They can add the artist's photo in the fact sheet.
5. Each group chooses a leader, who makes a presentation of their artist to the class.
6. The leader reads the fact sheet and plays some music by the artist to the class.

Game

Encuentra dónde estamos

Play this game to review the information about archaeological sites from *Capítulo 7*.

Players: entire class, playing in teams

Materials: slips of paper, a large world map, markers, pins or masking tape

Preparation: Prepare ahead. Draw with different color markers on the map the outlines of Mexico, Peru, Bolivia, Guatemala, and Isla de Pascua. On slips of paper, write the names of different ancient cities and indigenous groups described in *Capítulo 7, such as ruinas de Palenque, los aztecas, los mayas, ruinas de Cobá y Tulúm, ciudad de Teotihuacán, cabezas de los olmecas, Chichen Itzá, Líneas de Nazca, estatuas moai, indígenas quichés, ciudad de Machu Picchu, ciudad de Tiahuanaco.* Place the slips of paper in a bag.

Rules:

1. Students prepare for the game. Ask them to review *Capítulo 7*, paying attention to the location of the archaeological sites and the indigenous groups described.
2. Divide the class into teams. Each member of the team take turns taking a paper from the bag.
3. If the student places the note in the correct place on the map, the team receives 5 points.
4. If he or she can also give additional information, the team receives another 5 points.
5. The team with the most points when the bag is empty wins.

Variation: Names of indigenous groups from the United States can also be written on the slips of paper. In this case, the outline of the United States should be included.

21st Century Skills

Look for tips throughout Chapter 7 to enrich your teaching by integrating 21st Century Skills. Suggestions for the Project-Based Learning and Culture follow below.

Project-Based Learning

Modify the project with these suggestions:

ICT (Information, Communications and Technology) Literacy Encourage students to go online to their favorite Web sites to choose an indigenous group from the United States or Latin America. Then have them search for museum Web sites to view a variety of artwork from the indigenous group they have chosen.

Creativity and Innovation Encourage students with artistic interests to expand on the project's task by creating their own version of the indigenous artifacts in their presentation. Interested students can create their own tri-dimensional model of the artifact in different media, such as papier-maché, clay, or other materials, and share with the class their reasons for choosing it.

Communication As students prepare to present their project to the class, provide them with the handout "Give an Effective Presentation" to remind them of the importance of body language, tone of voice, eye contact, and other strategies for delivering an effective presentation.

Chapter Culture

Social and Cross-Cultural Skills Direct the students to the *Cultura* notes on pages 308 and 322. After reviewing the information in the notes, have them consider the similarities and differences between ancient and modern architecture. What functions do large construction projects have in a culture? Have students provide specific examples.

▶ **Technology: Videodocumentario**
View *¿Cómo se explican los misterios del mundo?* online with the class to learn more about the mysteries behind three ancient sites: Machu Picchu, Chichén Itzá and Teotihuacán.

Project-Based Learning

Cartel de arte indígena

Overview: Using the computer, students create an illustrated poster to show a piece of indigenous art. They research art of an indigenous group they know from the United States or Latin America and choose one or more images to create an interesting visual composition. Posters should include a message or two and a title. Students then present their poster to the class and describe what the art means, the indigenous group it belongs to, and why they chose those images.

Resources: digital or print photos, image editing and page layout software

Sequence: (suggestions for when to do each step are found throughout the chapter)

Step 1. Review instructions so students know what is expected of them. Share the rubric with the class.

Step 2. Students submit a sketch of their poster. Return the sketches with your suggestions.

Step 3. Students do layouts setting space for the messages. Encourage them to try different arrangements before placing their images.

Step 4. Students submit a draft of the messages and a paragraph for the presentation. Note your corrections and suggestions, then return drafts to students.

Step 5. Students make a brief presentation of their posters to the class.

Options

1. Students create a collage, using printed material.
2. Students make a brief presentation of the indigenous group they chose.

Assessment

Here is a detailed rubric for assessing this project:

Chapter 7 Project: Cartel de arte indígena

Rubric	Score 1	Score 3	Score 5
Your evidence of planning	You provide no poster layout or written draft.	You provide a layout and written draft, but they are not corrected.	You show evidence of corrected draft and layout.
Your use of illustrations	You include no art images, or they are not indigenous art.	You include images, but layout is not well organized.	Your poster is carefully done and images are consistent with text.
Your presentation	You include little of the required information.	You include most of the required information.	You include all of the required information.

AT A GLANCE

Objectives
- Listen and read about archeology and Pre-Columbian legends
- Talk and write about mysterious events
- Provide logical explanations for unexplained phenomena
- Mysteries of past civilizations in Latin America
- Provide explanations for Pre-Columbian myths
- Compare cultural products in an authentic audio recording about Machu Picchu

Vocabulary
- Discoveries
- Myths, legends, and unexplained phenomena
- Expressions of doubt
- Descriptions of the shapes and size of objects
- The universe

Grammar
- Present subjunctive and present perfect subjunctive with expressions of doubt
- Uses of **pero** and **sino**
- Subjunctive with adjective clauses

Culture
- Diego Rivera, p. 308
- Atlantis: Mystery or historical fact?, p. 316
- Inca trail to Machu Picchu, p. 322
- Mayan and Aztec cultures, pp. 326–327
- Aztec calendar, p. 328
- A Quiché legend, p. 330
- Easter Island, the Olmecs, and the Nazca lines, pp. 336–337
- Miguel de Cervantes Saavedra, p. 345

A ver si recuerdas...
- Architecture and materials
- Nature, animals, and places
- Negative constructions
- Adjectives used as nouns

Recycle
- Pronunciation of diphthong **ue**
- Pronouns **vosotros** and **vosotras**

Authentic Resources
- **Auténtico:** El secreto de Machu Picchu, pp. 346–347

RESOURCES

	FOR THE STUDENT	DIGITAL	PRINT	FOR THE TEACHER	DIGITAL	PRINT
A ver si recuerdas pp. 304–307						
Review	*A ver si recuerdas* with Remediation	•		*A ver si recuerdas* with Remediation	•	
	Guided WB, pp. 208–211	•	•	Teacher's Edition, pp. 304–307	•	•
	Core WB, pp. 91–92	•	•			
	Para hispanohablantes	•				
Introducción pp. 308–309						
Present	Student Edition, pp. 308–309	•	•	Teacher's Edition, pp. 308–309	•	•
	DK Reference Atlas	•		Teacher's Resource Materials	•	
	Videonovela: ¡Pura vida!	•		Mapa global interactivo	•	
	¡Pura vida! Video Activities	•				
	Para hispanohablantes	•				
Vocabulario en contexto pp. 310–313/324–327						
Present & Practice	Student Edition, pp. 310–313/324–327	•	•	Teacher's Edition, pp. 310–313/324–327	•	•
	Audio	•		Teacher's Resource Materials	•	
	Videohistoria	•		Vocabulary Clip Art	•	
	Flashcards	•		Technology: Audio	•	
	Instant Check	•		Video Program: Videohistoria	•	
	Guided WB, pp. 212–220/223–230	•	•			
	Core WB, pp. 93–94/98–99	•	•			
	Communication Activities	•				
	Para hispanohablantes	•				
Assess and Remediate				Pruebas 7–1, 7–4: Assessment Program, Assessment Program *Para hispanohablantes*	•	

RESOURCES

FOR THE STUDENT	DIGITAL	PRINT	FOR THE TEACHER	DIGITAL	PRINT
Vocabulario en uso pp. 314–317/328–330					
Present & Practice Student Edition, pp. 314–317/328–330	•	•	Interactive Whiteboard Vocabulary Activities	•	
Instant Check	•		Teacher's Edition, pp. 314–317/328–330	•	•
Communication Activities	•		Teacher's Resource Materials	•	
Para hispanohablantes	•		Technology: Audio	•	
Communication Activities	•		Videomodelos	•	
			Mapa global interactivo	•	
Assess and Remediate			Pruebas 7–2, 7–5 with Remediation	•	
			Pruebas 7–2, 7–5: Assessment Program, Assessment Program *Para hispanohablantes*	•	
Gramática pp. 318–323/331–335					
Present & Practice Student Edition, pp. 318–323/331–335	•	•	Interactive Whiteboard Grammar Activities	•	
Instant Check	•		Teacher's Edition, pp. 318–323/331–335	•	•
Tutorial Video: Grammar	•		Teacher's Resource Materials	•	
Canción de hip hop	•		Technology: Audio	•	
Guided WB, pp. 221–222/231–234	•	•	Videomodelos	•	
Core WB, pp. 95–97/100–102	•	•	Mapa global interactivo	•	
Communication Activities	•				
Para hispanohablantes	•				
Communicative Pair Activities	•				
Assess and Remediate			Pruebas 7–3, 7–6, 7–7 with Remediation	•	
			Pruebas 7–3, 7–6, 7–7: Assessment Program, Assessment Program *Para hispanohablantes*	•	
			Examen 1, Examen 2: Vocab. y gramática	•	
Aplicación pp. 336–347					
Apply Student Edition, pp. 336–347	•	•	Teacher's Edition, pp. 336–347	•	•
Authentic Resources Workbook	•	•	Teacher's Resource Materials	•	
Authentic Resources	•		Video Program: Videodocumentario	•	
Online Cultural Reading	•		Mapa global interactivo	•	
Guided WB, pp. 235–237	•	•	Authentic Resources Lesson Plans with scripts, answer keys	•	
Communication Activities	•				
Para hispanohablantes	•				
Videodocumentario	•				
Auténtico	•				
Repaso del capítulo pp. 348–351					
Review Student Edition, pp. 348–351	•	•	Teacher's Edition, pp. 348–351	•	•
Core WB, pp. 103–104	•	•	Teacher's Resource Materials	•	
Communication Activities	•		Technology: Audio	•	
Para hispanohablantes	•				
Instant Check	•				
Chapter Assessment					
Assess			Examen del capítulo 7: Assessment Program, Alternate Assessment Program, Assessment Program *Para hispanohablantes*	•	
			Technology: Audio Cap. 7, Examen	•	
			ExamView: Test Banks A and B (questions only online) Heritage Speaker Test Bank, Pre-AP® Test Bank	•	

LESSON PLAN

DAY	Warm-up / Assess	Preview / Present / Practice / Communicate		Wrap-up / Homework Options
1	**Warm-up** (10 min.) • Return Examen del capítulo: Capítulo 6	**Repaso** (35 min.) • A ver si recuerdas . . . • Actividades 1, 2, 4, 5, 7		**Wrap-up and Homework Options** (5 min.) • Core Practice 7-1, 7-2
2	**Warm-up** (10 min.) • Homework check	**Chapter Opener** (10 min.) • Objectives • Arte y cultura	**Vocabulario en contexto 1** (25 min.) • Presentation: Vocabulario y gramática en contexto • Actividades 1, 2, 3, 4, 5	**Wrap-up and Homework Options** (5 min.) • Clip Art Vocabulary
3	**Warm-up** (10 min.) • Homework check	**Vocabulario en contexto 1** (20 min.) • Presentation: Videohistoria • Después de ver	**Vocabulario en uso 1** (5 min.) • Interactive Whiteboard Vocabulary Activities • Actividades 4, 5	**Wrap-up and Homework Options** (5 min.) • Core Practice 7-3, 7-4 • Actividad 8 • Prueba 7-1: Vocabulary recognition
4	**Warm-up** (10 min.) • Homework check • **Formative Assessment** (10 min.) • Prueba 7-1: Vocabulary recognition	**Vocabulario en uso 1** (25 min.) • Actividades 6, 7, 9, 10 • Audio Activity • Ampliación del lenguaje		**Wrap-up and Homework Options** (5 min.) • Writing Activities • Prueba 7-2 with Remediation: Vocabulary production
5	**Warm-up** (15 min.) • Homework check • Communicative Pair Activity • **Formative Assessment** (10 min.) • Prueba 7-2 with Remediation: Vocabulary production	**Gramática y vocabulario en uso 1** (20 min.) • Presentation: Subjuntivo con expresiones de duda • Interactive Whiteboard Grammar Activities • Actividades 11, 12, 13		**Wrap-up and Homework Options** (5 min.) • Core Practice 7-5, 7-6, 7-7
6	**Warm-up** (10 min.) • Homework check	**Gramática y vocabulario en uso 1 (35 min.)** • Actividades 14, 15, 16 • Cultura		**Wrap-up and Homework Options** (5 min.) • Actividad 19
7	**Warm-up** (10 min.) • Homework check	**Gramática y vocabulario en uso 1** (35 min.) • Actividades 17, 18, 19 • Writing Activity • Communicative Pair Activity • En voz alta		**Wrap-up and Homework Options** (5 min.) • Writing Activity • Prueba 7-3 with Remediation: Subjuntivo con expresiones de duda
8	**Warm-up** (10 min.) • Homework check • **Formative Assessment** (10 min.) • Prueba 7-3 with Remediation: Subjuntivo con expresiones de duda	**Vocabulario en contexto 2** (25 min.) • Presentation: Vocabulario y gramática en contexto • Actividades 20, 21		**Wrap-up and Homework Options** (5 min.) • Clip Art Vocabulary • Examen: Vocabulario y gramática 1
9	**Warm-up** (5 min.) • Homework check • **Formative Assessment** (30 min.) • Examen: Vocabulario y gramática 1	**Vocabulario en contexto 2** (10 min.) • Presentation: Los mayas y los aztecas • Actividad 22		**Wrap-up and Homework Options** (5 min.) • Core Practice 7-8, 7-9 • Prueba 7-4: Vocabulary recognition
10	**Warm-up** (20 min.) • Homework check • **Formative Assessment** (10 min.) • Prueba 7-5: Vocabulary recognition	**Vocabulario en uso 2** (15 min.) • Actividades 23, 24, 25 • Interactive Whiteboard Vocabulary Activities		**Wrap-up and Homework Options** (5 min.) • Actividades 26, 27

LESSON PLAN

DAY	Warm-up / Assess	Preview / Present / Practice / Communicate		Wrap-up / Homework Options
11	**Warm-up** (15 min.) • Homework check	**Vocabulario en uso 2** (15 min.) • En voz alta • Audio Activity • Writing Activity • Communicative Pair Activity	**Gramática y vocabulario en uso 2** (15 min.) • Presentation: *Pero* y *sino* • Interactive Whiteboard Grammar Activities • Actividades 28, 29	**Wrap-up and Homework Options** (5 min.) • Core Practice 7-10 • Prueba 7-5 with Remediation: Vocabulary production
12	**Warm-up** (10 min.) • Homework check • **Formative Assessment** (10 min.) • Prueba 7-5 with Remediation: Vocabulary production	**Gramática y vocabulario en uso 2 (25 min.)** • Writing Activity 11 • Presentation: El subjuntivo en cláusulas adjetivas • Interactive Whiteboard Grammar Activities • Actividades 30, 31, 32		**Wrap-up and Homework Options** (5 min.) • Core Practice 7-11, 7-12 • Prueba 7-6 with Remediation: *Pero* y *sino*
13	**Warm-up** (10 min.) • Homework check • **Formative Assessment** (10 min.) • Prueba 7-6 with Remediation: *Pero* y *sino*	**Gramática y vocabulario en uso 2** (25 min.) • Actividades 33, 34, 35 • El español en el mundo del trabajo		**Wrap-up and Homework Options** (5 min.) • Writing Activity • Prueba 7-7 with Remediation: El subjuntivo en cláusulas adjetivas
14	**Warm-up** (10 min.) • Communicative Activity • Audio Activity • **Formative Assessment** (10 min.) • Prueba 7-7 with Remediation: El subjuntivo en cláusulas adjetivas	**Aplicación** (25 min.) • Puente a la cultura • ¿Comprendiste? • Investiga • Presentación oral: Step 1		**Wrap-up and Homework Options** (5 min.) • Examen: Vocabulario y gramática 2
15	**Warm-up** (10 min.) • Answer questions • **Formative Assessment** (20 min.) • Examen: Vocabulario y gramática 2	**Aplicación** (15 min.) • Presentación oral: Step 2		**Wrap-up and Homework Options** (5 min.) • Presentación oral: Step 3
16	**Warm-up** (15 min.) • Homework check	**Aplicación** (30 min.) • Presentación oral: Step 3 • Pre-AP® Integración 1, 2, 3		**Wrap-up and Homework Options** (5 min.) • Presentación escrita: Steps 1, 2
17	**Warm-up** (10 min.) • Homework check	**Aplicación** (35 min.) • Presentación oral: Step 3 • View Video • Video Activities 1, 2, 3 • Presentación escrita: Step 3		**Wrap-up and Homework Options** (5 min.) • Presentación escrita: Step 4 • Preparación para el examen: 1, 2
18	**Warm-up** (10 min.) • Homework check	**Aplicación** (25 min.) • Lectura • Interacción • Cultura • Auténtico **Repaso** (10 min.) • Preparación para el examen: Actividades 3, 4		**Wrap-up and Homework Options** (5 min.) • ¿Comprendiste? • Core Practice: Organizer 7-13, 7-14 • Instant Check
19	**Warm-up** (15 min.) • Homework check	**Repaso** (30 min.) • Preparación para el examen: Actividades 5, 6, 7 • Other review		**Wrap-up and Homework Options** (5 min.) • Examen del capítulo
20	**Warm-up** (5 min.) • Answer questions	• **Summative Assessment** (44 min.) • Examen del capítulo		**Wrap-up and Homework Options** (1 min.) • A ver si recuerdas: Capítulo 8

ALTERNATE LESSON PLAN

DAY	Warm-up / Assess	Preview / Present / Practice / Communicate	Wrap-up / Homework Options
1	**Warm-up** (35 min.) • Return Examen del capítulo: Capítulo 6 • A ver si recuerdas . . . • Homework check	**Chapter Opener** (10 min.) • Objectives • Arte y cultura **Vocabulario en contexto 1** (30 min.) • Presentation: Vocabulario y gramática en contexto • Actividades 1, 2, 3 • Presentation: Videohistoria • Después de ver **Vocabulario en uso 1** (10 min.) • Interactive Whiteboard Vocabulary Activities • Actividades 4, 5	**Wrap-up and Homework Options** (5 min.) • Core Practice 7-3, 7-4 • Clip Art Vocabulary • Prueba 7-1: Vocabulary recognition
2	**Warm-up** (15 min.) • Homework check • Actividades 6, 7 • **Formative Assessment** (15 min.) • Prueba 7-1: Vocabulary recognition	**Vocabulario en uso 1** (55 min.) • Actividades 8, 9, 10 • Ampliación del lenguaje • Audio Activity • Writing Activity • Communicative Pair Activity	**Wrap-up and Homework Options** (5 min.) • Prueba 7-2 with Remediation: Vocabulary production
3	**Warm-up** (5 min.) • Homework check • **Formative Assessment** (10 min.) • Prueba 7-2 with Remediation: Vocabulary production	**Gramática y vocabulario en uso 1** (70 min.) • Presentation: Subjuntivo con duda • Interactive Whiteboard Grammar Activities • Actividades 11, 12, 13, 14, 15, 16 • Cultura	**Wrap-up and Homework Options** (5 min.) • Cultura • Actividad 19 • Core Practice 7-5, 7-6, 7-7
4	**Warm-up** (10 min.) • Homework check	**Gramática y vocabulario en uso 1** (50 min.) • Actividades 17, 18 • Writing Activity • Communicative Pair Activity **Vocabulario en contexto 2** (25 min.) • Presentation: Vocabulario y gramática en contexto • Actividades 20, 21	**Wrap-up and Homework Options** (5 min.) • Prueba 7-3 with Remediation: El subjuntivo con duda • Examen: Vocabulario y gramática 1
5	**Warm-up** (10 min.) • Homework check • **Formative Assessment Options** (40 min.) • Prueba 7-3 with Remediation: El subjuntivo con duda • Examen: Vocabulario y gramática 1	**Vocabulario en contexto 2** (20 min.) • Presentation: Vocabulario y gramática en contexto • Actividad 22 **Vocabulario en uso 2** (15 min.) • Interactive Whiteboard Vocabulary Activities • Actividades 23, 24, 25	**Wrap-up and Homework Options** (5 min.) • Core Practice 7-8, 7-9 • Actividades 26, 27 • Clip Art • Prueba 7-4: Vocabulary recognition

ALTERNATE LESSON PLAN

DAY	Warm-up / Assess	Preview / Present / Practice / Communicate	Wrap-up / Homework Options
6	**Warm-up** (35 min.) • Homework check • En voz alta • Audio Activity • Writing Activity • **Formative Assessment** (10 min.) • Prueba 7-4: Vocabulary recognition	**Gramática y vocabulario en uso 2** (40 min.) • Presentation: *Pero* y *sino* • Interactive Whiteboard Grammar Activities • Actividades 28, 29 • Writing Activity 11	**Wrap-up and Homework Options** (5 min.) • Core Practice 7-10 • Pruebas 7-5, 7-6 with Remediations: Vocabulary production, *Pero* y *sino*
7	**Warm-up** (10 min.) • Writing Activity • Communicative Pair Activity • **Formative Assessment** (20 min.) • Pruebas 7-5, 7-6 with Remediations: Vocabulary production, *Pero* y *sino*	**Gramática y vocabulario en uso 2** (40 min.) • Presentation: Subjuntivo en cláusulas adjetivas • Interactive Whiteboard Grammar Activities • Actividades 30, 31, 32, 33, 34, 35 • El español en el mundo del trabajo **Aplicación** (15 min.) • Presentación oral: Steps 1, 2	**Wrap-up and Homework Options** (5 min.) • Core Practice 7-11, 7-12 • Writing Activity 12-13 • Prueba 7-7 with Remediation: El subjuntivo en cláusulas adjetivas • Presentación oral: Step 2 • Examen: Vocabulario y gramática 2
8	**Warm-up** (25 min.) • Homework check • Writing Activity • **Formative Assessment** (20 min.) • Prueba 7-7 with Remediation: El subjuntivo en cláusulas adjetivas	**Aplicación** (40 min.) • Presentación oral: Step 3 • Presentation: Misterios del pasado • ¿Comprendiste?	**Wrap-up and Homework Options** (5 min.) • ¿Comprendiste? • Investiga • Examen: Vocabulario y gramática 2
9	**Warm-up** (10 min.) • Homework check • **Formative Assessment** (25 min.) • Examen: Vocabulario y gramática 2	**Aplicación** (50 min.) • View Video • Video Activities • Pre-AP® Integración 1, 2, 3 • Presentación escrita: Step 1	**Wrap-up and Homework Options** (5 min.) • Presentación escrita: Step 2 • Preparación para el examen: Actividades 1, 2
10	**Warm-up** (20 min.) • Homework check • Presentación escrita: Step 3	**Aplicación** (35 min.) • Lectura • Interacción • ¿Comprendiste? • Cultura • Auténtico **Repaso** (30 min.) • Preparación para el examen: Actividades 3, 4, 6	**Wrap-up and Homework Options** (5 min.) • Presentación escrita: Step 4 • Core Practice: Organizer 7-13, 7-14 • Instant Check • Preparación para el examen: Actividades 5, 7 • Examen del capítulo
11	**Warm-up** (15 min.) • Homework check • **Summative Assessment** (45 min.) • Examen del capítulo	**Theme Game** (15 min.) **A ver si recuerdas – Capítulo 8** (10 min.) • Presentation: Vocabulario • Presentation: Gramática	**Wrap-up and Homework Options** (5 min.) • A ver si recuerdas – Capítulo 8 • Actividades 1–6 • Core Practice 8-1, 8-2

Vocabulario: Repaso

Standards: 1.1, 1.2

Suggestions: Before presenting the material in this review section, consider testing your students' command of the material by assigning the Prueba with Remediation. Students will automatically be given additional practice of the material they have not yet mastered, and you can focus your review based on the class's overall performance on the post-test.

Challenge students to create sentences that use vocabulary from as many categories as possible. For example: *Dentro de un palacio en el bosque, descubrimos una hermosa escultura de piedra.* This can be set up as a game. Students earn a point for every *Vocabulario* item used in a sentence that makes sense. Sentences in which items from all five categories are successfully used earn double, or ten, points. Sentences that don't make sense or are faultily constructed earn no points. The student who earns the most points wins.

Standards: 1.1, 1.2

Suggestions: In Step 1, encourage students to use the impersonal **se** when telling about what can be found in the various places. Provide a model such as *En la selva tropical de Honduras se pueden encontrar monumentos antiguos.*

Answers will vary.

Active Classroom

Group composition: Divide the class into groups of five. Each student is to begin a paragraph with a sentence that includes one of the negative expressions. Each student passes the paper with the first sentence to the student to his or her left. That student adds a sentence with a negative to the story. Pass to the left, again. Each student in turn adds a sentence to the story. When the paragraph returns to the first writer, have the group read each paragraph aloud to each other and determine the best "story." Have the group read the "best story" aloud for the class.

A ver si recuerdas

OBJECTIVES
▶ Talk and write about places you visited or would like to visit
▶ Make positive and negative statements

Vocabulario

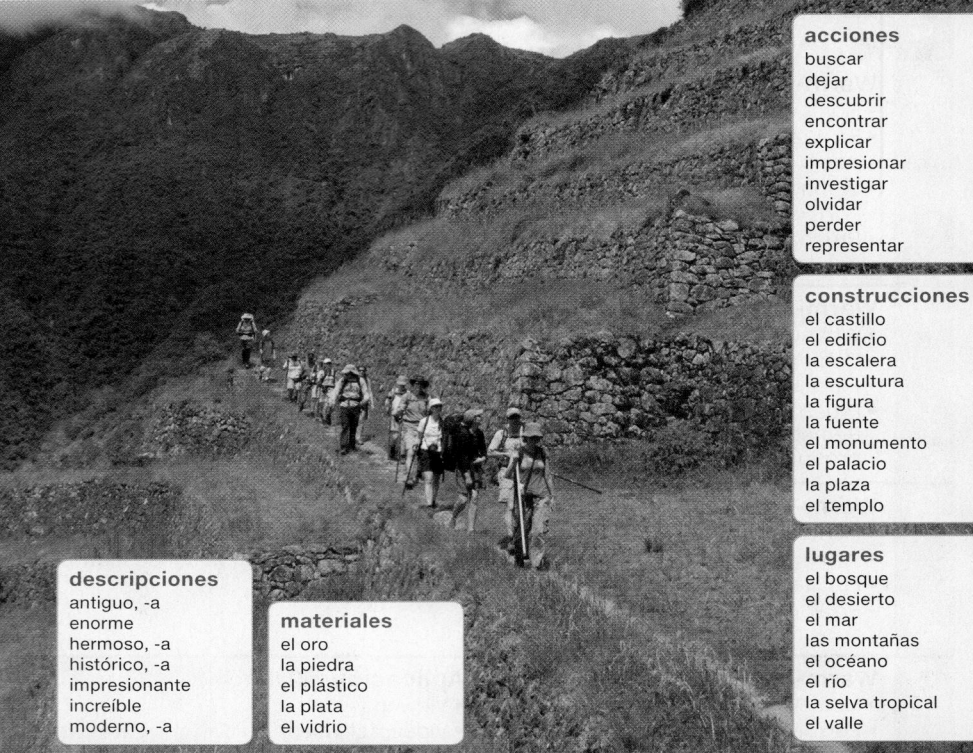

acciones
buscar
dejar
descubrir
encontrar
explicar
impresionar
investigar
olvidar
perder
representar

construcciones
el castillo
el edificio
la escalera
la escultura
la figura
la fuente
el monumento
el palacio
la plaza
el templo

lugares
el bosque
el desierto
el mar
las montañas
el océano
el río
la selva tropical
el valle

descripciones
antiguo, -a
enorme
hermoso, -a
histórico, -a
impresionante
increíble
moderno, -a

materiales
el oro
la piedra
el plástico
la plata
el vidrio

El viaje ideal

ESCRIBIR, HABLAR EN PAREJA

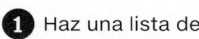

1 Haz una lista de:
- dos lugares que visitaste o te gustaría visitar
- dos construcciones que puedes encontrar en esos lugares
- tres palabras que describan cada lugar

2 Intercambia tu lista con un(a) compañero(a). Hablen sobre por qué escogieron esos lugares, cómo son y qué se encuentra allí.

304 trescientos cuatro • Capítulo 7 • ¿Mito o realidad?

Differentiated Instruction

Heritage Speakers

Have students who have lived in a heritage country create a travel brochure for that country. They may choose a place they know there or research another place. Encourage them to use words from the *Vocabulario* in order to create a vivid picture of the place.

Advanced Learners

Have students prepare an oral description of a famous monument. Ask them to give as many details as they can about the monument without naming it. Have them give their descriptions to the class who can guess which monument is being described. They can also tell which descriptive details helped them identify the monument.

Gramática

Las construcciones negativas

Here are some affirmative and negative words that you already know.
Remember that they are antonyms.

AFFIRMATIVE

alguien	someone
algo	something
alguno, alguna *(pron.)*	some
algún, alguna *(adj.)*	some
algunos, algunas *(pron., adj.)*	some
siempre	always
también	also

NEGATIVE

nadie	no one
nada	nothing
ninguno, ninguna *(pron.)*	none, not any
ningún, ninguna *(adj.)*	no, not any
ningunos, ningunas *(pron., adj.)*	none, not any
nunca	never
tampoco	neither, either

• *Alguno, alguna, algunos, algunas*, and *ninguno, ninguna* have the same number and gender as the noun they modify.

• When *alguno* and *ninguno* come before a masculine singular noun, they become *algún* and *ningún*.

• To make a sentence negative in Spanish, put *no* in front of the conjugated verb.

  No pudieron encontrar **nada**.

• If a sentence begins with a negative word, like *nunca* or *nadie,* you don't need to use the word *no* in front of the verb.

  Nunca investigaron bien el interior del templo.

Más recursos ONLINE

▶ **Tutorial:** Indefinite and Negative Expressions

2

¿Qué pasó?

🎤 **HABLAR EN PAREJA** Tu hermano vuelve a casa después de un viaje. Túrnate con tu compañero(a) para contestar sus preguntas en negativo.

▶ **Videomodelo**
A —¿Me llamó alguien por teléfono?
B —*No, nadie te llamó*.

1. ¿Pasó algo interesante?
2. ¿Vino algún amigo a verme?
3. Y Susana, ¿vino a verme?
4. ¿Llegó alguna carta para mí?

3

Una carta sin noticias

✎ **LEER** Escoge la expresión adecuada para este mensaje electrónico.

¡Hola Isabel!

¡Qué pena! No tengo __1.__ *(algo/nada)* para contarte. He estado estudiando y no ha pasado __2.__ *(nada/nadie)* interesante. No he visto a __3.__ *(alguien/nadie)*. No he ido a __4.__ *(nada/ninguna)* parte. ¡Estoy muy aburrida!

Saludos, Laura

Capítulo 7 • trescientos cinco 305

Gramática: Repaso

Standards: 4.1

Suggestions: Refer students who are having difficulty with indefinite and negative expressions to the online tutorials. Have pairs of students practice the words in the *Gramática* by asking negative questions and giving affirmative answers:

A: —¿No ves a nadie en la plaza?

B: —*Sí, veo a alguien.*

2

Standards: 1.1

Suggestions: Tell Student B to listen carefully for the affirmative word in the question in order to build the answer around its negative form.

Answers:

Wording of Student B's answers may vary. The following are likely results:

1. No, no pasó nada interesante.
2. No, ningún amigo vino a verte.
3. No, Susana tampoco vino a verte.
4. No, no llegó ninguna carta (ninguna carta llegó) para ti.

3

Standards: 1.2

Suggestions: Have students briefly review the *Gramática* before completing the activity and focus on which words are used for people, places, times, count nouns, and mass (collective) nouns.

Answers:

1. nada
2. nada
3. nadie
4. ninguna

Enrich Your Teaching

Teacher-to-Teacher

You can review vocabulary or structures that operate in pairs using the round-robin approach. Students need not form a circle; the process can also run up and down rows. To review the words in the *Gramática* on this page, for example, have the first student in a row say one of the words to the second student. The second student gives the opposite and says another word to the third student, and so on:

A: *Nadie.*
B: *Alguien. Siempre.*
C: *Nunca. Tampoco.*
D: *También….*

Vocabulario: Repaso

Standards: 1.1, 1.2

Suggestions: Have students make sentences using the expressions in the *para dar tu opinión* category and at least one word from another category. Remind them that when giving opinions, they might be using the subjunctive or indicative.

Standards: 1.1, 1.3

Suggestions: After pairs have worked together, ask students to tell the rest of the class about the animal that their partner chose.

Answers will vary.

Extension: Ask students to talk about any pets they now have or had in the past: *En mi casa tengo un pájaro. Es un canario amarillo que canta.*

Standards: 1.1

Suggestions: When students are writing their sentences about weather events, encourage them to use compound sentences with the imperfect and the preterite. Provide a model such as: *Llovía muy fuerte y de repente se oyó un trueno tremendo.*

Answers:

1. b	**3.** a
2. d	**4.** c

A ver si recuerdas

OBJECTIVES
▶ Talk and write about animals and nature
▶ Talk about similar people and things

Vocabulario

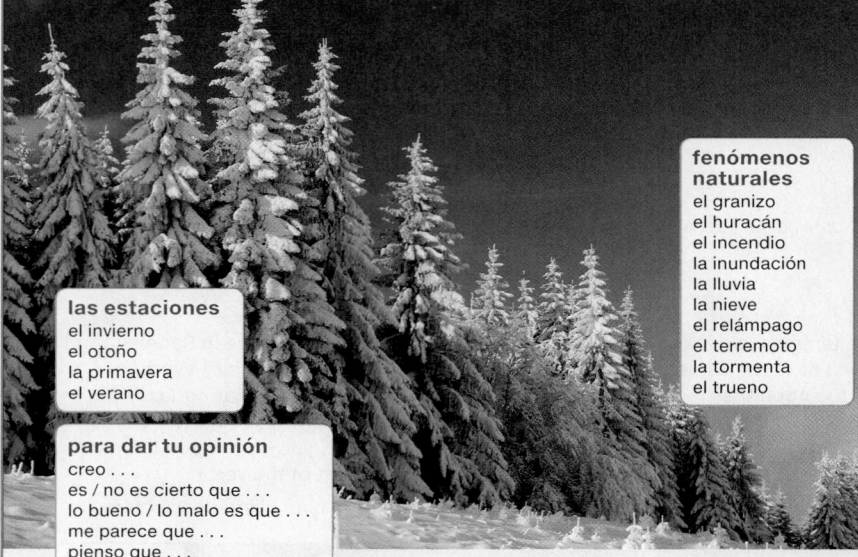

las estaciones
el invierno
el otoño
la primavera
el verano

fenómenos naturales
el granizo
el huracán
el incendio
la inundación
la lluvia
la nieve
el relámpago
el terremoto
la tormenta
el trueno

animales
la cebra
el elefante
el gato
el hipopótamo
la hormiga
el jaguar
el mono
la mosca
el mosquito
el oso
el pájaro
los peces
el perro
el tigre

sucesos
matar
morirse
nacer
ocurrir
pasar
suceder
tener lugar

para dar tu opinión
creo . . .
es / no es cierto que . . .
lo bueno / lo malo es que . . .
me parece que . . .
pienso que . . .

4

Una descripción

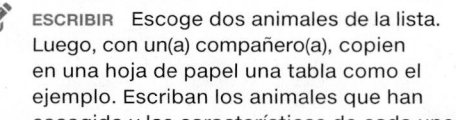

ESCRIBIR Escoge dos animales de la lista. Luego, con un(a) compañero(a), copien en una hoja de papel una tabla como el ejemplo. Escriban los animales que han escogido y las características de cada uno.

Animal favorito
Lugar donde vive
Fenómeno natural que lo afecta
Tu opinión sobre el animal

5

Dónde y cuándo

Trabaja con otro(a) estudiante para emparejar cada descripción con el fenómeno de la naturaleza que corresponde. Luego escoge dos de esos fenómenos y escribe una frase diciendo cuándo y dónde sucedió cada uno.

1. lluvia, truenos y relámpagos	**a.** trueno
2. luz muy viva producida en una tormenta	**b.** tormenta
3. ruido fuerte que se oye en una tormenta	**c.** huracán
4. viento muy fuerte y violento	**d.** relámpago

Differentiated Instruction

Heritage Speakers

Point out "nonstandard" or regional language use, such as substituting *lo* or *la* for *le* (*Lo hablé* instead of *Le hablé*) or adding *-s* to second-person singular preterite forms (¿*Ya fuistes?*). Explain that regional usage is acceptable in informal settings, but students should rely on "standard" usage in formal writing and speaking.

Students with Learning Difficulties

Write on the board pairs of nouns and adjectives. Have students follow a pattern to use the adjectives as nouns in complete sentences. For example, *pantalones/negros—*¿Pantalones? Yo prefiero los negros. *gatos/amarillos—*¿Gatos? Yo prefiero los amarillos.

Gramática

Los adjetivos usados como sustantivos

When you talk about two similar things in Spanish you can avoid repeating the noun by using the adjective as a noun.

> ¿Qué prefieres, los edificios antiguos o **los modernos?**
>
> ¿Quieres un gato blanco o **uno gris?**

- In both cases the noun is dropped in the second part of the sentence, and the definite (*el, la, los, las*) or indefinite article (*un, una, unos, unas*) comes before the adjective.

- The adjective agrees in gender and number just as if the noun were still there; also the indefinite article *un* becomes *uno* when it is not followed by the noun.

> No me gustan los edificios antiguos ni **los modernos.**
>
> No quiero un gato blanco ni **uno gris.**

- The same applies to a prepositional phrase beginning with *a, de,* or *para.*

> ¿Prefieres las esculturas de la derecha o **las de la izquierda?**
>
> ¿El informe es para esta semana o **para la próxima?**

A masculine singular adjective can be made into a noun by placing *lo* before it.

> **Lo bueno** del verano es que tenemos vacaciones.

 6

En el zoológico

LEER, ESCRIBIR   Dos amigos visitan el zoológico. Completa su conversación con *el, la, los, las* o *lo.*

A. —¿Vamos a la sección de los pájaros o a __1.__ de los reptiles?
B. —A mí me gusta más __2.__ de los reptiles.
A. —¡Mira ese cocodrilo! ¿No es impresionante?
B. —¿Cuál, __3.__ más grande?
A. —No, __4.__ pequeño. Para mí, __5.__ más interesante son sus dientes.
B. —A mí, __6.__ que más me interesa es no acercarme demasiado.

 7

Madre y niño

 HABLAR EN PAREJA   Una mamá le ofrece cosas a un niño, pero él quiere algo diferente. Con un(a) compañero(a) hagan los papeles de la mamá y del niño.

Videomodelo
querer / helado de chocolate / (vainilla)

A —*¿Quieres un helado de chocolate?*
B —*¡No, quiero uno de vainilla!*

1. comprar / el globo rojo / (azul)
2. conseguir / un perrito pequeño / (grande)
3. comer / los dulces de fresa / (de limón)
4. ponerse / los pantalones largos / (cortos)

Capítulo 7 • trescientos siete 307

Gramática: Repaso

Suggestions: Have students write one sentence in which they talk about two similar things. Ask them to take turns reading their sentences and have volunteers adapt the second part so that an adjective is used as a noun.

 6

Standards: 1.2

Suggestions: Remind students to pay attention to the gender and number of the noun they are referring to. Point out that sometimes they must refer to the previous sentence in order to do this.

Answers:

1. la	**4.** el
2. la	**5.** lo
3. el	**6.** lo

 7

Standards: 1.1

Suggestions: Encourage Student B to use exaggerated intonation for the child's role. Have pairs of students take turns performing one of the dialogues for the class.

Answers will vary. The following are likely results:

1. A—¿Compras el globo rojo?
   B—¡No, compro el azul!
2. A—¿Consigues un perrito pequeño?
   B—¡No, consigo uno grande!
3. A—¿Comes los dulces de fresa?
   B—¡No, como los de limón!
4. A—¿Te pones los pantalones largos?
   B—¡No, me pongo los cortos!

Additional Resources

 Technology: Online Resources
- *A ver si recuerdas* with Remediation
- Guided, Core, Audio, Writing practice
- *Para hispanohablantes*
Print
- Guided WB pp. 208–211
- Core WB pp. 91–92

Assessment

A ver si recuerdas **with Remedation (online only)**
After reviewing the material on these pages, assign the *A ver si recuerdas* with Remediation to evaluate students' mastery of the material. Additional practice is available online.

Enrich Your Teaching

Teacher-to-Teacher

Ask pairs of students to compare and contrast two pictures of similar items. Point out that they must determine a way to identify each picture. This might be simply the relative positions of the pictures themselves: **la rana de la izquierda** vs. **la de la derecha.**

21st Century Skills

ICT (Information, Communications and Technology) Literacy   Direct students to the online tutorials for self-directed review of the grammar topics recycled in this chapter. Students can expand their own learning by reviewing the related English grammar first then proceed to the new Spanish grammar point. Each tutorial is followed by a quick comprehension check.

Can-Do Statements

Read the Can-Do Statements in the chapter objectives with students. Then, have students read *Preparación para el examen* on page 350 to preview what they will be able to do at the end of the chapter.

Standards for Capítulo 7

To meet the Standards, students will:

COMMUNICATION

1.1 Interpersonal
- Talk about tourist sites, animals, natural phenomena
- Talk about muralist Diego Rivera
- Talk about archaeology and mysteries past and present
- Talk about shapes and measurements
- Talk about the 1938 "War of the Worlds" scare
- Talk about family and community
- Talk about pre-Columbian indigenous civilizations
- Talk about classified ads
- Talk about Cervantes and *Don Quijote de la Mancha*

1.2 Interpretive
- Read about tourist sites, animals, natural phenomena
- Read about muralist Diego Rivera
- Read and listen to information about archaeology and mysteries past and present
- Read about shapes and measurements
- Read about word families
- Read about the 1938 "War of the Worlds" scare
- Read and listen to information about pre-Columbian indigenous civilizations in America
- Read about Feliciano Sánchez Chan and his poetry
- Read about speech preparation and writing a legend
- Read about Cervantes and *Don Quijote de la Mancha*

1.3 Presentational
- Write and present information orally about tourist sites, animals, and natural phenomena
- Write and present information orally about archaeology and mysteries past and present
- Write and present orally about shapes and measurements
- Write and present information orally about a panic like the 1938 "War of the Worlds" scare
- Write about family and community
- Recite poetry by Feliciano Sánchez Chan
- Write about pre-Columbian indigenous civilizations
- Write classified ads and legends
- Write and present information orally about Cervantes and *Don Quijote de la Mancha*

CULTURE

2.1 Practices to Perspectives
- Describe the perspectives of muralist Diego Rivera
- Describe some practices and perspectives of pre-Columbian indigenous civilizations in America
- Interpret the perspectives of indigenous writers

¿Mito o realidad?

Country Connections Explorar el mundo hispano

Estados Unidos · España · México · Guatemala · Costa Rica · Perú · Bolivia · Chile

CHAPTER OBJECTIVES

Communication

By the end of the chapter you will be able to:
- Listen and read about archeology and Pre-Columbian legends
- Talk and write about mysterious events
- Provide logical explanations for unexplained phenomena

Culture

You will also be able to:
- Understand mysteries of past civilizations in Latin America
- Provide reasonable explanations for Pre-Columbian myths
- Compare cultural products in an authentic audio recording about Machu Picchu

You will demonstrate what you know and can do
- Presentación oral: Tu descubrimiento científico
- Presentación escrita: Tu leyenda

You will use

Vocabulary
- Discoveries
- Myths, legends, and unexplained phenomena
- Expressions of doubt
- Descriptions of the shapes and size of objects
- The universe

Grammar
- Present subjunctive and present perfect subjunctive with expressions of doubt
- Uses of *pero* and *sino*
- Subjunctive with adjective clauses

ARTE y CULTURA ‹ México

Diego Rivera, el gran pintor mexicano, basó su obra en temas políticos y sociales. Siempre tuvo un gran interés por la historia de su país, y muchas de sus pinturas representan elementos históricos. Estos elementos son una forma de honrar y preservar la herencia *(heritage)* cultural de las antiguas civilizaciones prehispánicas. En este caso, se puede apreciar un detalle del fresco "La civilización totonaca", que muestra a los jefes de los poztecas con las pirámides al fondo.

▶ ¿Qué construcciones indígenas conoces en los Estados Unidos? ¿Dónde están?

Detalle de "La civilización totonaca", (1950), Diego Rivera ▶
© 2009 Banco de México Diego Rivera & Frida Kahlo Museums Trust, México, D.F./Artists Rights Society (ARS), New York. Photo: Corbis.

308 trescientos ocho • Capítulo 7 • ¿Mito o realidad?

Enrich Your Teaching

The End in Mind

Have students preview the sample performance tasks on *Preparación para el examen,* p. 351, and connect them to the Chapter Objectives. Explain to students that by completing the sample tasks they can self-assess their learning progress.

Technology: Mapa global interactivo

Download the Mapa global interactivo files for Chapter 7 and preview the activities. Activity 1 explores Mexico City. Activity 3 visits Machu Picchu. Activity 5 looks at the Mayan empire. In Activity 6, discover the Nazca Lines.

Go **Online** to practice
PearsonSchool.com/Autentico

PEARSON
realize™

AUDIO   VIDEO   WRITING   SPEAK/RECORD   MAPA GLOBAL   AUTÉNTICO   FLASCHARDS   ETEXT 2.0   GAMES

Preview   7

Sitio arqueológico maya en San Bartolo, Guatemala

▶ Videonovela **¡Pura vida!**

Capítulo 7 • trescientos nueve **309**

- Interpret the work of the Academia de Español de Guatemala
- Interpret the perspectives of Miguel de Cervantes

2.2 Products to Perspectives
- Describe the work of muralist Diego Rivera
- Describe the contributions of ancient civilizations
- Discuss the fiction of Miguel de Cervantes

CONNECTIONS

3.1 Making Connections
- Discuss key facts about muralist Diego Rivera
- Discuss key facts about ancient civilizations
- Discuss facts about the "War of the Worlds" scare
- Discuss key facts about Mayan writer Sánchez Chan
- Discuss key facts about Antigua, Guatemala
- Discuss key facts about myths and legends
- Discuss key facts about Cervantes and his times
- Use language arts strategies: using illustrations, maintaining your focus, combining sentences, characters and actions

3.2 Acquiring information and Diverse Perspectives
- Read poetry by Feliciano Sánchez Chan
- Read fiction by Miguel de Cervantes

COMPARISONS

4.1 Language
- Compare pero and sino to English "but" and "but rather"
- Compare Spanish words to their English counterparts

4.2 Cultural
- Compare ancient myths with scientific explanations

COMMUNITIES

5.1 School and Global Communities
- Link to Web sites from the Spanish-speaking world

5.2 Lifelong Learning
- Develop an appreciation for fine art and literature
- Listen to an authentic Spanish-language audio recording

Chapter Opener

Resources: Regional maps

Suggestions: Introduce students to the chapter theme and objectives.

▶ **Technology: Videonovela ¡Pura vida!** View this stand-alone storyline video about five young adults in San José, Costa Rica with your class.

ARTE Y CULTURA ◀

Standards: 1.1, 1.2, 2.1, 2.2, 3.1, 5.2

Suggestions: After students read the information, ask comprehension questions.

Teaching with Art

Ask students: ¿Cuál es el significado de las pirámides en la pintura? ¿Qué está haciendo la gente? ¿Qué quiere mostrarnos Diego Rivera en esta pintura?

Project-Based Learning

Archaeological Mysteries

As students work through the chapter during the week, ask them to create a list of archaeological mysteries that are appealing to them based on what they have read. Have them write their own story about a mystery that has not been solved yet. Encourage them to use their imagination and to be very creative. Have them use this writing to complete the *Presentación escrita* on pages 340–341.

309

Vocabulario en contexto 1

Standards: 1.2

Resources: Teacher's Resource Materials: Input Script, Clip Art, Audio Script, Technology: Audio Cap. 7

Suggestions: You may want to use the Input Script from the *Teacher's Resource Materials* as a source of ideas for presentation of new vocabulary and comprehensible input. Meaning for vocabulary such as **calcular, medir, excavar, pesar,** and **trazar** can be clarified by pantomime. Visualized vocabulary, such as the various forms and measurements, can be taught using TPR commands.

Starter Activity

Show the painting on page 308. Read these true/false statements to the class. Have them respond on paper.

1. *La pintura representa una civilización del futuro.*
2. *Hay unos pájaros gigantescos que vuelan en el cielo.*
3. *Los indios preparan una cena muy especial.*
4. *La ropa de los indios es de muchos colores.*
5. *Vemos muchos árboles y ríos en la escena.*

(Answers: F, F, F, V, F)

Technology: Interactive Whiteboard

Vocabulary Activities 7-1 Use the whiteboard activities in your Teacher Resources as you progress through the vocabulary practice with your class.

Vocabulario en contexto 1

OBJECTIVES
Read, listen to, and understand information about
▸ What archeologists do
▸ Archeological mysteries of other civilizations

¡Visita México! ¡Es increíble!

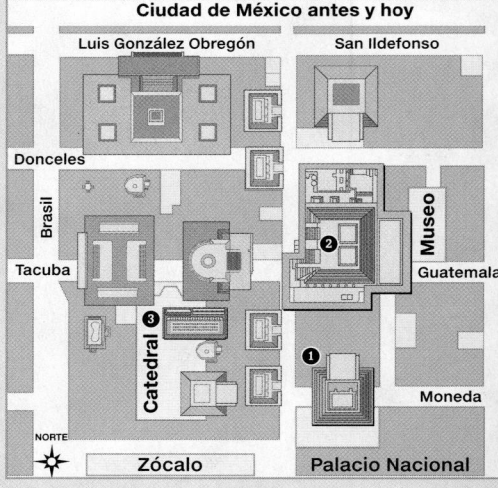

Ciudad de México antes y hoy

Mi papá es **arqueólogo**. Papá elige ciudades antiguas para explorar, **excavar** y descubrir cosas del pasado. Esta vez fuimos a la Ciudad de México. Caminamos por el Centro Histórico de la ciudad. Vimos muchas **ruinas**, a poca **distancia** una de otra. Ellas representan **una civilización** muy antigua, la azteca. Los aztecas son uno de los **pueblos** que **existieron** allí entre los años 1325 y 1521.

1

En 1988, allí se encontró el Cuauhxicalli de Moctezuma, una gran piedra en forma de **círculo** con **diseños geométricos**, de un gran **diámetro**. Me fascinó. Decidí **trazar** un dibujo en mi cuaderno para no olvidarlo. Su **función** era mostrar las conquistas de los aztecas. Esta piedra pesaba más de 24 **toneladas**.

2

Caminas un poco más y llegas al Museo de la Ciudad. En una de sus esquinas, puedes ver una cabeza de serpiente con un gran ojo en forma de **óvalo**. Para los aztecas, la serpiente era un dios.

310 trescientos diez • Capítulo 7 • ¿Mito o realidad?

Differentiated Instruction

Advanced Learners

First have students draw a simple design using one or two geometric shapes or lines. Ask them not to show their drawings to anyone. Then have partners sit back-to-back with pencils and pads, looking at their own drawings. Have them take turns using affirmative and negative commands to tell their partner, step by step, how to reproduce their drawing. When finished, have them compare the two drawings and discuss the reasons for any differences between them.

Go **Online** to practice

PEARSON
realize™

PearsonSchool.com/Autentico

AUDIO   SPEAK/RECORD

Interpretive   7

el alto
el ancho   el largo

❸

Más adelante aun, puedes ver el edificio de la Catedral. En 1790, en la Catedral, se encontró una figura de piedra que representaba Coatlicue, la madre de los dioses. Papá quiso calcular cuánto medía. Medía 250 **centímetros** de **alto** y 160 centímetros de **ancho**, con una base de 115 centímetros de **largo**.

¡Fue un viaje inolvidable! El año próximo iremos **al observatorio** de Chichén Itzá desde donde los aztecas miraban los movimientos del Sol y de **la Luna**. Allí visitaremos **las pirámides, estructuras** que parecen **triángulos** con **rectángulos** encima.

1

¿Qué hicieron Tomás y su padre?

 ESCUCHAR   En una hoja escribe los números del 1 al 6. Escucha las frases. Escribe *C* si la frase es cierta o *F* si la frase es falsa.

2

Somos arqueólogos

 ESCRIBIR, HABLAR EN PAREJA   Imagina que quieres ser arqueólogo(a). Con un compañero(a) desarrolla un plan que incluya adónde vas a ir y qué pasos debes seguir para completar una investigación sobre las civilizaciones antiguas. Luego, hablen sobre sus planes.

Modelo

A —*Voy a la ciudad de México. Visitaré el Templo Mayor, el museo y en la biblioteca buscaré información sobre los aztecas.*

B —*Voy a pedir un mapa en la casa de turismo y haré una lista de los lugares que quiero conocer.*

Capítulo 7 • trescientos once 311

1

Standards: 1.2

Resources: Teacher's Resource Materials: Audio Script, Technology: Audio Cap. 7

Suggestions: Before students listen, point out that the statements they will hear are related directly to the story about Tomás and his father on this and the previous page. Use the audio or read the text. Allow students to listen more than once.

 Technology: Audio Script and Answers

En una hoja escribe los números del 1 al 6. Escucha las frases. Escribe *C* si la frase es cierta o *F* si la frase es falsa. Vas a oír cada frase dos veces.

1. Tomás y su padre fueron a visitar el centro histórico de la Ciudad de México. *(C)*
2. Conocieron a un arquitecto en el Templo Mayor. *(F)*
3. Visitaron unas ruinas y vieron figuras de piedra. *(C)*
4. Tomás trazó algo en su cuaderno. *(C)*
5. Calcularon las medidas de la ciudad en el mapa. *(F)*
6. Visitaron las pirámides de Chichén Itzá. *(F)*

Extension: Ask students to correct the false statements. Have them do so by changing information, rather than making the false statement negative.

2

Standards: 1.1

Suggestions: As students talk together, encourage them to use gestures that show that they understand the meaning of the vocabulary items.

Answers will vary.

Enrich Your Teaching

Culture Note

The largest pyramid in the world by volume is located in Cholula, Mexico, two hours southeast of Mexico City. This colossal structure was only discovered in 1910 during the construction of a nearby building. Grassy vegetation had grown and covered the pyramid, making it look like a huge hill. A church was even built on it. Archaeologists have dug about five miles of tunnels inside the pyramid to study its history. The pyramid consists of several layers of construction that were built over ten centuries. Cholula was conquered by various tribes, including the Olmecs, the Toltecs, and the Aztecs, each building a larger pyramid around the existing one.

Vocabulario en contexto 1

Standards: 1.2

Resources: Teacher's Resource Materials: Input Script, Clip Art, Audio Script, Technology: Audio Cap. 7

Suggestions: Model the dialogue with a volunteer. Begin the reading again with volunteers playing the roles of the characters. Using the presentation, help students understand the new words in blue type.

Post-reading: Complete Actividad 3 to check comprehension.

3

Standards: 1.2

Suggestions: Have students discuss their responses. Encourage them to explain why the false statements are not true.

Answers:
1. C **2.** F **3.** F **4.** C

Pre-AP® Integration

- **Learning Objective:** Presentational Speaking
- **Activity:** Have students bring to class a picture of a single object (pre-Columbian statue, rocket ship, bridge, etc.). Taking turns, each student tells the class what his or her picture is and the dimensions of the object *(de ancho, de largo, de alto)*. The next student makes a comparative statement before continuing the activity. *(La Estatua de la Libertad que yo tengo es más alta que el Calendario Azteca que tú tienes.)*
- **Pre-AP® Resource Materials:** Comprehensive guide to Pre-AP® vocabulary skill development

Teacher-to-Teacher

Many students are intrigued by the mysteries associated with Latin American ruins. Encourage students to share their background knowledge about these places.

Project-Based Learning

Give students copies of the Project-Based Learning outline and rubric from the *Teacher's Resource Materials*. Explain the task and have them perform Step 1. (see p. 304-b.)

 Natalia es arqueóloga y está visitando las ruinas de Machu Picchu, en Perú. Le manda mensajes a su papá, quien también es arqueólogo.

Natalia **Papá**

Natalia: ¡Papá, no te imaginas lo que es ver esta **misteriosa** ciudad en persona! ☺

Papá: ¡Me imagino! El **misterio** que **cubre** a esta ciudad está sin **resolver.**

Natalia: Es **inexplicable** cómo los incas juntaron las piedras de sus estructuras, **ya que** no hay ninguna **evidencia** que muestre cómo lo hicieron. ☹

Papá: Hay personas que creen que los extraterrestres los ayudaron, ¡desde una **nave espacial**! A los científicos les parece muy **improbable.**

Natalia: Para mí, lo más **probable** es que los incas tuvieran una técnica secreta para construir. ¡Y tampoco me explico cómo construyeron los edificios **redondos**!

Papá: Sí, eso es un **fenómeno** muy **extraño,** y **dudo** que tú y yo vayamos a resolver el misterio en esta conversación.

Natalia: De acuerdo, papá. Voy a explorar más esta tarde. Hablamos mañana.

edificio redondo

3

 La visita de Natalia a Machu Picchu

 ESCRIBIR Lee las frases. Escribe *C* (cierto) si la frase es correcta o *F* (falso) si es incorrecta.

1. Natalia piensa que Machu Picchu es una ciudad misteriosa.
2. El papá de Natalia dice que hay evidencias de cómo se construyó la ciudad.
3. Natalia cree que una nave espacial llegó a Machu Picchu.
4. En Machu Picchu hay algunas estructuras redondas.

312 trescientos doce • Capítulo 7 • ¿Mito o realidad?

Differentiated Instruction

Heritage Speakers

As students use the new vocabulary, remind them to be careful with spellings of cognates, such as ***pirámide.***
Also remind them of differences in capitalization rules between English and Spanish: *The Incas versus **los incas.***

Students with Special Needs

Have partners describe the images in each photo so that visually impaired students can better understand the context.

La ciudad perdida

Antes de ver

Usar conocimientos previos Piensa en lo que ya sabes sobre las ruinas que han quedado de las grandes civilizaciones del pasado. Piensa también en cómo los artistas han ilustrado esas civilizaciones. Usa esos conocimientos para inferir palabras desconocidas y entender mejor la Videohistoria que verás.

Haz la actividad

Descripción Observa las fotos. Escribe un párrafo corto en el que describas lo que ves y cómo crees que se relacionan estas fotos con el tema de este capítulo.

Camila   Teo   Seba   Valentina   Ximena

▶ **Ve el video**

Seba llama a su grupo de amigos para compartir con ellos una gran noticia. ¿De qué se tratará?

Ve a **PearsonSchool.com/Autentico** para ver el video *La ciudad perdida.* También puedes leer el guión.

Después de ver

 ESCRIBIR   Contesta las siguientes preguntas:

1. ¿Qué noticia quería Seba darles a sus amigos?
2. Parafrasea lo que Seba cuenta sobre la Ciudad Perdida.
3. ¿Qué indígenas construyeron la Ciudad Perdida?
4. ¿Quién es Mabú? ¿Por qué lo creó Seba?
5. ¿Qué relación tiene Seba con los arhuacos?

Comparación cultural Piensa en una civilización real o mítica sobre la que has aprendido. Compárala con la civilización que Seba describe.

Capítulo 7 • trescientos trece **313**

Enrich Your Teaching

Cultural Note

The Arhuaco Indians live on the slopes of the Sierra Nevada de Santa Marta, a huge mountain range only 26 miles from the Caribbean coast in Colombia. They share this habitat with the Kogi, Wiwa and Kankuamo tribes—all descendants of the Tayronas. This ancient civilization was the builder of Tenuya, now known as Ciudad Perdida, or the Lost City. High in the sierra and surrounded by a dense jungle, this archeological site consists of a series of over 150 terraces carved into the mountainside by the Tayronas about 2,500 years ago. Many adventurous backpackers from around the world undertake the six day trek through the jungle to see the ancient terraces which once were the foundations for Tayrona houses, markets, and ritual sites.

Tecnología: Video

Standards: 1.2

Resources: Teacher's Resource Materials: Video Script

Antes de ver

Review the strategy and activity with students. Invite volunteers to share what they know about archeological sites. Also, discuss briefly how illustrators and artists depict ancient civilizations. Then, ask students to observe the photos and make a connection with the chapter's theme.

Ve el video

Show the video. Ask volunteers to paraphrase the main idea. Replay it, this time pausing to ask students about important details. Ask: *¿Qué dibujos les muestra Seba a sus amigos? ¿Cómo son los dibujos?* Ask students to use the images and the context to infer the meaning of unfamiliar words.

Después de ver

Standards: 1.2, 4.2

Suggestions: Invite students to work in pairs to paraphrase the main idea, theme, and details in the Videohistoria.

Answers: 1. que ganó un concurso de dibujo; **2.** está en Colombia, sus ruinas se descubrieron por accidente, tiene muchas terrazas, plazas y caminos de piedra; puede ser más vieja que Machu Picchu; **3.** un grupo de indígenas llamados arhuacos; **4.** un guerrero que lucha contra el mal; lo creó para ilustrar una composición; **5.** La abuela de su abuela era india arhuaca.

Comparación cultural: Answers will vary.

Have students go to **Realize** for additional video activities.

Additional Resources

 Technology: Online Resources
- Instant Check
- Guided, Core, Video, Audio
- *Para hispanohablantes*

Print
- Guided WB pp. 212–220
- Core WB pp. 93–94
- Authentic Resources Workbook

Assessment

Quiz: Vocabulary Recognition
- Prueba 7-1

4

Standards: 1.2, 3.1

Suggestions: Remind students that the items are presented as analogies. A single colon means "is to" and a double colon means "as."

Answers:

1. línea
2. medir
3. óvalo
4. astrónomo
5. centímetro
6. triángulo
7. arqueóloga

Starter Activity

Have volunteers talk about what archaeologists do when searching for new things.

5

Standards: 1.2

Suggestions: Remind students that reading through the entire announcement first will help them place their answers correctly.

Answers:

1. misterios
2. existen
3. que
4. cubría
5. se excavaron
6. extraños
7. redondas
8. arqueólogos
9. probable

Steps 2–3
Answers will vary.

Vocabulario en uso 1

OBJECTIVES
▶ Talk and read about archeology
▶ Discuss the legend of Atlantis

4

A recordar palabras

 LEER, ESCRIBIR Completa cada analogía con una palabra correcta del recuadro. Sigue el modelo.

triángulo	astrónomo	medir	centímetro
arqueóloga	línea	óvalo	

Modelo
cierta : verdad :: inexplicable : *improbable*

1. cortar : papel :: trazar : _____
2. kilo : pesar :: centímetro : _____
3. reloj : círculo :: huevo : _____
4. laboratorio : científico :: observatorio : _____
5. el peso : tonelada :: el largo : _____
6. puerta : rectángulo :: pared de una pirámide : _____
7. enseñar : maestra :: excavar : _____

5

¡A viajar!

 LEER, ESCRIBIR

1 Imagina que quieres irte de viaje con tu familia. Completa este anuncio de un viaje arqueológico usando las palabras del recuadro.

redondas	arqueólogos	que
se excavaron	probable	extraños
misterios	cubría	existen

2 ¿Qué otro misterio arqueológico te gustaría visitar? ¿Por qué?

3 Haz una lista de tres cosas interesantes que puedes ver en un viaje como éste.

Viaje Arqueológico

Los _1._ de los mayas

¿Sabías que. . .

. . .todavía _2._ muchas estructuras antiguas _3._ estaban construidas de piedra?

. . .la tierra _4._ muchos monumentos importantes haste que _5._ ?

. . .hay sitios misteriosos y _6._ con piedras perfectamente _7._ ?

Explora las ruinas del Yucatán y de Centroamérica con un equipo de _8._ en la selva tropical. Visita Cobá, uno de los sitios más antiguos de los mayas. Ve a Tulum y disfruta de las aguas azules del Caribe.

¡Es muy _9._ que te diviertas!

Viajes Paraíso
calle 55, esquina Lago
Ciudad de México, México

Differentiated Instruction

Students with Learning Difficulties

For *Actividad* 4, explain that to solve an analogy, students must find a word that completes the second pair. The first two words are always related; the second two must be related in the same way. Help students identify the relationship in order to solve the second analogy in each item.

Advanced Learners

Ask students to create more word analogies similar to the ones in *Actividad* 4. Have them refer to previous chapters for vocabulary sets.

6 Preguntas de arqueólogos

HABLAR EN PAREJA Un buen arqueólogo se hace muchas preguntas. Trabaja con un(a) compañero(a) para hablar de las fotos y los dibujos de los lugares en las páginas 310 a 313. Sigue el modelo.

Videomodelo
líneas de Nazca / ¿quiénes trazaron?
A —¿Quiénes trazaron las Líneas de Nazca?
B —Los extraterrestres las trazaron, según algunas personas.

Líneas de Nazca

Estudiante A

1. observatorio / ¿qué miraban?
2. la gran piedra de Moctezuma / ¿qué tipo de dibujos muestran?
3. el Cuauhxicalli / ¿cuánto pesa?
4. las paredes de la pirámide / ¿qué forma tienen?
5. Coaticlue, figura de piedra / ¿qué representaba?
6. las ruinas de Machu Picchu / ¿cuál era el misterio?

Estudiante B

triángulo
más de 24 toneladas
cómo unieron las piedras para formar las paredes
la madre de los dioses
diseños geométricos
los movimientos del Sol y de la Luna

7 Juego

ESCRIBIR, HABLAR EN GRUPO Tú y tus compañeros(as) van a jugar al juego de las veinte preguntas. Cada estudiante piensa en un objeto sin decir lo que es y sus compañeros tienen que hacerle preguntas que sólo pueden ser contestadas con *sí* o *no*.

❶ Cada estudiante escribe una descripción de un objeto de la sala de clases. Pueden usar las palabras del recuadro.

está hecho(a) de	pesa	mide	el ancho	el alto	el largo
óvalo	círculo	triángulo	rectángulo	redondo	sirve para

❷ Los estudiantes hacen preguntas para identificar el objeto. El (La) estudiante que identifica el objeto gana dos puntos.

Modelo
¿Tiene el objeto más de 20 centímetros de largo?
¿Tiene forma redonda?

Nota
Para expresar en español el largo, ancho o alto de un objeto, puedes usar estas mismas palabras precedidas por la preposición **de**. El monumento mide tres metros **de alto** y dos metros **de ancho.**

Capítulo 7 • trescientos quince **315**

6

Standards: 1.1

Suggestions: Point out to students that there will be more than one way to ask and answer the questions. Encourage them to use their language skills to create the most clear and efficient questions and answers possible.

Answers:

Questions and answers will vary. The following are suggestions:

1. A —¿Qué miraban en el observatorio?
   B —Miraban el movimiento del Sol y de la Luna.
2. A —¿Qué tipo de dibujos muestra la gran piedra de Moctezuma?
   B —Muestran diseños geométricos.
3. A —¿Cuánto pesa el Cuauhxicalli?
   B —Pesa más de 24 toneladas.
4. A —¿Qué forma tienen las paredes de la pirámide?
   B —Tienen la forma de un triángulo.
5. A —¿Qué representaba el Coaticlue, una figura hecha de piedra?
   B —La figura de piedra llamada Coaticlue representaba a la madre de los dioses.
6. A —¿Cuál era el misterio de las ruinas de Machu Picchu?
   B —El misterio era cómo unieron las piedras de las paredes.

7

Standards: 1.1

Suggestions: As students describe and ask about the objects, encourage them to include as much new shape and measurement vocabulary as they can.

Answers will vary.

Enrich Your Teaching

Teacher-to-Teacher

The game "Twenty Questions" is a tried-and-true language-teaching strategy. It is easily adaptable to all sorts of vocabulary and grammar teaching targets. Any variation that you can think of for the game (such as *Actividad* 7 on this page) will provide students with excellent real-life language practice. The game requires students to engage in question formation and a true exchange of information within any context you decide to apply.

Starter Activity

Remind students of the spelling changes in the preterite forms of verbs like **creer** and **leer.** On the board, begin a preterite conjugation of one or more of these verbs, supplying some of the preterite forms. Have volunteers finish the conjugation, including third-person, plural preterite forms like **creyeron** and **leyeron.**

8

Standards: 1.1, 1.2, 1.3, 3.1

Suggestions: First, have students read the article on their own and write their answers to the questions in Step 2. Have them share these answers when they meet in groups for Step 3. Doing so will help them address together any reading comprehension problems they may have.

Answers:

Wording of answers may vary. The following are likely results:

1. Trata del misterio de la Atlántida.
2. Atlántida es el nombre de una antigua civilización que se hundió rápidamente en el mar. Muchas personas creen que la historia de Atlántida es verdad. Otras no la creen.
3. Creta fue completamente cubierta por una ola gigantesca.
4. Los dos lugares fueron destruidos por el mar. La destrucción de los dos lugares ocurrió en la misma época.
5. Answers will vary.

Pre-AP® Integration

- **Learning Objective:** Interpretive: Print and Audio
- **Activity:** As a pre-reading activity, divide the students in groups of four. Write the first three questions from Actividad 8 on long strips of paper and distribute one strip to each of three of the group members. Have the fourth group member read the article about the Atlántida to his or her group members and have each share the answer to his or her question.
- **Pre-AP® Resource Materials:** Comprehensive guide to Pre-AP® communication skill development

---

8

La Atlántida

LEER, ESCRIBIR, HABLAR EN GRUPO

1 Lee el siguiente artículo sobre el misterio de la Atlántida.

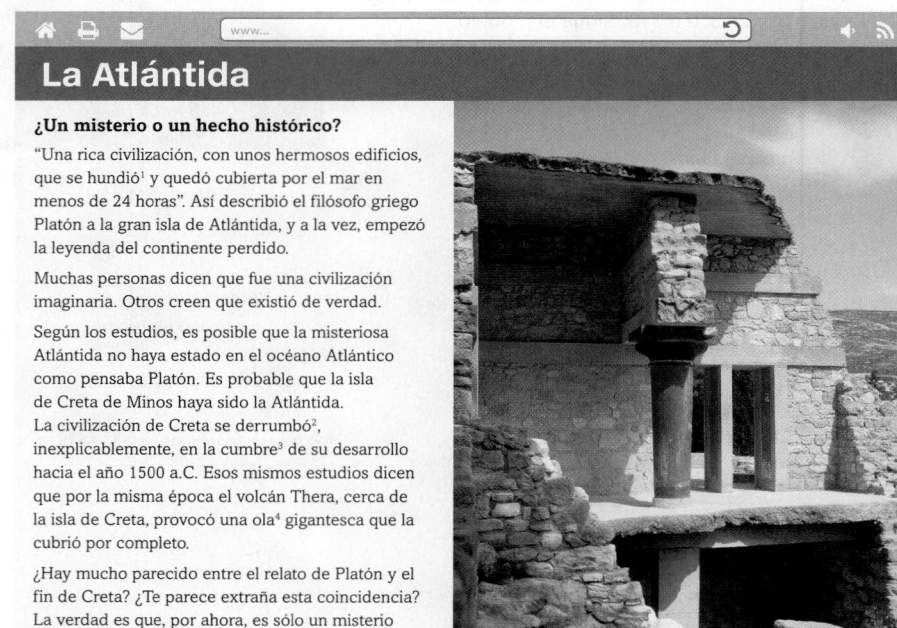

La Atlántida

¿Un misterio o un hecho histórico?

"Una rica civilización, con unos hermosos edificios, que se hundió[1] y quedó cubierta por el mar en menos de 24 horas". Así describió el filósofo griego Platón a la gran isla de Atlántida, y a la vez, empezó la leyenda del continente perdido.

Muchas personas dicen que fue una civilización imaginaria. Otros creen que existió de verdad.

Según los estudios, es posible que la misteriosa Atlántida no haya estado en el océano Atlántico como pensaba Platón. Es probable que la isla de Creta de Minos haya sido la Atlántida. La civilización de Creta se derrumbó[2], inexplicablemente, en la cumbre[3] de su desarrollo hacia el año 1500 a.C. Esos mismos estudios dicen que por la misma época el volcán Thera, cerca de la isla de Creta, provocó una ola[4] gigantesca que la cubrió por completo.

¿Hay mucho parecido entre el relato de Platón y el fin de Creta? ¿Te parece extraña esta coincidencia? La verdad es que, por ahora, es sólo un misterio más que sigue sin resolverse.

[1]sank [2]collapsed [3]peak [4]wave

2 Ahora contesta las preguntas sobre lo que dice el artículo.

1. ¿De qué trata el artículo?
2. ¿Qué es la Atlántida y qué creen las personas acerca de la Atlántida?
3. ¿Qué sucedió con Creta?
4. ¿En qué se relacionan Creta y la Atlántida?
5. ¿Habías visto o leído antes algo sobre la Atlántida, en películas, documentales, dibujos animados, libros o artículos? ¿Qué explicación se daba allí? ¿Era parecida a la de este artículo?

3 En grupo, comenten lo que dice la leyenda. ¿Cuántos creen que es cierta? ¿Creen que hay suficiente evidencia de que la Atlántida realmente existió?

316 trescientos dieciséis • Capítulo 7 • ¿Mito o realidad?

Differentiated Instruction

Students with Learning Difficulties

Point out to students that **a.C.** means **antes de Cristo.** Draw a timeline on the board. Label the points **1500 a.C., el año 1 (nacimiento de Jesucristo),** and **20xx** (the current year). Use this visual to demonstrate adding 1,500 years + 2,0(xx) years to determine how many years ago the civilization of Crete was destroyed.

Logical-Mathematical Learner

As the class completes *Actividad* 10, challenge students to convert answers to the metric system. Remind them that the metric system is used throughout Latin America, Spain, and many other countries. Provide them with the following information: 2.2 pounds = 1 kilogram; 3.3 feet = 1 meter; 1.6 miles = 1 km.

Go **Online** to practice
PEARSON
realize™
WRITING SPEAK/RECORD

PearsonSchool.com/Autentico

Interpersonal 7

9

Compara los misterios

HABLAR EN PAREJA, ESCRIBIR

1 Trabaja con un(a) compañero(a). Hagan una lista de los misterios que han estudiado hasta ahora en el capítulo. Añadan otros misterios que conozcan.

2 Escojan dos misterios y compárenlos. ¿En qué se parecen? ¿En qué se diferencian? Pueden usar un diagrama de Venn como el siguiente para compararlos.

3 Usando el diagrama de Venn, escriban frases para comparar los misterios.

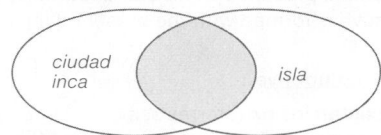

ciudad inca   isla

Machu Picchu   La Atlántida

10

Y tú, ¿qué dices?

ESCRIBIR, HABLAR

1. ¿Cuánto crees que pesa tu pupitre? ¿Y el escritorio del (de la) profesor(a)? ¿Y un árbol?
2. ¿Qué objeto o edificio en los Estados Unidos tiene el alto de una pirámide? ¿Qué río crees que es el más largo del mundo?
3. ¿Cuál es mayor, el diámetro de la Luna o el de la Tierra? ¿Y qué distancia crees que es mayor, la de la Tierra al Sol o la de la Tierra a la Luna?
4. Busca formas geométricas en la clase. ¿Qué cosas tienen forma de rectángulo, triángulo, círculo u óvalo?

Ampliación del lenguaje ▸ Familias de palabras

Muchas veces podemos averiguar el significado de una palabra si conocemos otras palabras de la misma familia. Observa la relación entre las siguientes palabras. Luego completa las frases.

1. La piedra es muy _____. _____ 20 kilos.
2. Nadie puede _____ ese fenómeno. Es _____.
3. Es _____ que él es el criminal. La _____ lo acusa.
4. Voy a participar en un concurso de _____. Debo _____ un coche súper moderno.

verbo	sustantivo	adjetivo
calcular	la calculadora	
cubrir		cubierto(a)
diseñar	el diseño	
dudar	a duda	dudoso(a)
	la evidencia	evidente
explicar	la explicación	inexplicable
	el fenómeno	fenomenal
funcionar	la función	
medir	la medida	
	el misterio	misterioso(a)
pesar	el peso	pesado(a)

Capítulo 7 • trescientos diecisiete **317**

Standards: 1.1, 1.3, 3.1

Suggestions: If students can't name other mysteries in Step 1, suggest well-known ones such as *las predicciones de Nostradamus* or *el Yeti*.

Answers will vary.

Standards: 1.1, 1.3

Suggestions: As students talk about their answers, they will be making comparisons. Model comparative and superlative structures as necessary.

Answers will vary.

AMPLIACIÓN DEL LENGUAJE

Standards: 1.2, 3.1

Suggestions: Ask pairs of students to build word families around other verbs such as **expresar** or **impresionar.**

Answers:
1. pesada; pesa
2. explicar; inexplicable
3. evidente; evidencia
4. diseño; diseñar

Additional Resources

🛜 **Technology: Online Resources**
• Guided, Core, Audio
• Communication Activities
Teacher Resources
• Teacher's Resource Materials: Audio Script, Technology: Audio Cap. 7, Communicative Pair Activity

Assessment

Prueba 7-2 with Remediation (online only)
Prueba: Aplicación del vocabulario 1
• Prueba 7-2

Enrich Your Teaching

Teacher-to-Teacher

A good way to draw students into a discussion is to use "faulty" questions. A "faulty" question is one that doesn't supply all the information necessary for it to be clearly answered. For example, a question such as: *¿Cuánto pesa un perro?* might elicit further comments, questions, and comparisons such as: *¿Qué clase de perro es?*

21st Century Skills

Critical Thinking and Problem Solving Have students research historical "lost civilizations," such as the Moche in Peru and the Anasazi in New Mexico. What explanations for their disappearance have been proposed? Have students compare them to the beliefs about Atlantis. Why does the idea of a "lost continent" continue to have such an influence in popular imagination, in their opinion?

Gramática

Standards: 4.1

Suggestions: Ask students to use the expressions in the *Gramática* in sentences with the subjunctive or the indicative, as appropriate. Encourage them to make comments about the mysteries already discussed in the chapter or about current events. If necessary, ask guiding questions such as: *¿Piensas que los extraterrestres ayudaron a los incas a construir su ciudad?*

 Technology: Interactive Whiteboard

Grammar Activities 7-1 Use the whiteboard activities in your Teacher Resources as you progress through the grammar practice with your class.

 11

Standards: 1.2

Suggestions: Remind students that these are complex sentences with more than one set of subject and verb. Tell them to carefully determine the subject of the subordinate clause before writing each answer, since their verb form must agree in person and number with that subject.

Answers:

1. excaven	4. calculen
2. pueda	5. pese/pesa
3. pesen	6. son

Gramática

OBJECTIVES
▸ Expressing doubt and uncertainty about facts
▸ Discuss mysterious phenomena

El presente y el presente perfecto del subjuntivo con expresiones de duda

To express doubt, uncertainty, or disbelief about actions in the present, you use the present subjunctive. To express doubt, uncertainty, or disbelief about actions in the past, you use the present perfect subjunctive. Recall that the present perfect subjunctive is formed with the present subjunctive of *haber* and a past participle.

doubt, uncertainty		subjunctive
Dudo que . . .		**existan** los extraterrestres
Es posible que . . .	**+**	*extraterrestrials **exist, do exist, will exist***
Es dudoso que . . .		

disbelief		
No creo que . . .	**+**	**hayan existido** los extraterrestres
Es imposible que . . .		*extraterrestrials **existed, have existed***

Expressions of belief, knowledge, or certainty are usually followed by the indicative.

Creo que . . .		
Estoy segura que . . .		
Es evidente que . . .		
Es verdad que . . .	**+**	ésas **son** ruinas mayas
Sabemos que . . .		
No dudo que . . .		

Más recursos ONLINE

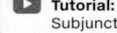 **Tutorial:** Use of Present Perfect Subjunctive

 Canción de hip hop: *La Atlántida*

11

 Lo dudo

 LEER, ESCRIBIR Jorge está leyendo en línea un artículo de arqueología. Completa lo que piensa con el presente del indicativo o el presente del subjuntivo.

1. Dudo que los arqueólogos _____ donde no exista evidencia de otras civilizaciones. (*excavar*)

2. Es improbable que una persona _____ trazar los diseños incas. (*poder*)

3. Es posible que las ruinas _____ muchas toneladas. (*pesar*)

4. No creo que los científicos _____ el diámetro de una estructura sin ver antes la evidencia. (*calcular*)

5. Es imposible que el antiguo observatorio _____ más que un edificio moderno. (*pesar*)

6. Estoy seguro de que los científicos _____ capaces de resolver misterios. (*ser*)

Differentiated Instruction

Students with Learning Difficulties

Point out that these sentences have two clauses, each with its own subject and verb that must agree. Provide models of different subjects with **haber** to form the present perfect subjunctive: *Es imposible que él haya creído esta leyenda. No creo que tú hayas visto un extraterrestre. Es dudoso que haya aterrizado una nave espacial.*

Challenge/Pre-AP®

Have students write three false statements about real-life events: *Shirley sacó una mala nota en el examen de inglés.* Have them exchange sentences with a partner and take turns commenting on each statement using the present perfect subjunctive: *Dudo que haya sacado una mala nota porque estaba muy bien preparada.*

12

¿Qué opinas?

 ESCRIBIR, HABLAR EN PAREJA Trabaja con un(a) compañero(a) para dar su opinión sobre algunas teorías sobre las pirámides y otras estructuras antiguas. Usen frases de las dos columnas en un correo electrónico.

Modelo
Los extraterrestres construyeron las pirámides en México.
*Dudo que los extraterrestres **hayan** construido las pirámides porque . . .*

Columna A

Los extraterrestres han transportado las piedras de Machu Picchu.

Los incas construyeron Machu Picchu para protegerse de las invasiones.

El Coaticlue está sentado en una nave espacial.

La piedra de Moctezuma tiene dibujos geométricos.

Atlántida fue en realidad la isla de Creta de Minos.

Columna B

Dudo que . . .

Creo que . . .

Estoy seguro(a) de que . . .

Es imposible que . . .

Es probable / improbable que . . .

13

Noticias increíbles

LEER, HABLAR EN GRUPO, ESCRIBIR Lee este artículo sobre algo que sucedió en 1938.

1 Contesta las preguntas.

   1. ¿De qué se trataba el programa de radio?

   2. ¿Qué causó el pánico?

   3. ¿Cree el señor en la calle que existen los extraterrestres?

   4. ¿Qué cree la señorita?

2 Trabaja con un grupo para pensar en un evento o un fenómeno que pueda causar pánico al público hoy día. Escriban entre todos un guión (*script*) de un programa sobre el evento o fenómeno.

3 "Transmitan" su programa a la clase.

---

31 de octubre, 1938

¡Pánico por supuesta invasión de marcianos!

Programa de radio causó gran revuelo[1]
Orson Welles adaptó y transmitió por radio ayer *La guerra de los mundos* de H. G. Wells, de manera tan realista que la gente creyó que estaba escuchando las noticias de una invasión extraterrestre. Aquí les damos la opinión del público en las calles cuando todo se aclaró.

Periodista: ¡Señor, señor! ¿Qué cree usted que ha sucedido? ¿Es posible que nos invadan los marcianos?

Señor en la calle: Quizas todos hayamos pensado que era verdad. Pero no creo que una invasión así sea posible.

Periodista: ¿Y usted, señorita?

Chica en la calle: Yo me asusté, pero en realidad, dudo que existan los marcianos.

[1]Commotion

Capítulo 7 • trescientos diecinueve **319**

12

Suggestions: Make sure partners switch roles in order to practice both halves of the dialogues. Encourage Student B to answer truthfully when expressing either doubt or certainty.

Answers will vary. The following are the possible combinations of expressions and verb forms:

doubt, uncertainty, disbelief

Dudo que; Es imposible que; Es probable/ improbable que/hayan transportado; hayan construido; esté sentado; sean; haya sido

certainty

Creo que; Estoy seguro(a) de que/han transportado (transportaron); construyeron; está sentado; son; fue

13

Suggestions: Remind students that when answering questions 3 and 4 in Step 1, they must use third-person verb forms. Encourage them to make an audio or video recording of their transmission for Step 3.

Answers: Wording of answers may vary. The following are likely results:
- Se trataba de una invasión de marcianos.
- El público creyó que la invasión era verdadera.
- Sí, el señor cree que existen los extraterrestres.
- La señorita duda que existan los extraterrestres.

Project-Based Learning

Students can perform Step 2 at this point. Be sure they understand your corrections and suggestions.
(For more information, see p. 304-b.)

Enrich Your Teaching

Teacher-to-Teacher

When students work on group projects, such as the creation of the transmission in *Actividad* 13, monitor them to make sure that everyone is contributing to the best of his or her ability. Whenever possible, allow them to organize themselves according to their skills. It will sometimes be necessary, however, to assign specific tasks to specific students. Those with stronger language skills might be given more of the writing task, for example, while those who are struggling might contribute to the more technical and hands-on parts of the task.

14

Suggestions: Tell students that Student A may interpret the images in more than one way in order to form the question. Student B should listen carefully and respond using a direct object pronoun that refers to the direct object that Student A used.

Answers:

Direct objects may vary. Direct object pronouns shown in Student B's answers replace the direct objects shown in Student A's questions.

1. A —¿Marcia ya excavó las ruinas?
   B —No, no creo que las haya excavado.
2. A —¿Tú ya pesaste las piedras?
   B —No, no creo que las haya pesado.
3. A —¿Carlos y Raúl ya trazaron las formas geométricas?
   B —No, no creo que las hayan trazado.
4. A —¿Usted ya calculó el diámetro del círculo?
   B —No, no creo que lo haya calculado.
5. A —¿Mateo ya estudió el monumento?
   B —No, no creo que lo haya estudiado.
6. A —¿Teresa y Emilio ya buscaron el templo?
   B —No, no creo que lo hayan buscado.

Active Classroom

After completing *Actividad* 15, divide students into groups of four. Have one student write out each of the expressions on a strip of paper. Place these face down in one pile. Then have students write on a a strip of paper a subject/verb combination: *El arqueólogo/encontrar* and place it in a second pile. One student selects a strip from each pile and creates a sentence combining both elements. The student receives one point if the sentence is correct and logical. Return the strips to the bottom of each pile. Continue play until each student gets three chances to create a sentence. The winner is the student with the most points.

14

Los arqueólogos

🎤 **HABLAR EN PAREJA** Imagina que estás trabajando en una excavación arqueológica. Algunos de tus compañeros se olvidaron de hacer sus tareas, y tú quieres confirmar que se han hecho. Observa las fotos, y con un(a) compañero(a) hagan y contesten preguntas según el modelo.

▶ **Videomodelo**
Pedro / medir
A —¿Pedro ya midió la pirámide?
B —No, no creo que la haya medido.

1. Marcia / excavar

2. tú / pesar

3. Carlos y Raúl / trazar

4. usted / calcular

5. Mateo / estudiar

6. Teresa y Emilio / buscar

Differentiated Instruction

Students with Learning Difficulties

Make sure students understand the scenario of *Actividad* 16. Then have them read the questions in part 2 to set a purpose for listening. Play the interview once for students to get the gist. Have them revisit the questions and answer any that they can. Play the interview two more times so they can listen for any answers they missed.

Students with Special Needs

In order to complete *Actividad* 14, students with visually impaired partners will need to describe the object illustrated for each sentence. For example: *La foto es de unas ruinas muy antiguas. Parece que una persona las está excavando.*

Go **Online** to practice

PEARSON
realize™

PearsonSchool.com/Autentico

VIDEO AUDIO SPEAK/RECORD

Interpersonal 7

15

Y tú, ¿qué crees?

ESCRIBIR, HABLAR EN PAREJA Escribe tres frases acerca de tu escuela, familia, comunidad o país, y léeselas a otro(a) estudiante. Tu compañero(a) debe responder usando las expresiones del recuadro.

(no) es cierto que	(no) dudar que	(no) creer que
es (im)probable que	es (im)posible que	(no) estar seguro(a) de que

▶ **Videomodelo**

A —*Creo que nuestro equipo de béisbol puede ganar el campeonato este año.*

B —*Estoy seguro de que nuestro equipo puede ganar el campeonato.*

o: —*Dudo que nuestro equipo pueda ganar este año porque Tomás Álvarez era el mejor jugador y acaba de romperse la muñeca.*

16

La civilización misteriosa

ESCUCHAR, HABLAR, ESCRIBIR

1 Un famoso arqueólogo ha descubierto las ruinas de una antigua ciudad de una misteriosa civilización. Escucha la entrevista que le hace una periodista al arqueólogo.

2 Ahora, usa las preguntas como guía y parafrasea la idea principal del audio. Incluye el tema y los detalles más importantes.

1. ¿Por qué no cree el Dr. Romero que haya existido esta civilización hace millones de años?

2. ¿El Dr. Romero cree que se puede calcular la edad de las ruinas?

3. ¿Qué formas geométricas se han usado en los diseños de los edificios?

4. Según el Dr. Romero, ¿quiénes fueron los habitantes de esta civilización?

3 Escribe un párrafo sobre cómo te imaginas tú que haya sido esta misteriosa civilización.

Capítulo 7 • trescientos veintiuno **321**

Enrich Your Teaching

Teacher-to-Teacher

Students intrigued by the mysteries mentioned in this chapter might wish to create their own "mystery." Encourage them to do so and suggest different formats. Some might write a story or a scene that takes place within a lost civilization. Others might prepare and record a news flash about the discovery of a mysterious object or structure.

21st Century Skills

Communication Have students do research on the Internet about the work of an archeologist working in the field today. Using the information and questions from *Actividad* 16 as a model, have students create a list of questions they would ask him or her. What would they be most interested in finding out during an interview?

15

Standards: 1.1, 1.3

Suggestions: Suggest that students write some sentences about things they are sure about and some about things they are unsure about. This way, expressions of both doubt and certainty can be used meaningfully in the speaking part of the activity.

Answers will vary.

16

Standards: 1.2, 1.3

Resources: Teacher's Resource Materials: Audio Script, Technology: Audio Cap. 7

Suggestions: Play the audio or read from the script. Then allow students two minutes to look over the comprehension questions. Allow them to listen again before they write their answers to the questions.

 Technology: Audio Script:

PERIODISTA: Doctor Romero, ¿cree que la misteriosa civilización haya existido hace millones de años?

DR. ROMERO: Dudo que esta civilización haya existido hace millones de años. Es imposible que la ciudad se haya conservado tan bien todos estos años.

PERIODISTA: ¿Es posible que los científicos calculen de qué año son las ruinas?

DR. ROMERO: Sí, estoy seguro de que lo pueden calcular.

PERIODISTA: ¿Qué diseño cree usted que han tenido los demás edificios de la ciudad?

DR. ROMERO: En los diseños se han usado círculos, óvalos y triángulos.

PERIODISTA: ¿Quiénes cree Ud. que eran los habitantes de esta civilización?

DR. ROMERO: Es posible que hayan sido extraterrestres, pero por ahora no tenemos evidencia de eso.

Answers:

1. Es imposible que la ciudad se haya conservado tan bien por tantos años. Además, dice que los seres humanos están en la Tierra desde hace sólo un millón de años.

2. Sí, está seguro de que se puede calcular.

3. Se han usado círculos, óvalos y rectángulos.

4. Dice que es posible que hayan sido extraterrestres, pero todavía esto no se puede saber.

Standards: 1.1, 1.2

Suggestions: Tell students to respond to the questions in Step 1 as though the excursion happened in the past. They should also practice the past tenses in Step 3 when telling about their discoveries.

Answers will vary.

CULTURA

Standards: 1.1, 1.2, 3.1, 5.2

Resources: Mapa global interactivo

Technology: Mapa global interactivo, Actividad 3 Travel the Inca Trail in Peru.

Suggestions: After students read the information, show *Mapa de América del Sur (parte norte)* on pp. xxviii–xxix. Ask a volunteer to show the extent of the *Camino del Inca* in relation to all of South America. Then ask comprehension questions such as: *¿Por qué recorren hoy en día muchos turistas el Camino del Inca?*

Answers will vary.

Project-Based Learning

Students can perform Step 3 at this point. (For more information, see p. 304-b.)

Teacher-to-Teacher

Have students search the Internet to find the official Peruvian government Web page for Machu Picchu. Have them look for information such as when the site is open, how to get there, and three things they will see when they visit. Have them write a report in Spanish in which they present the information they have learned.

322

La misteriosa civilización

✎ **HABLAR EN GRUPO, DIBUJAR**

1 Imagina que eres un(a) arqueólogo(a) y te envían a trabajar a un lugar misterioso. En grupos pequeños, imaginen cómo fue su viaje. Respondan a las siguientes preguntas. Recuerden que van a inventar una civilización y que deben ser creativos al responder a las preguntas.

1. ¿Adónde fueron? *(desierto, montaña, bosque, mar, playa, etc.)* ¿En qué país estaba ese lugar?

2. ¿Encontraron ruinas? ¿Cómo eran?

3. ¿Qué objetos encontraron? ¿Qué forma tenían esos objetos?

4. ¿Qué estructuras encontraron? ¿Qué creen que representan?

5. ¿Cómo se imaginan que era la civilización? ¿Creen que la crearon extraterrestres?

2 Ahora, dibujen lo que sucedió en el viaje. Pueden ilustrar las respuestas a las preguntas anteriores.

3 Cada grupo debe contar su viaje a la clase mientras muestran los dibujos que hicieron. Los estudiantes deben responderles usando diferentes expresiones del recuadro de gramática de la página 318.

CULTURA ‹ **El mundo hispano**

El Camino del Inca Antes de la llegada de los españoles, el imperio[1] inca iba desde lo que es hoy el norte de Chile hasta Colombia. Para poder comunicarse con todas las ciudades de este imperio tan inmenso, los incas construyeron más de 15,000 millas de caminos. El Camino Real, también llamado Camino del Inca, va desde Colombia hasta Chile y tiene 3,250 millas de largo. (Es más largo que el camino más largo construído por los romanos, que iba desde Jerusalén hasta Escocia). El camino pasa a través de montañas, selvas y desiertos, y llega a muchas de las antiguas ciudades del imperio.

Hoy en día, muchos turistas recorren[2] el Camino del Inca para visitar las ruinas de ciudades como Machu Picchu y también para ver los impresionantes paisajes de la geografía de América del Sur.

Camino del Inca a **Machu Picchu**

Huayna Picchu · Machu Picchu · Inti Punco · Wiñay Wayna · Chachabamba · Phuyupatamarca · Conchamarca · Sayacmarca · Machu Quente · Runcuraccay · Patallaca · Huillca Raccay · Cuzco

LEYENDA
Sitio arqueológico
Camino del Inca
Río Urubamba
Vía del tren

Pre-AP® Integration: Los temas económicos ¿Es importante la construcción de caminos en la sociedad actual? ¿Por qué?

Mapa global interactivo Explora una sección del Camino del Inca en Perú. Investiga la geografía del área, recorre parte de la ruta y compárala con otros senderos conocidos.

[1]empire [2]travel (along)

Differentiated Instruction

Students with Learning Difficulties

Provide questions for the last three bulleted items in *Actividad* 18 to guide students in looking for information. For the first of the questions, ask: *¿Qué dice la leyenda? ¿Hay diferentes versiones?* For the second, ask: *¿Qué parte de la leyenda está basada en la verdad? ¿Qué es todavía un misterio?* For the third, ask: *¿Qué crees tú?*

Advanced Learners

Have students read more about the Incan civilization in encyclopedias or on the Internet. Ask them to report two facts about the Incas not mentioned in the *Cultura*.

Go **Online** to practice

PearsonSchool.com/Autentico

PEARSON
realize™

WRITING   MAPA GLOBAL

Interpersonal   7

18

¿Cómo se explica?

 LEER, ESCRIBIR, HABLAR EN GRUPO ¿Te has preguntado alguna vez sobre los misterios? En grupos de tres o cuatro estudiantes investiguen y presenten ante la clase algunos misterios inexplicables del mundo.

Para decir más

el fantasma	*ghost*
el OVNI	*UFO*
la casa encantada	*haunted house*
el poltergeist	*poltergeist*
el amuleto	*amulet*

1 Investiguen uno de los misterios que estudiaron u otros fenómenos inexplicables. Deben:

- investigar en periódicos, revistas, libros o en la Red, cuándo, dónde y qué sucedió
- describir los cuentos populares y leyendas que haya sobre ese misterio
- incluir las explicaciones científicas
- dar la opinión que ustedes tienen sobre ese misterio

2 Luego, hagan una presentación a la clase. Incluyan todo lo que encontraron, defiendan sus opiniones y recomienden sitios en donde se puede investigar más sobre estos misterios.

19

Machu Picchu

 LEER, ESCRIBIR En 1911, el norteamericano Hiram Bingham descubrió unas ruinas en las montañas del Perú. Cuando se excavaron las estructuras cubiertas por la selva, se descubrió una ciudad maravillosa.

Conexiones ‹ **La historia**

Ubicado[1] a 2,400 metros sobre el nivel del mar, Machu Picchu es uno de los lugares más impresionantes del planeta. Esta ciudad de los incas, de casi un kilómetro de extensión, tenía aproximadamente 1,000 habitantes durante el siglo XV. Su diseño es extraordinario, y sus muros[2], acueductos y observatorios fueron perfectamente construidos sin usar ni cemento ni argamasa[3].

Machu Picchu es considerada uno de los monumentos arquitectónicos y arqueológicos más importantes del mundo, pero la historia y función de Machu Picchu siguen siendo un misterio. Algunos creen que era una fortaleza; otros creen que era un monasterio.

- ¿Por qué es un fenómeno arquitectónico Machu Picchu?
- ¿Cuál se cree que era la función de Machu Picchu?
- ¿Por qué crees que no se descubrieron las ruinas hasta 1911?

[1]located [2]walls [3]mortar

Capítulo 7 • trescientos veintitrés 323

Enrich Your Teaching

Culture Note

Part of the mystery of Machu Picchu is the skill with which it was constructed. Many of the buildings' stones weigh more than 50 tons. However, they are fitted together so exactly (without mortar) that even a thin knife blade will not fit between them.

21st Century Skills

Media Literacy Have students search the Internet for more information on the Incan civilization using the key words: *el Camino del Inca, Machu Picchu,* and *Cuzco.* Ask students to identify other important archeological sites along *el Camino del Inca.*

18

Standards: 1.2, 1.3, 3.1

Suggestions: Encourage students to do the initial research on their own. They can then work together to compile their notes, work them into a report, and decide which visuals to use and how to most effectively use them.

Answers will vary.

19

Standards: 1.1, 1.2, 2.1, 3.1, 5.2

Suggestions: Once students have read the information silently, ask comprehension questions before moving on to the discussion questions. For example: *¿Qué palabra en la primera frase es un sinónimo de "encontrado"? **(Ubicado)** Esta palabra nombra una estructura que se parece a un puente para el agua. ¿Qué palabra es? **(el acueducto)***

Answers:

- Es un fenómeno arquitectónico porque sus muros, acueductos y observatorios fueron perfectamente construidos sin cemento ni argamasa.
- Algunos creen que era una fortaleza; otros creen que era un monasterio.
- Answers will vary.

Additional Resources

Technology: Online Resources
- Instant Check
- Guided, Core, Audio
- *Para hispanohablantes*
- Teacher's Resource Materials: Audio Script, Technology: Audio Cap. 7, Communicative Pair Activity

Print
- Guided WB pp. 221–222
- Core WB p. 95–97

Assessment

Prueba 7-3 with Remediation (online only)
Prueba: El subjuntivo con expresiones de duda
- Prueba 7-3
Examen: Vocabulario y gramática 1
- Examen 1
- ExamView: Examen 1

Vocabulario en contexto 2

Standards: 1.2

Resources: Teacher's Resource Materials: Input Script, Clip Art, Audio Script, Technology: Audio Cap. 7

Suggestions: Have students read along as you present the new vocabulary by playing the audio or reading the text aloud. Some vocabulary, such as *leyenda* and *sagrada,* can be taught by explanation: *Una leyenda es una historia muy antigua de una cultura. La historia de Robin Hood es una leyenda inglesa. En nuestra cultura las sinagogas y las iglesias son lugares sagrados.* Other vocabulary, such as *brillaba* and *cualquier* can be taught by demonstration. For *brillar,* for example, look at a light, cover your eyes, squint, and say: *Esa lámpara brilla mucho.* For *cualquier,* present a student with cards as for a card trick and say: *Elige una carta, cualquier carta.* Finally, check comprehension by asking questions. See the Input Scripts in the *Teacher's Resource Materials* for specific questions.

Pre-AP® Integration

- **Learning Objective:** Interpretive: Print
- **Activity:** As a pre-reading activity for this reading, have students preview the title, the subtitles and the visuals, and then create a list of questions they believe will be answered in the reading. Have students follow along as you read the article out loud. Then, have them confirm their answers by reading the text.
- **Pre-AP® Resource Materials:** Comprehensive guide to Pre-AP® reading skill development.

Technology: Interactive Whiteboard

Vocabulary Activities 7-2 Use the whiteboard activities in your Teacher Resources as you progress through the vocabulary practice with your class.

Vocabulario en contexto 2

Vocabulario en contexto 2

OBJECTIVES
Read, listen to, and understand information about
▶ Myths and legends
▶ Contributions from ancient civilizations

🔊 Entrevista con una experta

Juan escribe para la revista de la escuela. Este mes entrevistó a la profesora Rita, experta en mitos y leyendas de los indígenas americanos.

Juan **Sra. Rita**

Máscara de oro de los incas

Tótem de los seminoles

Juan: ¿Por qué eran tan importantes los **mitos** y las **leyendas** para los antiguos **habitantes** de las Américas, como los incas, aztecas, hopi, mowhawk y seminoles?

Sra. Rita: Estas historias explicaban el mundo como hoy lo hacen las **teorías** científicas, o sea que expresaban las **creencias** de los pueblos sobre **el origen** de su cultura, del **universo** y de los fenómenos naturales.

Serpiente emplumada en el templo de Quetzalcóatl, Teotihuacán

Vía Láctea

Juan: ¿Puede darme un ejemplo?

Sra. Rita: En muchas culturas hay mitos sobre la Vía Láctea. ¿Has visto ese conjunto de estrellas? ¡Parecen miles de luces que alguien **arrojó** al cielo! Para los incas, esa inmensa cinta que **brillaba** en el cielo entre las sombras de la noche era un río de agua **sagrada**. Para los aztecas era una serpiente, pero no **cualquier** serpiente: era uno de sus principales **dioses**.

324 trescientos veinticuatro • Capítulo 7 • ¿Mito o realidad?

Differentiated Instruction

Students with Learning Difficulties

Before students begin to read, draw their attention to the boldface words in the text. Remind them that these are all vocabulary words that are listed at the end of the chapter. Encourage students to refer to the chapter vocabulary list as they read, if necessary.

Advanced Learners

On note cards or slips of paper, write several terms, such as *Quetzalcóatl, el mito de la Vía Láctea,* and *la leyenda de los seminoles.* Once students have read the selection, have them close their books. Place the cards or slips in a container and have students take turns drawing one at a time and explaining it in their own words.

Juan: ¿La mayoría de los mitos eran sobre el cielo?

Sra. Rita: No, había mitos muy variados. Por ejemplo, los hopi creían en una civilización de hombres-hormiga que vivían en el centro de **la Tierra**. Salían a nuestro mundo por el cráter del volcán Shasta. Los hopi hicieron dibujos en la roca que muestran a esos hombres.

Juan: ¿Y las leyendas sobre animales? ¿Son similares entre distintas culturas?

Sra. Rita: Similares y diferentes. Por ejemplo, muchas culturas relacionaban al **conejo** con la inteligencia para sobrevivir. La leyenda de los seminoles describe los **intentos** del conejo por robar el fuego para dárselo a los hombres. La leyenda de los mohawk es muy distinta. Es sobre un conejo gigante que **apareció** en el bosque cuando ellos estaban cazando. Los mohawk iban a atacarlo, pero el conejo comenzó a bailar. La situación de peligro **se convirtió** en celebración y ¡todos terminaron bailando! ¡Las leyendas son distintas, pero tienen muchos temas en común!

20

¿Qué sabes?

 ESCUCHAR Escribe en una hoja los números del 1 al 6. Escucha las frases. Escribe *C* (cierto) o *F* (falso) para cada frase.

21

¿Y el conejo?

 ESCRIBIR Según el relato del conejo, ¿en qué orden se sucedieron los siguientes sucesos? Numéralos del 1 al 5.

a. El conejo empezó a bailar.
b. Los mohawk quisieron atacarlo.
c. Todos terminaron bailando.
d. El conejo apareció en silencio.
e. Los mohawk estaban cazando en el bosque.

Capítulo 7 • trescientos veinticinco **325**

Enrich Your Teaching

Teacher-to-Teacher
Some students might be curious about the dance of the Big Rabbit in the story of the Mohawk. Invite them to do a research about a popular dance in Mexico called "Dance of the Deer". Ask them to find out details about its origins, its meaning, its music, and what costumes are used when it is performed.

21st Century Skills
ICT (Information, Communications and Technology) Literacy Have students use the digital technology within **Realize** to access and manage the audio files, videos, and activities that support learning the new vocabulary. Students can access the eText Audio to follow along with the *Entrevista con una experta* reading, then do additional vocabulary activities.

20

Standards: 1.2, 2.1, 2.2, 3.1

Resources: Teacher's Resource Materials: Audio Script, Technology: Audio Cap. 7

Suggestions: Before engaging students in the listening activity, give them a few minutes to read the information on these two pages silently and address any comprehension problems they may still have. Then play the audio or read from the script. Allow students to listen more than once.

Technology: Audio Script and Answers

Escribe en una hoja los números del 1 al 6. Escucha las frases. Escribe *C* (cierto) o *F* (falso) para cada frase. Vas a oír cada frase dos veces.
1. Las leyendas y los mitos son historias reales basados en el universo. *(F)*
2. Los mitos y las leyendas explican las creencias de los pueblos sobre el origen de las cosas. *(C)*
3. Los incas creían que la Vía Láctea era un río de agua sagrada. *(C)*
4. La serpiente era un dios muy importante en la civilización azteca. *(C)*
5. Los habitantes de las Américas no creían en dioses que fuesen animales. *(F)*
6. Los mohawk mataron al conejo para que no bailara más. *(F)*

Extension: Have students correct the answers they marked *false.* Have them do so by first making the original statement negative, then stating the correct fact: *Los habitantes de las Américas creían que algunos dioses eran animales.*

Starter Activity
Show the map of México on pp. xxii–xxiii. Point out the locations of *Popocatépetl* and *Iztaccíhuatl.* Ask a volunteer to remind the class which indigenous group of *México* is represented in the legend by these two volcanoes.

21

Standards: 1.2, 2.2, 3.1

Suggestions: If students have difficulty ordering the events, model for them how to scan the text on these two pages in order to reference each event.

Answers: 1-e; 2-d; 3-b; 4-a; 5-c

Vocabulario en contexto 2

Standards: 1.1, 1.2, 3.1, 5.2

Resources: Teacher's Resource Materials: Input Script, Clip Art, Audio Script, Technology: Audio Cap. 7

 Technology: Mapa global interactivo, Actividad 4 Compare the extent of the Aztec and Mayan empires.

Suggestions:

Pre-reading: Ask a volunteer to read aloud the main title. Say: *El título principal nos dice que esta lectura se trata de los mitos de dos culturas. ¿Cuáles son las dos culturas que van a compararse? (los mayas y los aztecas)* Point out new vocabulary items that are cognates: **astrónomos, planetas, eclipses,** and **símbolos.**

Reading: Allow students time to read the information on this page and the next silently first. Then play the audio or read the text and have students read along as they listen. Allow them to listen more than once. Demonstrate the meaning of **al igual que** by saying *Al igual que inglés, Uds. también hablan español.* Ask students what verb they think the noun **escritura** comes from. *(escribir)*

Post-reading: Check comprehension by asking questions. See the Input Script in the *Teacher's Resource Materials* for specific questions.

Starter Activity

Have students take a quick look at the illustrations on pages 326–327 without reading the captions. Ask them to make a list of the things that they see there.

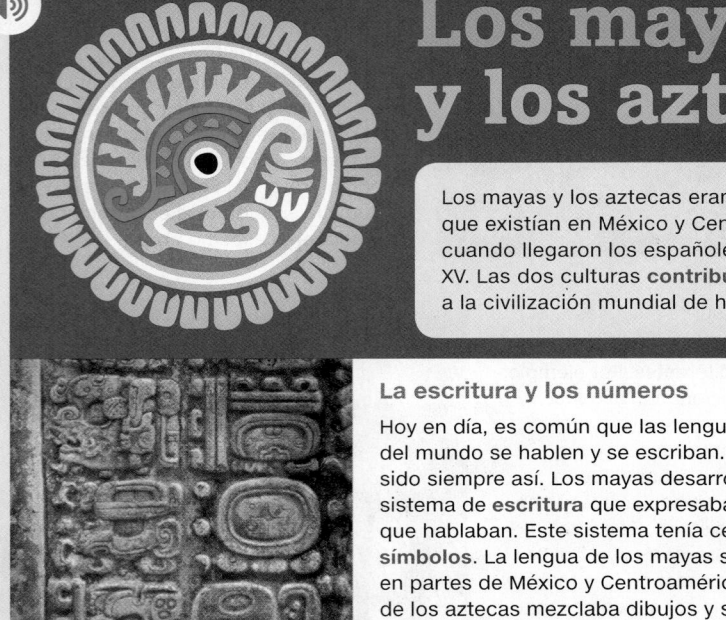

Los mayas y los aztecas

Los mayas y los aztecas eran dos pueblos que existían en México y Centroamérica cuando llegaron los españoles en el siglo XV. Las dos culturas **contribuyeron** mucho a la civilización mundial de hoy.

Algunos símbolos de la escritura azteca

La escritura y los números

Hoy en día, es común que las lenguas *(languages)* del mundo se hablen y se escriban. Pero no ha sido siempre así. Los mayas desarrollaron un sistema de **escritura** que expresaba la lengua que hablaban. Este sistema tenía cerca de 800 **símbolos.** La lengua de los mayas se habla todavía en partes de México y Centroamérica. La escritura de los aztecas mezclaba dibujos y símbolos. A veces, el número cinco era el dibujo de una mano, porque la mano tiene cinco dedos.

Los templos

Los mayas y los aztecas tenían pirámides como parte de su cultura. Como los dioses eran muy importantes, las dos civilizaciones construyeron sus templos sobre las pirámides.

"El Castillo", un templo maya sobre una pirámide en Chichén Itzá, en México

---

Differentiated Instruction

Heritage Speakers

Have students use the Internet to learn more about one of the topics presented in the reading. Invite them to present their findings orally to the class.

Students with Learning Difficulties

Read the introductory paragraph. Then draw students' attention to *Actividad* 22 and the chart that they will fill out after they read. Have students look at the headings in the reading and help them decide in which section they will probably find each piece of information.

Los números y el calendario

Los mayas fueron grandes matemáticos. Descubrieron el concepto del cero, un concepto fundamental en las matemáticas que usamos hoy día. Los aztecas, **al igual que** los mayas, eran grandes **astrónomos**. Los mayas observaron los movimientos del Sol desde que salía por la mañana hasta que **se ponía** por la noche. No solo estudiaron el Sol **sino** también las estrellas, **los planetas** y la Luna.

Los mayas y los aztecas tenían dos calendarios distintos. Uno, el sagrado, estaba basado en los dioses y la religión. El otro era como el que usamos nosotros, basado en el año solar de 365 días. Los mayas no sabían cómo ocurrían **los eclipses**, pero creían que cuando el Sol estaba oscuro era porque los dioses estaban enojados.

Observatorio "El Caracol (snail)", en la ciudad maya de Chichén Itzá

Calendario azteca, ▶ también llamado "Piedra del Sol"

22

¿Con qué contribuyeron?

✏️ **ESCRIBIR** Después de leer la información de estas páginas, completa el cuadro sobre lo que contribuyeron los mayas y los aztecas.

	Mayas	Aztecas
Astronomía		
Calendario		
Escritura		
Números		
Templos		

Capítulo 7 • trescientos veintisiete **327**

23

Standards: 1.2, 2.1, 2.2, 3.1

Suggestions: At first glance, students may think there is more than one correct answer for some items. Encourage them to scan the entire activity first and to use the process of elimination to determine the best answer for each item.

Answers:

1. leyendas
2. astrónomo
3. dioses
4. eclipse
5. símbolos

Starter Activity

Have students complete the following sentences by selecting the appropriate verb and conjugating it in the preterite or imperfect as needed.

1. Los mayas _____ (construir/desarrollar) un sistema de escritura.

2. Los aztecas _____ (tener/destruir) pirámides como parte de su cultura.

3. Los mayas _____ (descubrir/dibujar) el concepto del cero.

4. La escritura de los aztecas _____ (mezclar/convertir) dibujos y símbolos.

Answers: 1. desarrollaron 2. tenían
 3. descubrieron 4. mezclaba

24

Standards: 1.2, 2.1, 2.2, 3.1

Suggestions: Encourage students to scan the complete paragraph before they attempt to write their answers.

Answers:

1. se movían
2. planeta
3. dios
4. símbolos
5. creencia
6. habitantes

Active Classroom

After completing *En voz alta,* have students write a poem about nature modeled after the first verse in *Sueño cuarto (la luz).* Have students read their poem to a small group of students.

Vocabulario en uso 2

OBJECTIVES
▸ Read about ancient civilizations
▸ Discuss myths and legends

23

Un poco de todo . . .

 LEER Completa las siguientes frases con las palabras del recuadro.

dioses	leyendas	eclipse	astrónomo	símbolos

1. Los aztecas crearon _____ para explicar el origen del universo.
2. El _____ estudia los planetas y las estrellas desde el observatorio.
3. Las civilizaciones antiguas creían en muchos _____.
4. Durante un _____, la Luna cubre el Sol y la Tierra se queda a oscuras.
5. La escritura maya tiene una gran cantidad de _____.

24

El calendario azteca

 LEER Completa este párrafo con la palabra correcta que describe el calendario azteca.

El calendario azteca fue uno de los objetos más importantes de esa cultura. No sólo mostraba los días, sino que mostraba cómo __1.__ *(se movían / se convertían)* el Sol, la Luna y el __2.__ *(estrella / planeta)* Venus. El calendario es una piedra muy grande en forma de círculo y pesa 20 toneladas. En su centro está la cara de Tonatiuh, el __3.__ *(conejo / dios)* del sol que, rodeada[1] por otros __4.__ *(símbolos / mitos)*, representa el universo. Los aztecas tenían la __5.__ *(creencia / línea)* de que para mantener el orden del sistema del universo debían hacer ciertas ceremonias. Por ejemplo, los antiguos __6.__ *(sistemas / habitantes)* de la Ciudad de México ponían el calendario en posición horizontal como si fuera un espejo del cielo.

[1]surrounded

Differentiated Instruction

Students with Learning Difficulties

Have students break *Actividad* 25 into two tasks. First encourage them to identify which cue in column A matches the one in column B. Once students have identified these pairs, they can concentrate on the structure of their questions and answers.

Advanced Learners

Ask students to research and report interesting facts about our own Gregorian calendar. They can reference the Internet or other sources such as encyclopedias. Suggest that they look for information about such things as the creation of the calendar, the origins of month names, or the purpose of leap year.

Según la leyenda . . .

 HABLAR EN PAREJA Trabaja con tu compañero(a) para hablar sobre lo que están aprendiendo de las civilizaciones antiguas. Sigue el modelo.

Videomodelo

A —*Según una leyenda mexicana, dos volcanes eran antes unos novios, ¿no?*

B —*Sí, se casaron contra los deseos de sus padres.*

Estudiante A

Según una leyenda/un mito/una creencia . . .
1. la cinta de luces en el cielo era un río sagrado
2. unos extraterrestres construyeron el Machu Picchu
3. los hombres-hormiga vivían en el centro de la Tierra
4. los conejos existían en los tiempos de los mohawk
5. Atlántida fue una gran civilización en el Mediterráneo
6. Machu Picchu fue un centro comercial importante

Estudiante B

la erupción de un volcán causó su destrucción

los científicos no están seguros del origen de estas ruinas

lo hicieron para saber dónde aterrizar (land) sus naves espaciales

es la Vía Láctea

salían por el cráter del volcán

tienen un baile que los representa

¿Recuerdas?
In Spanish the diphthong *ue* is pronounced "*we*" as in "wet." Read and pronounce: *trueno, fuego*.

En voz alta

En México, muchos escritores de ascendencia maya escriben en el idioma nativo de sus antepasados[1]. Lo hacen para mantener vivos su idioma, cultura y para conservar los cuentos y las creencias que antes se trasmitían por tradición oral.

Feliciano Sánchez Chan nació en Yucatán, en 1960. Sus obras *Retazos*[2] *de vida* y *X-Marcela* han sido premiadas en concursos de literatura de la lengua maya.

Escucha el poema de Sánchez Chan y trata de repetirlo en voz alta.

- Nombra tres elementos naturales que se mencionan en el poema. ¿Crees que es importante la naturaleza en la cultura del poeta? ¿Por qué?

"Sueño cuarto (la luz)"
de Feliciano Sánchez Chan

Soy el trueno que ha venido
con su luz
de eternas profundidades
para alumbrar[3] el camino blanco
por donde transitan tus hijos, Madre.
. . .
El señor fuego es mi hermano mayor.
Hoy he venido
con mis cuatro hermanas:
la lluvia del oriente[4],
la lluvia del poniente[5],
la lluvia del norte
y la lluvia del sur.
. . .

[1]ancestors [2]snippets [3]to light [4]east [5]west

Capítulo 7 • ciento veintinueve 329

Standards: 1.1, 1.2

Suggestions: Explain that Student B must read to determine the correct cue and adapt it for his or her response.

Answers will vary. The following answers show the relationship between the comments of both partners:

1. A —Según una leyenda azteca, la cinta de luces en el cielo era un río sagrado, ¿no?
   B —Sí, era un río de agua sagrada, aunque en realidad es la Vía Láctea.
2. A —Según mucha gente, unos extraterrestres construyeron el Machu Picchu, ¿no?
   B —Sí, algunos dicen que lo hicieron para saber dónde aterrizar sus naves espaciales.
3. A —Según un mito, los hombres-hormiga...
   B —Sí, y salían por el cráter del volcán.
4. A —Según la leyenda de los mohawk, los conejos...
   B —Sí, y ahora tienen un baile...
5. A —Según mucha gente, Atlántida fue una gran civilización....
   B —Sí, pero la erupción de un volcán....
6. A —Según algunos arqueólogos, Machu Picchu fue....
   B —Sí, pero los científicos no están....

EN VOZ ALTA

Standards: 1.2, 1.3, 2.1, 2.2, 3.1, 3.2, 5.2

Resources: Teacher's Resource Materials: Audio Script, Technology: Audio Cap. 7

Suggestions: Have students practice reciting with a partner first, then ask volunteers to recite the poem fragment for the class.

Answers:

- el trueno, el rayo, la lluvia; Remainder of answer will vary.

Project-Based Learning

Students can perform Step 4 at this point. Be sure they understand your corrections and suggestions. (For more information, see p. 304-b.)

Enrich Your Teaching

Teacher-to-Teacher

Many books are available on the subject of ancient Latin American civilizations, and many among these contain beautiful pictures of ruins and artists' conceptions of what ancient cities may have been like. If possible, obtain such books from your local library. Have students sit with the books and talk about the pictures, using the vocabulary and structures they are now studying. When searching for books, look under topics such as archaeology and ancient Mesoamerica, as well as under the names of civilizations such as Inca, Maya, Olmec, and Aztec.

26

Suggestions: Remind students that they are to use their imaginations. Their explanations might resemble those in Mayan or Aztec legends, but they should invent their own.

Common Errors: Students will sometimes confuse *por qué* and *porque.* Remind them that the first is a question and the second an answer. Point out that they can use the accent mark in *por qué* as a reminder, since they know that accent marks appear in question words.

Answers will vary.

27

 Technology: Mapa global interactivo, Actividad 5 Look at rain forest habitat in Guatemala.

Suggestions: Have students read through the legend once on their own, then a second time with a partner. During the second reading, partners can help each other with difficult words or sentences.

Answers:
1. Quetzal era el hijo del cacique de una tribu quiché. Chiruma era el hermano del cacique (el tío de Quetzal).
2. Chiruma le robó la pluma de colibrí que lo protegía.
3. La pluma de colibrí es un símbolo de la buena suerte.

Additional Resources

 Technology: Online Resources
- Audio, Writing, Reading
- Communication Activities
- Teacher's Resource Materials: Audio Script, Communicative Pair Activities, Technology: Audio Cap. 7

Assessment

Prueba 7-5 with Remediation (online only)
Prueba: Aplicación del vocabulario 2
- Prueba 7-5

26

Mitos y leyendas

ESCRIBIR En los mitos y las leyendas la gente inventa razones para explicar ciertas cosas. Usa tu imaginación para escribir una frase sobre seis de los siguientes fenómenos de la naturaleza. Explica por qué . . .

Modelo
. . . hay truenos
Hay truenos porque los dioses están tocando los tambores.

1. . . . cae lluvia
2. . . . hace viento
3. . . . se pone el sol
4. . . . ocurre un eclipse
5. . . . aparecen sombras
6. . . . brillan las estrellas

27

Una leyenda quiché

LEER, ESCRIBIR Lee esta leyenda de los indígenas quichés de Guatemala sobre el pájaro quetzal, símbolo de la libertad y nombre de su moneda.

Quetzal nunca muere

Quetzal era el hijo del cacique[1] de una tribu[2] quiché[3]. Todos los habitantes lo admiraban y sabían que un día Quetzal se iba a convertir en el jefe de la tribu. Pero Chiruma, el hermano del cacique, estaba celoso de Quetzal.

Cuando Quetzal fue mayor, el adivino[4] le dijo: "No morirás nunca, Quetzal. Vivirás eternamente". Durante una lucha contra otra tribu, Chiruma se dio cuenta de que las flechas[5] que le arrojaban a Quetzal nunca lo herían[6]. Entonces Chiruma pensó que debía tener un amuleto. Esa noche, cuando Quetzal dormía, Chiruma entró en su cuarto y descubrió al lado de Quetzal una pluma de colibrí[7]. Recordó que el colibrí era un símbolo de la buena suerte[8] y robó la pluma.

Cuando murió el cacique, los ancianos escogieron a Quetzal para ser el nuevo jefe. Un día Quetzal caminaba por el bosque cuando de repente apareció un colibrí. El colibrí le dijo a Quetzal: "Soy tu protector y vengo a decirte que alguien quiere matarte".

De pronto oyó un silbido[9] y una flecha penetró en su pecho. Quetzal cayó sobre la hierba[10] verde y murió. Pero los dioses, que habían predicho una vida eterna, lo convirtieron en un hermoso pájaro. Su cuerpo tomó el color del césped, su pecho conservó el color de la sangre y el sol puso en su larga cola[11] muchos colores.

[1]chief [2]tribe [3]indigenous people of Guatemala [4]fortune-teller [5]arrows [6]wounded [7]hummingbird's feather [8]luck [9]whistling sound [10]grass [11]tail

¿Comprendiste?

1. ¿Quién es Quetzal? ¿Quién es Chiruma?
2. ¿Qué hizo Chiruma para vengarse *(get revenge)* cuando no lo escogieron para ser el cacique de la tribu?
3. ¿Qué representa el símbolo de la pluma de colibrí?

Mapa global interactivo Investiga una reserva dedicada a la protección del quetzal y compárala con áreas similares en tu estado o región.

Differentiated Instruction

Heritage Speakers

Encourage students to read Spanish-language materials recreationally for at least five to ten minutes per day. Allow them to read a book, magazine, or a newspaper of their choice. As students learn to enjoy reading recreationally in Spanish, they will improve their academic reading skills as well.

Linguistic Learner

Challenge students to pronounce the names of the Aztec gods in the Nahuatl language. When the letters *tl* occur together, they are pronounced as a single consonant, but not as a separate syllable (there is no vowel sound). Have students produce the sound by saying "nightly" without the final /i/ sound.

Gramática

OBJECTIVES
▶ Make negative statements
▶ Discuss and read about Aztec gods

Go **Online** to practice

PEARSON **realize**™

PearsonSchool.com/Autentico

VIDEO WRITING MAPA GLOBAL

Pero y sino

The word *pero* is usually the equivalent of the English conjunction *but*. However, there is another word in Spanish, *sino*, that also means *but*. *Sino* is used after a negative, in order to offer the idea of an alternative: *not this, but rather that*.

No voy a beber jugo de frutas **sino** agua.

• You can also use *sino* with *no solo. . . sino también. . . (not only . . . but also)*

Apareció **no solo** el sol **sino también** la luna.

• You use *sino que* instead of *sino* when there is a conjugated verb in the second part of the sentence.

No vendí mis libros **sino que** los regalé.

Más recursos ONLINE

▶ **Tutorial:** Use of *pero*, *sino* and *sino que*

28

¿Qué dice el artículo?

LEER Imagina que estás leyendo diferentes noticias y artículos. Decide si la palabra que completa cada frase es *pero* o *sino*.

1. Hizo varios intentos por convertirse en astrónomo _____ no lo consiguió.
2. No construirán un nuevo observatorio _____ que repararán el viejo.
3. No sólo se ven sombras en la Luna _____ también figuras oscuras.
4. Creía que el lugar era sagrado _____ ahora no estoy seguro.
5. Según la creencia, no fue un solo dios _____ todos.
6. Tenían no sólo información _____ también evidencia importante.

29

Dioses de los aztecas

LEER, HABLAR EN PAREJA Lee la lista de los dioses de los aztecas. Trabaja con otro(a) compañero(a) para hacer frases usando sino y pero.

Modelo
Quetzalcóatl no sólo era el dios del conocimiento sino también de la civilización.

Los DIOSES importantes de los AZTECAS

Coatlicue – La primera diosa: creó la Luna y las estrellas

Huitzilopochtli – Dios de la guerra y el Sol

Quetzalcóatl – Dios del conocimiento y la civilización

Ehecatl – Dios del viento

Mictlantecuhtle – Dios de los muertos

Tláloc – Dios de la lluvia

Xiuhtecuhtli – Dios del fuego

Capítulo 7 • trescientos treinta y uno **331**

Enrich Your Teaching

Teacher-to-Teacher

When talking about ancient civilizations, many unusual words appear, such as the names of gods in *Actividad* 29. Point out that these names come from ancient languages, but their spellings are based on the Spanish alphabet. Help students apply the Spanish phonics skills to sound out the words.

21st Century Skills

ICT (Information, Communications and Technology) Literacy Remind students of the various digital tools available in **Realize** to help them monitor their own understanding and learning needs, such as the online tutorials with comprehension check exercises, animated verbs, and additional grammar practice activities.

Interpersonal 7

Gramática

Standards: 4.1

Suggestions: Provide students with pairs of cues and ask them to make sentences like the models shown in *Gramática.* Tell them to make their sentences using past tenses. For example **ver la película en el cine/verla en casa:** *No vi la película en el cine sino que la vi en casa.*

 Technology: Interactive Whiteboard

Grammar Activities 7-2 Use the whiteboard activities in your Teacher Resources as you progress through the grammar practice with your class.

28

Standards: 1.2

Suggestions: Remind students that **no sólo** in the first part of a sentence is a hint telling them that they must use **sino también** in the second part.

Answers:

1. pero
2. sino
3. sino
4. pero
5. sino
6. sino

29

Standards: 1.2, 2.2, 3.1

Suggestions: Invite pairs of students to share their sentences with others. Encourage them to turn the sharing into a conversation by asking each other questions about the gods:

A —¿Tláloc era el dios del Sol?

B —Tláloc no era el dios del Sol sino de la lluvia.

Answers will vary.

Additional Resources

Technology: Online Resources
• Instant Check
• Guided, Core, Audio
• *Para hispanohablantes*
Print
• Guided WB pp. 231–232
• Core WB pp. 100

Assessment

Prueba 7-6 with Remediation (online only)
Prueba: *Pero y sino*
• Prueba 7-6

331

Gramática

Suggestions: By now, students have seen enough uses for the subjunctive to be able to begin to make subtle associations regarding its meaning. Ask them to give English equivalents for the Spanish models in the *Gramática*. Point out that the subjunctive mood often has the connotation of hypothesis, which can be translated by the English auxiliary verb "might." For this reason, *Busco un libro que tenga un artículo sobre los mayas* can be translated to "I'm looking for a book that might have an article about the Maya."

 Technology: Interactive Whiteboard

> **Grammar Activities 7-2** Use the whiteboard activities in your Teacher Resources as you progress through the grammar practice with your class.

30

Standards: 1.2

Suggestions: Remind students that the subjunctive is used when referring to something that only hypothetically exists. This is true when we refer to things we haven't found or aren't sure of yet. Once we begin talking about something or someone we definitely know of, we use the indicative.

Answers:

1. sea
2. hace
3. tiene
4. sepa
5. pueda
6. guste
7. sirva

Pre-AP® Integration

- **Learning Objective:** Interpersonal Writing
- **Activity:** Have students write an e-mail to a friend where they describe the qualities necessary for the perfect Spanish teacher. They can start their e-mail by completing the phrase, *"Busco un profesor de español que..."* and add a series of qualities. Be sure students ask their friend at least one question about their ideal Spanish teacher.
- **Pre-AP® Resource Materials:** Comprehensive guide to Pre-AP® writing skill development.

Gramática

OBJECTIVES
▶ Provide descriptions of people or things you know or you don't know
▶ Talk and write about a legend you know

El subjuntivo en cláusulas adjetivas

Sometimes you use an entire clause to describe a noun. This is called an adjective clause.

- When you have a specific person or thing in mind, you use the indicative.

  Este libro tiene un artículo **que habla** sobre los mayas.

- If you don't have a specific person or thing in mind, or if you are not sure the person exists, you use the subjunctive. Sometimes *cualquier(a)* is used in these expressions.

  Busco un libro **que tenga** un artículo sobre los mayas.
  Escoge **cualquier** cosa **que te guste**.

- You also use the subjunctive in an adjective clause when it describes a negative word such as *nadie, nada,* or *ninguno(a)*.

  No hay **nadie que conozca** los símbolos aztecas.

To refer to something or someone unknown in the past, you can use the present perfect subjunctive.

  Busco a una joven **que haya estudiado** arqueología.
  No hay nadie **que haya visto** un extraterrestre.

> **Más recursos** ONLINE
>
> ▶ **Tutorial:** Use of Subjunctive in Adjective Clauses
>
> 🔊 *Canción de hip hop:* Los misterios del mundo

30

El proyecto sobre culturas antiguas

 LEER Un grupo de estudiantes va a hacer un proyecto para representar algunos aspectos artísticos de las culturas antiguas. Están tratando de decidir a quiénes y qué necesitan para hacer su proyecto. Completa las siguientes frases con el presente del subjuntivo o del indicativo.

—Necesitamos encontrar a un estudiante que __1.__ *(ser)* muy artístico para hacer dibujos de los dioses.

—Yo conozco a una chica que __2.__ *(hacer)* dibujos bonitos.

—Fernando compró un libro que __3.__ *(tener)* diseños de la Pirámide del sol. Hagamos un modelo de ella. ¿Conocemos a alguien que __4.__ *(saber)* hacer construcciones de cerámica?

—No conozco ningún estudiante que __5.__ *(poder)* hacer un modelo de la pirámide.

—El calendario azteca es fascinante. Podemos dibujarlo y pintarlo como nos __6.__ *(gustar)*.

—Buena idea. Busquemos una foto que nos __7.__ *(servir)* de modelo.

Differentiated Instruction

Students with Learning Difficulties

Review how to form the present subjunctive and give examples: 1) form the first person singular in the present tense: ***hablo, vengo;*** 2) take away ***o: habl-, veng-;*** 3) add "opposite" endings (**-e** for **-ar** verbs and ***a*** for **-er** and **-ir** verbs): ***hable, venga;*** 4) make verbs agree with subjects: ***que yo hable, que ella venga.***

Challenge/Pre-AP®

Have students write three sentences that set up a situation in which there is a need. Have them trade sentences with a partner, who then makes a suggestion:

A —*Tengo que hacer una investigación sobre el calendario azteca, pero no sé cómo empezar.*
B —*Necesitas encontrar un sitio en el Internet que pueda ayudarte.*

31

Investigación sobre las culturas antiguas

LEER, ESCRIBIR Imagina que tienes que investigar acerca de las culturas antiguas. Usa tu imaginación y completa las frases usando la forma correcta del verbo. Añade detalles a cada frase.

Modelo
Busco una biblioteca que (*estar*). . .
Busco una biblioteca que esté cerca de mi casa.

1. Necesito un libro que (explicar). . .
2. Yo sé de un libro que (hablar). . .
3. No hay nadie que (conocer). . .
4. No hay nada que (decir). . .
5. Escogeré cualquier artículo que (gustar). . .
6. Quiero encontrar una página Web que (tener). . .
7. Mi amigo tiene varios artículos que (aparecer). . .
8. Tengo que hablar con las personas que (contribuir). . .

Museo Nacional de Antropología, ▲
Ciudad de México

32

¿A quién conoces que sepa . . . ?

HABLAR EN PAREJA Trabaja con otro(a) estudiante para identificar a personas de tu escuela o comunidad que hayan hecho o sepan hacer diferentes cosas.

Videomodelo
A —*¿Hay alguien en nuestra escuela que sepa hablar tres idiomas?*
B —*Sí, el padre de Berta sabe hablar español, italiano e inglés.*
o: —*No sé. No conozco a nadie que sepa hablar tres idiomas.*

Estudiante A

1. tener un coche deportivo
2. conocer a una persona famosa
3. haber ganado un campeonato de deportes
4. ser actor / actriz de cine
5. haber vivido en un país extranjero por más de un año
6. contribuir su tiempo como voluntario(a)

Estudiante B

¡Respuesta personal!

31

Standards: 1.2, 1.3

Suggestions: Remind students to stay within the context of the research project that is set up in the instructions. All of their completed sentences should make sense within that context.

Wording of sentences will vary. Students will use the following verb forms:

Answers:
1. explique
2. habla
3. conozca
4. diga
5. me guste
6. tenga
7. aparecen
8. contribuyen

32

Standards: 1.1

Suggestions: Point out that since Student A is asking if a certain kind of person exists, that person is only hypothetical, and so the subjunctive must be used in the question. If Student B doesn't know of anyone, then such a person remains hypothetical and the subjunctive continues to be used.

Answers:
Students will choose from among the following verb forms. Student A will always use the subjunctive in the question. Student B will use the indicative if he or she knows of a particular person, and the subjunctive if not.

1. tenga/tiene
2. conozca/conoce
3. haya ganado/ha ganado
4. sea/es
5. haya vivido/ha vivido (vivió)
6. contribuya/contribuye

Enrich Your Teaching

Teacher-to-Teacher
Students tend to have difficulty understanding the subjunctive since it has all but disappeared in English. Give them the example "If I were you...." Since the situation is hypothetical, we don't use the indicative "am." Instead, "were" acts as a vestige of the old English subjunctive.

21st Century Skills
Communication Have students work together to create a list of actions, skills, or experiences to use in *Actividad* 32 when asking specifically about the students in the class. *"¿Hay alguien en la clase que sepa...?"* Encourage students to come up with unique questions to ask their classmates.

Starter Activity

Briefly review with students vocabulary associated with jobs and job qualifications. This can be found in the *A ver si recuerdas* and *Vocabulario en contexto* sections of *Capítulos* 5 and 6.

33

Standards: 1.1, 1.3

Suggestions: Remind students to use the subjunctive in an adjective clause that modifies someone or something that they are searching for. If an adjective clause modifies something that is already known about, such as a course or a facility at a school, they must use the indicative.

Answers will vary.

El español en el mundo del trabajo

Standards: 1.2, 5.1

Suggestions: Once students have read the information, ask comprehension questions. For example: *¿Para qué profesiones dan cursos en español?* **(diferentes profesiones, incluyendo guías de turismo)** *En tus propias palabras, describe un paseo típico que da un profesor por la ciudad con sus estudiantes.*

33

Tu anuncio clasificado

 ESCRIBIR, HABLAR EN PAREJA

1 Imagina que decides aprender otro idioma o cambiar de trabajo. Escribe un anuncio clasificado para el periódico solicitando un(a) maestro(a) o una escuela de idiomas o pidiendo trabajo.

Modelo
Busco una escuela de idiomas que dé clases de chino.

2 Ahora, trabaja con otro(a) estudiante para intercambiar los anuncios que hicieron. Cada uno(a) debe responder al anuncio con un mensaje breve.

Videomodelo
A —*Busco una escuela de idiomas que dé clases de chino.*
B —*Yo conozco una escuela que da clases de chino.*

El español en el mundo del trabajo

Antigua, en Guatemala, es una de las ciudades más bellas de América Latina. Está llena de bellos edificios y plazas coloniales. También hay ruinas de edificios antiguos destruidos por los terremotos que ocurren en la región.

En esta ciudad se encuentra la Academia de Español de Guatemala. Allí se dan cursos de español especialmente diseñados para diferentes profesiones.

La escuela tiene cursos muy interesantes. Uno de ellos permite que los estudiantes salgan a pasear por la ciudad con el profesor mientras que él les enseña todas las palabras que deben saber para describir los edificios y las ruinas. Estos estudiantes aprenden a usar el español de manera útil e interesante.

Una Calle de Antigua

Differentiated Instruction

Heritage Speakers

Encourage students to take on the role of editor in *Actividad* 35. As group members suggest potential phrases and sentences, heritage speakers can offer more commonly used alternatives.

Students with Learning Difficulties

Remind students that in *Actividad* 33 they are composing an ad for a person or thing that they want to find. They can't be sure that the person or thing exists. So, as explained in the *Gramática* on p. 332, they need to put the verb in the subordinate clause in the subjunctive.

Juego

ESCRIBIR, HABLAR EN GRUPO

1 En grupos, piensen en algún programa de televisión, libro o película que trate sobre extraterrestres o fenómenos inexplicables. Completen una tabla como la siguiente sobre el programa, el libro o la película.

¿¿Extraterrestres??

Nombre del programa, libro o película
Argumento general
Ejemplos de fenómenos inexplicables
Personajes
¿Dónde ocurre?
¿Cuándo ocurre?
¿Cuál es el final?

2 Ahora, jueguen a adivinar qué programa de televisión, libro o película escogió cada grupo. Por turnos, cada grupo pasa al frente de la clase y relata de qué trata el programa, el libro o la película que escogió sin dar el título. Pero, para hacer el juego más divertido, tienen que cambiar uno de los elementos que pusieron en sus tablas. Por ejemplo, pueden cambiar el nombre de los personajes principales o el lugar donde ocurre la historia. Gana el grupo que haya adivinado más programas, libros o películas.

Estrategia
Cooperative learning
You might assign roles to each member of the group. These roles might include:
- secretary
- editor
- illustrator
- story-teller / presenter

35

¿Recuerdas la leyenda?

HABLAR EN GRUPO, ESCRIBIR Trabaja con un grupo para escribir con tus propias palabras una leyenda conocida.

1 Escojan una leyenda que conozcan.

2 Hagan una tabla con lo siguiente y complétenla con los datos de la leyenda que escogieron.

- el tema
- la situación
- los personajes
- el lugar y la época
- el conflicto
- cómo se resuelve el conflicto

3 Escriban la leyenda. No se olviden de escribir el título.

4 Pueden ilustrar la leyenda e incluir música.

Capítulo 7 • trescientos treinta y cinco **335**

34

Standards: 1.1, 1.3

Suggestions: Tell students to read the instructions for both steps before they begin their planning in Step 1. This way, they know that they will be using their information in a guessing game and devise more effective ways to disguise their TV show, book, or film.

Answers will vary.

35

Standards: 1.1, 1.3, 3.1

Suggestions: Before students begin, refer them to the *Estrategia.* Membership in groups should vary from activity to activity. Encourage students to devise quick, effective, and considerate ways to best use the talents of everyone in a group.

Answers will vary.

Project-Based Learning

Students can perform Step 5 at this point. Make audio or video recordings of their presentations for inclusion in their digital portfolios. (For more information, see p. 304-b.)

Additional Resources

📶 **Technology: Online Resources**
- Instant Check
- Guided, Core, Audio
- *Para hispanohablantes*
- Teacher's Resource Materials: Audio Script, Communicative Pair Activities, Technology: Audio Cap. 7

Print
- Guided WB pp. 233–234
- Core WB pp. 101–103

Assessment _____

Prueba 7-7 with Remediation (online only)
Prueba: El subjuntivo en cláusulas adjetivas
- Prueba 7-7
Examen: Vocabulario y gramática 2
- Examen 2
- ExamView: Examen 2

Enrich Your Teaching

Culture Note

When assigning *Actividad* 35, tell students an ancient Aztec legend called **La Llorona.** It is still told throughout Mexico and Guatemala today in several versions. Generally, the story is of a beautiful young woman who married a handsome man. They had two children, but eventually the man got tired of his wife. He continued to pay attention to his children but ignored the woman. Overcome by jealousy, she killed the children. Struck with remorse, she wandered the town at night, weeping and searching for her lost children. Parents warn their children that if they are out at night, the woman might mistake them for her own and take them away.

Puente a la cultura

Suggestions:

Pre-reading: Refer students to the *Estrategia*. Once they have read it, say: *Mira las fotos y los mapas. Basado en ellos, ¿qué predicciones puedes hacer sobre el contenido de esta lectura?* Ask students to write down their predictions in order to return to them later.

Reading: As students read, remind them to use background knowledge, cognates, and context clues to understand unfamiliar words and expressions. Help them resolve comprehension problems by asking ***sí/no*** questions.

Post-reading: Ask students to revisit their predictions. Ask: *¿Eran tus predicciones correctas? ¿Qué piensas de estos misterios?*

COUNTRY CONNECTION

 Technology: Mapa global interactivo, Actividad 6 Discover the mysterious statues on Easter Island off the coast of Chile.

Suggestions: Tell students that, although *la Isla de Pascua* is still the official Chilean name for the island (it is a province of Chile), most now refer to it by the name preferred by its inhabitants: Rapa Nui. Show students Rapa Nui on a map. Some, including the great Norwegian explorer and archaeologist Thor Hyerdahl, put forth the theory that the ancient inhabitants who placed the famous *moai* were from Peru. This was due to the statues' resemblance to Incan stonework. More recent archaeological evidence, however, leads us to believe that Polynesians discovered the island in about A.D. 400.

Online Cultural Reading

Suggestions: Encourage students to use a Venn diagram to help them compare the lifestyle in Teotihuacan with the lifestyle in a large metropolitan city today.

Puente a la cultura

Misterios del pasado

Cuando los europeos llegaron a las Américas en 1492, se encontraron con muchos pueblos indígenas. Hoy día no hay nadie que pueda explicar la desaparición de la cultura de algunos de estos pueblos.

La Isla de Pascua

En el medio del océano Pacífico se encuentra la Isla de Pascua, de unos 167 kilómetros cuadrados. Allí se encuentran los moai, unas estatuas enormes de piedra que representan enormes cabezas con orejas largas y torsos pequeños. Se encuentran en toda la isla y miran hacia el cielo como esperando a algo o alguien. Pero la pregunta es ¿cómo las construyeron y las movieron los habitantes indígenas a la isla? Se sabe que no conocían ni el metal ni la rueda. Cuando se les pregunta a los habitantes de hoy cómo llegaron las estatuas al lugar, ellos responden: —¡A pie!

Muchos esperan que aparezca la verdad acerca de estas estatuas. Hay quienes dicen que las estatuas representan a los primeros habitantes de la isla, que creen que eran polinesios. Otros dicen que representan a los dioses y muchos creen que eran extraterrestres. Quizás algún día descubramos el misterio de esta pequeña isla.

Estrategia

Using illustrations You can preview what you are about to read by looking at the illustrations or photos that accompany the text. You can also look at the illustrations to locate details while reading. Before starting to read, look at the photos on these pages and make a prediction about what the text is about. After you finish reading, check if your prediction was right.

Online Cultural Reading

Go to Auténtico ONLINE to read and understand a website with information about ancient civilizations in Mexico.

Los moai, en la Isla de Pascua

Differentiated Instruction

Heritage Speakers

Invite students with exemplary pronunciation to read short sections aloud as a model of fluency and pronunciation.

Advanced Learners

Ask students to research one of the mysteries they read about in the *Puente a la cultura.* Have them present brief oral reports to the class about their chosen mystery.

Los olmecas

Más de 1,500 años antes de los mayas y 25 siglos antes de los aztecas existieron los olmecas, la primera gran civilización de Mesoamérica. Entre sus ruinas se descubrieron unas cabezas de piedra gigantes que no sólo miden entre dos o tres metros de alto sino que pesan entre 11 y 24 toneladas. Pero en esa zona de México no existen piedras tan grandes. Se supone que[1] los olmecas tuvieron que mover esas piedras más de 129 kilómetros. ¿Cómo lo hicieron? Es un misterio.

Las Líneas de Nazca

En 1927, un arqueólogo que recorría[2] el sur del Perú observó unas largas líneas de muchas formas a los lados de la carretera. Observó las líneas desde una meseta, las dibujó en un papel y descubrió que un dibujo tenía la forma de un pájaro volando. Más tarde se encontraron en las pampas de Nazca, al sur del Perú, más de 30 dibujos que representan animales y figuras geométricas y humanas. Lo interesante de estos dibujos es que las formas solamente pueden verse desde el aire. ¿Para qué servían las líneas? ¿Cómo se hicieron?

[1]supposedly [2]travelled

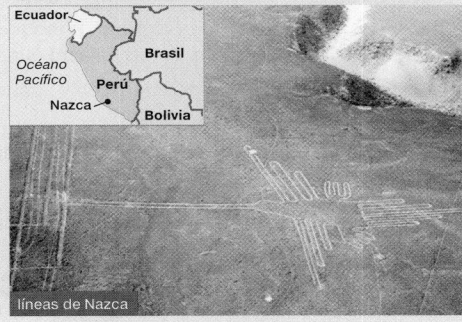
Cabeza olmeca

líneas de Nazca

¿Comprendiste?

1. ¿Qué son los moai? ¿Qué representan?
2. ¿Qué se descubrió entre las ruinas de los olmecas? ¿Por qué es un misterio?
3. ¿Qué descubrió un arqueólogo que recorría el sur del Perú?
4. ¿Qué representan los dibujos que forman las líneas de Nazca?
5. ¿Por qué es un misterio las líneas de Nazca?

Investiga

Busca en la biblioteca o en la Internet información sobre algún otro misterio del pasado, como el hombre de Palenque o la Atlántida. Escribe un pequeño párrafo que describa el misterio y expresa tu opinión sobre el tema con otro(a) estudiante por correo electrónico. Apoyen sus opiniones.

Videodocumentario ¿Cómo se explican los misterios del mundo?

Mapa global interactivo Explora la Isla de Pascua. Investiga su historia, sus misteriosos moai, y cómo la deforestación afectó el desarrollo de la cultura nativa. También explora las zonas ocupadas por los olmecas en México y las misteriosas líneas de Nazca en Perú.

Capítulo 7 • trescientos treinta y siete **337**

Enrich Your Teaching

Culture Note

One theory on the origin of the Nazca lines suggests that they indicate positions of the sun, moon, planets, and stars, and that they were used to determine the times of year for planting and harvesting. Another says that the animal figures represent the mountain gods' different animal forms.

21st Century Skills

Information Literacy Have students focus on the photographs that accompany the reading *Misterios del pasado.* Then ask students to use the Internet to locate additional images of the stone structures of the Olmec civilization, the *moai* from *Isla de Pascua,* or *las líneas de Nazca.* Have students share their images with the class and make new predictions about these ancient mysteries.

¿Comprendiste?

Standards: 1.2, 1.3

 Technology: Mapa global interactivo, Actividad 7 Discover the ancient Olmec civililzation.

Suggestions: Have students work in pairs to write their responses.

Answers:

1. Los moai son unas estatuas enormes de piedra. Representan cabezas con orejas largas y torsos pequeños.
2. Entre las ruinas se descubrieron unas cabezas de piedra gigantes. Es un misterio porque en esa zona de México no existen piedras tan grandes.
3. El arqueólogo observó unas largas líneas de muchas formas a los lados de la carretera.
4. animales, figuras geométricas y humanas
5. porque las formas solamente pueden verse desde el aire

 Technology: Mapa global interactivo, Actividad 8 Discover the mysteries of the Nazca Lines.

Investiga

Standards: 1.3, 5.1

Suggestions: Encourage students to use chapter vocabulary and structures in their paragraphs.
Answers will vary.

Digital Portfolio

Keep students' paragraphs from *Investiga* in their portfolios as a writing sample.

 Technology: Videodocumentario

Standards: 1.2

Resources: Teacher's Resource Materials: Video Script, Video Program: Cap. 7

View *¿Cómo se explican los misterios del mundo?* with the class. Access the video online in **Realize.** See the Video Teacher's Guide for suggestions.

Additional Resources

 Technology: Online Resources
• *Videodocumentario*
• Guided, Writing, Reading
• *Para hispanohablantes*
• Cultural Reading Activity
• Communication Activities
Print
• Guided WB p. 235

¿Qué me cuentas?

Standards: 1.1, 1.2, 1.3, 2.2, 3.1

Resources: Teacher's Resource Materials: Audio Script, Technology: Audio Cap. 7

AP® Skills: Integration of listening, reading, and writing to comprehend and synthesize information from spoken and written sources.

Suggestions: For Step 1, use the audio or read the descriptions aloud. Allow students to hear it twice through: the first time to write their answers, the second time to check them.

For Step 2, have students identify significant details as they read and then summarize the main points of the article.

For Step 3, encourage students to use each of the suggested expressions, and to support their arguments with specific information from both the listening in Step 1 and the reading in Step 2.

 Technology: Audio Script and Answers

Female Adult: Un arqueólogo fue de visita a la clase para hablar a los estudiantes de sus descubrimientos más recientes. Les contó que en su último trabajo en América Central, él y un grupo de arqueólogos descubrieron las ruinas de un antiguo palacio olmeca.

1. ¿Acerca de qué habló el arqueólogo en la clase?
2. ¿Cuál fue su descubrimiento más reciente?

Male Adult: La estructura que descubrieron era enorme. Estaba formada por bloques de piedra tan grandes como un autobús. Muchas tenían diseños geométricos, con círculos, óvalos y triángulos. Otras tenían símbolos y dibujos de soles y dioses. Midieron el alto, el largo y el ancho de todas las piedras y calcularon su peso. Cada piedra pesaba varias toneladas.

3. ¿Qué tipo de dibujos tenían las piedras?
4. ¿Qué hicieron los arqueólogos para saber el peso de las piedras?

Female Adult: Lo más extraño del descubrimiento fue un hombre misterioso que apareció un día. El hombre les dijo que había una leyenda sobre ese palacio olmeca entre los habitantes de la región. Sabían que esta estructura existía pero que nadie hablaba de ella ni se acercaba, porque creían que allí vivían extraterrestres.

5. ¿Qué fue lo más extraño del descubrimiento?
6. ¿Por qué no hablaban del palacio los habitantes de la región?

Step1

1. b **2.** b **3.** a **4.** b **5.** a **6.** b

Steps 2–3

Answers will vary.

Additional Resources

Technology: Online Resources
• *Para hispanohablantes*

Pre-AP®
Integración

OBJECTIVES
▶ Listen to and read descriptions of an archeological investigation
▶ Write a comparison of two excavations

◀)) ¿Qué me cuentas?: Ver para creer

¿Qué civilizaciones existían en las Américas antes de los aztecas, mayas e incas? Escucha a una persona que habla sobre una investigación. Anota las respuestas a las preguntas para usarlas en el paso 3.

1 Escucha las siguientes descripciones. Después de cada descripción, vas a oír dos preguntas. Escoge la mejor respuesta para cada pregunta.

1. a. del descubrimiento de América
   b. de su trabajo arqueológico

2. a. conocer a un grupo de arqueólogos
   b. las ruinas de un palacio olmeca

3. a. diseños geométricos y símbolos
   b. dibujos de animales

4. a. Leyeron las notas de los olmecas.
   b. Midieron las piedras.

5. a. un hombre misterioso les contó acerca de una leyenda
   b. que nadie sabía que esa estructura existiera

6. a. porque la leyenda decía que ese lugar no existía
   b. porque existía una leyenda y la creencia de que allí vivían extraterrestres

2 Lee este artículo sobre un descubrimiento arqueológico en América del Sur.

Ruinas de Caral, Perú.

CARAL, la ciudad más antigua de las Américas

América del Sur

Los descubrimientos de un equipo de arqueólogos peruanos revelaron que las ruinas de Caral en Perú, pertenecieron a[1] la civilización más antigua de las Américas. La evidencia indica que la ciudad prosperó por cinco siglos, aproximadamente desde el año 2627 a.C. Esto significa[2] que los habitantes de las comunidades alrededor del valle Supe fueron contemporáneos de las civilizaciones antiguas de la Mesopotamia y de Asia.

En el sitio de excavación, los arqueólogos ya desenterraron[3] ocho pirámides públicas, unas plataformas de forma circular que parecen plazas, seis unidades residenciales y cuatro sectores de la ciudad. En total la ciudad cubría un área de 150 ácres y se cree que fue un importante punto comercial.

[1]belonged to [2]means [3]unearthed

 3 Escribe una comparación de las dos excavaciones. ¿Qué encontraron en cada lugar? Mira la foto de Caral y revisa tus notas de la descripción de las ruinas en el paso 1. ¿En qué se parecen o se diferencian? ¿Qué importancia tienen estos descubrimientos? Usa las siguientes expresiones para conectar tus ideas.

al igual que	antes de	en contraste . . .	es similar a . . .
ya que	después de	me parece . . .	es diferente de . . .

Differentiated Instruction

Heritage Speakers

Have students periodically watch Spanish-language television programs or videos so that they also, along with their classmates, can benefit from exposure to different accents and language use.

Students with Learning Difficulties

Read the directions to the first task with students. Emphasize that they will: 1) hear a description; 2) hear two questions; 3) choose *a* or *b* to answer each question. Also before listening, have students read each pair of possible answers to help them focus on their listening task. Remind them to listen for one of the two choices.

Presentación oral

OBJECTIVES
▶ Demonstrate how to convince your class of a new scientific theory
▶ Maintain your focus for clarity

Tu descubrimiento científico

TAREA Eres científico(a) y creaste una teoría para explicar un fenómeno extraño. Tienes que convencer (*convince*) a la clase de que tu explicación tiene sentido.

Estrategia
Maintaining your focus It is important that when you are doing your speech you maintain your focus. Your focus is the message you want to communicate to your audience. Make sure your opinion is accompanied by supporting statements and is clearly understood by your audience. Avoid adding information not directly related to the topic that might interfere with the purpose of your speech.

❶ **Prepárate** Completa un organizador gráfico. Escribe el nombre y una descripción del fenómeno. A la derecha explica lo que sucedió. Puedes inventar el fenómeno y las teorías para tratar de explicarlo.

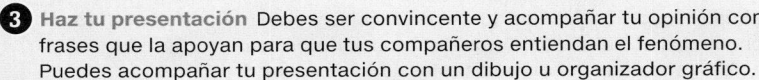

Fenómeno inexplicable: _____

❷ **Practica** Vuelve a leer el organizador. Practica tu presentación. Puedes usar tus notas para practicar, pero no al hablar ante la clase. Recuerda:

- explicar claramente de qué fenómeno estás hablando
- dar razones convincentes (*convincing*) que traten de explicarlo
- mirar directamente al público al hablar

Modelo
Nadie descubrió qué les sucedió a los habitantes de la Atlántida. En mi opinión unos extraterrestres aparecieron en la Atlántida y allí se quedaron. Dudo que el clima les haya gustado, por eso se mudaron a un pueblo de Alaska.

❸ **Haz tu presentación** Debes ser convincente y acompañar tu opinión con frases que la apoyan para que tus compañeros entiendan el fenómeno. Puedes acompañar tu presentación con un dibujo u organizador gráfico.

❹ **Evaluación** Tu profesor(a) utilizará la siguiente rúbrica para evaluarte.

Rubric	Score 1	Score 3	Score 5
How well you maintain your focus	Your theory is undeveloped. You miss important ideas.	You present a theory, but your ideas are disorganized.	Your theory is presented in a logical, organized way.
How convincing you are	Your supporting explanations are weak.	Your supporting explanations are somewhat convincing.	You use convincing explanations.
How effectively you deliver your speech	You read your speech and make no eye contact with your audience.	You make some eye contact and you use some intonation.	Your eye contact is good. Your intonation helps get the message across.

Capítulo 7 • trescientos treinta y nueve 339

Presentación oral

Standards: 1.2, 1.3, 3.1

Suggestions: Review the task and the four-step approach with students. Review the rubric with the class (see *Assessment* below) to explain how you will grade the performance task. Before students begin, direct their attention to the *Estrategia*. Point out that the key to maintaining their focus in a speech or in writing is to organize their ideas first. This is what they should do in Step 1. Draw a flowchart in the board and have students create a similar chart on their own paper, leaving out the rectangle farthest to the right. Model how to fill in a sample mysterious phenomenon and at least one explanation it. Encourage students to use their imaginations to create their own explanations which, although they may be invented, should be plausible.

Pre-AP® Integration

- **Learning Objective:** Presentational Speaking
- **Pre-AP® Resource Materials:** Comprehensive guide to Pre-AP® speaking skill development

Digital Portfolio

Make video or audio recordings of student presentations in class, or assign the Speak and Record activity so they can record their presentations online. Include the recording in their portfolios.

Additional Resources

📶 **Technology: Online Resources**
- *Para hispanohablantes*

Assessment _____

Presentación oral
- **Assessment Program:** Rubrics

Review the rubric with students. Go over the descriptions of the different levels of performance. After assessing students, help individuals understand how their performance could be improved. (See Teacher's Resource Materials for suggestions on using rubrics in assessment.)

Enrich Your Teaching

21st Century Skills

Collaboration Have students review the rubrics on pages 339 and 341. Ask them to work with a partner and discuss why their teacher gives them rubrics; how are they supposed to be used? Have them work with one of the rubrics to start with the outcome, figure out what they have to do to get the best grade possible, and develop a plan to achieve that goal.

Language Arts Connection: Persuasive Writing

Remind students that the subjunctive usually occurs in complex sentences. Point out that the sentences in which they learned to use **sino** in this chapter are compound sentences. Ask them to use their knowledge from their Language Arts courses to talk about the differences between compound and complex sentences.

Presentación escrita

Standards: 1.2, 1.3, 3.1

Suggestions: Begin by explaining the criteria you will use to evaluate students' compositions. (See Step 5, *Evaluación*, in the Student Edition, and *Assessment* on the following page.)

Direct students' attention to the *Estrategia*. Point out that in *Capítulo* 7, they have learned how to use the present perfect subjunctive and **sino,** as well as the subjunctive in adjective clauses. All three of these are valuable tools they can use to combine sentences more effectively. Then draw a four-column T-chart on the board. Fill in the left side of the chart and model for students how to add one or two pieces of information to the right side when they create their own charts.

Pre-AP® Integration

- **Learning Objective:** Presentational Writing
- **Pre-AP® Resource Materials:** Comprehensive guide to Pre-AP® writing skill development

---

Presentación escrita

OBJECTIVES
▶ Write a legend about something or someone from the past
▶ Combine sentences and use details to add interest to the story

Tu leyenda

 Usa tu imaginación y escribe una leyenda acerca de algún personaje o lugar imaginario. Puedes escribir acerca de una leyenda ya conocida pero añadiéndole detalles propios.

1 **Antes de escribir** Contesta las preguntas como ayuda para encontrar ideas para tu leyenda.

- ¿En dónde ocurre la historia?
- ¿Quién o quiénes son los protagonistas de tu historia?
- ¿Cuál es el misterio o fenómeno inexplicable principal? ¿Qué sucede?
- ¿El misterio o fenómeno inexplicable se resuelve?
- ¿Qué título tiene la leyenda?

Recuerda que una leyenda tiene la estructura de un cuento, con una introducción, un desarrollo y un final. Completa la tabla para ordenar tus ideas.

Título de la leyenda	La leyenda del extraterrestre del valle
Introducción	Un hombre estaba dando un paseo por el valle cuando de repente apareció un extraterreste . . .
Desarrollo	Se hicieron amigos y el hombre decidió acompañar al extraterrestre a su planeta . . .
Final	Nunca más se supo del hombre . . .

2 **Borrador** Escribe tu borrador utilizando la información de la tabla. Debes añadir todos los detalles que sean posibles y usar oraciones conectadas con elaboración para que los párrafos sean más interesantes. La leyenda debe ser misteriosa e interesante. Usa el vocabulario y la gramática que aprendiste en este capítulo.

Modelo

> Según cuenta la leyenda, un hombre estaba dando un paseo por el valle del pueblo cuando de repente apareció una figura muy extraña. Tenía una cabeza redonda sin pelo y sus ojos eran muy grandes y ovalados. "Dudo que existan extraterrestres", pensó el hombre en ese momento, "pero ahora no estoy tan seguro". . .

Topic sentence: Sets the story.

Description of a character: What did the stranger look like?

Estrategia

Combining sentences The paragraphs in your story may lose their impact if you use short, choppy sentences. To improve the flow of your paragraphs, combine sentences with conjunctions like *y, o,* or *pero.* For example, *"Todos los habitantes del pueblo conocen la leyenda pero ninguno habla de ella"* is more interesting than *"Todos los habitantes del pueblo conocen la leyenda. Ninguno habla de ella."* Likewise, *"El hombre no tenía ni familia ni amigos"* sounds better than *"El hombre no tenía familia. El hombre no tenía amigos."*

Differentiated Instruction

Heritage Speakers

Before students write final drafts of their legends, have them proofread for correct use of accent marks. Review frequently misspelled words that have homonyms, such as **como/cómo, que/qué, se/sé.**

Advanced Learners

Invite students to have a discussion in Spanish about other ways to create more varied and interesting sentences. Encourage them to talk about other types of subordinate clauses by helping them with vocabulary such as **cláusula adverbial** and **cláusula sustantiva.**

Go **Online** to practice
PEARSON
realize ™

PearsonSchool.com/Autentico

✎
WRITING

Presentational 7

> *El desconocido se le acercó y le dijo: "Es verdad, soy un extraterrestre, pero no tenga miedo. Yo solo busco un hombre que quiera ser mi amigo". El hombre le respondió que no tenía amigos pero que podía hacer una excepción. Después de hablar por muchas horas, el extraterrestre le ofreció llevarlo a conocer su planeta. El hombre aceptó la invitación. Entonces . . .*
>
> *Nunca más se supo del hombre . . .*

Development: What happened after the two characters met.

Conclusion: Explains the mystery or leaves it to the reader's imagination.

3 **Redacción/Revisión** Después de escribir el primer borrador de la leyenda, trabaja con otro(a) estudiante para intercambiar los trabajos y leerlos. Decidan qué aspectos son más efectivos. Fíjense en cómo el(la) escritor(a) del modelo incluyó detalles en su composición. Cada uno puede sugerir qué cambios hacer para mejorar las leyendas.

Haz lo siguiente: Verifica si usaste correctamente las formas del indicativo y del subjuntivo.

> *El desconocido se le acercó y le dijo : "Es*
> *soy*
> *verdad, ~~sea~~ un extraterrestre, pero no*
> *tenga*
> *~~tiene~~ miedo. Yo solo busco un hombre*
> *quiera*
> *que ~~quiere~~ ser mi amigo".*

4 **Publicación** Antes de hacer la versión final, lee de nuevo tu borrador y repasa lo siguiente:
- ¿La leyenda tiene un orden lógico?
- ¿Es interesante la introducción?
- ¿Incluí suficientes detalles que den un ambiente *(feeling)* a la historia?
- ¿Usé oraciones conectadas con detalles y elaboración?
- ¿Es misterioso el final de la leyenda?

Después de revisar el borrador, escribe tu composición en limpio.

5 **Evaluación** Se utilizará la siguiente rúbrica para evaluar tu presentación.

Rubric	Score 1	Score 3	Score 5
Completion of task	Your writing cannot be defined as a legend.	You present an idea for a legend, but you miss important elements.	Your writing is an interesting legend, containing all necessary elements.
Use of varied sentence structure	Your sentences are all the same length.	You combine some sentences but miss some opportunities.	Your sentences are varied, interesting, and effective.
Grammar, spelling, mechanics	Your grammar, spelling, and/or mechanics errors make for difficult reading.	You make some grammar, spelling, and/or mechanics errors. Your sentences are connected but may lack a few details or elaboration.	You make very few grammar, spelling, and/or mechanics errors. Your sentences are connected with details and elaboration.

Capítulo 7 • trescientos cuarenta y uno **341**

Enrich Your Teaching

21st Century Skills

Creativity and Innovation Students will have to use their written language for the purpose of creating a new legend. Have students review children's books or other legends they know from their own culture and choose one to adapt into Spanish. Students should retell the story and adapt its main features (characters, location, action) to fit into an ancient Spanish-speaking civilization.

Suggestions (Cont'd) Once students have a rough draft ready, read through the model on this page together. Help them see how information from the chart on the previous page was incorporated into this draft and to note the additional information that was added. Point out the use of the subjunctive in an adjective clause in the first paragraph: *Yo sólo busco un hombre **que quiera ser mi amigo.*** Encourage them to work toward similar organization, level of detail, and language use as they create their own drafts.

For Step 3, encourage students to experiment with various ways of combining sentences. Have them follow the suggestions shown.

Evaluation
Steps 4 and 5 overlap. Students will need evaluation by you, their peers, or self-evaluation to fine-tune and polish their drafts.

Digital Portfolio

Keep students' final drafts in their portfolios as a writing sample.

Teacher-to-Teacher

e-amigos: Have students send their *e-amigos* the legend they wrote for the *Presentación escrita.* Ask them to include an introduction in which they ask their *e-amigos* to critique the story. Encourage students to express their feelings in the form of constructive criticism. Have students print out their e-mails or send them to you for review.

Additional Resources

📶 **Technology: Online Resources**
- *Para hispanohablantes*

Assessment

Presentación escrita
- **Assessment Program:** Rubrics
Review the rubric with students. Go over the descriptions of the different levels of performance. After assessing students, help individuals understand how their performance could be improved. (See Teacher's Resource Materials for suggestions on using rubrics in assessment.)

Lectura

Standards: 1.2, 2.2, 3.1, 3.2, 5.2

Suggestions:

Pre-reading: Before reading, direct students' attention to the *Al leer* section. Have them begin a T-chart similar to the one on p. 345 and make sure they understand how they will use it. Also refer them to the *Estrategia.* Point out that their T-charts will help them keep track of the characters and their actions.

Reading: When reading together with students, pause frequently to address comprehension issues they may have and to allow them to fill in their charts for *Interacción con la lectura.* Here is an example: Point out that in Spanish, the noun to which a possessive adjective refers is not always immediately obvious. We have to use background knowledge and context clues in order to know. In the first paragraph, we know that **su escudero** means "his, her, or their squire." Since we learned earlier who Sancho Panza is, we can deduce that **su** refers to Don Quijote and not the guards or their prisoners.

COUNTRY CONNECTION

Resources: Mapa global interactivo

Suggestions: What was known as La Mancha in Cervantes' day is currently the **comunidad autónoma** called Castilla-La Mancha. Display *Mapa de España* on pp. xxxii–xxxiii and point out the region on the map. It is a large area in the central part of the country, east and southeast of Madrid. Before the **comunidades autónomas** were created, Spain was divided into smaller provinces named after important cities. Castilla-La Mancha is comprised of five of these older provinces called Guadalajara, Cuenca, Albacete, Ciudad Real, and Toledo.

Lectura

OBJECTIVES
▶ Read and understand a piece of fiction
▶ Understand the perspective of a character who lives his own fantasy
▶ Read about *Don Quijote's* author, Miguel de Cervantes Saavedra

Estrategia
Characters and actions Read the passage once through to understand the events of the story. When you have read through once, think about the characters in the story. What are they like? Then, re-read the story and write down the events.

Al leer

El personaje más famoso de la literatura española es Don Quijote de la Mancha, el protagonista de la novela del mismo nombre que escribió Miguel de Cervantes. La historia cuenta que el Quijote leyó tantos libros sobre caballeros andantes (*knights*), que un día perdió el juicio (*lost his mind*) y decidió ser uno de ellos. En la época en que él vive (el siglo XVII) ya no hay caballeros andantes, pero en su imaginación, el Quijote ve a las sirvientas (*maids*) como princesas, las posadas (*inns*) como castillos y los molinos (*windmills*) como gigantes contra los que tiene que pelear. El conflicto entre la fantasía del Quijote y la realidad produce situaciones cómicas que hacen reír.

El fragmento que vas a leer es una adaptación del Capítulo XXII, en el que Don Quijote y su escudero (*squire*) y amigo Sancho Panza se encuentran con unos prisioneros.

Copia la tabla de la página 345. Complétala mientras lees. Ésta te ayudará a contestar las preguntas que aparecen al final.

Fragmento de *Don Quijote de la Mancha* Capítulo XXII

Don Quijote vio que por el camino venían doce hombres atados[1] con una gran cadena[2] de hierro por el cuello, y todos con esposas[3] en las manos. Venían con ellos dos hombres a caballo y dos a pie. Su escudero Sancho Panza dijo:

—Ésta es una cadena de prisioneros, gente forzada[4] por el rey, que va a las galeras[5].

—¿Cómo gente forzada? —preguntó Don Quijote—. ¿Es posible que el rey haga fuerza a alguien?

—No digo eso —respondió Sancho—, son personas que, por sus crímenes, van condenadas a servir al rey en las galeras por fuerza.

---

[1]tied [2]chain [3]handcuffs [4]forced [5]galleys

Differentiated Instruction

Bodily-Kinesthetic Learner

Invite students to interpret the excerpt from *Don Quijote* by performing it as a skit for the class. They may use the excerpt as a script, adding inflection and gestures, or they may keep the general idea but improvise the lines. Have students work together to plan and perform their skit.

Students with Learning Difficulties

Have students read through the chart and comprehension questions on p. 345 before they begin to read the excerpt. They can use the questions to set a purpose for reading and to maintain a focus.

—Entonces —contestó Don Quijote— esta gente, aunque los llevan, van de por fuerza, y no porque ellos quieren.

—Así es —dijo Sancho.

—Pues —dijo su amo—, aquí puedo hacer mi tarea: deshacer fuerzas y ayudar a los miserables.

Don Quijote se acercó y le preguntó al primero que por qué crímenes iba a las galeras. Él le respondió que por enamorado.

—¿Por eso no más? —replicó Don Quijote—. Pues, si por enamorados echan a galeras, yo estaría en ellas desde hace tiempo.

—No son los amores como los que usted piensa —dijo el prisionero—; que los míos fueron que quise tanto a una cesta llena de ropa blanca, que la abracé conmigo tan fuertemente que, a no quitármela la justicia por fuerza, aún la tendría.

—Éste, señor, va por músico y cantor—, le dijeron.

—Pues, ¿cómo —repitió Don Quijote—, por músicos y cantores van también a galeras?

Pero uno de los guardas le explicó:

—Señor caballero, cantar es confesar en el tormento[6].

Luego al tercero que le preguntó Don Quijote, éste le dijo:

—Yo voy por cinco años porque me faltaron diez monedas de oro.

—Yo daré veinte de muy buena gana[7] —dijo Don Quijote— por libraros[8] de las galeras.

—Eso me parece —respondió el prisionero— como quien tiene dineros en mitad del mar y se está muriendo de hambre, sin tener adónde comprar lo que necesita. Si hubiera tenido el dinero necesario para cambiar la opinión del juez, hoy estaría paseando por la plaza de Toledo y no camino a las galeras.

Al final venía un hombre con más cadenas que los demás.

—¿Cuál es su crimen? —preguntó Don Quijote.

—Va por diez años por ladrón —replicó el guarda—. Este hombre tiene solo más crímenes que todos los otros juntos. Es el famoso Ginés de Pasamonte.

—Para servir a Dios y al rey, otra vez he estado cuatro años, —respondió Ginés—; y no me pesa mucho ir a ellas, porque allí tendré lugar de acabar de escribir mi libro.

Dijo entonces Don Quijote:

—De todo lo que me habéis dicho, he sacado en limpio que, aunque os han castigado[9] por vuestros crímenes, las penas que vais a padecer[10] no os dan mucho gusto, y que vais a ellas muy de mala gana y muy contra vuestra voluntad. Me parece duro caso hacer esclavos[11] a los que Dios y la naturaleza hizo libres. Estos pobres no han cometido nada contra vosotros, guardias. Pido que los dejéis libres pero si no lo hacen, por fuerza haré que lo hagáis.

[6]torture [7]willingly [8]*libraros* means *librarlos*; the ending -*os* is the pronoun corresponding to *vosotros* [9]punished [10]to suffer [11]slaves

Capítulo 7 • trescientos cuarenta y tres **343**

Enrich Your Teaching

Culture Note

Don Quijote de la Mancha is the most well-known work of literature in the Spanish language. It has been translated into more than 60 languages. Cervantes' novel is a comic satire, intended to poke fun at the popular chivalric romances of the time. The novel is entertaining, but it also carries a message. The author criticizes the greed, pride, and violence of society at the time. Don Quijote's insanity also demonstrates a form of wisdom. He sees humble people as noble, while the rich and members of the clergy are targets of his wrath.

Suggestions (Cont'd)

Reading: Here are some possible comprehension issues on this page for which you can provide some guidance:

- Tell students that **su amo** in line five refers to Don Quijote. Explain that **amo** means "master" here.
- Ask students to explain in their own words the real reason why the second prisoner is on his way to the galleys. If necessary, point out how both Spanish and English use the verb **cantar** (to sing) to mean "confess."
- Ask students what the third prisoner means by his analogy in which he refers to the sea. Guide students to understand that Don Quijote's offer of money comes too late for the man, since he's already been convicted of a crime—probably stealing.

Teacher-to-Teacher

Point out that reading a novel in Spanish may not be as difficult as students think. (Although most of those interested in doing so will probably want to start with a shorter and less complex one than *Don Quijote de la Mancha*.) Explain that in this short excerpt from Cervantes, there are indeed unfamiliar words and structures that may make the idea of reading a whole book seem daunting. Remind them that after a chapter or two in a book, however, such problems tend to level off, since the vocabulary used to tell a story doesn't usually keep changing. The hard work involved in reading a novel tends to be limited to the beginning.

Pre-AP® Integration

- **Learning Objective:** Presentational Speaking (Cultural Comparison)
- **Background:** This task prepares students for the Spoken Presentational Communication tasks that focus on cultural comparisons.
- **Activity:** Have students prepare a two-minute (maximum) presentation on the following topic: Different views of fantasy vs. reality are reflected in the literature of different times and cultures. Students may use the fragment they read from *Don Quijote de la Mancha* as a basis for the comparison. They should then comment on another work of literature from their own culture that also deals with fantasy vs. reality, explaining the similarities and differences between the two.
- **Pre-AP® Resource Materials:** Comprehensive guide to Pre-AP® speaking skill development

7 Interpretive Reading

Suggestions (Cont'd)

Reading: Here are some possible comprehension issues on this page for which you can provide some guidance:

- Refer students to the *¿Recuerdas?* Remind them that verb forms that look unfamiliar to them as they read might be **vosotros** forms.
- If students have difficulty understanding the paragraph that begins **—De gente bien educada...,** explain that Don Quijote sometimes uses archaic syntax when he speaks. Restate the first sentence using modern syntax: *La gente bien educada está siempre agradecida por los beneficios que recibe.*
- Ask students to work together to tell in their own words the sequence of events beginning the moment Don Quijote decides to free the prisoners.

Post-reading: Ask students to talk about the humor in the Cervantes excerpt. Guide them to talk about the situational irony of the character of Don Quijote, totally dedicated to his mission, a mission that has no place in the world in which he lives and which turns him into a clown, no matter how seriously he takes himself. Ask students to draw analogies to such a situation in the present day. For example, Don Quijote might be compared to a man who decides to dress like a cowboy hero and sets out to roam the streets of a modern city on a quest to help the downtrodden.

Starter Activity

Have the class brainstorm famous pieces of world literature that have been made into movies. Discuss briefly whether they most frequently think the book or the film is better. Mention the movie *The Man of La Mancha* made from the musical of the same name.

Active Classroom

After the class has read the excerpt from *Don Quijote,* create "story experts." Divide the story in four sections and give students numbers 1, 2, 3, or 4. This "expert" is to create five questions about his or her section of the story. Create groups of four students, each with a different "expert." Have them ask their questions to other members of the group.

Pero los guardias no hicieron caso y le dijeron:

— No ande buscando tres pies al gato[12].

—¡Vos sois el gato, y el ratón, y el bellaco! —respondió Don Quijote furioso y atacó[13] a los guardias. Sancho ayudó a dar la libertad a los prisioneros. Muy sorprendidos y asustados, los guardias se escaparon.

Don Quijote llamó entonces a los prisioneros y así les dijo:

—De gente bien educada es agradecer[14] los beneficios que reciben. Les pido que vayan a la ciudad del Toboso, y allí os presentéis ante la señora Dulcinea del Toboso y le digáis que su caballero, el de la Triste Figura, ha tenido esta famosa aventura.

Respondió por todos Ginés de Pasamonte, y dijo:

—Lo que vuestra merced[15] nos manda, señor y libertador nuestro, es imposible de toda imposibilidad cumplirlo. Lo que podemos hacer es rezar[16] por usted.

—¡No! —dijo Don Quijote furioso.

Pasamonte, que ya se había dado cuenta que Don Quijote no era muy cuerdo[17], empezó con los demás prisioneros a arrojarle piedras a Don Quijote, le quitaron la ropa a Sancho y huyeron[18]. Solos quedaron Sancho y Don Quijote; Don Quijote, muy triste de verse tan malparado[19] por los mismos a quien tanto bien había hecho.

[12]looking for a problem where there is none
[13]attacked [14]to thank
[15]archaic usage for *Usted*
[16]to pray [17]sane [18]fled
[19]left in such a sorry state

¿Recuerdas?

En el español antiguo, se utilizaban los pronombres personales *vosotros* y *vosotras*, y las formas verbales correspondientes. En la actualidad, estas formas casi no se usan en los países de habla hispana con excepción de España.

344 trescientos cuarenta y cuatro • Capítulo 7 • ¿Mito o realidad?

Differentiated Instruction

Students with Learning Difficulties

After students read the *¿Recuerdas?*, write on the board verbs from the text in the **vosotros** form. Demonstrate pronunciation of these words by comparing them to words that are familiar to students. For example, the vowels in the last syllables of **presentéis** and **vais** sound much like those in **seis** and **país.**

Advanced Learners

Invite students to read another excerpt from *Don Quijote de la Mancha,* such as his famous battle with the windmill giant, and tell about it in their own words.

Interacción con la lectura

1. Completa una tabla como la siguiente a medida que lees.

2. Trabaja con otro(a) compañero(a) para comparar la información de las tablas de cada uno(a). Añadan cualquier otro detalle interesante que recuerden.

Preguntas	Respuestas
1. ¿Cuál es la situación?	
2. ¿Qué piensa Don Quijote que ocurre?	
3. ¿Qué sucede en realidad?	
4. ¿Qué hace Don Quijote?	
5. ¿Qué resultados tiene su acción?	

¿Comprendiste?

1. Parafrasea la idea principal del cuento. Incluye el tema y los detalles más importantes.

2. Don Quijote escucha las historias de los prisioneros. ¿Cómo reacciona Don Quijote después de escucharlas? ¿Considera que el castigo (punishment) de los prisioneros es justo?

3. ¿Por qué quiere Don Quijote que los prisioneros ya libres vayan a ver a la señora Dulcinea? ¿Qué nos dice de su personalidad?

4. Don Quijote ve las cosas de manera diferente que los demás personajes. ¿Crees que él piensa que dice la verdad? ¿Crees que él ve las cosas como son? ¿Crees que Sancho ve las cosas como son?

5. Piensa en algún ejemplo de la vida real en el que dos personas vean una misma cosa de diferente forma y compáralo con la lectura. Di qué pueden hacer para ponerse de acuerdo.

6. En tu opinión, ¿qué quiere expresar el autor al escribir acerca de Don Quijote?

CULTURA ▸ España

Miguel de Cervantes Saavedra (1547–1616) nació en España, y antes de ser escritor participó en varias guerras. Como soldado (soldier), perdió el uso de la mano izquierda y poco después fue llevado a Argel como esclavo, donde estuvo cinco años. Buscando su libertad (freedom) trató de escapar cuatro veces. Un grupo de religiosos lo rescató y pudo regresar por fin a España. Trabajó para el gobierno (government) español, pero fue acusado de manejar mal el dinero a su cargo y fue encarcelado durante varios meses. Ya en libertad empezó a escribir novelas y comedias, entre ellas su más famosa novela, *Don Quijote de la Mancha*. Cervantes murió el mismo año que William Shakespeare.

Pre-AP® Integration: Los héroes y los personajes históricos ¿Cuál de los distintos momentos en la vida de Miguel de Cervantes

Miguel de Cervantes Saavedra

Saavedra te impresiona más? ¿De qué manera contribuyó Cervantes Saavedra a la cultura hispana?

Capítulo 7 • trescientos cuarenta y cinco **345**

Interacción con la lectura

Standards: 1.1, 1.2

Suggestions: After students finish and discuss their charts, encourage them to go back and read the excerpt again, now that they have a better understanding of Don Quijote's character and of Cervantes's use of language.

Answers will vary.

¿Comprendiste?

Standards: 1.3

Suggestions: Have students write the answers to the questions on their own first, then use them as a basis for class discussion.

Answers:

1. Don Quijote piensa que su misión es «deshacer fuerzas» y ayudar a los miserables.
2. Don Quijote reacciona con sorpresa y enojo. Piensa que los castigos son injustos.
3. Don Quijote quiere que los prisioneros vayan a decirle a Dulcinea el bien que ha hecho. Answers will vary.

4–6. Answers will vary.

CULTURA

Standards: 1.1, 1.2, 2.2, 3.1

Suggestions: After students have read the information silently, ask comprehension questions. For example: *¿Cuál fue la situación de Cervantes en Argel? (Fue llevado allí como esclavo.) ¿Por qué fue encarcelado Cervantes en España durante varios meses? (Lo acusaron de haber manejado mal el dinero a su cargo.) ¿En qué año murió William Shakespeare? (1616)*

Answers will vary.

Additional Resources

📶 **Technology: Online Resources**
- Guided, Writing, Reading
- Cultural Reading Activity
- Communication Activities
- Para hispanohablantes

Print
- Guided WB p. Lectura, pp. 236–237
- Literacy Skills WB

Enrich Your Teaching

Culture Note

Miguel de Cervantes Saavedra was shot in his left hand at the battle of Lepanto. He lost the use of this hand and was subsequently nicknamed **el manco** (the maimed) **de Lepanto.** He was proud of both his participation in the battle and his nickname. This nickname is still commonly associated with the author today.

21st Century Skills

ICT (Information, Communications and Technology) Literacy Remind students of the various digital tools available in **Realize** to access reading support. Computer corrected activities employ different strategies to help students build their vocabulary and progress at their own pace through the reading.

Auténtico

Standards: 1.2

Resources: Authentic Resources Wkbk, Cap. 7
Authentic Resources: Cap. 7: Audioscript
AP®Theme: *La belleza y la estética: La arquitectura*

Antes de oír

Discuss the *Estrategia* with students. Then, point to the photo and elicit a response from the students based on their previous knowledge. Have they seen a scene like this before in this chapter? Guide students to conclude that this is a photo of Machu Picchu, the mysterious city from the Inca civilization located in Peru. Then, review the key vocabulary with the class.

Technology: Oye el audio

Before starting the audio, direct students' attention to the *Mientras oyes* activity. Have them use the activity page from the *Authentic Resources Workbook.* Emphasize the difference between *viewing* a video and *listening* to an audio. Since there are no visual clues, they need to concentrate more and try to visualize what they hear described.

Play the audio once completely through, without pausing. Ask students how many people talked in the audio (three) and who gives the most important information (the woman called Ana María). Replay the audio, stopping as necessary to check comprehension. Play it a final time without pausing.

Haz las actividades

Mientras oyes

Standards: 1.2

Suggestions: Invite students to share and discuss their notes. What terms expressed on the audio are familiar to them? How did they use what they know to infer meaning of unfamiliar words?

Possible terms:

- Machu Picchu
- Camino del Inca
- selva
- turistas
- arqueólogos
- ciudad misteriosa

Auténtico

Partnered with **IDB**

El secreto de Machu Picchu

Antes de oír

Usa la estrategia: Usar el conocimiento previo

Observa la foto. Resume lo que ya sabes de Machu Picchu y úsalo para inferir el significado de términos nuevos. Piensas de sitios históricos de tu cultura y si están bien o mal preservados.

Lee el vocabulario clave

nivel del mar = sea level	**bajo tierra** = underground
sismos = earthquakes	**drenaje** = drainage
manantiales = springs	**ladera** = slope
picos nevados = snow-capped	**ceja de la selva** = rainforest edge

▶ Oye el audio

En casi todo el mundo hay ruinas de grandes ciudades y civilizaciones de la antigüedad. Algunas ruinas se han logrado preservar mejor que otras. ¿A qué crees que se debe esto?

Ve a **PearsonSchool.com/Autentico** para oír el audio **¿Sabes cuál es el secreto de la juventud eterna de Machu Picchu?**. Descubrirás por qué esta ciudad tan antigua sigue casi intacta después de tantos siglos.

Haz las actividades

Mientras oyes Mientras oyes el audio, trata de identificar palabras y términos que ya conocías sobre Machu Picchu. Haz una lista de las nuevas palabras o frases que aprendiste. ¿Cómo usaste lo que ya sabías para inferir su significado?

Differentiated Instruction

Heritage Speaker

Ask students who have lived in a heritage country to suggest names of archeological sites for their group to investigate. Once the group has selected a site, suggest they focus their research on the following: where the site is located, what culture or indigenous groups it represents, and what are the most impressive aspects of the site.

Advanced Learners

Have students write a paragraph describing how the structures of Machu Picchu have stood the test of time, earthquakes, and precipitation. To accomplish this task, students might need to listen to the audio one more time, paying special attention to the last part.

Después de oír

Standards: 1.2, 1.3, 4.2

Suggestions: Discuss each question with the class. Point out that the answer to the second question contains the audio's main idea.

Answers may vary:

1. Tema: Construcciones de civilizaciones antiguas. Idea principal: Cómo ha resistido Machu Picchu el paso del tiempo. Detalles: sistema bajo tierra; canales.
2. b: al sistema de edificaciones bajo tierra
3. mediante un sistema de canales de agua bajo tierra

For more Authentic Resources: Assign the Authentic Resources Workbook activities for homework, so that students can hear the audio on their own and complete the workbook activities at their own pace.

Pre-AP® Integration

Resources: Authentic Resources, Wkbk, Cap. 7
Authentic Resources: Cap. 7; Audioscript

Suggestions: Before completing the Pre-AP® activity, have students go to the workbook and complete the worksheets for the additional resources.

Integración de ideas

Demonstrate understanding of culturally authentic audio materials in a variety of contexts.

Comparación cultural

Suggestions: Guide students to research other Latin American archeological sites such as Teotihuacan in Mexico, Tikal in Peru, or Tiwanaku in Bolivia.

Integración

Después de oír Oye el audio una o dos veces más para poder contestar estas preguntas:

1. Parafrasea el tema, la idea principal y los detalles importantes del audio.
2. Según el audio, ¿a qué se debe la juventud eterna de Machu Picchu?
   a. a las rocas que se usaron para construirla
   b. al sistema de edificaciones bajo tierra
   c. al buen clima de la región
   d. a la manera en que Perú ha cuidado estas ruinas
3. ¿Cómo se llevaba el agua de la montaña a la ciudad de Machu Picchu?

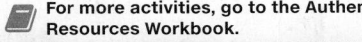 **For more activities, go to the Authentic Resources Workbook.**

Arquitectura y naturaleza

Expansión Busca otros recursos auténticos en *Auténtico* en línea y contesta las preguntas.

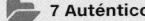 **7 Auténtico**

Integración de ideas ¿Cómo usaron los grandes constructores del pasado las formaciones naturales de la región para construir estructuras que resistieran el paso del tiempo? Respalda tu respuesta con hechos.

Comparación cultural ¿Conoces otro sitio histórico de importancia en tu cultura? Básate en lo que aprendiste sobre Machu Picchu para escribir una comparación entre las dos construcciones.

Enrich Your Teaching

Culture Note

As mentioned by the woman in the audio, Machu Picchu means *montaña vieja* in Quechua, the language of the indigenous people of the central Andes of South America. Quechua has been spoken in Peru since it became the language of the Inca Empire more than 600 years ago. Nowadays, it is the second most common language in Peru after Spanish.

Using Authentic Resources

Have students create a personal vocabulary list of terms related to the connection between architecture and nature. Suggest that they initiate their list with some of the key vocabulary featured in the audio: *curso del río, sistemas de drenaje, manantiales,* etc.

347

Review Activities

Descubrimientos/Mitos y leyendas/Para hablar de los fenómenos inexplicables: Have students number the items in these three categories. Ask them to write these numbers on slips of paper and put them into a hat or other container. Have students take turns drawing four numbers each, writing their numbers down, and then returning the slips to the hat or other container for the next person. Challenge students to write a sentence which uses the four words whose numbers they have drawn. Have them pass the hat more than once. Invite them to share their sentences.

Para describir objetos/Para indicar duda: Have students sketch the ruins of an imaginary ancient civilization and use as many words in this category as they can to label their sketch. Ask them to assume the role of archaeologists and show their sketch to their classmates, describing the ruins and telling what functions the various structures and monuments supposedly served.

El universo: Ask students to create a "size-line" on which they arrange the items in this category in a line from largest to smallest. They should show each item on the "size-line" using a simple sketch or symbol accompanied by a label.

Verbos: Ask students to invent a false definition for each of the verbs. Have them work in pairs and take turns defining the verbs. Students decide each time whether their definition will be the correct one or their invented false one. If the definition is correct, the partner says *Tienes razón.* If it is false, the partner says, for example: *No, trazar no significa "llenar," sino "dibujar."*

Otras palabras/Expresiones: Students can use these words and expressions as they go over the review activities for the other categories.

Additional Resources

Technology: Online Resources
- Instant Check
- Integrated Performance Assessment
- *Para hispanohablantes*
- Teacher's Resource Materials: Situation Cards, Clip Art

Repaso del capítulo

🔊 Vocabulario

descubrimientos

el / la arqueólogo(a)	archaeologist
la civilización	civilization
la escritura	writing
la pirámide	pyramid
las ruinas	ruins
sagrado, -a	sacred
el símbolo	symbol

mitos y leyendas

la creencia	belief
el / la dios(a)	god, goddess
la leyenda	legend
el mito	myth
la nave espacial	spaceship
el origen	origin

para hablar de los fenómenos inexplicables

la estructura	structure
la evidencia	proof, evidence
extraño, -a	strange
el fenómeno	phenomenon
la función	function
la imagen	image
inexplicable	inexplicable
el misterio	mystery
misterioso, -a	mysterious
la teoría	theory

para describir objetos

el alto	height
el ancho	width
el centímetro	centimeter
el círculo	circle
el diámetro	diameter
el diseño	design
la distancia	distance
geométrico, -a	geometric(al)
el largo	length
el óvalo	oval
el rectángulo	rectangle
redondo, -a	round
la tonelada	ton
el triángulo	triangle

otras palabras

el conejo	rabbit
cualquier, -a	any
el intento	attempt

para indicar duda

improbable	unlikely
probable	likely

el universo

el / la astrónomo(a)	astronomer
el eclipse	eclipse
el / la habitante	inhabitant
la Luna	moon
el observatorio	observatory
el planeta	planet
el pueblo	people
la sombra	shadow
la Tierra	Earth
el universo	universe

expresiones

al igual que	as, like
o sea que	in other words
sino	but
ya que	because, due to

verbos

aparecer (zc)	to appear
arrojar(se)	to throw (oneself)
brillar	to shine
calcular	to calculate, to compute
convertirse (en)	to turn (into), to become
contribuir (u→y)	to contribute
cubrir	to cover
dudar	to doubt
excavar	to excavate
existir	to exist
medir (e→i)	to measure
pesar	to weigh
ponerse (el sol)	to set (sun)
resolver (o→ue)	to solve
trazar	to trace, to draw

Differentiated Instruction

Verbal-Linguistic Learner

Remind students that many words in English come from Latin, with stops in Spanish and French along the way. Have students help their classmates by pointing out meaningful similarities between parts of Spanish and English words, such as "spaceship" and *(nave) espacial,* or "brilliant" and ***brillar.***

Advanced Learners

Have students use their creativity to make an audio or video recording about a group of archaeologists at the moment they discover an important find. Challenge them to use as much as they can of the chapter vocabulary in their script.

Gramática

El presente y el presente perfecto del subjuntivo con expresiones de duda

Use the present subjunctive after expressions of doubt, uncertainty, or disbelief.

Dudo que **haya** una nave espacial en el pueblo.

To express doubt, uncertainty, or disbelief about actions in the past, Spanish uses the present perfect subjunctive mode.

Es probable que los arqueólogos **hayan encontrado** nuevas evidencias.

Expressions starting with *creo, no dudo, estoy seguro(a)* are usually followed by the indicative since they do not express doubt, disbelief or uncertainty.

Estoy seguro de que aquellas piedras **pertenecen** a los mayas.

Pero y sino

The word *pero* is usually the equivalent of the English conjunction *but*. The word *sino* also means *but*. *Sino* is used when the idea being conveyed is *not this, but rather* that.

No voy a comer carne **sino** vegetales.

You can also use *sino* with *no sólo . . . sino también . . .*

Vino **no sólo** María **sino también** Ana.

You use *sino que* when there is a conjugated verb in the second part of the sentence.

No salí a pasear **sino que** me quedé en casa.

El subjuntivo en cláusulas adjetivas

You can use an entire clause to describe a noun. This is an adjective clause. When you have a specific person or thing in mind, you use the indicative.

Busco a la arqueóloga **que trabaja** con ruinas aztecas.

If you don't have a specific person or thing in mind, or if you are not sure the person exists, you use the subjunctive. To refer to something or someone in the past, you use the present perfect subjunctive.

Necesito un artículo **que hable** sobre las pirámides.
Busco a un joven **que haya estudiado** español.

You also use the subjunctive in an adjective clause when it describes a negative word such as *nadie, nada,* or *ninguno(a).*

No hay **nadie que tenga** tiempo libre.

You use the subjunctive in an adjective clause when it doesn't describe a specific person or thing, using words such as *cualquier* or *cualquiera.*

Escoge **cualquier** cosa **que quieras.**

El presente y el presente perfecto del subjuntivo con expresiones de duda: Ask students to think about the mysteries described in *Capítulo 7* as well as other mysteries and unanswered questions about our world or the universe in general. Have each student write on a slip of paper a statement of opinion about one mystery. Ask them to write their statement as though it were a fact, avoiding expressions of doubt. For example: *Los extraterrestres tenían una presencia en la civilización maya.* Mix the slips of paper. Have students take turns drawing one and giving their own opinion about the mystery, using an expression of certainty or uncertainty: *Es improbable que los extraterrestres hayan tenido una presencia en la civilización maya.*

Pero y sino: Ask students to comment on unexplained phenomena using **sino, sino que,** or **sino también.** For example: *Los extraterrestres no solo tenían una influencia en la civilización maya sino también en otras civilizaciones.*

El subjuntivo en cláusulas adjetivas: Ask students to pretend they are employment counselors. Have them write two sentences. In the first, they tell what type of position needs to be filled: *Se busca secretaria.* In the second, they tell about a desirable quality or skill needed for the job: *La secretaria tiene que ser organizada.* Have them trade pairs of sentences with a partner, who combines them into a single sentence with an adjective clause: Se busca una secretaria que sea organizada.

Digital Portfolio

Invite students to review the activities and projects they completed in this chapter. Have them select one or two items that they feel best demonstrate their achievements in Spanish. Include these products in students' portfolios.

Additional Resources

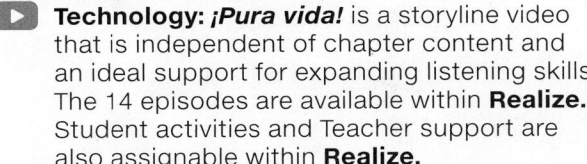 **Technology:** *¡Pura vida!* is a storyline video that is independent of chapter content and an ideal support for expanding listening skills. The 14 episodes are available within **Realize.** Student activities and Teacher support are also assignable within **Realize.**

Enrich Your Teaching

Teacher-to-Teacher

Make clear to students the value of using study groups to prepare for exams and other assessment activities. Encourage them to conduct all the activities of the group in Spanish. Besides sharing their knowledge about the vocabulary or grammatical structures under review, students in a study group must also use vital, everyday language necessary for the performance of group activities: taking turns, giving and following commands, offering suggestions and opinions, and so on.

Performance Tasks

Standards: 1.1, 1.2, 1.3, 2.1, 2.2, 3.1

Student Resource: *Para hispanohablantes*
Teacher Resources: Teacher's Resource Materials: Audio Script, Technology: Audio Cap. 7

1. Vocabulario

Suggestions: Encourage students to review the vocabulary from the *Vocabulario en contexto* sections on pp. 310–313 and 324–327 before they complete the activity.

Answers:

1. b	**5.** a
2. d	**6.** d
3. a	**7.** d
4. c	**8.** b

2. Gramática

Suggestions: Remind students of the main points of the grammar presentations in *Capítulo 7*:

- the present and present perfect subjunctive used with expressions of doubt
- the use of **pero** and **sino**
- the subjunctive in adjective clauses

Answers:

1. d	**5.** d
2. b	**6.** d
3. c	**7.** a
4. b	**8.** c

Repaso del capítulo

OBJECTIVE
▶ Demonstrate that you can perform the tasks on these pages

Preparación para el examen

❶ Vocabulario Escribe la letra de la palabra o expresión que mejor complete cada frase. Escribe tus respuestas en una hoja aparte.

1. Un huevo tiene forma de _____ .
   a. triángulo
   b. óvalo
   c. pirámide
   d. rectángulo

2. El arqueólogo midió _____ de la roca.
   a. el mito y el origen
   b. el planeta y el observatorio
   c. el fenómeno y el misterio
   d. el ancho y el largo

3. Cada civilización tenía sus teorías sobre el _____ del mundo.
   a. origen
   b. pueblo
   c. universo
   d. habitante

4. Los astrónomos mayas observaban _____ y los eclipses.
   a. las ruinas
   b. el símbolo
   c. los planetas
   d. el círculo

5. A un fenómeno extraño e inexplicable lo llamamos _____.
   a. misterio
   b. geométrico
   c. evidencia
   d. estructura

6. El arqueólogo _____ el diámetro del calendario azteca.
   a. cubrió
   b. dudó
   c. pesó
   d. midió

7. A las seis de la tarde se _____ el sol.
   a. excavó
   b. resolvió
   c. calculó
   d. puso

8. Los astrónomos _____ en la reunión con información sobre los planetas.
   a. brillaron
   b. contribuyeron
   c. se arrojaron
   d. existían

---

❷ Gramática Escribe la letra de la palabra o expresión que mejor complete cada frase. Escribe tus respuestas en una hoja aparte.

1. Dudo que _____ naves espaciales en el imperio maya.
   a. existió
   b. existirán
   c. existen
   d. hayan existido

2. Algunos creen que es probable que los extraterrestres _____ las Líneas de Nazca.
   a. trazaron
   b. hayan trazado
   c. trazan
   d. tracen

3. La arqueóloga está segura de que esta pirámide _____ a la civilización azteca.
   a. pertenecerá
   b. haya pertenecido
   c. pertenece
   d. pertenecerían

4. No conozco a ningún arqueólogo que _____ el nombre de todos los dioses aztecas.
   a. sabe
   b. sepa
   c. sabían
   d. supo

5. Necesitan a un científico que _____ la edad del templo.
   a. calcula
   b. calculen
   c. calculo
   d. calcule

6. Es improbable que los aztecas _____ a la Luna.
   a. han viajado
   b. viajan
   c. hayas viajado
   d. hayan viajado

7. No conozco a nadie que _____ para buscar ruinas de la cultura azteca.
   a. haya excavado
   b. excava
   c. han excavado
   d. hayan excavado

8. El sol no desapareció _____ que se puso.
   a. también
   b. pero
   c. sino
   d. sólo

Differentiated Instruction

Heritage Speakers

Have students review their past exams, portfolios, and pieces of writing on which you have given them feedback. Have them identify errors that they consistently make, including errors with accent marks and spelling. Guide them to make notes that will help them to not repeat these errors as they complete the writing portion of the exam.

Students with Learning Difficulties

Guide students to use the process of elimination by first determining which answers they are sure are incorrect and ignoring them. Help them begin by eliminating answers that do not agree in tense, person, or number with the rest of the sentence.

En el examen vas a . . .	Éstas son las tareas de práctica que te pueden ser útiles para el examen . . .	Para repasar, ve a tu libro de texto impreso o digital . . .
Interpretive		
3 ESCUCHAR Yo puedo escuchar y comprender una entrevista con un arqueólogo que acaba de regresar de una excavación.	Escucha una entrevista entre un locutor de una estación de radio y la famosa arqueóloga Dra. Cruz, y contesta a las siguientes preguntas: (a) ¿Qué civilización estudió? (b) ¿Qué excavó? (c) ¿Cómo explicó lo que encontró? (d) ¿El locutor cree que es un mito o la realidad?	pp. 310–313 *Vocabulario en contexto 1* p. 311 Actividad 1 p. 314 *Videohistoria* p. 321 Actividad 16 pp. 346–347 *Auténtico*
Interpersonal		
4 HABLAR Yo puedo hablar sobre un misterio o fenómeno inexplicable del pasado o del presente.	Piensa en un misterio o fenómeno inexplicable que te interese. Descríbelo y sugiere una explicación lógica de por qué existe o se produce dicho misterio o fenómeno.	p. 317 Actividad 9 p. 319 Actividad 13 p. 321 Actividad 16
Interpretive		
5 LEER Yo puedo leer y comprender una leyenda.	Lee este relato azteca. Según el relato, ¿cuál es la explicación para el principio de la lluvia? (a) A los dioses les gustaba el templo que los aztecas construyeron. (b) Para que lloviera, siete hombres cantaban cuatro canciones. (c) La Luna apareció por 28 días. *Cuenta el relato que los antiguos aztecas construyeron un templo a los dioses del fuego y de la lluvia en una montaña. Y siete hombres se reunían cuando llegaba el tiempo de sembrar la tierra, llamaban al dios de la lluvia y cantaban cuatro canciones, porque cuatro por siete es 28, y veintiocho días tiene el mes de la Luna. Poco después, comenzaba a llover.*	p. 316 Actividad 8 p. 323 Actividad 19 pp. 324–327 *Vocabulario en contexto 2* p. 330 Actividad 27 pp. 336–337 *Puente a la cultura*
Presentational		
6 ESCRIBIR Yo puedo escribir sobre un misterio arqueológico.	Escoge una de las ruinas misteriosas de las que se han hablado en este capítulo y escribe un párrafo sobre lo que piensas de ella. ¿Cuál crees que fue el origen y la función de esa construcción? ¿Está relacionada con algún mito o leyenda de esa civilización? ¿Crees que algún día se descubrirán sus misterios?	p. 316 Actividad 8 p. 317 Actividad 9 p. 321 Actividad 16 p. 323 Actividad 18 p. 330 Actividad 27 pp. 336–337 *Puente a la cultura*
Comparisons		
7 COMPARAR Yo puedo comparar un mito con una leyenda y buscar una explicación posible.	Compara una leyenda y un mito que has estudiado en este capítulo. Explica cómo los orígenes y las funciones que tenían son similares o diferentes.	p. 317 Actividad 9 p. 338 *¿Qué me cuentas?*

Capítulo 7 • trescientos cincuenta y uno **351**

Differentiated Assessment

Core Assessment
- Technology: Audio Cap. 7
- ExamView: Chapter Test, Test Banks A and B

Challenge/Pre-AP®
- ExamView: Pre-AP® Test Bank
- Pre-AP® Resource Materials

Extra Support
- Alternate Assessment Program: Examen del capítulo 7
- Technology: Audio Cap. 7

Heritage Speakers
- Assessment Program: Para hispanohablantes: Examen del capítulo 7
- ExamView Heritage Speaker Test Bank

3. Escuchar
Suggestions: Use the audio or read from the script.
Script
Escucha una entrevista entre un locutor de una estación de radio y la famosa arqueóloga Dra. Cruz, y responde a las siguientes preguntas: (a) ¿Qué civilización estudió? (b) ¿Qué excavó? (c) ¿Cómo explicó lo que encontró? (d) ¿El locutor cree que es un mito o la realidad? Vas a oír la entrevista dos veces.

(For the complete script, see Teacher's Resource Materials.)

Answers:
- **(a)** Estudió la civilización de los olmecas.
- **(b)** Excavó una roca con símbolos muy antiguos.
- **(c)** No son símbolos sino letras en un idioma muy extraño.
- **(d)** El locutor cree que los mitos muchas veces son realidad.

4. Hablar
Suggestions: Encourage students to use an expression of doubt or of certainty when giving their explanation for the phenomenon.
Answers will vary.

5. Leer
Suggestions: Tell students to refer to pp. 310–313 and 324–327 if they have questions about vocabulary in the review.
Answers:
b

6. Escribir
Suggestions: Encourage students to use subordinate clauses in their paragraphs in order to make their sentences varied and interesting.
Answers will vary.

7. Comparar
Suggestions: Ask students how their personal opinions regarding unexplained phenomena have changed, if at all, due to what they have learned in *Capítulo* 7. Ask them also to summarize the new information they have learned from the chapter.
Answers will vary.

Additional Resources
 Technology: Online Resources
- Instant Check
- *Para hispanohablantes*
Print
- Core WB pp. 103–104

CAPÍTULO 8

Chapter Overview

Interactions between different cultures

Vocabulary: fusion of cultures in Spain; fusion of cultures in the Americas

Grammar: conditional; imperfect subjunctive

Cultural Perspectives: the fusion of different cultures evidenced in the architecture and culture and lifestyles of Spain; Buenos Aires, a city where cultures, religions, and traditions mix; the Paraguayan harp and its European origin; Tex-Mex food, a mixture of two cultures; the missions of California

¡Pura vida!: Watch an engaging video episode about a group of young people in Costa Rica!

Chapter Support

Bulletin Boards

Theme: Mezcla de culturas en España

Ask students to cut out, copy, or download pictures showing evidence of the exchange between different cultures in Spain. They can include pictures of different architectural structures, musical instruments, writings, mathematical symbols, food, and other examples of how Spain assimilated elements from different cultures.

Hands-on Culture

Craft: Azulejo de maravilla

Students will imagine they are creating beautifully decorated *azulejos* (tiles) to be used in the construction of the Alhambra corridors and fountains.

Materials: Internet access or books and magazines about Moorish architecture in Spain (optional), tracing or drawing paper, carbon paper, 2 square or octagonal cardboard or plastic tiles per student, white or beige enamel, paint brushes, permanent markers in a variety of colors and tips

Directions:

1. Students cover each tile with one or two layers of enamel and let dry overnight.
2. Students either research in the Internet, books, or magazines for examples of Arab designs like the ones used in the tiles of the Alhambra and copy them on tracing paper, or make their own designs on drawing paper.
3. Once the enamel on the tiles dries, students transfer their designs by tracing their designs onto the top of each tile with a piece of carbon paper. They can use colored markers to decorate the design.

Game

Dominó de palabras

This domino game practices vocabulary about cultural exchange during the Spanish conquest of the Americas and the Middle Ages in Spain. Use it after students have practiced the vocabulary from the chapter.

Players: entire class

Materials: index cards, at least five per student, pens or markers

Rules:

1. Distribute five or more index cards to each student. Ask students to draw a vertical line on each card, dividing it in two halves, and write a vocabulary word on each half.
2. Collect the finished "domino" pieces, shuffle them, and redistribute them evenly.
3. Play! Students form a big circle and start playing domino with the cards. The criteria for matching domino halves will be that matching words should fall within the same category or be directly related to each other.
4. Students take turns setting one of their domino pieces on the table and arranging them in creative domino designs. If a student cannot match any of his or her pieces to the free ends of the domino, he or she skips the round and keeps the pieces. The objective is to be the first to set all the pieces on the table.

Variation: Instead of playing traditional domino, in which only one piece can be attached to each free end, students can attach up to three matching words to each word, thus making a multi-lineal design.

21st Century Skills

Look for tips throughout Chapter 8 to enrich your teaching by integrating 21st Century Skills. Suggestions for the Project-Based Learning and Culture follow below.

Project-Based Learning

Modify the project with these suggestions:

ICT (Information, Communications and Technology) Literacy Encourage students to access their favorite search engine to research the arrival of the Spaniards or other explorers in the Americas. Have them choose one particular explorer that interests them and search for reliable sources for their project. The handout "Search for Information on the Internet" can help them refine their search.

Creativity and Innovation Have students think about creative ways to organize and present their research. Ask students to come up with creative ways to arrange the information, such as time lines, maps, use of visuals with captions, or text.

Social and Cross-Cultural Skills

Have students work with partners to discuss the cultural backgrounds they represent. From where are their parents, grandparents, or other family members? What languages or cultural traditions do they use at home? What unique family traditions come from their cultural heritage?

Chapter Culture

Critical Thinking and Problem Solving

Direct students to the information in the *Cultura* on page 376 and *La fusión* on page 372. Have them compare their answers to the questions with classmates and promote a discussion about the fusion of cultures in Latin America. How is Tex-Mex cuisine representative of the fusion of local cultures in the Southwest? What are other examples of cultural fusion in Latin America or the U.S.?

▶ **Technology: Videodocumentario**
View *Unas herencias ricas* online with the class to learn more about how people of diverse cultural backgrounds can come together to share their cultures.

Project-Based Learning

Imágenes del encuentro entre culturas

Overview: Students create a Web page about the arrival of the Spaniards or other explorers in the Americas. They can focus on one of the many topics presented on pages 370–372. The Web page must feature labeled photos or illustrations related to the topic they have selected. Students then give an oral presentation describing briefly the culture they are showing and what happened during that period in history.

Resources: digital or print photos, image editing and page layout software

Sequence: (suggestions for when to do each step appear throughout the chapter)

Step 1. Review instructions so students know what is expected of them. Share the rubric with the class.

Step 2. Students choose their topic and submit a rough draft of their project. Return the drafts with your suggestions. For vocabulary and grammar practice, ask students to work in pairs and present their drafts to each other.

Step 3. Students do layouts. Encourage students to try different arrangements before writing descriptions.

Step 4. Students submit a draft of their descriptions. Note your corrections and suggestions, then return the drafts to students.

Step 5. Students complete and present their Web page to the class. They should describe one of the photos and give a brief summary of what is shown in the whole Web page.

Options

1. Instead of a Web page, students design a blog with similar information.
2. Students design a timeline beginning with the arrival of the Spaniards in Mexico up to and including the establishment of colonies.

Assessment

Here is a detailed rubric for assessing this project:

Chapter 8 Project: *Imágenes del encuentro entre culturas*

Rubric	Score 1	Score 3	Score 5
Your evidence of planning	You provide no preliminary proposal or descriptions.	Your preliminary proposal and descriptions are not revised.	You show evidence of corrected proposal and descriptions.
Your use of illustrations	Your photos or illustrations are incorrectly labeled.	Your photos or illustrations are disorganized.	Your photos or illustrations are organized. Your presentation is easy to read.
Your presentation	You do not include the required information.	You include most of the required information.	You include all of the required information.

AT A GLANCE

Objectives

- Listen and read about indigenous cultures
- Talk and write about cultural heritage
- Present a guided city tour
- Understand the historical context of Spanish missions in California
- Compare cultural practices in an authentic video about the Mapuche culture in Chile
- Express your opinion about cultural exchanges

Vocabulary

- Buildings
- The discovery of America
- Cultural exchanges

Grammar

- Conditional
- Imperfect subjunctive
- Imperfect subjunctive with *si*

Recycle

- The verb *haber* in the preterite
- The preterite of verbs
- Pronunciation of the letter *c* before *a*, *o*, and *u*

Culture

- Spain and Puerto Rico, pp. 358–360
- The Paraguayan harp, p. 369
- Aztecs and Hernán Cortés, pp. 370–371
- Spanish colonialism, pp. 372–373
- Empires, p. 375
- Tex-Mex food, p. 375
- The Aztec legend, *El Águila y el nopal*, p. 377
- The missions of California, pp. 384–385
- Aztec words used today, p. 393

A ver si recuerdas...

- Buildings, descriptions, and locations
- Conflicts and resolutions
- Interrogative words
- Verbs with changes in the preterite

Authentic Resources

- Auténtico: *Chile acepta la diversidad,* pp. 394–395

RESOURCES

	FOR THE STUDENT	DIGITAL	PRINT	FOR THE TEACHER	DIGITAL	PRINT
A ver si recuerdas PP. 352–355						
Review	*A ver si recuerdas* with Remediation	•		*A ver si recuerdas* with Remediation	•	
	Guided WB, pp. 352–355	•	•	Teacher's Edition, pp. 352–355	•	•
	Core WB, pp. 105–106	•	•			
	Para hispanohablantes	•				
Introducción PP. 356–357						
Present	Student Edition, pp. 356–357	•	•	Teacher's Edition, pp. 356–357	•	•
	DK Reference Atlas	•		Teacher's Resource Materials	•	
	Videonovela: *¡Pura vida!*	•		Mapa global interactivo	•	
	¡Pura vida! Video Activities	•				
	Para hispanohablantes	•				
Vocabulario en contexto PP. 358–361/370–373						
Present & Practice	Student Edition, pp. 358–361/370–373	•	•	Teacher's Edition, pp. 358–361/370–373	•	•
	Audio: Videohistoria	•		Teacher's Resource Materials	•	
	Flashcards	•		Vocabulary Clip Art	•	
	Instant Check	•		Technology: Audio	•	
	Guided WB, pp. 242–250/253–260	•	•			
	Core WB, pp. 107–108/112–113	•	•			
	Communication Activities	•				
	Para hispanohablantes	•				
Assess and Remediate				Pruebas 8–1, 8–4: Assessment Program, Assessment Program *Para hispanohablantes*	• •	

RESOURCES

	FOR THE STUDENT	DIGITAL	PRINT	FOR THE TEACHER	DIGITAL	PRINT
Vocabulario en uso pp. 362–365/374–377						
Present & Practice	Student Edition, pp. 362–365/374–377	•	•	Interactive Whiteboard Vocabulary Activities	•	
	Instant Check	•		Teacher's Edition, pp. 362–365/374–377	•	•
	Communication Activities	•		Teacher's Resource Materials	•	
	Para hispanohablantes	•		Technology: Audio	•	
	Communicative Pair Activities	•		Videomodelos	•	
Assess and Remediate				Pruebas 8–2, 8–5 with Remediation	•	
				Pruebas 8–2, 8–5: Assessment Program, Assessment Program *Para hispanohablantes*	•	
Gramática pp. 366–369/378–383						
Present & Practice	Student Edition, pp. 366–369/378–383	•	•	Interactive Whiteboard Grammar Activities	•	
	Instant Check	•		Teacher's Edition, pp. 366–369/378–383	•	•
	Animated Verbs	•		Teacher's Resource Materials	•	
	Tutorial Video: Grammar	•		Technology: Audio	•	
	Canción de hip hop	•		Videomodelos	•	
	Guided WB, pp. 251–252/261–264	•	•			
	Core WB, pp. 109–111/114–116	•	•			
	Communication Activities	•				
	Para hispanohablantes	•				
	Communicative Pair Activities	•				
Assess and Remediate				Pruebas 8–3, 8–6, 8–7 with Remediation	•	
				Pruebas 8–3, 8–6, 8–7: Assessment Program, Assessment Program *Para hispanohablantes*	•	
				Examen 1, Examen 2: Vocab. y gramática	•	
Aplicación pp. 384–395						
Apply	Student Edition, pp. 384–395	•	•	Teacher's Edition, pp. 384–395	•	•
	Authentic Resources Workbook	•	•	Teacher's Resource Materials	•	
	Authentic Resources	•		Video Program: *Videodocumentario*	•	
	Online Cultural Reading	•		Mapa global interactivo	•	
	Guided WB, pp. 265–267	•	•	Authentic Resources Lesson Plans with scripts, answer keys	•	
	Communication Activities	•				
	Para hispanohablantes	•				
	Videodocumentario	•				
	Auténtico	•				
Repaso del capítulo pp. 396–399						
Review	Student Edition, pp. 396–399	•	•	Teacher's Edition, pp. 396–399	•	•
	Core WB, pp. 117–118	•	•	Teacher's Resource Materials	•	
	Communication Activities	•		Technology: Audio	•	
	Para hispanohablantes	•				
	Instant Check	•				
Chapter Assessment						
Assess				Examen del capítulo 8: Assessment Program, Alternate Assessment Program, Assessment Program *Para hispanohablantes*	•	
				Technology: Audio Cap. 8, Examen	•	
				ExamView: Test Banks A and B (questions only online) Heritage Speaker Test Bank Pre-AP® Test Bank	• • •	

DAY	Warm-up / Assess	Preview / Present / Practice / Communicate		Wrap-up / Homework Options
		LESSON PLAN		
1	**Warm-up** (10 min.) • Return Examen del capítulo: Capítulo 7	**Repaso** (35 min.) • A ver si recuerdas . . . • Actividad 7		**Wrap-up and Homework Options** (5 min.) • Core Practice 8-1, 8-2
2	**Warm-up** (10 min.) • Homework check	**Chapter Opener** (10 min.) • Objectives • Arte y cultura	**Vocabulario en contexto 1** (25 min.) • Presentation: Vocabulario y gramática en contexto • Actividades 1, 2, 3, 4	**Wrap-up and Homework Options** (5 min.) • Clip Art Vocabulary
3	**Warm-up** (10 min.) • Homework check	**Vocabulario en contexto 1** (35 min.) • Presentación: Videohistoria *¡San Antonio te espera!* • View Videohistoria		**Wrap-up and Homework Options** (5 min.) • Core Practice 8-3, 8-4 • Actividad 6 • Prueba 8-1: Vocabulary recognition
4	**Warm-up** (10 min.) • Homework check • **Formative Assessment** (10 min.) • Prueba 8-1: Vocabulary recognition	**Vocabulario en uso 1** (25 min.) • Interactive Whiteboard Vocabulary Activities • Actividades 5, 7, 8, 9, 10 • Ampliación del lenguaje		**Wrap-up and Homework Options** (5 min.) • Writing Activities • Prueba 8-2 with Remediation: Vocabulary production
5	**Warm-up** (5 min.) • Homework check • **Formative Assessment** (10 min.) • Prueba 8-2 with Remediation: Vocabulary production	**Gramática y vocabulario en uso 1** (25 min.) • Presentation: El condicional • Interactive Whiteboard Grammar Activities • Actividades 12, 13, 14 • Writing Activity		**Wrap-up and Homework Options** (5 min.) • Core Practice 8-5
6	**Warm-up** (10 min.) • Actividad 11 • Homework check	**Gramática y vocabulario en uso 1** (35 min.) • Actividades 15, 16 • Audio or Writing Activity		**Wrap-up and Homework Options** (5 min.) • Core Practice 8-6, 8-7 • Writing Activity • Prueba 8-3 with Remediation: El condicional
7	**Warm-up** (10 min.) • Cultura • Homework check • **Formative Assessment** (10 min.) • Prueba 8-3 with Remediation: El condicional	**Gramática y vocabulario en uso 1** (10 min.) • Communicative Pair Activity	**Vocabulario en contexto 2** (25 min.) • Presentation: Vocabulario y gramática en contexto • Actividad 17	**Wrap-up and Homework Options** (5 min.) • Examen: Vocabulario y gramática 1
8	**Warm-up** (15 min.) • Writing Activity • Homework check • **Formative Assessment** (30 min.) • Examen: Vocabulario y gramática 1			**Wrap-up and Homework Options** (5 min.) • Writing Activity
9	**Warm-up** (5 min.) • Homework check • **Formative Assessment** (30 min.) • Examen: Vocabulario y gramática 1	**Vocabulario en contexto 2** (25 min.) • Presentation: La fusión y la herencia • Actividades 18, 19 • Audio and Writing Activities	**Vocabulario en uso 2** (15 min.) • Actividades 21, 22	**Wrap-up and Homework Options** (5 min.) • Core Practice 8-8, 8-9 • Prueba 8-4: Vocabulary recognition
10	**Warm-up** (15 min.) • Actividad 20 • Homework check • **Formative Assessment** (10 min.) • Prueba 8-4: Vocabulary recognition	**Vocabulario en uso 2** (20 min.) • Interactive Whiteboard Vocabulary Activities • Actividades 23, 24, 25		**Wrap-up and Homework Options** (5 min.) • Cultura • Prueba 8-5 with Remediation: Vocabulary production

LESSON PLAN

DAY	Warm-up / Assess	Preview / Present / Practice / Communicate	Wrap-up / Homework Options
11	**Warm-up** (10 min.) • Writing Activity • Homework check • **Formative Assessment** (10 min.) • Prueba 8-5 with Remediation: Vocabulary production	**Gramática y vocabulario en uso 2** (25 min.) • Presentation: El imperfecto del subjuntivo • Interactive Whiteboard Grammar Activities • En voz alta • Actividades 26, 27, 29 • Communicative Pair Activity	**Wrap-up and Homework Options** (5 min.) • Actividad 28 • Core Practice 8-10 • Prueba 8-6 with Remediation: El imperfecto del subjuntivo
12	**Warm-up** (10 min.) • Actividad 30 • Homework check • **Formative Assessment** (10 min.) • Prueba 8-6 with Remediation: El imperfecto del subjuntivo	**Gramática y vocabulario en uso 2** (25 min.) • El español en el mundo del trabajo • Presentation: El imperfecto del subjuntivo con *si* • Interactive Whiteboard Grammar Activities • Actividades 33, 34, 35	**Wrap-up and Homework Options** (5 min.) • Core Practice 8-11, 8-12 • Prueba 8-7 with Remediation: El imperfecto del subjuntivo con *si*
13	**Warm-up** (20 min.) • Actividades 31, 32, • Homework check • **Formative Assessment** (10 min.) • Prueba 8-7 with Remediation: El imperfecto del subjuntivo con *si*	**Gramática y vocabulario en uso 2** (15 min.) • Communicative Pair Activity	**Wrap-up and Homework Options** (5 min.) • Examen: Vocabulario y gramática 2
14	**Warm-up** (10 min.) • Writing Activity • **Formative Assessment** (10 min.) • Examen: Vocabulario y gramática 2	**Aplicación** (10 min.) • Presentación oral: Steps 1, 2	**Wrap-up and Homework Options** (5 min.) • Presentación oral: Step 2
15	**Warm-up** (10 min.) • Presentación oral: Step 2	**Aplicación** (35 min.) • Presentación oral: Step 3	**Wrap-up and Homework Options** (5 min.) • Las misiones de California • ¿Comprendiste?
16	**Warm-up** (15 min.) • Las misiones de California: ¿Comprendiste? • Homework check	**Aplicación** (30 min.) • Pre-AP® Integración 1, 2, 3 • View Video • Video Activities 1, 2, 3	**Wrap-up and Homework Options** (5 min.) • Presentación escrita: Steps 1, 2
17	**Warm-up** (10 min.) • Video Activity 4	**Aplicación** (15 min.) • Presentación escrita: Step 3 **Repaso** (20 min.) • Preparación para el examen: Actividades 3, 4	**Wrap-up and Homework Options** (5 min.) • Presentación escrita: Step 4
18	**Warm-up** (10 min.) • Homework check	**Aplicación** (35 min.) • Lectura • Interacción con la lectura • Cultura • Auténtico	**Wrap-up and Homework Options** (5 min.) • Core Practice: Organizer 8-13, 8-14 • Instant Check
19	**Warm-up** (20 min.) • Preparación para el examen: Actividades 1, 2 • Homework check	**Repaso** (25 min.) • Preparación para el examen: Actividades 5, 6, 7 • Other review	**Wrap-up and Homework Options** (5 min.) • Examen del capítulo
20	**Warm-up** (5 min.) • Answer questions • **Summative Assessment** (44 min.) • Examen del capítulo		**Wrap-up and Homework Options** (1 min.) • A ver si recuerdas: Capítulo 9

ALTERNATE LESSON PLAN

DAY	Warm-up / Assess	Preview / Present / Practice / Communicate		Wrap-up / Homework Options
1	**Warm-up** (25 min.) • Return Examen del capítulo: Capítulo 7 • A ver si recuerdas . . . • Actividad 7 • Homework check	**Chapter Opener** (10 min.) • Objectives • Arte y cultura **Vocabulario en contexto 1** (40 min.) • Presentation: Vocabulario y gramática en contexto • Actividades 1, 2, 3, 4 • Presentación: Videohistoria *¡San Antonio te espera!* • View Videohistoria	**Vocabulario en uso 1** (10 min.) • Actividad 7	**Wrap-up and Homework Options** (5 min.) • Core Practice 8-3, 8-4 • Clip Art Vocabulary • Prueba 8-1: Vocabulary recognition
2	**Warm-up** (15 min.) • Actividad 5 • Homework check • **Formative Assessment** (10 min.) • Prueba 8-1: Vocabulary recognition	**Vocabulario en uso 1** (60 min.) • Interactive Whiteboard Vocabulary Activities • Actividades 6, 8, 9, 10 • Ampliación del lenguaje • Communicative Pair Activity		**Wrap-up and Homework Options** (5 min.) • Writing Activities • Prueba 8-2 with Remediation: Vocabulary production
3	**Warm-up** (15 min.) • Writing Activity • Homework check • **Formative Assessment** (10 min.) • Prueba 8-2 with Remediation: Vocabulary production	**Gramática y vocabulario en uso 1** (60 min.) • Presentation: El condicional • Interactive Whiteboard Grammar Activities • Actividades 11, 12, 13, 14, 15, 16 • Cultura • Audio and Writing Activities		**Wrap-up and Homework Options** (5 min.) • Core Practice 8-5, 8-6, 8-7 • Prueba 8-3 with Remediation: El condicional
4	**Warm-up** (10 min.) • Writing Activity • Homework check • **Formative Assessment** (10 min.) • Prueba 8-3 with Remediation: El condicional	**Gramática y vocabulario en uso 1** (20 min.) • Communicative Pair Activity **Vocabulario en contexto 2** (40 min.) • Presentation: Vocabulario y gramática en contexto • Actividad 17 • Presentation: La fusión y la herencia • Actividades 18, 19		**Wrap-up and Homework Options** (5 min.) • Core Practice 8-8, 8-9 • Examen: Vocabulario y gramática 1
5	**Warm-up** (10 min.) • Actividad 19 • Homework check • **Formative Assessment Options** (30 min.) • Examen: Vocabulario y gramática 1	**Vocabulario en contexto 2** (20 min.) • Audio or Writing Activities **Vocabulario en uso 2** (25 min.) • Actividades 21, 22, 23 • En voz alta		**Wrap-up and Homework Options** (5 min.) • Actividades 20, 24 • Prueba 8-4: Vocabulary recognition

ALTERNATE LESSON PLAN

DAY	Warm-up / Assess	Preview / Present / Practice / Communicate	Wrap-up / Homework Options
6	**Warm-up** (20 min.) • Actividad 25 • Homework check • **Formative Assessment** (10 min.) • Prueba 8-4: Vocabulary recognition	**Gramática y vocabulario en uso 2** (55 min.) • Cultura • Presentation: El imperfecto del subjuntivo • Interactive Whiteboard Grammar Activities • Actividades 26, 27, 29, 30 • El español en el mundo del trabajo • Writing Activities	**Wrap-up and Homework Options** (5 min.) • Core Practice 8-10 • Pruebas 8-5, 8-6 with Remediation: Vocabulary production, El imperfecto del subjuntivo
7	**Warm-up** (10 min.) • Actividad 28 • Writing Activity • **Formative Assessment** (20 min.) • Pruebas 8-5, 8-6 with Remediation: Vocabulary production, El imperfecto del subjuntivo	**Gramática y vocabulario en uso 2** (40 min.) • Presentation: El imperfecto del subjuntivo con *si* • Interactive Whiteboard Grammar Activities • Actividades 31, 32, 33, 34, 35 **Aplicación** (15 min.) • Presentación oral: Steps 1, 2	**Wrap-up and Homework Options** (5 min.) • Presentación oral: Step 2
8	**Warm-up** (15 min.) • Writing Activity • Homework check • **Formative Assessment** (40 min.) • Presentación oral: Step 3	**Gramática y vocabulario en uso 2** (15 min.) • Communicative Pair Activity **Aplicación** (15 min.) • Presentation: Las misiones de California	**Wrap-up and Homework Options** (5 min.) • Core Practice 8-11, 8-12 • Prueba 8-7 with Remediation: El imperfecto del subjuntivo con *si* • Examen: Vocabulario y gramática 2
9	**Warm-up** (10 min.) • Homework check • **Formative Assessment Options** (30 min.) • Prueba 8-7 with Remediation: El imperfecto del subjuntivo con *si* • Examen: Vocabulario y gramática 2	**Aplicación** (45 min.) • Las misiones de California • ¿Comprendiste? • Pre-AP® Integración 1, 2, 3 • View Video • Video Activities • Presentación escrita: Step 1	**Wrap-up and Homework Options** (5 min.) • Presentación escrita: Step 2 • Preparación para el examen: Actividades 1, 2
10	**Warm-up** (20 min.) • Presentación escrita: Step 3 • Homework check	**Aplicación** (35 min.) • Lectura • Interacción con la lectura • Cultura • Auténtico **Repaso** (30 min.) • Preparación para el examen: Actividades 3, 4, 6	**Wrap-up and Homework Options** (5 min.) • Presentación escrita: Step 4 • Core Practice: Organizer 8-13, 8-14 • Instant Check • Preparación para el examen: Actividades 5, 7 • Examen del capítulo
11	**Warm-up** (15 min.) • Homework check • **Summative Assessment** (45 min.) • Examen del capítulo	**Theme Game** (15 min.) **A ver si recuerdas – Capítulo 9** (10 min.) • Presentation: Vocabulario • Presentation: Gramática	**Wrap-up and Homework Options** (5 min.) • A ver si recuerdas – Capítulo 9 • Actividades 1, 2, 3, 6, 8 • Core Practice 9-1, 9-2

Vocabulario: Repaso

Standards: 1.1

Suggestions: Before presenting the material in this review section, consider testing your students' command of the material by assigning the Prueba with Remediation. Students will automatically be given additional practice of the material they have not yet mastered, and you can focus your review based on the class's overall performance on the post-test.

Ask students to make a map of an imaginary neighborhood. Their map should include labels calling out several of the **construcciones** shown in the *Vocabulario*. Ask them to include some of the terms from the **para describir** and **en la ciudad** categories as well. Have students exchange maps with a partner and ask and answer questions about each other's maps:

A —¿*Cómo voy de la vieja sinagoga al nuevo museo?*

B —*Sal de la sinagoga y sigue por la Avenida Martín. Dobla a la derecha en la Calle del Museo. Camina dos cuadras y verás el museo.*

Standards: 1.1

Suggestions: Encourage students to invent Spanish names for places and buildings that are known by English names. Their Spanish names should be translations that are direct enough so that their partner can recognize them. If this proves too difficult, allow them to use the English name.

Answers will vary.

Active Classroom

Twenty Questions: Divide the class into groups of four or five to play "Twenty Questions." Each student will assume the identify of a person, living or dead. The group asks up to twenty questions to determine the identity of the mystery person.

A ver si recuerdas

OBJECTIVES
▶ Talk about landmarks and monuments in your town, city, or state
▶ Write and ask questions about cultural activities

Vocabulario

construcciones
el edificio histórico
la fuente
la iglesia
la mezquita
el monumento
el museo
el palacio
la plaza
el puente
la sinagoga
el teatro

para indicar el tiempo
¿Cuánto tiempo hace que . . . ?
desde
la fecha
hace . . . dos, tres, cuatro años
hace mucho / poco tiempo
recientemente

para indicar el lugar
a la derecha
a la izquierda
al lado de
cerca de
debajo de
delante de
detrás de
entre
lejos de

para describir
antiguo, -a
enorme
grande
horrible
moderno, -a
nuevo, -a
pequeño, -a
viejo, -a

en la ciudad
la avenida
la calle
la cuadra
la esquina

1

En tu ciudad

ESCRIBIR, HABLAR EN PAREJA

1 Haz una lista con tres lugares o edificios famosos de tu pueblo, de tu ciudad o de tu estado, por ejemplo: un monumento, una calle, un teatro o una plaza. En una tabla como la siguiente, escribe dónde quedan esos lugares o edificios, cómo son y cuándo los visitaste. Usa las palabras de la lista de vocabulario. NO escribas el nombre de la construcción.

	¿Qué es?	¿Dónde queda?	¿Cómo es?	¿Cuándo lo visitaste?
1.	[lugar o edificio]			
2.	[lugar o edificio]			

2 Hazle preguntas a otro(a) estudiante sobre los lugares de su lista. Pregúntale sobre la información que escribió y trata de identificar los lugares.

Videomodelo
A —*¿Cuándo visitaste el lugar?*
B —*Lo visité hace un año.*

Differentiated Instruction

Heritage Speakers

Ask students to share the names and types of buildings prevalent in, or specific to, their heritage country. Have them use specific vocabulary to describe some of the noteworthy structures found in their heritage country.

Advanced Learners

Have students write step-by-step directions in order to travel from one place in your community to another. Their directions should be clear and detailed enough so that a person following them would arrive at the destination. Have them read their directions to each other. Ask listeners to identify the destination.

Go **Online** to practice
PearsonSchool.com/Autentico
PEARSON
realize™
VIDEO   WRITING   SPEAK/RECORD

Recycle 8

Gramática

Las palabras interrogativas

Remember that you use interrogative words to ask questions. In Spanish, all interrogative words have a written accent mark.

The interrogative words *¿cómo?, ¿cuándo?, ¿dónde?, ¿adónde?, ¿qué?, ¿para qué?, ¿por qué?* are invariable—they do not change in gender or number.

¿Cuándo vas al museo?   **¿Por qué** vamos a la plaza?

The interrogative words *¿cuál? / ¿cuáles?*, and *¿quién? / ¿quiénes?* have both singular and plural forms, but do not change in gender.

¿Cuáles son tus amigos?   **¿Quién** es tu mejor amiga?

The interrogative words *¿cuánto? / ¿cuántos? / ¿cuánta? / ¿cuántas?* agree both in number (singular / plural) and gender (masculine / feminine) with the noun they modify.

¿Cuánto dinero?   **¿Cuántas** horas?

In Spanish, prepositions always precede interrogative words.

¿Para qué hiciste eso?   **¿Con quién** fuiste tú?

Just as in direct questions, interrogative words have a written accent when they are used in indirect questions.

Quiero saber **quiénes** van a la fiesta.   Me preguntó **cuál** era mi mochila.

Más recursos   ONLINE

▶ **Tutorial:** Questions with Interrogative Words

2

¿Cómo llegamos?

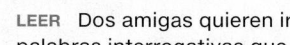 **LEER**   Dos amigas quieren ir al museo. Completa el diálogo con las palabras interrogativas que correspondan.

A. —¿ _1._ vamos al museo, en autobús o a pie?

B. —Depende . . . ¿tú sabes a _2._ cuadras de aquí está el museo?

A. —Creo que a unas veinte . . . ¿ _3._ no vamos en autobús?

B. —Sí, mejor. Estoy cansada. ¿Sabes _4._ está la parada del autobús?

A. —Aquí, paran cuatro autobuses. ¿ _5._ tomamos? ¿A _6._ le preguntamos?

3

Entrevista

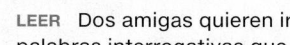 **ESCRIBIR, HABLAR EN PAREJA**   Tú y tu compañero(a) trabajan para una organización de turismo. Deben entrevistar a los turistas que visitan un centro cultural, un teatro o un museo. Escriban diez preguntas para hacerles y lean sus preguntas a la clase. Pueden representar la entrevista con otros(as) compañeros(as).

Modelo
¿De dónde es usted?
¿Por qué ha venido a . . . ?

Gramática: Repaso

Suggestions: Refer students who are having difficulty with interrogative words to the online tutorial.

Have students fold a sheet of paper in half to create a flashcard. On one side of the card, have them write a large accent mark. Tell them to leave the other side blank. Say sentences that contain the words reviewed in the *Gramática*. Some of your models should use the words to form questions, and others should use them in subordinate clauses in which no accent is required: *Cuando llegamos al museo, tú no estabas.* Have students flash the accent side their cards if they hear an interrogative word that requires an accent, and the blank side if a similar word they hear requires no accent.

2

Standards: 1.2

Suggestions: Have students scan the entire dialogue for meaning before they begin writing their answers.

Answers:

1. Cómo   4. dónde
2. cuántas   5. Cuál
3. Por qué   6. quién

Extension: Ask pairs of students to practice and present the dialogue for the class.

3

Standards: 1.3

Suggestions: Encourage students to ask questions that a tour agency might really ask in order to improve business.

Answers will vary.

Enrich Your Teaching

Teacher-to-Teacher

Challenge students to write sentences that contain many different types of information. For example: *La plaza vieja está a una distancia de tres cuadras de la plaza nueva. Jorge llegó allí a las seis con su hermana Gloria.* Have them trade sentences with a partner, who writes as many questions as possible about it. Here are some possible questions based on the sample sentences: *¿A qué distancia está la plaza vieja de la plaza nueva? ¿A cuántas cuadras está la plaza vieja de la plaza nueva? ¿Quién llegó a la plaza vieja? ¿Con quién llegó Jorge? ¿A qué hora llegaron Jorge y su hermana?*

Vocabulario: Repaso

Standards: 1.1

Suggestions: Ask students to write sentences using each of the verbs in the *reacciones* and *acciones* categories. In each of their sentences, challenge them to use items from at least one of the other categories as well.

4

Standards: 1.1, 1.2, 1.3

Suggestions: Once students have matched the items and written their definitions, ask them to identify prefixes and suffixes such as *des-* and *-ía* and explain how they are used.

Answers will vary.

1. b   4. a
2. c
3. d

5

Standards: 1.1, 3.1

Suggestions: As students discuss their word webs, ask them to explain how the solution to the conflict determines how we perceive its causes and reactions. Point out that when a conflict is not yet resolved, there is still confusion as to what its causes are and who is reacting to whom.

Answers will vary.

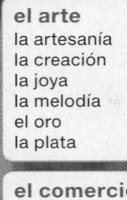

A ver si recuerdas

OBJECTIVES
▶ Discuss a conflict you had
▶ Talk about a movie you saw

Vocabulario

el arte
la artesanía
la creación
la joya
la melodía
el oro
la plata

el comercio
cambiar
comprar
el mercado
pagar
el producto
regatear
vender

reacciones
asustarse
enojarse
estar asustado, -a
estar enojado, -a
ponerse enojado, -a
temer
tener miedo de

las relaciones
colaborar
comunicarse
el conflicto
desconfiar
llevarse bien / mal
la pelea
pelearse
ponerse de acuerdo
reaccionar
relacionarse

acciones
atreverse
capturar
destruir
escaparse
luchar
matar
morirse
refugiarse
salvar

4

Definiciones

 LEER, ESCRIBIR, HABLAR EN PAREJA Empareja cada definición con la palabra correspondiente. Luego, escribe cuatro definiciones propias de las listas. Léelas a un(a) compañero(a) para que identifique las palabras apropiadas.

1. arte u obra con una marca personal   a. regatear
2. evitar un peligro   b. artesanía
3. no confiar   c. salvarse
4. discutir el precio de algo   d. desconfiar

5

Una vez yo . . .

 ESCRIBIR, HABLAR EN GRUPO Piensa en un conflicto que hayas tenido. Haz una red de palabras y complétala. Usa las palabras del vocabulario. Compara tu red con la de otros(as) compañeros(as). Hablen sobre las causas de los conflictos y sus soluciones.

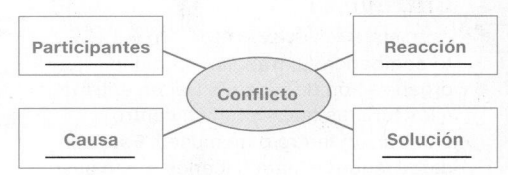

Differentiated Instruction

Logical Learner

Have students choose 8 to 10 words from the *Vocabulario* on pp. 352 and 354. Have them role-play a "walk around the city." Instruct students to meet their "neighbors" and chat about people, places, and reactions. Direct them to use each one of their chosen words before they can "stroll back home."

Students with Learning Difficulties

Students may have difficulty memorizing past forms of irregular verbs, especially verbs with irregular stems. Have students create their own reference cards for each of these verbs. On each card, students should list present, preterite, and imperfect forms. Encourage students to write clearly for quick reference.

Gramática

Verbos con cambios en el pretérito

Verbs like *oír, leer*, and *creer* change the *i* to *y* in the *Ud. / él / ella* and *Uds./ellos/ellas* forms: *leí, leíste, leyó, leímos, leísteis, leyeron*.

Stem-changing *-ir* verbs like *dormir, morir (o → ue), sentir, preferir (e → ie)*, and *pedir, repetir (e → i)* have changes in the *Ud. / él / ella* and the *Uds. / ellos / ellas* form of the preterite.

dormir: d**u**rmió, d**u**rmieron   sentir: s**i**ntió, s**i**ntieron

Some verbs, such as *decir, traer*, and *traducir* have irregular stems in the preterite but they share the same endings:

decir: dije, dijiste, dijo, dijimos, dijisteis, dijeron
traer: traje, trajiste, trajo, trajimos, trajisteis, trajeron
traducir: traduje, tradujiste, tradujo, tradujimos, tradujisteis, tradujeron

The following verbs also have irregular stems in the preterite and share the following endings: *-e, -iste, -o, -imos, isteis, -ieron*.

tener	estar	saber	poner	andar	poder	venir	hacer
tuv-	estuv-	sup-	pus-	anduv-	pud-	vin-	hic-*

*The *Ud./él/ella* form is *hizo*.

¿Recuerdas?

El verbo *haber* en el pretérito se conjuga *hubo*. Se usa para indicar que algo sucedió en el pasado en un momento específico en el tiempo, no algo que sucedía siempre.

Anoche *hubo* luna llena.

Más recursos ONLINE

▶ **Tutorial:** Stem-Changes in the Preterite

6

Un día ocupado

LEER Escribe la forma correcta del pretérito en este informe.

Ayer, ellos __1.__ *(tener)* muchas actividades. Primero, __2.__ *(andar)* por el parque. Después, sus amigos __3.__ *(venir)* a su casa. Luego, __4.__ *(estar)* en la biblioteca e __5.__ *(hacer)* sus tareas. __6.__ *(leer)* un cuento para la clase de inglés y __7.__ *(traducir)* algunas frases del español al inglés. Al salir, __8.__ *(querer)* llamar a Pablo pero no __9.__ *(poder)* porque su teléfono no funcionaba. __10.__ *(ir)* a un café y __11.__ *(pedir)* unos pasteles. ¡Una manera perfecta de terminar un día tan ocupado!

7

Al cine

HABLAR Entrevista a tu compañero(a) sobre la última película que fueron a ver sus amigos(as). Túrnense para hacer preguntas y contestarlas. Usen los siguientes verbos: *ir, estar, andar, dormir, preferir, comenzar, terminar*.

Modelo
ir
¿Qué película fueron a ver?

Gramática: Repaso

Suggestions: Refer students who are having difficulty with the preterite to the *GramActiva* videos from Level 2 Chapters 5A, 5B and 6A, and to the online tutorial. Have students use three different verbs from the *Gramática* in sentences with third-person singular or plural subjects. Ask volunteers to write their sentences on the board and point out the spellings of the irregular verb forms.

6

Standards: 1.2

Common Errors: Students may forget to use irregular preterite verb stems. Model the correct forms as necessary.

Suggestions: Remind students to pay particular attention to spelling, since that is the focus of the activity.

Answers:

1. tuvieron	7. tradujeron
2. anduvieron	8. quisieron
3. vinieron	9. pudieron
4. estuvieron	10. Fueron
5. hicieron	11. pidieron
6. Leyeron	

7

Standards: 1.1

Suggestions: Remind students that they are asking about a film their friends saw and should use the **Uds.** verb forms. Point out they should practice careful pronunciation, since many of the irregular verb forms contain spelling changes.

Answers will vary but may include:

fueron, estuvieron, anduvieron, durmieron, prefirieron, comenzaron, terminaron

Additional Resources

 Technology: Online Resources
• *A ver si recuerdas* with Remediation
• Guided, Core, Audio, Writing practice
• *Para hispanohablantes*
Print
• Guided WB pp. 238–241
• Core WB pp. 105–106

Assessment

A ver si recuerdas with Remediation (online only)
After reviewing the material on these pages, assign the *A ver si recuerdas* with Remediation to evaluate students' mastery of the material. Additional practice is available online.

Enrich Your Teaching

Teacher-to-Teacher

Ask students to talk about the histories of their family or the family of someone they know. Give them a few minutes to prepare what they plan to say. Encourage them to use verbs with irregular preterite forms: *Mis abuelos vinieron de Italia en 1930. Dejaron todo lo que tenían en Italia y trajeron muy poco con ellos.*

21st Century Skills

ICT (Information, Communications and Technology) Literacy Direct students to the online tutorials for self-directed review of the grammar topics recycled in this chapter. Students can expand their own learning by reviewing the related English grammar first then proceed to the new Spanish grammar point. Each tutorial is followed by a quick comprehension check.

Can-Do Statements

Read the Can-Do Statements in the chapter objectives with students. Then, have students read Preparación para el examen on pages 398–399 to preview what they will be able to do at the end of the chapter.

Standards for Capítulo 8

To meet the Standards, students will:

COMMUNICATION

1.1 Interpersonal
- Talk about city sights and their relative positions
- Talk about childhood and conflict resolution
- Talk about travel and favorite films
- Talk about Spanish painter Joaquín Sorolla y Bastida
- Talk about cultural and social interaction and fusion
- Talk about Spanish history, including colonial expansion
- Talk about Quechua music

1.2 Interpretive
- Read about city sights and their relative positions
- Read about conflict resolution
- Read about travel and daily activities
- Read about Spanish painter Joaquín Sorolla y Bastida
- Read and listen to information about cultural and social interaction and fusion
- Read about word families
- Read and listen to information about Spanish history
- Read about Quechua music
- Read a story by Elías Miguel Muñoz
- Read an Aztec legend
- Read about Houston's Museo de Salud y Ciencia
- Read about speech and composition preparation

1.3 Presentational
- Present information orally about travel and city sights
- Write about conflict resolution
- Write and present information orally about cultural and social interaction and fusion
- Write and present orally about Spanish history
- Present information orally about childhood

CULTURE

2.1 Practices to Perspectives
- Interpret cultural and social interaction and fusion
- Interpret cultural influences in Spanish history
- Interpret cultural perspectives in Quechua music

2.2 Products to Perspectives
- Describe the art of Joaquín Sorolla y Bastida and the fiction of Elías Miguel Muñoz
- Discuss cultural and social interaction and fusion
- Discuss Quechua music
- Discuss indigenous legends
- Discuss Spanish history, including colonial expansion

CAPÍTULO 8

Encuentro entre culturas

Country Connections Explorar el mundo hispano

Estados Unidos · España · México · Puerto Rico · Ecuador · Perú · Paraguay · Argentina

CHAPTER OBJECTIVES

Communication

By the end of the chapter you will be able to:
- Listen and read about indigenous cultures
- Talk and write about cultural heritage and fusion of cultures in Spain before 1492
- Present a guided city tour

Culture

You will also be able to:
- Understand the historical context of Spanish missions in California
- Express your opinion about cultural exchanges
- Compare cultural practices in an authentic video about the Mapuche culture in Chile

You will demonstrate what you know and can do
- Presentación oral: Una visita a . . .
- Presentación escrita: Mi experiencia con otras culturas

You will use

Vocabulary	Grammar
• Buildings	• Conditional
• The discovery of America	• Imperfect subjunctive
• Cultural exchanges	• Imperfect subjunctive with *si*

ARTE y CULTURA ⟩ España

Joaquín Sorolla y Bastida (1863–1923) fue un pintor español. Su obra refleja una gran habilidad para capturar los efectos de la luz. En este cuadro de Granada, Sorolla y Bastida captura la majestad de la Alhambra y de la Sierra Nevada usando el contraste entre la luz y la sombra.

▶ ¿Conoces a otros pintores que sean famosos por su uso de la luz? ¿Quiénes son?

"Granada", (1920), Joaquín Sorolla y Bastida ▶ Museo Sorolla, Madrid, Spain/Bridgeman Art Library.

Enrich Your Teaching

The End in Mind

Have students preview the sample performance tasks on *Preparación para el examen*, p. 399, and connect them to the Chapter Objectives. Explain to students that by completing the sample tasks they can self-assess their learning progress.

Technology: Mapa global interactivo

Download the *Mapa global interactivo* files for Chapter 8 and preview the activities. Use Act. 1 to travel to Spain. In Act. 2, visit Seville, in Act. 3, Toledo, and in Act. 4, Barcelona. In Act. 5, travel to Buenos Aires, Argentina. In Act. 6, travel the route from Río de la Plata to Paraguay. Act. 7 follows the route of Hernán Cortés. In Act. 8, visit California's historic missions. Act. 9 takes you to the Museo de Antropología in Mexico City.

Videonovela *¡Pura vida!*

La mezquita de Córdoba en España
es un ejemplo de fusión cultural.

Capítulo 8 • trescientos cincuenta y siete **357**

CONNECTIONS

3.1 Making Connections

- Discuss key facts about visual fine art, legends, fiction, music, and cuisine
- Discuss key facts about history and social studies
- Discuss Houston's Museo de Salud y Ciencia
- Use Language Arts strategies: fact and opinion, speaker's purpose, chronological ordering, skipping and guessing

3.2 Acquiring information and Diverse Perspectives

- Read a story by Miguel Muñoz and an Aztec legend

COMPARISONS

4.1 Language

- Compare the Spanish to the English conditional
- Compare Spanish use of the imperfect subjunctive with English if/then sentences
- Compare Spanish words to their English counterparts

4.2 Cultural

- Compare cultural fusion in the Spanish-speaking world with that in the United States
- Compare Tex-Mex and Latin American food with traditional fare in the United States
- Compare indigenous influence in Latin America with that in the United States

COMMUNITIES

5.1 School and global Comunities

- Link to Web sites from the Spanish-speaking world

5.2 Lifelong Learning

- Develop an appreciation for legends, fiction, and music

Chapter Opener

Suggestions: Introduce students to the theme of the chapter and go over the objectives. Point out that they will improve their ability to communicate on the topic of intermixing cultures. Use the maps to locate the countries featured.

▶ **Technology: Videonovela *¡Pura vida!*** View this stand-alone storyline video about five young adults in San José, Costa Rica with your class.

ARTE Y CULTURA ◀

Standards: 1.1, 1.2, 2.2, 3.1

Suggestions: After students read the information, ask comprehension questions.

Project-Based Learning

La historia de mi vida

As students go through the chapter during the week, ask them to create a timeline of their own lives beginning with Kindergarten. Ask them to mark the milestones during the past 10-12 years of their lives. Have them use this information to complete the *Presentación escrita* on pages 388–389.

Vocabulario en contexto 1

Standards: 1.2

Resources: Teacher's Resource Materials: Input Script, Clip Art, Audio Script, Technology: Audio: Cap. 8

 Technology: Mapa global interactivo, Actividad 1 Explore famous historic sites around Spain.

Focus: Presenting new vocabulary and using grammar lexically in context

Suggestions: Show the photos on pages 358 and 359. Say the names of visualized vocabulary items, have students repeat, and ask students to point to the appropriate image on their books. For non-visualized vocabulary such as *asimilaron, maravilla,* and *anteriormente,* use explanation, circumlocution, synonyms, antonyms, or gestures along with exaggerated intonation to clarify meaning: *Anteriormente significa antes. El Gran Cañón es una maravilla natural. La Alhambra en Granada es una maravilla de la arquitectura.* Ask students to point out cognates such as *influencia* and *invadieron* and challenge them to invent Spanish definitions for the words.

Starter Activity

As a class, have the students brainstorm a time line representing five important dates in U.S. history.

Active Classroom

My favorite place close to home: Divide the class into groups of three students. Have them create a new entry for an additional place in Melissa's blog. It can be a place in their community or in their state. Have them provide a brief description of the place and search for photos to share with the class.

 Technology: Interactive Whiteboard

> **Vocabulary Activities 8-1** Use the whiteboard activities in your Teacher Resources as you progress through the vocabulary practice with your class.

Vocabulario en contexto 1

OBJECTIVES
Read, listen to, and understand information about
▶ Interactions between cultures
▶ Fusion of different cultures in Spain before 1492

 ## El blog de los viajes de Melissa

 Viajar por España es una experiencia increíble. La historia de este país es una fusión de cuatro culturas y tres religiones. **Cristianos, musulmanes** y **judíos** se influyeron mutuamente y compartieron sus tesoros. ¡Ver **la influencia** de la cultura en la **arquitectura** de distintas construcciones es maravilloso!

Mensaje de Melissa: ¡España te amo!

Melissa Romano hace cinco minutos ✉ 📞 ★

Estos misteriosos **arcos** forman parte de un **acueducto**. **Los romanos** construyeron muchos acueductos en la época de su **conquista** de la Península Ibérica, alrededor de 300 a.C. De esa manera llevaban agua a las ciudades que **dominaban**. También trazaron caminos para permitir llegar su gobierno a todas las regiones del país, porque sabían que **la unidad** política era importante para sostener su **imperio**. Fueron los romanos quienes más tarde llevaron el cristianismo a España.

¿Les gustan los bosques? A mí también, pero no solo de árboles. ¡Lo que ven aquí es un bosque de más de mil columnas! Esta es la mezquita (*mosque*) de Córdoba, uno de los templos musulmanes que construyeron **los árabes** cuando **invadieron** y **conquistaron** la península ibérica en el siglo VIII. Muchas de sus mezquitas están en sitios donde **anteriormente** había iglesias. Los árabes **ocuparon** de 711 a 1492. Fue una **época** de convivencia, o sea armonía, entre las tres religiones.

Differentiated Instruction

Students with Learning Difficulties

Ask students to identify the main idea for each of Melissa's comments on her blog shown on pp. 358 and 359. Have them copy this main idea onto a card. Direct students to mix the cards, and then put each event with its corresponding picture in the right order.

Advanced Learners

Have students draw on their learning from social studies classes and tell what other countries besides Spain were influenced by the Roman Empire.

Miren esta foto. ¿No parece un castillo encantado de una película? En realidad es la Catedral de Sevilla. Sevilla fue **reconquistada** por los cristianos en 1248. Antes, en el lugar que ocupa la Catedral, había una mezquita. Lo **único** que quedó de la mezquita es **la torre** más alta, llamada La Giralda.

Sinagoga-Cordoba

A mí también me encantó esa mezcla de culturas. Miren la sinagoga de Córdoba. ¿No les recuerda a una mezquita? Es que los judíos de España **asimilaron** elementos del arte musulmán. Por eso aquí vemos una combinación de diseños árabes con inscripciones en hebreo, la lengua de los judíos. ☺

Pablo Pedrosa hace dos minutos   ✉ 📞 ★

¡Yo estuve en España el año pasado! Me contaron que los reyes católicos, quienes **gobernaban** España en 1492, **expulsaron** a los últimos musulmanes, pero conservaron muchos edificios de estilo árabe. Este es el Palacio de la Alhambra, en Granada. Era tan hermoso que los reyes no lo cambiaron. ¿No es **una maravilla**?

1

España y su cultura

 ESCUCHAR   En una hoja escribe los números del 1 al 6. Escucha las frases. Escribe *C* si la frase es cierta o *F* si la frase es falsa.

Capítulo 8 • trescientos cincuenta y nueve **359**

Enrich Your Teaching

Culture Note

The **Mezquita de Córdoba** was first built by Abd al-Rahman I in 785 A.D. on the site of the Visigoth Christian Church of St. Vincent, which had replaced a Roman pagan temple. In the sixteenth century, the mosque was converted to a cathedral and its tower was constructed directly over the Islamic Minaret.

21st Century Skills

Media Literacy Have students research Web sites in Spanish that give more information about the historical sites on pp. 358–359. What keywords will they use in their search? How can they decide which Web sites will give them reliable and accurate information? Are there other civilizations they have studied in other classes that may help them understand the fusion of cultures in Spain?

1

Standards: 1.2

Resources: Teacher's Resource Materials: Audio Script, Technology: Audio: Cap. 8

Suggestions: Before playing the audio or reading aloud the text, allow students to read over the information on pp. 358–359. Remind them to use familiar key words to help them comprehend what they hear. Allow them to listen more than once.

 **Technology: Audio Script and Answers**

Vas a oír cada frase dos veces.

1. Los acueductos servían para llevar agua a las ciudades. *(C)*
2. La mezquita de Córdoba tiene miles de árboles en su interior. *(F)*
3. La sinagoga de Córdoba tiene una torre llamada La Giralda. *(F)*
4. Los judíos de España adoptaron elementos musulmanes en su arquitectura. *(C)*
5. España es una fusión de culturas y religiones. *(C)*
6. Los musulmanes llevaron el cristianismo a España. *(F)*

Pre-AP® Integration

- **Learning Objective:** Interpersonal Writing
- **Activity:** Have students write an e-mail to a friend in which they choose a Spanish city to visit (Sevilla, Granada, Córdoba or another one). Have them say why they want to visit the city and what they want to see there, making sure they incorporate at least five new vocabulary words in their message. Students should ask their friend at least one question about which city they want to visit.
- *Pre-AP® Resource Materials:* Comprehensive guide to Pre-AP® vocabulary skill development

Vocabulario en contexto 1

Standards: 1.2

Resources: Teacher's Resource Materials: Input Script, Clip Art, Audio Script, Technology: Audio Cap. 8

Reading: Allow students time to read the dialogue silently first. Then play the audio or read the text, with students reading along as they listen. Allow them to listen more than once.

Post-reading: Complete Actividad 2 to check comprehension.

2

Standards: 1.3

Suggestions: Have students read each question and then re-read the dialogue, looking for key words to help them answer the questions.

Answers: **1.** El viejo San Juan **2.** española y árabe **3.** el Castillo de San Cristóbal

3

Standards: 1.1

Suggestions: Tell students to go back and reread the information on pages 358-360 before beginning their conversation.

Answers will vary.

4

Standards: 1.2

Suggestions: Use the audio or read the script aloud. Pause to check students' progress after each item.

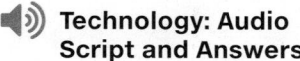 **Technology: Audio Script and Answers**

1. Tanto en España como en Puerto Rico hay influencia de otras culturas. *(C)*
2. En las calles del Viejo San Juan hay muchas mezquitas. *(F)*
3. En San Juan, Puerto Rico hay solo un castillo. *(F)*
4. El castillo de San Cristóbal está en Córdoba, España. *(F)*

Project-Based Learning

Give students copies of the Project-Based Learning outline and rubric from the *Teacher's Resource Materials*. Explain the task to them, and have them perform Step 1. (For more information, see p. 352-b.)

 Pablo acaba de regresar de San Juan, Puerto Rico. ¡Su prima Ana quiere saber todo sobre el viaje!

Pablo / Ana

Ana: Hola, primo. ¡Cuéntame cómo te fue en San Juan!

Pablo: ¡Fue un viaje **maravilloso**! Por fin pude conocer bien la ciudad en la que nací. Como me fui de allí cuando era pequeño, no recordaba casi nada.

Ana: ¿Qué fue lo que más te gustó?

Pablo: El Viejo San Juan, o la parte antigua. Caminé mucho por sus calles y tomé fotos de los **balcones** y las **rejas** de las casas. En su arquitectura **se integran** las influencias española y árabe.

Ana: Sí. Estas culturas **dejaron su huella** en las casas y calles de la ciudad.

Pablo: También me gustaron mucho los castillos. ¡El Castillo de San Cristóbal es **una construcción** impresionante!

Ana: ¿Y fuiste a la Casa de España como te recomendé? ¡Esa casa la **fundó** el padre de de nuestro abuelo!

Pablo: Sí. ¡Es hermosa! Me encantaron los **azulejos** que decoran muchas casas. Además, allí encontré información muy interesante sobre **el idioma** español de aquel tiempo y sobre **la población** y los **grupos étnicos** del país.

Ana: La próxima vez tenemos que ir juntos a Puerto Rico. ¡Nos falta mucho por conocer!

2

La visita de Pablo a San Juan

 ESCRIBIR Contesta las siguientes preguntas:

1. ¿Qué fue lo que más le gustó a Pablo de la ciudad?
2. ¿Qué influencias se integran en la arquitectura del Viejo San Juan?
3. ¿Qué edificio le pareció impresionante a Pablo?

3

¿A qué país prefieres ir?

 HABLAR EN PAREJAS Basándote en lo que has leído sobre España y Puerto Rico, dile a un(a) compañero(a) a cuál de estos dos países preferirías ir de vacaciones. Da razones que apoyen tu opinión.

4

España y Puerto Rico

 ESCUCHAR Escribe los números del 1 al 4 en una hoja de papel. Escucha cada frase y escribe *C* (cierta) si es correcta o *F* (falsa) si es incorrecta.

360 trescientos sesenta • Capítulo 8 • Encuentro entre culturas

---

Differentiated Instruction

Students with Learning Difficulties

Provide students with a graphic organizer to help support understanding of dialogue on p. 360. Have students create three columns on a piece of paper: ***ciudad, culturas, ejemplo de la mezcla de culturas.*** Then have them reread the selection to fill in the chart.

Students with Special Needs

You may wish to provide hearing-impaired students with a copy of the script so they may follow along and engage in post-viewing activities.

Go **Online** to practice
PearsonSchool.com/Autentico

PEARSON realize
AUDIO | VIDEO | WRITING | SCRIPT

¡San Antonio te espera!

Antes de ver

Usar las imágenes como contexto ¿Conoces una ciudad en la que haya mezcla de culturas o una gran diversidad cultural? Mira las fotos. Observa el tipo de arquitectura de los edificios y trata de identificar las huellas de otra cultura. Al ver el video, usa las imágenes como contexto para comprender mejor el diálogo.

Haz la actividad

Diversidad cultural Trabaja con un compañero(a). Hagan una lista de las cosas que muestran la diversidad cultural de una ciudad y su gente.

▶ Ve el video

Ximena está muy orgullosa de la ciudad en la que nació. ¿Quieres saber por qué?

Ve a **PearsonSchool.com/Autentico** para ver el video *¡San Antonio te espera!* También puedes leer el guión.

Camila | Teo | Seba
Valentina | Ximena

Después de ver

 ESCRIBIR Contesta las siguientes preguntas:

1. ¿Qué video les muestra Ximena a sus amigos? ¿Para qué hizo ese video?
2. ¿Qué lugares de la ciudad muestra Ximena en su video?
3. Parafrasea lo que dice Ximena sobre las influencias culturales en San Antonio.
4. ¿Qué tipos de festivales hay en San Antonio?

¿Cuál es tu impresión? Escribe un párrafo dando tu impresión sobre San Antonio. Di si te gustaría conocer esta ciudad y por qué. Justifica tu opinión con datos de la Videohistoria.

Capítulo 8 • trescientos sesenta y uno **361**

Enrich Your Teaching

Culture Note

There are other cities in the U.S. where the Spanish heritage is evident. Some of them are St. Augustine in Florida, San Diego and Sacramento in California, and Santa Fe and Alburquerque in New Mexico. The Spanish influence is clearly noticed in architectural structures such as churches, plazas, houses, monasteries, and forts.

21st Century Skills

Media Literacy Have students research Web sites in Spanish that give more information about the places mentioned on pp. 358–360. What key words will they use in their search? How can they decide which Web sites will give them reliable and accurate information?

Tecnología: Video

Standards: 1.2

Resources: Teacher's Resource Materials: Video Script

Antes de ver

Review the previewing strategy and activity with the class. Invite students to observe the photos and discuss the buildings they see. What architectural style do they think these buildings have? Do they perceive the influence of other cultures?

Ve el video

Show the video once without pausing. Guide students to infer the meaning of *embajadora turística* by using the main idea of the Videohistoria. Show the video again, asking students to pay attention to the images to get a better grasp of Ximena's descriptions and pausing to check comprehension. Show the video a final time without pausing.

Después de ver

Standards: 1.2

Suggestions: Guide students to summarize and paraphrase San Antonio's cultural influences as described by Ximena.

Answers

1. sobre San Antonio; para conseguir un trabajo como embajadora turística
2. plaza, catedral, tiendas, restaurantes
3. Answers may vary, but include that San Antonio has cultural influences from Spain and Mexico.
4. de música y baile, de comida, de libros, de flores

¿Cuál es tu impresión? Answers will vary.

Have students go to Realize for additional video activities.

Additional Resources

 Technology: Online Resources
• Instant Check
• Guided, Core, Video, Audio
• *Para hispanohablantes*
Print
• Guided WB pp. 242–250
• Core WB pp. 107–108

Assessment

Quiz: Vocabulary Recognition
• Prueba 8-1

Starter Activity

Briefly review rules for accent marks with students. On the board write words that require accent marks, but don't include them as you write. Ask students to say which letter in the word has an accent mark over it.

5

Standards: 1.2, 3.1

Suggestions: Tell students to complete the activity in three steps: 1. briefly read the word bank and the paragraph, 2. write the answers, 3. read the completed paragraph again.

Answers:

1. unidad
2. ocuparon
3. musulmanes
4. población
5. étnicos

6. judíos
7. maravillas
8. reconquistó
9. única
10. se integraron

6

Standards: 1.3, 2.2

Suggestions: Remind students to present their descriptions of the photo in a logical way. Suggest that they start with the foreground, continue with the background, and save their impressions for last.

Answers will vary.

Vocabulario en uso 1

OBJECTIVES
▶ Discuss and write about the cities of Toledo, Spain and Buenos Aires, Argentina
▶ Write about the history of Spain
▶ Talk about culture and architecture

5

¡Bienvenido a Toledo!

LEER, HABLAR EN PAREJA Completa la siguiente información con las palabras del recuadro. Después, habla con otro(a) compañero(a) y pregúntale si le gustaría visitar Toledo y por qué.

ocuparon	musulmanes	reconquistó	población	étnicos
judíos	maravillas	única	se integraron	unidad

Durante siglos, la ciudad de Toledo ha mantenido su __1.__ mientras recibía la influencia de muchas culturas y religiones. Los romanos entraron en la ciudad en 193 a.C. y la __2.__ Siglos después, los __3.__ que vinieron desde el sur de España y desde África conquistaron Toledo. Durante la Edad Media (*Middle Ages*), que se extendió aproximadamente desde el año 476 al 1492, Toledo fue un centro intelectual y artístico, con una gran __4.__ formada por varios grupos __5.__, como musulmanes, __6.__ y cristianos. El palacio musulmán, llamado El Alcázar, originalmente restaurado (*restored*) en el siglo XIII, fue modificado en 1535 como residencia de Carlos V. Es una de las verdaderas __7.__ de la ciudad. Más adelante, durante la Reconquista, el rey Alfonso VI __8.__ la ciudad en 1085 y volvieron a gobernar los reyes cristianos. Toledo no es la __9.__ ciudad de España donde __10.__ muchas culturas y religiones, pero es uno de los mejores ejemplos.

6

Un patio español

ESCRIBIR Observa la foto de un patio en España. Luego, escribe una descripción de lo que ves y tus impresiones. Incluye las palabras siguientes.

azulejos	arquitectura
construcción	maravilloso(a)
influencia	arco
rejas	musulmán

Patio antiguo, España ▶

Differentiated Instruction

Students with Learning Difficulties

Before students complete *Actividad* 5, have them separate the word choices into the following categories: people, things, descriptions, and actions. As students read through the paragraph, assist them in choosing the correct word by asking what type of word is missing.

Challenge/Pre-AP®

Ask students to write their own fill-in-the-blank vocabulary exercises. These can either be in paragraph form or presented as separate sentences. Have students number each blank and make an answer sheet. Have them exchange their work with a partner, complete each other's exercises, and check their answers together.

Go **Online** to practice

PearsonSchool.com/Autentico

PEARSON
realize™

VIDEO · WRITING · SPEAK/RECORD

Interpersonal 8

7 Una breve historia de España

LEER, HABLAR EN PAREJA Para entender bien las culturas de hoy, es importante que conozcas la historia de otros países. Lee la línea cronológica de esta página. Con otro(a) estudiante, habla de la historia de España. Trata de usar todos los verbos siguientes.

invadir	ocupar	asimilarse	llegar	contribuir
reconquistar	gobernar	expulsar	integrarse	dominar

Videomodelo
A —¿Qué pasó en el año 1085?
B —Los cristianos reconquistaron Toledo.

1236
Musulmanes: gobiernan desde La Alhambra de Granada

300 200 100   0   100 200 300 400 500 600 700 800 900 1000 1100 1200 1300 1400 1500

218 a.C.
Romanos: Conquista de España, construcción de puentes y acueductos

711
Llegada de los musulmanes del África; contribuciones en las matemáticas, las ciencias, el papel, los números que usamos hoy; integración de muchos grupos étnicos en España

1085
Cristianos: reconquista de Toledo

1496
Reyes Católicos: reconquista y ocupación de Granada; expulsión del último rey musulmán, Boabdil; expulsión de los judíos de España

Ampliación del lenguaje · Palabras árabes

Durante los ochocientos años en que los árabes estuvieron en España, muchas palabras del árabe pasaron a formar parte del español. Muchas de ellas entraron también en otros idiomas de Europa, incluyendo el inglés. Lee las palabras de la tabla y escoge las que mejor completan las frases.

1. En el _____ donde vivo hay una _____ adonde van los musulmanes.

2. El músico estaba tocando su _____ , pero cuando me vio me saludó diciendo "_____".

3. En mi casa tenemos una _____ en el piso que está hecha de _____ .

4. Todas las mañanas, mi mamá bebe una _____ de _____ y un jugo de _____ .

Palabras de origen árabe	
alcázar	¡hola!
algodón	jarabe
alfombra	limón
barrio	mezquita
baño	naranja
café	¡ojalá!
chisme	taza
guitarra	

Standards: 1.1, 1.2, 1.3

Recycle: Preterite tense verb forms, question formation

Suggestions: Once students have read and discussed the timeline together, open the question-and-answer session up to the whole class.

Answers will vary.

AMPLIACIÓN DEL LENGUAJE

Standards: 1.2, 3.1

Suggestions: First, address any comprehension issues students may have with the words in the table. Then, ask volunteers to supply definitions for the words.

Answers:
1. barrio; mezquita
2. guitarra; ¡hola!
3. alfombra; algodón
4. taza; café; naranja

Extension: Have students work in small groups and add to the list of words with Arabic roots. They can first guess at words they think come from Arabic and then check their guesses in a Spanish dictionary. Show them where to find the basic etymological information (just after the pronunciation) that most unabridged dictionaries provide.

Enrich Your Teaching

Culture Note

King Boabdil, known as the Boy King or **el Rey Chico,** was the last Islamic ruler of Granada. In 1492, Fernando and Isabel raised the flags of Christian Spain above the Alhambra. In the treaty of surrender, King Boabdil was sent into exile in the countryside along with his mother, Ayesha. Legend has it that as he turned back to look at the city, his mother chastised him severely. Seven years later the treaties were abrogated by Fernando and Isabel. Boabdil fled to Morocco, where he died in poverty.

Standards: 1.1, 1.2, 2.1, 3.1, 4.2, 5.2

 Technology: Mapa global interactivo, Actividad 5 Travel to Buenos Aires, Argentina.

Suggestions: First, have students silently read the article and answer questions 1–2 on their own. Invite them to share their answers to these questions in their small groups before they complete the chart for item 3.

Answers:

1. Answers to the first part will vary, but might include: los italianos, ingleses, judíos, rusos, árabes y bolivianos.
2. Es bueno porque hace que una ciudad sea multicultural y cosmopolita.
3. Answers will vary.

Mi Buenos Aires querido

 LEER, ESCRIBIR, HABLAR EN GRUPO ¿Has oído alguna vez hablar de la ciudad de Buenos Aires y su origen? Lee el siguiente artículo sobre Buenos Aires y contesta las preguntas.

Conexiones ‹ **Las ciencias sociales**

Buenos Aires

Desde que se fundó Buenos Aires en 1536, allí se han mezclado distintas culturas, religiones y tradiciones. Aunque el idioma oficial de Argentina es el español, en la ciudad hay barrios en los que a veces se escucha hablar el italiano, el inglés, el yiddish, el ruso o el árabe y donde se pueden ver mezquitas, sinagogas e iglesias. Anteriormente, la mayoría de los inmigrantes que llegaban a Buenos Aires venían de Europa, pero en los últimos tiempos la mayoría ha llegado de otros países latinoamericanos, sobre todo de Bolivia.

Esta inmigración de diferentes grupos étnicos ha hecho de Buenos Aires una ciudad multicultural y cosmopolita. En algunos casos los inmigrantes se han asimilado a la manera de vivir del lugar. Por ejemplo, aunque muchos hablan sus propios idiomas, la mayoría habla también español.

También puedes encontrar que en un mismo barrio se practican las religiones judía,

cristiana y musulmana, y se comen platos que vienen de muchos lugares, como la pasta de Italia o los guisos (*stews*) de España.

Buenos Aires no es la única ciudad de América del Sur con esta mezcla maravillosa de culturas pero es una de las más conocidas por su variedad.

1. ¿Cuáles son algunos de los inmigrantes y grupos étnicos que se establecieron en Buenos Aires?

2. ¿Por qué es bueno que muchas personas de diferentes culturas vivan en una misma ciudad?

3. Trabaja con tres estudiantes. Copien y completen esta tabla, y comparen su ciudad o comunidad con la ciudad de Buenos Aires.

	Buenos Aires	Mi ciudad / comunidad
¿Dónde está?		
¿Cuál es el idioma oficial?		
¿Qué religiones se practican?		
¿Hay muchos inmigrantes?		
¿De dónde son?		

 Mapa global interactivo Explora el área metropolitana de Buenos Aires, Argentina. Investiga su desarrollo, sistema de carreteras y relación con la vida urbana.

364 trescientos sesenta y cuatro • Capítulo 8 • Encuentro entre culturas

---

Differentiated Instruction

Heritage Speakers

After students have completed the table on p. 364 with reference to Buenos Aires and their own communities, ask them to answer the same questions with reference to their heritage country in general. What are some of the aspects of its culture?

Students with Learning Difficulties

Help students identify key words or phrases in each of the questions on p. 364. Instruct them to locate these words or phrases in the passage. Then have them reread around the key word or phrase to find the answer.

9

La cultura en la arquitectura

LEER, ESCRIBIR Puedes aprender sobre otras culturas al observar su arte y su arquitectura. Mira el anuncio y trabaja con otro(a) estudiante para hacer y contestar preguntas por correo électronico. Usa las siguientes preguntas como modelo.

1. ¿Sobre qué es la exposición *(exhibit)*?

2. ¿De dónde son los arquitectos? ¿Son todos de la misma cultura étnica?

3. ¿Crees que las construcciones que se presentan en la exposición van a ser similares? ¿Por qué? ¿Por qué no?

4. Imagina que puedes dejar una huella en tu comunidad. ¿Qué contribución te gustaría hacer? Haz un folleto como éste que la represente.

Museo Histórico Arqueológico y Museo Regional del Sur

PRESENTAN

HUELLAS DE IDENTIDAD:

Asimilación cultural en la arquitectura Chilena

23 de enero –12 de mayo

- 5 arquitectos de la época moderna
- diversas influencias étnicas
- construcciones únicas

Avenida de la Cruz, no. 32 Valparaíso

10

Y tú, ¿qué dices?

ESCRIBIR, HABLAR

1. ¿Qué cultura(s) representas tú? ¿De dónde eran tus abuelos y bisabuelos *(great-grandparents)*? ¿Qué idioma(s) hablaban? ¿Lo(s) siguen hablando? ¿Por qué?

2. ¿Qué culturas han contribuido a la cultura de los Estados Unidos? ¿Qué huellas han dejado?

3. ¿Alguna vez has tenido que integrarte a una nueva cultura o grupo? ¿Cuándo? ¿Cómo te sentiste? ¿Qué diferencias notaste entre tu manera de ser y la de ellos?

4. Imagina que hay un nuevo estudiante de otro país en tu clase. Di al menos cinco cosas que puedes hacer para ayudarle a integrarse.

9

Standards: 1.2

Suggestions: After students have read and discussed the ad, have them work in small groups to create their own ad for item 4.

Answers:

1. Es sobre la asimilación cultural en la arquitectura chilena.

2. Son de Chile. No. 3., 4. Answers will vary.

10

Standards: 1.1, 1.2, 4.2, 5.2

Suggestions: Many heritage speakers will have particularly insightful responses to question 4. Invite them to share these with the class.

Answers will vary.

Additional Resources

Technology: Online Resources
- Communication Activities
- Teacher's Resource Materials: Audio Script, Communicative Pair Activity, Technology: Audio Cap. 8

Assessment

Prueba 8-2 with Remediation (online only)
Prueba: Aplicación del vocabulario 1
- Prueba 8-2

Enrich Your Teaching

Teacher-to-Teacher

Take this opportunity to initiate a thoughtful and sensitive discussion with students on the topic of ethnic and cultural differences. Discuss how these differences can enrich our lives. Help students understand that ethnic stereotypes are inaccurate generalizations based on fear or a lack of knowledge.

21st Century Skills

Communication Encourage students to use their reading strategies when reading about Buenos Aires on p. 364. Working in small groups, students will compare Buenos Aires to their own town in *Actividad* 8. They can also compare Buenos Aires to Sevilla, Granada and Córdoba.

Starter Activity

Prepare students for the presentation of the conditional tense in the *Gramática* by briefly reviewing the formation of the future tense.

Gramática

Standards: 4.1

Suggestions: Ask students to practice the conditional tense by saying what they would do if the principal suddenly announced that school was canceled for the rest of the day.

 Technology: Interactive Whiteboard

Grammar Activities 8-1 Use the whiteboard activities in your Teacher Resources as you progress through the grammar practice with your class.

11

Standards: 1.2

Suggestions: Remind students to look over the entire paragraph first in order to get an idea of its meaning.

Common Errors: Students will often pronounce conditional tense forms of **querer** exactly like imperfect tense forms. Model the difference in sound between the rolled intervocalic **rr** in the conditional tense and the single **r** in the imperfect tense.

Answers:

1. sería   6. sabrían
2. comenzaría   7. podrían
3. irían   8. ayudarían
4. contribuirían 9. darían
5. podrían

Active Classroom

Divide students into pairs. Give each group two cubes. Have them write six infinitives from the list on p. 366 on one cube and six subject pronouns on the second. Each student "rolls the dice" and gives the conditional for the subjects/verbs on the cube.

Gramática

OBJECTIVES
▶ Write about things you would do
▶ Talk about activities you would do in a new community

El condicional

You use the conditional in Spanish to express what a person *would do* or what a situation *would be like.*

Me **gustaría** leer un libro sobre el budismo.   Yo le **pediría** ese libro a Tomás.

• As with the future tense, you form the conditional by adding the endings to the infinitive. The conditional endings are the same for all verbs. Here are the conditional forms of *hablar, ser,* and *ir.*

hablar		**ser**		**ir**	
hablar**ía**	hablar**íamos**	ser**ía**	ser**íamos**	ir**ía**	ir**íamos**
hablar**ías**	hablar**íais**	ser**ías**	ser**íais**	ir**ías**	ir**íais**
hablar**ía**	hablar**ían**	ser**ía**	ser**ían**	ir**ía**	ir**ían**

• All verbs that are irregular in the future tense have the same irregular stems in the conditional.

decir	**dir-**	poder	**podr-**	saber	**sabr-**	tener	**tendr-**
haber	**habr-**	poner	**pondr-**	salir	**saldr-**	querer	**querr-**
hacer	**har-**	componer	**compondr-**	venir	**vendr-**	contener	**contendr-**

Más recursos ONLINE

▶ **Tutorial:** Use of Conditional

🔊 *Canción de hip hop:*
Bienvenido a Toledo

11

La Ruta Quetzal

 LEER El año pasado tu amiga participó en la Ruta Quetzal, un viaje que muchos jóvenes hacen por España y América Latina. Tú quieres hacer el viaje el año próximo, y ella te cuenta cómo sería. Completa el párrafo con el condicional del verbo apropiado.

¿Te interesa participar en la Ruta Quetzal?

🏠 ✉ 💬

¿Te interesa participar en la Ruta Quetzal? Esta experiencia __1.__ (tener / ser) fantástica para ti. El viaje __2.__ (ocupar / comenzar) en España. Para decidir quiénes __3.__ (ir / poder), tú y los otros estudiantes __4.__ (contribuir / salir) ideas sobre los lugares que se __5.__ (fundar / poder) visitar. Al terminar la experiencia, Uds. __6.__ (saber / fundar) mucho más sobre la integración de la cultura española con la americana y __7.__ (poner / poder) apreciar más las dos culturas. Cuando yo fui, mis padres me dijeron que me __8.__ (ayudar / preferir) a juntar dinero. ¿Te __9.__ (saber / dar) dinero tus padres? ¡No importa! Tienes que ir.

Differentiated Instruction

Heritage Speakers

Ask students to model speech in the conditional tense. Ask them to speculate on what their life would be like if they were living in a different country. They might focus on their heritage country or another country with which they are familiar.

Advanced Learners

Have students write a paragraph telling what their daily routine would be if they lived in a place very unlike where they are. If you live in a city, have them tell what their routines would be if they lived in the countryside, or vice versa.

12 ¡Ganamos!

Go **Online** to practice
PearsonSchool.com/Autentico
PEARSON realize.
AUDIO VIDEO WRITING SPEAK/RECORD

HABLAR EN PAREJA Tu familia participa en un concurso para ganar una casa que se construiría según el estilo musulmán. Habla con otro(a) estudiante para describir lo que tu familia prefiere en su nueva casa.

Modelo
A —¿Qué prefiere tu mamá en la casa?
B —A ella le gustan los balcones. Tendría una ventana con un balcón.

Yo	tener	balcón
Nosotros	poner	rejas
Mis hermanos	construir	azulejos
Mi hermano(a)	gustar	flores
Mi mamá (o papá)	querer	fuente
Mis padres	pedir	arcos
¡Respuesta personal!	hacer	torre
	preferir	patio
	¡Respuesta personal!	jardín
		¡Respuesta personal!

13 No sabía que en . . .

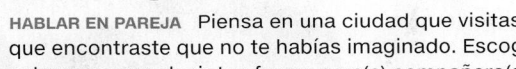

HABLAR EN PAREJA Piensa en una ciudad que visitaste y en las cosas que encontraste que no te habías imaginado. Escoge entre las cuatro columnas para decir tus frases a un(a) compañero(a).

Modelo
No me había dado cuenta de que vería grupos étnicos tan diferentes.

no podía creer que	haber	cosas tan . . .	divertido
no sabía que	encontrar	grupos étnicos tan . . .	interesante
no me di cuenta de que	ver	construcciones tan . . .	alto
nunca pensé que	comer	la influencia de . . .	impresionante
¡Respuesta personal!	escuchar	música tan . . .	diferente
	visitar	comida tan . . .	similar
	hacer	puntos de interés tan . . .	maravilloso
	¡Respuesta personal!	personas tan . . .	único
		¡Respuesta personal!	**¡Respuesta personal!**

Enrich Your Teaching

Teacher-to-Teacher

Invite students to use the conditional tense to write a description of the school of their dreams. Ask guiding questions as necessary. For example: *¿Cómo serían las aulas? ¿Qué cursos habría? ¿Cómo serían los profesores? ¿Qué harías durante un día típico? ¿En qué consistirían los almuerzos?* Invite students to share and discuss their completed descriptions.

12

Standards: 1.1

Suggestions: Point out to students that for the *respuesta personal,* they should use a verb of their own choosing that is different from the rest of those in the chart.

Answers will vary. Students will choose from among the following verb forms:

tendría/tendríamos/tendrían
pondría/pondríamos/pondrían
construiría/construiríamos/construirían
gustaría/gustarían
querría/querríamos/querrían
pediría/pediríamos/pedirían
haría/haríamos/harían
preferiría/preferiríamos/preferirían

13

Standards: 1.1

Suggestions: Remind students to make the adjectives in the fourth column agree in number and gender with the nouns they modify.

Answers will vary. Students will use the following verb forms:

habría	escucharía
encontraría	visitaría
vería	haría
comería	

Pre-AP® Integration

- **Learning Objective:** Presentational Writing
- **Activity:** Using *Actividad* 11 as a model, have students write a similar description of a nearby place of interest or well-known historical site. Include a picture, if possible. Share the description with classmates or display in the classroom.
- *Pre-AP® Resource Materials:* Comprehensive guide to Pre-AP® writing skill development,

Project-Based Learning

Students can perform Step 2 at this point. Be sure they understand your corrections and suggestions. (For more information, see p. 352–b.)

14

Suggestions: Ask students to complete the *Actividad* twice, switching roles. Student B's answers should be different each time.

Answers will vary. Students will use the following verb forms:

1. Viviría
2. podría
3. Sería
4. Tendría
5. encontraría
6. debería

15

Suggestions: If students have difficulty thinking of questions, ask them to consider things they like to do, list them, and use the list as a source of ideas for questions.

Answers will vary.

14

Conoce nuestra comunidad

 HABLAR EN PAREJA Imagina que un(a) estudiante de otro país te hace preguntas para informarse sobre tu comunidad y lo que tiene hacer durante su visita. Trabaja con otro(a) estudiante para hacer los papeles de estudiante y estudiante extranjero(a). Usen el condicional.

▶ **Videomodelo**

¿Qué (tener) que ponerme para ir el primer día de escuela?
A —*¿Qué **tendría** que ponerme para ir el primer día de escuela?*
B —*Podrías llevar jeans y una camiseta.*

Estudiante A

1. ¿*(Vivir)* en un barrio con muchos o pocos grupos étnicos?
2. ¿A qué lugares *(poder)* ir para ver la vida típica de los jóvenes en tu comunidad?
3. ¿*(Ser)* fácil o difícil asimilarme en tu escuela?
4. ¿*(Tener)* que hablar inglés todo el tiempo?
5. ¿Qué religiones diferentes *(encontrar)*?
6. ¿Qué más *(deber)* hacer para integrarme a la nueva cultura?

Estudiante B

¡Respuesta personal!

15

En un nuevo país

✎ **ESCRIBIR** Imagina que piensas ir a visitar a tu amigo que vive en Guatemala. Como quieres aprender más sobre su país, le envías un correo electrónico con preguntas. Usa una forma de escribir informal en un estilo apropiado. Incluye expresiones apropiadas.

Modelo

¿Adónde podría ir para encontrar jóvenes de mi edad? ¿Cómo debo saludarlos?

¿Cuál es el equipo de deportes más popular? ¿Cómo alientan a sus equipos?

¿Cuál es el restaurante más popular entre los jóvenes? ¿Debo esperar a que me sienten o elijo la mesa que me guste?

Plaza Mayor en Antigua, Guatemala

Trabaja con un grupo para escoger un mínimo de seis preguntas. Contesten las preguntas con sugerencias y úsenlas para escribir un breve párrafo en el que describan a Guatemala.

Modelo

Si quieres conocer a jóvenes de tu edad, podrías ir a la Plaza Mayor en Antigua. Puedes saludarlos dándoles la mano.

368 trescientos sesenta y ocho • Capítulo 8 • Encuentro entre culturas

---

Differentiated Instruction

Heritage Speakers

Ask students to comment on the musical traditions of their heritage country. Phrase questions so that they may be answered using the conditional tense. You might ask what kinds of instruments one would see, what kinds of sounds one would hear, or what kinds of locations one could visit to listen to music.

Musical Learner

Ask students who play a musical instrument to bring their instruments to share with the group. Ask them to research and discuss the history of their instruments, and the cultures in which they are prevalent. Have students play a short selection.

La música llegó por España

LEER, HABLAR Durante la conquista árabe, España se convirtió en la puerta por donde entraban a Europa las nuevas ideas y descubrimientos.

Conexiones ◄ La música

Durante la época en que los árabes ocuparon España, Europa recibió muchos instrumentos y conceptos musicales de ese pueblo.

Los árabes fundaron escuelas de música en España. Instrumentos musicales como la guitarra, el órgano y el laúd *(lute)* no se conocían en Europa hasta que los árabes los llevaron a España. Pero quizás la contribución más importante fue el concepto de armonía, que cambió la historia de la música europea.

• ¿Por qué crees que se dice que España era la puerta por donde entraban las nuevas ideas a Europa?

• ¿Cuáles fueron las contribuciones árabes a la música europea?

CULTURA ◄ España • Paraguay

El arpa paraguaya nació cuando se mezclaron dos culturas, la española y la guaraní, en el territorio que sería Paraguay. El arpa es originaria de Egipto y es uno de los instrumentos más antiguos que se conocen. Los exploradores españoles que viajaron por el Río de la Plata en 1526 fueron acompañados de un hombre que tocaba el arpa. Los guaraníes, que amaban la música, adoptaron el arpa, la cambiaron a su manera y la hicieron parte de su vida diaria. El resultado fue maravilloso: un instrumento ligero hecho de madera *(wood)* americana, y frecuentemente, con cuerdas *(strings)* de colores diferentes.

Los paraguayos de hoy enseñan a sus niños a tocar con una técnica propia que pasa de padres a hijos. La música que ha resultado de este instrumento, que llegó con los españoles y que ha sido integrada en la cultura indígena, es muy especial y bella.

 Mapa global interactivo Explora las rutas que tomaron los exploradores españoles para llegar a Paraguay desde el Río de la Plata.

Pre-AP® Integration: Las tradiciones y los valores ¿De qué manera influyó España en la música de Paraguay? ¿De qué manera influyeron la música de Paraguay y sus instrumentos en la música de los Estados Unidos?

Standards: 1.1, 1.2, 2.1, 3.1

Suggestions: Have students read the information on their own first, then discuss the questions with a partner. Invite partners to share their responses with the class.

Answers:

• Se dice esto porque España era el país que recibió la mayor cantidad de influencias importantes del mundo árabe.

• Los árabes contribuyeron con instrumentos musicales como la guitarra, el órgano y el laúd. La contribución más importante fue el concepto de armonía.

CULTURA ◄

Standards: 1.1, 1.2, 2.1, 2.2, 3.1, 5.2

Suggestions: After students have read the information, ask comprehension questions. For example: *¿Puedes nombrar a un pueblo indígena que vive en Paraguay? (los guaraníes) ¿Qué pasó en 1526? (Los españoles viajaron por el Río de la Plata.)*

Answers:

• España contribuyó con la idea del arpa, un elemento importante de la música paraguaya. Los guaraníes han cambiado los materiales que se usan para construir el arpa. También han adaptado la técnica de tocar ese instrumento.

• Answers will vary.

 Technology: Mapa global interactivo, Actividad 6 Travel the route from Río de la Plata to Paraguay.

Additional Resources

Technology: Online Resources
• Instant Check
• Guided, Core, Audio
• Teacher's Resource Materials: Audio Script, Communicative Pair Activity, Technology: Audio Cap. 8

Print
• Guided WB pp. 251–252
• Core WB pp. 109–111

Assessment

Prueba 8-3 with Remediation (online only)
Prueba: El condicional
• Prueba 8-3:
Examen: Vocabulario y gramática 1
• Examen 1:
• ExamView: Examen 1

Enrich Your Teaching

Culture Note

The harp is thought to have originally evolved from a hunter's bow. Variations can be found throughout the world: the Adunga from Uganda, Celtic harp, Chinese Konghou, Burmese Saung-Gauk, and the Paraguayan harp. The Veracruz harp, common throughout Mexico, came from Spain around the 1500s.

21st Century Skills

Information Literacy Have students search for information on the history of other instruments used in traditional Spanish or Latin American music, such as Spanish castanets, the Puerto Rican *cuatro*, or the accordion in Mexican *norteño* bands. Are any similar instruments used in music from their own culture?

Vocabulario en contexto 2

Standards: 1.2

Resources: Teacher's Resource Materials: Input Script, Clip Art, Audio Script, Technology: Audio Cap. 8

Suggestions: Ask volunteers to read the main title and the captions on these pages. Invite students to talk about what they see in the pictures. Have students point out cognates such as *europeos, colonia,* and *adoptaran* from among the new vocabulary. Play the audio or read the text and have students follow along. Check comprehension by asking questions. See the Input Script in the *Teacher's Resource Materials* for specific questions.

Pre-AP® Integration

- **Learning Objective:** Interpretive: Print and Audio
- **Activity:** Distribute Clip Art for new vocabulary presented on pp. 370–371. Have students prepare to retell some of the information in their own words. Then, each selects five of the pieces of clip art that could illustrate their summary. Now working in pairs, have one student tell his or her summary and the other arrange his or her partner's clip art on the desktop in the order it occurs in the summary.
- ***Pre-AP® Resource Materials:*** Comprehensive guide to Pre-AP® vocabulary skill development,

Active Classroom

Have each student write six *Cierto/Falso* statements from the information on pp. 370–371. Have them work in pairs and read statements to each other. The partner states whether the statement is *cierto* or *falso* and then corrects the information that is false.

 Technology: Interactive Whiteboard

> **Vocabulary Activities 8-2** Use the whiteboard activities in your Teacher Resources as you progress through the vocabulary practice with your class.

Vocabulario en contexto 2

Vocabulario en contexto 2

OBJECTIVES

Read, listen to, and understand information about
▶ Interaction between cultures
▶ Fusion of different cultures in the Americas after the arrival of the Europeans

 Sección: Paseos por la historia de México

La cultura mexicana nació del **encuentro** entre dos mundos. ¿Cómo pudieron mezclarse dos culturas con tan poca o ninguna **semejanza**? Estos paseos te darán alguna idea de cómo se hizo.

Ruinas de Tenochtitlán al lado de edificios modernos ▲

❶

Ruinas de Tenochtitlán (DF[1])

Tenochtitlán fue una gran ciudad construida por los aztecas, que **se establecieron** en la región durante el siglo XIV. Gracias al comercio, la agricultura y **la guerra**, los aztecas fundaron un **poderoso** imperio. **Al llegar** a esta **tierra**, en el siglo XVI, los españoles admiraron la **riqueza** de Tenochtitlán.

La ciudad fue destruida en 1521. Las ruinas no se descubrieron hasta 1978, cuando unos obreros que cavaban[2] la calle para hacer una instalación eléctrica las encontraron de casualidad[3]. ¡Puedes verlas en el centro del DF!

[1]DF = Distrito Federal, o sea Ciudad de México [2]dug up [3]by chance

❷

Caballos y armas

Aunque los guerreros aztecas se **enfrentaron** a los conquistadores valientemente en muchas **batallas**, los **soldados** españoles establecieron su **poder** gracias a dos elementos **desconocidos** en las Américas: las **armas** de fuego y los caballos.

370 trescientos setenta • Capítulo 8 • Encuentro entre culturas

---

Differentiated Instruction

Students with Learning Difficulties

Students may have difficulty with comprehension of the text on pp. 370 and 371. To help organize the information presented, have students find the dates mentioned in the reading. Then have them create a timeline with a simple caption for each year or century mentioned.

Advanced Learners

Ask students to write paraphrases for each of the four sections on these pages on separate sheets of paper. Collect and mix all the paraphrases. Have students arrange them into sets of four in chronological order and discuss similarities and differences among the different paraphrased versions.

Go **Online** to practice
PEARSON
realize.™
PearsonSchool.com/Autentico
AUDIO   MAPA GLOBAL

Interpretive   8

3

La noche triste (DF)

En 1519, cuando llegó Hernán Cortés, los aztecas **se rebelaron. Lucharon** contra los conquistadores y los vencieron en una famosa batalla. Los españoles la recuerdan como la "Noche triste", porque fue tan desastrosa que Cortés se sentó a llorar junto a un árbol. Ese árbol está en el centro del DF.

4

OAXACA: El Paseo de las Misiones

Los conquistadores triunfantes establecieron la **colonia** de Nueva España e iniciaron **un intercambio** de **mercancías** nuevas. Los **europeos** conocieron delicias como el café, el chocolate y el maíz, y los americanos probaron el pollo y el arroz.

Pero nada cambió tanto la vida de las Américas como las **misiones** católicas. Los franciscanos y dominicos las fundaron porque querían que los **indígenas adoptaran** la religión, la **lengua** y la cultura de España. Los principales conventos dominicos están en Oaxaca. Aunque ya no queda ningún **misionero** de aquella época, podrás apreciar los antiguos edificios de arquitectura europea.

17

Diferentes opiniones

 ESCUCHAR En una hoja escribe los números del 1 al 6. Escucha las frases. Escribe *C* si la frase es cierta o *F* si la frase es falsa.

Capítulo 8 • trescientos setenta y uno **371**

17

Standards: 1.2

Resources: Teacher's Resource Materials: Audio Script, Technology: Audio: Cap. 8

Suggestions: Before students listen, allow them a few minutes to silently read over the information on these two pages. Play the audio or read from the script. Allow students to listen more than once.

 Technology: Audio Script and Answers

Vas a oír cada frase dos veces.

1. Tecnochtitlán fue una ciudad construida por Hernán Cortés y sus hombres. *(F)*
2. La ciudad de Tecnochtitlán fue destruida en 1978. *(F)*
3. Los soldados españoles peleaban con armas de fuego y caballos. *(C)*
4. Los españoles conocieron el café y el chocolate en América. *(C)*
5. Las misiones católicas quisieron cambiar la religión y lengua de los indígenas. *(C)*
6. El convento dominico es un edificio antiguo de arquitectura azteca. *(F)*

Starter Activity

Have the students change these present tense verbs to the preterite:

> descubren
> van
> establecen
> construyen
> luchan

(**Answers:** descubrieron, fueron, establecieron, construyeron, lucharon)

Project-Based Learning

Students can perform Step 3 at this point. (For more information, see p. 352-b.)

Enrich Your Teaching

Teacher-to-Teacher

Use visuals on these pages to elicit as much language as possible from students. They can describe what they see, practice various tenses to say what happened, is happening, or will happen in a picture, or offer opinions or value statements based on their interpretation of a picture.

21st Century Skills

ICT (Information, Communications and Technology) Literacy Have students use the digital technology within **Realize** to access and manage the audio files and activities that support learning the new vocabulary. Students can access the eText Audio to hear the pronunciation of new vocabulary words of *Vocabulario en contexto*.

Vocabulario en contexto 2

Standards: 1.2

Resources: Teacher's Resource Materials: Input Script, Clip Art, Audio Script, Technology: Audio Cap. 8

Suggestions: Pre-reading: Point out cognates such as *descendencia, africana,* and *resultado* that will help students better understand the text as they read. Remind students that the information here is an extension of the historical treatment on pp. 370–371.

Reading: Allow students time to read the information on this and the next page silently first. Then play the audio and have students read along as they listen. Allow them to listen more than once.

Post-reading: Check comprehension by asking questions. For example: *¿La celebración del Día de los Muertos es una fusión de elementos de qué religiones? ¿La herencia de Sandra es una fusión de qué tres culturas?*

18

Standards: 1.2

Suggestions: Encourage students to review the material presented on pp. 370–373 before completing the activity.

Answers:
1. Se veía la influencia de los españoles, de los indígenas, y de los africanos.
2. Representa la combinación de las religiones católicas e indígenas.
3. La comida representa una mezcla de culturas.
4. La herencia cultural de Sandra representa las tradiciones de los españoles, de los africanos y de los indígenas.

Teacher-to-Teacher

Ask students to discuss how *La fusión* in Mexico has impacted life in the United States.

❧ LA FUSIÓN ❧

Durante la época colonial (1521–1821) se mezclaron diferentes **razas**, religiones y costumbres. No solo había gente de **descendencia** europea, sino también indígena y **africana**. Como **resultado** de esta **mezcla**, hay una gran **variedad** de tradiciones y culturas en América.

Celebración del Día de los Muertos ▲

1 Los indígenas influyeron en las prácticas religiosas cristianas que trajeron los españoles. En la celebración del Día de los Muertos, que tiene lugar el dos de noviembre para recordar a los familiares que han muerto, se combinan elementos de las religiones católicas e indígenas.

El mole poblano ▲

2 Una de las cosas en que se vio la influencia española fue la comida. Durante la época colonial, la alimentación de los indígenas cambió debido a los productos traídos por los españoles. Es en esta época que aparecen muchos de los platos mexicanos de hoy día. Por ejemplo, el mole poblano, una salsa típica de la cocina mexicana, fue creado por las monjas[1] de una misión utilizando productos mexicanos, asiáticos y europeos.

[1] nuns

18

Contestar

ESCRIBIR Contesta las preguntas con la información de las páginas 372–373.

1. En la fusión que tuvo lugar durante la época colonial, ¿se veía la influencia de qué tres tradiciones?

2. ¿La celebración del Día de los Muertos representa la combinación de elementos de qué religiones?

3. ¿Por qué dicen que la comida representa una fusión?

4. ¿Por qué representa la herencia de Sandra lo más noble de la historia de las Américas?

Differentiated Instruction

Heritage Speakers

Ask students to talk about traditional or typical foods in their heritage country. Ask them to discuss the history of these foods in the culture or in their own families. How did the recipes, ingredients, and traditions begin?

Students with Learning Difficulties

Students may have difficulty with the concept of analogies in *Actividad* 19. Provide students with visual clues to help establish the relationship between the first two words in the analogy. For example, for the first item, *europeo: Europa,* draw a person and a simple map.

Go **Online** to practice
PEARSON
realize™
PearsonSchool.com/Autentico

WRITING

Interpretive **8**

La herencia

Esta mezcla de culturas sigue presente hoy en día.

Sandra

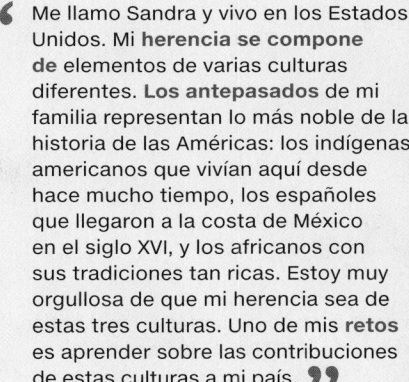

" Me llamo Sandra y vivo en los Estados Unidos. Mi **herencia se compone de** elementos de varias culturas diferentes. **Los antepasados** de mi familia representan lo más noble de la historia de las Américas: los indígenas americanos que vivían aquí desde hace mucho tiempo, los españoles que llegaron a la costa de México en el siglo XVI, y los africanos con sus tradiciones tan ricas. Estoy muy orgullosa de que mi herencia sea de estas tres culturas. Uno de mis **retos** es aprender sobre las contribuciones de estas culturas a mi país. "

19

Las analogías

 LEER, ESCRIBIR Escoge la mejor palabra para completar cada analogía.

africano	europeo	poderoso
luchar	desconocido	lengua

1. europeo: Europa; _____ : África
2. igual : diferente; _____ : débil
3. indígena : azteca; _____ : español
4. escribir : lápiz; _____ : arma
5. justo : injusto; _____ : familiar
6. volver : regresar; _____ : idioma

Enrich Your Teaching

Culture Note

The Aztecs and the Incas first cultivated the tomato as a crop around 700 A.D. The fruit was brought to Europe by explorers in the sixteenth century. The cuisines of France, Italy, and Spain quickly utilized the new ingredient. The French called it "the apple of love," and the Germans called it "the apple of paradise." As the tomato traveled north, however, its mystery increased. The British actually believed that the tomato was poisonous, a myth that traveled to the American colonies, and was believed by many until the nineteenth century.

19

Standards: 1.2, 3.1

Suggestions: Remind students that the items are presented as analogies. A single colon means "is to" and a double colon means "as."

Answers:
1. africano
2. poderoso
3. europeo
4. luchar
5. desconocido
6. lengua

Extension: After students complete the activity, ask them to point out words that are synonyms, such as *idioma* and *lengua,* and antonyms, such as *familiar* and *desconocido.*

Teacher-to-Teacher

Ask students to work in pairs to discuss how history described in *La herencia* has impacted Sandra's life in the United States.

Additional Resources

 Technology: Online Resources
- Instant Check
- Guided, Core, Audio, Writing practice
- *Para hispanohablantes*

Print
- Guided WB pp. 253–260
- Core WB pp. 112–113

Assessment

Prueba: Comprensión del vocabulario 2
- Prueba 8-4

20

Suggestions: Remind students that a valid definition of a word does not reuse the word or any other form of the word as part of the definition. Encourage them to consider which part of speech each word is before attempting to define it.

Answers will vary.

Starter Activity

Students will hear a combination of the imperfect and preterite tenses in *Actividad* 21. Briefly review the uses of the two tenses. Make statements that use both the imperfect and the preterite tenses. Have students tell why each tense was used.

21

Resources: Teacher's Resource Materials: Audio Script, Technology: Audio Cap. 8

Suggestions: Point out to students that the description they will hear is a running narrative rather than several independent sentences. Point to the painting in the activity as you play the audio or read from the script. Allow students to listen more than once.

Technology: Audio Script:

El conquistador Hernán Cortés entró a Tenochtitlán con sus caballos y sin usar sus armas, después de que Moctezuma enviara sus mensajeros para invitarlo a entrar en la ciudad. Los mensajeros le mostraron el camino que debía seguir pero como los aztecas eran desconocidos, Cortés desconfió de ellos y se fue por un camino diferente. Sin embargo, Cortés llegó al lugar donde lo esperaba el líder del imperio azteca. El encuentro de Cortés con Moctezuma fue en un enorme palacio donde Moctezuma vivía con miles de personas a su servicio. Moctezuma le regaló riquezas impresionantes.

Answers:
1. F; Cortés entró a Tenochtitlán después de que Moctezuma envió a sus mensajeros para invitarlo a entrar en la ciudad.
2. C
3. F; Cortés conoció a Moctezuma en Tenochtitlán.
4. C
5. F; Moctezuma le regaló riquezas importantes a Cortés.

Vocabulario en uso 2

20

 ¿Qué significa esta palabra?

✎ **ESCRIBIR** Trabaja con otro(a) estudiante para escribir definiciones de las palabras siguientes.

Modelo
poderoso
Una persona que es poderosa tiene mucha influencia.

1. la semejanza
2. el imperio
3. la riqueza
4. la batalla
5. el encuentro
6. el resultado
7. la mezcla
8. la mercancía
9. la misión
10. el reto

21

Cortés llega a Tenochtitlán

🔊 **ESCUCHAR, ESCRIBIR** Escucha una descripción de la entrada de Cortés a Tenochtitlán. Después, lee cada frase y escribe (*C*) si es cierta o (*F*) si es falsa. Si la frase es falsa, vuelve a escribirla para que diga algo cierto.

1. Cortés entró a Tenochtitlán después de una batalla contra los mensajeros de Moctezuma.

2. Los conquistadores no siguieron el camino a Tenochtitlán que les sugirieron los aztecas.

3. Cortés nunca llegó a conocer al líder del imperio azteca.

4. Moctezuma y Cortés se encontraron en un palacio muy grande.

5. Moctezuma le dio armas a Cortés como regalos.

▲ Primera entrada de Hernán Cortés y sus soldados en Tenochtitlán

Ahora usa las frases correctas para ayudarte a parafrasear la idea principal, el tema y los detalles del audio.

374 trescientos setenta y cuatro • Capítulo 8 • Encuentro entre culturas

---

Differentiated Instruction

Heritage Speakers

As students write their definitions for the vocabulary words in *Actividad* 20, ask them to also brainstorm a synonym for each word. Then have students discuss the subtle differences in meaning between the original word and its close relation.

Advanced Learners

Have students compare and contrast the two pictures of the encounter between Cortés and Moctezuma that accompany *Actividades* 21 and 22. Encourage them to paraphrase information they heard in *Actividad* 21 in order to talk about the events depicted.

Go **Online** to practice
PearsonSchool.com/Autentico

PEARSON
realize™
AUDIO WRITING SPEAK/RECORD

Interpersonal 8

22

¡A describir el cuadro!

 ESCRIBIR Mira este cuadro que representa el encuentro entre Cortés y los representantes de Moctezuma. Escríbele a un(a) compañero(a) por texto y hazle preguntas sobre lo que se ve en el cuadro. Él o ella responde con sus descripciones.

23

¿Qué es un imperio?

LEER, ESCRIBIR, HABLAR ¿Sabes qué es un imperio? Lee este párrafo para aprender qué es un imperio y cuáles son sus ventajas y desventajas.

Conexiones ◂ **Las ciencias sociales**

Un imperio es un grupo importante de territorios que dependen de un mismo gobierno. Los territorios que dependen del gobierno central se llaman colonias. Los ciudadanos de las colonias disfrutan por lo general de los mismos derechos y beneficios que los ciudadanos del país del gobierno central. Sin embargo, esto no ha sido siempre así. Como consecuencia, las colonias se han ido separando del gobierno central, creando sus propios gobiernos.

• ¿Cuáles son las características de un imperio? Trabaja con otro(a) estudiante para hacer una lista usando las palabras del recuadro.

componerse	poder	reto	variedad
riqueza	poderoso	luchar	establecer
invadir	batalla	soldado	intercambio

22

Standards: 1.1, 1.3

Suggestions: Point to the painting in the activity as students describe the picture.

Answers will vary.

23

Standards: 1.2, 1.3, 3.1

Suggestions: Ask students to share their background knowledge about colonies and colonial situations past and present. Challenge their critical thinking skills by asking: *Si los ciudadanos de las colonias disfrutan de los mismos derechos que los ciudadanos del gobierno central, ¿por qué siempre terminan votando o luchando por su libertad?*

Answers will vary.

Project-Based Learning

Students can perform Step 4 at this point. Be sure they understand your corrections and suggestions. (For more information, see p. 352-b.)

Teacher-to-Teacher

Have students discuss how the arrival of Cortés impacted historical and social events in Mexico and eventually, the present day United States.

Enrich Your Teaching

Culture Note

On September 15, 1821, five Latin American countries gained independence from Spain. They included Costa Rica, El Salvador, Guatemala, Honduras, and Nicaragua. September 15th is the national holiday of independence in each of these countries. For this reason, we now celebrate Hispanic Heritage Month from September 15th to October 15th. Mexico achieved its independence a few years earlier, but one day later, on September 16, 1810.

24

Standards: 1.2, 2.1, 2.2, 3.1, 3.2

Suggestions: As students read the information silently, ask them to note words or phrases at spots in which they have comprehension problems. Address these problem spots and have students read the material again before answering the questions.

Answers:

1. Su herencia está formada de tres culturas: la africana, la indígena y la española.
2. Sus antepasados son de África, la República Dominicana y España.
3. La cultura dominicana ha influido más en su vida.
4. Aprende sobre su cultura dominicana cuando visita la República Dominicana. También aprende mucho porque la cultura dominicana ha influido mucho en la Ciudad de Nueva York, donde vive.
5. Él se siente orgulloso de su herencia.
6. Answers will vary.

CULTURA

Standards: 1.1, 1.2, 2.1, 2.2, 3.1, 4.2

Suggestions: Before students read the information, ask them to share their background knowledge about Tex-Mex food. Then help them increase their knowledge by asking questions that have answers they will discover as they read. For example: *No solo dos sino tres culturas han influido en la comida texmex. ¿Cuáles son?*

Answers will vary.

Pre-AP® Integration

- **Learning Objective:** Interpretive: Print
- **Activity:** As a pre-reading activity, have students work with a partner who reads one of the two paragraphs in the narration, *Mi herencia africana* silently. Have each student write a one-sentence summary of his or her segment and share with the class.
- *Pre-AP® Resource Materials:* Comprehensive guide to Pre-AP® reading skill development,

---

24

Una mezcla de culturas

 LEER, ESCRIBIR   Lee la lectura y contesta las preguntas.

Mi herencia africana

Mi nombre es Norberto y nací en la ciudad de Santo Domingo, en la República Dominicana. Soy el resultado de una mezcla de razas y culturas. De mi padre recibí mi herencia africana. Los antepasados de mi madre eran españoles e indígenas. De niño, la cultura dominicana tuvo más influencia en mi vida. Ahora vivo en los Estados Unidos y me encanta ir a la República Dominicana, donde hay mucha riqueza cultural y donde lo paso muy bien con mi familia y mis amigos. Sin embargo, cuando estoy en la República Dominicana quiero volver a los Estados Unidos, porque también me identifico con este país.

Vivo en Nueva York, una ciudad donde se encuentran y se mezclan muchas culturas: la cultura dominicana, la estadounidense y la africana, entre otras. Para mí, en Nueva York es fácil aprender sobre mi herencia cultural. Voy a una iglesia dominicana, escucho cantantes dominicanos y españoles en la radio y voy a festivales de música y presentaciones de arte africano. Las culturas que forman mi herencia han influido mucho en la vida de toda la ciudad. Me siento orgulloso de mi herencia.

1. ¿De cuántas culturas está formada la herencia de Norberto? Di cuáles son.

2. ¿De dónde son los antepasados del autor?

3. ¿Cuál es la cultura que más ha influido en la vida del autor?

4. ¿Cómo aprende sobre su cultura dominicana?

5. ¿Cómo se siente él de su herencia?

6. ¿Hay una variedad de culturas en tu comunidad? Descríbelas.

CULTURA   Estados Unidos • México

¡Qué rica la comida texmex! El estado de Texas está en la frontera con México y allí se encuentran y se mezclan dos culturas, la estadounidense y la mexicana. Algunas personas hablan inglés con acento español o español con palabras del inglés.

La comida texmex es otro resultado de ese encuentro. Es una mezcla de la cocina mexicana y la texana, con influencia de la cocina cajún del Sur de los Estados Unidos. El arroz, los frijoles, el chile y las tortillas de maíz se mezclan con las cebollas texanas y los mariscos del Golfo, para lograr un resultado exquisito.

La comida texmex ya no se encuentra sólo en Texas; en todas las ciudades grandes de los Estados Unidos hay restaurantes de estilo texmex. La próxima vez que veas uno de ellos, no dejes de entrar.

Pre-AP® Integration: Los estilos de vida ¿Qué influencia tuvo la comida de origen mexicana en la texmex? Compara la comida texmex con la que generalmente comes en tu casa.

376 trescientos setenta y seis • Capítulo 8 • Encuentro entre culturas

---

Differentiated Instruction

Heritage Speakers

Have students share their own personal versions of **Una mezcla de culturas** in *Actividad* 24. Ask them to reread the passage, substituting their own information about their heritage country and culture. For example, *Mi nombre es ___ y nací en la ciudad de ___, en ___.*

Musical Learner

Divide students into small groups. Have each group rehearse a choral reading of **Calabó y bambú.** Instruct students to create their own rhythmic gestures and percussion accompaniment using hand claps, finger snaps, and knee slaps.

Go Online to practice
PearsonSchool.com/Autentico
PEARSON
realize™
AUDIO WRITING SPEAK/RECORD

Pronunciación ‹ En voz alta

Muchos poemas y cuentos indígenas pasaron a la forma escrita gracias a las personas bilingües que hablaban el idioma nativo y el español. Estas personas realizaron los escritos durante la colonización de las Américas para conservar la cultura y las creencias que antes se trasmitían por tradición oral.

La leyenda *El águila y el nopal*, redactada hacia el año 1600, explica los orígenes de la ciudad de Tenochtitlán, que hoy en día es la capital de México. Según la leyenda, los mexicas salieron del Norte y, guiados por el dios Huitzilopochtli, viajaron largas distancias buscando la señal que indicaría donde deberían construir su ciudad. El dios les dijo que verían un águila comiendo una serpiente encima de un nopal, un tipo de cactus. El encuentro entre los mexicas y el águila es un hecho de tanta importancia en la historia de México que es el único símbolo en la bandera.

Escucha la leyenda y trata de repetirla en voz alta.

• ¿Cómo apoya el tema de fusión de culturas esta leyenda?

> **¿Recuerdas?**
>
> Cuando la letra *c* va antes de *a, o* y *u*, se pronuncia como la *c* de *cat*.
>
> Cuando la *c* va antes de *e* o de *i*, se pronuncia como la *s* de *Sally*.
>
> Para mantener el sonido de la *c* de *cat* antes de la *e* y la *i*, las palabras se escriben con *qu: busqué, aquí*.

El Águila y el nopal

Llegaron al sitio donde se levanta el nopal salvaje allí al borde de la cueva[1], y vieron tranquila parada al Águila en el nopal salvaje: allí come, allí devora y echa a la cueva los restos[2] de lo que come.

Y cuando el Águila vio a los mexicanos, se inclinó profundamente. Y el Águila veía desde lejos. Su nido[3] y su asiento era todo él de cuantas finas plumas[4] hay; plumas de azulejos, plumas de aves rojas y plumas de quetzal. . .

Les habló el dios y les dijo: —¡Ah, mexicanos: aquí sí será! ¡México es aquí!

Y aunque no veían quién les hablaba, se pusieron a llorar y decían: —¡Felices nosotros, dichosos[5] al fin: hemos visto ya dónde ha de ser nuestra ciudad! ¡Vamos y vengamos a reposar aquí!

[1]cave [2]remains [3]nest [4]feathers [5]lucky

25 ¿De dónde venimos?

HABLAR EN PAREJA Trabaja con otro(a) estudiante para contestar las preguntas.

1. ¿Cómo se muestran las diferentes herencias culturales en tu comunidad? ¿Y en los Estados Unidos?

2. Intercambia tus preferencias personales sobre algunas celebraciones que tengan raíces *(roots)* culturales. ¿Qué te parece más atractivo? ¿En cuál preferías participar?

3. ¿Cómo se ve la influencia de diferentes herencias en la lengua que hablamos? ¿Puedes pensar en algún ejemplo?

4. ¿Hay influencia indígena en el lugar donde vives? ¿En qué cosas la ves?

5. ¿Qué grupo étnico te parece más interesante? ¿Por qué?

Capítulo 8 • trescientos setenta y siete **377**

EN VOZ ALTA ‹

Standards: 1.2, 1.3, 2.1, 2.2, 3.1, 3.2, 5.2

Resources: Teacher's Resource Materials: Audio Script, Technology: Audio Cap. 8

Suggestions: Have students read the information and the legend silently. Ask comprehension questions: *¿Cómo se escribieron en español la historia y las leyendas de las culturas indígenas? ¿Qué señal buscaban los mexicas? ¿Qué imagen está en la bandera de México?*

Before having students read the legend aloud, direct their attention to the information in the *¿Recuerdas?* Ask them to identify words with the hard and soft **c** sound and write them in a list. Allow them a few minutes to practice the words with a partner.

Answers will vary: Esta leyenda azteca ya es parte de la identidad nacional de México y contada en español.

25

Standards: 1.1, 1.3, 4.2

Suggestions: After students have answered the questions in item 3, ask *"¿Cómo se ve la influencia de diferentes **lenguas** en la lengua que hablamos?"* Have students give examples from various languages. Direct attention to the *Cultura* on p. 376 and have students identify words that have passed from Spanish into English. Have students tell you what they learned earlier about the influence of Latin and Arabic on Spanish.

Answers will vary.

Additional Resources

Technology: Online Resources
• Communication Activities
• Teacher's Resource Materials: Audio Script, Communicative Pair Activity, Technology: Audio Cap. 8

Assessment

Prueba 8-5 with Remediation (online only)
Prueba: Aplicación del vocabulario 2
• Prueba 8-5

Gramática

Suggestions: As you explain the points in the *Gramática,* point out to students the difference between the use of the ***presente perfecto del subjuntivo,*** which they learned in *Capítulo* 7, and the current lesson, the ***imperfecto del subjuntivo.*** We use the former when the main clause is in the present tense and expresses doubt or uncertainty about a situation in the past. We use the ***imperfecto del subjuntivo*** when the main clause is in one of the past tenses.

 Technology: Interactive Whiteboard

> **Grammar Activities 8-2** Use the whiteboard activities in your Teacher Resources as you progress through the grammar practice with your class.

26

Standards: 1.2, 3.1

Suggestions: As students complete the activity, ask them to focus on the clauses that make up each sentence. Remind them that in all cases, the main clause (containing an expression of emotion, doubt, or uncertainty) is in a past tense, thus requiring the imperfect subjunctive in the subordinate clause.

Answers:
1. fuera
2. tuvieran
3. pudiera
4. supieran

Active Classroom

Play the "Cube Game" with three cubes. In groups of two, give students three cubes. Cube 1: write six infinitives including some irregular verbs from p. 378. Cube 2: six expressions that use the subjunctive. Cube 3: subject pronouns. Have students roll the cubes and provide a sentence combining information on the three cubes: *Mi padre quería que yo estudiara.*

Gramática

OBJECTIVES
▶ Express doubts and wishes about family and cultural heritage in the past
▶ Talk about an important event in your childhood

El imperfecto del subjuntivo

You know that you use the subjunctive to persuade someone else to do something, to express emotions about situations, and to express doubt and uncertainty. If the main verb is in the present tense, use the present subjunctive. If the main verb is in the preterite or imperfect, use the imperfect subjunctive.

> Los indígenas **dudan** que los europeos **aprendan** su lengua.
> Los indígenas **dudaban** que los europeos **aprendieran** su lengua.

> El profesor **sugiere** que **aprendamos** los nombres de las colonias.
> El profesor **sugirió** que **aprendiéramos** los nombres de las colonias.

- To form the imperfect subjunctive, take the *Uds. / ellos / ellas* form of the preterite and replace the ending *-ron* with the imperfect subjunctive endings. Here are the forms of the imperfect subjunctive for *cantar, aprender,* and *vivir*.

cantar		aprender		vivir	
cant**ara**	cant**áramos**	aprend**iera**	aprend**iéramos**	viv**iera**	viv**iéramos**
cant**aras**	cant**arais**	aprend**ieras**	aprend**ierais**	viv**ieras**	viv**ierais**
cant**ara**	cant**aran**	aprend**iera**	aprend**ieran**	viv**iera**	viv**ieran**

- Note that the *nosotros* form has a written accent.

Irregular verbs, stem-changing verbs, and spelling-changing verbs follow the same rule for forming the imperfect subjunctive.

> **ir: fueron → fue-**   El rey les dijo que **fueran** al Nuevo Mundo.
> **haber: hubieron → hubie-**   Dudaba que **hubiera** semejanzas.
> **pedir: pidieron → pidie-**   No era necesario que **pidieran** tantas armas.
> **construir: construyeron → construye-**   Los europeos querían que los habitantes **construyeran** una iglesia.

> **Más recursos** ONLINE
> ▶ **Tutorial:** Use of Imperfect of Subjunctive

26

Historia de la conquista

 LEER, ESCRIBIR Bernal Díaz del Castillo (1492–1581) escribió uno de los libros más interesantes sobre la conquista de México. Completa estas opiniones de Bernal Díaz del Castillo con el imperfecto del subjuntivo del verbo apropiado.

1. Era impresionante que la capital de los aztecas *(ser / ver)* tan enorme.
2. Era increíble que los edificios de la ciudad *(tener / traer)* torres tan altas.
3. No podíamos creer que la gente *(creer / poder)* navegar por la ciudad.
4. Nos parecía interesante que los indígenas *(saber / decir)* cultivar el maíz en un lago.

378 trescientos setenta y ocho • Capítulo 8 • Encuentro entre culturas

---

Differentiated Instruction

Students with Learning Difficulties

Students may have difficulty grasping the distinction between the present subjunctive and past subjunctive. Before they attempt *Actividad* 26, provide them with additional examples. Provide a sentence utilizing the subjunctive in the present, discuss its meaning, and then transform that sentence using a past tense and the imperfect subjunctive.

Challenge/Pre-AP®

Ask students to revisit *Actividad* 11 on p. 318 in *Capítulo* 7. Challenge them to change the verbs in each item's main clause to the imperfect or preterite tense, and make the resulting change to the imperfect subjunctive in the subordinate clause.

27

Durante la conquista . . .

 LEER ESCRIBIR Imagina que estuviste presente cuando Cortés llegó a México. Tu trabajo era relatar lo que veías. Completa las siguientes oraciones con el imperfecto del subjuntivo del verbo apropiado.

ser	rebelarse	adoptar	comprender	establecer

1. Era imposible que los aztecas _____ la lengua de los españoles.
2. Los españoles esperaban que los indígenas _____ sus costumbres inmediatamente.
3. Los reyes querían que las colonias _____ un intercambio de mercancías.
4. Según los aztecas era posible que los españoles _____ enviados por sus antepasados.
5. Los españoles temían que los indígenas _____ contra ellos.

28

Nuestras raíces

ESCRIBIR Completa las frases de una manera original y conversa por texto con un amigo(a). Ofrece tus sugerencias y usa el imperfecto del subjuntivo de los verbos que están en el recuadro.

hablar	aprender	comer
adoptar	venir	ir
haber	sentirse	abandonar

Modelo
Papá quería que todos nosotros . . . (hablar)
*Papá quería que todos nosotros **habláramos** la lengua de nuestros antepasados.*

1. Mis padres preferían que mis hermanos y yo . . .
2. Mi mamá exigía que todos . . .
3. Mis padres no querían que yo . . .
4. Todos estábamos orgullosos que nuestros antepasados . . .
5. Mi hermana tenía miedo que nuestro hermano . . .
6. A mis abuelos no les gustaba que los jóvenes de la familia . . .
7. Nadie creía que . . .
8. Era importante que todos nosotros . . .

El español en el mundo del trabajo
Salud y ciencia . . . en español

La ciudad de Houston, en Texas, es la cuarta de los Estados Unidos con mayor número de hispanohablantes. Sin embargo, al abrir sus puertas en marzo de 1996, el Museo de Salud de Houston sólo tenía un trabajador bilingüe.

Actualmente el museo ofrece visitas guiadas en español. También hay videos educativos con subtítulos en español. Además, se publica una guía en español y el servicio telefónico de atención al público tiene menús bilingües.

Capítulo 8 • trescientos setenta y nueve **379**

27

Suggestions: Remind students to form the imperfect subjunctive beginning with the correct stem for regular verbs: the third-person plural stem from the preterite tense.

Answers:
1. comprendieran   4. fueran
2. adoptaran   5. se rebelaran
3. establecieran

28

Suggestions: Point out to students that number 7 provides no subject for the subordinate clause. They must choose their own subject and make the imperfect subjunctive form of the verb agree with it.

Answers will vary.

El español en la mundo del trabajo

Suggestions: Once students have read the information, ask comprehension questions. For example: *¿Cuántas ciudades estadounidenses tienen mayor número de hispanohablantes que Houston? (cuatro) ¿Quiénes ofrecen visitas guiadas en el Museo de Salud y Ciencia de Houston? (los profesionales bilingües)*

Enrich Your Teaching

Culture Note
The 2010 Census shows that the Spanish-speaking population in the United States is increasing quickly and dramatically. Since 2000, the Hispanic population in the United States has risen by 43 percent.

Teacher-to-Teacher
Invite students to practice the imperfect subjunctive in a discussion about their first year of high school. They can use sentences similar to those in *Actividad* 28, changing the subjects to ones such as **Los profesores, Los demás estudiantes,** or **Mis amigos.**

29

29

Standards: 1.1

Suggestions: Remind Student A to be careful to apply the rules for use of the preterite vs. the imperfect in the independent clause.

Answers will vary. Student B will most often use the nosotros forms of the imperfect subjunctive of the given verbs:

respetáramos	fuéramos
adoptáramos	durmiéramos
saliéramos	jugáramos
nos lleváramos	nos despertáramos

Extension: After students complete the activity, ask volunteers to spell aloud the verb forms used by Student B. Remind them to include the necessary accents in the *nosotros* forms as they spell.

Starter Activity

Have students unscramble these words to create logical sentences:

que/mi madre/fuera/yo/niño/quería

el viaje/dudaban/ellos/tanto/costara/que/ a España

(Answers: *Mi madre quería que yo fuera niño; Ellos dudaban que el viaje a España costara tanto.*)

30

Standards: 1.1

Suggestions: Tell students to keep sharpening their skills in the use of the subjunctive by making mental notes as they work on the types of expressions used in the independent clauses of sentences.

Answers will vary.

Additional Resources

 Technology: Online Resources
- Instant Check
- Guided, Core, Audio
- *Para hispanohablantes*

Print
- Guided WB pp. 261–262
- Core WB p. 114

Assessment

Prueba 8-6 with Remediation (online only)
Prueba: Imperfecto del subjuntivo
- Prueba 8-6

29

¿Qué querían que hicieras?

🎤 **HABLAR EN PAREJA** Piensa en las cosas que esperaban tus familiares u otras personas que hicieras de pequeño(a). Trabaja con otro(a) estudiante para hablar sobre lo que querían esas personas que hiciera cada uno(a) de pequeño(a). Añadan detalles a sus frases.

▶ **Videomodelo**
los maestros / querer / compartir
A —¿*Qué querían los maestros* de la escuela primaria?
B —*Los maestros querían que* **compartiéramos** *los materiales con nuestros compañeros.*

Estudiante A		**Estudiante B**
los maestros	querer	respetar
mi mamá	esperar	adoptar
mi papá	pedir	salir
mis padres / abuelos	decir	llevarse bien
mi(s) hermano(s)	prohibir	ir
mi(s) hermana(s)	aconsejar	dormir
el(la) director(a) de la escuela	sugerir	jugar
mi entrenador(a)	exigir	despertarse
¡Respuesta personal!		**¡Respuesta personal!**

30

¿Qué pasó?

✏️ **LEER, HABLAR** Piensa en un momento importante de tu niñez. Según lo que recuerdas, completa las siguientes frases.

1. Yo esperaba que . . .
2. Yo quería que . . .
3. [Nombre de un(a) amigo(a) o un familiar] quería que . . .
4. Era importante que . . .
5. (No) me sorprendió que . . .
6. Me gustó que . . .
7. Me molestó que . . .
8. Me pareció interesante que . . .

Differentiated Instruction

Heritage Speakers

Have students do *Actividad* 30 with a partner. After completing each sentence, have partners quiz each other on the correct spelling of the past subjunctive form used in the example. Instruct them to write down the verb form once they have agreed on the correct spelling.

Students with Learning Difficulties

Allow students time to brainstorm their responses before completing *Actividad* 30. Instruct them to write down the components of the clauses that they plan to add. For example, *Era importante que... (yo) (escuchar) (a mis padres).* Encourage students to use these notes to formulate their responses.

Gramática

> **OBJECTIVES**
> ▶ Talk about things you could do
> ▶ Discuss and write about cultural exchange

Go Online to practice
PEARSON **realize**™
AUDIO   VIDEO   WRITING   SPEAK/RECORD

PearsonSchool.com/Autentico

Interpersonal | **8**

El imperfecto del subjuntivo con *si*

Use the imperfect subjunctive after *si* when a situation is unlikely, impossible, or not true.

> **Si tuviera** tiempo, aprendería más sobre las misiones.
> ***If I had*** *time, I'd learn more about the missions.*

> **Si viviéramos** en México, adoptaríamos las costumbres del país.
> ***If we lived*** *in Mexico, we'd adopt the customs of the country.*

> Ese imperio sería más poderoso **si tuviera** oro.
> *That empire would be more powerful **if it had** gold.*

• Notice that you use the imperfect subjunctive form after *si,* and the conditional in the main clause.

After *como si* ("as if") you always use the the imperfect subjunctive regardless of the tense of the first verb in the sentence. Notice that the other verb can be in either the present or the past tense.

> Él se vestía **como si fuera** un rey.
> *He dressed **as if he were** a king.*

> Hablan **como si supieran** la lengua desde niños.
> *They speak **as if they knew** the language since childhood.*

> **Más recursos** ONLINE
>
> 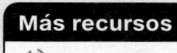 *Canción de hip hop:*
> *Una mezcla de culturas*

31

¡A pensar!

 LEER ESCRIBIR Imagina que has ido a ver un espectáculo de bailes tradicionales de América Latina. Completa el texto con el imperfecto del subjuntivo del verbo apropiado.

Si las personas que crearon los bailes __1.__ *(enfrentarse / vivir)* ahora, les gustaría ver a los bailarines interpretarlos. Ellos bailaban como si __2.__ *(estar / establecer)* en una gran fiesta. Las joyas que llevaban brillaban como si __3.__ *(ser / ir)* de oro. Si los antepasados los __4.__ *(ver / adoptar)* bailar, se emocionarían mucho. Si yo __5.__ *(poder / querer)*, aprendería más sobre las tradiciones y herencias de los países de América Latina. Me gustaría estudiar sobre los países que no __6.__ *(salir / tener)* muchas semejanzas con el mío.

Gramática

Standards: 4.1

Suggestions: Say clauses in which the verb is in the conditional: *...todos iríamos para ver el partido; ...aprenderías muy rápidamente el español.* Ask volunteers to supply subordinate *(si)* clauses that make sense. Point out the cause-and-effect relationship between the clauses in this type of complex sentence.

 Technology: Interactive Whiteboard

> **Grammar Activities 8-2** Use the whiteboard activities in your Teacher Resources as you progress through the grammar practice with your class.

31

Standards: 1.2

Suggestions: Have students complete the activity in pairs and discuss their reasoning behind each answer.

Answers:

1. vivieran
2. estuvieran
3. fueran
4. vieran
5. pudiera
6. tuvieran

Enrich Your Teaching

Teacher-to-Teacher

Have students imagine a situation in which everything goes wrong on what should be a dream vacation. Ask them to work with a partner and come up with as many sentences as they can, saying what they would do if things were different.

21st Century Skills

ICT (Information, Communications and Technology) Literacy Remind students of the various digital tools available in **Realize** to help them monitor their own understanding and learning needs about the imperfect subjunctive, such as the online tutorials with comprehension check exercises, animated verbs, and additional grammar practice activities.

Standards: 1.3

Suggestions: If students have difficulty, help them by telling them that they should use the expression *como si* in all the items.

Answers:

1. Antes de la obra el director les habló a los jóvenes como si supieran lo que estaban haciendo.
2. Las armas de los actores brillaron como si fueran de oro.
3. Los jóvenes lucharon como si participaran en una batalla.
4. El actor principal actuó como si fuera un rey de verdad.
5. El jóven que hizo el papel de misionero actuó como si sintiera compasión.
6. La actriz principal actuó como si estuviera enamorada del rey.
7. El público aplaudió como si hubiera visto una obra de teatro de Broadway.

33

Standards: 1.1, 1.3

Suggestions: Have students switch roles to practice writing both questions and responses.

Answers will vary.

32

Como si . . .

 ESCRIBIR En la escuela Gabriela Mistral los estudiantes están participando en una obra musical sobre la conquista de México. Describe lo que pasó usando expresiones de las dos columnas y el imperfecto del subjuntivo.

Modelo

Los estudiantes actuaron . . . / ser actores profesionales
Los estudiantes actuaron como si fueran actores profesionales.

Columna A

1. Antes de la obra el director les habló a los jóvenes . . .
2. Las armas de los actores brillaron . . .
3. Los jóvenes lucharon . . .
4. El actor principal actuó . . .
5. El jóven que hizo el papel de misionero actuó . . .
6. La actriz principal actuó . . .
7. El público aplaudió . . .

Columna B

estar enamorada del rey

sentir compasión

haber visto una obra de teatro de Broadway

ser un rey de verdad

ser de oro

saber lo que estaban haciendo

participar en una batalla

33

Nuestra sociedad

 ESCRIBIR Tú y tu amigo(a) intercambian mensajes de texto sobre las características y los problemas de la sociedad actual. Escribe cuatro ideas usando el imperfecto del subjuntivo con *si* y tu amigo(a) responde con cuatro ideas suyas.

Modelo

Si los niños y los adultos trataran de comprenderse mejor, no habría tantos conflictos en nuestras casas.
Sí, y si....

1. Si (encontrar)...
2. Si (tener)...
3. Si (hablar)...
4. Si no (perder)...
5. Si (comprar)...
6. Si (llegar)...
7. Si no (cerrar)...
8. Si (escuchar)...

Differentiated Instruction

Advanced Learners

Have students work in pairs to create two sets of cards. On one set they write only subordinate clauses with *si.* On the other they write corresponding main clauses that make sense with the *si* clauses. Have partners mix the cards in each set and exchange them with another pair of students. Students then match the sentence halves of the cards they have received. Some sentence halves may have more than one match. Have students discuss these instances with those who wrote the cards.

Go **Online** to practice
PearsonSchool.com/Autentico

PEARSON
realize™

WRITING

Interpersonal 8

34

Si pudiera . . .

LEER, HABLAR EN PAREJA

1 Lee el siguiente anuncio de una agencia de viajes y completa las frases.

Modelo
Si nada me parara . . .
Si nada me parara, **invitaría a** *mi mejor amigo(a) a un viaje a la Antártida.*

2 Ahora, trabaja con otro(a) estudiante para comparar lo que escribieron.

¡EXPLORAR ANTÁRTIDA!

- Si tuvieras todo el tiempo del mundo...
- Si tu sueño se hiciera realidad...
- Si la distancia no existiera...
- Si nada te parara... Si pudieras escoger...

¿QUÉ HARÍAS?

VIAJES INOLVIDABLES

REFORMA 400
TEL: 555-8900

35

Encuentros

HABLAR EN GRUPO, ESCRIBIR

1 En grupo, van a describir un encuentro de dos culturas del pasado. Pueden tomar ideas de este capítulo o de la clase de estudios sociales. Describan lo siguiente:

- ¿Qué culturas se encontraron?
- ¿Cuándo y dónde fue el encuentro?
- ¿Cómo fue el encuentro?
- ¿Exigía un grupo que el otro hiciera algo?
- ¿Cambió un grupo más que el otro?
- ¿Cuál fue el resultado del encuentro?

2 Compara el encuentro sobre el que escribieron con una situación del presente. Habla con otro(a) estudiante por texto. Pregúntale lo que deben hacer si hay algún conflicto y traten de llegar a una solución.

34

Standards: 1.1, 1.2, 1.3

Suggestions: Point out to students that they should complete all the sentences about themselves, using **yo** as the subject.

Common Errors: Students may mistakenly drop **-ar, -ir,** or **-er** infinitive endings when forming the conditional. Remind them that conditional endings are added to the complete infinitive forms of regular verbs.

Answers will vary.

Extension: After students complete step 2, ask them to use third-person forms to report on their partner's responses: **Si nada le parara, mi compañero(a)....**

35

Standards: 1.1

Suggestions: Encourage students to discuss current world events as they decide on and develop their present-day situation for Step 2.

Answers will vary.

Additional Resources

Technology: Online Resources
- Instant Check
- Guided, Core, Audio
- *Para hispanohablantes*
- Teacher's Resource Materials: Audio Script, Communicative Pair Activity, Technology: Audio Cap. 8

Print
- Guided WB pp. 263–264
- Core WB pp. 115–116

Project-Based Learning

Students can perform Step 5 at this point. Make audio or video recordings of their presentations for inclusion in their portfolios. (For more information, see p. 352-b.)

Assessment

Prueba 8-7 with Remediation (online only)
Prueba: Imperfecto del subjuntivo con *si*
- Prueba 8-7

Examen: Vocabulario y gramática 2
- Examen 2
- ExamView: Examen 2

Enrich Your Teaching

Teacher-to-Teacher

Help students develop their critical thinking skills. Invite them to research current or recent events for information that will add to class discussions about encounters between different cultures. Besides obtaining information from encyclopedias, newspapers, magazines, personal interviews, and the Internet, they might use information they learned from discussions in their Social Studies courses. Encourage them to synthesize information they glean from a variety of sources, both English and Spanish, in order to verify their facts and develop objective opinions.

8 Culture

Puente a la cultura

Standards: 1.1, 1.2, 2.1, 2.2, 3.1, 5.1, 5.2

Suggestions

Pre-reading: Refer students to the *Estrategia.* Show a T-chart with the two columns labeled *los hechos* and *las opiniones.* Have students set up a similar chart on their own paper and use it to record facts and opinions as they read the selection.

Reading: As students read, remind them to use background knowledge, cognates, and context clues to understand unfamiliar words and expressions. Help them resolve comprehension problems by asking *sí/no* or embedded-answer questions.

Post-reading: After students have read the selection, allow them to complete their *los hechos/las opiniones* charts and share the information they recorded there. Use the information from the *las opiniones* column as a springboard to discuss the cultural encounter between the Spanish colonizers and the indigenous peoples of California.

COUNTRY CONNECTION

Standards: 3.1

Resources: Mapa global interactivo

 Technology: Mapa global interactivo, Actividad 8 Visit California's historic missions.

Suggestions: Use *Mapa de Estados Unidos* and the map on p. 385 to show the relative location of the *Camino Real.* Explain to students that some of the California missions developed into modern-day cities, the names of which still retain at least part of the name of the original missions. The largest of these are Los Angeles and San Francisco. Smaller cities include Santa Barbara and San Luis Obispo. Other missions, such as San Antonio de Padua, never grew into cities, and today they remain isolated in rural areas.

Online Cultural Reading

Standards: 2.1, 4.2

Suggestions: After doing the online activity, ask students to list the cultures that are part of their background, and to tell how those cultures shaped their families nowadays.

Puente a la cultura

OBJECTIVES
▶ Read about Spanish missions and learn about their role in California's history
▶ Distinguish between fact and fiction

Estrategia
Fact and opinion
As a critical reader, you must distinguish between the facts and opinions of your source to judge the information's reliability. As you read, try to determine if any of the information presented is the opinion of the author, or whether it is based on facts.

Las misiones de California

Durante el siglo XVIII, los españoles colonizaron el territorio de California. En 1767, el gobierno español y la Iglesia Católica les dieron la tarea a los padres franciscanos de construir misiones y encargarse de ellas.

Las misiones fueron creadas no solo para enseñar la religión cristiana a los indígenas sino también para enseñarles tareas que pudieran realizar en la nueva sociedad española. Asimismo[1] tenían la función de recibir y alimentar a las personas que viajaban a través del territorio desconocido de California.

Las misiones incluían una iglesia, cuartos para los sacerdotes, depósitos, casas para mujeres solteras, barracas para los soldados, comedores y talleres. Los indígenas casados vivían en una villa cerca de la misión.

[1]likewise

Online Cultural Reading

Go to Auténtico ONLINE to read and understand a website about the different civilizations and religions that have existed in Spain during the last 2000 years.

Estrategia Use prior knowledge: As you explore the website, ask yourself if the cultural practices are similar to those in your area.

¡Inténtalo! Read the website. Are the festivals celebrated in Toledo similar to those you know? Do the restaurants feature cuisine you enjoy?

Estatua del Fray *(Brother)* Junípero Serra

Misión de San Diego de Alcalá, la más antigua de las misiones

384 trescientos ochenta y cuatro • Capítulo 8 • Encuentro entre culturas

---

Differentiated Instruction

Students with Learning Difficulties

Provide students with a concept web to help support their comprehension of *Las misiones de California.* Use the question words **¿Qué? ¿Quién? ¿Cuándo? ¿Dónde?** and **¿Por qué?** as the components of the web. After students have read the passage, have them supply information relevant to each of the question words.

Advanced Learners

Invite students to search the Internet for more information about one or more of the missions along the *Camino Real.* Ask them to present the information they find in a brief report to the class. Encourage them to show downloaded photos and share a few facts that are specific to each mission.

El Camino Real

California

Iglesia de la Misión de Santa Bárbara, también llamada "Reina de las Misiones", pues es la más grande de todas

San Rafael
San Francisco de Solano
San José
San Francisco de Asís
Santa Clara
Santa Cruz
San Juan Bautista
San Carlos de Monterey
Soledad
San Antonio
San Miguel
San Luis Obispo
La Purísima
Santa Inés
Santa Bárbara
San Buenaventura
San Fernando Rey
San Gabriel
San Juan Capistrano
San Luis Rey
San Diego

océano Pacífico

Fray Junípero Serra fue escogido por los españoles para fundar las misiones. Serra fundó nueve misiones en California: se encuentran en el Camino Real, una ruta que va desde San Diego hasta la Bahía de San Francisco. Muchas personas recorren hoy el Camino Real para visitar las misiones y aprender sobre su historia.

 ¿Comprendiste?

1. ¿Para qué fueron creadas las misiones?
2. ¿Qué hizo Fray Junípero Serra?
3. ¿Conoces otros edificios que representen el encuentro entre distintas culturas? Explica tu respuesta.

 Mapa global interactivo Explora las misiones franciscanas de California. Investiga su historia, sus ubicaciones y estilos, y compáralas con otras instituciones similares en los Estados Unidos.

 Videodocumentario *Unas herencias ricas*

Capítulo 8 • trescientos ochenta y cinco **385**

¿Qué me cuentas?

Standards: 1.1, 1.2, 1.3

Resources: Teacher's Resource Materials: Audio Script, Technology: Audio: Cap. 8

AP® Skills: Integration of listening, reading, and writing to comprehend and synthesize information from spoken and written sources.

Suggestions: For Step 1, use the audio or read the descriptions aloud. Allow students to hear it twice through: the first time to write their answers, the second time to check them.

For Step 2, have students identify significant details as they read and then summarize the main points of the article.

Encourage students to express their own opinions and to cite specific information from Steps 1 and 2 in their written responses for Step 3.

 Technology: Audio

(For the complete script, see Teacher's Resource Materials.)

Answers:

Step 1

1. b	**3.** c	**5.** c
2. a	**4.** b	**6.** c

Step 2–3

Answers will vary.

Additional Resources

 Technology: Online Resources
* *Para hispanohablantes*

Pre-AP®
Integración

OBJECTIVES
▶ Listen to and read about a legend and an Inca temple
▶ Discuss the relation between indigenous and European cultures

¿Qué me cuentas?: De leyendas y ciudades

¿Qué resultados trajo el encuentro entre los españoles y los indígenas en las Américas? Escucha una leyenda. Anota las respuestas a las preguntas y guárdalas para usarlas en el paso 3.

 1 Escucha la leyenda. Después de cada párrafo vas a oír dos preguntas. Escoge la mejor respuesta para cada pregunta.

1. a. una mercancía	**b.** un bolso lleno de oro	**c.** un azulejo
2. a. devolvérselo a su dueño	**b.** llevárselo a su familia	**c.** comprar muchas cosas
3. a. en el bolso no había ninguna moneda	**b.** en el bolso había cuarenta monedas	**c.** faltaban dos monedas en el bolso
4. a. al rey	**b.** al representante del rey	**c.** a sus amigos
5. a. porque le contó su historia	**b.** porque compró pocas cosas con el oro	**c.** porque devolvió el bolso
6. a. al señor español	**b.** al mensajero	**c.** al señor azteca

2 Ahora, lee este artículo sobre una construcción colonial.

Destinos andinos

Koricancha: Templo e iglesia

El Templo del Sol de Koricancha en la ciudad de Cusco, Perú fue la construcción más impresionante del imperio inca. Estaba decorado totalmente con oro. Había páneles, figuras religiosas y altares de oro, y en el interior había colgado un enorme disco dorado que reflejaba el sol. Durante la conquista, los incas utilizaron gran parte de este oro para pagar la fianza[1] de Atahualpa, el líder capturado por los españoles. Los españoles sacaron lo que quedaba del oro cuando conquistaron Cusco. Después, ellos construyeron el convento y la iglesia de Santo Domingo encima del templo, integrando los muros[2] incaicos de piedra en la base del edificio. El resultado fue una mezcla única de arquitectura colonial.

◀ Vista del muro incaico en la Iglesia de Santo Domingo, Cusco.

[1]ransom [2]walls

 3 Habla con un(a) compañero(a) sobre la relación entre la cultura indígena y la europea en las Américas. ¿Cómo crees que se sentían los indígenas y españoles? ¿Cómo se refleja la fusión de las culturas en la leyenda y en la iglesia? Compara este encuentro entre culturas con lo que pasó en España. Usa las siguientes expresiones para conectar tus ideas.

antes de	anteriormente	también	durante	para ilustrar

Differentiated Instruction

Heritage Speakers

After each oral presentation, ask students to play the part of tourists in the city. Encourage them to ask follow-up questions of the tour guide, and to discuss how this city compares to other cities with which they are familiar, perhaps in their heritage country.

Students with Learning Difficulties

Encourage students to organize and record the information for their oral presentations on index cards. Remind them not to read from their cards, but to refer to their notes during the course of the presentation.

Presentación oral

OBJECTIVES
▶ Demonstrate how to give a guided city tour
▶ Identify a purpose to improve your presentation

Go **Online** to practice
PearsonSchool.com/Autentico
PEARSON
realize™
🔊 AUDIO 🎤 SPEAK/RECORD

Una visita a . . .

TAREA Eres guía turístico(a) en una ciudad multicultural. Planeas una visita a los lugares más importantes de la ciudad.

1 **Prepárate** Escoge la ciudad que te gustaría visitar. Completa una tabla con sus características.

nombre de la ciudad
herencia cultural
religiones
restaurantes típicos
edificios históricos

Puedes dibujar un plano de la ciudad y marcar con una flecha *(arrow)* los lugares sobre los que hablarás.

2 **Practica** Vuelve a leer la información que anotaste en la tabla. Practica tu presentación. Puedes usar tus notas para practicar, pero no al hablar ante la clase. Recuerda:

- describir con detalles la parte de la ciudad de la que hablas
- añadir detalles sobre cómo se relacionan entre sí los diferentes grupos culturales de la ciudad
- mirar directamente al público
- usar el vocabulario y la gramática del capítulo

Estrategia

Speaker's purpose Before giving an oral presentation, you must think what the purpose of your speech is. Do you want to inform, persuade, or entertain your audience?

In this case, your purpose will be to inform. You need your audience—the tourists—to be both interested in the tour and informed. Use interesting facts about the city and present them in an engaging way.

Modelo

Hoy visitaremos el centro de la ciudad de San Francisco de Quito.
La ciudad tiene herencia cultural española e indígena. La religión de sus habitantes es la cristiana, por eso tiene muchas iglesias . . .

3 **Haz tu presentación** Imagina que tus compañeros de clase son los turistas. Explícales cómo es la ciudad, como si estuvieran allí.

4 **Evaluación** Tu profesor(a) utilizará la siguiente rúbrica para evaluar tu presentación.

Rubric	Score 1	Score 3	Score 5
How clearly you state your purpose	Your purpose is not stated or evident.	You hint at a purpose but don't clearly state it.	You clearly state your purpose at the beginning.
How well you organize and present information	You give very little information.	You lack important information. You do not organize your information.	Your information is complete, interesting, and well-organized.
How effectively you deliver your speech	Your speech is read. You make no eye contact with the audience.	You make some eye contact with the audience.	You make good eye contact with the audience.

Enrich Your Teaching

21st Century Skills

Creativity and Innovation Have students think about the purpose of a guided tour. What are the most interesting features of a city and how would they present them to an audience of fellow students? What are the most interesting ways to promote each visit? Encourage students to be creative in the way they present their city tour using visuals, maps, artifacts, or personal anecdotes.

Presentación oral

Standards: 1.2, 1.3, 3.1

Suggestions: Review the task and the four-step approach with students. Review the rubric with the class (see *Assessment* below) to explain how you will grade the performance task. Before students begin, direct their attention to the *Estrategia*. Then ask a volunteer to read the *Modelo* in Step 2. Ask students if they think the speaker's purpose is evident in this sample speech introduction. Tell them that they should not only clarify their purpose in their own minds but make it clear to their audience as well by stating it at the beginning of their speech.

Pre-AP® Integration

- **Learning Objective:** Presentational Speaking
- **Activity:** Remind students to gather as many interesting facts about their city as possible in order to make their presentation informative and interesting. Students should focus on the presentational speaking skills used in this task such as fluency, pronunciation, and comprehensibility.
- **Pre-AP® Resource Materials:** Comprehensive guide to Pre-AP® speaking skill development,

Digital Portfolio

Make video or audio recordings of student presentations in class, or assign the Speak and Record activity so they can record their presentations online. Include the recording in their portfolios.

Additional Resources

 Technology: Online Resources
  - *Para hispanohablantes*

Assessment

Presentación oral

- **Assessment Program:** Rubrics
  Review the rubric with students. Go over the descriptions of the different levels of performance. After assessing students, help individuals understand how their performance could be improved. (See Teacher's Resource Materials for suggestions on using rubrics in assessment.)

Language Arts Connection: Expository Writing

Standards: 3.1

Have students consult models of narratives they have encountered in their Social Studies courses, including narratives they themselves may have created. Ask them to focus on how chronological order was used in those narratives and the transitions that were used to connect ideas. Have them incorporate successful organizational strategies from these models into their narrative compositions.

Presentación escrita

Standards: 1.2, 1.3, 3.1

Suggestions: Begin by explaining the criteria you will use to evaluate students' compositions. (See Step 5, *Evaluación,* in the Student Edition, and *Assessment* on the following page.)

Direct students' attention to the *Estrategia.* Ask them to share additional background information they have learned in Language Arts courses about chronological order. Use a four-column T-chart to model brainstorming and recording ideas for a personal experience narrative. Have students create a similar chart on their own paper, adding a fifth column.

Pre-AP® Integration

- **Learning Objective:** Presentational Writing
- ***Pre-AP® Resource Materials:*** Comprehensive guide to Pre-AP® writing skill development,

---

Presentación escrita

OBJECTIVES
▶ Narrate a personal experience
▶ Order facts chronologically
▶ Add details to make a story more interesting

✏ Mi experiencia con otras culturas

¿Cómo sería ir a vivir a otro país? ¿Te mudaste de país? ¿Tus padres nacieron en otro país? ¿Conservan en tu familia tradiciones de sus antepasados? ¿Conoces a alguna persona que haya nacido en otro país y esté viviendo aquí? Escribe un episodio *(episode)* autobiográfico sobre una experiencia personal, o inventa una historia. Puedes relatar cómo te sentiste cuando llegaste al país, qué piensas de la integración con otras culturas o qué tradiciones conserva tu familia.

1 Antes de escribir Piensa en ideas para tu episodio y hazte estas preguntas:
- ¿Con qué claridad recuerdo o me imagino la experiencia?
- ¿Estoy listo(a) para compartirla con otros?
- ¿Qué aprendí o aprendería de la experiencia?

Ordena tus ideas completando una tabla como esta.

Estrategia

Chronological ordering Putting events in chronological order means listing them in the order they occurred. This usually means starting with the first event and continuing to the last. You can also use reverse chronological order if it's more appropriate for the story you are telling. Remember to use signal words that indicate chronological order, like *primero, luego, después, segundo, finalmente, por último.*

Personajes	Lo que sucedió	Época	Lugar	Pensamientos/Sentimientos
yo, mamá, papá, abuela	mudarnos a Estados Unidos	cinco años atrás	Nueva York	• triste por dejar a mis amigos • nervioso por ir a un país desconocido

2 Borrador Al escribir el borrador, ordena tus ideas lógicamente para que el relato sea fácil de leer. Añade todos los detalles necesarios e incluye tus preferencias y recomendaciones. Recuerda usar expresiones apropiadas. Escribe en un estilo formal y apropiado para tu audiencia.

Modelo

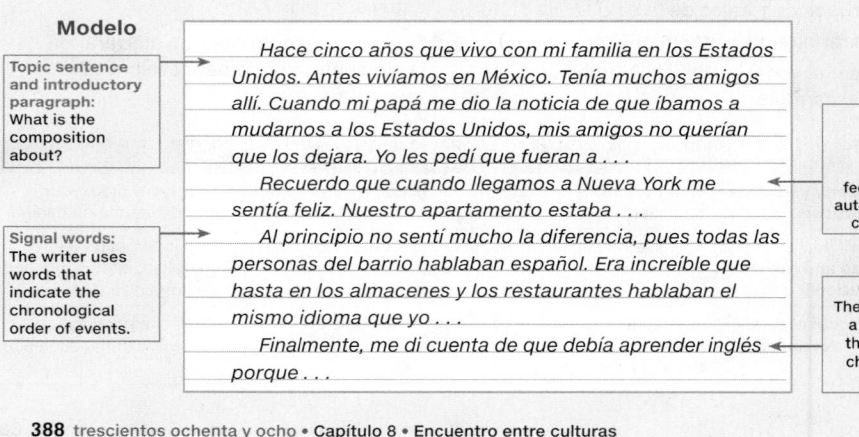

Topic sentence and introductory paragraph: What is the composition about?

> Hace cinco años que vivo con mi familia en los Estados Unidos. Antes vivíamos en México. Tenía muchos amigos allí. Cuando mi papá me dio la noticia de que íbamos a mudarnos a los Estados Unidos, mis amigos no querían que los dejara. Yo les pedí que fueran a . . .

Details: The writer expresses his or her feelings in the autobiographic composition.

> Recuerdo que cuando llegamos a Nueva York me sentía feliz. Nuestro apartamento estaba . . .

Signal words: The writer uses words that indicate the chronological order of events.

> Al principio no sentí mucho la diferencia, pues todas las personas del barrio hablaban español. Era increíble que hasta en los almacenes y los restaurantes hablaban el mismo idioma que yo . . .

Conclusion: The writer uses a signal word that indicates chronological order.

> Finalmente, me di cuenta de que debía aprender inglés porque . . .

Differentiated Instruction

Heritage Speakers

Ask willing students to serve as interviewees for other students. Encourage them to share their own experiences or those of family members. Have the interviewers show their questions to you first, and remind all participants to conduct these personal interviews with respect and consideration.

Advanced Learners

Invite students to write a short story or dramatic scene. Their story or scene should convey the emotional impact that arises from an encounter between two cultures. Encourage students to limit the number of characters in their story or scene to two or three.

Go **Online** to practice

PEARSON
realize™

PearsonSchool.com/Autentico

WRITING

3 **Redacción/Revisión** Después de escribir el primer borrador, trabaja con otro(a) estudiante para intercambiar los trabajos y leerlos. Luego, hagan sugerencias para mejorar sus composiciones.

Haz lo siguiente: Subraya con una línea los verbos en pretérito o en imperfecto y con dos líneas los verbos en imperfecto del subjuntivo.

• ¿Siguieron el plan de la tabla que hicieron?
• ¿Organizaron la información en orden cronológico?
• ¿Están empleados correctamente el pretérito, el imperfecto y el imperfecto del subjuntivo?

> *Cuando mi papá me dio la noticia de que íbamos*
>
> *a mudarnos a los Estados Unidos, mis amigos*
>
> *   dejara   pedí*
> *no querían que los deje. Yo les pediré que*
>
> *fueran a . . .*

4 **Publicación** Antes de escribir la versión final, lee de nuevo tu borrador y repasa los siguientes puntos:
• ¿Incluí detalles para expresar mis preferencias y recomendaciones?
• ¿Estoy relatando un episodio interesante?
• ¿Refleja la integración con otras culturas?

Después de revisar el borrador, escribe en limpio tu composición.

5 **Evaluación** Se utilizará la siguiente rúbrica para evaluar tu presentación.

Rubric	Score 1	Score 3	Score 5
Completion of task	Your idea is not stated or is unclear. There is little or no development of it.	Your main idea is hinted at, but your development of it is weak.	Your main idea is clear and interestingly developed.
Use of chronological order and transitions	You present too few events and use no transitions.	Some of your events are out of order or lacking helpful transitions.	You sequence events and use effective transitions.
Sentence structure/ grammar, spelling, mechanics	Sentences run on or are fragmented. You make many grammar, spelling, and/or mechanics errors.	You use sentences consistently. You make some grammar, spelling, and/or mechanics errors.	Your sentence structure is correct and varied. You make few grammar, spelling, and/or mechanics errors.

Suggestions (Cont'd): Once students have a rough draft ready, read through the model on this page together. Help them see how information from the chart on p. 388 was incorporated into this draft and to note transitions that were used. Ask them to identify uses of the imperfect subjunctive. Encourage them to work toward a similar level of organization, detail, and language use, even if they have chosen a different chronological order for their own personal experience narratives.

For Step 3, encourage students to focus on sentence structure, transitions, and use of the imperfect subjunctive. Have them follow the suggestions shown.

Evaluation

Steps 4 and 5 overlap. Students will need evaluation by you, their peers, or self-evaluation to fine-tune and polish their drafts.

Digital Portfolio

Keep students' final drafts in their portfolios as a writing sample.

Additional Resources

📶 **Technology: Online Resources**
• *Para hispanohablantes*

Assessment

Presentación escrita
• **Assessment Program:** Rubrics
Review the rubric with students. Go over the descriptions of the different levels of performance. After assessing students, help individuals understand how their performance could be improved. (See Teacher's Resource Materials for suggestions on using rubrics in assessment.)

Enrich Your Teaching

21st Century Skills

Creativity and Innovation Students will use their written language for the purpose of narrating a personal cross-cultural experience. Have them think of creative ways to express their personal reactions to the experience. How did they feel? What was their first reaction? What did they learn from the experience? They can also include the reaction of others in their narration.

Lectura

Standards: 1.2, 2.1, 2.2, 3.1, 3.2, 5.2

 Technology: Mapa global interactivo, Actividad 9 Discover the Museo de Antropología in Mexico City.

Suggestions

Pre-reading: Before reading, direct students' attention to the *Al leer* section. Have them copy the graphic organizer from p. 393 and make sure they understand how they will use it. If necessary, use a four-column T-chart to model setting up a similar chart, leaving one of the columns empty. Explain that **Antes** refers to the point at which the story begins or before, and **Ahora** refers to the end of the story. Point out the relationship between the five questions in *Al leer* and the information in the left column of the chart. Also refer them to the *Estrategia.* Remind them to follow the suggestions there and to read the selection the first time without stopping.

Reading: Allow students time to read the entire selection on their own silently. You might assign this task for homework. This will allow you to capitalize on class time to read it again together with students. When reading together, pause frequently to address comprehension issues they may have and to allow them to fill in their **Cambios en la narración** charts from p. 393. Here are some possible comprehension issues on this page for which you can provide some guidance:

- Explain that the first, italicized paragraph is a summary. It is important to understand this summary of who the characters Daniel and Chalchi are in order to follow the rest of the story.
- *¿En qué tiempo está la narración del cuento, en el presente o en el pasado? (el presente)*
- *¿Daniel se da cuenta de qué cambios en su situación mientras se despierta? (Su ropa y su cama han cambiado.)*
- *¿A quién se parece la mujer que está llamando a Daniel? (Se parece a su novia Chalchi.)*
- *¿Qué nombre es una forma corta de Chalchiunenetl? (Chalchi)*

Lectura

OBJECTIVES
- ▸ Read and understand a story based on historical facts
- ▸ Use context to guess the meaning of unfamiliar words
- ▸ Learn about Aztec heritage and borrowed words

Estrategia
Skipping and guessing When reading for pleasure, you may try to skip unfamiliar words. If the word is truly essential to the meaning of the passage, try to guess the word's meaning. If you guess correctly, the text will make sense!

Al leer

¿Alguna vez has sentido que nadie te entiende? Vas a leer un cuento de Elías Miguel Muñoz, un destacado novelista y cuentista cubano que reside en los Estados Unidos. Al leer este cuento te verás transportado(a) a otro mundo, el mundo del México antiguo, Tenochtitlán. Lee el cuento una primera vez sin pararte. No te preocupes por las palabras que no conozcas. Trata de adivinarlas. Cuando leas el cuento por segunda vez, mira los significados para ver si las entendiste. Mientras lees, presta atención a los siguientes puntos para que puedas llenar la tabla que aparece al final de la lectura:

- quiénes son los personajes
- dónde ocurre la acción, cómo cambia
- cómo cambia la relación de los personajes
- cómo reacciona el narrador
- cómo se siente el narrador al final de la lectura

Universidad Nacional Autónoma de México

390 trescientos noventa • Capítulo 8 • Encuentro entre culturas

El último sol
Fragmento adaptado

*D*aniel, el protagonista de "El último sol" *es un joven que estudia en la Ciudad de México. A Daniel le encanta compartir pasajes de la historia de México con su novia Chalchi. Un día Daniel se queda dormido y sueña con la Piedra del Sol, el calendario azteca que había visto en el Museo de Antropología. Cuando se despierta, Daniel se encuentra en un mundo diferente . . .*

"¡Tozani!" Escucho una voz de mujer que viene de lejos. "¡Tozani!" Trato de despertar, pero me pesan los párpados[1]. Siento mucho frío. "¡Tozani!" La voz se hace más fuerte. Abro por fin los ojos y veo mi cuerpo, casi desnudo. Sólo llevo un taparrabo[2] y estoy acostado en una cama que no es la mía; es un petate[3]. Busco a la dueña de la voz y por fin la veo, parada frente a mí.

—Despierta ya —me dice ella.

Habla un idioma extraño que yo, de una manera también muy extraña, puedo comprender. Sus palabras llegan a mí como filtradas por el aire frío de este cuarto.

—Despierta —repite—. Es hora de ir al lago.

La observo. Es una muchacha joven, hermosa. Tiene el cabello atado atrás, con dos trenzas[4] sobre la frente. Lleva un vestido largo, blanco; en la cintura, un amplio cincho[5] bordado. Sus ojos son de un verde intenso. Se parece tanto a Chalchi que la llamo por ese nombre, Chalchiunenetl, y ella responde . . .

—Sí. Has dormido mucho, Tozani.

—Levántate ya, esposo.

[1]eyelids [2]loincloth [3]bedroll [4]braids [5]belt

Differentiated Instruction

Students with Learning Difficulties

Students may be confused by the main character's own confusion in **El último sol.** To help clarify the plot, assign small groups of students different sections of the excerpt. Have each group choose a narrator and the necessary characters. Give students the opportunity to quickly rehearse and present their dramatic interpretation of events.

Students with Special Needs

Provide visually impaired students with partners to describe the illustrations on pp. 391 and 392. Instruct these partners to provide details regarding the setting, calendar, and dress shown. How do these images differ from what Daniel must have been used to?

¡Me ha llamado esposo! Miro a mi alrededor y descubro que no estoy en casa de mis padres. Este lugar es mucho más grande; las paredes son blancas y a lo largo de cada una hay tiestos⁶ enormes con flores de varios tipos y colores. Los muebles son escasos pero hermosos, de madera densa: un pequeño armario, una mesa baja y dos sillas. Hay una armonía total en este sitio. La puerta que da a la calle está inundada de luz.

¿Dónde estoy?

———————

Trato de ordenar mis pensamientos. Debo estar soñando. Cierro los ojos. Me golpeo la cara para despertar, ¡una, dos, tres veces! Y escucho la voz asustada de Chalchi; sus manos sujetan las mías.

—¡Tozani! —exclama—. ¡¿Qué haces?! ¿Por qué te golpeas?

No puedo contestarle. Algo en la garganta me impide hablar.

—Estabas soñando, esposo —me dice ella, mientras me acaricia.

—¿Soñando? —le pregunto, incrédulo.

—Sí. Pero ya, por fin, empiezas a despertar.

Me muevo. Respiro. Tengo los ojos muy abiertos. Sí. Estoy despierto.

—Cuando regreses del lago, comeremos —me dice Chalchi. Y se va a otro cuarto.

El lago. ¿Qué tendré que hacer en el lago? Me acuesto otra vez en el petate incómodo. ¿Cómo explicar todo esto?

⁶flowerpots

 Mapa global interactivo Explora el famoso Museo Nacional de Antropología e investiga la zona cerca del museo en Ciudad de México. Compara el museo con instituciones similares en los Estados Unidos

Capítulo 8 • trescientos noventa y uno **391**

Suggestions (Cont'd):

Reading: Here are some possible comprehension issues on this page for which you can provide some guidance:

- *En el primer párrafo, hay una palabra que significa lo mismo que harmony en inglés. Adivina qué palabra es. (armonía)*

- *¿Cuáles son los muebles que Daniel ve? (un armario, una mesa y dos sillas) ¿Estos son muchos o pocos muebles? (pocos) Entonces, ¿qué quiere decir la palabra "escasos": "muchos" o "pocos"? (pocos)*

- *¿Por qué no puede hablar Daniel? (Algo en su garganta le impide.) ¿Qué palabra en inglés significa lo mismo que "impide"? (impede)*

Starter Activity
Ask students to look at the painting on page 374 for twenty seconds. With the books closed, ask the students five true/false statements.

Teacher-to-Teacher
When having students read selections aloud, try assigning roles to volunteers. In this story, you could choose one or more narrators, who rotate reading paragraphs of the narration. Two other volunteers can assume the roles of Daniel-Tozani and Chalchiunenetl.

Suggestions (Cont'd):

Reading: Here are some possible comprehension issues on this page for which you can provide some guidance:

- *¿Cuál es la fecha, exactamente, en el calendario moderno?* (el 29 de junio de 1519)
- *Moctezuma quiere que Daniel-Tozani sea responsable de una misión importante. ¿Qué verbo usa Chalchi que significa "hacer responsable"?* (encomendar)
- *¿Qué expresión usa Chalchi para decir que los seres blancos son altos?* (son grandes de estatura)

Post-reading: Have students complete their ***Cambios en la narración*** charts, referring to the story as necessary. Ask volunteers to read aloud or paraphrase parts of the story that support their choices for the chart.

Pre-AP® Integration

- **Learning Objective:** Interpretive: Print
- **Activity:** Have students create a series of drawings to represent scenes in this story. Use the form of a *códice*. (A *códice* is a book that describes a story with colorful drawings that can be symbols or realistic scenes.) The pages of the book are not separated; each page is long and horizontal, folded like an accordion, between one scene and another. Students should include five scenes. Then, have volunteers tell their story to the class using the *códice* to illustrate it.
- ***Pre-AP® Resource Materials:*** Comprehensive guide to Pre-AP® reading skill development,

Active Classroom

Expert Groups: After the class has read the story, give each student the number 1, 2, or 3. The story is divided into three sections. Indicate to the students which section they are to focus on. Each student is to write eight questions about their section. Then divide the class into groups of three, with a number 1, 2, and 3 in each group. Have each student read his or her questions starting with the 1s. If a student needs assistance with a particular section, he or she can "ask the expert."

—¡Chalchi! —la llamo, y ella aparece ante mí.

—Estoy amasando *tlaxcalli*[7], preparando tu *atolli*[8]. ¿Por qué no te has ido al lago?

—¡Porque no sé para qué tengo que ir al lago!

—¿Estás soñando otra vez, querido mío? —ella me dice, sonriendo—. Tienes que ir al lago para bañarte, claro. Luego te vestirás de guerra para asistir al Templo Mayor. No olvides que el Reverendo Padre quiere verte.

—¿El Reverendo Padre?

—Sí. El señor emperador, Moctezuma.

—¡¿Quién?!

—Pobre de ti. Ese sueño de anoche te obsesiona.

—¿En qué año estamos, Chalchi?

—Acatl. El año 1-Caña[9], el día de 2-Casas.

Trato de recordar el calendario azteca. Un escalofrío[10] me invade el cuerpo cuando por fin descifro el significado de aquella fecha. *Acatl*, equivalente al año 1519 del calendario cristiano. El día 2-Casas, o sea, el 29, probablemente del mes de junio. Un mes antes de la entrada de Hernán Cortés en Tenochtitlán.

—Chalchi, ¿por qué quiere verme Moctezuma?

Ella me mira como diciéndome, "despierta ya, querido esposo". Exasperada y sin comprender mi pregunta, me explica:

—El reverendo señor Moctezuma, *Huey-Tlatoani* de los aztecas, quiere encomendarte una misión muy importante . . .

—¿Qué misión es?

—¿Tampoco lo recuerdas? ¡Ese sueño de anoche te ha convertido en otro hombre, Tozani!

—Mi misión tiene que ver con los "dioses blancos", ¿verdad?

—Sí. En la última reunión del consejo gobernante, nuestro emperador decidió enviar una comisión para recibir a los seres blancos, para llevarles regalos y guiarlos

hasta nuestra ciudad. El consejo te escogió a ti para encabezar la comisión.

—Esos seres no son dioses, Chalchi.

—¿Cómo lo sabes?

—Lo sé. Simplemente lo sé.

Chalchi se queda pensativa unos minutos. Luego me dice, agitada:

—Los mensajeros de Moctezuma que han visto a esos seres, cuentan que son grandes de estatura, que tienen la cara cubierta de cabello. Y algunos de ellos tienen cuatro patas enormes y dos cabezas, una de animal y otra de hombre . . .

—Son los españoles, Chalchi —le digo, sabiendo que no me entenderá. Repito: —Son los soldados de Cortés.

—Los soldados . . . ¿de quién?

—De Cortés, un hombre que viene a destruirnos.

—¡No! Moctezuma dice que son dioses. Dice que nuestro creador, Quetzalcóatl, ha regresado para recuperar su reino.

—¡Está loco el emperador!

---

[7]corn tortillas [8]corn gruel [9]1-Reed, represents a month in the Aztec calendar [10]chill

Differentiated Instruction

Heritage Speakers

Ask students to choose an interesting and/or important historical event from their heritage country. Have students briefly discuss what it would be like to return to that event. Who would they wish to be? How might their perspective on the event be different given their present-day knowledge?

Advanced Learners

Have students choose one word or expression from the story that they consider new or difficult and write it on a slip of paper. Mix the slips and have students take turns drawing one. Ask them to use background knowledge or reference materials to write a definition or explanation of the item they drew.

Interacción con la lectura

Interpretive Reading

8

1 Llena la tabla con la información del cuento.

CAMBIOS EN LA NARRACIÓN		
	Antes	Ahora
Nombre de los dos personajes principales		
Cuándo ocurre la acción		
Lugar donde ocurre la acción		
Cuál es la relación entre los personajes		
Cómo se sienten los personajes		

2 Trabaja con un grupo de estudiantes para comentar lo que escribieron en sus tablas y contestar las siguientes preguntas.

- ¿Qué le ha ocurrido a Daniel? ¿Cómo lo sabes?
- ¿Cómo es la nueva vida de Daniel?

- ¿Por qué es importante la fecha? ¿Quiénes son esos seres con dos cabezas y cuatro patas?
- ¿Qué tarea le ha encargado el emperador a Daniel?
- ¿Qué sabe Daniel que nadie más sabe?
- ¿Daniel puede cambiar lo que ocurrirá?

3 Trabaja con tu grupo para describir a los personajes en el mundo azteca: ¿Cómo se vestían? ¿Qué comían? Usa el vocabulario de la lectura.

4 Conocemos el final de la historia: Hernán Cortés conquistó el imperio Azteca. ¿Qué crees que hizo Daniel? ¿Trató de prevenir *(warn)* a los demás? ¿Trató de parar a los españoles? Comenta tus ideas con tus compañeros.

CULTURA ▸ México

La herencia azteca Aunque el mundo de los aztecas desapareció con la llegada de Hernán Cortés en 1519, en México todavía se siente la herencia azteca. En México todavía usan petates para acostarse en el campo y tanto los niños como los adultos toman atole. Además, en todo el mundo se usan las palabras tomate, chocolate, chile, coyote. Las otras lenguas americanas de Norteamérica, el Caribe y Sudamérica también han contribuido con palabras que se usan hoy en todo el mundo: *caimán, canoa, caribú, cóndor, gaucho, huracán, iglú, iguana, jaguar, maíz, mocasín, papaya, poncho, puma.* Generalmente, estas palabras se refieren a objetos que se desconocían en Europa antes del descubrimiento de América.

- ¿Conoces más palabras como éstas?
- ¿Qué tipos de palabras pasan de una lengua a otra? ¿Por qué?
- ¿Tú usas palabras nuevas o distintas a las que usan los demás? ¿De dónde vienen? ¿Por qué las usas?

Capítulo 8 • trescientos noventa y tres 393

Interacción con la lectura

Standards: 1.1, 1.2, 3.1

Suggestions: Explain that the last piece of information in the chart in Step 1, ***Cómo se siente el personaje,*** refers to Daniel-Tozani.

Answers:

Step 1
Daniel/Tozani; Chalchi/Chalchiunenetl
hoy en día/en el año 1519
Ciudad de México/Tenochtitlán
novios/esposos
Answers for how Daniel-Tozani feels will vary.

Step 2
- Daniel se ha despertado en otro mundo. En la introducción es un joven de la Ciudad de México de hoy en día. De repente se encuentra en el mundo precolonial de los aztecas.
- Su vida es muy distinta a la vida de un joven azteca de hace 500 años.
- Es una fecha importante porque es un mes antes de la llegada de los europeos. Son soldados españoles montados a caballo.
- El emperador ha encargado a Daniel con la tarea de recibir a los europeos.
- Daniel sabe que los seres blancos no son dioses sino los españoles.
- Answers will vary.

Steps 3–4
Answers will vary.

CULTURA ◂

Standards: 1.1, 1.2, 2.1, 2.2, 3.1

Suggestions: After students have read the information silently, ask them to work in pairs or small groups and develop lists of other words borrowed from indigenous American languages and used in either English or Spanish. Remind them of the many place names in the United States that come from indigenous languages. Encourage them to find out what some of these names mean in their original languages.

Answers will vary.

Additional Resources

 Technology: Online Resources
- Guided, Writing, Reading
- *Para hispanohablantes*
- Cultural Reading Activity

Print
- Guided WB pp. 266–267
- Literacy Skills

Enrich Your Teaching

Culture Note

Today maize is the third most planted field crop in the world (first and second being wheat and rice). Maize is actually a domesticated grass first cultivated and developed by the Aztecs. A chief staple of their diet, maize also played an important religious role. Of the Aztecs' many gods, **Xilonen** was the god of the "young maize ear." The name maize, however, is not an indigenous word. It's thought to have evolved from Columbus' entourage encountering Tahino people, and their **mahis,** which means "source of life." **Mahis** developed into the word **maíz.**

Interpret Authentic Resources

Auténtico

Standards: 1.2

Resources: Authentic Resources Wkbk, Cap. 8
Authentic Resources: Cap. 8: Videoscript
AP®Theme: *Las identidades personales y públicas: La identidad nacional y la identidad étnica*

Antes de ver

Discuss the video still with students. Guide them to conclude that it depicts a group of children with indigenous attire. Then refer students to the *Estrategia.* Tell them that by paraphrasing the main idea, details and theme they will get a better grasp of the concepts presented. Then review the key vocabulary with the class.

Technology: Ve el video

Before starting the video, direct students' attention to the *Mientras ves* activity. Have them complete the activity page from the Authentic Resources Workbook.

Play the video withouth pausing, asking students to focus on the visuals and the text that appear on the screen. Replay the video, stopping as necessary for students to paraphrase what is being said in each section. Show the video a final time without pausing.

Haz las actividades

Mientras ves

Standards: 1.2

Suggestions: Tell students that at the beginning of the video they will hear a song in an indigenous language. As they continue watching, guide them to infer the meaning of phrases they hear by paying special attention to the visuals and the text.

Answers may vary:

- tener una identidad
- educación intercultural bilingüe
- sabiduría ancestral
- mostrar valores mapuches
- enseñar tradición
- escuchar, aprender

Auténtico

Partnered with IDB

Chile y la diversidad

Antes de ver

Usa la estrategia: Parafrasear

Mira la imagen. ¿Cómo se relaciona con el tema de este capítulo? Al ver el video, haz pausas para parafrasear lo que has aprendido. Recuerda que no es necesario entender todas las palabras para entender la idea. Toma notas de los comentarios importantes y lee el texto que sale en la pantalla.

Lee el vocabulario clave

fortalecer = to strengthen
saberes ancestrales = ancestral knowledge
sabiduría = wisdom
ruca = Mapuche hut
mapundungu = Mapuche language
raíces = roots

▶ Ve el video

¿Qué crees que se puede hacer para que los indígenas de un país no se sientan excluidos de la sociedad moderna? ¿Y qué se puede hacer para que toda la sociedad conozca y aprecie mejor las tradiciones indígenas?

Ve a **PearsonSchool.com/Autentico** para ver el video **Chile acepta la diversidad.** Conocerás un programa de integración para los mapuches, un grupo de indígenas que viven en algunas regiones de América del Sur.

Haz las actividades

Mientras ves Algunas partes del video te pueden parecer confusas por el acento con el que hablan las personas. Trata de concentrarte en lo que entiendes y usa las imágenes y el texto escrito como ayuda. A medida que ves el video, trata de identificar a cada una de las personas de la siguiente lista y anota dos o tres palabras claves *(key words)* que te recuerden lo que dice o hace esa persona:

- el niño mapuche
- la profesora (educadora) joven
- el coordinador general
- la profesora vieja
- el director de la escuela
- la niña mapuche

Differentiated Instruction

Heritage Speakers

Invite students to do some research on indigenous languages from their heritage country. Encourage them to share their findings with the class using maps, video clips, illustrations and other aids. You may want to create an exhibit entitled *Lenguas indígenas* with the students' contributions.

Students with Learning Difficulties

To help students with paraphrasing, provide them with a graphic organizer such as a concept web. Encourage them to write the main idea in the center of the web and the details in the surrounding ovals. They can then use the web to answer question 1 on page 395.

Nutram
Kallfü
Wenüy
Dungü

Fücha
Rali
Antü
Fachantü

Después de ver

Standards: 1.2, 1.3, 4.2

Suggestions: To assist students with the questions, you may want to provide a script of some speech that is unclear in the video, specially the part of the older educator. Ask volunteers to respond to each question to evaluate overall understanding. Answers may vary based on their comprehension.

Answers:

1. diversidad cultural; en Chile hay un programa para integrar a los mapuches; se da a conocer la sabiduría mapuche, se integra a los mapuche.
2. fortalece la cultura, la lengua y las tradiciones indígenas
3. con su sabiduría ancestral
4. que aprendan a valorar su cultura e identidad

For more Authentic Resources: Assign the Authentic Resources Workbook activities for homework, so that students can play the video on their own and complete the workbook activities at their own pace.

Pre-AP® Integration

Resources: Authentic Resources, Wkbk, Cap. 8
Authentic Resources: Cap. 8: Videoscript
Suggestions: Before completing the Pre-AP® activity, have students go to the workbook and complete the worksheets for the additional resources.

Comparación cultural

Suggestions: Ask students to provide specific examples of the challenges faced by the indigenous cultures.

Integración

Después de ver Vuelve a ver el video una o dos veces más y después contesta estas preguntas:

1. Parafrasea el tema, la idea principal y los detalles importantes del video.

2. Según la profesora joven, ¿por qué es importante la educación intercultural bilingüe?

3. ¿Cómo pueden los indígenas contribuir a la sociedad moderna?

4. ¿Qué es lo que la profesora vieja quiere que aprendan los niños mapuche?

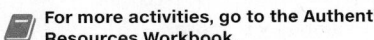 **For more activities, go to the Authentic Resources Workbook.**

Identidad étnica y vida contemporánea

Expansión Busca estos recursos en *Auténtico* en línea y contesta las preguntas.

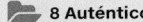 **8 Auténtico**

Integración de ideas ¿Crees que los indígenas y otros grupos étnicos pueden integrarse a la vida contemporánea sin perder su identidad étnica? ¿Por qué?

Comparación cultural Identifica un grupo de indígenas nativos de Estados Unidos y comenta los retos de vivir en medio de la sociedad moderna. Compara los retos que ese grupo tiene con los retos de los mapuches.

Enrich Your Teaching

Culture Note

The Mapuche Indians, whose name means "people of the land," are one of the few tribes in the Americas who have preserved many of their traditions. They are one of the three surviving tribes of the ancient *araucanos* who lived in Chile and Argentina before the Incas.

Using Authentic Resources

Have students create a personal vocabulary list with terms related to cultural identity, indigenous groups and assimilation.

Review Activities

Para hablar de construcciones: Ask students to work in pairs to quiz each other. Have them take turns sketching and identifying the various items.

Para hablar del descubrimiento de América: Have students work in groups to create a summary of the discovery and early contact in the Americas. Their summary should include all of the words in the category. Invite them to present their summaries orally. Have the class discuss differences and similarities between the various summaries they hear.

Para hablar del encuentro de culturas: Ask students to prepare brief oral reports about a cultural encounter of their choice, past or present. Encourage each student to base the report on his or her own cultural heritage. Their reports should include as many of the words in the category as possible. Ask students to be prepared to field questions from the audience after their report.

Verbos: Have students choose any five of the verbs and use them in the imperfect subjunctive in complex sentences. Then have students share their sentences.

Otras expresiones y palabras: Students can use these words and expressions as they go over the review activities for the other categories.

Additional Resources

 Technology: Online Resources
- Instant Check
- Integrated Performance Assessment
- *Para hispanohablantes*

Teacher Resources
- Teacher's Resource Materials: Situation Cards, p. 201, Clip Art, pp. 202–209
- **Assessment Program:** Chapter Checklist and Self-Assessment Worksheet

---

Repaso del capítulo

◀)) Vocabulario

para hablar de construcciones

el acueducto	aqueduct
el arco	arch
la arquitectura	architecture
el azulejo	tile
el balcón, *pl.* los balcones	balcony
la construcción	construction
la reja	railing, grille
la torre	tower

para hablar de la llegada a las Américas

anteriormente	before
el arma, *pl.* las armas	weapon
la batalla	battle
la colonia	colony
la conquista	conquest
el imperio	empire
el / la indígena	native
la maravilla	marvel, wonder
la misión	mission
el / la misionero(a)	missionary
la población	population
el poder	power
poderoso, -a	powerful
el reto	challenge
la riqueza	wealth
el / la soldado	soldier
la tierra	land

para hablar del encuentro de culturas

africano, -a	African
el antepasado	ancestor
el / la árabe	Arab
cristiano, -a	Christian
la descendencia	descent, ancestry
desconocido, -a	unknown
el encuentro	meeting
la época	time, era
europeo, -a	European

la guerra	war
el grupo étnico	ethnic group
la herencia	heritage
el idioma	language
la influencia	influence
el intercambio	exchange
el / la judío(a)	Jew
la lengua	language
la mercancía	merchandise
la mezcla	mix
el musulmán, la musulmana	Muslim
el / la romano(a)	Roman
la raza	race
el resultado	result, outcome
la semejanza	similarity
la unidad	unity
la variedad	variety

verbos

adoptar	to adopt
asimilar(se)	to assimilate
componerse de	to be formed by
conquistar	to conquer
dejar huellas	to leave marks, traces
dominar	to dominate
enfrentarse	to face, to confront
establecer (zc)	to establish
expulsar	to expel
fundar(se)	to found
gobernar (ie)	to rule, to govern
integrarse	to integrate
invadir	to invade
luchar	to fight
ocupar	to occupy
rebelarse	to rebel, to revolt
reconquistar	to reconquer

otras expresiones y palabras

al llegar	upon arriving
maravilloso, -a	wonderful
único, -a	only

Differentiated Instruction

Students with Learning Difficulties

Divide students into pairs. Instruct them to use the vocabulary on p. 396 as a guide. One partner should choose a word and read it aloud. The other partner should review the chapter to locate a picture of, or reference to, that word. Have students use the information they have found to formulate a sentence using the word.

Advanced Learners

Have students assume the role of a politician, either local, national, or international. Ask them to prepare and deliver a brief message in which they suggest one or more ways to improve relations between two cultures. Tell them that their message can be created as though it were part of a longer speech.

Gramática

el condicional

Use the conditional to express what you would do or what a situation would be like.

hablar

hablaría	hablaríamos
hablarías	hablaríais
hablaría	hablarían

ser

sería	seríamos
serías	seríais
sería	serían

ir

iría	iríamos
irías	iríais
iría	irían

Verbs that are irregular in the future tense have the same irregular stems in the conditional.

tener

tendría	tendríamos
tendrías	tendríais
tendría	tendrían

future and conditional stems of other irregular verbs:

decir	dir-	poder	podr-	saber	sabr-
haber	habr-	poner	pondr-	salir	saldr-
hacer	har-	querer	querr-	venir	vendr-

el imperfecto del subjuntivo

Use the subjunctive to say what one person asks, hopes, tells, insists, or requires someone else to do. If the main verb is in the preterite or imperfect tense, use the imperfect subjunctive.

cantar

cantara	cantáramos
cantaras	cantarais
cantara	cantaran

aprender

aprendiera	aprendiéramos
aprendieras	aprendierais
aprendiera	aprendieran

vivir

viviera	viviéramos
vivieras	vivierais
viviera	vivieran

el imperfecto del subjuntivo con *si*

Use the imperfect subjunctive after *si* when a situation is unlikely, impossible, or not true. Use the conditional in the main clause.

Si hablaras más, **tendrías** muchos amigos.
Si Marcos **no fuera** tan travieso, lo **llevaría** de paseo.

After *como si* you always use the imperfect subjunctive.

Ella se sentía **como si estuviera** en un lugar desconocido.

El condicional: Tell students that Mateo is a very popular boy. Everyone always needs to talk to him or has something to do with him. Ask students to think of at least two questions concerning Mateo that they might ask a friend, such as: *¿Hablarás con Mateo hoy?* The friend responds using the conditional, saying that he or she would do that thing, but Mateo is not to be found: *Le hablaría, pero no lo encuentro.* Another example might be: *¿Harás tu tarea con Mateo hoy? La haria con él, pero no lo encuentro.* Have partners take turns asking and answering each other's questions.

El imperfecto del subjuntivo: Ask students to think of five wishes they have always had. On the board write the sentence starter **Siempre he querido que....** Have students use the sentence starter five times to write their wishes: *Siempre he querido que el año escolar no fuera tan largo.*

El imperfecto del subjuntivo con si: Challenge students to write comparisons using complex sentences with **como si:** *Entró en el cuarto como si fuera una reina.* Encourage them to make their comparisons humorous: *Estaba tan alegre como si fuera una tortuga con patines.*

Digital Portfolio

Invite students to review the activities they completed in this chapter, including written reports, posters or other visuals, recordings of oral presentations, and other projects. Have them select one or two items that they feel best demonstrate their achievements in Spanish. Include these products in students' portfolios. Have them include this with the Chapter Checklist and Self-Assessment Worksheet.

Additional Resources

 Technology: *¡Pura vida!* is a storyline video that is independent of chapter content and an ideal support for expanding listening skills. The 14 episodes are available within **Realize.** Student activities and Teacher support are also assignable within **Realize.**

Enrich Your Teaching

Teacher-to-Teacher

Have students create a practice test covering the vocabulary and grammar structures. Encourage them to use multiple choice, true/false, or short answer questions. Have them exchange tests with a partner or compile the questions and answer them in a game show format.

21st Century Skills

ICT (Information, Communications and Technology) Literacy Remind students of the various digital tools available in **Realize** to help them monitor their own understanding and learning needs as they prepare for chapter tests, such as the online tutorials with comprehension check exercises, interactive puzzles, and flashcards.

Performance Tasks

Standards: 1.1, 1.2, 1.3, 3.1

Student Resource: *Para hispanohablantes*
Teacher Resources: Teacher's Resource Materials: Audio Script, Technology: Audio: Cap. 8

1. Vocabulario

Suggestions: Encourage students to review the vocabulary from the *Vocabulario en contexto* sections on pp. 358–359 and 370–371 before they complete the activity.

Answers:

1. b	**5.** d
2. c	**6.** d
3. b	**7.** b
4. c	**8.** c

2. Gramática

Suggestions: Remind students of the main points of the grammar presentations in *Capítulo* 8:

- the conditional
- the imperfect subjunctive
- the imperfect subjunctive with *si*

Answers:

1. c	**5.** a
2. b	**6.** b
3. c	**7.** a
4. a	**8.** d

Additional Resources

 Technology: Online Resources
- Instant Check
- *Para hispanohablantes*

Print
- Core WB pp. 117–118

Preparación para el examen

1 Vocabulario Escribe la letra de la palabra o expresión que mejor complete cada frase. Escribe tus respuestas en una hoja aparte.

1. Un ejemplo de un _____ fue el pueblo romano, porque tuvo tanto poder que pudo decidir el futuro de otros pueblos.
   a. misionero c. arte
   b. imperio d. arma

2. Empezó un intercambio de _____ entre Europa y las Américas.
   a. riquezas c. mercancías
   b. banderas d. libertad

3. Cuando un país invade a otro país y se queda allí por muchos años, decimos que lo _____.
   a. expulsa c. lucha
   b. ocupa d. permite

4. Como resultado de la mezcla de españoles, indígenas y africanos hay una gran _____ de culturas en América.
   a. batalla c. variedad
   b. reja d. mercancía

5. La Mezquita de Córdoba es un ejemplo de la arquitectura árabe porque tiene muchos _____, igual que la Alhambra, en Granada.
   a. caballos c. budistas
   b. retos d. arcos

6. Los misioneros tenían opiniones diferentes sobre _____ de los españoles en la vida de los indígenas.
   a. la semejanza c. la arquitectura
   b. el azulejo d. la influencia

7. España era un imperio _____ en la época de la conquista de América.
   a. único c. débil
   b. poderoso d. africano

8. Cuando los cristianos reconquistaron Sevilla, muchos árabes se habían _____ con los españoles.
   a. rebelado c. asimilado
   b. reconquistado d. expulsado

2 Gramática Escribe la letra de la palabra o expresión que mejor complete cada frase. Escribe tus respuestas en una hoja aparte.

1. Yo _____ con Luisa por teléfono todos los días si tuviera tiempo, pero estoy muy ocupada.
   a. hablo c. hablaría
   b. he hablado d. hablaba

2. Nosotros _____ al balcón, pero hace mucho frío y está lloviendo.
   a. saldremos c. salíamos
   b. saldríamos d. saldrían

3. El arquitecto le dijo al dueño de la casa que _____ el azulejo de color amarillo porque era mejor.
   a. compré c. comprara
   b. compró d. compras

4. El rey de España lo miró como si _____ que estaba mintiendo.
   a. creyera c. creía
   b. crea d. creerá

5. La madre le dijo al niño que _____ a la escuela después de comprar la comida.
   a. vendría c. vinieron
   b. vienen d. viene

6. Si _____ todas tus riquezas, te regalaría mis caballos, le dijo el español al indígena.
   a. me das c. me diste
   b. me dieras d. me dieron

7. Aprenderíamos otros idiomas, como el chino, si _____ la oportunidad de estudiarlos en la escuela.
   a. tuviéramos c. tuvieran
   b. tuvimos d. tuvieras

8. Los misioneros querían que los indígenas _____ su religión.
   a. adoptáramos c. adoptamos
   b. adoptaron d. adoptaran

Differentiated Instruction

Heritage Speakers

Ask students to identify a writing skill that they would like to improve. Examples might include spelling, punctuation, or organization. Have students create a draft of an essay based on the topic on p. 399. Then, have them revise their drafts, focusing on the skill they are trying to improve.

Students with Learning Difficulties

Direct students to focus on the verb(s) in each example of the *Gramática* review. Help them establish the time frame of each sentence. Then, instruct students to choose the verb form that corresponds to both the time frame and meaning of the sentence.

Assessment 8

En el examen vas a . . .	Éstas son las tareas de práctica que te pueden ser útiles para el examen . . .	Para repasar, ve a tu libro de texto impreso o digital . . .
Interpretive		
❸ ESCUCHAR Yo puedo escuchar y comprender la descripción de una visita a un pueblo indígena	La visitante describe su visita a un pueblo. Parafrasea la idea principal, el tema y los detalles más importantes del audio.	**pp. 358–361** *Vocabulario en contexto 1* **p. 361** Videohistoria **p. 371** Actividad 17 **pp. 394–395** *Auténtico*
Interpersonal		
❹ HABLAR Yo puedo presentar una visita guiada para conocer una ciudad	Escoge una ciudad que te guste. Imagina que le hablas de esta ciudad a un recién llegado. Tu amigo(a) te pregunta sobre lo que tiene hacer en la ciudad. Responde y menciona (a) los edificios históricos, (b) las culturas y religiones, (c) una breve historia de la ciudad y (d) lugares donde los jóvenes se divierten.	**p. 364** Actividad 8 **p. 368** Actividad 14 **p. 387** *Presentación oral*
Interpretive		
❺ LEER Yo puedo leer y comprender un cuento	Lee este párrafo sobre las aventuras de un indígena azteca y di (a) ¿En qué ciudad crees que se despierta Maco? ¿En qué época sería? (b) ¿Qué lengua habla la gente? (c) ¿Crees que es un sueño o es la realidad? *Un día, Maco, un joven indígena, cerró sus ojos y cuando los abrió se vio en medio de una ciudad muy diferente a la que habitaba. La gente era alta con los cabellos claros. Llevaban ropas largas y zapatos. Hablaban una lengua familiar, parecida a la de las personas que habían llegado a su tierra hacía poco tiempo. La gente lo miraba, pero nadie se paraba a hablarle...*	**pp. 390–393** *Lectura*
Presentational		
❻ ESCRIBIR Yo puedo escribir una reseña sobre la herencia cultural	Escribe una reseña sobre qué cosas pueden hacer las familias para mantener sus raíces culturales y las tradiciones de sus antepasados. Sugiere qué pueden hacer para mantener el idioma, las comidas y otras tradiciones familiares.	**p. 365** Actividad 9 **p. 366** Actividad 11 **pp. 388–389** *Presentación escrita*
Comparisons		
❼ COMPARAR Yo puedo comparar ejemplos de intercambio cultural en el mundo de hoy y decir si son positivos o no	Da un ejemplo de un intercambio entre culturas en el mundo de hoy en día. Di por qué crees que ese intercambio es positivo o crea conflictos. ¿Crees que ayuda a que las personas se integren o no?	**p. 364** Actividad 8 **p. 376** Actividad 24 **pp. 384–385** *Puente a la cultura*

Capítulo 8 • trescientos noventa y nueve **399**

Differentiated Assessment

Core Assessment
- Technology: Audio: Cap. 8
- ExamView: Chapter Test, Test Banks A and B

Advanced/Pre-AP®
- ExamView: Pre-AP® Test Bank
- Pre-AP® Resource Materials

Extra Support
- Alternate Assessment Program: Examen del capítulo 8
- Technology: Audio: Cap. 8

Heritage Speakers
- Assessment Program: Para hispanohablantes: Examen del capítulo 8
- ExamView: Heritage Speaker Test Bank

3. Escuchar

Suggestions: Use the audio or read from the script.

🔊 **Technology: Audio**

Script:

Llegamos a Valle de Bravo el viernes por la tarde. El pueblo tiene una arquitectura que es resultado de la influencia española durante la colonia. En las calles hay casas con enormes rejas y balcones. La población es principalmente indígena y el pueblo es famoso por su maravillosa artesanía. En la oficina de turismo, nos sugirieron que fuéramos al mercado. ¡Nunca he visto tantas mercancías juntas en un lugar! No tenía nada en común con lo que yo había visto antes. Vendían hamacas, joyas de plata y cerámica y también canoas. La semejanza de ese mercado con el que describió Hernán Cortés en sus Cartas de relación era impresionante. Los vestidos de las mujeres eran de hermosos colores y ellas conversaban muy animadas. Era fácil imaginar a sus antepasados haciendo lo mismo.

Answers: Wording of answers will vary.
- **a.** Es famoso por su maravillosa artesanía. Dice que la arquitectura es un resultado de la influencia española durante la colonia.
- **b.** Le impresiona más la variedad de las mercancías. El mercado le recuerda de lo que describió Hernán Cortés en sus Cartas de relación.
- **c.** Hamacas, joyas de plata y cerámica y canoas.
- **d.** Lo compara con un mercado de hace siglos.

4. Hablar

Standards: 1.1

Suggestions: Encourage students to combine ideas into complex sentences as they describe their city.
Answers will vary.

5. Leer

Suggestions: Tell students to refer to pp. 358–361 and 370–373 for vocabulary review.
Answers:
- **a.** Cities named should be major Spanish cities. Es la época moderna.
- **b.** La gente habla español.
- **c.** Answers will vary between *sueño* and *realidad*.

6. Escribir

Suggestions: Encourage students to work in pairs or groups to gather ideas for their *reseñas.*
Answers will vary.

7. Comparar

Suggestions: Ask students to consider how their thoughts about cultural fusion have changed.
Answers will vary.

Chapter Support

Bulletin Boards

Theme: Animales en peligro de extinción

Ask students to cut out, copy, or download photos or pictures of animals in danger of extinction. Place photos around a world map with leader lines from animals to their habitats. Add captions explaining why these animals are in danger of extinction.

Game

En las noticias

Play this game with the entire class to review *Capítulo 9* vocabulary.

Materials: index cards, pen

Rules:

1. On index cards, write vocabulary words, expressions, and verbs from *Capítulo 9*. Place the cards in a box.
2. Have a student write a word in an index card and begin a story for a news article, using that word in a sentence. Write the sentence on the board. Ask the class to make any corrections.
3. Call on another volunteer to pick a card and to continue the story, doing the same thing until the class feels the story has reached a logical conclusion. If every student has not had the chance to contribute, begin a second story.

   Student 1: (drew **capa de ozono**) *El problema del agujero en la capa de ozono es grave.*

   Student 2: (drew **disminuir**) *Si no disminuimos el uso de aerosoles, podrían producirse más agujeros en la capa de ozono.*

Hands-on Culture

Art: Un adorno móvil de mariposas

Mobiles of butterflies are a decoration in homes throughout the Spanish-speaking world.

Materials: construction paper, pencil, scissors, hole punch, pipe cleaners, thread, large upholstery needle, 3 twigs (about 1 ft long each), markers or crayons, glitter glue, etc.

1. Fold a piece of construction paper in half and cut along the fold. (This will make 2 butterflies.) You will need to make 4 or more butterflies for the mobile.
2. Fold one of these pieces of paper in half. Draw half of a butterfly along the fold line.
3. Fold a small piece of black or brown paper in half. Draw the body and head of a butterfly on it. Make it the same length as your butterfly. Cut them out. Glue a body on each side of your butterfly.
4. Using a hole punch, make two holes in the butterfly's head. Cut a pipe cleaner in half. Thread it through the holes in the butterfly's head as antennae.
5. Decorate both sides of your butterfly using crayons, markers, glitter, or glitter glue.
6. Using a needle, pull a short length of knotted thread through the balancing point of the butterfly (near its middle). Tie the other end of the thread to the end of a twig.
7. On the other end of the twig, attach another butterfly in the same way.
8. Tie a thread to the middle of this twig and attach it to the end of another twig. Attach a butterfly to the end of this twig.
9. Using a short length of thread, attach what you've made to the end of another twig. Attach a butterfly to the other end of this twig.
10. Tie a longer length of thread to the top twig. If you want the twigs to remain horizontal, tie the thread where the mobile will balance.

21st Century Skills

Look for tips throughout Chapter 9 to enrich your teaching by integrating 21st Century Skills. Suggestions for the Project-Based Learning and Culture follow below.

Project-Based Learning

Modify the project with these suggestions:

Media Literacy Encourage students to go online and research national parks in Central or South America. The handout "Search for Information on the Internet" will help them find reliable sources to help them choose a park and find the information and images to use in their brochure.

Creativity and Innovation Have students be as creative as possible with the layout of their brochure. Ask students to come up with different ways to arrange and label the information, such as flora and fauna, conservation programs, activities to do, things to see, etc.

Critical Thinking and Problem Solving Discuss with students the purpose of a brochure. What is the best media to express their message and attract more visitors to the national park? Who is the target audience? What words, expressions, or images would they use to interest potential visitors? What other media might they use?

Chapter Culture

Social and Cross-Cultural Skills Direct students to review the *Cultura* notes on pages 412 and 425. Have them compare with a partner their opinions about the environmental problems in Latin America and the U.S. Promote a discussion about cultural perspectives regarding pollution, endangered animals, or natural environmental disasters.

▶ **Technology: Videodocumentario** View *Exploremos la naturaleza fascinante* online with the class to learn more about how several Latin American countries are balancing economic needs and environmental protection.

Project-Based Learning

Visita un parque nacional

Overview: Students create a digital or print brochure for a national park in Central or South America featuring the flora and fauna of the area, as well as conservation programs sponsored by the park. They should include illustrations of some species found in the area accompanied by a brief description of each. Illustrations can be obtained from magazines, travel brochures, or downloaded from the Web. Students then give an oral presentation of their brochure describing the park and trying to convince their listeners to support the conservation program sponsored by the park.

Resources: digital or print photos, image editing and page layout software, and/or construction paper, magazines, travel brochures, scissors, glue, colored pencils and markers

Sequence: (suggestions for when to do each step appear throughout the chapters)

Step 1. Review instructions so students know what is expected of them. Share the rubric with the class.

Step 2. Students submit a rough sketch of their brochure. Return the sketches with your suggestions. For vocabulary and grammar practice, ask students to work in pairs and present their sketches to each other.

Step 3. Students create layouts. Encourage students to work in pencil first and to try different arrangements before writing the contents of the brochure.

Step 4. Students submit a draft of their brochure. Note your corrections and suggestions, then return the drafts to students.

Step 5. Students complete and present their brochure to the class, trying to convince their fellow students to support the conservation program sponsored by the park.

Options

1. Students create a poster for the national park instead of a brochure.
2. Students write an article for the school newspaper about a national park.

Assessment

Here is a detailed rubric for assessing this project:

Chapter 9 Project: *Visita un parque nacional*

Rubric	Score 1	Score 3	Score 5
Your evidence of planning	You provide no written draft or page layout.	Your draft and layout are provided, but not corrected.	You show evidence of corrected draft and layout.
Your use of illustrations	You include no photos or visuals.	You include photos or visuals, but your layout is disorganized.	Your brochure is easy to read, complete, and accurate.
Your presentation	You include little of the required information.	You include some of the required information. You attempted to convince.	You include all of the required information. You convinced us to support the program.

AT A GLANCE

Objectives

- Listen and read about pollution and other environmental issues
- Talk and write about environmental problems and solutions
- Make suggestions to protect the environment
- Understand the causes of environmental issues in Latin America
- Compare an environmental problem in Latin America with one in the U.S.
- Demonstrate understanding of a culturally authentic audio recording about reducing trash production

Vocabulary

- Pollution
- Natural resources
- Animals
- The environment

Grammar

- Conjunctions used with the subjunctive and the indicative tenses
- Relative pronouns *que, quien, lo que*

Culture

- Diego Rivera, p. 404
- Restrictions on driving cars, p. 412
- Punta Arenas, Chile, p. 422
- National Park of Guanacaste, Costa Rica, p. 423
- Magellanic penguins, p. 425
- Tropical forest of Costa Rica, p. 426
- The Vaquita porpoise
- Galapagos Islands, pp. 432–433
- Monarch Butterfly Festival, p. 441

A ver si recuerdas...

- Recycling and community
- Places and natural phenomena
- Verbs like *gustar*
- Uses of the definite article

Recycle

- Syllabication

Authentic Resources

- **Auténtico:** ¿Cuánta basura generas?, pp. 442–443

RESOURCES

	FOR THE STUDENT	DIGITAL	PRINT	FOR THE TEACHER	DIGITAL	PRINT
A ver si recuerdas pp. 400–403						
Review	*A ver si recuerdas* with Remediation	•		*A ver si recuerdas* with Remediation	•	
	Guided WB, pp. 268–271	•	•	Teacher's Edition, pp. 400–403	•	•
	Core WB, pp. 119–120	•	•			
	Para hispanohablantes	•				
Introducción pp. 404–405						
Present	Student Edition, pp. 404–405	•	•	Teacher's Edition, pp. 404–405	•	•
	DK Reference Atlas	•		Teacher's Resource Materials	•	
	Videonovela: *¡Pura vida!*	•				
	¡Pura vida! Video Activities	•				
	Para hispanohablantes	•				
Vocabulario en contexto pp. 406–409/420–423						
Present & Practice	Student Edition, pp. 406–409/420–423	•	•	Teacher's Edition, pp. 406–409/420–423	•	•
	Audio	•		Mapa global interactivo	•	
	Videohistoria	•				
	Flashcards	•		Teacher's Resource Materials	•	
	Instant Check	•		Vocabulary Clip Art	•	
	Guided WB, pp. 272–280/285–292	•	•	Technology: Audio	•	
	Core WB, pp. 121–122/126–127	•	•	Video Program: Videohistoria	•	
	Communication Activities	•				
	Para hispanohablantes	•				
Assess and Remediate				Pruebas 9–1, 9–5: Assessment Program, Assessment Program *Para hispanohablantes*	•	

RESOURCES

	FOR THE STUDENT	DIGITAL	PRINT	FOR THE TEACHER	DIGITAL	PRINT
Vocabulario en uso pp. 410–413/424–427						
Present & Practice	Student Edition, pp. 410–413/424–427	•	•	Interactive Whiteboard Vocabulary Activities	•	
	Instant Check	•		Teacher's Edition, pp. 410–413/424–427	•	•
	Communication Activities	•		Teacher's Resource Materials	•	
	Para hispanohablantes	•		Technology: Audio	•	
	Communicative Pair Activities	•		Mapa global interactivo	•	
				Videomodelos	•	
Assess and Remediate				Pruebas 9–2, 9–6 with Remediation	•	
				Pruebas 9–2, 9–6: Assessment Program, Assessment Program *Para hispanohablantes*	•	
Gramática pp. 414–419/428–431						
Present & Practice	Student Edition, pp. 414–419/428–431	•	•	Interactive Whiteboard Grammar Activities	•	
	Instant Check	•		Teacher's Edition, pp. 414–419/428–431	•	•
	Tutorial Video: Grammar	•		Teacher's Resource Materials	•	
	Canción de hip hop	•		Technology: Audio	•	
	Guided WB, pp. 281–284/293–294	•	•	Videomodelos	•	
	Core WB, pp. 123–125/128–130	•	•			
	Communication Activities	•				
	Para hispanohablantes	•				
	Communicative Pair Activities	•				
Assess and Remediate				Pruebas 9–3, 9–4, 9–7 with Remediation	•	
				Pruebas 9–3, 9–4, 9–7: Assessment Program, Assessment Program *Para hispanohablantes*	•	
				Examen 1, Examen 2: Vocab. y gramática	•	
Aplicación pp. 432–443						
Apply	Student Edition, pp.432–443	•	•	Teacher's Edition, pp. 432–443	•	•
	Authentic Resources Workbook	•	•	Teacher's Resource Materials	•	
	Authentic Resources	•		Video Program: Videodocumentario	•	
	Online Cultural Reading	•		Mapa global interactivo	•	
	Guided WB, pp. 295–297	•	•	Authentic Resources Lesson Plans with scripts, answer keys	•	
	Communication Activities	•				
	Para hispanohablantes	•				
	Videodocumentario	•				
Repaso del capítulo pp. 444–447						
Review	Student Edition, pp. 444–447	•	•	Teacher's Edition, pp. 444–447	•	•
	Core WB, pp. 131–132	•	•	Teacher's Resource Materials	•	
	Communication Activities	•		Technology: Audio	•	
	Para hispanohablantes	•				
	Instant Check	•				
Chapter Assessment						
Assess				Examen del capítulo 9: Assessment Program, Alternate Assessment Program, Assessment Program *Para hispanohablantes*	•	
				Technology: Audio, Cap. 9, Examen	•	
				ExamView: Test Banks A and B (questions only online) Heritage Speaker Test Bank, Pre-AP® Test Bank	•	

LESSON PLAN

DAY	Warm-up / Assess	Preview / Present / Practice / Communicate	Wrap-up / Homework Options
1	**Warm-up** (10 min.) • Return Examen del capítulo: Capítulo 8	**Repaso** (35 min.) • A ver si recuerdas . . . • Actividades 1–8	**Wrap-up and Homework Options** (5 min.) • Core Practice 9-1, 9-2
2	**Warm-up** (10 min.) • Homework check	**Chapter Opener** (10 min.) • Objectives • Arte y cultura **Vocabulario en contexto 1** (25 min.) • Presentation: Vocabulario y gramática en contexto • Actividades 1, 2 • Presentación: Videohistoria: Heroína del medio ambiente • View: Videohistoria	**Wrap-up and Homework Options** (5 min.) • Clip Art Vocabulary
3	**Warm-up** (10 min.) • Homework check	**Vocabulario en uso 1** (35 min.) • Presentation: ¿Cómo cuidas tu planeta?; Cómo proteger el medio ambiente • Actividad 3	**Wrap-up and Homework Options** (5 min.) • Core Practice 9-3, 9-4 • Actividad 4 • Prueba 9-1: Vocabulary recognition
4	**Warm-up** (10 min.) • Homework check • **Formative Assessment** (10 min.) • Prueba 9-1: Vocabulary recognition	**Vocabulario en uso 1** (25 min.) • Interactive Whiteboard Vocabulary Activities • Actividades 6, 7, 8, 9	**Wrap-up and Homework Options** (5 min.) • Actividades 5, 10 • Writing Activities • Prueba 9-2 with Remediation: Vocabulary production
5	**Warm-up** (10 min.) • Homework check • **Formative Assessment** (10 min.) • Prueba 9-2 with Remediation: Vocabulary production	**Gramática y vocabulario en uso 1** (25 min.) • Cultura • Presentation: Conjunciones que se usan con el subjuntivo y el indicativo • Interactive Whiteboard Grammar Activities • Actividades 11, 12 • Ampliación del lenguaje	**Wrap-up and Homework Options** (5 min.) • Core Practice 9-5
6	**Warm-up** (10 min.) • Actividad 13 • Homework check	**Gramática y vocabulario en uso 1** (35 min.) • Actividades 14, 15, 16 • Communicative Pair Activity • Presentation: Los pronombres relativos *que, quien* y *lo que* • Interactive Whiteboard Grammar Activities • Actividad 18	**Wrap-up and Homework Options** (5 min.) • Writing Activity • Prueba 9-3 with Remediation: Conjunciones que se usan con el subjuntivo y el indicativo
7	**Warm-up** (10 min.) • Actividad 17 • Homework check • **Formative Assessment** (10 min.) • Prueba 9-3 with Remediation: Conjunciones que se usan con el subjuntivo y el indicativo	**Gramática y vocabulario en uso 1** (25 min.) • Actividad 19 • Communicative Pair Activity	**Wrap-up and Homework Options** (5 min.) • Core Practice 9-6, 9-7 • Prueba 9-4 with Remediation: Los pronombres relativos *que, quien* y *lo que*
8	**Warm-up** (15 min.) • Writing Activity • Homework check • **Formative Assessment** (10 min.) • Prueba 9-4 with Remediation: Los pronombres relativos *que, quien* y *lo que*	**Vocabulario en contexto 2** (20 min.) • Presentation: Vocabulario y gramática en contexto • Actividades 20, 21	**Wrap-up and Homework Options** (5 min.) • Clip Art Vocabulary • Examen: Vocabulario y gramática 1
9	**Warm-up** (5 min.) • Homework check • **Summative Assessment** (30 min.) • Examen: Vocabulario y gramática 1	**Vocabulario en contexto 2** (10 min.) • Presentation: Punta Arenas • Presentation: El Parque Nacional de Guanacaste	**Wrap-up and Homework Options** (5 min.) • Actividad 22 • Core Practice 9-8, 9-9 • Prueba 9-5: Vocabulary recognition
10	**Warm-up** (10 min.) • Actividad 23 • Homework check • **Formative Assessment** (10 min.) • Prueba 9-5: Vocabulary recognition	**Vocabulario en uso 2** (25 min.) • Interactive Whiteboard Vocabulary Activities • Actividades 26, 27 • Cultura	**Wrap-up and Homework Options** (5 min.) • Actividades 24, 25 • Prueba 9-6 with Remediation: Vocabulary production

LESSON PLAN

DAY	Warm-up / Assess	Preview / Present / Practice / Communicate	Wrap-up / Homework Options
11	**Warm-up** (10 min.) • Writing Activity • Homework check • **Formative Assessment** (10 min.) • Prueba 9-6 with Remediation: Vocabulary production	**Vocabulario en uso 2** (25 min.) • Actividades 28, 29 • Communicative Pair Activity	**Wrap-up and Homework Options** (5 min.) • Actividad 30 • Writing Activity
12	**Warm-up** (10 min.) • Homework check	**Gramática y vocabulario en uso 2** (35 min.) • Presentation: Más conjunciones que se usan con el subjuntivo y el indicativo • Interactive Whiteboard Grammar Activities • Actividades 31, 32, 34 • En voz alta	**Wrap-up and Homework Options** (5 min.) • Actividad 33 • Core Practice 9-11, 9-12 • Prueba 9-7 with Remediation: Conjunciones con el subjuntivo y el indicativo
13	**Warm-up** (10 min.) • Homework check • **Formative Assessment** (10 min.) • Prueba 9-7 with Remediation: Conjunciones con el subjuntivo y el indicativo	**Gramática y vocabulario en uso 2** (25 min.) • Actividades 35, 36, • El español en el mundo del trabajo • Communicative Pair Activity	**Wrap-up and Homework Options** (5 min.) • Examen: Vocabulario y gramática 2
14	**Warm-up** (8 min.) • Writing Activity • **Formative Assessment** (30 min.) • Examen: Vocabulario y gramática 2	**Aplicación** (10 min.) • Presentación oral: Steps 1, 2	**Wrap-up and Homework Options** (2 min.) • Presentación oral: Step 2
15	**Warm-up** (10 min.) • Presentación oral: Step 2	**Aplicación** (35 min.) • Presentación oral: Step 3	**Wrap-up and Homework Options** (5 min.) • Galápagos: el encuentro con la naturaleza • ¿Comprendiste?
16	**Warm-up** (15 min.) • Galápagos: el encuentro con la naturaleza: ¿Comprendiste? • Homework check	**Aplicación** (30 min.) • Pre-AP® Integración 1, 2, 3 • View Video • Video Activities 1, 2, 3	**Wrap-up and Homework Options** (5 min.) • Presentación escrita: Steps 1, 2
17	**Warm-up** (10 min.) • Video Activity 4	**Aplicación** (15 min.) • Presentación escrita: Step 3 **Repaso** (20 min.) • Preparación para el examen: Actividades 3, 4	**Wrap-up and Homework Options** (5 min.) • Presentación escrita: Step 4
18	**Warm-up** (10 min.) • Homework check	**Aplicación** (35 min.) • Lectura • Interacción con la lectura • Cultura • Auténtico	**Wrap-up and Homework Options** (5 min.) • Core Practice: Organizer 9-13, 9-14 • Instant Check
19	**Warm-up** (20 min.) • Preparación para el examen: Actividades 1, 2 • Homework check	**Repaso** (25 min.) • Preparación para el examen: Actividades 5, 6, 7 • Other review	**Wrap-up and Homework Options** (5 min.) • Examen del capítulo
20	**Warm-up** (5 min.) • Answer questions • **Summative Assessment** (44 min.) • Examen del capítulo		**Wrap-up and Homework Options** (1 min.) • A ver si recuerdas: Capítulo 10

ALTERNATE LESSON PLAN

DAY	Warm-up / Assess	Preview / Present / Practice / Communicate	Wrap-up / Homework Options
1	**Warm-up** (35 min.) • Return Examen del capítulo: Capítulo 8 • A ver si recuerdas . . . • Actividades 4, 5, 7 • Homework check	**Chapter Opener** (10 min.) • Objectives • Arte y cultura **Vocabulario en contexto 1** (30 min.) • Presentation: Vocabulario y gramática en contexto • Actividades 1, 2, 3 • Presentación: Videohistoria: Heroína del medio ambiente **Vocabulario en uso 1** (10 min.) • Actividades 7, 8	**Wrap-up and Homework Options** (5 min.) • Core Practice 9–3, 9–4 • Clip Art Vocabulary • Prueba 9–1: Vocabulary recognition
2	**Warm-up** (15 min.) • Actividad 4 • Homework check • **Formative Assessment** (10 min.) • Prueba 9–1: Vocabulary recognition	**Vocabulario en uso 1** (60 min.) • Interactive Whiteboard Vocabulary Activities • Actividades 5, 6, 9, 10 • Communicative Pair Activity	**Wrap-up and Homework Options** (5 min.) • Writing Activities • Prueba 9–2 with Remediation: Vocabulary production
3	**Warm-up** (10 min.) • Writing Activity • Homework check • **Formative Assessment** (15 min.) • Prueba 9–2 with Remediation: Vocabulary production	**Gramática y vocabulario en uso 1** (60 min.) • Presentation: Conjunciones con el subjuntivo y el indicativo • Interactive Whiteboard Grammar Activities • Actividades 11, 12, 13, 14, 15 • Ampliación del lenguaje • Audio and Writing Activities	**Wrap-up and Homework Options** (5 min.) • Core Practice 9–5 • Prueba 9–3 with Remediation: Conjunciones con el subjuntivo y el indicativo
4	**Warm-up** (10 min.) • Actividad 16 • Homework check • **Formative Assessment** (10 min.) • Prueba 9–3 with Remediation: Conjunciones con el subjuntivo y el indicativo	**Gramática y vocabulario en uso 1** (50 min.) • Presentation: Los pronombres relativos *que, quien* y *lo que* • Interactive Whiteboard Grammar Activities • Actividades 17, 18, 19 • Communicative Pair Activity **Vocabulario en contexto 2** (15 min.) • Presentation: Vocabulario y gramática en contexto • Actividades 20, 21	**Wrap-up and Homework Options** (5 min.) • Core Practice 9–6, 9–7 • Prueba 9–4 with Remediation: Los pronombres relativos *que, quien* y *lo que* • Examen: Vocabulario y gramática 1
5	**Warm-up** (10 min.) • Writing Activity • Homework check • **Formative Assessment Options** (40 min.) • Prueba 9–4 with Remediation: Los pronombres relativos *que, quien* y *lo que* • Examen: Vocabulario y gramática 1	**Vocabulario en contexto 2** (20 min.) • Presentation: Punta Arenas: miedo al sol • Actividad 22 • Presentation: El Parque Nacional de Guanacaste • Actividad 23 **Vocabulario en uso 2** (15 min.) • Interactive Whiteboard Vocabulary Activities • Actividades 26, 27 • Cultura	**Wrap-up and Homework Options** (5 min.) • Core Practice 9–8, 9–9 • Prueba 9–5: Vocabulary recognition
6	**Warm-up** (20 min.) • Actividades 24, 25 • Homework check • **Formative Assessment** (10 min.) • Pruebas 9–5: Vocabulary recognition	**Gramática y vocabulario en uso 2** (55 min.) • Actividades 28, 29, 30 • Presentation: Más conjunciones que se usan con el subjuntivo y el indicativo • Interactive Whiteboard Grammar Activities • Actividades 31, 32, 33 • En voz alta • Writing Activities	**Wrap-up and Homework Options** (5 min.) • Core Practice 9–10 • Prueba 9–6 with Remediation: Vocabulary production

ALTERNATE LESSON PLAN

DAY	Warm-up / Assess	Preview / Present / Practice / Communicate	Wrap-up / Homework Options
7	**Warm-up** (10 min.) • Homework check • **Formative Assessment** (10 min.) • Prueba 9-6 with Remediation: Vocabulary production	**Gramática y vocabulario en uso 2** (45 min.) • Actividades 34, 35, 36 • El español en el mundo del trabajo • Communicative Pair Activity **Aplicación** (20 min.) • Presentación oral: Steps 1, 2	**Wrap-up and Homework Options** (5 min.) • Presentación oral: Step 2
8	**Warm-up** (15 min.) • Writing Activity • Homework check • **Formative Assessment** (40 min.) • Presentación oral: Step 3	**Aplicación** (30 min.) • Presentation: Galápagos: el encuentro con la naturaleza • ¿Comprendiste?	**Wrap-up and Homework Options** (5 min.) • Core Practice 9-11, 9-12 • Prueba 9-7 with Remediation: Conjunciones con el subjuntivo y el indicativo • Examen: Vocabulario y gramática 2
9	**Warm-up** (10 min.) • Homework check • **Formative Assessment Options** (40 min.) • Prueba 9-7 with Remediation: Conjunciones con el subjuntivo y el indicativo • Examen: Vocabulario y gramática 2	**Aplicación** (35 min.) • Pre-AP® Integración 1, 2, 3 • Presentación escrita: Step 1 • View Video • Video Activities	**Wrap-up and Homework Options** (5 min.) • Presentación escrita: Step 2 • Preparación para el examen: Actividades 1, 2
10	**Warm-up** (20 min.) • Presentación escrita: Step 3 • Homework check	**Aplicación** (35 min.) • Lectura • Interacción con la lectura • Cultura • Auténtico **Repaso** (30 min.) • Preparación para el examen: Actividades 3, 4, 6	**Wrap-up and Homework Options** (5 min.) • Presentación escrita: Step 4 • Core Practice: Organizer 9-13 9-14 • Instant Check • Preparación para el examen: Actividades 5, 7 • Examen del capítulo
11	**Warm-up** (15 min.) • Homework check • **Summative Assessment** (45 min.) • Examen del capítulo	**Theme Game** (15 min.) **A ver si recuerdas – Capítulo 10** (10 min.) • Presentation: Vocabulario • Presentation: Gramática	**Wrap-up and Homework Options** (5 min.) • A ver si recuerdas – Capítulo 10 • Core Practice 10-1, 10-2

Vocabulario: Repaso

Standards: 1.1, 1.2

Suggestions: Before presenting the material in this review section, consider testing your students' command of the material by assigning the Prueba with Remediation. Students will automatically be given additional practice of the material they have not yet mastered, and you can focus your review based on the class's overall performance on the post-test.

Number the categories of the *Vocabulario* from 1 to 6, proceeding from left to right on the page: *la basura* is number 1, *la comunidad* is number 2, and so on. Have students roll a numbered cube three times and write down the numbers that they roll. These pertain to the categories of the *Vocabulario*. Ask them to write a sentence using one word from each of the three categories they rolled. Have them roll and write as often as possible in an amount of time that you set.

 1

Standards: 1.1

Suggestions: Allow students to convert some of the sentences they wrote for the *Suggestions* above to questions for this *Actividad*.

Answers will vary.

Extension: Have students report to the class about what is important to their partner. Remind them to use third-person verb forms and indirect object pronouns.

 2

Suggestions: Remind students that antonyms sometimes work well to define words. Have them use the sentence starter **Es lo contrario de...** when using an antonym to define a word.

Answers will vary.

A ver si recuerdas

OBJECTIVES
▸ Discuss and write about the environment
▸ Express likes and dislikes

Vocabulario

la basura
la campaña
el centro de reciclaje
la contaminación
el medio ambiente
reciclar
recoger
separar

la comunidad
la avenida
el barrio
la calle
la carretera
la gente
el lago
el parque
la plaza
el pueblo
el río
los vecinos

para reciclar
la botella
el cartón
la lata
el plástico
el vidrio

el tráfico
la ambulancia
el camión
el coche
el peatón
la sirena
la zona escolar
la zona de
construcción

actividades
adoptar
arrojar
beneficiar
colaborar
contar con
establecer
evitar
mejorar
obligar
prevenir
reducir

opiniones
me encanta(n)
me gusta(n)
me importa(n)
me interesa(n)
me molesta(n)
me parece(n)
me preocupa(n)

1

Opiniones

 ESCRIBIR, HABLAR EN PAREJA ¿Te importa el medio ambiente? Escribe cinco preguntas que le puedes hacer a un(a) compañero(a) para saber si le importa a él / ella. Luego, trabaja con tu compañero(a) para hacer preguntas y contestarlas.

▶ **Videomodelo**
A —¿Te importa reciclar el vidrio?
B —Sí, me importa mucho. Mi familia y yo siempre reciclamos.

2

Definiciones

  ESCRIBIR, HABLAR EN PAREJA Trabaja con otro(a) estudiante para escribir definiciones de las palabras siguientes. Lean sus definiciones a otros estudiantes para ver si pueden identificar las palabras correctas.

1. tráfico
2. carretera
3. arrojar
4. botella
5. peatones
6. evitar
7. sirena
8. vecinos

Differentiated Instruction

Spatial Learner
Have students create a map of a fictional community that is environmentally conscious. Instruct them to include the items listed in *la comunidad, el tráfico*, and *para reciclar*. Have students label the areas and objects shown on their maps using the vocabulary.

Advanced Learners
Have students list five *Vocabulario* items from any of the categories except **opiniones** and exchange lists with a partner. Partners have three minutes to create a drawing that includes all of the items in the list, complete with labels. Then have partners talk about their drawings.

Go **Online** to practice
PEARSON
realize™
VIDEO   WRITING   SPEAK/RECORD

PearsonSchool.com/Autentico

Recycle   **9**

Gramática

Verbos como *gustar*

You know that *gustar* is used to talk about likes and dislikes. When you use *gustar*, the subject of the sentence is what is liked or disliked. You use the singular form *gusta* when what is liked is a singular noun or an action (an infinitive). You use the plural form *gustan* when what is liked is a plural noun.

Nos **gusta** este barrio.   Le **gusta** trabajar para la comunidad.
Me **gustan** las calles de este barrio.

Use the indirect object pronoun to indicate to whom something is pleasing.

Me gustaría participar en la campaña de reciclaje.

Other Spanish verbs that often follow the same pattern as *gustar* are:

doler *to ache, to be painful*	importar *to matter*	parecer *to seem*
encantar *to love*	interesar *to interest*	preocupar *to worry*
faltar *to lack, to be missing*	molestar *to bother*	quedar (bien / mal) *to fit*

• The personal *a* plus a pronoun or a person's name can be used for emphasis, or to make clear to whom you are referring.

A nosotros nos preocupa la contaminación del aire.
¿Le interesaron **a Sergio** los libros?

Más recursos   ONLINE

▶ **Tutorial:** *Gustar* and Similar Verbs

3

Escoger

 LEER, ESCRIBIR Unos vecinos escribieron un correo electrónico al periódico. Usa *preocupar, interesar* o *molestar* para completarlo.

Estimado Sr. Director:

Le escribimos porque __1.__ el tráfico en la calle Ramos. Aunque a todos nosotros __2.__ que se construya un nuevo centro médico, la construcción __3.__ A nosotros __4.__ también la basura que se está acumulando en el lugar. Favor de mejorar la situación.

Atentamente,

Los vecinos de la calle Ramos

4

Según ellos

 HABLAR EN PAREJA Tu compañero(a) describe a sus amigos y a su familia usando las palabras siguientes. Responde con ejemplos de tu propia experiencia.

▶ **Videomodelo**
A mi hermano(a) y a mí (molestar) . . .
A —*A nosotros(as)* **nos molesta el frío.**
B —*A mis hermanos(as) no* **les molesta nada el frío.**

1. A mí *(molestar)*
2. A mi compañero(a) *(interesar)*
3. A mis amigos(as) *(preocupar)*
4. A mi madre (padre) no *(gustar)*
5. A mí *(faltar)*
6. A mi mejor amigo(a) *(encantar)*

Capítulo 9 • cuatrocientos uno **401**

Gramática: Repaso

Standards: 4.1

Suggestions: Refer students who are having difficulty with *gustar* to the *GramActiva* video from Level 1 Chapter 1A, and to the online tutorial. Ask students to write three questions they can ask a partner, using three of the verb phrases from the *Gramática*. Have partners take turns asking and answering questions. Then have them report to the class on their partner's answers.

3

Standards: 1.3

Suggestions: Point out the use of the expressions ***Estimado*** and ***Atentamente*** in the salutation and closing of the letter. Remind students that these are good expressions to use in more formal letters.

Answers:
1. nos preocupa
2. nos importa
3. nos molesta
4. nos molesta

4

Standards: 1.1

Suggestions: Encourage students to listen to each other and to be inventive with their responses. Explain that using the cues to create a natural, flowing conversation is preferable to a rigid A-B-A-B exchange.

Answers will vary. Students will use the following verb forms and indirect object pronouns:

1. me molesta(n)	4. le gusta(n)
2. le interesa(n)	5. me falta(n)
3. les preocupa(n)	6. le encanta(n)

Enrich Your Teaching

Teacher-to-Teacher

Fill your classroom with posters, advertisements, displays, photos, signs, and anything you can find that corresponds to the environmental theme. Provide students with a center containing articles, suggested Web sites, magazines, and books to browse on the topic.

A classroom environment that is linguistically rich and full of information will enhance learning and provide students with interesting facts and details they can use to contribute to class discussions.

Vocabulario: Repaso

Standards: 1.1, 1.2

Suggestions: Have students sit in a circle. Give one student a foam ball and have him or her give a definition of a vocabulary item from one of the lists. That student tosses the ball to another and names a term from a different *Vocabulario* category. Whoever catches the ball gives a brief definition of that term and tosses the ball to another student, and so on.

5

Standards: 1.1

Common Errors: Even with regular review, students may make verbs like *gustar* agree with the indirect object rather than the subject. Remind them that **gustar** means "to please" rather than "to like," and provide models as necessary.

Suggestions: Encourage students to consider all five senses when talking about why they are or are not partial to the various places.

Answers will vary.

6

Standards: 1.2

Suggestions: Remind students that since the items are headlines, their structure is different from that of complete sentences.

Answers:

1. Incendio; árboles
2. mosquitos; insectos
3. inundaciones; lluvias
4. océano; peces

A ver si recuerdas

OBJECTIVES
▶ Talk and write about places and natural phenomena
▶ Refer to people, places and addresses

Vocabulario

fenómenos naturales
la explosión
el huracán
el incendio
la inundación
la lluvia
la nieve
el relámpago
el terremoto
la tormenta
el trueno

acciones
capturar
cuidar
eliminar
matar
permitir
prohibir
proteger
rescatar
salvar

lugares
el bosque
el campo
el desierto
el fondo del mar
las montañas
el océano
el parque nacional
la selva tropical
la sierra
los valles

animales
el caballo
la cebra
el conejo
el elefante
el gato
el hipopótamo
la hormiga
los insectos
el jaguar
el mono
la mosca
el mosquito
el oso
el pájaro
los peces
el perro
el tigre

5

Lugares interesantes

HABLAR EN PAREJA, ESCRIBIR Decide con tu compañero(a) qué lugares de la lista les interesan más y cuáles les interesan menos y por qué. Hagan una tabla como la siguiente y compartan los resultados con la clase.

Nos gustan más ...	Porque ...	Nos gustan menos ...	Porque ...
1. las montañas		1. el desierto	
2. el océano		2. las sierras	

6

Titulares

LEER, ESCRIBIR Lee con un(a) compañero(a) los siguientes titulares y anuncios de periódicos y luego complétenlos con las palabras o expresiones del recuadro.

insectos	océano	mosquitos	árboles
incendio	inundaciones	peces	lluvias

1. ¡_____ en el bosque! Se quemaron miles de _____.
2. Si quiere que los _____ se mantengan lejos, use el repelente de _____.
3. Grandes _____ en Zamora a causa de las _____ recientes.
4. Una exploración del _____ descubre nuevas especies de _____.

402 cuatrocientos dos • Capítulo 9 • Cuidemos nuestro planeta

---

Differentiated Instruction

Heritage Speakers

Ask students to model additional examples of cases in which the definite article is used in Spanish, but not in English. Then, have students create a short "fill in the blank" exercise for their peers.

Students with Learning Difficulties

Help students reinforce the vocabulary presented on p. 402. Encourage them to create small picture clues for words that are unfamiliar. Ask students to share their picture clues with the group, and have other students guess the word indicated.

Go **Online** to practice
PEARSON
realize™

PearsonSchool.com/Autentico

WRITING

Recycle 9

Gramática

Usos del artículo definido

In general, the definite article (el, la, los, las) is used in Spanish the same way it is in English. In the following cases, however, it is used in Spanish but not in English.

When people are referred to by name and an accompanying title, preceding the title (but not when people are addressed directly using a title):

La profesora Estévez enseña ciencias.   Buenas tardes, **doctor Zabala**.

Before the name of a street, avenue, park, or other proper names:

Los vecinos de **la calle Ramos** se quejaron.

Before any noun representing an entire species, institution, or general concept:

El perro es el mejor amigo del hombre.   **La educación** es muy importante.

With certain time expressions:

Llegó a **las siete** de la tarde. *(hours)*   Me encanta **la primavera**. *(seasons)*
Van a reunirse **el lunes** próximo. *(days)*   Salió de su país a **los diez años**. *(age)*

When it is an inseparable part of the name of a country, such as *El Salvador* and of some cities, such as *El Cairo, La Habana, El Havre, La Haya, La Paz*.

The words *al* and *del* result from contracting the prepositions *a* and *de* with the article *el*, but there is no contraction when *El* is part of a proper name.

Vamos **al** parque. Venimos **del** bosque.   Vamos a **El Paso**. Venimos de **El Paso**.

7

Practicar

 ESCRIBIR Con un(a) compañero(a) escriban sustantivos (con el artículo definido) para completar las frases.

Modelo
_____ es bueno para la salud.
El aire puro / El ejercicio / El jugo de naranja es bueno para la salud.

1. _____ Romero nos recibirá a las cuatro.
2. _____ es / no es un país de Asia.
3. _____ son / no son muy caros.
4. Generalmente _____ por la tarde voy al club.

8

Un diálogo

 ESCRIBIR Completa los diálogos con artículos definidos o con las contracciones *al* o *del*. Si el artículo no es necesario, deja el espacio en blanco.

1. —Lo siento, ya son _____ siete y debo irme.
   —Claro, Carmen, nos vemos _____ miércoles. Recuerda que es _____ reunión.
2. — ¡Mira! Aquí llega _____ doctora López.
   —¿Cómo está, _____ doctora López?

Capítulo 9 • cuatrocientos tres **403**

Enrich Your Teaching

Teacher-to-Teacher

Applying the correct gender to nouns is one of the more difficult skills that English-speaking learners of Spanish must master. Encourage students to invent their own mnemonic devices for remembering genders. One way is to associate the noun with an oft-heard, tell-tale modifier: **Buenos Aires, Santa Fe, sangre fría**.

21st Century Skills

ICT (Information, Communications and Technology) Literacy Direct students to the online tutorials for self-directed review of *gustar* and similar verbs recycled in this chapter. Students can expand their own learning by reviewing the related English grammar first, then proceed to the new Spanish grammar point. Each tutorial is followed by a quick comprehension check.

Gramática: Repaso

Standards: 4.1

Suggestions: Refer students who are having difficulty with indefinite articles to the online tutorial. Have students write five sentences or parts of sentences in which they incorrectly use a definite article. Collect their papers and shuffle and redistribute them. Have them correct the errors and discuss their reasoning behind the corrections.

7

Standards: 1.1

Suggestions: Ask students which rule from the *Gramática* applies to each use of the definite article.

Answers will vary. Students may use articles and nouns such as the following:

1. El ingeniero/La doctora/La señorita
2. El Salvador/La República Dominicana/Los Estados Unidos
3. Los coches/Los zapatos/Los discos compactos
4. los fines de semana/los sábados/los domingos

8

Standards: 1.2

Suggestions: Remind students to read through each item first before attempting to write their answer.

Answers:

1. las; el; la
2. la; leave blank

Additional Resources

 Technology: Online Resources
• *A ver si recuerdas* with Remediation
• Guided, Core, Audio, Writing practice
• *Para hispanohablantes*
Print
• Guided WB pp. 268–271
• Core WB pp. 119–120

Assessment

***A ver si recuerdas* with Remediation (online only)**
After reviewing the material on these pages, assign the *A ver si recuerdas* with Remediation to evaluate students' mastery of the material. Additional practice is available online.

Can-Do Statements

Read the Can-Do Statements in the chapter objectives with students. Then, have students read *Preparación para el examen* on pages 446–447 to preview what they will be able to do at the end of the chapter.

Standards for Capítulo 9

To meet the Standards, students will:

COMMUNICATION

1.1 Interpersonal
- Talk about neighborhoods, regions, and weather
- Talk about Diego Rivera, José Martí, and their work
- Talk about environmental issues and endangered species
- Talk about post-high-school plans
- Talk about the Galapagos Islands and butterflies
- Talk about a festival in Michoacán, Mexico

1.2 Interpretive
- Read about neighborhoods, regions, and weather
- Read about Diego Rivera, José Martí, and their work
- Read and listen to information about environmental issues and endangered species
- Read about word families
- Read about the Galapagos Islands, Monarch butterflies, and Magellanic penguins
- Read about *turrones*
- Read about Latin American rescue teams
- Read about a festival in Michoacán, Mexico
- Read about speech prep. and persuasive letters

1.3 Presentational
- Write and present information orally about environmental issues and endangered species
- Write and present information orally about the Galapagos Islands and Monarch butterflies

CULTURE

2.1 Practices to Perspectives
- Interpret Latin American perspectives and practices regarding the environment and endangered species
- Describe Latin American rescue operations
- Describe Ecuador's policies regarding the Galapagos
- Describe Mexican events spurred by butterfly migration

2.2 Products to Perspectives
- Discuss Diego Rivera, José Martí, and their work
- Describe a Puerto Rican recycling program
- Describe Ecuadorian national parks

CONNECTIONS

3.1 Making Connections
- Discuss key facts about Diego Rivera and José Martí
- Discuss key facts about ecological science, biology, and demographics

---

CAPÍTULO 9
Cuidemos nuestro planeta

Country Connections Explorar el mundo hispano

CHAPTER OBJECTIVES

Communication
By the end of the chapter you will be able to:
- Listen and read about pollution and other environmental issues
- Talk and write about environmental problems and solutions
- Make suggestions to protect the environment

Culture
You will also be able to:
- Demonstrate understanding of a culturally authentic audio recording about reducing trash production
- Understand the causes of environmental issues in Latin America
- Compare an environmental problem in Latin America with one in the U.S.

You will demonstrate what you know and can do
- Presentación oral: Campaña para limpiar la comunidad
- Presentación escrita: Cuidemos nuestros océanos

You will use
Vocabulary
- Pollution
- Natural resources
- Animals
- The environment

Grammar
- Conjunctions used with the subjunctive and the indicative tenses
- Relative pronouns *que, quien, lo que*

ARTE y CULTURA ▸ México

Diego Rivera (1886–1957) En 1921, el pintor Diego Rivera conoció a José Vasconcelos, que estaba a cargo del Ministerio de Educación de México. Una de las ideas de Vasconcelos era crear murales en edificios públicos para educar al pueblo. En 1922, Vasconcelos le encomendó (*commissioned*) a Rivera su primer mural. Este mural se llamó "Creación". En este mural Rivera combina elementos de la tradición indígena, como se ve en el dibujo del jaguar, con elementos religiosos e intelectuales basados en el arte clásico europeo.

▸ ¿Qué otras cosas asocias con la tradición indígena mexicana?

"Creación", (1922–1923), Diego Rivera ▸
© 2014 Banco de México Diego Rivera & Frida Kahlo Museums Trust, México, D.F./Artists Rights Society (ARS), New York. Photo: © Art Resource, NY.

404 cuatrocientos cuatro • Capítulo 9 • Cuidemos nuestro planeta

---

Enrich Your Teaching

The End in Mind

Have students preview the sample performance tasks on *Preparación para el examen*, p. 447, and connect them to the Chapter Objectives. Explain to students that by completing the sample tasks they can self-assess their learning progress.

Technology: Mapa global interactivo

Download the *Mapa global interactivo* files for Chapter 9 and preview the activities. Use Activity 1 to explore Santiago, Chile. Activity 2 takes you to Punta Arenas, Chile. In Activity 3, visit penguin nesting areas in Chile and Argentina. In Activity 4, explore the Islas Galápagos. Activity 5 follows monarch butterflies to Mexico.

Guacamayas rojas

▶ Videonovela ¡Pura vida!

Capítulo 9 • cuatrocientos cinco **405**

- Discuss key geographical facts about Puerto Rico, Chile, Mexico, Costa Rica, and Ecuador
- Discuss key facts about emergency organizations
- Use Language Arts Strategies: using topic sentences, finding good details, good conclusions, context clues

3.2 Acquiring information and Diverse Perspectives
- Read poetry by José Martí

COMPARISONS

4.1 Language
- Compare use of Spanish verbs like *gustar* to that of their English counterparts
- Compare Spanish and English pronouns and conjunctions
- Compare Spanish words to their English counterparts

4.2 Cultural
- Compare Latin American environmental and recycling problems and programs to those in the United States
- Compare nature-based festivals in Mexico and the U.S.

COMMUNITIES

5.1 School and Global Communities
- Link to Web sites from the Spanish-speaking world
- Describe urban vehicle restriction laws

5.2 Lifelong Learning
- Develop an appreciation for poetry and the visual arts
- Discuss ecological trends and possibilities for community involvement
- Listen to an authentic Spanish-language recording

Chapter Opener

Resources: Mapa global interactivo: Regional maps

Suggestions: Introduce students to the theme of the chapter and go over the objectives. Point out that they will improve their ability to talk and write about environmental concerns.

▶ **Technology: Videonovela *¡Pura vida!*** View this stand-alone storyline video about five young adults in San José, Costa Rica with your class, online.

ARTE Y CULTURA ◀

Standards: 1.1, 1.2, 2.2, 3.1, 4.1, 5.2

Suggestions: After students read the information, ask comprehension questions. For example: *¿Cuál era la idea de José Vasconcelos? (Su idea era crear unos murales para educar al pueblo.)*

Answers will vary.

Project-Based Learning

Una escuela limpia

As students go through the chapter during the week, ask them to come up with an imaginary campaign to keep their school clean, and to help protect the environment from contamination.

Ask students to put their ideas in a word web, and share it with the rest of the class. Have them use this information to complete the *Presentación oral* on page 435.

Vocabulario en contexto 1

Standards: 1.2

Resources: Teacher's Resource Materials: Input Script, Clip Art, Audio Script, Technology: Audio Cap. 9

Suggestions: You may want to use the Input Script from the *Teacher's Resource Materials* as a source of ideas for presentation of new vocabulary and comprehensible input. While presenting the vocabulary, capitalize on cognates, such as **contaminadas, petróleo**, and **conservar**. Since most of the vocabulary is not visualized, encourage students to use context clues to help themselves understand the meanings of new words and expressions.

Starter Activity

Have students complete this chart from the board:

	Verbo	Sustantivo	Profesión
1.	vender	venta	
2.		baile	bailarín
3.	cocinar		cocinero

Answers: 1. *vendedor*   2. *bailar*   3. *cocina*

 Technology: Interactive Whiteboard

> **Vocabulary Activities 9-1** Use the whiteboard activities in your Teacher Resources as you progress through the vocabulary practice with your class.

Vocabulario en contexto 1

OBJECTIVES
Read, listen to, and understand information about
▶ environmental issues
▶ what we can do to protect the environment

🔊 **Así conservamos y protegemos nuestros recursos naturales**

NUESTRO MUNDO

El estado del medio ambiente **depende de** cómo tratamos nuestros recursos naturales. Si no los cuidamos, **se agotarán**. Somos responsables de los **desperdicios** que **echamos** en los ríos y mares, y de la tierra y del aire **contaminados debido al** uso de productos **químicos** o **pesticidas**. Pero hay grupos en Latinoamérica que están **tomando medidas** para resolver estos problemas.

ARGENTINA

En Patagonia, la población **crece** y **amenaza** la calidad del agua de los ríos y lagos. Algunos científicos trabajan con grupos allí para **fomentar** la conservación de los ecosistemas. **La escasez** de agua limpia es un **grave** problema en algunas regiones del mundo.

MÉXICO

El **gobierno** está a **cargo de** un programa llamado *ProAire* que ha mejorado el aire de la Ciudad de México. Cerraron una refinería de **petróleo** y limitaron la circulación de autos. Además, construyeron un edificio con un exterior especial que puede reducir la **contaminación** del aire.

406 cuatrocientos seis • Capítulo 9 • Cuidemos nuestro planeta

---

Differentiated Instruction

Advanced Learners

Have students research a picture or bring in an object that represents one kind of threat to the environment. Ask them to use the picture or object as the basis for a short oral presentation about one kind of pollution. They can tell why they chose that particular picture or object, what kind of environmental problem it represents, their feelings about the seriousness of the problem, and then offer one or more possible solutions to the problem.

Go **Online** to practice

PearsonSchool.com/Autentico

AUDIO

PEARSON
realize™

Interpretive 9

CHILE

En ciudades como Santiago, hay programas que exigen a **las fábricas** que protejan los recursos naturales. Algunos procesos industriales producen **venenos**, como mercurio o arsénico. Si el gobierno encuentra algún problema, las industrias tienen que resolverlo **tan pronto como** sea posible o serán **castigados**.

un río contaminado

PANAMÁ

Un proyecto organizado por El Cuerpo de Paz es la construcción de estufas **económicas** para personas que normalmente cocinan sobre un fuego abierto. Habrá menos contaminación y mejorará la vida de la comunidad. Además ayudará **la protección** de los bosques porque usan menos leña.

1
El medio ambiente

🔊 ESCUCHAR   Escribe los números del 1 al 6 en una hoja de papel. Escucha lo que dice cada persona y di si es cierto *(C)* o falso *(F)*.

2
¿De qué hablan?

🔊 ESCUCHAR   Escucha lo que dicen los jóvenes e identifica el país del que hablan indicándolo en la página.

Capítulo 9 • cuatrocientos siete **407**

Enrich Your Teaching

Culture Note

As urbanization and development increase, motor vehicles are quickly becoming the main source of air pollution in Latin America. Air pollution can lead to such health problems as coughing, bronchitis, and lung cancer. The air in Mexico City, for example, was ranked the most contaminated by the World Health Organization.

21st Century Skills

ICT (Information, Communications and Technology) Literacy Have students use the digital technology within **Realize** to access and manage the audio files and activities that support learning the new vocabulary. Students can access the eText Audio to hear the pronunciation of new vocabulary words of *Vocabulario en contexto*, or they can use the Flashcards to study the vocabulary, then do some additional vocabulary activities.

1

Standards: 1.2

Resources: Teacher's Resource Materials: Audio Script, Technology: Audio Cap. 9

Suggestions: Before students listen, give them a few minutes to review the information on these two pages. Use the audio or read the text. Allow students to listen more than once.

🔊 **Technology: Audio Script and Answers**

Vas a oír cada frase dos veces.

1. Debemos cuidar los recursos naturales para que no se agoten. *(C)*
2. Los productos químicos y pesticidas limpian el aire y la tierra. *(F)*
3. En la Ciudad de México cerraron fábricas que producían venenos como el mercurio o arsénico. *(F)*
4. El uso de estufas económicas ayudará a proteger los bosques en Panamá. *(C)*
5. El crecimiento de la población en la Patagonia, es una amenaza para el agua de ríos y lagos. *(C)*
6. El gobierno de Chile tiene un programa llamado ProAire que se ocupa del petróleo. *(F)*

Extension: Ask students to correct the false statements. Have them do so by changing information, rather than making the false statement negative. For example: *Los pesticidas no limpian, sino contaminan el aire y la tierra.*

2

Standards: 1.2

Suggestions: Before students listen, allow them a few minutes to silently read over the information on these two pages. Play the audio or read from the script. Allow students to listen more than once.

🔊 **Technology: Audio Script and Answers**

Vas a oír cada frase dos veces.

1. Para reducir la contaminación de aire, limitaron la circulación de autos en la ciudad. *(México)*
2. El gobierno castiga a las fábricas que producen venenos, como mercurio o arsénico. *(Chile)*
3. Cocinar en estufas económicas reduce la contaminación y mejora la vida de la gente. *(Panamá)*
4. Los científicos trabajan para fomentar la conservación de los ecosistemas. *(Argentina)*

Vocabulario en contexto 1

Standards: 1.2

Resources: Teacher's Resource Materials: Input Script, Clip Art, Audio Script, Technology: Audio Cap. 9

Suggestions

Pre-reading: Point out that all of the information on this page is an interview.

Reading: Have students read the interview first and then present the new vocabulary to them. After the new vocabulary has been presented, play the audio or read aloud as students follow along. Allow them to listen more than once.

Post-reading: Check comprehension by asking questions, for example: *¿Cómo puedes ayudar a evitar la contaminación del aire y el agua?*

Starter Activity

Briefly review the present perfect tense and ask students what they have done, eaten, heard, and seen today.

Pre-AP® Integration

- **Learning Objective:** Interpersonal Writing
- **Activity:** Have students draft an email to the Environment Protection Center Director requesting ideas for conservation initiatives that could be implemented in their own school.
- **Pre-AP® Resource Materials:** Comprehensive guide to Pre-AP® vocabulary skill development

3

Standards: 1.2, 1.3, 3.1

Suggestions: Allow students to silently review the dialogue before completing the writing activity.

Answers:

1. F 3. C
2. C 4. F

Active Classroom

After students read the interview on page 408, discuss what other questions should Julia, the reporter, ask the Director of the Environmental Protection Center.

Performanced-Based Learning Project

Give students copies of the Chapter Project outline and rubric from the *Teacher's Resource Materials*. Explain the task to them, and have them perform Step 1. (For more information, see p. 400-b.)

Julia escribe para el periódico de su escuela. Hoy entrevista al director de un centro de protección del medio ambiente.

Julia / Director

Julia:	¿Cuáles son los objetivos de este centro?
Director:	Queremos **promover** la protección del medio ambiente y reducir la contaminación **ambiental**.
Julia:	¿Qué recomendaciones le hace el centro a la población en general?
Director:	Todos debemos tomar medidas para evitar que se agoten nuestros recursos. Para comenzar, debemos tener **suficiente** información sobre lo que **daña** al medio ambiente, como la contaminación del aire y del agua y el mal uso de nuestros recursos.
Julia:	¿Qué medidas específicas sugiere?
Director:	Cada persona puede ayudar desde su casa. Hay que enseñarles a los niños a no **desperdiciar** el papel y a apagar las luces para ahorrar **electricidad**. Hay que **deshacerse** de la basura del modo apropiado y **colocar** las cosas de plástico en los **recipientes** de reciclaje. Y lo más importante: hay que **limitar** el uso de productos que contaminen el medio ambiente. Por ejemplo, **en vez de** usar detergentes, debemos usar productos naturales, como el vinagre.
Julia:	¿Alguna otra recomendación?
Director:	¡Sí! Olvidé algo que casi nadie hace: **las pilas** viejas no se deben botar con el resto de la basura porque contaminan el suelo. Hay sitios especiales donde se pueden llevar las pilas viejas.
Julia:	Muchas gracias. Su información me ha servido mucho.

3

Proteger al medio ambiente

 ESCRIBIR Lee las frases. Escribe *C* (cierto) si la frase es correcta o *F* (falso) si la frase es incorrecta.

1. Julia habló con el director de un centro que protege plantas y animales.
2. El director del centro dice que debemos usar bien los recursos.
3. Un modo de proteger el ambiente es usar vinagre en vez de detergentes.
4. Las pilas se deben botar con el papel en los recipientes de reciclaje.

408 cuatrocientos ocho • Capítulo 9 • Cuidemos nuestro planeta

---

Differentiated Instruction

Heritage Speakers

Ask students to briefly debate the issues presented in the interview. Are there reasons one might not turn off a light or use recycled paper? Perhaps there are security or cost concerns. Encourage students to consider possible arguments and discuss them fully.

Students with Learning Difficulties

Assign the interview script on p. 408 to a pair or small group of students. Direct students to act out the questions and answers. Encourage them to provide two versions of the action. For example, have them act out turning off the lights.

Heroína del medio ambiente

Antes de ver

Determinar el propósito Al ver la Videohistoria, piensa en el propósito de las personas que la hicieron. ¿Qué mensaje te quieren transmitir? Usa el título, las imágenes y los diálogos para determinar el propósito y el tema.

Haz la actividad

Tipos de problemas Observa las fotos. Escribe una descripción del tipo de problema ambiental que representa cada una.

▶ Ve el video

Valentina ha encontrado la historia perfecta para su informe sobre el medio ambiente. ¿De qué se tratará?

Ve a **PearsonSchool.com/Autentico** para ver el video *Heroína del medio ambiente.* También puedes leer el guión.

Camila · Teo · Seba · Valentina · Ximena

Después de ver

 ESCRIBIR Contesta las siguientes preguntas:

1. Valentina narró la historia de Érica Fernández. Parafrasea los detalles que expliquen qué ha hecho Érica por el medio ambiente.

2. Infiere el significado de esta frase de Seba: "El planeta nos va a castigar por no conservar los recursos naturales".

3. Parafrasea la idea principal y el tema de esta Videohistoria.

¿Qué pasará? Habla con un(a) compañero(a). Comenten qué podrá pasar si continúa aumentando la contaminación.

Enrich Your Teaching

Culture Note

Pronaturaleza is a Peruvian non-profit organization that works to protect Peru's natural heritage for the benefit of future generations. Among its efforts, this entity has a socio-environmental program that trains local community representatives to monitor the environmental and social performance of industries. In the field of education, *Pronaturaleza* has a special school program to promote participation of students in the conservation effort.

21st Century Skills

Social and Cross-Cultural Skills
Invite students to write a short essay in Spanish on today's main environmental menace and how they perceive themselves as active participants in the worldwide cause to solve it. What actions can they take to make a difference in the future of the planet?

Tecnología: Video

Standards: 1.2

Resources: Teacher's Resource Materials: Video Script

Antes de ver

Review the previewing strategy and activity with students. Point out that thinking about the purpose of the video may help them with comprehension. Based on the pictures, generate a brief discussion about the possible theme of the selection and its connection with this chapter.

Ve el video

Show the video once without pausing. Ask volunteers to paraphrase the main idea. Show it again, stopping at key points to ask specific details about the video. Show the segment a final time without pausing.

Después de ver

Standards: 1.2, 1.3

Suggestions: For the first question, invite volunteers to paraphrase Érica Fernández's actions in favor of the environment.

Answers

1. organizó protestas; ayudó a detener la contaminación de un proyecto minero
2. de una niebla tóxica que flota por muchas ciudades
3. Answers will vary, but should demonstrate an understanding of the phrase.
4. Idea principal: una chica ayudó a detener la contaminación en su ciudad. Tema: medio ambiente.

¿Qué pasará? Answers will vary.

Have students go to Realize for additional video activities.

Additional Resources

 Technology: Online Resources
- Instant Check
- Guided, Core, Video, Audio
- *Para hispanohablantes*

Print
- Guided WB pp. 272–280
- Core WB pp. 121–122
- Authentic Resources Workbook

Assessment

Quiz: Vocabulary Recognition
- Prueba 9-1

4

Standards: 1.2, 3.1

Suggestions: Remind students that in each item, both possible answers are the correct part of speech, but only one makes sense in the sentence. They must choose their answer based solely on meaning.

Answers:

1. castiga
2. en vez de/la pila
3. contaminado/grave
4. coloca
5. energía
6. escasez/conservar

Extension: After students complete the activity, ask volunteers to summarize what they have learned about some environmental problems and solutions in a few countries.

Starter Activity

Have students brainstorm a list of items that could be recycled.

5

Standards: 1.1, 1.2, 1.3, 3.1

Recycle: *por* and *para*, imperatives

Suggestions: Encourage students to read the entire poster before answering any questions. Have them work with a partner to resolve comprehension problems.

Answers:

Step 1

1. No usar más bolsas de las que se necesitan, comprar productos en recipientes grandes, evitar los productos desechables.
2. Reciclar es devolver a las fábricas todos los materiales que se pueden volver a usar.
3. El objetivo es educar a la gente sobre las tres "R".

Step 2

Answers will vary.

Step 3

Answers will vary.

Vocabulario en uso 1

OBJECTIVES
▶ Read and write about environmental issues and solutions
▶ Discuss pollution and the shortage of natural resources
▶ Read and write about population growth

4

Problemas y soluciones del medio ambiente

 LEER, ESCRIBIR Lee las siguientes frases que describen problemas del medio ambiente y las soluciones. Escoge la palabra que mejor complete cada frase.

1. En la capital de Chile, se *(castiga / desperdicia)* con una multa a las personas que echan basura en la calle.

2. En España, reciclan los teléfonos celulares *(en vez de / a cargo de)* echarlos a la basura, pero primero se separa *(el veneno / la pila)* del teléfono.

3. En la Ciudad de México, el aire *(contaminado / económico)* es un problema tan *(químico / grave)* que se prohíbe el uso del coche ciertos días de la semana.

4. En Perú, para reciclar, se *(agota / coloca)* el vidrio y el papel en un recipiente especial.

5. Argentina tiene mucho gas natural, que sirve para producir *(desperdicios / energía)*.

6. Debido a la *(escasez / medida)* en la Ciudad de México, hay que *(promover / conservar)* el agua.

5

Un cartel ecológico

 LEER, ESCRIBIR

1 Lee el cartel y responde a las preguntas.

1. ¿Qué consejos da el cartel para reducir la basura?
2. Según el cartel, ¿qué es reciclar?
3. ¿Cuál es el objetivo de este cartel?

2 Piensa en las tres "R"s de las que habla el cartel. Escribe otros dos consejos sobre cosas específicas que la gente pueda hacer para reducir, reciclar y reutilizar.

3 Escribe un correo electrónico a un(a) compañero(a) y hazle preguntas sobre las tres "R"s. Él o ella te responderá con lo que debes hacer, incluyendo sus razones.

Modelo

A —Me interesa reutilizar las botellas de plástico. ¿Cómo lo hago?

B —Deberías lavarlas y usarlas de nuevo. Así les darás todo el uso posible.

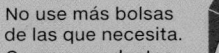

Reducir
• No use más bolsas de las que necesita.
• Compre productos en recipientes grandes.
• Evite los productos desechables[1].

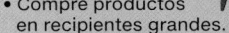

Reciclar
• Reciclar es devolver a las fábricas todos los materiales que se pueden volver a usar, como el cartón y el vidrio.

Reutilizar
• Dé a cada producto todo el uso posible antes de considerarlo basura.
• Es importante ser consumidores responsables y pedir a las empresas que vendan productos que se puedan reutilizar.

[1] disposable

410 cuatrocientos diez • Capítulo 9 • Cuidemos nuestro planeta

---

Differentiated Instruction

Heritage Speakers

The level of recycling activity and awareness varies greatly depending on country and community. Ask students who have lived in a heritage country to comment on recycling in that country. Were the programs and awareness more or less developed than in their current communities?

Advanced Learners

Invite students to work in a small group to create a Spanish-language poster about environmental programs in your community. If the technology is available in your school, have them generate the poster using computer software. Then they can obtain permission to create multiple copies and post them.

Go **Online** to practice
PearsonSchool.com/Autentico
PEARSON
realize™
VIDEO   WRITING   SPEAK/RECORD

Interpersonal   9

6

Las cosas que contaminan

LEER, ESCRIBIR En cada grupo de palabras busca algo que contamina el medio ambiente. Después, escribe frases que describan cómo esas cosas contaminan el medio ambiente. Además, sugiere una solución al problema.

Modelo
el petróleo
El petróleo que se usa en los coches contamina mucho.
Tenemos que inventar coches que no usen petróleo.

1. a. el reciclaje   b. las medidas   c. los productos químicos
2. a. el recipiente   b. el gobierno   c. los pesticidas
3. a. el veneno   b. la protección   c. la electricidad
4. a. las verduras   b. la energía   c. la pila
5. a. la población   b. los desperdicios   c. los derechos
6. a. la basura   b. lo suficiente   c. el ambiente

7

En el futuro

HABLAR EN PAREJA Muchos jóvenes se preocupan por el futuro, pues no saben cómo se resolverán los problemas de contaminación y la escasez de recursos naturales que tenemos hoy. Con un(a) compañero(a), hagan y contesten preguntas acerca de las soluciones posibles. Expresen sus opiniones.

Videomodelo
A —*En el futuro, ¿crees que se fomentará el uso del transporte público?*
B —*Sí, porque es mucho más económico.*

fomentar

Estudiante A

1 dañar
2 fomentar
3 limitar
4 agotarse
5 ¡Respuesta personal!

Estudiante B

económico(a)
grave
medida
escasez
¡Respuesta personal!

6

Standards: 1.3

Suggestions: After students make their selections, have them check their work with a partner before writing sentences for the second part of the activity.

Answers: Choices for the first part are as follows. Sentences for the second part will vary:
1. c   4. c
2. c   5. b
3. a   6. a

7

Standards: 1.1

Suggestions: As you go over the model with students, point out the use of **porque** as a transition in Student B's response. Encourage students to be creative with their language and vary the way in which they respond to each other's comments.

Answers will vary. Student A will use the following vocabulary and future forms of verbs:
1. las fábricas/dañarán
2. la energía solar/fomentará
3. los pesticidas/se limitarán
4. el agua/se agotará

Enrich Your Teaching

Culture Note
Extended Producer Responsibility is the concept that a manufacturer's responsibility for the environmental effects of its product does not end when the product is sold. Rather, producers retain a role in the recycling, reuse, or disposal of the product and/or its packaging. In 2000, Peru became the first Latin American country to institute a packaging take-back law. Started in response to a landfill crisis in Germany in 1991, take-back programs require producers to accept responsibility for the waste management of their packaging, even after the product has been sold to and used by the consumer.

Standards: 1.1, 1.2, 1.3

Recycle: impersonal **se**, pronoun placement

Suggestions: Have students copy the chart to their own paper. Use a four-column chart to model adding one other problem to the chart. Leave the right column empty on the chart.

Answers will vary.

Standards: 1.1, 1.3

Suggestions: Students may wish to consult each other or a bilingual dictionary for pertinent vocabulary to add to the discussion.

Answers will vary.

CULTURA

Standards: 1.1, 1.2, 2.1, 3.1, 4.2

Suggestions: After students have read the information, ask comprehension questions. For example: *¿Por qué han establecido la "restricción vehicular" en Santiago? (La han establecido porque el aire está muy contaminado.)*

Answers will vary.

Technology: Mapa global interactivo, Actividad 1 Explore geographical limits to Santiago, Chile's expansion.

Para proteger el futuro

ESCRIBIR, HABLAR EN PAREJA

1 Piensa en los problemas del medio ambiente y lo que se puede hacer para protegerlo. Copia la tabla y complétala con, por lo menos, cuatro problemas.

2 Trabaja con otro(a) estudiante. Hablen de las medidas que indicaron en sus tablas y expliquen quiénes deben estar a cargo de tomar esas medidas.

el problema	lo que se puede hacer	quiénes están a cargo
contaminación del océano	*no echar basura*	*los ciudadanos*
los desperdicios industriales		

 Videomodelo
proteger el océano

A —*¿Qué medidas se pueden tomar para proteger el océano de la contaminación?*

B —*No debemos echar basura ni desperdicios al océano.*

A —*¿Quiénes están a cargo de protegerlo?*

B —*Todos los ciudadanos podemos proteger el océano al no echar basura.*

3 Ahora, hagan una presentación para explicar a la clase los problemas y las soluciones de los que han hablado. Usen oraciones conectadas con detalles y elaboración.

Y tú, ¿qué dices?

 ESCRIBIR, HABLAR

1. ¿Qué problemas ambientales existen en tu comunidad?

2. ¿Qué medidas toman tú, tu familia y tu comunidad para proteger el medio ambiente?

3. ¿Qué pueden hacer que no estén haciendo ya?

4. Nombra al menos una cosa que quieras no desperdiciar, promover, limitar o conservar.

CULTURA ‹ Chile

Restricción de vehículos El aire en la ciudad de Santiago de Chile está muy contaminado. El problema es tan grave, que el gobierno ha tenido que establecer la "restricción vehicular". Eso quiere decir que algunos días de la semana no puedes usar tu coche en la ciudad. El día depende del último número de la patente *(license plate)* del coche y el color de sello.

Pre-AP® Integration: Los temas del medio ambiente La "restricción vehicular" es una solución al problema del aire contaminado en Santiago de Chile. ¿Cuáles son otras posibles soluciones?

 Mapa global interactivo Investiga la geografía de Santiago de Chile y conecta esta información con el tráfico de la ciudad y la contaminación del aire.

412 cuatrocientos doce • Capítulo 9 • Cuidemos nuestro planeta

---

Differentiated Instruction

Heritage Speakers

Ask students who have lived in a heritage country to discuss the issues of vehicular traffic and water availability in those countries. Are there specific problems or programs in place? If these issues are not at the forefront, are there other, more pressing environmental concerns?

Students with Learning Difficulties

Encourage students to plan out their responses for *Actividad* 9. Before they write their answers, have them record possible ideas in list form. Then, help them use elements of the question and their lists to formulate a complete response.

La población crece

LEER, ESCRIBIR

1 Lee la tabla y contesta las preguntas.

1. Según la tabla, ¿en qué siglo creció más la población?

2. ¿Qué problemas crees que ha causado este gran aumento en la población?

2 Ahora, lee el artículo siguiente y contesta las preguntas.

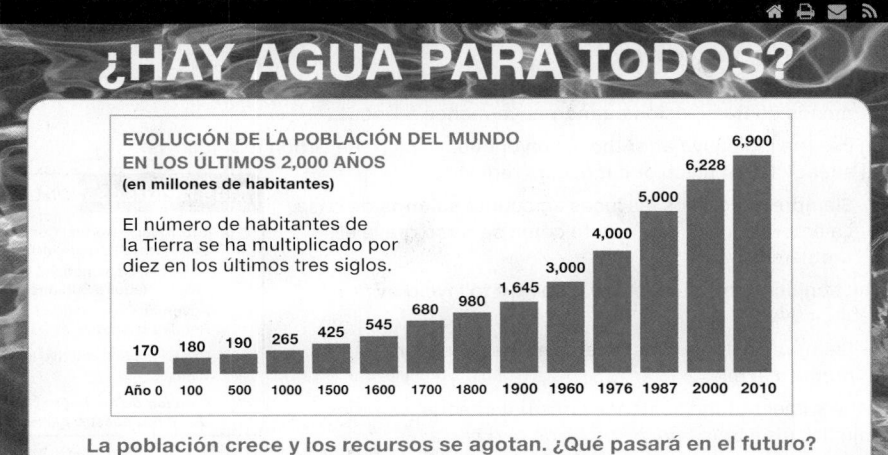

¿HAY AGUA PARA TODOS?

EVOLUCIÓN DE LA POBLACIÓN DEL MUNDO EN LOS ÚLTIMOS 2,000 AÑOS
(en millones de habitantes)

El número de habitantes de la Tierra se ha multiplicado por diez en los últimos tres siglos.

Año 0	100	500	1000	1500	1600	1700	1800	1900	1960	1976	1987	2000	2010
170	180	190	265	425	545	680	980	1,645	3,000	4,000	5,000	6,228	6,900

La población crece y los recursos se agotan. ¿Qué pasará en el futuro?

¿Qué pasará en el futuro si la población sigue creciendo? Los científicos no tienen una respuesta.

Uno de los problemas más graves que tendremos que resolver es la escasez de agua. Hoy día 783 millones de personas no tienen acceso a agua potable. Es estimado que la población del mundo crecerá de 7 billones a 9.6 billones en 2050. En el año 2050, el 52 por ciento de la población

mundial tendrá problemas para conseguir el agua que necesita. Además muchas fuentes de agua están contaminadas debido al uso de los pesticidas.

Esto hace aun más grave el problema, pues la agricultura es la mayor fuente de alimentos del planeta, su principal recurso nutritivo. El trigo *(wheat)*, el arroz y el maíz son los alimentos más consumidos en todo el planeta.

¿Comprendiste?

1. ¿Cuál será uno de los problemas más graves si la población sigue creciendo?

2. ¿Cuáles son los alimentos más consumidos en todo el planeta?

3. En tu opinión, ¿quién debe tomar medidas para resolver estos problemas: los gobiernos de cada comunidad, los gobiernos de cada país, las Naciones Unidas o los ciudadanos?

Capítulo 9 • cuatrocientos trece **413**

10

Standards: 1.2, 1.3, 3.1

Suggestions: In addition to answering the questions in Step 1, encourage students to comment on the rate of population growth over the years.

Answers:

Step 1

1. La población creció más en el siglo XX.

2. Answers will vary.

Step 2

1. Uno de los problemas más graves será la escasez de agua.

2. Los alimentos más consumidos en el planeta son el trigo, el arroz y el maíz.

3. Answers will vary.

Active Classroom

Inside-Outside Circles. Have students go through the information on pp. 406–413. Have each student create a question and write it on a sheet of paper. Have students count off as 1 or 2. All number 1s form the outside circle. All number 2s form the inside circle, facing out. Each student should be paired. Have each student ask their questions and then the outside circle moves two people to the left. Each partner asks the questions again. Rotate until the class rotates back to the original partner.

Additional Resources

 Technology: Online Resources
- Guided, Core, Audio
- Communicative Pair Activity

Teacher Resources
- Teacher's Resource Materials: Audio Script
- Technology: Audio Cap. 9; Comm. Audio Act. 1

Assessment

Prueba 9-2 with Remediation (online only)
Prueba: Aplicación del vocabulario 1
- Prueba 9-2

Enrich Your Teaching

Culture Note

Because of its geography, Santiago suffers from greater air pollution even compared to cities with similar vehicle emissions levels. Located between two mountain ranges, the Andes and the *Cordillera de la Costa*, the air pollution tends to remain over the city.

21st Century Skills

Media Literacy Have students research Web sites in Spanish that give more information about environmental problems in Latin American cities, such as pollution, scarce natural resources, and population, among others. What keywords will they use in their search? How can they decide which Web sites will give them reliable and accurate information?

Starter Activity

Briefly review with students the formation and use of the subjunctive before beginning the next *Gramática* presentation and series of *Actividades*.

Gramática

Standards: 4.1

Suggestions: In random order, call out the conjunctions shown in the *Gramática* and ask volunteers to use them in sentences. Make sure students understand that the two rules given after the word bank apply to all the conjunctions shown in the word bank, not just to those shown in sample sentences.

 Technology: Interactive Whiteboard

Grammar Activities 9-1 Use the whiteboard activities in your Teacher Resources as you progress through the grammar practice with your class.

11

Standards: 1.2

Suggestions: Have students read the entire dialogue for meaning before they write their answers.

Answers:

1. tome
2. eche
3. se agoten
4. estén
5. sepan

Project-Based Learning

Students can perform Step 2 at this point. Be sure they understand your corrections and suggestions. (For more information, see p. 400-b.)

Gramática

OBJECTIVES
▶ Talk and write about events that have happened and that have not yet happened
▶ Discuss measures that could be taken against pollution

Conjunciones que se usan con el subjuntivo y el indicativo

Certain conjunctions related to time are followed by either the indicative or the subjunctive.

después (de) que *after*	**mientras** *while, as long as*	**cuando** *when*
en cuanto *as soon as*	**tan pronto como** *as soon as*	**hasta que** *until*

You use the subjunctive after these conjunctions when the action that follows has not yet taken place.

> Van a seguir contaminando **hasta que** el gobierno los castigue. Habrá menos contaminación **cuando haya** menos fábricas.

You use the indicative after these conjunctions when the action that follows has already taken place or if it occurs regularly.

> Siempre apagamos las luces en cuanto **salimos** de casa. La empresa cerró tan pronto como **se puso** grave el problema.

- The conjunction *antes de que* is always followed by the subjunctive.

> Siempre se agotan los boletos **antes de que yo compre** el mío.

- If the subject of the sentence does not change, use the infinitive after *antes de, después de* and *hasta*:

> **Después de visitar** (nosotros) la fábrica, debemos escribir el informe.
> Marisa no piensa descansar **hasta resolver** (ella) el problema.

Más recursos ONLINE

▶ **Tutorials:** Adverbial Conjunctions that Always Require Indicative
Adverbial Conjunctions that Always Require Subjunctive
Adverbial Conjunctions that may Require Indicative or Subjunctive

Use of the Subjunctive in Noun Clauses

◀)) *Canción de hip hop:*
Cuidemos nuestro planeta

11

La contaminación

 LEER, ESCRIBIR Dos amigos están dialogando sobre la contaminación. Completa el diálogo con el presente del subjuntivo del verbo apropiado del recuadro.

estar	echar	saber
tomar	agotarse	

💬

🌐 La contaminación es un problema muy grave. Va a seguir aumentando hasta que el gobierno __1.__ medidas serias.

✌ Sí, seguro. Mientras la gente __2.__ desperdicios en lugares públicos, no vamos a resolver el problema.

🌐 La gente debe saber que tan pronto como los recursos naturales __3.__, no vamos a tener lo suficiente para poder vivir.

✌ ¡Debemos hacer algo!

🌐 Sí. Podemos hacer una campaña en la escuela. Mientras los estudiantes __4.__ en recreo, pueden informarse sobre cómo conservar los recursos naturales.

✌ Después de que nuestros compañeros __5.__ más sobre el tema, todos van a querer colaborar.

Differentiated Instruction

Students with Learning Difficulties

Lead students through *Actividad* 11 step by step. First, ask them to select the correct verb for the sentence based on meaning. Then, have them create the present subjunctive form of that verb. Last, ask them to explain why the subjunctive is necessary given the conjunction used and the time frame of the sentence.

Advanced Learners

Ask students to write two ways in which people commonly hurt the environment or waste resources. Have them read their sentences to a partner, who responds using a time-related conjunction: A —*Mucha gente no conserva el agua cuando se ducha.* B —*Verdad. Conservaremos el agua tan pronto como desaparezca.*

Ampliación del lenguaje   Familias de palabras

Las familias de palabras son grupos de palabras relacionadas por tener una misma raíz. Lee las familias de palabras de la tabla. Piensa en palabras que conoces que pertenezcan a esas familias. Escribe en una hoja de papel las palabras que faltan para llenar los recuadros.

Sustantivos	Adjetivos	Verbos
1. desperdicios	desperdiciado(a)	
2. contaminación		contaminar
3.	protegido(a)	proteger
4. amenaza	amenazante	
5. agotamiento	agotado(a)	
6. economía		economizar

 **12**

¿Cuándo?

 **HABLAR EN PAREJA**   Tu compañero(a) quiere saber cuándo se van a reconocer las amenazas del futuro. Responde a sus preguntas usando las conjunciones *antes de que, cuando, tan pronto como, después de que, mientras, hasta que, en cuanto.*

▶ **Videomodelo**

el gobierno *(tomar)* medidas para fomentar la protección de la Tierra / reducir los recursos naturales

A —*¿Cuándo va a tomar medidas el gobierno para fomentar la protección de la Tierra?*

B —*Cuando se reduzcan los recursos naturales.*

Estudiante A

1. las fábricas *(deshacerse)* de los desperdicios sin contaminar
2. voluntarios *(fomentar)* el cuidado de la comunidad
3. *(promoverse)* leyes para proteger los recursos naturales
4. los ciudadanos *(colocar)* los objetos reciclables en lugares apropiados
5. las compañías que producen coches *(limitar)* el uso de petróleo

Estudiante B

castigarlas el gobierno
poder organizarse y recibir fondos
agotarse los recursos naturales
ser fácil y económico hacerlo
dejar de comprar coches ineficientes
tener más influencia los ciudadanos que las empresas
reconocer que el problema es grave

AMPLIACIÓN DEL LENGUAJE

Standards: 1.2

Suggestions: Ask pairs of students to build word families around other words such as ***conservar*** or ***fábrica***.

Answers:

1. desperdiciar   4. amenazar
2. contaminado(a)   5. agotar
3. protección   6. económico(a)

12

Standards: 1.1

Suggestions: Point out that Student B has a choice of more responses than there are questions. Students should choose responses that reflect their opinions and make sense.

Answers will vary. The following are some likely results.

1. **A** —¿Cuándo van a deshacerse las fábricas de los desperdicios sin contaminar?
   B —Tan pronto como el gobierno las castigue.
2. **A** —¿Cuándo fomentarán los voluntarios el cuidado de la comunidad?
   B —En cuanto se puedan organizar y recibir fondos.
3. **A** —¿Cuándo se promoverán leyes para proteger los recursos naturales?
   B —No hasta que tengan más influencia los ciudadanos que las empresas.
4. **A** —¿Cuándo colocarán los ciudadanos los objetos reciclables en lugares apropiados?
   B —En cuanto sea fácil y económico hacerlo.
5. **A** —¿Cuándo van a limitar las compañías que producen coches el uso de petróleo?
   B —Después de que se agoten los recursos naturales.

Enrich Your Teaching

Teacher-to-Teacher

Have students prepare interviews which they can conduct with local business people, merchants, farmers, or community leaders who speak Spanish. Tell students that the purpose of their interviews should be to find out more about what people in your community are doing to protect the environment and conserve natural resources. Ask students to prepare a draft of several questions, then convene in a group to exchange ideas and correct any grammar errors their questions may have. Ask students to conduct their interviews and report back to the class with the results.

13

Standards: 1.2, 1.3, 3.1

Suggestions: Have students read the brochure silently. Ask them to identify and give brief definitions of new vocabulary items it contains.

Answers:

1. La fábrica se deshace de su basura en nuestras aguas y en nuestro aire.
2. El gobierno ha promovido leyes para la protección de la comunidad, pero la fábrica no las obedece.
3. Los ciudadanos pueden dejar de comprar pesticidas y exigir que la fábrica use recipientes adecuados para sus productos químicos.
4. Los ciudadanos pueden participar en una marcha frente a la fábrica, o pueden firmar una petición contra la persona que está a cargo.
5. Answers will vary.

14

Standards: 1.1, 1.3

Suggestions: As students make their suggestions in Step 2, encourage them to add comments using verbs of emotion and the subjunctive: *Es importante que hagamos....* Refer them to *Capítulo* 4, p. 154, for information about this use of the subjunctive.

Answers will vary. Students will use subjunctive verb forms after the time-related conjunctions in Step 1.

Pre-AP® Integration

- **Learning Objective:** Interpretive: Print and Audio
- **Activity:** As a pre-reading activity, have students work in pairs. One student opens the textbook and reads the article in *Actividad* 13 to the partner. Then the partner opens the textbook and, while covering the article, looks at questions 1–4 as the other re-reads the article. The second student answers the questions aloud. If he or she is not able to answer the questions, the student who reads the article may re-read the particular section of the article where the answer is found. Finally, both students discuss question 5.
- **Pre-AP® Resource Materials:** Comprehensive guide to Pre-AP® communication skill development

---

13

¡No a la contaminación!

 LEER, ESCRIBIR Lee el siguiente folleto *(brochure)* sobre una fábrica de tu comunidad y responde a las preguntas que aparecen a continuación.

MARCHA EN CONTRA DE LA CONTAMINACIÓN

¿Sabías que la fábrica de pesticidas no respeta el medio ambiente? Contamina el agua del río con los desperdicios y también contamina el aire. Aunque el gobierno ha promovido leyes para la protección de la comunidad, la fábrica continúa deshaciéndose de su basura en nuestras aguas y en nuestro aire.

Mientras fábricas como ésta no respeten las medidas de protección, van a dañar cada vez más a nuestro planeta. ¡Debemos exigir que la fábrica coloque sus desperdicios en lugares apropiados antes de que sea demasiado tarde! Juntos, podemos fomentar un cambio. ¡Toma medidas para proteger al planeta! ¡Deja de comprar los pesticidas! ¡Exige que la fábrica use recipientes apropiados para sus productos químicos!

Para mostrar tu apoyo, puedes participar en la marcha frente a la fábrica, o puedes firmar una petición en contra de la persona que está a cargo. *La protecció de la comunidad depende de ti.*

1. ¿Cómo contamina el medio ambiente la fábrica de pesticidas?
2. ¿Existen leyes para proteger a la comunidad? ¿Las obedece la fábrica?
3. ¿Qué medidas pueden tomar los ciudadanos? Nombra dos medidas.
4. ¿Cómo pueden apoyar la causa los ciudadanos?
5. Escribe un texto al organizador de la marcha. Pregúntale qué se debe hacer para apoyar la causa. Un(a) compañero(a) juega el papel del organizador y te responde para decir lo que debes hacer, incluyendo sus razones.

14

Problemas y soluciones

 ESCRIBIR, HABLAR

1 Con otro(a) estudiante, escribe cinco frases que identifiquen amenazas en tu comunidad respecto al medio ambiente y soluciones posibles, usando las conjunciones *antes de que, cuando, tan pronto como, después de que, mientras, hasta que.*

Modelo
Los ciudadanos no ahorran electricidad. Hasta que los ciudadanos hagamos un esfuerzo por ahorrar electricidad tendremos problemas.

2 Cada pareja va a compartir sus ideas con la clase. Para cada problema que se menciona, la clase va a sugerir soluciones. Prepárense para defender sus recomendaciones y opiniones.

Differentiated Instruction

Heritage Speakers

Ask students to model the use of the time-related conjunctions in *Actividad* 15. After they have written their responses, have them go back and circle each verb that follows a conjunction. Ask students to confirm and explain why each verb requires the indicative or the subjunctive. Also, have students confirm the spelling of these verb forms.

Students with Learning Difficulties

Encourage students to circle a key word in each of the questions following the brochure in *Actividad* 13. Instruct students to search for these key words in the text to help locate the information required to answer each question.

Go **Online** to practice   PearsonSchool.com/Autentico
PEARSON
realize™
VIDEO   WRITING   SPEAK/RECORD

15

En cuanto podamos . . .

ESCRIBIR, HABLAR EN PAREJA

❶ Trabaja con otro(a) estudiante. Imaginen que se reunieron para hablar sobre lo que harán después de graduarse de la escuela. Hagan una lista de cosas que pueden hacer.

❷ Escojan una idea de su lista y hablen de sus planes y de los pasos necesarios para realizarla, usando las siguientes conjunciones.

Modelo
- ir a la universidad
- buscar un trabajo
- viajar

después de que	tan pronto como	después de	mientras
cuando	hasta que	en cuanto	

▶ **Videomodelo**
ir a la universidad
A —*En cuanto me gradúe iré a la universidad.*
B —*Me quedaré con mis padres hasta que empiecen las clases.*

16

La lluvia ácida

LEER, ESCRIBIR Lee el siguiente artículo sobre la lluvia ácida y contesta las preguntas que aparecen a continuación.

Conexiones ‹ **Las ciencias**

En más de una docena de países europeos está ocurriendo una corrosión acelerada en los edificios y monumentos históricos. Así, por ejemplo, el Partenón ha sufrido más el efecto de la erosión en los últimos 30 años que durante los 2,400 años anteriores, y en España las pinturas del museo del Prado se han estado deteriorando a causa de la contaminación.

Todo ello es debido a las emisiones de dióxido de azufre *(sulfur)* y óxidos de nitrógeno, que se convierten en ácidos fuertes y atacan tanto a edificios antiguos como nuevos. Los más afectados son los objetos y estructuras de materiales fácilmente degradables, como la piedra caliza *(limestone)* y la arenisca *(sandstone)*.

- ¿Qué otros ejemplos de corrosión por lluvia ácida conoces?

- ¿Hay corrosión por lluvia ácida en tu comunidad? Descríbela.

Capítulo 9 • cuatrocientos diecisiete **417**

15

Standards: 1.1

Suggestions: Point out that the future activities in the model are suggestions only. Encourage students to talk about their actual plans after high school.

Answers will vary.

16

Standards: 1.1, 1.2, 3.1

Suggestions: Have students read the information silently. Help them address any comprehension problems they may have. Ask them to share background knowledge they may have about the major causes of acid rain.

Answers will vary.

Active Classroom

After completing p. 417, have students write five *Cierto/Falso* statements about *Actividad* 13 or 15. Ask them to work with a partner and ask each other their questions.

Additional Resources

 Technology: Online Resources
- Instant Check
- Guided, Core, Audio, Writing, Reading
- *Para hispanohablantes*
Print
- Guided WB pp. 281–282
- Core WB p. 123

Assessment

Prueba 9-3 with Remediation (online only)
Prueba: Conjunciones con el subjuntivo
- Prueba 9-3

Enrich Your Teaching

Culture Note

In the Mexico City basin, acid rain is eroding the Aztec ruins of Tenochtitlán. In the Yucatán Peninsula, it is accelerating the erosion of the Mayan ruins. In Peru, it is attacking the Nazca Lines. Projects and studies around the world are dedicated to solving the problem of acid rain, but many of them lack funds.

21st Century Skills

Information Literacy Remind students that whenever they do a speaking activity, as in *Actividad* 15, they will have the opportunity to first watch and listen to native speakers in the *Videomodelos*. This way, they can use a native-speaker model to monitor their own progress.

Gramática

Standards: 4.1

Suggestions: Say two short sentences referring to the same thing or person: *La señora Martínez es profesora. Hablé con la señora Martínez ayer.* Ask students to combine the two sentences using a relative pronoun from the *Gramática: La señora Martínez es la profesora con quien hablé ayer.*

 Technology: Interactive Whiteboard

> **Grammar Activities 9-1** Use the whiteboard activities in your Teacher Resources as you progress through the grammar practice with your class.

 17

Standards: 1.2

Suggestions: Suggest that students follow three steps to complete the activity. First, read and understand the sentence. Second, locate the noun that will be replaced by the relative pronoun. Third, choose the correct relative pronoun.

Common Errors: Some students will follow English grammatical logic and use **quien** to refer to people, even when the pronoun doesn't follow a preposition: *Melina es una persona quien conozco.* Remind them that in Spanish, **que** is used to refer to both things and people unless a preposition precedes the relative pronoun: *Melina es una persona que conozco.*

Answers:

1. que	**3.** quien	**5.** que
2. Lo que	**4.** que	**6.** quienes

18

Standards: 1.1

Suggestions: Point out that students are creating complex sentences. The relative pronoun serves as the subject of the subordinate clause. They must supply the verb phrase for that clause.

Answers will vary.

Gramática

OBJECTIVES
▸ Describe people and issues related to the environment
▸ Read and write about environmental disasters

Los pronombres relativos *que, quien y lo que*

You use relative pronouns to combine two sentences or to give clarifying information. The most common relative pronoun in Spanish is *que*. It can mean "that," "which," "who," or "whom," and it may refer either to persons or to things.

> Ésta es la fábrica **que** visité ayer. La fábrica, **que** hace productos químicos, fomenta la protección del medio ambiente. El Sr. Ríos es el profesor **que** nos llevó a la fábrica.

After a preposition, use *que* to refer to things and *quien(es)* to refer to people.

> No encuentro el papel **en que** escribí tu dirección.
> El problema **del que** te hablé ocurrió en otro barrio.
> La señora **a quien** te presenté trabaja en una fábrica de recipientes.

• Use the relative phrase *lo que* to refer to a situation, concept, action, or object not yet identified.

> No recuerdo **lo que** me dijo.
> **Lo que** más me gusta es estar a cargo del proyecto.

Más recursos ONLINE

▶ **Tutorial:** Relative Pronouns

17

El medio ambiente

 LEER, ESCRIBIR Muchas de las noticias del periódico hablan sobre el medio ambiente. Completa las frases con los pronombres relativos *que, quien(es)* o *lo que*.

1. El gobierno anunció las medidas _____ limitan el uso de pesticidas.
2. _____ más amenaza a la población es la escasez de recursos.
3. La persona de _____ habla el artículo tira los desperdicios en el río.
4. Las medidas _____ fueron tomadas por el gobierno no resuelven los problemas más graves.
5. El petróleo _____ se echa en el océano produce contaminación.
6. Las personas a _____ ayudó el gobierno viven ahora en una zona sin contaminación.

18

Lo que a mí me parece es . . .

 HABLAR Conversa con un compañero(a). Completa las frases siguientes con sus opiniones personales.

1. Lo que más me molesta de la contaminación es . . .
2. El gobierno es la organización que . . .
3. Nuestros padres son las personas con quienes . . .
4. (Nombres) son las personas que . . .
5. No estoy de acuerdo con lo que . . .

Differentiated Instruction

Challenge/Pre-AP®

On the board, write questions that ask for identifying information that students can supply: *¿Quién es el señor Harler? ¿Qué es la lluvia ácida?* Then answer the questions with complex sentences containing relative pronouns: *El señor Harler es el profesor que enseña matemáticas.*

La lluvia ácida es un problema que destruye los monumentos antiguos. Have students write three similar questions and exchange them with a partner, who answers them using complex sentences with relative pronouns.

El petróleo

LEER, ESCRIBIR, HABLAR EN GRUPO

1 En grupo, lean el siguiente artículo sobre el petróleo en el mar.

Petróleo en el mar

En nuestra sociedad, el petróleo y sus derivados son imprescindibles[1] como fuente de energía y para la fabricación[2] de productos químicos, alimentos, medicinas, etc.

Por otro lado, alrededor del 0.1% al 0.2% de la producción mundial de petróleo termina en el mar. Esto produce la contaminación de las aguas y daña el ecosistema marino. Aves[3] y mamíferos mueren constantemente a causa del petróleo en sus cuerpos.

¿Cómo llega el petróleo al mar? El petróleo debe ser transportado muchas millas por el mar hasta llegar al lugar donde se va a usar. En el camino se producen a veces accidentes que pueden ser muy graves. Pero, la mayor parte del petróleo que termina en el mar procede de la tierra, de desperdicios de las casas, automóviles, combustible, fábricas, etc.

En la actualidad[4] se usan productos de

limpieza especiales para limpiar el petróleo, pero evitar la contaminación es la única solución verdaderamente aceptable.

[1]indispensable, essential [2]manufacture
[3]Birds [4]currently, today

2 Decidan cuáles son las ideas más importantes del artículo. Escríbanlas en una lista y añadan detalles.

Modelo
Necesitamos el petróleo como fuente de energía.

3 Usen las ideas que anotaron para pensar en una propuesta sobre cómo resolver el problema del petróleo en el mar y en cómo se puede evitar la contaminación de las aguas. Pueden usar la Internet o la biblioteca para investigar sobre el tema.

Modelo
*Cuando se transporta el petróleo por mar,
se deben usar barcos que sean más modernos.*

4 Usen las ideas que anotaron para informar a la clase. Presenten sus ideas usando oraciones conectadas con detalles y elaboración.

Capítulo 9 • cuatrocientos diecinueve **419**

Standards: 1.1, 1.2, 1.3, 3.1

Suggestions: For Steps 2–3, encourage students to use a graphic organizer, such as a three-column chart, to record the main ideas and important details of the article. They can write their proposed solutions in the third column.

Answers will vary.

Project-Based Learning

Students can perform Step 3 at this point. (For more information, see p. 400-b.)

Additional Resources

 Technology: Online Resources
- Instant Check
- Guided, Core, Audio
- *Para hispanohablantes*
- Technology: Audio Cap 9: Comm. Audio Act. 2
- Communicative Pair Activity
- Teacher's Resources Material

Print
- Guided WB pp. 283–284
- Core WB pp. 124–125

Assessment

Prueba 9-4 with Remediation (online only)
Prueba: Pronombres relativos: *que, quien, lo que*
- Prueba 9-4

Examen: Vocabulario y gramática 1
- Examen 1
- ExamView: Examen 1

Enrich Your Teaching

Culture Note

Oil was first discovered in Venezuela in 1921. In 1960, the country became a founding member of OPEC. In 1976, the oil industry was nationalized. Oil is undoubtedly the lifeblood of the Venezuelan economy. The oil industry accounts for about 80 percent of Venezuela's export earnings.

21st Century Skills

Critical Thinking and Problem Solving Working in small groups, have students discuss recent oil spill disasters in this country and in the world. Where have the recent oil spill disasters occurred? What companies and countries are involved? What are the biggest problems facing oil companies, environmentalists, and governments?

Vocabulario en contexto 2

Standards: 1.2

Resources: Teacher's Resource Materials: Input Script, Clip Art, Audio Script, Technology: Audio Cap. 9

Suggestions: Have students look over the four reading sections on these pages. Ask questions to help them achieve a general idea of what they will read. For example: *¿Piensas que esta lectura se trata más de la literatura o de las ciencias?* **(las ciencias)** Ask students to describe what they see in the photos. Encourage them to use background knowledge from their science and other courses in this discussion. Use **sí/no** or embedded answer questions to elicit new vocabulary from students. Then have students read along as you present the new vocabulary by playing the audio or reading the text aloud. Check for comprehension by asking questions. See the Input Scripts in the *Teacher's Resource Materials* for specific questions.

Starter Activity

Have the students complete the sentences from the board with the name of the appropriate animal.

1. *La _____ tiene rayas negras y blancas.*
2. *El _____ es un mamífero muy grande.*
3. *Al _____ le gusta nadar en el océano.*
4. *El mejor amigo del hombre es el _____.*
5. *Cuando hacemos un picnic, las _____ nos visitan.*

(**Answers:** *cebra; elefante/hipopótamo; pez; perro; hormigas/moscas*)

🔲 Technology: Interactive Whiteboard

Vocabulary Activities 9-2 Use the whiteboard activities in your Teacher Resources as you progress through the vocabulary practice with your class.

Vocabulario en contexto 2

OBJECTIVES
Read, listen to, and understand information about
▶ environmental issues and endangered species
▶ measures to protect the environment and endangered species

🔊 La feria de ciencias

Nuestra clase de ciencias organizó una feria sobre los problemas más graves del mundo de hoy y sus posibles soluciones. Mi tema era los animales **en peligro de extinción**. Yo creo que hay tres razones importantes de por qué están en peligro muchos animales: **la caza, la falta** de hábitat y el cambio climático.

plumas

el águila calva

La caza

Los humanos de este planeta siempre han cazado **las aves**, o para comerlas o para usar sus **plumas**. Pero si no dejamos de **explotar** los animales, sus números van a **disminuir** o desaparecer por completo. Casi se extinguió **el águila calva** en Estados Unidos. La protección del gobierno la salvó.

Los peligros

Algunas especies marinas, como las **focas** y **ballenas** también están amenazadas por la caza, así como por los **derrames de petróleo**. En 2010, por ejemplo, hubo un gran derrame en el Golfo de México. Muchos voluntarios tuvieron que ayudar en **el rescate** de animales y en **la limpieza** de las plumas y **la piel** de los animales.

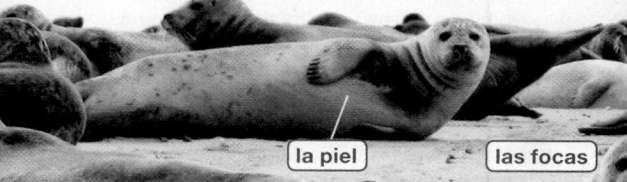

la ballena

la piel

las focas

Differentiated Instruction

Students with Learning Difficulties

Before students write their definitions for *Actividad* 21, instruct them to locate each word in the reading. Model for students how to use context clues in the reading to come up with a definition for each word.

Advanced Learners

Have students search for information about the greenhouse effect and based on what they find, help them create a diagram. Ask them to include labels in it. Have them use the diagram as a visual aid for a brief oral presentation about *el efecto invernadero*.

El clima

Un peligro aún mayor es **el recalentamiento global**. Cuando la **atmósfera** contiene cantidades **excesivas** de gases como CO_2, que se **produce** cuando quemamos gasolina en los aviones y automóviles, **atrapa** el calor del sol. Esto se llama **el efecto invernadero**, y hace que suba la temperatura del planeta. **La selva tropical** absorbe mucho CO_2 y por esto su **preservación** es tan importante. **En cuanto** suba la temperatura, por ejemplo, **el hielo** en los polos norte y sur **se derrite**, dejando menos hábitat para los animales **salvajes**.

la selva tropical

el hielo

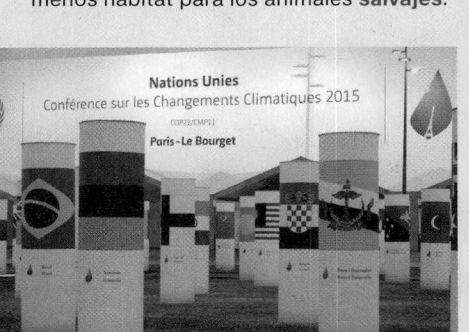

El futuro

Según muchos científicos, el problema del recalentamiento global es uno de los más graves de este siglo. **A menos que** lo **detengamos**, no solo van a sufrir los animales y las plantas sino todos nosotros. Es por esto que 195 países firmaron el acuerdo sobre **el clima** de París de diciembre de 2015. Podemos preservar la vida del planeta y de todos sus habitantes **con tal de** que todos los países trabajen juntos.

Como dijeron en la Conferencia: **¡Viva el planeta! ¡Viva la humanidad! ¡Viva la vida!**

20 ¿Será cierto?

 ESCUCHAR Escribe los números del 1 al 6 en una hoja. Escucha cada frase y escribe *C* o *F*. En el caso de las falsas, vuelve a escribir la frase para que sea cierta.

21 ¿Qué quiere decir?

 ESCUCHAR, ESCRIBIR Trabaja con otro(a) estudiante para escribir definiciones de estas palabras y expresiones. Luego, escriban frases usando tres de las palabras y expresiones del recuadro.

el efecto invernadero	la caza	derretir	el rescate	disminuir

Go **Online** to practice
PearsonSchool.com/Autentico
PEARSON **realize**
AUDIO WRITING

20

Standards: 1.2

Resources: Teacher's Resource Materials: Audio Script, Technology: Audio Cap. 9

Suggestions: Allow students to listen to the audio once through first. Then play it again, pausing after each item, so they can write their answers.

Technology: Audio Script and Answers

Vas a oír cada frase dos veces.

1. Cuando se produce un derrame de petróleo, muchos peces y otros animales marinos pueden morir. *(C)*
2. Si no detenemos el recalentamiento global, muchas ciudades se quedarán sin agua. *(F)*
3. Muchas especies están en peligro a causa de la falta de sol. *(F)*
4. La caza y la pesca excesivas han puesto a muchos animales en peligro de extinción. *(C)*
5. El fenómeno llamado efecto invernadero ha hecho que las temperaturas aumenten. *(C)*
6. Las selvas tropicales han sido explotadas sin control. *(C)*

21

Standards: 1.1, 1.3

Suggestions: Allow students to use phrases and sentence fragments to define the words and expressions in the first part of the activity. This way they can focus on meaning.

Answers: Sentences and wording of definitions will vary. Definitions should contain the following basic information:

1. el calor del sol que queda atrapado en la atmósfera
2. el acto de seguir a los animales para matarlos
3. calentar el hielo para hacerlo líquido
4. liberación del peligro
5. hacer menos

Enrich Your Teaching

Teacher-to-Teacher

Many of your students are already well versed in the area of pollution and other environmental problems. Encourage them to draw on this information and use their Spanish skills and reference materials such as bilingual dictionaries to synthesize it for discussions and writing in Spanish.

21st Century Skills

Critical Thinking and Problem Solving Divide the class into four teams. Each team will do additional research about one of the environmental issues (greenhouse gases; oil spills; endangered species; global warming) described on pp. 420–421. Have students hold a round table discussion in class to summarize their findings and propose solutions to the problems.

Vocabulario en contexto 2

Resources: Teacher's Resource Materials: Input Script, Clip Art, Audio Script

Suggestions

Pre-reading: Before reading, point out that *ozono, aerosoles*, and *afecta* are cognates. Show how removing the initial *a-* from the verb *amenazar* makes it closely resemble the English verb "menace," and explain that the meaning is the same. Have volunteers read aloud the titles on this and the next page to help students focus on the main ideas of the two readings.

Reading: Allow students time to read the information on this and the next page silently first. Then play the audio or read the text and have students read along as they listen. Allow them to listen more than once.

Post-reading: Check comprehension by asking questions, including those in *Actividad* 22. See the Input Script in the *Teacher's Resource Materials* for other questions.

22

 Technology: Mapa global interactivo, Actividad 2 Look at the proximity of Punta Arenas, Chile to the South Pole.

Suggestions: Have students answer the questions on their own. Then invite them to share their responses.

Answers:

1. La capa de ozono es importante porque nos protege de los rayos ultravioleta del sol. Si no la cuidamos, afectará nuestra vida diaria.
2. Punta Arenas está en Chile. Está en la región con el agujero más grande de la capa de ozono.
3. Los habitantes pueden llevar ropa que protege todo el cuerpo, ponerse anteojos de sol y loción protectora para el sol.
4–5. Answers will vary.

Punta Arenas: Miedo al sol

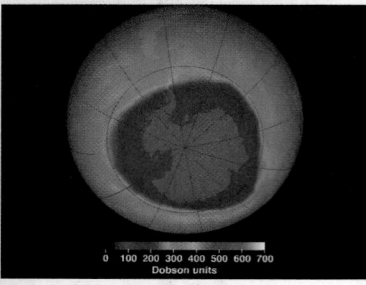

¿Has oído hablar de **la capa de ozono?** El ozono es un gas que forma una capa en la atmósfera que nos protege de los rayos ultravioleta del sol. A veces esta capa contiene **agujeros** a causa del uso excesivo de productos que usamos todos los días, como **los aerosoles.** Es importante **tomar conciencia** de este problema, ya que **afecta** nuestra vida diaria.

Punta Arenas, en Chile, es una de las ciudades más cercanas al polo Sur. Y es en esa región donde está el agujero más grande de la capa de ozono.

Desde hace años, los habitantes de Punta Arenas viven bajo **la amenaza** de los rayos ultravioleta y ajustan *(adjust)* sus vidas a los niveles de ozono de la atmósfera. Si las noticias del tiempo indican que los niveles de ozono son muy altos, se recomienda llevar ropa que proteja todo el cuerpo, ponerse anteojos de sol y loción protectora para el sol.

Los científicos no saben aún cómo afectará este fenómeno en el futuro a los habitantes de esta ciudad.

22

La amenaza del sol

 LEER, ESCRIBIR Parafrasea la idea principal, el tema y los detalles del artículo. Luego, contesta las preguntas.

1. ¿Por qué es importante la capa de ozono? ¿Qué pasará si no la cuidamos?
2. ¿Dónde está Punta Arenas? ¿Qué problema hay allí?
3. ¿Qué pueden hacer los habitantes de Punta Arenas para protegerse de los rayos ultravioleta?
4. ¿Cómo crees que se sentirán los habitantes de esa ciudad viviendo bajo esta amenaza todos los días?
5. ¿Qué podemos hacer para que la gente tome conciencia de la importancia que tiene cuidar nuestro medio ambiente?

 Mapa global interactivo Explora la geografía de Punta Arenas, Chile, e investiga el agujero en la capa de ozono.

Differentiated Instruction

Heritage Speakers

Students may not be familiar with specific scientific vocabulary. Have them read through the passages on pp. 422 and 423 to find terms with which they are not familiar. Then, have them create a simple scientific glossary with explanations of each of these terms.

Students with Special Needs

Help students with visual impairments experience the images of *El Parque Nacional de Guanacaste*. Locate a recording that features some of the sounds one would hear at a Costa Rican nature preserve. These might include the sounds of the weather, birds, and animals.

El Parque Nacional de Guanacaste

Go Online to practice
PearsonSchool.com/Autentico

PEARSON
realize.

WRITING   MAPA GLOBAL

Interpretive   9

En los últimos años se ha hecho muy popular el ecoturismo. Los turistas ecológicos no solo quieren visitar lugares hermosos, sino que desean aprender sobre la fauna y la flora de la región, las características del terreno *(terrain)* y su clima. Este tipo de turista desea ayudar a cuidar y preservar la naturaleza.

Costa Rica

 1

Uno de los países que promueve el ecoturismo es Costa Rica. El Parque Nacional de Guanacaste, en la región del Pacífico Norte, por ejemplo, es un refugio para muchos animales y plantas, pero también uno de los lugares favoritos de los ecoturistas. En los años 80, se creó un Programa de Ecoturismo para que los visitantes pudieran disfrutar de los hermosos paisajes mientras participan en los programas educativos.

Lagartija verde, Guanacaste

2

Guanacaste es una **reserva natural** para muchos animales y plantas, pues en sus **tierras** hay varios tipos de bosques. Según los científicos, este parque tiene 3,000 tipos de plantas, 300 especies de aves y mamíferos, como el armadillo, el puma y el mono de cara blanca, y 5,000 especies de mariposas.

23

Cuando vaya a Guanacaste . . .

 ESCRIBIR, HABLAR EN PAREJA Pregunta a otro(a) estudiante sobre los esfuerzos que deben hacer en un parque nacional de Costa Rica por proteger el medio ambiente. Él/ella debe incluir sus razones.

Capítulo 9 • cuatrocientos veintitrés **423**

Enrich Your Teaching

Culture Note

Although Costa Rica faces the same development concerns as many other countries, including a growing population and high deforestation, the small Central American country has taken a leadership role in the development of ecotourism. With only .03 percent of the world's total land mass, Costa Rica is home to 6 percent of the globe's biodiversity. Currently, national parks and

reserves constitute approximately 25 percent of the country's area. Hundreds of thousands of ecotourists visit each year to view, study, and appreciate Costa Rica's natural resources, and these numbers are projected to grow. In 2010 an estimated 2.1 million foreign tourists visited Costa Rica.

23

Standards: 1.1, 1.2, 3.1

Suggestions: Explain to students that most of the **esfuerzos** they list and talk about should be a product of their own background knowledge and critical thinking skills.

Answers will vary.

Extension: After students compare and discuss their lists, encourage them to research ecotourism in **El Parque Nacional de Guanacaste** or other **parques nacionales** and collect facts about efforts there to protect wildlife and the environment.

Pre-AP® Integration

- **Learning Objective:** Interpersonal Speaking
- **Activity:** Have pairs of students turn their questions and answers from Activity 23 into an interview. One student will play the role of an ecotourism guide from Guanacaste Park. The other will be a tourist interested in finding out details about the park's ecology and the government's conservation initiatives. Encourage students to use information they have learned throughout the chapter to expand the interview. Have students present their dialogues in front of the class.
- **Pre-AP® Resource Materials:** Comprehensive guide to Pre-AP® vocabulary skill development

Project-Based Learning

Students can perform Step 4 at this point. Be sure they understand your corrections and suggestions. (For more information, see p. 400-b.)

Additional Resources

 Technology: Online Resources
- Instant Check
- Guided, Core, Audio, Writing practice
- *Para hispanohablantes*

Print
- Guided WB pp. 285–292
- Core WB pp. 126–127

Assessment

Prueba: Comprensión del vocabulario 2
- Prueba 9-5

24

Recycle: definite articles, relative pronouns

Suggestions: After students have written their answers on their own, suggest that they repeat the activity orally in pairs. One partner reads the definitions in the left column to the other, who has his or her book closed and answers from memory.

Answers:

1. e	**5.** d
2. g	**6.** c
3. h	**7.** b
4. f	**8.** a

Starter Activity

Use Clip Art (see the *Teacher's Resource Materials*) for the animals found on p. 421 and have the students arrange them on their desktop in order of size. Have partners discuss their arrangements.

25

Suggestions: Encourage students to scan the complete conversation before they attempt to write their answers.

Answers:

1. efecto invernadero	**5.** los aerosoles
2. la atmósfera	**6.** una amenaza
3. el clima	**7.** el recalentamiento global
4. la capa de ozono	

Extension: After students have completed the activity, have pairs assume the roles of Tomás and Ana. Ask them to practice speaking the conversation and present all or part of it to the class.

Vocabulario en uso 2

24

Definiciones ambientales

LEER, ESCRIBIR Indica a qué palabra se refiere cada definición. Luego, escribe un párrafo en el que usas por lo menos tres de las palabras.

1. mamífero *(mammal)* enorme que vive en el agua
2. animal con piel que vive en el mar y en la tierra
3. acción de limpiar
4. cubre el cuerpo del ave
5. hacer o causar algo
6. parar
7. agua sólida
8. ave que representa un símbolo de los Estados Unidos

a. el águila calva
b. el hielo
c. detener
d. producir
e. la ballena
f. la pluma
g. la foca
h. la limpieza

25

El efecto invernadero

LEER, ESCRIBIR Completa esta conversación entre Tomás y Ana con las palabras del recuadro.

una amenaz	el recalentamiento global	la capa de ozono	los aerosoles
el clima	efecto invernadero	la atmósfera	

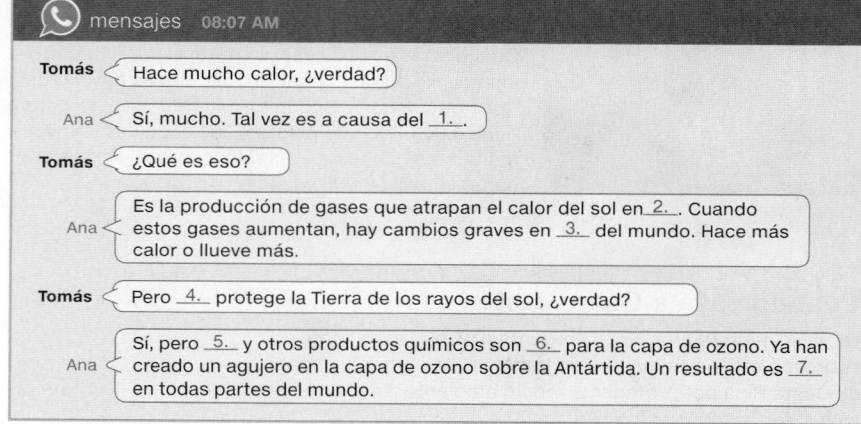

mensajes 08:07 AM

Tomás Hace mucho calor, ¿verdad?

Ana Sí, mucho. Tal vez es a causa del __1.__

Tomás ¿Qué es eso?

Ana Es la producción de gases que atrapan el calor del sol en __2.__ Cuando estos gases aumentan, hay cambios graves en __3.__ del mundo. Hace más calor o llueve más.

Tomás Pero __4.__ protege la Tierra de los rayos del sol, ¿verdad?

Ana Sí, pero __5.__ y otros productos químicos son __6.__ para la capa de ozono. Ya han creado un agujero en la capa de ozono sobre la Antártida. Un resultado es __7.__ en todas partes del mundo.

Differentiated Instruction

Students with Learning Difficulties

Have students label the words in *Actividad* 24 with one of the following codes: *an (animal), c (cosa)*, or *ac (acción)*. Then ask students to determine whether each definition applies to an animal, a thing, or an action. Have them choose the correct word from the smaller group of choices.

Advanced Learners

Have pairs or small groups of students use vocabulary from *Actividades* 24 and 25 to write and present their own conversations. Encourage them to create situations in which the vocabulary would arise naturally, such as a conversation between ecotourists and a park ranger, or between a museum guide and museum goers.

Go **Online** to practice

PearsonSchool.com/Autentico

PEARSON
realize™

VIDEO   WRITING   SPEAK/RECORD

26

Peligros

ESCRIBIR, HABLAR EN PAREJA

1 Escribe una lista de cinco cosas que pueden afectar la vida y la salud de los animales y de los seres humanos. Puedes usar las palabras del recuadro.

2 Luego, intercambia tu lista con otro(a) estudiante y comenten qué se debe hacer para solucionar los problemas. Hablen de posibles soluciones.

▶ **Videomodelo**
la pesca excesiva
A—*La pesca excesiva es una amenaza a la población de peces.*
B—*Podemos establecer leyes en contra de la pesca excesiva.*

escasez
derretir
contaminado(a)
capa de ozono
derrame de petróleo
especia
caza excesiva
falta
explotar
amenaza

27

Un rescate problemático

LEER, HABLAR EN PAREJA   Imagina que hay un derrame de petróleo y tienes que llevar a la otra orilla *(bank)* del río a una anaconda, un cocodrilo y un ave. En el barco hay lugar solo para ti y uno de ellos. Como no puedes dejarlos juntos en ninguna orilla porque la anaconda se comería al cocodrilo o el cocodrilo se comería al ave, ¿cómo podrías rescatar a todos sin problemas? Con un(a) compañero(a), hagan y contesten preguntas acerca de las soluciones posibles.

CULTURA Argentina • Chile

Pingüinos magallánicos Los pingüinos magallánicos son los pingüinos más grandes de las zonas templadas. Reciben su nombre de Fernando de Magallanes, quien los vio por primera vez en 1519. Estos pingüinos tienen plumas negras y blancas en la cara, el cuello y el pecho. Viven en las costas rocosas del sur de Argentina y Chile y comen calamares[1] y peces pequeños. Aunque actualmente son numerosos los pingüinos magallánicos, se consideran amenazados porque las aguas donde comen están expuestas[2] al peligro de derrames de petróleo y algunas veces los pingüinos quedan atrapados en las redes de los pescadores[3].

▶ **Pre-AP® Integration: Los temas del medio ambiente** ¿Qué peligros hay en las aguas donde viven los pingüinos y cuáles son algunas de sus posibles soluciones?

Mapa global interactivo Explora los hábitats de los pingüinos magallánicos en Chile y Argentina y compara los esfuerzos que se hacen para protegerlos con los programas de protección similares en los Estados Unidos.

[1]squid [2] exposed [3] fishermen's nets

Capítulo 9 • cuatrocientos veinticinco **425**

26

Standards: 1.1, 3.1

Suggestions: Remind students that the vocabulary in the word bank is there to give them ideas. Encourage them to use the word bank, but to go beyond it as well, and use other pertinent vocabulary they may already know.

Answers will vary.

27

Standards: 1.1, 1.2, 3.1

Suggestions: Suggest strategies in which students take two animals across, leave one, and return with the other to pick up the third.

Answers will vary.

CULTURA

Standards: 1.1, 1.2, 3.1

Suggestions: After students have read and discussed the information, ask: *¿Qué sabes de los otros animales que viven en la tierra o en el mar en la parte sur de América del Sur? ¿Cómo se llaman? ¿Qué información interesante puedes decir sobre ellos?*

Answers will vary.

🌐 **Technology: Mapa global interactivo, Actividad 3** Visit penguin nesting areas along the coastlines of Chile and Argentina.

Enrich Your Teaching

Culture Note

Magellanic penguins are not the only things in the Southern Atlantic to receive the name of Fernando de Magallanes. The Strait of Magellan is the name of the body of water that separates the island of Tierra del Fuego from the tip of South America. Today, ecotours and cruises are available in and around the "land of fire."

Teacher-to-Teacher

Problem-solving activities like *Actividad 27* are an excellent way to get groups of students speaking in Spanish. Many books are available containing such activities. Although the problems you find will most likely be in English, they can readily be converted and solved in Spanish.

Starter Activity

Before students complete *Actividad* 28, briefly review the uses of **por** and **para**. The *Gramática* presentation for these is in *Capítulo* 4 on p. 177.

28

Standards: 1.1, 1.2, 1.3. 3.1, 5.2

Suggestions: For the slogans or announcements in Step 3, encourage students to make their message more effective by using poetic devices such as rhyme or alliteration.

Answers:

Step 2

1. Se cortan los árboles para hacer cosas de madera y tener tierras libres para que coman las vacas.
2. El gobierno ayuda al Instituto Costarricense de Turismo.
3. Nelly recomienda educar a la gente para que no contamine la atmósfera.

Step 3

Answers will vary.

Extension: After students have completed the activity, ask pairs of volunteers to perform a dramatic reading of the interview with Nelly Anderson.

28

Las selvas tropicales de Costa Rica

 LEER, HABLAR EN PAREJA, ESCRIBIR

1 Lee la siguiente entrevista de Nelly Anderson, una estudiante de Costa Rica que se dedica a la preservación de la flora y la fauna de su país.

Entrevista con Nelly Anderson

¿Por qué te interesa la ecología?

Porque Costa Rica tiene muchas especies de plantas y animales salvajes.

¿Cuáles son los problemas que afectan las selvas tropicales y la naturaleza en el mundo?

Muchos países han explotado las selvas sin control. Se cortan los árboles para hacer cosas de madera[1] y tener tierras libres para que coman las vacas[2]. Ahora hay una escasez de recursos naturales.

¿Quién debe ejercer[3] este control?

El gobierno y todos los habitantes de países como Costa Rica. Además, los agricultores no deben cortar tantos árboles y deben respetar la naturaleza.

¿Qué hace el gobierno de Costa Rica ante este problema?

El gobierno ayuda al Instituto Costarricense de Turismo. Los turistas vienen a Costa Rica por su flora y fauna. Por lo tanto, el gobierno trata de fomentar más interés por la ecología.

¿Qué se puede hacer para que los niños y los adultos tomen conciencia del medio ambiente?

Pienso que la gente no tiene suficiente información. Por eso usan productos como aerosoles y pesticidas, que contaminan la atmósfera. Hay que educarlos.

[1] wood [2] cows [3] to exercise

2 Contesta las preguntas sobre la entrevista.

1. ¿Por qué se cortan muchos árboles?
2. ¿Qué hace el gobierno de Costa Rica para apoyar la causa de Nelly?
3. ¿Qué recomienda Nelly para que la gente tome conciencia del problema?

3 Trabaja con un(a) compañero(a) para crear un lema *(slogan)* o un anuncio que ayude a la gente a tomar conciencia de la importancia de no destruir las selvas tropicales.

426 cuatrocientos veintiséis • Capítulo 9 • Cuidemos nuestro planeta

---

Differentiated Instruction

Heritage Speakers

Ask students who have lived in a heritage country if they would volunteer to be interviewed. As the topic, ask them to identify a natural resource or geographic area of the heritage country. Have other students model their questions on those posed to Nelly Anderson in *Actividad* 28.

Spatial Learner

Once students have chosen the theme that concerns them the most in *Actividad* 30, have them create a public awareness poster or pamphlet. How could they use art and design to inform the public and improve the situation?

29

Para el futuro

 HABLAR EN GRUPO, ESCRIBIR

1 En grupos de tres o cuatro estudiantes escojan uno de estos temas. Hagan una lista de todas las palabras o expresiones relacionadas con ese tema.

- los derrames de petróleo
- se disminuyen los árboles en las selvas tropicales
- los animales que están en peligro de extinción
- el agujero en la capa de ozono
- el recalentamiento global
- la falta de preservación de la flora del planeta

2 Luego diseñen un cartel para que la gente de su comunidad tome conciencia del problema que han escogido. Indiquen qué cosas hace la gente diariamente que producen el problema y lo que se puede hacer para mejorar la situación. Usa oraciones conectadas con detalles y elaboración.

Cada vez que usas una botella de plástico en vez de un recipiente reutilizable, creas basura que no es necesaria.

30

Y tú, ¿qué dices?

 LEER, ESCRIBIR, HABLAR

Contesta las preguntas:

1. ¿Puedes nombrar animales en el mundo que estén en peligro de extinción? Usa un diccionario para buscar los nombres en español. ¿Por qué es importante salvar a los animales que están en peligro de extinción?

2. ¿Cómo han cambiado la Tierra las personas? Escribe un párafo e incluye cuatro o cinco cosas que han hecho. Usa oraciones conectadas con detalles y elaboración.

3. ¿Qué te preocupa más? Pon en orden la lista de temas, de lo más a lo menos serio, en tu opinión. Después explica por qué te preocupa el tema que escogiste como el más serio.

a. el recalentamiento global

b. la amenaza de una guerra nuclear

c. la destrucción de las selvas tropicales

d. la caza excesiva

e. la falta de recursos naturales

f. la contaminación de las aguas

g. el derretimiento de los glaciares

h. las nuevas enfermedades

i. la violencia en la sociedad

4. ¿De qué se preocupan tus compañeros(as)? Haz una encuesta en tu clase para conocer la opinión de los demás estudiantes. Comenta los resultados con el resto de la clase.

Capítulo 9 • cuatrocientos veintisiete **427**

29

Standards: 1.1, 1.2, 1.3

Suggestions: Allow students to use and expand upon their slogans or ads from *Actividad* 28 in the posters they create here.

Answers will vary.

30

Standards: 1.1, 1.2, 3.1

Recycle: present perfect tense

Suggestions: Have groups compile the information that they wrote in item 2. Encourage them to use some of this information, as well as the prioritizing they did in item 3, when they conduct their interviews in item 4.

Answers will vary.

Active Classroom

Total the individual class results for *Actividad* 30, item 3. Determine the top three environmental concerns. Ask students to write whether they agree or disagree with the top choices. Have each student present their opinion to the class.

Additional Resources

Technology: Online Resources
- Technology: Audio Cap 9: Comm. Audio Act. 3
- Communicative Pair Activity
- Audio Program, Cap 9

Print
Teacher's Resource Materials: Audio Script

Assessment

Prueba 9-6 with Remediation (online only)
Prueba: Aplicación del vocabulario 2
- Prueba 9-6

Enrich Your Teaching

Culture Note

In 1998, the Costa Rican Tourism Institute developed a "Certification for Sustainable Tourism." Tourism companies, from guides to hotels, apply to be rated on a scale from 0 to 5; 0 being unsustainable and 5 being the most sustainable. Companies are rated according to their management of natural, cultural, and social resources.

21st Century Skills

Critical Thinking and Problem Solving Have students work in pairs or small groups to discuss the most serious environmental problems that, in their opinion, will challenge the world most in 50 years. Use the list of environmental concerns in *Actividad* 30, item 3 as a point of departure, then add future concerns to that list.

Gramática

Standards: 4.1

Suggestions: Point out to students that here, just as in past *Gramática* presentations concerned with the subjunctive, the key to understanding its use is the concept of hypothetical actions or situations. If a situation has not yet occurred, or is only being considered as a possibility, the subjunctive is used.

 Technology: Interactive Whiteboard

> **Grammar Activities 9-2** Use the whiteboard activities in your Teacher Resources as you progress through the grammar practice with your class.

31

Standards: 1.2

Suggestions: Ask students to complete the activity on their own. Then have them share their answers and discuss their reasons for choosing the subjunctive or the indicative.

Answers:
1. sepamos
2. se molesten
3. haya
4. desaparezcan

32

Standards: 1.1, 1.2

Suggestions: Encourage students to refer back to the rules in the *Gramática* as often as necessary in order to complete the activity.

Answers will vary. Students will use subjunctive verb forms in the subordinate clauses.

Gramática

OBJECTIVES
▸ Express intentions, purpose, and uncertainty
▸ Discuss intentions to deal with environmental issues

Más conjunciones que se usan con el subjuntivo y el indicativo

The following conjunctions are usually followed by the subjunctive to express the purpose or intention of an action:

a menos que *unless*	**para que** *so that*
sin que *without*	**aunque** *although, even though*
con tal (de) que *provided (that)*	

> Te doy este libro **para que** tengas más información sobre la capa de ozono.

If the subject of the sentence does not change, use the infinitive after *para* and *sin*.

> No puedes saber el final **sin ver** la película.

With the conjunction *aunque*, use the subjunctive to express uncertainty. Use the indicative when there is no uncertainty. Compare the following:

Aunque llueve, vamos a la reserva natural.	*Although it is raining, we're going to the nature preserve.*
Aunque llueva, vamos a la reserva natural.	*Although it may rain, we're going to the nature preserve.*

Más recursos ONLINE

▶ **Tutorial:** Adverbial Conjunctions that Require Indicative or Subjunctive

🔊 *Canción de hip hop: Animales en peligro de extinción*

31

En el zoológico

 LEER, ESCRIBIR Completa las frases con el subjuntivo del verbo apropiado.

1. Nos han dado información para que (nosotros) (*producir / saber*) más.

2. El guardia del zoológico limpia el lugar de las focas sin que (*ellas*) (*molestarse / derretirse*).

3. Aunque (*explotar / haber*) contaminación el río parece limpio.

4. Se construyen reservas para que los animales salvajes no (*desaparecer / afectar*).

32

El rescate

 ESCRIBIR, HABLAR Imagina que se produjo un derrame de petróleo. Pregunta a otros lo que se debe hacer para rescatar los animales. Completa las frases de una manera lógica.

1. Nosotros vamos a trabajar hasta tarde con tal de que Uds. . . .

2. No pueden tocarles la piel a las focas a menos que . . .

3. Leonardo y María, Uds. deben limpiar el área sin . . .

4. Escribe un informe sobre el rescate para que la gente . . .

428 cuatrocientos veintiocho • Capítulo 9 • Cuidemos nuestro planeta

---

Differentiated Instruction

Challenge/Pre-AP®

On separate slips of paper, have students write three subordinate clauses beginning with conjunctions taught in the *Gramática* on this page. If they use ***aunque***, allow them to use either the infinitive or the subjunctive in the clause. Collect the strips, mix them, and place them in a container.

Have students meet in a circle, take turns drawing one subordinate clause at a time, and completing a complex sentence by inventing a suitable independent clause.

¡Delicioso!

 LEER, ESCRIBIR Una empresa que crea anuncios para revistas necesita tu ayuda. Completa los anuncios usando la conjunción apropiada de la página 428. Usa como modelo el anuncio sobre el turrón, un alimento dulce en forma de tableta típico de España.

¡No conocerás el mejor turrón, a menos que pruebes el turrón Real!

1. El chocolate . . . cómelo _____ te sientas más dulce.

2. ¡No manejes este coche _____ todos lleven su cinturón de seguridad (*seat belts*)!

3. El único teléfono celular que funciona _____ estés bajo tierra.

4. El reloj que sigue funcionando durante un año _____ cambies la pila.

5. ¡Salgan de casa! Vengan de viaje con nosotros . . . ¡_____ tengan un niñero!

En voz alta

🔊 José Martí (1853–1895) fue una de las grandes figuras históricas y literarias de América. Además de escribir poesía, artículos periodísticos y muchísimos ensayos, Martí dedicó su vida a la lucha por la libertad de Cuba. Fue uno de los fundadores del modernismo, un estilo literario que se caracteriza por su interés en la belleza y el estilo. La poesía de Martí es directa y clara. *Versos sencillos,* del cual las siguientes estrofas representan una pequeña parte, refleja la visión que tenía del mundo. Escucha las estrofas y luego contesta las preguntas.

• Según el poema, ¿cómo es el poeta?

• ¿Cómo le da importancia el poeta a la naturaleza en el poema?

De *Versos sencillos,* 1891
José Martí

Yo soy un hombre sincero
de donde crece la palma,
y antes de morirme, quiero
echar mis versos del alma.[1]

Yo vengo de todas partes,
y hacia todas partes voy:
arte soy entre las artes,
en los montes,[2] monte soy.

[1]soul [2]forests

¿Recuerdas?
Generalmente se divide una palabra en sílabas después de una vocal o entre las consonantes. Cada línea de estas estrofas de *Versos sencillos* tiene ocho sílabas. Escribe el poema en una hoja de papel y divide las palabras en sílabas.

Standards: 1.2

Suggestions: Students will enjoy sharing their responses for these items. After they complete the activity, invite them to do so in round-robin fashion.

Answers
1. para que
2. a menos que
3. aunque
4. sin que
5. Answers will vary.

EN VOZ ALTA

Standards: 1.1, 1.2, 2.2, 3.1, 3.2, 5.2

Resources: Teacher's Resource Materials: Audio Script, Technology: Audio Cap. 9

Suggestions: After students read the poem, encourage them to write a few lines of poetry to describe themselves and their relationship with nature.

Answers:
• Es un hombre sincero que quiere escribir poesía.
• Dice que, en los montes, el poeta es monte también; por lo tanto, el poeta es parte de la naturaleza.

Extension: José Martí is an AP® Literature author. You may want to suggest that students read additional works by this poet.

Enrich Your Teaching

Culture Note

Turrón, translated as "nougat," is a Spanish sweet with Arabic origins. The traditional recipe calls for almonds, honey, and eggs. These ingredients can be combined to form **alicante**, a hard nougat with whole almonds, or **jijona**, a soft nougat with crushed almonds. **Turrones** are traditionally eaten at Christmas time, especially after Christmas dinner with coffee.

Today, many varieties of the traditional candy are available, including nougats made with peanuts, hazelnuts, coconut, or covered in chocolate.

9 Communication

34

Standards: 1.1

Suggestions: Remind students that the model shows just one possible way to use the cues. Encourage Student A to begin the questions in other ways. Suggest other possibilities, such as: *¿Seremos capaces de parar...?* or *¿Qué se puede hacer con respecto a...?*

Answers will vary. Student B will use the subjunctive after the conjunction.

35

Standards: 1.1, 1.2

Suggestions: Point out to students that not all of the subordinate clauses they write must begin with *tú*. It is a given in items 2 and 6, but in the other items they can use different subjects.

Answers will vary. Students will use the subjunctive in the subordinate clauses, with the possible exception of number 5.

Project-Based Learning

Students can perform Step 5 at this point. Make audio or video recordings of their presentations for inclusion in their portfolios. (For more information, see p. 400-b.)

Teacher-to-Teacher

e-amigos: Have students write their *e-amigos* a list of what they feel are the four most important environmental problems facing their generation. Have them respond to the messages by giving possible solutions to the problems. Have students print out their e-mails or send them to you for review.

Pre-AP® Integration

- **Learning Objective:** Presentational Writing
- **Activity:** Have students write a conclusion for the article in *Actividad 36*. Have students include the following in their texts: 1. a statement to summarize the personal opinion of the author on the topic, and 2. a possible long-term solution to the problem.
- **Pre-AP® Resource Materials:** Comprehensive guide to Pre-AP® writing skill development

---

34

Cómo cuidar el planeta

 HABLAR EN PAREJA Imagina que vas a una conferencia sobre cómo cuidar el planeta en que vivimos. En ella se habla sobre diferentes temas ambientales. Trabaja con un(a) compañero(a) para hacer preguntas y respuestas sobre los temas de la conferencia. Usen las expresiones apropiadas para la conversación, que es seria pero informal.

¡Cuidemos el planeta!
Conferencia sobre el medio ambiente
Sábado 3 de mayo

- **Oportunidades para hacer trabajo voluntario**
- **Ideas para tu comunidad**
- **Nuevos productos para proteger el planeta**

Proyecto Limpieza

▶ **Videomodelo**

el recalentamiento global / a menos que

A —¿Qué va a suceder con el recalentamiento global?

B —A menos que los gobiernos no tomen conciencia del problema, el recalentamiento global aumentará cada año.

Estudiante A

1. la caza excesiva
2. la destrucción de árboles en la selva tropical
3. la capa de ozono
4. las reservas naturales del planeta
5. la contaminación de los ríos
6. la extinción de algunos animales
7. los derrames de petróleo

Estudiante B

a menos que
para que
sin que
con tal (de) que
aunque
sin

35

Ecoturismo en Chile

 LEER, HABLAR Imagina que vas a hacer ecoturismo a Chile con un(a) amigo(a). Como él (ella) todavía no ha llegado, le cuentas tus planes por teléfono. Completa las frases de una manera apropiada.

1. Visitaremos varias reservas naturales a menos que . . .
2. No saldré hasta que tú . . .
3. Iremos a una conferencia sobre la capa de ozono con tal que . . .
4. Sacaremos fotos de las especies del lugar para que . . .
5. Nos quedaremos en un pueblo cerca del océano aunque . . .
6. No haré nada sin que tú . . .
7. Planearemos nuestras excursiones en cuanto . . .

Differentiated Instruction

Students with Learning Difficulties

Before students read **La vaquita está en peligro** on p. 431, ask them to preview the questions. Have them record a "shorthand" for the main idea of each question. For example: 1) *¿reglas o recomendaciones?* 2) *¿implementar nuevos métodos de pesca o buscar un lugar donde observar a los delfines?* Remind students to consider these notes as they read the passage.

Advanced Learners

Have students create an adapted version of *Actividad 35*. In their version, ask them to include information about an actual ecotourism spot in Latin America. They can research this information on the Internet.

36

La vaquita en peligro

LEER, ESCRIBIR

1 Lee el artículo en línea acerca del reporte del Comité Internacional para la Recuperación de la Vaquita (CIRVA).

2 Ahora, contesta las preguntas.

1. En el artículo se habla de imponer regulaciones. ¿Qué quiere decir la palabra *regulaciones*?

2. ¿Qué recomendaciones hace el Comité?

3. ¿Qué se lograría con las recomendaciones?

4. ¿Has ido alguna vez a un lugar donde se pueda observar delfines o marsopas como la vaquita? Descríbelo.

3 Trabaja con un(a) compañero(a). Uno escribe un correo electrónico al editor del periódico con su opinión del artículo sobre la vaquita. El otro estudiante (el editor) responde con su opinión o posibles consecuencias. Usen el subjuntivo cuando sea posible.

La vaquita está en peligro

La vaquita, una marsopa *(porpoise)*, está en peligro de extinción. Vive únicamente en una zona del Golfo de California en México y es uno de los mamíferos más amenazados del mundo. La estimación es que la vaquita se extinguirá posiblemente en el año 2018. Pero eso puede ocurrir antes si no se elimina inmediatamente su captura con redes de pesca. México es el líder en los esfuerzos para salvar la vaquita y formó el Comité Internacional para la Recuperación de la Vaquita (CIRVA). Este comité recomienda que el gobierno de México imponga regulaciones de emergencia. La pesca ilegal se ha incrementado y la vigilancia en el mar no es suficiente. Es necesario eliminar el uso, posesión o transporte de redes de pesca en la zona de la vaquita. Además el Comité quiere que el gobierno introduzca otros métodos de pesca.

El español en el mundo del trabajo

Rescatista internacional en Sudamérica

En los países de habla hispana existen brigadas de rescate que ayudan a las víctimas de tragedias como, por ejemplo, la de los 33 mineros que quedaron atrapados en una mina el 5 de agosto de 2010 en Copiapó, Chile. Para desempeñar *(perform)* este trabajo se necesita entrenamiento, equipo y conocimiento del idioma para comunicarse y coordinarse con los demás rescatistas *(rescuers)*. No importa cuál sea la especialidad del rescatista: primeros auxilios, excavación, demolición o control de incendios, hablar español le permite al rescatista trabajar en equipo con las otras organizaciones nacionales. Hoy en día, existen numerosos grupos, tanto oficiales como no oficiales, que desempeñan esta labor tan importante.

• ¿Conoces a algún grupo de rescatistas?

• ¿Te gustaría trabajar como rescatista?

Capítulo 9 • cuatrocientos treinta y uno **431**

36

Suggestions: Have students note down their ideas for responses to the questions on their own. Tell them their notes do not have to be in the form of complete sentences. Have them use these notes as they discuss the questions with a partner or in a group.

Answers:

1. reglas
2. El gobierno de México necesita imponer regulaciones de inmediato e introducir nuevos métodos de pesca.
3. Posiblemente salvaría la vaquita de extinción.
4. Answers will vary.

El español en el mundo del trabajo

Suggestions: Once students have read the information, ask comprehension questions. For example: *¿Cuáles son algunas especialidades de los rescatistas? (Son primeros auxilios, excavación, demolición y control de incendios.)*

Answers will vary.

Additional Resources

📶 **Technology: Online Resources**
• Instant Check
• Guided, Core, Audio
• Para hispanohablantes
• Technology: Audio Cap 9: Comm. Audio Act. 4–5
• Communicative Pair Activity

Print
• Teacher's Resource Materials: Audio Script
• Guided WB pp. 293–294
• Core WB p. 128–130

Assessment

Prueba 9-7 with Remediation (online only)
Prueba: Más conjunciones con el subjuntivo
• Prueba 9-7
Examen: Vocabulario y gramática 2
• Examen 2
• ExamView: Examen 2

Enrich Your Teaching

Culture Note

In 1998, Brazil and Argentina proposed a South Atlantic whale sanctuary, stretching from the equator to Antarctica, and from South America to Africa. Before whaling, there were 100,000 humpbacks in these waters, but due to exploitation the numbers dwindled to 10,000. Today, after strong recovery efforts, there are close to 60,000 humpbacks in the South Atlantic.

21st Century Skills

Creativity and Innovation Have students working in small groups come up with a creative idea for a product to protect the planet, as announced in the conference brochure in *Actividad* 34. Have a representative from each group describe the benefits of their environmentally-friendly product as if they were participants in the conference.

Puente a la cultura

Standards: 1.2, 3.1

Suggestions

Pre-reading: Refer students to the *Estrategia* and have them read the topic sentences from the selection in order to better understand the information. Ask them to share background knowledge they may have about the function of topic sentences from their Language Arts courses.

Reading: Help students resolve comprehension problems by asking *sí/no* or embedded-answer questions: *En el siglo XVI, ¿los barcos españoles fueron atacados por los piratas ingleses o por los piratas peruanos? (por los piratas ingleses) ¿El exceso de tortugas es uno de los problemas que enfrenta las islas Galápagos? (No, pero un problema es el exceso de la población humana.)*

Post-reading: Ask volunteers to tell in their own words about the important details that support the topic sentence in each paragraph of the selection.

COUNTRY CONNECTION

Standards: 3.1

Resources: Mapa global interactivo

 Technology: Mapa global interactivo, Actividad 4 Explore the Islas Galápagos off the coast of Ecuador.

Suggestions: Ecuador's official name for the Galapagos Islands is the ***Archipiélago de Colón***. Before the historical events presented on these pages, it is thought that people from the northern part of the Incan Empire, the Chimu, were present here. The islands were "discovered" by Europeans in 1535, when the Bishop of Panama's ship was blown off course on its way to Peru. The archipelago consists of eight major islands, thirteen smaller ones, and forty islets. Besides the turtles mentioned in the reading selection, the islands are famous for their iguanas, of which there are two types: the sea iguana and the land iguana.

Online Cultural Reading

Standards: 2.1, 4.2

Suggestions: After doing the online activity, ask students to name an animal that they think should be included in the list of protected animals and explain why they selected it.

Puente a la cultura

OBJECTIVES
▶ Read about the history of the Galapagos Islands
▶ Learn about the endangered species of the Galapagos
▶ Use topic sentences to increase comprehension

Galápagos: El encuentro con la naturaleza

Las islas Galápagos son un archipiélago de más de cincuenta islas que se encuentran en el Océano Pacífico a 800 kilómetros de la costa del Ecuador. Estas islas, que forman una provincia del Ecuador, son de origen volcánico y se ubican[1] directamente en la línea ecuatorial. Las islas son famosas por sus tortugas gigantes, que pueden vivir más de 100 años.

A finales del siglo XVI los piratas ingleses se establecieron en el archipiélago para atacar los barcos españoles que traían riquezas del Perú. Los piratas descubrieron que la carne de las tortugas gigantes era una excelente fuente de alimentos. Además, las tortugas podían vivir en los barcos, sin comida ni agua, por muchos meses.

A finales del siglo XVIII llegaron los balleneros. Pronto comenzaron a cazar las tortugas con la misma velocidad con que cazaban las ballenas. Se cree que mataron alrededor de 200,000 tortugas.

En 1835, un joven inglés de 22 años llamado Charles Darwin llegó a las islas en el barco *HMS Beagle* y pasó cinco semanas estudiando su fauna. Las ideas centrales de su libro fundamental, *El origen de las especies*, nacieron a partir de su viaje en el *Beagle*. La teoría propone[2] que las tortugas son las especies más fuertes que sobreviven[3] a través del tiempo.

[1]they are located [2]proposes [3]survive

Estrategia

Using topic sentences to orient you In this text, you will read about the history of a particular place. As you read, notice how the topic sentence of each paragraph helps orient you. Each topic sentence contains a date, and the paragraph then discusses a particular period in history. As you read, think about what other information the topic sentence provides to set the scene for the rest of the paragraph.

Online Cultural Reading

Go to Auténtico ONLINE to read and understand a website about an environmental organization.

Estrategia Use prior knowledge: As you read the website, ask yourself whether what you find is similar to what you already know.

¡Inténtalo! Explore the website. What organizations in your culture are similar to or different from the one in the website? Do they have similar goals, publications, and events?

Differentiated Instruction

Students with Learning Difficulties

Assign each paragraph of the reading to a small group of students. Direct each group to create a picture based on the main idea of their paragraph. Then, have students arrange their pictures by date to create a pictorial timeline of the reading's main ideas.

Advanced Learners

Ask students to research a Galapagos animal on the Internet. Have them present brief oral reports in which they present a few interesting facts about their chosen animal.

En 1935 el gobierno ecuatoriano decidió establecer una reserva natural de flora y fauna en las islas. En esa época, 3 de las 14 especies de tortugas habían desaparecido junto con algunos mamíferos y aves del lugar. En 1959 se creó la Fundación Charles Darwin para las islas Galápagos. Su trabajo de investigación y protección de los animales logró salvar varias especies que estaban por desaparecer.

El turismo organizado comenzó en 1970, pero se han implementado estrictas reglas para el cuidado de la fauna del lugar. Hoy en día las islas enfrentan muchos problemas, como el exceso de población y la falta de recursos del gobierno ecuatoriano para proteger su flora y fauna. Pero muchos colaboran para preservar este lugar único . . . y sus tortugas gigantes.

¿Comprendiste?

1. Usando las frases que empiezan cada párrafo, dibuja una línea de tiempo identificando los períodos de tiempo en la historia de las islas Galápagos de los que habla el artículo. Usa la línea de tiempo para parafrasear el tema, la idea principal y los detalles.

2. ¿A qué país pertenecen las islas Galápagos? ¿Dónde se encuentran?

3. ¿Por qué se establecieron en Galápagos los piratas ingleses?

4. ¿Qué logró la Fundación Charles Darwin para las islas Galápagos?

5. ¿Qué problemas enfrentan hoy en día las islas?

 Videodocumentario Exploremos la naturaleza fascinante.

 Mapa global interactivo Explora las islas Galápagos en Ecuador y analiza el papel que las islas jugaron en las investigaciones científicas.

Suggestions: Have students write their responses to the questions on their own. For item 1, ask them to write a brief identifying detail at each point on their time line.

Answers:

1. Siglo XVI, piratas ingleses descubren las tortugas gigantes; siglo XVIII, llegada de los balleneros; 1835, llegada de Charles Darwin; 1935, creación de la reserva natural; 1959, Fundación Charles Darwin para las islas Galápagos; 1970, comienzo del turismo organizado

2. Las islas Galápagos forman una provincia del Ecuador. Se ubican directamente en la línea ecuatorial en el Océano Pacífico, a 800 kilómetros de la costa del Ecuador.

3. Los piratas ingleses se establecieron en Galápagos porque querían atacar los barcos españoles que traían riquezas del Perú.

4. La Fundación Charles Darwin logró salvar varias especies que estaban por desaparecer.

5. Hoy en día las islas enfrentan muchos problemas, como el exceso de población y la falta de recursos del gobierno ecuatoriano para proteger su flora y fauna.

Digital Portfolio

Keep students' responses to the *¿Comprendiste?* questions in their portfolios as a writing sample.

 Technology: Videodocumentario

Standards: 1.2

Resources: Teacher's Resource Materials: Video Script, Video Program, Cap. 9

View *Exploremos la naturaleza fascinante* with the class to learn more about the economic use and environmental protection of natural resources in the Spanish-speaking world. Access the video online in **Realize**. See the *Video Teacher's Guide* for additional suggestions.

Additional Resources

Technology: Online Resources
• *Videodocumentario*
• Guided, Writing, Reading
• *Para hispanohablantes*
• Cultural Reading Activity
Print
• Guided WB p. 295

Enrich Your Teaching

Culture Note

The Galapagos Islands are part of Ecuador's national park system. The human population lives in roughly five percent of the islands' area that is not a park. One of the main challenges facing the wildlife of the islands today is the introduction by humans of animals such as pigs and goats, which destroy natural habitats, and rats, which prey on the young of wild animals.

21st Century Skills

Information Literacy Have students research Web sites in Spanish that give more information about the Galapagos Islands. Have them find photos of the unique endangered species that live there. What keywords will they use in their search? How can they decide which Web sites will give them reliable and accurate information?

¿Qué me cuentas?

Standards: 1.1, 1.2, 1.3

Resources: Teacher's Resource Materials: Audio Script, Technology: Audio Cap. 9

AP® Skills: Integration of listening, reading, and writing to comprehend and synthesize information from spoken and written sources.

Suggestions: For Step 1, use the audio or read the descriptions aloud. Allow students to hear the descriptions and true/false statements twice.

For Step 2, have students identify significant details as they read and then summarize the main points.

Have students review the rules on pages 414 and 428 before they begin Step 3. Encourage them to use each of the suggested expressions.

 Technology: Audio Script and Answers

Cuando estaba de vacaciones en Chile, Catalina pasó un día entero en el sol sin llevar crema protectora. Su piel estaba completamente roja y el cuerpo le hervía. Sus amigas se asustaron mucho y decidieron llevarla al hospital. Allí la revisó una doctora, quien le dijo que se había quemado demasiado a causa del sol. La doctora le explicó que en esa zona del planeta existía un agujero en la capa de ozono y el sol era muy peligroso para la piel.

1. Catalina se quemó a causa del sol en España. *(F)*
2. La doctora le dijo que el sol en Chile era peligroso para la piel. *(C)*

La doctora también le dijo a Catalina que usara siempre crema protectora para que el sol no la quemara. Le aconsejó que por unos días no fuera a la playa a menos que usara ropa que le cubriera todo el cuerpo. Catalina tuvo que hacer lo que le dijo la doctora. Le tomó unos cuantos días recuperarse sin ir a la playa.

3. La doctora le aconsejó que usara crema protectora y cubriera la cara si fuera a la playa. *(C)*
4. Carolina decidió no ir a la playa. *(C)*

Esas vacaciones cambiaron la forma en que Catalina pensaba acerca del medio ambiente. Hasta ese momento, Catalina no había pensado en la preservación del planeta. Su experiencia en Chile le hizo tomar conciencia del peligro de los agujeros en la capa de ozono. Después del viaje, Catalina decidió limitar su uso de aerosoles y empezó a hacer un esfuerzo para conservar los recursos naturales de su comunidad.

5. Catalina empezó a tomar más importancia en la preservación del planeta después de sus vacaciones. *(C)*
6. Para conservar los recursos naturales ella empezó a usar menos aerosoles. *(F)*

Steps 2–3: Answers will vary.

Additional Resources

Technology: Online Resources
• *Para hispanohablantes*

Pre-AP®
Integración

OBJECTIVES
▶ Listen to and read about a vacation that teaches you about global warming
▶ Write about the environment and how to take care of it

¿Qué me cuentas?: Unas vacaciones inolvidables

 1 Escucha estas descripciones de las vacaciones de Catalina. Después de cada párrafo vas a oír dos declaraciones. Escucha cada declaración y escribe *C* (Cierta) o *F* (Falsa).

2 Ahora lee el artículo que Catalina escribió para su periódico escolar.

Recalentamiento global

Además del uso de productos aerosoles, hay otros factores que amenazan la capa de ozono: el recalentamiento global y el efecto invernadero causado por los gases que se quedan en la atmósfera, sobre todo el CO_2. Este gas se queda en la parte inferior de la atmósfera y atrapa el calor, que contribuye al recalentamiento global. Y cuando menos calor pasa de la parte inferior a la parte superior de la atmósfera, donde está la capa de ozono, la parte superior más se enfría. Resulta que mientras más se enfríe, más se dañará la capa de ozono.

El uso de energía produce CO_2. Por eso cada uno de nostros debe reducir la energía que usamos. O sea, reducir nuestra "huella de carbono."[1]

A continuación se indican las fuentes mayores de uso de energía en el país y en las viviendas. ¿Cómo puedes ayudar y usar menos energía?

[1] carbon footprint

Fuentes de emisiones que más contribuyen al recalentamiento global en EE.UU.

- Electricidad
- Transporte
- Industria
- Comercio y residencial
- Agricultura

9% · 12% · 31% · 21% · 27%

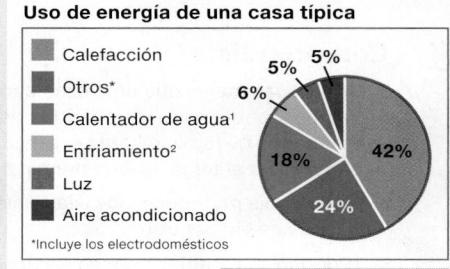

Uso de energía de una casa típica

- Calefacción
- Otros*
- Calentador de agua[1]
- Enfriamiento[2]
- Luz
- Aire acondicionado

5% · 5% · 6% · 42% · 18% · 24%

*Incluye los electrodomésticos

[1] water heater [2] cooling

 3 Escribe un artículo sobre la experiencia que motivó a Catalina a estudiar sobre el medio ambiente y las recomendaciones que ella hace. ¿Qué pueden hacer tú y tus compañeros y por qué? Usa las expresiones para conectar tus ideas.

| antes de que | tan pronto como | hasta que | sin que | para que |

Differentiated Instruction

Social Learner

Encourage students to follow through on the topics of their oral presentations. Have students form action teams based on their areas of interest, and give them an opportunity to bring their message to the wider school audience through posters or announcements.

Students with Learning Difficulties

Students may have difficulty recalling and utilizing new vocabulary. Refer them to the vocabulary lists on pp. 400 and 402. Have students identify and copy words that would be useful to their oral presentations.

Presentación oral

	OBJECTIVES
	▸ Demonstrate how to organize a campaign to keep your community clean
	▸ Use details to improve your presentation

Go **Online** to practice
PEARSON
realize™

PearsonSchool.com/Autentico

🔊 AUDIO   ✍ WRITING   🎤 SPEAK/RECORD

Campaña para limpiar la comunidad

TAREA Vas a organizar una campaña para limpiar tu comunidad. Tienes que convencer a tus compañeros de que es necesario mantener limpia la ciudad para evitar la contaminación. Haz un discurso persuasivo para presentar tus ideas.

❶ Prepárate Completa una red de palabras como la siguiente.

¿Por qué hay que mantener limpia la comunidad?

> **Estrategia**
> **Finding good details** When giving a speech, you need to include appropriate details in order to make sense when talking about your topic. Interesting details add color and life to what you talk about and give it more substance. A good way to choose the right details to include is to ask these questions: *Who? What? Where? Why? When? How?*

❷ Practica Vuelve a leer la red de palabras. Practica tu presentación para recordar los detalles. Puedes usar tus notas para practicar. Recuerda:

- explicar cada razón usando oraciones conectadas con detalles y elaboración
- presentar un plan a tus compañeros de lo que deben hacer
- mirar al público y hablar con voz clara y persuasiva

Modelo

Existen muchas razones para que mantengamos limpia nuestra comunidad. Es importante que sepamos que la contaminación se puede evitar. Cada uno de nosotros puede contribuir con la tarea.

❸ Haz tu presentación Imagina que tus compañeros de clase van a ayudar a limpiar la comunidad. Explícales por qué es importante.

❹ Evaluación Se utilizará la siguiente rúbrica para evaluar tu presentación.

Rubric	Score 1	Score 3	Score 5
How well you organize information	The information you present is not well organized.	Your information is somewhat organized but hard to follow.	Your information is well organized and easy to follow.
How well you use details	You do not include details that make your speech interesting.	Your details are too few; some do not belong with your main idea.	Your details are interesting and support your main idea.
How well you deliver your speech	You read your speech and make no eye contact.	You make some eye contact, and use some intonation.	Your eye contact is good. Your intonation helps you persuade.

Capítulo 9 • cuatrocientos treinta y cinco **435**

Enrich Your Teaching

21st Century Skills

Collaboration Have students review the rubrics on pp. 435 and 437. Have them work in partners and discuss why their teacher gives them rubrics; how are they supposed to be used? Have them work with one of the rubrics to start with the outcome, figure out what they have to do to get the best grade possible, and develop a plan to achieve that goal.

Presentación oral

Standards: 1.1, 1.2, 1.3, 3.1, 5.1

Suggestions: Review the task and the four-step approach with students. Review the rubric with the class (see *Assessment* below) to explain how you will grade the performance task. Before students begin, direct their attention to the *Estrategia*. Remind them of how the inclusion of details made for interesting reading in the *Puente a la cultura* section on pp. 432–433. Draw a word web on the board and have students create a similar word web on their own paper. Model how to include some details related to the topic that would make for an interesting and persuasive speech, i.e. details about a litter problem or a clean-up program at your school.

Pre-AP® Integration

- **Learning Objective:** Presentational Speaking
- **Pre-AP® Resource Materials:** Comprehensive guide to Pre-AP® speaking skill development

Digital Portfolio

Make video or audio recordings of student presentations in class, or assign the Speak and Record activity so they can record their presentations online. Include the recording in their portfolios.

Additional Resources

 Technology: Online Resources
- *Para hispanohablantes*

Self Assessment

Presentación oral
- **Assessment Program:** Rubrics
Review the rubric with students. Go over the descriptions of the different levels of performance. After assessing students, help individuals understand how their performance could be improved. (See Teacher's Resource Materials for suggestions on using rubrics in assessment.)

Language Arts Connection: Persuasive Writing

Standards: 3.1

Encourage students to draw on background knowledge they have from their Language Arts courses about introductions and conclusions in formal speaking and writing. Remind them that introductions and conclusions act as signposts to prepare the reader for the information presented and to summarize the information so it is easier to remember.

Presentación escrita

Standards: 1.3, 3.1

Suggestions: Begin by explaining the criteria you will use to evaluate students' compositions. (See Step 5, *Evaluación*, in the Student Edition, and *Assessment* on the following page.)

Direct students' attention to the *Estrategia*. Remind them that an effective conclusion of a composition or letter almost always restates the main idea in other words. For this assignment, it should also help persuade. Draw a T-chart on the board. Model filling in information like that shown in the chart on this page, and have students follow along on their own paper. Have them continue adding ideas to their charts that will help them develop their own compositions. Encourage them to do some outside research in order to find additional facts and interesting details that will improve their compositions.

Pre-AP® Integration

- **Learning Objective:** Presentational Writing
- **Pre-AP® Resource Materials:** Comprehensive guide to Pre-AP® writing skill development

---

Presentación escrita

Cuidemos nuestros océanos

Trabajas como voluntario(a) en una asociación para la preservación de los océanos. Tienes que escribir un correo electrónico a una empresa petrolera para que tome conciencia de los problemas que producen los derrames de petróleo y qué cosas se pueden hacer para evitarlos. Puedes concentrarte en los problemas que producen en su flora y fauna y las consecuencias para las personas.

Estrategia

Good conclusions It's always a good idea to end what you write with a good conclusion that draws your main ideas together. For example, your conclusion can review ideas you introduced earlier and give a few sentences that tie them together. Your conclusion can also summarize your main idea in other words, or it can close with an interesting comment that leaves your reader wanting to know more about your topic.

① Antes de escribir Completa una tabla como la siguiente para reunir datos sobre los problemas que producen los derrames de petróleo en las aguas de los océanos.

Problemas que causan los derrames	Cómo se pueden evitar
• destrucción de las plantas	• tener cuidado
• contaminación del alimento de los peces	• tomar conciencia de los peligros
•	•
•	•

② Borrador Escribe tu borrador. Expresa tu opinión y defiéndela con una explicación de cómo afectan los derrames de petróleo a los océanos. Incluye tus recomendaciones de qué se puede hacer para evitarlos. Añade todos los detalles necesarios. Recuerda que debes usar el vocabulario y la gramática de este capítulo.

Modelo

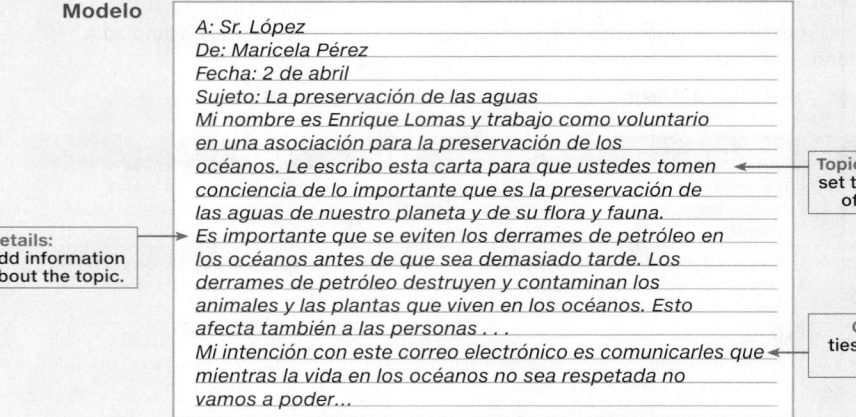

A: Sr. López
De: Maricela Pérez
Fecha: 2 de abril
Sujeto: La preservación de las aguas
Mi nombre es Enrique Lomas y trabajo como voluntario en una asociación para la preservación de los océanos. Le escribo esta carta para que ustedes tomen conciencia de lo importante que es la preservación de las aguas de nuestro planeta y de su flora y fauna.
Es importante que se eviten los derrames de petróleo en los océanos antes de que sea demasiado tarde. Los derrames de petróleo destruyen y contaminan los animales y las plantas que viven en los océanos. Esto afecta también a las personas . . .
Mi intención con este correo electrónico es comunicarles que mientras la vida en los océanos no sea respetada no vamos a poder...

Details: add information about the topic.

Topic sentence: set the purpose of the e-mail.

Conclusion: ties everything together.

Differentiated Instruction

Heritage Speakers

Students may have difficulty organizing their writing into formal, cohesive paragraphs. Have students write the topic sentence of each paragraph they plan to include at the top of an index card. Then have them add supporting details below. Remind them that each card will constitute one paragraph.

Advanced Learners

Encourage students to experiment with more than one attempt at a concluding paragraph for their letters. They might simply summarize the ideas presented in the body of the composition, restate the introduction in other words, or ask a question or two that will keep their readers thinking about the implications of what they have said.

Go **Online** to practice
PEARSON
realize.

PearsonSchool.com/Autentico

WRITING

Presentational 9

3 **Redacción/Revisión** Después de escribir el primer borrador, trabaja con otro(a) compañero(a) para intercambiar los trabajos y leerlos. Decidan qué aspectos son más efectivos. Luego, hagan sugerencias para mejorar sus composiciones. Fíjense si:

- ¿Se usó correctamente el subjuntivo o el indicativo después de las conjunciones?
- ¿Están conectadas las oraciones con detalles y elaboración?
- ¿Hay concordancia *(agreement)* entre los sujetos y los verbos?
- ¿Existen errores de ortografía?

En caso de algún error, corríjanlo.

> *Le escribo esta carta para que ustedes*
> *tomen*
> *~~toman~~ conciencia de lo importante*
> *es   preservación*
> *que ~~son~~ ~~la preservasión~~ de las aguas de*
>
> *nuestro planeta y de su flora y fauna.*

4 **Publicación** Antes de hacer la versión final, lee de nuevo tu borrador y repasa los siguientes puntos:

- ¿Muestra el correo electrónico mi punto de vista respecto al tema?
- ¿Incluí detalles y recomendaciones con mi opinión?
- ¿Refleja la importancia de comprender el problema?
- ¿Presenta una conclusión interesante?

Después de revisar el borrador, escribe una copia en limpio.

5 **Evaluación** Se utilizará la siguiente rúbrica para evaluar tu presentación.

Rubric	Score 1	Score 3	Score 5
Completion of task	Important parts of your e-mail are missing.	Parts of your e-mail are missing or disorganized.	You include and organize all the parts needed for a persuasive e-mail.
Effective conclusion	Your e-mail lacks an effective conclusion.	Your e-mail has a conclusion, but it is not effective.	You include an effective conclusion that helps persuade your readers.
Grammar, spelling, mechanics	You make many errors in grammar, spelling, and punctuation.	You make some errors in grammar, spelling, and punctuation.	You make very few errors in grammar, spelling, and punctuation.

Suggestions (Cont'd):

In Step 2, students should concentrate on how to develop and organize their ideas from the chart from Step 1 into an effective sequence. This is also the step in which they should focus on an effective conclusion for their persuasive letter. Encourage them to work toward organization, level of detail, and language use similar to that shown in the model.

For Step 3, encourage students to experiment with various ways of combining sentences. Remind them that this often entails use of the subjunctive. Have them follow the revision suggestions shown.

Evaluation

Steps 4 and 5 overlap. Students will need evaluation by you, their peers, or self-evaluation to fine-tune and polish their drafts.

Digital Portfolio

Keep students' final drafts in their portfolios as a writing sample

Additional Resources

 Technology: Online Resources
- *Para hispanohablantes*

Self Assessment

Presentación escrita
- **Assessment Program:** Rubrics

Review the rubric with students. Go over the descriptions of the different levels of performance. After assessing students, help individuals understand how their performance could be improved. (See Teacher's Resource Materials for suggestions on using rubrics in assessment.)

Enrich Your Teaching

21st Century Skills

Communication Students will use their written language for the purpose of petitioning a corporation about an environmental problem. They will need to use formal language in a business letter format. Have them work in small groups and determine the desired format for a business letter and the appropriate language to use when addressing a company's representative. What is a proper way to begin and end a business letter?

Lectura

Suggestions

Pre-reading: Before reading, direct students' attention to the *Estrategia* and *Al leer* sections. Have them begin a T-chart similar to the one on p. 441 and make sure they understand how they will use it. Point out that their T-charts will help them keep track of important details related to the points listed in *Al leer*. Have a volunteer read the subtitles of the passage aloud, so that the class can get an idea of how the information about Monarch butterflies will be presented.

Reading: Allow students time to read the selection on their own silently. Consider assigning this task for homework. This will allow you to capitalize on class time to read it again together with students. When reading together, pause frequently to address comprehension issues they may have and to allow them to fill in their ***Mariposa monarca*** charts from p. 441. Ask comprehension questions to help them focus on the main idea and important details in sections of the reading. Suggestions for these begin on the next page.

COUNTRY CONNECTION

Resources: Mapa de México

 Technology: Mapa global interactivo, Actividad 5 Follow monarch butterfly migrations to Mexico.

Suggestions: The state of Michoacán lies to the west of the state of México, (where Ciudad de México is located). Since it extends from the center of Mexico to the Pacific coast, Michoacán has a variety of climactic zones and terrains. It is primarily an agricultural and livestock-raising zone, specializing in lemons, corn, cotton, sugar cane, beef cattle, and pigs. The capital of Michoacán is Morelia, a city with a population of nearly one million.

Lectura

Al leer

Vas a leer un artículo sobre la mariposa monarca. Como ocurre casi siempre en los textos de no ficción, encontrarás palabras relacionadas con el tema de las mariposas que quizás no conozcas. Recuerda que debes tratar de determinar su significado a partir del contexto antes de consultar el diccionario o pedir ayuda a otra persona. Antes de leer, copia la tabla que aparece al final de la lectura. Mientras lees, complétala para que puedas contestar las preguntas sobre la lectura. Presta atención a los siguientes puntos:

• la migración de la mariposa monarca
• características que diferencian a esta mariposa de las demás
• los problemas que amenazan a la mariposa monarca

La mariposa monarca

Tres cuartas partes de los animales que viven en la tierra son insectos. De todos los insectos, quizás el más hermoso sea la mariposa monarca. Este insecto, además de ser increíblemente bello, es un importante agente polinizador[1] y un factor de equilibrio ecológico.

Las mariposas, en general, viven alrededor de 24 días; sin embargo, la mariposa monarca puede llegar a vivir 8 meses, es decir, 12 veces más que las otras especies de mariposas. Además, es muy resistente a las condiciones del clima.

[1] pollen carrier

Differentiated Instruction

Heritage Speakers

Ask students to read ***La mariposa monarca*** aloud. Have them model pronunciation, and encourage them to follow the rules of punctuation in their reading. They should briefly pause at each comma, and pause a bit longer at each period.

Students with Learning Difficulties

Students may have difficulty organizing the wealth of information provided in the non-fiction passage. Have them create their own concept webs around the theme of ***La mariposa monarca***. As they encounter interesting facts in the reading, instruct them to record the information on their webs.

La ruta de las mariposas monarca

Llegada a México

Cada año, millones de mariposas monarca vuelan desde Canadá, lugar de donde provienen[2], hasta México. Llegan a fines de octubre a la zona entre Michoacán y el Estado de México y a mediados[3] de abril comienzan el viaje de regreso al norte. Es un viaje de más de 4,000 kilómetros.

En el camino, las mariposas se alimentan de asclepias[4], unas plantas que contienen una sustancia que es venenosa para otras especies. Esta sustancia le da a la mariposa un sabor y un olor desagradables, y esto le sirve de protección contra otros animales. La mariposa monarca también ayuda a la asclepia, pues es su agente de polinización.

Las condiciones de las montañas michoacanas son ideales para las mariposas: hay mucho oxígeno, están protegidas del viento y la temperatura es casi siempre agradable. Por otra parte, gracias a que los millones de mariposas que llegan a esta zona son agentes de polinización, hay una gran variedad de plantas en esta región.

[2]come from [3]in the middle of [4]milkweed

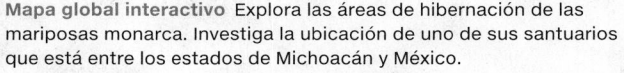

Mapa global interactivo Explora las áreas de hibernación de las mariposas monarca. Investiga la ubicación de uno de sus santuarios que está entre los estados de Michoacán y México.

Hibernación

Durante mucho tiempo se pensó que la mariposa monarca pasaba el invierno en zonas tropicales; pero nadie sabía adónde iban. Fue un misterio hasta 1975, en que después de décadas de investigación se encontró su lugar de hibernación. Para sorpresa de muchos, estaba en una zona donde las temperaturas normales están cerca de cero grados centígrados, en una región boscosa[5] entre valles y montañas. Esta región tiene una altitud promedio[6] de 3,300 metros sobre el nivel del mar, y se encuentra en la majestuosa Sierra Madre de México, entre Michoacán y el Estado de México.

Como la mariposa es un insecto de sangre fría, puede ajustar[7] la temperatura de su cuerpo al medio ambiente, lo que le permite conservar una gran cantidad de energía y grasa para su largo viaje de regreso.

Migración

Las mariposas monarca deben migrar en invierno porque el clima de Canadá es extremadamente frío durante esa estación. Para asegurar su sobrevivencia[8], las mariposas comienzan a desplazarse[9] al sur a medida que se acerca el invierno. Al llegar a las zonas de hibernación entre los estados de México y Michoacán, las mariposas buscan los lugares con la mejor temperatura para hibernar.

El número de mariposas que llega a los diferentes refugios del Estado de México y Michoacán está entre los 100 y los 140 millones, de acuerdo con las condiciones de su hábitat de verano en Canadá y los Estados Unidos.

[5]wooded [6]average [7]to adjust [8]survival [9]travel

Capítulo 9 • cuatrocientos treinta y nueve **439**

Go Online to practice
PEARSON
realize.™

PearsonSchool.com/Autentico

MAPA GLOBAL

Suggestions (Cont'd):

Reading: Here are some possible comprehension issues on pp. 438–439 for which you can provide some guidance:

p. 438

- After reading the first sentence of the selection, ask a volunteer to write on the board the numerical percentage of earth's animals that are insects. (75%)
- After reading the second paragraph, ask a volunteer to write an arithmetical sentence that shows the calculation of how long a Monarch butterfly lives compared to most other butterflies. (Possible response: 24 días mariposa típica X 12 veces más = 288 días ó 9.6 meses.)

p. 439

- *¿De dónde vienen las mariposas monarca? (de Canadá)*
- *¿En qué meses del año se quedan las mariposas monarca en su lugar en México? (desde octubre hasta abril)*
- *¿A los demás animales les gusta comer las mariposas monarca? (No. Las mariposas tienen un sabor y un olor desagradables para los demás animales.)*
- *¿Qué fue un misterio hasta 1975 sobre las mariposas monarca? (el lugar donde se hibernan)*
- *¿Cuál tiene más influencia sobre la hibernación de las mariposas monarca, la presión atmosférica o la temperatura? (la temperatura)*

Pre-AP® Integration

- **Learning Objective:** Interpretive: Print
- **Activity:** Have students work in groups of five. Assign each student in the group one of the five subtitled sections of this article. Ask that they create three multiple-choice questions for their section. While sitting in a circle, each student passes their three questions to the person on their left. The person assigned the first section, *Llegada a México*, reads the section aloud to the group. The person to his or her left asks one of the three questions to each of the other three students. Rotate around the circle in the same way until all sections have been read and all questions answered.
- **Pre-AP® Resource Materials:** Comprehensive guide to Pre-AP® reading skill development

---

Enrich Your Teaching

Teacher-to-Teacher

Monarch butterflies are present in many parts of the United States during one part of the year or another. Invite students to talk about personal sightings of Monarch butterflies. If milkweed grows nearby, ask volunteers to bring in samples and tell where they found them. Interested students may wish to create a ***Centro de mariposas monarca*** in which they display photos and other information.

21st Century Skills

ICT (Information, Communications and Technology) Literacy Remind students of the various digital tools available in **Realize** to access extra reading support. Computer corrected activities use different reading strategies to help students build their vocabulary and progress at their own pace through the reading.

Suggestions (Cont'd):

Reading: Here are some possible comprehension issues on this page for which you can provide some guidance:

- *Mira la sección **Refugios**. Sabemos ya el significado de la palabra "lado." Basado en esto y las claves de contexto, adivina qué palabra en este párrafo significa "el lado de una montaña"? (ladera)*

- *Mira la sección **Peligros**. Usa claves de contexto para contestar la pregunta siguiente. ¿Qué significa la palabra "esfuerzo", ministro o intento? (intento)*

Post-reading: Have students refer to their *Mariposa monarca* charts. Ask them to skim through the selection again to verify the information they have written there.

Sobrevivir[10] el invierno es una tarea difícil para las monarcas. También es importante el papel que juegan los depredadores[11], aves y pequeños mamíferos, ya que de las mariposas muertas el 50% muestra mutilaciones y señales de ataque. La mortalidad natural en invierno se acerca al 35% aunque cambia de acuerdo a las condiciones del clima.

Refugios

Los refugios son lugares donde se reúnen las monarcas para pasar el invierno y reproducirse; se trata de bosques localizados en las laderas de las montañas y que están resguardados[12] del aire polar y de los cambios del clima. Los refugios se localizan entre los 2,700 y 3,200 metros de altitud sobre el nivel del mar, dependiendo de las condiciones del clima de cada año.

Peligros

En los últimos años, el mayor problema de las monarcas es la desaparición[13] de su hábitat. El uso de pesticidas en las cosechas[14] agrícolas y la tala[15] de árboles hacen que desaparezca la planta asclepias, donde estas mariposas ponen huevos.

Otro problema para las mariposas es el clima en Norteamérica. Las variaciones extremas del clima, como la sequía[16] o las tormentas, han afectado la migración. De acuerdo con el *Center for Biological Diversity*, la población de las mariposas monarca ha disminuido en un 90 por ciento. Pero en 2015 hubo buenas noticias: los científicos registraron por primera vez, en los últimos 4 años, un aumento en el número de mariposas monarca migrando de Estados Unidos a México. Sin embargo, ese número es el penúltimo más bajo desde que empezó el registro en 1994. Se considera incluir la mariposa monarca en la lista de especies en peligro de extinción. En febrero de 2015, el presidente Obama de Estados Unidos, el presidente Peña Nieto de México y el primer Ministro Harper de Canadá acordaron coordinar los esfuerzos para preservar el hábitat de la mariposa monarca en toda Norteamérica.

Las mariposas monarca son insectos bellos, útiles y resistentes. Debemos hacer todo lo posible para proteger los increíbles habitantes que comparten este planeta con nosotros.

[16]drought

[10]to survive [11]predators [12]protected
[13]disappearance [14]crops [15]tree felling

Differentiated Instruction

Students with Learning Difficulties

Model for students how to transform each question into the base for their answer. For example: *¿Cuáles son los principales problemas que enfrentan las mariposas monarca? Los principales problemas que enfrentan las mariposas monarca son...*

Advanced Learners

Invite students to research and prepare brief reports on another kind of butterfly common to your area. Encourage them to make comparisons between the butterfly they research and the Monarch.

Go Online to practice

PEARSON
realize™

PearsonSchool.com/Autentico

WRITING

Interpretive Reading

9

Interacción con la lectura

1. Trabaja con un grupo de estudiantes para comentar lo que escribieron en sus tablas.

   • ¿En qué se diferencia la mariposa monarca de las demás mariposas?

   • ¿Conoces otros animales que migran para pasar el invierno en otras zonas? ¿En qué se diferencian esos animales de las mariposas monarca?

   • ¿Por qué podemos decir que las mariposas monarca no son solamente hermosas sino también muy útiles?

   • ¿Cuáles son los principales problemas que enfrentan las mariposas monarca? ¿Qué podemos hacer para protegerlas?

2. Trabaja con tu grupo para buscar palabras de la lectura que no conocías. Hablen sobre cómo infirieron el significado de esas palabras para entender la lectura.

3. Y tú, ¿qué piensas? ¿Crees que las mariposas monarca son animales extraordinarios o no? ¿Qué otro animal conoces que te parece extraordinario? Habla de ese animal a tu grupo.

Mariposa monarca	
¿Dónde vive?	
¿Cuánto tiempo vive?	
¿De qué se alimenta?	
Otras características importantes	
¿Qué peligros la amenazan?	

CULTURA ▸ México

Festival Cultural de la Mariposa Monarca Desde hace más de 20 años, en los pueblos de Michoacán cercanos a los lugares donde hibernan las mariposas monarca, se celebra el Festival Cultural de la Mariposa Monarca. El Festival tiene como objetivo promover las artes de esos pueblos y el ecoturismo en la región oriental del estado de Michoacán.

La fiesta incluye música, danza, pintura y artesanías. La sede central del festival es Angangueo, ciudad que se hizo famosa desde que en 1976 se descubrió cerca de allí el primer santuario de las mariposas monarca. Durante los 16 días del festival, los artesanos trabajan en las plazas de los pueblos y venden sus obras a sus visitantes.

• Compara el festival de la mariposa en México con algún otro festival que conozcas. ¿Qué música, danzas u otras actividades incluye el festival?

Capítulo 9 • cuatrocientos cuarenta y uno **441**

Interacción con la lectura

Standards: 1.1, 1.2, 1.3, 3.1

Suggestions: As students work together in Step 2, ask them to use their combined knowledge and context clues to resolve comprehension problems. Encourage them to use dictionaries as a last resort.

Answers:

Step 1

• La mariposa monarca se diferencia de las demás mariposas porque vive 12 veces más que las otras especies. Además es muy resistente a las condiciones del clima.

• Answers will vary.

• Las mariposas monarca no son solamente hermosas sino también muy útiles porque son un importante agente polinizador y un factor de equilibrio ecológico.

• Los principales problemas que enfrentan son el clima, los depredadores y los incendios. The remainder of this answer will vary.

Steps 2-3

• Answers will vary.

CULTURA ◂

Standards: 1.1, 1.2, 2.1, 3.1, 4.2

Suggestions: After students have read the information and answered the question, invite them to draft a letter to festival organizers in Mexico, telling them about a festival in your area that celebrates some plant or animal. In their letter, they should compare and contrast features of the *Festival Cultural de la Mariposa Monarca* and your local festival.

Answers will vary.

Additional Resources

Technology: Online Resources
  • Guided, Writing, Reading
  • Cultural Reading Activity
  Print
  • Guided WB pp. 296–297

Enrich Your Teaching

Culture Note

One of the greatest threats to the Monarch butterfly is to its natural environment. The forests in Michoacán offer a unique ecosystem. Hanging from fir trees, the Monarchs achieve the perfect temperature for their winter hibernation. Unfortunately, this forest ecosystem only constitutes 2% of the total forest area in Mexico. In addition, there are people who depend on the logging and development of these areas for economic reasons. In 1986, the *Reserva de la Biosfera Mariposa Monarca* created two zones within the butterfly's habitat. In the "nuclear zone," no logging is allowed; in the "buffer zone," only limited logging is permitted.

Auténtico

Standards: 1.2

Resources: Authentic Resources Wkbk, Cap. 9
Authentic Resources: Cap. 9: Audioscript
AP®Theme: *Los desafíos mundiales: Los temas del medio ambiente*

Antes de oír

Direct students to the photo of the landfill. Guide them to make the connection between the photo and the theme of the chapter. Then discuss the *Estrategia* with students. Explain that they will hear some terms previously learned in this chapter. You may wish to ask students to revisit the *Vocabulario en uso 1,* where the terms *reciclar, reducir,* and *reutilizar* are practiced. Then, review the key vocabulary with the class.

Technology: Oye el audio

Before starting the audio, direct student's attention to the *Mientras oyes* activity. Have them use the activity page from the *Authentic workbook.*

Play the audio once completely through, without pausing. Ask students what kind of audio is this (*una entrevista*). Who is being interviewed and on what subject? (*un experto en basura*). Replay the audio, stopping as necessary to check students' comprehension. Play the audio a final time without pausing.

Haz las actividades

Mientras oyes

Standards: 1.2

Suggestions: Explain that the chart only asks for certain figures that are listed on the audio. Ask the class to be very attentive to those figures.

Figures to complete the chart:

1. 0,63 kilogramos
2. 17,2 toneladas
3. 70 toneladas

Auténtico

Partnered with  IDB

¿Cuánta basura generas?

Antes de oír

Usa la estrategia: Conocimiento previo

Mira la foto. ¿Cómo se relaciona con el tema de este capítulo? Al oír el audio, pon atención a los términos que te parezcan familiares. Usa tus conocimientos previos para inferir el significado de palabras desconocidas y así entender mejor lo que dice el experto.

Lee el vocabulario clave

desafíos = challenges
saneamiento de residuos = handling waste
generar = to generate
domiciliarios = *adj.* household
a nivel de hogar = at the household level
asciende = reaches
rellenos sanitarios = landfills
vida útil = lifespan

🔊 Oye el audio

Todos sabemos que el exceso de basura es un gran problema ambiental. Pero, ¿te has puesto a pensar cómo puedes ayudar a combatir ese problema? Piensa en qué hace tu propia comunidad para combatirlo.

Ve a **PearsonSchool.com/Autentico** para oír el audio **¿Sabes cuánta basura generas en un día?** y saber qué cantidad de desperdicios produce una persona en promedio *(average)* en América Latina. ¿Se compara esto con otro país? ¿Cuál?

Haz las actividades

Mientras oyes En este audio escucharás muchas cifras *(numbers)* sobre la cantidad de basura que se produce en América Latina. Copia esta tabla y úsala para anotar las cifras sobre la cantidad de basura que se produce en esta región del mundo. Escucha el audio cuantas veces necesites para completar la tabla. Recuerda que en español no se dice "cinco punto tres" (5.3) sino "cinco coma tres" (5,3) para decir 5.3.

1. Cantidad de basura que genera una persona en un día	
2. Cantidad de basura que genera una persona en 75 años	
3. Cantidad de basura que genera una familia de 4 en 75 años	

Differentiated Instruction

Heritage Speakers

Invite groups of students to gather a list of variants for the term *garbage can* in different Spanish speaking countries (*cubo de basura, bote de basura, caneca, zafacón, tacho.*) Ask them to decide which of these variants would be the most universally understood by Spanish speakers. You may want to extend the activity to other domestic utensils such as *mop* (*trapero, trapeador, trampazo, mapo, mopa, coleto*) and dishcloth (*paño de cocina, limpión, trapo*).

Advanced Learners

Ask pairs of students to write a script in Spanish for a radio interview with the owner of a landfill. Make suggestions for the script, such as the owner alerting citizens that the landfill will have to be shut down in the near future if the municipality continues sending the same amount of garbage each year. Invite students to play role the interview based on their script.

Suggestions: Invite volunteers to answer the first question. Use their responses as a vehicle for a short discussion in Spanish on their personal responsibility to stop the increasing amount of trash they generate.

Answers:

1. advertir sobre el exceso de basura
2. la basura que producen las casas y comercios.
3. reducir: evitar producir basura; reusar: volver a usar algo; reciclar: transformar algo para volverlo a usar
4. porque incrementa la vida útil de los rellenos sanitarios; esto trae beneficios financieros y ambientales

For more Authentic Resources: Assign the Authentic Resources Workbook activities for homework, so that students can hear the audio on their own and complete the workbook activities at their own pace.

Pre-AP® Integration

Resources: Authentic Resources, Wkbk, Cap. 9
Authentic Resources: Cap. 9: Audioscript

Suggestions: Before completing the Pre-AP® activity, have students go to the workbook and complete the worksheets for the additional resources.

Comparación cultural

Suggestions: Have students fill out a Venn diagram with details from the audio and data about trash production in the United States to show where they differ and where they are similar.

Integración

Después de oír Vuelve a oír el audio y después contesta estas preguntas:

1. ¿Cuál crees que es el objetivo de este audio?

2. ¿Qué es la basura municipal? Explica cómo usaste tu conocimiento previo para inferir el significado de la frase.

3. ¿Cuáles son las tres formas de contribuir a que no se produzca tanta basura? Parafrasea en qué consiste cada una.

4. ¿Por qué es importante evitar que llegue tanta basura a los rellenos sanitarios? ¿Qué beneficios trae esto?

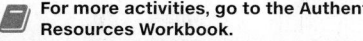 **For more activities, go to the Authentic Resources Workbook.**

Medio ambiente y conciencia social

Expansión Busca estos recursos en *Auténtico* en línea y contesta las preguntas.

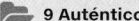 **9 Auténtico**

Integración de ideas ¿Qué impacto puede tener la conciencia social *(social awareness)* en la protección del medio ambiente?

Comparación cultural Según el audio, en Estados Unidos se produce casi un kilogramo más de basura municipal al día que en América Latina. ¿A qué crees que se debe esto? Justifica tu respuesta con ejemplos concretos.

Enrich Your Teaching

Culture Note

Spain is one of the European champions in recycling efforts. Whether it is a big metropolis like Madrid or a small town in the mountains, people will find recycling bins coded by color: blue for paper and cardboard, yellow for plastic, and green for glass. In some places you will also find orange bins for recycling used cooking oil.

Using Authentic Resources

Have students create a personal vocabulary list of terms related to the connection between consumer behavior and environmental protection. Suggest that they initiate their list with some of the key vocabulary featured in the audio: *reducir, reusar, reciclar, patrones de consumo*.

Review Activities

Sobre la contaminación/Sobre el medio ambiente: Have students prepare their own Spanish definition for each vocabulary item in these categories. Then have teams of two students play against each other in a game of "Password." One student on a team gives his or her partner a definition. The partner must name the vocabulary item defined to earn a point. If he or she cannot, the other team gets a chance at the same definition. The team that correctly matches the greatest number of definitions and vocabulary items wins.

Sobre los recursos naturales: On their own, have students write three other words or expressions that are clearly associated with each item in this category. For example, for **la protección**, a student might write **un santuario ballenero, una ley**, and **una reserva natural**. Have students conduct the next part of the activity in round-robin fashion. One student says a word that he or she has written. The next student says which **recursos naturales** word it is associated with and explains the association.

Animales/Sobre los animales: Have students create their own fill-in-the-blanks exercises for these words. Tell them to create answer keys as well. Have them exchange exercises with a partner, complete each other's exercise, and check their answers together.

Otras palabras y expresiones: Students can use these words and expressions as they go over the review activities for the other categories and in the grammar review activities on the next page.

Verbos: Ask students to perform actions that they think portray the meanings of the verbs. Those watching must guess which verb is being acted out. Some verbs, such as **derretir** and **castigar** will be easy and fun to act out. Others like **fomentar** and **promover** present more of a challenge.

Repaso del capítulo

🔊 Vocabulario

sobre la contaminación

el aerosol	aerosol
la contaminación	pollution
contaminado, -a	polluted
el derrame de petróleo	oil spill
el desperdicio	waste
la fábrica	factory
el pesticida	pesticide
el petróleo	oil
la pila	battery
químico, -a	chemical
el recipiente	container
el veneno	poison

sobre los recursos naturales

económico, -a	economical
la protección	protection
el recurso natural	natural resource
suficiente	enough

verbos

afectar	to affect
agotar(se)	to exhaust, to run out
amenazar	to threaten
atrapar	to catch, to trap
castigar	to punish
colocar	to put, place
conservar	to preserve
crecer	to grow
dañar	to damage
depender de	to depend on
derretir	to melt
deshacerse de	to get rid of
desperdiciar	to waste
detener	to stop
disminuir	to decrease, to diminish
echar	to throw (away)
explotar	to exploit, to overwork
fomentar	to encourage
limitar	to limit
producir	to produce
promover (ue)	to promote

sobre los animales

la caza	hunting

(en) peligro de extinción	(in) danger of extinction, endangered
la piel	skin
la pluma	feather
salvaje	wild

otras palabras y expresiones

el agujero	hole
la amenaza	threat
a menos que	unless
con tal que	provided that, as long as
debido a	due to
la electricidad	electricity
en cuanto	as soon as
la escasez	shortage
estar a cargo de	to be in charge of
excesivo, -a	excessive
la falta	lack
el gobierno	government
grave	serious
la limpieza	cleaning
tan pronto como	as soon as
tomar conciencia de	to become aware of
tomar medidas	to take steps (to)

sobre el medio ambiente

la atmósfera	atmosphere
la capa de ozono	ozone layer
el clima	weather
el efecto invernadero	greenhouse effect
el hielo	ice
la preservación	conservation
el recalentamiento global	global warming
el rescate	rescue
la reserva natural	nature preserve
la selva tropical	tropical forest
la tierra	land

animales

el ave	bird
el águila calva, pl. las águilas calvas	bald eagle
la ballena	whale
la especie	species
la foca	seal

Differentiated Instruction

Heritage Speakers

Have students provide examples of sentences utilizing each of the conjunctions reviewed on p. 445. Ask them to explain why they used the indicative or the subjunctive following each conjunction. Then have them write down their examples focusing on the spelling of the appropriate verb forms.

Advanced Learners

Invite students to create and exchange word-search puzzles using the chapter vocabulary. Remind them that the words hidden in their grids of letters can be written vertically, horizontally, or diagonally. Remind them to blend in the Spanish letters **ñ** and **ll** throughout their word-search grids.

Gramática

Conjunciones que se usan con el subjuntivo y el indicativo

Certain conjunctions related to time are followed by either the indicative or the subjunctive.

en cuanto	tan pronto como	cuando
mientras	hasta que	después (de) que

You use the subjunctive after these conjunctions when the action that follows has not yet taken place. You use the indicative with these conjunctions when the action that follows has already taken place or if it occurs regularly.

Van a producir petróleo **hasta que** se agote.
En cuanto salgo del cuarto, siempre apago las luces.

• The conjunction *antes de que* is always followed by the subjunctive.

Pon el helado en el refrigerador **antes de que** se derrita.

• If the subject of a sentence does not change, use the infinitive after *antes de, después de, hasta*.

Después de salir del trabajo, voy a visitar a mi amigo Juan.

Más conjunciones que se usan con el subjuntivo y el indicativo

The following conjunctions are usually followed by the subjunctive to express the purpose or intention of an action:

a menos que	para que	sin que	con tal (de) que	aunque

No haré la limpieza de la casa **a menos que** me ayudes.

• If the subject of the sentence does not change, use the infinitive after *para* and *sin*.

Debemos dejar de usar aerosoles **para** detener la destrucción de la capa de ozono.

• With the conjunction *aunque*, use the subjunctive to express uncertainty. Use the indicative when there is no uncertainty.

Aunque produzcan más petróleo no podrán depender de este recurso por mucho tiempo.
No quiero ver ese programa sobre las ballenas **aunque** todos dicen que es muy bueno.

Los pronombres relativos *que*, *quien* y *lo que*

You use relative pronouns to combine two sentences or to give clarifying information. The most common relative pronoun in Spanish is *que*. It can mean "that," "which," "who," or "whom," and it may refer either to persons or to things.

El artículo **que** salió en el periódico habla sobre la contaminación.

After a preposition, use *que* to refer to things and *quien(es)* to refer to people.

El problema **del que** te hablé es muy grave.   La persona **de quien** te hablé se llama Adriana.

Use the relative phrase *lo que* to refer to a situation, concept, action, or object not yet identified.

Te cuento **lo que** me explicó el científico.

Conjunciones que se usan con el subjuntivo y el indicativo: In this activity, students can review the conjunctions from both the first and second grammar explanations on this page. On their own, have students use each of the eleven conjunctions in a written sentence. Tell them to use the subjunctive or indicative incorrectly in about half of their sentences and to randomly mix these incorrect sentences in with the rest. Then have students trade papers. Ask them to mark the correct sentences they see with a **C**, and to correct any errors they see in the use of the subjunctive versus the indicative. Have them read the corrected sentences aloud to their partners and explain the corrections they made.

***Los pronombres relativos* que, quien *y* lo que:** Have students use the pronouns to create definitions of the chapter vocabulary on the previous page. For example: *Una selva tropical es un bosque cerca del ecuador que recibe una gran cantidad de lluvia. Los senadores son unas personas a quienes podemos escribir sobre la protección del medio ambiente. Crecer es lo que hacen las plantas en la primavera.*

Digital Portfolio

Invite students to review the activities and projects they completed in this chapter. Have them select one or two items that they feel best demonstrate their achievements in Spanish. Include these products in students' portfolios with their Chapter Checklist and Self-Assessment Worksheet.

Additional Resources

 Technology: Online Resources
  • *Para hispanohablantes*
  Teacher Resources
  • Teacher's Resource Materials: Situation Cards, Clip Art

▶ **Technology: ¡Pura vida!** is a storyline video that is independent of chapter content and an ideal support for expanding listening skills. The 14 episodes are available within **Realize**. Student activities and Teacher support are also assignable within **Realize**.

Enrich Your Teaching

Teacher-to-Teacher

Play "Concentration." Prepare twenty note cards. On ten, write an indicative form of one of the verbs from the list on p. 444. On the other ten, write a the corresponding subjunctive form. A sample pair might be **coloca/coloque**. Number the cards randomly 1–20 on the reverse side. Tape them to the board in numerical order in a grid.

Divide students into two teams. A player from Team A chooses two cards, which are turned over and read aloud. If they match, they are removed from the grid. Team A scores a point and goes again. If the cards don't match, they are returned to their positions and it is Team B's turn.

Performance Tasks

Standards: 1.1, 1.2, 1.3, 3.1

Student Resource: *Para hispanohablantes*
Teacher Resources: Teacher's Resource Materials: Audio Script, Technology: Audio Cap. 9

1. Vocabulario

Suggestions: Encourage students to review the vocabulary from the *Vocabulario en contexto* sections on pp. 406–409 and 420–423 before they complete the activity.

Answers:

1. b	**3.** b	**5.** b	**7.** a
2. c	**4.** a	**6.** d	**8.** b

2. Gramática

Suggestions: Remind students of the main points of the grammar presentations in *Capítulo* 9:

- conjunctions that use the subjunctive and the indicative
- the relative pronouns *que, quien,* and *lo que*

Answers:

1. a	**3.** d	**5.** d	**7.** c
2. a	**4.** a	**6.** a	**8.** b

3. Escuchar

Suggestions: Use the audio or read from the script.

🔊 **Technology: Audio Script:**

Female adult: Mucha gente no se da cuenta que la contaminación de nuestros ríos es un problema muy grave. La causa mayor de esta contaminación son las fábricas de pesticidas que echan venenos y productos químicos al agua. Si el gobierno no toma medidas apropiadas para castigar a las fábricas que continúan echando desperdicios al agua, no habrá más peces y no podremos disfrutar de agua pura.

Male adult: Otro problema que sufre el planeta es el recalentamiento global. Si la nieve y el hielo de los polos se derrite, muchas ciudades quedarán bajo el agua. También se destruirán los recursos naturales de los cuales dependemos y la vida animal y vegetal. Creo que el gobierno debe informar a la población sobre estas consecuencias graves. Mi propuesta sería hacer una campaña mundial, en todos los países, para buscar soluciones a este problema.

Answers:

(a) El problema de la contaminación de los ríos.

(b) Que el gobierno tome las medidas apropiadas para castigar a las fábricas que continúan echando desperdicios al agua.

Repaso del capítulo

OBJECTIVE
▶ Demonstrate that you can perform the tasks on these pages

Preparación para el examen

❶ Vocabulario Escribe la letra de la palabra o expresión que mejor complete cada frase. Escribe tus respuestas en una hoja aparte.

1. Muchos animales salvajes están en peligro de _____ a causa de la caza.
   a. preservación   c. población
   b. extinción   d. amenaza

2. El uso excesivo de _____ puede destruir la capa de ozono.
   a. venenos   c. aerosoles
   b. derrames   d. recipientes

3. Es muy peligroso cuando las fábricas arrojan _____ al río.
   a. peces   c. recursos
   b. desperdicios   d. medidas

4. ¿Qué haremos cuando se acaben los recursos naturales como _____?
   a. el petróleo   c. el terreno
   b. la energía   d. el clima

5. El número de ballenas ha disminuido a causa de _____ de petróleo.
   a. la contaminación   c. la piel
   b. los derrames   d. la electricidad

6. Hay que buscar nuevas maneras de _____ de la basura.
   a. depender   c. promover
   b. castigar   d. deshacerse

7. El _____ es un fenómeno que ocurre cuando las temperaturas suben.
   a. efecto invernadero c. producto químico
   b. derrame de petróleo d. medio ambiente

8. Muchos se dedican a la caza de las focas para usar sus _____.
   a. alimentos   c. plumas
   b. pieles   d. dientes

❷ Gramática Escribe la letra de la palabra o expresión que mejor complete cada frase. Escribe tus respuestas en una hoja aparte.

1. No van a parar de tirar desperdicios hasta que los _____.
   a. castiguen   c. castigaran
   b. castigaron   d. castigan

2. Mientras la gente no _____ conciencia de los problemas de la contaminación, no podrán disminuirla.
   a. tome   c. haya tomado
   b. tomará   d. toma

3. Después de _____ los ríos, tendremos que tomar medidas para reducir el número de fábricas.
   a. limpiemos   c. limpiaremos
   b. limpiamos   d. limpiar

4. Mientras no _____ leyes más justas no voy a contribuir a su campaña.
   a. promuevan   c. promoviendo
   b. promueven   d. promovieron

5. Allí está el refugio de vida silvestre _____ visitamos el año pasado.
   a. quien   c. lo que
   b. del que   d. que

6. _____ más le molesta a la gente es el recalentamiento global.
   a. Lo que   c. Que
   b. El que   d. En que

7. La señora _____ te hablé trabaja en una reserva natural.
   a. a quien   c. de quien
   b. del que   d. que

8. Siempre _____ las luces en cuanto salimos de casa.
   a. apaguemos   c. apagaron
   b. apagamos   d. apaguen

Differentiated Instruction

Heritage Speakers

Encourage students to review the standard format for a business or professional letter on p. 437. Discuss how a letter to the editor of a newspaper or to an environmental group would differ in form and content from a casual letter to a friend or family member.

Students with Learning Difficulties

Have students identify and copy the conjunction used in each sentence of the *Gramática* review. Have them refer to the chart on p. 445 to review the rules for each conjunction. Then direct them to apply the appropriate rule to select the correct choice.

Más recursos — PearsonSchool.com/Autentico

Games · Flashcards · Instant check · Tutorials

En el examen vas a . . .	Éstas son las tareas de práctica que te pueden ser útiles para el examen . . .	Para repasar, ve a tu libro de texto impreso o digital . . .
Interpretive		
3 ESCUCHAR Yo puedo escuchar y comprender unas descripciones sobre la contaminación.	Escucha a una persona que llama al locutor de un programa popular en la radio. Quiere expresar sus opiniones sobre los problemas y las soluciones del medio ambiente. Identifica a) el problema que menciona, y b) la solución que sugiere.	**pp. 406–409** *Vocabulario en contexto 1* **p. 412** Actividades 8–9
Interpersonal		
4 HABLAR Yo puedo hacer unas sugerencias sobre cómo proteger el medio ambiente.	Trabajas para un centro comunitario y te piden que hables con un grupo de jóvenes sobre qué se debe hacer para proteger el medio ambiente. Incluye razones. Diles qué deben hacer en a) casa, b) la escuela y c) la comunidad. Usa expresiones y palabras apropiadas para la conversación, que es seria pero informal.	**p. 410** Actividad 5 **p. 412** Actividades 8–9 **p. 416** Actividad 13 **p. 435** *Presentación oral*
Interpretive		
5 LEER Yo puedo leer y comprender declaraciones sobre los problemas del medio ambiente.	Lee este artículo di a) ¿dónde tuvo lugar el derrame?, b) ¿por qué ha sido un desastre para el turismo?, c) ¿qué medidas deberían tomarse para prevenir estos accidentes? **El derrame de petróleo cerca de la costa de Galicia, en España, ha causado grandes problemas. El gobierno ha gastado millones de euros en la limpieza de las playas y el rescate de la fauna marina. Miles de peces y otras especies marinas han desaparecido. A menos que no haya leyes más estrictas para prevenir desastres de este tipo, la vida marina y el turismo seguirán amenazados.**	**pp. 420–423** *Vocabulario en contexto 2* **p. 426** Actividad 28 **p. 431** Actividad 36
Presentational		
6 ESCRIBIR Escribe un correo electrónico sobre los problemas del medio ambiente.	Escribe un correo electrónico a los jóvenes de tu zona para que tomen conciencia de lo que pueden hacer para proteger la comunidad. Describe por lo menos dos problemas y explica las consecuencias si no se toman las medidas necesarias. Al final, diles qué pueden hacer ellos para ayudar.	**p. 410** Actividad 5 **p. 412** Actividad 9 **p. 416** Actividad 14 **p. 427** Actividad 29 **pp. 436–437** *Presentación escrita*
Comparisons		
7 COMPARAR Yo puedo comparar los problemas ecológicos de los Estados Unidos y los de otros países del mundo.	Piensa en uno de los problemas y su solución mencionados en el capítulo. Descríbelo y piensa si en los Estados Unidos existe o no ese problema y cómo lo resolverías tú.	**p. 425** Cultura **p. 441** Cultura

Capítulo 9 • cuatrocientos cuarenta y siete **447**

4. Hablar

Standards: 1.1

Suggestions: Encourage students to use in their answer at least one of the conjunctions studied in this chapter that take either the subjunctive or the indicative.

Answers will vary.

5. Leer

Suggestions: Tell students to refer to pp. 406–409 and 420–423 if they have questions about vocabulary in the review.

Answers:

a. El derrame tuvo lugar cerca de la costa de Galicia, en España.

b. Ha causado grandes problemas para el turismo porque ha ensuciado las playas.

c. Debe haber leyes más estrictas para prevenir desastres de este tipo.

6. Escribir

Suggestions: Remind students of what they learned about effective conclusions in this chapter's *Presentación escrita*. Have them apply that learning to their writing here.

Answers will vary.

7. Comparar

Suggestions: Encourage students to review current events on the Internet or in your local newspaper in light of what they have learned about the environment in *Capítulo* 9.

Answers will vary.

Additional Resources

 Technology: Online Resources
- Instant Check
- Puzzles
- Guided, Core, Audio, Writing, Reading

Print
- Core WB pp. 131–132

Differentiated Assessment

Core Assessment
- Technology: Audio Cap. 9
- ExamView: Chapter Test, Test Banks A and B

Advanced/Pre-AP®
- ExamView: Pre-AP® Test Bank
- Pre-AP® Resource Materials

Students Needing Extra Help
- Alternate Assessment Program: Examen del capítulo 9
- Technology: Audio Cap. 9

Heritage Speakers
- Assessment Program: Para hispanohablantes: Examen del capítulo 9
- ExamView: Heritage Speaker Test Bank

CAPÍTULO **10**

¿Cuáles son tus derechos y deberes?

Rights and responsibilities

Vocabulary: rights and responsibilities at home and in school; rights in society guaranteed by the Constitution

Grammar: passive voice; present perfect subjunctive and imperfect subjunctive; pluperfect subjunctive; conditional perfect

Cultural Perspectives: find out what young people think about their rights and world problems; interpret cultural perspectives on rights and responsibilities; heroes of the Latin American independence movement

¡Pura vida!: Watch an engaging video episode about a group of young people in Costa Rica!

Chapter Support

Bulletin Boards

Theme: Derechos y deberes

Have students work in pairs to brainstorm about their rights and duties at home, at school, and with their friends, and then collect magazine clippings to illustrate them. The class then arranges the information on the bulletin board under *Derechos* and *Deberes*.

Hands-on Culture

Recipe: Queso fundido

This is an authentic recipe to help you celebrate Mexican Independence Day. This delicious fondue takes only about 20 minutes to make. It serves six and can be served on *tortillas* or scooped up with chips.

Ingredients:

1 lb. Mexican *queso Cacique* or any other *queso blanco* (light white cheese), cut into small chunks

3 to 4 cloves garlic, minced juice of 4 limes, or 1/4 cup lime juice

6 to 8 drops of Tabasco, or other hot pepper sauce

Directions:

1. Slowly melt cheese in a medium saucepan over slow heat. Stir continuously with a wooden spoon.
2. When almost melted, add the garlic, lime, and Tabasco, and heat through.
3. Serve immediately with *tortillas* or chips.

Game

Derechos contra obligaciones

Play this game to review the objectives and the vocabulary from *Capítulo* 10.

Players: entire class

Materials: pens, paper, a stopwatch

Rules:

1. Divide the class into two teams: *los derechos* and *las obligaciones*. *Los derechos* team generates a list of rights of parents, children, and teachers. *Las obligaciones* group generates a list of responsibilities for those same categories.
2. Teams have ten minutes to generate their lists.
3. When time is up, toss a coin to determine which team begins the game.
4. The team member who plays first tells a *derecho/obligación* from the list. For example, a *derechos* player says: *Un niño tiene derecho a jugar todos los días.*
5. The member of the opposite team should tell an obligation the same child should have. For example, *Un niño debe cumplir con sus deberes de la escuela todos los días.*
6. Play continues until a team is stumped and cannot think of a reply.
7. No repeated sentences are allowed.

Variation: Apply the game to rights of animals, communities, or countries.

21st Century Skills

Look for tips throughout Chapter 10 to enrich your teaching by integrating 21st Century Skills. Suggestions for the Project-Based Learning and Culture follow below.

Project-Based Learning

Modify the project with these suggestions:

Media Literacy Encourage students to access a variety of Web sites to use as a model for the design of their own music-sharing club site. Have them evaluate the format, organization, use of visuals and text, and layout of various sites to gather ideas. What is the best way to attract fans to their music-sharing club?

Creativity and Innovation Have students develop their own timeline for accomplishing different stages of the project. They should study the rubric in order to figure out in advance the grammar and vocabulary tools they will need to successfully accomplish the tasks. The handout "Solve Problems" can help them develop a plan of action.

Collaboration Encourage students to work together in small groups and assume shared responsibility for researching and creating their Web site project. Provide them with the handout "Work in Teams" to help them organize their group and divide the tasks.

Chapter Culture

Social and Cross-Cultural Skills Direct students to review the *Cultura* notes on pages 461 and 471. Promote a discussion about young people's different cultural perspectives about their student rights and responsibilities or the importance of a good education.

▶ **Technology: Videodocumentario**
View *Gran trabajo para la comunidad* online with the class to learn more about a Latino political organization in Massachusetts.

Project-Based Learning

Web pages for Club Los Ruidosos

Overview: Students work in teams of four to create illustrated pages for a Web site of fans and members of a music-sharing club. The home page should include an introduction and an index to three pages.

Resources: digital or print photos, image editing and page layout software; if computers are not available, poster boards, magazines, markers, glue, scissors

Sequence: (suggestions for when to do each step appear throughout the chapter)

Step 1. Review instructions so students know what is expected of them. Share the rubric with the class.

Step 2. Students submit sketches of their Web pages. Return the sketches with your suggestions.

Step 3. Students do layouts of Web pages. Encourage them to try different arrangements before adding illustrations.

Step 4. Students submit a draft of the texts for each page. Note your corrections and suggestions, then return drafts to students.

Step 5. Students complete and present their Web pages to the class, reading and / or describing all the information featured in the pages.

Options

Students create Web pages for a club of book fans.

Assessment

Here is a detailed rubric for assessing this project:

Chapter 10 Project: *Web pages for Club Los Ruidosos*

Rubric	Score 1	Score 3	Score 5
Your evidence of planning	You provide no layout or written draft.	Your layout and written draft are provided, but not corrected.	You show evidence of corrected draft and layout.
Your use of illustrations	You include no images and little of the required information.	You include images, but your layout is disorganized.	Your Web pages are carefully done and images are consistent with text.
Your presentation	You include little of the required information.	You include most of the required information.	You include all the required information.

Objectives
- Listen and read about rules and government
- Write about rights and responsibilities
- Talk about citizen and animal rights
- Understand the historical context of the Latin American independence movement
- Express your opinion on children's rights
- Compare cultural practices in an authentic video about building girls' leadership skills and confidence through sports

Vocabulary
- Rights and responsibilities
- At home and at school
- Citizens' and people's rights

Grammar
- Passive voice
- Present perfect subjunctive and imperfect subjunctive
- Pluperfect subjunctive
- Conditional perfect

Recycle
- Pronunciation of diphthong *ue*
- Pronouns *vosotros* and *vosotras*

Culture
- Francisco de Goya, p. 453
- *Consulta infantil y juvenil 2000, p. 461*
- Teenagers and world problems, pp. 468–469
- José Vasconcelos, politician and educator, p. 471
- Juan Lovera, painter, p. 473
- Latin American heroes, pp. 480–481
- Domitila Barrios de Chungara, p. 489

A ver si recuerdas
- Rights and obligations
- People and organizations
- Conflicts and solutions
- Preterite vs. imperfect
- Verbs with different meanings in the imperfect and preterite tenses

Authentic Resources
- Auténtico: *Niñas con altura,* pp. 491–492

FOR THE STUDENT	DIGITAL	PRINT	FOR THE TEACHER	DIGITAL	PRINT
A ver si recuerdas pp. 448–451					
Review — A *ver si recuerdas* with Remediation	•		A *ver si recuerdas* with Remediation	•	
Guided WB, pp. 298–301	•	•	Teacher's Edition, pp. 448–451	•	•
Core WB, pp. 133–134	•	•			
Para hispanohablantes	•				
Introducción pp. 452–453					
Present — Student Edition, pp. 452–453	•	•	Teacher's Edition, pp. 452–453	•	•
DK Reference Atlas	•		Teacher's Resource Materials	•	
Videonovela: ¡Pura vida!	•				
¡Pura vida! Video Activities	•				
Para hispanohablantes	•				
Vocabulario en contexto pp. 454–457/466–469					
Present & Practice — Student Edition, pp. 454–457/466–469	•	•	Teacher's Edition, pp. 454–457/466–469	•	•
Audio	•		Teacher's Resource Materials	•	
Videohistoria	•		Vocabulary Clip Art	•	
Flashcards	•		Technology: Audio	•	
Instant Check	•		Video Program: Videohistoria	•	
Guided WB, pp. 302–310/315–322	•	•			
Core WB, pp. 135–136/140–141	•	•			
Communication Activities	•				
Para hispanohablantes	•				
Assess and Remediate			Pruebas 10-1, 10-5: Assessment Program, Assessment Program *Para hispanohablantes*	•	

	FOR THE STUDENT	DIGITAL	PRINT	FOR THE TEACHER	DIGITAL	PRINT
Vocabulario en uso pp. 458–461/470–473						
Present & Practice	Student Edition, pp. 458–461/470–473	•	•	Interactive Whiteboard Vocabulary Activities	•	
	Instant Check	•		Teacher's Edition, pp. 458–461/470–473	•	•
	Communication Activities	•		Teacher's Resource Materials	•	
	Para hispanohablantes	•		Technology: Program	•	
	Communicative Pair Activities	•		Videomodelos	•	
Assess and Remediate				Pruebas 10-2, 10-6 with Remediation	•	
				Pruebas 10-2, 10-6: Assessment Program, Assessment Program *Para hispanohablantes*	•	
Gramática pp. 462–465/474–479						
Present & Practice	Student Edition, pp. 462–465/474–479	•	•	Interactive Whiteboard Grammar Activities	•	
	Instant Check	•		Teacher's Edition, pp. 462–465/474–479	•	•
	Animated Verbs	•		Teacher's Resource Materials	•	
	Tutorial Video: Grammar	•		Technology: Audio	•	
	Canción de hip hop	•		Videomodelos	•	
	Guided WB, pp. 311–315/323–326	•	•			
	Core WB, pp. 137–139/142–144	•	•			
	Communication Activities	•				
	Para hispanohablantes	•				
	Communicative Pair Activities	•				
Assess and Remediate				Pruebas 10-3, 10-4, 10-7, 10-8 with Remediation	•	
				Pruebas 10-3, 10-4, 10-7, 10-8: Assessment Program, Assessment Program *Para hispanohablantes*	•	
				Examen 1, Examen 2: Vocab. y gramática	•	
Aplicación pp. 480–491						
Apply	Student Edition, pp. 480–491	•		Teacher's Edition, pp. 480–491	•	•
	Authentic Resources Workbook	•	•	Teacher's Resource Materials	•	
	Authentic Resources	•	•	Video Program: Videodocumentario	•	
	Online Cultural Reading	•		Mapa global interactivo	•	
	Guided WB, pp. 327–329	•	•	Authentic Resources Lesson Plans with scripts, answer keys	•	
	Communication Activities	•				
	Para hispanohablantes	•				
	Videodocumentario	•				
Repaso del capítulo pp. 492–495						
Review	Student Edition, pp. 492–495	•	•	Teacher's Edition, pp. 492–495	•	•
	Core WB, pp. 145–146	•	•	Teacher's Resource Materials	•	
	Communication Activities	•		Technology: Audio	•	
	Para hispanohablantes	•				
	Instant Check	•				
Chapter Assessment						
Assess				Examen del capítulo 10: Assessment Program, Alternate Assessment Program, Assessment Program *Para hispanohablantes*	•	
				Technology: Audio Cap. 10, Examen	•	
				ExamView: Test Banks A and B (questions only online) Heritage Speaker Test Bank, Pre-AP® Test Bank	•	

RESOURCES

LESSON PLAN

DAY	Warm-up / Assess	Preview / Present / Practice / Communicate		Wrap-up / Homework Options
1	**Warm-up** (10 min.) • Return Examen del capítulo: Capítulo 9 • Homework check	**Repaso** (35 min.) • A ver si recuerdas . . . • Actividades 1–8		**Wrap-up and Homework Options** (5 min.) • Core Practice 10-1, 10-2
2	**Warm-up** (10 min.) • Homework check	**Chapter Opener** (10 min.) • Objectives • Arte y cultura	**Vocabulario en contexto 1** (25 min.) • Presentation: Vocabulario y gramática en contexto • Actividades 1, 2	**Wrap-up and Homework Options** (5 min.) • Clip Art Vocabulary
3	**Warm-up** (10 min.) • Homework check	**Vocabulario en contexto 1** (35 min.) • Presentación: Videohistoria: *¡Bienvenido al grupo!* • Presentation: Derechos • Actividades 3, 4	**Vocabulario en uso 1** (25 min.) • Actividades 5, 6	**Wrap-up and Homework Options** (5 min.) • Core Practice 10-3, 10-4 • Actividad 4 • Prueba 10-1: Vocabulary recognition
4	**Warm-up** (10 min.) • Homework check • Audio or Writing Activity • **Formative Assessment** (10 min.) • Prueba 10-1: Vocabulary recognition	**Vocabulario en uso 1** (25 min.) • Interactive Whiteboard Vocabulary Activities • Actividades 7, 8, 9, 10 • Cultura		**Wrap-up and Homework Options** (5 min.) • Actividad 11 • Writing Activities • Prueba 10-2 with Remediation: Vocabulary production
5	**Warm-up** (15 min.) • Homework check • Communicative Activity • **Formative Assessment** (10 min.) • Prueba 10-2 with Remediation: Vocabulary production	**Gramática y vocabulario en uso 1** (20 min.) • Presentation: La voz pasiva • Interactive Whiteboard Grammar Activities • Actividades 12, 13 • Writing Activity		**Wrap-up and Homework Options** (5 min.) • Core Practice 10-5
6	**Warm-up** (10 min.) • Homework check	**Gramática y vocabulario en uso 1** (35 min.) • Presentation: El presente y el imperfecto del subjuntivo • Interactive Whiteboard Grammar Activities • Actividades 14, 15, 16, 17		**Wrap-up and Homework Options** (5 min.) • Core Practice 10-6, 10-7 • Writing Activity • Prueba 10-3 with Remediation: La voz pasiva
7	**Warm-up** (10 min.) • Homework check • **Formative Assessment** (10 min.) • Prueba 10-3 with Remediation: La voz pasiva	**Gramática y vocabulario en uso 1** (25 min.) • Writing Activity • Communicative Pair Activity • En voz alta		**Wrap-up and Homework Options** (5 min.) • Writing Activity • Prueba 10-4 with Remediation: El presente y el imperfecto del subjuntivo
8	**Warm-up** (10 min.) • Homework check • **Formative Assessment** (10 min.) • Prueba 10-4 with Remediation: El presente y el imperfecto del subjuntivo	**Vocabulario en contexto 2** (25 min.) • Presentation: Vocabulario y gramática en contexto • Actividades 18, 19		**Wrap-up and Homework Options** (5 min.) • Clip Art Vocabulary • Examen: Vocabulario y gramática 1
9	**Warm-up** (5 min.) • Homework check • **Formative Assessment** (30 min.) • Examen: Vocabulario y gramática 1	**Vocabulario en contexto 2** (10 min.) • Presentation: Jóvenes por el desarrollo y la paz • Actividades 20, 21		**Wrap-up and Homework Options** (5 min.) • Actividad 22 • Core Practice 10-8, 10-9 • Prueba 10-5: Vocabulary recognition
10	**Warm-up** (20 min.) • Homework check • **Formative Assessment** (10 min.) • Prueba 10-5: Vocabulary recognition	**Vocabulario en uso 2** (20 min.) • Interactive Whiteboard Vocabulary Activities • Actividades 23, 24, 25 • Cultura		**Wrap-up and Homework Options** (5 min.) • Actividades 29, 30

LESSON PLAN

DAY	Warm-up / Assess	Preview / Present / Practice / Communicate	Wrap-up / Homework Options
11	**Warm-up** (10 min.) • Homework check	**Vocabulario en uso 2** (20 min.) • Actividades 26, 27, 28 • Audio Activity • Writing Activity **Gramática y vocabulario en uso 2** (15 min.) • Presentation: El pluscuamperfecto del subjuntivo • Interactive Whiteboard Grammar Activities • Actividades 31, 32	**Wrap-up and Homework Options** (5 min.) • Core Practice 10-10 • Prueba 10-6 with Remediation: Vocabulary production
12	**Warm-up** (10 min.) • Homework check • Communicative Pair Activity • **Formative Assessment** (10 min.) • Prueba 10-6 with Remediation: Vocabulary production	**Gramática y vocabulario en uso 2** (25 min.) • Actividades 33, 34 • Writing Activity • Presentation: El condicional perfecto • Interactive Whiteboard Grammar Activities • Actividades 35, 36	**Wrap-up and Homework Options** (5 min.) • Core Practice 10-11, 10-12 • Prueba 10-7 with Remediation: El pluscuamperfecto del subjuntivo
13	**Warm-up** (10 min.) • Homework check • **Formative Assessment** (10 min.) • Prueba 10-7 with Remediation: El pluscuamperfecto del subjuntivo	**Gramática y vocabulario en uso 2** (25 min.) • Actividades 35–40 • Audio Activity • Writing Activity	**Wrap-up and Homework Options** (5 min.) • Prueba 10-8 with Remediation: El condicional perfecto
14	**Warm-up** (10 min.) • Communicative Pair Activity • **Formative Assessment** (10 min.) • Prueba 10-8 with Remediation: El condicional perfecto	**Aplicación** (25 min.) • Puente a la cultura: Héroes de América Latina • ¿Comprendiste? • Cronología • Presentación oral: Step 1	**Wrap-up and Homework Options** (5 min.) • Examen: Vocabulario y gramática 2
15	**Warm-up** (5 min.) • Answer questions • **Formative Assessment** (25 min.) • Examen: Vocabulario y gramática 2	**Aplicación** (15 min.) • Presentación oral: Step 2	**Wrap-up and Homework Options** (5 min.) • Presentación oral: Step 3
16	**Warm-up** (5 min.) • Homework check	**Aplicación** (30 min.) • Presentación oral: Step 3 (half class) • Pre-AP® Integración 1, 2, 3	**Wrap-up and Homework Options** (5 min.) • Presentación escrita: Steps 1, 2
17	**Warm-up** (10 min.) • Homework check	**Aplicación** (35 min.) • Presentación oral: Step 3 (half class) • View Video • View Activities 1, 2, 3 • Presentación escrita: Step 3	**Wrap-up and Homework Options** (5 min.) • Presentación escrita: Step 4 • Preparación para el examen: 1, 2
18	**Warm-up** (10 min.) • Homework check	**Repaso** (10 min.) • Preparación para el examen: Actividades 3, 4 **Aplicación** (25 min.) • Lectura • Interacción • ¿Comprendiste? • Cultura • Auténtico	**Wrap-up and Homework Options** (5 min.) • ¿Comprendiste? • Core Practice: Organizer 10–13, 10–14 • Instant Check
19	**Warm-up** (15 min.) • Homework check	**Repaso** (30 min.) • Preparación para el examen: Actividades 5, 6, 7 • Other review	**Wrap-up and Homework Options** (5 min.) • Examen del capítulo
20	**Warm-up** (5 min.) • Answer questions • **Summative Assessment** (45 min.) • Examen del capítulo		

ALTERNATE LESSON PLAN

DAY	Warm-up / Assess	Preview / Present / Practice / Communicate	Wrap-up / Homework Options
1	**Warm-up** (35 min.) • Return Examen del capítulo: Capítulo 9 • A ver si recuerdas . . . • Homework check	**Chapter Opener** (10 min.) • Objectives • Arte y cultura **Vocabulario en contexto 1** (30 min.) • Presentation: Vocabulario y gramática en contexto • Actividades 1, 2 • Presentation: Derechos • Actividades 3, 4 • Presentación: Videohistoria: *¡Bienvenido al grupo!* **Vocabulario en uso 1** (10 min.) • Interactive Whiteboard Vocabulary Activities • Actividades 5, 6, 7	**Wrap-up and Homework Options** (5 min.) • Core Practice 10-3, 10-4 • Clip Art Vocabulary • Prueba 10-1: Vocabulary recognition
2	**Warm-up** (15 min.) • Homework check • Actividades 8, 9 • **Formative Assessment** (10 min.) • Prueba 10-1: Vocabulary recognition	**Vocabulario en uso 1** (60 min.) • Actividades 10, 11 • Fondo cultural • Ampliación del lenguaje • Audio Activity • Writing Activity • Communicative Pair Activity	**Wrap-up and Homework Options** (5 min.) • Prueba 10-2 with Remediation: Vocabulary production
3	**Warm-up** (5 min.) • Homework check • **Formative Assessment** (10 min.) • Prueba 10-2 with Remediation: Vocabulary production	**Gramática y vocabulario en uso 1** (70 min.) • Presentation: La voz pasiva • Interactive Whiteboard Grammar Activities • Actividades 12, 13 • Presentation: El presente y el imperfecto del subjuntivo • Interactive Whiteboard Grammar Activities • Actividades 14, 15 • Writing Activity	**Wrap-up and Homework Options** (5 min.) • Core Practice 10-5 • Prueba 10-3 with Remediation: La voz pasiva
4	**Warm-up** (10 min.) • Homework check • **Formative Assessment** (10 min.) • Prueba 10-3 with Remediaiton: La voz pasiva	**Gramática y vocabulario en uso 1** (50 min.) • Actividades 16, 17 • En voz alta • Writing Activity • Communicative Pair Activity **Vocabulario en contexto 2** (15 min.) • Presentation: Vocabulario y gramática en contexto • Actividades 18, 19	**Wrap-up and Homework Options** (5 min.) • Core Practice 10-6, 10-7 • Prueba 10-4 with Remediation: El presente y el imperfecto del subjuntivo • Examen: Vocabulario y gramática 1
5	**Warm-up** (10 min.) • Homework check • **Formative Assessment** (40 min.) • Prueba 10-4 with Remediation: El presente y el imperfecto del subjuntivo • Examen: Vocabulario y gramática 1	**Vocabulario en contexto 2** (20 min.) • Presentation: Jóvenes por el desarrollo y la paz • Actividades 20, 21, 22 **Vocabulario en uso 2** (15 min.) • Interactive Whiteboard Vocabulary Activities • Actividades 23, 24	**Wrap-up and Homework Options** (5 min.) • Core Practice 10-8, 10-9 • Actividad 25 • Clip Art • Prueba 10-5: Vocabulary recognition
6	**Warm-up** (35 min.) • Homework check • Cultura • Actividades 26, 27, 28 • Audio Activity • Writing Activity • Communicative Pair Activity • **Formative Assessment** (10 min.) • Pruebas 10-5: Vocabulary recognition	**Gramática y vocabulario en uso 2** (40 min.) • Presentation: El pluscuamperfecto del subjuntivo • Interactive Whiteboard Grammar Activities • Actividades 31, 32, 33, 34 • El español en la comunidad	**Wrap-up and Homework Options** (5 min.) • Actividades 29, 30 • Core Practice 10-10 • Pruebas 10-6, 10-7 with Remediation: Vocabulary production, El pluscuamperfecto del subjuntivo

ALTERNATE LESSON PLAN

DAY	Warm-up / Assess	Preview / Present / Practice / Communicate	Wrap-up / Homework Options
7	**Warm-up** (10 min.) • Homework check • **Formative Assessment** (20 min.) • Pruebas 10-6, 10-7 with Remediation: Vocabulary production, El pluscuamperfecto del subjuntivo	**Gramática y vocabulario en uso 2** (40 min.) • Presentation: El condicional perfecto • Interactive Whiteboard Grammar Activities • Actividades 35, 36, 37, 38, 39, 40 • Audio Activity • Writing Activity **Aplicación** (15 min.) • Presentación oral: Steps 1, 2	**Wrap-up and Homework Options** (5 min.) • Core Practice 10-11, 10-12 • Prueba 10-8 with Remediation: El condicional perfecto • Presentación oral: Step 2
8	**Warm-up** (15 min.) • Homework check • Communicative Pair Activity • **Formative Assessment** (20 min.) • Prueba 10-8 with Remediation: El condicional perfecto	**Aplicación** (35 min.) • Presentación oral: Step 3 **Aplicación** (15 min.) • Presentation: Héroes de América Latina • ¿Comprendiste?	**Wrap-up and Homework Options** (5 min.) • ¿Comprendiste? • Cronología • Examen: Vocabulario y gramática 2
9	**Warm-up** (10 min.) • Homework check • **Formative Assessment** (30 min.) • Examen: Vocabulario y gramática 2	**Aplicación** (45 min.) • Pre-AP® Integración 1, 2, 3 • Presentación escrita: Step 1 • View Video • Video Activities	**Wrap-up and Homework Options** (5 min.) • Presentación escrita: Step 2 • Preparación para el examen: Actividades 1, 2
10	**Warm-up** (20 min.) • Homework check • Presentación escrita: Step 3	**Aplicación** (35 min.) • Lectura • Interacción • ¿Comprendiste? • Cultura • Auténtico **Repaso** (30 min.) • Preparación para el examen: Actividades 3, 4, 6	**Wrap-up and Homework Options** (5 min.) • Presentación escrita: Step 4 • Core Practice: Organizer 10-13, 10-14 • Instant Check • Preparación para el examen: Actividades 5, 7 • Examen del capítulo
11	**Warm-up** (20 min.) • Homework check • **Summative Assessment** (45 min.) • Examen del capítulo	**Theme Game** (25 min.)	

Vocabulario: Repaso

Standards: 1.1, 1.2

Suggestions: Before presenting the material in this review section, consider testing your students' command of the material by assigning the Remediation. Students will automatically be given additional practice of the material they have not yet mastered, and you can focus your review based on the class's overall performance on the post-test.

Have students copy the names of the five categories to their own paper. Allow them to look at the list of words in each category for a few minutes. Then, with books closed, have students work in pairs and list as many words and expressions as they can remember in each category.

1

Standards: 1.1, 1.2, 1.3

Suggestions: Remind students to consider parts of speech when completing the matching activity. Explain that a definition beginning with a verb is most likely matched with a verb; one that begins with a noun is mostly likely matched with a noun.

Answers:
1. f. proteger
2. d. injusto
3. e. los vecinos
4. c. permitir
5. a. cumplir
6. b. la ley
7. g. encargarse

2

Standards: 1.1, 1.3

Suggestions: Point out to students that when listing permitted or prohibited activities, they can use either the impersonal *se* or *estar* + past participle: *se prohíbe/está prohibido.*
Answers will vary.

Active Classroom

Have students write five questions, each using a different vocabulary word from the vocabulary review. Have them ask a partner the questions.

A ver si recuerdas

OBJECTIVES
▶ Talk and write about permitted and prohibited activities
▶ Write a story in the past

Vocabulario

la sociedad
la comunidad
la costumbre
los/las demás
la escuela
la familia
el hermano, la hermana
los padres
la sociedad
el vecino, la vecina

condiciones
la edad
injusto, -a
justo, -a
libre
mayor
menor

derechos y obligaciones
el derecho
la injusticia
la ley
las medidas
la obligación
las reglas
la responsabilidad
la seguridad
las tareas

actividades
alcanzar
beneficiar
conseguir
cumplir (con)
disfrutar (de)
encargarse (de)
luchar
obtener
proteger

expresiones
a favor
de niño
de pequeño
en contra
(me) parece justo/ injusto
se permite
se prohíbe

1

Emparejar

 HABLAR EN PAREJA, ESCRIBIR Trabaja con otro(a) estudiante para emparejar cada definición con la palabra correspondiente. Luego, escoge 4 palabras y escribe un cuento.

1. cuidar a alguien de cualquier tipo de peligro
2. lo contrario de justo
3. las personas que viven en el mismo barrio
4. lo contrario de prohibir
5. hacer lo que se debe
6. la regla establecida por una autoridad
7. tomar la responsabilidad de hacer algo

a. cumplir
b. la ley
c. permitir
d. injusto
e. los vecinos
f. proteger
g. encargarse

2

Actividades

 ESCRIBIR, HABLAR EN PAREJA Haz una lista de tres actividades que se prohíban y tres actividades que se permitan en tu casa o en tu escuela. Compara la lista con la de un(a) compañero(a). Escriban una frase entre los (las) dos para expresar su opinión. Compartan su opinión con la clase.

Modelo
En la escuela se prohíbe hablar mientras la profesora habla. Nos parece justo para mantener el orden en la clase.

Differentiated Instruction

Heritage Speakers
After the class writes their accounts of experiences in *Actividad* 4, have them exchange papers. Ask students with strong grammar skills to identify errors they see in their partners' work without correcting them. Then have the writers revise their work based on this feedback.

Advanced Learners
Challenge students to create sentences that use vocabulary from as many categories as possible. For example: *En mi familia, los niños mayores disfrutan de más derechos que los niños menores.*

Gramática

Pretérito vs. imperfecto

Remember that when speaking in Spanish about the past, you can use either the preterite or the imperfect, depending on the sentence and the meaning you want to convey. Compare:

El sábado pasado me **permitieron** llegar tarde a casa.
De niño nunca me **permitían** llegar tarde.

Use the preterite:

• to tell about past actions that happened and are complete.

Las mujeres **protestaron** para obtener los mismos derechos.

• to give a sequence of actions in the past.

Llegamos al restaurante, **nos sentamos** y **comimos.**

Use the imperfect:

• to tell about habitual actions in the past.

Ellas no **tenían** los mismos derechos que los hombres.

• to give background details such as time, location, weather, mood, age, and physical and mental descriptions.

Era tarde, **hacía** frío y **estábamos** cansados.

• when two or more actions are taking place simultaneously in the past.

Nosotros **comíamos** y ellos **se peleaban.**

Use the preterite and the imperfect together when an action (preterite) interrupts another that is taking place in the past (imperfect).

Estábamos comiendo cuando **llegó** mi hermano.

Más recursos ONLINE

▶ **Tutorial:** Summary of Uses of Preterit and Imperfect

3

Completar

 LEER, ESCRIBIR   Esteban se asustó ayer por la noche al volver a su casa. Para saber qué le pasó, completa estas frases con el tiempo verbal correcto.

> Ayer __1.__ *(eran/fueron)* las once de la noche cuando Esteban __2.__ *(regresó/regresaba)* a su casa. __3.__ *(Estaba/Estuvo)* muy oscuro y no se __4.__ *(vio/veía)* nada. De repente __5.__ *(se escuchó/se escuchaba)* un extraño ruido en la noche. Esteban __6.__ *(salió/salía)* corriendo y __7.__ *(se escondió/se escondía)* detrás de un árbol. ¿ __8.__ *(Fue/Era)* un fantasma quien __9.__ *(se acercó/se acercaba)*? ¡No! __10.__ *(Fue/Era)* un gato que __11.__ *(tuvo/tenía)* hambre y __12.__ *(buscó/buscaba)* algo para comer.

4

Relatar

 ESCRIBIR, HABLAR EN GRUPO   Con un(a) compañero(a) escribe un relato sobre algo que les haya sucedido, usando el pretérito y el imperfecto. Primero, escojan algo en lo que los (las) dos participaron. Luego, formen frases sobre:

• la causa de lo que sucedió

• la hora de llegada y una descripción del ambiente

• qué hacía la gente

• algo que pasó

Usen oraciones conectadas con detalles y elaboración para describir los eventos y compartan su relato con otros(as) compañeros(as).

Modelo
Era el cumpleaños de [nombre] y él (ella) hizo una fiesta.

Gramática: Repaso

Suggestions: Refer students who are having difficulty with preterite vs. imperfect contrast to the *GramActiva* videos from Level 2 Chapters 4B, 5A, and 5B, and to the online tutorial. Have students write three sentences using past tenses. Encourage them to use more than one verb in each sentence. Have them take turns reading their sentences aloud and explaining their reason for using the preterite tense or the imperfect tense in each case.

3

Standards: 1.2

Suggestions: Have students number the rules in the *Gramática* from 1 to 6. As they complete *Actividad* 3, have them write the rule number that applies beside each sentence.

Answers:

1. eran	**7.** se escondió
2. regresó	**8.** Era
3. Estaba	**9.** se acercó
4. veía	**10.** Era
5. se escuchó	**11.** tenía
6. salió	**12.** buscaba

4

Standards: 1.1, 1.3

Suggestions: Before students begin writing, encourage them to decide which tense they think should be used with each of the four cues that are given. Point out that the verbs in the clues provide some guidance on which tenses they should use.

Answers will vary.

Enrich Your Teaching

Teacher-to-Teacher

Correct use of the imperfect tense vs. the preterite tense is a difficult skill for language learners to master. Remind them that mastery comes through patience and practice. Whenever students are engaged in oral communication, correct errors that they may make by modeling the correct usage and having them repeat.

Better yet, create a cue card with *imperfecto* written on one side and *pretérito* on the other. Flash the appropriate side of this card when you hear an error, and have the student self-correct.

Vocabulario: Repaso

Standards: 1.1, 1.2

Suggestions: Ask students to create sentences that use items from at least three of the categories in the *Vocabulario*. For example: *El juez resolvió el problema entre los dos ciudadanos.*

5

Standards: 1.2

Suggestions: Have students read the sentences first and make tentative decisions about how they will use the words in the word bank. Remind them to complete the items about which they are the most certain first.

Answers:
1. manifestación
2. habitantes; gobierno
3. víctimas; juez
4. campaña; población
5. beneficios

6

Standards: 1.1, 3.1

Suggestions: As students discuss their conflicts in Step 2, remind them to use the preterite and the imperfect tenses appropriately.

Answers will vary.

A ver si recuerdas

OBJECTIVES
▶ Write about government and conflicts
▶ Express ideas in the past

Vocabulario

conflictos
acusar
arrestar
capturar
el conflicto
desconfiar
limitar
mentir
molestar
la pelea
pelearse
el problema
quejarse
rebelarse
temer
la víctima

expresiones
decir la verdad
tener la culpa
tener razón

soluciones
los beneficios
la confianza
confiar
garantizar
obedecer
perdonar
resolver
reunirse
solicitar

personas y organizaciones
la campaña
el ciudadano, la ciudadana
la gente
el gobierno
el/la habitante
la manifestación
la organización
la población
la reunión
el sistema

profesiones
el abogado, la abogada
el juez, la jueza
el/la policía

5

Titulares

 LEER, ESCRIBIR Lee los titulares y anuncios y complétalos con las palabras del recuadro.

campaña	gobierno	beneficios
juez	habitantes	víctimas
manifestación	población	

1. ¡Arrestaron a quince personas en la _____ de ayer!

2. El conflicto entre los _____ del valle causa problemas al _____.

3. Las _____ del accidente aparecen ante (*before*) el _____.

4. La _____ de limpieza de la plaza Tribunales cuenta con el apoyo de la _____ de ese lugar.

5. Los ciudadanos quieren garantizar _____ para los ancianos.

6

Un conflicto

 ESCRIBIR, HABLAR EN PAREJA

1 Piensa en un conflicto que haya sucedido en tu familia, escuela o comunidad recientemente. Luego, copia esta tabla en una hoja y complétala.

¿Quiénes participaron?	¿Qué hicieron?	¿Por qué?	¿Tenían o no razón?
_____	_____	_____	_____

2 Usa la información de la tabla y cuéntale a otro(a) estudiante la historia.

450 cuatrocientos cincuenta • Capítulo 10 • ¿Cuáles son tus derechos y deberes?

Differentiated Instruction

Students with Learning Difficulties

Students may have difficulty establishing the contexts in *Actividades* 7 and 8. Give them the opportunity to act out the events described in both activities. This will help them grasp each situation, which will in turn help them choose correct answers.

Advanced Learners

Ask students to model using the vocabulary in context. Give them time to think about the words, then ask them to create a fictional story about a courtroom scene that uses as many of the words as possible.

Go **Online** to practice
PEARSON
realize. PearsonSchool.com/Autentico
WRITING SPEAK/RECORD

Gramática

Verbos con distinto sentido en el pretérito y en el imperfecto

A few Spanish verbs have different meanings in the imperfect and the preterite tenses.

	IMPERFECT	PRETERITE
saber	*knew* ¿**Sabías** que Ángel Suárez había ganado?	*found out, learned* Sí, lo **supe** esta mañana.
conocer	*knew (somebody)* Mi padre lo **conocía** cuando era pequeño.	*met (somebody) for the first time* Ellos se **conocieron** en la escuela.
(no) querer	*wanted to* Mi hermana **quería** ir a la manifestación.	*tried to* Yo también **quise** hacerlo pero no pude.
	didn't want to No **querían** decir la verdad.	*refused to* No **quisieron** decir la verdad.
poder	*was able to, could* Ella **podía** encontrar la solución.	*managed to, succeeded in* Ella **pudo** encontrar la solución.

7 Completar

LEER, ESCRIBIR Completa esta conversación con el pretérito o el imperfecto del verbo apropiado.

conocer	poder	querer	saber

A— ¿Pudiste estudiar el sábado por la tarde?

B— No, no __1.__. Pablo y Agustín estuvieron en casa toda la tarde.

A— ¡Ah! Pablo es el chico que yo __2.__ el verano pasado, ¿no?

B— No, tú no lo __3.__.

A— Bueno, yo __4.__ conocerlo, pero no __5.__ conocerlo en persona. Lo __6.__ por teléfono.

B— ¿Tú hablaste por teléfono con él? ¡No lo __7.__! ¡Qué bien!

8 Escoger

LEER, ESCRIBIR Completa el correo electrónico con el verbo apropiado.

¡Hola Mónica!

Hoy __1.__ *(conocí/conocía)* a un chico guapísimo. Julia y yo __2.__ *(quisimos/queríamos)* ir al cine, pero no __3.__ *(pudimos/podíamos)*. No había más entradas para la película que __4.__ *(quisimos/queríamos)* ver. Al salir nos encontramos con el chico guapísimo. Yo no lo __5.__ *(conocí/conocía)*, pero Julia me contó que ella lo __6.__ *(conoció/conocía)* en una fiesta. Él __7.__ *(quiso/quería)* ir a tomar algo pero Julia no __8.__ *(quiso/quería)*.

Enrich Your Teaching

Teacher-to-Teacher

A great way to get students on-task at the beginning of the class is to put a short written exercise on the board. Stand at the door as students enter and hand them copies of the accompanying activity to complete and have them begin immediately. These should be short activities.

21st Century Skills

ICT (Information, Communications and Technology) Literacy Direct students to the online tutorials for self-directed review of the grammar topics recycled in this chapter. Students can review the related grammar first and then proceed to the new Spanish grammar point. Each tutorial is followed by a quick comprehension check.

Gramática: Repaso

Standards: 4.1

Suggestions: Have students write question-and-answer dialogues practicing the verbs in the preterite tense: —¿*Jorge escribió su composición?* —*Quiso escribirla pero dice que era demasiado difícil.*

 7

Standards: 1.2

Common Errors: Some students may spell preterite forms of ***querer*** with ***-c-*** instead of ***-s-*** in the middle. On the board, model as necessary the correct spellings of the forms of this irregular verb.

Suggestions: Remind students that the items in the activity are part of a dialogue. They need to keep track of the meaning of what has already been said in order to better know which verb form to use.

Answers:

1. pude
2. conocí
3. conociste
4. quería
5. pude
6. conocí
7. sabía

 8

Standards: 1.2

Suggestions: Remind students to read the entire diary entry before attempting to write their answers.

Answers:

1. conocí
2. queríamos
3. pudimos
4. queríamos
5. conocía
6. conoció
7. quería
8. quiso

Additional Resources

Technology: Online Resources
- *A ver si recuerdas* with Remediation
- Guided, Core, Audio, Writing practice
- *Para hispanohablantes*

Print
- Guided WB pp. 298–301
- Core WB pp. 133–134

Assessment

A ver si recuerdas **with Remediation (online only)**
After reviewing the material on these pages, assign the *A ver si recuerdas* with Remediation to evaluate students' mastery of the material. Additional practice is available online.

¿Cuáles son tus derechos y deberes?

Country Connections Explorar el mundo hispano

España · Florida · Cuba · México · Venezuela · Perú · Bolivia · Paraguay

---

Can-Do Statements

Read the Can-Do Statements in the chapter objectives with students. Then, have students read *Preparación para el examen* on page 494 to preview what they will be able to do at the end of the chapter.

Standards for Capítulo 10

To meet the Standards, students will:

COMMUNICATION

1.1 Interpersonal
- Talk about rights, responsibilities, the role of government
- Talk about Goya, Barrero, Lovera, and their work
- Talk about Peruvian schools and a Mexican referendum
- Talk about famous people who fought for justice
- Talk about heroes of Latin American independence

1.2 Interpretive
- Read and listen to information about problems, rights, responsibilities, and the role of government
- Read about Goya, Barrero, Lovera, and their work
- Listen to information about Peruvian schools
- Read about a Mexican referendum
- Read about the suffix *-miento*
- Read about famous people who fought for justice
- Read about Spanish-language campaigns in the U.S.
- Read about heroes of Latin American independence
- Read about Barrios de Chungara's struggle for justice

1.3 Presentational
- Write and present information orally about problems, rights, responsibilities, and the role of government
- Recite poetry by Hilario Barrero
- Write a news report
- Write and present orally about famous people
- Write about heroes of Latin American independence
- Write about Barrios de Chungara's struggle for justice

CULTURE

2.1 Practices to Perspectives
- Interpret the cultural perspectives of important artists
- Interpret student rights in Spain and Peru
- Interpret the vision of José Vasconcelos
- Interpret the perspectives of heroes of Latin America

2.2 Products to Perspectives
- Discuss the work of Goya, Barrero, Lovera
- Discuss Latin American independence movements
- Discuss a book about Domitila Barrios de Chungara

CONNECTIONS

3.1 Making Connections
- Discuss key facts about art, poetry and literature
- Discuss key social and geographical facts about many Latin American countries and Spain

---

CHAPTER OBJECTIVES

Communication

By the end of the chapter you will be able to:
- Listen and read about rules and government
- Write about rights and responsibilities
- Talk about citizen and animal rights

Culture

You will also be able to:
- Compare cultural practices in an authentic video about building girls' leadership skills and confidence through sports
- Understand the historical context of the Latin American independence movement
- Express your opinion on children's rights

You will demonstrate what you know and can do
- Presentación oral: Los derechos de los estudiantes
- Presentación escrita: ¿Cuáles son sus derechos?

You will use

Vocabulary
- Rights and responsibilities
- At home and at school
- Citizens' and people's rights

Grammar
- Passive voice
- Present perfect subjunctive and imperfect subjunctive
- Pluperfect subjunctive
- Conditional perfect

ARTE y CULTURA ▸ España

Escenas de la vida La obra de Francisco de Goya (1746–1828) cubrió un período de más de 60 años. En su juventud, cuando pintó este cuadro, Goya aceptó felizmente el mundo tal como era.

Años más tarde, Goya comenzó a sentirse desilusionado con la gente y la sociedad. Como resultado, pintó escenas que criticaban la política de la época. Su selección de temas es evidencia de que creía en el derecho del artista de pintar el mundo tal como lo veía.

▸ ¿Crees que un artista debe tener el derecho de pintar lo que le dé la gana? ¿Por qué? ¿Por qué no?

"El baile a orillas del Manzanares", (1777), ▸ Francisco de Goya y Lucientes
© 2003 SCALA/Art Resource, New York.

452 cuatrocientos cincuenta y dos • Capítulo 10 • ¿Cuáles son tus derechos y deberes?

Enrich Your Teaching

The End in Mind

Have students preview the sample performance tasks on *Preparación para el examen,* p. 493, and connect them to the Chapter Objectives. Explain to students that by completing the sample tasks they can self-assess their learning progress.

Technology: Mapa global interactivo

Download the *Mapa global interactivo* files for Chapter 10 and preview the activities. In Activity 1, look at the countries liberated by Bolívar, Martí, and Hidalgo. In Activity 2, travel to the mountains of Bolivia.

Manifestación de
jóvenes en Lima, Perú

▶ Videonovela ¡Pura vida!

Capítulo 10 • cuatrocientos cincuenta y tres **453**

- Discuss key facts about civics and social studies
- Use Language Arts Strategies

3.2 Acquiring information and Diverse Perspectives
- Read a pamphlet from Spain
- Read a transcript of an interview with a Peruvian student
- Read poetry by Hilario Barrero
- Read a testimonial by Domitila Barrios de Chungara

COMPARISONS

4.1 Language
- Compare the passive voice in Spanish and English
- Compare the use of como si with "as if"
- Compare the Spanish conditional perfect with English
- Compare Spanish words with their English counterparts

4.2 Cultural
- Compare student rights and responsibilities in Spain and Mexico with those in the United States
- Compare Venezuelan historical art with that of the U.S.
- Compare Latin American independence movements
- Compare a Bolivian civil rights movement with one in the United States

COMMUNITIES

5.1 School and Global Communities
- Link to Web sites from around the Spanish-speaking world

5.2 Lifelong Learning
- Develop an appreciation for visual art, and literature
- Discuss the individual's place in society

Chapter Opener

Suggestions: Introduce students to the theme and objectives of the chapter.

▶ **Technology: Videonovela ¡Pura vida!** View this stand-alone storyline video about five young adults in San José, Costa Rica with your class.

ARTE Y CULTURA

Standards: 1.1, 1.2, 2.1, 2.2, 3.1

Suggestions: After students read the information, ask: ¿Cómo comenzó a sentirse Goya durante la segunda parte de su vida?

Teaching with Art

Suggestions: After students read the information, ask: ¿Qué muestra Goya en este cuadro? ¿Cómo crees que se sentía cuando lo pintó?

Project-Based Learning

Entrevistas

As students work through the chapter during the week, have them interview people of different ages about their knowledge of the rights of United States citizens. Direct them to use the questions in item 1 on p. 484. Explain that they will use the interviews to complete the editorial essay for *Presentación escrita* on pp. 484–485.

Vocabulario en contexto 1

Standards: 1.2

Resources: Teacher's Resource Materials: Input Script, Clip Art, Audio Script; Technology: Audio Cap. 10

Focus: Presenting new vocabulary and using grammar lexically in context

Suggestions: You may want to use the Input Script from the *Teacher's Resource Materials* as a source of ideas for presentation of new vocabulary and comprehensible input. While presenting the vocabulary, point out cognates, such as *adolescentes, injusticia, libertad, respeto,* and *tolerancia.* Since most of the vocabulary is not visualized, encourage students to use context clues to help themselves understand the meanings of new words and expressions.

Active Classroom

Divide the class into two sections. Have students from one half work in groups of three and create three additional *derechos de los adolescentes.* Have the other half work in threes and write three additional *derechos de los padres.* Ask each group to present their statements to the groups. Write different *derechos* on the board and have the class vote on the best three.

Culture Note

According to UNICEF statistics, an average of 1 in 3 students between the ages of 13 and 15 worldwide have been bullied on a regular basis.

 Technology: Interactive Whiteboard

Vocabulary Activities 10-1 Use the whiteboard activities in your Teacher Resources as you progress through the vocabulary practice with your class.

Vocabulario en contexto 1

OBJECTIVES
Read, listen to, and understand information about
▶ Bullying at school, on line, and by text and how to cope
▶ Children's rights and responsibilities

🔊 **¡ALTO al bullying/maltrato!**

BULLYING

¿Qué es?
El "bullying" es el **maltrato** e intimidación de una persona o un grupo de personas por otra persona. Muchos **adolescentes**, o sea los jóvenes de 12 a 18 años, son víctimas de esta situación en la escuela o a través de correos, páginas personales, llamadas por teléfono celular o mensajes de texto.

¿Qué puedes hacer si alguien no te *trata* con respeto y te sientes víctima?

1. Ignóralo. **De ese modo** quitas el control del agresor.

2. Si ese paso no es **adecuado**, pide ayuda y **apoyo** de tus padres. **Ambos** te querrán ayudar y juntos van a encontrar una solución.

3. Tienes que reportar **la injusticia** al consejero(a) de tu escuela. Recuerda que no es una situación normal y no debes aceptarla.

4. Nunca olvides que eres una persona especial. Nadie puede **obligarte** a hacer algo que no quieres hacer. Tienes derecho a tus **libertades** y a tu **felicidad**.

Differentiated Instruction

Advanced Learners

Ask students to work in a small group to compare and contrast the rights and responsibilities they and their classmates have at home. They can begin by telling about their own rights and responsibilities in round-robin fashion, and then commenting on similarities and differences among them. Encourage them to compile information on the group in a T-chart with the two headings *nuestros derechos en casa* and *nuestras responsabilidades en casa.* Invite the group to share their findings with the rest of the class.

Go **Online** to practice
PearsonSchool.com/Autentico

PEARSON
realize™

🔊
AUDIO

Interpretive 10

Consejos para los que *maltratan*

Primero, tienes **el deber,** o responsabilidad, de tratar a otras personas con respeto y **tolerancia.**

Tu comportamiento no es aceptable. Tienes que hacer un esfuerzo para cambiar. Te sentirás mejor cuando actúes amablemente con los demás.

¿Cómo puedes ayudar a las víctimas?

Esperamos que nunca hayas tenido experiencia personal con este **asunto,** pero si observas que alguien es víctima, ayúdalo y sé amable. Acércate a él o ella. Háblale. Intenta acompañar a la persona, por ejemplo, invitándola a almorzar con tus amigos.

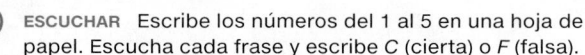

1

Un asunto triste

 ESCUCHAR Escribe los números del 1 al 5 en una hoja de papel. Escucha cada frase y escribe *C* (cierta) o *F* (falsa).

2

¿Quiénes hablan?

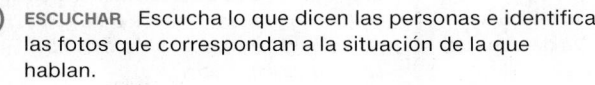 ESCUCHAR Escucha lo que dicen las personas e identifica las fotos que correspondan a la situación de la que hablan.

Enrich Your Teaching

Culture Note

Many families in Spanish-speaking countries still take the time to discuss daily events, make plans, and resolve conflicts in a conversation around the table after dinner. There is even a name for this custom of after-dinner conversation: *la sobremesa.* Depending on the household, dessert and coffee may remain on the table during *la sobremesa,* or other foods, such as fruit or cheeses, may be served. On special days, when guests are invited to the house, *la sobremesa* may last for hours. *Una sobremesa* after a Sunday lunch, for example, may last right into dinnertime!

1

Standards: 1.2

Resources: Teacher's Resource Materials: Audio Script; Technology: Audio Cap. 10

Suggestions: Remind students to listen for key words that will help them determine the answers. Use the audio or read the script. Allow students to listen more than once.

 Technology: Audio Script and Answers

1. Eres una víctima solo si la persona te maltrata en persona. (*F*)
2. Si sufres una injusticia repetida tienes el deber de reportarla. (*C*)
3. Una manera de quitar el control del agresor es ignorarlo. (*C*)
4. Las personas entre los 12 y 18 años son adolescentes. (*C*)
5. Si eres el agresor y no tratas con respeto a los demás tienes que cambiar. (*C*)

2

Standards: 1.2

Have students take a good look at each of the photos on pp. 454 and 455 before listening to the audio. Read the script or play the audio and allow students to listen more than once.

Technology: Audio Script and Answers

1. No entiendo porque Julia me manda estos mensajes por mi celular. Son horribles. Tengo que reportar el asunto a la directora. (Photo 1)
2. El pobre de Manuel fue víctima de las injusticias de un grupo de muchachos por varias semanas. Pero ahora está con nosotros y vamos a cambiar la situación. (Photo 4)
3. Ay Mamá, ¡no sé qué hacer! No me dejan en paz. Todos los días me mandan correos electrónicos o textos diciendo que me van a pegar. En la escuela me hacen caras y dicen cosas muy feas. (Photo 2)
4. De niño yo era un bully. Pero aprendí que me siento mejor cuando soy una persona amable y trato a las personas con respeto. (Photo 3)

Vocabulario en contexto 1

Standards: 1.2

Resources: Teacher's Resource Materials: Input Script, Clip Art, Technology: Audio Cap. 10

Suggestions: Pre-reading: Explain to students that the readings on these two pages are separate and will be read and discussed individually.

Reading: After students read the dialogue on this page, have them complete *Actividad* 3 and *Actividad 4*.

Post-reading: After an initial reading of the dialogue, clarify the meaning of new vocabulary as necessary. Point out cognates such as *satisfactoria* and *abusos.* Ask a volunteer to read aloud the definition for *estado* that is included in the dialog on p. 456. *(el gobierno)* Use circumlocution, synonyms, antonyms, and demonstrations to teach the meanings of other non-visualized words and expressions.

3

Standards: 1.3

Suggestions: Have students answer the questions in their own words. Then invite them to share their responses with the class.

Answers
1. El estado es responsable de aplicar las leyes que protegen a los niños.
2. vivir en paz y no sufrir de abusos ni maltratos
3. Tienen que respetar la autoridad y tener una conducta satisfactoria.

4

Standards: 1.1

Suggestions: Remind students that they should make personal recommendations and to respond appropriately with their opinions in the e-mail. The response should contain statements that support their opinions and recommendations.

Answers will vary.

 Juanita tiene que hacer un informe sobre los derechos y deberes de los niños. Su tío Carlos, quien es abogado, la está orientando.

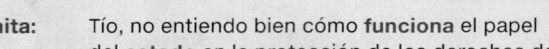

Juanita | Tío Carlos

Juanita: Tío, no entiendo bien cómo **funciona** el papel del **estado** en la protección de los derechos de los niños.

Tío: El estado, o sea el gobierno, es responsable de **aplicar** las leyes que protegen a los niños. Es **la razón** por la que tenemos una **enseñanza gratuita** en las escuelas públicas.

Juanita: ¿Eso quiere decir que debe haber **igualdad** en la enseñanza?

Tío Carlos: Así es. Ningún niño debe ser **discriminado** por ningún **motivo**. Todos tienen derecho a vivir en **paz** y no **sufrir** de **abusos** ni **maltratos**. **La niñez** debe ser un tiempo para **gozar de** la vida.

Juanita: ¡Y los niños que viven en medio de la **pobreza** tienen derecho a vivir mejor!

Tío: Así es. Muchos niños **están sujetos** a condiciones de vida terribles. Por eso hay que **votar** por leyes que garanticen comida, vivienda y educación para todos los niños.

Juanita: **En cuanto a** los deberes de los niños y adolescentes en la escuela, ¿qué me puedes decir?

Tío Carlos: Ese es otro asunto importante. Tú lo sabes mejor que yo: el primer deber es respetar **la autoridad** de los maestros y tener una conducta **satisfactoria**.

Juanita: ¡Ah, claro! Por eso hay un cartel en **el armario** de cada estudiante con el **código de vestimenta** y de conducta.

Tío Carlos: Y no se te olvide otro deber básico: respetar **el pensamiento** de todos tus compañeros, sin **discriminar**.

3

Deberes y derechos de los niños

 ESCRIBIR Contesta las siguientes preguntas:
1. ¿ Quién debe aplicar las leyes que protegen a los niños?
2. ¿Cuáles son dos de los derechos de los niños?
3. ¿Cuáles son dos de los deberes de los niños y adolescentes en la escuela?

4

El código de vestimenta

 ESCRIBIR Escribe a un(a) compañero(a) un texto con tus recomendaciones sobre un código de vestimenta de tu escuela. Él o ella responde con sus ideas. Da detalles de apoyo que expliquen las razones.

Modelo
A —*Creo que todos los estudiantes deben usar uniforme para tener menos problemas.*
B —*No estoy de acuerdo. Así no tenemos libertad de expresión.*

456 cuatrocientos cincuenta y seis • Capítulo 10 • ¿Cuáles son tus derechos y deberes?

Differentiated Instruction

Advanced Learners

Invite students to create an "official" ***Panfleto de los deberes y derechos de los estudiantes*** for your school. If they have computer software available to them, encourage them to design the pamphlet for reproduction and posting in the classroom or, with permission, in other parts of the school. Interested students may want to bring the contents of their pamphlet before your school's student council for consideration.

Videohistoria

Go **Online** to practice
PEARSON realize™
AUDIO VIDEO WRITING SCRIPT
PearsonSchool.com/Autentico

Interpretive | 10

¡Bienvenido al grupo!

Antes de ver

Usar experiencias previas Mira las fotos. ¿Cómo se relacionan con las reglas y responsabilidades que tú tienes que respetar todos los días? Usa tus propias experiencias para inferir palabras o frases desconocidas en el video.

▶ Ve el video

Daniel, el hermano menor de Seba, fue aceptado en el grupo de voluntarios *Codo a Codo*. ¿Qué le dirán los chicos mayores a Daniel sobre esta organización?

Ve a **PearsonSchool.com/Autentico** para ver el video *¡Bienvenido al grupo!* También puedes leer el guión.

Haz la actividad

¿Qué diferencia hay? Trabaja con un compañero(a). Comenten qué diferencia hay entre una regla y una responsabilidad. Hagan una lista de algunas reglas y una lista de algunas responsabilidades.

Camila · Seba · Valentina · Teo · Ximena

Después de ver

 ESCRIBIR Contesta estas preguntas:

1. ¿Qué intención tiene el grupo de amigos al hablar con Daniel?

2. ¿Por qué causas sociales podrá luchar Daniel en *Codo a Codo*? Parafrasea los detalles de la conversación entre los chicos.

3. Los chicos hablan sobre algunas reglas de la organización. Identifica las reglas que son "en broma" *(in jest).*

Responsabilidades sociales Escribe un párrafo corto en el que expliques qué responsabilidades crees que tú tienes con la sociedad.

Enrich Your Teaching

Teacher to Teacher

As a follow up activity to evaluate general comprehension, you may want to invite students to underline those sections of the video script that contain the most significant information. Emphasize that greetings, jokes, and trivial comments between the characters make the video interesting but are not important to grasp the general idea.

21st Century Skills

Communication Have pairs of students discuss the guidelines for the members of a volunteer organization. Why is important to establish rules and assign responsibilities in a volunteer job? Should those rules and responsibilities be as strict as in a paid job?

Tecnología: Video

`Standards: 1.2`

Resources: Teacher's Resource Materials: Video Script

Antes de ver

Review the previewing strategy and activity with students. Point out that using their prior knowledge will help them with comprehension. Brainstorm with students a list of rules and responsibilities they have at home, school, and other activities.

Ve el video

Show the video once without pausing. Lead students to infer that the organization mentioned in this video, *Codo a Codo*, is the same introduced in one of the earlier Videohistorias. For the second viewing, pause the video and invite volunteers to paraphrase de important details. Show the segment a final time without pausing.

Después de ver

`Standards: 1.2, 1.3`

Suggestions: For the third question, guide students to perceive the joking tone group of friends.

Answers

1. Possible answers: darle la bienvenida; darle detalles sobre Codo a Codo; hacerlo sentir bien
2. ayudar a gente que lo necesita; servir a los demás
3. dar un "like" en las redes sociales; bailar

Responsabilidades sociales:

Answers will vary.

Have students go to Realize for additional video activities.

Additional Resources

 Technology: Online Resources
- Instant Check
- Guided, Core, Video, Audio
- *Para hispanohablantes*

Print
- Guided WB pp. 302–310
- Core WB pp. 135–136
- Authentic Resources Workbook

Assessment

Quiz: Vocabulary Recognition
- Prueba 10-1

5

Standards: 1.2, 1.3, 3.1

Suggestions: Tell students that for some items, such as *el deber,* there may be a rationale for placing them in either category.

Answers will vary. The following are likely results. Some items have been placed in both categories:

lo positivo
la libertad, el respeto, la felicidad, el deber, la tolerancia, el apoyo, gratuito(a), la paz, la igualdad, adecuado(a)

lo negativo
el abuso, el deber, discriminar, maltratar, sufrir, el maltrato, la injusticia, adecuado(a)

Extension: After they complete the activity, ask students to explain their reasoning behind the placement of items such as *el deber, el apoyo,* and *adecuado(a).*

6

Standards: 1.1, 1.2, 2.1, 3,1

Resources: Teacher's Resource Materials: Audio Script, Technology: Audio Cap. 10

Suggestions: Play the audio or read the script once through entirely. Allow students to listen again, pausing after each item, so they can write their answers. Allow them to listen a third time to check their answers.

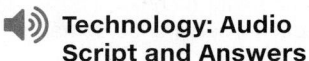 **Technology: Audio Script and Answers**

1. En Perú, en los colegios del estado, ¿las familias tienen que pagar la educación o ésta es gratuita? (*Los colegios del estado son gratuitos.*)
2. ¿Hay un uniforme nacional para las escuelas de Perú o cada escuela tiene su propio uniforme? (*Cada escuela tiene su propio uniforme.*)
3. ¿Qué son las postas médicas? ¿Qué servicios tienen? (*Son centros médicos pequeños. Ofrecen consultas y dan vacunas.*)

Pre-AP® Integration

- **Learning Objective:** Presentational Writing
- **Activity:** Have students write a blog about the rights and responsibilities of the students in their school. Have them complete the phrases, *Los estudiantes tienen el deber de:* and *Los estudiantes tienen derecho a:* with their lists of action items. Have them use vocabulary words in their lists of student rights and responsibilities.
- **Pre-AP® Resource Materials:** Comprehensive guide to *Pre-AP®* writing skill development

---

Vocabulario en uso 1

OBJECTIVES
▸ Listen to and talk about students' rights and responsibilities at school
▸ Discuss social issues in your country
▸ Write and draw about people's rights and responsibilities

5

Lo positivo y lo negativo

 LEER, ESCRIBIR   En una hoja de papel, copia esta tabla. Lee las palabras y escríbelas en la columna apropiada. Luego, escribe frases con tres de las palabras.

lo positivo	lo negativo

la libertad	el respeto	la felicidad	el abuso
el deber	discriminar	la tolerancia	el apoyo
maltratar	sufrir	el maltrato	gratuito(a)
la paz	la injusticia	la igualdad	adecuado(a)

6

Entrevista con una joven peruana

 LEER, ESCUCHAR

1 Lee esta entrevista con Viviana Gallegos, una adolescente del Perú.

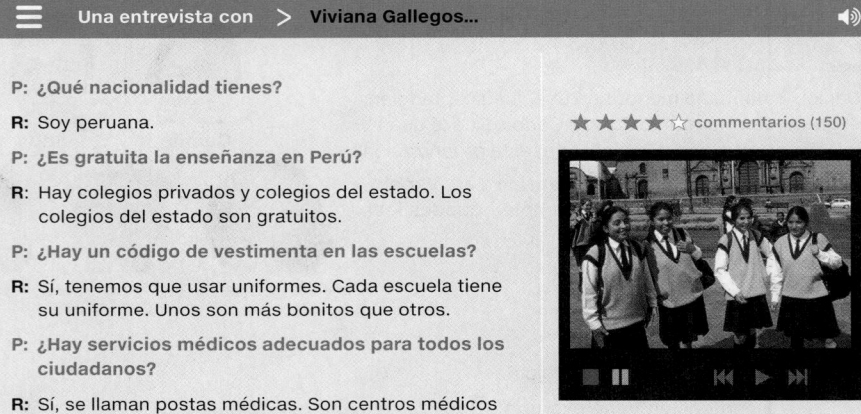

> **Una entrevista con > Viviana Gallegos...**
>
> P: ¿Qué nacionalidad tienes?
>
> R: Soy peruana.
>
> P: ¿Es gratuita la enseñanza en Perú?
>
> R: Hay colegios privados y colegios del estado. Los colegios del estado son gratuitos.
>
> P: ¿Hay un código de vestimenta en las escuelas?
>
> R: Sí, tenemos que usar uniformes. Cada escuela tiene su uniforme. Unos son más bonitos que otros.
>
> P: ¿Hay servicios médicos adecuados para todos los ciudadanos?
>
> R: Sí, se llaman postas médicas. Son centros médicos pequeños. Ofrecen consultas con médicos y dan vacunas (*vaccinations*). Ambos servicios son gratuitos.

★ ★ ★ ★ ☆ commentarios (150)

▲ En la Plaza de Armas, Cuzco, Perú

 2 Ahora, escucha las preguntas y contéstalas en clase.

Differentiated Instruction

Heritage Speakers

Ask students who have lived in a heritage country if they would let others interview them on the topic of schools and the educational system in the heritage country. Interviewers can base their questions on the interview with Viviana Gallegos in *Actividad* 6.

Students with Learning Difficulties

Help students grasp the abstract concepts listed in *Actividad* 8. Provide them with photographs or icons that represent each of the issues described. For example, a photograph of people protesting might represent *la libertad de expresión y pensamiento.*

7

Los derechos en nuestra escuela

 LEER, ESCRIBIR, HABLAR EN PAREJA Túrnate con un(a) compañero(a) para indicar si estás de acuerdo o no con las frases siguientes sobre tu escuela, y explícale por qué. Tu compañero(a) va a tomar apuntes sobre lo que dices, y luego ambos van a compartir sus ideas con la clase.

1. No es necesario seguir un código de vestimenta en esta escuela.
2. Los adolescentes deben tratar a los maestros con más respeto y, de ese modo, respetar su autoridad.
3. En nuestras clases, los chicos tienen más libertad que las chicas.
4. La enseñanza en esta escuela es adecuada para prepararme para lo que voy a hacer en el futuro.
5. Todos los estudiantes tienen derecho a gozar de libertad de expresión.
6. Los profesores deben tener la autoridad y el deber de registrar los armarios.
7. Todos los estudiantes deben estar sujetos a las mismas reglas.

8

En nuestro país

 ESCRIBIR, HABLAR

1 Piensa en estos temas sociales. ¿Cuál es el más importante? ¿Y el menos importante? Ponlos en orden de importancia.

1. la libertad de expresión y pensamiento
2. la igualdad entre los hombres y las mujeres
3. cómo tratar a los animales
4. los servicios médicos
5. el apoyo a los niños
6. la pobreza
7. las reglas para manejar
8. los deberes del estado

2 Dile tu opinión a un(a) compañero(a) sobre los temas mencionados en la parte anterior. Usa las palabras del recuadro.

adecuado(a)	satisfactorio(a)	injusticia	en cuanto a
abuso	respeto	gratuito(a)	ambos(as)

 Videomodelo
la alimentación
A —*La alimentación en nuestro país es satisfactoria.*
B —*Pues yo no estoy de acuerdo. La gente come demasiada comida basura y . . .*

Capítulo 10 • cuatrocientos cincuenta y nueve 459

7

Standards: 1.1, 1.2, 1.3

Suggestions: Remind students that when they report on their pair work, they will change verb forms frequently in order to tell about what their partner said.

Answers will vary.

8

Standards: 1.1, 1.2

Recycle: conjunctions that take the subjunctive or the indicative

Suggestions: For Step 1, tell students to copy each item entirely for writing practice, rather than using numbers to order the items.

Answers will vary.

Project-Based Learning

Give students copies of the Project-Based Learning outline and rubric from the *Teacher's Resource Materials*. Explain the task to them, and have them perform Step 1. (For more information, see p. 430-b.)

Enrich Your Teaching

Teacher-to-Teacher

Invite students who have cameras to create photo essays about student rights and responsibilities in your school. They can take pictures of their friends studying, participating in extracurricular activities, having lunch in the cafeteria, taking breaks, making visits to their lockers, interacting with faculty and administration, and so on. Have them assemble the photos in a visual display, complete with a title, a brief statement about the purpose of the display, and a caption for each photo, explaining how it represents a student right or responsibility.

9

Standards: 1.1, 1.3, 3.1

Suggestions: This activity can be conducted with the whole class. Project or draw the chart on the board, and have students follow along on their own paper. Use guiding questions to elicit from students the information to record on the chart. Record it there yourself or have a volunteer do so as the class follows along.

Answers will vary.

10

Standards: 1.1

Suggestions: Encourage students to use background knowledge they have gained in their Language Arts or Social Studies classes to answer the questions.

Answers will vary.

AMPLIACIÓN DEL LENGUAJE

Standards: 1.2, 3.1

Suggestions: After students complete the chart, encourage them to experiment using ***-miento*** to form other nouns from verbs. They can use a dictionary to check their work.

Answers:

Chart

3. pensamiento
4. mejoramiento
5. conocimiento
6. comportamiento
7. descubrimiento
8. movimiento

Sentences

1. descubrimiento; descubrir
2. mejorar; mejoramiento

9

Derechos y responsabilidades

HABLAR EN GRUPO, ESCRIBIR

1. Ser adolescente quiere decir tener muchos derechos pero también responsabilidades. En grupo, completen una tabla como la de la derecha con los derechos y responsabilidades que tienen los adolescentes.

Derechos	Responsabilidades
1.	1.
2.	2.
3.	3.

2. ¿Cómo se comparan los derechos y responsabilidades de los adolescentes con los de los adultos? Usen sus tablas para responder.

10

Y tú, ¿qué dices?

ESCRIBIR, HABLAR

1. ¿Por qué crees que hay códigos de vestimenta en muchas escuelas? ¿Crees que es buena idea tener un código de vestimenta? ¿Por qué?
2. Describe el asunto de tu comunidad que sea más importante para ti. ¿Cómo se debe resolver ese asunto?
3. En tu opinión, ¿por qué la gente discrimina? ¿Tiene motivos personales? Explica.
4. ¿Hasta qué punto piensas que en nuestra sociedad hay igualdad?

Ampliación del lenguaje El sufijo *-miento*

Un sustantivo que termina en el sufijo *–miento* tiene como base un verbo. Para formar sustantivos, a los verbos en infinitivo que terminan en *-ar*, quítales la *r* y añádeles el sufijo *-miento (tratar → trata**miento**)*, y a los que terminan en *-er* y en *-ir*, quítales la terminación y agrégales una *i* antes del sufijo *(vencer → venc**imiento**)*. Los sustantivos con *-miento* son masculinos. Copia la tabla y escribe los sustantivos. Luego, completa las frases.

verbo	sustantivo
1. funcionar	funcionamiento
2. nacer	nacimiento
3. pensar	
4. mejorar	
5. conocer	
6. comportar	
7. descubrir	
8. mover	

1. El ____ de la electricidad hizo que la vida de mucha gente fuera más fácil. Pero ____ la electricidad tomó mucho tiempo.
2. Muchos científicos trabajan juntos para ____ el medio ambiente. El ____ del medio ambiente es importante.

460 cuatrocientos sesenta • **Capítulo 10 • ¿Cuáles son tus derechos y deberes?**

Differentiated Instruction

Heritage Speakers

Ask students who have lived in a heritage country to comment on the issue of equality in that country. Do they feel equality exists? If not, along which lines do inequalities appear? Invite all students to compare these descriptions to the situation in their present community.

Students with Learning Difficulties

Before students speak about their opinions in *Actividad* 10, give them the opportunity to brainstorm and plan their responses. Suggest that students write down a few notes on each of the topics.

Go **Online** to practice

PEARSON
realize™

PearsonSchool.com/Autentico

WRITING   SPEAK/RECORD

Interpersonal 10

11

Una tarjeta especial

Igualdad para todos.

Todos tenemos derechos.

ESCRIBIR, DIBUJAR Vas a entrar en un concurso para hacer tarjetas que digan algo sobre los derechos y las responsabilidades de la gente. Dibuja una tarjeta con una recomendación o derecho. Por medio de textos, intercambia recomendaciones con otro(a) estudiante.

Modelo

A —*Yo recomiendo que todos los ciudadanos voten.*

B —*Sí, estoy de acuerdo. Es importante para proteger los derechos de todos.*

CULTURA ◄ Iberoamérica

En defensa de nuestros derechos

La **Convención Iberoamericana de Derechos de los Jóvenes** fue firmada en 2005 por casi todos los países miembros de la OIJ (Organización Iberoamericana de la Juventud). En sus 44 artículos se reconocen derechos fundamentales para los ciudadanos de 15 a 24 años. Estos son algunos ejemplos:

Aspecto de la vida	Tipo de artículo	Contenido
Civil y político	Derecho	a la vida a tener identidad propia
	Libertad	de pensamiento de expresión
Económico, social y cultural	Derecho	a la educación a la cultura y el arte a la salud

La firma de los países es solo el primer paso, ya que también se necesita el acuerdo de los parlamentos. Una vez que los parlamentos de 5 países han aceptado todos los artículos, cualquier joven de Iberoamérica puede usarlos como evidencia para defender sus derechos.

• ¿Por qué crees que es importante reconocer los derechos de los jóvenes?

Pre-AP® Integration: La conciencia social ¿Qué diferencias y similitudes encuentras entre los derechos reconocidos para los jóvenes iberoamericanos y los estadounidenses?

Capítulo 10 • cuatrocientos sesenta y uno **461**

11

Standards: 1.1, 1.3

Suggestions: Allow students time to exchange ideas and recommendations before drawing their greeting cards. Encourage students to research greeting card stores or the Internet to find creative ideas for their cards.

Answers will vary.

CULTURA ◄

Standards: 1.1, 1.2, 2.1, 3.1, 4.1

Suggestions: After students have read the information, ask: *¿Para quiénes son dirigidos los derechos fundamentales (ciudadanos de 15 a 24 años), ¿Cuáles son algunos derechos? (a la vida, a tener identidad propia, a la educación, a la cultura y arte y a la salud) ¿Para qué sirven los artículos? (para defender los derechos)*

Answers will vary.

Additional Resources

 Technology: Online Resources
- Guided, Core, Audio, Writing practice
- Technology: Audio Cap. 10: Comm Audio Activity 1, p. 134
- Audio script
- Communicative Pair Activity

Assessment

Prueba 10-2 with Remediation (online only)
Prueba: Aplicación del vocabulario 1
- Prueba 10-2

Enrich Your Teaching

Teacher-to-Teacher

The **Convención Iberoamericana de Derechos de los Jóvenes** contains 5 chapters and 44 articles. Its purpose is to implement the rights and freedoms of adolescents throughout every nation.

21st Century Skills

Communication As an expansion of *Actividad* 11, have students write an e-mail to their local representative in Congress in which they express their concerns about student rights and responsibilities. Have them take a stand on an issue that is important to them.

Gramática

Suggestions: Ask questions about what students do to elicit the passive voice: —¿*Por quién fue cerrada la puerta?* —*La puerta fue cerrada por* (nombre).

 Technology: Interactive Whiteboard

> **Grammar Activities 10–1** Use the whiteboard activities in your Teacher Resources as you progress through the grammar practice with your class.

12

Resources: Teacher's Resource Materials: Audio Script, Technology: Audio Cap. 10

Suggestions: Pause the audio after each item, so students can write their answers.

 Technology: Audio

Script:
1. Un perro fue maltratado por su dueño esta mañana.
2. Varios jóvenes fueron discriminados en un restaurante de la ciudad.
3. Los dueños de una fábrica fueron acusados de abuso y maltrato.
4. Dos adolescentes fueron obligados a devolver un televisor robado.
5. La víctima fue apoyada por los abogados que la defendieron.
6. Un hombre fue criticado por otros ciudadanos por expresar sus opiniones.
7. Los criminales fueron perdonados por el juez.
8. Una empleada fue acusada por el dueño de la compañía de esconder dinero.

Answers:
1. un perro; fue maltratado; su dueño
2. varios jóvenes; fueron discriminados; no se sabe
3. los dueños de una fábrica; fueron acusados; no se sabe
4. dos adolescentes; fueron obligados; no se sabe
5. la víctima; fue apoyada; los abogados
6. un hombre; fue criticado; otros ciudadanos
7. los criminales; fueron perdonados; el juez
8. una empleada; fue acusada; el dueño de la compañía

13

Suggestions: Have students switch roles, so everyone has a chance to practice.

Answers: Passive subjects will vary. The following are possible results.
1. —¿Quién curó a los niños?
   —Fueron curados por....
2. —¿Quién respetó la igualdad?
   —La igualdad fue respetada por....

Gramática

La voz pasiva: *ser* + participio pasado

In a sentence, the subject usually performs the action. This is called active voice. Sometimes, the subject does not "do" the action but rather has the action "done to it" or receives the action. This is called passive voice.

> Santiago **estableció** las reglas del club.
> Las reglas del club **fueron establecidas** por Santiago.

In Spanish, like in English, you form the passive voice by using *ser* + past participle. Since the past participle is an adjective, it agrees in number and gender with the subject.

> Las reglas **son aplicadas** por el estado.

• If you mention "who" or "what" performs the action, you use *por* to mean "by."

• You often use the impersonal *se* when the subject is unknown.

> **Se necesita** una persona para trabajar en el centro comunitario.

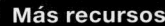 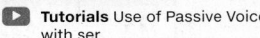
Más recursos ONLINE

 Tutorials Use of Passive Voice with ser

Canción de hip hop: *Los derechos y los deberes*

12

 ### Las noticias del día

ESCUCHAR, ESCRIBIR, HABLAR Imagina que enciendes la radio y escuchas las noticias del día. Para cada frase que escuches, escribe las respuestas a estas preguntas: ¿Quién(es) fue(ron) afectado(s)? ¿Qué le(s) pasó? ¿Por quién(es)? Después, usa tus notas para narrar la situación a la clase. Usa oraciones conectadas con detalles y elaboración.

Modelo
*Un niño **fue asustado** por **un oso** que había escapado del zoológico.*

13

 ### ¿Quién lo hizo?

HABLAR EN PAREJA Con un(a) compañero(a), comenta por quién o quiénes fueron hechas estas cosas.

▶ **Videomodelo**
escribir / artículo
A —¿Quién escribió el artículo sobre la adolescencia?
B —El artículo fue escrito por un reportero.

Estudiante A
1. curar / niños
2. respetar / igualdad
3. leyes / aplicar
4. leer / discurso
5. entrevistar / adolescentes
6. (nombre) / escoger
7. promover / paz
8. evitar / injusticias

Estudiante B
autoridades
gobierno
estudiantes
maestro(a)
médico(a)
reportero(a)
juez

Differentiated Instruction

Students with Learning Difficulties

Before students make their choices in *Actividad* 14, first have them identify the verb in the main clause of each sentence. Second, ask them to determine the tense based on that verb. Third, have them choose the correct answer based on that tense.

Challenge/Pre-AP®

Have students prepare brief news reports about current events. Tell them to use at least one sentence in the passive voice for each report.

Gramática

OBJECTIVES
▶ Discuss and read about school and students' responsibilities
▶ Discuss and write about life as a teenager today

Go Online to practice
PearsonSchool.com/Autentico
PEARSON realize™
 AUDIO   VIDEO   WRITING SPEAK/RECORD

El presente y el imperfecto del subjuntivo

Use the present or the present perfect subjunctive when the verb in the main clause is in the:

Present	**Espero** que **hayan votado**.
Command form	**Dile** que **vote** mañana en las elecciones.
Present perfect	No **hemos establecido** ninguna regla que **sea** injusta.
Future	El sistema **funcionará** mejor cuando **se cambien** las leyes.

Use the imperfect subjunctive when the verb in the main clause is in the:

Preterite	Mi mamá me **pidió** que **tratara** con más respeto a mi hermano.
Imperfect	Mis padres **querían** que mi hermano y yo **nos lleváramos** bien.
Pluperfect	El profesor nos **había exigido** que ambos **tuviéramos** más tolerancia.
Conditional	Al jefe le **gustaría** que los empleados **llegaran** a tiempo.

14

Responsabilidades como estudiante

 LEER, ESCRIBIR Lee el blog de la Sra. Lupe que habla de las responsabilidades que tenía cuando iba a la escuela. Completa el párrafo con el tiempo correcto del subjuntivo de los verbos.

 **El blog de Lupe**

Cuando era joven, el director de la escuela quería que los estudiantes __1.__ *(sigan / siguieran)* un código de vestimenta. A mí no me gustaba que __2.__ *(tenga / tuviera)* que usar ropa especial para ir a clases. Yo quería que nosotros __3.__ *(gocemos / gozáramos)* de la libertad de vestirnos de cualquier manera. ¡Tú tienes suerte! Los maestros no pueden prohibir que __4.__ *(lleves / llevaras)* pantalones rotos ni zapatos viejos. Siempre me ha sorprendido que ahora los maestros no __5.__ *(obliguen / obligaran)* a los estudiantes a sentarse cuando empieza la clase. Es curioso que tampoco les __6.__ *(pidan / pidieran)* la tarea todos los días. En mis clases era común que todas las semanas nos __7.__ *(den / dieran)* un examen, así hacían que __8.__ siempre *(estudiáramos /estudiemos)*. También querían que __9.__ *(hagamos / hiciéramos)* proyectos especiales después de la escuela. Hoy, el sistema de enseñanza menos formal funciona bien, a menos que los jóvenes __10.__ *(se rebelen / se rebelaran)*. Ojalá no __11.__ *(pase / pasara)* eso. Sería triste que los estudiantes __12.__ *(sufran / sufrieran)* por una falta de organización en la escuela.

Capítulo 10 • cuatrocientos sesenta y tres **463**

Enrich Your Teaching

Teacher-to-Teacher

Have students interview a family member from an earlier generation about similarities and differences between family dynamics when they were adolescents and now. Ask students to report on the comments. To practice the subjunctive, include that person's value judgments or opinions.

21st Century Skills

ICT (Information, Communications and Technology) Literacy Remind students of the various digital tools available in **Realize** to help them monitor their own understanding and learning needs about the present and imperfect subjunctive, such as the online tutorials with comprehension check exercises, animated verbs, and additional grammar practice activities.

---

13 (cont'd)

3. —¿Quién aplicó las leyes?
   —Las leyes fueron aplicadas por....
4. —¿Quién leyó el discurso?
   —El discurso fue leído por....
5. —¿Quién entrevistó a los adolescentes?
   —Los adolescentes fueron entrevistados por....
6. —¿Quién escogió...?
   —...fue escogido por...
7. —¿Quién promovió la paz?
   —La paz fue promovida por....
8. —¿Quién evitó las injusticias?
   —Las injusticias fueron evitadas por....

Starter Activity

Before completing the next *Gramática* presentation and accompanying series of activities, briefly review with students the formation of the imperfect subjunctive.

Gramática

Suggestions: Have students invent sentences to demonstrate their understanding of each of the rules for use of the present subjunctive, present perfect subjunctive, and imperfect subjunctive.

 Technology: Interactive Whiteboard

> **Grammar Activities 10-1** Use the whiteboard activities in your Teacher Resources as you progress through the grammar practice with your class.

14

Standards: 1.2

Suggestions: Remind students to focus on the verb in the main clause of each sentence in order to determine which tense to use in the subordinate clause.

Answers:

1. siguieran
2. tuviera
3. gozáramos
4. lleves
5. obliguen
6. pidan
7. dieran
8. estudiáramos
9. hiciéramos
10. se rebelen
11. pase
12. sufrieran

Assessment

Prueba 10-3 with Remediation (online only)
Prueba: La voz pasiva con *ser*
• Prueba 10–3

15

Suggestions: Tell students to use one of the words or expressions from Column B in the sentence about the past as well as in the one about the present.

Answers will vary.

16

Suggestions: Students can begin their preparation in Step 1 by writing a key word or two about something they would like to ask their interview subject. Then they can determine which verbs they will use and begin to construct the questions.

Answers will vary.

Pre-AP® Integration

- **Learning Objective:** Interpersonal Writing
- **Activity:** Have students write an e-mail to a friend in which they give their opinion on the most important issue facing teenagers today. They can start their e-mail by completing the phrase, "*Nos importa que...*" with their most important issue. Be sure students ask their friend at least one question about important issues facing them.
- **Pre-AP® Resource Materials:** Comprehensive guide to Pre-AP® writing skill development

Active Classroom

Cube Game with *Actividad* 15: Divide the class into groups of three. Give each group two game cubes or two small six-sided boxes. Have students write on each side of one cube a word from Column A. Then have them write one verb from Column B on each side of the other box. Have each student roll the cubes and create a sentence combining the words that show face-up on the cubes.

Teacher-to-Teacher

e-amigos: Have students write their *e-amigos* describing the basic needs of teenagers. Ask them to respond to the messages by outlining the steps required to satisfy at least two of those needs. Have students send their e-mails to you for review.

 15

Los primeros años . . .

HABLAR EN PAREJA ¿Cómo fueron tus primeros años de escuela? Con un(a) compañero(a), comparen las responsabilidades que tenían en sus primeros años de escuela con las que tienen ahora. Usen palabras de las dos columnas.

Modelo
Antes, la maestra prefería que yo hiciera la tarea con mis padres. Ahora, mis profesores quieren que haga la tarea solo(a).

Columna A	Columna B
mis padres	exigir
mis maestros(as)	dudar
mis profesores(as)	aconsejar
mis amigos(as)	ser común que
mi entrenador(a)	querer
mis hermanos(as)	sugerir
mis compañeros(as) de clase	preferir
	recomendar
	ser importante que

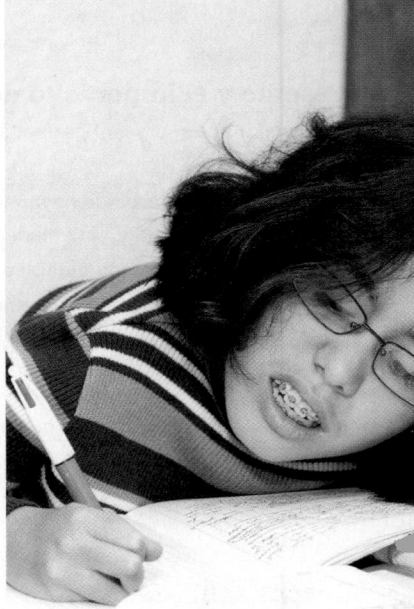

16

Una biografía

ESCRIBIR, HABLAR EN PAREJA Imagina que intercambias correos electrónicos con un(a) compañero(a) en los que lo entrevistas sobre su vida.

1 Escribe cinco preguntas que le puedes hacer a tu compañero(a) sobre su niñez y sobre cómo es diferente hoy por las experiencias que ha tenido.

 Videomodelo
A —¿De qué tenías miedo cuando eras niño(a)?
B —Tenía miedo de que mis padres me castigaran.
A —Y ahora, ¿de qué tienes miedo?
B —Ahora tengo miedo de que las clases de la universidad sean más difíciles.

2 Haz las preguntas a tu compañero(a) y toma apuntes mientras las contesta. Luego, intercambien papeles.

3 Usa tus notas para escribir una biografía breve.

Differentiated Instruction

Heritage Speakers

Before partners complete *Actividad* 16, ask students who have lived in a heritage country to serve as models. Ask questions that highlight the differences between childhood in the heritage country and childhood in the United States.

Musical/Rhythmic Learner

In small groups, have students rehearse choral readings of Hilario Barrero's ***Subjuntivo.*** Discuss how punctuation, word choice, and line breaks impact the rhythm of the poem. Have students compare and contrast the different interpretations they hear.

Los adolescentes en el mundo de hoy

 HABLAR EN GRUPO, ESCRIBIR Tu clase va a escribir un informe sobre los adolescentes de hoy.

1 Para juntar información, trabajen en grupos de cuatro estudiantes y completen las siguientes frases con tres diferentes respuestas.

- Nos importa que . . .
- Nos sorprende que . . .
- Queremos que . . .
- Nos alegramos de que . . .
- Es una lástima que . . .
- Nos molesta que . . .

2 Compartan sus respuestas con los otros grupos. Escojan las respuestas que más se repitieron y digan en qué orden de importancia las colocarían.

3 Ahora, imaginen que pueden hablar con las autoridades del gobierno para informarles cómo se sienten ustedes como adolescentes. Deben presentarles una propuesta *(proposal)* sobre cuáles son los temas más importantes para los adolescentes. Escríbanlos en forma de frase, dando buenas razones de por qué son importantes.

Modelo
Nos parece injusto que no podamos votar hasta los 18 años. Tenemos . . .

En voz alta

Escucha el poema que escribió Hilario Barrero (Toledo, 1948–), un escritor, traductor y poeta español que vive en Nueva York. Trata de repetir el poema en voz alta. Luego, contesta las preguntas.

- ¿Por qué dice el poeta que el maestro les roba su tiempo a los estudiantes?

- ¿Crees que los estudiantes están interesados en lo que les quiere enseñar el profesor? Repite alguna de las frases del poema para dar un ejemplo.

- ¿Te parece que para el autor es fácil o difícil enseñar a los estudiantes? ¿Por qué?

"Subjuntivo"
de Hilario Barrero

Y tener que explicar de nuevo el subjuntivo,
. . . cuando lo que desean es (. . .)
olvidarse del viejo profesor que les roba
su tiempo inútilmente.
Mientras copian los signos del lenguaje,
emotion, doubt, volition, fear, joy . . .,
y usando el subjuntivo de mi lengua de humo[1]
mi deseo es que tengan un amor como el nuestro,
pero sé que no escuchan la frase
que les pongo para ilustrar su duda
ansiosos como están de usar el indicativo.
(. . .)

[1]smoke

Capítulo 10 • cuatrocientos sesenta y cinco **465**

Go Online to practice PearsonSchool.com/Autentico

PEARSON realize™ AUDIO VIDEO WRITING SPEAK/RECORD

17

Standards: 1.1, 1.3

Suggestions: For Step 1, ask: *¿En qué tiempo estarán los verbos que escriben Uds? (en el presente o el presente perfecto del subjuntivo)*
Answers will vary.

EN VOZ ALTA

Standards: 1.1, 1.2, 1.3, 2.1, 2.2, 3.1, 3.2, 5.2

Suggestions: Before students read the poem, prepare them by saying: *Este poema se trata de los pensamientos de un profesor de español.* When they recite the poem, encourage them to use expression appropriate to the professor's thoughts.
Answers will vary.

Project-Based Learning

Students can perform Step 2 at this point. Be sure they understand your corrections and suggestions. (For more information, see p. 448-b.)

Additional Resources

Technology: Online Resources
- Instant Check
- Guided, Core, Audio
- *Para hispanohablantes*
- Teacher's Resource Materials: Audio Script
- Technology: Audio Cap 10, Comm. Audio Act. 2
- Communicative Pair Activity
Print
- Guided WB pp. 313–314
- Core WB p. 138–139

Assessment

Prueba 10-4 with Remediation (online only)
Prueba: El presente y el imperfecto del subjuntivo
- Prueba 10-4
Examen: Vocabulario y gramática 1
- Examen 1
- ExamView: Examen 1

Enrich Your Teaching

Culture Note

Hilario Barrero's poetry has won awards and been published in numerous anthologies and literary magazines. Besides writing poetry and teaching Spanish, Barrero has translated to Spanish the poetry of Robert Frost, Jane Kenyon, and Donald Hall, among others.

21st Century Skills

Leadership and Responsibility In preparation for *Actividad* 17, have students clearly define and assign the tasks for each person in their group. Teams work well together if they know what they want to accomplish and when each person has an equal role.

Vocabulario en contexto 2

Standards: 1.2

Resources: Teacher's Resource Materials: Input Script, Clip Art, Audio Script; Technology: Audio Cap. 10

Suggestions: Have students read along as you present the new vocabulary by playing the audio or reading the text aloud. Use the pictures on pages 466–467 and questions with embedded answers to elicit the vocabulary from students: *¿Una persona que da testimonio en el corte es un testigo o un sospechoso? (testigo) ¿Lo contrario de inocente es acusado o culpable? (culpable)* Check for comprehension by asking other questions. See the Input Scripts in the *Teacher's Resource Materials* for specific questions.

Technology: Interactive Whiteboard

Vocabulary Activities 10-2 Use the whiteboard activities in your Teacher Resources as you progress through the vocabulary practice with your class.

Vocabulario en contexto 2

OBJECTIVES
Read, listen to, and understand information about
▶ Individual rights in society
▶ The role of government

🔊 La Constitución: Los estudiantes de la Sra. Rivera preparan la dramatización de un **juicio**

Libertad de expresión

Sra. Rivera: Elena, ¿quieres ser la **testigo**?

Elena: Sí, claro. ¿Quién es el **acusado**?

Sra. Rivera: Es Alfredo. Hace el papel de un estudiante que volvía de una manifestación pacífica. Fue detenido como **sospechoso** cuando pasaba por un lugar cercano donde destruyeron tiendas y automóviles, pero es **inocente**.

La detención del sospechoso

Tomás: ¿La testigo vio todo eso?

Sra. Rivera: Sí, es una trabajadora de **prensa** que también volvía de la manifestación. Ella lo vio salir de la manifestación, **de modo que** sabe que no es **culpable**.

Mercedes: Entonces el abogado dirá que el arresto **ha violado** derechos **fundamentales**, como la libertad de reunión y expresión. En una sociedad **libre** y **democrática**, no se puede **detener** a una persona solo porque estaba en el lugar equivocado, en el momento equivocado.

466 cuatrocientos sesenta y seis • Capítulo 10 • ¿Cuáles son tus derechos y deberes?

Differentiated Instruction

Students with Learning Difficulties

Before students read or listen to the text on pp. 466–467, ask them to preview the dialogue to look for cognates. Some examples might include *garantía, fundamentales, justicia,* or *democrática.* Discuss how these words can help students decipher meaning from the text.

Advanced Learners

Have students search newspapers, magazines, and the Internet for pictures of such things as the Bill of Rights, trials, juries, defendants, and judges. Have them work together in a group to assemble these visuals into a display, complete with captions and labels, about individual rights and the role of government.

El jurado en la corte

Julián: ¿El acusado será **juzgado** por **jurado**?

Sra. Rivera: Sí, porque ahora estamos estudiando la **garantía** constitucional que dice que el acusado tiene derecho a un juicio rápido y que no se permiten **castigos** crueles.

La testigo

Eduardo: ¿Los que hacen de jurado también son estudiantes de la clase?

Sra. Rivera: No. Seleccionaremos a personas de otras clases para **asegurar** que **lleguen a** su conclusión sin saber la situación antes.

Alfredo: Me parece una buena idea. Un jurado real tiene que basar su **punto de vista** en lo que oye en la corte. El derecho a **la igualdad** también asegura que todos podamos opinar en cuestiones de **justicia**.

18

Nuestros derechos y deberes

 ESCUCHAR En una hoja escribe los números del 1 al 6. Escucha las frases. Escribe *C* si la frase es cierta o *F* si la frase es falsa.

19

Un buen jurado

 ESCRIBIR Escribe tres cosas importantes que crees que debe tener un buen jurado. Puedes usar las que aparecen en estas páginas u otras que conozcas.

Capítulo 10 • cuatrocientos sesenta y siete **467**

18

Standards: 1.2

Resources: Teacher's Resource Materials: Audio Script; Technology: Audio Cap. 10

Suggestions: Allow students to silently review the material on these two pages before they complete the listening activity. Use the audio or read from the script. Allow students to listen more than once.

🔊 **Technology: Audio Script and Answers**

1. Un testigo es la persona que viola la libertad. (*F*)
2. El jurado es un grupo de sospechosos. (*F*)
3. Un trabajador de prensa trabaja para un periódico o revista. (*C*)
4. El acusado no tiene que ir al juicio. (*F*)
5. Una persona es inocente hasta que se pruebe que es culpable. (*C*)
6. La constitución garantiza igualdad y justicia para todos. (*C*)

19

Standards: 1.3

Suggestions: Point out to students that they need not use the word ***derecho*** in each item in their list. Have them study the material on these two pages as a model for how to express various rights.

Answers will vary.

Vocabulario en contexto 2

Standards: 1.2

Resources: Teacher's Resource Materials: Input Script, Clip Art, Audio Script; Technology: Audio Cap. 10

Suggestions: Pre-reading: Present the readings on this and the next page one at a time, along with their respective activities.

Reading: Allow students time to read each presentation silently first before they listen to the audio.

Post-reading: Check comprehension by asking questions. See the *Teacher's Resource Materials* for specific questions.

20

Standards: 1.3

Suggestions: Encourage students to think of problems they consider important and list them with the problems on this page.

Answers will vary.

Pre-AP® Integration

- **Learning Objective:** Interpersonal Speaking
- **Activity:** Have students focus on one problem presented on this page and allow them two minutes to think of a specific way they would propose to solve it. Then have students work in pairs and tell each other the problem they have chosen along with their proposed solution. Allow each student to talk for one minute. Request that they offer suggestions to each other to improve their mini-talk.
- **Pre-AP® Resource Materials:** Comprehensive guide to Pre-AP® vocabulary skill development

Active Classroom

Have students work in pairs and rank the problems from most to least serious. Have each group report back on their top four. Use the results to create a class summary.

Jóvenes por el desarrollo y la paz

Los jóvenes tienen gran fuerza en el mundo de hoy. El desarrollo de los países depende, entre otras cosas, de la participación de los jóvenes. Hay organizaciones internacionales, como la Red de Jóvenes de las Américas, que reúnen grupos de jóvenes de distintos países. Allí **intercambian** sus ideas y hacen **propuestas** sobre los diferentes **modos** de resolver sus propios problemas y los de otros jóvenes.

Manifestación por la paz en España

A medida que participan en estas reuniones, los jóvenes aprenden a respetar la diferencia de opiniones de otros grupos. Juntos **proponen** soluciones a sus problemas y a los problemas del mundo.

Estos son algunos problemas que enfrentan los jóvenes:

- **las desigualdades** sociales, económicas y políticas
- **el desempleo**
- la discriminación por sexo
- los jóvenes sin hogar
- los conflictos **mundiales**
- la contaminación ambiental
- las enfermedades, el hambre y la mala nutrición
- los problemas en la familia
- **la falta de** oportunidades de educación y entrenamiento

Un participante

20

Problemas de los jóvenes

ESCRIBIR   Haz una lista de los problemas que tienen los jóvenes de hoy. Empieza con los que creas que son más importantes y termina con los menos importantes.

Differentiated Instruction

Heritage Speakers

Ask students who have lived in a heritage country to share their views on the biggest problems facing the youth in that country. Are the issues similar to or different from those faced by young people in the United States?

Students with Learning Difficulties

Ask students to provide each other with brief definitions or explanations of each of the issues listed on p. 468. For example: *¿Qué es el desempleo? ¿Cuáles son algunos ejemplos de problemas en la familia?*

Go **Online** to practice

PearsonSchool.com/Autentico

PEARSON realize ™

AUDIO WRITING

☰ Blog > ¿Qué proponen los jóvenes?

★ ★ ★ ★ ☆ comentarios (129)

Lydia, *de San Luis Obispo, California.*
Ella quiere ser representante **ante** la Organización de las Naciones Unidas.

❝**En lugar de** pensar solo en nosotros mismos, somos responsables de hablar por los jóvenes del mundo que llevan una vida difícil. Ellos también tienen derecho a lograr sus **aspiraciones**❞.

Mark, *de Atlanta, Georgia.*
Mark dice que trabajará en el gobierno.

❝**El fin** de la democracia es que tengamos más libertad para expresar sin miedo lo que **opinamos.** La libertad de expresión es **un valor** democrático fundamental❞.

Yamiko y Alicia, *de Providence, Rhode Island.* Ellas quieren ser consejeras de estudiantes.

❝Si la gente se reúne con fines **pacíficos** e intercambia opiniones cuando no está de acuerdo, puede encontrar soluciones a muchos problemas. Así, habrá menos guerras y también menos problemas en las escuelas❞.

21

Hagamos algo

ESCUCHAR Escucha las frases. Después de oír cada frase, di quién de los estudiantes de esta página crees que dijo cada cosa.

22

Y tú, ¿qué propones?

ESCRIBIR Imagina que te invitan a representar a los jóvenes de tu país, o de otro país que conozcas, en alguna organización internacional. Prepara un correo electrónico con cinco ideas y envíaselo a un representante de esa organización. El representante te da recomendaciones para que tú puedas ayudar. Apoya las ideas y recomendaciones.

Capítulo 10 • cuatrocientos sesenta y nueve **469**

Enrich Your Teaching

Culture Note

La Red de Jóvenes y Estudiantes, mentioned on p. 468, belongs to the Mexican section of Amnesty International, and some of its campaigns are operated through that organization. Their mission is to encourage youth involvement in the promotion and defense of human rights. Each year, Amnesty International unites the energy and ideas of young Mexicans of ***la Red*** with other young people all over the world in a unified action. They call attention to one place in the world in which human rights are in jeopardy and put pressure on authorities and organizations in that place to respect human rights.

21

Standards: 1.2

Resources: Teacher's Resource Materials: Audio Script; Technology: Audio Cap. 10

Suggestions: Remind students that the comments they will hear are by the four people shown on this page.

 Technology: Audio

Script:
1. La responsabilidad de la Naciones Unidas es la de hablar por los jóvenes del mundo.
2. La libertad de expresión es un derecho fundamental.
3. Es importante escuchar a otras personas aunque no estés de acuerdo con ellas.
4. Yo necesito expresar mis opiniones sin miedo.
5. Los jóvenes del mundo tienen el derecho de lograr sus aspiraciones.

Answers:
1. Lydia
2. Mark
3. Yamiko y Alicia
4. Mark
5. Lydia

22

Standards: 1.3

Suggestions: Once students have written their five problems and solutions, invite them to share them in a class discussion.

Answers will vary.

Project-Based Learning

Students can perform Step 3 at this point. (For more information, see p. 448-b.)

Additional Resources

Technology: Online Resources
- Instant Check
- Guided, Core, Audio, Writing practice
- *Para hispanohablantes*

Print
- Guided WB pp. 315–322
- Core WB pp. 140–141

Assessment

Prueba: Comprensión del vocabulario 2
- Prueba 10-5

23

Standards: 1.2

Suggestions: Make sure students are given adequate writing practice by having them write the entire answer and not just the corresponding letter.

Answers:

1. c
2. b
3. a
4. c
5. a
6. b
7. c (a)

24

Standards: 1.2, 1.3

Suggestions: After students have completed the activity, have them share their work, reading each item as a complete sentence.

Answers:

1. dar a cada persona lo que es de esa persona
2. cuando todos participan en el gobierno de un país
3. cuando la policía le quita la libertad a una persona porque cree que es sospechosa
4. las da el estado cuando asegura derechos para todos sus ciudadanos
5. las cosas que los ciudadanos pueden hacer o exigir de acuerdo con la ley
6. no respetar una ley

Vocabulario en uso 2

OBJECTIVES
- Read and write about justice
- Express your opinions about rights and responsibilities
- Discuss and write about democracy

23

En la sala de justicia

LEER ¿Quién dijo cada frase en la sala de justicia?

1. Hay que prometer decir la verdad, solo la verdad.
   a. el inocente   **b.** el juicio   **c.** el juez

2. Desde donde yo estaba, pude ver muy bien lo que hizo el criminal.
   a. el sospechoso   **b.** el testigo   **c.** la acusada

3. Lo siento, señor juez, pero esa mujer no ha dicho la verdad. Yo no lo hice.
   a. el acusado   **b.** el jurado   **c.** la víctima

4. No hay suficiente información. ¡El acusado es inocente!
   a. la justicia   **b.** la policía   **c.** la abogada

5. Sí, soy inocente. ¡Tienen que creerme!
   a. el acusado   **b.** el juicio   **c.** el castigo

6. Hemos decidido quién es culpable.
   a. el inocente   **b.** el jurado   **c.** la acusada

7. El jurado deberá juzgar al acusado con justicia.
   a. el juez   **b.** los valores   **c.** la prensa

24

¿Qué quieren decir?

LEER, ESCRIBIR Para poder defender nuestros derechos, es importante saber lo que quieren decir las palabras de la Declaración de derechos. Empareja cada palabra con su significado. Luego, escribe dos frases usando cuatro palabras de la primera columna.

1. la justicia — dar a cada persona lo que es de esa persona

2. democrático(a) — no respetar una ley

3. detener — las cosas que los ciudadanos pueden hacer o exigir de acuerdo con la ley

4. las garantías — cuando todos participan en el gobierno de un país

5. los derechos — cuando la policía le quita la libertad a una persona porque cree que es sospechosa

6. violar — las da el estado cuando asegura derechos para todos sus ciudadanos

470 cuatrocientos setenta • Capítulo 10 • ¿Cuáles son tus derechos y deberes?

Differentiated Instruction

Students with Learning Difficulties

Assign students the roles outlined in *Actividad* 23, and provide each character with a label card. Ask them to stand at the front of the class, holding their label card. Read the quotes from the activity and ask students to call out the character who would say those words.

Advanced Learners

Have students write sentences containing the unused words from *Actividad* 23. Ask them to read their sentences to each other and listen to make sure the words are used correctly.

25 ¿Qué dicen los titulares?

Go **Online** to practice
PearsonSchool.com/Autentico
PEARSON realize.
WRITING

ESCRIBIR, HABLAR EN PAREJA

1 Usa elementos de cada columna para escribir titulares (headlines).

El Sol

Santiago   23 de septiembre

Presidente asegura derechos a todos los niños.

1. la Organización de las Naciones Unidas	detener	puntos de vista con fines pacíficos
2. la policía	votar	competencia mundial de atletismo
3. el Congreso	asegurar	garantías y derechos de los ciudadanos
4. el juez	proponer	el castigo del culpable
5. la declaración	reunirse	los valores democráticos
6. el presidente del club atlético	defender	los sospechosos
7. el grupo para la defensa de los niños	intercambiar	el derecho a la educación y la alimentación

2 Imagina que eres reportero(a). Trabaja con otro(a) estudiante para escribir tres frases sobre uno de los titulares.

CULTURA ‹ México

Políticos y educadores ¿Sabías que muchos líderes políticos en los países hispanohablantes fueron educadores o maestros? Un político famoso, el mexicano José Vasconcelos (1882–1959), también fue educador, además de filósofo, abogado, historiador y escritor. Después de luchar en la Revolución Mexicana, fue rector de la Universidad Nacional y creó la Secretaría de Educación Pública. La dividió en cuatro departamentos: el de Escuelas, el de Bibliotecas, el de Bellas Artes y el de Enseñanza indígena. En su época, miles de campesinos y obreros aprendieron a leer y a escribir y se dio el más importante avance de la educación en México. Los estudiantes lo llamaron "Maestro de la juventud de América".

Vasconcelos, además, creó la orquesta sinfónica de México y promovió la pintura mural y la obra de los grandes muralistas Diego Rivera y José Clemente Orozco.

▲ José Vasconcelos

• ¿Por qué es importante que los políticos sean maestros?

Pre-AP® Integration: Los héroes y los personajes históricos ¿De qué manera puede contribuir un maestro en un puesto de gobierno?

25

Standards: 1.1, 4.1

Suggestions: Remind students that the structure of a *titular* is different from that of a complete sentence. Point out the model *titular* at the top of the page, and ask them to use it as a model.
Answers will vary.

CULTURA ‹

Standards: 1.1, 1.2, 3.1

Suggestions: After students have read and discussed the information, ask comprehension questions. For example: *¿Cuáles eran las profesiones de José Vasconcelos? (político, educador, filósofo, abogado, historiador, escritor) ¿Cuáles eran los cuatro departamentos de la Secretaría de Educación Pública que él creó? (los departamentos de Escuelas, Bibliotecas, Bellas Artes y Enseñanza indígena)*
Answers will vary.

Enrich Your Teaching

Culture Note
José Vasconcelos considered it one of his most important missions as a leader to reach out to the indigenous peoples of Mexico through education. As part of this mission, he started the "muralist movement," which helped launch the artistic careers of Diego Rivera, José Clemente Orozco, and Alfaro Siqueiros.

21st Century Skills
Critical Thinking and Problem Solving
Have students do further research about José Vasconcelos and his accomplishments in education, art, and government in Mexico. Ask them to look up a list of his major writings. What do the titles indicate about Vasconcelos' interests and concerns as educator and politician?

26

Standards: 1.2

Resources: Teacher's Resource Materials: Audio Script; Technology: Audio Cap. 10

Suggestions: Before students listen, tell them that they will hear five separate, short news reports. Encourage them to write their responses in their own words.

 Technology: Audio Script:

1. En Santa Ana, acusaron a un grupo de personas de tratar de robar un banco. El testigo principal en el juicio será un joven de 18 años de edad.
2. En Ciudad Luna, en lugar de no hacer nada para solucionar el problema del tráfico, todas las personas hicieron una manifestación pacífica frente al congreso.
3. Representantes de la organización internacional Los Amigos fueron a varios países para hablar de los derechos y los valores democráticos.
4. Y ahora las noticias locales. La policía dijo que hay tres nuevos sospechosos en la desaparición de 200 cajas de juguetes de la tienda Alegría.
5. A pesar de que muchos se quejaron, el alcalde Marino dijo que se castigará a quien viole la ley contra el ruido.

Answers: Wording of answers will vary. The following contain the main ideas:
1. está acusado de tratar de robar un banco.
2. pidiendo una solución al problema del tráfico.
3. fueron a varios países para hablar de los derechos y los valores democráticos.
4. de la tienda Alegría.
5. castigaría a quien viole la ley contra el ruido.

27

Standards: 1.1

Recycle: subjunctive with verbs of emotion or doubt

Suggestions: Have students take turns being the one to launch each interchange.

Answers will vary.

28

Standards: 1.1, 1.3

Recycle: preterite and imperfect tenses

Suggestions: Encourage students to present their report as though it were part of a real news program. The narrator should introduce the witness.

Answers will vary.

26

Escucha la radio

 ESCUCHAR, ESCRIBIR A veces parece que las noticias siempre son malas. Escucha la radio y completa las frases para hacer un resumen de las noticias.

1. En Santa Ana, un grupo de personas . . .
2. En Ciudad Luna, hubo una manifestación . . .
3. Representantes de la organización mundial Los Amigos . . .
4. Desaparecieron 200 cajas de juguetes . . .
5. El alcalde Marino dijo que . . .

27

¿Qué opinas? o "la libertad de opinión"

 LEER, HABLAR EN PAREJA Trabaja con otro(a) estudiante. Usa tu derecho a la libertad de opinión y di si estás de acuerdo o no con las siguientes frases. Usa expresiones como: *creo que, me parece que, me preocupa que, dudo que.*

 Videomodelo
(no) proteger los derechos fundamentales
A —*Debemos proteger los derechos fundamentales.*
B —*Creo que debemos proteger los derechos fundamentales para no perderlos.*

1. (no) detener a los sospechosos
2. los testigos de un crimen (no) ayudar a la víctima
3. (no) ser culpables los padres de jóvenes desobedientes
4. (no) apoyar la participación de jóvenes en manifestaciones pacíficas
5. (no) luchar contra la falta de justicia en otros países
6. (no) construir más carreteras
7. (no) controlar lo que pueden hacer los jóvenes
8. (no) proponer soluciones pacíficas

28

El noticiero

 HABLAR EN PAREJA, ESCRIBIR Con un(a) compañero(a), escribe un breve reportaje sobre "el misterio de la desaparición de una bicicleta" para el programa de noticias. Usa oraciones conectadas con detalles y elaboración. Describe lo que pasó e incluye un comentario de un testigo. Pueden usar las palabras del recuadro. Presenten su reportaje a otra pareja. Uno(a) es reportero(a) del noticiero y otro(a) es testigo.

| el / la testigo | culpable | en lugar de | sospechoso(a) |
| inocente | detener | el punto de vista | opinar |

Differentiated Instruction

Students with Learning Difficulties

For *Actividad* 28, help students first note down ideas for events involved in the theft of a bicycle. Have them use a flow chart or other graphic organizer for this purpose. Ask what would happen: first the discovery that the bicycle is missing, then asking family members or neighbors, and so on. Guide them to use the vocabulary in the word bank.

Students with Special Needs

You may need to provide impaired students with a copy of the script in order for them to complete listening activities like *Actividad* 26.

Momentos históricos

 LEER, HABLAR En todas las épocas hay artistas que representan momentos históricos de la vida de sus países y de sus héroes. Uno de esos momentos es cuando se firman *(sign)* documentos fundamentales, como las declaraciones de independencia y las constituciones. Lee sobre un pintor de la historia de Venezuela y contesta las preguntas.

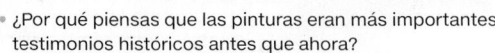 **Conexiones** **Las artes**

Juan Lovera (1776–1841) es un pintor que inició el género de pintura histórica en Venezuela. En su obra, "El 5 de julio de 1811", retrata a más de cien personajes y deja testimonio de un suceso de gran importancia para Venezuela, la firma de la declaración de independencia de España. La pintura muestra con detalles y de manera fiel a los hechos la ropa y la posición de los criollos *(native born)* de esa época. Además de los dibujos de cada uno de los personajes principales, tiene escritos sus nombres. Esta obra muestra la misión de las artes para preservar la historia.

▲ "El 5 de julio de 1811",
Juan Lovera, (Venezuela)

• ¿Por qué piensas que las pinturas eran más importantes testimonios históricos antes que ahora?

• ¿Recuerdas alguna pintura que muestre un momento de la historia de los Estados Unidos?

30

Y tú, ¿qué respondes?

 HABLAR EN PAREJA, ESCRIBIR

1 Imagina que estás en tu clase de educación cívica. En una conversación, haz y contesta estas y otras preguntas originales con un(a) compañero(a). Apoya tus opiniones o recomendaciones y usa expresiones apropiadas.

1. En tu opinión, ¿qué debe garantizar el gobierno a los ciudadanos?

2. ¿Qué debe garantizar el(la) director(a) de tu escuela a los(as) estudiantes?

3. ¿Conoces países donde no respetan el punto de vista de la gente? ¿Puedes mencionar algunos de esos países?

4. ¿El desempleo existe en todos los países del mundo? ¿Cómo crees que afecta a las familias que sufren debido al desempleo?

5. ¿Qué organizaciones mundiales conoces que tengan fines pacíficos? Descríbelas.

6. ¿Conoces países que aseguran una educación gratuita para los ciudadanos?

2 Escribe un párrafo sobre lo que significa para ti la democracia de los Estados Unidos.

Capítulo 10 • cuatrocientos setenta y tres **473**

Enrich Your Teaching

Culture Note

Juan Lovera is Venezuela's most outstanding artist of the school known as **arte republicana,** which portrayed historical events. He eventually became known as **El pintor de los Próceres.** His paintings on a grand scale like **El 5 de julio de 1811** are known for their composition and perspective.

21st Century Skills

Communication As a warm-up to *Actividad* 30, have students brainstorm a list of expressions in Spanish they would use when giving their personal opinion or when taking a stand on an important issue. What words or expressions do they use to persuade others to agree with them? Have them choose one of the questions in this activity, then prepare to debate the issue with their classmates.

29

Standards: 1.1, 1.2, 2.2, 3.1, 4.2

Suggestions: Have students read the information about Juan Lovera in pairs and help each other with any comprehension problems they may have. Guide students in their comparisons of the role art has played in cultural practices in the past and present.

Answers will vary.

30

Standards: 1.1, 1.3

Recycle: subjunctive, country names

Suggestions: For Step 2, encourage students to consider and comment on their partner's opinions as well as their own.

Answers will vary.

Active Classroom

After completing *Actividad* 30 #2, have each student write on the board one statement from his or her paragraph. Use these ideas as a brainstorm. Have each student take these ideas and write a new paragraph. Select the top two paragraphs and send them to a local Spanish newspaper to be published or submit them to the school literary magazine.

Additional Resources

 Technology: Online Resources
• Teacher's Resource Materials: Audio Script
• Technology: Audio Cap. 10, Comm. Audio Activity 3
• Communicative Pair Activity

Assessment

Prueba 10-6 with Remediation (online only)
Prueba: Aplicación del vocabulario 2
• Prueba 10-6

Starter Activity

Briefly review with students other tenses they have learned that use the auxiliary verb **haber:** the **presente perfecto** and the **pluscuamperfecto.**

Gramática

Standards: 4.1

Suggestions: On the board, write sentence frames consisting of a verb in the preterite, the imperfect, or the past perfect tense, followed by **que,** followed by an infinitive. The three parts should be able to work together as building blocks for a complex sentence. Here are some examples:

dudó + que + terminar

quería + que + invitar

habíamos pedido + que + servir

Challenge students to put the parts together to make complex sentences using the pluperfect subjunctive. Tell them they can use whatever subject they wish in the subordinate clause. The above frames might result in sentences like the following:

Papá dudó que Benito hubiera terminado el maratón antes de la puesta del sol.

Yo quería que tú me hubieras invitado.

Habíamos pedido que Ud. nos hubiera servido antes.

 Technology: Interactive Whiteboard

Grammar Activities 10-2 Use the whiteboard activities in your Teacher Resources as you progress through the grammar practice with your class.

31

Standards: 1.2

Suggestions: In addition to forming the pluperfect subjunctive for the correct verb, encourage students to think about the time relationships in the sentences.

Answers:

1. hubiera detenido
2. hubieran destruido
3. hubiera castigado
4. hubieran sido
5. hubiera garantizado
6. hubiera opinado

Gramática

OBJECTIVES
▶ Talk and write about events that happened prior to other past events
▶ Discuss the achievements of a famous person

El pluscuamperfecto del subjuntivo

You use the pluperfect subjunctive to describe actions in the past, when one action takes place before the other. In such cases, the action that takes place before is in the pluperfect subjunctive, and the action that takes place after is in the preterite, the imperfect or the pluperfect of the indicative.

> Carlos **se sorprendió** que su amigo **hubiera comprado** todos los materiales.
> **Esperaba** que **hubieran ido** a la fiesta con los niños.
> Yo **había querido** que mis hermanos **hubieran venido** a la casa de la abuela.

You form the pluperfect subjunctive using the past subjunctive of *haber* + the past participle of the verb.

hub**iera** sal**ido**	hub**iéramos** sal**ido**
hub**ieras** sal**ido**	hub**ierais** sal**ido**
hub**iera** sal**ido**	hub**ieran** sal**ido**

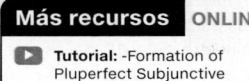
Más recursos ONLINE

▶ **Tutorial:** -Formation of Pluperfect Subjunctive

• You also use the pluperfect subjunctive when the verb in the main clause is in the conditional.

> **¿Sería** posible que Teresa **hubiera terminado** el informe?

• Note that since the expression *como si* (as if) always refers to something that is contrary to the truth, or unreal, it must always be followed by the subjunctive, either the imperfect subjunctive or the pluperfect subjunctive.

> Estaba tan cansada **como si hubiera corrido** todo el día.
> Sergio descansa **como si no tuviera** nada que hacer.

31

Las noticias del día

 LEER, ESCRIBIR Imagina que estás leyendo el periódico. Completa las siguientes frases con la forma correcta del verbo en el pluscuamperfecto del subjuntivo.

1. Fue una sorpresa que el gobierno _____ (detener/proponer) a tantas personas en el aeropuerto.

2. Los ciudadanos se sorprendieron que los aerosoles _____ (opinar/destruir) tanto el medio ambiente.

3. Los estudiantes dudaban que la policía _____ (castigar/asegurar) al presidente de la universidad.

4. Los testigos esperaban que las noticias _____ (estar/ser) más positivas.

5. Los ciudadanos de ese país esperaban que el gobierno _____ (garantizar/juzgar) la libertad de prensa y de expresión.

6. Me sorprendía que el juez _____ (opinar/violar) de esa manera.

Differentiated Instruction

Advanced Learners

On separate slips of paper, have students write three subordinate clauses beginning with conjunctions taught in the *Gramática* on this page. If they use **aunque,** allow them to use either the indicative or the subjunctive in the clause. Collect the strips, mix them, and place them in a container.

Have students meet in a circle, take turns drawing one subordinate clause at a time, and completing a complex sentence by inventing a suitable main clause.

32

En tu comunidad

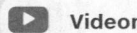

HABLAR EN PAREJA Imagina que te encuentras con un(a) amigo(a) y conversan sobre las cosas que sucedieron en tu barrio. Trabaja con un(a) compañero(a). Tu compañero(a) te dice lo que pasó en el barrio y tú le respondes cómo te hizo sentir, usando las expresiones apropiadas, un verbo de emoción y el pluscuamperfecto del subjuntivo.

Videomodelo

Roberto / celebrar su cumpleaños
A —*Roberto celebró su cumpleaños.*
B —*Me alegré mucho que hubiera celebrado su cumpleaños.*

Estudiante A

1. la abuela de Pedro / enfermarse
2. los hijos de Ana / cambiarse de escuela
3. la familia Ortiz / irse de viaje
4. el dueño del supermercado / acusar al vecino
5. los padres de Luisa/comprarse una casa

Estudiante B

Me alegré . . .
Fue una lástima . . .
Me sorprendió . . .
Me enojó . . .
Fue maravilloso . . .

El español en la comunidad

El español y las campañas electorales

Cada día más, en las campañas electorales en los Estados Unidos los candidatos dedican tiempo a comunicarse en español con la comunidad hispanohablante. Además de que ya hay boletas para votar traducidas al español, hoy día los candidatos usan la radio, la televisión y páginas de Internet en español para trasmitir sus mensajes y dar entrevistas

en español. Pero esta idea no es nueva; el presidente John F. Kennedy fue el primero que grabó mensajes en español durante su campaña, en 1960.

Como la población de hispanohablantes está creciendo en los Estados Unidos, se espera que durante las campañas presidenciales próximas, los candidatos usarán aún más el español para convencer *(convince)* a los hispanohablantes de votar por ellos. Es probable que entonces quienes puedan hablar los dos idiomas, ¡tendrán más posibilidades de ganar!

El bilingüismo es importante en las campañas electorales de varios países del mundo.

Capítulo 10 • cuatrocientos setenta y cinco **475**

32

Suggestions: Make sure both partners have a chance to assume the role of Student B.

Answers: Student B's choices of verbs of emotion will vary. The following are likely results:

1. —La abuela de Pedro se enfermó.
   —Fue una lástima que ella se hubiera enfermado.
2. —Los hijos de Ana se cambiaron de escuela.
   —Me sorprendió que ellos se hubieran cambiado de escuela.
3. —La familia Ortiz se fue de viaje.
   —Fue maravilloso que ellos se hubieran ido de viaje.
4. —El dueño del supermercado acusó al vecino.
   —Me enojó que él lo hubiera acusado.
5. —Los padres de Luisa se compraron una casa.
   —Fue maravilloso que ellos se hubieran comprado una casa.

El español en la comunidad

Suggestions: Once students have read the information, ask comprehension questions. For example: *¿De qué manera se comunican los candidatos con la comunidad? (Hay boletas para votar traducidas al español. Usan la radio, la televisión y el Internet para transmitir sus mensajes. Se entrevistan en programas de la televisión en español.)*

Answers will vary.

Project-Based Learning

Students can perform Step 4 at this point. Be sure they understand your corrections and suggestions. (For more information, see p. 448-b.)

Enrich Your Teaching

Culture Note

Business leaders and politicians from the Spanish-speaking community in the United States have made great progress in broadcasting their messages in the past thirty years. Besides many Spanish-language media tools, such as radio stations and TV channels at their disposal throughout the country, there is also Hispanic Heritage Month. It runs from September 15 to October 15 of each year and celebrates contributions to United States society from anyone in the Spanish-speaking community. It was originally approved by Congress as National Hispanic Heritage Week in 1968, and was expanded to an entire month in 1988.

33

Standards: 1.1

Suggestions: Conduct the activity with the whole class, calling on volunteers randomly for each item.

Answers:

1. El vecino actuó como si no le hubiera importado nada.
2. El contador respondió como si hubiera estado loco.
3. La vendedora pareció como si hubiera escondido algo.
4. La dueña habló como si se hubiera enojado con la vendedora.
5. El cliente se rio como si se hubiera asustado con las preguntas.

34

Standards: 1.1, 1.3, 3.1

Suggestions: Encourage students to check back to the rules in the *Gramática* as often as necessary in order to complete the activity. Remind them that the most likely way to use the pluperfect subjunctive is to talk about the reactions others had to what their famous person did or said.

Answers will vary.

Additional Resources

 Technology: Online Resources
• Instant Check
• Guided, Core, Audio
• *Para hispanohablantes*
Print
• Guided WB pp. 323–324
• Core WB p. 142

Assessment

Prueba 10-7 with Remediation (online only)
Prueba: El pluscuamperfecto del subjuntivo
• Prueba 10-7

 33

El culpable

 ESCRIBIR Imagina que eres un(a) detective que investigó un robo en una tienda. Entrevistaste a diferentes personas y su comportamiento fue muy sospechoso. Usa la expresión *como si* y el pluscuamperfecto del subjuntivo para explicar cómo actuaron.

Modelo
el chofer *(reaccionar)* / *estar* enojado con la dueña
*El chofer **reaccionó como si hubiera estado** enojado con la dueña.*

1. el vecino *(actuar)* / no importarle nada
2. el contador *(responder)* / estar loco
3. la vendedora *(parecer)* / esconder algo
4. la dueña *(hablar)* / enojarse con la vendedora
5. el cliente *(reírse)* / asustarse con las preguntas

34

Por una sociedad mejor

HABLAR EN GRUPO, ESCRIBIR

1 En grupo, investiguen sobre la vida de una persona famosa que luchó o que lucha por una sociedad más justa. Pueden buscar información en la biblioteca o en la Red. La persona puede ser:

• un(a) presidente(a)   • un héroe o una heroína
• un(a) escritor(a)   • un(a) científico(a)
• un(a) pintor(a)

2 Preparen un cuestionario que incluye detalles y elaboración sobre la vida de la persona que escogieron, por ejemplo, dónde nació, cómo fue su niñez, a qué se dedicaba, cuáles eran o son sus razones para luchar por una sociedad mejor, qué logró hacer. Escriban en una hoja de papel aparte las respuestas a las preguntas del cuestionario.

Modelo
¿Cómo reaccionó el país cuando se murió Lincoln?
El país se sorprendió de que el presidente Lincoln hubiera muerto.

3 Intercámbiense los cuestionarios entre los grupos para responderlos. Luego, devuélvanlos al grupo que los hizo para que revise las respuestas.

4 Corrijan las respuestas y compartan su información sobre la persona famosa con el resto de la clase.

476 cuatrocientos setenta y seis • Capítulo 10 • ¿Cuáles son tus derechos y deberes?

Differentiated Instruction

Heritage Speakers

For *Actividad* 34, encourage students who have lived in a heritage country to suggest famous persons from that country for their group to investigate. They can provide valuable cultural insight on the famous person's achievements.

Advanced Learners

Have students use the pluperfect subjunctive to tell about three outstanding events in their lives and their reactions—or the reactions of others—to those events. Provide an example, such as: *Mis padres no pudieron creer que yo hubiera ganado el concurso de poesía.*

Gramática

OBJECTIVES
▶ Express what would or should have happened
▶ Discuss possible outcomes
▶ Exchange information about animal rights

Go **Online** to practice
PearsonSchool.com/Autentico
PEARSON realize™
AUDIO VIDEO WRITING

Interpersonal 10

El condicional perfecto

You use the conditional perfect to express what would or should have happened at some point in the past.

Y tú, ¿qué **habrías dicho** en esa situación?
*And you, what **would you have said** in that situation?*

Yo le **habría dado** un buen consejo.
*I **would have given** him(her) good advice.*

You form the conditional perfect using the conditional of *haber* + the past participle of the verb.

habría trabajado	habríamos trabajado
habrías trabajado	habríais trabajado
habría trabajado	habrían trabajado

Más recursos ONLINE

▶ **Tutorial:** Formation of Conditional Perfect

🔊 *Canción de hip hop:*
¿Qué habrías dicho?

- The conditional is used with *si* clauses to say what might have been if things had been different. In these sentences you use the past perfect subjunctive and the conditional perfect together.

  Si **hubiera sabido** que estabas interesada, te **habría invitado** a la reunión.
  *If I had **known you were** interested, I **would have invited** you to the meeting.*

  Si **no hubieran venido** a este país, **no los habrías conocido**.
  *If they **hadn't come** to this country, you **would not have met** them.*

35

Lo habrían hecho pero, . . .

 LEER Muchas personas quieren resolver problemas, pero no siempre pueden. Completa las frases con el condicional perfecto del verbo apropiado.

1. Yo (*participar / detener*) en la reunión, pero no pude porque estaba enferma.

2. Los profesores (*obligar / asegurar*) el respeto a los derechos de los estudiantes si hubieran ido a la manifestación.

3. Si las personas no hubieran actuado mal, la policía no los (*detener / intercambiar*).

4. Si yo fuera el profesor, (*decir / proponer*) otro código de vestimenta.

5. Si ellos no hubieran tenido problemas, no (*aceptar / sufrir*) nuestra ayuda.

6. Si hubiera tenido problemas como tú, yo (*buscar / asegurar*) el apoyo de mis padres.

7. Con un buen traductor, la confusión entre los dos países (*proponerse / resolverse*).

Capítulo 10 • cuatrocientos setenta y siete **477**

Gramática

Standards: 4.1

Suggestions: To help students become familiar with using the past perfect subjunctive and the conditional perfect together, write on the board English sentences like the examples in the second part of the *Gramática* and have students translate them to Spanish.

🔌 **Technology: Interactive Whiteboard**

Grammar Activities 10-2 Use the whiteboard activities in your Teacher Resources as you progress through the grammar practice with your class.

35

Standards: 1.2

Common Errors: Some students will confuse verb forms of *haber* when working with the past perfect subjunctive and the conditional perfect. Write the forms of *haber* for the former tense on the left side of the board and those for the latter tense on the right side, and allow students to refer to them as they complete the activities.

Suggestions: Once students have written the answers on their own, invite them to take turns reading the completed sentences aloud.

Answers:

1. habría participado
2. habrían asegurado
3. habría detenido
4. habría propuesto
5. habrían aceptado
6. habría buscado
7. se habría resuelto

Enrich Your Teaching

Teacher-to-Teacher

If you use a predictable system for calling on volunteers, such as going up and down rows, some students will determine which item they are going to be held responsible for and "drop out" of the activity until it is their turn. When conducting activities together with the whole class, randomize the way you choose volunteers.

21st Century Skills

ICT (Information, Communications and Technology) Literacy Remind students of the various digital tools available in **Realize** that can provide extra practice with verb conjugations. Students can access grammar tutorial with comprehension check exercises and additional grammar practice activities.

36

Standards: 1.3

Suggestions: Encourage students to use humor in some of their responses.

Answers will vary. Students will use *habría* in all main clauses, since they are talking about themselves. Pluperfect subjunctive forms for the subordinate *(si)* clauses follow:

1. hubiera estado	**6.** hubiera empezado
2. hubiera perdido	**7.** hubiera encontrado
3. hubiera llegado	**8.** hubiera tenido
4. hubiera ganado	**9.** hubiera visto
5. hubiera sido	**10.** hubiera tenido

37

Standards: 1.1

Recycle: past participle formation, reflexive verbs

Suggestions: Encourage students to answer honestly and completely in order to practice useful, real-world vocabulary.

Answers will vary. Students will use the following pluperfect subjunctive forms:

1. hubieras ido
2. hubieras perdido
3. hubiera ocurrido
4. te hubieran invitado
5. te hubiera detenido
6. hubiera desaparecido
7. te hubieras enterado
8. te hubieran ignorado

 38

Standards: 1.1, 1.3

Suggestions: For Step 2, encourage students to talk about their partners as well as themselves in order to practice different verb forms.

Answers will vary.

Project-Based Learning

Students can perform Step 5 at this point. Make audio or video recordings of their presentations for inclusion in their portfolios. (For more information, see p. 448-b.)

478

 36

¿Qué habrías hecho?

ESCRIBIR Imagina que te sucedieran las siguientes cosas. Escribe frases sobre lo que habrías hecho si hubieras estado en estas situaciones.

Modelo
ser testigo
*Si **hubiera sido** testigo en un juicio, **me habría olvidado de todo lo que sabía.***

1. estar acusado	**6.** empezar a trabajar
2. perder (una cosa)	**7.** encontrar (una cosa)
3. llegar tarde	**8.** tener derecho a (algo)
4. ganar un premio	**9.** ver un extraterrestre
5. ser sospechoso(a)	**10.** tener conocimiento de (una cosa)

 37

¿Qué habría hecho yo?

 HABLAR EN PAREJA Habla con un(a) compañero(a) de lo que habrías hecho si hubieran pasado las siguientes cosas. Usen la información para hacer la pregunta *¿Qué habrías hecho si . . .?* y contéstenla. Apoyen sus opiniones.

▶ **Videomodelo**
mudarse nuevos vecinos a tu barrio
A —*¿Qué habrías hecho si se hubieran mudado nuevos vecinos a tu barrio?*
B —*Yo habría ido a conocerlos. Siempre es bueno hacer nuevas amistades.*

1. (no) ir de vacaciones	**5.** detenerte la policía
2. perder mucho dinero	**6.** desaparecer tu coche
3. ocurrir un accidente en la calle	**7.** enterarte de un crimen
4. invitarte a ir a una fiesta	**8.** ignorarte tus amigos

 38

Cómo me habría gustado

HABLAR EN PAREJA, ESCRIBIR

1 ¿Qué habrías hecho para mejorar la vida de los jóvenes de tu país y del mundo en el siglo XX? Trabaja con otro(a) estudiante preguntándole qué habría hecho él sobre los siguientes temas:

- la escuela
- la comunidad
- los países pobres
- el gobierno

Modelo
A: *¿Cómo habrías ayudado a los países pobres?*
B: *Habría enviado comida todos los meses.*

2 Ahora, cada pareja debe presentar y defender sus recomendaciones a la clase. La clase debe hacer comentarios y preguntas sobre las recomendaciones.

Differentiated Instruction

Students with Learning Difficulties

Use English and basic physical demonstrations to point out to students the cause-and-effect nature of situations that require the conditional perfect. For example, drop a piece of chalk and say, "The chalk broke. Why? Because I dropped it. If I hadn't dropped the chalk, it wouldn't have broken."

Challenge/Pre-AP®

Invite students to talk about how things would have turned out differently if certain events had or had not happened in the past. Encourage them to mention world as well as local events: *Si no hubieran inventado el Internet, yo no me habría comunicado tanto con mi tía de España.*

39

En otro país

ESCRIBIR, HABLAR EN PAREJA

1 Imagina cómo habría sido tu vida si hubieras nacido en otro país. Piensa en un país que te interese. Investiga cómo vive la gente en ese lugar. Escribe un párrafo describiendo cómo habría sido tu vida en ese país. Usa oraciones conectadas con detalles y elaboración.

Modelo
Si yo hubiera nacido en España, habría hablado español. Me habría gustado la comida con pescado y mariscos, así como . . .

2 Trabaja con otro(a) estudiante. Lean los párrafos que escribieron y digan por qué eligieron ese lugar. Añadan detalles de ese país, como el clima, los lugares que pueden visitar, la comida, el idioma y la música.

▲ Madrid, España

40

Por los derechos de los animales

LEER, ESCRIBIR, HABLAR EN GRUPO

1 Lee el siguiente correo electrónico que se repartió en una manifestación en España a favor de los derechos de los animales.

2 Responde a las siguientes preguntas sobre el correo electrónico.

1. Según el correo electrónico, ¿cuál es la situación de los perros en España? ¿Cómo ayudan los suizos?

2. ¿Cuál habría sido tu reacción si hubieras recibido este correo electrónico?

3. ¿Qué opinas sobre los derechos de los animales? ¿Piensas que todos los animales deben gozar de los mismos derechos? ¿Por qué?

3 En grupo, comparen sus respuestas a las preguntas anteriores. Piensen qué otras cosas se podrían hacer para proteger a los animales. Escriban un correo electrónico para proponer sus ideas y explicar por qué la gente debe cuidar a los animales.

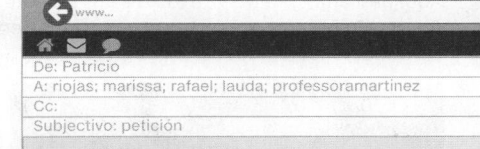
De: Patricio
A: riojas; marissa; rafael; lauda; professoramartinez
Cc:
Subjectivo: petición

Situación de los perros en España

Estoy obligado a escribir esto, después de toda la información que he recibido sobre el maltrato que dan a muchos animales en España. Ahora vivo en Zurich (Suiza), y me sorprende que la gente de este país tenga que solucionar nuestros problemas. Cada semana, llegan perros de España que son salvados de su sacrificio o rescatados de alguna otra situación difícil.

Por favor, firmen esta petición de apoyo.

—Amante de los animales

Capítulo 10 • cuatrocientos setenta y nueve **479**

39

Standards: 1.1, 1.2, 1.3

Suggestions: In Step 2, encourage students to make suggestions to their partner on what else he or she might have done: *Habrías visitado la ciudad de...; Habrías ido a un concierto de....*
Answers will vary.

40

Standards: 1.1, 1.2, 1.3, 2.1

Suggestions: Display students' leaflets from Step 3 around the classroom.
Answers will vary.

Pre-AP® Integration

- **Learning Objective:** Presentational Writing
- **Activity:** As a variation for *Actividad* 39, ask that students write the paragraph describing how their life would have been if they had been born in another time. However, do not include the time period referenced. Then, have students read their paragraph to a partner and allow the partner to guess the time period.
- **Pre-AP® Resource Materials:** Comprehensive guide to Pre-AP® communication development

Additional Resources

Technology: Online Resources
- Instant Check
- Guided, Core, Audio
- *Para hispanohablantes*
- Teacher's Resource Materials: Audio Script;
- Technology: Audio Cap. 10, Comm. Activities 4–5
- Communicative Pair Activity

Print
- Guided WB pp. 325–326
- Core WB pp. 143–144

Assessment

Prueba 10-8 with Remediation (online only)
Prueba: El condicional perfecto
- Prueba 10-8

Examen: Vocabulario y gramática 2
- Examen 2
- ExamView: Examen 2

Enrich Your Teaching

Culture Note

The notion of animal rights has been gaining popularity. Animal rights groups in Spanish-speaking countries include *Alternativa de la Liberación Animal* in Spain, *Ánima* and *Asociación para la Defensa de los Derechos del Animal* in Argentina, and Mexico's *Conservación de Mamíferos Marinos de México.*

21st Century Skills

Critical Thinking and Problem Solving Have students write a blog about animal rights in this country. Have students complete the phrase, *Los animales tienen el derecho a:* or *Los animales no tienen derecho a:* with their list of action items. Have them use vocabulary from this chapter and apply it to animals. Have students take sides and see which side has a stronger argument.

Puente a la cultura

Standards: 1.1, 1.2, 2.1, 2.2, 3.1, 4.1

Suggestions:

Pre-reading: Refer students to *Estrategia*. Then, based on a brief survey of the selection's main title, subtitles, pictures, and captions, ask: *Si vamos a crear una línea cronológica, ¿de qué se tratará: la historia social y política en América Latina o el desarrollo de las artes en América Latina? (la historia social y política en América Latina)*

Reading: Encourage students to read through the entire passage once silently, without stopping at problem words or to ask questions. Then, for the second time through, ask volunteers to read sections aloud. Remind students to use background knowledge, cognates, and context clues to help them understand unfamiliar words and expressions as they read.

Post-reading: Ask students to paraphrase the main accomplishments of each of the three heroes mentioned in the reading.

COUNTRY CONNECTION

Standards: 3.1

 Mapa global interactivo, Actividad 1 Look at the countries liberated by Simón Bolívar, José Martí, and Miguel Hidalgo.

Venezuela's large size and latitudinal location result in a variety of topographies and climates. The country has four main climactic zones, all of which fall under the main category of "tropical." These include rain forest (a large part of the Amazon) in the south, savannah in the center and northwest, semi-arid tropical regions along the coasts, and highlands. The different areas—some of them huge—as well as the difficulty of overland travel, have given rise to many different indigenous cultures throughout the country. These, along with strong Spanish and African influences, are what create Venezuela's incredibly rich blend of dialects, foods, music, and folklore.

Online Cultural Reading

Standards: 2.1

After doing the online activity, ask students to discuss the injustices that occurred to José Martí and the indigenous people in Mexico.

Puente a la cultura

Héroes de América Latina

Durante la época colonial, España dominaba un territorio desde California hasta el Cabo de Hornos, al extremo sur de Sudamérica. Este territorio tenía aproximadamente 17 millones de habitantes y estaba dividido en cuatro virreinatos, o unidades políticas. Los representantes de la Corona[1] española controlaban no solo la política en las colonias sino también los impuestos[2], el comercio, y así la vida de los habitantes.

Los habitantes de las colonias en América criticaban a España por su gran poder, pero en 1808, la monarquía española tuvo una crisis. Al sentir que la monarquía estaba débil, los criollos, o hijos de españoles nacidos en América, se rebelaron contra la Corona, iniciando así un movimiento de independencia en las colonias. Este movimiento resultó en la independencia de los países de América Latina.

Aquí hablamos de tres de los héroes de este movimiento. Aunque la historia de cada uno es my diferente, sus sueños de crear naciones independientes en América son muy similares.

Estrategia
Creating a timeline Graphic aids are always useful to show data in a visual way. *Timelines* are graphic aids used to organize data in chronological order. Use them when you have historical information to organize and compare.

Online Cultural Reading
Go to Auténtico ONLINE to read and understand a website about laws against discrimination on the basis of nationality.

◀ Simón Bolívar

Simón Bolívar: El Libertador de América

Simón Bolívar (1783–1830) nació en Caracas, Venezuela. Su sueño era liberar las colonias españolas y unirlas en una gran patria[3]. Casi lo logró en 1819 cuando, después de muchos éxitos militares, creó la República de la Gran Colombia y fue su presidente. La Gran Colombia incluía los territorios que hoy forman Colombia, Venezuela, Panamá y Ecuador. Hacia 1826, Bolívar ya era también jefe supremo del Perú y presidente de Bolivia. Pero Bolívar murió sin realizar su sueño. Nunca pudo unir las repúblicas hispanoamericanas ya que había divisiones entre ellas. Bolivia se independizó en 1825 y Venezuela se separó de Colombia.

[1] (Spanish) crown [2] taxes [3] homeland

480 cuatrocientos ochenta • Capítulo 10 • ¿Cuáles son tus derechos y deberes?

Differentiated Instruction

Students with Learning Difficulties

Help students focus on the theme of national heroes by asking them to talk briefly about heroes they know of from United States history. Connect this to the reading by saying: *En América Latina también hay héroes. Ellos lucharon por la independencia de sus países. Esta lectura se trata de ellos.*

Advanced Learners

Ask students to do further research on one of the figures from the selection, or on another of their choice from Latin American history, such as José de San Martín.

Go **Online** to practice
PEARSON
realize™
PearsonSchool.com/Autentico

VIDEO WRITING MAPA GLOBAL

Interpretive **10**

José Martí: El apóstol de la independencia cubana

Además de gran poeta e intelectual, José Martí (1853–1895) es el héroe nacional y el apóstol de la independencia de Cuba. Desde los dieciséis años, ya participaba en la vida política y estuvo en prisión por haber escrito en publicaciones contra las autoridades coloniales españolas. Lo deportaron a España y de allí, fue a Nueva York, donde escribió la mayoría de sus obras. Luego, fundó el Partido Revolucionario Cubano en 1892. Regresó a Cuba cuando comenzó la guerra por la independencia en 1895 y murió en una batalla.

José Martí ▶

Miguel Hidalgo: El precursor de la independencia de México

Miguel Hidalgo se destaca en la historia de México como uno de los precursores de la independencia de ese país. Muchos lo criticaron porque era miembro del clero[1] y tenía ideas revolucionarias. En 1810, durante un sermón, llamó al pueblo a luchar. Miles de indígenas que habían sufrido largos años de maltrato y explotación, decidieron seguirlo junto con los criollos. Miguel Hidalgo y su representante, el general Allende, organizaron el movimiento que llevó a la independencia en 1821.

[1]clergy

▲ Miguel Hidalgo

 ### ¿Comprendiste?

1. ¿En qué siglo se iniciaron los movimientos de independencia de las naciones hispanohablantes de América y cuáles fueron sus causas?

2. ¿Qué tienen en común los héroes del artículo? Da dos ejemplos.

3. Menciona dos héroes de otros países y di quiénes eran y qué hicieron.

4. Compara el movimiento de independencia de los Estados Unidos con el de las naciones hispanohablantes. Di cuáles son sus semejanzas y diferencias.

Cronología de la independencia latinoamericana

Copia la línea cronológica y complétala con la información del texto que leíste. Úsala para parafrasear la idea principal, el tema y los detalles del artículo.

1808	1810	1819	1821	1825	1826	1895
_____	Movimiento de independencia de México	_____	_____	Independencia de Bolivia	_____	_____

 Mapa global interactivo Describe los territorios que Simón Bolívar, José Martí y Miguel Hidalgo ayudaron a liberar en Latinoamérica e investiga sus luchas.

 Videodocumentario Gran trabajo para la comunidad

Enrich Your Teaching

Culture Note

José Martí was unwelcome in many countries because of his political outspokenness. He had a variety of jobs, including editor, journalist, and foreign correspondent for several magazines. He even worked as a Spanish teacher at New York's Central High School. The popular song ***Guantanamera*** is based on Martí's poetry.

21st Century Skills

Information Literacy To expand on their knowledge of Latin American independence movements, have student research the role played by women such as Manuela Sáenz or Mariana Bracetti in these struggles. Have students compare them to female figures in their own culture who have played similar historical roles.

¿Comprendiste?

Standards: 1.1, 1.2, 1.3, 2.1, 2.2, 3.1, 4.2

Suggestions: Before discussing, have students write the answers on their own.

Answers:

1. Se iniciaron en el siglo XIX.
2. La causa de Bolívar era unir a las colonias en una gran patria. La de Martí era la independencia de Cuba. Hidalgo luchaba contra la esclavitud y por los derechos de los indígenas.

3–4. Answers will vary.

Cronología de la independencia latinoamericana

Standards: 1.2, 1.3

Suggestions: Have students complete their time lines together in pairs or groups.

Answers will vary, but should include:

1808: Rebelión de los criollos latinoamericanos
1819: Creación de la República de la Gran Colombia por Bolívar
1821: Organización del movimiento independentista mexicano
1826: Bolívar: jefe supremo en Perú, presidente en Bolivia
1895: Muere José Martí

Digital Portfolio

Keep students' responses and their time lines in their portfolios as writing samples.

 Technology: Videodocumentario

Standards: 1.2

Resources: Teacher's Resource Materials: Video Script, Technology: Video Program, Cap. 10

View *Gran trabajo para la comunidad* to learn about a political organization for the Spanish-speaking community. Access the video online in **Realize.** See the *Video Teacher's Guide* for suggestions.

Additional Resources

Technology: Online Resources
- *Videodocumentario*
- Guided, Writing, Reading
- *Para hispanohablantes*
- Cultural Reading Activity

Print
- Guided WB p. 327

¿Qué me cuentas?

Standards: 1.1, 1.2, 1.3

Resources: Teacher's Resource Materials: Audio Script, p. 304; Technology: Audio Cap. 10

Focus: Practicing listening and reading comprehension of new vocabulary and grammar; using information to write a cohesive and coherent reaction.

AP® Skills: Integration of listening, reading, and writing to comprehend and synthesize information from spoken and written sources.

Suggestions: For Step 1, use the audio or read the script aloud. Allow students to hear it twice through: the first time to write their answers, the second time to check them.

For Step 2, have students identify significant details as they read and then summarize the main points of the article.

Encourage students to express their own opinions and to cite specific information from Steps 1 and 2 in their written responses for Step 3.

 Technology: Audio

Script:

For the complete script, see Teacher's Resource Materials.

Answers:

1. b	**3.** b	**5.** c
2. a	**4.** a	**6.** c

Steps 2–3

Answers will vary.

Additional Resources

Technology: Online Resources
  • *Para hispanohablantes*

Pre-AP® Integración

OBJECTIVES
▶ Listen to and read about the legal system in Mexico
▶ Compare the old and new Mexican legal systems with the current legal system in the U.S.

¿Qué me cuentas?: Justicia para todos

Compara el sistema legal de México con el sistema de los Estados Unidos. Primero escucha la conversación. Anota las respuestas a las preguntas y guárdalas para usarlas en el paso 3.

1 Escucha el siguiente diálogo entre Sergio y su padre. Después de cada sección del diálogo vas a oír tres preguntas. Escoge la mejor respuesta para cada pregunta.

1. a. a una propuesta
   b. a un juicio
   c. a un castigo

2. a. un jurado, un juez y testigos
   b. una secretaria y dos policías
   c. un representante del estado

3. a. un libro
   b. un video
   c. una obra de teatro

4. a. gozarían de igualdad
   b. todos serían culpables
   c. no podría haber testigos

5. a. el juez
   b. el abogado
   c. el estado

6. a. es interesante
   b. es divertido
   c. es muy necesario

2 Ahora lee sobre el sistema legal de México.

México Hoy   20 de junio

Aplicación del nuevo sistema penal

CIUDAD DE MÉXICO. En 2016 venció el plazo para aplicar en todo el país el nuevo Sistema de Justicia Penal. La reforma es ley desde 2008, pero los 32 estados tenían un plazo de ocho años para adaptarse a las nuevas condiciones. En el nuevo sistema, los acusados de un crimen son inocentes hasta que se compruebe su culpabilidad en un juicio oral. En el sistema anterior, el juez leía el caso y evaluaba las evidencias a solas. Eran juicios escritos que duraban de 6 a 8 meses. Con el sistema reformado, el juez escucha el caso delante del acusado, los abogados y el público en un juicio que dura solo de 2 a 3 meses.

---

 3 En parejas, comparen el sistema legal antiguo de México con el sistema nuevo. Luego, conversen sobre cuál de los dos sistemas se parece más al sistema estadounidense que describen Sergio y su padre. Consideren estas preguntas: ¿Creen que una persona acusada bajo el sistema antiguo de México hubiera sido considerada culpable o inocente antes del juicio? ¿Y ahora? ¿Qué sistema trata mejor a los acusados y asegura sus derechos? ¿Qué ventajas y desventajas habrían en un juicio escrito y cerrado? ¿Y en un juicio abierto? Usen oraciones conectadas con detalles y elaboración y las siguientes u otras expresiones apropiadas para conectar sus ideas.

cuando	con tal que	antes de	mientras	aunque	después de

Differentiated Instruction

Students with Learning Difficulties

For the *Presentación* oral, allow students the option of describing rules and regulations your school already has.

Students with Special Needs

Make a recording of the article in Step 2 of *¿Qué me cuentas?* for visually impaired students. They can then perform the task on their own, including for homework.

Presentación oral

OBJECTIVES
▶ Demonstrate how to present new rules and rights for your school
▶ Make a plan to improve your performance

Go **Online** to practice
PearsonSchool.com/Autentico
PEARSON realize™
🔊 AUDIO   🎤 SPEAK/RECORD

🎤 Los derechos de los estudiantes

TAREA El director de la escuela ha decidido que los estudiantes propongan qué reglas y derechos les gustaría tener en su escuela. Prepara un discurso para presentar tus recomendaciones.

① Prepárate Completa una tabla como la siguiente con las reglas y los derechos que quieres proponer.

Reglas de la escuela	Derechos de los estudiantes

② Practica Vuelve a leer la información que anotaste en la tabla. Practica varias veces tu discurso. Presenta razones por las que crees que estos derechos y reglas son beneficiosos. Usa tus notas para practicar, pero no al hablar ante la clase. Recuerda:

- explicar cada regla y derecho en forma clara y persuasiva
- presentar las situaciones y razones por las que serían beneficiosos
- mirar directamente al público y hablar con voz clara

Modelo

Los estudiantes deberíamos tener derecho a vacaciones más largas. Si hubiéramos tenido antes más tiempo para relajarnos, habríamos aprendido más y mejor. También la escuela debería tener derecho a exigir que . . .

③ Haz tu presentación Imagina que tus compañeros son los que van a analizar las reglas y los derechos que recomiendes. Debes convencerlos de tu opinión y de que tus recomendaciones beneficiarán tanto a los estudiantes como a los profesores. Recuerda usar oraciones conectadas con detalles y elaboración.

④ Evaluación Tu profesor(a) utilizará la siguiente rúbrica para evaluar tu presentación.

Estrategia

Think, plan, then speak Before proposing a list of rules, think about what you're going to include. Make a plan and use a table or graphic to organize your thoughts. Then, speak using the information that you have gathered.

Rubric	Score 1	Score 3	Score 5
How well you use organizers	Your speech includes no organizers.	You use one or more organizers, but they contain little useful information.	You use organizers effectively to plan your speech.
How convincing you are	You miss important arguments. Your arguments are weak and lack details and elaboration.	You present some convincing arguments, but your speech lacks some details.	You present convincing arguments. Your sentences are connected and contain details and elaboration.
How effectively you deliver your speech	You read your speech and make no eye contact with your audience.	You make some eye contact, and you use some intonation.	Your eye contact is good. Your intonation helps get your message across.

Capítulo 10 • cuatrocientos ochenta y tres **483**

Presentación oral

Standards: 1.2, 1.3, 3.1

Suggestions: Review the task and the four-step approach with students. Review the rubric with the class (see *Assessment* below) to explain how you will grade the performance task. Before students begin, direct their attention to the *Estrategia.* Have them create a word chart on their own paper. Model how to include in the chart an idea or two for proposed student rules and rights. Encourage them to use other graphic organizers as well, such as concept webs, that they may find beneficial in developing their speeches. Remind them that they will submit and be evaluated on their use of one or more organizers.

Pre-AP® Integration

- **Learning Objective:** Presentational Speaking
- **Pre-AP® Resource Materials:** Comprehensive guide to Pre-AP® speaking skill development

Digital Portfolio

Make video or audio recordings of student presentations in class, or assign the Speak and Record activity so they can record their presentations online. Include the recording in their portfolios.

Additional Resources

 Technology: Online Resources
- *Para hispanohablantes*

Assessment _____

Presentación oral
- **Assessment Program:** Rubrics
Review the rubric with students. Go over the descriptions of the different levels of performance. After assessing students, help individuals understand how their performance could be improved. (See Teacher's Resource Materials for suggestions on using rubrics in assessment.)

Enrich Your Teaching

21st Century Skills

Communication As a warm-up to the *Presentación oral,* have students brainstorm a list of expressions in Spanish that they would use when proposing new school rules and advocating student rights.

What expressions can be used to convince or persuade the audience to agree? Have students list the verbs they would use, then conjugate them in the conditional.

Language Arts Connection: Expository Writing

Standards: 3.1

Encourage students to draw on background knowledge they have from their Language Arts courses about introductions used in writing. Remind them that an effective introduction provides readers with a context for what is to follow—a kind of mental "shelf" on which to place the information they will read. Without an effective introduction, an essay is bound to quickly lose readers' attention.

Presentación escrita

Standards: 1.2, 1.3, 3.1

Suggestions: Begin by explaining the criteria you will use to evaluate students' compositions. (See Step 5, *Evaluación,* in the Student Edition, and *Assessment* on the following page.)

Direct students' attention to the *Estrategia.* Suggest than another idea for a snappy introduction for this particular essay might be to include an interesting comment from one of the people interviewed. Such a comment should catch readers' attention and give an idea of what the subject of the essay will be. Then show a T-chart. Model filling in part of a column with information like that shown in the chart on this page. Have students begin a similar columnar chart on their own paper. Tell them to use one column for the responses of each person that they interview, and to interview at least two people.

Pre-AP® Integration

- **Learning Objective:** Presentational Writing
- **Pre-AP® Resource Materials:** Comprehensive guide to Pre-AP® writing skill development

---

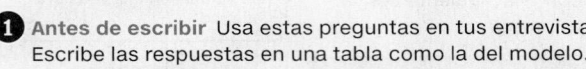

Presentación escrita

OBJECTIVES
▸ Write an editorial essay for a newspaper
▸ Present other people's opinions about a subject
▸ Use an interesting fact to capture the audience's attention

✎ ¿Cuáles son sus derechos?

Eres reportero(a) y escribes un ensayo editorial sobre lo que saben los ciudadanos de los Estados Unidos acerca de los derechos y las garantías que tienen según la Constitución. Entrevista *(interview)* a personas de diferentes edades y usa sus respuestas.

Estrategia
Snappy introductions
An interesting introduction will get your reader involved in your essay immediately. One good way to begin is to ask a question to pique his or her curiosity. Another way to hook your reader is to start with an interesting fact or incident related to your story.

1 **Antes de escribir** Usa estas preguntas en tus entrevistas. Escribe las respuestas en una tabla como la del modelo.

1. ¿Es ciudadano(a) de los Estados Unidos?
2. ¿A qué se dedica?
3. ¿Sabe qué derechos y garantías tiene?
4. ¿Cómo usa usted sus libertades?
5. ¿Cómo compara su situación en este país con respecto a otros países?

Entrevista a: Ingrid Ramírez
1. ciudadana de los Estados Unidos
2. maestra en Nueva York
3. derecho a la libertad de expresión, libertad de prensa, libertad de religión
4. "Trabajo, me expreso y viajo libremente; tengo la religión que quiero".
5. muy buena situación

Entrevista a: Jorge Ríos
1. ciudadano de los Estados Unidos
2. mecánico en Miami
3. derecho a la libertad de decir lo que uno quiere
4. "Puedo tener una vida cómoda, trabajar y viajar".
5. mejor situación que en otros países

2 **Borrador** Escribe tu borrador. Presenta las opiniones de las personas entrevistadas. Añade todos los detalles necesarios con oraciones conectadas con detalles y elaboración. Recuerda usar el vocabulario y la gramática de este capítulo.

Modelo

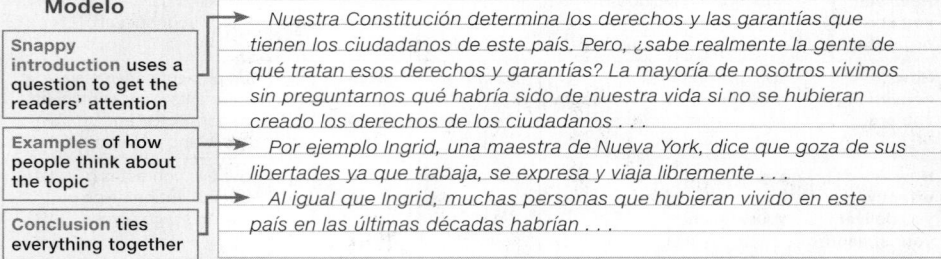

Snappy introduction uses a question to get the readers' attention	Nuestra Constitución determina los derechos y las garantías que tienen los ciudadanos de este país. Pero, ¿sabe realmente la gente de qué tratan esos derechos y garantías? La mayoría de nosotros vivimos sin preguntarnos qué habría sido de nuestra vida si no se hubieran creado los derechos de los ciudadanos . . .
Examples of how people think about the topic	Por ejemplo Ingrid, una maestra de Nueva York, dice que goza de sus libertades ya que trabaja, se expresa y viaja libremente . . .
Conclusion ties everything together	Al igual que Ingrid, muchas personas que hubieran vivido en este país en las últimas décadas habrían . . .

Differentiated Instruction

Students with Learning Difficulties

Suggest that students interview their Social Studies teachers for the *Presentación escrita.* If possible, meet with the teachers beforehand and tell them what type of research students are doing, so that they can provide guidance to students during the interviews.

Advanced Learners

Have students prepare and present orally their own Spanish paraphrases of the ten amendments to the United States Constitution in the Bill of Rights.

Go **Online** to practice

PEARSON realize. TM

PearsonSchool.com/Autentico

WRITING

3 **Redacción/Revisión** Después de escribir el primer borrador, trabaja con otro(a) compañero(a) para intercambiar los trabajos y leerlos. Decidan qué aspectos son más interesantes. Luego, hagan sugerencias para mejorar sus composiciones y corregir los errores.

- ¿Se usó correctamente el pluscuamperfecto del subjuntivo y el condicional perfecto?
- ¿Existen errores de ortografía?

> mayoría
> La ~~mayorías~~ de nosotros vivimos sin
>
> habría
> preguntarnos qué ~~habrían~~ sido de nuestra
>
> hubieran
> vida si no se ~~hubiera~~ creado los derechos
>
> de los ciudadanos . . .

4 **Publicación** Antes de hacer la versión final, lee de nuevo tu borrador y repasa los siguientes puntos:

- ¿Presenta el ensayo una idea clara sobre el tema?
- ¿Incluí opiniones de otras personas para explicar el tema?
- ¿Incluí razones que apoyan y defienden las opiniones?
- ¿Usé oraciones conectadas con detalles y elaboración?
- ¿Muestra el ensayo la importancia del tema?
- ¿Presenta una conclusión interesante?

Después de revisar el borrador, escribe una copia en limpio de tu composición.

5 **Evaluación** Se utilizará la siguiente rúbrica para evaluar tu presentación.

Rubric	Score 1	Score 3	Score 5
Completion of task	Important parts of your essay are missing.	Information in your essay is disorganized and hard to follow.	You include and organize all the parts needed for an effective essay.
Effective introduction	Your essay lacks an introduction.	You attempt an introduction, but it is not effective.	Your introduction is effective, attracting and orienting readers.
Grammar, spelling, mechanics	You make many errors in grammar, spelling, and punctuation.	You make some errors in grammar, spelling, and punctuation.	You make very few errors in grammar, spelling, and punctuation.

Capítulo 10 • cuatrocientos ochenta y cinco **485**

Enrich Your Teaching

21st Century Skills

Critical Thinking and Problem Solving Students will use their written language for the purpose of writing an editorial essay. For this, they will need to play several roles; first they will gather information as they interview people about their opinions on their Constitutional rights, then they will present these opinions in an editorial essay and provide their own conclusion. Remind students that they will need to adapt to these different roles in the project.

Suggestions (Cont'd): For Step 1, encourage students to interview at least one Spanish-speaking person, if possible. Help them agree upon effective English translations of the five interview questions to use when interviewing people in English. Remind them that they must convert the information gained in English interviews to Spanish.

In Step 2, students should concentrate on developing the information they obtained in their interviews into a rough draft. This is also the step in which they should focus on an effective introduction for their essay. Encourage them to work toward organization, level of detail, and language use similar to that shown in the model.

For Step 3, encourage students to experiment with various ways of combining sentences. Suggest that they use the pluperfect subjunctive and the conditional perfect at least once by mentioning how some aspect of United States society would have developed differently without the rights guaranteed by the Constitution and the Bill of Rights.

Evaluation

Steps 4 and 5 overlap. Students will need some evaluation by you, their peers, or self-evaluation to fine-tune and polish their drafts.

Digital Portfolio

Keep students' final drafts in their portfolios as a writing sample.

Additional Resources

Technology: Online Resources
- *Para hispanohablantes*

Assessment

Presentación escrita
- **Assessment Program:** Rubrics

Review the rubric with students. Go over the descriptions of the different levels of performance. After assessing students, help individuals understand how their performance could be improved. (See Teacher's Resource Materials for suggestions on using rubrics in assessment.)

Lectura

Standards: 1.2, 2.1, 3.1, 3.2, 5.2

Suggestions

Pre-reading: Before reading, direct students' attention to the *Estrategia* and *Al leer* sections. Have them copy the T-chart on p. 489 to their own paper and make sure they understand how they will use it. Explain that, since this reading is based on an oral account, the language used is more informal than in other readings. Point out as examples of this the use of **Bueno** at the outset of the reading and the frequent use of informal and creative diminutives, such as **otrita** and **cajoncito** in the first paragraph. Ask students to pay attention to other examples of informal language as they read.

Reading: When reading together with students, pause frequently to address comprehension issues they may have and to allow them to fill in their charts from p. 489. Here are some suggestions for providing comprehension guidance on this page:

* Ask: *¿En qué año empieza la historia? (1954)*
* Ask: *En tus propias palabras, describe qué verías si la joven Domitila y sus hermanas te pasaran en la calle delante de la escuela.*

COUNTRY CONNECTION

Standards: 3.1

 Mapa global interactivo, Actividad 2 Travel to the mountains of Bolivia.

Suggestions: After students have read the *Al leer* section, show a map of South America and ask a volunteer to point out Bolivia. Explain to students that historically mining was the most important attraction that the country held for Europeans. At the end of the sixteenth century, for example, the city of Potosí was the largest urban center in South America, due to its surrounding silver mines. Those mines are now depleted.

Lectura

OBJECTIVES
▶ Read and understand an autobiographical account
▶ Understand the author's reasons for writing the selection
▶ Read about a Bolivian social activist and give your opinion about social rights movements

Al leer

Este fragmento es parte de una historia oral basada en las experiencias de Domitila Barrios de Chungara en las minas de cobre *(copper mines)* de Bolivia que fue recogida y escrita por Moema Viezzer. En este fragmento, Domitila cuenta cómo tenía que luchar para quedarse en la escuela y continuar su educación. Su testimonio revela a una joven cuyo coraje y determinación lograron vencer los obstáculos y prejuicios que formaban parte de la vida diaria de las mujeres en los pueblos mineros. Mientras lees este relato, presta atención a los siguientes puntos y luego completa la tabla que aparece en la página 489 con la siguiente información:

* el ambiente de pobreza en el hogar de la protagonista
* los errores que cometió y cómo logró superarlos
* los obstáculos que tuvo que enfrentar
* la actitud del padre de Domitila

Estrategia

Investigate the author's reasons Authors must decide which materials are most appropriate for describing the events they want to include in the narration of their experiences. The setting, the selection of special memories and how they affected the author's life, the use of particular details to describe feelings and personal opinions and the inclusion of anecdotes to liven up the narration will give you clues to the author's reasons for writing.

Si me permiten hablar . . . Testimonio de Domitila Barrios, por Moema Viezzer (Fragmento)

Bueno, en el 54 me fue difícil regresar a la escuela después de las vacaciones, porque nosotros teníamos una vivienda que consistía en una pieza pequeñita donde no teníamos patio y no teníamos dónde ni con quiénes dejar a las wawas[1]. Entonces consultamos al director de la escuela y él dio permiso para llevar a mis hermanitas conmigo. El estudio se hacía por las tardes y por las mañanas. Yo tenía que combinar todo: casa y escuela. Entonces yo llevaba a la más chiquita cargada y a la otra agarrada de la mano y Marina llevaba las mamaderas[2] y las mantillas[3] y mi hermana la otrita llevaba los cuadernos. Y así todas nos íbamos a la escuela. En un rincón teníamos un cajoncito donde dejábamos a la más chiquita mientras seguíamos estudiando. Salía de la escuela, tenía que cargarme la niñita, nos íbamos a la casa y tenía yo que cocinar, lavar, planchar, atender a las wawas. Me parecía muy difícil todo eso. ¡Yo deseaba tanto jugar! Y tantas otras cosas deseaba, como cualquier niña.

Dos años después, ya la profesora no me dejó llevar a mis hermanitas porque ya metían bulla[4]. Mi padre no podía pagar a una sirvienta, pues no le alcanzaba su sueldo ni para la comida y la ropa de nosotras. En la casa, por ejemplo, yo andaba siempre descalza, usando los zapatos solamente para ir a la escuela.

---

[1]small children [2]baby bottles [3]diapers [4]made noise

Differentiated Instruction

Heritage Speakers

When the class reads the Bolivian slang term **wawas,** ask students to mention other slang terms for children that they may know. They may wish to comment on other elements of Domitila Barrios' informal style of narration, as well.

Students with Learning Difficulties

Write a paragraph-by-paragraph paraphrase of the reading selection for students, using language suitable to their level. Consider jigsawing this task and assigning paragraphs or sections to interested Advanced Learners.

Bueno, como la profesora me había dado aquella orden, entonces yo empecé a irme sola a la escuela. Echaba llave a la casa y tenían que quedarse las wawas en la calle, porque la vivienda era oscura, no tenía ventana y les daba mucho terror cuando se la cerraba. Era como una cárcel[5], solamente con una puerta. Y no había dónde dejar a las chicas, porque en ese entonces vivíamos en un barrio de solteros, donde no había familias, puros hombres vivían allí.

Entonces mi padre me dijo que dejara la escuela, porque ya sabía leer y leyendo podía aprender otras cosas. Pero yo no acepté y me puse fuerte[6] y seguí yendo a la escuela.

Mi padre gestionó[7] en la empresa minera de Pulacayo para que le diera una vivienda con patiecito, porque era muy difícil vivir donde estábamos. Y el gerente, a quien mi papá le arreglaba sus trajes, ordenó que le diera una vivienda más grande con un cuarto, una cocina y un corredorcito donde se podía dejar a las chicas.

Sufríamos hambre a veces y no nos satisfacían los alimentos porque era poco lo que podía comprar mi papá. Ha sido duro vivir con privaciones y toda clase de problemas cuando pequeñas. Pero eso desarrolló algo en nosotras: una gran sensibilidad, un gran deseo de ayudar a toda la gente. Nuestros juegos de niños siempre tenían algo relacionado con lo que vivíamos y con lo que deseábamos vivir. Además, en el transcurso de nuestra infancia habíamos visto eso: mi madre y mi padre, a pesar de que teníamos tan poco, siempre estaban ayudando a algunas familias de Pulacayo. Entonces, cuando veíamos pobres por la calle mendigando[8], yo y mis hermanas nos poníamos a soñar. Y soñábamos que un día íbamos a ser grandes, que íbamos a tener tierras, que íbamos a sembrar y que a aquellos pobres les íbamos a dar de comer.

Y bueno, así era nuestra vida. Yo tenía entonces 13 años. Mi padre siempre insistía en que no debía seguir en la escuela. Pero yo le iba rogando[9], rogando y seguía yendo. Claro, siempre me faltaba material escolar[10]. Entonces, algunos maestros me comprendían, otros no.

---

[5]jail [6]got stubborn [7]negotiated [8]begging [9]pleading [10]school supplies

Capítulo 10 • cuatrocientos ochenta y siete **487**

Suggestions (Cont'd):

Reading: Here are some suggestions for providing comprehension guidance on this page:

- After reading the second paragraph, write on the board in English:
  A. "In the sixth grade I had a great teacher who knew how to understand me."
  B. "In the sixth grade I had a great teacher who learned how to understand me."
  Then ask: *¿Cuál es la mejor traducción de la primera frase de este párrafo, A o B? ¿Por qué? (B. El pretérito de* saber *quiere decir "learned.")*
- After reading the first column, ask: *¿Qué significa la expresión "a la salida": "en la puerta del aula" o "después de la clase"? (después de la clase)*
- After reading the second column, ask: *¿Creían los vecinos de Domitila en educar a las niñas? (No. Creían que no se debe eseñar a leer a las mujeres.)*
- *¿Tenía Domitila un hermano? ¿Qué parte del texto te lo dice? (No tenía hermano. "cinco mujeres, ningún varón")*

Post-reading: When students finish reading, ask: *¿Qué inferencia podemos hacer al fin de la historia? ¿Qué decidió hacer el maestro de Domitila? (Parece que decidió darle a Domitila el material escolar que necesitaba.)* Then ask them to go back and identify other examples of informal language they can find in the reading.

Interacción con la lectura

Standards: 1.1, 1.2, 1.3

Suggestions: Have students work together to complete their charts in Step 1. Encourage them to help each other paraphrase the pertinent parts of the text.

Answers will vary.

Additional Resources

 Technology: Online Resources
- *Para hispanohablantes*

El problema es que habíamos hecho un trato[11] mi papá y yo. Él me había explicado que no tenía dinero, que no me podía comprar material, que no podía dar nada para la escuela. Y de ahí que me arreglaba como podía. Y por eso tenía yo problemas.

En el sexto curso tuve como profesor a un gran maestro que me supo comprender. Era un profesor bastante estricto, y los primeros días que no llevé el material completo, me castigó severamente. Tuve que irme a la casa, llorando. Pero al día siguiente, volví. Y de la ventana miraba lo que estaban haciendo los chicos.

En uno de esos momentos, el profesor me llamó.

—Seguramente no ha traído su material —me dijo. Yo no podía contestar y me puse a llorar.

—Entre. Ya pase, tome su asiento. Y a la salida se ha de quedar usted.

A la salida me quedé y entonces él me dijo:

—Mira, yo quiero ser tu amigo, pero necesito que me digas qué pasa con vos[12]. ¿Es cierto que no tienes tu mamá?

—Sí, profesor.

—¿Cuándo se murió?

—Cuando estaba todavía en el primer curso.

—Y tu padre, ¿dónde trabaja?

—En la policía minera, es sastre[13].

—Bueno, ¿qué es lo que pasa? Mira, yo quiero ayudarte, pero tienes que ser sincera. ¿Qué es lo que pasa?

Yo no quería hablar, porque pensé que iba a llamar a mi padre como algunos profesores lo hacían cuando estaban enojados. Pero el profesor me hizo otras preguntas y entonces le conté todo. También le dije que podía hacer mis tareas, pero que no tenía mis cuadernos, porque éramos bien pobres y mi papá no podía comprar y que, años atrás, ya mi papá me había querido sacar de la escuela porque no podía hacer ese gasto más. Y que con mucho sacrificio y esfuerzo había yo podido llegar hasta el sexto curso. Pero no era que mi papá no quisiera, sino porque no podía, porque, incluso, a pesar de toda la creencia que había

en Pulacayo de que a la mujer no se le debía enseñar a leer, mi papá siempre quiso que supiéramos por lo menos eso.

Sí, mi papá siempre se preocupó por nuestra formación[14]. Cuando murió mi mamá, la gente nos miraba y decía: "Ay, pobrecitas, cinco mujeres, ningún varón . . . ¿Para qué sirven? . . . Mejor si se mueren". Pero mi papá muy orgulloso decía: "No, déjenme a mis hijas, ellas van a vivir". Y cuando la gente trataba de acomplejarnos[15] porque éramos mujeres y no servíamos para gran cosa, él nos decía que todas las mujeres tienen los mismos derechos que los hombres. Y decía que nosotras podíamos hacer las hazañas[16] que hacen los hombres. Nos crió siempre con esas ideas. Sí, fue una disciplina muy especial. Y todo eso fue muy positivo para nuestro futuro. Y de ahí que nunca nos consideramos mujeres inútiles.

El profesor comprendía todo esto, porque yo le contaba. E hicimos un trato de que yo le iba a pedir todo el material que necesitaba. Y así pude terminar mi último año escolar.

---

[11]deal [12]with you [13]tailor [14]education [15]make us feel bad [16]feats

Vista de La Paz, Bolivia

 Mapa global interactivo Describe la historia de Bolivia y su industria minera. Investiga la geografía de la región.

Differentiated Instruction

Heritage Speakers
Ask students who have lived in heritage countries to share what they know about student-teacher relations in schools there.

Advanced Learners
Invite students to compare Domitila Barrios Chungara's account with readings from past *Capítulos*. Can they find a similar theme of overcoming obstacles in the other readings? What are the obstacles? How are they overcome?

Go **Online** to practice
PEARSON
realize™
PearsonSchool.com/Autentico
WRITING MAPA GLOBAL

Interpretive
Reading

10

Interacción con la lectura

1 Completa la tabla siguiente para investigar por qué Domitila Barrios de Chungara escribió este relato autobiográfico.

Razones de Domitila	Ejemplos
describir las condiciones en que ella y su familia vivían	vivienda pobre, pasar hambre
analizar sus errores para prevenirlos en el futuro	
explicar su actitud frente a los obstáculos que tenía que enfrentar	
explicar el comportamiento de sus maestros	
explicar el comportamiento de su padre	

2 Trabaja con otro(a) compañero(a) para analizar la información de las tablas de cada uno(a). Usa esa información para ayudarte a parafrasear la idea principal del relato. Incluye el tema y los detalles más importantes. Luego, comenten cuáles son las razones principales que llevaron a Domitila Barrios de Chungara a escribir este relato.

¿Comprendiste?

1. ¿Por qué dice Domitila que le fue difícil regresar a la escuela después de las vacaciones de 1954?

2. ¿Qué quiere decir Domitila cuando dijo que tenía que vivir con privaciones? ¿Qué aspecto positivo surgió de las privaciones?

3. ¿Cuál era la actitud del pueblo de Pulacayo hacia las mujeres?

4. ¿Qué piensas de la actitud del padre hacia los derechos de las mujeres?

5. ¿Piensas que Domitila logró superar los obstáculos que tuvo que enfrentar? Explica tu respuesta.

CULTURA ◀ Bolivia

Domitila Barrios De Chungara (1937–2012) se crió en Pulacayo, un pueblo minero de Bolivia. Recogió sus memorias de este pueblo en su obra *Si me permiten hablar . . . .* Desde muy pequeña, Domitila estaba consciente del sufrimiento de su pueblo. Su ambición era mejorar las condiciones de vida de los campesinos y mineros de Bolivia. En 1952 se casó con un minero y empezó a participar en el Comité de Amas de Casa *(Homemakers)* del Distrito Minero Siglo XXI, y después, fue nombrada su Secretaria General. Su participación en las protestas contra las injusticias del gobierno causó que la encarcelaran *(jailed)*. Después tuvo que exiliarse *(go into exile)* en Europa. A pesar de estas experiencias, Domitila siguió su campaña por los derechos humanos y fue nombrada para el Premio Nobel de la Paz en 2005.

• Parafrasea la idea principal de la biografía. Incluye el tema y los detalles más importantes.

Mujeres mineras protestan en Bolivia.

Capítulo 10 • cuatrocientos ochenta y nueve **489**

¿Comprendiste?

Standards: 1.1, 1.2, 1.3

Suggestions: Have students first write the answers to the questions on their own. Then invite them to share their answers as a basis for discussion of the reading.

Answers:
1. Fue difícil porque tenía que llevar a sus hermanitas a la escuela. Después de la clase, tenía que cargar a sus hermanitas a la casa, cocinar, lavar, planchar y atender a las niñas.
2. Ella desarrolló una sensibilidad y un deseo de ayudar a los demás.
3. Ellos no creían en la educación de las mujeres.
4–5. Answers will vary.

CULTURA ◀

Standards: 1.1, 1.2, 3.1

Suggestions: After students have read the information, ask: *¿Cuál fue el resultado de las protestas de Domitila Barrios de Chungara contra las injusticias del gobierno? (La encarcelaron y tuvo que exiliarse en Europa.)*

Answers will vary.

Pre-AP® Integration

• **Learning Objective:** Interpretive: Print
• **Activity:** Before reading the story together as a class, divide students into groups of five. Assign to each student in each group one of the *¿Comprendiste?* questions found on this page. As the story is read, each student focuses specifically on the answer to his or her question. After reading the story, each student shares his or her answer, points out where it is found in the selection, and offers support and personal opinions as appropriate.
• **Pre-AP® Resource Materials:** Comprehensive guide to Pre-AP® reading skill development.

Additional Resources

Enrich Your Teaching

Teacher-to-Teacher

Invite interested students to research and report more about Domitila Barrios de Chungara. Encourage them to read her book, the full title of which is *Si me permiten hablar... testimonio de Domitila Barrios*, by Moema Viezzer. It has also been translated to English and given the title *Let Me Speak* (Monthly Review Press, Boulder, 1978).

21st Century Skills

ICT (Information, Communications and Technology) Literacy Remind students of the various digital tools available in **Realize** to access extra reading support. Computer corrected activities use different reading strategies to help students build their vocabulary and progress at their own pace through the reading.

Auténtico

Auténtico
Partnered with 🔵IDB

Standards: 1.2

Resources: Authentic Resources Wkbk, Cap. 10
Authentic Resources: Cap. 10: Videoscript
AP®Theme: *Los desafíos mundiales: El bienestar social*

Antes de ver

Have students look at the image from the video. Ask what relation there might be between a girl playing soccer and the theme of equality. Help them make the connection by explaining that in some countries girls have been traditionally excluded from certain sports. Then, discuss the *Estrategia.* Say that the images and the text will be of great help to understand some parts of the speech that could be unclear. Then discuss the key vocabulary with the class.

Technology: Ve el video

Before starting the video, direct students' attention to the *Mientras ves* activity. Have them complete the activity page from the Authentic Resources Workbook.

Play the video completely through once, without pausing. Tell students that they won't understand every word, but that they should listen and watch for overall understanding. After the first viewing, ask volunteers to express the general ideas that they were able to grasp. Replay the video, stopping after each new speaker so students can paraphrase what each one says. Show the video a final time without pausing.

Haz las actividades

Mientras ves

Standards: 1.2

Suggestions: Guide students to identify key details at the beginning of the video that will be essential to understand it as a whole. Ask them to pay attention to the setting. Also, point to the introductory text and help students' understanding if necessary.

Answers:
- El Alto; es la ciudad más joven de Bolivia.
- En promedio, los hombres estudian 2 años más que las mujeres. (Interpretation: Las mujeres tienen menos oportunidades educativas en esta ciudad.)

Niñas con altura

Antes de ver

Usa la estrategia: Claves visuales y contexto

Mira la imagen. ¿Qué relación tendrá con este capítulo? Al ver el video, usa las imágenes y el texto para entender lo que dicen las personas. Fíjate en sus gestos. ¿Sonríen o no? ¿Mueven las manos o la cabeza al hablar?

Lee el vocabulario clave

altura = height; altitude	**en promedio** = on average
varón = man	**dama** = woman
cancha = sports field	
contextos masculinos = male settings	
arma secreta = secret weapon	
aula de clase = classroom	
trabajo en equipo = team work	
autoestima = self-esteem	

▶ Ve el video

En este capítulo viste que la igualdad es fundamental para que haya una sociedad justa. Piensa en qué pasa cuando no hay igualdad de oportunidades para hombres y mujeres. ¿Cómo se puede solucionar esa desigualdad?

Ve a **PearsonSchool.com/Autentico** para ver el video **Niñas viviendo con altura** y conocer un programa que lucha por la equidad de género *(gender equality)* en Bolivia.

Haz las actividades

Mientras ves Mientras ves el video, es importante que no solo oigas lo que dicen las personas sino que leas el texto que aparece en la pantalla y las palabras que identifican a cada persona. Pon atención a los detalles importantes que te ayudarán a entender el resto del video. Anota estos datos:
- ¿Qué ciudad aparece en el video y qué tipo de ciudad es?
- Parafrasea el texto que aparece al comienzo del video. ¿Qué puedes inferir de este texto?

Differentiated Instruction

Heritage Speakers

Encourage students to choose a women in their heritage country who holds or has held an important job once reserved to men. For example, Chile, Argentina, Brazil, Costa Rica, Panama, and Nicaragua have had female presidents. Other women are part of the presidential cabinet or occupy important positions in the private sector. Ask students to write a short bio in Spanish of the woman they chose and invite them to share it with the class.

Advanced Learners

Invite students to work in small groups to identify a type of discrimination that they consider specially unfair and to propose a way to solve it. The program in the video uses sports as a vehicle to give girls more visibility and opportunities. What vehicle do students propose to reduce the type of discrimination that they identified? Ask them to write a couple of paragraphs in Spanish answering this question.

Integración

Después de ver Vuelve a ver el video para poder contestar estas preguntas:

1. Parafrasea lo que dice el entrenador sobre cómo se discriminaba a las mujeres hace unos años.

2. Parafrasea las metas de las niñas que hablan en el video.

3. Resume qué busca el programa a través de la estrategia del deporte.

4. ¿Por qué crees que el video se llama *Niñas viviendo con altura*?

 For more activities, go to the Authentic Resources Workbook.

La igualdad y el bienestar social

Expansión Busca estos recursos en *Auténtico* en línea y contesta las preguntas.

🗂 **10 Auténtico**

Integración de ideas ¿De qué manera la equidad de género contribuye al bienestar *(well-being)* social de un país? Antes de escribir, conversa sobre este asunto con un(a) compañero(a). Recuerda usar gestos apropiados al exponer tus ideas.

Comparación cultural Compara la discriminación de la que se habla en el video con un tipo de discriminación que veas en Estados Unidos. Da ejemplos.

Enrich Your Teaching

Teacher to Teacher

So that the video doesn't generate stereotyping about the subordinate role of women in Latin American countries, emphasize that the kind of gender inequality that the video shows is characteristic of small towns and cities everywhere that are geographically and culturally isolated. In most big cities in Latin America, women have reached high levels of social and political visibility, much as they have in Europe and the United States.

Using Authentic Resources

Have students create a personal vocabulary list with terms from the authentic resources that are related to human's rights.

Después de ver
Standards: 1.2, 1.3, 4.2

Suggestions: Before asking students to answer the questions, you might need to repeat in a clear voice some portions of the video's speech, especially what the coach says. Discuss each question and invite volunteers to answer each one. For the last question guide students to infer the double connotation of the video's title.

Answers:

1. lavaban platos y cocinaban mientras los niños hacían deporte.
2. participar en deportes, estudiar y triunfar
3. darles a las niñas los mismos derechos que a los niños y ayudarles a desarrollarse más.
4. Double connotation: Porque las niñas alcanzan metas muy altas a través del deporte; porque las niñas viven en una ciudad que se llama El Alto. (Write *alto/altura* on the board.)

For more Authentic Resources: Assign the Authentic Resources Workbook activities for homework, so that students can play the video on their own and complete the workbook activities at their own pace.

Pre-AP® Integration

Resources: Authentic Resources Wkbk, Cap. 10
Authentic Resources: Cap. 10: Videoscript

Suggestions: Before completing the Pre-AP® activity, have students go to the workbook and complete the worksheets for the additional resources.

Comparación cultural
Interpretive: Compare and contrast cultural practices from authentic audiovisual materials.
Suggestions: Tell students to focus on one specific type of discrimination and describe what their community is doing to improve the situation. Have them use that information to compare with the discrimination outlined in the video.

491

Repaso del capítulo

OBJECTIVE
▶ Review the vocabulary and grammar

Review Activities

Sobre tus derechos y responsabilidades/ Sobre los derechos de los ciudadanos/Sobre los derechos de todas las personas: On strips of paper, have students write a phrase or sentence using each word in these three categories. You can divide this task among small groups. Students' phrases or sentences should connote either a right or a responsibility. For example: ***que los niños no sufran*** or ***Gozamos de una prensa libre.*** Collect all strips and place them in a container. Have students sit in a circle. They take turns drawing one slip at a time, reading it aloud, and stating whether the phrase or sentence connotes a **derecho** or a **responsabilidad.**

En el hogar: Have students work in pairs and play *hangman* using the words and expressions in this category.

En la escuela: Play charades using the words and expressions in this category. Write them on slips of paper and place them in a container. Students take turns drawing an expression and getting its meaning across to the others any way they can without speaking or writing. Use body language and strategies of traditional charades such as tugging at the ear to mean **suena como** or holding up two fingers to mean **dos palabras**—or invent your own rules.

Otros adjetivos y expresiones: Students can use these words and expressions in the grammar review activities on the next page.

Pre-AP® Integration

- **Learning Objective:** Interpersonal speaking
- **Pre-AP® Resource Materials Activity Sheets, Cap. 10:** After students complete their Venn diagrams, call on volunteers to present their hero comparisons.

Additional Resources

 Technology: Online Resources
- Instant Check
- *Para hispanohablantes*

Teacher Resources
- Teacher's Resource Materials: Situation Cards, Clip Art
- **Assessment Program:** Chapter Checklist and Self-Assessment Worksheet

 Technology: ¡Pura vida! is a storyline video that is independent of chapter content and an ideal support for expanding listening skills. The 14 episodes are available within **Realize**. Student activities and Teacher support are also assignable within **Realize**.

Vocabulario

sobre tus derechos y responsabilidades

aplicar (las leyes)	to apply (the law)
discriminado, -a	discriminated
discriminar	to discriminate
funcionar	to function
gozar (de)	to enjoy
maltratar	to mistreat
obligar	to force
sufrir	to suffer
tratar	to treat
votar	to vote

en el hogar

el abuso	abuse
el / la adolescente	adolescent
el apoyo	support
la libertad	liberty
la niñez	childhood
la pobreza	poverty

en la escuela

el armario	locker
la autoridad	authority
el código de vestimenta	dress code
el deber	duty
la enseñanza	teaching
la igualdad	equality
el maltrato	mistreatment
el motivo	cause
el pensamiento	thought
la razón	reason
el respeto	respect

otros adjetivos y expresiones

adecuado, -a	adequate
ambos	both
de ese modo	in that way
en cuanto a	with respect to, as for
estar sujeto(a) a	to be subject to
gratuito, -a	free (no cost)
satisfactorio, -a	satisfactory

sobre los derechos de los ciudadanos

el / la acusado(a)	accused, defendant
asegurar	to assure
el castigo	punishment

la desigualdad	inequality
el desempleo	unemployment
detener	to detain
el estado	the state
la felicidad	happiness
fundamental	fundamental, vital
la injusticia	injustice
el juicio	judgement
el jurado	jury
la justicia	justice
juzgar	to judge
la paz	peace
la prensa	the press
la propuesta	proposal
sospechoso, -a	suspicious
el / la testigo	witness
la tolerancia	tolerance
violar	to violate

sobre los derechos de todas las personas

la aspiración	aspiration
el fin	purpose
la garantía	guarantee
la igualdad	equality
intercambiar	to exchange
libre	free
mundial	worldwide
opinar	to think
pacífico, -a	peaceful
proponer	to propose, to suggest
el punto de vista	point of view
el valor	value

otros adjetivos y expresiones

a medida que	as
ante	before
culpable	guilty
democrático, -a	democratic
de modo que	so, so that
el modo	the way
en lugar de	instead of
la falta de	lack of
inocente	innocent
llegar a	to reach, to get to

Differentiated Instruction

Students with Learning Difficulties

For additional vocabulary practice, have students make vocabulary flashcards for the vocabulary words. Tell them to write the word on one side of the card, and on the other to include a photo, sketch, synonym, antonym, or whatever other clue helps them remember the word. Have pairs of students quiz each other using their cards.

Advanced Learners

Invite students to create and trade crossword puzzles using the chapter vocabulary. Tell them they can be creative with their clues, but they must be accurate. You may wish to provide or have students use computer software to make the crossword puzzles.

Más recursos PearsonSchool.com/Autentico

▣ Games   ✎ Flashcards   ✎ Instant check

▶ Tutorials

Gramática

La voz pasiva: ser + participio pasado

Form the passive voice by using *ser* + past participle. The past participle is an adjective, so it agrees in number and gender with the subject. However, use the impersonal *se* when the subject is unknown.

Las reglas **son aplicadas** por el estado.   **Se necesita** una persona para trabajar con nosotros.

El presente y el imperfecto del subjuntivo

Use the present subjunctive when the verb in the main clause is in the present, present perfect, command or future tense.

Dile que **vote** mañana en las elecciones.   Armando cantará cuando **se lo pidan**.
No hemos dicho que ella **sea** nuestra amiga.

Use the imperfect subjunctive when the verb in the main clause is in the preterite, imperfect, pluperfect or conditional.

Mi maestra me pidió que **bailara**.   El adolescente había tratado que **nos conociéramos**.
El presidente quería que todos **votaran**.   Le gustaría a mamá que **llegáramos** a tiempo.

pluscuamperfecto del subjuntivo

Use the pluperfect subjunctive when the verb of the main clause is in the preterite, the imperfect or the pluperfect of the indicative.

Esperaba que **hubieran ido** a la fiesta con los niños.
Carlos no pensó que Juan **hubiera intercambiado** su pluma.
Había querido que la prensa **hubiera dicho** la verdad.

To form the pluperfect subjunctive use the past subjunctive of *haber* + the past participle of the verb.

hubiera	salido	hubiera	salido	hubierais	salido
hubieras	salido	hubiéramos	salido	hubieran	salido

Also use the pluperfect subjunctive when the verb in the main clause is in the conditional.

¿**Sería** posible que él **hubiera terminado** la tarea?

After the expression *como si* (as if), use either the imperfect subjunctive or the pluperfect subjunctive.

Estaba tan alegre **como si hubiera dormido**.   El niño descansa **como si no tuviera** nada que hacer.

El condicional perfecto

Form the conditional perfect using the conditional of *haber* + the past participle of the verb.

habría	trabaj**ado**	habría	trabaj**ado**	habríais	trabaj**ado**
habrías	trabaj**ado**	habríamos	trabaj**ado**	habrían	trabaj**ado**

In sentences with *si* clauses, use the past perfect subjunctive and the conditional perfect together.

Si **hubieras ido** a la fiesta, te **habrías divertido**.   Si **hubieran venido** aquí, no **habrían estudiado**.

Enrich Your Teaching

Teacher-to-Teacher

As students read more and more in Spanish, help them improve their skills in dictionary use by offering this suggestion. Tell them that each time they look up a word in their own dictionary, they should place a small dot beside the entry. If they look up a word and find a dot already there, they know this is the second time they have looked up the word. If they see two dots beside a word, they know it is one that they need frequently, and they should take steps to internalize it.

La voz pasiva: **ser + *participio pasado*:** Ask students to write five sentences that contain a transitive verb and a direct object. Have them exchange sentences with a partner, who converts them to the passive voice: *Tina leyó un libro sobre los derechos de la gente./Un libro sobre los derechos de la gente fue leído por Tina.*

El presente y el imperfecto del subjuntivo: Ask students to write two opinions they have about rights and responsibilities. Encourage them to begin each opinion with an expression that requires the subjunctive and to sign their opinions. For example: *Es importante que el gobierno asegure la protección de los niños—Pedro.* Have them place these in a "time capsule." Pretend that 100 years have passed and the class is opening the time capsule. Students read the opinions, converting them to the past tense: *Pedro dijo que era importante que el gobierno asegurara la protección de los niños.*

El pluscuamperfecto del subjuntivo: Have students write humorous expressions using *como si* and the pluperfect subjunctive: *La muchacha bailó como si hubiera tenido alitas en los tobillos.*

El condicional perfecto: Have students write five things to tell a partner that he or she should have done. For example: *Deberías haber ido a la fiesta.* Ask them to take turns reading their statements to a partner, who asks *¿Por qué?* The first student then responds with a suitable sentence using the conditional perfect: *Habrías bailado mucho.*

Digital Portfolio

Invite students to review the activities they completed in this chapter, including written reports, posters or other visuals, recordings of oral presentations, and other projects. Have them select one or two items that they feel best demonstrate their achievements in Spanish. Include these products in students' portfolios. Have them include this with the Chapter Checklist and Self-Assessment Worksheet.

Performance Tasks

Standards: 1.1, 1.2, 1.3, 3.1

Student Resource: *Para hispanohablantes*
Teacher Resources: Teacher's Resource Materials: Audio Script; Technology: Audio Cap. 10

1. Vocabulario

Suggestions: Encourage students to review the vocabulary from the *Vocabulario en contexto* sections on pp. 454–455 and 466–467 before they complete the activity.

Answers:

1. c	**5.** a
2. d	**6.** a
3. c	**7.** c
4. b	**8.** b

2. Gramática

Suggestions: Remind students of the main points of the grammar presentations in *Capítulo* 10:

- the passive voice
- the present and imperfect subjunctive
- the pluperfect subjunctive
- the conditional perfect

Answers:

1. d	**5.** a
2. c	**6.** d
3. c	**7.** c
4. a	**8.** d

Repaso del capítulo

OBJECTIVE
▶ Demonstrate that you can perform the tasks on these pages

Preparación para el examen

① Vocabulario Escribe la letra de la palabra o expresión que mejor complete cada frase. Escribe tus respuestas en una hoja aparte.

1. El _____ de las opiniones de los demás ayuda a que la gente viva de manera pacífica.
   a. valor   c. respeto
   b. código de vestimenta d. maltrato

2. Antes, era muy difícil recibir las noticias _____ si vivías en un pueblo pequeño.
   a. inocentes   c. enseñanzas
   b. propuestas   d. mundiales

3. La justicia y la paz son _____ que tienen los países de todo el mundo.
   a. democráticas   c. aspiraciones
   b. injusticias   d. castigos

4. A medida que le hacían preguntas, el sospechoso de _____ la ley se asustaba más.
   a. intercambiar   c. opinar
   b. violar   d. proponer

5. En los libros que usan los abogados encontrarás frecuentemente las palabras juicio, _____ y juzgar.
   a. jurado   c. desempleo
   b. armario   d. felicidad

6. Cuando pasan de _____ , muchos adolescentes creen que pueden hacer todo sin avisar a sus padres.
   a. la niñez   c. la injusticia
   b. la pobreza   d. la libertad

7. La policía tiene _____ de detener a las personas cuando existe un motivo.
   a. la igualdad   c. el deber
   b. la tolerancia   d. el pensamiento

8. _____ guardar para sus estudios el dinero que ganó con el premio, lo gastó en divertirse.
   a. A pesar de   c. Ante
   b. En lugar de   d. Debido a

② Gramática Escribe la letra de la palabra o expresión que mejor complete cada frase. Escribe tus respuestas en una hoja aparte.

1. Luis no esperaba que su jefe lo _____ a quedarse trabajando toda la noche.
   a. obligará   c. habrá obligado
   b. habían obligado   d. hubiera obligado

2. Las leyes que prohiben maltratar a los animales _____ en muchas ciudades.
   a. aplicarán   c. están aplicadas
   b. son aplicados   d. son aplicadas

3. Si _____ una educación adecuada, todos los jóvenes se habrían graduado.
   a. tienen   c. hubieran tenido
   b. tenían   d. han tenido

4. La acusada hablaba sobre el asunto como si _____ la autoridad para acusar a otros durante su propio juicio.
   a. hubiera gozado de c. habría gozado de
   b. han gozado de   d. ha gozado de

5. Dile al candidato que te _____ que va a luchar contra la desigualdad.
   a. asegure   c. asegura
   b. asegurará   d. ha asegurado

6. Si _____ sujeto a todos los problemas que sufrió ese adolescente, tu punto de vista sería muy distinto.
   a. estabas   c. hubiste estado
   b. estás   d. hubieras estado

7. Ambos estudiantes le pidieron al profesor que _____ de convencer a toda la clase para que votaran por su candidata.
   a. tratará   c. tratara
   b. hubiera tratado   d. trataría

8. Su amigo le _____ el apoyo que necesitaba si él no lo hubiera tratado así.
   a. sería dado   c. había dado
   b. habrá dado   d. habría dado

494 cuatrocientos noventa y cuatro • Capítulo 10 • ¿Cuáles son tus derechos y deberes?

Differentiated Instruction

Students with Learning Difficulties

Refer students to their portfolios. Have them look at chapter exams from past chapters. Lay three or four exams side-by-side and point out the similarities in structure between them. Remind students that knowing how a test is laid out helps them know what to expect next and reduces stress.

Advanced Learners

Provide students with additional vocabulary practice by asking them to use the incorrect answers from performance task 1 in sentences.

En el examen vas a . . .	Éstas son las tareas que te pueden ser útiles para el examen . . .	Para repasar, ve a tu libro de texto impreso o digital . . .
Interpretive		
❸ **ESCUCHAR** Yo puedo escuchar y comprender la descripción de las reglas de un club deportivo.	Responde a las preguntas sobre las reglas del Club Deportivo Veloz. (a) ¿Respetar el código de vestimenta es un derecho o un deber de los miembros? (b) ¿Qué significa que los miembros tendrán derecho de opinar? (c) ¿Qué les pasa a los que no obedecen las reglas? (d) ¿Crees que hay igualdad entre los derechos y los deberes de los miembros? Di por qué.	**pp. 454–457** *Vocabulario en contexto 1* **p. 462** Actividad 12 **p. 482** *Pre-AP® Integración*
Presentational		
❹ **HABLAR** Yo puedo hacer una presentación para explicar por qué los animales también tienen derechos.	Haz una presentación a los jóvenes del barrio sobre lo que deben hacer para cuidar a los animales. Usa oraciones conectadas con detalles y elaboración que incluye: (a) una explicación de los problemas que sufren los animales, (b) qué derechos deberían tener, (c) lo que pueden hacer los jóvenes para protegerlos.	**p. 479** Actividad 40 **p. 483** *Presentación oral*
Interpretive		
❺ **LEER** Yo puedo leer y comprender un párrafo de un ensayo editorial.	Lee un párrafo de un ensayo editorial sobre el mar y Chile. (a) ¿Qué solución propone el autor para desarrollar al país? (b) ¿Quién es el libertador de Chile? (c) ¿De qué depende Chile? *Ante lo que he dicho antes, propongo que hagamos una campaña para que Chile vuelva a mirar hacia el mar como solución para desarrollar al país. Para terminar, debemos recordar a nuestro libertador, Don Bernardo O'Higgins, quien dijo que el pueblo de Chile, "desde siempre y para siempre, depende del mar".*	**pp. 466–468** *Vocabulario en contexto 2* **p. 473** Actividad 29 **pp. 486–489** *Lectura*
Presentational		
❻ **ESCRIBIR** Yo puedo escribir un cuestionario sobre cómo hacer uso de un parque.	En un parque sembraron césped y flores y construyeron un camino para bicicletas, pero la gente no está de acuerdo en cómo usarlos. Escribe un cuestionario para preguntarles cómo habrían usado el parque si hubiera sido de ellos. Incluye (a) el horario, (b) las obligaciones y los derechos, (c) lo que debe garantizar la ciudad.	**p. 460** Actividad 9 **p. 465** Actividad 17 **p. 478** Actividades 36, 38
Comparisons		
❼ **COMPARAR** Yo puedo comparar algunos problemas que enfrentan los jóvenes.	Compara los problemas de la juventud en tu comunidad con algunos de los problemas de la lista de *Vocabulario en contexto 2*, p. 468.	**p. 481** *¿Comprendiste?* #4

Capítulo 10 • cuatrocientos noventa y cinco **495**

Differentiated Assessment

Core Assessment
- Technology: Audio Cap. 10
- ExamView: Chapter Test, Test Banks A and B

Challenge/Pre-AP®
- ExamView: Pre-AP® Test Bank
- Pre-AP® Resource Materials

Extra Support
- Alternate Assessment Program: Examen del capítulo 10
- Technology: Audio Cap. 10

Heritage Speakers
- Assessment Program: Para hispanohablantes: Examen del capítulo 10
- ExamView: Heritage Speaker Test Bank

3. Escuchar

Suggestions: Use the audio or read from the script.

🔊 **Technology: Audio**

Script:
1. Los miembros deberán tener respeto por el código de vestimenta al hacer ejercicio.
2. Las decisiones sobre todas las actividades que se organicen serán democráticas y los miembros tendrán derecho a opinar.
3. Quienes violen las reglas la primera vez, serán castigados sin usar los equipos deportivos durante un mes. La segunda vez que no respeten las reglas, deberán salir del club.
4. No habrá tolerancia para los que violen las reglas.

Answers:
a. un deber
b. podrán votar
c. serán castigados
d. Answers will vary.

4. Hablar

Suggestions: Encourage students to use sentences in which they say what will happen to the animals if they are not cared for and protected.

Answers will vary.

5. Leer

Suggestions: Tell students to refer to pp. 454–457 and 466–469 if they have questions about vocabulary in the review

Answers:
a. Propone una campaña para que el país use el mar.
b. Don Bernardo O'Higgins
c. Chile depende del mar.

6. Escribir

Suggestions: Remind students of what they learned about effective introductions in this chapter's *Presentación escrita*. Have them apply that learning to their writing here.

Answers will vary.

7. Comparar

Suggestions: Encourage students to review the reading on pp. 486–488 before they make their recommendations.

Answers will vary.

Additional Resources

 Technology: Online Resources
- Instant Check
Print
- Core WB pp. 145–146

Vocabulario adicional

Capítulo 1

El equipo para ir de cámping
el abrelatas can opener
la balsa raft
el bote inflable inflatable boat
la cantimplora canteen
la caña de pescar fishing rod
el casco helmet
el chaleco salvavidas life jacket
los fósforos matches
la leña firewood
el remo oar, paddle

Para indicar cuándo sucede algo
el amanecer dawn
el atardecer dusk
el mediodía noon
la puesta del sol sunset
la salida del sol sunrise

Expresiones para los deportes
empatar to tie (a game)
la cancha (sports) field
el podio podium

Capítulo 2

Los materiales
la acuarela watercolor
el barro clay
el caballete easel
el lienzo canvas
el óleo oleo (paint)
la témpera tempera

Las expresiones de teatro
la escenografía set design
la iluminación lighting

la ovación ovation
poner en escena (una obra) to stage (a play)
el telón curtain
la utilería props
el vestuario wardrobe

Los instrumentos musicales
el arpa harp
el contrabajo double bass
la flauta flute
el instrumento de cuerda string instrument
el instrumento de percusión percussion instrument
el instrumento de viento wind instrument
el violoncelo cello

La literatura
la autobiografía autobiography
la biografía biography
el ensayo essay
la estrofa stanza
la ficción fiction
la prosa prose
la rima rhyme

Capítulo 3

Las expresiones para la salud
el análisis clínico laboratory test
el / la especialista specialist
el estetoscopio stethoscope
el medicamento medicine
los minerales minerals
la presión arterial blood pressure
los primeros auxilios first aid
la respiración breathing
el síntoma symptom
el termómetro thermometer

Las máquinas de ejercicio
la caminadora treadmill
la máquina de remar rowing machine
la máquina de subir escaleras stair climber
las pesas libres free weights

Los condimentos
la mayonesa mayonnaise
la mostaza mustard
la salsa de tomate ketchup

Otro tipo de comidas
los fideos noodles

Capítulo 4

Los estados de ánimo
ansioso, -a anxious
abrumado, -a overwhelmed
agotado, -a exhausted
rendido, -a worn out

Las relaciones con los demás
agradecer to thank
chismear to gossip
disculpar to excuse
insultar to insult
opinar to give / to have an opinion
querer (a alguien) to love (someone)
soportar to tolerate

Capítulo 5

Expresiones para el empleo y trabajo voluntario
comunitario, -a community related
la destreza skill
los estudios (cursados) studies (completed)

el patrón / la patrona boss

los recursos humanos human resources

el / la supervisor(a) supervisor

sin fines de lucro nonprofit

Capítulo 6

Otras profesiones

el / la aprendiz apprentice

el / la camarógrafo(a) cameraman, camerawoman

el / la cirujano(a) surgeon

el /la intérprete interpreter

el / la jardinero(a) gardener

el / la modista(a) dressmaker, designer

el /la oculista eye doctor

Las ciencias

la astronomía astronomy

la física physics

la química chemistry

La tecnología

la energía nuclear nuclear energy

el facsímil fax

la fotocopiadora copier

inalámbrico, -a wireless

el microscopio electrónico electronic microscope

el rayo / la luz láser laser beam / light

el telescopio telescope

Capítulo 7

La arqueología

abandonar to abandon

el / la antropólogo(a) anthropologist

avanzado, -a advanced

los datos data, information

la desaparición disappearance

descifrar to decipher

desenterrar to unearth

la evolución evolution

el / la geólogo(a) geologist

el jeroglífico hieroglyph

la prueba proof

el significado meaning

surgir to arise

Para hablar del universo

la constelación constellation

la galaxia galaxy

intergaláctico, -a intergalactic

el sistema solar solar system

Otras formas geométricas

el cuadrado square

la circunferencia circumference

el cubo cube

la esfera sphere

la rueda wheel

Capítulo 8

La arquitectura

la capilla chapel

la cúpula dome

el muro wall

la muralla (de la ciudad) wall (of a city)

Expresiones para la historia de América

la armadura armor

las armas de fuego firearms

el arribo arrival

cabalgar to ride a horse

la carabela caravel

el escudo shield

la lanza spear

la nave (a vela) sailboat

la pólvora gunpowder

unificar to unify

el yelmo helmet

Capítulo 9

Expresiones sobre el cuidado del planeta

la atmósfera atmosphere

la biosfera biosphere

descomponer(se) to decompose

los desechos industriales industrial waste

el /la ecólogo(a) ecologist

la erosión erosion

la radioactividad radioactivity

radiactivo,-a radiactive

la superpoblación overpopulation

la sustancia substance

la tala de bosques felling of forests

Capítulo 10

Las leyes y los derechos

apelar to appeal

el congreso congress

la Declaración de Derechos Bill of Rights

la democracia democracy

los derechos civiles civil rights

los derechos humanos human rights

encarcelar to put in jail

las enmiendas amendments

el himno nacional national anthem

la monarquía monarchy

la patria homeland

el patriotismo patriotism

el senado senate

Adjectives describe nouns: *a **red** car.*

Adverbs usually describe verbs: *He read it **quickly.*** Adverbs can also describe adjectives or other adverbs: ***very tall, quite well.***

Articles are words in Spanish that can tell you whether a noun is masculine, feminine, singular, or plural. In English, the articles are ***the, a,*** and ***an.***

Commands are verb forms that tell people to do something: ***Work!***

Comparatives compare people or things: *more . . . than.*

Conditional tense is used to express what a person would do or what a situation would be like: *I **would like** to write a book.*

Conjugations are verb forms that add endings to the stem in order to tell who the subject is and what tense is being used: *escrib**o**, escrib**iste**.*

Conjunctions join words or groups of words. The most common ones are ***and, but,*** and ***or.***

Direct objects are nouns or pronouns that receive the action of a verb: *I read **the book.** I read **it.***

Future tense is used to talk about actions in the future: *Tomorrow we **will begin** working.*

Gender in Spanish tells you whether a noun, pronoun, or article is masculine or feminine.

Imperfect tense is used to talk about actions that happened repeatedly in the past; to describe people, places, and situations in the past; to talk about a past action or situation where no beginning or end is specified; and to describe an ongoing action in the past.

Imperfect progressive tense is used to describe something that was taking place over a period of time in the past: *He **was skiing** when he broke his leg.*

Indicative mood refers to present, past or future actions or states based on reality: *It **snowed** all night. **It's snowing** right now. **Will it snow** tomorrow?*

Indirect objects are nouns or pronouns that tell you to whom / what or for whom / what something is done: *I gave **him** the book.*

Infinitives are the basic forms of verbs. In English, infinitives have the word "to" in front of them: ***to walk.***

Interrogatives are words that ask questions: ***What** is it? **Who** is he?*

Nouns name people, places, or things: ***students, Mexico City, books.***

Number tells you if a noun, pronoun, article, or verb is singular or plural.

Past participles are verb forms that are used with forms of *haber* to form compound tenses: ***He escrito** una carta.* When a participle is used with *estar*, it functions as an adjective: *La mesa **está puesta.***

Prepositions show relationship between their objects and another word in the sentence: *He is **in** the classroom.*

Present tense is used to talk about actions that always take place, or that are currently happening: *I always **take** the bus; I **study** Spanish.*

Present perfect tense is used to say what a person *has done: We **have seen** the new movie.*

Present progressive tense is used to emphasize that an action is happening *right now: I **am doing** my homework; he **is finishing** dinner.*

Preterite tense is used to talk about actions that were completed in the past: *I **took** the train yesterday.*

Pronouns are words that take the place of nouns: ***She** is my friend.*

Reflexive verbs are used to say that people do something to or for themselves: *I **wash my** hair.* Reflexive verbs often describe a change in emotional or physical state, and express the idea that someone "gets" or "becomes": *They **became** angry.*

Subjects are the nouns or pronouns that perform the action in a sentence: ***John** sings.*

Subjunctive mood is used to say that one person influences the actions of another: ***I recommend that you study** more.* It is also used after verbs and expressions of doubt or uncertainty: ***It's possible that there's** enough food.*

Verbs show action or link the subject with a word or words in the predicate (what the subject does or is): *Ana **writes;** Ana **is** my sister.*

Nouns, Number, and Gender

Nouns refer to people, animals, places, things, and ideas. Nouns are singular or plural. In Spanish, nouns have gender, which means that they are either masculine or feminine.

Singular Nouns	
Masculine	**Feminine**
libro	carpeta
pupitre	casa
profesor	noche
lápiz	ciudad

Plural Nouns	
Masculine	**Feminine**
libros	carpetas
pupitres	casas
profesores	noches
lápices	ciudades

Definite Articles

El, la, los, and *las* are definite articles and are the equivalent of "the" in English. *El* is used with masculine singular nouns; *los* with masculine plural nouns. *La* is used with feminine singular nouns; *las* with feminine plural nouns. When you use the words *a* or *de* before *el,* you form the contractions *al* and *del: Voy al centro; Es el libro **del** profesor.*

Masculine		Feminine	
Singular	**Plural**	**Singular**	**Plural**
el libro	los libros	la carpeta	las carpetas
el pupitre	los pupitres	la casa	las casas
el profesor	los profesores	la noche	las noches
el lápiz	los lápices	la ciudad	las ciudades

Indefinite Articles

Un and *una* are indefinite articles and are the equivalent of "a" and "an" in English. *Un* is used with singular masculine nouns; *una* is used with singular feminine nouns. The plural indefinite articles are *unos* and *unas.*

Masculine		Feminine	
Singular	**Plural**	**Singular**	**Plural**
un libro	unos libros	una revista	unas revistas
un baile	unos bailes	una mochila	unas mochilas

Pronouns

Subject pronouns tell who is doing the action. They replace nouns or names in a sentence. Subject pronouns are often used for emphasis or clarification: *Gregorio escucha música. **Él** escucha música.*

A *direct object* tells who or what receives the action of the verb. To avoid repeating a direct object noun, you can replace it with a *direct object pronoun.* Direct object pronouns have the same gender and number as the nouns they replace: *¿Cuándo compraste **el libro? Lo** compré ayer.*

An indirect object tells to whom or for whom an action is performed.

Indirect object pronouns are used to replace an indirect object noun: ***Les** doy dinero. (I give money to them.)* Because *le* and *les* have more than one meaning, you can make the meaning clear, or show emphasis, by adding *a* + the corresponding name, noun, or pronoun: ***Les** doy dinero a **ellos.***

When two object pronouns are used together, the indirect object pronoun comes before the direct object pronoun: *Si necesitas este libro, **te lo** doy.*

The indirect object pronoun *le* or *les* becomes *se* before the direct object pronoun *lo, la, los,*

The Personal a

When the direct object is a person, a group of people, or a pet, use the word *a* before the object. This is called the "personal *a*": *Visité **a** mi abuela. Busco **a** mi perro, Capitán.*

or *las: María quiere escuchar esta canción. **Se la** voy a cantar.*

A *reflexive pronoun* is used to show that someone does an action to or for themselves. Each reflexive pronoun corresponds to a different subject and always agrees with the subject pronoun: *Todos los días **me ducho** y **me arreglo** el pelo.*

Subject Pronouns		Direct Object Pronouns		Indirect Object Pronouns		Reflexive Pronouns		Objects of Prepositions	
Singular	**Plural**	**Singular**	**Plural**	**Singular**	**Plural**	**Singular**	**Plural**	**Singular**	**Plural**
yo	nosotros, nosotras	me	nos	me	nos	me	nos	(para) mí, conmigo	nosotros, nosotras
tú	vosotros, vosotras	te	os	te	os	te	os	(para) ti, contigo	vosotros, vosotras
usted (Ud.), él, ella	ustedes (Uds.), ellos, ellas	lo, la	los, las	le	les	se	se	Ud., él, ella	Uds. ellos, ellas

Adjectives

Words that describe people and things are called adjectives. In Spanish, most adjectives have both masculine and feminine forms, as well as singular and plural forms. Adjectives must agree with the noun they describe in both gender and number. When an adjective describes a group including both masculine and feminine nouns, use the masculine plural form.

Masculine		Feminine	
Singular	**Plural**	**Singular**	**Plural**
alto	altos	alta	altas
inteligente	inteligentes	inteligente	inteligentes
trabajador	trabajadores	trabajadora	trabajadoras
fácil	fáciles	fácil	fáciles

Shortened Forms of Adjectives

When placed before masculine singular nouns, some adjectives change into a shortened form.

bueno	→ buen chico
malo	→ mal día
primero	→ prímer trabajo
tercero	→ tercer plato
grande	→ gran señor

One adjective, **grande,** changes to a shortened form before any singular noun: *una* **gran** *señora, un* **gran** *libro.* In these cases, **gran** means "great."

Possessive Adjectives and Pronouns

Possessive adjectives are used to tell what belongs to someone or to show relationships. Like other adjectives, possessive adjectives agree in number with the nouns that follow them.

Only *nuestro* and *vuestro* have different masculine and feminine endings. *Su* and *sus* can have many different meanings: *his, her, its, your,* or *their.*

The long forms of possessive adjectives agree in number and gender with the noun. They are used for emphasis and come *after*

Singular	Plural	Singular	Plural
mi	mis	mío/mía	míos/mías
tu	tus	tuyo/tuya	tuyos/tuyas
su	sus	suyo/suya	suyos/suyas
nuestro, -a	nuestros, -as	nuestro/nuestra	nuestros/nuestras
vuestro, -a	vuestros, -as	vuestro/vuestra	vuestros/vuestras
su	sus	suyo/suya	suyos/suyas

the noun. They may also be used without a noun: *¿Esta chaqueta es* **tuya?** *Sí, es* **mía.**

Possessive pronouns use the long form of possessive adjectives preceded by the definite article. *Tu cuarto es grande.* **El mío** *es pequeño.*

Demonstrative Adjectives and Pronouns

Demonstrative adjectives are used to point out people or things that are nearby and farther away. A demonstrative adjective agrees in gender and number with the noun that follows it.

Use *este, esta, estos, estas* ("this" / "these") before nouns that name people or things that are close to you. Use *ese, esa, esos, esas* ("that" / "those") before nouns that name people or things that are at some distance from you.

Use *aquel, aquella, aquellos,* or *aquellas* ("that one [those] over there") before nouns that name

people or things that are far from both you and the person you are speaking to.

Demonstrative adjectives can be used as pronouns to replace

nouns. Accents are no longer required on demonstrative pronouns as of 2010. Anything written before 2009 will include accents on demonstratives.

	Close to you		Closer to the person you are talking to		Far from both of you	
Adjectives	este	estos	ese	esos	aquel	aquellos
	esta	estas	esa	esas	aquella	aquellas
Pronouns	éste	éstos	ése	ésos	aquél	aquéllos
	ésta	éstas	ésa	ésas	aquélla	aquéllas

Interrogative Words

You use interrogative words to ask questions. When you ask a question with an interrogative word, you put the verb before the subject. All interrogative words have a written accent mark.

¿Adónde?	**¿Cuándo?**	**¿Dónde?**
¿Cómo?	**¿Cuánto, -a?**	**¿Por qué?**
¿Con quién?	**¿Cuántos, -as?**	**¿Qué?**
¿Cuál?	**¿De dónde?**	**¿Quién?**

Comparatives and Superlatives

Comparatives Use *más . . . que* or *menos . . . que* to compare people or things: *más interesante que . . . , menos alta que . . . .*

When talking about number, use *de* instead of *que: Tengo más de cien monedas en mi colección.*

To compare people or things that are equal, use *tan . . . como: tan popular como . . . . Tanto / tanta . . . como* is used to say "as much as" and *tantos / tantas . . . como* is used to say "as many as": *tanto dinero como . . . tantas amigas como . . . . Tanto* and *tanta*

match the number and gender of the noun to which they refer.

Superlatives Use this pattern to express the idea of "most" or "least."

el
la + *noun* + más / menos + *adjective*
los
las

Es la chica más seria de la clase.

Son los perritos más pequeños.

Several adjectives are irregular when used with comparisons and superlatives.

older	mayor
younger	menor
better	mejor
worse	peor

Affirmative and Negative Words

To make a sentence negative in Spanish, *no* usually goes in front of the verb or expression. To show that you do not like either of two choices, use *ni . . . ni.*

Alguno, alguna, algunos, algunas and *ninguno, ninguna* match the number and gender of the noun to which they refer. *Ningunos* and *ningunas* are rarely used. When *alguno* and *ninguno* come before a masculine singular noun, they change to *algún* and *ningún.*

Affirmative	Negative
algo	nada
alguien	nadie
algún	ningún
alguno, -a, -os, -as	ninguno, -a, -os, -as
siempre	nunca
también	tampoco

Adverbs

To form an adverb in Spanish, *-mente* is added to the feminine singular form of an adjective. The *-mente* ending is equivalent to the "-ly" ending in English. If the adjective has a written accent, such as *rápida, fácil,* and *práctica,* the accent appears in the same place in the adverb.

general	→ generalmente
especial	→ especialmente
fácil	→ fácilmente
feliz	→ felizmente
rápida	→ rápidamente
práctica	→ prácticamente

Past Participles

Past participles are used with forms of the verb *haber* to form compound tenses: **Había escrito** *un poema muy hermoso.* They can also be used as adjectives: *El espejo estaba* **roto**. *To* form a past participle, add *-ado* to the root of *-ar* verbs and *-ido* to the root of *-er* and *-ir* verbs.

Some past participles are irregular.

decorar decorado	conocer conocido	preferir preferido

abrir: abierto	morir: muerto
cubrir: cubierto	poner: puesto
decir: dicho	resolver: resuelto
descubrir: descubierto	romper: roto
escribir: escrito	ver: visto
hacer: hecho	volver: vuelto

Por and *para*

Both *por* and *para* are prepositions. Their usages are quite different.

Use *por* to indicate:	
length of time or distance	Caminamos por dos horas.
where an action takes place	El perro corría por la playa.
an exchange	Le doy diez pesos por ese dibujo.
an action on behalf of someone or something	Vamos a la marcha por la paz.
a means of communication or transportation	Lo vimos por televisión.

Use *por* in certain expressions:
por ejemplo
por eso (tanto)
por la (mañana, tarde, noche)
por favor
por lo general
por primera (segunda, tercera, última) vez
por supuesto

Use *para* to indicate:	
purpose	Como frutas para obtener vitaminas.
destination	Hace una hora salieron para la playa.
a point in time	Para mañana ya tendrás lo que encargaste.
use	¿Dónde hay una cuchara para sopa?
opinion	Para los niños el helado es muy rico.

Pero and *sino*

The word *pero* is usually the equivalent of the English conjunction *but*. The word *sino* also means *but*.

> **Sino is used after a negative, to convey the idea of an alternative: "not this, but rather that."**
>
> **No compré pastel *sino* helado.**
>
> **Yo can also use *sino* with *no sólo . . . sino* también.**
>
> **Me regaló *no sólo* dulces *sino* también flores.**
>
> **You use *sino que* when there is a conjugated verb in the second part of the sentence.**
>
> **No fuimos a la ciudad *sino que* salimos a navegar.**

Relative Pronouns *que*, *quien*, and *lo que*

You use relative pronouns to combine two sentences or to give clarifying information. The most common relative pronoun in Spanish is *que*. It can mean *that, which, who*, or *whom*, and it may refer either to persons or to things.

*El artículo **que** salió en el periódico habla sobre la contaminación.*

> **After a preposition, use *que* to refer to things and *quien(es)* to refer to people.**
>
> > **El problema del que te hablé es muy grave.**
> > **La persona de quien te hablé se llama Adriana.**
>
> **Use the relative phrase *lo que* to refer to a situation, concept, action, or object not yet identified.**
>
> > **Te cuento lo que me explicó el científico.**

Conjunctions Used with the Subjunctive and the Indicative

Certain conjunctions related to time are followed by either the indicative or the subjunctive:

> | antes de que | tan pronto como | cuando | en cuanto |
> |---|---|---|---|
> | después (de) que | hasta que | mientras | |
>
> **You use the subjunctive after these conjunctions when the action that follows has not yet taken place. You use the indicative with these conjunction when the action that follows has already taken place or if it occurs regularly.**
>
> > **Van a producir petróleo hasta que se agote.**
> > **En cuanto salgo del cuarto, siempre apago las luces.**
>
> **The conjunction *antes de que* is always followed by the subjunctive.**
>
> > **Pon el helado en el refrigerador antes de que se derrita.**
>
> **If the subject of a sentence does not change, use the infinitive after *antes de, después de* and *hasta*.**
>
> > **Voy a salir después de terminar la tarea.**

The following conjunctions are usually followed by the subjunctive to express the purpose or intention of an action:

> | a menos que | para que | sin que |
> |---|---|---|
> | a fin de que | aunque | con tal (de) que |
>
> **No haré la limpieza de la casa a menos que me ayudes.**
>
> **If the subject of the sentence does not change, use the infinitive after *para* and *sin*.**
>
> > **Debemos dejar de usar aerosoles para detener la destrucción de la capa de ozono.**
>
> **With the conjunction *aunque*, use the subjunctive to express uncertainty. Use the indicative when there is no uncertainty.**
>
> > **Aunque produzcan más petróleo, no podrán depender de este recurso por mucho tiempo.**
> > **No quiero ver ese programa sobre las ballenas aunque todos dicen que es muy bueno.**

Verbos

Regular Verbs

Here are the conjugations for regular -ar, -er, and -ir verbs in the indicative (present, preterite, imperfect, future, and conditional) and the present and imperfect subjunctive.

Infinitive Present Participle Past Participle	Present		Preterite		Imperfect	
estudiar estudiando estudiado	estudio estudias estudia	estudiamos estudiáis estudian	estudié estudiaste estudió	estudiamos estudiasteis estudiaron	estudiaba estudiabas estudiaba	estudiábamos estudiabais estudiaban
correr corriendo corrido	corro corres corre	corremos corréis corren	corrí corriste corrió	corrimos corristeis corrieron	corría corrías corría	corríamos corríais corrían
vivir viviendo vivido	vivo vives vive	vivimos vivís viven	viví viviste vivió	vivimos vivisteis vivieron	vivía vivías vivía	vivíamos vivíais vivían

Present Progressive and Imperfect Progressive

Progressive tenses are formed with a form of *estar* and the present participle.

Present Progressive	Present Participle	Imperfect Progressive	Present Participle
estoy estás está estamos estáis están	estudiando corriendo viviendo	estaba estabas estaba estábamos estabais estaban	estudiando corriendo viviendo

Reflexive Verbs

Infinitive and Present Participle	Present	Preterite	Subjunctive
lavarse lavándose	me lavo te lavas se lava nos lavamos os laváis se lavan	me lavé te lavaste se lavó nos lavamos os lavasteis se lavaron	me lave te laves se lave nos lavemos os lavéis se laven

Regular Verbs (continued)

Future		Conditional		Present Subjunctive		Imperfect Subjunctive	
estudiaré	estudiaremos	estudiaría	estudiaríamos	estudie	estudiemos	estudiara	estudiáramos
estudiarás	estudiaréis	estudiarías	estudiarías	estudies	estudiéis	estudiaras	estudiarais
estudiará	estudiarán	estudiaría	estudiaría	estudie	estudien	estudiara	estudiaran
correré	correremos	correría	correríamos	corra	corramos	corriera	corriéramos
correrás	correréis	correrías	correríais	corras	corráis	corrieras	corrierais
correrá	correrán	correría	correrían	corra	corran	corriera	corrieran
viviré	viviremos	viviría	viviríamos	viva	vivamos	viviera	viviéramos
vivirás	viviréis	vivirías	viviríais	vivas	viváis	vivieras	vivierais
vivirá	vivirán	viviría	vivirían	viva	vivan	viviera	vivieran

Perfect Tenses

Perfect tenses are formed with an auxiliary verb *(haber)* and a past participle.

Present Perfect		Pluperfect		Future Perfect		Present Perfect Subjunctive		Past Perfect Subjunctive		Conditional Perfect	
he		había		habré		haya		hubiera		habría	
has	estudiado	habías	estudiado	habrás	estudiado	hayas	estudiado	hubieras	estudiado	habrías	estudiado
ha	corrido	había	corrido	habrá	corrido	haya	corrido	hubiera	corrido	habría	corrido
hemos	vivido	habíamos	vivido	habremos	vivido	hayamos	vivido	hubiéramos	vivido	habríamos	vivido
habéis		habíais		habréis		hayáis		hubierais		habríais	
han		habían		habrán		hayan		hubieran		habrían	

Stem-changing Verbs

Here is a list of stem-changing verbs. Only conjugations with changes are shown.

Infinitive in -ar

Infinitive	Present Indicative		Present Subjunctive	
pensar (e→ie)	pienso piensas piensa	pensamos pensáis piensan	piense pienses piense	pensemos penséis piensen
Verbs like pensar: calentar, comenzar, despertar(se), empezar, recomendar, tropezar				
contar (o→ue)	cuento cuentas cuenta	contamos contáis cuentan	cuente cuentes cuente	contemos contéis cuenten
Verbs like contar: acostar(se), almorzar, costar, encontrar(se), probar(se), recordar				
jugar (u→ue)	juego juegas juega	jugamos jugáis juegan	juegue juegues juegue	juguemos juguéis jueguen

Infinitive in -er

	Present Indicative		Present Subjunctive	
entender (e→ie)	entiendo entiendes entiende	entendemos entendéis entienden	entienda entiendas entienda	entendamos entendáis entiendan
Verbs like entender: encender, perder				
devolver (o→ue) past participle: devuelto	devuelvo devuelves devuelve	devolvemos devolvéis devuelven	devuelva devuelvas devuelva	devolvamos devolváis devuelvan
Verbs like devolver: mover(se), resolver, torcer(se), volver (past participle: vuelto)				

Stem-changing Verbs (continued)

Infinitive in *-ir*

	Indicative				Subjunctive	
	Present		**Preterite**		**Present**	
pedir (e→i) (e→i) present participle: pidiendo	pido pides pide	pedimos pedís piden	pedí pediste pidió	pedimos pedisteis pidieron	pida pidas pida	pidamos pidáis pidan
Verbs like pedir: conseguir, despedir(se), repetir, seguir, servir, vestir(se)						
preferir (e→ie) (e→i) present participle: prefiriendo	prefiero prefieres prefiere	preferimos preferís prefieren	preferí preferiste prefirió	preferimos preferisteis prefirieron	prefiera prefieras prefiera	prefiramos prefiráis prefieran
Verbs like preferir: divertir(se), hervir, mentir, sugerir						
dormir (o→ue) (o→u) present participle: durmiendo	duermo duermes duerme	dormimos dormís duermen	dormí dormiste durmió	dormimos dormisteis durmieron	duerma duermas duerma	durmamos durmáis duerman
Verbs like dormir: morir(se) (past participle: muerto)						

Spelling-changing Verbs

These verbs have spelling changes in the present, preterite, and/or the subjunctive tenses. The spelling changes are indicated in boldface.

Infinitive Present Participle Past Participle	Present		Preterite		Subjunctive	
almorzar (z→c) almorzando almorzado	See stem-changing verbs		almorcé almorzaste almorzó	almorzamos almorzasteis almorzaron	almuerce almuerces almuerce	almorcemos almorcéis almuercen
buscar (c→qu) buscando buscado	See regular *-ar* verbs		busqué buscaste buscó	buscamos buscasteis buscaron	busque busques busque	busquemos busquéis busquen
comunicarse (c→qu) comunicándose	See reflexive verbs		See reflexive verbs and buscar		See reflexive verbs and buscar	
conocer (c→zc) conociendo conocido	conozco conoces conoce	conocemos conocéis conocen	See regular *-er* verbs		conozca conozcas conozca	conozcamos conozcáis conozcan
creer (i→y) creyendo creído	See regular *-er* verbs		creí creíste creyó	creímos creísteis creyeron	See regular *-er* verbs	
empezar (z→c) empezando empezado	See stem-changing verbs		empecé empezaste empezó	empezamos empezasteis empezaron	See stem-changing verbs	
enviar (i→í) enviando enviado	envío envías envía	enviamos enviáis envían	See regular *-ar* verbs		envíe envíes envíe	enviemos enviéis envíen
escoger escogiendo escogido	escojo escoges escoge	escogemos escogéis escogen	See regular *-er* verbs		escoja escojas escoja	escojamos escojáis escojan
esquiar (i→í) esquiando esquiado	See enviar		See regular *-ar* verbs		See enviar	
jugar (g→gu) jugando jugado	See stem-changing verbs		jugué jugaste jugó	jugamos jugasteis jugaron	See stem-changing verbs	
leer (i→y) leyendo leído	See regular *-er* verbs		See creer		See regular *-er* verbs	
obedecer (c→zc) obedeciendo obedecido	See conocer		See regular *-er* verbs		See conocer	

Spelling-changing Verbs (continued)

Infinitive Present Participle Past Participle	Present		Preterite	Subjunctive	
ofrecer (c→zc) ofreciendo ofrecido	See conocer		See regular -er verbs	See conocer	
pagar (g→gu) pagando pagado	See regular -ar verbs		See jugar	pague pagues pague	paguemos paguéis paguen
parecer (c→zc) pareciendo parecido	See conocer		See regular -er verbs	See conocer	
practicar (c→qu) practicando practicado	See regular -ar verbs		See buscar	See buscar	
recoger (g→j) recogiendo recogido	recojo recoges recoge	recogemos recogéis recogen	See regular -er verbs	See escoger	
sacar (c→qu) sacando sacado	See regular -ar verbs		See buscar	See buscar	
tocar (c→qu) tocando tocado	See regular -ar verbs		See buscar	See buscar	

Irregular Verbs

These verbs have irregular patterns.

	1		2		3		4	
Infinitive Present Participle Past Participle			**Present**		**Preterite**		**Imperfect**	
dar dando dado	doy das da	damos dais dan	di diste dio	dimos disteis dieron	daba dabas daba	dábamos dabais daban
decir diciendo dicho	digo dices dice	decimos decís dicen	dije dijiste dijo	dijimos dijisteis dijeron	decía decías decía	decíamos decíais decían
estar estando estado	estoy estás está	estamos estáis están	estuve estuviste estuvo	estuvimos estuvisteis estuvieron	estaba estabas estaba	estábamos estabais estaban
haber habiendo habido	he has ha	hemos habéis han	hube hubiste hubo	hubimos hubisteis hubieron	había habías había	habíamos habíais habían
hacer haciendo hecho	hago haces hace	hacemos hacéis hacen	hice hiciste hizo	hicimos hicisteis hicieron	hacía hacías hacía	hacíamos hacíais hacían
ir yendo ido	voy vas va	vamos vais van	fui fuiste fue	fuimos fuisteis fueron	iba ibas iba	íbamos ibais iban
oír oyendo oído	oigo oyes oye	oímos oís oyen	oí oíste oyó	oímos oísteis oyeron	oía oías oía	oíamos oíais oían
poder pudiendo podido	puedo puedes puede	podemos podéis pueden	pude pudiste pudo	pudimos pudisteis pudieron	podía podías podía	podíamos podíais podían
poner poniendo puesto	pongo pones pone	ponemos ponéis ponen	puse pusiste puso	pusimos pusisteis pusieron	ponía ponías ponía	poníamos poníais ponían

Irregular Verbs (continued)

5		6		7		8	
Future		**Conditional**		**Present Subjunctive**		**Imperfect Subjunctive**	
daré	daremos	daría	daríamos	dé	demos	diera	diéramos
darás	daréis	darías	daríais	des	deis	dieras	dierais
dará	darán	daría	darían	dé	den	diera	dieran
diré	diremos	diría	diríamos	diga	digamos	dijera	dijéramos
dirás	diréis	dirías	diríais	digas	digáis	dijeras	dijerais
dirá	dirán	diría	dirían	diga	digan	dijera	dijeran
estaré	estaremos	estaría	estaríamos	esté	estemos	estuviera	estuviéramos
estarás	estaréis	estarías	estaríais	estés	estéis	estuvieras	estuvierais
estará	estarán	estaría	estarían	esté	estén	estuviera	estuvieran
habré	habremos	habría	habríamos	haya	hayamos	hubiera	hubiéramos
habrás	habréis	habrías	habríais	hayas	hayáis	hubieras	hubierais
habrá	habrán	habría	habrían	haya	hayan	hubiera	hubieran
haré	haremos	haría	haríamos	haga	hagamos	hiciera	hiciéramos
harás	haréis	harías	haríais	hagas	hagáis	hicieras	hicierais
hará	harán	haría	harían	haga	hagan	hiciera	hicieran
iré	iremos	iría	iríamos	vaya	vayamos	fuera	fuéramos
irás	iréis	irías	iríais	vayas	vayáis	fueras	fuerais
irá	irán	iría	irían	vaya	vayan	fuera	fueran
oiré	oiremos	oiría	oiríamos	oiga	oigamos	oyera	oyéramos
oirás	oiréis	oirías	oiríais	oigas	oigáis	oyeras	oyerais
oirá	oirán	oiría	oirían	oiga	oigan	oyera	oyeran
podré	podremos	podría	podríamos	pueda	podamos	pudiera	pudiéramos
podrás	podréis	podrías	podríais	puedas	podáis	pudieras	pudierais
podrá	podrán	podría	podrían	pueda	puedan	pudiera	pudieran
pondré	pondremos	pondría	pondríamos	ponga	pongamos	pusiera	pusiéramos
pondrás	pondréis	pondrías	pondríais	pongas	pongáis	pusieras	pusierais
pondrá	pondrán	pondría	pondrían	ponga	pongan	pusiera	pusieran

Irregular Verbs (continued)

1 Infinitive Present Participle Past Participle	2 Present		3 Preterite		4 Imperfect	
querer queriendo querido	quiero quieres quiere	queremos queréis quieren	quise quisiste quiso	quisimos quisisteis quisieron	quería querías quería	queríamos queríais querían
saber sabiendo sabido	sé sabes sabe	sabemos sabéis saben	supe supiste supo	supimos supisteis supieron	sabía sabías sabía	sabíamos sabíais sabían
salir saliendo salido	salgo sales sale	salimos salís salen	salí saliste salió	salimos salisteis salieron	salía salías salía	salíamos salíais salían
ser siendo sido	soy eres es	somos sois son	fui fuiste fue	fuimos fuisteis fueron	era eras era	éramos erais eran
tener teniendo tenido	tengo tienes tiene	tenemos tenéis tienen	tuve tuviste tuvo	tuvimos tuvisteis tuvieron	tenía tenías tenía	teníamos teníais tenían
traer trayendo traído	traigo traes trae	traemos traéis traen	traje trajiste trajo	trajimos trajisteis trajeron	traía traías traía	traíamos traíais traían
venir viniendo venido	vengo vienes viene	venimos venís vienen	vine viniste vino	vinimos vinisteis vinieron	venía venías venía	veníamos veníais venían
ver viendo visto	veo ves ve	vemos veis ven	vi viste vio	vimos visteis vieron	veía veías veía	veíamos veíais veían

Irregular Verbs (continued)

	5 Future		6 Conditional		7 Present Subjunctive		8 Imperfect Subjunctive	
querré	querremos	querría	querríamos	quiera	queramos	quisiera	quisiéramos
querrás	querréis	querrías	querríais	quieras	queráis	quisieras	quisierais
querrá	querrán	querría	querrían	quiera	quieran	quisiera	quisieran
sabré	sabremos	sabría	sabríamos	sepa	sepamos	supiera	supiéramos
sabrás	sabréis	sabrías	sabríais	sepas	sepáis	supieras	supierais
sabrá	sabrán	sabría	sabrían	sepa	sepan	supiera	supieran
saldré	saldremos	saldría	saldríamos	salga	salgamos	saliera	saliéramos
saldrás	saldréis	saldrías	saldríais	salgas	salgáis	salieras	salierais
saldrá	saldrán	saldría	saldrían	salga	salgan	saliera	salieran
seré	seremos	sería	seríamos	sea	seamos	fuera	fuéramos
serás	seréis	serías	seríais	seas	seáis	fueras	fuerais
será	serán	sería	serían	sea	sean	fuera	fueran
tendré	tendremos	tendría	tendríamos	tenga	tengamos	tuviera	tuviéramos
tendrás	tendréis	tendrías	tendríais	tengas	tengáis	tuvieras	tuvierais
tendrá	tendrán	tendría	tendrían	tenga	tengan	tuviera	tuvieran
traeré	traeremos	traería	traeríamos	traiga	traigamos	trajera	trajéramos
traerás	traeréis	traerías	traeríais	traigas	traigáis	trajeras	trajerais
traerá	traerán	traería	traerían	traiga	traigan	trajera	trajeran
vendré	vendremos	vendría	vendríamos	venga	vengamos	viniera	viniéramos
vendrás	vendréis	vendrías	vendríais	vengas	vengáis	vinieras	vinierais
vendrá	vendrán	vendría	vendrían	venga	vengan	viniera	vinieran
veré	veremos	vería	veríamos	vea	veamos	viera	viéramos
verás	veréis	verías	veríais	veas	veáis	vieras	vierais
verá	verán	vería	verían	vea	vean	viera	vieran

Affirmative and Negative Commands

To form an affirmative *tú* command, use the present-tense indicative
Ud. / él / ella form. This rule also applies to stem-changing verbs. Some
verbs have an irregular affirmative *tú* command.

To form a command with *Ud.,* remove the *-s* from a negative *tú* command
form. To form a command with *Uds.,* replace the *-s* of a negative *tú*
command with an *-n*.

Regular and stem-changing verbs, and verbs ending in *-car, -gar,* and *-zar*

Infinitive	Tú	Negative tú	Usted	Ustedes
estudiar	estudia	no estudies	(no) estudie	(no) estudien
volver	vuelve	no vuelvas	(no) vuelva	(no) vuelvan
abrir	abre	no abras	(no) abra	(no) abran
sacar	saca	no saques	(no) saque	(no) saquen
llegar	llega	no llegues	(no) llegue	(no) lleguen
cruzar	cruza	no cruces	(no) cruce	(no) crucen

Irregular verbs

Infinitive	Tú	Negative tú	Usted	Ustedes
decir	di	no digas	(no) diga	(no) digan
hacer	haz	no hagas	(no) haga	(no) hagan
ir	ve	no vayas	(no) vaya	(no) vayan
mantener	mantén	no mantengas	(no) mantenga	(no) mantengan
poner	pon	no pongas	(no) ponga	(no) pongan
salir	sal	no salgas	(no) salga	(no) salgan
ser	sé	no seas	(no) sea	(no) sean
tener	ten	no tengas	(no) tenga	(no) tengan
venir	ven	no vengas	(no) venga	(no) vengan

Placement of Pronouns with Commands

Attach reflexive or object pronous at the end of affirmative commands.
With negative commands, place them after the word *no*.

Toma esas vitaminas.
¡Tómalas ahora mismo!
*No **las** tomes*.

Expresiones útiles para conversar

Making an Apology

Perdóname. Forgive me.

Lo siento mucho. I'm very sorry.

Fue un malentendido. It was a misunderstanding.

Hagamos las paces. Let's make up.

Reconciliémonos. Let's reconcile.

Te pido perdón. I'm asking for your forgiveness.

Estoy equivocado, -a. I'm wrong.

Pongámonos de acuerdo. Let's come to an agreement.

Yo tengo la culpa. It's my fault.

Talking about Friendship

Tenemos mucho en común. We have a lot in common.

Te acepto tal como eres. I accept you just the way you are.

Tengo celos. I'm jealous.

No me hace caso. He / She doesn't pay any attention to me.

Sólo piensa en sí mismo, -a. He / She only thinks about himself / herself.

Confío en ti. I trust you.

Cuento contigo. I count on you.

Sé guardar un secreto. I can keep a secret.

Resolvamos este conflicto. Let's resolve this conflict.

Tenemos una diferencia de opinión. We disagree.

Me identifico contigo. I identify with you.

De hoy en adelante . . . From now on . . .

Ten en cuenta . . . Keep in mind . . .

Tengo derecho a . . . I have a right to . . .

Expressing Disagreement

Qué va. No way.

Yo no fui. I didn't do it.

No es cierto que . . . It's not true that . . .

No es verdad que . . . It's not true that . . .

No estoy de acuerdo. I disagree.

Me parece que no tienes razón. I think you're wrong.

Expressing Interest

Me es posible. I can.

Me gustaría . . . I'd like to . . .

Me encantaría . . . I'd love to . . .

Expressing Certainty or Possibility

Es cierto que . . . It's true that . . .

Estoy seguro, -a que . . . I'm sure that . . .

Es probable que . . . It's probable that . . .

Puede ser que . . . It's possible that . . .

Es posible que . . . It's possible that . . .

Es evidente que . . . It's clear that . . .

Quizás . . . Perhaps . . .

Expressing Doubt or Uncertainty

Dudo que . . . I doubt that . . .

No creo que . . . I don't think that . . .

No estoy seguro, -a que . . . I'm not sure that . . .

Es imposible que . . . It's impossible that . . .

Talking about How You Feel Physically

Me siento fatal. I feel awful.

Me caigo de sueño. I'm exhausted.

Estoy resfriado, -a. I have a cold.

Tengo tos. I have a cough.

Estornudo mucho. I'm sneezing a lot.

Tengo gripe. I have the flu.

Tengo fiebre. I have a fever.

Tengo alergia a . . . I'm allergic to . . .

Talking about How You Feel Emotionally

Estoy en la luna. I'm daydreaming.

No puedo concentrarme. I can't concentrate.

No aguanto más. I can't take it anymore.

Estoy de buen humor. I'm in a good mood.

Estoy de mal humor. I'm in a bad mood.

Estoy estresado, -a. I'm stressed out.

Me preocupo por . . . I'm worried about . . .

Me emociono mucho. I'm very emotional.

Estoy orgulloso, -a de . . . I'm proud of . . .

Estoy animado, -a. I'm excited.

Tengo confianza en mí mismo, -a. I have confidence in myself.

Me vuelvo loco, -a. I'm going crazy.

He cambiado de opinión. I've changed my mind.

Me doy cuenta de que . . . I realize that . . .

Me vuelvo . . . I'm getting / becoming . . .

Haré lo que me dé la gana. I'll do whatever I want.

Talking about Personal Goals

Alcancé mi meta. I achieved my goal.

Hice un esfuerzo. I made an effort.

Salí campeón. I won (I was the winner).

¡Felicitaciones! Congratulations!

Eres mi fuente de inspiración. You're my inspiration.

Describing Things or People

Se parece a . . . It / He / She looks like . . .

Suena a . . . It / He / She sounds like . . . .

Está basado, -a en . . . It's based on . . .

Se destaca. It / He / She stands out.

Está a cargo de . . . He / She is in charge of . . .

Vocabulario
español-inglés

The *Vocabulario español-inglés* contains all active vocabulary from the text, including vocabulary presented in the grammar sections.

A dash (—) represents the main entry word. For example, **pasar la —** after **la aspiradora** means **pasar la aspiradora.**

The number following each entry indicates the chapter in which the word or expression is presented. A Roman numeral (I) indicates that the word was presented in AUTÉNTICO 1. A Roman numeral (II) indicates that the word was presented in AUTÉNTICO 2.

The following abbreviations are used in this list: *adj.* (adjective), *dir. obj.* (direct object), *f.* (feminine), *fam.* (familiar), *ind. obj.* (indirect object), *inf.* (infinitive), *m.* (masculine), *pl.* (plural), *prep.* (preposition), *pron.* (pronoun), *sing.* (singular).

A

a to (*prep.*) (I)

— **... le gusta(n)** he / she likes (I)

— **... le encanta(n)** he / she loves (I)

— **casa** (to) home (I)

— **causa de** because of (II)

— **favor de** in favor of (5-2)

— **la derecha (de)** to the right (of) (I)

— **la izquierda (de)** to the left (of) (I)

— **la parrilla** on the grill (II)

— **la una de la tarde** at one (o'clock) in the afternoon (I)

— **las ocho de la mañana** at eight (o'clock) in the morning (I)

— **las ocho de la noche** at eight (o'clock) in the evening, at night (I)

— **mano** by hand (II)

— **medida que** as (10-2)

— **menos que** unless (9-2)

— **menudo** often (I)

— **pesar de** despite (10-2)

— **mí también.** I do (like to) too. (I)

— **mí tampoco.** I don't (like to) either. (I)

¿— **qué hora?** (At) what time? (I)

— **tiempo** on time (II)

— **tiempo completo** full time (5-1)

— **tiempo parcial** part time (5-1)

— **través de** through (2-1)

— **veces** sometimes (I)

— **ver.** Let's see. (I)

abdominales crunches (3-2)

abierto, -a open (II)

el **abogado, la abogada** lawyer (II, 6-1)

abordar to board (II)

abrazar(se) to hug (II)

el **abrigo** coat (I)

abril April (I)

abrir to open (I)

abstracto, -a abstract (2-1)

el **abuelo, la abuela** grandfather, grandmother (I)

los **abuelos** grandparents (I)

aburrido, -a boring (I)

aburrir to bore (I)

aburrirse to get bored (II)

me aburre(n) it bores me (they bore me) (I)

el **abuso** abuse (10-1)

acabar de + *inf.* to have just... (I)

el **accidente** accident (II)

el **aceite** cooking oil (II)

aceptar to accept (4-1)

— **tal como (soy)** to accept (me) the way (I am) (4-1)

acercarse a to approach (1-1)

acompañar to accompany (II)

aconsejar to advise (3-2)

acostarse (o → ue) to go to bed (II)

las **actividades extracurriculares** extracurricular activities (II)

el **actor** actor (I)

la **actriz,** *pl.* **las actrices** actress (I)

la **actuación** acting (II)

actuar to perform (2-2)

el **acueducto** aqueduct (8-1)

acuerdo:

Estoy de —. I agree. (I)

No estoy de —. I don't agree. (I)

el **acusado, la acusada** accused (10-2)

acusar to accuse (4-2)

adecuado, -a adequate (10-1)

además de in addition to, besides (II, 6-1)

¡Adiós! Good-bye! (I)

la **adolescencia** adolescence (10-1)

el / la **adolescente** adolescent (10-1)

¿Adónde? (To) where? (I)

adoptar to adopt (8-2)

la **aduana** customs (II)

el **aduanero, la aduanera** customs officer (II)

el **aeropuerto** airport (II)

el **aerosol** aerosol (9-2)

afectar to affect (9-2)

afeitarse to shave (II)

el **aficionado, la aficionada** fan (II)

afortunadamente fortunately (II)

africano, -a African (8-2)

la **agencia de viajes** travel agency (II)

el / la **agente de viajes** travel agent (II)

agitado, -a agitated (II)

agosto August (I)

agotar(se) to exhaust, to run out (9-1)

agradable pleasant (5-1)

el **agricultor, la agricultora** farmer (II)

el **agua** *f.* water (I)

   el **— de colonia** cologne (II)

el **aguacate** avocado (II)

aguantar to endure, to tolerate (3-2)

el **águila calva,** *pl.* **las águilas calvas** bald eagle (9-2)

el **agujero** hole (9-2)

ahora now (I)

ahorrar to save (II, 6-1)

el **aire acondicionado** air conditioner (II)

el **ajedrez** chess (II)

el **ajo** garlic (II)

al *(a + el),* **a la** to the (I)

   — aire libre outdoors (II)

   — amanecer at dawn (1-1)

   — anochecer at dusk (1-1)

   — final at the end (II)

   — horno baked (II)

   — igual que as, like (7-2)

   — lado de next to (I)

   — llegar upon arriving (8-2)

   — principio at the beginning (1-2)

alcanzar to reach (1-2)

alegrarse to be delighted (4-1)

alegre happy (II)

la **alergia** allergy (3-1)

la **alfombra** rug (I)

algo something (I)

   ¿**— más?** Anything else? (I)

el **algodón** cotton (II)

alguien someone, anyone (II)

algún, alguno, -a some (II)

   — día some day (II)

algunos, as any (II)

la **alimentación** nutrition, feeding (3-1)

los **alimentos** food (3-1)

allí there (I)

   una vez — once there (1-1)

el **almacén,** *pl.* **los almacenes** department store (I)

almorzar (o → ue) to have lunch (II)

el **almuerzo** lunch (I)

en el — for lunch (I)

alquilar to rent (II)

alrededor de around (II)

alto, -a tall (I); high (II)

el **alto** height (7-1)

amable kind, nice (4-1)

amanecer:

   al — at dawn (1-1)

amarillo, -a yellow (I)

ambicioso, -a ambitious (6-1)

ambiental environmental (9-2)

ambos both (10-1)

la **ambulancia** ambulance (II)

la **amenaza** threat (9-2)

amenazar to threaten (9-1)

la **amistad** friendship (4-1)

el **amor** love (II)

añadir to add (II)

anaranjado, -a orange (I)

ancho, -a wide (II)

el **ancho** width (7-1)

el **anciano, la anciana** elderly man, elderly woman (I)

los **ancianos** the elderly (I)

andar to walk, to move (1-1)

el **anillo** ring (I)

animado, -a excited (1-2)

el **animador, la animadora** cheerleader (II)

el **animal** animal (I)

el **aniversario** anniversary (II)

anoche last night (I)

anochecer:

   al — at dusk (1-1)

ante before (10-1)

los **anteojos de sol** sunglasses (I)

el **antepasado, la antepasada** ancestor (8-2)

anteriormente before (8-1)

antes de before (I, II)

el **antibiótico** antibiotic (3-1)

antiguo, -a old, antique (II)

anunciar to announce (II)

el **anuncio** announcement (II)

   el **— clasificado** classified ad (5-1)

el **año** year (I)

   el **— pasado** last year (I)

   ¿**Cuántos —s tiene(n)...?** How old is / are...? (I)

   Tiene(n)...—s. He / She is / They are...(years old). (I)

apagar to put out *(fire)* (II); to turn off (II)

el **aparato** gadget (6-2)

aparecer (zc) to appear (1-1, 7-2)

el **apartamento** apartment (I)

aplaudir to applaud (II)

el **aplauso** applause (2-2)

aplicar (las leyes) to apply (the law) (10-1)

apoyar(se) to support, to back (each other) (4-1)

el **apoyo** support (10-1)

aprender (a) to learn (I)

   — de memoria to memorize (II)

apretado, -a tight (II)

apropiado, -a appropriate (3-1)

aproximadamente approximately (II)

aquel, aquella that one (over there) (II)

aquellos, aquellas those (over there) (II)

aquí here (I)

el / la **árabe** Arab (8-1)

el **árbol** tree (I)

el **arco** arch (8-1)

los **aretes** earrings (I)

el **argumento** plot (II)

el **arma,** *pl.* **las armas** weapon (8-2)

el **armario** closet, locker (I, II, 10-1)

la **armonía** harmony (4-2)

el **arqueólogo, la arqueóloga** archaeologist (7-1)

el **arquitecto, la arquitecta** architect (II, 6-1)

la **arquitectura** architecture (8-1)

arreglar (el cuarto) to straighten up (the room) (I)

arreglarse (el pelo) to fix (one's hair) (II)

arrestar to arrest (II)

arrojar (se) to throw (7-2)

el arroz rice (I)

el arte:

    la clase de — art class (I)

    la obra de — work of art (2-1)

    las artes the arts (II)

    las — marciales martial arts (II)

la artesanía handicrafts (II)

el artículo article (II)

el / la artista artist (II)

artístico, -a artistic (I)

asado, -a grilled (II)

asar to grill (II)

el ascensor elevator (II)

asco:

    ¡Qué —! How awful! (I)

asegurar to assure (10-2)

así this way (1-1)

    — que therefore (6-1)

el asiento seat (II)

asimilar(se) to assimilate (8-1)

asistir a to attend (II)

la aspiración aspiration (10-2)

la aspirina aspirin (3-1)

el astrónomo, la astrónoma astronomer (7-2)

el asunto matter (10-1)

asustado, -a frightened (II)

asustar to scare (1-1)

atender to help, to assist (5-1)

atento, -a attentive (II)

el / la atleta athlete (II)

la atmósfera atmosphere (9-2)

la atracción, *pl.* **las atracciones** attraction (I)

atrapar to catch, trap (9-2)

atreverse to dare (4-2)

atrevido, -a daring (I)

la audición, *pl.* **las audiciones** audition (II)

el auditorio auditorium (II)

aumentar to increase (6-2)

aunque despite, even when (3-1)

el autobús, *pl.* **los autobuses** bus (I)

la autoridad authority (10-1)

el autorretrato self-portrait (2-1)

el / la auxiliar de vuelo flight attendant (II)

el avance advance (6-2)

el ave bird (9-2)

la avenida avenue (II)

averiguar to find out (6-1)

el avión airplane (I)

¡Ay! ¡Qué pena! Oh! What a shame / pity! (I)

ayer yesterday (I)

la ayuda help (II)

ayudar to help (I)

el azúcar sugar (I)

azul blue (I)

el azulejo tile (8-1)

B

bailar to dance (I)

el bailarín, la bailarina dancer (II)

el baile dance (I)

bajar to go down (II)

bajar (información) to download (I)

bajo, -a short *(stature)* (I); low (II)

la planta baja ground floor (I)

el balcón, *pl.* **los balcones** balcony (8-1)

la ballena whale (9-2)

el banco bank (II)

la banda (musical) band (II)

la bandera flag (I)

el banquero, la banquera banker (6-1)

bañarse to take a bath (II)

el baño bathroom (I)

    el traje de — swimsuit (I)

barato, -a inexpensive, cheap (I)

el barco boat, ship (I)

el barrio neighborhood (I)

¡Basta! Enough! (II)

el básquetbol:

    jugar al — to play basketball (I)

bastante enough, rather (I)

basura:

    sacar la — to take out the trash (I)

la batalla battle (8-2)

batir to beat (II)

el / la bebé baby (II)

beber to drink (I)

las bebidas drinks (I)

béisbol: jugar al — to play baseball (I)

bello, -a beautiful (II)

beneficiar to benefit (5-2)

los beneficios benefits (II, 5-1)

besar(se) to kiss (II)

la biblioteca library (I)

bien well (I)

    — educado, -a well-behaved (II)

    pasarlo — to have a good time (1-1)

bienvenido, -a welcome (II)

bilingüe bilingual (II)

los binoculares binoculars (1-1)

el bistec steak (I)

blanco, -a white (I)

los bloques blocks (II)

la blusa blouse (I)

la boca mouth (I)

la boda wedding (II)

el boleto ticket (I)

el bolígrafo pen (I)

los bolos:

    jugar a los — to bowl (II)

la bolsa bag, sack (I)

el bolso purse (I)

el bombero, la bombera firefighter (II)

bonito, -a pretty (I)

el bosque wood, forest (II, 1-1)

las botas boots (I)

el bote:

    pasear en — to go boating (I)

    el — de vela sailboat (II)

la botella bottle (I)

el brazo arm (I)

brillar to shine (7-2)

la brújula compass (1-1)

bucear to scuba dive, to snorkel (I)

bueno (buen), -a good (I)

Buenas noches. Good evening. (I)

Buenas tardes. Good afternoon. (I)

Buenos días. Good morning. (I)

buscar to look for, to search (for) (I)

la **búsqueda** search (II)

    hacer una — to do a search (II)

el **buzón,** *pl.* **los buzones** mailbox (II)

C

el **caballo:**

    montar a — to ride horseback (I)

la **cabeza** head (I)

    cada día every day (I)

la **cadena** chain (I)

    caer granizo to hail (1-1)

    caerse to fall (II)

      — de sueño to be exhausted, sleepy (3-2)

      (yo) me caigo I fall (II)

      (tú) te caes you fall (II)

el **café** coffee; café (I)

la **caja** box (I); cash register (II)

el **cajero, la cajera** cashier (II)

    el — automático ATM (II)

el **calambre** cramp (3-2)

los **calcetines** socks (I)

el **calcio** calcium (3-1)

la **calculadora** calculator (I)

    calcular to calculate, to compute (7-1)

el **caldo** broth (II)

la **calefacción** heat (II)

    calentar (e → ie) to heat (II)

    caliente hot (II)

la **calle** street, road (I)

    calor:

      Hace —. It's hot. (I)

      tener — to be warm (I)

la **cama** bed (I)

    hacer la — to make the bed (I)

la **cámara** camera (I)

    la — digital digital camera (I)

el **camarero, la camarera** waiter, waitress (I)

el **camarón,** *pl.* **los camarones** shrimp (II)

    cambiar to change, to exchange (II)

      — de opinión to change one's mind (4-1)

    caminar to walk (I)

la **caminata** walk (II)

    dar una — to take a walk (II)

el **camión,** *pl.* **los camiones** truck (II)

la **camisa** shirt (I)

la **camiseta** T-shirt (I)

el **campamento** camp (I)

la **campaña** campaign (5-2)

el **campeón, la campeona,** *pl.* **los campeones** champion (II)

el **campeonato** championship (II)

el **campo** countryside, field (I, 6-2)

el **canal** (TV) channel (I)

la **canción,** *pl.* **las canciones** song (I, II)

    canoso: pelo — gray hair (I)

    cansado, -a tired (I)

el / la **cantante** singer (II)

    cantar to sing (I)

la **capa de ozono** ozone layer (9-2)

    capaz able (6-1)

    capturar to capture (II)

la **cara** face (II)

    cara a cara face-to-face (I)

    caramba good gracious (II)

el **carbohidrato** carbohydrate (3-1)

    cariñoso, -a loving, affectionate (4-1)

la **carne** meat (I)

    la — de res beef (II)

el **carnet de identidad** I.D. card (II)

    caro, -a expensive (I)

la **carpeta** folder (I)

    la — de argollas three-ring binder (I)

la **carrera** race (II, 1-2); career (II)

la **carretera** highway (II)

la **carta** letter (I, II)

    echar una — to mail a letter (II)

el **cartel** poster (I)

la **cartera** wallet (I)

el **cartero, la cartera** mail carrier (II)

el **cartón** cardboard (I)

la **casa** home, house (I)

    a — (to) home (I)

    en — at home (I)

    — de cambio money exchange (II)

    casado, -a married (6-1)

    casarse (con) to get married to (II)

    casi almost (I, II)

    castaño:

      pelo — brown (chestnut) hair (I)

    castigar to punish (9-1)

el **castigo** punishment (10-2)

el **castillo** castle (II)

la **catedral** cathedral (II)

    catorce fourteen (I)

la **causa** cause (II)

la **caza** hunting (9-2)

la **cebolla** onion (I)

    celebrar to celebrate (I)

    celos:

      tener celos to be jealous (4-1)

    celoso, -a jealous (4-1)

la **cena** dinner (I)

    centígrado

      el grado — centigrade degree (3-1)

el **centímetro** centimeter (7-1)

el **centro** center, downtown (I, II)

    el — comercial mall (I)

    el — de la comunidad community center (5-2)

    el — de reciclaje recycling center (I)

    el — de rehabilitación rehabilitation center (5-2)

el — recreativo recreation center (5-2)

cepillarse (los dientes) to brush (one's teeth) (II)

el cepillo brush (II)

el — de dientes toothbrush (II)

la cerámica pottery (2-1)

cerca (de) close (to), near (I)

el cerdo pork (II)

la chuleta de — pork chop (II)

el cereal cereal (I)

la ceremonia ceremony (1-2)

la cereza cherry (II)

cero zero (I)

cerrado, -a closed (II)

cerrar to close (II)

el certificado certificate, diploma (1-2)

la cesta basket (II)

el champú shampoo (II)

la chaqueta jacket (I)

charlar to chat (II)

el cheque:

cobrar un — to cash a check (II)

el — de viajero traveler's check (II)

el — personal personal check (II)

la chica girl (I)

el chico boy (I)

chismoso, -a gossipy (4-1)

chocar con to crash into, to collide with (II)

la chuleta de cerdo pork chop (II)

el cielo sky (II)

cien one hundred (I)

las ciencias:

la clase de — naturales science class (I)

la clase de — sociales social studies class (I)

el científico, la científica scientist (II, 6-1)

(es) cierto (it is) true (II)

cinco five (I)

cincuenta fifty (I)

el cine movie theater (I)

la cinta adhesiva adhesive tape (II)

el cinturón, *pl.* **los cinturones** belt (II)

el círculo circle (7-1)

la cita date (II)

la ciudad city (I)

la ciudadanía citizenship (5-2)

el ciudadano, la ciudadana citizen (5-2)

la civilización civilization (7-1)

claro, -a light *(color)* (II)

la clase class (I)

la sala de clases classroom (I)

¿Qué — de...? What kind of...? (I)

clásico, -a classical (2-2)

el cliente, la clienta client (5-1)

el clima weather (9-2)

el club, *pl.* **los clubes** club (II)

el — atlético athletic club (II)

cobrar un cheque to cash a check (II)

el coche car (I)

la cocina kitchen (I)

cocinar to cook (I)

el cocinero, la cocinera cook (6-1)

el código de vestimenta dress code (10-1)

el codo elbow (II)

colaborar to collaborate (4-2)

la colección, *pl.* **las colecciones** collection (II)

coleccionar to collect (II)

el colegio secondary school, high school (II)

la colina hill (II)

el collar necklace (I)

colocar to put, place (9-1)

la colonia colony (8-2)

el color, *pl.* **los colores** (I)

¿De qué — ...? What color...? (I)

la comedia comedy (I)

el comedor dining room (I)

el — de beneficencia soup kitchen (5-2)

el comentario commentary (II)

comenzar (e → ie) to start (II)

comer to eat (I)

cómico, -a funny, comical (I)

la comida food, meal (I)

la — basura junk food (3-1)

como like, as (I)

— si fuera as though it were (6-2)

¿Cómo?:

¿— eres? What are you like? (I)

¿— es? What is he / she like? (I)

¿— está Ud.? How are you? *formal* (I)

¿— estás? How are you? *fam.* (I)

¿— lo pasaste? How was it (for you)? (I)

¿— se dice...? How do you say...? (I)

¿— se escribe...? How is... spelled? (I)

¿— se hace...? How do you make...? (II)

¿— se llama? What's his / her name? (I)

¿— se va a...? How do you go to...? (II)

¿— te llamas? What is your name? (I)

¿— te queda(n)? How does it (do they) fit you? (I)

¡Cómo no! Of course! (II)

la cómoda dresser (I)

cómodo, -a comfortable (II)

la compañía firm, company (5-1)

compartir to share (I)

el compás rhythm (2-2)

la competencia competition (II)

competir (e → i) to compete (II)

complicado, -a complicated (I, II)

componerse de to be formed by (8-2)

el comportamiento behavior (4-2)

la composición, *pl.* **las composiciones** composition (I)

comprar to buy (I)

   — recuerdos to buy souvenirs (I)

comprender to understand (I)

comprensivo, -a understanding (4-1)

la computación computer science (5-1)

la computadora computer (I)

   la — portátil laptop computer (I)

   usar la — to use the computer (I)

comunicarse to communicate (I, 6-2)

   (tú) te comunicas you communicate (I)

   (yo) me comunico I communicate (I)

la comunidad community (I)

con with (I)

   — destino a going to (II)

   — mis / tus amigos with my / your friends (I)

   — tal de que provided that (9-2)

   ¿— qué se sirve? What do you serve it with? (II)

   ¿— quién? With whom? (I)

concentrarse to concentrate (3-2)

el concierto concert (I)

el concurso contest (II)

   el — de belleza beauty contest (II)

el conductor, la conductora driver (II)

el conejo rabbit (7-2)

confianza trust (4-1)

   — en sí mismo, -a self-confidence (3-2)

confiar (i → í) to trust (4-1)

el conflicto conflict (4-2)

congelado, -a frozen (II)

el conjunto band (2-2)

conmigo with me (I)

conocer to know, to be acquainted with (I, II)

los conocimientos knowledge (5-1)

la conquista conquest (8-1)

conquistar to conquer (8-1)

conseguir (e → i) to obtain (II)

el consejero, la consejera counselor (5-1)

el consejo advice (3-2)

consentido, -a spoiled (II)

conservar to conserve (II, 9-1)

considerado, -a considerate (4-1)

la construcción construction (8-1)

construir (i → y) to build (5-2)

el consultorio doctor's / dentist's office (II)

el contador, la contadora accountant (II, 6-1)

la contaminación pollution (II, 9-1)

contaminado, -a polluted (II, 9-1)

contaminar to pollute (6-2)

contar (chistes) (o → ue) to tell (jokes) (II)

   — con to count on (4-1)

contener to contain (3-1)

contento, -a happy (I)

contestar to answer (II)

contigo with you (I)

contra against (II, 1-2)

   en — (de) against (5-2)

contribuir (u → y) to contribute (7-2)

convertirse (en) to turn (into), to become (7-2)

el corazón heart (3-2)

la corbata tie (I)

el coro chorus, choir (II)

el correo post office (II)

el correo electrónico e-mail (I)

   escribir por — to write e-mail (I)

correr to run (I)

cortar to cut (I, II)

   — el césped to mow the lawn (I)

   —se to cut oneself (II)

   —se el pelo to cut one's hair (II)

cortés, pl. corteses polite (II)

las cortinas curtains (I)

corto, -a short (length) (I)

   los pantalones —s shorts (I)

la cosa thing (I)

costar (o → ue) to cost (I)

   ¿Cuánto cuesta(n)...? How much does (do)...cost? (I)

la costumbre custom (II)

crear to create (I)

   — una página Web to create a Web page (II)

crecer to grow (9-1)

la creencia belief (7-2)

creer:

   Creo que... I think... (I)

   Creo que no. I don't think so. (I)

   Creo que sí. I think so. (I)

el crimen crime (II)

el / la criminal criminal (II)

el cristiano, la cristiana Christian (8-1)

criticar to criticize (4-2)

el crítico, la crítica critic (II)

el cruce de calles intersection (II)

cruzar to cross (II)

el cuaderno notebook (I)

la cuadra block (II)

el cuadro painting (I)

¿Cuál? Which? What? (I)

   ¿— es la fecha? What is the date? (I)

la cualidad quality (4-1)

cualquier, -a any (7-2)

¿Cuándo? When? (I)

¿Cuánto?:

   ¿— cuesta(n)...? How much does (do)...cost? (I)

   ¿— tiempo hace que...? How long (has)...? (II)

¿Cuántos, -as? How many? (I)

   ¿—s años tiene(n)...? How old is / are...? (I)

cuanto:

   en — a with respect to, as for (10-1)

   en — as soon as (9-1)

cuarenta forty (I)

cuarto, -a fourth (I)

   y — quarter past *(in telling time)* (I)

el cuarto room (I)

cuatro four (I)

cuatrocientos, -as four hundred (I)

cubrir to cover (7-1)

la cuchara spoon (I)

la cucharada tablespoon(ful) (II)

el cuchillo knife (I)

el cuello neck (II)

la cuenta bill (I)

   tener en — to take into account (6-2)

la cuerda rope (II)

el cuero leather (II)

cuidadoso, -a careful (6-1)

cuidar a to take care of (II)

culpable guilty (10-2)

el cumpleaños birthday (I)

   ¡Feliz —! Happy birthday! (I)

cumplir años to have a birthday (II)

cumplir con to carry out, to perform (5-1)

el cupón de regalo, *pl.* los cupones de regalo gift certificate (II)

curar to cure (6-2)

el curso:

   tomar un curso to take a course (I)

D

la danza dance (2-2)

dañar to damage (9-1)

dar to give (I)

   — + *movie or TV program* to show (I)

   — de comer al perro to feed the dog (I)

   — puntadas to stitch *(surgically)* (II)

   — un discurso to give a speech (II)

   — un paseo to take a walk, to stroll (1-1)

   — una caminata to take a walk (II)

dar(se) la mano to shake hands (II)

darse cuenta de to realize (1-2)

de of, from (I)

   — acuerdo. OK. Agreed. (II)

   — algodón cotton (II)

   — cuero leather (II)

   ¿— dónde eres? Where are you from? (I)

   — ida y vuelta round trip (II)

   — la mañana / la tarde / la noche in the morning / afternoon / evening (I)

   — lana wool (II)

   — negocios business (II)

   — niño as a child (II)

   — oro gold (II)

   — pequeño as a child (II)

   — plata silver (II)

   — plato principal as a main dish (I)

   — postre for dessert (I)

   — prisa in a hurry (II)

   ¿— qué color...? What color...? (I)

   ¿— qué está hecho, -a? What is it made of? (II)

   — repente suddenly (II)

   — seda silk (II)

   — sólo un color solid-colored (II)

   — tela sintética synthetic fabric (II)

   ¿— veras? Really? (I)

   — vez en cuando once in a while (II)

debajo de underneath (I)

deber should, must (I)

el deber duty (10-1)

debido a due to (9-1)

débil weak (3-2)

decidir to decide (I)

décimo, -a tenth (I)

decir to say, to tell (I)

   — la verdad to tell the truth (II)

   ¿Cómo se dice...? How do you say...? (I)

dime tell me (I)

¡No me digas! You don't say! (I)

¿Qué quiere —...? What does...mean? (I)

Quiere — ... It means... (I)

Se dice... You say..., people say... (I)

las decoraciones decorations (I)

decorar to decorate (I)

dedicado, -a dedicated (5-1)

dedicarse a to dedicate oneself to (6-1)

el dedo finger (I)

Déjame en paz. Leave me alone. (II)

dejar to leave, to let (II)

   — de to stop (doing something) (1-1)

   — huellas to leave marks, traces (8-1)

   no dejes don't leave, don't let (II)

delante de in front of (I)

delicioso, -a delicious (I)

la demanda demand (6-2)

los / las demás others (I)

demasiado too (I)

democrático, -a democratic (10-2)

el / la dentista dentist (II)

dentro de inside (II)

depende it depends (II)

depender de to depend on (9-1)

el dependiente, la dependienta salesperson (I)

deportista athletic, sports-minded (I)

derecha:

   a la — (de) to the right (of) (I)

derecho straight (II)

el derecho *(study of)* law (II)

los derechos rights (5-2)

el derrame de petróleo oil spill (9-2)

derretir to melt (9-2)

desafortunadamente unfortunately (1-2)

desanimado, -a discouraged (1-2)

desaparecer to disappear (6-2)

desarrollar to develop (3-2)

el **desarrollo** development (6-2)

el **desayuno** breakfast (I)

en el — for breakfast (I)

descansar to rest, to relax (I)

la **descendencia** descent, ancestry (8-2)

desconfiar to mistrust (4-1)

desconocido, -a unknown (8-2)

descubrir to discover (6-2)

los **descuentos:**

la **tienda de** — discount store (I)

desde from, since (II)

desear to wish (I)

¿Qué desean (Uds.)? What would you like? *formal* (I)

desempeñar un cargo to hold a position (6-1)

el **desempleo** unemployment (10-2)

el **desfile** parade (II)

deshacerse de to get rid of (9-1)

el **desierto** desert (II, 1-1)

la **desigualdad** inequity (10-2)

desobediente disobedient (II)

el **desodorante** deodorant (II)

desordenado, -a messy (I)

despacio slowly (II)

el **despacho** office, study (home) (I)

despedirse (e → i) de to say good-bye (II)

el **despertador** alarm clock (I)

desperdiciar to waste (9-1)

el **desperdicio** waste (9-1)

despertarse (e → ie) to wake up (II)

después (de) afterwards, after (I)

destacar(se) to stand out (2-2)

la **destrucción** destruction (II)

destruir (i → y) to destroy (II)

el / la **detective** detective (II)

detener to detain (10-2), to stop (9-2)

detrás de behind (I)

devolver (o → ue) (un libro) to return (a book) (II)

el **día** day (I)

Buenos —s. Good morning. (I)

cada — every day (I)

el — festivo holiday (II)

¿Qué — es hoy? What day is today? (I)

todos los —s every day (I)

el **diámetro** diameter (7-1)

la **diapositiva** slide (I)

dibujar to draw (I)

el **diccionario** dictionary (I)

diciembre December (I)

diecinueve nineteen (I)

dieciocho eighteen (I)

dieciséis sixteen (I)

diecisiete seventeen (I)

los **dientes** teeth (II)

cepillarse — to brush one's teeth (II)

el cepillo de — toothbrush (II)

la **dieta** diet (3-1)

diez ten (I)

la **diferencia de opinión** difference of opinion (4-2)

difícil difficult (I)

digital:

la **cámara** — digital camera (I)

dime tell me (I)

el **dinero** money (I)

— **en efectivo** cash (II)

el **dinosaurio** dinosaur (II)

el **dios, la diosa** god, goddess (7-2)

la **dirección,** *pl.* **las direcciones** direction (II)

la — **electrónica** e-mail address (I)

directo, -a direct (II)

el **director, la directora** (school) principal (II)

el **disco compacto** compact disc (I)

grabar un — to burn a CD (I)

discriminado, -a discriminated (10-1)

discriminar to discriminate (10-1)

el **discurso** speech (II)

discutir to discuss (II)

el **diseñador, la diseñadora** designer (II, 6-1)

diseñar to design (6-1)

el **diseño** design (7-1)

disfrutar de to enjoy (II)

disminuir (i→y) to decrease, to diminish (9-2)

la **distancia** distance (7-1)

divertido, -a amusing, fun (I)

divertirse (e → ie) to have fun (II)

doblar to turn (II)

doce twelve (I)

el **documento** document (I)

doler (o → ue) to hurt (I, II)

el **dolor** pain (II)

dominar to dominate (8-1)

domingo Sunday (I)

donar to donate (5-2)

dónde:

¿—? Where? (I)

¿De — eres? Where are you from? (I)

dormido, -a asleep (II)

dormir (o → ue) to sleep (I)

—se to fall asleep (II)

el saco de — sleeping bag (1-1)

el **dormitorio** bedroom (I)

dos two (I)

los / las **dos** both (I)

doscientos, -as two hundred (I)

el **drama** drama (I)

la **ducha** shower (II)

ducharse to take a shower (II)

dudar to doubt (II, 7-1)

el **dueño, la dueña** owner (II, 5-1)

dulce sweet (II)

los **dulces** candy (I)

durante during (I)

durar to last (I, II)

el durazno peach (II)

duro, -a hard (1-2)

E

echar to throw (away) (9-1)

— una carta to mail a letter (II)

el eclipse eclipse (7-2)

ecológico, -a ecological (II)

económico, -a economical (II, 9-1)

la edad age (3-1)

el edificio de apartamentos apartment building (II)

la educación física:

la clase de — physical education class (I)

educar to educate (5-2)

efecto:

el — invernadero greenhouse effect (9-2)

los efectos especiales special effects (II)

eficiente efficient (II, 6-1)

egoísta selfish (4-1)

el ejercicio:

hacer — to exercise (I)

ejercicios aeróbicos aerobics (3-2)

el m. sing. the (I)

él he (I)

la electricidad electricity (II, 9-1)

los electrodomésticos:

la tienda de — household-appliance store (I)

electrónico, -a:

la dirección — e-mail address (I)

elegante elegant (II)

eliminar to eliminate (II, 1-2)

ella she (I)

ellas f. they (I)

ellos m. they (I)

emocionado, -a excited, emotional (II)

emocionante touching (I)

emocionarse to be moved (1-2)

el empate tie (II)

empezar (e → ie) to begin, to start (I, II)

el empleado, la empleada employee (II)

emprendedor, -a enterprising (6-1)

la empresa business (6-1)

en in, on (I)

— + vehicle by, in, on (I)

— casa at home (I)

— contra (de) against (5-2)

— cuanto as soon as (9-1)

— cuanto a with respect to (10-1)

— la…hora in the…hour (class period) (I)

— la Red online (I)

— lugar de instead of (10-2)

— medio de in the middle of (II)

— punto exactly (II)

¿— qué puedo servirle? How can I help you? (I)

— realidad really (II)

— seguida right away (II)

— vez de instead of (9-2)

enamorado, -a de in love with (II)

enamorarse (de) to fall in love (with) (II)

encantado, -a delighted (I)

encantar to please very much, to love (I)

a él / ella le encanta(n) he / she loves (I)

me encantaría I would love to… (5-2)

me / te encanta(n)… I / you love… (I)

encargarse (de) (g → gu) to be in charge (of) (5-1)

encender (e → ie) to turn on, to light (II)

encima de on top of (I)

encontrar (o → ue) to find (II)

el encuentro meeting (8-2)

la energía energy (II, 3-1)

la fuente de — energy source (6-2)

enero January (I)

la enfermedad illness (6-2)

el enfermero, la enfermera nurse (II)

enfermo, -a sick (I)

enfrentarse to face, to confront (8-2)

enlatado, -a canned (II)

enojado, -a angry (II)

enojarse to get angry (II)

enorme enormous (II)

la ensalada salad (I)

la — de frutas fruit salad (I)

ensayar to rehearse (II)

el ensayo rehearsal (II)

la enseñanza teaching (10-1)

enseñar to teach (I)

entender (e → ie) to understand (II)

enterarse to find out (6-2)

entonces then (I)

la entrada entrance (II), ticket (2-2)

entrar to enter (I)

entre among, between (II)

la entrega de premios awards ceremony (1-2)

entregar to turn in (II)

— la tarea a tiempo to turn in homework on time (II)

el entrenador, la entrenadora coach, trainer (II)

el entrenamiento training (1-2)

entrenarse to train (1-2)

la entrevista interview (II, 5-1)

entrevistar to interview (II)

entrometido, -a meddlesome, interfering (4-1)

entusiasmado, -a excited (II)

el entusiasmo enthusiasm (2-2)

enviar to send (I, II)

la época time, era (8-1)

equilibrado, -a balanced (3-1)

el equipaje luggage (II)

facturar el — to check luggage (II)

el equipo team (II)

    el — de sonido sound (stereo) system (I)

    el — deportivo sports equipment (II)

¿Eres...? Are you...? (I)

es is; (he / she / it) is (I)

    — cierto it's true (II)

    — el *(number)* **de** *(month)* it is the... of... *(in telling the date)* (I)

    — el primero de *(month)*. It is the first of... (I)

    — la una. It is one o'clock. (I)

    — necesario. It's necessary. (I)

    — un(a)... It's a... (I)

la escala stopover (II)

escalar to climb (a rock or mountain) (1-1)

la escalera stairs, stairway (I); ladder (II)

escaparse to escape (II)

la escasez shortage (9-1)

la escena scene (II)

el escenario stage (2-2)

escoger to choose (II)

esconder(se) to hide (oneself) (II)

escribir: to write (I)

    ¿Cómo se escribe...? How is...spelled? (I)

    — cuentos to write stories (I)

    — por correo electrónico to write e-mail (I)

    — un informe sobre... to write a report about...

    Se escribe... It's spelled... (I)

el escritor, la escritora writer (II, 2-2)

el escritorio desk (I)

la escritura writing (7-2)

escuchar música to listen to music (I)

la escuela primaria primary school (I)

la escuela técnica technical school (II)

el escultor, la escultora sculptor (2-1)

la escultura sculpture (2-1)

ese, esa that (I, II)

    de ese modo in that way (10-1)

eso:

    por — that's why, therefore (I)

esos, esas those (I, II)

el espacio (outer) space (II)

los espaguetis spaghetti (I)

la espalda back (II)

el español:

    la clase de — Spanish class (I)

especial special (II)

especialmente especially (I)

la especie species (9-2)

el espectáculo show (2-2)

el espejo mirror (I)

    esperar to hope (for) (4-1); to wait (II)

la esposa wife (I)

el esposo husband (I)

el esquí acuático water-skiing (II)

    esquiar to ski (I)

la esquina corner (II)

    Está hecho, -a de... It is made of... (II)

    establecer (zc) to establish (8-2)

la estación, *pl.* **las estaciones** season (I)

    la — de servicio service station (II)

el estadio stadium (I)

el estado state (10-1)

el estante shelf, bookshelf (I)

estar to be (I)

    ¿Cómo está Ud.? How are you? *formal* (I)

    ¿Cómo estás? How are you? *fam.* (I)

    — + *present participle* to be + *present participle* (I)

    — a cargo de to be in charge of (9-1)

    — basado, -a en to be based on (II)

    — de buen / mal humor to be in a good / bad mood (3-2)

    — de moda to be in fashion (II)

    — en la luna to be daydreaming (3-2)

    — en línea to be online (I)

    — enamorado, -a de to be in love with (II)

    — equivocado, -a to be mistaken (4-2)

    — orgulloso / orgullosa de to be proud of (1-2)

    — resfriado, -a to have a cold (3-1)

    — seguro, -a to be sure (II)

    — sujeto, -a a to be subject to (10-1)

Estoy de acuerdo. I agree. (I)

No estoy de acuerdo. I don't agree. (I)

la estatua statue (II)

la estatura height (3-1)

este, esta this (I, II)

    esta noche this evening (I)

    esta tarde this afternoon (I)

    este fin de semana this weekend (I)

el estilo style (II)

estirar to stretch (3-2)

el estómago stomach (I)

estornudar to sneeze (3-1)

estos, estas these (I, II)

Estoy de acuerdo. I agree. (I)

la estrategia strategy (6-2)

estrecho, -a narrow (II)

la estrella (del cine) (movie) star (II)

el estrés stress (3-2)

estresado, -a stressed out (3-2)

la estructura structure (7-1)

el / la estudiante student (I)

estudiar to study (I)

estudioso, -a studious (I)

la estufa stove (II)

estupendo, -a stupendous, wonderful (II)

europeo, -a European (8-2)

la evidencia proof, evidence (7-1)

el evento especial special event (II)

evitar to avoid (3-1)

exagerado, -a outrageous (II)

exagerar to exaggerate (2-2)

examinar to examine, to check (II)

excavar excavate (7-1)

excesivo, -a excessive (9-2)

exigir to demand (3-2)

existir to exist (7-1)

el éxito success (II)

    tener — to be successful (II)

la excursión, *pl.* **las excursiones** excursion, short trip (II)

la experiencia experience (I)

la explicación explanation (4-2)

explicar to explain (II)

la explosión, *pl.* **las explosiones** explosion (II)

explotar to exploit, to overwork (9-2)

expresar(se) to express (oneself) (2-1)

expulsar to expel (8-1)

extracurricular extracurricular (II)

extinción:

    (en) peligro de — (in) danger of extinction, endangered (9-2)

extranjero, -a foreign (II)

extraño, -a strange (7-1)

el / la extraterrestre alien (II)

F

la fábrica factory (6-2)

fácil easy (I)

facturar (el equipaje) to check (luggage) (II)

la falda skirt (I)

la falta lack (9-2)

    la — de lack of (10-2)

faltar to be missing (I)

famoso, -a famous (II, 2-1)

fantástico, -a fantastic (I)

la farmacia pharmacy (II)

fascinante fascinating (I)

fascinar to fascinate (II)

favorito, -a favorite (I)

febrero February (I)

la fecha:

    ¿Cuál es la —? What is the date? (I)

    la — de nacimiento date of birth (5-1)

la felicidad happiness (10-1)

    ¡Felicidades! Congratulations! (II)

    ¡Felicitaciones! Congratulations! (1-2)

felicitar to congratulate (II)

    ¡Feliz cumpleaños! Happy birthday! (I)

fenomenal phenomenal (II)

el fenómeno phenomenon (7-1)

feo, -a ugly (I)

la fibra fiber (3-1)

la fiebre fever (3-1)

la fiesta party (I)

    la — de sorpresa surprise party (II)

la figura figure (2-1)

el fin, *pl.* **los fines** purpose (10-2)

el fin de semana:

    este — this weekend (I)

    los fines de semana on weekends (I)

las finanzas finance (6-1)

flexible flexible (5-1)

flexionar to flex, to stretch (3-2)

flexiones:

    hacer — to do push-ups

flojo, -a loose (II)

la flor, *pl.* **las flores** flower (I)

la foca seal (9-2)

la fogata bonfire (II)

fomentar to encourage (9-1)

el fondo background (2-1)

el fósforo match (II)

la foto photo (I)

la fotografía photography (II)

el fotógrafo, la fotógrafa photographer (II)

el fracaso failure (II)

frecuentemente frequently (II)

el fregadero sink (II)

freír (e → í) to fry (II)

las fresas strawberries (I)

fresco, -a fresh (II)

los frijoles beans (II)

el frío:

    Hace —. It's cold. (I)

    tener — to be cold (I)

frito, -a fried (II)

fue it was (I)

    — un desastre. It was a disaster. (I)

el fuego fire (II)

los fuegos artificiales fireworks (II)

la fuente fountain (II); source (II)

    la — de energía energy source (6-2)

    la — de inspiración source of inspiration (2-1)

fuera (de) outside (II)

fuerte strong (3-1)

la fuerza strength (3-2)

la función function (7-1)

funcionar to function, to work (II, 10-1)

fundamental fundamental, vital (10-2)

fundar to found (8-1)

furioso, -a furious (II)

el fútbol:

    jugar al — to play soccer (I)

el fútbol americano:

    jugar al — to play football (I)

el futuro future (II)

G

el galán leading man (II)

la galleta cookie (I)

ganar to win; to earn *(money)* (II)

    — se la vida to make a living (II)

la ganga bargain (II)

el garaje garage (I)

la garantía guarantee (10-2)

garantizar to guarantee (5-2)

la gasolina gasoline (II)

gastar to spend (II)

el gato cat (I)

el gel gel (II)

el gen *pl.* **los genes** gene (6-2)

generalmente generally (I)

generoso, -a generous (II)

la genética genetics (6-2)

¡Genial! Great! (I)

la gente people (I)

    la — sin hogar homeless people (5-2)

geométrico, -a geometric(al) (7-1)

el / la gerente manager (II, 5-1)

el gesto gesture (2-2)

la gimnasia gymnastics (II)

el gimnasio gym (I)

el globo balloon (I)

gobernar (ie) to rule, to govern (8-1)

el gobierno government (9-1)

el gol goal *(in sports)* (II)

    meter un — to score a goal (II)

el golf:

    jugar al — to play golf (I)

la gorra cap (I)

gozar (de) to enjoy (10-1)

grabar to record (II)

    — un disco compacto to burn a CD (I)

gracias thank you (I)

gracioso, -a funny (I)

el grado centígrado centigrade degree (3-1)

la graduación, *pl.* **las graduaciones** graduation (II)

graduarse (u → ú) to graduate (II, 6-1)

los gráficos computer graphics (I)

grande large (I)

el granizo hail (1-1)

    caer — to hail (1-1)

la grapadora stapler (II)

grasoso, -a greasy (II)

gratuito, -a free (10-1)

grave serious (II, 9-1)

la gripe flu (3-1)

gris gray (I)

gritar to scream (II)

el grupo étnico ethnic group (8-1)

los guantes gloves (I)

guapo, -a good-looking (I)

guardar (un secreto) to keep (a secret) (4-1)

la guardería infantil day-care center (II)

la guerra war (II, 8-2)

el / la guía guide (II)

la guía guidebook (II)

los guisantes peas (I)

gustar:

    a él / ella le gusta(n) he / she likes (I)

    (A mí) me gusta... I like to... (I)

    (A mí) me gusta más... I like to...better (I prefer to...) (I)

    (A mí) me gusta mucho... I like to...a lot (I)

    (A mí) no me gusta... I don't like to... (I)

    (A mí) no me gusta nada... I don't like to...at all. (I)

    Le gusta... He / She likes... (I)

    Me gusta... I like... (I)

    Me gustaría... I would like... (I)

    Me gustó. I liked it. (I)

    No le gusta... He / She doesn't like... (I)

    ¿Qué te gusta hacer? What do you like to do? (I)

    ¿Qué te gusta hacer más? What do you like to do better / prefer to do? (I)

    Te gusta... You like... (I)

    ¿Te gusta...? Do you like to...? (I)

    ¿Te gustaría...? Would you like...? (I)

    ¿Te gustó? Did you like it? (I)

H

haber to have *(as an auxiliary verb)* (II)

había there was / there were (II)

la habilidad skill (5-1)

la habitación, *pl.* **las habitaciones** room (II)

    la — doble double room (II)

    la — individual single room (II)

el / la habitante inhabitant (7-2)

el hábito alimenticio eating habit (3-1)

hablar to talk (I)

    — por teléfono to talk on the phone (I)

habrá there will be (II)

hacer to do (I)

    hace + *time expression* ago (I)

    Hace + *time* + **que...** It has been... (II)

    Hace calor. It's hot. (I)

    Hace frío. It's cold. (I)

    Hace sol. It's sunny. (I)

    — bicicleta to use a stationary bike (3-2)

    — caso to pay attention, to obey (4-2)

    — cinta to use a treadmill (3-2)

    — ejercicio to exercise (I)

    — el papel de to play the role of (II)

    — escala to stop over (II)

    — flexiones to do push-ups (3-2)

    — gimnasia to do gymnastics (II)

    — la cama to make the bed (I)

    — la maleta to pack the suitcase (II)

    — las paces to make peace with (4-2)

    — ruido to make noise (II)

    — un esfuerzo to make an effort (1-2)

    — un picnic to have a picnic (II)

    — un proyecto to do a project (II)

    — un viaje to take a trip (II)

    — un video to videotape (I)

    — una búsqueda to do a search (II)

— una gira to take a tour (II)

— una parrillada to have a barbecue (II)

— una pregunta to ask a question (II)

haz *(command)* do, make (I)

¿Qué hiciste? What did you do? (I)

¿Qué tiempo hace? What is the weather like? (I)

(tú) haces you do (I)

(yo) hago I do (I)

hacerse to become (6-1)

hacia toward (1-1)

hambre:

Tengo —. I'm hungry. (I)

la hamburguesa hamburger (I)

haré lo que me dé la gana I'll do as I please (6-1)

la harina flour (II)

has visto you have seen (II)

hasta until (II); as far as, up to (II)

— luego. See you later. (I)

— mañana. See you tomorrow. (I)

hay there is, there are (I)

— que one must (I)

haya *(subjunctive)* there is, there are (II)

he visto I have seen (II)

el helado ice cream (I)

la herencia heritage (8-2)

herido, -a injured (II)

el herido, la herida injured person (II)

el hermanastro, la hermanastra stepbrother, stepsister (I)

el hermano, la hermana brother, sister (I)

los hermanos brothers, brother(s) and sister(s) (I)

hermoso, -a beautiful (1-1)

el héroe hero (II)

la heroína heroine (II)

hervir (e → ie) (e → i) to boil (II)

el hielo ice (9-2)

el hierro iron (3-1)

el hijo, la hija son, daughter (I)

los hijos children, sons (I)

histórico, -a historical (II)

el hockey hockey (II)

hogar:

el — de ancianos home for the elderly (5-2)

la gente sin — homeless people (5-2)

la hoja de papel sheet of paper (I)

¡Hola! Hello! (I)

el hombre man (I)

el — de negocios businessman (II, 6-1)

el hombro shoulder (II)

honesto, -a honest (4-1)

la hora:

en la... — in the...hour (class period) (I)

¿A qué —? (At) what time? (I)

el horario schedule (I)

la hormiga ant (II)

el horno oven (II)

al — baked (II)

horrible horrible (I)

el horror:

la película de — horror movie (I)

el hospital hospital (I)

la hospitalidad hospitality (6-2)

el hotel hotel (I)

hoy today (I)

de — en adelante from now on (6-2)

hubo there was (II)

el hueso bone (II)

los huevos eggs (I)

el humo smoke (II)

el huracán, *pl.* **los huracanes** hurricane (II)

I

ida y vuelta round trip (II)

identificarse con to identify oneself with (2-2)

el idioma language (II)

la iglesia church (I)

ignorar to ignore (4-2)

igual: al — que as, like (7-2)

la igualdad equality (10-1)

igualmente likewise (I)

la imagen image (2-1)

impaciente impatient (I)

el imperio empire (8-1)

importante important (I)

importar: me importa(n) it matters (it's important) / they matter to me (II)

impresionante impressive (I)

impresionar to impress (1-1)

improbable unlikely (7-1)

el incendio fire (II)

incluir to include (3-1)

increíble incredible (I)

el / la indígena native (8-2)

la industria industry (6-2)

inexplicable inexplicable (7-1)

infantil childish (I)

la influencia influence (8-1)

influir (i → y) to influence (2-1)

la información information (I)

la informática information technology (6-2)

el informe report (I, II)

el ingeniero, la ingeniera engineer (II, 6-1)

el inglés:

la clase de — English class (I)

el ingrediente ingredient (II)

la injusticia injustice (10-1)

injusto, -a unfair (5-2)

inmediatamente immediately (II)

inocente innocent (10-2)

inolvidable unforgettable (I)

inscribirse to register (1-2)

la inscripción registration (1-2)

insistir en to insist (II)

la inspección, *pl.* **las inspecciones de seguridad** security checkpoint (II)

inspirar to inspire (2-1)

integrarse to integrate (8-1)

inteligente intelligent (I)

el intento attempt (7-2)

intercambiar to exchange (10-2)

el intercambio exchange (8-2)

el interés interest (II)

interesante interesting (I)

interesar to interest (I)

me interesa(n) it interests me (they interest me) (I)

me interesaría I would be interested... (5-2)

la interpretación interpretation (2-2)

interpretar to interpret (2-2)

íntimo, -a intimate (4-1)

la inundación, *pl.* **las inundaciones** flood (II)

invadir to invade (8-1)

inventar to invent (6-2)

el invento invention (6-2)

investigar to investigate (II)

el invierno winter (I)

la inyección, *pl.* **las inyecciones** injection, shot (II)

ir to go (I)

— **a** + *inf.* to be going to + *verb* (I)

— **a la escuela** to go to school (I)

— **a pie** to go on foot (II)

— **de cámping** to go camping (I)

— **de compras** to go shopping (I)

— **de pesca** to go fishing (I)

— **de vacaciones** to go on vacation (I)

¡Qué va! No way! (4-2)

¡Vamos! Let's go! (I)

el itinerario itinerary (II)

la izquierda:

a la — (de) to the left (of) (I)

el jabón soap (II)

el jarabe syrup (3-1)

el jardín garden, yard (I)

los jeans jeans (I)

el jefe, la jefa boss (6-1)

joven *adj.* young (I)

el / la joven young man, young woman (I)

los jóvenes young people (II)

las joyas (de oro, de plata) (gold, silver) jewelry (II)

la joyería jewelry store (I)

las judías verdes green beans (I)

el judío, la judía Jew(ish) (8-1)

jueves Thursday (I)

el juez, la jueza, *pl.* **los jueces** judge (II, 6-1)

el jugador, la jugadora player (II)

jugar (a) (u → ue) to play *(games, sports)* (I)

— **a los bolos** to bowl (II)

— **al básquetbol** to play basketball (I)

— **al béisbol** to play baseball (I)

— **al fútbol** to play soccer (I)

— **al fútbol americano** to play football (I)

— **al golf** to play golf (I)

— **al tenis** to play tennis (I)

— **al vóleibol** to play volleyball (I)

— **videojuegos** to play video games (I)

el jugo:

el — de manzana apple juice (I)

el — de naranja orange juice (I)

el juguete toy (I)

el juicio trial (10-2)

julio July (I)

junio June (I)

juntar fondos to fundraise (5-2)

juntarse to join (II)

juntos, -as together (4-1)

el jurado jury (10-2)

la justicia justice (10-2)

justo, -a fair (5-2)

juzgar to judge (10-2)

la the *f. sing.* (I); it, her *f. dir. obj. pron.* (I)

los labios lips (II)

el laboratorio laboratory (I, II)

el lado:

al — de next to (I)

el ladrón, la ladrona, *pl.* **los ladrones** thief (II)

el lago lake (I)

la lámpara lamp (I)

la lana wool (II)

el lápiz, *pl.* **los lápices** pencil (I)

largo, -a long (I)

el largo length (7-1)

las the *f. pl.;* them *f. dir. obj. pron.* (I)

— **dos, los dos** both (I)

lástima:

¡Qué —! What a shame! (II)

lastimarse to hurt oneself (II)

la lata can (I)

lavar to wash (I)

— **el coche** to wash the car (I)

— **la ropa** to wash the clothes (I)

— **los platos** to wash the dishes (I)

—**se la cara** to wash one's face (II)

le (to / for) him, her, it, *(formal)* you *sing. ind. obj. pron.* (I)

— **gusta...** He / She likes... (I)

— **traigo...** I will bring you... (I)

No — gusta... He / She doesn't like... (I)

la lección, *pl.* **las lecciones de piano** piano lesson (class) (I)

la leche milk (I)

la lechuga lettuce (I)

el lector DVD DVD player (I)

leer revistas to read magazines (I)

lejos (de) far (from) (I)

la lengua language (8-2)

lentamente slowly (II)

la leña firewood (II)

les (to / for) them, *(formal)* you *pl. ind. obj. pron.* (I)

la letra lyrics (2-2)

el letrero sign (II)

levantar pesas to lift weights (I)

levantarse to get up (II)

la ley law (II, 5-2)

la leyenda legend (7-2)

la libertad liberty (10-1)

libre free (10-2)

la librería bookstore (I)

el libro book (I)

la liga league (II)

limitar to limit (9-1)

la limonada lemonade (I)

limpiar el baño to clean the bathroom (I)

la limpieza cleaning (9-2)

limpio, -a clean (I)

la línea:

    estar en — to be online (I, II)

    la — aérea airline (II)

la linterna flashlight (1-1)

la liquidación, *pl.* **las liquidaciones** sale (II)

listo, -a ready (II)

llamar:

    — por teléfono to call on the phone (II)

    ¿Cómo se llama? What's his / her name? (I)

    ¿Cómo te llamas? What is your name? (I)

    Me llamo... My name is... (I)

la llave key (II)

el llavero key chain (I)

la llegada arrival (II)

llegar to arrive

    al — upon arriving (8-2)

    — a to reach, to get to (10-2)

    — tarde to arrive late (II)

llenar (el tanque) to fill (the tank) (II)

lleno, -a full (3-1)

llevar to wear (I); to take, to carry, to bring (I)

llevarse bien / mal to get along well / badly (II)

llorar to cry (II)

llover (o → ue) to rain (II)

Llueve. It's raining. (I)

la lluvia rain (II)

lo que what (II)

lo it, him *m. dir. obj. pron.* (I)

    — siento. I'm sorry. (I)

el locutor, la locutora announcer (II)

lograr to achieve (6-1)

los the *m. pl.* (I); them *m. dir. obj. pron* (I)

    — dos, las dos both (I)

    — fines de semana on weekends (I)

    — lunes, los martes... on Mondays, on Tuesdays... (I)

luchar to fight (II, 8-2)

luego then (II)

el lugar place (I)

    en — de instead of (10-2)

    tener — to take place (1-2)

la Luna the Moon (II, 7-1)

lunes Monday (I)

los lunes on Mondays (I)

la luz, *pl.* **las luces** light (I)

M

la madrastra stepmother (I)

la madre (mamá) mother (I)

maduro, -a mature (6-1)

el maíz corn (II)

mal bad, badly (I)

    pasarlo — to have a bad time (1-1)

el malentendido misunderstanding (4-2)

la maleta suitcase (II)

malo, -a bad (I)

maltratar to mistreat (10-1)

el maltrato mistreatment (10-1)

manejar to drive (II)

la manera way, manner (II, 3-1)

la manifestación demonstration (5-2)

la mano hand (I)

    darse la — to shake hands (II)

mantener:

    para — la salud to maintain one's health (I)

la mantequilla butter (I)

la manzana apple (I)

    el jugo de — apple juice (I)

mañana tomorrow (I)

la mañana:

    a las ocho de la — at eight (o'clock) in the morning (I)

    de la — in the morning (I)

el maquillaje make-up (II)

la máquina machine (6-2)

el mar sea (I)

la maravilla marvel, wonder (8-1)

maravilloso, -a wonderful (8-1)

la marca brand (II)

la marcha march (5-2)

los mariscos shellfish (II)

marrón brown (I)

martes Tuesday (I)

los martes on Tuesdays (I)

marzo March (I)

más:

    ¿Qué —? What else? (I)

    — ...que more...than (I)

    — de more than (I)

    — o menos more or less (I)

matar to kill (II)

las matemáticas:

    la clase de — mathematics class (I)

los materiales supplies, materials (II)

mayo May (I)

la mayonesa mayonnaise (II)

mayor, *pl.* **mayores** *adj.* older (I)

los mayores grown-ups (II)

la mayoría the majority (6-2)

me me *dir. obj. pron.,* (to / for) me *ind. obj. pron.* (I)

    — aburre(n) it / they bore(s) me (I)

    — encantaría I would love to... (5-2)

    — es imposible It is impossible for me... (5-2)

    — estás poniendo nervioso, -a. You are making me nervous. (II)

    — falta(n)... I need... (I)

— **gustaría** I would like (I)

— **gustó.** I liked it. (I)

— **interesa(n)** it / they interest(s) me (I)

— **interesaría** I would be interested... (5-2)

— **llamo...** My name is... (I)

— **importa(n)** it matters (it's important) / they matter to me (II)

— **parece** it seems to me (II)

— **queda(n) bien / mal.** It / They fit(s) me well / poorly. (I)

— **quedo en casa.** I'm staying at home. (I)

¿— **trae...?** Will you bring me...? *formal* (I)

el mecánico, la mecánica mechanic (II)

la medalla medal (1-2)

media, -o half (I)

y — thirty, half past (I)

mediano, -a medium (II)

la medicina medicine (II)

el médico, la médica doctor (II)

el medio ambiente environment (II, 5-2)

los medios de comunicación media (6-2)

medir (e → i) to measure (7-1)

mejor:

el / la —, los / las —es the best (I)

—(es) que better than (I)

mejorar to improve (II, 4-2)

la melodía melody (2-2)

el melón, *pl.* **los melones** melon (II)

menor younger (I)

menos:

a — que unless (9-2)

más o — more or less (I)

— ...que less / fewer...than (I)

— de less / fewer than (I)

el mensajero, la mensajera messenger (5-1)

mentir (e → ie) to lie (II)

el menú menu (I)

menudo:

a — often (I)

el mercadeo marketing (6-2)

el mercado market (II)

la mercancía merchandise (8-2)

la merienda snack (3-1)

el mes month (I)

la mesa table (I)

poner la — to set the table (I)

la mesita night table (I)

la meta goal (1-2)

meter:

meter un gol to score a goal (II)

el metro subway (II)

la mezcla mix (8-2)

mezclar to mix (II)

la mezquita mosque (I)

mi, mis my (I)

mí:

a — también I do (like to) too (I)

a — tampoco I don't (like to) either (I)

para — in my opinion, for me (I)

el micrófono microphone (2-2)

el microondas microwave (II)

el miedo: tener — (de) to be scared (of), to be afraid (of) (I)

el miembro member (II)

ser miembro to be a member (II)

mientras (que) while (II)

miércoles Wednesday (I)

mil thousand (I)

militar *(adj.)* military (II)

un millón de / millones de a million / millions of (II)

mío, -a, -os, -as mine (II)

mirar to look (at) (I)

la misión mission (8-2)

el misionero, la misionera missionary (8-2)

mismo, -a same (I)

pensar en sí — to think of oneself (4-2)

el misterio mystery (7-1)

misterioso, -a mysterious (7-1)

el mito myth (7-2)

la mochila bookbag, backpack (I)

los modales manners (II)

el modo the way (10-2)

de ese — in that way (10-1)

de — que so, so that (10-2)

mojado, -a wet (II)

molestar to bother (II)

el momento:

un — a moment (I)

la moneda coin (II)

el mono monkey (I)

las montañas mountains (I)

montar:

— a caballo to go (horseback) riding (I)

— en bicicleta to ride a bicycle (I)

— en monopatín to skateboard (I)

el monumento monument (I)

morado, -a purple (I)

morirse to die (II)

la mosca fly (II)

la mostaza mustard (II)

mostrar (ue) to show (2-1)

el motivo cause (10-1)

la moto acuática personal watercraft (II)

moverse (o → ue) to move (II)

el movimiento movement (2-1)

mucho, -a a lot (I)

— gusto pleased to meet you (I)

muchos, -as many (I)

mudarse to move (house) (6-1)

los muebles furniture (II)

muerto, -a dead (II)

la naturaleza muerta still life (2-1)

la mujer woman (I)

la — de negocios businesswoman (II, 6-1)

las muletas crutches (II)

la multa ticket (II)

mundial worldwide (10-2)

el mundo world (II)

la muñeca doll (II); wrist (II)

el muñeco action figure (II)

el mural mural (2-1)

el músculo muscle (II, 3-2)

el museo museum (I)

el músico, la música musician (II)

el musulmán, la musulmana Muslim (8-1)

muy very (I)

— **bien** very well (I)

N

nacer to be born (II)

nada nothing (I)

(A mí) no me gusta — ... I don't like to...at all. (I)

nadar to swim (I)

nadie no one, nobody (II)

la naranja:

el jugo de — orange juice (I)

la nariz, *pl.* **las narices** nose (I)

la natación swimming (II)

natural:

la reserva — nature preserve (9-2)

la naturaleza nature (II, 1-1)

la — **muerta** still life (2-1)

la nave espacial spaceship (7-1)

navegar to sail, to navigate (II)

— **en la Red** to surf the Web (I, II)

necesario:

Es —. It's necessary. (I)

necesitar:

necesitas you need (I)

necesito I need (I)

los negocios business (II)

el hombre de — businessman (II, 6-1)

la mujer de — businesswoman (II, 6-1)

negro, -a black

el pelo — black hair (I)

nervioso, -a nervous (II)

nevar (e → ie) to snow (II)

Nieva. It's snowing. (I)

ni...ni neither...nor, not...or (I)

ningún, ninguno, -a no, none (II)

el niñero, la niñera babysitter (5-1)

la niñez childhood (10-1)

el niño, la niña young boy, young girl (I)

los niños children (I)

el nivel level (3-1)

No comas. Don't eat. (II)

No dejes Don't leave, don't let (II)

No escribas. Don't write. (II)

No estoy de acuerdo. I don't agree. (I)

No hables. Don't speak. (II)

¡No me digas! You don't say! (I)

no...todavía not yet (II)

la noche:

a las ocho de la — at eight (o'clock) in the evening, at night (I)

Buenas —**s.** Good evening. (I)

de la — in the evening, at night (I)

esta — this evening (I)

nos us *dir. obj. pron.*, (to / for) us *ind. obj. pron.* (I)

¡ — **vemos!** See you later! (I)

nosotros, -as we (I)

la nota grade, mark (in school) (II)

sacar una buena — to get a good grade (II)

el noticiero newscast (II)

novecientos, -as nine hundred (I)

noveno, -a ninth (I)

noventa ninety (I)

noviembre November (I)

el novio, la novia boyfriend, girlfriend (I)

la nube cloud (II)

nuestro, -a, -os, -as our (I)

nueve nine (I)

nuevo, -a new (I)

el número shoe size (II)

nunca never (I)

nutritivo, -a nutritious (3-1)

O

o or (I)

— **sea que** in other words (7-2)

obedecer to obey (II)

obediente obedient (II)

obligar to force (10-1)

la obra:

la — **de arte** work of art (2-1)

la — **de teatro** play (I)

observar to observe (II)

el observatorio observatory (7-1)

obtener to obtain, to get (1-2)

ochenta eighty (I)

ocho eight (I)

ochocientos, -as eight hundred (I)

el ocio free time (6-2)

octavo, -a eighth (I)

octubre October (I)

ocupado, -a busy (I)

ocupar to occupy (8-1)

ocurrir to occur (II)

ofender to offend (II)

la oficina office (II)

ofrecer to offer (II)

el oído ear (3-1)

oír to hear (II)

ojalá I wish (4-1)

el ojo eye (I)

la olla pot (II)

el olor odor (II)

olvidarse de to forget about (II)

no te olvides de don't forget about (II)

once eleven (I)

opinar to think (10-2)

la oportunidad opportunity (II)

ordenado, -a neat (I)

organizar to organize (5-2)

el origen origin (7-2)

el oro gold (II)

la orquesta orchestra (II)

os you *pl. fam. dir. obj. pron.*, (to / for) you *pl. fam. ind. obj. pron.* (I)

oscuro, -a dark (II)

el oso de peluche teddy bear (II)

el **otoño** fall, autumn (I)

otro, -a other, another (I)

otra vez again (I)

el **óvalo** oval (7-1)

¡Oye! Hey! (I)

ozono:

la **capa de —** ozone layer (9-2)

P

la **paciencia** patience (II)

tener — to be patient (II)

paciente *adj.* patient (I)

pacífico, -a peaceful (10-2)

el **padrastro** stepfather (I)

el **padre (papá)** father (I)

los **padres** parents (I)

pagar (por) to pay (for) (I)

la **página Web** Web page (I)

el **país** country (I)

el **paisaje** landscape (1-1)

el **pájaro** bird (I)

la **palabra** word (II)

el **palacio** palace (II)

la **paleta** palette (2-1)

el **palo de golf** golf club (II)

el **pan** bread (I)

el **— tostado** toast (I)

la **pantalla** (computer) screen (I)

los **pantalones** pants (I)

los **— cortos** shorts (I)

las **papas** potatoes (I)

las **— fritas** French fries (I)

el **papel** role (II)

el **— picado** cut-paper decorations (I)

hacer el — de to play the role of (II)

la **hoja de —** sheet of paper (I)

la **papelera** wastepaper basket (I)

para for (I)

— + *inf.* in order to (I)

— la salud for one's health (I)

— mantener la salud to maintain one's health (I)

— mí in my opinion, for me (I)

¿ — qué sirve? What's it (used) for? (I)

— ti in your opinion, for you (I)

parado, -a to be standing (2-1)

el **paramédico, la paramédica** paramedic (II)

parar to stop (II)

pararse to stand up (2-2)

parecer:

me parece que it seems to me (II)

¿Qué te parece? What do you think? / How does it seem to you? (II)

parecerse a to look, to seem (like) (2-2)

la **pared** wall (I)

los **parientes** relatives (II)

el **parque** park (I)

el **— de diversiones** amusement park (I)

el **— nacional** national park (I)

la **parrilla** grill (II)

el / la **participante** participant (1-2)

participar (en) to participate (in) (II)

el **partido** game, match (I)

el **pasajero, la pasajera** passenger (II)

el **pasaporte** passport (II)

pasar to pass, to go (II)

¿Cómo lo pasaste? How was it (for you)? (I)

— la aspiradora to vacuum (I)

— tiempo con amigos to spend time with friends (I)

¿Qué pasa? What's happening? (I)

¿Qué te pasó? What happened to you? (I, II)

pasarlo bien / mal to have a good time / bad time (1-1)

el **pasatiempo** pastime (II)

pasear en bote to go boating (I)

el **pasillo** aisle (II)

el **paso** step (2-2)

la **pasta dental** toothpaste (II)

pastel *adj.* pastel (colors) (II)

el **pastel** cake (I)

los **pasteles** pastries (I)

las **pastillas** pills (II)

patinar to skate (I)

los **patines** skates (II)

el **patio de recreo** playground (II)

el **pavo** turkey (II)

la **paz** peace (II, 10-1)

hacer las paces to make peace (with) (4-2)

el **peatón,** *pl.* **los peatones** pedestrian (II)

el **pecho** chest (3-1)

el **pedazo** piece, slice (II)

pedir (e → i) to order, to ask for (I)

— ayuda to ask for help (II)

— prestado, -a (a) to borrow (from) (II)

— perdón to ask for forgiveness (4-2)

el **peine** comb (II)

pelar to peel (II)

la **pelea** fight (4-2)

pelearse to fight (II)

la **película** film, movie (I)

la **— de acción** action film (II)

la **— de ciencia ficción** science fiction movie (I)

la **— de horror** horror movie (I)

la **— policíaca** detective movie, mystery (I)

la **— romántica** romantic movie (I)

ver una — to see a movie (I)

peligro:

(en) peligro de extinción (in) danger of extinction, endangered (II, 9-2)

peligroso, -a dangerous (II)

pelirrojo, -a red-haired (I)

el **pelo** hair (I, II)

    el **— canoso** gray hair (I)

    el **— castaño** brown (chestnut) hair (I)

    el **— negro** black hair (I)

    el **— rubio** blond hair (I)

la **pelota** ball (II)

el **peluquero,** la **peluquera** hairstylist (6-1)

el **pensamiento** thought (10-1)

pensar (e → ie) to plan, to think (I)

    — en sí mismo(a) to think of oneself (4-2)

peor:

    el / la —, los / las —es the worst (I)

    —(es) que worse than (I)

pequeño, -a small (I)

perder (e → ie) to lose (II)

    — el equilibrio to lose one's balance (1-1)

perderse to get lost (1-1)

Perdón. Excuse me. (I)

perdonar to forgive (4-2)

perezoso, -a lazy (I)

el **perfume** perfume (I)

el **periódico** newspaper (I)

el **permiso de manejar** driver's license (II)

permitir to permit, to allow (II)

pero but (I)

el **perrito caliente** hot dog (I)

el **perro** dog (I)

la **persona** person (I)

el **personaje principal** main character (II)

pesar to weigh (7-1)

    a — de despite (10-2)

pesas:

    levantar — to lift weights (I)

el **pescado** fish *(as a food)* (I)

el **peso** weight (3-1)

el **pesticida** pesticide (9-1)

el **petróleo** oil (9-1)

    el derrame de — oil spill (9-2)

el **pez,** *pl.* **los peces** fish (II)

picante spicy (II)

picar to chop (II)

el **picnic** picnic (II)

el **pie** foot (I)

la **piedra** rock (II)

la **piel** skin (9-2)

la **pierna** leg (I)

la **pila** battery (9-1)

el / la **piloto** pilot (II)

la **pimienta** pepper (I)

el **pincel** brush (2-1)

    pintarse (las uñas) to paint, to polish (one's nails) (II)

el **pintor,** la **pintora** painter (II)

la **pintura** painting (2-1)

la **piña** pineapple (II)

la **piñata** piñata (I)

la **pirámide** pyramid (7-1)

la **piscina** swimming pool (I)

el **piso** story, floor (I)

    primer — second floor (I)

    segundo — third floor (I)

la **pizza** pizza (I)

    planear to plan (II)

el **planeta** planet (7-2)

la **planta** plant (II)

la **planta baja** ground floor (I)

el **plástico** plastic (I)

la **plata** silver (II)

el **plátano** banana (I)

el **plato** plate, dish (I)

    de — principal as a main dish (I)

    el — principal main dish (I)

la **playa** beach (I)

la **plaza** plaza (II)

la **pluma** feather (9-2)

la **población** population (8-1)

    pobre poor (I)

    pobrecito, -a poor thing (II)

la **pobreza** poverty (10-1)

    poco:

        un — (de) a little (I)

    poder to be able to (I)

        (tú) puedes you can (I)

        (yo) puedo I can (I)

el **poder** power (8-2)

    poderoso, -a powerful (8-2)

el **poema** poem (2-2)

el / la **poeta** poet (2-2)

el / la **policía** police officer (II)

    policíaca:

        la película — detective movie, mystery (I)

la **política** politics (II)

el **político,** la **política** politician (II)

el **pollo** chicken (I)

    poner to put, to place (I)

        pon *(command)* put, place (I)

        — la mesa to set the table (I)

        — una multa to give a ticket (II)

        (tú) pones you put (I)

        (yo) pongo I put (I)

    ponerse to apply, to put on *(clothing, make up, etc.)* (II); to become (II)

        — de acuerdo to reach an agreement (4-2)

        — el sol to set (the sun) (7-2)

por for (how long) (II); by, around, along, through (II)

    — ejemplo for example (II)

    — eso that's why, therefore (I)

    — lo general in general (II)

    — lo tanto therefore (6-1)

    ¿— qué? Why? (I)

    — supuesto of course (I)

    —...vez for the...time (II)

porque because (I)

portarse bien / mal to behave well / badly (II)

la **posesión,** *pl.* **las posesiones** possession (I)

el **postre** dessert (I)

    de — for dessert (I)

la **práctica** practice (II)

    practicar deportes to play sports (I)

    práctico, -a practical (I)

el **precio** price (I, II)

    predecir to predict (6-2)

    preferir (e → ie) to prefer (I)

(tú) prefieres you prefer (I)

(yo) prefiero I prefer (I)

la **pregunta** question (II)

    hacer una — to ask a question (II)

el **premio** prize (II)

la **prensa** the press (10-2)

preocuparse worry (3-2)

preparar to prepare (I)

    —se to get ready (II)

la **presentación,** *pl.* **las presentaciones** presentation (I)

el **presentador, la presentadora** presenter (II)

presentarse to apply for a job (5-1)

la **preservación** conservation (9-2)

prestar atención to pay attention (II)

la **primavera** spring (I)

primer (primero), -a first (I)

    — piso second floor (I)

    el — plano foreground (2-1)

el **primo, la prima** cousin (I)

los **primos** cousins (I)

prisa hurry (II)

    tener — to be in a hurry (II)

probable likely (7-1)

probar (o → ue) to taste, to try (II)

probarse (o → ue) to try on (II)

el **problema** problem (I)

producir to produce (9-2)

el **producto** product (6-2)

la **profesión,** *pl.* **las profesiones** profession (II)

el **profesor, la profesora** teacher (I)

el **programa** program, show (I)

    el — de concursos game show (I)

    el — de dibujos animados cartoon (I)

    el — de entrevistas interview program (I)

    el — de estudios course of studies (II)

    el — de la vida real reality program (I)

    el — de noticias news program (I)

    el — deportivo sports program (I)

    el — educativo educational program (I)

    el — musical musical program (I)

el **programador, la programadora** programmer (6-1)

prohibir: se prohíbe it is forbidden (II)

prolongar to prolong, to extend (6-2)

promover (ue) to promote (9-1)

pronto soon (II)

    tan — como as soon as (9-1)

la **propina** tip (II)

propio, -a own (I)

proponer to propose, to suggest (10-2)

la **propuesta** proposal (10-2)

la **protección** protection (9-1)

proteger to protect (II, 5-2)

la **proteína** protein (3-1)

próximo, -a next (6-1)

el **proyecto** project (II)

    el — de construcción construction project (I)

el **público** audience (II)

el **pueblo** people (7-1); town (II)

puedes:

    (tú) — you can (I)

puedo:

    (yo) — I can (I)

el **puente** bridge (II)

la **puerta** door (I)

    la — de embarque departure gate (II)

pues well *(to indicate pause)* (I)

el **puesto** position (5-1); food stand (II)

la **pulsera** bracelet (I)

el **reloj** watch (I)

las **puntadas** stitches (II)

    dar — to stitch *(surgically)* (II)

el **punto de vista** point of view (10-2)

puntual punctual (II, 5-1)

el **pupitre** desk (I)

puro, -a pure (II)

Q

que who, that (I)

qué:

    ¿Para — sirve? What's it (used) for? (I)

    ¡— + *adj.!* How...! (I)

    ¡— asco! How awful! (I)

    ¡— buena idea! What a good / nice idea! (I)

    ¿— clase de...? What kind of... ? (I)

    ¿— desean (Uds.)? What would you like? *formal* (I)

    ¿— día es hoy? What day is today? (I)

    ¿— es esto? What is this? (I)

    ¿— hiciste? What did you do? (I)

    ¿— hora es? What time is it? (I)

    ¡— lástima! What a shame! (II)

    ¿— más? What else? (I)

    ¿— pasa? What's happening? (I)

    ¡— pena! What a shame / pity! (I)

    ¿— quiere decir... ? What does...mean? (I)

    ¿— tal? How are you? (I)

    ¿— tal es...? How is (it)...? (II)

    ¿— te gusta hacer? What do you like to do? (I)

    ¿— te gusta hacer más? What do you like to do better / prefer to do? (I)

    ¿— te parece? What do you think? / How does it seem to you? (I, II)

    ¿— te pasó? What happened to you? (I, II)

    ¿— tiempo hace? What's the weather like? (I)

    ¡— va! No way! (4-2)

quedar to fit, to be located (I, II)

quedarse to stay (II)

el **quehacer (de la casa)** (household) chore (I)

quejarse to complain (3-2)

quemar(se) to burn (oneself), to burn up (II)

querer (e → ie) to want (I)

¿Qué quiere decir...? What does...mean? (I)

Quiere decir... It means... (I)

quisiera I would like (I)

(tú) quieres you want (I)

(yo) quiero I want (I)

¿Quién(es)? Who? (I)

químico, -a chemical (9-1)

quince fifteen (I)

quinientos, -as five hundred (I)

quinto, -a fifth (I)

el quiosco newsstand (II)

quisiera I would like (I)

quitar to take away, to remove (II)

— el polvo to dust (I)

quizás maybe (I)

R

la radiografía X-ray (II)

rápidamente quickly (I, II)

la raqueta de tenis tennis racket (II)

un rato a while (1-1)

el ratón, *pl.* **los ratones** (computer) mouse (I)

la raza race (8-2)

razón reason (10-1)

tener — to be correct (I)

reaccionar to react (4-2)

la realidad virtual virtual reality (6-2)

realista realistic (I)

realizar to perform, to accomplish (2-2)

rebelarse to rebel, to revolt (8-2)

el recalentamiento global global warming (9-2)

la recepción reception desk (II)

el / la recepcionista receptionist (5-1)

la receta prescription (II); recipe (II)

recetar to prescribe (II)

recibir to receive (I)

reciclar to recycle (I)

recientemente recently (II)

el recipiente container (9-1)

recoger to collect, to gather (I)

recomendar (e →ie) to recommend (II)

reconciliarse to become friends again (4-2)

reconocer (c → zc) to admit, recognize (4-2)

reconquistar to reconquer (8-1)

recordar (o → ue) to remember (II)

el rectángulo rectangle (7-1)

los recuerdos souvenirs (I)

comprar — to buy souvenirs (I)

el recurso natural natural resource (9-1)

la Red:

en la — online (I)

navegar en la — to surf the Web (I)

el redactor, la redactora editor (6-1)

redondo, -a round (7-1)

reducir (zc) to reduce (II, 6-2)

reemplazar to replace (6-2)

la referencia reference (5-1)

el refresco soft drink (I)

el refrigerador refrigerator (II)

refugiarse to take shelter (1-1)

el refugio refuge, shelter (1-1)

regalar to give (II)

el regalo gift, present (I)

regatear to bargain (II)

registrar to inspect, to search *(luggage)* (II)

la regla rule (II)

regresar to return (I)

regular okay, so-so (I)

la reina queen (II)

reírse (e → í) to laugh (II)

la reja grate (8-1)

relajar(se) to relax (3-2)

el relámpago lightning (1-1)

el reloj clock (I)

el — pulsera watch (I)

reparar to repair (5-1)

el repartidor, la repartidora delivery person (5-1)

repartir to deliver (5-1)

el repelente de insectos insect repellent (1-1)

repetir (e → i) to repeat (II)

el reportero, la reportera reporter (II)

el / la representante representative (1-2)

representar to represent (2-1)

el requisito requirement (5-1)

la res cattle (II)

rescatar to rescue (II)

el rescate rescue (9-2)

la reseña review (2-2)

la reserva natural nature preserve (9-2)

la reservación, *pl.* **las reservaciones** reservation (II)

reservado, -a reserved, shy (I)

resolver (o → ue) to resolve (4-2); to solve (II)

respetar to respect (II)

el respeto respect (10-1)

respirar to breathe (3-2)

la responsabilidad responsibility (5-2)

responsable responsible (5-1)

el restaurante restaurant (I)

el resultado result, outcome (8-2)

resultar to result, to turn out (II)

el reto challenge (8-2)

el retraso delay (II)

el retrato portrait (2-1)

la reunión, *pl.* **las reuniones** meeting, gathering (II)

reunirse (u → ú) to meet (II)

el rey king (II)

rico, -a rich, tasty (I)

el río river (I)

la riqueza wealth (8-2)

el ritmo rhythm (2-2)

robar to rob, to steal (II)

la roca rock (1-1)

la rodilla knee (II)

rojo, -a red (I)

el romano, la romana Roman (8-1)

romántico, -a:

la película — romantic movie (I)

romper to break (I)

   —se to break, to tear (II)

la ropa:

   la tienda de — clothing store (I)

rosado, -a pink (I)

roto, -a broken (II)

rubio, -a blond (I)

el ruido noise (II)

las ruinas ruins (II, 7-1)

S

sábado Saturday (I)

saber to know (how) (I, II)

   (tú) sabes you know (how to) (I)

   (yo) sé I know (how to) (I)

el sabor taste (II)

sabroso, -a tasty, flavorful (I)

el sacapuntas, *pl.* **los sacapuntas** pencil sharpener (I)

sacar:

   — fotos to take photos (I)

   — la basura to take out the trash (I)

   — un libro to take out, to check out a book (II)

   — una buena nota to get a good grade (II)

el saco de dormir sleeping bag (1-1)

sagrado, -a sacred (7-2)

la sal salt (I)

la sala living room (I)

   la — de clases classroom (I)

   la — de emergencia emergency room (II)

el salario (*o* **el sueldo)** salary (II, 5-1)

la salchicha sausage (I)

la salida exit (II); departure (II)

salir to leave, to go out (I)

   — campeón, campeona to become the champion (1-2)

el salón de belleza, *pl.* **los salones de belleza** beauty salon (II)

los salones de chat chat rooms (II)

la salsa salsa, sauce (II)

   la — de tomate ketchup (II)

saltar:

   — a la cuerda to jump rope (II)

   — una comida to skip a meal (3-1)

la salud:

   para la — for one's health (I)

   para mantener la — to maintain one's health (I)

saludable healthy (3-1)

saludar(se) to greet (II)

salvaje wild (9-2)

salvar to save (II)

el / la salvavida lifeguard (5-1)

la sandía watermelon (II)

el sándwich de jamón y queso ham and cheese sandwich (I)

la sangre blood (II)

la sartén frying pan (II)

satélite:

   vía satélite via satellite (6-2)

satisfactorio, -a satisfactory (10-1)

se abre opens (II)

se cierra closes (II)

se me olvidó I forgot (II)

se murieron they died (II)

se prohíbe... it's forbidden... (II)

se puede you can (II)

sé:

   (yo) — I know (how to) (I)

el secador blow dryer (II)

secarse to dry (II)

seco, -a dry (II)

el secretario, la secretaria secretary (II)

el secreto secret (4-1)

sed:

   Tengo —. I'm thirsty. (I)

la seda silk (II)

seguir (e → i) to follow, to continue (II)

   — (*+ gerund***)** to keep on (doing) (5-1)

   — una carrera to pursue a career (II, 6-1)

según according to (I)

   — mi familia according to my family (I)

segundo, -a second (I)

   — piso third floor (I)

seguro, -a sure (II)

seis six (I)

seiscientos, -as six hundred (I)

el sello stamp (II)

la selva tropical tropical rainforest (II, 9-2)

el semáforo stoplight (II)

la semana week (I)

   este fin de — this weekend (I)

   la — pasada last week (I)

   los fines de — on weekends (I)

sembrar (ie) to plant (5-2)

la semejanza similarity (8-2)

el sendero trail (II)

sentado, -a to be seated (2-1)

el sentimiento feeling (2-1)

sentirse (e → ie) to feel (II)

   — fatal to feel awful (3-2)

la señal sign (II)

   la — de parada stop sign (II)

señor (Sr.) sir, Mr. (I)

señora (Sra.) madam, Mrs. (I)

señorita (Srta.) miss, Miss (I)

separar to separate (I)

septiembre September (I)

séptimo, -a seventh (I)

ser to be (I)

   ¿Eres...? Are you...? (I)

   es he / she is (I)

   fue it was (I)

   no soy I am not (I)

   — miembro to be a member (II)

   soy I am (I)

ser:

   será it, he, she will be (II)

serio, -a serious (I)

el servicio service (6-2)

   el — social social service (5-2)

la servilleta napkin (I)

servir (e → i) to serve, to be useful (I)

¿En qué puedo —le? How can I help you? (I)

¿Para qué sirve? What's it (used) for? (I)

sirve para it is used for (I)

sesenta sixty (I)

setecientos, -as seven hundred (I)

setenta seventy (I)

sexto, -a sixth (I)

si if, whether (I)

sí yes (I)

siempre always (I)

siento:

　Lo —. I'm sorry. (I)

la sierra sierra, mountain range (1-1)

siete seven (I)

el siglo century (2-1)

siguiente next, following (II)

la silla chair (I)

　la — de ruedas wheelchair (II)

el símbolo symbol (7-2)

simpático, -a nice, friendly (I)

sin without (I)

　— duda without a doubt (II)

　— embargo however (1-2)

la sinagoga synagogue (I)

sincero, -a sincere (4-1)

sino but (7-2)

el sitio Web Web site (I)

sobre about (I)

sociable sociable (I)

la sociedad society (5-2)

¡Socorro! Help! (II)

el software software (I)

el sol:

　Hace —. It's sunny. (I)

　los anteojos de — sunglasses (I)

　tomar el — to sunbathe (I)

solar solar (II)

el / la soldado soldier (8-2)

soler (ue) to usually do something (5-1)

solicitar to request (5-1)

la solicitud de empleo job application (5-1)

sólo only (I)

solo, -a alone (I)

soltero, -a single (6-1)

la sombra shadow (7-2)

Son las... It is... *(in telling time)* (I)

sonar (ue) (a) to sound like (2-2)

sonreír (e → í) to smile (II)

la sopa de verduras vegetable soup (I)

sorprender(se) to (be) surprise(d) (4-1)

la sorpresa surprise (II)

sospechoso, -a suspicious (10-2)

el sótano basement (I)

soy I am (I)

su, sus his, her, your *formal,* their (I)

subir to go up (II)

suceder to occur (1-1)

sucio, -a dirty (I)

la sudadera sweatshirt (I)

el suelo ground, floor (II)

sueño: tener — to be sleepy (I)

el suéter sweater (I)

suficiente enough (9-1)

sufrir to suffer (10-1)

sugerir (e → ie) to suggest (II)

el supermercado supermarket (II)

supuesto: por — of course (I)

el surf de vela windsurf (II)

T

tal: ¿Qué — ? How are you? (I)

tal vez maybe, perhaps (II)

talentoso, -a talented (I)

la talla size (II)

el taller workshop (2-1)

también also, too (I)

　a mí — I do (like to) too (I)

el tambor drum (2-2)

tampoco:

　a mí — I don't (like to) either (I)

tan so (II)

　— + *adj.* so + *adj.* (II)

　— + *adj.* + como as + *adj.* + as (II)

— pronto como as soon as (9-1)

el tanque tank (II)

el tanteo score (II)

tanto so much (I)

　por lo — therefore (6-1)

tantos, -as + *noun* + **como** as much / many + *noun* + as (II)

tarde late, afternoon (I)

　a la una de la — at one (o'clock) in the afternoon (I)

　Buenas —s. Good afternoon. (I)

　de la — in the afternoon (I)

　esta — this afternoon (I)

　llegar — to arrive late (II)

la tarea homework (I)

la tarjeta card (I, II)

　la — de crédito credit card (II)

　la — de embarque boarding pass (II)

　la — postal postcard (II)

la taza cup (I)

te you *sing. dir. obj. pron.*, (to / for) you *sing. ind. obj. pron.* (I)

　¿— gusta...? Do you like to...? (I)

　¿— gustaría...? Would you like...? (I)

　¿— gustó? Did you like it? (I)

　— importa(n) it matters (it's important), they matter to you (II)

　— ves (bien) you look (good) (II)

el té tea (I)

　el — helado iced tea (I)

el teatro theater (I)

　la obra de — play (2-1)

el teclado (computer) keyboard (I)

el técnico, la técnica technician (II)

la tecnología technology / computers (I)

　la clase de — technology / computer class (I)

tecnológico, -a technological (6-2)

la tela sintética synthetic fabric (II)

la telenovela soap opera (I)

el televisor television set (I)

el tema subject (2-1)

temer to fear (4-1)

el templo temple, Protestant church (I)

temprano early (I)

el tenedor fork (I)

tener to have (I)

    ¿Cuántos años tiene(n)...? How old is / are...? (I)

    — calor to be warm (I)

    — celos to be jealous (4-1)

    — cuidado to be careful (II)

    — en común to have in common (4-1)

    — en cuenta to take into account (6-2)

    — éxito to succeed, to be successful (II)

    — frío to be cold (I)

    — la culpa to be guilty (4-2)

    — lugar to take place (1-2)

    — miedo (de) to be scared (of), to be afraid (of) (I)

    — paciencia to be patient (II)

    — prisa to be in a hurry (II)

    — razón to be correct (I)

    — sueño to be sleepy (I)

Tengo hambre. I'm hungry. (I)

Tengo que... I have to... (I)

Tengo sed. I'm thirsty. (I)

Tiene(n)...años. He / She is / They are...(years old). (I)

el tenis:

    jugar al — to play tennis (I)

la teoría theory (7-2)

tercer (tercero), -a third (I)

terminar to finish, to end (I)

el terremoto earthquake (II)

el / la testigo witness (10-2)

    ti you *fam. after prep.*

    ¿Y a —? And you? (I)

    para — in your opinion, for you (I)

el tiempo:

    a — on time (II)

    a — completo full time (5-1)

    a — parcial part time (5-1)

    el — libre free time (I)

    pasar — con amigos to spend time with friends (I)

    ¿Qué — hace? What's the weather like? (I)

la tienda store (I)

    la — de acampar tent (1-1)

    la — de descuentos discount store (I)

    la — de electrodomésticos household-appliance store (I)

    la — de ropa clothing store (I)

Tiene(n)...años. He / She is / They are...(years old). (I)

la Tierra Earth (II, 7-2); **la tierra** land (8-2)

las tijeras scissors (II)

    tímido, -a timid (II)

    típico, -a typical (II)

el tío, la tía uncle, aunt (I)

los tíos uncles, aunt(s) and uncle(s) (I)

    tirar to spill, to throw away (II)

    no tires don't spill, don't throw away (II)

la toalla towel (II)

el tobillo ankle (II)

    tocar la guitarra to play the guitar (I)

el tocino bacon (I)

    todavía still (II)

    todo el mundo everyone (II)

    todos, -as all (I)

    — los días every day (I)

la tolerancia tolerance (10-1)

    tomar to take, to drink (3-1)

    — conciencia de to become aware of (9-2)

    — decisiones to make decisions (6-1)

    — el sol to sunbathe (I)

    — lecciones to take lessons (II)

    — un curso to take a course (I)

los tomates tomatoes (I)

la tonelada ton (7-1)

    tonto, -a silly, stupid (I)

torcerse (o → ue) to twist, to sprain (II)

la tormenta storm (II)

la torre tower (8-1)

la tortuga turtle (II)

la tos cough (3-1)

    trabajador, -ora hardworking (I)

    trabajar to work (I)

el trabajo work, job (I)

    el — voluntario volunteer work (I)

    traducir to translate (6-1)

el traductor, la traductora translator (6-1)

traer:

    Le traigo... I will bring you... (I)

    ¿Me trae...? Will you bring me...? *formal* (I)

el tráfico traffic (II)

el traje suit (I)

    el — de baño swimsuit (I)

    tranquilo, -a calm (II)

    tratar to treat (10-1)

    — de to try to (II)

    tratarse de to be about (II)

    travieso, -a naughty, mischievous (II)

    trazar to trace, to draw (7-1)

    trece thirteen (I)

    treinta thirty (I)

    treinta y uno thirty-one (I)

    tremendo, -a tremendous (I)

el tren train (I)

    el — eléctrico electric train (II)

    tres three (I)

    trescientos, -as three hundred (I)

el triángulo triangle (7-1)

el triciclo tricycle (II)

    triste sad (I)

el trofeo trophy (1-2)

la trompeta trumpet (2-2)

    tropezar (e → ie) (con) to trip (over) (II)

el trueno thunder (1-1)

    tu, tus your (I)

    tú you *fam.* (I)

el / la **turista** tourist (II)
tuyo, -a, -os, -as yours (II)

U

Ud. (usted) you *formal sing.* (I)
Uds. (ustedes) you *formal / informal pl.* (I)
¡Uf! ugh!, yuck! (I)
último, -a the last / final (II)
un, una a, an (I)
— **poco (de)** a little (I)
la **una:**
a la — at one o'clock (I)
único, -a only (8-1)
la **unidad** unity (8-1)
la **universidad** university (II)
el **universo** universe (7-2)
uno one (I)
unos, -as some (I)
las **uñas** nails (II)
usado, -a used (I)
usar la computadora to use the computer (I)
el **uso** use (6-2)
usted (Ud.) you *formal sing.* (I)
ustedes (Uds.) you *formal / informal pl.* (I)
las **uvas** grapes (I)

V

las **vacaciones: ir de** — to go on vacation (I)
vacío, -a empty (3-1)
valiente brave (II)
el **valle** valley (II, 1-1)
el **valor** value (10-2)
¡Vamos! Let's go! (I)
vanidoso, -a vain, conceited (4-1)
la **variedad** variety (8-2)
varios, -as various, several (II)
el **vaso** glass (I)
el **vecino, la vecina** neighbor (II)
veinte twenty (I)
veintiuno (veintiún) twenty-one (I)

la **vela** sail (II)
vencer to beat (1-2)
la **venda** bandage (II)
el **vendedor, la vendedora** vendor (II)
vender to sell (I)
el **veneno** poison (9-1)
venir to come (I)
la **ventana** window (I)
la **ventanilla** (airplane) window (II)
ver to see (I)
a — ... Let's see... (I)
¡Nos vemos! See you later! (I)
— **la tele** to watch television (I)
— **una película** to see a movie (I)
el **verano** summer (I)
veras:
¿De —**?** Really? (I)
la **verdad** truth (II)
¿Verdad? Really? (I)
verde green (I)
el **vestido** dress (I)
vestirse (e → i) to get dressed (II)
el **veterinario, la veterinaria** veterinarian (II)
la **vez,** *pl.* las **veces:**
a veces sometimes (I)
en — **de** instead of (10-1)
otra — again (I)
una — **allí** once there (1-1)
vía satélite via satellite (6-2)
viajar to travel (I)
el **viaje** trip (I)
la **víctima** victim (II)
la **vida** life (II)
el **video** video (I)
los **videojuegos: jugar** — to play video games (I)
el **vidrio** glass (I)
viejo, -a old (I)
viernes Friday (I)
el **vinagre** vinegar (II)
violar to violate (10-2)
la **violencia** violence (II)
violento, -a violent (I)

visitar to visit (I)
— **salones de chat** to visit chat rooms (I, II)
la **vitamina** vitamin (3-1)
la **vivienda** housing (6-2)
vivir to live (I)
vivo, -a bright *(color)* (II); living, alive (II)
el **vóleibol: jugar al** — to play volleyball (I)
el **voluntario, la voluntaria** volunteer (I)
volver (o → ue) to return (II)
— **se loco, -a** to go crazy (II)
volverse (ue) to become (2-1)
vosotros, -as you *fam. pl.* (I)
votar to vote (10-1)
la **voz,** *pl.* las **voces** voice (II)
el **vuelo** flight (II)
vuestro, -a, -os, -as your (I)

Y

y and (I)
¿ — **a ti?** And you? (I)
— **cuarto** quarter past (I)
— **media** thirty, half-past *(in telling time)* (I)
¿ — **tú?** And you? *fam.* (I)
¿ — **usted (Ud.)?** And you? *formal* (I)
ya already (I, II)
— **que** because, due to (7-1)
el **yeso** cast (II)
yo I (I)
¡Yo no fui! It was not me! (4-2)
el **yoga** yoga (3-2)
el **yogur** yogurt (I)

Z

las **zanahorias** carrots (I)
la **zapatería** shoe store (I)
los **zapatos** shoes (I)
el **zoológico** zoo (I)

English–Spanish Vocabulary

The *English-Spanish Vocabulary* contains all active vocabulary from the text, including vocabulary presented in the grammar sections.

A dash (—) represents the main entry word. For example, **to play —** after **baseball** means **to play baseball.**

The number following each entry indicates the chapter in which the word or expression is presented. A Roman numeral (I) indicates that the word was presented in AUTÉNTICO 1. A roman numeral II indicates the word was presented in AUTÉNTICO 2.

The following abbreviations are used in this list: *adj.* (adjective), *dir. obj.* (direct object), *f.* (feminine), *fam.* (familiar), *ind. obj.* (indirect object), *inf.* (infinitive), *m.* (masculine), *pl.* (plural), *prep.* (preposition), *pron.* (pronoun), *sing.* (singular).

A

a, an un, una (I)

a little un poco (de) (I)

a lot mucho, -a (I)

a while un rato (1-1)

able capaz (6-1)

able:

    to be — to poder (o ➔ ue) (I)

about sobre (I)

abstract abstracto, -a (2-1)

abuse el abuso (10-1)

to accept aceptar (4-1)

    — (me) the way (I am) aceptar tal como (soy) (4-1)

accident el accidente (II)

to accompany acompañar (II)

to accomplish realizar (2-2)

according to según (I)

    — my family según mi familia (I)

accountant el contador, la contadora (II, 6-1)

to accuse acusar (4-2)

accused el acusado, la acusada (10-2)

to achieve lograr (6-1)

acquainted:

    to be — with conocer (I, II)

acting la actuación (II)

action figure el muñeco (II)

actor el actor (I)

actress la actriz, *pl.* las actrices (I)

to add añadir (II)

address:

    e-mail — la dirección electrónica (I)

adequate adecuado, -a (10-1)

adolescence la adolescencia (10-1)

adolescent el / la adolescente (10-1)

to adopt adoptar (8-2)

advance el avance (6-2)

advice el consejo (3-2)

to advise aconsejar (3-2)

aerobics ejercicios aeróbicos (3-2)

aerosol el aerosol (9-2)

to affect afectar (9-2)

affectionate cariñoso, -a (4-1)

afraid:

    to be — (of) tener miedo (de) (I)

African africano, -a (8-2)

after después de (I)

afternoon:

    at one (o'clock) in the afternoon a la una de la tarde (I)

    Good —. Buenas tardes. (I)

    in the — de la tarde (I)

    this — esta tarde (I)

afterwards después (I)

again otra vez (I)

against contra (II, 1-2), en contra de (5-2)

age la edad (3-1)

agitated agitado, -a (II)

ago hace + *time expression* (I)

agree:

    I —. Estoy de acuerdo. (I)

    I don't —. No estoy de acuerdo. (I)

Agreed. De acuerdo. (II)

air conditioner el aire acondicionado (II)

airline la línea aérea (II)

airplane el avión (I)

airport el aeropuerto (II)

aisle el pasillo (II)

alarm clock el despertador (I)

alien el / la extraterrestre (II)

alive vivo, -a (II)

all todos, -as (I)

allergy la alergia (3-1)

almost casi (I, II)

alone solo, -a (I)

along por (II, II)

already ya (I)

also también (I)

always siempre (I)

am:

    I — (yo) soy (I)

    I — not (yo) no soy (I)

ambitious ambicioso, -a (6-1)

ambulance la ambulancia (II)

among entre (II)

amusement park el parque de diversiones (I)

amusing divertido, -a (I)

ancestor el antepasado, la antepasada (8-2)

ancestry la descendencia (8-2)

and y (I)

    — you? ¿Y a ti? *fam.* (I); ¿Y tú? *fam.* (I); ¿Y usted (Ud.)? *formal* (I)

angry enojado, -a (II)

to **get** — enojarse (II)

animal el animal (I)

ankle el tobillo (II)

anniversary el aniversario (II)

another otro, -a (I)

to **announce** anunciar (II)

announcement el anuncio (II)

announcer el locutor, la locutora (II)

to **answer** contestar (II)

ant la hormiga (II)

antibiotic el antibiótico (3-1)

antique antiguo, -a (II)

any algunos, -as (II); cualquier, -a (7-2)

anyone alguien (II)

Anything else? ¿Algo más? (I)

apartment el apartamento (I)

— **building** el edificio de apartamentos (II)

to **appear** aparecer (zc) (1-1, 7-2)

to **applaud** aplaudir (II)

applause el aplauso (2-2)

apple la manzana (I)

— **juice** el jugo de manzana (I)

to **apply for a job** presentarse (5-1)

to **apply (the law)** aplicar (las leyes) (10-1)

to **approach** acercarse a (1-1)

appropriate apropiado, -a (3-1)

approximately aproximadamente (II)

April abril (I)

aqueduct el acueducto (8-1)

Arab el / la árabe (8-1)

arch el arco (8-1)

archaeologist el arqueólogo, la arqueóloga (7-1)

architect el arquitecto, la arquitecta (II, 6-1)

architecture la arquitectura (8-1)

Are you...? ¿Eres...? (I)

arm el brazo (I)

around por (II); alrededor de (II)

to **arrest** arrestar (II)

arrival la llegada (II)

to **arrive late** llegar tarde (II)

art class la clase de arte (I)

article el artículo (II)

artist el artista, la artista (II)

artistic artístico, -a (I)

arts las artes (II)

martial — las artes marciales (II)

as como (I), al igual que (7-2), a medida que (10-2)

— **a child** de niño (II); de pequeño (II)

— **a main dish** de plato principal (I)

— **far as, up to** hasta (II)

— **soon as** en cuanto, tan pronto como (9-1)

— **though it were** como si fuera (6-2)

as much / many + noun + as tantos, -as + noun + como (II)

as + adj. + as tan + adj. + como (II)

to **ask for** pedir (e → i) (I)

to — **forgiveness** pedir perdón (4-2)

— **help** pedir ayuda (II)

to **ask a question** hacer una pregunta (II)

asleep dormido, -a (II)

aspiration la aspiración (10-2)

aspirin la aspirina (3-1)

astronomer el astrónomo, la astrónoma (7-2)

to **assimilate** asimilar(se) (8-1)

to **assist** atender (5-1)

to **assure** asegurar (10-2)

at:

— **dawn** al amanecer (1-1)

— **dusk** al anochecer (1-1)

— **eight (o'clock)** a las ocho (I)

— **eight (o'clock) at night** a las ocho de la noche (I)

— **eight (o'clock) in the evening** a las ocho de la noche (I)

— **eight (o'clock) in the morning** a las ocho de la mañana (I)

— **home** en casa (I)

— **one (o'clock)** a la una (I)

— **one (o'clock) in the afternoon** a la una de la tarde (I)

— **the beginning** al principio (1-2)

— **the end** al final (II)

— **what time?** ¿A qué hora? (I)

ATM el cajero automático (II)

atmosphere la atmósfera (9-2)

attempt el intento (7-2)

to **attend** asistir a (II)

attentive atento, -a (II)

athlete el / la atleta (II)

attraction(s) la atracción, pl. las atracciones (I)

audience el público (II)

audition la audición, pl. las audiciones (II)

auditorium el auditorio (II)

August agosto (I)

aunt la tía (I)

aunt(s) and uncle(s) los tíos (I)

authority la autoridad (10-1)

autumn el otoño (I)

avenue la avenida (II)

avocado el aguacate (II)

to **avoid** evitar (3-1)

awards ceremony la entrega de premios (1-2)

B

baby el / la bebé (II)

babysitter el niñero, la niñera (5-1)

back la espalda (II)

to **back (each other)** apoyarse (4-1)

background el fondo (2-1)

backpack la mochila (I)

bacon el tocino (I)

bad malo, -a (I); mal (I)

badly mal (I)

bag la bolsa (I)

baked al horno (II)

balanced equilibrado, -a (3-1)

balcony el balcón, *pl.* los balcones (8-1)

bald eagle el águila calva, *pl.* las águilas calvas (9-2)

ball la pelota (II)

balloon el globo (I)

banana el plátano (I)

band *(musical)* la banda (II), el conjunto (2-2)

bandage la venda (II)

bank el banco (II)

banker el banquero, la banquera (6-1)

bargain la ganga (II)

to **bargain** regatear (II)

baseball:

  to play — jugar al béisbol (I)

basement el sótano (I)

basket la cesta (II)

basketball:

  to play — jugar al basquétbol (I)

bathroom el baño (I)

battery la pila (9-1)

battle la batalla (8-2)

to **be** ser (I); estar (I)

  He / She is / They are... (years old). Tiene(n)... años. (I)

  How old is / are...? ¿Cuántos años tiene(n)...? (I)

  to — + *present participle* estar + *present participle* (I)

  to — a member ser miembro (II)

  to — able to poder (o → ue) (I)

  to — about tratarse de (II)

  to — acquainted with conocer (I)

  to — afraid (of) tener miedo (de) (I)

to — based on estar basado, -a en (II)

to — born nacer (II)

to — cold tener frío (I)

to — correct tener razón (I)

to — daydreaming estar en la luna (3-2)

to — delighted alegrarse (4-1)

to — exhausted caerse de sueño (3-2)

to — formed by componerse de (8-2)

to — going to + *verb* ir a + *inf.* (I)

to — guilty tener la culpa (4-2)

to — in a good / bad mood estar de buen / mal humor (3-2)

to — in charge of encargarse (5-1), estar a cargo de (9-1)

to — in fashion estar de moda (II)

to — in love with estar enamorado, -a de (II)

to — jealous tener celos (4-1)

to — located quedar (I, II)

to — mistaken estar equivocado, -a (4-2)

to — moved emocionarse (1-2)

to — online estar en línea (I)

to — proud of estar orgulloso, -a de (1-2)

to — scared (of) tener miedo (de) (I)

to — sitting sentado, -a (2-1)

to — sleepy tener sueño (I), caerse de sueño (3-2)

to — standing parado, -a (2-1)

to — subject to estar sujeto, -a a (10-1)

to — sure estar seguro, -a (II)

to — surprised sorprenderse (4-1)

to — useful servir (I)

to — warm tener calor (I)

beach la playa (I)

beans los frijoles (II)

bear el oso (I)

to **beat** batir (II), vencer (1-2)

beautiful bello, -a (II), hermoso, -a (1-1)

beauty salon el salón de belleza, *pl.* los salones de belleza (II)

because porque (I), ya que (7-1)

  — of a causa de (II)

to **become** ponerse (II), volverse (ue) (2-1), hacerse (6-1), convertirse (en) (7-2)

  to — aware of tomar conciencia de (9-2)

  to — friends again reconciliarse (4-2)

  to — the champion salir campeón/campeona (1-2)

bed la cama (I)

  to make the — hacer la cama (I)

bedroom el dormitorio (I)

beefsteak el bistec (I)

before antes de (I), anteriormente (8-1), ante (10-1)

to **begin** empezar (e → ie) (I)

to **behave well / badly** portarse bien / mal (II)

behavior el comportamiento (4-2)

behind detrás de (I)

belief la creencia (7-2)

belt el cinturón, *pl.* los cinturones (II)

to **benefit** beneficiar (5-2)

benefits los beneficios (II, 5-1)

best:

  the — el / la mejor, los / las mejores (I)

better than mejor(es) que (I)

between entre (II)

bicycle:

  to ride a — montar en bicicleta (I)

bilingual bilingüe (II)

bill la cuenta (I)

binder:
    three-ring — la carpeta de argollas (I)

binoculars los binoculares (1-1)

bird el pájaro (I), el ave (9-2)

birthday el cumpleaños (I)
    Happy —! ¡Feliz cumpleaños! (I)

black hair el pelo negro (I)

block la cuadra (II)

blocks los bloques (II)

blond hair el pelo rubio (I)

blood la sangre (II)

blouse la blusa (I)

blow dryer el secador (II)

blue azul (I)

to board abordar (II)

boat el barco (I)
    sail— el bote de vela (II)

boating:
    to go — pasear en bote (I)

to boil hervir (e → ie) (II)

bone el hueso (II)

bonfire la fogata (II)

book el libro (I)

bookbag la mochila (I)

bookshelf el estante (I)

bookstore la librería (I)

boots las botas (I)

to bore aburrir (I)
    it / they bore(s) me me aburre(n) (I)
    to get bored aburrirse (II)

boring aburrido, -a (I)

to borrow (from) pedir prestado, -a (a) (II)

boss el jefe, la jefa (6-1)

both los dos, las dos (I), ambos (10-1)

to bother molestar (II)

bottle la botella (I)

to bowl jugar a los bolos (II)

box la caja (I)

boy el chico (I)
    young — el niño (I)

boyfriend el novio (I)

bracelet la pulsera (I)

brand la marca (II)

brave valiente (II)

bread el pan (I)

to break romper (I); romperse (II)

breakfast el desayuno (I)
    for — en el desayuno (I)

to breathe respirar (3-2)

bridge el puente (II)

bright (color) vivo, -a (II)

to bring traer (I); llevar (I)
    I will — you... Le traigo... (I)
    Will you — me... ? ¿Me trae... ? (I)

broth el caldo (II)

brother el hermano (I)

brothers; brother(s) and sister(s) los hermanos (I)

brown marrón (I)
    — (chestnut) hair el pelo castaño (I)

brush el cepillo (II), el pincel (2-1)
    tooth— el cepillo de dientes (II)

to brush (one's teeth) cepillarse (los dientes) (II)

to build construir (i → y) (5-2)

to burn a CD grabar un disco compacto (I)

to burn (oneself), to burn up quemar(se) (II)

bus el autobús, *pl.* los autobuses (I)

business los negocios (II), la empresa (6-1)
    —man el hombre de negocios (II, 6-1)
    —woman la mujer de negocios (II, 6-1)

busy ocupado, -a (I)

but pero (I), sino (7-2)

butter la mantequilla (I)

to buy comprar (I)
    — souvenirs comprar recuerdos (I)

by por (II)
    — + *vehicle* en + *vehicle* (I)
    — hand a mano (II)

C

café el café (I)

cake el pastel (I)

calcium el calcio (3-1)

to call:
    to — on the phone llamar por teléfono (II)

to calculate calcular (7-1)

calculator la calculadora (I)

calm tranquilo, -a (II)

camera la cámara (I)
    digital — la cámara digital (I)

camp el campamento (I)

campaign la campaña (5-2)

can la lata (I)

can:
    I — (yo) puedo (I)
    you — (tú) puedes (I)

candy los dulces (I)

canned enlatado, -a (II)

cap la gorra (I)

to capture capturar (II)

car el coche (I)

carbohydrate el carbohidrato (3-1)

card la tarjeta (I)
    credit — la tarjeta de crédito (II)
    post— la tarjeta postal (II)

cardboard el cartón (I)

career la carrera (II)

careful cuidadoso, -a (6-1)

carrots las zanahorias (I)

to carry llevar (I)
    — out cumplir con (5-1)

cartoon el programa de dibujos animados (I)

cash el dinero en efectivo (II)
    to cash a check cobrar un cheque (II)

cash register la caja (II)

cashier el cajero, la cajera (II)

cast el yeso (II)

castle el castillo (II)

cat el gato (I)

to catch atrapar (9-2)

cathedral la catedral (II)

cattle la res (II)

cause la causa (II), el motivo (10-1)

CD:

    to burn a — grabar un disco compacto (I)

to celebrate celebrar (I)

center, downtown el centro (I, II)

centigrade degree el grado centígrado (3-1)

centimeter el centímetro (7-1)

century el siglo (2-1)

cereal el cereal (I)

ceremony la ceremonia (1-2)

certificate el certificado (1-2)

chain la cadena (I)

chair la silla (I)

    wheel— la silla de ruedas (II)

challenge el reto (8-2)

champion el campeón, la campeona, pl. los campeones (II)

to become the — salir campeón, campeona (1-2)

championship el campeonato (II)

to change cambiar (II)

    to — one's mind cambiar de opinión (4-1)

channel (TV) el canal (I)

to chat charlar (II)

chat rooms los salones de chat (II)

cheap barato, -a (I)

check:

    to cash a — cobrar un cheque (II)

    traveler's — el cheque de viajero (II)

    personal — el cheque personal (II)

to check (luggage) facturar (el equipaje) (II)

to check out a book sacar (II)

cheerleader el animador, la animadora (II)

chemical químico, -a (9-1)

cherry la cereza (II)

chess el ajedrez (II)

chest el pecho (3-1)

chicken el pollo (I)

childhood la niñez (10-1)

childish infantil (I)

children los hijos (I); los niños (I)

to chop picar (II)

chore:

    household — el quehacer (de la casa) (I)

chorus, choir el coro (II)

to choose escoger (II)

Christian el cristiano, la cristiana (8-1)

church la iglesia (I)

    Protestant — el templo (I)

circle el círculo (7-1)

citizen el ciudadano, la ciudadana (5-2)

citizenship la ciudadanía (5-2)

city la ciudad (I)

civilization la civilización (7-1)

class la clase (I)

classical clásico, -a (2-2)

classified ad el anuncio clasificado (5-1)

classroom la sala de clases (I)

clean limpio, -a (I)

to clean the bathroom limpiar el baño (I)

cleaning la limpieza (9-2)

client el / la cliente / a (5-1)

to climb (a rock or mountain) escalar (1-1)

clock el reloj (I)

to close cerrar (II)

close (to) cerca (de) (I)

closed cerrado, -a (II)

closes se cierra (II)

closet el armario (I)

clothing store la tienda de ropa (I)

club el club, pl. los clubes (II)

    athletic — el club atlético (II)

coach el entrenador, la entrenadora (II)

coat el abrigo (I)

coffee el café (I)

coin la moneda (II)

cold:

    It's —. Hace frío. (I)

    to be — tener frío (I)

to collaborate colaborar (4-2)

to collect recoger (I)

to collect coleccionar (II)

collection la colección, pl. las colecciones (II)

to collide with chocar con (II)

cologne el agua de colonia (II)

colony la colonia (8-2)

color:

    What — ... ? ¿De qué color ... ? (I)

    —s los colores (I)

comb el peine (II)

to come venir (I)

comedy la comedia (I)

comfortable cómodo, -a (II)

comical cómico, -a (I)

commentary el comentario (II)

to communicate comunicarse (I, 6-2)

    I — (yo) me comunico (I)

    you — (tú) te comunicas (I)

community la comunidad (I)

    — center el centro de la comunidad (5-2)

compact disc el disco compacto (I)

    to burn a — grabar un disco compacto (I)

company la compañía (5-1)

compass la brújula (1-1)

to compete competir (e → i) (II)

competition la competencia (II)

to complain quejarse (3-2)

complicated complicado, -a (I, II)

composition la composición, pl. las composiciones (I)

to compute calcular (7-1)

computer la computadora (I)

    — graphics los gráficos (I)

    — keyboard el teclado (I)

— **mouse** el ratón (I)

— **screen** la pantalla (I)

— **science** la computación (5-1)

—**s / technology** la tecnología (I)

laptop — la computadora portátil (I)

to use the — usar la computadora (I)

conceited vanidoso, -a (4-1)

to **concentrate** concentrarse (3-2)

concert el concierto (I)

conflict el conflicto (4-2)

to **confront** enfrentarse (8-2)

to **congratulate** felicitar (II)

Congratulations! ¡Felicidades! (II), ¡Felicitaciones! (1-2)

to **conquer** conquistar (8-1)

conquest la conquista (8-1)

conservation la preservación (9-2)

to **conserve** conservar (II)

considerate considerado, -a (4-1)

construction la construcción (8-1)

— **project** el proyecto de construcción (I)

to **contain** contener (3-1)

container el recipiente (9-1)

contest el concurso (II)

beauty — el concurso de belleza (II)

to **contribute** contribuir (u → y) (7-2)

cook el cocinero, la cocinera (6-1)

to **cook** cocinar (I)

cookie la galleta (I)

cooking oil el aceite (II)

corn el maíz (II)

corner la esquina (II)

correct:

to be — tener razón (I)

to **cost** costar (o → ue) (I)

How much does (do)... —? ¿Cuánto cuesta(n)? (I)

cotton el algodón (II)

cough la tos (3-1)

counselor el consejero, la consejera (5-1)

to **count on** contar con (4-1)

country el país (I)

countryside el campo (I)

course:

to take a — tomar un curso (I)

— **of studies** el programa de estudios (II)

cousin la prima, el primo (I)

—**s** los primos (I)

to **cover** cubrir (7-1)

cramp el calambre (3-2)

to **crash into** chocar con (II)

to **create** crear (I)

to — **a Web page** crear una página Web (II)

crime el crimen (II)

— **movie** la película policíaca (I)

criminal el / la criminal (II)

critic el crítico, la crítica (II)

to **criticize** criticar (4-2)

to **cross** cruzar (II)

crunches los abdominales (3)

crutches las muletas (II)

to **cry** llorar (II)

cup la taza (I)

to **cure** curar (6-2)

curtains las cortinas (I)

custom la costumbre (II)

customs la aduana (II)

customs officer el aduanero, la aduanera (II)

to **cut** cortar (I, II)

to — **oneself** cortarse (II)

to — **one's hair** cortarse el pelo (II)

to — **the lawn** cortar el césped (I)

cut-paper decorations el papel picado (I)

to **damage** dañar (9-1)

dance el baile (I), la danza (2-2)

to **dance** bailar (I)

dancer el bailarín, la bailarina (II)

dangerous peligroso, -a (II)

to **dare** atreverse (4-2)

daring atrevido, -a (I)

dark oscuro, -a (II)

date:

What is the —? ¿Cuál es la fecha? (I)

date la cita (II)

date of birth la fecha de nacimiento (5-1)

daughter la hija (I)

day el día (I)

every — todos los días (I); cada día (I)

What — **is today?** ¿Qué día es hoy? (I)

day-care center la guardería infantil (II)

dead muerto, -a (II)

December diciembre (I)

to **decide** decidir (I)

to **decorate** decorar (I)

decorations las decoraciones (I)

to **decrease** disminuir (9-2)

to dedicate oneself to dedicarse a (6-1)

dedicated dedicado, -a (5-1)

delay el retraso (II)

delicious delicioso, -a (I)

delighted encantado, -a (I)

to **deliver** repartir (5-1)

delivery person el repartidor, la repartidora (5-1)

demand la demanda (6-2)

to **demand** exigir (3-2)

democratic democrático, -a (10-2)

demonstration la manifestación (5-2)

dentist el / la dentista (II)

department store el almacén, *pl.* los almacenes (I)

departure gate la puerta de embarque (II)

to **depend on** depender de (9-1)

deodorant el desodorante (II)

descent la descendencia (8-2)

desert el desierto (II, 1-1)

design el diseño (7-1)

to **design** diseñar (6-1)

designer el diseñador, la diseñadora (II, 6-1)

desk el pupitre (I); el escritorio (I)

despite aunque (3-1), a pesar de (10-2)

dessert el postre (I)

for — de postre (I)

to **destroy** destruir (i → y) (II)

destruction la destrucción (II)

to **detain** detener (10-2)

detective el / la detective (II)

detective movie la película policíaca (I)

to **develop** desarrollar (3-2)

development el desarrollo (6-2)

diameter el diámetro (7-1)

dictionary el diccionario (I)

Did you like it? ¿Te gustó? (I)

to **die** morirse (II)

diet la dieta (3-1)

difference of opinion la diferencia de opinión (4-2)

difficult difícil (I)

digital camera la cámara digital (I)

to **diminish** disminuir (9-2)

dining room el comedor (I)

dinner la cena (I)

dinosaur el dinosaurio (II)

diploma el certificado (1-2)

direct directo, -a (II)

direction la dirección, pl. las direcciones (II)

dirty sucio, -a (I)

to **disappear** desaparecer (zc) (6-2)

disaster:

It was a —. Fue un desastre. (I)

discount store la tienda de descuentos (I)

discouraged desanimado, -a (1-2)

to **discover** descubrir (6-2)

to **discriminate** discriminar (10-1)

to **discuss** discutir (II)

dish el plato (I)

as a main — de plato principal (I)

main — el plato principal (I)

disobedient desobediente (II)

distance la distancia (7-1)

to **do** hacer (I)

— (command) haz (I)

— you like to ... ? ¿Te gusta ... ? (I)

I — (yo) hago (I)

to — a project hacer un proyecto (II)

to — a search hacer una búsqueda (II)

to — gymnastics hacer gimnasia (II)

to — push-ups hacer flexiones (3-2)

to — the laundry lavar la ropa (I)

you — (tú) haces (I)

What did you —? ¿Qué hiciste? (I)

doctor el médico, la médica (II)

doctor's / dentist's office el consultorio (II)

document el documento (I)

dog el perro (I)

to feed the — dar de comer al perro (I)

doll la muñeca (II)

to **dominate** dominar (8-1)

to **donate** donar (5-2)

Don't eat. No comas. (II)

Don't leave, Don't let No dejes (II)

Don't speak. No hables. (II)

Don't write. No escribas. (II)

door la puerta (I)

to **doubt** dudar (II, 7-1)

to **download** bajar (información) (I)

drama el drama (I)

to **draw** dibujar (I)

dress el vestido (I)

— code el código de vestimenta (10-1)

dresser la cómoda (I)

to **drink** beber (I), tomar (3-1)

drinks las bebidas (I)

to **drive** manejar (II)

driver el conductor, la conductora (II)

driver's license el permiso de manejar (II)

drum el tambor (2-2)

dry seco, -a (II)

to **dry** secarse (II)

due to ya que (7-1), debido a (9-1)

during durante (I)

to **dust** quitar el polvo (I)

duty el deber (10-1)

DVD player el lector DVD (I)

E

e-mail:

— address la dirección electrónica (I)

to write — escribir por correo electrónico (I)

ear el oído (3-1)

early temprano (I)

to **earn (money)** ganar (II)

Earth la Tierra (II, 7-2)

earthquake el terremoto (II)

earrings los aretes (I)

easy fácil (I)

to **eat** comer (I)

eating habit el hábito alimenticio (3-1)

eclipse el eclipse (7-2)

ecological ecológico, -a (II)

economical económico, -a (II, 9-1)

editor el redactor, la redactora (6-1)

to **educate** educar (5-2)

educational program el programa educativo (I)

efficient eficiente (II, 6-1)

eggs los huevos (I)

eight ocho (I)

eight hundred ochocientos, -as (I)

eighteen dieciocho (I)

eighth octavo, -a (I)

eighty ochenta (I)

either tampoco (I)

    I don't (like to) — a mí tampoco (I)

elbow el codo (II)

elderly man, woman el anciano, la anciana (I)

the elderly los ancianos (I)

electricity la electricidad (II, 9-1)

elegant elegante (II)

elevator el ascensor (II)

eleven once (I)

to eliminate eliminar (II, 1-2)

else:

    Anything —? ¿Algo más? (I)

    What —? ¿Qué más? (I)

emergency room la sala de emergencia (II)

empire el imperio (8-1)

employee el empleado, la empleada (II)

empty vacío, -a (3-1)

to encourage fomentar (9-1)

to end terminar (I)

endangered (en) peligro de extinción (9-2)

to endure aguantar (3-2)

energy la energía (II, 3-1)

    — source la fuente de energía (6-2)

engineer el ingeniero, la ingeniera (II, 6-1)

English class la clase de inglés (I)

to enjoy disfrutar de (II), gozar (de) (10-1)

enormous enorme (II)

enough bastante (I), suficiente (9-1)

Enough! ¡Basta! (II)

to enter entrar (I)

enterprising emprendedor, -a (6-1)

enthusiasm el entusiasmo (2-2)

entrance la entrada (II)

environment el medio ambiente (II, 5-2)

environmental ambiental (9-2)

equality la igualdad (10-1)

era la época (8-1)

to escape escaparse (II)

especially especialmente (I)

establish establecer (zc) (8-2)

ethnic group el grupo étnico (8-1)

European europeo, -a (8-2)

even when aunque (3-1)

evening:

    Good —. Buenas noches. (I)

    in the — de la noche (I)

    this — esta noche (I)

every day cada día (I), todos los días (I)

everyone todo el mundo (II)

evidence la evidencia (7-1)

exactly en punto (II)

to exaggerate exagerar (2-2)

to examine, to check examinar (II)

to excavate excavar (7-1)

excessive excesivo, -a (9-2)

exchange el intercambio (8-2)

to exchange cambiar (II)

to exchange intercambiar (10-2)

excited entusiasmado, -a, emocionado, -a (II), animado, -a (1-2)

excursion, short trip la excursión, *pl.* las excursiones (II)

Excuse me. Perdón. (I)

to exercise hacer ejercicio (I)

to exhaust agotar(se) (9-1)

to exist existir (7-1)

exit la salida (II)

to expel expulsar (8-1)

expensive caro, -a (I)

experience la experiencia (I)

to explain explicar (II)

explanation la explicación (4-2)

to exploit explotar (9-2)

explosion la explosión, *pl.* las explosiones (II)

to express (oneself) expresar(se) (2-1)

to extend prolongar (6-2)

extinction:

    in danger of — en peligro de extinción (9-2)

extracurricular extracurricular

    — activities las actividades extracurriculares (II)

eye el ojo (I)

F

face la cara (II)

to face enfrentarse (8-2)

face-to-face cara a cara (I)

factory la fábrica (6-2)

failure el fracaso (II)

fair justo, -a (5-2)

fall el otoño (I)

to fall caerse (II)

    I — (yo) me caigo (II)

    to — asleep dormirse (II)

    to — in love (with) enamorarse (de) (II)

    you — (tú) te caes (II)

famous famoso, -a (II, 2-1)

fan el aficionado, la aficionada (II)

fantastic fantástico, -a (I)

far (from) lejos (de) (I)

farmer el agricultor, la agricultora (II)

to fascinate fascinar (II)

fascinating fascinante (I)

fast rápidamente (I)

father el padre (papá) (I)

favorite favorito, -a (I)

to fear temer (4-1)

feather la pluma (9-2)

February febrero (I)

to feed the dog dar de comer al perro (I)

to feel sentirse (e → ie) (II)

    to — awful sentirse fatal (3-2)

feeling el sentimiento (2-1)

fever la fiebre (3-1)

fewer:

    — ...than menos... que (I)

    — than... menos de... (I)

fiber la fibra (3-1)

field el campo (6-2)

fifteen quince (I)

fifth quinto, -a (I)

fifty cincuenta (I)

fight la pelea (4-2)

to fight luchar (II, 8-2), pelearse (II)

figure la figura (2-1)

to fill (the tank) llenar (el tanque) (II)

film la película (I)

final último, -a (II)

finance las finanzas (6-1)

to find encontrar (o → ue) (II)

    — out averiguar (6-1), enterarse (6-2)

finger el dedo (I)

to finish terminar (I)

fire el incendio (II); el fuego (II)

firefighter el bombero, la bombera (II)

firewood la leña (II)

fireworks los fuegos artificiales (II)

firm la compañía (5-1)

first primer (primero), -a (I)

fish el pescado (I); el pez, *pl.* los peces (II)

    to go —ing ir de pesca (I)

to fit:

    It / They —(s) me well / poorly. Me queda(n) bien / mal. (I)

five cinco (I)

five hundred quinientos, -as (I)

to fix (one's hair) arreglarse (el pelo) (II)

flag la bandera (I)

flashlight la linterna (1-1)

flavorful sabroso, -a (I)

to flex flexionar (3-2)

flexible flexible (5-1)

flight el vuelo (II)

flight attendant el / la auxiliar de vuelo (II)

flood la inundación, *pl.* las inundaciones (II)

floor el piso (I); el suelo (II)

    ground — la planta baja (I)

    second — el primer piso (I)

    third — el segundo piso (I)

flour la harina (II)

flower la flor, *pl.* las flores (I)

flu la gripe (3-1)

fly la mosca (II)

folder la carpeta (I)

to follow seguir (e → i) (II)

following siguiente (II)

food la comida (I), los alimentos (3-1)

food stand el puesto (II)

foot el pie (I)

football:

    to play — jugar al fútbol americano (I)

for para (I)

    — breakfast en el desayuno (I)

    — lunch en el almuerzo (I)

    — me para mí (I)

    — you para ti (I)

for (how long) por (II)

    — example por ejemplo (II)

    — the ... time por ... vez (II)

forbidden:

    It is —. Se prohíbe. (II)

to force obligar (10-1)

foreground el primer plano (2-1)

forest el bosque (II, 1-1)

to forget about olvidarse de (II)

    don't — no te olvides de (II)

to forgive perdonar (4-2)

fork el tenedor (I)

fortunately afortunadamente (II)

forty cuarenta (I)

to found fundar (8-1)

fountain la fuente (II)

four cuatro (I)

four hundred cuatrocientos, -as (I)

fourteen catorce (I)

fourth cuarto, -a (I)

free gratuito, -a (10-1), libre (10-2)

free time el tiempo libre (I), el ocio (6-2)

French fries las papas fritas (I)

frequently frecuentemente (II)

fresh fresco, -a (II)

Friday viernes (I)

fried frito, -a (II)

friendly simpático, -a (I)

friendship la amistad (4-1)

frightened asustado, -a (II)

from de (I); desde (II)

    — now on de hoy en adelante (6-2)

    Where are you —? ¿De dónde eres? (I)

frozen congelado, -a (II)

fruit salad la ensalada de frutas (I)

frying pan la sartén (II)

full lleno, -a (3-1)

    — time a tiempo completo (5-1)

fun divertido, -a (I)

function la función (7-1)

to function, to work funcionar (II, 10-1)

fundamental fundamental (10-2)

to fundraise juntar fondos (5-2)

funny gracioso, -a (I); cómico, -a (I)

furious furioso, -a (II)

furniture los muebles (II)

future el futuro (II)

G

gadget el aparato (6-2)

game el partido (I)

game show el programa de concursos (I)

garage el garaje (I)

garden el jardín (I)

garlic el ajo (II)

gasoline la gasolina (II)

to **gather** recoger (I)

gathering la reunión, *pl.* las reuniones (II)

gel el gel (II)

gene, genes el gen, *pl.* los genes (6-2)

generally generalmente (I)

generous generoso, -a (II)

genetics la genética (6-2)

geometric(a) geométrico, -a (7-1)

gesture el gesto (2-2)

to **get** obtener (1-2)

   to — **a good grade** sacar una buena nota (II)

   to — **along well / badly** llevarse bien / mal (II)

   to — **dressed** vestirse (e → i) (II)

   to — **lost** perderse (1-1)

   to — **married (to)** casarse (con) (II)

   to — **ready** prepararse (II)

   to — **rid of** deshacerse de (9-1)

   to — **up** levantarse (II)

gift el regalo (I)

gift certificate el cupón de regalo, *pl.* los cupones de regalo (II)

girl la chica (I)

   young — la niña (I)

girlfriend la novia (I)

to **give** dar (I); regalar (II)

   to — **a speech** dar un discurso (II)

   to — **a ticket** poner una multa (II)

glass el vaso (I); el vidrio (I)

global warming el recalentamiento global (9-2)

gloves los guantes (I)

to **go** ir (I); pasar (II)

   Let's —! ¡Vamos! (I)

   to be —ing to + *verb* ir a + *inf.* (I)

   to — **to bed** acostarse (o → ue) (II)

   to — **boating** pasear en bote (I)

   to — **camping** ir de cámping (I)

   to — **crazy** volverse loco (II)

   to — **down** bajar (II)

   to — **fishing** ir de pesca (I)

   to — **on foot** ir a pie (II)

   to — **on vacation** ir de vacaciones (I)

   to — **out** salir (I)

   to — **shopping** ir de compras (I)

   to — **to school** ir a la escuela (I)

   to — **up** subir (II)

goal *(in sports)* el gol (II); la meta (1-2)

   to score a — meter un gol (II)

god, goddess el dios, la diosa (7-2)

going to con destino a (II)

gold el oro (II)

golf:

   — **club** el palo de golf (II)

   to play — jugar al golf (I)

good bueno (buen), -a (I)

   — **afternoon.** Buenas tardes. (I)

   — **evening.** Buenas noches. (I)

   — **gracious** caramba (II)

   — **morning.** Buenos días. (I)

Good-bye! ¡Adiós! (I)

good-looking guapo, -a (I)

gossipy chismoso, -a (4-1)

to **govern** gobernar (8-1)

government el gobierno (9-1)

grade *(in school)* la nota (II)

   to get a good — sacar una buena nota (II)

to **graduate** graduarse (u → ú) (II, 6-1)

graduation la graduación, *pl.* las graduaciones (II)

grandfather el abuelo (I)

grandmother la abuela (I)

grandparents los abuelos (I)

grapes las uvas (I)

grate la reja (8-1)

gray gris (I)

   — **hair** el pelo canoso (I)

greasy grasoso, -a (II)

Great! ¡Genial! (I)

green verde (I)

   — **beans** las judías verdes (I)

   —**house effect** el efecto invernadero (9-2)

to **greet** saludar(se) (II)

to **grill** asar (II)

grill la parrilla (II)

grilled asado, -a (II)

ground floor la planta baja (I)

ground el suelo (II)

to **grow** crecer (9-1)

grown-ups los mayores (II)

guarantee la garantía (10-2)

to **guarantee** garantizar (5-2)

guide el / la guía (II)

guidebook la guía (II)

guilty culpable (10-2)

guitar:

   to play the — tocar la guitarra (I)

gym el gimnasio (I)

gymnastics la gimnasia (II)

H

hail granizo (1-1)

   to hail caer granizo (1-1)

hair el pelo (I)

   black — el pelo negro (I)

   blond — el pelo rubio (I)

   brown (chestnut) — el pelo castaño (I)

   gray — el pelo canoso (I)

hair stylist el peluquero, la peluquera (6-1)

half media, -o (I)

   — **past** y media *(in telling time)* (I)

ham and cheese sandwich el sándwich de jamón y queso (I)

hamburger la hamburguesa (I)

hand la mano (I)

   to shake —s darse la mano (II)

handicrafts la artesanía (II)

happiness la felicidad (10-1)

happy contento, -a (I); alegre (II)

   — **birthday!** ¡Feliz cumpleaños! (I)

harmony armonía (4-2)

hardworking trabajador, -ora (I)

to **have** tener (I)

   I — to... tengo que + *inf.* (I)

   to — a barbecue hacer una parrillada (II)

   to — a birthday cumplir años (II)

   to — a cold estar resfriado, -a (3-1)

   to — a good / bad time pasarlo bien / mal (1-1)

   to — a picnic hacer un picnic (II)

   to — fun divertirse (e → ie) (II)

   to — in common tener en común (4-1)

   to — just... acabar de + *inf.* (I)

   to — lunch almorzar (o → ue) (II)

to **have** haber *(as an auxiliary verb)* (II)

he él (I)

he / she is es (I)

He / She is / They are... (years old). Tiene(n) ... años. (I)

head la cabeza (I)

health:

   for one's — para la salud (I)

   to maintain one's — para mantener la salud (I)

healthy saludable (3-1)

to **hear** oír (II)

   heart el corazón (3-2)

   heat la calefacción (II)

to **heat** calentar (e → ie) (II)

   height la estatura (3-1), el alto (7-1)

   Hello! ¡Hola! (I)

   help la ayuda (II)

to **help** ayudar (I), atender (5-1)

   How can I — you? ¿En qué puedo servirle? (I)

   her su, sus *possessive adj.* (I); la *dir. obj. pron.* (I); le *ind. obj. pron.* (I)

   here aquí (I)

   heritage la herencia (8-2)

   hero el héroe (II)

   heroine la heroína (II)

   Hey! ¡Oye! (I)

to **hide (oneself)** esconder(se) (II)

   high alto, -a (II)

   high school el colegio (II)

   highway la carretera (II)

   hill la colina (II)

   him lo *dir. obj. pron.* (I); le *ind. obj. pron.* (I)

   his su, sus (I)

   historical histórico, -a (II)

   hockey el hockey (II)

to **hold a position** desempeñar un cargo (6-1)

   hole el agujero (9-2)

   holiday el día festivo (II)

   home: la casa (I)

     at — en casa (I)

     — **for the elderly** el hogar de ancianos (5-2)

     — **office** el despacho (I)

     (to) — a casa (I)

   homeless people la gente sin hogar (5-2)

   homework la tarea (I)

   honest honesto, -a (4-1)

to **hope (for)** esperar (4-1)

   horrible horrible (I)

   horror movie la película de horror (I)

horseback:

   to ride — montar a caballo (I)

hospital el hospital (I)

hospitality la hospitalidad (6-2)

hot caliente (II)

   — **dog** el perrito caliente (I)

   It's —. Hace calor. (I)

hotel el hotel (I)

hour:

   in the ... — en la ... hora *(class period)* (I)

house la casa (I)

household:

   — **appliance store** la tienda de electrodomésticos (I)

   — **chore** el quehacer (de la casa) (I)

housing la vivienda (6-2)

how!

   — + *adj.*! ¡Qué + *adj.*! (I)

   — **awful!** ¡Qué asco! (I)

How? ¿Cómo? (I)

   — **are you?** ¿Cómo está Ud.? *formal* (I); ¿Cómo estás? *fam.* (I); ¿Qué tal? *fam.* (I)

   — **can I help you?** ¿En qué puedo servirle? (I)

   — **do you go to...?** ¿Cómo se va...? (II)

   — **do you make ...?** ¿Cómo se hace ...? (II)

   — **do you say... ?** ¿Cómo se dice... ? (I)

   — **does it (do they) fit (you)?** ¿Cómo te queda(n)? (I)

   — **does it seem to you?** ¿Qué te parece? (II)

   — **is ... spelled?** ¿Cómo se escribe ...? (I)

   — **is (it)...?** ¿Qué tal es...? (II)

   — **long...?** ¿Cuánto tiempo hace que...? (II)

   — **many?** ¿Cuántos, -as? (I)

   — **much does (do) ... cost?** ¿Cuánto cuesta(n) ... ? (I)

   — **old is / are ... ?** ¿Cuántos años tiene(n) ... ? (I)

   — **was it (for you)?** ¿Cómo lo pasaste? (I)

however sin embargo (1-2)

to hug abrazar(se) (II)

hundred:

    one — cien (I)

hungry:

    I'm —. Tengo hambre. (I)

hunting la caza (9-2)

hurricane el huracán, *pl.* los huracanes (II)

to hurt doler (o → ue) (I, II)

to hurt oneself lastimarse (II)

hurry prisa (II)

    to be in a — tener prisa (II)

husband el esposo (I)

I

I yo (I)

    — am soy (I)

    — am not no soy (I)

    — do too a mí también (I)

    — don't either a mí tampoco (I)

    — don't think so. Creo que no. (I)

    — forgot se me olvidó (II)

    — have seen he visto (II)

    — 'll do as I please haré lo que me dé la gana (6-1)

    —'m hungry. Tengo hambre. (I)

    —'m sorry. Lo siento. (I)

    —'m thirsty. Tengo sed. (I)

    — stay at home. Me quedo en casa. (I)

    — think ... Creo que ... (I)

    — think so. Creo que sí. (I)

    — will bring you ... Le traigo ... (I)

    — wish ojalá (4-1)

    — would like Me gustaría (I); quisiera (I)

    — would be interested ... Me interesaría ... (5-2)

    — would love to ... Me encantaría ... (5-2)

ice el hielo (9-2)

ice cream el helado (I)

iced tea el té helado (I)

I.D. card el carnet de identidad (II)

to identify oneself with identificarse con (2-2)

if si (I)

to ignore ignorar (4-2)

illness la enfermedad (6-2)

image la imagen (2-1)

immediately inmediatamente (II)

impatient impaciente (I)

important importante (I)

impress impresionar (1-1)

impressive impresionante (I)

to improve mejorar (II, 4-2)

in en (I)

    — addition to además de (6-1)

    — danger of extinction (en) peligro de extinción (II)

    — favor of a favor de (5-2)

    — front of delante de (I)

    — general por lo general (II)

    — love with enamorado, -a de (II)

    — my opinion para mí (I)

    — other words o sea que (7-2)

    — order to para + *inf.* (I)

    — that way de ese modo (10-1)

    — the ... hour en la ... hora (class period) (I)

    — the middle of en medio de (II)

    — your opinion para ti (I)

include incluir (3-1)

to increase aumentar (6-2)

incredible increíble (I)

industry industria (6-2)

inequity la desigualdad (10-2)

inexpensive barato, -a (I)

inexplicable inexplicable (7-1)

influence la influencia (8-1)

to influence influir (i → y) (2-1)

information la información (I)

    — technology la informática (6-2)

ingredient el ingrediente (II)

inhabitant el / la habitante (7-2)

injection, shot la inyección, *pl.* las inyecciones (II)

injured herido, -a (II)

injured person el herido, la herida (II)

injustice la injusticia (10-1)

innocent inocente (10-2)

insect repellent el repelente de insectos (1-1)

inside dentro de (II)

to insist insistir en (II)

to inspect registrar (II)

to inspire inspirar (2-1)

instead of en vez de (9-1), en lugar de (10-2)

to integrate integrarse (8-1)

intelligent inteligente (I)

interest el interés (II)

to interest interesar (I)

    it / they interest(s) me me interesa(n) (I)

interesting interesante (I)

interfering entrometido, -a (4-1)

to interpret interpretar (2-2)

interpretation la interpretación (2-2)

intersection el cruce de calles (II)

interview la entrevista (II, 5-1)

    — program el programa de entrevistas (I)

to interview entrevistar (II)

intimate íntimo, -a (4-1)

to invade invadir (8-1)

to invent inventar (6-2)

invention el invento (6-2)

to investigate investigar (II)

iron el hierro (3-1)

is es (I)

    he / she — es (I)

    it — true es cierto (II)

it la, lo *dir. obj. pron.* (I)

— **depends** depende (II)

— **fits (they fit) me well / poorly.** Me queda(n) bien / mal. (I)

— **has been...** Hace + *time* + que... (II)

— **is ...** Son las *(in telling time)* (I)

— **is forbidden...** Se prohíbe... (II)

— **is impossible for me...** Me es imposible... (5-2)

— **is made of...** Está hecho, -a de... (II)

— **is one o'clock.** Es la una. (I)

— **is the ... of ...** Es el *(number)* de *(month)* (in telling the date)* (I)

— **is the first of ...** Es el primero de *(month).* (I)

— **seems to me** me parece que (II)

— **was** fue (I)

—**was not me!** ¡Yo no fui! (4-2)

— **was a disaster.** Fue un desastre. (I)

—**'s a ...** es un / una ... (I)

—**'s cold.** Hace frío. (I)

—**'s hot.** Hace calor. (I)

—**'s necessary.** Es necesario. (I)

—**'s raining.** Llueve. (I)

—**'s snowing.** Nieva. (I)

—**'s sunny.** Hace sol. (I)

it / he / she will be ser: será (II)

itinerary el itinerario (II)

J

jacket la chaqueta (I)

January enero (I)

jealous celoso, -a (4-1)

jeans los jeans (I)

jewelry (gold, silver) las joyas (de oro, de plata) (II)

jewelry store la joyería (I)

Jew(ish) el judío, la judía (8-1)

---

job el trabajo (I)

— **application** la solicitud de empleo (5-1)

to join juntarse (II)

judge el juez, la jueza, *pl.* los jueces (II, 6-1)

to judge juzgar (10-2)

juice:

apple — el jugo de manzana (I)

orange — el jugo de naranja (I)

July julio (I)

to jump (rope) saltar (a la cuerda) (II)

June junio (I)

junk food la comida basura (3-1)

jury el jurado (10-2)

just:

to have — ... acabar de + *inf.* (I)

justice la justicia (10-2)

K

to keep (a secret) guardar un secreto (4-1)

to keep on (doing) seguir (+ present participle) (5-1)

ketchup la salsa de tomate (II)

key la llave (II)

key chain el llavero (I)

keyboard (computer) el teclado (I)

to kill matar (II)

kind:

What — of ... ? ¿Qué clase de ... ? (I)

kind amable (4-1)

king el rey (II)

to kiss besar(se) (II)

kitchen la cocina (I)

knee la rodilla (II)

knife el cuchillo (I)

to know saber (I); conocer (I, II)

I — (yo) conozco (I)

I — (how to) (yo) sé (I)

---

you — (tú) conoces (I)

you — (how to) (tú) sabes (I)

knowledge los conocimientos (5-1)

L

laboratory el laboratorio (I)

lack la falta (9-2)

ladder la escalera (II)

lake el lago (I)

lamp la lámpara (I)

language el idioma (II)

land la tierra (8-2)

landscape el paisaje (1-1)

language la lengua (8-2)

laptop computer la computadora portátil (I)

large grande (I)

last último, -a (II)

last:

— **night** anoche (I)

— **week** la semana pasada (I)

— **year** el año pasado (I)

to last durar (II)

late tarde (I)

to arrive — llegar tarde (II)

later:

See you — ¡Hasta luego!; ¡Nos vemos! (I)

to laugh reírse (e → í) (II)

laundry:

to do the — lavar la ropa (I)

law *(study of)* el derecho (II)

law la ley (II, 5-2)

lawyer el abogado, la abogada (II, 6-1)

lazy perezoso, -a (I)

leading man el galán (II)

league la liga (II)

to learn aprender (a) (I)

leather el cuero (II)

to leave salir (I), dejar (II)

don't — no dejes (II)

to — marks / traces dejar huellas (8-1)

Leave me alone. Déjame en paz. (II)

left:

    to the — (of) a la izquierda (de) (I)

leg la pierna (I)

legend la leyenda (7-2)

lemonade la limonada (I)

length el largo (7-1)

less:

    — ... than menos ... que (I)

    — than menos de (I)

to let dejar (II)

    don't — no dejes (II)

Let's go! ¡Vamos! (I)

Let's see ... A ver ... (I)

letter la carta (I, II)

    to mail a — echar una carta (II)

lettuce la lechuga (I)

level el nivel (3-1)

liberty la libertad (10-1)

library la biblioteca (I)

to lie mentir (e → ie) (II)

    life la vida (II)

    lifeguard el / la salvavida (5-1)

to lift weights levantar pesas (I)

to light encender

    light (color) claro, -a (II)

    light la luz, *pl.* las luces (I)

to light encender (e → ie) (II)

    lightning el relámpago (1-1)

    like como (I)

to like:

    Did you — it? ¿Te gustó? (I)

    Do you — to ...? ¿Te gusta ... ? (I)

    He / She doesn't — ... No le gusta ... (I)

    He / She —s ... Le gusta ... (I); A él / ella le gusta(n) ... (I)

    I don't — to ... (A mí) no me gusta ... (I)

    I don't — to ... at all. (A mí) no me gusta nada ... (I)

    I — ... Me gusta ... (I)

    I — to ... (A mí) me gusta ... (I)

    I — to ... a lot (A mí) me gusta mucho ... (I)

    — to ... better (A mí) me gusta más ... (I)

    I —d it. Me gustó. (I)

    I would — Me gustaría (I); quisiera (I)

    What do you — to do? ¿Qué te gusta hacer? (I)

    What do you — to do better / prefer to do? ¿Qué te gusta hacer más? (I)

    What would you — ? ¿Qué desean (Uds.)? (I)

    Would you —? ¿Te gustaría? (I)

    You — ... Te gusta ... (I)

likely probable (7-1)

likewise igualmente (I)

to limit limitar (9-1)

lips los labios (II)

to listen to music escuchar música (I)

little:

    a — un poco (de) (I)

to live vivir (I)

living vivo, -a (II)

living room la sala (I)

locker el armario (I, II, 10-1)

long largo, -a (I)

to look:

    to — (at) mirar (I)

    to — for buscar (I)

    to — like parecerse a (2-2)

loose flojo, -a (II)

to lose perder (e → ie) (II)

    — one's balance perder el equilibrio (1-1)

lot:

    a — mucho, -a (I)

to love encantar (I)

    He / She —s ... A él / ella le encanta(n) ... (I)

    I / You — ... Me / Te encanta(n)... (I)

love el amor (II)

loving cariñoso, -a (4-1)

low bajo, -a (II)

luggage el equipaje (II)

    to check — facturar el equipaje (II)

lunch el almuerzo (I)

    for — en el almuerzo (I)

lyrics la letra (2-2)

M

machine máquina (6-2)

madam (la) señora (Sra.) (I)

magazines:

    to read — leer revistas (I)

majority la mayoría (6-2)

mail:

    — carrier el cartero, la cartera (II)

    —box el buzón, *pl.* los buzones (II)

    to — a letter echar una carta (II)

main:

    — character el personaje principal (II)

    — dish el plato principal (I)

    as a — dish de plato principal (I)

to maintain one's health para mantener la salud (I)

to make:

    — (command) haz (I)

    to — a living ganarse la vida (II)

    to — an effort hacer un esfuerzo (1-2)

    to — decisions tomar decisiones (6-1)

    to — the bed hacer la cama (I)

    to — noise hacer ruido (II)

    to — peace with hacer las paces (4-2)

    You are making me nervous. Me estás poniendo nervioso, -a. (II)

make-up el maquillaje (II)

mall el centro comercial (I)

man el hombre (I)

    business— el hombre de negocios (II)

    elderly — el anciano (I)

manager el / la gerente (II, 5-1)

manner la manera (II)

manners los modales (II)

many muchos, -as (I)

    How —? ¿Cuántos, -as? (I)

March marzo (I)

march la marcha (5-2)

mark *(in school)* la nota (II)

    to get a good — sacar una buena nota (II)

market el mercado (II)

marketing el mercadeo (6-2)

married casado, -a (6-1)

marvel la maravilla (8-1)

match el partido (I); el fósforo (II)

materials los materiales (II)

mathematics class la clase de matemáticas (I)

matter el asunto (10-1)

mature maduro, -a (6-1)

May mayo (I)

maybe quizás (I)

mayonnaise la mayonesa (II)

me me *dir. obj. pron., ind. obj. pron.* (I)

    for — para mí (I), me (I)

    it matters / they matter to — me importa(n) (II)

    it seems to — me parece que (II)

    — too a mí también (I)

    to — me (I)

    with — conmigo (I)

meal la comida (I)

to mean:

    It —s ... Quiere decir ... (I)

    What does ... —? ¿Qué quiere decir ... ? (I)

to measure medir (i) (7-1)

meat la carne (I)

mechanic el mecánico, la mecánica (II)

medal la medalla (1-2)

media los medios de comunicación (6-2)

medicine la medicina (II)

medium mediano, -a (II)

meddlesome entrometido, -a (4-1)

to meet reunirse (u → ú) (II)

    meeting la reunión, *pl.* las reuniones (II), el encuentro (8-2)

melody la melodía (2-2)

melon el melón, *pl.* los melones (II)

to melt derretir (9-2)

member el miembro (II)

    to be a — ser miembro (II)

to memorize aprender de memoria (II)

menu el menú (I)

merchandise la mercancía (8-2)

messenger el mensajero, la mensajera (5-1)

messy desordenado, -a (I)

microphone el micrófono (2-2)

microwave el microondas (II)

military *(adj.)* militar (II)

milk la leche (I)

million un millón (II)

    —s of millones de (II)

mine mío, -a, -os, -as (II)

mirror el espejo (I)

Miss (la) señorita (Srta.) (I)

missing:

    to be — faltar (I)

mission la misión (8-2)

missionary el misionero, la misionera (8-2)

to mistreat maltratar (10-1)

mistreatment el maltrato (10-1)

to mistrust desconfiar (4-1)

misunderstanding el malentendido (4-2)

mix la mezcla (8-2)

to mix mezclar (II)

moment:

    a — un momento (I)

Monday lunes (I)

    on —s los lunes (I)

money el dinero (I)

money exchange la casa de cambio (II)

monkey el mono (I)

month el mes (I)

monument el monumento (I)

moon la Luna (II)

more:

    — ... than más ... que (I)

    — or less más o menos (I)

    — than más de (I)

morning:

    Good —. Buenos días. (I)

    in the — de la mañana (I)

mosque la mezquita (I)

mother la madre (mamá) (I)

mountain range sierra (1-1)

mountains las montañas (I)

mouse (computer) el ratón (I)

mouth la boca (I)

to move moverse (o → ue) (II), andar (1-1); *(house)* mudarse (6-1)

movement el movimiento (2-1)

movie la película (I)

    action — la película de acción (II)

    — theater el cine (I)

    to see a — ver una película (I)

to mow the lawn cortar el césped (I)

Mr. (el) señor (Sr.) (I)

Mrs. (la) señora (Sra.) (I)

much:

    so — tanto (I)

mural el mural (2-1)

muscle el músculo (II)

museum el museo (I)

music:

    to listen to — escuchar música (I)

    —al program el programa musical (I)

musician el músico, la música (II)

Muslim el musulmán, la musulmana (8-1)

must deber (I)

   one — hay que (I)

mustard la mostaza (II)

my mi (I); mis (I)

   — **name is ...** Me llamo ... (I)

mysterious misterioso, -a (7-1)

myth el mito (7-2)

mystery la película policíaca (I); el misterio (7-1)

N

name:

   My — is ... Me llamo ... (I)

   What is your —? ¿Cómo te llamas? (I)

   What's his / her —? ¿Cómo se llama? (I)

nails las uñas (II)

napkin la servilleta (I)

narrow estrecho, -a (II)

native el / la indígena (8-2)

naughty travieso, -a (II)

national park el parque nacional (I)

natural preserve la reserva natural (9-2)

natural resource el recurso natural (9-1)

nature la naturaleza (II, 1-1)

near cerca (de) (I)

neat ordenado, -a (I)

necessary:

   It's —. Es necesario. (I)

neck el cuello (II)

necklace el collar (I)

to need

   I — necesito (I)

   I — ... Me falta(n) ... (I)

   you — necesitas (I)

neighbor el vecino, la vecina (II)

neighborhood el barrio (I)

neither ... nor ni ... ni (I)

nervous nervioso, -a (II)

never nunca (I)

new nuevo, -a (I)

news program el programa de noticias (I)

newscast el noticiero (II)

newspaper el periódico (I)

newsstand el quiosco (II)

next siguiente (II), próximo (6-1)

   — **to** al lado de (I)

nice simpático, -a (I), amable (4-1)

night:

   at — de la noche (I)

   last — anoche (I)

night table la mesita (I)

nine nueve (I)

nine hundred novecientos, -as (I)

nineteen diecinueve (I)

ninety noventa (I)

ninth noveno, -a (I)

No way! ¡Qué va! (4-2)

nobody nadie (II)

noise el ruido (II)

none ningún, ninguno, -a (II)

nose la nariz, *pl.* las narices (I)

not:

   — **yet** no...todavía (II)

   — **... or** ni ... ni (I)

notebook el cuaderno (I)

nothing nada (I)

November noviembre (I)

now ahora (I)

nurse el enfermero, la enfermera (II)

nutrition la alimentación (3-1)

nutritious nutritivo, -a (3-1)

O

obedient obediente (II)

to obey obedecer to (II); hacer caso (4-2)

   observatory el observatorio (7-1)

to observe observar (II)

to obtain conseguir (e → i) (II), obtener (1-2)

to occupy ocupar (8-1)

to occur ocurrir (II), suceder (1-1)

   o'clock:

      at eight — a las ocho (I)

      at one — a la una (I)

   October octubre (I)

   odor el olor (II)

   of de (I)

      — **course** por supuesto (I)

   What is it made —? ¿De qué está hecho, -a? (II)

to offend ofender (II)

to offer ofrecer (II)

   office (home) el despacho (I)

   office la oficina (II)

   often a menudo (I)

   Oh! What a shame / pity! ¡Ay! ¡Qué pena! (I)

   oil el petróleo (9-1)

      — **spill** el derrame de petróleo (9-2)

   okay regular (I)

   old viejo, -a (I); antiguo, -a (II)

      He / She is / They are ... years —. Tiene(n) ... años. (I)

      How — is / are ... ? ¿Cuántos años tiene(n) ... ? (I)

      —**er** mayor, *pl.* mayores (I)

   on en (I)

      — **Mondays, on Tuesdays ...** los lunes, los martes ... (I)

      — **the grill** a parrilla (II)

      — **time** a tiempo (II)

      — **top of** encima de (I)

      — **weekends** los fines de semana (I)

   once there una vez allí (1-1)

   one uno (un), -a (I)

      at — (o'clock) a la una (I)

      — **hundred** cien (I)

      — **must** hay que (I)

   onion la cebolla (I)

   online en la Red (I)

      to be — estar en línea (I)

   only sólo (I), único, -a (8-1)

to **open** abrir (I)

open abierto, -a (II)

opens se abre (II)

opinion:

   in my — para mí (I)

opportunity la oportunidad (II)

or o (I)

orange anaranjado, -a (I)

   — juice el jugo de naranja (I)

orchestra la orquesta (II)

to **order** pedir (e → i) (I)

to **organize** organizar (5-2)

origin el origen (7-2)

other otro, -a (I)

others los / las demás (I)

our nuestro(s), -a(s) (I)

outcome el resultado (8-2)

outdoors al aire libre (II)

outer space el espacio (II)

outrageous exagerado, -a (II)

outside fuera (de) (II)

oval el óvalo (7-1)

oven el horno (II)

to **overwork** explotar (9-2)

own propio, -a (I)

owner el dueño, la dueña (II, 5-1)

ozone layer la capa de ozono (9-2)

P

to **pack the suitcase** hacer la maleta (II)

pain el dolor (II)

to **paint (one's nails)** pintarse (las uñas) (II)

painter el pintor, la pintora (II)

painting el cuadro (I), la pintura (2-1)

palace el palacio (II)

palette la paleta (2-1)

pants los pantalones (I)

paper:

   sheet of — la hoja de papel (I)

parade el desfile (II)

paramedic el paramédico, la paramédica (II)

parents los padres (I)

park el parque (I)

   amusement — el parque de diversiones (I)

   national — el parque nacional (I)

part time a tiempo parcial (5-1)

participant el / la participante (1-2)

to **participate (in)** participar (en) (II)

party la fiesta (I)

   surprise — la fiesta de sorpresa (II)

to **pass** pasar (II)

passenger el pasajero, la pasajera (II)

passport el pasaporte (II)

pastel *(colors)* pastel *adj.* (II)

pastime el pasatiempo (II)

pastries los pasteles (I)

patience la paciencia (II)

patient paciente (I)

   to be — tener paciencia (II)

to **pay (for)** pagar (por) (I)

to **pay attention** prestar atención (II)

   — to hacer caso a (4-2)

peace la paz (II, 10-1)

peaceful pacífico, -a (10-2)

peach el durazno (II)

peas los guisantes (I)

pedestrian el peatón, *pl.* los peatones (II)

to **peel** pelar (II)

pen el bolígrafo (I)

pencil el lápiz, *pl.* los lápices (I)

   — sharpener el sacapuntas, *pl.* los sacapuntas (I)

people la gente (I); el pueblo (7-1)

   elderly — los ancianos (I)

pepper la pimienta (I)

to **perform** realizar (2-2); actuar (2-2); cumplir con (5-1)

perfume el perfume (I)

to **permit, to allow** permitir (II)

person la persona (I)

personal watercraft la moto acuática (II)

pesticide el pesticida (9-1)

pharmacy la farmacia (II)

phenomenal fenomenal (II)

phenomenon el fenómeno (7-1)

phone:

   to talk on the — hablar por teléfono (I)

photo la foto (I)

   to take —s sacar fotos (I)

photographer el fotógrafo, la fotógrafa (II)

photography la fotografía (II)

physical education class la clase de educación física (I)

piano lesson (class) la lección de piano (I)

picnic el picnic (II)

piece el pedazo (II)

pills las pastillas (II)

pilot el / la piloto (II)

piñata la piñata (I)

pineapple la piña (II)

pink rosado, -a (I)

pizza la pizza (I)

place el lugar (I)

to **place** poner (I), colocar (9-1)

to **plan** pensar (e → ie) (I)

plant la planta (II)

to **plant** sembrar (5-2)

plastic el plástico (I)

plate el plato (I)

play la obra de teatro (I)

to **play** jugar (a) (u → ue) *(games, sports)* (I); tocar *(an instrument)* (I)

   to — baseball jugar al béisbol (I)

   to — basketball jugar al básquetbol (I)

   to — football jugar al fútbol americano (I)

   to — golf jugar al golf (I)

   to — soccer jugar al fútbol (I)

to — **sports** practicar deportes (I)

to — **tennis** jugar al tenis (I)

to — **the guitar** tocar la guitarra (I)

to — **the role of** hacer el papel de (II)

to — **video games** jugar videojuegos (I)

to — **volleyball** jugar al vóleibol (I)

player el jugador, la jugadora (II)

playground el patio de recreo (II)

plaza la plaza (II)

pleasant agradable (5-1)

to **please very much** encantar (I)

pleased to meet you mucho gusto (I)

plot el argumento (II)

poem el poema (2-2)

poet el / la poeta (2-2)

point of view el punto de vista (10-2)

poison el veneno (9-1)

police officer el / la policía (II)

to **polish (one's nails)** pintarse (las uñas) (II)

polite cortés, pl. corteses (II)

politician el político, la política (II)

to **pollute** contaminar (6-2)

polluted contaminado, -a (II, 9-1)

pollution la contaminación (II, 9-1)

pool la piscina (I)

poor pobre (I)

— **thing** pobrecito, -a (II)

population la población (8-1)

pork el cerdo (II)

— **chop** la chuleta de cerdo (II)

portrait el retrato (2-1)

position el puesto (5-1)

possession la posesión, pl. las posesiones (I)

post office el correo (II)

poster el cartel (I)

pot la olla (II)

potatoes las papas (I)

pottery la cerámica (2-1)

poverty la pobreza (10-1)

power el poder (8-2)

powerful poderoso, -a (8-2)

practical práctico, -a (I)

practice la práctica (II)

to **predict** predecir (6-2)

to **prefer** preferir (e → ie) (I)

I — (yo) prefiero (I)

I — to ... (a mí) me gusta más ... (I)

you — (tú) prefieres (I)

to **prepare** preparar (I)

to **prescribe** recetar (II)

prescription la receta (II)

present el regalo (I)

presentation la presentación, pl. las presentaciones (I)

presenter el presentador, la presentadora (II)

to **preserve** conservar (9-1)

press la prensa (10-2)

pretty bonito, -a (I)

price el precio (I)

principal (of a school) el director, la directora (II)

primary school la escuela primaria (I)

prize el premio (II)

problem el problema (I)

to **produce** producir (9-2)

product el producto (6-2)

profession la profesión, pl. las profesiones (II)

program el programa (I)

programmer el programador, la programadora (6-1)

project el proyecto (II)

to **prolong** prolongar (6-2)

to **promote** promover (ue) (9-1)

proposal la propuesta (10-2)

to **propose** proponer (10-2)

proof la evidencia (7-1)

protein la proteína (3-1)

Protestant church el templo (I)

to **protect** proteger (II, 5-2)

protection la protección (9-1)

provided that con tal que (9-2)

punctual puntual (II, 5-1)

to **punish** castigar (9-1)

punishment el castigo (10-2)

pure puro, -a (II)

purple morado, -a (I)

purpose el fin, pl. los fines (10-2)

purse el bolso (I)

to **pursue a career** seguir una carrera (II, 6-1)

to **put** poner (I), colocar (9-1)

— (command) pon (I)

I — (yo) pongo (I)

to — on (clothing, make-up, etc.) ponerse (II)

to — out (fire) apagar (II)

you — (tú) pones (I)

pyramid la pirámide

Q

quality cualidad (4-1)

quarter past y cuarto (I)

queen la reina (II)

question la pregunta (II)

to ask a — hacer una pregunta (II)

quickly rápidamente (I)

R

rabbit el conejo (7-2)

race la carrera (II, 1-2), la raza (8-2)

rain la lluvia (II)

to **rain** llover (o → ue) (II)

It's —ing. Llueve. (I)

rather bastante (I)

to **reach** alcanzar (1-2), llegar a (10-2)

— **an agreement** ponerse de acuerdo (4-2)

to **react** reaccionar (4-2)

to **read magazines** leer revistas (I)

ready listo, -a (II)

realistic realista (I)

reality program el programa de la vida real (I)

to **realize** darse cuenta de (1-2)

Really? ¿Verdad? (I); ¿De veras? (I)

really en realidad (II)

reason la razón (10-1)

to **rebel** rebelarse (8-2)

receptionist el recepcionista, la recepcionista (5-1)

to **receive** recibir (I)

recently recientemente (II)

reception desk la recepción (II)

recipe la receta (II)

to **recommend** recomendar (e → ie) (II)

to **reconquer** reconquistar (8-1)

to **record** grabar (II)

recreation center el centro recreativo (5-2)

rectangle el rectángulo (7-1)

to **recycle** reciclar (I)

recycling center el centro de reciclaje (I)

red rojo, -a (I)

— **-haired** pelirrojo, -a (I)

to **reduce** reducir (zc) (II), (6-2)

reference la referencia (5-1)

refrigerator el refrigerador (II)

refuge el refugio (1-1)

to **register** inscribirse (1-2)

registration la inscripción (1-2)

rehabilitation center el centro de rehabilitación (5-2)

rehearsal el ensayo (II)

to **rehearse** ensayar (II)

relatives los parientes (II)

to **relax** descansar (I), relajar(se) (3-2)

to **remember** recordar (o → ue) (II)

to **rent** alquilar (II)

to **repair** reparar (5-1)

to **repeat** repetir (e → i) (II)

to **replace** reemplazar (6-2)

report el informe (I)

reporter el reportero, la reportera (II)

to **represent** representar (2-1)

representative el / la representante (1-2)

to **request** solicitar (5-1)

requirement el requisito (5-1)

rescue el rescate (9-2)

to **rescue** rescatar (II)

reservation la reservación, pl. las reservaciones (II)

reserved reservado, -a (I)

to **resolve** resolver (o → ue) (4-2)

respect el respeto (10-1)

to **respect** respetar (II)

responsibility la responsabilidad (5-2)

responsible responsable (5-1)

to **rest** descansar (I)

restaurant el restaurante (I)

result el resultado (8-2)

to **result** resultar (II)

to **return** regresar (I, II)

to — **a book** devolver (o → ue) (un libro) (II)

review la reseña (2-2)

to **revolt** rebelarse (8-2)

rhythm el ritmo, el compás (2-2)

rice el arroz (I)

rich rico, -a (I)

to **ride:**

to — **a bicycle** montar en bicicleta (I)

to — **horseback** montar a caballo (I)

right:

to the — **(of)** a la derecha (de) (I)

— **away** en seguida (II)

rights los derechos (5-2)

ring el anillo (I)

river el río (I)

road la calle (I)

to **rob** robar (II)

rock la piedra (II), la roca (1-1)

role el papel (II)

to play the — **of** hacer el papel de (II)

Roman romano, -a (8-1)

romantic movie la película romántica (I)

room el cuarto (I); la habitación, pl. las habitaciones (II)

double occupancy — la habitación doble (II)

single occupancy — la habitación individual (II)

to straighten up the — arreglar el cuarto (I)

rope la cuerda (II)

round redondo, -a (7-1)

round-trip ida y vuelta (II)

ruins las ruinas (II, 7-1)

rug la alfombra (I)

rule la regla (II)

to **rule** gobernar (8-1)

to run correr (I)

to — **out** agotar(se) (9-1)

S

sack la bolsa (I)

sacred sagrado, -a (7-2)

sad triste (I)

sail la vela (II)

to **sail** navegar (II)

salad la ensalada (I)

fruit — la ensalada de frutas (I)

salary el salario (II, 5-1)

sale la liquidación, pl. las liquidaciones (II)

salesperson el dependiente, la dependienta (I)

salsa la salsa (II)

salt la sal (I)

same mismo, -a (I)

sandwich:

ham and cheese — el sándwich de jamón y queso (I)

satisfactory satisfactorio, -a (10-1)

Saturday sábado (I)

sausage la salchicha (I)

to save ahorrar (II, 6-1)

to save salvar (II)

to say decir (I)

    How do you —? ¿Cómo se dice? (I)

    to — good-bye despedirse (e → i) de (II)

    You — ... Se dice ... (I)

    You don't —! ¡No me digas! (I)

to scare asustar (1-1)

    scared:

        to be — (of) tener miedo (de) (I)

scene la escena (II)

schedule el horario (I)

science:

    — class la clase de ciencias naturales (I)

    — fiction movie la película de ciencia ficción (I)

scientist el científico, la científica (II, 6-1)

scissors las tijeras (II)

to score (a goal) meter un gol (II)

    score el tanteo (II)

to scream gritar (II)

    screen:

        computer — la pantalla (I)

to scuba dive bucear (I)

sculpture escultura (2-1)

sculptor el escultor, la escultora (2-1)

secret el secreto (4-1)

sea el mar (I)

seal la foca (9-2)

to search (for) buscar (I)

    search la búsqueda (II)

    to do a — hacer una búsqueda (II)

    to — (luggage) registrar (II)

season la estación, *pl.* las estaciones (I)

seat el asiento (II)

second segundo, -a (I)

— floor el primer piso (I)

secretary el secretario, la secretaria (II)

security checkpoint la inspección, *pl.* las inspecciones de seguridad (II)

to see ver (I)

    Let's — A ver ... (I)

    — you later! ¡Nos vemos!; Hasta luego. (I)

    — you tomorrow. Hasta mañana. (I)

    to — a movie ver una película (I)

to seem like parecerse a (2-2)

self-confidence confianza en sí mismo, -a (3-2)

self-portrait el autorretrato (2-1)

selfish egoísta (4-1)

to sell vender (I)

to send enviar (I, II)

to separate separar (I)

September septiembre (I

serious serio, -a (I), grave (9-1)

to serve servir (e → i) (I)

    service el servicio (6-2)

    — station la estación de servicio (II)

to set (sun) ponerse (el sol) (7-2)

    to set the table poner la mesa (I)

seven siete (I)

seven hundred setecientos, -as (I)

seventeen diecisiete (I)

seventh séptimo, -a (I)

seventy setenta (I)

shadow la sombra (7-2)

shake hands dar(se) la mano (II)

shame:

    What a —! ¡Qué lástima! (II)

shampoo el champú (II)

to share compartir (I)

to shave afeitarse (II)

    she ella (I)

sheet of paper la hoja de papel (I)

shelf el estante (I)

shellfish los mariscos (II)

shelter el refugio (1-1)

to shine brillar (7-2)

ship el barco (I)

shirt la camisa (I)

    T-— la camiseta (I)

shoe store la zapatería (I)

shoes los zapatos (I)

shoe size el número (II)

short bajo, -a *(stature);* corto, -a *(length)* (I)

shortage la escasez (9-1)

shorts los pantalones cortos (I)

should deber (I)

shoulder el hombro (II)

show el programa (I); el espectáculo (2-2)

to show + *movie or TV program* dar (I); mostrar (ue) (2-1)

shower la ducha (II)

shrimp el camarón, *pl.* los camarones (II)

shy reservado, -a (I)

sick enfermo, -a (I)

sierra la sierra (1-1)

sign el letrero (II); la señal (II)

    stop — la señal de parada (II)

silk seda (II)

silly tonto, -a (I)

silver la plata (II)

similarity la semejanza (8-2)

since desde (II)

sincere sincero, -a (4-1)

to sing cantar (I)

singer el / la cantante (II)

single soltero, -a (6-1)

sink el fregadero (II)

sir (el) señor (Sr.) (I)

sister la hermana (I)

site:

    Web — el sitio Web (I)

six seis (I)

six hundred seiscientos, -as (I)

sixteen dieciséis (I)

sixth sexto, -a (I)

sixty sesenta (I)

size la talla (II)

to skate patinar (I)

to skateboard montar en monopatín (I)

skates los patines (II)

to ski esquiar (I)

skill la habilidad (5-1)

skin la piel (9-2)

to skip (a meal) saltar (una comida) (3-1)

skirt la falda (I)

sky el cielo (II)

to sleep dormir (I)

sleeping bag el saco de dormir (1-1)

sleepy:

    to be — tener sueño (I)

slice el pedazo (II)

slide la diapositiva (I)

slowly lentamente (II); despacio (II)

small pequeño, -a (I)

to smile sonreír (e → í) (II)

smoke el humo (II)

snack la merienda (3-1)

to sneeze estornudar (3-1)

to snorkel bucear (I)

to snow: nevar (e → ie) (II)

    It's —ing. Nieva. (I)

so tan (II), de modo que (10-2)

    — + *adj*. tan + *adj*. (II)

    — much tanto (I)

    so-so regular (I)

    — that de modo que (10-2)

soap el jabón (II)

soap opera la telenovela (I)

soccer:

    to play — jugar al fútbol (I)

sociable sociable (I)

social service el servicio social (5-2)

social studies class la clase de ciencias sociales (I)

society la sociedad (5-2)

socks los calcetines (I)

soft drink el refresco (I)

software el software (I)

solar solar (II)

soldier el / la soldado (8-2)

solid-colored de sólo un color (II)

to solve resolver (o → ue) (II)

some unos, -as (I); algún, alguno, -a (II)

    some day algún día (II)

someone alguien (II)

something algo (I)

sometimes a veces (I)

son el hijo (I)

    —s; —(s) and daughter(s) los hijos (I)

song la canción, *pl.* las canciones (I,II)

soon pronto (II)

sorry:

    I'm —. Lo siento. (I)

sound (stereo) system el equipo de sonido (I)

to sound like sonar (ue) a (2-2)

soup:

    vegetable — la sopa de verduras (I)

soup kitchen el comedor de beneficencia (5-2)

source la fuente (II)

    — of inspiration la fuente de inspiración (2-1)

souvenirs los recuerdos (I)

    to buy — comprar recuerdos (I)

spaceship la nave espacial (7-1)

spaghetti los espaguetis (I)

Spanish class la clase de español (I)

special especial (II)

    special effects los efectos especiales (II)

    special event el evento especial (II)

    species la especie (9-2)

speech el discurso (II)

to spell:

    How is ... spelled? ¿Cómo se escribe ... ? (I)

    It's spelled ... Se escribe ... (I)

to spend gastar (II)

    to — time with friends pasar tiempo con amigos (I)

spicy picante (II)

to spill tirar (II)

    don't — no tires (II)

spoiled consentido, -a (II)

spoon la cuchara (I)

sports:

    — equipment el equipo deportivo (II)

    — -minded deportista (I)

    — program el programa deportivo (I)

    to play — practicar deportes (I)

spring la primavera (I)

stadium el estadio (I)

stage el escenario (2-2)

stairs, stairway la escalera (I)

stamp el sello (II)

to stand:

    — out destacarse (2-2)

    — up pararse (2-2)

stapler la grapadora (II)

star:

    movie — la estrella (del cine) (II)

to start empezar (e → ie) (I); comenzar (e → ie) (II)

state el estado (10-1)

statue la estatua (II)

to stay: quedarse (II)

    I — at home. Me quedo en casa. (I)

steak la carne de res (II), el bistec (I)

to steal robar (II)

step el paso (2-2)

stepbrother el hermanastro (I)

stepfather el padrastro (I)

stepmother la madrastra (I)

stepsister la hermanastra (I)

stereo system el equipo de sonido (I)

still todavía (II)

still life la naturaleza muerta (2-1)

to **stitch** *(surgically)* dar puntadas (II)

stitches las puntadas (II)

stomach el estómago (I)

to **stop** parar (II), detener (9-2)

    — doing something dejar de (1-1)

    — over hacer escala (II)

stoplight el semáforo (II)

stopover la escala (II)

store la tienda (I)

    book— la librería (I)

    clothing — la tienda de ropa (I)

    department — el almacén, *pl.* los almacenes (I)

    discount — la tienda de descuentos (I)

    household-appliance — la tienda de electrodomésticos (I)

    jewelry — la joyería (I)

    shoe — la zapatería (I)

stories:

    to write — escribir cuentos (I)

storm la tormenta (II)

story el piso (I)

stove la estufa (II)

straight derecho (II)

to **straighten up the room** arreglar el cuarto (I)

strange extraño, -a (7-1)

strategy la estrategia (6-2)

strawberries las fresas (I)

street la calle (I)

strength la fuerza (3-2)

stress el estrés (3-2)

stressed out estresado, -a (3-2)

to **stretch** estirar (3-2)

to **stroll** dar un paseo (1-1)

strong fuerte (3-1)

structure la estructura (7-1)

student el / la estudiante (I)

studious estudioso, -a (I)

to **study** estudiar (I)

stupendous estupendo, -a (II)

stupid tonto, -a (I)

style el estilo (II)

subject el tema (2-1)

subway el metro (II)

success el éxito (II)

    to be —ful tener éxito (II)

suddenly de repente (II)

to **suffer** sufrir (10-1)

sugar el azúcar (I)

to **suggest** sugerir (e → ie) (II), proponer (10-2)

suit el traje (I)

suitcase la maleta (II)

summer el verano (I)

to **sunbathe** tomar el sol (I)

Sunday domingo (I)

sunglasses los anteojos de sol (I)

sunny:

    It's —. Hace sol. (I)

supermarket el supermercado (II)

supplies los materiales (II)

support el apoyo (10-1)

to **support (each other)** apoyarse (4-1)

sure seguro, -a (II)

to **surf the Web** navegar en la Red (I)

surprise la sorpresa (II)

suspicious sospechoso, -a (10-2)

sweater el suéter (I)

sweatshirt la sudadera (I)

sweet dulce (II)

to **swim** nadar (I)

swimming la natación (II)

swimsuit el traje de baño (I)

symbol el símbolo (7-2)

synagogue la sinagoga (I)

synthetic fabric la tela sintética (II)

syrup el jarabe (3-1)

T

T-shirt la camiseta (I)

table la mesa (I)

    to set the — poner la mesa (I)

to **take** llevar (I), tomar (3-1)

    to — a bath bañarse (II)

    to — a course tomar un curso (I)

    to — a shower ducharse (II)

    to — a tour hacer una gira (II)

    to — a trip hacer un viaje (II)

    to — a walk dar una caminata (II), dar un paseo (1-1)

    to — away quitar (II)

    to — care of cuidar a (II)

    to — into account tener en cuenta (6-2)

    to — lessons tomar lecciones (II)

    to — out the trash sacar la basura (I)

    to — photos sacar fotos (I)

    to — place tener lugar (1-2)

    to — shelter refugiarse (1-1)

talented talentoso, -a (I)

to **talk** hablar (I)

    to — on the phone hablar por teléfono (I)

tall alto, -a (I)

tank el tanque (II)

taste el sabor (II)

to **taste** probar (o → ue) (II)

tasty sabroso, -a (I); rico, -a (I)

tea el té (I)

    iced — el té helado (I)

to **teach** enseñar (I)

teacher el profesor, la profesora (I)

teaching la enseñanza (10-1)

team el equipo (II)

to **tear** romperse (II)

technical school la escuela técnica (II)

technician el técnico, la técnica (II)

technological tecnológico, -a (6-2)

technology / computers la tecnología (I)

technology / computer class la clase de tecnología (I)

teddy bear el oso de peluche (II)

teeth los dientes (II)

  to brush one's — cepillarse los dientes (II)

television:

  to watch — ver la tele (I)

television set el televisor (I)

to tell decir (I)

  — me dime (I)

  to — jokes contar (chistes) (o → ue) (II)

  to — the truth decir la verdad (II)

temple el templo (I)

ten diez (I)

tennis:

  to play — jugar al tenis (I)

tent la tienda de acampar (1-1)

tennis racket la raqueta de tenis (II)

tenth décimo, -a (I)

thank you gracias (I)

that que (I); ese, esa (I)

  —'s why por eso (I)

that one (over there) aquel, aquella (II)

the el, la, los, las (I)

  — best el / la mejor, los / las mejores (I)

  — worst el / la peor, los / las peores (I)

theater el teatro (I)

  movie — el cine (I)

their su, sus (I)

them las, los *dir. obj. pron.* (I), les *ind. obj. pron.* (I)

then entonces (I)

then luego (II)

theory la teoría (7-2)

there allí (I)

  — is / are hay (I); haya *(subjunctive)* (II)

  — was hubo (II)

  — was / — were había (II)

  — will be habrá (II)

therefore por eso (I), así que (6-1), por lo tanto (6-1)

these estos, estas (I)

they ellos, ellas (I)

they died se murieron (II)

thief el ladrón, la ladrona, *pl.* los ladrones (II)

thing la cosa (I)

to think pensar (e → ie) (I), opinar (10-2)

  I don't — so. Creo que no. (I)

  I — ... Creo que ... (I)

  I — so. Creo que sí. (I)

  to — of oneself pensar en sí mismo, -a (4-2)

  What do you — (about it)? ¿Qué te parece? (I)

third tercer (tercero), -a (I)

third floor el segundo piso (I)

thirsty:

  I'm —. Tengo sed. (I)

thirteen trece (I)

thirty treinta (I); y media *(in telling time)* (I)

thirty-one treinta y uno (I)

this este, esta (I)

  — afternoon esta tarde (I)

  — evening esta noche (I)

  — way así (1-1)

  — weekend este fin de semana (I)

  What is — ? ¿Qué es esto? (I)

those esos, esas (I)

those (over there) aquellos, aquellas (II)

thought el pensamiento (10-1)

thousand:

  a — mil (I)

threat la amenaza (9-2)

to threaten amenazar (9-1)

three tres (I)

three hundred trescientos, -as (I)

three-ring binder la carpeta de argollas (I)

through por (II), a través de (2-1)

to throw arrojar(se) (7-2)

  to — away tirar (II), echar (9-1)

thunder el trueno (1-1)

Thursday jueves (I)

ticket el boleto (I), la entrada (2-2)

ticket la multa (II)

tie la corbata (I); el empate (II)

tight apretado, -a (II)

tile el azulejo (8-1)

time la época (8-1)

time:

  At what —? ¿A qué hora? (I)

  free — el tiempo libre (I)

  on — a tiempo (II)

  to spend — with friends pasar tiempo con amigos (I)

  What — is it? ¿Qué hora es? (I)

timid tímido, -a (II).

tip la propina (II)

tired cansado, -a (I)

to a *prep.* (I)

  in order — para + *inf.* (I)

  — the a la, al (I)

  — the left (of) a la izquierda (de) (I)

  — the right (of) a la derecha (de) (I)

toast el pan tostado (I)

today hoy (I)

together juntos, -as (4-1)

tolerance la tolerancia (10-1)

to tolerate aguantar (3-2)

tomatoes los tomates (I)

tomorrow mañana (I)

  See you —. Hasta mañana. (I)

ton la tonelada (7-1)

too también (I); demasiado (I)

  I do (like to) — a mí también (I)

  me — a mí también (I)

toothbrush el cepillo de dientes (II)

toothpaste la pasta dental (II)

top:

  on — of encima de (I)

touching emocionante (I)

tourist el / la turista (II)

toward hacia (1-1)

towel la toalla (II)

tower la torre (8-1)

town el pueblo (II)

toy el juguete (I)

to **trace** trazar (7-1)

traffic el tráfico (II)

trail el sendero (II)

train el tren (I)

    electric — el tren eléctrico (II)

to **train** entrenarse (1-2)

training el entrenamiento (1-2)

trainer el entrenador, la entrenadora (II)

to **translate** traducir (zc) (6-1)

translator el traductor, la traductora (6-1)

transparent tape la cinta adhesiva (II)

to **trap** atrapar (9-2)

to **travel** viajar (I)

    travel agency la agencia de viajes (II)

    travel agent el / la agente de viajes (II)

to **treat** tratar (10-1)

tree el árbol (I)

tremendous tremendo, -a (I)

trial el juicio (10-2)

triangle el triángulo (7-1)

tricycle el triciclo (II)

trip el viaje (I)

to **trip (over)** tropezar (e → ie) (con) (II)

trophy el trofeo (1-2)

tropical rain forest la selva tropical (II, 9-2)

truck el camión, *pl.* los camiones (II)

true:

    it's true es cierto (II)

trumpet la trompeta (2-2)

trust la confianza (4-1)

to **trust** confiar (i → í) (4-1)

truth la verdad (II)

to **try on** probarse (o → ue) (II)

to **try to** tratar de (II)

Tuesday martes (I)

    on —s los martes (I)

turkey el pavo (II)

to **turn** doblar (II)

    to — in entregar (II)

    to — in homework on time entregar la tarea a tiempo (II)

    to — into convertirse en (7-2)

    to — off apagar (II)

    to — on encender (e → ie) (II)

    to — out resultar (II)

turtle la tortuga (II)

TV channel el canal (I)

twelve doce (I)

twenty veinte (I)

twenty-one veintiuno (veintiún) (I)

to **twist** torcerse (o → ue) (II)

two dos (I)

two hundred doscientos, -as (I)

typical típico, -a (II)

U

Ugh! ¡Uf! (I)

ugly feo, -a (I)

uncle el tío (I)

uncles; uncle(s) and aunt(s) los tíos (I)

underneath debajo de (I)

to **understand** comprender (I); entender (e → ie) (II)

understanding comprensivo, -a (4-1)

unemployment el desempleo (10-2)

unfair injusto, -a (5-2)

unfortunately desafortunadamente (1-2)

unity la unidad (8-1)

universe el universo (7-2)

university la universidad (II)

unforgettable inolvidable (I)

unknown desconocido, -a (8-2)

unless a menos que (9-2)

unlikely improbable (7-1)

until hasta (II)

upon arriving al llegar (8-2)

us nos *dir. obj. pron.* (I)

    (to / for) — nos *ind. obj. pron.* (I)

to **usually do something** soler (ue) (5-1)

use el uso (6-2)

to **use:**

    to — a stationary bike hacer bicicleta (3-2)

    to — a treadmill hacer cinta (3-2)

    to — the computer usar la computadora (I)

    What's it —d for? ¿Para qué sirve? (I)

used usado, -a (I)

    it's — for sirve para (I)

useful:

    to be — servir (I)

V

vacation:

    to go on — ir de vacaciones (I)

to **vacuum** pasar la aspiradora (I)

vain vanidoso, -a (4-1)

valley el valle (II), (1-1)

value el valor (10-2)

variety la variedad (8-2)

various varios, -as (II)

vegetable soup la sopa de verduras (I)

vendor el vendedor, la vendedora (II)

very muy (I)

    — well muy bien (I)

veterinarian el veterinario, la veterinaria (II)

via satellite via satélite (6-2)

victim la víctima (II)

video el video (I)

video games:

    to play — jugar videojuegos (I)

to **videotape** hacer un video (I)

vinegar el vinagre (II)

to **violate** violar (10-2)

violence la violencia (II)

violent violento, -a (I)

virtual reality la realidad virtual (6-2)

to **visit** visitar (I)

    to — **chat rooms** visitar salones de chat (I)

vital fundamental (10-2)

vitamin la vitamina (3-1)

voice la voz, *pl.* las voces (II)

volleyball:

    to **play** — jugar al vóleibol (I)

volunteer el voluntario, la voluntaria (I)

    — **work** el trabajo voluntario (I)

to **vote** votar (10-1)

W

to **wait** esperar (II)

waiter, waitress el camarero, la camarera (I)

to **wake up** despertarse (e → ie) (II)

to **walk** caminar (I), andar (1-1)

    to **take a** — dar una caminata (II)

wall la pared (I)

wallet la cartera (I)

to **want** querer (e → ie) (I)

    I — (yo) quiero (I)

    you — (tú) quieres (I)

war la guerra (II, 8-2)

warm:

    to **be** — tener calor (I)

was fue (I)

to **wash** lavar (I)

    to — **the car** lavar el coche (I)

    to — **the clothes** lavar la ropa (I)

    to — **the dishes** lavar los platos (I)

    to — **one's face** lavarse la cara (II)

waste el desperdicio (9-1)

to **waste** desperdiciar (9-1)

wastepaper basket la papelera (I)

watch el reloj pulsera (I)

    to **watch television** ver la tele (I)

water el agua (I)

watermelon la sandía (II)

waterskiing el esquí acuático (II)

way la manera (II, 3-1), el modo (10-2)

we nosotros, -as (I)

weak débil (3-2)

wealth la riqueza (8-2)

to **wear** llevar (I)

    weapon el arma, *pl.* las armas (8-2)

weather el clima (9-2)

    What's the — **like?** ¿Qué tiempo hace? (I)

Web:

    to **surf the** — navegar en la Red (I)

    — **page** la página Web (I)

    — **site** el sitio Web (I)

Wednesday miércoles (I)

wedding la boda (II)

week la semana (I)

    last — la semana pasada (I)

weekend:

    on —**s** los fines de semana (I)

    this — este fin de semana (I)

to **weigh** pesar (7-1)

weight el peso (3-1)

welcome bienvenido, -a (II)

well bien (I); pues ... *(to indicate pause)* (I)

    very — muy bien (I)

    — **-behaved** bien educado, -a (II)

wet mojado, -a (II)

whale la ballena

What? ¿Cuál? (I)

    — **a shame!** ¡Qué lástima! (II)

    — **are you like?** ¿Cómo eres? (I)

    (At) — **time?** ¿A qué hora? (I)

    — **color ... ?** ¿De qué color ... ? (I)

    — **day is today?** ¿Qué día es hoy? (I)

    — **did you do?** ¿Qué hiciste? (I)

    — **do you like to do better / prefer to do?** ¿Qué te gusta hacer más? (I)

    — **do you like to do?** ¿Qué te gusta hacer? (I)

    — **do you think (about it)?** ¿Qué te parece? (I, II)

    — **does ... mean?** ¿Qué quiere decir ... ? (I)

    — **else?** ¿Qué más? (I)

    — **happened to you?** ¿Qué te pasó? (I, II)

    — **is she / he like?** ¿Cómo es? (I)

    — **is the date?** ¿Cuál es la fecha? (I)

    — **is this?** ¿Qué es esto? (I)

    — **is your name?** ¿Cómo te llamas? (I)

    — **kind of ... ?** ¿Qué clase de... ? (I)

    — **time is it?** ¿Qué hora es? (I)

    — **would you like?** ¿Qué desean (Uds.)? (I)

    — **'s happening?** ¿Qué pasa? (I)

    — **'s his / her name?** ¿Cómo se llama? (I)

    — **'s it (used) for?** ¿Para qué sirve? (I)

    — **'s the weather like?** ¿Qué tiempo hace? (I)

what!:

    — **a good / nice idea!** ¡Qué buena idea! (I)

    — **a shame / pity!** ¡Qué pena! (I)

what lo que (II)

When? ¿Cuándo? (I)

Where? ¿Dónde? (I)

    — **are you from?** ¿De dónde eres? (I)

    (To) —**?** ¿Adónde? (I)

whether si (I)

Which? ¿Cuál? (I)

while mientras (que) (II)

once in a — de vez en cuando (II)

white blanco, -a (I)

who que (I)

Who? ¿Quién? (I)

Why? ¿Por qué? (I)

wide ancho, -a (II)

width el ancho (7-1)

wife la esposa (I)

wild salvaje (9-2)

Will you bring me ... ? ¿Me trae ... ? (I)

window la ventana (I)

window *(airplane)* la ventanilla (II)

windsurf el surf de vela (II)

winter el invierno (I)

with con (I)

   — me conmigo (I)

   — my / your friends con mis / tus amigos (I)

   — respect to en cuanto a (10-1)

   — whom? ¿Con quién? (I)

   — you contigo (I)

   What do you serve it —? ¿Con qué se sirve? (II)

without sin (I)

   — a doubt sin duda (II)

   witness el / la testigo (10-2)

woman la mujer (I)

   business— la mujer de negocios (II)

   elderly woman la anciana (I)

wonder la maravilla (8-1)

wonderful estupendo, -a (II), maravilloso, -a (8-1)

wood el bosque (1-1)

wool la lana (II)

word la palabra (II)

work el trabajo (I)

   — of art la obra de arte (2-1)

   volunteer — el trabajo voluntario (I)

to work trabajar (I)

workshop el taller (2-1)

world el mundo (II)

worldwide mundial (10-2)

to worry preocuparse (3-2)

worse than peor(es) que (I)

worst:

   the — el / la peor, los / las peores (I)

Would you like? ¿Te gustaría? (I)

wrist la muñeca (II)

to write:

   to — e-mail escribir por correo electrónico (I)

   to — stories escribir cuentos (I)

writer el escritor, la escritora (II, 2-2)

writing la escritura (7-2)

X-ray la radiografía (II)

yard el jardín (I)

year el año (I)

   He / She is / They are ... —s old. Tiene(n) ... años. (I)

   last — el año pasado (I)

yellow amarillo, -a (I)

yes sí (I)

yesterday ayer (I)

yoga el yoga (3-2)

yogurt el yogur (I)

you *fam. sing.* tú (I); *formal sing.* usted (Ud.) (I); *fam. pl.* vosotros, -as (I); *formal and informal pl.* ustedes (Uds.) (I); *fam. after prep.* ti (I); *sing. dir. and ind. obj. pron.* te (I); *sing. formal dir. obj. pron.* lo, la (I); *pl. fam. ind. obj. pron.* os (I); *ind. obj. pron.* le, les (I)

   And —? ¿Y a ti? (I)

   for — para ti (I)

   it matters (it's important), they matter to — te importa(n) (II)

   to / for — *fam. pl.* os (I)

   to / for — *fam. sing.* te (I)

   with — contigo (I)

   — can se puede (II)

   — don't say! ¡No me digas! (I)

   — have seen has visto (II)

   — know conocen (II)

   — look (good) te ves (bien) (II)

   — say ... Se dice ... (I)

young joven (I)

   — boy / girl el niño, la niña (I)

   — man el joven (I)

   — people los jóvenes (II)

   — woman la joven (I)

   —er menor, *pl.* menores (I)

your *fam.* tu (I); *fam. pl.* tus, vuestro(s), -a(s) (I); *formal* su, sus (I)

yours tuyo, -a, -os, -as (II)

yuck! ¡Uf !(I)

zero cero (I)

zoo el zoológico (I)

Grammar Index

Structures are often presented first in *Vocabulario en contexto*, where they are practiced lexically in conversational contexts. They are then explained in a *Gramática* section or are placed as reminders in a *¿Recuerdas?* or *Nota*. Lightface numbers refer to the pages where these structures are initially presented lexically or, after explanation, where student reminders occur. Lightface numbers also refer to pages that review structures first presented in Level 2. **Boldface numbers** refer to pages where new structures are explained.

Acknowledgments

Cover Fitopardo/Moment/Getty Images

Front Matter **xix:** Dikobrazik/Fotolia; **xix:** Noche/Fotolia; **xxiii:** Noche/Fotolia; **xxii-xxiii:** frans lemmens/Alamy Stock Photo; **xxii-xxiii:** Frans Lemmens/Alamy Stock Photo; **xxivBC:** Noche/Fotolia; **xxivBL:** Noche/Fotolia; **xxivBR:** Noche/Fotolia; **xxiv-xxv:** Joakim Lloyd Raboff/Shutterstock; **xxixBC:** Globe Turner/Shutterstock; **xxixBL:** Noche/Fotolia; **xxixBR:** Noche/Fotolia; **xxvBC:** Esancai/Fotolia; **xxvi:** Gary Ives/Shutterstock; **xxviBC:** Noche/Fotolia; **xxviBL:** Noche/Fotolia; **xxviBR:** Vector Icon/Fotolia; **xxviiiBL:** Noche/Fotolia; **xxviiiBR:** Noche/Fotolia; **xxx:** Noche/Fotolia; **xxxiBC:** Noche/Fotolia; **xxxiBL:** Noche/Fotolia; **xxxiBR:** Noche/Fotolia; **xxxiiB:** incamerastock/Alamy Stock Photo; **xxxiii:** Javier Gil/Photoshot/Newscom; **xxxiiiBL:** Noche/Fotolia; **xxxiiiBR:** Stakes/Shutterstock; **xxxv:** Noche/Fotolia

Para Empezar **000:** Kim Karpeles/Alamy Stock Photo; **001:** Carlos Mora/Alamy Stock Photo; **002B:** Jim Lane/Alamy Stock Photo; **002T:** Image Source/Photodisc/Getty Images; **004:** Monkey Business/Fotolia; **006B:** Andreas Pollok/The Image Bank/Getty Images; **006T:** Tracy Frankel/The Image Bank/Getty Images; **008B:** Ted Foxx/Alamy Stock Photo; **008C:** Bst2012/Fotolia; **008T:** Jim West/Alamy Stock Photo; **010B:** Monart Design/Fotolia; **010C:** Svyatoslav Lypynskyy/Fotolia; **010CL:** Ajr Images/Fotolia; **010T:** Ajr Images/Fotolia; **013:** Pearson Education, Inc; **013:** Pearson Education, Inc.; **014B:** Joe McBride/Corbis; **014T:** Katja Heinemann/Aurora Photos/Alamy Stock Photo; **015:** Monkey Business/Fotolia

Chapter 01 **016:** Image Source/Photodisc/Getty Images; **018:** Cathy Yeulet/123RF; **020:** Artists Rights Society; **021:** Prisma Bildagentur AG/Alamy Stock Photo; **022BL:** Michael Marquand/Lonely Planet Images/Getty Images; **022BR:** Rickszczechowski/iStock/Getty Images; **022MC:** Design Pics Inc/Alamy Stock Photo; **022ML:** Juan Carlos Muñoz/AGE Fotostock/Alamy Stock Photo; **022MR:** Trevor Chriss/Alamy Stock Photo; **022T:** Pearson Education, Inc.; **022TR:** Daniel Pangbourne/Dorling Kindersley Ltd; **022TR:** Daniel Pangbourne/Dorling Kindersley, Ltd.; **023C:** Andrea Jemolo/Encyclopedia/Corbis; **023L:** e54/ZUMA Press/Newscom; **023R:** Traveller Martin/Shutterstock; **024BL:** Mark Romesser/Alamy Stock Photo; **024BR:** Gerault Gregory/Hemis/Alamy Stock Photo; **024TL:** Pearson Education, Inc.; **024TR:** Kim Smith/Alamy Stock Photo; **025C:** Tucapress/LatinContent Editorial/Getty Images; **025L:** Patrick J. Endres/Alamy Stock Photo; **025R:** Adrian hepworth/Alamy Stock Photo; **026BCL:** Trevor Chriss/Alamy Stock Photo; **026BCR:** Lawrence Manning/Corbis; **026BL:** Susanna Price/DK Images; **026BL:** Susanna Price/Dorling Kindersley, Ltd.; **026BR:** Lawrence Manning/Keepsake RF/Corbis; **026ML:** Daniel Pangbourne/Dorling Kindersley Ltd; **026ML:** Daniel Pangbourne/Dorling Kindersley, Ltd.; **026MR:** Design Pics Inc/Alamy Stock Photo; **027B:** Jorisvo/Shutterstock; **027BC:** Kevin Schafer/Encyclopedia/Corbis; **027T:** Kevin Schafer/Encyclopedia/Corbis; **027TC:** Michael Marquand/Lonely Planet Images/Getty Images; **027TL:** Juan Carlos Muñoz/AGE Fotostock/Alamy Stock Photo; **027TR:** Andrea Jemolo/Encyclopedia/Corbis; **028:** Ostrs Zdravko/Chromorange/Alamy Stock Photo; **029:** Luke Dodd/Science Source.; **030:** Gregory G. Dimijian, M.D./Science Source; **033BL:** Juan Carlos Muñoz/AGE Fotostock/Alamy Stock Photo; **033BR:** Susanna Price/Dorling Kindersley, Ltd.; **033T:** Monkey Business Images/Corbis; **034:** Jacques Jangoux/Science Source; **035:** SeBuKi/Alamy Stock Photo; **036BCL:** BillionPhotos.com/Fotolia; **036BCR:** Mega Pixel/Shutterstock; **036BL:** D.Nakashima/Aflo Co. Ltd/Alamy Stock Photo; **036BR:** Chones/Shutterstock; **036TR:** Anna Moskvina/Fotolia; **037B:** PJPhoto69/E+/Getty Images; **037T:** Andrew Rich/E+/Getty images; **038BR:** IPG Gutenberg UK Ltd/iStock/Getty Images; **038TR:** A.J.D. Foto Ltd./Alamy Stock Photo; **039C:** Inti St Clair/DigitalVision/Getty Images; **039L:** Inti St Clair/DigitalVision/Getty Images; **039R:** Inti St Clair/DigitalVision/Getty Images; **041B:** Alamy; **041CL:** Africa Studio/Shutterstock; **041CR:** PhlllStudio/Shutterstock; **041ML:** Hundreddays/iStock/Getty Images; **041MR:** Mega Pixel/Shutterstock; **043:** Todd Warnock/Digital Vision/Getty Images; **045B:** Tanya Constantine/Blend Images/Alamy Stock Photo; **045T:** Jiro Mochizuki/Image of Sport/Newscom; **047BCL:** CaiaImageJV/OJO+/Getty Images; **047BL:** Ted Foxx/Alamy Stock Photo; **047TCL:** Rafael Ramirez Lee/Shutterstock; **047TCR:** Desiree Navarro/Everett Collection/Alamy Stock Photo; **047TL:** Dmitrij Skorobogatov/Shutterstock; **047TR:** Jiri Hubatka/ImageBroker/Newscom; **048:** Reproduction of Map of Routes of St. James of Compostel, originally engraved by D.Serveaux 1648, French School, (17th century) (after)/Private Collection/Archives Charmet/Bridgeman Images; **048L:** Jennie Hart/Alamy Stock Photo; **048R:** Leandro Hermida/Alamy Stock Photo; **049R:** James Sturcke/Alamy Stock Photo; **050:** Tony Waltham/Robertharding/Getty Images; **054:** Blend Images/SuperStock, Inc.; **055:** Diego Rivera/Art Resource; **055:** Diego Rivera/Art Resource, NY; **055:** The Culture of Totonaken, detail of Totonac nobility trading with Aztec merchants, 1950 (mural), Rivera, Diego (1886-1957)/Palacio Nacional, Mexico City, Mexico/

Bridgeman Images; **056:** Detail from 'The Great City of Tenochtitlan', from the 'Pre-Hispanic and Colonial Mexico' cycle, 1945 (fresco) (see also 136705 and 277723), Rivera, Diego (1886-1957)/Palacio Nacional, Mexico City, Mexico/Bridgeman Images; **057:** Marco Regalia/Shutterstock; **58-59:** Univision

Chapter 02 "Amigos" from Mientras Mas lo Pienso… Tu, by Juan Luis Guerra. Copyright ©1995 Karen Publishing Co. Reprinted by permission.; **00BR:** Dina Bursztyn; **064:** Collection OAS AMA/Art Museum of the Americas; **066:** Ted Foxx/Alamy Stock Photo; **068:** Photo: © The Museum of Modern Art/Scala/Art Resource, NY; **069:** Graham Jeremy/Dbimages/ Alamy Stock Photo; **070BC:** Painting/Alamy Stock Photo; **070L:** Massimo Sestini/Mondadori Portfolio/ Getty Images; **070TC:** Leo Bild/Alamy Stock Photo; **070TL:** Fine Art Images/Heritage Image Partnership Ltd/Alamy Stock Photo; **071BR:** Street Art/Alamy Stock Photo; **071L:** Jeff Greenberg/Alamy Stock Photo; **071TR:** David Lyons/Alamy Stock Photo; **072:** AGE Fotostock/Alamy Stock Photo; **073C:** DEA/G. DAGLI ORTI/De Agostini Picture Library/ Getty Images; **073L:** Glow Images/Getty Images; **073R:** World History Archive/Alamy Stock Photo; **074BCL:** Alex.pin/Fotolia; **074BCR:** Olllinka2/Fotolia; **074BR:** G-stockstudio/Shutterstock; **074T:** Dinga/ Shutterstock; **075B:** Erich Lessing/Art Resource, NY; **075T:** Naturaleza Muerta/Alfonso Fernandez; **076:** SuperStock; **076L:** SuperStock; **076R:** Dennis Hallinan/Alamy Stock Photo; **077:** Digital Image ©The Museum of Modern Art/Licensed by SCALA/ Art Resource, NY; **079:** ©2009 VEGAP, Madrid/Artists Rights Society; **080B:** Schalkwijk/Art Resource, NY; **082B:** Walker Art Center; **083T:** ChameleonsEye/ Shutterstock; **084BL:** Piotr & Irena Kolasa/Alamy Stock Photo; **084BR:** CaiaImageJV/OJO+/Getty Images; **084C:** Myrleen Pearson/Alamy Stock Photo; **084L:** Steve Debenport/iStock/Getty Images; **084TR, C:** Myrleen Pearson/Alamy Stock Photo; **085:** Ted Foxx/ Alamy Stock Photo; **085BL:** Tushin Anton Itar-Tass Photos/Newscom; **085TL:** Lifestylepics/Alamy Stock Photo; **086B:** Holger Leue/LOOK Die Bildagentur der Fotografen GmbH/Alamy Stock Photo; **086T:** Michael Owen Baker/ZUMA Press/Newscom; **087:** Janet Mayer/ Splash News/Newscom; **088:** David Friedman/Reuters; **091:** Leanna Rathkelly/Photographer's Choice/Getty Images; **093:** Ingolf Pompe/LOOK Die Bildagentur der Fotografen GmbH/Alamy Stock Photo; **094:** Clasos/ CON/Latin Content Editorial/Getty Images; **095T:** CTK/ Alamy Stock Photo; **096:** Scala/Art Resource, NY; **096R:** NewsCom; **097B:** Goya y Lucientes, Francisco Jose de (1746-1828)/Bibliotheque Nationale, Paris, France/Archives Charmet/Bridgeman Images; **097T:** Erich Lessing/Art Resource, NY; **098L:** Schalkwijk/Art Resource; **098R:** Salvador Dali Museum; **099:** Daniel

DeSlover/ZUMA Press/Newscom; **103:** Anne-Christine Poujoulat/AFP/Getty Images; **105:** Angel M. Rivera/ STAFF/El Nuevo Dia de Puerto Rico/Newscom; **106:** Dorothy Alexander / Alamy; **106-107:** GV Cruz/ WireImage/Getty Images; **108-109:** Univision

Chapter 03 "Cambia tus hábitos!" from 15 a 20 by Danae Salazar. August 2. Reprinted by permission.; **112:** Michelle D. Bridwell/PhotoEdit, Inc.; **114:** Jaume Gaul/age fotostock/Getty Images; **116:** Christie's Images/Fine Art/Corbis; **116:** USDA; **117:** Terry Williams/Photographer's Choice/Getty Images; **118BL:** David Buffington/Blend Images/Getty Images; **118BR:** Hinterhaus Productions/DigitalVision/Getty Images; **118C:** B. BOISSONNET/BSIP SA/Alamy Stock Photo; **118TL:** Wavebreakmedia Micro/Fotolia; **118TR:** Pearson Education, Inc.; **118TR:** Rob/Fotolia; **119B:** Melissa Vis/123RF; **119C:** Asha Yoganandan/Flickr Flash/Getty Images; **119T:** Obak/iStock/Getty Images; **121C:** Marsan/Shutterstock; **121L:** whiteaster/Fotolia; **121R:** ISchmidt/Shutterstock; **122CL:** MBI/Alamy Stock Photo; **122CR:** Russell Underwood/Upper Cut Images/Getty Images; **122L:** David Buffington/ Blend Images/Getty Images; **122R:** Lorena Natalia Fernandez/Getty Images; **123BL:** Pearson Education, Inc.; **123BR:** B. BOISSONNET/BSIP SA/Alamy Stock Photo; **123CL:** EPF/Alamy Stock Photo; **123T:** Catalin Petolea/Alamy Stock Photo; **124:** Patsy Michaud/ Shutterstock; **125:** Viktor/Fotolia; **126T:** Helen Norman/ Corbis; **127:** Dotshock/Shutterstock; **128:** Melissa Vis/123RF; **130BC:** Moodboard/Getty Images Plus/ Getty Images; **130BL:** Andersen Ross/Blend Images/ Getty Images; **130BR:** Image Source Plus/Alamy Stock Photo; **130TL:** Brocreative/Shutterstock; **130TR:** Dotshock/123RF; **131BL:** Yew! Images/Image Source/Getty Images; **131BR:** Jozef Polc/123RF; **131TL:** Brocreative/Shutterstock; **131TR:** Andresr/ Shutterstock; **133CR:** Andres Rodriguez/Fotolia; **135BC:** Andersen Ross/Blend Images/Getty Images; **135BL:** Image Source Plus/Alamy Stock Photo; **135BR:** Yew! Images/Image Source/Getty Images; **135TC:** Moodboard/Getty Images Plus/Getty Images; **135TL:** Brocreative/Shutterstock; **135TR:** Dotshock/123RF; **137B:** John Alves/Mystic Wanderer Images; **137T:** Yellow Dog Productions/Iconica/Getty Images; **138:** Andres Rodriguez/Fotolia; **140BCL:** Moodboard/Getty Images; **140BCR:** Blend Images/Getty Images; **140L:** EPF/Alamy Stock Photo; **140R:** Catalin Petolea/Alamy Stock Photo; **140T:** Implementar Films/Alamy Stock Photo; **143:** Gavin Rodgers/Alamy Stock Photo; **144:** Erich Lessing/Art Resource, NY; **145B:** Heritage Image Partnership Ltd/Alamy Stock

Photo; **145C:** Dorling Kindersley, Ltd.; **145T:** Macduff Everton/Encyclopedia/Corbis; **146:** Foodcollection RF/ Getty Images; **148:** Susanna Price/Dorling Kindersley, Ltd.; **150:** Russell Underwood/Upper Cut Images/Getty

Images; **151B:** Aksenova Natalya/Shutterstock; **151T:** Jonathan Kantor Studio/Photodisc/Getty Images; **152:** ©Michael Prince/Flirt/Corbis; **152:** Michael Prince/Flirt/Corbis; **152T:** Susanna Price/Dorling Kindersley Ltd; **153:** David R. Frazier/Danita Delimont Photography/Newscom; **156-157:** NBC Learn videos.

Chapter 04 "Homenaje a los Padres Chicanos" from It's Cold: 52 Cold Thought Poems of Abelardo by Abelardo Delgado. Copyright (c) 1974 Barrio Publications. Reprinted by permission.; "Como tú" Autor: Roque Dalton. Reproducido con permiso de acuerdo e asta contrato.; "Poema 15" from VEINTE POEMAS DE AMOR Y UNA CANCIÓN DESESPERADA ©1924, Fundación Publo Neruda.; **160:** Lucky Images/Shutterstock; **160:** LuckyImages/Shutterstock; **162:** Pearson Education, Inc.; **164:** RMN-Grand Palais/Art Resource, NY; **165:** Blend Images/Alamy Stock Photo; **166B:** Daniel M Ernst/Shutterstock; **166MR:** Blend Images/Shutterstock; **166TL:** Jennie Hart/Alamy Stock Photo; **166TR:** Yellow Dog Productions/Taxi/Getty Images; **167:** Image Source/Photodisc/Getty Images; **168:** Image Source/Photodisc/Getty Images; **169L:** Ariel Skelley//Blend Images/Getty Images; **169R:** KidStock/Blend Images/Getty Images; **170BL:** Emyerson/Getty Images; **170BR:** Gelpi JM/Shutterstock; **170C:** Rubberball/Fotolia; **170CL:** Necip Yanmaz/iStock/Getty Images; **170CR:** Daniel M Ernst/Shutterstock; **170T:** Erik Isakson/Blend Images/Getty Images; **173:** Eurobanks/Shutterstock; **175:** Ghislain & Marie David de Lossy/Cultura/Getty Images; **176:** Ronnie Kaufman/Blend Images/Alamy Stock Photo; **180BL:** Diego Cervo/iStock/Getty Images; **180BR:** Emyerson/Getty Images; **180T:** Hill Street Studios/Blend Images/Getty Images; **181BL:** Hill Street Studios/Blend Images/Getty Images; **181MR:** E.Myerson/Getty Images; **181T:** Juanmonino/E+/Getty Images; **182:** Pearson Education Inc; **182:** Pearson Education, Inc.; **183:** Myrleen Pearson/PhotoEdit, Inc.; **184:** Victor Chavez/WireImage/Getty Images; **185:** Wolfgang Dietze/Carmen L. Garza; **186:** Art Resource, NY; **189BC:** Igor Mojzes/Fotolia; **189BL:** Purestock/AGE Fotostock; **189BR:** Minerva Studio/Fotolia; **189T:** PT Images/Getty Images; **191:** Jack Hollingsworth/Corbis; **192:** Tony Freeman/PhotoEdit, Inc.; **193:** Bill Ross/Flirt/Corbis; **194:** Rubberball/Mike Kemp/Getty Images; **198:** Kurt Stier/Corbis; **199:** Enzo Figueres/Moment/Getty Images; **200:** Album/Art Resource, NY; **200:** Woman in Spanish Costume (La Salchichona) (1917) by Pablo Picasso/Giraudon/Art Resource, NY; **201:** Philip Scalia/Alamy Stock Photo; **202-203:** Jose Luis Pelaez Inc/Blend Images/Getty Images; **202-203:** Univision

Chapter 05 00: Pearson Education, Inc.; **208:** Sturti/E+/Getty Images; **210:** Tetra Images/Brand X Pictures/Getty Images; **212:** Girl with Sunflowers,

1941 (oil on masonite), Rivera, Diego (1886-1957)/Private Collection/Photo ©Christie's Images/Bridgeman Images; **213:** RosaIreneBetancourt 8/Alamy Stock Photo; 214 TC: Tyler Olson/123RF; **214BL:** Nicolas McComber/E+/Getty Images; **214BL:** NicolasMcComber/E+/Getty Images; **214BR:** Hero Images/DigitalVision/Getty Images; **214TL:** Daniel Dempster Photography/Alamy Stock Photo; **214TR:** Andresr/Shutterstock; **215BL:** Gareth Boden/Pearson Education Ltd; **215BL:** Gareth Boden/Pearson Education, Inc.; **215BR:** Antonio Diaz/Fotolia; **215TL:** Echo/Cultura/Getty Images; **215TR:** sturti/E+/Getty Images; **216L:** Jason Stitt/Shutterstock; **216R:** Pearson Education, Inc.; **217C:** RosaIreneBetancourt 9/Alamy Stock Photo; **217L:** RosaIreneBetancourt 2/Alamy Stock Photo; **217R:** RosaIreneBetancourt 5/Alamy Stock Photo; 219 BL: Daniel Dempster Photography/Alamy Stock Photo; 219 CCR: Nicolas McComber/E+/Getty Images; 219 TL: Hero Images/DigitalVision/Getty Images; **219BCL:** Claudia Veja/Shutterstock; **219BR:** Antenna/Getty Images; **219CCR:** Inmagineasia/Getty Images; **219CL:** Tetra Images/Shutterstock; **219CR:** Kablonk Micro/Fotolia; **220:** Moxie Productions/Blend Images/Getty Images; **224:** Paul Froggatt/Alamy Stock Photo; **226:** Tyler Olson/123RF; **227:** Detroit Industry, north wall, 1933 (fresco) (detail), Rivera, Diego (1886-1957)/Detroit Institute of Arts, USA/Bridgeman Images; **228:** Pamela Moore/iStockphoto/Getty Images; **229BL:** KidStock/Blend Images/Getty Images; **229BR:** Enigma/Alamy Stock Photo; **229T:** Steve Debenport/iStock/Getty Images Plus/Getty Images; **230:** Jennifer Paley/Pearson Education Inc.; **231B:** ERproductions Ltd/Blend Images/Getty Images; **231T:** Monkey Business/Fotolia; 233 BC: KidStock/Blend Images/Getty Images; 233 BL: Enigma/Alamy Stock Photo; 233 CC: Steve Debenport/iStock/Getty Images Plus/Getty Images; 233 CL: Pamela Moore/iStockphoto/Getty Images; **233T:** Wavebreak Media Micro/Fotolia; **236:** Dwayne Newton/PhotoEdit, Inc.; **237B:** Jari Hindstrom/123RF; **237C:** Andres Rodriguez/Fotolia; **237T:** Myrleen Pearson/Alamy Stock Photo; **238:** Alejandro Zepeda/Corbis Wire/Corbis; **239:** Julio Etchart/Alamy Stock Photo; **240:** CD1 WENN Photos/Newscom; **241B:** epa european pressphoto agency ./Alamy Stock Photo; **241C:** CD1 WENN Photos/Newscom; **241T:** Alvarado Construction Inc.; **246:** G. Kiner/Getty Images; **247:** DEA / G. KINER/De Agostini/Getty Images; **248:** Stephen Clarke/123RF; **249:** Tia Chucha's Centro Cultural; **250-251:** Hero Images/Getty Images

Chapter 06 "Rosa" by Angel Balzarino. Reprinted by permission.; **256:** Ariel Skelley/Blend Images/Getty Images; **258:** Carolyn Brown/The Image Bank/Getty Images; **260:** CNAC/MNAM/Dist. RMN-Grand Palais/Art Resource, NY; **261:** Right Perspective

Images/Alamy Stock Photo; **262BC:** Wavebreakmedia/ Shutterstock; **262BL:** Wavebreak Media Ltd/123RF; **262BR:** Andersen Ross/Blend Images/Getty Images; **262CC:** ImageSource/Photodisc/Getty Images; **262CL:** West Coast Surfer/Glow Images; **262TC:** LL28/E+/ Getty Images; **262TL:** Jetta Productions/Iconica/ Getty Images; **262TR:** Karan Kapoor/Compassionate Eye Foundation/DigitalVision/Getty Images; **263C:** Bill Aron/PhotoEdit, Inc.; **263L:** Agnormark/Fotolia; **263R:** Diego Cervo/123RF; **264B:** moodboard/Cultura/Getty Images; **264L:** Agencja Fotograficzna Caro/Alamy Stock Photo; **264R:** Blend Images/Alamy Stock Photo; **265C:** Greenshoots Communications/Alamy Stock Photo; **265L:** Andrew Brookes/Cultura Exclusive/Getty Images; **265R:** Greenshoots Communications/Alamy Stock Photo; **267B:** Dev Carr/Cultura Creative/Alamy Stock Photo; **272:** Congressional Hispanic Caucus Institute; **273:** Monkey Business Images/Shutterstock; **275:** Timothy Oleary/ShutterStock; **276B:** Misha/ Fotolia; **276C:** Leungchopan/Shutterstock; **276CR:** Leezsnow/iStock/Getty Images Plus/Getty Images; **276TL:** Pearson Education; **276TL:** Pearson Education, Inc.; **276TR:** Pearson Education; **276TR:** Pearson Education, Inc.; **277BL:** Nicola Tree/The Image Bank/ Getty Images; **277L:** Nataliya Hora/Fotolia; **277T:** Comaniciu Dan/123RF; **278B:** John Cogill/AP Images; **278C:** Bob Thomas/The Image Bank/Getty Images; **278T:** Erik Isakson/Glow Images; **279:** Jamie Grill/JGI/ Blend Images/Getty Images; **280:** Paul Fleet/123RF; **281:** Jim Weber/The Commercial Appeal/ZUMAPRESS. com/Newscom; **282:** Carol and Mike Werner/Alamy Stock Photo; **284:** Car Culture/Getty Images; **285:** Digital Art/Corbis; **286:** Alex Segre/Alamy Stock Photo; **287:** Science and Society/SuperStock; **288C:** Andy Selinger/AGE Fotostock/Getty Images; **288L:** Jan Butchofsky/Encyclopedia/Corbis; **288R:** Randy Faris/Flirt/Corbis; **289:** John Anderson/Fotolia; **291:** Blend Images/Alamy Stock Photo; **292:** Paul Barton/ Corbis; **296-297:** La banca del futuro, Inter- American Development Bank.

Chapter 07 "Sueño Cuarto" from Los Siete Sueños by Feliciano Sánchez Chan. Reprinted by permission.; **294:** Kotenko Oleksandr/Shutterstock; **294:** National Geographic RF/Getty Images; **296:** Charles & Josette Lenars/Fine Art/Corbis; **304:** Anthony Haigh/Alamy Stock Photo; **308:** Charles & Josette Lenars/Fine Art/ Corbis; **309:** Danita Delimont/Alamy Stock Photo; **310BR:** John Mitchell/Alamy Stock Photo; **310TL:** Dea Picture Library/Getty Images; **311:** Sean White/Design Pics/Newscom; **311BL:** Yiming Chen/Moment/Getty Images; **311BR:** Jo Ann Snover/Shutterstock; **311TL:** World History Archive/Alamy Stock Photo; **312L:** Bill Bachmann/PhotoEdit, Inc.; **312R:** Terex/Fotolia; **312TL:** George Wada/Fotolia; **312TR:** Bikeriderlondon/ Shutterstock; **313L:** Maxime Dube/Gallo Images/Alamy

Stock Photo; **313R:** Danita Delimont/Gallo Images/ Getty Images; **315:** Kevin Schafer/Encyclopedia/ Corbis; **316:** Michael Nicholson/Fine Art/Corbis; **320BC:** Joe Sohm Visions of America/Newscom; **320BL:** Gianni Dagli Orti/Fine Art/Corbis; **320BR:** Akg/Bildarchiv Steffens/Newscom; **320C:** Dariya Maksimova/123RF; **320CL:** La Venta/Sygma/Corbis; **320T:** Danny Lehman/Terra/Corbis; **324:** James L. Amos/Latitude/Corbis; **324BL:** Glow Images/ Getty Images; **324BR:** Khlongwangchao/Fotolia; **324CL:** Carlos Santa Maria/Fotolia; **324CR:** David Lyons/Alamy Stock Photo; **324TL:** Maria Teijeiro/ Photodisc/Getty Images; **324TR:** Christopher Meder/ Shutterstock; **325BR:** Native American - Indian culture/Alamy Stock Photo; **325TL:** Chris Boswell/ Fotolia; **325TR:** Joseph Ryczaj/iStock/Getty Images Plus/Getty Images; **326TL:** Charles & Josette Lenars/Encyclopedia/Corbis; **330:** Kevin Schafer/ Photographer's Choice/Getty Images; **333:** John Neubauer/PhotoEdit, Inc.; **334:** Terrance Klassen/AGE Fotostock; **335:** Mary Evans Picture Library/Alamy Stock Photo; **336:** Shin/Shutterstock; **337B:** Charles & Josette Lenars/Encyclopedia/Corbis; **337T:** Gianni Dagli Orti/Fine Art/Corbis; **338:** Pasquale Sorrentino/ Science Source; **342:** Heritage Images/Hulton Fine Art Collection/Getty Images; **343:** Walker Art Library/ Alamy Stock Photo; **344:** Heritage Image Partnership Ltd/Alamy Stock Photo; **345:** Falkensteinfoto/Alamy Stock Photo; **346-347:** Adwo/Fotolia; Darrell Gulin/ Dembinsky Photo Associates; **348-349:** ¿Sabes cuál es el secreto de la juventud eterna de Machu Pichu?, Inter- American Development Bank

Chapter 08 "Uno" from Viajes Fantásticos by Miguel Elías Muñoz. Copyright ©1999 McGraw-Hill Education. Reprinted by permission.; **338:** gvictoria/ Shutterstock; **340:** Piumatti Sergio/Prisma Bildagentur AG/Alamy Stock Photo; **342:** Granada, 1920, Sorolla y Bastida, Joaquin (1863-1923)/Museo Sorolla, Madrid, Spain/Index/Bridgeman Images; **343:** HP Canada/Alamy Stock Photo; **348:** Charlie Wait/ The Image Bank/Getty Images; **349:** Really Easy Star/ Salvatore Pipia/Alamy Stock Photo; **350:** Pearson Education, Inc.; **350:** Sonderegger Christof/Prisma Bildagentur AG/Alamy Stock Photo; **351:** Gunter Hartnage/Moment Open/Getty Images; **353:** John Mitchell/Alamy Stock Photo; **354:** Cecilia Colussi Stock/Alamy Stock Photo; **358B:** Barone Firenze/ Shutterstock; **358TL:** Pearson Education, Inc.; **358TR:** Patrick Ward/Corbis; **359:** Jordan Chastang; **359BR:** Jon Arnold/Jon Arnold Images Ltd/Alamy Stock Photo; **359C:** PHB.cz(Richard Semik)/Shutterstock; **359T:** Stuart Black/Robertharding/Alamy Stock Photo; **360:** Bridgeman-Giraudon/Art Resource, NY; **360B:** Triocean/iStock/Getty Images; **360C:** Olga Kolos/ Alamy Stock Photo; **360TL:** Pearson Education, Inc.;

Grateful acknowledgement is made to the following for copyrighted material:

ACTFL

World Readiness Standards for Language Learners by The American Council on the Teaching of Foreign Languages. Copyright ©ACTFL. Used by permission.

Agencia Literaria Carmen Balcells

"Poema 15" from *Veinte Poemas De Amor Y Una Canción Desesperada*. Copyright ©1924 Fundación Publo Neruda. Used by permission.

Angel Balzarino

"Rosa" by Angel Balzarino. Copyright ©Angel Balzarino. Used by permission.

Barrior Publications

"Homenaje a los Padres Chicanos" from *It's Cold: 52 Cold Thought Poems of Abelardo by Abelardo* Delgado. Copyright ©1974 Barrio Publications. Used by permission.

Da Capo Press

From *When I Was Puerto Rican* by Esmeralda Santiago, copyright (c) 1993. Reprinted by permission of Da Capo Press, an imprint of Perseus Books, a division of PBG Publishing, LLC, a subsidiary of Hachette Book Group, Inc.

Feliciano Sánchez Chan

"Sueño Cuarto" from *Los Siete Sueños* by Feliciano Sánchez Chan. Copyright ©Feliciano Sánchez Chan. Used by permission.

Hilario Barrero

"Subjuntivo" by Hilario Barrero. Copyright ©Hilario Barrero. Used by permission.

Karen Publishing

"Amigos" from *Mientras Mas lo Pienso...Tu,* by Juan Luis Guerra. Copyright ©1995 Karen Publishing Co. Used by permission.

McGraw-Hill Education

"Uno" from *Viajes Fantásticos* by Miguel Elías Muñoz. Copyright ©1999 McGraw Hill Education. Used by permission..

Moema Viezzer

"Si me permiten hablar..." from *Si me permiten hablar...Testimonio de Domitila: Una Mujer de las Minas de Bolivia* by Moema Viezzer. Copyright (c) 1977 Siglo XXI Editores S.A. Used by permission.

Notmusa S.A. de C.V.

"Cambia tus hábitos!" from *15 a 20, Agoato, 2002* by Danae Salazar. Copyright ©Notmusa, S.A. de C.V. Used by permission.

Estate of Roque Dalton

"Como tú" from *Poetry Like Bread* by Roque Dalton. Reproducido con permiso de acuerdo e asta contrato. Copyright ©Estate of Roque Dalton. Used by permission.

Vintage Espanol

Excerpt from *Cuando Era Puertorriqueña* by Esmeralda Santiago, translation copyright ©1994 by Penguin Random House LLC. Used by permission of Vintage Espanol, an imprint of the Knopf Doubleday Publishing Group, a division of Penguin Random House LLC. All rights reserved.

Note: Every effort has been made to locate the copyright owner of material reproduced in this component. Omissions brought to our attention will be corrected in subsequent editions.